Dictionary of Literary Biography

1 *The American Renaissance in New England*, edited by Joel Myerson (1978)

2 *American Novelists Since World War II*, edited by Jeffrey Helterman and Richard Layman (1978)

3 *Antebellum Writers in New York and the South*, edited by Joel Myerson (1979)

4 *American Writers in Paris, 1920-1939*, edited by Karen Lane Rood (1980)

5 *American Poets Since World War II*, 2 parts, edited by Donald J. Greiner (1980)

6 *American Novelists Since World War II, Second Series*, edited by James E. Kibler Jr. (1980)

7 *Twentieth-Century American Dramatists*, 2 parts, edited by John MacNicholas (1981)

8 *Twentieth-Century American Science-Fiction Writers*, 2 parts, edited by David Cowart and Thomas L. Wymer (1981)

9 *American Novelists, 1910-1945*, 3 parts, edited by James J. Martine (1981)

10 *Modern British Dramatists, 1900-1945*, 2 parts, edited by Stanley Weintraub (1982)

11 *American Humorists, 1800-1950*, 2 parts, edited by Stanley Trachtenberg (1982)

12 *American Realists and Naturalists*, edited by Donald Pizer and Earl N. Harbert (1982)

13 *British Dramatists Since World War II*, 2 parts, edited by Stanley Weintraub (1982)

14 *British Novelists Since 1960*, 2 parts, edited by Jay L. Halio (1983)

15 *British Novelists, 1930-1959*, 2 parts, edited by Bernard Oldsey (1983)

16 *The Beats: Literary Bohemians in Postwar America*, 2 parts, edited by Ann Charters (1983)

17 *Twentieth-Century American Historians*, edited by Clyde N. Wilson (1983)

18 *Victorian Novelists After 1885*, edited by Ira B. Nadel and William E. Fredeman (1983)

19 *British Poets, 1880-1914*, edited by Donald E. Stanford (1983)

20 *British Poets, 1914-1945*, edited by Donald E. Stanford (1983)

21 *Victorian Novelists Before 1885*, edited by Ira B. Nadel and William E. Fredeman (1983)

22 *American Writers for Children, 1900-1960*, edited by John Cech (1983)

23 *American Newspaper Journalists, 1873-1900*, edited by Perry J. Ashley (1983)

24 *American Colonial Writers, 1606-1734*, edited by Emory Elliott (1984)

25 *American Newspaper Journalists, 1901-1925*, edited by Perry J. Ashley (1984)

26 *American Screenwriters*, edited by Robert E. Morsberger, Stephen O. Lesser, and Randall Clark (1984)

27 *Poets of Great Britain and Ireland, 1945-1960*, edited by Vincent B. Sherry Jr. (1984)

28 *Twentieth-Century American-Jewish Fiction Writers*, edited by Daniel Walden (1984)

29 *American Newspaper Journalists, 1926-1950*, edited by Perry J. Ashley (1984)

30 *American Historians, 1607-1865*, edited by Clyde N. Wilson (1984)

31 *American Colonial Writers, 1735-1781*, edited by Emory Elliott (1984)

32 *Victorian Poets Before 1850*, edited by William E. Fredeman and Ira B. Nadel (1984)

33 *Afro-American Fiction Writers After 1955*, edited by Thadious M. Davis and Trudier Harris (1984)

34 *British Novelists, 1890-1929: Traditionalists*, edited by Thomas F. Staley (1985)

35 *Victorian Poets After 1850*, edited by William E. Fredeman and Ira B. Nadel (1985)

36 *British Novelists, 1890-1929: Modernists*, edited by Thomas F. Staley (1985)

37 *American Writers of the Early Republic*, edited by Emory Elliott (1985)

38 *Afro-American Writers After 1955: Dramatists and Prose Writers*, edited by Thadious M. Davis and Trudier Harris (1985)

39 *British Novelists, 1660-1800*, 2 parts, edited by Martin C. Battestin (1985)

40 *Poets of Great Britain and Ireland Since 1960*, 2 parts, edited by Vincent B. Sherry Jr. (1985)

41 *Afro-American Poets Since 1955*, edited by Trudier Harris and Thadious M. Davis (1985)

42 *American Writers for Children Before 1900*, edited by Glenn E. Estes (1985)

43 *American Newspaper Journalists, 1690-1872*, edited by Perry J. Ashley (1986)

44 *American Screenwriters, Second Series*, edited by Randall Clark, Robert E. Morsberger, and Stephen O. Lesser (1986)

45 *American Poets, 1880-1945, First Series*, edited by Peter Quartermain (1986)

46 *American Literary Publishing Houses, 1900-1980: Trade and Paperback*, edited by Peter Dzwonkoski (1986)

47 *American Historians, 1866-1912*, edited by Clyde N. Wilson (1986)

48 *American Poets, 1880-1945, Second Series*, edited by Peter Quartermain (1986)

49 *American Literary Publishing Houses, 1638-1899*, 2 parts, edited by Peter Dzwonkoski (1986)

50 *Afro-American Writers Before the Harlem Renaissance*, edited by Trudier Harris (1986)

51 *Afro-American Writers from the Harlem Renaissance to 1940*, edited by Trudier Harris (1987)

52 *American Writers for Children Since 1960: Fiction*, edited by Glenn E. Estes (1986)

53 *Canadian Writers Since 1960, First Series*, edited by W. H. New (1986)

54 *American Poets, 1880-1945, Third Series*, 2 parts, edited by Peter Quartermain (1987)

55 *Victorian Prose Writers Before 1867*, edited by William B. Thesing (1987)

56 *German Fiction Writers, 1914-1945*, edited by James Hardin (1987)

57 *Victorian Prose Writers After 1867*, edited by William B. Thesing (1987)

58 *Jacobean and Caroline Dramatists*, edited by Fredson Bowers (1987)

59 *American Literary Critics and Scholars, 1800-1850*, edited by John W. Rathbun and Monica M. Grecu (1987)

60 *Canadian Writers Since 1960, Second Series*, edited by W. H. New (1987)

61 *American Writers for Children Since 1960: Poets, Illustrators, and Nonfiction Authors*, edited by Glenn E. Estes (1987)

62 *Elizabethan Dramatists*, edited by Fredson Bowers (1987)

63 *Modern American Critics, 1920-1955*, edited by Gregory S. Jay (1988)

64 *American Literary Critics and Scholars, 1850-1880*, edited by John W. Rathbun and Monica M. Grecu (1988)

65 *French Novelists, 1900-1930*, edited by Catharine Savage Brosman (1988)

66 *German Fiction Writers, 1885-1913*, 2 parts, edited by James Hardin (1988)

67 *Modern American Critics Since 1955*, edited by Gregory S. Jay (1988)

68 *Canadian Writers, 1920-1959, First Series*, edited by W. H. New (1988)

69 *Contemporary German Fiction Writers, First Series*, edited by Wolfgang D. Elfe and James Hardin (1988)

70 *British Mystery Writers, 1860-1919*, edited by Bernard Benstock and Thomas F. Staley (1988)

71 *American Literary Critics and Scholars, 1880-1900*, edited by John W. Rathbun and Monica M. Grecu (1988)

72 *French Novelists, 1930-1960,* edited by Catharine Savage Brosman (1988)

73 *American Magazine Journalists, 1741-1850,* edited by Sam G. Riley (1988)

74 *American Short-Story Writers Before 1880,* edited by Bobby Ellen Kimbel, with the assistance of William E. Grant (1988)

75 *Contemporary German Fiction Writers, Second Series,* edited by Wolfgang D. Elfe and James Hardin (1988)

76 *Afro-American Writers, 1940-1955,* edited by Trudier Harris (1988)

77 *British Mystery Writers, 1920-1939,* edited by Bernard Benstock and Thomas F. Staley (1988)

78 *American Short-Story Writers, 1880-1910,* edited by Bobby Ellen Kimbel, with the assistance of William E. Grant (1988)

79 *American Magazine Journalists, 1850-1900,* edited by Sam G. Riley (1988)

80 *Restoration and Eighteenth-Century Dramatists, First Series,* edited by Paula R. Backscheider (1989)

81 *Austrian Fiction Writers, 1875-1913,* edited by James Hardin and Donald G. Daviau (1989)

82 *Chicano Writers, First Series,* edited by Francisco A. Lomelí and Carl R. Shirley (1989)

83 *French Novelists Since 1960,* edited by Catharine Savage Brosman (1989)

84 *Restoration and Eighteenth-Century Dramatists, Second Series,* edited by Paula R. Backscheider (1989)

85 *Austrian Fiction Writers After 1914,* edited by James Hardin and Donald G. Daviau (1989)

86 *American Short-Story Writers, 1910-1945, First Series,* edited by Bobby Ellen Kimbel (1989)

87 *British Mystery and Thriller Writers Since 1940, First Series,* edited by Bernard Benstock and Thomas F. Staley (1989)

88 *Canadian Writers, 1920-1959, Second Series,* edited by W. H. New (1989)

89 *Restoration and Eighteenth-Century Dramatists, Third Series,* edited by Paula R. Backscheider (1989)

90 *German Writers in the Age of Goethe, 1789-1832,* edited by James Hardin and Christoph E. Schweitzer (1989)

91 *American Magazine Journalists, 1900-1960, First Series,* edited by Sam G. Riley (1990)

92 *Canadian Writers, 1890-1920,* edited by W. H. New (1990)

93 *British Romantic Poets, 1789-1832, First Series,* edited by John R. Greenfield (1990)

94 *German Writers in the Age of Goethe: Sturm und Drang to Classicism,* edited by James Hardin and Christoph E. Schweitzer (1990)

95 *Eighteenth-Century British Poets, First Series,* edited by John Sitter (1990)

96 *British Romantic Poets, 1789-1832, Second Series,* edited by John R. Greenfield (1990)

97 *German Writers from the Enlightenment to Sturm und Drang, 1720-1764,* edited by James Hardin and Christoph E. Schweitzer (1990)

98 *Modern British Essayists, First Series,* edited by Robert Beum (1990)

99 *Canadian Writers Before 1890,* edited by W. H. New (1990)

100 *Modern British Essayists, Second Series,* edited by Robert Beum (1990)

101 *British Prose Writers, 1660-1800, First Series,* edited by Donald T. Siebert (1991)

102 *American Short-Story Writers, 1910-1945, Second Series,* edited by Bobby Ellen Kimbel (1991)

103 *American Literary Biographers, First Series,* edited by Steven Serafin (1991)

104 *British Prose Writers, 1660-1800, Second Series,* edited by Donald T. Siebert (1991)

105 *American Poets Since World War II, Second Series,* edited by R. S. Gwynn (1991)

106 *British Literary Publishing Houses, 1820-1880,* edited by Patricia J. Anderson and Jonathan Rose (1991)

107 *British Romantic Prose Writers, 1789-1832, First Series,* edited by John R. Greenfield (1991)

108 *Twentieth-Century Spanish Poets, First Series,* edited by Michael L. Perna (1991)

109 *Eighteenth-Century British Poets, Second Series,* edited by John Sitter (1991)

110 *British Romantic Prose Writers, 1789-1832, Second Series,* edited by John R. Greenfield (1991)

111 *American Literary Biographers, Second Series,* edited by Steven Serafin (1991)

112 *British Literary Publishing Houses, 1881-1965,* edited by Jonathan Rose and Patricia J. Anderson (1991)

113 *Modern Latin-American Fiction Writers, First Series,* edited by William Luis (1992)

114 *Twentieth-Century Italian Poets, First Series,* edited by Giovanna Wedel De Stasio, Glauco Cambon, and Antonio Illiano (1992)

115 *Medieval Philosophers,* edited by Jeremiah Hackett (1992)

116 *British Romantic Novelists, 1789-1832,* edited by Bradford K. Mudge (1992)

117 *Twentieth-Century Caribbean and Black African Writers, First Series,* edited by Bernth Lindfors and Reinhard Sander (1992)

118 *Twentieth-Century German Dramatists, 1889-1918,* edited by Wolfgang D. Elfe and James Hardin (1992)

119 *Nineteenth-Century French Fiction Writers: Romanticism and Realism, 1800-1860,* edited by Catharine Savage Brosman (1992)

120 *American Poets Since World War II, Third Series,* edited by R. S. Gwynn (1992)

121 *Seventeenth-Century British Nondramatic Poets, First Series,* edited by M. Thomas Hester (1992)

122 *Chicano Writers, Second Series,* edited by Francisco A. Lomelí and Carl R. Shirley (1992)

123 *Nineteenth-Century French Fiction Writers: Naturalism and Beyond, 1860-1900,* edited by Catharine Savage Brosman (1992)

124 *Twentieth-Century German Dramatists, 1919-1992,* edited by Wolfgang D. Elfe and James Hardin (1992)

125 *Twentieth-Century Caribbean and Black African Writers, Second Series,* edited by Bernth Lindfors and Reinhard Sander (1993)

126 *Seventeenth-Century British Nondramatic Poets, Second Series,* edited by M. Thomas Hester (1993)

127 *American Newspaper Publishers, 1950-1990,* edited by Perry J. Ashley (1993)

128 *Twentieth-Century Italian Poets, Second Series,* edited by Giovanna Wedel De Stasio, Glauco Cambon, and Antonio Illiano (1993)

129 *Nineteenth-Century German Writers, 1841-1900,* edited by James Hardin and Siegfried Mews (1993)

130 *American Short-Story Writers Since World War II,* edited by Patrick Meanor (1993)

131 *Seventeenth-Century British Nondramatic Poets, Third Series,* edited by M. Thomas Hester (1993)

132 *Sixteenth-Century British Nondramatic Writers, First Series,* edited by David A. Richardson (1993)

133 *Nineteenth-Century German Writers to 1840,* edited by James Hardin and Siegfried Mews (1993)

134 *Twentieth-Century Spanish Poets, Second Series,* edited by Jerry Phillips Winfield (1994)

135 *British Short-Fiction Writers, 1880-1914: The Realist Tradition,* edited by William B. Thesing (1994)

136 *Sixteenth-Century British Nondramatic Writers, Second Series,* edited by David A. Richardson (1994)

137 *American Magazine Journalists, 1900-1960, Second Series,* edited by Sam G. Riley (1994)

138 *German Writers and Works of the High Middle Ages: 1170-1280,* edited by James Hardin and Will Hasty (1994)

139 *British Short-Fiction Writers, 1945-1980,* edited by Dean Baldwin (1994)

140 *American Book-Collectors and Bibliographers, First Series,* edited by Joseph Rosenblum (1994)

141 *British Children's Writers, 1880-1914,* edited by Laura M. Zaidman (1994)

142 *Eighteenth-Century British Literary Biographers,* edited by Steven Serafin (1994)

143 *American Novelists Since World War II, Third Series,* edited by James R. Giles and Wanda H. Giles (1994)

144 *Nineteenth-Century British Literary Biographers,* edited by Steven Serafin (1994)

145 *Modern Latin-American Fiction Writers, Second Series,* edited by William Luis and Ann González (1994)

146 *Old and Middle English Literature,* edited by Jeffrey Helterman and Jerome Mitchell (1994)

147 *South Slavic Writers Before World War II,* edited by Vasa D. Mihailovich (1994)

148 *German Writers and Works of the Early Middle Ages: 800-1170,* edited by Will Hasty and James Hardin (1994)

149 *Late Nineteenth- and Early Twentieth-Century British Literary Biographers,* edited by Steven Serafin (1995)

150 *Early Modern Russian Writers, Late Seventeenth and Eighteenth Centuries,* edited by Marcus C. Levitt (1995)

151 *British Prose Writers of the Early Seventeenth Century,* edited by Clayton D. Lein (1995)

152 *American Novelists Since World War II, Fourth Series,* edited by James R. Giles and Wanda H. Giles (1995)

153 *Late-Victorian and Edwardian British Novelists, First Series,* edited by George M. Johnson (1995)

154 *The British Literary Book Trade, 1700-1820,* edited by James K. Bracken and Joel Silver (1995)

155 *Twentieth-Century British Literary Biographers,* edited by Steven Serafin (1995)

156 *British Short-Fiction Writers, 1880-1914: The Romantic Tradition,* edited by William F. Naufftus (1995)

157 *Twentieth-Century Caribbean and Black African Writers, Third Series,* edited by Bernth Lindfors and Reinhard Sander (1995)

158 *British Reform Writers, 1789-1832,* edited by Gary Kelly and Edd Applegate (1995)

159 *British Short-Fiction Writers, 1800-1880,* edited by John R. Greenfield (1996)

160 *British Children's Writers, 1914-1960,* edited by Donald R. Hettinga and Gary D. Schmidt (1996)

161 *British Children's Writers Since 1960, First Series,* edited by Caroline Hunt (1996)

162 *British Short-Fiction Writers, 1915-1945,* edited by John H. Rogers (1996)

163 *British Children's Writers, 1800-1880,* edited by Meena Khorana (1996)

164 *German Baroque Writers, 1580-1660,* edited by James Hardin (1996)

165 *American Poets Since World War II, Fourth Series,* edited by Joseph Conte (1996)

166 *British Travel Writers, 1837-1875,* edited by Barbara Brothers and Julia Gergits (1996)

167 *Sixteenth-Century British Nondramatic Writers, Third Series,* edited by David A. Richardson (1996)

168 *German Baroque Writers, 1661-1730,* edited by James Hardin (1996)

169 *American Poets Since World War II, Fifth Series,* edited by Joseph Conte (1996)

170 *The British Literary Book Trade, 1475-1700,* edited by James K. Bracken and Joel Silver (1996)

171 *Twentieth Century American Sportswriters,* edited by Richard Orodenker (1996)

172 *Sixteenth-Century British Nondramatic Writers, Fourth Series,* edited by David A. Richardson (1996)

173 *American Novelists Since World War II, Fifth Series,* edited by James R. Giles and Wanda H. Giles (1996)

174 *British Travel Writers, 1876-1909,* edited by Barbara Brothers and Julia Gergits (1997)

175 *Native American Writers of the United States,* edited by Kenneth M. Roemer (1997)

176 *Ancient Greek Authors,* edited by Ward W. Briggs (1997)

177 *Italian Novelists Since World War II, 1945-1965,* edited by Augustus Pallotta (1997)

178 *British Fantasy and Science-Fiction Writers Before World War I,* edited by Darren Harris-Fain (1997)

179 *German Writers of the Renaissance and Reformation, 1280-1580,* edited by James Hardin and Max Reinhart (1997)

180 *Japanese Fiction Writers, 1868-1945,* edited by Van C. Gessel (1997)

181 *South Slavic Writers Since World War II,* edited by Vasa D. Mihailovich (1997)

182 *Japanese Fiction Writers Since World War II,* edited by Van C. Gessel (1997)

183 *American Travel Writers, 1776-1864,* edited by James J. Schramer and Donald Ross (1997)

184 *Nineteenth-Century British Book-Collectors and Bibliographers,* edited by William Baker and Kenneth Womack (1997)

185 *American Literary Journalists, 1945-1995, First Series,* edited by Arthur J. Kaul (1998)

186 *Nineteenth-Century American Western Writers,* edited by Robert L. Gale (1998)

187 *American Book Collectors and Bibliographers, Second Series,* edited by Joseph Rosenblum (1998)

188 *American Book and Magazine Illustrators to 1920,* edited by Steven E. Smith, Catherine A. Hastedt, and Donald H. Dyal (1998)

189 *American Travel Writers, 1850-1915,* edited by Donald Ross and James J. Schramer (1998)

190 *British Reform Writers, 1832-1914,* edited by Gary Kelly and Edd Applegate (1998)

191 *British Novelists Between the Wars,* edited by George M. Johnson (1998)

192 *French Dramatists, 1789-1914,* edited by Barbara T. Cooper (1998)

193 *American Poets Since World War II, Sixth Series,* edited by Joseph Conte (1998)

194 *British Novelists Since 1960, Second Series,* edited by Merritt Moseley (1998)

195 *British Travel Writers, 1910-1939,* edited by Barbara Brothers and Julia Gergits (1998)

196 *Italian Novelists Since World War II, 1965-1995,* edited by Augustus Pallotta (1999)

197 *Late-Victorian and Edwardian British Novelists, Second Series,* edited by George M. Johnson (1999)

198 *Russian Literature in the Age of Pushkin and Gogol: Prose,* edited by Christine A. Rydel (1999)

199 *Victorian Women Poets,* edited by William B. Thesing (1999)

200 *American Women Prose Writers to 1820,* edited by Carla J. Mulford, with Angela Vietto and Amy E. Winans (1999)

201 *Twentieth-Century British Book Collectors and Bibliographers,* edited by William Baker and Kenneth Womack (1999)

202 *Nineteenth-Century American Fiction Writers,* edited by Kent P. Ljungquist (1999)

203 *Medieval Japanese Writers,* edited by Steven D. Carter (1999)

204 *British Travel Writers, 1940-1997,* edited by Barbara Brothers and Julia M. Gergits (1999)

205 *Russian Literature in the Age of Pushkin and Gogol: Poetry and Drama,* edited by Christine A. Rydel (1999)

206 *Twentieth-Century American Western Writers, First Series,* edited by Richard H. Cracroft (1999)

207 *British Novelists Since 1960, Third Series,* edited by Merritt Moseley (1999)

208 *Literature of the French and Occitan Middle Ages: Eleventh to Fifteenth Centuries,* edited by Deborah Sinnreich-Levi and Ian S. Laurie (1999)

209 *Chicano Writers, Third Series,* edited by Francisco A. Lomelí and Carl R. Shirley (1999)

210 *Ernest Hemingway: A Documentary Volume,* edited by Robert W. Trogdon (1999)

211 *Ancient Roman Writers,* edited by Ward W. Briggs (1999)

212 *Twentieth-Century American Western Writers, Second Series,* edited by Richard H. Cracroft (1999)

213 *Pre-Nineteenth-Century British Book Collectors and Bibliographers,* edited by William Baker and Kenneth Womack (1999)

214 *Twentieth-Century Danish Writers,* edited by Marianne Stecher-Hansen (1999)

215 *Twentieth-Century Eastern European Writers, First Series,* edited by Steven Serafin (1999)

216 *British Poets of the Great War: Brooke, Rosenberg, Thomas. A Documentary Volume,* edited by Patrick Quinn (2000)

217 *Nineteenth-Century French Poets,* edited by Robert Beum (2000)

218 *American Short-Story Writers Since World War II, Second Series,* edited by Patrick Meanor and Gwen Crane (2000)

219 *F. Scott Fitzgerald's* The Great Gatsby: *A Documentary Volume,* edited by Matthew J. Bruccoli (2000)

220 *Twentieth-Century Eastern European Writers, Second Series,* edited by Steven Serafin (2000)

221 *American Women Prose Writers, 1870-1920,* edited by Sharon M. Harris, with the assistance of Heidi L. M. Jacobs and Jennifer Putzi (2000)

222 *H. L. Mencken: A Documentary Volume,* edited by Richard J. Schrader (2000)

223 *The American Renaissance in New England, Second Series,* edited by Wesley T. Mott (2000)

224 *Walt Whitman: A Documentary Volume,* edited by Joel Myerson (2000)

225 *South African Writers,* edited by Paul A. Scanlon (2000)

226 *American Hard-Boiled Crime Writers,* edited by George Parker Anderson and Julie B. Anderson (2000)

227 *American Novelists Since World War II, Sixth Series,* edited by James R. Giles and Wanda H. Giles (2000)

228 *Twentieth-Century American Dramatists, Second Series,* edited by Christopher J. Wheatley (2000)

229 *Thomas Wolfe: A Documentary Volume,* edited by Ted Mitchell (2001)

230 *Australian Literature, 1788-1914,* edited by Selina Samuels (2001)

231 *British Novelists Since 1960, Fourth Series,* edited by Merritt Moseley (2001)

232 *Twentieth-Century Eastern European Writers, Third Series,* edited by Steven Serafin (2001)

233 *British and Irish Dramatists Since World War II, Second Series,* edited by John Bull (2001)

234 *American Short-Story Writers Since World War II, Third Series,* edited by Patrick Meanor and Richard E. Lee (2001)

235 *The American Renaissance in New England, Third Series,* edited by Wesley T. Mott (2001)

236 *British Rhetoricians and Logicians, 1500-1660,* edited by Edward A. Malone (2001)

237 *The Beats: A Documentary Volume,* edited by Matt Theado (2001)

238 *Russian Novelists in the Age of Tolstoy and Dostoevsky,* edited by J. Alexander Ogden and Judith E. Kalb (2001)

239 *American Women Prose Writers: 1820-1870,* edited by Amy E. Hudock and Katharine Rodier (2001)

240 *Late Nineteenth- and Early Twentieth-Century British Women Poets,* edited by William B. Thesing (2001)

Documentary Series

1 *Sherwood Anderson, Willa Cather, John Dos Passos, Theodore Dreiser, F. Scott Fitzgerald, Ernest Hemingway, Sinclair Lewis,* edited by Margaret A. Van Antwerp (1982)

2 *James Gould Cozzens, James T. Farrell, William Faulkner, John O'Hara, John Steinbeck, Thomas Wolfe, Richard Wright,* edited by Margaret A. Van Antwerp (1982)

3 *Saul Bellow, Jack Kerouac, Norman Mailer, Vladimir Nabokov, John Updike, Kurt Vonnegut,* edited by Mary Bruccoli (1983)

4 *Tennessee Williams,* edited by Margaret A. Van Antwerp and Sally Johns (1984)

5 *American Transcendentalists,* edited by Joel Myerson (1988)

6 *Hardboiled Mystery Writers: Raymond Chandler, Dashiell Hammett, Ross Macdonald,* edited by Matthew J. Bruccoli and Richard Layman (1989)

7 *Modern American Poets: James Dickey, Robert Frost, Marianne Moore,* edited by Karen L. Rood (1989)

8 *The Black Aesthetic Movement,* edited by Jeffrey Louis Decker (1991)

9 *American Writers of the Vietnam War: W. D. Ehrhart, Larry Heinemann, Tim O'Brien, Walter McDonald, John M. Del Vecchio,* edited by Ronald Baughman (1991)

10 *The Bloomsbury Group,* edited by Edward L. Bishop (1992)

11 *American Proletarian Culture: The Twenties and The Thirties,* edited by Jon Christian Suggs (1993)

12 *Southern Women Writers: Flannery O'Connor, Katherine Anne Porter, Eudora Welty,* edited by Mary Ann Wimsatt and Karen L. Rood (1994)

13 *The House of Scribner, 1846-1904,* edited by John Delaney (1996)

14 *Four Women Writers for Children, 1868-1918,* edited by Caroline C. Hunt (1996)

15 *American Expatriate Writers: Paris in the Twenties,* edited by Matthew J. Bruccoli and Robert W. Trogdon (1997)

16 *The House of Scribner, 1905-1930,* edited by John Delaney (1997)

17 *The House of Scribner, 1931-1984,* edited by John Delaney (1998)

18 *British Poets of The Great War: Sassoon, Graves, Owen,* edited by Patrick Quinn (1999)

19 *James Dickey,* edited by Judith S. Baughman (1999)

See also DLB 210, 216, 219, 222, 224, 229, 237

Yearbooks

1980 edited by Karen L. Rood, Jean W. Ross, and Richard Ziegfeld (1981)

1981 edited by Karen L. Rood, Jean W. Ross, and Richard Ziegfeld (1982)

1982 edited by Richard Ziegfeld; associate editors: Jean W. Ross and Lynne C. Zeigler (1983)

1983 edited by Mary Bruccoli and Jean W. Ross; associate editor Richard Ziegfeld (1984)

1984 edited by Jean W. Ross (1985)

1985 edited by Jean W. Ross (1986)

1986 edited by J. M. Brook (1987)

1987 edited by J. M. Brook (1988)

1988 edited by J. M. Brook (1989)

1989 edited by J. M. Brook (1990)

1990 edited by James W. Hipp (1991)

1991 edited by James W. Hipp (1992)

1992 edited by James W. Hipp (1993)

1993 edited by James W. Hipp, contributing editor George Garrett (1994)

1994 edited by James W. Hipp, contributing editor George Garrett (1995)

1995 edited by James W. Hipp, contributing editor George Garrett (1996)

1996 edited by Samuel W. Bruce and L. Kay Webster, contributing editor George Garrett (1997)

1997 edited by Matthew J. Bruccoli and George Garrett, with the assistance of L. Kay Webster (1998)

1998 edited by Matthew J. Bruccoli, contributing editor George Garrett, with the assistance of D. W. Thomas (1999)

1999 edited by Matthew J. Bruccoli, contributing editor George Garrett, with the assistance of D. W. Thomas (2000)

Concise Series

Concise Dictionary of American Literary Biography, 7 volumes (1988-1999): *The New Consciousness, 1941-1968; Colonization to the American Renaissance, 1640-1865; Realism, Naturalism, and Local Color, 1865-1917; The Twenties, 1917-1929; The Age of Maturity, 1929-1941; Broadening Views, 1968-1988; Supplement: Modern Writers, 1900-1998.*

Concise Dictionary of British Literary Biography, 8 volumes (1991-1992): *Writers of the Middle Ages and Renaissance Before 1660; Writers of the Restoration and Eighteenth Century, 1660-1789; Writers of the Romantic Period, 1789-1832; Victorian Writers, 1832-1890; Late-Victorian and Edwardian Writers, 1890-1914; Modern Writers, 1914-1945; Writers After World War II, 1945-1960; Contemporary Writers, 1960 to Present.*

Concise Dictionary of World Literary Biography, 10 volumes projected (1999-   ): *Ancient Greek and Roman Writers; German Writers; African, Carribbean, and Latin American Writers; South Slavic and Eastern European Writers.*

Dictionary of Literary Biography® • Volume Two Hundred Forty

Late Nineteenth- and Early Twentieth-Century British Women Poets

Dictionary of Literary Biography® • Volume Two Hundred Forty

Late Nineteenth- and Early Twentieth-Century British Women Poets

Edited by
William B. Thesing
University of South Carolina

ST. PHILIP'S COLLEGE LIBRARY

A Bruccoli Clark Layman Book
The Gale Group
Detroit • San Francisco • London • Boston • Woodbridge, Conn.

Advisory Board for
DICTIONARY OF LITERARY BIOGRAPHY

John Baker
William Cagle
Patrick O'Connor
George Garrett
Trudier Harris
Alvin Kernan
Kenny J. Williams

Matthew J. Bruccoli and Richard Layman, Editorial Directors
C. E. Frazer Clark Jr., Managing Editor
Karen L. Rood, Senior Editor

Printed in the United States of America

The paper used in this publication meets the minimum requirements
of American National Standard for Information Sciences–Permanence
Paper for Printed Library Materials, ANSI Z39.48-1984. ∞™

This publication is a creative work fully protected by all applicable copyright laws, as well as by misappropriation, trade secret, unfair competition, and other applicable laws. The authors and editors of this work have added value to the underlying factual material herein through one or more of the following: unique and original selection, coordination, expression, arrangement, and classification of the information.

All rights to this publication will be vigorously defended.

Copyright © 2001 by The Gale Group
27500 Drake Road
Farmington Hills, MI 48331

All rights reserved including the right of reproduction in
whole or in part in any form.

Library of Congress Cataloging-in-Publication Data

Late nineteenth- and early twentieth-century British women poets / edited by William B. Thesing.
    p. cm.–(Dictionary of literary biography: v. 240)
"A Bruccoli Clark Layman book."
Includes bibliographical references and index.
ISBN 0-7876-4657-1 (alk. paper)
1. English poetry–Women authors–Bio-bibliography–Dictionaries. 2. Women and literature–Great Britain–History–19th century–Dictionaries. 3. Women and literature–Great Britain–History–20th century–Dictionaries. 4. English poetry–19th century–Bio-bibliography–Dictionaries. 5. English poetry–20th century–Bio-bibliography–Dictionaries. 6. Poets, English–19th century–Biography–Dictionaries. 7. Poets, English–20th century–Biography–Dictionaries. 8. Women poets, English–Biography–Dictionaries. I. Thesing, William B. II. Series.

PR115L345 2001
821'.8099287'03–dc21
[B]   2001018968

---

10 9 8 7 6 5 4 3 2 1

For Jane I. and Amy K. Thesing
and
for Becky W. Lewis and Denis W. Thomas

Contents

Plan of the Series xv
Introduction xvii

Bertha Leith Adams (Mrs. Leith Adams,
Mrs. R. S. de Courcy Laffan) (1837?-1912) 3
   Amanda Jo Pettit

Louisa Baldwin (Mrs. Alfred Baldwin)
(1845-1925) 9
   Linda A. Julian

Mary Butts (1890-1937) .14
   Roslyn Reso Foy

Frances Cornford (1886-1960) 23
   Ashley Brown

Camilla Toulmin Crosland
(Mrs. Newton Crosland) (1812-1895) 29
   Kathleen McCormack

Nancy Cunard (1896-1965) 36
   Chris Hopkins

Olive Custance (Lady Alfred Douglas)
(1874-1944) 46
   Michelle L. Whitney

Toru Dutt (1856-1877) 54
   Alpana Sharma

Michael Field (Katherine Harris Bradley [1846-1914]
and Edith Emma Cooper [1862-1913]) 61
   Ed Madden

Eva Gore-Booth (1870-1926) 69
   John C. Hawley

Mary Anne Hearn (Marianne Farningham,
Eva Hope) (1834-1909) 79
   Linda A. Julian

Laurence Hope (Adela Florence Cory Nicolson)
(1865-1904) 88
   Edward Marx

Nora Hopper (Mrs. Nora Chesson) (1871-1906) . . .94
   Siobhan Craft Brownson

Mary Catherine Hume-Rothery (1824-1885) 100
   Kathleen McCormack

Violet Jacob (1863-1946) 107
   Florence Boos

Eliza Keary (1827-1918) .113
   Naomi Hetherington

May Kendall (1861-1943) 118
   Marion Thain

Lucy Knox (1845-1884) .124
   Kirsten E. Escobar

Emily Lawless (The Hon. Emily Lawless)
(1845-1913) 128
   Richard Tobias

Amy Levy (1861-1889) .134
   Rebecca Shapiro

Annie Matheson (1853-1924) 142
   Florence Boos

Susan Miles (Ursula Wyllie Roberts)
(1888-1975) 150
   Becky W. Lewis

Alice Milligan (1866-1953) 158
   Eugenie Celeste Martin

Rosa Harriet Newmarch (1857-1940) 164
   Lee Anna Maynard

Charlotte Grace O'Brien (1845-1909) 172
   Lisa Kerr

Ellen O'Leary (1831-1889) 178
   Rose Novak

Bessie Rayner Parkes (Madame Belloc)
(1829-1925) 183
   Constance M. Fulmer

Dollie Radford (1858-1920) 191
   LeeAnne Marie Richardson

A. Mary F. Robinson (Madame James Darmesteter,
Madame Mary Duclaux) (1857-1944) 201
   Cynthia E. Huggins

Christina Rossetti (1830-1894) 210
   Mary Arseneau

Lady Margaret Sackville (1881-1963) 232
   Whitney Womack

Alicia Anne Scott (Lady John Scott)
(1810-1900) 240
   Susannah Clements

Catharine Amy Dawson Scott (1865–1934). 246
Tonya L. Wertz-Orbaugh

Dora Sigerson Shorter (1866–1918). 252
Deborah A. Logan

Flora Thompson (1876–1947). 261
John Ferns

Katharine Tynan (1861–1931). 268
Michele Martinez

Evelyn Underhill (1875–1941). 283
James Whitlark

Helen Waddell (1889–1965). 293
Susan T. Harrington

Anna Louisa Walker (Mrs. Harry Coghill)
(circa 1836–1907). 299
Bettina Tate Pedersen

Anna Letitia Waring (1823–1910). 305
Crys Armbrust

Rosamund Marriott Watson (Graham R. Tomson)
(1860–1911) 308
Linda K. Hughes

Lucy Webling (Lucy Betty MacRaye) (1877–1952) and
Peggy Webling (Arthur Weston) (1871–1949) 321
Jeanie Grant Moore

Augusta Webster (1837–1894) 332
Kathleen Hickok

Anna Wickham (Edith Alice Mary Harper)
(1883–1947). 345
Ann Vickery

Margaret L. Woods (1855–1945) 352
Martha S. Vogeler

Checklist of Further Readings. 361
Contributors 365
Cumulative Index 369

Plan of the Series

...Almost the most prodigious asset of a country, and perhaps its most precious possession, is its native literary product—when that product is fine and noble and enduring.

Mark Twain*

The advisory board, the editors, and the publisher of the *Dictionary of Literary Biography* are joined in endorsing Mark Twain's declaration. The literature of a nation provides an inexhaustible resource of permanent worth. Our purpose is to make literature and its creators better understood and more accessible to students and the reading public, while satisfying the needs of teachers and researchers.

To meet these requirements, *literary biography* has been construed in terms of the author's achievement. The most important thing about a writer is his writing. Accordingly, the entries in *DLB* are career biographies, tracing the development of the author's canon and the evolution of his reputation.

The purpose of *DLB* is not only to provide reliable information in a usable format but also to place the figures in the larger perspective of literary history and to offer appraisals of their accomplishments by qualified scholars.

The publication plan for *DLB* resulted from two years of preparation. The project was proposed to Bruccoli Clark by Frederick G. Ruffner, president of the Gale Research Company, in November 1975. After specimen entries were prepared and typeset, an advisory board was formed to refine the entry format and develop the series rationale. In meetings held during 1976, the publisher, series editors, and advisory board approved the scheme for a comprehensive biographical dictionary of persons who contributed to literature. Editorial work on the first volume began in January 1977, and it was published in 1978. In order to make *DLB* more than a dictionary and to compile volumes that individually have claim to status as literary history, it was decided to organize volumes by topic, period, or genre. Each of these freestanding volumes provides a biographical-bibliographical guide and overview for a particular area of literature. We are convinced that this organization—as opposed to a single alphabet method—constitutes a valuable innovation in the presentation of reference material. The volume plan necessarily requires many decisions for the placement and treatment of authors. Certain figures will be included in separate volumes, but with different entries emphasizing the aspect of his career appropriate to each volume. Ernest Hemingway, for example, is represented in *American Writers in Paris, 1920–1939* by an entry focusing on his expatriate apprenticeship; he is also in *American Novelists, 1910–1945* with an entry surveying his entire career, as well as in *American Short-Story Writers, 1910–1945, Second Series* with an entry concentrating on his short fiction. Each volume includes a cumulative index of the subject authors and articles.

Since 1981 the series has been further augmented by the *DLB Yearbooks,* which update published entries, add new entries to keep the *DLB* current with contemporary activity, and provide articles on literary history. There have also been nineteen *DLB Documentary Series* volumes which provide illustrations, facsimiles, and biographical and critical source materials for figures works, or groups judged to have particular interest for students. In 1999 the *Documentary Series* was incorporated into the *DLB* volume numbering system beginning with *DLB 210, Ernest Hemingway.*

We define literature as the *intellectual commerce of a nation:* not merely as belles lettres but as that ample and complex process by which ideas are generated, shaped, and transmitted. *DLB* entries are not limited to "creative writers" but extend to other figures who in their time and in their way influenced the mind of a people. Thus the series encompasses historians, journalists, publishers, book collectors, and screenwriters. By this means readers of *DLB* may be aided to perceive literature not as cult scripture in the keeping of intellectual high priests but firmly positioned at the center of a nation's life.

DLB includes the major writers appropriate to each volume and those standing in the ranks behind them. Scholarly and critical counsel has been sought in

*From an unpublished section of Mark Twain's autobiography, copyright by the Mark Twain Company

deciding which minor figures to include and how full their entries should be. Wherever possible, useful references are made to figures who do not warrant separate entries.

Each *DLB* volume has an expert volume editor responsible for planning the volume, selecting the figures for inclusion, and assigning the entries. Volume editors are also responsible for preparing, where appropriate, appendices surveying the major periodicals and literary and intellectual movements for their volumes, as well as lists of further readings. Work on the series as a whole is coordinated at the Bruccoli Clark Layman editorial center in Columbia, South Carolina, where the editorial staff is responsible for accuracy and utility of the published volumes.

One feature that distinguishes *DLB* is the illustration policy–its concern with the iconography of literature. Just as an author is influenced by his surroundings, so is the reader's understanding of the author enhanced by a knowledge of his environment. Therefore *DLB* volumes include not only drawings, paintings, and photographs of authors, often depicting them at various stages in their careers, but also illustrations of their families and places where they lived. Title pages are regularly reproduced in facsimile along with dust jackets for modern authors. The dust jackets are a special feature of *DLB* because they often document better than anything else the way in which an author's work was perceived in its own time. Specimens of the writers' manuscripts and letters are included when feasible.

Samuel Johnson rightly decreed that "The chief glory of every people arises from its authors." The purpose of the *Dictionary of Literary Biography* is to compile literary history in the surest way available to us–by accurate and comprehensive treatment of the lives and work of those who contributed to it.

The DLB Advisory Board

Introduction

Dictionary of Literary Biography volume 240: *Late Nineteenth- and Early Twentieth-Century British Women Poets* is the second of two volumes on British women poets who wrote between 1832 and 1928; the first was *DLB 199: Victorian Women Poets* (1999). The scope of the present volume is the two final decades of the reign of Queen Victoria (1880-1901); the reign of her successor, King Edward VII (1901-1910); and all but the last eight years of the reign of King George V (1910-1936). Only four of the subjects treated in this volume (Amy Levy, Christina Rossetti, Katharine Tynan, and Augusta Webster) and four of those in *DLB 199* (Emily Brontë, Elizabeth Barrett Browning, Dora Greenwell, and Adelaide Anne Procter) appear in *DLB 32: Victorian Poets Before 1850* (1984) or *DLB 35: Victorian Poets After 1850* (1985). That the seventy-five other poets in *DLB 199* and *DLB 240* were not covered in the earlier volumes is an indication of increased scholarly interest in women writers: many of these poets have only recently been rediscovered or given fresh critical attention. In their introduction to *Nineteenth-Century Women Poets: An Oxford Anthology* (1996) Isobel Armstrong and Joseph Bristow write:

> Over the last two decades, researchers have gradually begun to rediscover the work of women poets of the nineteenth and earlier centuries. This process of rediscovery has been one of the most intellectually exciting developments within the field of literary history, and its significance cannot be underestimated. As a consequence, the contours of the literary past begin to change as new relations emerge, both between newly read poems and the largely male canon, and between women poets themselves.

The reigns of Victoria, Edward VII, and George V encompassed significant improvements in women's rights. The introduction to *DLB 199* discusses developments in the earlier part of Victoria's reign, such as the Infant Custody Bill of 1839, the Divorce and Matrimonial Causes Act of 1857, and the Married Women's Property Acts of 1870 and 1882. Throughout the second half of the nineteenth century and continuing through the years of World War I, women found increasing opportunities for education. At the University of Cambridge, Girton College for women was founded in 1869. The Women's Education Union was founded in 1871; in 1872 the Slade School of Art was opened to women. The London Medical College for Women was established in 1874. In 1878 women were admitted to lectures at Oxford, and London University degrees were opened to women. Two Oxford colleges for women, Lady Margaret Hall and Somerville Hall, were established in 1879. In 1893 the requirement that women students be chaperoned to lectures at Oxford was dropped. In 1921 the poet Evelyn Underhill became the first woman to lecture on religion at Oxford.

One of the most important rights obtained by women during the period was the right to vote. The Women's Franchise League, founded in the 1880s, advocated aggressive methods to obtain votes for women. Not all women, to be sure, approved of these developments: Queen Victoria herself regarded campaigns for woman suffrage as "dangerous and unchristian and unnatural," and Christina Rossetti was one of more than a hundred prominent women who signed a public protest letter against the suffrage movement that was published in the periodical *Nineteenth Century* in 1889. Of the poets treated in this volume, Mary Anne Hearn, Camilla Toulmin Crosland, and Margaret L. Woods were also opposed to woman suffrage, while "Michael Field" (Katherine Harris Bradley and Edith Emma Cooper), Eva Gore-Booth, Lucy Knox, Susan Miles, and Bessie Rayner Parkes were active in the campaign for votes for women. In 1903 Emmeline Pankhurst founded the National Women's Social and Political Union. In 1913 there were many suffragette demonstrations in London, and violence loomed; Pankhurst, for instance, was sentenced for inciting rioters to plant explosives in the home of Prime Minister David Lloyd George. Suffragette activities ceased in the summer of 1914, when the assassination of Austrian archduke Francis Ferdinand in Sarajevo led to the outbreak of World War I. After the war ended in 1918, Parliament granted the vote to women aged thirty and above. In 1919 Nancy Witcher Shaw, Lady Astor, became the first woman elected to Parliament. In 1928 the voting age for women was lowered to twenty-one.

The term "the New Woman," coined in 1894 by the novelist Sarah Grand, was used from the 1890s until shortly before the beginning of World War I to describe the new fashions and lifestyles that came into vogue for women during the period. Women were seen riding bicycles on public streets; in 1909 the first permanent waves were given by London hairdressers to women bold enough to experiment with the new artificial look; by 1917 the even more daring style of bobbed hair swept the women's fashion world. The New Woman was unmarried and worked in a middle-class job rather than in domestic service or a factory. Smoking and drinking in public and the wearing of un-Victorian fashions were part of the New Woman's image. Antifeminists often added negative images of stubbornness, irresponsibility, and promiscuity to the concept. The foremost examples of "New Women" in this volume are Michael Field, May Kendall, and Dollie Radford.

In the latter part of the nineteenth century, women often held important editorial positions. Augusta Webster, for example, served as poetry editor of the influential periodical *The Athenaeum*. Several of the poets in this volume were regular contributors to the decadent magazine *The Yellow Book,* including Radford, Olive Custance, Nora Hopper, Rosamund Marriott Watson, and Gore-Booth. Rosa Harriet Newmarch contributed to various journals. In Paris, Nancy Cunard operated her own small publishing firm, The Hours Press.

As the central figure in *DLB 199* was Elizabeth Barrett Browning, in *DLB 240* it is Christina Rossetti. With the exception of the handful who were born a few years before Rossetti's birth in 1830–Crosland, Parkes, Mary Catherine Hume-Rothery, Eliza Keary, Alicia Anne Scott, and Anna Letitia Waring–all of the poets in this volume were born after Rossetti; and all except Cunard, who was born in 1896, were born before Rossetti's death in 1894. Rossetti's immediate circle included Parkes, Annie Matheson, and Katharine Tynan; through the Portfolio Society, these poets exchanged their poems, met regularly, and offered mutual support. Many of the other subjects treated in this volume knew and respected Rossetti's work.

In 1897 Arthur Symons wrote that Rossetti "possessed, in union with a profoundly emotional nature, a power of artistic self-restraint which no other woman who has written in verse, except the supreme Sappho, has ever shown." When Alfred Tennyson died in 1892, there was much speculation about who would succeed him as poet laureate. Lewis Carroll was a firm supporter of Rossetti: "If only the Queen would consult *me* as to whom to make Poet Laureate: I would say 'For once, Madam, take a *lady!*'" (Alfred Austin was named the next poet laureate in 1896.) Rossetti's popularity continued into the twentieth century, with an important edition of her poems published by her brother William Michael Rossetti in 1904. But an anti-Victorian reaction began in the 1920s, and her reputation declined. Between 1930 and 1979 few books or articles were written about her work or life; but in the latter year her poem "Goblin Market" (1862) was the subject of a key chapter in the influential feminist study *The Madwoman in the Attic: The Woman Writer and the Nineteenth-Century Literary Imagination,* by Sandra Gilbert and Susan Gubar, and the poem was freshly viewed as an allegory about the difficulties faced by women in breaking through the barriers erected by male editors and publishers. A variorum edition of Rossetti's poetry, edited by Rebecca W. Crump, was published in 1980. An impressive amount of scholarly work on Rossetti by major critics such as Gilbert, Nina Auerbach, Sandra Margaret Homans, Jerome McGann, Antony H. Harrison, and Dorothy Mermin appeared in the 1980s and 1990s. Feminist literary criticism, in particular, has allowed readers to see new voices, strategies, and subversive turns in her work. In 1994, the centennial of Rossetti's death, the journal *Victorian Poetry* published a special double issue of essays on her, and *Christina Rossetti: A Literary Biography,* by Jan Marsh, appeared. Harrison, whose *Christina Rossetti in Context* was published in 1988, has been editing the multivolume *Collected Letters of Christina Rossetti* since 1997.

While Rossetti is the towering figure of the period under consideration in this volume, the other subjects are by no means devoid of interest. Their poetry ranges widely in theme and style. Kendall, Peggy Webling, and Frances Cornford, the granddaughter of Charles Darwin, wrote about science, including the controversial topic of evolution. Animal-rights and antivivisectionist concerns can be found in the poetry of Bertha Jane Adams and Michael Field, as well as in that of Rossetti. Environmental issues (especially pollution) are treated by Matheson in her poetry. Some women poets devoted their verse to the causes of Irish and Scottish nationalism during this period. Poets who wrote about Irish nationalism or who were considered Irish Revivalists include Gore-Booth, Hopper, Tynan, Emily Lawless, Alice Milligan, Ellen O'Leary, Althea Gyles, Charlotte Grace O'Brien, and Dora Sigerson Shorter. Noted Scottish poets include Violet Jacob and Alicia Anne Scott.

Sexual passion was a major theme in poetry by women throughout Queen Victoria's reign, and some of the poems on the topic were treasured by the queen herself. Peggy and Lucy Webling and Knox explore relationships between men and women, while Michael Field, Custance, and Amy Levy write of lesbian love.

Women poets of the late Victorian, Edwardian, and Georgian periods used a variety of poetic forms, including the lyric, the dramatic monologue, and the sonnet sequence. They sometimes held conversational-style dialogues with one another on literary issues. Examples include Levy's "To Vernon Lee," Field's "To Christina Rossetti," and Parkes's "For Adelaide" (addressed to Procter). Writers of hymns—an enormously popular form in the Victorian era—include Rossetti, Waring, Hearn, Underhill, and Annie Louisa Walker.

Kendall and Peggy Webling used humor to satirize the restraints and hypocrisies of Victorian society, while Adams, Crosland, Underhill, Hearn, Knox, Matheson, and Louisa Baldwin used serious verse to agitate for reform of the conditions of the poor. Adams, Gyles, and Hearn advocated educational reforms in their verse.

Thus, *DLB 240*, taken together with *DLB 199*, fills a need by bringing to the reader the results of the most recent scholarship on a group of female writers who lived in a time of enormous progress for women and who, in many cases, were instrumental in helping to bring about that progress through their work. That work is, however, of interest not only for its connections with social and political developments but also in its own right as literature. The purpose of these volumes will have been fulfilled if they inspire readers to make the effort to seek out the writings of some of these fascinating women.

—William B. Thesing

Acknowledgments

This book was produced by Bruccoli Clark Layman, Inc. Karen L. Rood is senior editor. Philip B. Dematteis and Teresa D. Tynes were the in-house editors.

Production manager is Philip B. Dematteis.

Administrative support was provided by Ann M. Cheschi, Amber L. Coker, and Angi Pleasant.

Accounting supervisor is Ann-Marie Holland.

Copyediting supervisor is Phyllis A. Avant. The copyediting staff includes Brenda Carol Blanton, Allen E. Friend Jr., Melissa D. Hinton, William Tobias Mathes, Rebecca Mayo, Nancy E. Smith, and Elizabeth Jo Ann Sumner.

Editorial associates are Andrew Choate and Michael S. Martin.

Database manager is José A. Juarez.

Layout and graphics supervisor is Janet E. Hill. The graphics staff includes Karla Corley Brown and Zoe R. Cook.

Office manager is Kathy Lawler Merlette.

Photography supervisor is Paul Talbot. Photography editors are Charles Mims and Scott Nemzek.

Permissions editor is Jeff Miller.

Digital photographic copy work was performed by Joseph M. Bruccoli.

The SGML staff includes Frank Graham, Linda Dalton Mullinax, Jason Paddock, and Alex Snead.

Systems manager is Marie L. Parker.

Typesetting supervisor is Kathleen M. Flanagan. The typesetting staff includes Patricia Marie Flanagan, Mark J. McEwan, Pamela D. Norton, and Alison Smith. Freelance typesetters are Wanda Adams and Vicki Grivetti.

Walter W. Ross did library research. He was assisted by Steven Gross and the following librarians at the Thomas Cooper Library of the University of South Carolina: circulation department head Tucker Taylor; reference department head Virginia W. Weathers; Brette Barclay, Marilee Birchfield, Paul Cammarata, Gary Geer, Michael Macan, Tom Marcil, Rose Marshall, and Sharon Verba; interlibrary loan department head John Brunswick; and interlibrary loan staff Robert Arndt, Hayden Battle, Barry Bull, Jo Cottingham, Marna Hostetler, Marieum McClary, Erika Peake, and Nelson Rivera.

The editor would like to thank the following graduate students at the University of South Carolina who worked on this book as research assistants: Sarah Barnhart, Brian Gregory, Jason McCullough, Michelle Whitney, and Leean Hawkins. He is also grateful to Patrick G. Scott for gathering photos and materials from the rare books collection at Thomas Cooper Library of the University of South Carolina.

Dictionary of Literary Biography® • Volume Two Hundred Forty

Late Nineteenth- and Early Twentieth-Century British Women Poets

Dictionary of Literary Biography

Bertha Leith Adams
(Mrs. Leith Adams, Mrs. R. S. de Courcy Laffan)
(1837? – 5 September 1912)

Amanda Jo Pettit
University of South Carolina

BOOKS: *Nancy's Work: A Church Story,* as the Author of "Keane Malcombe's Pupil" (B. L. A.) (London & Oxford: Mowbray, 1876);

Winstowe: A Novel, as Mrs. Leith Adams (3 volumes, London: Hurst & Blackett, 1877; 1 volume, New York: Harper, 1877);

Georgie's Wooer: A Novelette, as Mrs. Leith-Adams (New York: Harper, 1878);

Madelon Lemoine, as Mrs. Leith Adams, 3 volumes (London: Hurst & Blackett, 1879); republished as *Madelon Lemoine: A Novel,* 1 volume (Philadelphia: Lippincott, 1879);

My Land of Beulah and Other Stories, as Mrs. Leith-Adams (3 volumes, London: Tinsley, 1880); republished as *My Land of Beulah,* 1 volume (Philadelphia: Lippincott, 1891)–comprises "My Land of Beulah," "Georgie's Wooer," and "Mabel Meredith's Love Story";

Aunt Hepsy's Foundling: A Novel (1 volume, New York: Munro, 1880; 3 volumes, London: Chapman & Hall, 1881);

Expiated: By Mrs. Leith Adams. And Other Stories (London: Groombridge, 1881);

Lady Deane, and Other Stories, as Mrs. Leith Adams, 3 volumes (London: Chapman & Hall, 1882);

Cosmo Gordon: A Novel, as Mrs. Leith Adams, 3 volumes (London: Chapman & Hall, 1882);

Geoffrey Stirling: A Novel, as Mrs. Leith Adams (3 volumes, London: Chapman & Hall, 1883; 1 volume, Philadelphia: Lippincott, 1887);

My Brother Sol Etc., as Mrs. Leith-Adams, 3 volumes (London: Tinsley, 1883);

Bertha Leith Adams

A Song of Jubilee and Other Poems, as Mrs. R. S. de Courcy Laffan (Mrs. Leith-Adams) (London: Kegan Paul, Trench, 1887);

Louis Draycott: The Story of His Life. A Novel, as Mrs. R. S. de Courcy Laffan (Mrs. Leith-Adams), 2 volumes (London: Chapman & Hall, 1890 [i.e., 1889]);

Bonnie Kate: A Story from a Woman's Point of View, as Mrs. Leith Adams (Mrs. R. S. De Courcy Laffan), 3 volumes (London: Kegan Paul, Trench, Trübner, 1891);

The Cruise of the "Tomahawk": The Story of a Summer's Holiday in Prose and Rhyme. By Mrs. R. S. de Courcy Laffan (Mrs. Leith-Adams), Assisted by "Stroke" and "Bow" (London: Eden, Remington, 1892);

A Garrison Romance, as Mrs. Leith-Adams (Mrs. R. S. de Courcy Laffan) (London: Eden, Remington, 1892);

The Peyton Romance, as Mrs. Leith Adams (Mrs. R. S. De Courcy Laffan), 3 volumes (London: Kegan Paul, Trench, Trübner, 1892);

Colour Sergeant No. 1 Company, as Mrs. Leith Adams (Mrs. R. S. De Courcy Laffan), 2 volumes (London: Jarrold, 1894);

The Old Pastures: A Story of the Woods and Fields, as Mrs. Leith-Adams (Mrs. R. S. De Courcy Laffan) (London: Kegan Paul, Trench, Trübner, 1895);

Accessory after the Fact, as Mrs. Leith-Adams (Mrs. de Courcy Laffan) (London: Digby, Long, 1899);

The Prince's Feathers: A Story of Leafy Warwickshire in the Olden Times. A Novel, as Mrs. Leith-Adams (Mrs. De Courcy Laffan) (London: Digby, Long, 1899);

Cruel Calumny, and Other Stories, as Mrs. Leith-Adams (Mrs. De Courcy Laffan) (London: Digby, Long, 1901);

What Hector Had to Say, and Other Stories, as Mrs. Leith-Adams (Mrs. De Courcy Laffan) (London, Digby, Long, 1902);

The Dream of Her Life, and Other Stories, as Mrs. Leith-Adams (Mrs. De Courcy Laffan) (London: Digby, Long, 1902);

The Vicar of Dale End: A Study, as Mrs. Leith-Adams (Mrs. De Courcy Laffan) (London: Digby, Long, 1906);

Poems, as Mrs. De Courcy Laffan (Edinburgh & London: Foulis, 1907);

Dreams Made Verity: Stories, Essays and Memories, as Mrs. De Courcy Laffan (London: Elkin Mathews, 1910);

The Story of the Brotherhood of Hero Dogs, as Mrs. De Courcy Laffan (London: Madgwick, Houlston, 1910);

A Book of Short Plays and a Memory, as Mrs. De Courcy Laffan (London: Stanley Paul, 1912).

OTHER: David Grant, *Metrical Tales, and Other Poems,* edited by Adams as Mrs. Leith-Adams (Sheffield: W. C. Leng, 1880).

SELECTED PERIODICAL PUBLICATIONS–UNCOLLECTED: "Keane Malcombe's Pupil," *All the Year Round,* 15 (February–March 1876);

"Through the Ranks," *All the Year Round,* 10–11 (July 1893–January 1894).

A prolific writer, Bertha Leith Adams was primarily a novelist; she published only two volumes of verse, one in 1887 and the other in 1907. Her poems are by no means innovative in style, but they suggest great feeling and reveal a sensitivity to her surroundings and an active interest in the issues and people of her day.

Bertha Jane Grundy was born, probably in 1837, in the town of Mottram in Longdale, Cheshire. Her father, Frederick Grundy, was a solicitor. In 1859 she married army surgeon Andrew Leith Adams of the First Battalion Cheshire, with whom she began the travels that became the source for much of her writing. The first six months of their marriage were spent in Ireland, during which time Bertha Adams was introduced to the Irish viceregal court and attended parties at the home of the prominent physician Sir Henry Marsh, where she met many of the literary men in Dublin. The whirl of life in Ireland came to an end when the regiment moved to Malta, where the couple's first son, Francis, was born in 1862. Adams sent her son to England during a cholera epidemic that swept through Malta in 1865–1866; but instead of leaving with him, she remained to tend the sick in the battalion. In 1867 the regiment moved to New Brunswick. The Adamses relocated to Guernsey in 1871 and then moved back to Ireland. Finally, Andrew Leith Adams took a staff appointment in the recruiting office at the Horse Guards in London. He retired from the army in 1873 and was appointed professor of zoology at the College of Science in Dublin.

A member of the Royal Society and the author of several natural histories, including *Field and Forest Rambles, with Notes and Observations on the Natural History of Eastern Canada* (1873), Andrew Leith Adams associated with many of the intelligentsia of England, including the famous biologist and Darwinian Thomas Henry Huxley. Bertha Adams called her experiences with the Royal Society a "liberal education." She later told Helen C. Black, author of *Notable Women Authors of the Day* (1893), that at the society's soirées she "used to delight in meeting all the talent of this and many another country," and she held the "very strongest opinions as to the unspeakable advantage that it is to a woman to listen to highly gifted and deeply learned men discussing questions and knowledge of the greatest and most vital importance."

Adams submitted the manuscript for her first story, "Keane Malcombe's Pupil," to Charles Dickens, who accepted it for publication in his *All the Year Round* in 1876. The work began her long connection with the periodical, in which many of her novels first appeared, for the most part anonymously. Her first three-volume novel, *Winstowe*, was published in 1877. *Winstowe* was followed in 1879 by *Madelon Lemoine*, a novel that the *Pall Mall Gazette* found to have "lifelike" characters. In 1879–1880 Adams edited *Kensington Magazine*, in which she published at least one poem by her son Francis, "A Lay of Shrewsberry School." Her *Aunt Hepsy's Foundling* (1880) drew on her experiences with her husband's regiment in New Brunswick; *The Saturday Review* called it "an almost perfect novel of its kind," and the book quickly went into a second edition.

Andrew Leith Adams took a position as a professor of natural history at Queen's College, Cork, in 1878. He died of tuberculosis in 1882. The following year Bertha Leith Adams married the Reverend Robert Stuart de Courcy Laffan, who became headmaster of the King Edward VI Grammar School and Chaplain of the Guild in Stratford-upon-Avon in 1885.

Adams's first book of verse, *A Song of Jubilee and Other Poems*, was published in 1887. The title poem refers to the fiftieth anniversary of Queen Victoria's accession to the throne, which was being celebrated that year. The poem praises Victoria and her empire in a tone that is both reverent and joyful:

> Bringing greeting to our Lady–England's Queen for fifty years;
> Fifty years of strong endeavor, fifty years of purpose high
> Wrought out slowly to fulfilment, years whose record cannot die
> While within one English bosom still the love abideth sure
> Of whatever things are noble, and whatever things are pure.

Throughout the poem Adams presents her nationalism in a religious light, focusing on the queen as the prayerful servant of her nation. As virtuous virgin, wife, and widow, Adams says, Victoria has been the "Royal Lady" of the empire.

Several other poems in the book display a religious reverence in their portrayal of characters in difficult circumstances. "In Time of War" draws on Adams's experience as a soldier's wife to depict the plight of women left behind during battles. Though the refrain says that the "Women are left to weep and pray," the verses show them bravely going on with their lives without their husbands and the fathers of their children. "At the Call of God. A Lay of St. Anne's Lifeboat" also shows women sending their husbands to answer the call of duty. Adams says that the husbands and wives both *"understand"* what must be done "at the call of God": the men who die trying to save the people in the lifeboat are heroes, but so are the women who stay awake through the night, watching and praying.

Two poems are taken from Adams's previously published novels: "Harvest-Tide: A Song" from *Madelon Lemoine* and "Carol" from *Geoffrey Stirling* (1883). Many of the poems in the collection are love poems. "Love's Awakening: An Idyl" dwells on the delights of a kiss, "the new, fond thoughts, and passionate, sweet joy." The speaker slept, and even in her dreams "you kissed me still." She longed to be outside and alone, for she was "stifled with sweet thoughts, and love / ran riot" in her heart. In "Always" the male speaker reminisces about his first meeting with his wife: "About her web of golden hair / The wanton breezes played, / Ah! in that misty evening air / The twilight landscape glimmered fair, / But fairer still the maid." Though both of these poems seem initially to be about the onset of young love, they actually deal with the enduring quality of love as they depict couples walking "hand in hand through life."

A

SONG OF JUBILEE

AND

OTHER POEMS.

BY

MRS. R. S. DE COURCY LAFFAN

(MRS. LEITH-ADAMS).

LONDON
KEGAN PAUL, TRENCH, & CO.
1 PATERNOSTER SQUARE.
1887.

Title page for the first of Adams's two volumes of poetry

In pressing steadily toward the town, she had ignored the wound inflicted by one of the arrows that the robbers shot at her. The heroine resembles Queen Victoria of "A Song of Jubilee" in her willingness to set herself aside for the virtue of her country. Like the queen, she "proved herself true woman," "toiling for the nation's welfare . . . and never weary till the task in hand was done."

A Song of Jubilee and Other Poems was the usually prolific Adams's first publication in four years; her next book did not appear for another two years. Black asserts that bereavements and unstable health contributed to this fallow time. This period also corresponds with the moves of both of her sons, Francis and Harry Beardoe Adams, to Australia. Francis, a journalist, novelist, and poet, had relocated shortly after his first marriage in 1884 because of his health; Harry, a physician, followed in 1888. Francis returned to England in 1889. Harry Adams died in 1892, and in 1893 Francis committed suicide after suffering a hemorrhage brought on by tuberculosis and throat cancer.

Adams's husband developed the boarding side of the King Edward VI School; Black records that boys and young men were constantly in and out of Adams's sitting room. Laffan also widened the curriculum, adding more language and science courses, and he also restored the medieval buildings; with these improvements the enrollment more than doubled, from fewer than forty to more than one hundred. Adams, a pianist, organized evening concerts for the teachers and pupils; she designed the costumes for the plays performed on the annual speech day, and in the early 1890s she wrote a play for the junior boys and composed the accompanying music. In 1889 she published the novel *Louis Draycott: The Story of His Life,* which is obviously influenced by her work at the school. A critic for *The Athenaeum* wrote, "We turn with pleasure to the tender spell and purity of purpose in *Louis Draycott.*" The work was followed in 1891 by *Bonnie Kate: A Story from a Woman's Point of View,* which suggests that the "truest life-dramas" occur after marriage. A reviewer in *The St. James Gazette* noted that there is "something very delightful" in the book. In 1892 Adams, her husband, and a friend collaborated on *The Cruise of the "Tomahawk": The Story of a Summer's Holiday in Prose and Rhyme.* The small volume is a collection of prose, poetry, and illustrations. *A Garrison Romance* (1892) and *Colour Sergeant No. 1 Company* (1894), two of her more popular works, draw on her experiences as a military wife.

In 1889 Adams, who was active in the cause of education for the working class, began giving lectures on literature. She delivered the first, "Fiction Viewed in Relation to Christianity," to the Church Congress at Cardiff. At the Ladies' College in Cheltenham in April

Adams's son Francis, a journalist, novelist, and poet, who moved to Australia in 1884 and committed suicide in 1893

The final poem in the volume, "The Ladey's Ride: A Legend of Brittany," seems to be a companion piece to the first. It relates the legend of a woman who fasts, prays, and pleads with her husband to pardon a group of men who beat his herald. She finally gains his pity, but he gives her the responsibility of reaching the town before the men are executed. She asks some of her knights to accompany her; though they love her, none is willing to risk the "night when the spirits of Hell / Have power o'er earth and sky." As she rides through the night she is followed by the "spirits of hell," but she outrides them. She is then attacked by robbers; she readily gives them her jewels and gold but must ward off further assault. Getting past them at last, she reaches the town at dawn:

> She waves the Pardon high in air
>   (Sunlight flood o'er the ocean shed),
> She hath brought them hope in their despair—
> Then Lady and roan in the castle square
>   Together fall down dead.

1897 she delivered the lecture "Literature as a Profession for Women." Later that year she delivered similar lectures at the Sesame and Pioneer Clubs, both titled "Fictional Literature as a Calling for Women." In October 1897 she spoke at the Cheltenham Workingmen's Club on "The Freedom of the Mind." The late 1890s and early 1900s brought the publication of several more novels and a few collections of short stories. In 1904 Adams had a one-act play, *Their Experiment,* produced, and in 1905 a dramatized version of *Geoffrey Stirling* was performed at the Fulham Theatre.

In 1907 Adams published *Poems,* which includes almost all of the poems from her previous collection and thirty-five new poems and songs; two of the poems not republished in the later collection are "A Song of Jubilee" and "The Ladey's Ride." The volume is divided into four sections. Part 1, "Poems," includes twelve pieces from the previous collection, but the first four poems are new and comprise a group. Though seemingly on different topics, the theme of all four is that of peace or prayers for peace. The first poem, "The Nation's Prayer," while it concerns Queen Victoria, has a strikingly different tone from that of "A Song of Jubilee." Instead of being exultant, the poem is sorrowful, presumably mourning the state of England during the Boer War. The persona speaks for the nation, which takes Victoria's troubles as its own:

> Queen of the tender heart and sympathetic hand—
> A hand stretched out to touch the sorrows of the Land. . . .
> We take *thy* sorrow as if it were our own. . . .
>   The cruel hurt
> That wounds thy gentle heart must wound us too—
> For all thy Nation's love for thee is true
>   And every heart uplifts a prayer to Heaven.

The nationalistic fervor of "The Nation's Prayer" is representative of many of the poems in the volume, and, as in the earlier collection, patriotism is mixed with religious sentiments. "New Years Eve: 1903–4" is another prayer for peace, and the obvious connotation of "Christmas Dawning" is of peace as well. The fourth poem in the set, "The New Century," begs the 1900s to bring "the perfect, shining gift of Heavenly Peace." Adams wants the earth to become fruitful once more after the Boer War: "Let the grass grow above the bare, red earth, / Red with the blood of heroes." While Adams is distressed by the empire's troubles, she does not criticize England's imperialistic policies.

Two of the poems in part 1, "Roses" and "Despairing Grief," are expressions mourning for Adams's dead sons. In "Roses," written the year of Harry Adams's death, the speaker commands the roses she puts on the grave to "do him so much grace," then: "I go my way, and leave him here– / I shed no tear– /

POEMS

BY

MRS DE COURCY LAFFAN

T. N. FOULIS
EDINBURGH AND LONDON
1907

Title page for Adams's second poetry collection

Sorrow like mine is past all speech." Unlike the speaker of "Roses," that of "Despairing Grief" weeps; but, like the other, she hopes to see one day those whom she has lost.

Two poems in part 1 condemn cruelty to animals. In "The Cry of the Dying Vivisector" the speaker is haunted by the memory of the animals on which he has experimented: "Having steeled my heart to their piercing cries," he now wants to "cover their eyes–cover their eyes." Eventually, however, he is touched by the eyes and wants to spare the animals. Before he can "end this cruelty," however, death takes him. "The Coster's Question" tells of a peddler who is jailed for two weeks for beating his already injured donkey. On his way home after his release, the peddler picks up a newspaper and reads a story about a deer that was hunted down and killed. The article details the "cruel chase" and condemns the "idle rich" for their "glorious *sport*." The coster gathers his friends together and says,

> "Mates all, I've got a word to siy," and slid
> His hand across his stubbly head,—"I'll speak out stright. They did
> That spotted moke most shimeful cruel, gentry though they be—
> An' now I arst you this—**What be's the odds 'twixt them an' me**?"

Part 2 of *Poems,* "In Shakespeare Land," includes several poems written for the occasion of William Shakespeare's birthday. During their years in Stratford, Adams and her husband began the annual ceremony of laying flowers on Shakespeare's grave on the anniversary of his birth; what started as a simple institutional event is now an international occasion. Verses such as "God's Twofold Gift," "The Poet's Birthday," and "To the Poet—Greeting!" were probably read at the ceremony. Another poem in this section, "Friends across the Sea," was read by the actor Sir Henry Irving at the opening of a fountain that was given to Stratford-upon-Avon by a Mr. Child.

"A Garland of Song," part 3 of the volume, includes many of Adams's songs, some of which were quite popular. "Goodbye Daddy," circulated during the Boer War, is a touching piece about a boy bidding farewell to his soldier father. The child prides himself in being a "soldier's kiddy every inch," but prays, "Oh God take care of Daddy—Daddy—Goodbye! Goodbye!" In the companion song "Daddy's Coming Home!" the child beats the drum his father gave him before leaving and sings, "Daddy's coming, / Coming—coming home to me!" In "The Hooligan Brigade" a group of soldiers sing a "wild, Imperial song": "Gather them in, / Gather them in! / They're sure to win, / They're sure to win!" The "hooligans" are slum dwellers who have been given the chance to become soldiers for the queen; all they need is "discipline." "Train them and teach them, then give them their fling," the song joyfully declares.

The last section of *Poems,* "In Memoriam," commemorates some of Adams's dead contemporaries—Irving, the musician Charles Hallé, and various statesmen and military officers—as "knights," "beacons," "gallant sons," and "Warrior-Saints." She says that Irving, who was apparently a close friend, had

> The soul of a true knight indeed,
> That gave and gave to every need,
> Largesse of god—and, what should be
> More precious yet—of sympathy?

Adams produced only a few more works between the publication of *Poems* and her death on 5 September 1912. Her obituary in *The Times* (London) said that she died after a long illness and noted a few of her more popular novels, her more recent volume of poetry, and her contributions to *All the Year Round.* While Adams's novels, poems, and songs touched many people of the Victorian and Edwardian periods, she is all but forgotten today.

Biography:

Helen C. Black, "Mrs. Leith Adams," in her *Notable Women Authors of the Day* (Glasgow: Bryce, 1893), pp. 286–298.

References:

"Shakespeare's School: A Brief History of the Grammar School Stratford-upon-Avon," in *William Shakespeare of Stratford-upon-Avon: Brief History, Times and References* <http://www.stratford-upon-avon.co.uk/soawshst.htm>, April 1999;

John Sutherland, "Adams, Mrs. [Bertha Jane] Leith," in his *The Stanford Companion to Victorian Fiction* (Stanford, Cal.: Stanford University Press, 1989), pp. 7–8;

Meg Tasker, *Francis Adams: A Bibliography,* Victorian Fiction Research Guides, no. 24 (Queensland, Australia: Department of English, University of Queensland, 1996).

Louisa Baldwin
(Mrs. Alfred Baldwin)
(8 August 1845 – 16 May 1925)

Linda A. Julian
Furman University

BOOKS: *A Martyr to Mammon,* as L. Baldwin, 3 volumes (London: Swan, 1886);

The Story of a Marriage, as Mrs. Alfred Baldwin, 3 volumes (London: Ward & Downey, 1889; revised edition, London: Dent, 1895);

Where Town and Country Meet, as Mrs. Alfred Baldwin (London: Longmans, Green, 1891);

Richard Dare, as Mrs. Alfred Baldwin, 2 volumes (London: Smith Elder, 1894);

The Shadow on the Blind and Other Ghost Stories, as Mrs. Alfred Baldwin (London: Dent / New York: Macmillan, 1895);

A Chaplet of Verse for Children, as L. Baldwin (London: Elkin Mathews, 1904);

From Fancy's Realm, as Mrs. Louisa Baldwin (London & Edinburgh: Chambers, 1905);

Afterglow, as L. Baldwin (London: Methuen, 1911);

The Pedlar's Pack, as Mrs. Alfred Baldwin (London & Edinburgh: Chambers / New York: Stokes, 1925).

Louisa Baldwin

Louisa Baldwin's early and sustained connection to the Pre-Raphaelite circle and her role as the mother of Prime Minister Stanley Baldwin and the aunt of Rudyard Kipling ensure Baldwin a position of interest to literary critics and historians today. Her novels, stories, and poems give her a more tenuous hold on fame, although they will continue to claim the attention of literary and cultural historians. Her works, many of them for children, include strokes of imagination, inspiration, and technical proficiency, but they also embody heavy-handed moralism, coincidence-riddled plots, wrenched poetic lines, and clichéd figurative language. A third of her poems treat religious subjects less likely to interest modern readers than they did her contemporaries. As a whole, however, her works offer useful insight into the social issues of her day, especially the interaction among social classes and the treatment and roles of women.

Baldwin and three of her older sisters distinguished themselves not only through their accomplishments but also by their rise from the relatively poor household of a Methodist minister to affluence and acclaim through their marriages to talented and influential men. Louisa Macdonald married Alfred Baldwin, whose family owned ironworks, worsted mills, and a tin factory; her eldest sister, Alice, married John Lockwood Kipling, sculptor, writer, archaeologist, linguist, and eventually curator of the Central Museum and head of the School of Industrial Arts at Lahore, India; Georgiana married Edward Burne-Jones, the Pre-Raphaelite artist; and Agnes married Sir Edward Poynter, who became director of the National Gallery of Art and president of the Royal Academy.

Born in Wakefield on 8 August 1845, Louisa, called Louie, was reportedly so named because she was born on St. Louis King Day, while her father was reading about Louis XVI. She was the eighth of eleven children born to the Reverend George Browne Macdonald and his second wife, Hannah, née Jones. A Methodist minister, the Reverend Macdonald was moved every three years–to Sheffield, Manchester, Bristol, back to Sheffield, Birmingham, Leeds, Wakefield, Huddersfield, back to Birmingham, and to London. Among the goods moved each time was the Reverend Macdonald's library of about two thousand volumes.

The children were given a strict Methodist upbringing, their mother even more rigid in her beliefs than their father. The family believed in education, thrift, and worship. Idleness was considered sinful, so the children were kept busy with housework. They were encouraged to read and write, and their mother, who suffered from melancholy, even found time to write verse and prose. They read religious books but also ones by Charles Kingsley, Sir Walter Scott, Charles Dickens, William Makepeace Thackeray, Edward Bulwer Lytton, and Alfred Tennyson. They also treasured copies of the *Quarterly Review, Blackwood's Magazine,* and *Chambers's Journal.* William Shakespeare's plays were unsuitable, however, and the theater was considered wicked. The family did enjoy music, believing song to be a pillar of Methodism, and occasionally they visited museums. Their social life revolved around the Methodist Society.

Her brothers and sisters doted on young Louisa. A nearsighted and somewhat frail child, she was slow in beginning to read and write. She dictated her first story "The History of the Piebald Family," to her older sister when she was about seven. In *The Macdonald Sisters* (1960), a family memoir by her great-grandson, A. W. Baldwin, her brother Fred recounts Louisa's first lines of poetry, the beginning phrases of two unfinished poems: "And down the shady path that devil walked" and "Crash, crash, my soul, like a thunderbolt over the rocks." These lines embody the tone and subject matter of much of her later poetry. By age nine she was at last able to write her own letters, stories, and poems. At the age of ten she was showing her precociousness, sharing with her brother Harry her thoughts on a poem by Tennyson: "I have read Maud through though not carefully; it requires hours of careful study if one wishes to comprehend it."

In 1852 Harry brought home two friends from King Edward's School Birmingham–Edward Jones (later Sir Edward Burne-Jones) and William Morris, both of whom quickly became fond of Louie and remained close to her for the rest of their lives. Burne-Jones often took Macdonald to London's Red Lion Square, where he shared rooms with Morris. There, while Macdonald drew her pictures, Morris would read aloud his work, though she thought he read too loudly and dramatically. Morris paid her a compliment by using her name for one of the four women in his poem "The Blue Closet," a work inspired by a painting of the same name by Dante Gabriel Rossetti. On her eleventh birthday Morris and Burne-Jones took her to call on Rossetti, who presented her with a copy of a sketch by Holman Hunt, inscribed to her for the occasion. In her *Memorials of Edward Burne-Jones* (1904) Georgiana Burne-Jones recalled that to Macdonald, Burne-Jones "talked and wrote in a way that the differences in their age would have seemed to make impossible." In an 1862 letter to her, Edward Burne-Jones encouraged her study of art: "Keep up the drawing. The whole time though, say at the least half the day, and let it be from nature–faces, best of all, because hardest." Inspired by the art of Burne-Jones and Morris, she continued to work hard on her drawing. In 1864 Burne-Jones painted her, Agnes, Georgiana, and Morris's wife, Jane, at Red House, the Morrises' home, in a pastoral watercolor he titled *Green Summer*. Macdonald must also have been working hard at her writing; according to A. W. Baldwin's memoirs, she had one of her stories turned down for publication by a London magazine because it was too long, but in September 1865 *Victoria Magazine* published one of her stories.

On 9 August 1866, in a double ceremony, Agnes married Edward Poynter and Louisa married Alfred Baldwin. Though the grandson of a Methodist minister, Baldwin considered himself a "high church" Anglican. Louisa was less concerned about his religious practice, however, than the fact that he was involved in business, which she considered worldly. Furthermore, she knew that her parents did not particularly like him. Although she had known Baldwin only a month when she agreed to marry him, the marriage remained a strong and happy one. Their only child, Stanley, the future prime minister, was born in August 1867.

For the next sixty years Louisa Baldwin endured lengthy periods of ill health that were never clearly diagnosed. Her husband steadfastly supported her many trips to London physicians and European spas. She had relied on her mother, who lived nearby, to help her with her household during her illness, but when her mother died in 1875, her youngest sister, Edith, came to help manage the Baldwin house. During the late 1860s and the 1870s she worked on novels, sharing her manuscripts with others, including Georgiana and Morris, but it was many years before they were published.

Much of Baldwin's fiction, especially her four novels, concerns the issue of social class. In her first published novel, *A Martyr to Mammon* (1886), an orphan, who has grown up in the care of her late father's ruthless business partner, is tricked into marrying him even though she has fallen in love with his architect. In *The Story of a Marriage* (1889), an upper-class advocate of intermarriage between the classes marries the daughter of a market gardener, forsaking a woman of his own class. When the marriage fails, he is forced to admit he has badly erred. *Where Town and Country Meet* (1891) continues the theme of class intermarriage as an affluent farmer, who has grown bitter and withdrawn over the years, falls in love with one of his young workers. Not yet able to trust another, he tests her honesty, and when she passes his test, he admits remorse and proposes marriage. In *Richard Dare* (1894) a man escapes the humiliations suffered at the hands of his alcoholic blacksmith father, changes his name, and becomes a famous London surgeon. The following year Baldwin's first collection of short stories appeared, and while most of the characters in *The Shadow on the Blind and Other Ghost Stories* are drawn from the middle and upper classes, one story centers on a lower-class farm couple whose son is gifted with clairvoyance.

Baldwin's first book of poetry appeared in 1904. *A Chaplet of Verse for Children* consists of forty-two poems, many of them whimsical celebrations of animals, play, or nature; and others, serious verses about moral issues and religion. Ranging in length from one brief stanza to several pages, all of the poems are rhymed, and most are in either four- or six-line iambic tetrameter. A dog, the months, coins, the seasons, and fairies serve as the voices of some of the poems, though most are from the point of view of a child.

One of the more serious poems is "In War Time," about the Boer War. The poem, four four-line stanzas of rhyming heptameter couplets, repeats the same phrase at the beginning of each stanza; and the four stanzas fill out the first lines with descriptions of battle and patriotic sentiments: "They are fighting hard in Africa and the great guns roar," "They are fighting hard in Africa, and the sharp swords gleam," "They are fighting hard in Africa, Boer and Briton brave," and "They are fighting hard in Africa; when we've won our place / And paid in precious blood, the fighting then will cease." The poem ends with the expectation that after the war Briton and Boer will "learn to know each other as they never knew before." Other poems of a serious nature include "Untaught Thanksgiving," a four-stanza prayer thanking God for nature, food, pets,

Baldwin's husband, Alfred Baldwin, whom she married in 1866

and family; "The End of Search," a three-stanza poem about the needlessness of looking for happiness far away when it is at hand; "Nettle and Dock," a two-stanza warning not to give sick friends plants for medicine, because many are poisonous; and "Spirit of Love," a three-stanza exhortation to Love to "Make me thy dwelling-place!" and "clothe me with thy grace."

In "Fluff's Funeral" Baldwin handles a poem with a serious subject matter in a comic way in order to ease the pain a child might feel on the death of a beloved pet. The poem, with fifteen four-line stanzas of alternating iambic tetrameter and trimeter, rhyming *abab*, details the funeral "in state" of a pet kitten. The children make a coffin, enclose a bit of herring, and take turns carrying the cat to her grave, the coffin "Beneath a girlish pall of white, / For dear Fluff died unmarried." They bemoan the fact that none of Fluff's family attend "Because both relative and friend / Were busy hunting rats."

The longest of the poems is the twenty-five-page "A Masque of the Months," complete with costuming directions for children portraying each of the months. For example, January wears two masks under a hood; February is dressed like a woodcutter; April wears green and has a white lamb at her side; and July wears flame-colored clothes and carries a basket of fruit. Each month speaks in rhymed couplets—some heroic, some tetrameter, and some dimeter—describing nature and

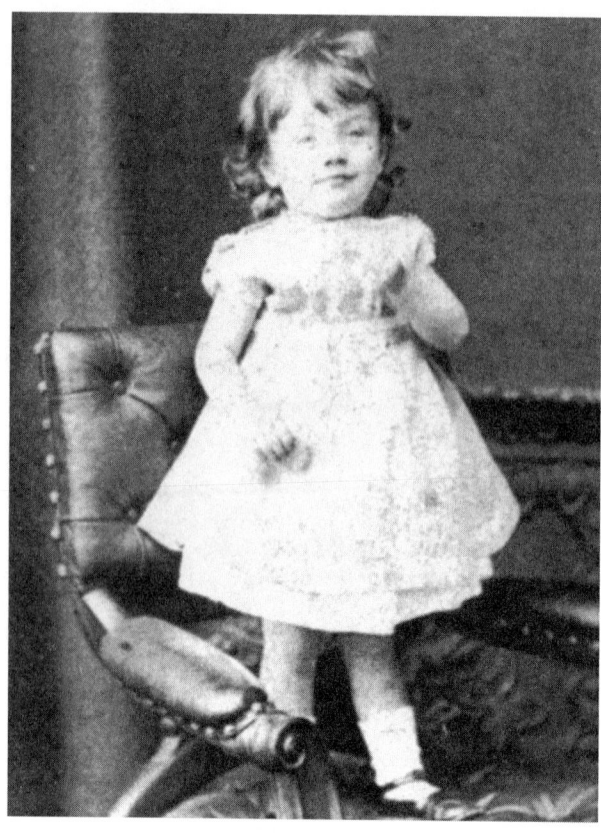

Baldwin's son, Stanley, the future prime minister, at age three

human activities appropriate to the season and generally praising rural life. The December section ends by reminding readers that they should be generous and loving to the poor and needy because "Christ was born on Christmas Day." A reviewer for the December 1904 *The Academy and Literature* praised the book as "full of true 'childishness,' with touches of unstrained sentiment such as a child often shows."

This book of verse was followed by *From Fancy's Realm* (1905), consisting of two long children's stories. "The Giant Baby" is the tale of a farming family's discovery of a giant's baby and their subsequent hardships in taking care of it. "Hubert the Shepherd" recounts the adventures of a boy who vows to give up his firstborn son in exchange for the ability to speak the language of all animals.

Afterglow, Baldwin's only book of poetry for adults, appeared in 1911. The sixty-three poems display uneven competence with several verse types, notably the sonnet, and limited and somewhat predictable subjects. According to A. W. Baldwin's memoirs, she sent several of her sonnets to her famous nephew, Rudyard Kipling, for his critique; he tactfully suggested changes, including the advice to rewrite one of them completely. The poem was not included in the volume. A reviewer writing for *The Athenaeum* (30 December 1911) commented that most of the volume consisted of "rhymed prose, the purport whereof is now didactic, now descriptive." Characterizing the sonnets as "rather heavy" and the humorous poems not "very mirth provoking," the reviewer, nevertheless, identified three of the pieces as "poems indeed": "A Sacrificial Death," "The Speeded Guest," and "Wind and Wave." The eleven heroic couplets of "A Sacrificial Death" describe the death in childbirth of a woman married only a year: she "made an altar of her dying bed, / Whereon she offered up her life to give / Her infant life, and died that it might live." The three-stanza "The Speeded Guest," twelve lines of iambic and anapestic feet, in alternating tetrameter and trimeter (rhyming *abcb*), functions as an extended metaphor that equates the guest at a banquet with a person on life's journey and the "Lord of the feast" with God. The host tells the guest it is time to leave, though the guest is yet unsatisfied: "Though whither I know not I turn me away, / And fearless set forth in the dark." "Wind and Wave," one of the few unrhymed poems in the volume, playfully describes the incoming waves as horses–"Springing, foam-footed, through fields of the sea."

Two poems of biographical interest are those Baldwin wrote in memory of her husband and her sister Agnes. Agnes, who died of cancer in 1906, was commemorated in "Hail and Farewell," included in the first printing of *Afterglow* but not subsequent ones. The sonnet "Afterglow," the first poem in the volume, reveals the author's grief at the sudden death of her husband in February 1908. This English sonnet describes the speaker's desolation and fear and then, in the final seven lines, the coming of hope in the presence of "one arrayed in white" who says that although the brightness of day has been taken, "behold, thou shalt have light enow, / To walk illumined by the afterglow." The failure of this sonnet to yoke the content to the form is common to most of the nineteen other sonnets. Although Baldwin writes in both Italian and English forms and experiments with variations of these, only rarely is there tension between the octave and sestet or resolution in a couplet. One sonnet that does take advantage of the structure is "The Sun God," where the three quatrains explain why the speaker does not worship the sun as he rises in the east or climbs high at noon, and the couplet surprises the reader with "Then as he sinks to his appointed rest, / Then would I bow before the flaming west."

Nine of the sonnets are religious; five are about love or sorrow; and one comments on social issues. One of the most noteworthy poems–because it was written by a woman–is "The Unwilling Warrior," an irregular sonnet equating life to a battle in which the "sword is forced and I must join the fray." Commenting on her own society in "Then and Now," Baldwin devotes ten lines to an idealized view of the courage, integrity, and bravery of leaders in years past, and in the final four lines she condemns the typical leader of her own day as "glib-tongued" and cowardly, adding that "There is no penalty for stirring faction, / He is left basely free as madmen be / To shout wild words that lead to wilder action."

The sonnets appear in a separate section in the middle of the book, surrounded by poems of other forms. Four of the best are "England," "New Style, 1752," "The Pigeon's Feather," and "Creed of the Dull Soul." "England," six four-line stanzas of alternating tetrameter and trimeter iambic feet, rhyming *abab*, expresses the speaker's love of country. This apostrophe to her country says that "With ashes of our hallowed dead, / Flesh of our flesh art thou" and ends by praising the English folk, "Whose strength has passed into the oak, / Whose blood has dyed the rose." In a starkly different tone, "New Style, 1752" is a dramatic exchange between Dick and Tom about the calendar change that year that moved 2 September directly to 14 September, thus eliminating eleven days. In one hundred lines of rhyming iambic tetrameter couplets, the two characters comically question and lament the loss of these days, arguing that the leisured classes who do not mind wasting time should not take it from the hardworking poor: "Why that's no reason they should steal / From them that hasn't time enough / To sneeze or take a pinch o' snuff."

Comprising 298 lines of heroic couplets, "The Pigeon's Feather" is the longest poem in the volume. Believing the superstition that "a sick man cannot die so long as there is a pigeon's feather in his pillow," the ailing protagonist promises the feathers of other birds—which are "Devoid of beauty, freedom, grace / And stifling in this breathless place, / Beneath an aching fevered head"—that if he can obtain a pigeon feather and be cured, he will release them from the pillow. Mysterious circumstances supply the feather, and on his recovery he has the nurse cut open the pillow and scatter the feathers to the winds. Not as odd but also humorous, "Creed of a Dull Soul" is an epistolary exchange in rhyming tetrameter couplets between a man and woman who are arguing about the differences in their philosophies. A businessman who eschews poetry and poetic feeling, he says, "Where you see visions I seek facts. / The rainbow is a fact, *au reste*, / I like my facts uncoloured best." To his assertion that "The world can do without the poet," she replies that she cannot imagine living "Where never fruit of fancy grows, / To beautify your barren facts, / Lending a grace to common acts." She concludes that he has surely exaggerated his depiction of himself and that she wants "to see you bow the knee, / Before the power of poesy."

After her husband's death Baldwin occupied herself with reading to schoolchildren, doing needlework, writing letters and poems, and visiting spas. She lived to see her son's rise to prime minister in 1923. Her final book, *The Pedlar's Pack*, a collection of nine children's stories that includes the two tales of *From Fancy's Realm*, appeared two years later. Most of the tales involve well-known fairy-tale motifs, such as the king who disguises himself to take a vacation, the princess made ugly by a spell not to be broken until an unselfish man finds her, and the king who falls in love with a statue.

Baldwin died on 16 May 1925. At her husband's death she had commissioned a Burne-Jones stained-glass window of Joshua for Wilden Church. To commemorate her own life she had selected a Burne-Jones preliminary sketch of Margaret of Scotland to be executed and installed beside her husband's window; but Morris and Company could not get the colored glass needed for the design, and Morris's window of briar roses was substituted.

Biographies:

A. W. Baldwin, Earl Baldwin of Bewdley, *The Macdonald Sisters* (London: Davies, 1960);

Ina Taylor, *Victorian Sisters* (Bethesda, Md.: Adler & Adler, 1987).

References:

"Baldwin's Mother Dead," *New York Times*, 17 May 1925, p. 17;

Virginia Blain, Patricia Clements, and Isobel Grundy, *The Feminist Companion to Literature in English: Women Writers from the Middle Ages to the Present* (New Haven: Yale University Press, 1990), p. 53;

Georgiana Burne-Jones, *Memorials of Edward Burne-Jones*, 2 volumes (London: Macmillan, 1904);

Keith Middlemas and John Barnes, *Baldwin* (London: Weidenfeld & Nicolson, 1969);

"Mrs. Alfred Baldwin," *Times* (London), 18 May 1925, p. 21.

Mary Butts

(13 December 1890 – 5 March 1937)

Roslyn Reso Foy
University of New Orleans

BOOKS: *Speed the Plough and Other Stories* (London: Chapman & Hall, 1923);

Ashe of Rings (Paris: Contact Editions Three Mountain Press, 1925; London: Wishart, 1933);

Imaginary Letters, illustrated by Jean Cocteau (Paris: Titus, 1928);

Armed with Madness (London: Wishart, 1928; New York: Boni, 1928);

Death of Felicity Taverner (London: Wishart, 1932);

Several Occasions (London: Wishart, 1932);

Traps for Unbelievers (London: Harmsworth, 1932);

Warning to Hikers (London: Wishart, 1932);

The Macedonian (London: Heinemann, 1933);

Scenes from the Life of Cleopatra (London: Heinemann, 1935);

The Crystal Cabinet: My Childhood at Salterns (London: Methuen, 1937; enlarged edition, Boston: Beacon, 1988; Manchester: Carcanet, 1988);

Last Stories (London: Brendin, 1938);

With and without Buttons and Other Stories (Manchester: Carcanet, 1991);

From Altar to Chimney-piece: Selected Stories (Kingston, N.Y.: McPherson, 1992);

Ashe of Rings and Other Writings (Kingston, N.Y.: McPherson, 1998).

Editions and Collections: *Imaginary Letters* (Vancouver: Talonbooks, 1979);

The Crystal Cabinet: My Childhood at Salterns, foreword by Camilla Bagg, afterword by Barbara Wagstaff (Boston: Beacon, 1988; Manchester: Carcanet, 1988);

The Taverner Novels: Armed with Madness and Death of Felicity Taverner (Kingston, N.Y.: McPherson, 1992);

The Classical Novels: The Macedonian / Scenes from the Life of Cleopatra (Kingston, N.Y.: McPherson, 1998).

OTHER: "Corfe," in *An "Objectivists" Anthology,* edited by Louis Zukofsky (LeBeausset, France: Two Publishers, 1932), pp. 36-39.

SELECTED PERIODICAL PUBLICATIONS—
UNCOLLECTED: "The Heavenward Side," *Outlook,* 83 (30 June 1906): 504;

Mary Butts

"Vision," *Egoist,* 5 (September 1918): 111;

"Pythian Ode," *Transatlantic Review,* 2, no. 3 (1924): 235-239;

"Two Poems" ("Give Bread and Drink"; "On Vexui [*sic*]"), *Larus,* 1 (May 1927): 10-13;

"Picus Martius," *Hound & Horn,* 3 (January-May 1930): 230-233;

"Heartbreak House," *Pagany,* 1 (July–September 1930): 1–4;

"Thinking of Saints and Petronius Arbiter," *Pagany,* 2 (January–March 1931): 95–97;

"Rites of Passage," *Pagany,* 2 (July–September 1931): 62–63;

"Douarnenez," *Soma,* 3 (1932): 45–46;

"On An American Wonder-Child Who Translated Homer at Eight Years Old," *Seed,* 1 (January 1933): 9–10;

"House Rhymes by Cecil and Mary" ("The Douglas Credit System," "Hutson's Meals," "Love," "The Bath"), by Butts and Cecil Maitland, edited by Robert H. Byington and Glen E. Morgan, *Art and Literature,* 7 (Winter 1965): 167–169;

"Two Ways of Not Seeing the World," "Parenthesis," and "Avenue Montaigne," *Antaeus,* 12 (Winter 1973): 140, 143, 151–152.

Growing up in Edwardian England under the influence of a Victorian mother, Mary Butts underwent a struggle for identity that mirrored those of other young women of the period. In her review of Mark Perugini's *Victorian Days and Ways,* which appeared in *The Bookman* (May 1932), she wrote,

> To many women I have known, "growing-up" in Edwardian England implied an agonised, ridiculous, exhausting, confusing, nerve-wrecking, complex-forming struggle for the right to grow into the kind of person that she was. . . . And it is a paradox of that extraordinary age, of which the girl's war was one of the death-throes, that it produced the greatest intellectual statement of women's rights to be human beings that the world has ever known. Yet it was not John Stuart Mill, but the European War that did the trick.

Rebelling against her mother, Butts made her own intellectual statement through her writing, one that is often elliptical and difficult and assumes knowledge and attention on the part of the reader. Like William Butler Yeats and H.D. (Hilda Doolittle), she dabbled in the occult; like T. S. Eliot, she intertwined her knowledge of classical mythology with contemporary issues; like James Joyce and Virginia Woolf, she pursued imaginative expression of consciousness. She shared with D. H. Lawrence an interest in primitive religions and nature mysticism and like him, examined relationships that ignored gender boundaries. Butts believed herself to be something of a seer, a mystic who sought to discover what she called "a perception of the nature of the universe as yet unknown to man." Through the use of ritual, myth, and mysticism, Butts's sibylline prose establishes her place among the moderns.

Mary Francis Butts was born 13 December 1890 in Dorset, England, the first child of retired Army officer Captain Frederick John Butts and Mary Jane Briggs, a woman thirty years his junior. For Captain Butts, a widower, it was his second marriage. His first wife and their two sons had died, and in marrying Mary Jane Briggs, he hoped to rebuild a family. Butts's great-grandfather was Captain Thomas Butts, patron and friend of the poet William Blake, and Salterns, her family's home near Poole Harbour, Dorset, housed a collection of Blake's watercolors, engravings, and sketches. She writes in *The Crystal Cabinet* that as a young girl she drew inspiration from these images and became immersed in "the kind of seeing that there was in William Blake." Growing up affluent, Butts would nevertheless exaggerate the social status of her family throughout her life, characterizing it as aristocratic with a pedigree dating back to the twelfth century, a questionable lineage.

Salterns was the center of Butts's early life, and the surrounding Poole Harbour and countryside became her primary source of inspiration. Her father was central to his daughter's early education. Butts attended two local schools, The Haven and Sandecotes, but it was her father who instilled in her a love of learning, provided an education in the classics, and established a passion for the land and a sense of her place within the class of country gentry. He helped create an independence of mind that would later infuse her work and her attitudes toward life.

From an early age Butts recognized her poetic calling. As a young girl, she recalled in *The Crystal Cabinet,* she knew poetry "was the alpha and omega of all writing." The Blake paintings offered her a way to look beyond the external world into an "unseen world" that would help define her poetic and artistic vision. As a young woman, however, she still contended with the constraints of late-Victorian values and expectations, especially from her mother. In one of her early poems from 1909, she aligns herself with mermaids rather than with humans. This identification with the natural world and all its elements and powers began early in her artistic and intellectual career.

When Butts was eleven, her brother Anthony Bacon Drury (Tony) was born. When she was fourteen, her father died, and fifteen months later her mother married Francis Frederick Musgrove Colville-Hyde, an old friend of the captain's. The family adopted the name Colville-Hyde. Butts was fond of her stepfather (she later called him Tiger-Tiger). Yet, her mother, whom Butts considered a different social and intellectual class from her father and who had brought with her a conventional sense of womanhood and women's education that even as a child Butts found

Butts's first husband, John Rodker, whom she married in 1918

offensive, accused her of impropriety with her stepfather. Whether this was true or not (Butts denied the accusation and was profoundly hurt by it), it created a deeper breach between mother and daughter. She was soon sent to boarding school at St. Leonard's School for Girls in St. Andrews, Scotland, where she experienced severe emotional hardship. Accustomed to her own solitude, she had difficulty relating to the interests and concerns of the other girls, yet she was grateful to receive one of the best educations a girl could expect at the time.

The publication of the essay "The Poetry of Hymns" and her poem "The Heavenward Side" in *The Outlook* (1906) marked the beginning of Butts's writing career and revealed the early influence of Blake. "The Heavenward Side" examines the soul of a man passing from life into death who, "in the new country of the soul," discovers a "radiance of bloom." He meets an angel who explains that the bloom is "the heavenward side of your grief," watered with "the bitter dew of tears" on earth. In this early sonnet, Butts lays a spiritual foundation that will permeate all her writing. The relationship between the "seen" and the "unseen" world, the connection between one's "clay tenement" and the "rapture" of a heavenly world are essential concerns that identify the Butts style and mirror the early influence both of Blake (and the Romantic poets William Wordsworth and Percy Bysshe Shelley) and Butts's childhood immersion in the world of nature.

After becoming estranged from her mother and brother, mainly over issues of money, Butts moved to London. She studied at Westfield College from 1909–1912 and continued to write poetry, much of it dealing with her feelings for and relationships with women and the biases of contemporary society concerning sexuality. Butts's biographer Nathalie Blondel notes that between July 1911 and February 1914 Butts filled a notebook with poems written by Mark Drury, a pen name she adopted due to the Sapphic nature of the work. These poems, although not published, marked a significant period in Butts's life. Examining her own Sapphic inclinations in "Ad Maiorem Margaritae Gloriam" (1909), Butts writes about her love for a *flaneuse,* a "child of the streets." This poem examines the attitudes of society toward the sexual openness of such creatures: "They turn their eyes away and murmur 'Bold!'" In 1910 she wrote "A Fragment from Sappho" describing how the "ancient desire / swept and held me." Other poems blend her love of classical literature with the new feelings she was exploring with several close women friends in London.

Much of her poetry at the time also addresses the lack of power possessed by women. In "Vacation Christmas 1911" she juxtaposes the freedom of men who "may go apart" with the "nice poise of small issues" offered to women. Other poems were inspired either by her reading or by her travels to the Continent–Milan, Florence, Venice, and Rome–with her Aunt Ada, apparently to help her forget her unrequited love for Gwen Ingram, a member of the nonresident staff at Westfield College. The sense of rebellion, combined with a unique spirituality, rings loudly in this early, unpublished work.

Butts attended the London School of Economics from 1912 to 1914, graduating with a social-science certificate. She worked with the London County Council, the Children's Care Committee (with the Australian painter Stella Bowen), and the National Council Against Conscription during the early years of World War I. During this time Butts had an affair with Eleanor Rogers and also started her twenty-one years of journal writing, beginning 21 July 1916.

While involved with Rogers and working for the National Council Against Conscription (which in 1916 was changed to the National Council for Civil Liberties), Butts met poet and publisher John Rodker, a conscientious objector and son of Jewish immigrants. She eventually broke things off with Eleanor, married Rodker in 1918, and worked with him at his Ovid Press, whose publications included Ezra Pound's *Hugh Selwyn Mauberley* and Eliot's second book of poetry, *Ara Vos Prec*. In 1918 her second published poem, "Vision," appeared in *The Egoist*. An odd prose poem that reinforces her interest in the mystical and supernatural through the agency of a mouse, "a chinoiserie of the imagination," "Vision" records a moment of insight or lifting of the "liquid veil" before the ring of the telephone jars the narrator back into reality. Her poetry would continue to appear intermittently in many little magazines, including *Transatlantic Review, Larus,* and *The Hound and Horn*. Many of the titles from 1924 through 1933 employ classical images to reflect her continuing interest in classical and anthropological themes such as "Pythian Ode" (1924), "On Vexui" [sic] (1927), "Picus Martius" (1930), and "Thinking of Saints and Petronius Arbiter" (1931).

In 1918 Butts had a failed pregnancy, whether from miscarriage or abortion is unclear, and although she disliked the feeling of being pregnant, she recognized the stirrings of the mystical while in this state. By the end of the year, Butts had met Pound, Wyndham Lewis, Ford Madox Ford, and Roger Fry. She felt herself falling in love with Fry but refrained from sexual infidelity to Rodker. In 1920 she met Cecil Maitland, a Scottish artist and Joyce critic who had been wounded, both physically and psychically, in the war, and he became the major love of her life.

Maitland possessed an interest in magic and the occult that struck a chord in Butts, yet the relationship remained unconsummated because by the end of February 1920, Butts was again pregnant. Her marriage to Rodker was in trouble, and her fascination with Maitland increased. Camilla, Butts's only child, was born on 7 November 1920. Motherhood proved difficult for Butts and for her work; she was also now preoccupied with Maitland's drugs, despondency, and his attempted suicide. By December, Butts and Maitland became lovers. In January 1921, while in Spain, Rodker read a 1920 entry from Mary's diary and discovered her affair with Maitland. When Rodker moved out of their apartment, Butts waited three days, settled Camilla with a friend (Camilla was shuffled around during her early childhood but was finally raised by her great-aunt Ada), and left with Maitland for Paris. Butts had already dabbled with drugs, but Maitland helped deepen her involvement, introducing her to opium, cocaine, heroin, and hashish. He also introduced her to "The Great Beast," Aleister Crowley. After a brief encounter with Crowley's occult group in Cefalu, Italy, Butts became disenchanted with Crowley; however, in spite of the fact that they disliked each other, Crowley respected Butts's knowledge of magic and the occult.

Butts and Maitland spent the next few years traveling, practicing magic, taking drugs, and writing. Butts's daughter and Blondel agree that her personal habits did not interfere with her work. By 1922 her short stories had begun to appear in little magazines. "Speed the Plough," a story about a shell-shocked World War I soldier, was published in the annual anthology, *Georgian Stories*. In 1923, Chapman & Hall published her first book, *Speed the Plough and Other Stories*. Reviews at the time were mixed, as they were with much of her work, but many recognized her mastery of the short story. Glenway Wescott likened the stories to Joyce's *Dubliners* with their emphasis on familial and societal discord, primitive invocation, sharp realities, and oblique style. Included in the collection were "In Bayswater," examining relationships among a mad mother, son, daughter, and lodger that reflect Homeric tragic waste, and "Madonna of the Magnificat," reinterpreting and modernizing the Annunciation of the coming of Christ. Zelda and F. Scott Fitzgerald praised the latter story as one of their favorites, though Butts claimed she wrote it as filler to enlarge the collection at the publisher's request. This collection introduced the complex style that was to define her work, one that would capture the essence of London and Paris in the 1920s and 1930s.

Maitland and Butts pursued their bohemian life in London and Paris until their separation in February 1925. Butts had been writing steadily, and *Ashe of Rings* (1925) appeared from Robert McAlmon's Contact Press in the same year. Written between 1916 and 1919, her first novel, which Butts would later describe as a "war-fairy-tale," merges war with the fairy tale genre to create the major metaphor of the work. With war at the center, Butts mixes autobiographical elements with the world of fantasy, and although she tells us, in the "Afterword" of the 1933 edition, that as a "fairy-story it had to end happily," she recognizes that this ideal would "very likely never have happened." Reviewers once again were not sure what to make of this budding writer's abilities but they compared her to Fyodor Dostoevsky, Joyce, Lawrence, and Dorothy Richardson in an attempt to categorize her work.

Juxtaposing symbols of female transcendence with those of female subversion (along with witchcraft and the occult), Butts creates an uncommon novel that examines the effects of war on the young. Separated into three chronological sections, the novel parallels

Butts with her lover, Scottish artist and critic Cecil Maitland, circa 1921

much of Butts's own childhood and family difficulties. In telling the story of Vanna Elizabeth Ashe's birth, her growth into young womanhood, and her later life in London 1917, Butts reaches back into an enchanted past to resolve terrors of war and to introduce characters who would appear in much of her later work. In the novel, Vanna, an ancient priestess who practices white magic, and her foil, Judy Marston, a practicioner of black magic and witchcraft, battle over the soul of Serge, a white Russian emigré. In the struggle between black and white magic, Butts establishes the thread that will run throughout most of her work—a union of Christian and pagan symbolism that recognizes the power of the authentic adept, a true initiate with an authority drawn from her cultural and racial past. Incorporating ancient myth, ritual, and mysticism, along with the spirituality found in the natural world, Butts creates her modernist vision, one that is consistently optimistic in the midst of a culture flawed by circumstances.

After her separation from Maitland in 1925, Butts continued to live the bohemian life in London, Paris, and Villefranche, accounts of which appear in many memoirs of the time. She moved easily among her fellow modernists but never identified herself with any particular group. A free spirit with bright red hair (which she called "scarlet") and pale skin, Butts made her mark in this avant-garde society.

Her behavior shocked even those whose habits were similar. Letters between H.D. and Bryher, both of whom were good friends of Butts's, acknowledge that her behavior at times amazed many who crossed her path. She continued to write, and at this time she began her novel *Armed with Madness* (1928).

At the Hotel Welcome in Villefranche, a resort on the French Riviera, Butts encountered many artists and writers, including Paul Robeson, Isadora Duncan, and Jean Cocteau. Cocteau became a close friend and illustrated her next novel *Imaginary Letters* (1928); a note by Edward W. Titus, the publisher, states that "it is the first book not written by himself that Cocteau consented to illustrate." An epistolary novel of letters, never sent and never intended to be sent, to the mother of a white Russian emigré, *Imaginary Letters* records the writings of a young woman in Paris. Boris, her love interest, is homosexual, lost, and unavailable. The young letter writer is driven by her fascination with the mixture of cruelty, pain, madness, and beauty that she observes in the lost boy, finding in him a "state of imagination" that somehow initiates the creative process. The letter writer seeks to join with the young boy to heal or penetrate his pain; in doing so, she may find an answer to her own suffering in the wake of World War I. Here Butts writes about homosexuality with an openness and compassion that was not prevalent at the time. She indicates her dislike for Bolshevism and establishes a distinct compassion for those who live outside the norms of accepted society, whether through homosexuality, madness, or simple terror of existence. Butts wrote in her diary that she was interested in finding someone "psychically sick" and discovering a way to heal this illness. She equates healing, dealt with openly and honestly, with the power of her art and gender to transform experience and fuel the imagination.

Armed with Madness also appeared in 1928. Butts's 1927 journal entry states that this novel "might well have been called 'The Wasteland.' Eliot always anticipates my titles. . . . Eliot and I are working on a parallel." A modern retelling of the Grail quest, *Armed with Madness* also comments on postwar modern society. Butts, like Eliot, draws on the themes of death and rebirth central to Jessie L. Weston's *From Ritual to Romance* (1920) the connection between Christianity and paganism, and the power of myth in creating order within the chaos of the modern world. The focus in this novel, set on the Cornwall coast, is the search for spiritual truth as a group of friends discover a jade cup and embark on their quest of mythic proportions. Scylla Taverner, the major female character, and her companions have lived through the war, but they mourn the loss of their privileged social and economic security. They live in a reality whose adventures, as Scylla observes, "are like patterns of another adventure going on somewhere else all the time. . . . For another of its names is intellectual beauty, and another, the peace of God." Frozen in a sacred game and isolated from the events of World War I, the characters are living inside a work of art in an attempt to escape from the real world. Their only armor is madness.

As in *Ashe of Rings* and many of her short stories, Butts reveals her knowledge of ancient mysteries and ritual practice, one that she had acquired in her study of Greek and Latin, the work of Jane Ellen Harrison and the Cambridge Ritualists, and Sir James Frazer's *The Golden Bough* (1890). While one contemporary review found it a failure as an attempt to integrate the Grail myth into modern literature, poet Marianne Moore recognized its worth and acknowledged Butts's ability to sympathize with the souls of a lost generation.

During 1928 Butts returned to London, intermittently saw her daughter, Camilla; visited her old school, The Haven (which she wanted Camilla to attend); took short trips to Bruges, and continued to write essays and work on her novels and short stories. Butts was recovering from a relationship with Sergei Maslenikof, a Russian exile and a homosexual (probably the source of the character Boris in *Imaginary Letters*). By 1929 she returned to Paris and renewed a relationship with Mireille Havet, a French poet and writer she had met in Villefranche earlier that year, and she helped Havet through his excessive drug addiction. She also encountered Gabriel Aitken, an English artist, alcoholic, and a homosexual, whom she had met earlier in Paris and again in Villefranche. Butts's own drug habit had progressed from opium to heroin and was beginning to take its toll on her health. She had, however, been working steadily for months. Aitken invited her to St. Malo, a medieval harbor town on the coast of Brittany, and during her stay and slow recovery, she fell in love with him. The natural landscape of the town, combined with her own fascination with mana (the elemental force that one tries to acquire from a totem animal or god) and magic, helped refresh her imagination.

Physically handsome, Aitken had a history of difficulties with constancy, but for a brief time Butts's affair with Aitken was passionate and physical. In her diary she records praying at the Cathedral in St. Malo that their love would survive. Aitken needed the encouragement and devotion that Butts supplied. By the end of 1929, both of them were having difficulties with family inheritances. She returned to Paris, spent time in London visiting her mother, her brother, Tony, Camilla, and Rodker. She corresponded with Aitken during this time, disagreed with her mother and brother over the proceeds of a sale of a Hans Holbein painting that was part of her family's estate, returned to Paris on 1 January 1930, and spent the next five months in Paris. Though Aitken's alcoholism strained their relationship, Butts continued working on her poetry, short stories, and her next novel, *Death of Felicity Taverner* (1932). Both had troubles with money and depression; drugs offered only temporary respite and increased their depression. Saved from a total breakdown by visits from friends, including Rodker, Butts became increasingly ill and dunned by creditors. Her mother tried to convince her to enter a nursing home, but eventually Butts returned to England to stay with her in London. Butts's reviews, poetry, and stories continued to appear in many little magazines including *The Egoist*, *Transatlantic Review*, *Pagany*, *The Little Review*, *The Dial*, and *The Hound & Horn*.

By the middle of 1930 Butts had nearly completed *Death of Felicity Taverner*. Although she recognized that her mother had saved her life, they soon quarreled once again. On 29 October 1930, she and Aitken were married in London. Spending six months in the house of a friend in east Sussex, they started their married life together, and while she worked diligently on her writing, she slowly began to heal physically. She and Aitken traveled within England for the next few months though money was still a concern. In mid 1931, Aitken underwent a tuberculosis cure in Switzerland and then returned to England. The couple apparently got on well except for certain indiscretions of Aitken's supposedly homosexual encounters.

They traveled to Newcastle in July 1931, where Butts found inspiration for her pamphlet, *Warning to Hikers* (1932), calling for conservation of the English countryside. Also in Newcastle she finished several stories, assembled a list of possible stories for an upcoming collection, and wrote several reviews for Hugh Ross Williamson, editor of *The Bookman*. She also wrote *Traps for Unbelievers* (1932), a pamphlet about the state of religion in her contemporary world. At the end of 1931 she discovered that Eliot at Faber and Faber had rejected her manuscript on the life of Alexander the Great, *The Macedonian* (1933), because, in spite of its obvious merits, it would not draw a large enough public.

In January 1932 Butts and Aitken moved to Sennen Cove in Cornwall, near Land's End, where she lived for the rest of her life. That year several of

Butts on Dancing Ledge, Dorset, in 1922

her works were published. *Death of Felicity Taverner,* a sequel to *Armed with Madness,* again explored the power of the female spirit, this time in the character of Felicity Taverner. In this detective story about the death of the title character, Butts invokes primitive ritual as an answer to her characters' confusion and pain. As the novel opens, Felicity, although dead, is at the center of the plot that involves a complicated struggle between her family and Felicity's husband, Nick Kralin, a Bolshevik, a blackmailer, and a Jew. After a struggle over Felicity's inheritance of land sacred to the Taverners and a threat from Kralin to destroy the purity of her image and the purity of the land itself, the plot shifts to myth and ancient ritual as a way to justify the murder of Kralin, the "Grey Thing" that threatens all that is good and pure. Imbuing her novel once again with the work of Frazer and Harrison, Butts creates an allegory of good versus evil in an attempt to protect the community and the past. The fear of technological progress, the menace of commercial development of the land, and the threat of destruction of the "bosom of Nature" all combine to express Butts's concerns for the sacredness of the English countryside–the same ideas that she communicates in her pamphlet *Warning to Hikers.*

The year 1932 also marked the publication of her second book of short stories, *Several Occasions.* This collection included several strong stories about life in the 1920s: "In Bloomsbury," "The House Party," "Widdershins," "Brightness Falls," and "Friendship's Garland." Most of her stories employ mythic themes to enhance and examine the world in which she moved. John Ashbery, Robin Blaser, Robert Duncan, and other poets have commented on the strength of her short stories, claiming that their cinematic and elliptical style makes her work contemporary with the 1990s.

In mid-May of 1932, Butts's trustees bought her and Aitken a bungalow that Butts dubbed "Tebel-Vos," a Cornish name meaning something like "House of Magic." She came to equate this area near Sennen Cove in Cornwall with her childhood home at Salterns. Her poetry continued to appear, including the important poem "Corfe," a poem about Corfe Castle in Dorset that Louis Zukofsky included in *An "Objectivists" Anthology* (1932). Although written some time in the 1920s, this poem resonates with nearly all of Butts's major concerns. The qualities of Corfe Castle–its history and ability to endure the ravages of time–represent the same ideas Butts promotes in *Death of Felicity Taverner* and *Warning to Hikers:* "God keep the Hollow Land from all wrong! / God keep the Hollow Land going strong." Anticipating the destruction of the natural world with the intrusion of tourists and technology, Butts offers a call to embrace the past, present, and eternity. The influence of Blake, Yeats, and Wordsworth all meet in her apocalyptic vision of the future, and she pleads for preserving or stopping time. The lines "sea orchestrates / The still dance in the cup" anticipate Eliot's "still point in the turning world" (which would not appear until "Burnt Norton" in 1935).

In February of 1932 Butts received word that her novel on Alexander the Great was again rejected, this time by Cape; however, by mid-April she learned that Heinemann would publish the newly titled *The Macedonian* the following year. During the summer of 1932, she also made up a list of stories for a third collection to be published by Wishart. She continued writing reviews and produced an article on supernatural fiction. Also in 1932 she received word that an article she had started in 1928, "Ghosties and Ghoulies," would be published the following year in four installments of *The Bookman.* (It was republished in book form in *Ashe of Rings and Other Writings* [1998].) With the appearance of her two pamphlets, a second collection of short stories, and *Death of Felicity Taverner* by the end of 1932, the year had proved one of her most productive.

Though she was enjoying professional success, conflicts with her mother and her brother, Tony, continued over money and the sale of a portion of her family's estate. Meanwhile her daughter, Camilla, was growing up under the care of her mother and her aunt. Camilla had not spent much time with either of her parents, but Butts managed to find time for a summer visit at Sennen Cove. Camilla had a difficult relationship with her mother, who offered the child little motherly care and who considered writing her first priority. Butts was usually exhausted by a visit from the child and after any extended stay, eager for her departure. The emotional neglect that Camilla received from her mother and her father were, at least in most important ways, soothed by her relationship with her great-aunt and her grandmother.

Although Butts was making many friends during this time and producing some of her best work, her marriage with Aitken was failing. She was constantly disappointed with his lack of commitment to his art, his alcoholism, and his general weakness of character. In March 1933, *The Macedonian* appeared to good reviews, but in the same month, Aitken left Tebel-Vos for a visit north, and by the end of 1934 they were no longer living together as husband and wife. By March of 1934, Butts had finished her second historical novel, *Scenes from the Life of Cleopatra* (1935). Both novels were a success and pursued ideas that would have moved the writer in a new direction had she lived.

Butts's reconstruction and reinterpretation of historical figures reflected not only her unique vision of classical ideals but also projected a modern view of how history should be written. Her scholarship is clearly obvious, while her vision of these great figures emphasizes their spirituality and historical inheritance. If *The Macedonian* explores Alexander the Great's recognition and acceptance of a spiritual force within himself, her *Scenes from the Life of Cleopatra* presents a woman who uses her inheritance and her sexuality as a road to power and independence, an obvious connection and identification with Butts herself and her racial inheritance. In the 1935 appendix to *Scenes from the Life of Cleopatra*, Butts writes, "men–historians or not–do not like to think, and so refuse to believe, in an active woman alone, enjoying the use of power." Her Cleopatra is a clever queen conscious of her power and position as female and goddess, one connected, like Alexander the Great, to myth and divinity.

As early as 1933 Mary Butts had rediscovered faith. Though she continued her drug habit, she attended the church at Sennen Cove and befriended Father Bernard Walke, the vicar of the church of St. Hilary. Butts took on the battle to save the church for Father Walke and the community. Her remaining years were extremely productive. Her longtime friendships with Scottish writer Angus Davidson, American writer Harcourt Wesson Bull, and writer and musician Frank Baker would be important ones until her death.

Early in 1935 she was busy writing the autobiography of her childhood, *The Crystal Cabinet: My Childhood at Salterns*. Taking its name from a poem by William Blake, *The Crystal Cabinet* records the events of Butts's early life, the happy years with her father until his death, the difficulties between her and her mother, the love of and growing estrangement from her brother, and her identity with her sacred Dorset home. In 1935 she also began a third historical narrative about Julian the Apostate, but she was unable to complete it. *Scenes from the Life of Cleopatra* appeared this same year and received a good deal of attention for what some reviewers identified as her "woman's angle."

The following year was a difficult one with periods of ill health, continued family disagreements, and problems with publication of *The Crystal Cabinet* (Heinemann turned it down supposedly for fear of libel action from Butts's family). Butts quarreled with the few friends she had made in Sennen Cove. She did, however, write many reviews and several essays, one insightful account of "Bloomsbury," and continued work on a book on Julian the Apostate. Her health was failing again, she had a recurring knee problem that gave her trouble walking around Cornwall, and she was in serious need of money. The Holbein painting had been sold, but her mother made a settlement that stipulated the money could come to her only after the death of her younger brother and his children, if he had any. This decision increased Butts's antagonism toward her mother. Her attempt to save St. Hilary for Father Walke and the High Church services also failed, but she continued to attend services for the fun of the squabble among the parishioners. Sennen Cove was beginning to be commercially developed, as she had so clearly foreseen in *Death of Felicity Taverner*, and her health continued to deteriorate. Still she proceeded to write short stories and to develop ideas for other works in progress.

Butts also continued to write and publish poetry through her later years, some of it parodies of Eliot's work, such as "Thinking of Saints and of Petronius Arbiter" (1973). The poem "Two Ways of Not Seeing the World" suggests the American poet Wallace Stevens's "Thirteen Ways of Looking at a Blackbird." Although Blondel gives no date for "Two Ways of Not Seeing the World" and Stevens's poem appeared in 1917, Camilla Bagg is certain that Butts knew the work of Stevens. Most of her poetry, however, reflects her concerns of the dual nature of existence, the reality of two worlds ("seen" and "unseen"), and the power of mana–that energy or life force central to all of her work.

Butts found solace in her final days by returning to her past and to the English landscape. One journal entry from 1927 best reflects her lifelong desires: "What apart from the specific work of writing is what interests me? Nothing but spiritual development, the soul living at its fullest capacity. That is the lever, the new synthesis, or vision or faith." This "new synthesis" resounds throughout her writing, cradled in her unique and enigmatic style.

In January 1937 she made out her will, although there was no sign of imminent death from her illnesses. She was still smoking opium and began drinking Champagne Wine Nerve Tonic. She asked her mother for a loan to go to London, but Mary Colville-Hyde refused, having been asked far too often. In February, T. S. Eliot rejected a story, "Mappa Mundi," for *The Criterion* but expressed interest in a collection of short stories for Faber and Faber. She answered Eliot's request and offered to send him a selection of stories. Meanwhile, she wrote to Aitken, from whom she had separated but had not divorced, expressing regret that he had never offered hope for reconciliation.

Butts collapsed at Tebel-Vos and was rushed to West Cornwall Hospital in Penzance, where she died on 5 March 1937 after an operation for a gastric ulcer. Aitken registered her age as forty-four; she was actually forty-six. On 22 March 1937, Davidson, Butts's literary executor, sent thirteen complete stories to Butts's literary agent, Leonard Moore, who was then to forward them to Faber and Faber. Davidson also sent a list of the stories to Eliot, saying that the stories themselves would soon follow. Eliot acknowledged receipt of Davidson's letter, but Blondel, Butts's biographer, explains that there is no record of the stories ever arriving at Faber and Faber or of Eliot's rejection. Had Faber and Faber published Butts's stories, there is no doubt that her reputation would have been secured.

In 1938 Bryher, who owned the Brendin Publishing Company, published Butts's thirteen stories, which had been collected for Faber and Faber, as *Last Stories*. This collection included two of her best stories, "From Altar to Chimney-piece" and "With and without Buttons"; neither story had previously appeared in print, but each became the title selections of the two volumes of her stories published in the 1990s. "From Altar to Chimney-piece" is Butts's scathing indictment of Gertrude Stein and her salon. "With and without Buttons" is a delightful tale that lures its readers to question the reality of the supernatural. In 1945 Camilla Rodker Bagg inherited her mother's papers and journals, which Butts had kept from 1916 until her death in 1937. After several years of wrangling, Camilla refused Norman Holmes Pearson's request to place the papers at the Beinecke Rare Book and Manuscript Library at Yale University–along with those of other major modernists, including Pound, H.D., Eliot, and Stein. It was only in 1998 that Camilla finally agreed to have the papers go to the Beinecke after all. Along with the journals and letters there is an unpublished novel titled "Unborn Gods" about men and sex, additional poetry, and the unfinished "Julian the Apostate." Interest in her work continues to grow, and with the recent reissuing of her novels, stories, essays, and autobiography, her place in literature seems assured.

References:

Nathalie Blondel, *Mary Butts: Scenes from the Life* (Kingston, N.Y.: McPherson, 1998);

Roslyn Reso Foy, *Ritual, Myth, and Mysticism in the Work of Mary Butts: Between Feminism and Modernism* (Fayetteville, Ark.: University of Arkansas Press, 2000);

Marianne Moore, "A House Party," *Dial,* 85 (September 1928): 258–260;

Christopher Wagstaff, ed., *A Sacred Quest: The Life and Writings of Mary Butts* (Kingston, N.Y.: McPherson, 1995).

Papers:

Mary Butts's papers are in the Beinecke Rare Book and Manuscript Library at Yale University.

Frances Cornford
(30 March 1886 – 19 August 1960)

Ashley Brown
University of South Carolina

BOOKS: *Poems* (Hampstead, London: Priory, 1910);
Death and the Princess; a morality (Cambridge: Bowes, 1912);
Spring Morning (London: Poetry Bookshop, 1915);
Autumn Midnight (London: Poetry Bookshop, 1923);
Different Days (London: Hogarth Press, 1928);
Mountains and Molehills (Cambridge: Cambridge University Press, 1934);
Travelling Home and Other Poems (London: Cresset, 1948);
Collected Poems (London: Cresset, 1954);
On a Calm Shore (London: Cresset, 1960).

TRANSLATIONS: *Poems from the Russian,* translated by Cornford and Esther Polianowsky Salaman (London: Faber & Faber, 1943);
Paul Eluard, *The Dour Desire to Endure,* translated by Stephen Spender (Philadelphia: Grey Falcon Press / London: Trianon, 1950);
Fifteen Poems from the French (Edinburgh: Tragara Press, 1976).

Although Frances Cornford essentially remained a Georgian poet through a career that lasted half a century, she was sometimes associated with literary figures of the modernist generation and their successors. She was, after all, a contemporary of T. S. Eliot and Ezra Pound, Marianne Moore and H.D. (Hilda Doolittle)–the latter born in the same year, 1886. These poets were Americans who lived in London mainly to make poetry new (in Pound's famous phrase), whereas Frances Cornford was born and grew up in a brilliant intellectual milieu in Cambridge University. In their youth both she and Virginia Woolf were close friends of Rupert Brooke, a glamorous Cambridge poet who died in 1915, but Cornford and Woolf lived in different worlds. Their chief association seems to have been in the late 1920s, when Leonard and Virginia Woolf published Cornford's fourth volume of verse, *Different Days* (1928), through their Hogarth Press. Woolf knew John Maynard Keynes, the economist and a prominent member of the

Frances Cornford

Bloomsbury group, while Cornford was closer to his brother, Sir Geoffrey Keynes, a distinguished surgeon and an authority on William Blake. He wrote Cornford's obituary for the *Dictionary of National Biography* based on his personal knowledge of her.

Cornford's family connections linked her with several famous people, mostly from Cambridge. Born

Frances Crofts Darwin on 30 March 1886, she was, on her father's side, a granddaughter of Charles Darwin; her father, Sir Francis Darwin, was a reader in botany at Cambridge University. Her mother, Ellen Wordsworth Crofts, was a great-niece of the poet William Wordsworth and a lecturer at Newnham, one of the first women's colleges at Cambridge. Ellen Darwin died when Frances was seventeen. One might suppose that Frances would have followed her parents into an academic career, but she was privately educated, according to Geoffrey Keynes, and did not attend the university. Her education was thus much the same as Virginia Woolf's. The idyllic world of the Darwins and their friends in Cambridge was described many years later by her cousin Gwen Raverat in a charming memoir titled *Period Piece* (1952), which is dedicated to Frances.

In the summer of 1908 Frances Darwin assisted in a production of John Milton's *Comus* (1637) at Christ's College as part of a Milton tercentenary celebration. There she became romantically involved with the actor playing the lead, Francis D. Cornford, a fellow of Trinity College and later professor of ancient philosophy in the university. Twelve years older than Frances Darwin, he was one of the great classical scholars of his time. The couple were married in 1909. According to Keynes, their home in Cambridge became a center of hospitality for such intellectual figures as Bertrand Russell and Goldsworthy Lowes Dickinson, as well as the setting for their family life, which would include five children.

Cornford had been writing poetry since she was a young girl, and her creativity was encouraged by her family. At the same time she accepted the criticism that her friends, especially Brooke, one year younger, offered her. Both planned to publish their first books in 1910, but Frances's appeared first. Perhaps her quiet domestic existence in Cambridge gave her the advantage. Brooke, at this point in his life, traveled widely. He was certainly more ambitious, and his early death during World War I made him a celebrity. In 1915 the Cornfords named their first son, Rupert John Cornford, after him; this boy would himself become a poet who was killed in another war and who had a small posthumous fame.

Frances Cornford's first book, titled simply *Poems*, was published by a small press in Hampstead in northern London. In her *Collected Poems* of 1954 these earliest poems are titled "Juvenilia," and she remarks in the preface of the book that the first of the eight poems that she preserved from this early volume–"Autumn Morning in Cambridge"–was written in 1902, when she was only sixteen. Even though the poem is a slight production, it has some of the recurrent features of the verse that she would write during the remainder of her life:

I ran out in the morning, when the air was clean and new
And all the grass was glittering and grey with autumn dew,
I ran out to an apple-tree and pulled the apple down,
And all the bells were ringing in the old grey town.

Cornford almost invariably wrote rhymed stanzas, frequently in the form of couplets, but after this first poem she nearly always used shorter lines than these hexameters. Cambridge is the setting for many of her poems, and autumn is a favorite season, suggesting a typically elegiac tone. The versification is competent; for instance, "old grey town" with its three successive stresses is good work for a sixteen-year-old.

Frances Cornford's finest verse was written in short forms, similar to those used by Walter Savage Landor (1775–1864), and these poems have survived best in anthologies. One of her earliest, simply titled "Youth," has had a certain fame, because it describes Brooke as he appeared to the poet around 1907:

A young Apollo, golden-haired,
   Stands dreaming on the verse of strife,
Magnificently unprepared
   For the long littlements of life.

No biography of Brooke would be complete without this epigram, which is included in Cornford's *Poems*. In retrospect it seems ironic that the youth should be "on the verge of strife," since he would die within a few years against the background of World War I–although not in battle.

Another short poem from the first volume, "To a Fat Lady Seen from a Train," has been frequently anthologized, sometimes in the category of light verse:

O why do you walk through the fields in gloves,
   Missing so much and so much?
O fat white woman whom nobody loves,
Why do you walk through the fields in gloves,
When the grass is soft as the breast of doves
   And shivering-sweet to the touch?
O why do you walk through the fields in gloves,
   Missing so much and so much?

As the poet notes below the title, this is a triolet, a verse form that she favored; she returned to it occasionally in her last books. It came into English from medieval French, and indeed it would probably be easier to write in French because of the strict form. Composed of eight lines, the triolet consists of only two rhymes, always used in the way that Cornford uses them here. The intricate rhyming pattern presents a slight difficulty, partly because the rhymes could be obtrusive. To write a graceful triolet would be something of a challenge. The old form fell out of use after the fifteenth century but was revived by late-nineteenth-century poets in

France and then by Robert Bridges in England during Cornford's youth. Her quiet humor, a frequent feature of her work, and a certain sympathy for the woman in the fields are revealed in this, her most famous poem.

Another French (originally Italian) verse form that Cornford occasionally used was the villanelle, which is even more demanding than the triolet. Its structure is based on five tercets and a quatrain, during the course of which two lines are repeated three times. The repeated lines carry the weight of the poem, and they obviously must have a certain resonance and take on a slightly different meaning with each repetition. Cornford had already mastered this form by 1908, the date of "London Streets," one of her few urban poems. One of the repeated lines is taken from a phrase in prose by her grandfather, Charles Darwin: "The blundering and cruel ways of nature." This phrase is the only instance in her poetry where the famous ancestor figures. The Darwins and the Crofts belonged to the liberal intelligentsia of the nineteenth century, and in theological matters they tended to be agnostic. Consequently, the phrase from Darwin has a certain ambiguity about it. In his obituary of her, Keynes states that Cornford "had not been christened as a child and was brought up without religion." He also refers to her cousin Raverat's *Period Piece*, noting that "Frances began to suffer at an early age from doubts, and long before death had accepted with deep conviction the faith of the Church of England." This early villanelle is the personal statement of a young person who is trying to find her bearings in a congenial but demanding intellectual milieu. As a formal achievement, her villanelle is remarkable for 1908. In a later generation William Empson, W. H. Auden, and Dylan Thomas would write famous villanelles, and eventually so would Elizabeth Bishop, but one should give credit to Frances Cornford for being a precursor.

Her second volume, *Spring Morning*, was published in 1915 by the Poetry Bookshop in London. The establishment had recently been founded by poet Harold Monro to promote and publish the work of the Georgians, poets of a deliberately pastoral tendency even though they may have lived in central London and enjoyed the countryside only on weekends. Monro had somewhat eclectic interests, and his Poetry Bookshop was a gathering place for a few of the Americans who had been living in London, such as Conrad Aiken. Cornford must have been introduced to many literary figures at the Poetry Bookshop; the most notable was Sir Edward Marsh, a man of letters who moved in public circles and at one time served for many years as secretary to Winston Churchill. In the 1910s and 1920s he included her

Cornford (center) with her family in 1928; on left, her husband, Francis, holding their daughter Clare; behind them, their daughter Helena; on right (from top), their sons John, Christopher, and Hugh

work in his *Georgian Poetry* series. Cornford dedicated her *Collected Poems* of 1954 to Marsh's memory.

Collected Poems retains only four brief poems from *Spring Morning*. Cornford may have been rather severe in editing her early verse. Her skill in versification, however, is evident in the first of three quatrains in "A Waster Day":

I spoiled the day;
Hotly, in haste,
All the calm hours
I gashed and defaced.

Lines in iambic dimeter are not easy to write effectively in English, even in a poem of only twelve lines. Cornford, however, has only one regular line, the first, after which she syncopates the rhythm in various ways. The strongest word in the poem, "gashed," is not the true monosyllable because its cluster of consonants must be forced into one syllable, but it successfully brings out the theme of the poem. At this time poets in the United States, such as Wallace Stevens and William Carlos Williams, were experimenting with a kind of controlled free verse in their short poems. Cornford now and then seems to approach this form, but she always uses traditional means of varying her rhythmic base. For some British poets in her generation, who usually had an excellent classical education, the so-called Greek anthology of short elegiac poems was a model. She refers to it in poems in her last book, *On a Calm Shore* (1960). In 1907 a selection of the poems had been translated by J. W. Mackail.

The ten poems that survive from *Autumn Midnight*, her third collection, published by the Poetry Bookshop in 1923, show no remarkable change in theme and technique. The book includes well-wrought short poems, a villanelle, the title poem in iambic pentameter couplets, and "A Lodging for the Night," a somewhat bold dramatic monologue in hexameters. The speaker, an old woman, imagines that the spirit of a recently dead child has come to her for comfort, but in the morning he has gone. The situation may have some strong personal meaning for Cornford, the mother of five children, even if it is projected into the genre of the ghost story.

The only poem that refers, even indirectly, to World War I is dated 1915. When published in *Autumn Midnight* it was called "No Immortality?," but in the *Collected Poems* it is titled "Contemporaries." The poem concerns the death of Brooke, who is never mentioned by name, and the poet's true feelings about him. In his autobiography, *The Gates of Memory* (1981), Geoffrey Keynes includes an earlier version of the poem in manuscript titled "Rupert Brooke." Cornford wrote the poem in April 1915, soon after Brooke's death that month. (He died of blood poisoning on a troopship and was buried on one of the Greek islands.) One might have guessed, knowing that Cornford was closely associated with Brooke, that he is the youth being celebrated in the poem, even though the revised version, by its successive changes of title, seems to put a certain distance between her and Brooke. Running twenty-three lines, the revised poem is superior to the manuscript version. In both versions the poet invents an anonymous Greek boy who dies (perhaps in the vicinity of Brooke's grave) a thousand years ago. The poem concludes with the lines:

> Of him
> Now we know nothing, nothing is altered now
> Because of all he was. Most loved, on you
> Can such oblivion fall? Then, if it can
> How futile, how absurd the life of man.

Over the years Cornford found more of her work that she deemed suitable for perpetuating in the *Collected Poems*. In 1928 Leonard and Virginia Woolf published her collection *Different Days*, sixteen of the poems that she included in the later collection. She continued to write poems about Cambridge, and autumn was still her favorite season. Two poems—"Mediterranean Morning" and "A Stranger in Provence"—celebrate the landscapes of the world that the wife of a great classical scholar would have found familiar. One fine poem, "Words for Music," celebrates the Elizabethan musician John Dowland, and indeed she works up her poem in ten quatrains from lines by Dowland himself: "Time stands still / With gazing on her face." The title anticipates a series of poems that William Butler Yeats composed under the heading of *Words for Music Perhaps* (1933). Yeats may have taken the idea for this sequence from Cornford; he knew her work well.

By the early 1930s Cornford had a competitor in her own family: her eldest son, John (he never used his first name, Rupert), who was a godson of Keynes. This talented boy was drawn by the age of fifteen to both politics and poetry. He was, according to Keynes, strong-willed and unusually independent in his views: "no godfather could have diverted his drift into the ranks of the Communist Party, culminating in his death in the Spanish Civil War in 1936." A collection of John Cornford's writing was published as early as 1938. In 1966 another collection, edited by Jonathan Galassi, was published.

Galassi's collection includes poems, essays, and more than sixty letters, most of them between John and his mother, beginning around 1930 and ending shortly before his death in Spain. Considerable affection is displayed between mother and son, but John's independence in literary matters is already clear in the title of his first poem in the collection: "This Is the Way the World Ends," with its title borrowed from Eliot's "The Hollow Men" and its imagery partly taken from *The Waste Land* (1922). In his first letter to his mother he expresses his dislike of Alfred Tennyson and Robert Browning, evidently among her favorite poets. Before long, mother and son were exchanging their poems for criticism almost as soon as they were written, and John was the more forthright of the two. In 1931, when he was sixteen, he started a letter by stating about a new poem of hers: "I have just finished reading 'The Tapestry Song' which I did not like in the least." No doubt the poem went through a certain amount of revision, but Cornford did include it in *Mountains and Molehills* (1934) and later in the *Collected Poems*. In the manner of Tennyson's "The Lady of Shalott" (1832), the poem is clearly the sort of poetry that John Cornford would reject. For a few years her son played the same role in her verse writing that Brooke fulfilled twenty years earlier.

Mountains and Molehills, dedicated to her husband, was Cornford's last collection for fourteen years. The

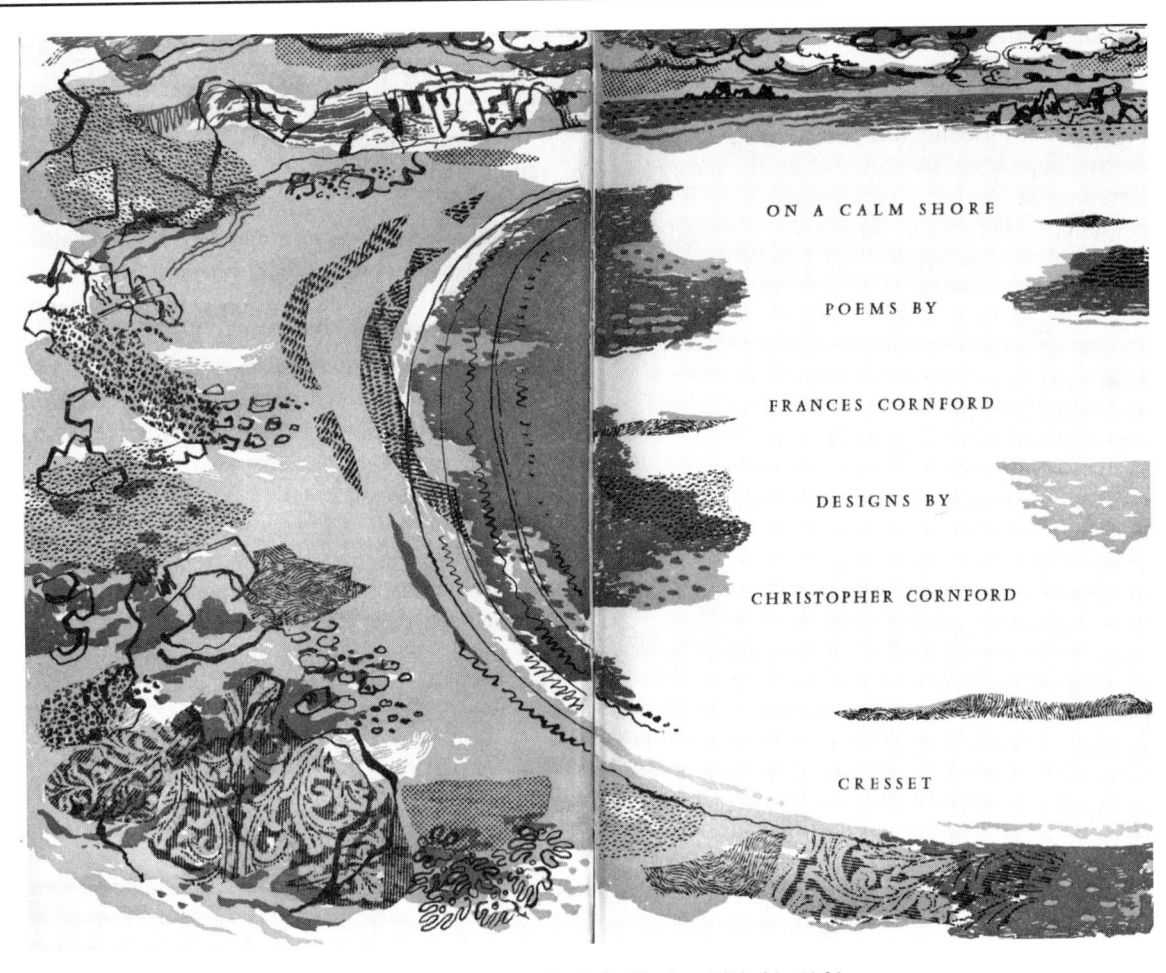

Two-page title for Cornford's final book, published in 1960

title refers to the structure of the book: three long poems set off by sixteen short poems, two of which consist of a single quatrain.

"Cambridge Autumn," which is three pages long, is written in blank verse with only occasional rhymes. The poem harkens back to the themes of her youthful "Autumn Morning in Cambridge," but this poem demonstrates her growing maturity as a poet. The poem opens:

> For long, so long, this timeless afternoon
> My body has lain in sun-receiving fields
> On the wood's border, by the bounteous elms,
> An unbeliever in approaching night
> And the cold, winter-prophesying dew,
> Heedless of all, forgetting all but now.

This stanza is verse as living speech. The calculated irregularities (for instance, the sprung rhythm of "on the wood's border") give a vitality to the language, similar to what Pound had observed in Yeats's poetry in 1914. "Cambridge Autumn" is one of Frances Cornford's more ambitious poems; she seldom wrote one as long as three pages. Its relative spaciousness allows her to experiment with different kinds of lines, and the middle section of the poem is done entirely in couplets. By this time she had moved away from the predictable sentiments and technical procedures of Georgian poetry. All the same, she usually favored a rural setting, as was the case with most Georgian poets, while modernist poets, beginning with Charles Baudelaire, typically dealt with the psychological experience of living in great cities.

"Ode on the Whole Duty of Parents," the second lengthy poem in the collection, was written by a woman with much experience in parenting, but it does not have quite the focus of most of Cornford's poetry, and the experiment in short lines alternating with pentameters does not work as well as it does in "Cambridge Autumn." "Fairy-Tale Idyll for Two Voices" is another Tennysonian poem with some attractive lines. The short poems, however, are more impressive, and the rest of her career she seldom wrote poems more than a page in length. Indeed, she seemed happy with epigrams of a single quatrain on a variety of subjects, literary and personal.

Cornford's husband died in 1943. The period covered by the pieces in her next book, *Travelling Home and Other Poems* (1948), includes the years of World War II, but public events have little part in Cornford's poetry. Living in Cambridge, she would have been aware of the Allied airfields in East Anglia, and in one poem she mentions them:

> How strange it was to see
> In the soft Cambridge sky our Squadron's wings,
> And hear the huge hum in the familiar grey.

Keynes, who characterizes her poetry as "unpretentious," summarizes her work: "Her aim was to express only what she truly felt, and she was able to catch and fix with economy of words her passing emotions or moments of experience realized with visual acuity and often with quiet humor." She never published any "major" poems, but many of her short pieces are pleasing, similar in fashion to poems by Thomas Campion or Robert Herrick. These Renaissance poets wrote according to certain recognized conventions or fictions. Cornford, like her ancestor Wordsworth, did not have this advantage, and she wrote poems in which sincerity and truth to experience greatly mattered.

Cornford's *Collected Poems* includes thirty-five poems composed after 1948. In 1960 she published a volume of seventy-two poems titled *On a Calm Shore*, illustrated by her son Christopher. She died on 19 August of that year.

One of Cornford's last poems, "Waiting in Hospital," carries an epigraph from *The Waste Land*–"These fragments have I shored against my ruin":

> This dominant machine,
> These forms, these files,
> This self-assured routine,
> Cylinderred oxygen for gasping breath,
> White antiseptic tiles,
> Clattering heels and smiles,
> Each fragment of this regulate hour
> Innocent man has shored against the power
> Of ruinous death.

In the preface to *On a Calm Shore* Cornford thanks John Hayward for "his kind scrutiny" of these poems. Hayward had performed the same service for Eliot's late poems and plays. Cornford, Geoffrey Keynes observed, owed little to Eliot, but at certain moments she approached his formulation of experience; a poem such as "Waiting in Hospital" is far removed from the typical work of the Georgians.

Another way Cornford moved away from her usual subjects was through her work in translation. In 1943 she had collaborated on *Poems from the Russian*. Consisting of work by eleven Russian poets from Aleksandr Pushkin to Anna Akhmatova and Aleksander Blok, with a preface by Cornford, the book went through at least four printings by 1946. She also collaborated with Stephen Spender in translating *Le dur désir de durer* (1946), a long poem by Paul Eluard, written by the French poet during the German occupation. Titled *The Dour Desire to Endure,* the translation was published in 1950 in a limited edition that reproduced the illustrations by Marc Chagall that had appeared in the original. In the preface Spender wrote that Cornford was "one of the best translators living." Finally, she translated a collection of fifteen poems from French writers, ranging from Pierre de Ronsard to Louis Aragon. *Fifteen Poems from the French* (1976) includes several works by the modernist poet Guillaume Apollinaire. This posthumous volume, published in a limited edition in Edinburgh, shows the range of her literary interests.

Frances Cornford's books have never been published in the United States, but she is known to a few American readers here through her brief appearances in anthologies. Oscar Williams included two of her poems in the light verse section of the widely read *A Little Treasury of Modern Poetry* (1947). Allen Tate and David Cecil include two poems in their *Modern Verse in English* (1958), the early "Autumn Morning at Cambridge" and "Susan to Diana," a villanelle from *Autumn Midnight*. Cornford would be best served by a selected poetry collection that could include a few of her translations from the French. She was a fine poet whose best work might be set beside that of H.D., her contemporary. The two exemplify the different modes of poetry explored by many British and American poets in the twentieth century.

References:

John Cornford, *Collected Writing,* edited by Jonathan Galassi (Manchester: Carcanet, 1986);

Geoffrey Keynes, *The Gates of Memory* (New York: Oxford University Press, 1981);

Keynes, obituary of Frances Cornford, *Dictionary of National Biography Supplement 1951–1966* (London: Oxford University Press, 1971), pp. 256–257;

Gwen Raverat, *Period Piece* (New York: Norton, 1953);

Peter Stansky and William Abraham, *Journey to the Frontier* (Boston: Little, Brown, 1966).

Papers:

The major collection of Frances Cornford's papers is in the British Library in London.

Camilla Toulmin Crosland
(Mrs. Newton Crosland)
(9 June 1812 – 16 February 1895)

Kathleen McCormack
Florida International University

BOOKS: *The Little Berlin Wool Worker: or Cousin Caroline's Visit* (London: Orr, 1844);

Lays and Legends Illustrative of English Life (London: How, 1845);

Poems (London: Orr, 1846);

Partners for Life: A Christmas Story (London: Orr, 1846; Philadelphia: Moore, 1848);

Toil and Trial. A Story of London Life. To Which Are Added The Iron Rule; and A Story of the West End (London: Hall & Virtue, 1849);

Stratagems: A Story (London: Hall & Virtue, 1849);

The Young Lord and Other Tales to Which Is Added Victorine Durocher by Mrs. Sherwood (And . . . Mrs. Streeten) (London: Darton, 1849, 1850);

Lydia: A Woman's Book (London: Groombridge, 1852; Boston: Ticknor, Reed & Fields, 1852);

English Tales and Sketches (Boston: Ticknor, Reed & Fields, 1853);

Stray Leaves from Shady Places (London: Routledge, 1853);

Memorable Women: The Story of Their Lives (London: David Bogue, 1854; Boston: Ticknor, Reed & Fields, 1854);

Hildred, the Daughter (London: Routledge, 1855);

Light in the Valley: My Experiences of Spiritualism (London & New York: Routledge, 1857);

Is It Meekness or Vanity? [A Tale], Miniature Library, volume 6 (Edinburgh: Chambers, 1858);

The Gentleman of the Family. A Tale, Miniature Library, volume 8 (Edinburgh: Chambers, 1858);

The Neglected Child, Miniature Library, volume 12 (Edinburgh: Chambers, 1858);

Mrs. Blake: A Story of Twenty Years, 3 volumes (London: Hurst & Blackett, 1862);

The Island of the Rainbow. A Fairy Tale; and Other Fancies (London: Routledge, 1865);

The Diamond Wedding, a Doric Story; and Other Poems (London: Houlston, 1871);

Hubert Freeth's Prosperity, 3 volumes (London: Hurst & Blackett, 1873; Philadelphia: Lippincott, 1874);

Summer Night: A Cantata for Treble Voices, music by Emanuel Aquilar (London: Hutchings & Romer, 1876);

Stories of the City of London, Retold for Youthful Readers (London: W. H. Allen, 1880);

Landmarks of a Literary Life (London: Sampson Low, Marston, 1893; New York: Scribners, 1893).

TRANSLATION: Victor Hugo, *Dramatic Works of Victor Hugo,* translated by Crosland and Frederick L. Slous (London: G. Bell, 1887).

The nineteenth-century restoration of St. Albans Cathedral in Hertfordshire, which rescued the decaying Norman structure from accelerating deterioration, included new stained-glass windows ranging in size from one to five panels wide. One of the smaller windows, on the east side of the south transept, commemorates "a sincere Christian . . . distinguished in literature," the versatile Victorian author Camilla Toulmin. It pictures St. Catherine of Siena, who wears a pensive expression under her crown and a deep red robe clasped over a deep blue gown. Her golden hair curls over her right shoulder down to her elbow, and she holds a sword in one hand, a book in the other.

The literary achievement commemorated in this striking memorial includes fifty-five years of writing fiction, children's stories, biography, translations, and essays, but poetry launched Toulmin's long writing career when "The Parting" appeared in the 1838 *Book of Beauty*. Soon afterward, Marguerite Gardiner, Countess of Blessington (Lady Blessington), the editor of *Book of Beauty*, welcomed her new contributor into the group associated with the annuals, and Toulmin spent twenty years writing poems for them and for eventual publication in collections. When this market waned, Toulmin demonstrated her versatility by finding others, and though she varied the genres in which she worked according to market demands, she continued producing poetry for nearly forty years.

The daughter of a solicitor with connections in France, Camilla Dufour Toulmin began writing professionally in her twenties after a Louisa May Alcott–type of girlhood spent struggling to maintain middle-class appearances on little money. Born in the City near St. Paul's on 9 June 1812, the infant Camilla soon moved with her parents to Fitzroy Square just south of Euston Road. For her first eight years she enjoyed security in a neighborhood of comfortable houses and flower-filled balconies. Her parents took her to the theater and encouraged her precocity by mapping out an education for her that included Latin and Greek.

The Toulmins maintained an active social life, some of it centering on whist. Sarah Wright Toulmin gave card parties for which she dressed her little girl in her prettiest short frocks and showed her off to the company. The precocious child was learning music, thriving at her school, and, even then, writing. In Toulmin's diaries, portions of them reprinted in her husband's *Rambles Round My Life: An Autobiography (1819–1896)* (1898), she reports that she learned her letters by eighteen months and was reading at three years. In her own *Landmarks of a Literary Life* (1893) she dates her first memories from the day of the Battle of Waterloo, which she remembered not because she heard news of the momentous events occurring in Belgium but because of a Sunday visit to her cousins in the country.

Then in 1820 William Toulmin died, leaving his family completely unprovided for. Newly poor, Sarah Wright Toulmin spent the next four years trying to support herself and her two children by keeping a boardinghouse. Friends subscribed to a fund that permitted the purchase and furnishing of an attractive property on Burton Crescent just east of Tavistock Square. The neighbors, mostly "wealthy merchants and professional men," included the veteran Radical M.P. John Cartwright, for whom the street was eventually renamed Cartwright Gardens. Toulmin's diary describes the routine sights of the neighborhood, in particular Cartwright: "a thin, venerable-looking old man" whose passage elicited negative comments from Tory houses, including, one assumes, her own. Whether or not the residents shared their politics, they all held keys to the "exquisite" crescent-shaped garden that fit into the curve of the street. Under the eyes of a watchful beadle, Camilla and the other children who played in the garden took care not to harm its flowers and shrubs.

But the boardinghouse on the garden crescent did not succeed financially, and in 1824 the widow had to sell all her furniture and move to a far humbler neighborhood south of the Thames. Although her daughter found her school near Burton Crescent inferior to the one she had attended during her father's lifetime, the opportunity to board there kept the child in her old neighborhood and enabled her to escape some of the distress her mother and younger brother endured: "Clothed mainly by gifts, and fed but poorly, we nevertheless contrived to keep up a certain position and to visit a little." Later, in the 1830s, their fortunes declined still further. Young Camilla left school at thirteen, and the family went to live in "humble lodgings in London, I visiting about, staying with relatives and friends and moving in very good middle-class circles, where my real destitution was often little suspected." Finally, the small family moved back north of the Thames not far from Burton Crescent, just off Lamb's Conduit Street. Teaching jobs and needlework allowed them to survive while Toulmin tackled the periodical marketplace. Although she believed her submission to the *Book of Beauty* launched her as a professional poet and, later, editor, the monetary rewards still did not match the expenses incurred by the Toulmin family.

Experiences of poverty not only impelled Toulmin to choose a writing career but also helped shape her choices in poetic subject matter. Many of the poems published in periodicals and collected in 1846 in Toulmin's first volume of poetry concern such struggles. "Spring Is Coming" points out how winter exacerbates hunger and other suffering. "Song of a Flower Sprite" attacks the poorhouses and argues that poverty plus ignorance cause crime. "The Death of the Pauper Peasant" attributes such conditions to a national greed and indifference: "England is bleak to the poor and old, / She knoweth no worth but the worth of gold." As time went on, Toulmin wrote both poetry and prose about poor relations, and she dedicated her early books to relatives in whose homes she had visited.

Living and working in 1840s London, Toulmin sought her inspiration as well as her markets close at hand. Because the annuals and magazines wanted upbeat works as well as indignation and sentimentality, she found occasions for her happier poems in English history, current events, and the activities of the royal family. She also celebrated the joys and achievements of London life. Indeed, when "London by Moonlight" appeared in *Bentley's Miscellany,* it led to her discovery by the Chambers brothers, William and Robert. She became one of their most reliable authors, and they published her poetry, fiction, and essays literally until the day she died, both in *Chambers's Edinburgh Journal* and as separate books.

The poems Toulmin set in London, including the pivotal "London by Moonlight," sometimes take an embattled stance. In "A Defence of London," the persona responds to "surprise expressed that poets should live there" by pointing out that "the imperial two" (William Shakespeare and John Milton) both lived in London. She pointed to the inspiration provided by other Londoners famous in history–explorers who departed on their voyages from the Thames and leaders buried in Westminster Abbey, also figures in "London by Moonlight." At the same time Toulmin continued to emphasize urban poverty. "London by Moonlight" contrasts a "burst of revelry that breaks / Upon the solemn stillness of the hour" with the quiet in nearby streets where "Gaunt Famine stalks, and holds the shrivell'd hand." Less typically of her times, she celebrated the achievements of urban industrialism. "The Railway Whistle" inspires positive feelings because

> It bringeth glad words from–some sick friend,
>   And they are so newly writ,
> Ye forget the terrors that time might send
>   For the ink is pallid yet!

Her article about the opening of the Thames Tunnel led to a happy meeting with the engineer who designed the tunnel, Marc Isambard Brunel, who became both an acquaintance and one of her heroes.

Additional poems in the 1846 volume sustain the desired positive tone by mentioning other inspirational historical figures. In "The Mighty Dead" Toulmin quotes George Gordon, Lord Byron, and says that he

Newton Crosland, who married Camilla Toulmin in 1848

and other greats, "rule us from their tombs." "Josephine" is set on Napoleon's wedding day to Marie Louise and creates a nobly unselfish voice for the rejected empress. "The Death of Leonardo Da Vinci" takes its inspiration from "the fine engraving of Mr. Fisk's exquisite picture" of Da Vinci dying in the arms of Francis I. Frequently, Toulmin wrote poems about famous people to accompany engravings, the expensive pictures that, to some degree, determined the poetic content of the periodicals. The illustrations in the books and periodicals in which she published her writing both stimulated and limited her creativity as she designed both poetry and prose during the 1840s to take advantage of opportunities to write about the illustrations.

Toulmin's poetry suggests she remained undaunted by the rigid formal requirements imposed by the poems that editors needed to accompany portrait engravings of beautiful women. Each poem had to praise the beauty of the subject and propose some more-or-less original connection between this beauty and life in general. For *Friendship's Offering,* the *Book of Beauty,* and the *Keepsake,* Toulmin wrote many poems, including "Lady There Is a Beauty that Doth Claim," "Lines on the Portrait of Miss Lucy B.," and "On the Portrait of Mrs. Maher." Royal portraits also prompted poems. "On the Marriage of the Queen Feb 10 1840," describes the happiness of the young queen's subjects:

>   They see thee not in regal splendour shining,–
>   They feel that thou art woman, young and fair,
>   And joy to think, that thou this day art twining
>   Love's Roses in the Crown thy head must wear!

Another poem, "Written to Illustrate the Frontispiece to 'Friendship's Offering' for 1843, Representing Her Majesty, H.R.H. Prince Albert, the Prince of Wales, and the Princess Royal," assures Queen Victoria a place among her predecessors, the ancient kings who welcome her to their line, but advises the Princess Royal that she should take joy that she will, because of her gender, avoid assuming her mother's responsibilities.

Toulmin's first prose work outside of a periodical also includes illustrations, in this case embroidery instruction patterns and representations of finished embroidered articles. Written two years before her book *Poems* (1846), *The Little Berlin Wool Worker* (1844) reflects the knowledge of needlework likely in women struggling to maintain middle-class status. This prose work integrates fictional narrative with needlework history and instructions. Its protagonist, a child named Emily, loves her needle, her mother, and her Cousin Caroline, whose embroidering talents inspire her as she learns them. Cousin Caroline intersperses hints on the challenges of various stitches with historical anecdotes concerning the tapestries of Bayeux and Gobelin, creating a book whose usefulness and entertainment value compensate for its excessive didacticism.

Illustrations also appear prominently in Toulmin's more-poetic second book, *Lays and Legends of English Life* (1845). Dozens of engraved pictures supplement the text in which Toulmin narrates the history of a country family in Devon. In this format, each event of Trevalyan family history occasions the interpolation of a "Legend" or a "Lay," all of them written by Toulmin and concerned with English traditions–the Maypole, for example, or the story of Sir Francis Drake and the forests of England. "A Song of the Trees," one of the "Lays," celebrates the usefulness of one English species after another: oak and pine supply wood for building ships, while laurel crowns successful heads. *Lays and Legends of English Life* went into a second edition in 1852.

By 1846 Toulmin had published three full-length works as well as countless poems and tales for the annuals. As subeditor of *Friendship's Offering* from 1842 through 1844, she did a large portion of the writing herself. To the 1842 volume, for example, she contributed six pieces, while the following year she wrote three poems and three short stories under assumed names.

During this active decade of her long life, while still living with her mother in Bloomsbury, Toulmin formed friendships with her colleagues among London authors and editors. In addition to Lady Blessington, she knew Thomas Moore, William and Mary Howitt, and Dinah Mulock. She visited among all these, and in 1845 she spent a month in Scotland alternating as the guest of Robert, then William Chambers, enjoying Edinburgh as well as the other sights. Her social circle widened in 1846 with the addition of Newton Crosland, a chief clerk to a wine merchant, who liked to write and publish an occasional essay or review and had at one point helped to launch a little magazine. Recently promoted, Crosland reports in his *Rambles Round My Life* that he decided he wanted to marry. Soon he found himself attracted to two women he met through his literary friends–Toulmin, then thirty-four, and her best friend, Mulock, ten years younger. In *Rambles Round My Life* he confesses, "I hope I shall not lose caste among my fair friends when I make the frank confession that I was captivated by both ladies at the same time, and paid them both devoted attention, and both were favourable to my advances. . . . I wanted the qualities of both to be combined in one individual; but as that desire was not realisable, I decided to make overtures to Miss Toulmin, as I considered that somehow my honour was implicated in her favour, although youth and beauty were on the side of Miss Mulock." Only after the engagement did he discover the debt and frail health of his fiancée, and at that point he felt obliged but also pleased to rescue both her and her mother from their genteel poverty.

In a wedding one friend described as a "surprise," Toulmin and Crosland married on 22 July 1848 at St. Pancras New Church with Mulock as bridesmaid. After their honeymoon on the southern coast, Newton Crosland moved his bride out of the center of London to 3 Hyde Vale Cottages in Greenwich, a comfortable but not luxurious neighborhood, which curves up the western side of the slope crowned by Flamsteed House and the Royal Observatory. He chose the location carefully. Born in America, he had happy memories of Greenwich, where, as a teenager, he first landed in England: "My first experience of English life was going into the park, where the deer took food from my hand. This incident was to me such a novelty that it inspired me with the most lively delight." The Crosland household included Sarah Wright Toulmin, at last returned through the kindness of her son-in-law to the securely middle-class status she had been feigning, especially for her daughter's sake, for more than twenty years.

Despite the financial rescue provided by her marriage, Camilla Crosland continued to write as if her survival depended upon it. Her husband described the difficulties she encountered when writing: "If a letter came in the morning and required an answer, she was unfit for any literary composition for the rest of the day. The noise of a hurdy-gurdy, or barrel-organ, drove her almost frantic, and I should say dissipated nine-tenths of her ideas. I could not sympathise with this nervous condition, as none of those disturbing elements which affected her had the slightest effect upon me." Nevertheless, he demonstrated his pride in his wife's achievements and concluded his autobiography with a pleased description of the St. Albans stained-glass window. Meanwhile, Camilla Crosland's lavish output belies her husband's description of her fragility.

Although *Friendship's Offering* had by this time folded, Crosland continued to contribute poems to the *Keepsake* and the *Book of Beauty* while bringing out short prose works: *Partners for Life: A Christmas Story* (1846), *Stratagems, a Story* (1849), *Toil and Trial* (1849), *The Young Lord and Other Tales* (1849), and *Lydia: A Woman's Book* (1852). In 1848 she assumed the editorship of the *New Monthly Belle Assemblée* and retained this post as the fashion periodical went through various incarnations and several names. Described by a friend as attractive and well dressed, Crosland could also draw on her French background to edit sections on "Gossip from Paris" and "The Toilet," which always pictured hooped and ruffled gowns from France.

Like the periodicals she edited, Crosland's most popular book from this period, a group of profiles called *Memorable Women: The Story of Their Lives* (1854) also appealed to a female audience. Crosland took pride in her dislike for what she called "the shrieking sisterhood," but she also acknowledged that feminists did good work in getting women access to employment. She pointed to her own girlhood experience of job seeking to justify this gratitude. The periodicals she edited did not advocate changes in the conditions of women's lives, and *Memorable Women* emphasizes the heroism of its subjects in terms of their acts as wives and mothers. Within this plan, however, Crosland's book includes three authors–Fanny Burney d'Arblay, Hester Thrale Piozzi, and Margaret Fuller Ossoli.

In the mid 1850s, the Croslands acquired a provocative new interest to share and a new subject to write about. At Greenwich, they had many visitors, including Nathaniel Hawthorne and in 1854 Anna Savage Shipton, just back from America, who introduced them to spiritualism. Newton Crosland resisted for a time, but his wife began a series of séances at their home behind his back while she and her medium monitored her husband's potential reaction through contacts with the spirits. After six months, while returning home on the train one night, Newton Crosland sat next to a man who convinced him simultaneously of his good sense and his sincere belief in spiritualism. Converted, Newton Crosland informed his wife of his encounter. She admitted her secret, and he undertook a yearlong study of spiritualist beliefs. For two years the couple together hosted séances conducted by their favorite medium in their home at Hyde Vale Cottages.

Newton Crosland's autobiography reports that these practices cost them friends, acquaintances, dignity, the entire staff of his wine business, and six hundred pounds in one year. But they also gained slightly in that both sold writing about their experiences. Crosland's *Light in the Valley: My Experiences of Spiritualism* (1857) describes séances, and its illustrations reproduce drawings and writings produced by a medium who believed that her hand was directed by departed spirits. Meanwhile, still attentive to her audience, Crosland kept spiritualism rigorously out of the poetry she was still writing for the *Keepsake* on such conventional topics as "The Bride," "The Poor Cousin," "On the Portrait of the Viscountess Sydney," and "A Soldier's Nurse."

Although Newton Crosland comments that his wife's writing earned little, his prosperous business gave him leisure to sustain his own desultory literary pursuits. The couple traveled, sometimes together, sometimes independently. In 1854 Newton Crosland went to Oxford, where he attended a huge party hosted by the mayor. That same year he also went by himself on his first trip to France. Writing home to his wife, he promised her a similar jaunt: "My journey, I hope, will render me more satisfied with my own home than I ever was before; and when you visit Paris next year–a treat I hope to give you–I think it will raise your own notions of self-importance, for your eyes and figure ought to make a sensation in Paris." In April 1862 Newton Crosland joined a party of male friends on the Isle of Wight, and his *Rambles Round My Life* reveals how they remained all afternoon at the Crab and Lobster near Ventnor, largely because of the warm welcome from the barmaid, "one of the most lovely girls I had ever seen."

For her part, Crosland made a journey to Italy without her husband in 1857 in the company of her sister-in-law and a young heiress, Maria Russell, who financed the trip and for whom Crosland acted as chaperone. Russell complicated the experience for all three of them through her romance with Pierre de Gendre, who followed the party as they moved from Rome to Florence to Naples. Finally, the young couple formed an engagement and succeeded in marrying, though they divorced eventually, and the Countess de Gendre resumed her birth name. During the breakup, the Croslands sheltered the wife from her violent husband in their home outside of London.

Although chaperoning Russell in Italy demanded all Crosland's ingenuity, especially when the wealthy young traveler proposed to marry her lover without arranging a financial settlement, Crosland did manage to enjoy herself when not distracted by the couple's passionate imprudence. She took lessons in Italian, and her letters of introduction to artists and literati provided a range of amusement. She attended the Anglican Church in Florence along with many of the expatriates who lived in Bellosguardo and Fiesole. When she visited at Casa Guidi, she found herself impressed with the company, and she joined the many Victorian women poets who addressed poems to Elizabeth Barrett Browning.

The Italian journey helped return Crosland to poetry by providing her with fresh material. Again, like many nineteenth-century women poets, she found inspiration in the Risorgimento. "The Austrian Goliath: On the Outbreak of War in 1859" calls for Italy to pursue freedom in the names of its immortal authors and painters. In "The King of Italy on the Title Being First Proclaimed" the persona creates lines full of local detail to stress that "the king of many palaces" still lacked the two needed to complete Garibaldi's victories, Venice and Rome. But another Italian-inspired poem takes a novel approach in its pleasure at the installation of electric wire along the Appian Way. The ancient Romans who built the road "set costly tombs along the public way" that consecrated the "Sub-Urban miles." Past them traveled a typically Roman procession of patricians, legions, priests, captives, wild beasts, and "flower-crowned oxen, white without a stain." The persona contrasts this past with a present in which

> the marble mounds, like giant beads,
> Seem hung on beauty's neck; for lo! The threads
> Of fine electric wire pass tremblingly
> Along the sombre rows.

Despite the fervor of the Italian poems, Crosland's personae remain convinced of the superiority of England. Written in 1861, "The Talking Fire" concludes that despite the weather, England is best.

In 1862, after fourteen years in Hyde Vale Cottages, Sarah Wright Toulmin died, and the Croslands, who never had children, moved across Greenwich Park to Vanbrugh Park Road, a neighborhood of larger houses. Their street opened out onto Greenwich Park just where it meets Blackheath, and they named their large new home Lynton Lodge. As the decade went on, Crosland was concentrating most of her energy on a three-volume novel, but unlike many active authors with long careers, she did not yet give up poetry.

The Italian poems written after her 1857 journey appeared in her last full-length collection of poetry, *The Diamond Wedding*, published in 1871. It includes a total of seventy-six poems—fifty-two lyrics and narratives, along with special sections of eleven songs and thirteen sonnets. *Diamond Wedding* begins with the title poem, a blank-verse saga of a country family with many children. Crosland divides it into dated sections, supplying scenes that occur on silver (1830), golden (1855), and diamond (1865) anniversaries. As the couple age, they find forgiveness and compensations for the troubles their children suffer. At the seaside, celebrating their diamond wedding, for example, they happen on a ship named for their heroic son Henry, lost in a wreck during which he had saved two other vessels. Another son becomes an M.P. A daughter dies. Crosland's rural setting unifies the poem and establishes its pastoralism. In the final lines, the passage of time has wiped out the domestic setting, including the site of the "quiet, quaint pagoda," where in earlier sections of the poem the family members gathered but where now "the Railway Engine hissing, pants and halts." This melancholy closure creates the railway, which elsewhere Crosland's poetry praises, as an unexpectedly monstrous factor in the otherwise benign passage of time.

Like "The Diamond Wedding," other poems in the collection acknowledge the effects of the passage of time. In "The Heart's Awakening" time matures a young girl into womanhood, while "Lost! Lost!" suggests that "Faith" provides the vision by which "Is seen Youth's wealth . . . Restored and glorified." "Day by Day" observes that gradual changes can occur in both positive and negative directions. This collection also includes poems dating back to the 1840s.

Additional continuity with Crosland's own past occurs in the new poems on royal topics. "He Giveth His Beloved Sleep" consoles Queen Victoria upon Albert's death, while "Epithalamium" celebrates the engagement of the Prince of Wales and the arrival of his betrothed from across the sea. The collection also ends with timely material. "An Invocation" prays that God will make France see its error in engaging in the Franco-Prussian War. A New Year's Eve poem, "Eighteen Hundred and Seventy-One," also mentions the war as it acknowledges the problems of the departing year.

Although by the time of their move across Greenwich Park the Croslands had given up séances, their pursuits never became conventional. Perhaps inspired by proximity to the Royal Observatory, Newton Crosland continued depending on astrology to make many decisions. His wife, who in 1846 had published a poem in which she personified astrology and alchemy as the venerable parents of astronomy and chemistry, apparently shared her husband's interest in the stars. Newton Crosland mentions in *Rambles Round My Life* that before her eyesight began deteriorating, his wife could "see the satellites of Jupiter with the naked eye"; she wrote a poem on the mapping of the constellations called "A Night Thought." Newton Crosland favored founding a school for study of the "science" of astrology, and he revealed that both he and his wife believed in receiving auguries from birds that paid them particular attention.

In 1872 the couple weathered Newton Crosland's conviction for libel. In 1871 he had written a pamphlet, *The Eltham Tragedy Reviewed,* which questioned the verdict in a local murder. His public criticism earned him a fine of £50, but an enthusiastic group, described as "friends and neighbors" in the inscription on the silver inkstand they gave him, compensated him for the sum. They also honored him with a testimonial dinner at Lynton Lodge.

The pathos of the last years of Crosland's long life proceeds from her illness and her return to humble circumstances similar to the conditions she spent her youth disguising and attempting to escape. She began to deteriorate with asthma, heart problems, and incipient blindness in 1874. For six years the couple continued at Vanbrugh Park Road. Then, at age sixty-seven, Newton Crosland retired, sold his business, and moved his seventy-three-year-old wife to small quarters on Ondine Road in East Dulwich. Here he coped with her debility: "Under the influence of illness, it is not surprising that she lost a good deal of her 'optimism' and if she became somewhat irritable and exigent, she must be forgiven, for these abnormal symptoms were not ingrained in her disposition; they were mere blemishes on the surface of a noble nature which had been tried and schooled by no ordinary discipline of worldly care. Attacks of asthma, weakness of the heart's action and failure of sight, all gathered about her at once with increased persistence and intensity." Still, she wrote. She took up translating the works of Victor Hugo and completed her autobiographical *Landmarks of a Literary Life* at the age of eighty, two years before she died. Her husband claimed that at the very moment of her death on 16 February 1895, the postman rang their door with an issue of *Chambers's Edinburgh Journal,* which included her last publication, an essay on "Politeness."

In 1853 a reviewer in the *Morning Advertiser* ranked Crosland (Toulmin) among "the female poets who have formed a bright constellation for themselves in the heaven of modern English poesy–Joanna Baillie, Felicia Hemans, Caroline Bowles, LEL, Mary Howitt, Mrs. Norton, Agnes Strickland, Camilla Toulmin, and Elizabeth Barrett Browning." Her husband placed her poetry in "the school" of Elizabeth Barrett Browning and Alfred Tennyson, and her frequent adoption of both the "Locksley Hall" and "In Memoriam" stanza forms suggests that she deliberately evoked the latter comparison. Currently unanthologized, however, neither her poetry nor her prose has sustained its appeal. Nevertheless, Crosland's longevity, productivity, and versatility make her a key figure in the history of publishing during one of its most active periods. But because she could and did write a poem about just about anything needed or sought after, her poetry is commercial and conventional as opposed to inspired and original.

Although Crosland's long London life began in Bloomsbury, she spent most of it, nearly forty years, in the mild exile of the suburbs: Greenwich, Blackheath, and East Dulwich. Nevertheless, she filled her life with London people and activities and often chose London settings for her prose and poetry. After her death, however, the need for stained-glass windows during the restoration of St. Albans Cathedral resulted in the placement of the most striking monument to Crosland's life in an area she did not frequent. The window creates a small mystery because, although Newton Crosland mentions it in his autobiography, the couple's modest circumstances in East Dulwich, living in quarters no more than a third the size of Lynton Lodge, suggest that he could not, at that point in his life, have paid for it. Although the cathedral has no record of its buyer, the window pictures St. Catherine of Siena, a saint commemorated for her mysticism.

References:

Andrew Boyle, *An Index to the Annuals,* volume 1 (Worcester: Andrew Boyce, 1967);

Newton Crosland, *Rambles Round My Life: An Autobiography (1819–1896)* (London: E. W. Allen, 1898).

Nancy Cunard

(10 March 1896 – 16 March 1965)

Chris Hopkins
Sheffield Hallam University

BOOKS: *Outlaws* (London: Elkin Mathews, 1921);
Sublunary (London & New York: Hodder & Stoughton, 1923);
Parallax (London: Hogarth Press, 1925);
Poems (Two) 1925 (London: Aquila, 1930);
Black Man and White Ladyship: An Anniversary (Toulon: Privately printed, 1931);
The White Man's Duty: An Analysis of the Colonial Question in the Light of the Atlantic Charter, by Cunard and George Padmore (London: W. H. Allen, 1942);
Men-Ship-Tank-Plane (London: New Books, 1944);
Relève into Maquis (Derby: Grasshopper Press, 1944);
Grand Man: Memories of Norman Douglas (London: Secker & Warburg, 1954);
GM: Memories of George Moore (London: Hart-Davis, 1956);
These Were the Hours: Memories of My Hours Press, Réanville and Paris, 1928–1931, edited by Hugh Ford (Carbondale: Southern Illinois University Press, 1966);
Thoughts about Ronald Firbank, foreword by Miriam J. Benkovitz (New York: Albondocani Press, 1971).

OTHER: *Wheels: An Anthology of Verse,* edited by Edith Sitwell, contributions by Cunard (Oxford: Blackwell, 1916);
Negro Anthology, Made by Nancy Cunard, 1931–1933, edited by Cunard (London: Published by Nancy Cunard at Wishart & Co., 1934; New York: Negro Universities Press, 1969);
Les Poètes du monde défendant les peuple espagnols, edited by Cunard and Pablo Neruda (La Chapelle-Réanville: Printed by Nancy Cunard, 1937);
Authors Take Sides on the Spanish War, edited by Cunard (London: Left Review, 1937);
Poems for France, Written by Poets on France since the War, with Biographical Notes of the Authors, edited by Cunard (Paris: La France Libre, 1944); selections translated by Cunard as *Poèmes à la France, 1939–1944, réunis et traduits de l'anglais, avec une préface, des notes biographiques et le portrait des auteurs* (Paris: Seghers, 1946);
Raymond Michelet, *African Empires and Civilization,* foreword by Cunard, International African Service Bureau Publications, no. 4 (London: Panaf Service, 1945).

Nancy Cunard was an important and notoriously bohemian figure in avant-garde literary, artistic, and political circles from 1916 on and throughout the 1920s and 1930s. Between 1928 and 1931 she operated the Hours Press in La Chapelle-Réanville, France, publishing some significant modernist works. She was well known for her passionate interests in, and commitment to, African and African American culture and for her opposition to fascism. She created a monumental celebration of black achievement in *Negro Anthology, Made by Nancy Cunard, 1931–1933* (1934). Her poetry, influenced by Georgian and emerging modernist traditions, was widely known in the interwar period and was initially well received, but it has been largely neglected until recently. Her prose and her personality are more often discussed than her poetry.

Clara Nancy Cunard was born at Nevill Holt, a country house in Leicestershire, on 10 March 1896. Her father, Sir Bache Cunard, was a grandson of Samuel Cunard, originally of Philadelphia, who founded the Cunard shipping line in 1840. Her mother, Maud, née Burke, was an American; as Lady Cunard, she renamed herself Emerald. While Sir Bache was devoted to the countryside, to his role as a member of the gentry, and to his hobby, ornamental metalworking, Lady Cunard sought fame in London society. She cultivated both political and literary circles, entertaining politicians such as Arthur James Balfour, Herbert Henry Asquith, and F. E. Smith, and writers such as Alfred Austin, Francis Meynell, and W. Somerset Maugham. The novelist George Moore, a lifelong friend of mother and daughter, was said to be Lady Cunard's lover, and Nancy was rumored to be his daughter. Cunard was

Nancy Cunard in the late 1920s (photograph by Curtis Moffat)

fond of her unassuming father but antagonistic toward her mother for most of her life.

Whatever the exact nature of her relationship with Moore might have been, it is certain that in 1910 Lady Cunard became the lover of the orchestra conductor Sir Thomas Beecham. She left Nevill Holt to live with him in London, taking Nancy with her. The breach between mother and daughter seems to date from this period, and it resulted as much from Cunard's resentment of her mother's betrayal of Moore as from the treatment of her father. Cunard's attitudes toward authority and conformity stemmed from what she saw as her mother's hypocrisy: Lady Cunard was socially ambitious and inclined to regard the demands of society as of high importance, in spite of her own somewhat bohemian approach to life.

Cunard was sent to a private school in London, then studied in Germany and at a finishing school in Paris in 1912-1913. At eighteen, Cunard followed the custom of her class by "coming out" into society and being presented at court. At this time she became a friend of the daughter of the actor Sir Herbert Beerbohm Tree, Iris Tree, who later became a poet. With Tree, Cunard began to move in artistic circles of the younger generation—circles that partly overlapped and partly rivaled those cultivated by her mother. Cunard met or saw, often at her mother's parties, figures such as Osbert Sitwell, Ezra Pound, and Wyndham Lewis.

While Cunard was wildly unconventional for most of her life, she reacted quite conventionally to World War I, which broke out in August 1914: as her biographer Anne Chisholm points out, "gallant wounded officers were the center of attention" for Cunard and her friends. In 1915 Cunard met Sydney Fairburn, who was home on leave after being wounded at Gallipoli; they were married in November 1916. As Chisholm observes, the extremely conventional Fairburn seemed an unlikely match. Cunard's mother was opposed to the marriage, which almost certainly confirmed Cunard in her determination to go through with it. Besides, marriage offered her an escape from her mother. Cunard was, in her own later account, relieved when Fairburn's convalescent leave ended in July 1918 and he was posted to France. She had fallen in love with one of his friends, Broughton Adderley, but Adderley was killed in France in October 1918. When Fairburn returned home in January 1919, Cunard told him that she could not continue with the marriage. A legal separation was arranged, though they were not divorced until 1925.

During this often miserable period, Cunard's interest in poetry developed (one of her dissatisfactions with Fairburn was that she had found it impossible to write poetry when he was at home). She had published her first poem in 1915 in the *Eton Chronicle*, a school journal edited by her cousin Victor Cunard. In 1916 her first professionally published poems appeared in the first of a series of six annual anthologies published by Edith Sitwell between 1916 and 1921. The series was titled *Wheels;* the first volume included seven poems by Cunard, including the one from which the anthology took its title:

> I sometimes think that all our thoughts are wheels,
> Rolling forever through a painted world:
> Moved by the cunning of a thousand clowns
> Dressed paper-wise, with blatant rounded masks,
> That take their multi-coloured caravans
> From place to place, and act and leap and sing,
> Catching the spinning hoops when cymbals clash.
> And one is dressed as Fate and one as Death;
> The rest that represent Love, Joy and Sin,
> Join hands in solemn stage-learnt ecstasy,
> While Folly beats a drum with golden pegs,
> And mocks that shrouded jester called Despair.

Reviewers of *Wheels* often pointed to this poem as characteristic of the aesthetic of the whole volume. As C. K. Stead points out, some reviews were as interested in the gossip-worthiness of the contributors as they were in the poetry. *The Observer,* noting that the contributors included the colorful Sitwell siblings, Aldous Huxley, Iris Tree, and Cunard, commented that "their names are enough to secure a second edition." The publicity value of the contributors was not irrelevant to the poetics of the volumes, for, as critics then and since have pointed out, the anthology was clearly intended to mark an escape from the previous generation—the generation of the contributors' "society" parents. As John Press writes, it was "to be an act of defiance, a deliberate rebellion against the stuffy canons of respectable, conservative society." Some reviewers, members of the "establishment" who saw their standards being attacked, were hostile: one of them characterized the anthology as "conceived in morbid eccentricity and executed in fierce fictitious gloom." Other critics of the older generation, particularly the anonymous reviewer for the 11 April 1911 issue of *The Athenaeum,* pointed out that this "new" poetry was not really all that new but noted a shift from Georgian "simplicity" to an emphasis on "intelligence." Some younger critics, while pointing out weaknesses in the poetry of *Wheels,* also gave some support to its attempts to move away from the exhausted language of Georgianism toward a new modernist language. Thus, T. S. Eliot commented in the March 1918 issue of *The Egoist* that "instead of rainbows, cuckoos, daffodils, and timid hares, they give us garden-gods, guitars and mandolins." Reviewers also noted that the volume suggested a world- and war-weariness, features that can be seen in Cunard's poem. The extended "wheels" metaphor suggests a world that goes through the motions but is empty of uniqueness or authentic value.

The dissolution of her marriage threatened the independence that had been Cunard's major motivation for becoming a poet. She had no home of her own and was forced to return to live with her mother, but she stayed with friends as often as possible. In 1919 Cunard contracted the Spanish flu, which was then epidemic; her health was impaired for several years afterward. In January 1920 she left England for Paris, determined never to return to the conventionality of English life. That winter she had several major operations, including a hysterectomy and an appendectomy.

On a visit to London in the spring of 1920 Cunard met an Armenian, Dikran Kouyoumdjian, who soon became a best-selling novelist under the pseudonym Michael Arlen. Their relationship continued for several years, and some of the characters in Arlen's novels are partly based on Cunard.

In 1921 Cunard's first volume of poems, *Outlaws,* was published. It included five poems from *Wheels* along with thirty-one new pieces. The style of the new poems is similar to that of the earlier ones, though some development is visible. A mixture of late-Victorian, Georgian, and early-modernist features is present both within individual poems and across the collection. Much of the diction, however, has a noticeably Keatsian feel. This feature is no doubt drawn partly from the general persistence of John Keats's influence, but it also may stem more specifically from Wilfred Owen's use of Keatsian elements (some of Owen's poems were first published in the *Wheels* series). Thus, the title poem, a seven-sonnet sequence, has an air of Keats's "Ode on a Grecian Urn" (1820) about it, as can be seen in the last poem in the sequence:

> One thinks to hear them crying in the wind:
> "Life was so bitter to us—but we chose
> The living, stressful moments from this close
> Denying existence . . .
>
> . . . You cannot part
> Our twin minds from each other, and we sail
> Proud and forever on the clutching sea,
> Grown element again; the heaven's breath
> Makes clear our souls with space; life does not fail
> As we have used it." . . . They shall ever be;
> Summer has set upon them but not death.

As in "Wheels," a lack of faith in the value of ordinary life is manifest, but the sensibility here is hardly a modernist one.

Other poems use more contemporary voices, in part or whole. Thus, "Poor-Streets," while mainly written in a quite traditional poetic diction, has a more

Cunard's parents, Maude Alice Burke and Sir Bache Cunard, at the time of their marriage in 1895

modern close: "And know the ending of your day will be / The desolate despair of public-houses." The influence of William Butler Yeats that is detectable here can also be seen in "The Last of Pierrot": Pierrot "sits and shivers on a tattered stool" and draws "life-blood from out his painted heart; / Forgetting that its texture is but paper." "Mood" suggests a different kind of modern voice—a precursor to certain veins of poetry of the later 1920s and the 1930s:

> Smoke-stacks, coal-stacks, hay-stacks, slack,
> Colourless, scentless, pointless, dull,
> Railways, highways, roadways black,
> Grantham, Birmingham, Leeds, and Hull.
> . . . .
> What can these ever mean to me?

The keynote of the volume is the emptiness of contemporary experience, a theme first introduced in "Wheels," and Cunard makes considerable use of images deployed in that poem—particularly clowns, wheels, paper clothes and masks, and signs of emptiness.

Outlaws was well reviewed on the whole, though most critics expressed reservations. Some reviews stressed a lack of consistency; thus, *The Nation* said,

"Miss Cunard's poems are of unequal quality, due rather to a wavering technique than any poverty of central fires." Edgell Rickword in *The New Statesman* made a related point in a more positive way: "one can feel the pulse of an original mind beating through a rather uncongenial medium." Cunard was particularly pleased by a careful and encouraging review by Moore in *The Observer* (27 February 1921).

Cunard became acquainted with many of the expatriate avant-garde artists and writers in Paris, while retaining her contacts with English writers. She soon counted among her circle important modernists such as Eliot, Pound, Richard Aldington, Samuel Beckett, Bryher (Annie Winifred Ellerman), Sylvia Beach, Janet Flanner, and H.D. (Hilda Doolittle). Cunard had met Pound as part of her mother's circle in 1915, but she introduced herself in her own right by sending him a poem (it is not clear which) for possible publication in *The Dial*. Pound replied with a critique of the poem, which Cunard kept in her scrapbook. She referred to it in an angry letter written to Pound on 11 June 1946 denouncing his support of fascism: "in 1921 you helped me greatly with your criticism of poetry (of my poetry of then too)." Pound's 1921 letter echoes more bluntly the criticisms made by the reviewers of *Outlaws:*

I will take the poem to the Dial this evening, but my dear, why, why the devil do you write in that obsolete dialect and with the cadences of the late Alfred Tennyson. What is good in the poem is that you have not tried to lie or to exaggerate, and as in other poems of yours that I have seen, you do hunt about for a visual accurate adjective. It is not Georgian, at least that is a gain.

Pound also advises her to stop using the "motion of pentameter dragging with it the Victorian or Elizabethan 'poetic' word order."

In addition to this helpful, if frank, advice from Pound, 1921 also brought a less constructive poetic/critical reaction from Eliot that is generally supposed to refer to Cunard. The draft typescript for *The Waste Land* (1922) that Eliot gave Pound in January 1921 included in "The Fire Sermon" section a vicious sixty-nine-line portrait of a woman poet named Fresca. The section was in the style of Alexander Pope, and the first half is based mainly on various of Pope's and Jonathan Swift's verse depictions of women. A literary patron, "Lady Kleinwurm," may be based on Cunard's mother. In the second half of the section misogynistic attention is turned to Fresca's personality, sexual behavior, and poetry, all of which are represented as strongly linked:

Fresca! In other time or place had been
A meek and lowly weeping Magdalene
. . . .
For varying forms, one definition's right:
Unreal emotions and real appetite.
Women grown intellectual grow dull
. . . .
Fresca was baptised in a soapy sea
Of Symonds—Walter Pater—Vernon Lee.
The Scandinavians bemused her wits,
The Russians thrilled her to hysteric fits.
From such chaotic misch-masch potpourri

What are we to expect but poetry?
. . . .
And on those nights when Fresca lies alone,
She scribbles verse of such a gloomy tone
That cautious critics say, her style is quite her own.
Not quite an adult, and still less a child,
By fate misbred, by flattering friends beguiled,
Fresca's arrived (the Muses nine declare)
To be a sort of can-can salonniere.

Though scurrilous—partly as a result of the misogyny of his eighteenth-century satirical models—Eliot's comments on "Fresca" are similar to those on Cunard made by more conventional critics. There is the criticism of the combination of poetic traditions, particularly Victorian, with recent innovations (the Russian reference is presumably to the modernist impact of Sergey Diaghilev's Ballets Russes, rather than to the influence of any Russian writers). There is also the accusation that the poet is a rich and fashionable, if depressed, amateur whose poems contain "unreal emotions" created from boredom, hysteria, and flattery. There is, presumably, an implicit contrast with the "authentic" (masculine) work of real innovators in poetry, such as Eliot and Pound.

Pound insisted that the Fresca section be cut on artistic grounds—though he may also have felt some concern for the feelings of Cunard and her mother. As well as providing a critical reaction to Cunard's poetry and image, the excised lines show that she had her enemies among the younger artistic circles.

Not yet firmly settled in Paris, Cunard moved frenetically around France and Italy, renting apartments or staying in hotels or with friends. She gathered still more friends in avant-garde circles, including Tristan Tzara, Man Ray, and M. Constantin Brancusi. Ray photographed her; Tzara dedicated to her his dadaist play *Mouchoir de Nuages* (Handkerchief of Clouds, 1924); and Brancusi sculpted a wooden image of her, *Jeune Fille Sophistiquée* (Sophisticated Young Girl). She also met Louis Aragon, who later tried to reconcile Surrealism with communism. Cunard was thus linked with the new and particularly French Surrealist movement. In 1923 she was introduced to a figure from an older generation, the travel writer Norman Douglas; they remained friends for the rest of his life.

Cunard's second volume of poems, *Sublunary,* was published in London in 1923. It comprised sixty-five new works. The style—or mixture of styles—is not, overall, much different from that in *Outlaws,* though some poems show signs of new powers. Reviewers reacted much as they had to the previous volume, but the reservations were more heavily weighted, perhaps because of a sense that the "promise" of the first collection had not been realized in the second. *The Manchester Guardian* said that the new volume showed "promise rather than achievement." The 26 July 1923 *TLS* considered the collection "thoroughly acceptable" but noted "a tendency to be thin and wordy." *The Spectator* alluded to Cunard's image and reputation by saying that the poetry had a "permeating sense of effort not to be young lady-ish." In fact, some of the poems are still far from unconventional; the title poem is wistful and as reminiscent of Robert Browning as it is of more-recent poets:

They are met at midnight in the windy tower,
Alchemist and students of alchemy,
Beneath a failing moon's reluctance; dark

Other poems, however, draw more clearly on Cunard's Paris milieu and hint at a liberation from social, if not poetic, convention. "In a Café" suggests the independent manner of life of a "New Woman" of the 1920s, though quite negatively, as it questions what is reality, and what is appearance:

Pale-face, turn round and look at me:
From out the shimmer of your glass
Are gone the indifferent that pass
Your fragile face. They cannot see,
Mark as I do, your weariness
Bowed to the music of this hour,
Unconscious, pensive as a flower.
Suppose I took for happiness
(All of a moment) your white face

One or two poems begin to attempt a more contemporary voice of the kind advised by Pound. "I Am Not One for Expression" uses some sharply delineated and self-contained images before going on to explore the difficulty of writing and the situation of the modern poet. It begins:

I am not one for expression;
The fish leaps in the stream,
The bird rends the air sharply,
But I linger as if underground
In a web of escaping thoughts.
I have laughed,
Applauded, marvelled, thrilled at others' emotion—
After these what is left in my hand to-morrow but the feel of a vanished leaf?

This opening suggests, along imagist lines, the organic purity of authentic poetry. But the poet persona cannot easily achieve this kind of creation and is overawed by coming after generations of more-fruitful writers:

Now at the end of your fruition—
All of you
Had keys to expression, went up and opened the doors
On glamour, romance and soul's philosophy. . . .

The last line suggests that this achievement is that of a premodernist poetry. The speaker has no such "wealth" in "the currency of your riches." Her belatedness leaves her in the position of the modernist writer who must forge a language for herself from difficult materials:

I am the pilgrim of lost paths,
The gleaner in the empty harvest-field
. . . .
Till I sit again, aloof
Like a cross-legged tailor stitching in his small shop,
Handling thoughts that are the ghosts of deeds,
(Ghosts and precursors)
Hammering cold words
On ill-shaped anvils

The poem is one of Cunard's best: it uses the poetic traditions she knows to form a precise and specific vision of her own experience.

"Adolescence" ends less certainly than "I Am Not One for Expression" but has a similar quality of engagement and exploration:

Cunard and her father at Nevill Holt, their country house in Leicestershire, in 1912

I am in years almost the century's child
At grips with still the same uncertainty
That was attendant to me at school.
The classics set before us, twenty voices
Took up enunciation, I was dumb.

The poem expresses Cunard's alienation from tradition and passes through her sense of liberation as a young adult before World War I, but it ends with a sense that she has not yet found a new identity for herself:

Then had I thought of aftermaths, and stood
Uncertainly between the opened gates
Scanning the crossroads of a violent world

In 1924 Cunard acquired an apartment of her own in Paris; but she still spent a good part of her time traveling, especially in the south of France. Her third volume of poetry, *Parallax,* was published in 1925. It is a single long poem of some five hundred lines. Anne Chisholm thinks that it is Cunard's best poem, and some contemporary reviewers were also impressed. Edgell Rickword, writing for the *TLS,* thought that "it has a grasp of reality and complexity which is so frequently lacking from women's poetry." *The Manchester Guardian* reviewer saw the complexity but valued it negatively, saying that the poem was "almost a study in obscurity." Other reviews criticized the poem for being obviously derivative of *The Waste Land,* a work that had, indeed, deeply impressed Cunard. The *Daily News* called the poem "a rather delirious echo of Mr. T. S. Eliot's *The Waste-Land.*" This criticism was repeated in Laura Riding and Robert Graves's influential *A Survey of Modernist Poetry* (1929), which defined *Parallax* as an "imitation of T. S. Eliot" and Cunard as an "Eliotite"–a borrower of the authentic master's "stage-properties." When *Parallax* is mentioned at all in more-recent surveys of modernist poetry, similar comments are usually made.

Unquestionably, *Parallax* is heavily influenced by *The Waste Land.* Eliot's poem offered Cunard a poetic voice that expressed the tenor of her previous collections: a sense of being adrift in a world that was itself adrift. The recognition of the suitability of this modernist voice perhaps overwhelmed the mixed voices through which she had begun to express her own sense of her situation in *Sublunary.* (The mixture of voices in Eliot's work was probably one of its attractions for Cunard.) *Parallax* is less personal than her previous collection: its domination by Eliot is shown in its style, its fragmentation, and its imagery, but also, most significantly, in its lack of any specifically feminine view of the state of the modern world: one of the poem's voices–perhaps the central one–is clearly male. Nevertheless, it is a substantial and accomplished poem, showing continuity with Cunard's earlier work in its sense of an old world left behind and a new one not yet achieved: "I have changed my prisons."

In 1925 Cunard's father died, leaving her a substantial inheritance that helped to support her artistic and political activities for some years. In 1926 she became interested in African art–probably via the general avant-garde interest in the value of non-European, tribal, and "primitive" cultures–and began buying "ivory, gods, masks, fetishes" as she wrote to Janet Flanner 11 March 1926. Soon her collection of African carved ivory bracelets became her trademark, as gossip columnists observed: "Ivory shackles: one thing Nancy Cunard did while in London was to create a new fashion in ivory bracelets." While she was not averse to finding ways of marking out her individuality, Cunard's interest in African art was genuine and not merely that of a dilettante.

In 1927 Cunard was occupied with her troubled relationship with Aragon and with buying a house in La Chapelle-Réanville in Normandy. By the summer of 1928 she had decided to use some of the extensive outbuildings there to house her own press, which would be dedicated to the handprinting and publication of contemporary poetry. She bought an old handpress and engaged a professional printer to teach her the craft. She learned quickly, and soon the Hours Press began producing high-quality small editions of works of prose and poetry in which commercial publishers were unlikely to be interested. Between 1928 and 1931 the Hours Press published new works by such writers as Moore, Beckett, Graves, Pound, Riding, and Aldington. The best known was Beckett's poem *Whoroscope,* which won The Hours Press prize of £10 for the best poem on the topic of time in 1930.

During a trip to Venice in the summer of 1928 Cunard's often violent relationship with Aragon ended after he attempted suicide. At a Venice hotel Cunard met Henry Crowder, who was playing there in a black American jazz quartet called the Alabamians–an unusual sight and sound in Europe at the time. Cunard and Crowder soon became lovers, and when the quartet's contract with the hotel ended, Crowder remained with Cunard. Italy, however, was a Fascist state, and the two felt that their being together was viewed with hostility. Even outside Italy such an interracial pairing was regarded as extraordinary and as breaking a profound taboo. Lady Cunard viewed the relationship with shocked distaste, and the breach between mother and daughter became absolute.

Crowder rejoined the Alabamians in Paris and continued to see Cunard. In 1929 he became unemployed and moved in with Cunard at La Chapelle-Réanville, where he helped with the Hours Press. Their relationship was not an easy one; Cunard's bohemian ideas about sexual and other behavior were not Crowder's. Sometimes she urged him to be "more African," and he protested, "But I ain't African, I'm American." In 1931 Crowder returned to the United States, relieved to get away from the unpredictable Cunard. But he soon returned, hoping for better job prospects in Europe.

Through her conversations with Crowder, Cunard learned much about the lives of African Americans. She was appalled by his accounts of racism, especially in the South, and she began to think about putting together an anthology that would represent the creativity of African and African American culture. Her determination to celebrate and defend black culture was particularly focused by the Scottsboro Boys case, which became a focal point for protest against racial injustice in the United States. In March

1931 nine black youths were sentenced to death in Scottsboro, Alabama, for raping two white girls who had been riding the rails with them in a boxcar; the charges were unfounded. Cunard did everything she could to publicize the case. She and Crowder went to New York (against his better judgment, since he feared—correctly—that they would be targets of white hostility) so that Cunard could make contacts with writers who could contribute to her anthology, lend support to the Scottsboro protests, and see conditions in the United States for herself. Crowder did not return to Europe with her. In 1932 Cunard traveled to Boston, returning to France via Jamaica so that she could observe Britain's treatment of its black colonial subjects. She continued to commission articles and poems for the anthology, for which her ambitions were vast: it was to cover the social and political conditions and the cultural achievements of people of African descent throughout the world. "It is primarily for the Coloured people," she had said in announcing the volume in 1931.

By 1934 Cunard had assembled a bulky typescript, and she began approaching publishers. Those who were at all interested asked her to scale down the book, but she refused to do so. Finally, the London communist firm Wishart and Company agreed to publish the book if Cunard funded it: the publishers were sympathetic to the cause the book was intended to advance but did not feel able to bear the cost of producing such a long and complex work. This method of publication meant that Cunard retained total control over the book, and the expense was partly met by libel cases she won against several British newspapers who attacked her in racist articles.

Negro Anthology, Made by Nancy Cunard, 1931–1933 was published in 1934. It was 855 pages in length and included many photographs, as well as scores for African music. The articles covered topics ranging from ethnography, linguistics, and poetry to political commentary and analysis. Contributors included such well-known black writers as Sterling Brown, Langston Hughes, and Zora Neale Hurston. Cunard contributed to the section "By White Poets" a ninety-six-line poem titled "Southern Sheriff." The savagely ironic monologue spoken by the title character is unlike anything Cunard had written previously:

> White Folks don't kill each other in the South
> Ho no, not with so many niggers around.
> It's the wrong end of the stick you got, englishman.
> You say: "here's a murder, find the criminal"
> *We* say: "too many niggers around with uppity ideas"
> So we jus' take one or two along for murder

The American jazz musician Henry Crowder, who became Cunard's lover in Venice in 1928

Cunard also wrote six essays for the volume, one of them about the Scottsboro Boys case.

Though clearly a landmark in retrospect, at the time *Negro Anthology* did not have the impact for which Cunard hoped. The book was not widely reviewed, even in activist journals. Part of the problem was the wide range of contributors to the book: it had pieces by moderate liberal black leaders, as well as by Communist Party writers. Though Cunard's introduction made it clear that she supported the Communist Party line that revolution was the only way to end racism, other writers had reservations about Communist orthodoxy. Thus, if there was something to please a variety of African American opinions, there was equally something to offend everyone. Additionally, the book was expensive and cumbersome to handle, so that it did not have much chance of selling even to activists, let alone to ordinary readers. The anthology did receive good reviews in Britain from the Communist *Daily Worker* and from *The New Statesman,* but Cunard had expected a wider response, especially in the United States. The book was banned as seditious in the British West Indies and in several British colonies in Africa.

After publishing *Negro Anthology* Cunard turned her attention to Europe, where fascism was making increasing inroads. Adolf Hitler had become chancellor of Germany in 1933. In 1935 Benito Mussolini invaded

Cunard in Paris in the spring of 1930 with her Hours Press books

Abyssinia (Ethiopia) as part of his plan to establish the empire that he regarded as Italy's due. Cunard's response to the invasion united her detestation of fascism with her determination to defend black culture throughout the world. She became a correspondent for the Associated Negro Press in Geneva, where she reported on the fruitless efforts of the League of Nations to deter Mussolini's aggression.

On 17 July 1936 the Spanish Civil War broke out when fascist army units calling themselves "Nationalists" rebelled against the mainly left-of-center coalition "Republican" government that had been elected on 16 February. General Francisco Franco gradually assumed the leadership of the Nationalist forces. Determined to contribute to the struggle on the Republican side, Cunard traveled to Spain several times as a reporter for the Associated Negro Press and wrote articles about the war. In Madrid she met the Chilean consul, the poet Pablo Neruda. Together they planned a series of pamphlets on the war to raise money for the Republican side, which she would print on the handpress that she still owned from the Hours Press days. They published six in 1937 under the title *Les Poètes du monde defendant les peuple espagnols* (Poets of the World Defend the Spanish People), comprising poems in English, French, and Spanish.

Cunard had an idea for another way to promote the characteristic 1930s ideal of a united front between writers and activists: certain that all writers of distinction must be opposed to fascism, she planned to send to all noted English authors a letter asking for their views on the Spanish Civil War; the answers would be published as a volume to demonstrate the consensus of the forces of civilization. Together with eleven other writers, including Tzara, W. H. Auden, and Stephen Spender, she composed a short preface that culminated:

> This is the question we are asking you:
> Are you for, or against, the legal Government and the People of Republican Spain?
> Are you for, or against, Franco and Fascism?
> For it is impossible any longer to take no side.

Clearly, the answer expected was "for." Using her handpress, Cunard printed "The Question" on a large sheet of paper and sent it out. Most of the replies were, indeed, in favor of the Republic, though Eliot, Pound, and H. G. Wells declined to take sides, and Edmund Blunden and Evelyn Waugh's answers were put into the "against" category. The completed exercise was published as a pamphlet by the periodical *Left Review* in 1937 and sold well.

In January 1939 the Republican government was defeated. On 24 August, Germany and the Soviet Union signed a nonaggression pact, and on 1 September the two countries invaded Poland; on 3 September, Britain and France declared war on Germany. Four months later Cunard left France for Chile. She soon wished to return to Britain, but under wartime conditions it was not easy to do so. In 1941, via Trinidad (where she was hailed by the black press as the creator of the banned *Negro*) and New York, she crossed to Liverpool. She lived in London throughout the war, picking up some journalistic commissions and working as a translator and secretary for a Free French organization. In 1944 she edited a collection, *Poems for France, Written by Poets on France since the War,* designed to show support for the Resistance.

When Cunard returned to La Chapelle-Réanville in 1945, she found that her house had been ransacked by German troops and by some of her French neighbors. Her collection of African bracelets had been stolen, and her African sculptures and various modernist paintings had been vandalized. Cunard could no longer stand to live there, and after a period of restlessness she bought a house in the Dordogne in 1949. Though she wrote poetry until the end of her life, none of it found its way into print. In 1954, however, she published the first of three books in which she looked back over aspects of her life: *Grand Man: Memories of Norman Douglas*. It was followed by *GM: Memories of George Moore* (1956) and the posthumously published *These Were the Hours: Memories of My Hours Press, Réanville and Paris, 1928–1931* (1966).

Throughout her life Cunard drank heavily and pursued casual sexual adventures, usually in tandem with longer-term relationships. She was, thus, often involved in complicated and sometimes violent episodes. Toward the end of her life she had periods of drunken paranoia. She was particularly ill between 1958 and 1960, when she was arrested in Spain and in London, in the latter instance throwing her shoes at the police. A London magistrate remanded her for psychiatric examination, and she was judged to be suffering from a mental disorder combined with alcoholism. She was treated for four months at the Holloway Sanatorium in Virginia Water, where she recovered much of her mental equilibrium. She never changed any of the opinions she had developed during the 1930s and 1940s, however, and sometimes they surfaced in inappropriate ways. Thus, while traveling across France by train shortly before her death, she was asked for her ticket by the conductor; but Cunard associated uniforms with fascism and ate the ticket rather than surrender it to this "enemy." She died in a Paris hospital on 16 March 1965.

Cunard's reputation as an outrageous breaker of rules was well deserved. She had no use for social conventions; if this attitude began as a rebellion against her mother, it developed into a lifelong commitment to fighting injustice. Her reputation is better remembered than her poetry, but her life and work are closely linked: both show a progression from a wish to shock and a rejection of old meanings to a search for new and valuable insights. She began her career as a poet by searching for a voice with which to express her rejection of exhausted conventions. Her best poetry was produced in the 1920s; thereafter, she found passionately engaging causes that led her, first, to make her poetry an expression of her political activism and, in the end, to abandon poetry as her main interest. If her verse never quite established a secure and distinctive voice of its own, it is, nevertheless, worth reading for the insights it offers into the aesthetic and political possibilities of poetry in the period 1916 to 1940. Furthermore, her creation of *Negro Anthology* stands alongside her own writing as a significant achievement.

Biographies:

Daphne Fielding, *Those Remarkable Cunards: Emerald and Nancy. Lady Cunard and Her Daughter* (London: Eyre & Spottiswoode, 1968; New York: Atheneum, 1968);

Hugh Ford, ed., *Nancy Cunard: Brave Poet, Indomitable Rebel, 1896–1965* (Philadelphia: Chilton, 1968);

Charles Burkhart, *Herman and Nancy and Ivy: Three Lives in Art* (London: Gollancz, 1977);

Anne Chisholm, *Nancy Cunard* (London: Sidgwick & Jackson, 1979).

References:

Sheri Benstock, *Women of the Left Bank: Paris, 1900–1940* (Austin: University of Texas Press, 1986), p. 346;

Valentine Cunningham, *British Writers of the Thirties* (Oxford: Oxford University Press, 1989);

Jane Dowson, ed., *Women's Poetry of the 1930s–A Critical Anthology* (London: Routledge, 1996), pp. 51–54;

Hugh Ford, *Published in Paris–American and British Writers, Printers and Publishers in Paris, 1920–1939* (London: Garnstone, 1975), pp. 253–268, 269–281, 287–289;

Paul Fussell, *Abroad: British Literary Travelling between the Wars* (Oxford: Oxford University Press, 1980), pp. 121, 123, 166, 187;

Bonnie Kime-Scott, *The Gender of Modernism–A Critical Anthology* (Bloomington & Indianapolis: Indiana University Press, 1990), pp. 63–84;

Kime-Scott, *The Women of 1928,* volume 1 of her *Refiguring Modernism* (Bloomington & Indianapolis: Indiana University Press, 1990), pp. xxv, 91, 94, 103, 185;

Janet Montefiore, *Men and Women Writers of the 1930s: The Dangerous Flood of History* (London: Routledge, 1996), pp. 2–6, 21, 24, 114, 116–118, 158, 183;

John Press, *A Map of Modern English Verse* (Oxford: Oxford University Press, 1969), p. 156;

Laura Riding and Robert Graves, *A Survey of Modernist Poetry* (London: Heinemann, 1929), pp. 165, 201;

C. K. Stead, *The New Poetic: From Yeats to Eliot* (London: Athlone Press, 1998), p. 112;

Tory Young, "The Reception of Nancy Cunard's *Negro,*" in *Women Writers of the 1930s: Gender, Politics and History,* by Maroula Joannou (Edinburgh: Edinburgh University Press, 1999), pp. 113–122.

Papers:

The Harry Ransom Humanities Research Center, University of Texas at Austin, has a large holding of Nancy Cunard's correspondence, holograph and typescript works, and works by authors associated with Cunard. The Library of Congress has some items, including photographs. Morris Library at Southern Illinois University, Carbondale, has some holdings.

Olive Custance
(Lady Alfred Douglas)
(7 February 1874 – 12 February 1944)

Michelle L. Whitney
University of South Carolina

BOOKS: *Opals* (London & New York: John Lane, 1897);

Rainbows (London & New York: John Lane, 1902);

The Blue Bird (London: Marlborough, 1905);

The Inn of Dreams (London & New York: John Lane, 1911).

Collections: *The Selected Poems of Olive Custance,* edited by Brocard Sewell (London: Cecil Woolf, 1995);

Opals; with, Rainbows, edited by R. K. R. Thorton and Ian Small (Poole, U.K. & New York: Woodstock, 1996).

Olive Custance is best known for her association with some of the decadent era's most notable people: the publisher John Lane, the poet Richard Le Gallienne, the artist Aubrey Beardsley, and one of the most notorious men of the 1890s—her husband, Lord Alfred Douglas. Nevertheless, she earned moderate success with her poetry. Her poems appeared in periodicals such as Lane's *The Yellow Book,* to which she was a frequent contributor, and between 1897 and 1911 she published four volumes of poetry. Reviewers pointed to her simplistic, almost childish themes, trite language, and exaggerated use of punctuation. But even the most severe critics acknowledged that Custance's poems had an ineffable charm and moments that pointed toward a bright potential. Despite her classification as a minor poet, Custance has been mentioned or anthologized in many works dealing with the fin de siècle.

Olive Eleanor Custance was born on 7 February 1874, the oldest child of Colonel Frederic Hambledon Custance and Eleanor Constance Custance, née Jolliffe, of Weston Hall, Norfolk. The Custances and Jolliffes were distinguished aristocratic families: Olive's grandfather, Sir Hambledon Francis Custance, was a high sheriff of the County of Norfolk; her father served as a justice of the peace and commanded a battalion in the Boer War. While the father could be kindly and good-natured, his partial deafness and austerity could

Olive Custance (Lady Alfred Douglas)

make him irascible. His eldest daughter lived most of her life under the shadow of his domineering presence.

As an adult, Custance wrote in her diary that she had been "a naughty . . . funny . . . fat little child, with pink cheeks and short brown hair, and big blue eyes."

What she called her "wild spirits" and her waywardness sent a succession of nurses through the Custance household. While adults often misunderstood her headstrong temperament, it was also the source of her early creative energy. Custance recorded in her diary on 17 February 1899: "My great amusement was 'acting' . . . pretending to be someone else. . . . And it was not only one person that I acted but a whole crowd. The first thing I remember acting was Robin Hood and his merry men. I did not do it as a play. . . . I entered as it were into the words."

In 1884 Custance was a bridesmaid at the wedding of Rachel Montgomery, a cousin of Douglas's, although later they did not recall having met each other there. When she was sixteen she met the twenty-five-year-old poet John Gray, the model for Dorian in Oscar Wilde's *The Picture of Dorian Gray* (1891), at a party and fell in love with him almost immediately. Though she did not see him again, they frequently corresponded about literary matters. In 1892 she wrote a poem for him titled "The Prince of Dreams"; she later renamed it "Ideal" and published it in her first book of poetry, *Opals* (1897). The poem describes her frustration when he "passed me carelessly in the throng" at a party and is laden with her characteristic romantic embellishments: "You were indifferent . . . and I may forget / Your profound eyes, your heavy hair, your voice / So clear, yet deep and low with tenderness." As the poem implies, Gray was unmoved by her charms: he remained unmarried and became a Roman Catholic priest in 1901. He sent Custance a copy of his *Silverpoints* (1893), and she sent him a manuscript for sixteen poems that later appeared in her first two books. In her diary entry for 10 February 1895 Custance recorded some advice on writing poetry Gray offered her in a recent letter:

> At a certain time one is apt to want to live for grace. Soon the better ideal comes to live well and chance the grace. And is it not so with poetry? Have you come to the determination to write *well* at every risk? to put more fire into your work than anyone else could ever find out.

The circumstances of Custance's life kept her from following Gray's advice to the fullest.

According to her biographer, Brocard Sewell, Custance was not shy about writing to people whose work she admired, and in the early 1890s she began a correspondence with another well-known poet, Le Gallienne. Sewell describes "a certain 'kittenish' quality in Olive at this time, which used to show itself in lengthy letters to her friends, written somewhat breathlessly, with erratic and idiosyncratic punctuation, and a plethora of dashes and dots." Le Gallienne was charmed by Custance, whose "flower-like loveliness" he describes in his *The Romantic '90s* (1926). She wrote often of him in her diary, nicknaming him "Narcissus." In May 1894 Le Gallienne's wife died of typhoid fever; Custance recorded in her diary on 19 June 1894: "I could read between the lines and see how sad he was—though he scarcely spoke of his sorrow: indeed his beautiful soul always seems to be thinking of others. . . ." She received an early copy of Le Gallienne's *Prose Fancies* (1894) inscribed "Olive Custance from Mildrech S. R. Le Gallienne: June 15." The book was forwarded to her by his publisher, Lane.

Lane was well known for publishing the works of many of the decadent writers of the 1890s; he also published the short-lived and controversial literary journal *The Yellow Book,* to which Le Gallienne, Beardsley, and Max Beerbohm were regular contributors. In a diary entry for June 1894 Custance describes meeting Le Gallienne and Lane for the first time when she and her governess, "Tannie," had tea with them at Lane's office: "We were both very shy, Tannie and I, as we stood in John Lane's little sitting room waiting for him to come in . . . John Lane was shy too, I think, when he shook hands." Custance's first published poem, "Twilight," appeared in the October 1894 issue of *The Yellow Book*. On 21 November she recorded in her diary that she received a "charming letter from John Lane" with a payment, which she describes as "wonderful, 'fairy gold,'" for the publication of her poem. She had seven more poems published in *The Yellow Book;* her poetry also appeared in *Savoy, Living Age,* and *The Academy*.

In 1897 Beardsley designed a bookplate for Custance and became another victim of her correspondence. In a 7 June 1897 letter to his publisher, Leonard Smithers, he calls her "Silly little O."; a month later he tells Smithers that he received "Eleven pages from Olive this morning plus two pages of verse."

In 1897 Lane published Custance's first volume of poems. The book was titled *Opals* because she had a particular love of the stone, which some say brings bad luck, and "Opal" was one of the nicknames she called herself. Some critics deemed the title appropriate because the poems had much in common with the delicate, shimmering gems. Le Gallienne called the book "the best poetry written by a woman in a long time." He commended Custance's depiction of simple yet "rich and subtle" themes, such as "the sound of the rain," "the beauty of the morning sky," and "the sudden wonderful face of love." In typically decadent fashion he argued that it was not important for Custance to "trouble her head" about moral issues or literary arguments; more crucial was that she "instinctively understands some of the secrets of the use of words." While her simple, intuitive approach was a strength of her

47

The poet John Gray—the model for Oscar Wilde's Dorian Gray—with whom Custance fell in unrequited love in 1884

poetry, however, it was also a weakness. "A Lament for the Leaves" demonstrates Custance's pretty, but often vacuous, style:

> The trees look sad—sad—I long for the leaves,
> Green leaves that shimmer—and shelter the nests that the
>   song-birds make,
> The earth is glad—glad—but my spirit grieves.
> Break forth from your buds and awake
>   O! leaves!

In addition, critics were quick to point out her overzealous use of punctuation: her poetry, like her letters and diaries, is saturated with dashes and dots. Using the British expression for *period,* the reviewer for *The Times Literary Supplement* (*TLS,* 25 July 1902) offered a "word of trivial advice": "if Miss Custance will realize that one full stop can do quite as much work as three, the look of her pages would be improved."

While Custance's first collection has an overall "girlish" tone, it includes many moments that hint at a developing maturity. "The Poet's Picture" seems to be a self-portrait: the "brow half hid with curling hair" and "wistful eyes a flight" that she attributes to her poet can be seen in photographs of Custance. Her frustration at being a "girl-poet," as Le Gallienne called her, is evident when she pits the "pent-up passion" of the female poet against the "whole wide sorrow of the world."

"The Music of Dvorák" is one of the few decadent pieces in Custance's oeuvre. The poem depicts the frenzied and sensuous movement of girls dancing themselves into trancelike states—the "flutter of loose robes," "the rhythmic beat of drums," and "the clash of cymbals" paint a vibrant, stirring picture. The trance brought on by music and dancing is "ever as the shadow of soft wings / Shutting away all sense of sordid things, / All sight of that inscrutable Sphinx called 'Life.'" The poem embraces the aestheticist notion that beauty in art can help to shut out the ugliness of ordinary life.

In 1900 Custance wrote to yet another young, handsome poet, introducing herself and praising his poetry. The poet was Lord Alfred Bruce Douglas, son of John Sholto Douglas, the eighth Marquess of Queensberry. Known as "Bosie," Alfred Douglas received some notice for his sonnets but was better known for his connection with Oscar Wilde. In 1895 the marquess, who vehemently opposed his son's relationship with the celebrated literary figure, left his calling card, with the inscription "for Oscar Wilde posing as Somdomite [*sic*]," at Wilde's club. After losing a libel suit against Queensberry, Wilde was tried for sodomy and sentenced to two years' hard labor in Reading Gaol. It was to Alfred Douglas that Wilde bitterly addressed his confessional letter *De Profundis,* which was published posthumously in 1905. He died on 30 November 1900, three years after his release from prison. For the rest of his life Douglas was tainted by his association with Wilde.

Douglas's reputation did not deter Custance from corresponding with him. On receiving a response to her first letter, of 20 June 1900, she sent him a bunch of flowers and a copy of *Opals*. He responded four days later that her poems were "wonderfully beautiful" and sent a photograph of himself. They began a romantic correspondence, Douglas signing himself "Your loving Prince" and Custance "Your Page." Early in 1901 they agreed to meet at the South Kensington Museum (now the Victoria and Albert Museum), but Douglas entered through the wrong door and missed her. To his surprise, she appeared at his lodgings on Duke Street, chaperoned by her maid. According to Douglas's autobiography, it was "love at first sight." Douglas had already decided that he needed to marry, but his bride would have to be "well born, beautiful and outstandingly attractive," as well as "intellectual and appreciative of poetry and literature." He thought that the odds against his finding such a perfect woman were too great—"Yet there she was!" The two seemed perfect for each other. The bisexual Douglas was attracted to her handsome, rather boyish appearance, and she seems to have been attracted to his feminine good looks. Douglas said in his autobiography that he believed that "almost everyone is more or less bi-sexual" and that the "obscure psychology of sex" drew him and Custance to each other.

As passionate as Custance and Douglas were for each other, marriage seemed to be out of the question: Custance's father would never tolerate the notorious Douglas as his son-in-law; and Douglas needed money—he could not afford to marry for love. Consequently, in September 1901 he sailed for the United States to look for an heiress to marry. Before leaving he gave Custance a heart-shaped locket that held a lock of his hair. She thanked him in a letter: "My own Prince, the little heart is sweet and I shall wear it even when you have forgotten all about me and married the beautiful rich princess who will give you all those lovely things you ought to have." She added that she hoped that one day Douglas would "come back to 'him'"—that is, to his page boy. Continuing the gender-switching theme, Douglas asked her in September, "Why can't you dress up as a boy and come with me?"

Some scholars have pointed to this facet of Custance's relationship with Douglas and to her friendship with the Paris-based American lesbian writer Natalie Clifford Barney as evidence of Custance's homosexual tendencies. Custance had been introduced to Barney around the time she met Douglas. On a visit to London, Barney had been given a copy of *Opals* by Lane. When she returned to Paris, Barney began a correspondence with Custance. In one letter Custance included a poem she had written for Barney. The poem has never been published in its entirety, but a fragment has often been quoted for its hints of lesbianism:

> For I would dance to make you smile, and sing
> Of those who with some sweet mad sin have played,
> And how Love walks with delicate feet afraid
>   'Twixt maid and maid.

Custance first met Barney face to face while Douglas was in the United States. She had gone to Paris with her mother and Freddie Manners-Sutton, whom Custance's mother hoped she would marry. Unhappy with Manners-Sutton's attentions, Custance told her friend about the situation, and Barney is supposed to have said, "Tell him I'm in love with you!" To escape Manners-Sutton, Custance persuaded her mother to allow her to travel with Barney to Venice. During their time together Barney wrote several love poems to Custance; one of them, "How Do I Love You," includes the lines: "Of all my cruel loves I love you most, / and since I love you most–ah sweet love me!" Aware of Custance's love for Douglas, Barney–who was herself an American heiress–suggested that she marry Douglas so that they could all live together in a ménage à trois. Custance knew that the plan would not work; she returned to England, and Barney returned to her former girlfriend.

Although Douglas bragged that several American heiresses were interested in him, his time overseas was unhappy. He found that the Wilde affair had not been forgotten in the United States; in addition, he was in love with Custance. In January 1902 he returned to England, tired and discouraged, only to discover that Custance had become engaged to someone else. To make matters worse, the fiancé was George Montagu (later the ninth Earl of Sandwich), a former Winchester College classmate and possible love interest of Douglas's. Montagu's family had pressured him to disassociate himself from Douglas so that his chance to run for Parliament would not be harmed by rumors of homosexuality. Douglas's resentment of Montagu's renunciation of their friendship inspired him to write "The Traitor," published in his *Collected Poems* (1919).

Custance had not been aware of Douglas's hatred of Montagu; she only knew that Montagu had known Douglas at school and could tell interesting stories about him and do amusing "Bosie imitations." Clearly, she was not in love with Montagu; she may have been pressured into the relationship by her family or may have been trying to make Douglas jealous. If the latter was the case, her plan succeeded. In his autobiography Douglas says: "When I returned from America and found that he was engaged to marry 'my girl' the blood of a hundred Douglas ancestors surged up, and I said in my heart: 'No, you don't!'" He arranged to meet Custance, asked her to elope with him, and she agreed. While she was visiting Montagu's family at their country house, Douglas obtained a special marriage license. On the morning of 4 March 1902 she sneaked out of the house and met Douglas at Saint George's Church in Hanover Square. Only Custance's maid and Douglas's mother were aware of their plans. According to Douglas's autobiography, Lady Queensberry gave the couple "£200, her fondest blessing, a diamond ring for Olive, and the promise of an allowance."

Custance's father was less understanding: on learning that his daughter had eloped and run away to Paris, Colonel Custance went to Scotland Yard and demanded that the police do something about the situation. But nothing could be done: the couple was legally married. Custance's father soon reconciled himself to the marriage, and when the new couple came to visit at Weston Hall, he taught his son-in-law how to fly-fish.

Custance's future husband, Lord Alfred Douglas (right), with Oscar Wilde at Oxford in 1893

The Douglases' son, Raymond Wilfrid Sholto Douglas, was born on 17 November 1902.

That same year Custance published *Rainbows,* her second volume of poetry. A reviewer for the *TLS* (18 July 1902) described the book as "short love poems, ardent, musical, and showing considerable nervous sensibility." Another critic, writing in the 26 July issue of *The Academy and Literature,* commended the "markedly sincere" emotions in her poetry but also pointed out many strained and unrealistic metaphors and phrases, such as "monstrous daffodil" and "crimson meadows." Overall, however, *Rainbows* shows significant growth in poetic style and thematic content. Among the new themes are disillusionment with love, gender roles within relationships, and self-analysis.

Custance dedicated the book "To the Fairy Prince"—her husband—and many of the poems deal with their relationship. "A Song to Beauty" is addressed to Douglas and speaks of "the troubled beauty of your great blue eyes, / The wild-rose whiteness of your body fair." Referring obliquely to his former homosexual companions, the poem tells of his "pale lovers" who watched him "pass them by" to be with her. Custance apparently wrote the poem while Douglas was in the United States, since it mentions the "long leagues of land, broad wastes of shining sea" between them. She describes herself as the pursuer in the relationship, calling her heart a "princely hunter"; but in the next stanza her heart is a "song-bird" that is "tangled in Love's snare."

A similar pattern emerges in "Songs of a Fairy Princess," a five-poem series that retells the fairy-tale formula of a "proud" princess waiting for her handsome prince to rescue her. In these poems the female is again both the aggressor and the victim of aggression. The speaker warns the princess that she must keep the prince captive: "hold him fast / with slim white hands, each kiss may be the last." But at the same time, the princess is herself a captive: she is forced to watch from "behind her bars" for the prince's approach. One of the poems mentions "a little page from Love's own court," evidently referring to Custance's nickname for herself in her relationship with Douglas. Custance's verse often takes on a masculine tone: the princess's description of her lover—"your great blue eyes," "dreams of your dear mouth," and "golden like your hair"—sound more like a man wooing a woman in traditional Petrarchan terms than like a woman describing her husband. Years later Douglas wrote in his autobiography:

> even if I had known then what I know now, I could only have prolonged the agony of our love. But how could I know or guess that the very thing she loved in me was that which I was always trying to suppress and keep under: I mean the feminine part of me? As soon as I was married I deliberately tried to be more and more manly. The more manly I became the less attractive I was to Olive.

Some of the poems in *Rainbows* hint at Custance's growing disillusionment with the superficiality of fin-de-siècle life. "The Masquerade" laments the falseness of modern relationships, comparing people to "masked dancers" at a ball who are afraid to reveal their true identities. Normally, a masquerade ball would call up images of colorful costumes and lively partygoers; but here the dancers move "wearily together" through predetermined steps as if in a trance. The metaphor is an apt one for the tired, lackluster close of the vibrant 1890s. "The Masquerade" recalls Custance's earlier poem, "The Music of Dvořák," but the trance induced by dancing is no longer a blissful state: instead, it is a type of imprisonment.

The final piece in *Rainbows,* "The Girl in the Glass," examines disillusionment of a more personal nature: "Girl in the Glass! You smile, and yet / Your eyes are full of a vague regret." In fact, Custance was starting to regret her marriage to Lord Douglas. The couple was having money troubles, and they quarreled frequently. In 1904 they moved to Lake Farm in Wiltshire, where they lived until 1907. Custance's diary of this period details arguments with Douglas, chronic illness, and many days in which she rose from bed only to eat dinner. She wrote little during this time, commenting in her 6 October 1906 diary entry: "I wrote a poem today! The first for a year . . . I am in what I call the poet's mood!"

Custance's third volume of poems, *The Blue Bird* (1905), mostly comprises material she had written earlier. Unlike the first two, this book was published not by Lane but by Thomas William Henry Crosland's Marlborough Press; many of the poems had appeared in Crosland's journal, *The English Review*. The change in publishers was not a profitable decision. Although Crosland offered Custance royalties of 20 percent, she received no money and wound up purchasing the unsold copies from him for £5. Nevertheless, Custance graciously offered Crosland "A thousand thanks for the charming little birds" and invited him to dinner. The critics again commented on the dashes and dots, strained language, and lack of depth in the poems; and again they also pointed to a few moments in the work that, as the reviewer for *The Athenaeum* (17 February 1906) wrote, "possess that quality which distinguishes poetry from verse."

The Blue Bird opens with a quotation from Wilde's *Intentions* (1891) about a bluebird who sings "of beautiful and impossible things, of things that / are lovely and that never happen, of things / that are not and that should be." On the opposite page is the poem "To My Husband," which ends, "And now, O poet passionate and brave, / O lover with the beautiful sad face, / Like a shy child I bring you all my songs." The poems in *The Blue Bird*, however, are not the childishly innocent love poems of her earlier two volumes. The unhappiness and regret that were hinted at in *Rainbows* have grown into disillusionment; the theme of love grown bitter is repeated throughout the collection. In "Hyacinthus," for example, "Love is blind and cruel, and the end / Of every joy is sorrow and distress." In the bittersweet "A Memory" Custance recalls the days of her and Douglas's budding romance. While Douglas's side of the story of the disintegration of their marriage has been told by his biographers and by Douglas himself in his autobiography, "A Memory" may be one of the few places in which Custance makes her position known:

> You never saw the prisoned soul
> Behind the windows of my eyes,
> Frantic to break from fate's control
> And charm you with her flatteries . . .
> And show you, your cold heart to move,
> The shining treasure of her love.

Custance's friend and possible lover, the American expatriate writer Natalie Clifford Barney

In "A Dream" the speaker and her lover walk together down a road lined with poplar trees. It is a beautiful summer day, and the talk between the two is "delicate and shy." The speaker is, however, all too aware that a quarrel lurks just below the surface: "though in that cage of words wild thoughts were / pent."

A yearning for peace becomes a morbid obsession with death in "I am Weary, Let Me Sleep," one of Custance's more eloquent works. The speaker is exhausted from the constant struggle of life: "I am weary, let me sleep / In some great embroidered bed. / Let me dream that I am dead, / Nevermore to wake and weep."

Despite their marital problems, Douglas and Custance were still deeply in love. In 1907 Douglas composed a six-sonnet series titled "To Olive"; the poems, which are among his best-known works, were published in *Sonnets by Lord Alfred Douglas* (1909). The fifth sonnet includes the line "I loved you as a tired child loves sleep."

material also shows how little she was writing as her marriage neared its end. The critics were quick to point out that the vitality and innocence had faded from her poetry. As the reviewer for *TLS* (7 December 1911) wrote:

> The earlier volumes of Lady Alfred Douglas had a freshness, a gaiety, a swift play of lights and shadows like an April day, which were full of charm. . . . In her new book the utterance is still her own . . . but the years have taken away the freshness and the buoyancy without bringing depth to the tone or richness to the thought.

The reviewer added, "Youth passes and leaves us shivering and forlorn: and only a very little good poetry can be made out of that." If her first two books exuded the childish innocence of youth, and her third expressed growing disillusionment, Custance's final volume detailed the despair of adult life.

Two poems in particular exemplify the despondency that underlies *The Inn of Dreams*. In "The Prisoner of God" the speaker's spirit is compared to a bird whose wings and voice bring delight. But for an unspecified reason God has decided to take away the speaker's "spirit wings," leaving her a hopeless captive: "Once long and long ago I did rejoice, / But now I am a stone that falls and falls. / A prisoner, cursing the blank prison walls." "The Storm" presents an even bleaker picture; the stormy winds have chased away joy, leaving only a dark, enveloping despair: "And my soul is heavy and dark with a great / distress, / For heaven is far away and hope is / dead." This was the unhappiest point in her life: she was trapped between her father's demands and her husband's accusations of betrayal. In "Opal Song" she defends herself against the latter: "I come back to you, / Never doubt my loyalty."

For two years Douglas bombarded his father-in-law with letters and telegrams protesting the colonel's interference with his wife and child, and on 26 February 1913 Frederic Custance had Douglas arrested for criminal libel. Around this time Olive Custance left her husband and returned to live with her father at Weston Hall. On 29 April, Douglas, realizing that he would lose the libel case, offered an official apology to his father-in-law.

From 1914 through 1915 Douglas and Colonel Custance fought in the courts for custody of Raymond. Each time, Olive Custance took her father's side. On 14 January she wrote to her mother-in-law, Lady Queensberry:

> My father is angry all the time because I love Bosie still—and I am utterly miserable. But would it do Bosie any good if I am turned out to starve? I am utterly

Custance and Douglas's son, Raymond, who became the object of a custody battle between his parents and Custance's father

Custance's father had never been completely reconciled to his daughter's choice of husband, and after the death of his wife in 1908 his relationship with his son-in-law worsened. When Douglas converted to Roman Catholicism in 1911, Frederic Custance persuaded Olive to resettle her inheritance rights on her son, Raymond. He sought thereby both to control his grandson's upbringing and to prevent Alfred Douglas from having access to the Custance property after his death. Against the advice of her husband, Olive Custance agreed to give up her inheritance in exchange for a monthly allowance of £600. She entered into the agreement without a written promise from her father to pay the allowance. Frederic Custance then threatened to stop the monthly payments unless Raymond was turned over to him. The situation caused even more strain in the Douglases' relationship.

In 1911 Lane published Custance's final book of poetry, *The Inn of Dreams*. Of the thirty-nine poems in the volume, twenty were repeated from *The Blue Bird*, probably because that book had done so poorly with Crosland's Marlborough Press. The lack of new

helpless since I made those settlements. Perhaps it would be better for Bosie to divorce me for desertion? I only wish I had enough courage to kill myself.

The court finally ordered that Raymond spend three-fifths of his school holidays with his grandfather at Weston Hall. In 1915 Custance was reconciled with her husband, and on 30 June they applied together for custody of Raymond. The court, however, reaffirmed its original decision.

Custance left her husband again, this time permanently. In 1920 she moved away from her father, as well, relocating to a cottage in Bembridge on the Isle of Wight. Sewell cites a report that an inscription on the cottage gate read, "Safe haven, after a stormy passage." In 1924, the year her father died, she became a Catholic, but she left the faith three years later. Also in 1927 her son suffered a mental breakdown. Raymond was diagnosed as "schizo-effective" and placed in St. Andrew's Hospital, where he spent most of the rest of his life.

In 1930 Custance moved to London and in 1932 to a cottage in Hove in East Sussex. Douglas had been living in an apartment nearby since 1927. Although they knew that they could not live together, they remained close friends and saw each other almost every day. Marie Carmichael Stopes, a friend of Douglas's in later life, asked him why he and his wife did not live together. She reports that he replied with a laugh, "Poets are difficult to live with, and I am a specially difficult poet."

Throughout most of 1943 Custance was increasingly ill and suffered from delusions. On 11 February 1944 Douglas spent many hours by his wife's bedside; she was only semiconscious. The next morning the maid called to tell him that Custance was dead; she had died of a cerebral hemorrhage. Douglas wrote to a friend, "My darling little Olive died this morning." He survived his wife by a little more than a year, dying at seventy-four on 20 March 1945 of congestive heart failure. Custance's instructions for the disposition of her remains were not carried out until 1950, when her ashes were scattered in the sea near Brighton.

Although Olive Custance has long been considered a minor poet, recent scholarship has brought her poetry and her life renewed attention. Her poems have been included as representatives of the fin de siècle in several anthologies, and Douglas Murray's *Bosie: A Biography of Lord Alfred Douglas* (2000) has disclosed some previously unpublished information about her marriage. With the increased critical attention, Custance's status as a "girl-poet" of the 1890s is likely to change.

Bibliography:

Nancy J. Hawkey, "Olive Custance Douglas: An Annotated Bibliography of Writings about Her," *English Literature in Transition (1880–1920)*, 15 (1972): 49–56.

Biography:

Brocard Sewell, *Olive Custance: Her Life and Work* (London: Eighteen Nineties Society, 1975).

References:

Aubrey Beardsley, *The Letters of Aubrey Beardsley,* edited by Henry Maas, J. L. Duncan, and W. G. Good (Rutherford, N.J.: Fairleigh Dickinson University Press, 1970), pp. 240–377;

Patrick Braybrooke, *Lord Alfred Douglas: His Life and Work* (London: Cecil Palmer, 1931);

W. Sorley Brown, *The Life and Genius of T. W. H. Crosland* (London: Cecil Palmer, 1928), pp. 183–192;

Rupert Croft-Cooke, *Bosie: Lord Alfred Douglas, His Friends and Enemies* (Indianapolis: Bobbs-Merrill, 1963);

Lord Alfred Douglas, *The Autobiography of Lord Alfred Douglas* (London: Secker, 1929);

Douglas, *Oscar Wilde and Myself* (London: John Long, 1932);

William Freeman, *The Life of Lord Alfred Douglas: Spoilt Child of Genius* (London: Herbert Joseph, 1948);

H. Montgomery Hyde, *Lord Alfred Douglas: A Biography* (London: Methuen, 1984);

Mark Samuels Lasner, *The Yellow Book: A Checklist and Index* (London: Eighteen Nineties Society, 1998);

Richard Le Gallienne, "A New Woman Poet," in his *Sleeping Beauty and Other Prose Fancies* (London: John Lane, 1900), pp. 161–169;

Le Gallienne, *The Romantic '90s* (London: Putnam, 1926), pp. 96–97, 100–105;

Katherine Lyon Mix, *The Study in Yellow: The Yellow Book and Its Contributors* (Lawrence: University of Kansas Press, 1960), pp. 186–188;

Douglas Murray, *Bosie: A Biography of Lord Alfred Douglas* (New York: Hyperion Press, 2000);

Marie Carmichael Stopes, *Lord Alfred Douglas: His Poetry and Personality* (London: Richards, 1949).

Papers:

Olive Custance's letters and diaries are in the Henry A. and Albert W. Berg Collection of the New York Public Library, along with many of her husband's letters and manuscripts. The collection also includes the manuscript for her sixteen poems dedicated to John Gray.

Toru Dutt

(4 March 1856 – 30 August 1877)

Alpana Sharma
Wright State University

BOOK: *Le Journal de Mademoiselle d'Arvers* (Paris: Didier, 1879).

TRANSLATIONS: *A Sheaf Gleaned in French Fields* (Bhowanipore: Saptahik Sambad Press, 1876; London: Kegan Paul, 1880);
Ancient Ballads and Legends of Hindustan, with an introduction by Edmund Gosse (London: Kegan Paul, Trench, 1882).

SELECTED PERIODICAL PUBLICATIONS–UNCOLLECTED: "Essay: Henry Vivian Derozio" and "Essay: Leconte de Lisle," *Bengal Magazine* (December 1874);
"A Scene from Contemporary History," *Bengal Magazine* (June–July 1875);
"Bianca, or The Young Spanish Maiden," *Bengal Magazine* (January–April 1878).

In the course of a brief life punctuated by painful illness, Toru Dutt generated an impressive body of work in the confines of her father's two houses in Bengal, India (a British colony at the time), the most notable of which are *A Sheaf Gleaned in French Fields* (1876), a translation of French verse into English, and the posthumously published *Ancient Ballads and Legends of Hindustan* (1882), a translation of Sanskrit verse into English. Dutt also wrote essays for *The Bengal Magazine* and had two novels published posthumously: "Bianca, or The Young Spanish Maiden" (1878) and *Le Journal de Mademoiselle d'Arvers* (1879), the former of which is incomplete and was published in *The Bengal Magazine*.

Why the Indian-born Dutt was so prolific in English, French, and, to a lesser extent, Sanskrit, was no doubt owing to her extraordinary family background and upbringing. Dutt was born on 4 March 1856 to Govin Chunder Dutt and his wife Kshetramoni; she was the youngest of three children. The Dutt family was landed, prosperous, highly educated in English, and steeped in European culture. Dutt's father had a profoundly formative influence on his daughter.

Toru Dutt

He worked briefly for the colonial government but resigned due to the lack of promotion opportunity for Indians in government jobs; later in life, he became an honorary magistrate, justice of the peace, and a fellow of the University in Calcutta. Govin Chunder Dutt was a convert to Christianity along with his brothers, following the oldest brother's mystical vision of the other world while on his deathbed; the remaining brothers and their families were all baptized in 1862. In his spare time he wrote poetry fashioned after his favorite Romantic poet, William Wordsworth. The young Dutt was twelve years old when she went with her family to Europe; she learned French in Nice, music in London, and, in 1871, she attended the Higher Lectures for Women in Cambridge. According to her biographer Harihar Das, the Dutt women were the first Bengali women to have visited Europe. The family returned to Calcutta in 1873, and two years later Dutt had undertaken a study of Sanskrit with her father. By 1875 she had also lost both of her siblings, Abju and Aru, the latter to tuberculosis, and knew from her own early symptoms that she might share her sister's fate. To her identity as a British colonial subject, her vast reading interests, and her linguistic dexterity at such a young age, should be added the fact that all her fame derives posthumously; indeed, in her short life of twenty-one years, only four of which were spent abroad, she seldom left her city house in Rambagan except for summer vacations at Baugmaree, the family's country house.

While in England, Dutt began her collection of translated verse from French to English, compiled in *A Sheaf Gleaned in French Fields,* her only book to appear in print in her lifetime. It includes almost two hundred poems and eighty authors, biocritical notes on many of the authors, and occasional corresponding or analogous lines from British literature. Eight of the poems are translations by her sister Aru Dutt. Toru Dutt's interest in French Romantic poetry is evinced from her choice of nineteenth-century poets: Victor Hugo, Gérard de Nerval, Emile Deschamps, Théodore de Banville, Leconte de Lisle, Charles Baudelaire, Joseph Soulary, Louis Bouilhet, Sully Prudhomme, Victor de Laprade, Alfred de Musset, and Jules Lefevre-Deumier, among others. Her poetic rhythm follows the original meter as closely as possible, but her translations are often loose, sometimes surprisingly so. For instance, Hugo's memorable antiroyalist lines in "Napoleon le Petit"–"Toi, tu te noyeras dans la fange, / Petit, petit!"–are rendered as "Thou too shalt drown, but drown in slime, / Tom Thumb, Tom Thumb!" Of the knowledge of European poetry emerging from the notes, critics have commented that it is sometimes astonishing and sometimes limited: she could detect a plagiarism in Baudelaire but she thought Alexander Smith, the Scottish poet, was still alive (Smith had died in 1867.) Critics agree, however, that Dutt made extraordinary use of limited resources given her geographical isolation, producing a book that not only acquainted English readers with some previously unknown French verse but also, in the process, placed her among the ranks of contemporary authors in Britain.

Dutt contributed her translations to *The Bengal Magazine* from 1874 to 1877. In 1876 the Saptahik Sambad Press in Bhowanipore collected and published all of her translated verse under the title *A Sheaf Gleaned in French Fields.* It was not read by many Indians, and if it had not fallen into the hands of André Theuriet in France and Edmund Gosse in England, it would most likely not have come to the attention of European readers. Theuriet gave it a glowing review in *Revue des Deux Mondes* (1 February 1877) as did Gosse in *The Examiner* (26 August 1876). A second edition, also by Saptahik Press, came out in May 1878, this one containing a frontispiece portrait of the two sisters and a biographical note by their father. The third edition was published in London in 1880 by Kegan Paul. An autographed copy Dutt gave to Chevalier de Châtelain, the French translator of Shakespeare, is now housed in the British Museum Library. Dutt's other contributions to *The Bengal Magazine* consist of prose pieces: critical essays on Anglo-Indian and French poets (Henry Vivian Derozio and Leconte de Lisle) and translations of the political speeches of Victor Hugo and Louis Adolphe Thiers ("A Scene from Contemporary History").

Having already come in contact with Dutt through his review of *A Sheaf Gleaned in French Fields,* Gosse was a good candidate to present to the English-speaking world Dutt's second volume of poetry, *Ancient Ballads and Legends of Hindustan.* Dutt's fame largely rests on this collection of loose translations, from Sanskrit to English, of Hindu stories based on epic and folklore. In 1875, approximately two years after returning from Europe, Dutt started studying Sanskrit with her father. Her study of Sanskrit lasted less than a year, terminated by her untimely death, but critics agree that the resulting translations mark the height of her poetic abilities. Nine poems were originally planned for what she called her second "sheaf gleaned in Indian fields." The poems emerge out of Dutt's readings in the Hindu religious texts of the *Puranas,* the *Mahabharata,* and the *Ramayana.* Two early experiments were published in Calcutta periodicals: "The Legend of Dhruva" in *The Bengal Magazine* in October 1876; and "The Royal Ascetic and the Hind" in *The Calcutta Review* in January 1877. Of the planned nine poems, two were either missing or not yet written upon Dutt's death. Her father made up for the missing poems by adding "The Legend of Dhruva" and "The Royal Ascetic and the Hind" to the existing seven, hence producing *Ancient Ballads and Legends of Hindustan.* The book was published in 1882 in London with an introductory memoir by Edmund Gosse. In it Gosse predicted–rightly, as it turns out–that on these poems would rest the weight of Dutt's poetic legacy.

Dutt (right) at seventeen, with her nineteen-year-old sister, Aru, who died of tuberculosis two years later

Ancient Ballads and Legends of Hindustan was received with positive reviews in England. Even English readers earmarked for praise what they perceived to be a genuinely Indian sensibility expressing itself in the medium of English. What current criticism overwhelmingly agrees upon is, first, a simplicity of expression that is modern yet does not anglicize Hindu stories for the sake of a Western audience and, second, the promise Dutt showed in the mastery of narrative and descriptive verse. For Indian readers in particular, *Ancient Ballads and Legends of Hindustan* restores Dutt's cultural identity as decidedly Indian. Dutt herself notes in a letter to her friend Mary Martin that her mother's evening chanting of Hindu hymns almost always brought the young girl to tears. This deep emotional response encapsulates for readers of a nationalistic bent Dutt's link with her "mother land" through the immediate link with her mother. Of the nine ballads and legends, the ones most consistently singled out for critical commentary are "Savitri," "Lakshman," and "Jogadhya Uma." Critics seem agreed that the others ("Buttoo," "Sindhu," "Prahlad," "Sita," and the two previously published poems) lack the narrative and stylistic force so amply evidenced in the first three. All nine poems employ the octosyllabic meter of traditional English ballads; there are two blank-verse experiments ("The Legend of Dhruva" and "The Royal Ascetic and the Hind"), an exercise in pentameter ("Sita"), and a variation on octosyllabic verse ("Sindhu").

"Savitri" derives from a legend in the epic *Mahabharata* that celebrates the archetypal figure of the self-sacrificing wife so central to Hindu thought. In the poem Dutt narrates the heroic and ultimately successful efforts a wife, Savitri, makes to bring her husband, Satyavan, back from the realm of the dead. The salient points of the original story are as follows: Savitri was the beautiful daughter of Asvapati, king of Mudra, born to him after many years of praying for a son to the goddess Savitri. Considered an impossible challenge by eligible bachelors in the neighboring provinces, Savitri set out to find her own husband, finding him in the figure of a young man who turned out to have a grim forecast: he was destined to die within a year. Savitri, who quickly proved an exceptional wife and daughter-in-law, determined to avert her husband's destiny through fasting, dedication, and perseverence. On the appointed day and time, when the figure of death, Yama, appeared to carry Satyavan's body to his kingdom, Savitri's persistent pleading broke Yama down to the point of granting her the ultimate boon—the restoration of her dead husband's life.

While Hindu tradition emphasizes in this story the wifely qualities of self-sacrifice and devotion, Dutt chooses to emphasize other aspects—Savitri's freedom, mobility, individuality, and right to self-determination:

> In those far-off primeval days
>   Fair India's daughters were not pent
> In closed zenanas. On her ways
>   Savitri at her pleasure went
> Whither she chose . . .
> . . . .
>   In boyish freedom. . . .

While Dutt was influenced by British views on Indian culture (in particular, their critical stance on restrictive Indian customs relating to women, surfacing in the poem in the lines "In those far-off primeval days / Fair India's daughters were not pent / In closed zenanas"), it is difficult to align her purely with the British. She remained Indian in their eyes; Gosse, for instance, refers to her as a "Hindu poetess" in his introductory essay even though he knew she was a Christian convert. Dutt herself began increasingly to see herself as Indian. Early letters to her friend Mary Martin, written shortly after the Dutt family had arrived back in Calcutta, made frequent mention of Indians as "natives." On Martin's surprise at her use of this alienating word, Dutt expressed regret and began to practice a touching self-censorship: "the reproof is just, and I stand corrected. I shall take care and not call them natives again. It is indeed a term only used by prejudiced Anglo-Indians, and I am really ashamed to have used it." Later letters show her growing political consciousness about imperialism in India; many of these angrily describe the one-sided workings of colonial law in events involving injustice, brutality, and wanton murders of Indians at the hands of British judges and officers. Hence, it would be more accurate to say that Dutt's Savitri was neither an exclusively British nor an exclusively Indian creation but, rather, Dutt's attempt at constructing her own ideal of womanhood.

"Lakshman" is a poem written in a casual and conversational tone. It employs dramatic dialogue to tell a story from the *Ramayana,* one of the great Hindu epics in which a prince, Rama, his wife Sita and his brother Lakshman are exiled from their kingdom. During their exile in the forest, Rama is lured away by a golden deer who in actuality is a demoness taking revenge on Rama for his spurning of her advances. Sita, who in the first place had asked Rama to follow the beautiful deer and bring it to her, hears what sounds like Rama's voice calling out as if in pain to her and Lakshman. The poem begins in medias res ("'Hark! Lakshman! Hark, again that cry!'"), and while it is termed a dramatic dialogue, it seems to read as a series of dramatic monologues embedded within a dialogue: first Sita speaks, then Lakshman responds; Sita speaks again, then Lakshman responds again. Sita's pleas to Lakshman to go to Rama's aid turn into taunts, and Lakshman reluctantly disobeys his brother's orders by leaving her by herself; but before he sets out he draws a magic circle around the hermitage with his arrow, and enjoins Sita not to cross the circle. His departure is accompanied by ill omens.

Of particular interest are the character delineations of Lakshman and Sita. According to Das and A. N. Dwivedi, they display a psychological depth that, while still basic and experimental, hints at what Dutt was beginning to master. Lakshman is not simply a type of an ideal brother but is given certain "real" attributes, as he vacillates in uneasy response to Sita's pleas and taunts. More so than Lakshman, Sita is a complicated creature, both subject, in the sense of engendering action–she goads Lakshman to go after Rama against Rama's own express command–and object, in that she cannot fend for herself and knows she is dependent on male protection. Within a few pages, Dutt takes readers beyond the reductive questions of right and wrong derived from a prewritten script; her characters act not merely as they are expected to but as they themselves seem driven to, by their own torn allegiances, instincts, and weaknesses.

"Jogadhya Uma," unlike the majority of poems in *Ancient Ballads,* is based on folklore rather than religious verse in Sanskrit. It was originally narrated to the young Toru by Suchee, the family nurse who was a devout Hindu to whom all the Dutt children were close. Dutt pays homage to Suchee at the end of her poem:

> Absurd may be the tale I tell,
>   Ill-suited to the marching times,
> I loved the lips from which it fell,
>   So let it stand among my rhymes.

Hence, it would be safe to say that the poem's grounding in popular appeal and oral tradition of storytelling secures for it, more than any other poem in the collection, the status of ballad, that is, the poetic narration of a popular legend. "Jogadhya Uma" is a poem that moves from scene to vivid scene in a dreamlike way. A peddler crying out his wares (shell bracelets) advances down a misty road that runs "straight, a red, red line" in the early morning, arriving at a "Pellucid lake-like tank." There, on the marble steps leading to the water, sits a beautiful young girl who dons one of the bracelets and refers the peddler for payment to her father's house. The location she describes is exact: the money is to be found in a small "bright vermillion" box by the shrine (her father is priest of a temple). The peddler, dazzled by her beauty, finds the temple and the priest, who insists he has no daughter. Together, they find the red box and wonderingly find in it the exact amount for the bracelet. The priest realizes the maiden the peddler saw was the same goddess whose vision he himself had been seeking all these years. They rush back to the water tank but, to their disappointment, find nothing: "The landscape lay in slumber's chain, / E'en Echo slept within her cell." Then a braceleted arm rises out of the water and just as quickly sinks down. From this day onward, descendants of the peddler pay the temple shell bracelets as an annual tribute to the goddess.

Appended to the ballads are seven "Miscellaneous Poems" that are autobiographical and personal. Dutt began them during her stay in England (1870 to 1873), and they end a few months before her death on 30 August 1877. "The Tree of Life," written closest to her death, tells of a mystic vision received by the poet of a "dead silver and live gold tree" by the side of which

The Cedars of Lebanon
A. De Lamartine

Eagles that wheel above our crests
Say to the storms that round us blow,
They cannot harm our gnarlèd breasts
Firm rooted as we are, below.
Their utmost efforts we defy!
They lift the sea-waves to the sky,
But when they wrestle with our arms
Nervous and gaunt, or lift our hair,
Balanced within its cradle fair
The tiniest bird has no alarms.

Sons of the rock, no mortal hand
Here planted us, God-sown we grew.
We're the diadem green and grand
On Eden's summit that He threw
When waters in a deluge rose
Our hollow flanks could well enclose
Awhile, the whole of Adam's race;
And children of the patriarch
Within our forest built the Ark
Of covenant, foreshadowing grace.

Fair copy manuscript for a poem by Dutt (from Harihar Das, Life and Letters of Toru Dutt, *1921)*

He saw the tribes as captives led,
He saw them back return anon;
As rafters have our branches dead
Covered the porch of Solomon.
And later, when the Word made Man
Came down in God's salvation-plan
To pay for sin the ransom price,
The beams that formed the Cross we gave,
These, red in blood of power to save,
Were altars of the Sacrifice

In memory of such great events,
Men come to worship our remains,
Kneel down in prayer within our tents,
And kiss our old trunks' weather-stains
The saint, the poet, and the sage
Hear, and shall hear from age to age
Sounds in our foliage like the voice
Of many waters In these shades
Their burning words are forged like blades,
While their uplifted souls rejoice

                Toru Dutt.
1st November 1876.   Calcutta.

stands an angel. The angel plucks some of the leaves and crowns the poet's head with them whereupon her fever abates. But when she asks the angel to do the same to her father, who is seated next to her, the angel gently refuses. The vision reveals itself to be a premonition of death.

Three poems invariably singled out for critical commentary among the miscellaneous poems are "Baugmaree," "The Lotus," and "Our Casuarina Tree," the first two of which are sonnets. "Baugmaree" describes in glorious detail Dutt's beloved family garden, a riot of natural beauty and color, its flowers "Red, –red, and startling like a trumpet's sound." "The Lotus" relates how the lotus was born as a way to end the quarrel about which flower was the loveliest, the rose or the lily; it is cited as an excellent example both of Dutt's mastery of the sonnet form and of her special ability to celebrate nature in verse. "Our Casuarina Tree" also celebrates nature in poetic description but even more elaborately so; here, the natural object being described in loving detail is a large and beautiful tree which is a repository of the poet's happy childhood memories. The poem experiments in the form of an eleven-line stanza with the unusual rhyming scheme *a b b a, e d d e, e e e,* and critics conclude that it is both novel and successful. The first two stanzas are a literal description of all the flora and fauna thriving on the tree's trunk and branches: a creeper with its crimson flowers winding around like "a huge Python," a gray baboon sitting "statue-like alone," its stillness contrasting with the frenetic activities of its playful offspring. The third stanza marks a transition in which the tree begins to bear symbolic meaning, standing for the poet's fondly remembered "sweet companions" from childhood and her beloved "native clime," and the fifth stanza culminates in the hope that her mortal verse might secure for the tree immortality: ". . . though weak the verse / That would thy beauty fain, oh fain rehearse, / May Love defend thee from Oblivion's curse."

The remaining posthumous works of Dutt are two prose texts. The unfinished romance novel *Bianca, or The Young Spanish Maiden* was published by Dutt's father in serialized form in *The Bengal Magazine* (January–April 1878). The French novel *Le Journal de Mademoiselle d'Arvers,* Dutt's only complete prose narrative, was published in Paris in 1879. It includes a preface by one of Dutt's European correspondents, Clarisse Bader, and received reviews that viewed Dutt's linguistic achievement as unprecedented. On the basis of these prose texts, Das summarizes: "We question if, in the whole of the history of literature, another such example can be found of a foreign language being so completely mastered in so short a time that the production of an entire book in that tongue was possible, and that too in the finished style which this book displays."

Letters:

Harihar Das, *Life and Letters of Toru Dutt* (London: Oxford University Press, 1921).

Biography:

Harihar Das, *Life and Letters of Toru Dutt* (London: Oxford University Press, 1921).

References:

Meena Alexander, "Outcaste Power: Ritual Displacement and Virile Maternity in Indian Women Writers," *Journal of Commonwealth Literature,* 24 (August 1989): 12–29;

A. N. Dwivedi, *Toru Dutt* (New Delhi: Heinemann, 1977);

Padmini Sen Gupta, *Toru Dutt* (New Delhi: Sahitya Academi, 1968);

Amaranatha Jha, "Introductory Memoir," in Dutt's *Ancient Ballads and Legends of Hindustan* (Allahabad: Kitabistan, 1941), pp. 7–36;

Susie Tharu, "Tracing Savitri's Pedigree: Victorian Racism and the Image of Women in Indo-Anglian Literature," in *Recasting Women: Essays in Colonial History,* edited by Kumkum Sangari and Sudesh Vaid (New Delhi: Kali for Women, 1989), pp. 254–268.

Michael Field
(Katherine Harris Bradley)
(27 October 1846 – 26 September 1914)

and

(Edith Emma Cooper)
(12 January 1862 – 13 December 1913)

Ed Madden
University of South Carolina

BOOKS: *The New Minnesinger and Other Poems,* by Bradley, as Arran Leigh (London: Longmans, Green, 1875);

Bellerophôn, by Bradley and Cooper, as Arran and Isla Leigh (London: Kegan Paul, Trench, 1881);

Callirrhoë; Fair Rosamund (London: Bell / Clifton: Baker, 1884; New York: Holt, 1885);

The Father's Tragedy; William Rufus; Loyalty or Love? (London: Bell / Clifton: Baker, 1885; New York: Holt, 1886);

Brutus Ultor (London: Bell / Clifton: Baker, 1886);

Canute the Great; The Cup of Water (London: Baker, 1887);

Long Ago (London: Bell, 1889; Portland, Me.: Mosher, 1897);

The Tragic Mary (London: Bell, 1890);

Stephania: A Trialogue (London: Elkin Mathews & John Lane, 1892);

Sight and Song (London: Elkin Mathews & John Lane, 1892);

A Question of Memory: A Play in Four Acts Produced at the Independent Theatre, London, on Friday October the 27th 1893 (London: Elkin Mathews & John Lane, 1893);

Underneath the Bough: A Book of Verses (London: Bell, 1893; revised and shortened, 1893; revised and enlarged edition, Portland, Me.: Mosher, 1898);

Attila, My Attila! A Play (London: Elkin Mathews, 1896);

The World at Auction (London: Hacon & Ricketts, 1898);

Anna Ruina (London: Nutt, 1899);

Noontide Branches: A Small Sylvan Drama Interspersed with Songs and Invocations (Oxford: Printed by H. Daniel, 1899);

The Race of Leaves (London: Hacon & Ricketts / New York: John Lane, 1901);

Michael Field (Katherine Harris Bradley and Edith Emma Cooper)

Julia Domna (London: Hacon & Ricketts / New York: John Lane, 1903);

Borgia: A Period Play, anonymous (London: Bullen, 1905);

Queen Mariamne, as the author of "Borgia" (London: Sidgwick & Jackson, 1908);

Wild Honey from Various Thyme (London: Unwin, 1908);

The Tragedy of Pardon; Diane, as the author of "Borgia" (London: Sidgwick & Jackson, 1911);

The Accuser; Tristan de Léonois; A Messiah, as the author of "Borgia" (London: Sidgwick & Jackson, 1911);

Poems of Adoration (London: Sands, 1912);

Mystic Trees (London: Nash, 1913);

Whym Chow, Flame of Love (London: Eragny Press, 1914);

Dedicated: An Early Work of Michael Field (London: Bell, 1914);

Deirdre, A Question of Memory, and Ras Byzance (London: Poetry Bookshop, 1918);

In the Name of Time: A Tragedy (London: Poetry Bookshop, 1919);

The Wattlefold: Unpublished Poems by Michael Field, edited by Emily C. Fortey (Oxford: Blackwell, 1930);

Works and Days: From the Journal of Michael Field, edited by T. and D. C. Sturge Moore (London: Murray, 1933).

Editions and Collections: *Fair Rosamund* (London: Hacon & Ricketts, 1897);

A Selection from the Poems of Michael Field, edited by Mary Sturgeon and T. Sturge Moore (London: Poetry Bookshop, 1923; Boston: Houghton Mifflin, 1925);

Sight and Song, with Underneath the Bough, introduction by R. K. R. Thornton and Ian Small (Oxford & New York: Woodstock, 1993).

PLAY PRODUCTION: *A Question of Memory,* London, J. T. Grein's Independent Theatre, Opera Comique, 27 October 1893.

"Michael Field" is the pseudonym of Katherine Harris Bradley and Edith Emma Cooper, an aunt and niece who together wrote twenty-eight plays (twenty-seven tragedies and one masque) and eight volumes of poetry. They also produced a journal of thirty volumes that documents their life together in daily entries, drafts of poetry, and transcribed letters; a small portion of this voluminous work, which is now housed in the British Library, was compiled by their literary executor, T. Sturge Moore and his son, Daniel, and published in 1933. Everything they wrote after 1884 was published under the Field pen name; they continued to use the name after their dual authorship was made public and also for later volumes of poetry that were primarily the work of one writer rather than of both.

The publications of Michael Field were praised by reviewers until it was revealed that the supposed singular male author was, in fact, two women. Their biographer Mary Sturgeon points out that the Victorian mind found something "obscurely repellent" in the act of literary collaboration. In their journals and in letters Bradley insisted that the fact that they were women was also a hindrance to their literary and critical success.

Critics disagree about the exact nature of Bradley's and Cooper's affection for each other. The journals are silent or, at least, evasive on the subject. Lillian Faderman believes that the two poets had a paradigmatic Victorian "romantic friendship"—that is, a loving but probably nonsexual alliance. On the other hand, Chris White, Emma Donoghue, and Angela Leighton claim that the variety of voices and languages Bradley and Cooper use to express desire confirms that their relationship was a sexual one, and evidence exists for such an interpretation. For example, after visiting their friend Robert Browning in the mid 1880s, Bradley wrote in her 18 May 1886 journal entry about the relationship of Robert and Elizabeth Barrett Browning: "Those two poets, man and wife, wrote alone; each wrote, but did not bless or quicken one another at their work," and added about herself and Cooper, "*we are closer married.*" Their *Canute the Great* (1887), a play that addresses ideas about social and cultural evolution, includes a scene of affection between two women that David J. Moriarty reads as a figure for their own love. Sturgeon considers the poem "It was deep April and the morn" in *Underneath the Bough* (1893) their marriage vow: on the morning of William Shakespeare's birthday the speaker says, "My Love and I took hands and swore, / Against the world, to be / Poets and lovers ever more." Bradley and Cooper's friends were aware of their love for one another, although they appear to have been unclear as to its precise character. Browning called them his "two dear Greek women"—indicating their interest in antiquity but also, perhaps, referring to their affection in euphemistic terms. Whether Bradley and Cooper were an unusually close aunt and niece, intimate friends, or lesbian lovers, it is clear that for them poetry was at once an act of rebellion, an aesthetic labor, and a vow of mutual devotion.

Bradley was born on 27 October 1846 in Birmingham to Charles Bradley, a tobacco manufacturer, and Emma Harris Bradley. Her father died of cancer when she was two. Bradley, her mother, and her older sister, Emma, moved to the suburbs of Birmingham; they were supported by profits from the father's factory, which provided Bradley a small income for the rest of her life. Around 1860 Emma married James Robert Cooper; Katherine Bradley and her mother moved to Kenilworth, Warwickshire, to live with them in 1865. Edith Cooper was born on 12 January 1862. Bradley developed a maternal attachment to her niece that became even stronger when Emma Cooper became a permanent invalid at the birth of her second daughter, Amy, in 1864.

After the death of her mother in May 1868 Bradley began a serious pursuit of education, beginning in October with a brief attendance at College de France, and then, in 1875, taking courses at Newnham College, Cambridge. In Paris she fell in love with a young Frenchman, the brother of a friend; after his sudden death she returned to Kenilworth, where she continued her education by reading widely in German and French literature and philosophy. Although she had been composing poetry since childhood, at this time she began to see writing as her vocation. She published her first collection, *The New Minnesinger and Other Poems,* in 1875 under the pen name Arran Leigh–apparently an androgynous echo of Elizabeth Barrett Browning's *Aurora Leigh.* The volume, which opens with the poem "Think of Womanhood, and thou be a woman," calls for the poet to be faithful to the "unrecorded life" of women, focuses on a woman's aptitude for poetry and for love, and suggests a developing feminist sensibility. During this period Bradley began a philosophical correspondence with the essayist and critic John Ruskin, which ended in disappointment in 1880 when he rejected her professed atheism as well as her poetry.

Bradley and Cooper moved to Bristol in 1878 to attend University College. They were known at the school for their daring and flowing clothes in the aesthetic style, their interest in "pagan" culture, and their penchant for archaic language. Their idiosyncracies included a prolific use of nicknames for their friends and themselves; their pen name is a combination of their nicknames for each other: Bradley was "Michael," and Cooper was "Field" (and later "Henry"). They attended classics and philosophy classes together and developed some proficiency in languages, Bradley in Greek and both women in Latin.

Bradley and Cooper's first joint book of poetry was *Bellerophôn,* which they published in 1881 under the names Arran and Isla Leigh. Uneven and largely juvenile works, neither *The New Minnesinger and Other Poems* nor *Bellerophôn* has received much critical attention.

The career of Michael Field was inaugurated in 1884 with the publication in one volume of two plays, *Callirrhoë* and *Fair Rosamund. Callirrhoë,* which attracted the admiration of Robert Browning, centers on the worship of Dionysus, a religion of sacrifice and ecstasy–two themes that appear in Michael Field's poetry and drama. Ecstatic joy, in the form of physical and artistic pleasure, fills the poetry of the authors and also played a role in their daily lives: in their journals they repeatedly invoke Bacchus, Dionysus, and Eros to describe the pleasure they take in art, flowers, food, wine, companionship, and each other.

In the next three years Bradley and Cooper published seven more plays under the Field pseudonym. They also became involved in issues of the day, actively supporting the woman suffrage and antivivisectionist movements. Although all but one of their plays are

Binding for the first book Bradley and Cooper published under their pseudonym. This 1889 collection of poems that elaborate on fragments from Sappho is widely considered to be their best work.

based on historical or legendary themes, the issues of the "New Woman" are much in evidence: marriage as an economic and social (and sometimes loveless) contract, the right of women to their own loves and desires outside the bounds or expectations of family and culture, and the role of women in the evolution of culture and the defeat of oppressive conventions. Women in the plays often resist the marital or social roles expected of them and forge new relationships of their own.

Most of the plays, especially the early Elizabethan-style five-act tragedies, are static, cumbersome, and ornate closet dramas; many are considered unstageable. Only one of the plays–*A Question of Memory* (1893), which concludes, rather shockingly for the time, with two men and a woman deciding to spend their lives together–was ever staged, and it received predominantly negative reviews. Though the later plays approach the economy of symbolist drama, they have been rejected as less accomplished than the poetry. Except for isolated songs and monologues, the plays fail as verse drama; their meter, ostensibly iambic pentameter, is uneven and variable. The plays, however, deserve attention from historians of Victorian culture and also

Pendant with miniature of Cooper by Charles Ricketts (from Emma Donoghue, We Are Michael Field, *1998)*

for their relationship to the poetry of Michael Field: many themes, such as the exploration of female romantic and sexual love, appear in both genres, and many of the songs in the plays reappear in the poetry volumes.

When Browning wrote to what he assumed was the male playwright about *Callirrhoë,* Cooper responded, on 29 May 1884, revealing Michael Field's true identities and explaining the nature of the collaboration. She described her and Bradley's writing as "like mosaic-work—the mingled, various product of our two brains," in which each wrote, cut, added, gathered, and spliced words, lines, and scenes. "I think if our contributions were disentangled and one subtracted from the other, the amount would be almost even. . . . This happy union of two in work and aspiration is sheltered and expressed by 'Michael Field.'" Similarly, in "A Girl," which is simultaneously an *ars poetica* and a love poem in *Underneath the Bough,* they claim to have "souls so knit" together that one may leave a half-written page out for the other to complete: "The work begun / Will be to heaven's conception done, / If she come to it." In another poem, "When high Zeus first peopled earth," in *Underneath the Bough,* they say: "We are bound by such close ties / None can tell of either breast / The native sigh / Who try / To learn with whom the Muse is guest." When, in May 1886, their friend the sexologist Havelock Ellis asked about their collaboration, Bradley used matrimonial imagery in her reply: "As to our work, let no man think he can put asunder what God has joined." Their friends and biographers repeatedly describe Bradley and Cooper in complimentary terms: emotion and intellect, lyrical and dramatic, surface and depth, and light and dark, and the two portray themselves in their journals as interrelated parts of one body: for example, Cooper ties Bradley's poetic power to "blood," while "all my power is in the nerves." "If two individuals of exactly the same nature are joined together," Bradley wrote to Browning in November 1884, "they make up a single individual, doubly stronger than each alone." She added, "Edith and I make a *veritable Michael.*"

A few months after Cooper had revealed their identity, Bradley wrote to beg Browning to keep their identity a secret and "to set the critics on a wrong track." The revelation of their dual authorship "would indeed be utter ruin to us; but the report of lady authorship will dwarf and enfeeble our work at every turn." They would "be stifled in drawing-room conventionalities," she feared; and, "We have many things to say that the world will not tolerate from a woman's lips." When an anonymous review of the second edition of *Callirrhoë* in *Athenaeum* referred to the author as "She," Bradley and Cooper assumed Browning had revealed their gender, because he was the only person who knew their identities. Years later, in 1897, Bradley wrote in her journal: "What good times men have, what pipes, what deep communings! . . . Yet if women seek to learn their art from life, instead of what the angels bring down to them in dishes, they simply get defamed."

In 1888 Bradley and Cooper moved from Bristol to Reigate, south of London. Their first book of poetry under the "Michael Field" pseudonym, *Long Ago* (1889), a collection of poems that elaborate on fragments of the ancient Greek poet Sappho, is considered their best and has received the most attention from critics. Henry Thornton Wharton's *Sappho: Memoir, Text, Selected Readings and a Literal Translation* (1885) had restored the female addressee of some of the love poems, and several of Bradley and Cooper's poems emphasize the lesbian possibilities of Sappho's verse. Passion—women's passion, in particular—is the theme of the volume, as the poets point out in the introduction: referring to the "passionate pleasure" of reading Wharton's book, they invoke "the one woman who has dared to speak unfalteringly of the fearful mastery of love." One poem in *Long Ago,* which Moore and Sturgeon republished in their 1923 edition of Michael Field's selected poems under the title "Sweeter Far than the Harp, More Gold than Gold," makes the mother-daughter relationship of Demeter and Persephone an analogy for Sapphic love; the relationship echoes the age difference between Bradley and Cooper, who regarded their own love as both maternal and matrimonial. Michael Field's work is part of an important cultural moment when many late-Victorian and "decadent" writers were exploring languages of female sexual desire and seeking alternative languages of sexuality, including same-sex sexuality.

A poem in *Long Ago* that was praised by Browning and singled out by Moore in his introduction to the 1923 edition retells the classical myth of Tiresias's change from female to male, his subsequent blinding by the goddess Hera for declaring that women take greater pleasure in sex than men, and Zeus's bestowal on him of the gift of prophecy in recompense. Bradley and Cooper locate Tiresias's prophetic power in the female consciousness, with its "finer sense for bliss and dole," that he seems to retain: "Thou hast been woman and can'st see / Therefore into futurity." Although the two poets wrote under a male pseudonym, they insisted that their poetic power was tied to their gender; accordingly, White has called Michael Field "the Tiresian poet."

In the late 1880s Bradley and Cooper traveled extensively in Germany, France, and Italy, visiting museums and attending Wagnerian operas. This tour inspired Michael Field's second volume of poetry, *Sight and Song* (1892), a series of poems based on famous paintings. The authors say in their preface that they are attempting to "translate" into poetry the lines and colors of painting, which they further imagine as a kind of music. Although the paintings are of a wide range of classical and religious subjects, the poems pay consistent attention to the bodies and faces of women, as in a sonnet on *La Gioconda* that seems to have been inspired by Walter Pater's passages on the painting in his *Studies in the History of the Renaissance* (1873).

Three poems deal with paintings of St. Sebastian, a figure often associated with homoeroticism; in one poem he appears against a sky of "Hyacinthine hue," alluding to another homoerotic icon, Hyacinthus, the beloved of Apollo. (Images of Sebastian also appear in the journals, particularly in a section from 1891 devoted to Cooper's illness in Germany and a nurse's unwelcome physical attentions and "fleshly love" for Cooper. Cooper writes of Sebastian's "reproachful" face facing heaven, asking "Why am I denied what I was made for?" She adds, "That picture was constantly with me." The section also mentions Cooper's boyish haircut and her nickname "Henry" and includes her comparison of herself to another homoerotic icon: Hadrian's lover, the adolescent Antinous.) More frequently noted by critics is "Sleeping Venus," based on a painting by Giorgione: the voyeuristic and sensual poem suggests female sexual pleasure—and, some claim, lesbian and autoerotic sensuality.

In Reigate, Bradley and Cooper began to develop the literary and cultural contacts that informed the rest of their lives. They continued their friendship with Browning's family after his death in 1889 and became acquainted with Ellis; their future literary executor, Moore; Oscar Wilde, who fascinated them; the lesbian poet Vernon Lee; Elkin Mathews and John Lane, publishers of the infamous literary periodical *The Yellow Book*, from which the scandalized Bradley and Cooper withdrew their submissions; the artist William Rothenstein; the art critic Bernard Berenson; the poet and, later, priest John Gray; William Butler Yeats, who included nine of their poems (four of them Sapphics) in the 1936 edition of *The Oxford Book of Modern Verse*; and, most important of all, the artists Charles Ricketts and Charles Shannon, publishers of *The Dial*, who remained their close friends until the end of their lives.

Although Ricketts and Shannon were admirers of Bradley and Cooper's work since at least 1890, when they bought a copy of *The Tragic Mary*—which they appreciated as much for its Selwyn Image cover as for its text—they did not actually meet the women until early 1894, when Bradley and Cooper visited them at their home, The Vale, in the Chelsea section of London. The friendship of the four developed rapidly and included the exchange of meals, flowers, artwork, poetry, and literary criticism. Ricketts commented on several of Bradley and Cooper's works, contributed cover and interior illustrations for their books, and designed and printed four of their plays at his Vale Press. He also gave Bradley and Cooper jewelry he designed, including a pendant enclosing a miniature portrait of Cooper and a "Sabbatai" ring, based on a character in their play *A Messiah*. In 1898 Ricketts and Shannon moved to Richmond; a year later Bradley and Cooper followed, and No. 1 The Paragon remained their home until their deaths. Ricketts and Shannon moved away in 1902; later Ricketts looked back on the four years in Richmond as one of the happiest periods of his life. In her journals Bradley compared her relationship with Cooper, a union of life, work, and love, to that of Ricketts and Shannon. Some biographers have interpreted both of these "passionate friendships" as nonsexual, while other scholars have examined the relationships in the context of developing understandings of homosexuality.

During the 1890s Michael Field published eight plays and had one play staged, but only one more book of poetry appeared before the turn of the century. *Underneath the Bough* actually appeared three times: the first edition in the spring of 1893; a revised and short-

Bradley with her and Cooper's beloved dog, Whym Chow

ened edition in the fall of that year in which Bradley and Cooper responded to criticisms made by their friends; and another revised edition in 1898, in which they restored some of the deleted poems. *Underneath the Bough*—the title alludes to Edward FitzGerald's translation of the *Rubáiyát of Omar Khayyám* (1859)—incorporates poems written at various periods. Most are love poems, though a few are about the death of Cooper's mother (19 August 1889), songs (frequently love songs) from their plays, and a scattered motif of Greek fauns and bacchantes cavorting through pastoral imagery. The book includes pastoral and nature poems, but as critics point out, nature is rarely sentimentalized—more often than not, the nature imagery is of fecundity or of bleak, impersonal, and elemental forces. When fused with the predominant love theme, such imagery suggests, according to Leighton, an "unsocialized love," an "elemental Darwinism of the heart." The most important series of poems, the third of the four "Books of Songs" into which the volume is divided, seems to be addressed by Bradley to Cooper; it includes "It was deep April and the morn," which Sturgeon considers their "marital" pledge of poetry and love.

The year 1906 marked a profound turning point in the lives of Bradley and Cooper: the death of their beloved chow dog, Whym Chow. Many of their friends considered their deep grief and prolonged mourning for the pet extravagant; Ricketts, in particular, was exasperated by their overwrought expressions of bereavement. Cooper wrote in her journal that it was the worst loss of her life. The poets were already considered somewhat eccentric, but this behavior intensified their isolation. In 1907 the two converted to Roman Catholicism; their biographers attribute this conversion to their extreme sense of loss over the death of Whym Chow—Leighton notes ironically that they lost their dog and gained a God. Cooper entered the Catholic faith at St. Elizabeth's in Richmond; Bradley did so in Edinburgh, where she was received by their old friend, Father John Gray.

Like *Underneath the Bough,* Michael Field's subsequent book of poetry, *Wild Honey from Various Thyme* (1908), for which Ricketts designed the cover, is marked by an imagistic lyricism and some formal experimentation. The title *Wild Honey from Various Thyme* denotes, through the pun on *thyme/time,* the wide range of dates and contexts of composition of the poems in the book, which is even greater than in *Underneath the Bough.* Again, love poems, natural imagery, and classical themes—including "Penetration," a seductive sonnet spoken by Syrinx to Pan—predominate; but there is also a whiff of late-Victorian orientalism in poems about Egyptian mummies. Several sonnets address the fate of Cooper's father, who fell to his death while hiking in the Alps in 1897, his body lying undiscovered for months; others express Bradley and Cooper's love for Whym Chow, who seems at times to personify Eros or Bacchus. Leighton claims that the death of Whym Chow represented for Bradley and Cooper the death of their own pagan past.

In 1911 Cooper was diagnosed with cancer. In 1913 Bradley received the same diagnosis, but she kept her illness secret so as not to trouble her companion. Both poets refused to take morphine so that they could keep their minds clear for writing. The themes of the plays they published after the turn of the century, most of which had been drafted if not finished before 1907, move from the fall of the Roman Empire—a critical motif for decadent writers—to the Holy Land, religious faith and corruption, and legendary love affairs such as those of Tristan and Isolde, Celtic Deirdre and Naisi, and, in *Queen Mariamne* (1908), Herod and Salome, a fin-de-siècle obsession. They may have revised some of the plays, but they focused their attention on two volumes of devotional verse—*Poems of Adoration* (1912), predominantly the work of Cooper, and *Mystic Trees* (1913), of which all but one or two poems are Bradley's—and on *Whym Chow, Flame of Love* (1914), a collection of elegies for their pet.

The religious books have received little serious attention. Sturgeon and Leighton compare Bradley and Cooper's religious devotions to those of seventeenth-century poets–Sturgeon with faint praise, Leighton dismissively–but most readers reject the works as doctrinal expositions in overwrought verse. Cooper knew that she was dying when she wrote *Poems of Adoration;* the book traces her explorations of faith and her physical and spiritual crises but also recalls, if only slightly, some of the exoticism, sensuality, and baroque nonconformity of her earlier work. In "Desolation" Bacchus has been replaced by Christ, who appears as a lonely wine-treader preparing for the paschal cup rather than drunken revelry. Yet, Salome and John the Baptist's severed head appear in a symbolist evocation of gesture, whiteness, silence, and ice reminiscent of Stéphane Mallarmé's "Hérodiade" (Herodias) (1870), and Cooper's poem of irregular rhyme and meter only recovers a doctrinal focus in the last stanza, a formal quatrain apostrophe to "Holy John."

Likewise, although Sturgeon dismisses Bradley's work as even more doctrinal than Cooper's, *Mystic Trees* is filled with unconventional figurations of Christian imagery refocused through pagan myth or her love for Cooper. The first part, "Hyssop," addresses the life of Christ; the second, "Cedar," focuses on the Virgin Mary; the third, "Sward," turns to the religious devotion of the "folk"; and a short section of religious love poems written for Cooper concludes the book. In "They Took Jesus" and "Thou Comest Down to Die," Bradley compares Jesus to Venus rising from the sea as he "broke forth from the flowers" and likens his feet to those of Hermes, "fleet" in a task's completion. Imagining her soul beside Christ in heaven in "The Homage of Death," she compares herself to the beggar maid loved by King Cophetua (a familiar story in Victorian poetry and painting) and wonders about the "caprice" of Christ's thus romanticized "worship" of her–a highly unconventional reversal. More strangely, Bradley imagines Cooper, coughing on her deathbed, as a bird singing from the "tree" of Golgotha, and at times the "he" or "Bridegroom" who calls to the speaker seems as easily to be Cooper as Christ.

Cooper died on 13 December 1913; Bradley suffered a hemorrhage on the day of the funeral. At the time of Cooper's death Bradley was compiling *Whym Chow, Flame of Love* and *Dedicated: An Early Work of Michael Field* (1914), a collection of Cooper's early poetry. She published *Whym Chow, Flame of Love* in an edition of twenty-seven copies at Lucien Pissaro's Eragny Press and distributed it to close friends. Here the dog is not presented sentimentally but as a bacchic

Father John Gray, the priest and former poet who received Bradley into the Roman Catholic faith in Edinburgh in 1906

figure of "potency," "joy," and "lust." *Dedicated* ends with the last poem Bradley wrote, "Fellowship," which suggests a nostalgic return to her and Cooper's old styles of passion and art, that of the pagan and aesthete: "In the old accents I will sing," she writes, "with pagan might."

Bradley died in Hawksyard Priory, Straffordshire, on 26 September 1914, collapsing on her way to mass. In 1923 Ricketts designed a tombstone for Cooper's grave; the inscription commemorated both women. Three years later the stone cracked and was removed.

After Bradley's death there was a brief attempt to renew interest in the work of Michael Field. Harold Monro of The Poetry Bookshop published several of their plays, as well as *A Selection from the Poems of Michael Field* (1923), edited by Moore. A. J. A. Symons included some of their poems in his *Anthology of "Nineties" Verse* (1928). Emily C. Fortey edited *The Wattlefold: Unpublished Poems by Michael Field* (1930), an uneven collection of previously unpublished work. The title alludes to a ballad from *Underneath the Bough* in which a queen who loved a murdered shepherd boy becomes a shepherdess to escape her murderous and class-bound society. The poets left their journals, spanning the years 1888 to 1914, to Moore, with instructions to open them at the end of 1929. He published a small selection from the journals, along with some letters, in 1933 as *Works and Days: From the Journal of Michael Field.*

Until near the end of the twentieth century Michael Field's poetry lingered only in tiny selections in anthologies of 1890s verse, such as Karl Beckson's *Aesthetes and Decadents of the 1890s* (1981), or in volumes of gay and lesbian poetry, such as Stephen Coote's *The Penguin Book of Homosexual Verse* (1983). But critics of Victorian poetry have effected a recovery of their work, and anthologies of Victorian women's poetry have facilitated renewed attention to it. Although their original texts are not easily available, since most were published by small presses in limited editions, *Sight and Song* and *Underneath the Bough* have been reprinted together in facsimile (1993). Their plays continue to be ignored, and further exploration needs to be made of the interactions of Ricketts and Shannon with Bradley and Cooper and of the other cultural contexts that inform Michael Field's work: the Victorian literary and sexual subcultures, woman suffrage and antivivisectionism, sexology, and Catholic aestheticism. Lesbian and feminist criticism have done much to enrich the understanding of Bradley and Cooper's lives and work, especially in their focus on *Long Ago* and the place of Sapphic classicism in Victorian culture and the lesbian literary heritage. Michael Field is being recognized as a writer of significant literary and cultural importance in the Victorian tradition.

Letters:

Some Letters from Charles Ricketts and Charles Shannon to "Michael Field," edited by J. G. Paul Delaney (Edinburgh: Tragara Press, 1979);

Letters from Charles Ricketts to "Michael Field," edited by Delaney (Edinburgh: Tragara Press, 1981).

Biographies:

Mary Sturgeon, *Michael Field* (London: Harrap, 1922);

Charles Ricketts, *Michael Field,* edited by Paul Delaney (Edinburgh: Tragara Press, 1976);

Emma Donoghue, *We Are Michael Field* (Bath: Absolute Press, 1998).

References:

J. G. Paul Delaney, *Charles Ricketts: A Biography* (Oxford: Clarendon Press, 1990);

Lillian Faderman, *Surpassing the Love of Men: Romantic Friendship and Love between Women from the Renaissance to the Present* (New York: Morrow, 1981; London: Women's Press, 1985);

Holly Laird, "Contradictory Legacies: Michael Field and Feminist Restoration," *Victorian Poetry,* 33 (Spring 1995): 111–128;

Angela Leighton, *Victorian Women Poets: Writing against the Heart* (New York & London: Harvester Wheatsheaf, 1992);

Jerusha Hall McCormack, *John Gray: Poet, Dandy, Priest* (Hanover, N.H. & London: Brandeis University Press, 1991);

David J. Moriarty, "'Michael Field' (Edith Cooper and Katherine Bradley) and Their Male Critics," in *Nineteenth-Century Women Writers of the English-Speaking World,* edited by Rhoda B. Nathan (Westport, Conn. & London: Greenwood Press, 1986), pp. 121–142;

Yopie Prins, "A Metaphorical Field: Katherine Bradley and Edith Cooper," *Victorian Poetry,* 33 (Spring 1995): 129–148;

Prins, "Sappho Doubled: Michael Field," *Yale Journal of Criticism* (Spring 1995): 165–186;

Mary Sturgeon, *Studies of Contemporary Poets,* revised and enlarged edition (London: Harrap, 1920) pp. 347–367;

Martha Vicinus, "The Adolescent Boy: Fin de Siècle Femme Fatale," *Journal of the History of Sexuality,* 5 (July 1994): 90–114;

Chris White, "'Poets and lovers evermore': The Poetry and Journals of Michael Field," in *Sexual Sameness: Textual Differences in Lesbian and Gay Writing,* edited by Joseph Bristow (London & New York: Routledge, 1992), pp. 26–43;

White, "The Tiresian Poet: Michael Field," in *Victorian Women Poets: A Critical Reader,* edited by Leighton (Cambridge, Mass.: Blackwell, 1996), pp. 148–161.

Papers:

The major collection of Katherine Harris Bradley and Edith Emma Cooper's papers and manuscripts is at the British Library. It includes the thirty volumes of their journal, covering the years 1888 to 1914, along with Bradley's journal for 1868–1869.

Eva Gore-Booth
(22 May 1870 – 30 June 1926)

John C. Hawley
Santa Clara University

BOOKS: *Poems* (London: Longmans, Green, 1898);
The One and the Many (London: Longmans, Green, 1904);
Unseen Kings (London: Longmans, Green, 1904);
Women Workers and Parliamentary Representation (Manchester: Lancashire and Cheshire Women Textile and Other Workers' Representation Committee, 1904);
The Three Resurrections and The Triumph of Maeve (London: Longmans, Green, 1905);
The Egyptian Pillar (Dublin: Maunsel, 1907);
The Sorrowful Princess (London: Longmans, Green, 1907);
Women's Right to Work (Manchester & Salford: Women's Trade and Labour Council, 1908);
The Agate Lamp (London: Longmans, Green, 1912);
The Perilous Light (London: Macdonald, 1915);
Religious Aspects of Non-Resistance (London: League for Peace and Freedom, 1915);
Broken Glory (Dublin: Maunsel, 1918);
The Sword of Justice (London: Headley, 1918);
Select Passages Illustrating Florentine Life in the Thirteenth and Fourteenth Centuries, Texts for Students, no. 19 (London: Society for Promotion of Christian Knowledge, 1920);
A Psychological and Poetic Approach to the Study of Christ in the Fourth Gospel (London: Longmans, Green, 1923);
The Shepherd of Eternity (London: Longmans, Green, 1925);
The House of Three Windows (London: Longmans, Green, 1926);
The Inner Kingdom (London: Longmans, Green, 1926);
The World's Pilgrim (London: Longmans, Green, 1927);
Poems of Eva Gore-Booth (London: Longmans, Green, 1929);
The Buried Life of Deirdre (London: Longmans, Green, 1930);
Prison Letters of Countess Markievicz (London: Longmans, Green, 1934);
The Plays of Eva Gore-Booth, edited by Frederick S. Lapisardi (San Francisco: Mellen, 1991).

Eva Gore-Booth

OTHER: *New Songs, A Lyric Selection*, edited by A. E. (George William Russell) (Dublin: O'Donoghue, 1904);
"The women's suffrage movement among trade unionists," in *The Case for Women's Suffrage*, edited by Brougham Villers (London: Unwin, 1907).

SELECTED PERIODICAL PUBLICATION–UNCOLLECTED: "Women and the Suffrage: A Reply," *Living Age,* 259 (1908): 140.

Eva Selena Gore-Booth was born in Lissadell in County Sligo, Ireland, on 22 May 1870, the third child of Sir Henry and Georgina (Hill) Gore-Booth. The daughter of Anglo-Irish landowners, she had a privileged childhood and was educated by governesses. Her sister, Constance, two years her senior, later gained fame as Countess Markievicz, imprisoned for her involvement in the 1916 Easter Rebellion. Gore-Booth published nine books of poems, seven plays, many pamphlets on feminist and political questions, several collections of spiritual essays, and a lengthy analysis of the New Testament Gospel written by St. John.

Three incidents from her childhood, as she recounts in "The Inner Life of a Child" (published posthumously in 1929), suggest the memories that structured Gore-Booth's characteristic literary themes. The first was the death of her grandmother, Lady Hill, the sister of the Earl of Scarbrough, when Gore-Booth was nine. In an action that came to typify her life, Gore-Booth sought to understand the event by walking in the forest. Speaking of herself in the third person, she writes:

> On that January day she had realized clearly and practically the fact of death, a fact that up till then had been as remote as the blue Galway mountains over the bay.... As she stood in the cold wind, under the blue and sunny sky, shining above her in floods of transparent colour, she gradually became conscious of a strong intuitive feeling, a flash of sudden freedom and power, of strange happiness, an uplifting of the soul, a sense of something swift and free, of life in some world beyond the slavery of the senses, some aether beyond the air.... This she did not understand at the time, but she put it into clumsy words that half-shocked herself—"Now I understand it all, and it's delightful to die, and wonderful to think of anyone being dead." She was conscious of a vast comradeship, of unseen hands held out to her, of kindness, of power, of happiness everywhere.

Thus, her first vivid impression in childhood was an optimistic, even mystical, embrace of a reality that could be read in nature, but which transcended it. This insight would dominate her spiritual writing and inform most of her poetry.

The second significant event was her response to a gift that she received as a child. In the cold dark hours of a December morning, she recalls, she opened a parcel containing a statuette:

> Out of a bundle of brown paper and straw emerged a face, a beautiful white gleaming face, such a face as she had never seen in her conscious life; and yet in a moment a mad, struggling throng of associations, of dreams, of thoughts jostled together in her mind. She was overwhelmed by a flood of new emotions. The door of all the mysteries opened in the air, and she is not ashamed to own that there and then she flung herself down on her knees by the school-room table, and prayed with all her heart to a cast of Apollo. Yet not to the cast, but to the Divine idea of beauty, the symbol of the conquering soul.

Such highly attuned sensitivity to beauty in a schoolgirl is remarkable, reflecting a poetic nature that would sustain her throughout a life of political activity. That she could describe beauty as the conquering strength of the soul suggests the happy conflation of worldly concerns and eternal mysteries that she carried with her, whether in the streets of Manchester or in a quiet meadow.

The third incident demonstrated her unwavering faith in human intuition as a door to greater truths. For many years following her grandmother's death she sensed her presence. "It was many years," she writes, "before she ever dreamt of questioning or doubting the actual presence of the death woman." Later, however, with more education, she became aware of the theories that "you must not trust your senses, because you could see anything, whether it was there or not, provided you imagined it enough." To test the theory, she lay awake many nights trying to imagine that the closed window blind was really open, but to no avail. As shaky as the science may have been, her conclusions had a great impact on her future writing: "It was through this experience," she records, "that in her inmost self she gradually lost a practical belief in the power of the imagination to materialize what has no existence, and grew to look upon the faculty that goes by that name, as simply a subtler and keener perception of things that are really there." Her later interest in theosophy and the mysticism of her poetry took their root in this simple childhood experiment. "If you can once get at your soul behind your brain," she writes, "you will get at the truth of everything. But the brain is the old deceiver, the confuser of issues, always able and willing to blind the eyes of the incarnate spirit with handfuls of dust."

Gore-Booth's inner life, clearly, was eventful. In recalling her former pupil, her governess wrote that the twelve-year-old "was a very fair, fragile-looking child, most unselfish and gentle with the general look of a Burne-Jones or Botticelli angel . . . and a little lonely mentally. . . . Eva was of course presented in her turn and a good deal admired but society of the fashionable kind did not, I think, ever appeal much to her." Gore-Booth led an otherwise sheltered life that nurtured independent thinking and creative self-expression. The family property in "Yeats country" extended over 25,000 acres, and Gore-Booth's brother, Josslyn, ultimately became the first of the Anglo-Irish to sell his estates to his tenants after the 1903 Land Act; he also favored home rule. All three children looked to the Irish radical politician, Feargus O'Connor, for inspiration in defining the new Celtic revival, and the two sisters reminded each other that several generations of poets called O'Daly had lived at Lissadell before them. When famine came to Ireland in 1879, soon after her grandmother's death, Gore-Booth and her sister helped their parents in the distribution of food and clothing to the many poor who lived on their land.

For all her raised consciousness regarding death and social responsibility, however, one of the first pieces that Gore-Booth wrote was a burlesque for family guests titled *A Daughter of Eve, or Alphonso's Bride* (1891, unpublished). Just twenty-one years old, she pokes fun at the self-important politicians who were rattling their sabers and threatening to overturn the social order in which the Gore-Booths had prospered. Just a few years later, however, in the poem "The Land to a Landlord" (*The One and the Many,* 1904), she wrote: "You hug to your soul a handful of dust / And you think the round world your sacred trust / But the sun shines, and the wind blows / And nobody cares and nobody knows . . . . Over your head the sky gleams blue / Not a cloud or a star belongs to you." For all the fun that she had within the family compound, the socialism that was to influence her brother was clearly at work in her as well.

In 1895 after visiting Lissadell, William Butler Yeats wrote a letter to Olivia Shakespear about Gore-Booth, recognizing the burgeoning poet's raw but undisciplined talent. "I'm always ransacking Ireland for people to set at writing Irish things," he notes. "She does not know that she is the last victim—but is deep in some books of Irish legends I sent her and might take fire." He was correct, in some respects. Though she would move to England, she would also be identified sufficiently with the Celtic revival to be included in the Dublin 1904 volume *New Songs,* made up of poems from a host of Irish writers. Yeats recognizes that she had "some literary talent, and much literary ambition," but "she needs . . . like all Irish literary people, a proper respect for craftsmanship." George Russell later made a similar assessment of her technical slips, but was far more approving than Yeats in describing her as a "tall slim defiant girl."

Gore-Booth's view of the world broadened when she traveled with her father in 1894 to the West Indies and North America, and then with her mother to Germany and Italy. In Venice, however, she developed the asthmatic condition and consumption that plagued her the rest of her life, and she was advised to

Gore-Booth and her sister, Constance, in their early twenties

spend more time near the Mediterranean. This was to be a recommendation with significant ramifications. Gore-Booth's public life began to come into focus when, in 1896, she returned to Italy and met Esther Roper, a women's suffrage activist and the woman who would become her lifelong companion. Based upon the pair's subsequent writings denigrating sexuality, it seems unlikely that their relationship ever developed beyond a deep friendship. Much like the "Boston marriages" of the time, however, the two women lived in every other respect as partners for the rest of their lives. Although Gore-Booth was to live another thirty years, this long life expectancy did not at first seem to be the case, and in 1900 she wrote her will, giving her entire estate to Roper. In 1898 the two moved to Manchester, where Roper further schooled Gore-Booth in the great political causes of the day and then stepped back and allowed the poet to take the spotlight.

Where Gore-Booth was a member of the Anglo-Irish aristocracy, Roper was the daughter of a clergyman. Though her father had died when Roper was only nine, the same familiarity with the poor, hard work, and zeal that had helped him rise from the slums of Manchester to become a missionary to Africa also shaped his daughter. She, in turn, offered Gore-Booth her practical skills in organizing communities around causes that had already become important to the young poet. The two women were among the first suffragists who advocated extending the vote not only to women of property, but to working-class women as well.

Where Roper did most of her organizing in factories, Gore-Booth saw her initial mission as educational and cultural. She offered classes in poetry to working women, and eventually wrote her several plays as a means of educating and entertaining this audience. At the Manchester University Settlement, founded in the slums of Ancoats in 1895, Gore-Booth formed a dramatic society for women machinists and staged amateur performances of William Shakespeare and of her own plays. Among these was *Unseen Kings* (1904) which, while finally produced at the Abbey Theatre 25 January 1912, was presented by the Independent Theatre Company, run by her sister's husband, Casimir Markievicz, rather than the Abbey Theatre's resident Irish National Theatre Society. Dublin critics panned the production, and this was Gore-Booth's only play to be performed at the Abbey.

Markievicz's company also performed *The Buried Life of Deirdre* (1930) in December of 1911 at another theater. Just as the young Gore-Booth and her siblings had occasionally put on plays in Sligo for charity entertainment, so now the writing of these plays and their production were envisioned by the poet as didactic vehicles rather than as major literary works for the stage. *The Buried Life of Deirdre,* with its strong pacificist theme that was later used as a protest to World War I, may have been the closest to Gore-Booth's heart, since she returned to work on it late in life. She did much the same with another of her early plays, *The Triumph of Maeve* (1905), which she republished in 1916. The principal theme here was a sort of transcendent and nonpossessive love, and the timing of the second edition, which included her sister's illustrations, was designed to offer support to her sister's political struggles during the Easter Uprising. The headline in *The New York Times Magazine* announcing the production ignores the play's literary qualities to focus on the personal: "Irish Rebel Illustrates Nonresistance Play: Countess Markievicz, in Jail for Life for Her Part in Dublin Uprising, Makes Mystic Drawings for Sister's Poetic Drama."

As surprised and dismayed as Gore-Booth's family was to hear that she was moving in 1898 from their enormous estate to live in a row house in Manchester with Roper and her younger brother Reginald Roper, she herself seemed content in her new life. The industrial city, however, had little to recommend itself to one so schooled in rural beauty, and Gore-Booth's early poetry is nostalgic for all that she had given up. Thus, in her first collection, *Poems* (1898), she writes, in the ironically titled "Spring in Manchester": "Poor battered crocus, feebly fair / Smutty and stained and crouching down / Half stifled by the smoky air / And murky coldness of the town"; and in "From a Far Country" she writes: "I have such longing to be home again / 'Tis lucky that the Muse / Doth still refuse / To visit me on winged Pegasus / For if she came to see me riding thus / I might be tempted with prosaic force / To steal her horse." Nonetheless, Gore-Booth's great-uncle Henry was a clergyman in Manchester for her first six years in the city, and his philanthropic work in a slum parish, along with the Booth Trust which had been founded by a family member in the seventeenth century, inspired her to labor selflessly. Thus, her poem continues: "Goddess of Drudgery, to thee / I dedicate my hopes and all my days / Knowing that labour brings no earthly praise / Nor heavenly bliss for guerdon / Only this: / The promise of a higher life, to be– / The lightening of life's burden / Of satiety."

By the time she published her next volume of poems, *The One and the Many,* her nostalgia has been replaced by an angry commitment to social change. Typical of this collection is the following, titled "The City":

On through the iron day each stone-bound square
The soul of the green grass entombed hides,
The buried Spirit of the Wise and Fair
Imprisoned in the earth's heart still abides.

Then evening passes cool hands o'er the town,
Making a dream, against the conquering skies,
Of giant Labour-houses that crush down
The buried Spirit of the Fair and Wise.

As prisoners count the ray of sunshine dear
That filters dimly through their prison bars;
So my heart burns to feel the twilight near,
And the far presence of the inviolate stars.

Then does the Spirit of the Wise and Fair
Break from her sepulchre and walk the town,
The iron bonds are loosened everywhere–
No pavement gray can crush the green grass down.

In 1900, with textile worker Sarah Dickenson, Gore-Booth became co-secretary of the Manchester and Salford Women's Trade Union Council, which ultimately had a great influence on the formation of forty

Dust jacket for a 1907 political book to which Gore-Booth contributed

other women's unions. Dickenson later wrote of Gore-Booth that "she is remembered by thousands of working women in Manchester for her untiring efforts to improve their industrial conditions, for awakening and educating their sense of political freedom, and for social intercourse." In 1903 Gore-Booth became the union's representative on the Technical Instruction Committee of the City Council, where she fought to extend scholarships to women at the Municipal School of Technology and, in general, to shape a view of both sexes as being equally qualified for most types of work.

Themes of sexual liberation and equality came increasingly to dominate her poetry, especially in 1907 with the publication of *The Egyptian Pillar*. Thus, in "Man and Woman" she recounts the meeting of Solomon and Sheba and notes that, for all the magnificence of the former, when Sheba returned to her own land and reflected upon his manly strength she nonetheless "bade her goldsmiths cut and grave / For him an agate ring. / 'This too will pass'–the Queen's reply / From her dark jewel shone." In response to the prime minister's recommendation to the Women's Franchise Deputation on 19 May 1906, to "Have patience!" Gore-Booth wrote "Women's Trades on the Embankment," in which she looks at Cleopatra's Needle and concludes: "Long has submission played a traitor's part– / Oh human soul, no patience any more / Shall break your wings and harden Pharaoh's heart / And keep you lingering on the Red Sea shore." In "Women's Rights" she notes that "where men in office sit / Winter holds the human wit." Why not, therefore, give women a chance to govern? "Men have got their pomp and pride– / All the green world is on our side." She had long associated masculinity with mechanical rigidity and unthinking force and increasingly associated the feminine character with nature and instinctive love. She was not averse to making a row, if that were what was necessary to melt the masculine winter. It is no great surprise that some of the workers described her as a "liquid pool of spontaneous combustion."

Little wonder, either, that she attracted the attention of some of the other early voices for women's voting rights, and foremost among these was Christabel Pankhurst. Though Pankhurst also came from a privileged background in 1901 she joined Gore-Booth's poetry class at the Manchester University Settlement and described her mentor as "sybil-like." Christabel's mother, Sylvia, apparently did not approve of her daughter's new attachment. In any event, it was not to last long. Three years later, the younger woman decided that more raucous means were necessary than those that Gore-Booth embraced, and Pankhurst soon led a breakaway group that disrupted public meetings of all sorts by loudly demanding the views of speakers on women's suffrage, regardless of the announced topic of the day. Impatient with her mentor, Pankhurst described her as "just temperament without direction." Gore-Booth never spoke harshly of the younger woman, but the strain may have played a role in the sad tone of many of the poems in *The One and the Many,* which were composed during the breakdown: "I was the light that made you wise / I was the Dream that broke your heart– / Now the tears are dry in your eyes / Though I depart– though I depart." This poem, titled "The Soul to the Body," is the last in the volume and suggests that Gore-Booth was struggling even as a thirty-year-old to transcend any earthly ties, whether of fame or human dependence.

As if to remind herself that there was more to life than the political struggle, in 1912 Gore-Booth published a collection titled *The Agate Lamp,* which is remarkably aesthetic in its themes, with poems on Leonardo da Vinci and other Italian painters, on Auguste Rodin, and on Holman Hunt. "Free to all souls the hidden beauty calls," she writes. But even in this sonnet she notes that "God made a garden, it was men built walls." In a remarkably belletristic piece she transforms a Keats-like vision into a bold warning to her female readers by titling it "The Anti-Suffragist":

> The princess in her world-old tower pined
> A prisoner, brazen-caged, without a gleam
> Of sunlight, or a windowful of wind;
> She lived but in a long lamp-lighted dream.
>
> They brought her forth at last when she was old;
> The sunlight on her blanched hair was shed
> Too late to turn its silver into gold.
> "Ah, shield me from this brazen glare!" she said.

The poem would remind her readers of the sharp exchange in *The Times* on 8 March 1907 between Gore-Booth and Mrs. Humphry Ward, who the following year founded the National League for Opposing Women Suffrage.

Between the years of 1906 and 1911 Gore-Booth's political work focused on the voting question, but also on the rights of various women workers: florists' assistants, pit-brow workers, barmaids, women gymnasts, and circus performers, among others. She represented the Lancashire Working Women's Societies at the 1906 deputation to the Liberal Prime Minister, Henry Campbell-Bannerman, and made the point on that occasion that "the number of women who are engaged at this time in producing the wealth of this country is double the population of Ireland." Pankhurst's more strident voice was soon in the ascendant, but she did not seem to speak for working women in the evangelistic way that had become Gore-Booth's custom. Gore-Booth wrote to Millicent Fawcett, head of the conservative National Union of Women's Suffrage Societies, to affirm her opposition to Pankhurst's strategies, assuring her that "we feel we must tell you this as we are in great difficulties because our members in all parts of the country are so outraged at the idea of taking part in such proceedings that everywhere for the first time they are shrinking from public demonstrations. . . . It is not the rioting, but the *kind* of rioting."

This political caution suggests the rationale not only for Gore-Booth's fading prominence in the struggle for suffrage, when compared to the Pankhursts, but also the markedly different course her life took with regard to Irish home rule. Gore-Booth had become a pacifist by the time of World War I, but her sister, who chose a more militant path, respected her views. Referring to the involvement of Countess Markievicz in the Sinn Fein movement, Gore-Booth writes, "She did not speak much to us of the revolutionary side of her life, though, of course, I saw numbers of Fianna boys at her house." In fact, she and Roper thought the whole enterprise appeared too ragtag to be taken seriously as a plot for revolution. When her sister, however, was sentenced to death on 6 May 1916 for her role in the Easter Rebellion, Gore-Booth appealed to Prime Minister Herbert Asquith, and the sentence was commuted to a life sentence in penal servitude. As it happens, Markievicz would outlive her sister by one year.

The next two collections of Gore-Booth's poems, *The Perilous Light* (1915) and *Broken Glory* (1918), deal with World War I, the rebellion, her concern for Constance, and the violence that had replaced the western world's faith in transcendent truths. In "To J. W. In Winchester Prison," for example, she concludes: "Outside men's maniac fury shrieks and raves / And dark submission chained in sunlight dwells, / The only free souls in a race of slaves / Live in strange solitudes and prison cells." And she asks, in "An Experience," "Shall my sad heart be prisoned evermore / In a dark cave behind a barrèd door?" In "To Constance–In Prison" she imagines herself literally behind bars: "Yours is that inner Ireland beyond green fields and brown"; and in "To C. M. On Her Prison Birthday" she paradoxically describes her sister as "free in a prison cell." It is in these two collections, perhaps, that she most closely parallels Yeats's conflicted relationship with Ireland and with the rebellion. Like him, she celebrates those who gave their lives, as in "Easter Week": "Grief for the noble dead / Of one who did not share their strife / And mourned that any blood was shed / Yet felt the broken glory of their state / Their strange heroic questioning of Fate / Ribbon with gold the rags of this our life." Also, like Yeats, she ponders her role as "The Artist in War Time" and angrily condemns those who resort to force in the name of God and with the voice of "black and stupid guns": "Labourers in mad mechanic purpose bound / They dig in vain Immortal Beauty's grave / And bury the very starlight underground / And crash above the song of wind and wave / Their monstrous rhythms of fire and steel and lead." As willing as she is to honor those who gave their lives fighting for Irish freedom, she lavishes her most heartfelt praise on Francis Sheehy-Skeffington, a pacifist who attempted to intervene between both sides in the strife and who was shot dead by Captain Bowen-Colthurst: "Crown him with olive who was not afraid / To join the desolate unarmed ranks of life / Who did not fear to die, yet feared to slay, / A leader in the war that shall end war." She offered similar support for Sir Roger Casement, a homosexual who had enlisted German support for Irish independence. "I dream of the hatred of men," she writes, after his execution, "Their lies against him who knew nothing of lying, / Nor was there fear in his mind."

The years in which Gore-Booth maintained pacifism in the face of the Easter Rebellion and World War I, and in which she attended the trials of conscientious objectors for the No-Conscription Fellowship, took their toll on her already fragile health. She and Roper went to Italy to help restore her health, but to little avail. They involved themselves in other campaigns, such as the League for the Abolition of Capital Punishment, vegetarianism, and antivivisection. She devoted most of the final six years of her life to the two causes that had always focused her attention and undergirded her work on behalf of suffrage and pacifism: the theoretically questionable division of the sexes, and the importance of the spiritual life.

The religious themes were revealed in Gore-Booth's final two books of poems, *The Shepherd of Eternity* (1925) and *The House of Three Windows* (1926). The latter is introduced by Evelyn Underhill, the famous writer on mysticism, who describes Gore-Booth as "a true mystic" who was enthralled by natural beauty. Thus, Gore-Booth never lost "that close contact with the visible world which the mystic needs so greatly if he is to escape a dangerous aloofness from the simplic-

Gore-Booth (left) and her longtime companion, Esther Roper (center), with unidentified friends, 1920

ities of human life." Seeking to ground the transcendent in the imminent, "she persistently and instinctively sought a sacramental expression for spiritual truth." Underhill notes that mystics generally follow one of two possible routes of development. On the one hand, they may begin with a personal anthropomorphic view of God and move to one that is abstract, or, and this was the route followed by Gore-Booth, "they may begin with the diffuse and impersonal—with some sort of 'cosmic consciousness,' or 'nature-mysticism,' or other type of philosophic abstraction—and thence move to a more and more concentrated, concrete and personal, and thus more rich and fruitful relationship." Underhill accurately categorizes Gore-Booth's early poetic volumes, with their "innate sense of 'otherness'" and interest in Celtic legends, as manifesting a "strongly Platonic bent" and the "emergence of a spiritual outlook which might almost be called pantheistic." But in her later collections of poems, *The Shepherd of Eternity* and *The House of Three Windows,* and in her outright religious essays and dialogues, like the lengthy *A Psychological and Poetic Approach to the Study of Christ in the Fourth Gospel* (1923) and *The Inner Kingdom* (1926), Underhill writes, "the essence of her teaching will be found: a teaching which has special value for a generation only too ready to mistake spiritual haziness for spiritual truth." Underhill characterizes that "teaching" as

Christian Platonism, in which "love and its redemptive and creative power, its obligation of unlimited mercy and forgiveness, is ever the meaning."

The title poem for *The Shepherd of Eternity* reads like a Christian response to Algernon Charles Swinburne's "Hymn to Proserpine," even imitating the general sound of his meter. "Joyful and swift, who led / The souls of the dead / In a shadowy band / To the Twilight land, / Surely deaf wert thou to our crying, / In silence conceivèd, in darkness dying, / And we wept as we went / Down the dark descent." In the two volumes she often takes significant moments, objects, or characters from biblical parables and uses them, as she did with nature in her earlier work, as occasions to pause and reflect on greater mysteries. In the poem "Higher Criticism" from *The House of Three Windows*, she reflects on all the images of Christ that are offered by the various writers of the gospels. Comparing their struggling descriptions with Plato's cave dwellers, she avoids the relativist cynicism of many of her contemporaries and instead celebrates the prismatic nature of such self-expression:

> Yet must we love these pictures painted on the wall
> Of every brother's mind, however worn or faint.
> For everywhere he passed and let his shadow fall
> Some flower grew, some dream arose, some light was shed.
> Ah, how shall we restore lost outlines, fading paint—
> How shall we know which were the words he really said,
> Entangled in men's fancies, memories, faults, desire
> That turns all things to its own likeness, foul or fair?
> As easy tell the moonlight shining on the waves
> From the sea's darkness, or the stars' far-coloured fire
> From broken shadows wandering in night-haunted caves.
> Where love is perfect, full, unfaltering, he is there.
> Love fills the lost and broken outlines of his face,
> Yea, all the light in all this world of ours is one.
> Mercy is his whole soul, God has no other grace,
> Do we know Light from darkness, we who have seen the Sun?

The long prose work, *A Psychological and Poetic Approach to the Study of Christ in the Fourth Gospel,* reiterates the insight that informs this poem and so many others in these final two volumes: a heartfelt trust in the insight of individuals, as opposed to a heavily rational science that, in Eva Gore-Booth's view, leads to mechanistic and masculine domination.

The condemnation of that stark delineation of the sexes found its most strikingly modern expression in *Urania*, a privately circulated magazine that Gore-Booth printed when she and Roper moved to London in the 1920s. In the journal Gore-Booth offered this challenge: "There is a vista before us of a Spiritual progress which far transcends all political matters. It is the abolition of the 'manly' and the 'womanly.' Will you not help to sweep them into the museum of antiques? Don't you care for the union of all fine qualities in one splendid ideal?" Though she was writing in 1924, her words still seem controversial: "Urania," she suggests, "denotes the company of those who are firmly determined to ignore the dual organisation of humanity in all its manifestations. They are convinced that this duality has resulted in the formation of two warped and imperfect types." "Sex," she writes, "is an accident," whereby society imposes roles in much the same way as a playwright. Far from leading to anything resembling sexual promiscuity, however, Gore-Booth's writings revealed another manifestation of her drive toward transcendence. "The emancipated modern girl," she writes, "interprets her freedom as freedom to enslave herself to men. . . . The acceptance of her biological destiny takes precedence of the fulfillment of her soul—to her utter degradation. . . . The 'frankness' and 'realism' and 'candour' of the present day spell, not freedom, but Enslavement of the Spirit, to a purgatory of physiology."

Physiology ultimately plagued Gore-Booth. Always frail, and always, as she notes in many places, fearful of death, she seems to have had some sort of mystic vision in her final days that removed this fear. "There was a radiance all around," she told Roper, "and I was filled with an extraordinary feeling of joy, the greatest I have ever known." Gore-Booth died of intestinal cancer in London on 30 June 1926. Evelyn Underhill wrote the obituary for *The Times*. Esther Roper describes her friend's final hour: "At the end she looked up with that exquisite smile that always lighted up her face when she saw one she loved, then closed her eyes and was at peace." Roper, having edited Gore-Booth's remaining works and seeing them through to publication, died in April of 1938. The two women are buried in the same grave, marked with a verse from Sappho.

Frederick Lapisardi, musing on why the poems are not well remembered nor much anthologized, concludes that "she missed the Modernist boat, and drifted off into some Tennysonian fog." A look at the poetry, however, while surely demonstrative of a Wordsworthian insight into humanity's place in nature and possibly suggestive of a less than adventuresome poetics, is far freer than the comparison with Tennyson might suggest. "Among the spiritual adventures of childhood," Gore-Booth had written in *The Inner Life of a Child*, "there is nothing that brings us closer to the ante-natal mystery, than the shock of the child's clear, instant and untaught perception of abstract truths. . . . Thus does one strive to find again one's own soul and the visions that surrounded

Page from the manuscript for Gore-Booth's posthumously published play, The Buried Life of Deirdre *(1930), with her illustrations (Collection of Josslyn Gore-Booth)*

one in the enchanted forests of childhood before the hemlock grew." Richard M. Fox, writing in 1935, is perhaps too enthusiastic but nonetheless closer to the mark in concluding that "among Irish poets she has been ranked next to W. B. Yeats, and critics have written of the magic, glamour, distinction, melody, classic quality and dramatic intensity of her poetry." For all Yeats's overstated concern for her lack of care in crafting her poems, Eva Gore-Booth deserves a far more prominent place in the canon of British literature of the early twentieth century.

Biographies:

Gifford Lewis, *Eva Gore-Booth and Esther Roper: A Biography* (London: Pandora, 1988);

Rosangela Barone, *The Oak Tree and the Olive Tree: The True Dream of Eva Gore-Booth* (Bari, Italy: Edizioni Dal Sud, 1991).

References:

L. Bather, "Manchester and Salford Trades Council from 1880," unpublished dissertation, Manchester University, 1956;

Michael Begnal, "Eva Gore-Booth on Behalf of Roger Casement, an unpublished appeal," *Eire-Ireland*, 6.1 (1971): 11–16;

S. M. Bryan, "The Women's Suffrage Question in the Manchester Area 1890–1906," unpublished M.A. thesis, Manchester University, 1977;

Richard M. Fox, *Rebel Irish Women* (Dublin: Progress House, 1935);

Roger Fulford, *Votes for Women* (London: Faber & Faber, 1958);

Sandra Stanley Holton, *Feminism and Democracy: Women's Suffrage and Reform Politics in Britain 1900–1918* (Cambridge: Cambridge University Press, 1986);

Leslie Parker Hume, *The National Union of Women's Suffrage Societies 1897–1914* (New York: Garland, 1982), pp. 17–19;

Jill Liddington and Jill Norris, *One Hand Tied Behind Us* (London: Virago, 1978);

Glenda Norquay, *Voices and Votes: A Literary Anthology of the Women's Suffrage Campaign* (Manchester & New York: Manchester University Press, 1995), pp. 34–39, 90–91, 310;

Andrew Rosen, *Rise Up Women, The Militant Campaign of the Women's Social and Political Union 1903–1914* (London: Routledge & Kegan Paul, 1974), pp. 24–27;

Constance Rover, *Women's Suffrage and Party Politics in Britain 1866–1914* (London: Routledge & Kegan Paul, 1967).

Mary Anne Hearn
(Marianne Farningham, Eva Hope)
(17 December 1834 – 16 March 1909)

Linda A. Julian
Furman University

BOOKS: *Lays and Lyrics of the Blessed Life, Consisting of Light from the Cross and Other Poems,* as Marianne Farningham (London: Clarke, 1860);

Life Sketches and Echoes from the Valley, as Farningham, nos. 1–3 (London, 1861–1871);

Poems, as Farningham (London: Clarke, 1866);

Listening for the Bells. A Round of Stories, etc., as Farningham (N.p., 1867);

Chats by the Sea, as Farningham (London, 1868);

Little Tales for Little Readers, as Farningham (London, Ipswich, 1869);

Home Life, as Farningham (London, 1869);

Girlhood, as Farningham (London, 1869; revised, 1895);

Boyhood, as Farningham (London, 1870);

The Cathedral's Shadow, as Farningham (London, 1871);

The Sunday Schools of the Future, as Farningham (London, 1871);

Out of the Depths. A Round of Stories, as Farningham (N.p., 1872);

Leaves from Elim, as Farningham (London, 1873);

Brothers and Sisters, as Farningham (London, 1873);

Sunday Afternoons with Jesus. Bible Readings on the Life of Christ, as Farningham (London, 1874);

Dell's New Year, as Farningham (London, 1875);

Grace Darling: Heroine of the Farne Islands, her life and its lessons, as Eva Hope (London: Scott, 1875);

The Summer and Autumn of Life, as Farningham (London, 1876);

What of the Night? A Temperance Tale of the Times, as Farningham (London, 1876);

Will You Take It? The History of a Young Women's Class. To Which Is Added a Paper On Young Women's Classes in the Provinces, as Farningham (London: Chilworth, 1877);

The Children's Holidays: Out-of-door Stories for the Little Ones, as Farningham (London: Clarke, 1878);

Songs of Sunshine, as Farningham (London: Clarke, 1878);

Mary Anne Hearn

The Story of the Years: A text-book and diary, with verses by Farningham, selected by her father, as Farningham (London: Clarke, 1880);

Life of General Gordon, as Hope (London: Scott, 1884);

Homely Talks About Homely Things, as Farningham (London: Clarke, 1886);

England Under Victoria: A Complete and Authentic History of Our Times, Religious, Social, Literary, Artistic, Scientific, Political, and Commercial. With Lives of Our Queen and Royal Family, by Hope and Stephen Albert Swaine (West Bromwich, U.K.: Eld & Blackman, 1886);

Our Queen: A Sketch of the Life and Times of Victoria, Queen of Great Britain and Ireland, as Hope (London: Scott, 1887);

New World Heroes: Presidents Lincoln and Garfield, as Hope (London: Scott, n.d.); revised as *New World Heroes: Lincoln and Garfield: the Life-story of Two Self-Made Men Whom the People Made Presidents* (London: Scott, 1887)

Stanley and Africa, as Hope (London: Scott, 1890);

Famous Women Authors, as Hope (London: Scott, 1890);

Spurgeon: The People's Preacher, as Hope (London: Scott, 189–?);

Nineteen Hundred? A Forecast and a Story, as Farningham (London: Clarke, 1892);

A Story of Fifty Years: A Souvenir of the Ministerial Jubilee of the Rev. J. T. Brown, as Farningham (London: Clarke, 1893);

In Evening Lights, as Farningham (London: Clarke, 1897);

A Window in Paris, as Farningham (London: Clarke, 1898);

Harvest Gleanings and Gathered Fragments, as Farningham (London: Clarke, 1903);

Women and Their Saviour. Thoughts of a Minute for a Month of Mornings, as Farningham (London: Clarke, 1904);

Women and Their Work: Wives and Daughters of the Old Testament, as Farningham (London: Clarke, 1906);

A Working Woman's Life: An Autobiography, as Farningham (London: Clarke, 1907);

Lyrics of the Soul, as Farningham (London: Clarke, 1908);

Songs of Joy and Faith, as Farningham (London: Clarke, 1909).

OTHER: *Poetical Works of William Cowper,* preface by Hearn, as Hope (London & Newcastle-on-Tyne: Scott, 1885);

The Poetical Works of John Greenleaf Whittier, preface by Hearn, as Hope (London: Scott, 1886);

Poems of Henry Wadsworth Longfellow, preface by Hearn, as Hope (London: Scott, 1886).

The title of Mary Anne Hearn's 1907 autobiography—*A Working Woman's Life*—precisely describes Hearn's life and alludes to one of her lifelong themes, the importance of work. Never married, Hearn devoted her life to writing more than forty books and tracts, hundreds of articles in Christian publications, lecturing to large audiences, teaching, and serving her community. Her life of independence, usefulness, and unending work exemplified the kind of life her poems and sketches advocated for the hundreds of thousands of readers she reached over her fifty-two years as a writer for *The Christian World* and twenty-four years as an editor of *The Sunday School Times.*

Hearn deserves attention as one of the most prolific religious writers of the second half of the nineteenth century, though her poems, sketches, and biographies have little literary merit to modern readers. On the other hand, as her work appealed mainly to the working classes, it reveals much about the relationship between nonconformist religion and social class as well as the relationships among nonconformist sects. Those interested in social issues such as poverty, women's lives, and education, especially the importance of Sunday schools, will also find her work of value.

None of her work was published under her own name. In her autobiography, Hearn said she felt that writing in her own name would be "presumptuous" for one of such lowly upbringing, and at the suggestion of the Reverend Jonathan Whittemore, her minister and founder of *The Christian World,* she settled on the surname Farningham, the name of the village where she grew up. In 1875, when she was asked to write a series of biographies for another publisher, she chose the pseudonym Eva Hope, because she felt that Marianne Farningham belonged to *The Christian World* and its publisher, James Clarke & Company.

This self-effacing attitude that led her to these pseudonyms originated in the tenets of the Particular Baptist Church, to which her family belonged. This sect, which appeared first in England in 1633, taught a combination of Baptist and Calvinist beliefs, and like other nonconformist churches, it incurred some abuse by members of other sects as well as the Church of England. In her autobiography Hearn recalls, "Those were hard days for Dissent, and I think our people were pretty badly persecuted." Her grandmother was pelted by stones from a mob as she returned home from her baptism. Although as an adult Hearn worked for understanding among nonconformist sects, her early religious experiences were strict and narrow. Her fear of sin was great from an early age, and hell was so real for her that she was afraid of a place called Whitepost Hill, because she thought it was an entrance to hell that would swallow her up. She remembers, "Much of the religious teaching of the day was far more sombre than it should have been, and I rejoice to think that only the happier side of Christian life and theology is presented to the children of to-day."

Born on 17 December 1834 in Farningham, Kent, to Joseph and Rebecca Bowers Hearn, Mary Anne Hearn was the first of five children, and she was to outlive all of her siblings. Her father was a shoemaker and the village postmaster, and her mother was the daughter of a papermaker who was also a preacher. Both were Sunday school teachers at the Eynsford chapel attended by the family. The family was poor but Hearn's memories of her childhood reveal a lively, hardworking mother who "loved to see us play and to play with us" and a father who was kind and enjoyed fun. Hearn was taught to read by her maternal grandmother, and by age six she could read the Bible. Fairy tales were prohibited, but the children delighted in religious verse and nursery rhymes. She describes herself as "a rollicking, mischievous child, often getting into trouble." Hearn's father always prayed for each child during Sunday evening lessons, and she said his prayers for her suggested that she was not pretty and was likely to have a difficult future.

Because none of the schools nearby were nonconformist and the family could not afford boarding school, Hearn did not attend school until age nine or ten, when the British and Foreign School Society built a school at Eynsford, about a mile from Farningham. Before attending school, however, she had been taught to write by a neighbor and by imitating the handwriting on the letters she helped her father sort as postmaster. Her first attempt at poetry was a rhyme she delivered as an epitaph for a dead toad, although she could not yet write, and before she began school, she had been inspired by Felicia Hemans's poem, "The Better Land," which she found in a sailing magazine at home. Hearn's mother would not allow her to read until evenings when she had finished her household chores. She delighted in school, but her happiness was short-lived. When she was twelve her mother died on Christmas Day, and she had to stay at home to look after her brother and sisters and do the housework. This death was the second Hearn had experienced: her brother Alfred had died when she was younger. A short time later, her father said that she would have to pay room and board, because he could not afford to house her; but he hired her to do shoe-binding, allowing her to attend school part-time.

When Hearn was seventeen she formed a friendship that would transform her life. Reverend Whittemore became the minister at Eynsford chapel, though he continued to work in publishing in London during the week. He offered advice on her

Hearn (on floor) with her brother Tom; her father, Joseph; and her sister, Hephzibah

poems and gave her William Shakespeare's works and Charlotte Brontë's *Jane Eyre* (1847), the first mainstream literature she had seen. Even so, they were regarded as wicked by some of her acquaintances. Whittemore helped her strengthen her poetry. One of Hearn's poems, "Music in Heaven," was published in *The Gospel Magazine*. Also in her seventeenth year, she moved to Bristol to assist the mistress of the Durdham Down school. After a year there she was called home to help nurse her sister Rebecca, who was suffering from consumption. A doctor told the family that if Rebecca could be taken to the south of France, she might live a few years rather than the few months she would have at home, and Hearn writes in her autobiography, "Of course that was utterly impossible, and so we had that very common experience of the poor." The family simply had to watch her die. The effect of poverty on families coping with illness is a theme that appears in many of Hearn's later poems.

In 1857 Whittemore founded *The Christian World*, and the first issue, as well as subsequent ones, included a poem by Hearn. Eighteen months later he hired Hearn to write some prose pieces, hymn lyrics, and more poems for the journal. She would be a member of the staff for the next fifty-one years. *The Christian World* included the week's news, readings for Sundays at home, and a collection of sketches, stories, and poems for leisure reading, including a section for children. In her autobiography Hearn recalls that its most important section was the "Chronicle of the Churches," which "taught people to know and understand each other better, and therefore to look with more love than suspicion upon the character and doings of the various denominations." The publication was evangelical but not sectarian, and it advocated peace and progress. In January 1860 Whittemore also founded *The Sunday School Times and Home Educator,* which reached a circulation of twenty-five thousand in its first year. Hearn also began to contribute pieces for children to this journal, though she refused to move to London where it and *The Christian World* were published. In 1859 Hearn moved to Northampton as headmistress of a school for young children, a position that she held for the next seven years. She remained in Northampton for the rest of her life.

In 1860, at Whittemore's urging, Hearn collected her poems and published her first volume, *Lays and Lyrics of the Blessed Life.* The book went through five editions in the next six years. The two hundred poems range in length from brief works of a stanza or two to the fourteen-page "Light from the Cross," which opens the book and contains her prayer that light from the cross "will gild my page, / Irradiate my mind, and nerve my hand / To write." In the poem, Hearn writes, "God is the source of art, and Calvary's beams / Give it a glory never seen before." In the poem she alludes to England as the nation that will progress because it is a Christian one, and she incorporates the idea of empire by mentioning Africa and India, along with Greenland and Mexico.

All but a handful of the poems in this first volume rhyme, and though her rhymes are fairly predictable, Hearn uses a variety of rhyme schemes. Her verse ranges from alternating dimeter/trimeter lines to hexameter couplets. Some poems address the reader directly, some have a first-person speaker, a few are in the third person, and some are apostrophes to God. Every poem is religious, most overtly so, and eighty-eight have biblical quotations as epigraphs, drawing on twenty-eight books of the Bible. Many of the poems about nature praise the Creator, but the major themes are dying and preparation for death, the need to work hard, and the importance of unselfish usefulness to others. Throughout she speaks particularly to the poor, urging them to bear their sufferings on earth in expectation of Heaven's riches. The most commonly used techniques are personification and repetition of a line or part of a line throughout the poem, and she uses metaphor and symbol, but in trite ways.

An anti-Catholic narrative poem, "The Convert," consists of twelve eight-line stanzas of alternating tetrameter/trimeter verse (rhyming *ababcdcd*). The poem features the story of an eighteen-year-old girl worshiping in a "Romanist" service who begins to question the need for Latin and for rote responses from the congregation: "O, what a mockery it is, / To worship God like this!" She begins to read the Bible and discovers the truth for herself. When she starts to talk about her conversion, she is threatened with burning at the stake; but she steadfastly wins many to God, withstanding all persecution. Among the poems exhorting the poor to be content with their lot is "The Useful," where readers are told that "Christ-like spirits will not wish for scenes of wealth and pride / They are *really useful* who, with humble, reverent heart, / Unseen by earth's admirers, seek to do their secret part." As might be expected, many poems describe the delights of Heaven, including "The Countless Multitude," "A Glimpse of Heaven," and "Heaven." Poems that teach the reader to accept death include "Holy Living and Dying," "The Dying Christian," and "The Christian's Lot," where the reader learns that "The Christian's lot may not be high or great, / His earthly friends may all be poor or low."

After the death of Whittemore in 1860, James Clarke, the publisher of *The Christian World,* assumed the editorship, and he expanded it and invited even more submissions from Hearn. He also doubled her salary. In 1866, she published a second volume, *Poems,* a collection of 231 works. The first poem, "Gilbert: A Tale of the Times," is one of the few narrative poems and one of two anti-Catholic pieces. Gilbert, who gives in to monastic life out of despair, is about to take orders as a monk when God's voice tells him to go forth and do good and not spend his life in fasting and "aimless prayer." In the other anti-Catholic poem, "A Passage in a Noble Life," Farningham praises the heroism of Joan of Arc at a point when she is ministering to the needs of the suffering but ends by criticizing her for becoming a martyr out of "ignorance."

Like the poems in her first collection, these are mostly rhymed, and they are all religious, though they lack Bible verses as epigraphs. The title page, however, has as an epigraph some lines by Henry

Wadsworth Longfellow, for whose collection of poems she would later write a preface. Several poems stand out because of their less-predictable rhymes and line lengths. In "Let There Be Light" the seven four-line stanzas have a tetrameter triplet followed by a trimeter line varied slightly from stanza to stanza. In one of her most delicate poems, "In the Night," five eight-line stanzas beginning with the line "Solemnly, silently," describe physical sleep, comparing it to death in alternating trimeter and dimeter lines, thus creating a haunting effect. "Falling Leaves," in hexameter couplets, begins with a physical description of nature, as is the case with many of Hearn's poems, but quickly moves to a symbolic level: in autumn one can perceive the physical death that comes to all people and see it as a sacred season born of grief but one to be celebrated as an assurance that God "doeth all things well." Several poems describe the deaths of children; "Dying" describes the simultaneous deaths of a child of wealth and a child of poverty. The two boys become friends in Heaven, though "the happier one, I ween, / Is the one who came from the heap of straw / Which his dying bed had been."

In 1867 Clarke asked Hearn to write full-time, so she gave up her teaching position. By then she had published a series of sketches, *Life Sketches and Echoes from the Valley* (1861–1871), that she had written for *The Christian World*. In the next three years a children's book, *Chats by the Sea* (1868), and two books for older children, *Girlhood* (1869) and *Boyhood* (1870), were published, all collections of work written for the journals. Hearn said in her autobiography that *Girlhood* "proved by far my most successful book." This collection of brief essays addressed to adolescents discusses the perils that might keep a young girl from living a useful, Christian life. She tells her readers to educate themselves even though they may be manual laborers: "It is possible to be a hard worker with the hands, and yet to be cultivated and well-informed. Work need never debase anyone." She advises them to cultivate a healthy self-respect as an important defense against temptation, and she urges them to work hard for their employers, avoiding the temptation to steal in the form of wasting time that belongs to the employer. Similarly, *Boyhood* tells readers: "There is no disgrace in work, but on the contrary, he who works skillfully and conscientiously and well does a worthy thing. The disgrace is in idleness and uselessness and self-indulgence."

In 1871 Hearn's sister Hephzibah and her husband and children moved to Northampton, and Hearn went to live with them. Her sister's house

Title page for a 1903 volume of poems published under one of Hearn's pseudonyms

became the meeting place for her Sunday school class, which she had started teaching in 1867 and which would continue until 1901. By 1882 this class, which numbered 180 to 200 young women, would move again to a classroom built by friends, a room that later had its own organ and library. Associated with the College Street Baptist Church, the class was interdenominational, and its members were mostly factory workers, along with a few pupil teachers, music teachers, artists, and servants. Throughout her work with the class, Hearn sought not only a close spiritual relationship with the women but also a personal one. She arranged annual holidays for those who could afford it, taking them to such places as Brighton, Edinburgh, and Barmouth. Many had never seen the sea, and Hearn, who loved the sea, delighted in outings to the coast. She also developed a thrift society to enable the women to save money and to make loans to those in the group in need. Though the initial amount was small, Hearn convinced a friend to pay 5 percent interest on their funds. Finally, however, when the fund grew to more than £1,000, the friend said he could no longer afford to pay the interest, and the society was discontinued. Establishing the organization was one of the steps Hearn took to help young women become independent, and although Hearn's writing seems to disparage women's rights, her actions seem to have fostered the spirit of independence and self-reliance among women.

Hearn's novel, *The Cathedral's Shadow,* an anti-Catholic story, appeared in 1871. Hearn recognized that she could not write novels, and in her autobiography she says she had often wished she could write them as well as hymns. A third large volume of poems, *Leaves from Elim,* appeared in 1873. Hearn's techniques are the same as in earlier volumes, but the tone of these poems is lighter. Most of the 323 poems have the same themes, but they emphasize suffering less and praise for God more, especially through the beauties of nature. The poem ends with the plea that "God in mercy spare our Daisy / Many, many years." "When the Wind Blows" contrasts the warmth of the family circle to cold, blowing wind sweeping across the moors. Although several poems use night as a metaphor for encroaching death, two of them, "The Joy of the Night" and "Songs in the Night," portray it as a time to feel especially close to God. Other poems, for example, "After the Night" and "To the Night," depict night as a time of struggle in which we can perceive the will of God. Some poems use the metaphor of the Christian pilgrim on a journey, and several equate Christians to soldiers in battle, an ironic choice of metaphor considering Hearn's antiwar beliefs.

Unusual in her work, the poem "Daisy" whimsically describes a little girl by that name who is a "chatterbox," a "busy-body," the "greatest-tease," and a "merry-maker / Of her happy home." Two other poems differ in subject matter from the rest: "The Queen's Thanksgiving" celebrates the recovery of the health of one of Queen Victoria's sons, and "Pity the Nations" argues against war. "The Queen's Thanksgiving," presumably referring to the near death of the Prince of Wales from typhoid fever in December 1871, has a stately tone and rhythm, as the last of the five stanzas shows:

So sing the sweet anthems, and ring out the bells,
   While thousands of hearts their deep loyalty prove;
And all lands unite in the glad song that swells
   For the Prince who is saved and the Queen whom we love,
     To our Father above.

"Pity the Nations" prays that God pity those dying in war as well as the families that will be left fatherless and that God "Give peace in our time again."

Hearn's writing took a new direction in 1875 when she was asked by Adam & Company to write a series of biographies, beginning with the life of Grace Darling, the daughter of a lighthouse-keeper in the Farne Islands. Dismissing the extreme danger to themselves, Darling and her father rowed out among the rocks in a pounding storm and heroically saved nine people from the shipwrecked *Forfarshire,* though only five survived. The wreck occurred in September 1838, and at least sixty lives were lost. Hearn's book, the first under her pseudonym Eva Hope, begins by addressing the topic of what is appropriate work for women and concludes that women must do what they see needs doing. The 312-page book holds up the life of Grace Darling as a model for women to follow. Here, as elsewhere, she urges young women to learn about the outdoors, and to be strong and healthy by walking so that they will be able to perform God's will. She cautions young women not to waste their time reading novels: "Another thing is morally certain, and it is, that Grace Darling had not read many novels. The effect of doing this is to make girls dream, rather than do." Other biographies followed in the next two decades, including those of the American presidents Abraham Lincoln and James Garfield (1884), General Charles George Gordon (1885), Queen Victoria (1887), Henry Stanley (1890), and the popular Baptist preacher, Charles H. Spurgeon (189–?). The volume containing the biographies of Lincoln and Garfield was directed at boys, and the lessons to be learned are summarized at the end of the volume: poor youths can attain wealth and success through hard work, but success requires strong character. For her, the greatest men were Christians. In 1890 Hearn published *Famous Women Authors,* a book that included biographies of Mary Somerville, Harriet Martineau, Elizabeth Barrett Browning, Charlotte Brontë, George Eliot, and Felicia Hemans. Hearn wrote large sections of these biographies in the reading room in the British Museum.

Beginning in 1877 Hearn wrote and delivered hundreds of lectures, often under the auspices of Sunday school unions or other groups that could benefit from sharing the fees she earned. She was invited to speak in towns all over the country and drew crowds of up to two thousand to hear such lectures as "Help-Meets and Hinderers," "The Women of the Bible," and "The Rush and Hush of Life," which she gave more than two hundred times. Giving more than one hundred lectures each year brought her enough money to buy her own house in Northampton. She continued to lecture for the next decade.

In 1879 Hearn's father came to live with her in Northampton, and he became active in the church life, enthusiastically leading the singing at services. He lived with Hearn for ten years, until his death in April 1889. Because she did not sleep well, Hearn would begin writing at 5 A.M., working for a couple of hours, and then again in the evening, taking long walks in between. At this time she also developed the habit of traveling several times a year to observe places and people that might enrich the subject matter of her articles, stories, and poems. At the request of a woman she met on a lecture tour, Hearn accompanied her to the Holy Land. She paid Hearn's expenses on the tour, which included a group of twenty. Four years later, Hearn went to Switzerland to recover from influenza. In 1889 she traveled to Italy, spending Easter at St. Peter's in Rome, and then seeing Perugia, Florence, Bologna, Padua, Milan and Venice, where her visit to St. Mark's Cathedral was especially meaningful. In her autobiography she writes, "no church that I have ever seen made me feel so much as St. Mark's."

In 1878 *Songs of Sunshine* was published, a book that included 220 of Hearn's poems. Like the previous collection, this one has a less somber tone than the first books of poetry. Though it certainly has many poems with heavy-handed Christian injunctions and many based on characters in the Bible, it includes some nature poems in which God is only mentioned at the end or, in one or two cases, not at all. Several poems describe particular ruins and castles that reflect Hearn's travels. This volume also includes a political poem, a rare kind for Hearn, whose political comments in poetry are generally confined to the topic of peace. In fact, Hearn said that she was not interested in politics, though she was interested in social causes such as temperance, education, and the protection of children. In this volume she writes about hunger in India. In "The Indian Famine," Hearn contrasts the "scorching plains" and "shrieks of agony" of famine-torn India with the "food-wealth" of the English storehouses. She asks "Shall we heap up wealth in our selfishness, / Nor our Indian brothers help to bless?" She concludes that because "They have made us rich with their wealth before," England must share its bounty because God sees all of humanity as one people. The volume also features an antiwar poem, "A Prayer for the Times (Written During the Late War)," and one titled "Many Happy Returns" commemorating the

Photograph of Hearn used as the frontispiece for her autobiography, published in 1907

birthday of Queen Victoria, whom Hearn greatly admired.

This volume also reflects Hearn's love of the sea. In "By the Sea-Side" Hearn observes scenes on the beach: "Scarce a cave, sea-washed and shady, / But is sheltering some lady, / Or a beach but has its myriads of glad children at their play." She describes the people as they "Sit and lie on sand or shingle, and enjoy their well-earned rest" and the sea "as it dashes / On the rocks, and gently splashes / World-worn faces. . . ." Then she tells readers that the beauty of the scene comes from God. In the poem "Seaward" she describes the "whispering waters" and "the leaping, gladsome billows," and urges the reader to leave work behind and "learn how bright and gladsome / Summer holidays can be." In the last of five stanzas Hearn says that being in nature in this way can help us feel the presence of God. Several other nature poems in the volume are among her best poems, for example, "The Snowdrops," "First Violets," and "The Robin in May." These are less trite, less ponderous in their references to religion, and more delicate in their observation of nature than most of the others. Particularly strong are several poems about autumn: "Autumn Winds," "October," "The Reapers," and "Violets in November." "Autumn Winds" shows a keen observation of nature and a playful spirit rare in Hearn's poems. Hearn describes the winds as lifting "the veil from the sun's bright face," calling boys out to play and then pelting the boys "With the apple showers that fall," and sweeping the yellow leaves "down with a mighty blast." In "October" Hearn says "the trees blush deeply crimson when they feel the North wind's breath." "The Reapers" is particularly interesting in light of poems in earlier volumes that present a somber view of the reapers as those whom God will eventually harvest. Here, "The Reapers," which begins the last four of its six stanzas with "Good Speed to the reapers!," depicts the work of the reapers in a cheerful tone and concludes with a lightly handled reference to the speaker's bringing home the harvest "In the autumn that yet shall be."

Also notable in this volume are poems about real places including "Shakespeare's House at Stratford," "Sir Walter Scott at Kenilworth," "By Charlotte Brontë's Grave, in Haworth Church," "Montgomery's Tomb," "Nottingham Cemetery," "In Grasmere Churchyard," and "Furness Abbey." In "Shakespeare's House at Stratford," the many visitors to the house "Are bound together by love of him / Whose genius the whole world knows," and it makes clear that God is the source of Shakespeare's genius. "In Grasmere Churchyard" emphasizes the simplicity of Wordsworth's grave; the banners waving over his grave are "Only loving hearts whose pain / Has been soothed by the sweet strain / Of the man below." In "By Charlotte Brontë's Grave, in Haworth Church" the speaker describes climbing down from the hills around Haworth and attending a service in the church where Brontë is buried: "While we joined in the words of the Evening Prayer / We knew that we knelt by the silent grave / Of a faithful woman whose heart was brave." The poem concludes with the assurance that Brontë now understands "The things that were dim in this darker land."

Writing as Eva Hope, Hearn wrote the prefaces for three volumes of the Canterbury Poets series published by Walter Scott. Her prefaces to the works of William Cowper, John Greenleaf Whittier, and Henry Wadsworth Longfellow offer more biographical information than comments on the poetry; and the criticism that does appear is unsophisticated and sometimes sentimental. For example, commenting on Cowper's line "England, with all they faults, I love thee still," Hearn comments, "His apostrophe has deepened or awakened true patriotism in many hearts." She praises Longfellow for the contribution his "Poems on Slavery" made to the antislavery movement: "'Psalm of Life' and 'Excelsior' have been like stirring battle marches to those who are entering life, with its possibilities before them." Hearn concludes that if Longfellow were "not the greatest of poets he was one of the sweetest; if he led us into the calms rather than the storms of imagination, he gave the world what it wanted."

During this same period Hearn added to her already heavy literary responsibilities by agreeing to edit *The Sunday School Times*. Because of the improvements in day schools, Hearn thought the journal would need to be even more discriminating if it were to play an important role in education. Not only did Hearn review the more than five hundred manuscripts sent to her annually for publication, she also continued to write for the journal. One article that she wrote for it was published in 1898 as the book *A Window in Paris*. The 358-page work, written to promote peace, describes the experiences of a couple and their daughter who lived through the Franco-Prussian War in Paris in 1870. Discussing this work in *A Farningham Childhood: Chapters from the Life of Marianne Farningham* (1988), Shirley Burgoyne Black argues that Hearn's vocabulary limited her ability to convey the terrors of the situation, though she commends Hearn for taking on a story that was bound to unsettle the minds of readers. *Harvest Gleanings and Gathered Fragments*, a collection of 170 poems, appeared in 1903. The most-engaging poems are the twenty-five nature poems that she grouped under the heading "Songs of Out-of-Doors," and the twenty-three under the heading "Songs of Men and Places." This latter section includes poems on Whittier and Ruskin as well as poems that reflect Hearn's travel: "Lake Nauchatel," "Jungfrau," "A Memory of Lake Como," "Trummelbach Waterfall," and "Lake Brienz and Giessbach."

By the late 1880s Hearn was at last able to afford a place by the sea. She rented a cottage at the Mawddach Estuary at Barmouth in Wales, and through her connections there she became acquainted with John Ruskin as well as Frances Power Cobbe, who worked on behalf of the Married Woman's Property Act and the conferring of university degrees to women. Hearn also mourned the deaths of her two remaining siblings as well as that of her longtime editor and friend, James Clarke, in 1888. Her brother had gone to South Africa, where he died in 1889, and her sister died in 1893, two years after her return to England from South Africa.

Hearn's autobiography was published in 1907, followed the next year by *Lyrics of the Soul,* a collection of 169 poems. These poems are grouped under the headings "Divine Goodness and Care," "Divine Grace and Companionship," "Lessons from Nature," "Life and Duty," "Times and Seasons," "Gains of Experience," "Of Fatherland," "Home and the Human Brotherhood," and "Of Men and Movements." The poem "National Assets" argues for the care and protection of children, and "Florence Nightingale" praises the nurse for her work and legacy—the "Women of skill and tenderness" who "Perpetuate your fame."

The autobiography, *A Working Woman's Life,* is probably the most widely known of Hearn's books, and seems to have been the only one reviewed in the mainstream journals. A brief anonymous review in *The London Quarterly Review* from 1908 describes it as "delightfully unconventional," a work in which "Simple sincerity, joy in doing good, unfailing interest in nature and travel, mark it throughout." Recent critics such as Deborah Gorham and Mary Ann T. Leiby have been interested in Hearn's conception of femininity, and Ursula Howard has explored ways in which writing empowered Hearn into having a productive life through a community of others who shared his values.

Hearn died at Barmouth on 16 March 1909 following a prolonged illness. Her final volume of verse, *Songs of Joy and Faith,* appeared posthumously in September 1909. This 208-page collection of 113 poems includes a few new poems along with ones from earlier collections.

Hearn will never be regarded as a great poet. In *A Farningham Childhood* Black argues that Hearn's religious upbringing, with its emphasis on telling the truth and denying the imagination, negatively affected her work, as did her limited education and small vocabulary. Black also points out that many of the weaknesses in her poetry and prose result from the severely limited time left to her writing by her many other responsibilities. One might argue, on the other hand, that since Hearn was reading Shakespeare, Brontë, Longfellow, Cowper, and other writers, she did understand the power of the imagination and that she may have chosen simple language and simple forms to reach the working class, her primary audience. Still, modern readers will continue to read Hearn's work as a way of understanding nonconformist denominations, the lives of working-class women, and the relationship between Sunday schools and nineteenth-century education.

References:

Shirley Burgoyne Black, *A Farningham Childhood: Chapters from the Life of Marianne Farningham* (Sevenoaks, Kent, U.K.: Darenth Valley, 1988);

Deborah Gorham, *The Victorian Girl and the Feminine Ideal* (London: Croom Helm, 1982);

Ursula Howard, "Self, Education, and Writing in Nineteenth-Century Communities," in *Writing in the Community,* edited by David Barton and Ivanic Roz (Newberry Park, Cal.: Sage, 1991), pp. 78–108;

R. M. Julian, "In Memoriam: Marianne Farningham," *Christian World* (18 March 1909): 195–197;

Thomas Walter Laqueur, *Religion and Respectability: Sunday Schools and Working Class Culture 1780–1850* (New Haven: Yale University Press, 1976);

Mary Ann T. Leiby, "The 'Respectables' and the 'Roughs': Subjectivity and Class in the Academy and Victorian Women's Writing," dissertation, University of Florida, 1995.

Laurence Hope
(Adela Florence Cory Nicolson)
(9 April 1865 – 4 October 1904)

Edward Marx
Kyoto University

BOOKS: *The Garden of Káma, and Other Love Lyrics from India, Arranged in Verse by Laurence Hope* (London: Heinemann, 1901); republished as *India's Love Lyrics: Collected & Arranged in Verse by Laurence Hope* (New York: John Lane, 1902);

Stars of the Desert (London: Heinemann / New York: John Lane, 1903);

Indian Love (London: Heinemann / New York: John Lane, 1905); republished as *Last Poems: Translations from the Book of Indian Love* (New York: John Lane, 1905);

Laurence Hope's Poems (New York: Reynolds / London: Heinemann, 1907.

Editions and Collections: *Songs from the Garden of Kama* (London: Heinemann, 1908);

The Garden of Kama, and Other Love Lyrics from India, Arranged in Verse by Laurence Hope (London: Heinemann / New York: John Lane, 1914);

Selected Poems from the Indian Love Lyrics of Laurence Hope, edited by Malcolm Josceline Nicolson (London: Heinemann, 1922);

Selected Love Lyrics: Containing Poems from India's Love Lyrics, Stars of the Desert, Last Poems (New York: Dodd, Mead, 1929);

Complete Love Lyrics, Including India's Love Lyrics, Stars of the Desert, Last Poems (New York: Dodd, Mead, 1937);

Selected Love Lyrics, Including India's Love Lyrics, Stars of the Desert, Last Poems (New York: Dodd, Mead, 1968).

Laurence Hope (courtesy of The Lilly Library, Indiana University)

Among the most popular poets of the Edwardian era, Adela Florence Cory Nicolson rose to fame on a wave of interest in the exotic with her racy Indian love lyrics published under the pseudonym "Laurence Hope." A female rival to Rudyard Kipling, though with a sensibility more akin to the Decadent poets, Nicolson was recognized by contemporary poets, including Thomas Hardy, Arthur Symons, James Elroy Flecker, and Edith Thomas, who admired her passion, sincerity, and abundant, if often uncontrolled, lyrical gifts. Although her brief literary career was cut short by suicide in 1904, her poetry remained popular for decades, and, though critically neglected for many years, her unconventional life and poetry have experienced a revival of interest in recent years.

Laurence Hope was born Adela Florence Cory in Gloucestershire on 9 April 1865 to Arthur Cory, an officer in the Bengal Army, and Fanny Elizabeth Griffin

Cory. Adela was the second of three daughters. Her father was on leave in England at the time of her birth, and while his wife was preparing for the event, Captain (later Colonel) Cory was taking advantage of "an interval of unwonted leisure" to compose a lengthy and now deservedly forgotten epic poem, *The Reconquest: A Love Story* (1865). Like Kipling, her contemporary, Cory was left in England to be raised, in her case, by relatives, while her father finished out his army years in northwest India. In her teens she was sent to school abroad, where she began to write poetry, recording her impressions of Italian art and culture.

At sixteen Cory joined her parents in Lahore, where her father, who by then had retired, had co-edited the *Civil and Military Gazette* since 1877. It was a short visit, for in November 1882 the colonel–the author of a somewhat controversial and militaristic treatise titled *The Eastern Menace* (1881)–left his position on the paper to return to England, citing illness. (Earlier that year, a fellow Lahorean and sometime-contributor to the *Gazette,* Lockwood Kipling, had made arrangements for his son, Rudyard, to step in as assistant editor.)

The family returned to India, this time to the rapidly developing port city of Karachi, where the father took the position of editor of the *Sind Gazette*. Little is known about Adela's life in this period, but some sources claim she assisted her father on the paper, along with her elder sister, Isabell Edith, and probably her younger sister, Annie Sophie, as well. (All three Cory daughters were destined for literary careers: Isabell, as the editor of the *Gazette* after her father's death in 1903; Annie Sophie, as the controversial novelist "Victoria Cross," achieving success and notoriety in the field of fiction; and Adela, making her name in poetry as Laurence Hope.)

In 1889 Cory married Colonel Malcolm H. Nicolson, a Bombay army officer renowned for having crossed Karachi's famous crocodile-infested tank by hopping from the back of one crocodile to another. Colonel Nicolson–at forty-six, nearly twice her age–was the commander of a native regiment then stationed in the area. He was a veteran of the Second Afghan War and proficient in the Baluchi language spoken by his troops, as well as in Persian, Pashto, and Brahui.

The Nicolsons' relationship was said, by those who knew the couple, to be a happy one, but clearly it took a deep toll on Adela–or Violet, as she preferred to be called–emotionally. Hardy, who met her in 1903, observed that "the impression of her personality was that of one whose nature was not sufficiently renunciative to be likely to encounter the ordinary shocks of life without exceptional perturbation, distress, and rebellion." The "ordinary shocks of life" with a commander of an Indian army regiment on the Afghan frontier, however, even one without Colonel Nicolson's taste for adventure, would have been considerable. She is said to have accompanied her husband on a military expedition into Afghanistan's Zhob Valley a year after their marriage, disguised as a Pathan boy. (A poem evidently based on the experience, "Camp Follower's Song: Gomal River" appears in her first volume.) Her poetry, however, reveals that such adventures, which she relished, could only partially compensate for the long periods of solitude and frequent displacements that exacerbated her loneliness and depression.

In 1893 the nomadic period came to an end when Malcolm was promoted to general and made commanding officer of Deesa, a small backwoods station where they spent the next two years. In 1895 General Nicolson was given command of the important Mhow district in the native state of Indore (now part of Madhya Pradesh). He held the post for five years.

"Mhow is noted as the place where Laurence Hope wrote her hectic verse," wrote Mrs. Walter Tibbits in her travelogue, *Veiled Mysteries of India* (1929). The Scottish writer Violet Jacob, whose husband was also stationed at Mhow, was friendly with the Nicolsons. In her writings collected as *Violet Jacob: Diaries and Letters from India 1895–1900* (1990) she gives her first impression of Nicolson: "a tiny, fair, very strange woman, vilely and impossibly clothed in a short skirt like a schoolgirl and a little round cape; her hair hangs down just touching her shoulders and is cut square on her forehead." Flora Annie Steel, an old friend of Nicolson's husband, was also shocked by her attire. She recalled in her autobiography, "unconventional as I was, I felt a little embarrassed at having to sit beside her striking figure, dressed in a low-necked, short-sleeved, pink satin gown, in an open victoria in broad daylight." As Steel and Jacob were far less bound to convention than most of their compatriots, the general opinion of the wayward Nicolson must have been scathing. "Everyone mocks at her and I can't help doing it myself sometimes at the really absurd figure she makes," Jacob confessed, but then, Nicolson was the *burra memsahib* of Mhow, and, in any case, no woman afraid of scandal could have written the poems she wrote.

The poems first appeared in 1901, in England, as *The Garden of Káma, and Other Love Lyrics from India, Arranged in Verse by Laurence Hope*. ("*Káma,*" glossed in the title poem as "the Indian Eros," lost its accent in later editions). In the United States the collection appeared the following year as *India's Love Lyrics: Collected & Arranged in Verse by Laurence Hope*. Hardy noted that the poems' "tropical luxuriance and Sapphic fervour attracted the attention of so many readers that a second and third edition of the book were demanded."

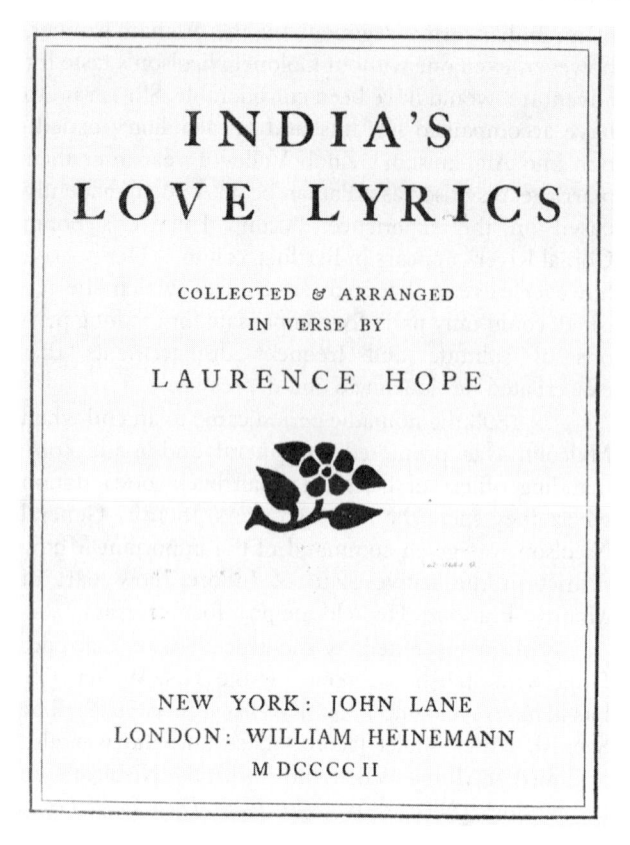

Title page for the second edition of Hope's first and best-known collection of poems (courtesy of The Lilly Library, Indiana University)

Dozens of reprintings and two lavishly illustrated posthumous editions followed. The phenomenal success of the book owed much to the popularity of Amy Woodforde-Finden's musical arrangements of a selection of the poems as *Four Indian Love Lyrics* in 1902. The best known of the four, "Kashmiri Song," is a melancholy remembrance of the "Pale hands I loved beside the Shalimar," ending on the masochistic note, "I would rather have felt you round my throat, / Crushing out life, than waving me farewell!"

At the end of the general's term at Mhow the Nicolsons traveled to Bombay, where Violet gave birth to their only child, Malcolm Josceline. They then returned to England. In 1902, leaving the infant in the care of relatives, they traveled to North Africa, where the general purportedly hoped to find employment in Morocco, with French sovereignty in the region still several years off. There Nicolson wrote many of the poems for her second book, *Stars of the Desert* (1903).

Returning to London in 1903, Nicolson made some tentative forays into literary society. Although the identity of the poet was still not widely known, as early as June 1902 Jeannette Gilder revealed in *The Critic* that "Laurence Hope is said to be the pen name of Mrs. Malcolm Nicolson, wife of Lieutenant-General Nicolson, late of the Indian army." She met Hardy at a literary salon hosted by Blanche Crackanthorpe. W. Somerset Maugham recorded in his *A Writer's Notebook* (1949) that the Crackanthorpe circle concluded that the poems were "obviously not addressed to her husband." Maugham later made this observation the basis for his story, "The Colonel's Lady," included in his collection *Creatures of Circumstance* (1947). In November 1903 Nicolson sat for society photographer G. C. Beresford, a session that produced the frontispiece for her next book.

Home for Nicolson, however, was no longer England. "I want the lonely, level sands / Stretched out beneath the sun, / The sadness of the old, old lands, / Whose destiny is done," she wrote in "Trees of Wharncliffe House." In 1904 the Nicolsons returned to India, this time to the Madras region. The general may have planned to seek a new post, but for the moment they settled on the Malabar coast, in Cannanore and Feroke, where a fellow resident recalled their "charming bungalow on a hill-top." Nicolson was evidently pleased with the arrangement: "Heart, my heart, thou hast found thy home!," she wrote in "Song of the Parao."

> Thou hast returned to thy dear delights;
>   The golden glow of the quivering days,
> The silver silence of tropical nights,
>   No more to wander in alien ways.

But even in these happy days, there were unhappy thoughts. Despair remained a recurrent theme. In her poem "Feroke," she wrote:

> The current brought a stranger yesterday,
>   And laid him on the sand beneath a palm,
> His worn young face was partly torn away,
>   His eyes, that saw the world no more, were calm.
>
> We could not close his eyelids, stiff with blood,—
>   But, oh, my brother, I had changed with thee!
> For I am still tormented in the flood,
>   Whilst thou hast done thy work, and reached the sea.

On 7 August 1904 Malcolm Nicolson died while undergoing a minor prostate operation in Madras. On the afternoon of 4 October, having revised her will the previous day, Violet Nicolson swallowed mercury perchloride, a corrosive poison. General Sir Norman Stewart, a friend of her late husband's with whom she was staying in Madras, quickly discovered her and called a doctor, but she died several hours later. Another friend, W. Francis Grahame, wrote to Hardy that Nicolson had "never got over the death of her husband, over which she brooded with an intensity which became deeper and deeper as time passed by." Grahame wrote that Nicolson blamed herself for not dissuading him from the operation and "also became possessed of the thought that it was 'disloyal' to him that she should remain in this world 'enjoying life.'" Her suicidal intentions had been apparent, but constant surveillance had seemed, according to Grahame, unjustifiable. The coroner's verdict of suicide while in a state of temporary insanity allowed her to be buried alongside her husband in St. Mary's Cemetery.

The suicide note "Dedication to Malcolm Nicolson," which prefaces her posthumously published third volume of verse, indicated how she wished her last act to be read:

> I, who of lighter love wrote many a verse,
>   Made public never words inspired by thee,
> Lest strangers' lips should carelessly rehearse
>   Things that were sacred and too dear to me.
>
> Thy soul was noble; through these fifteen years
>   Mine eyes familiar, found no fleck nor flaw,
> Stern to thyself, thy comrades' faults and fears
>   Proved generosity thine only law.
>
> Small joy was I to thee; before we met
>   Sorrow had left thee all too sad to save.
> Useless my love—as vain as this regret
>   That pours my hopeless life across thy grave.

The volume, titled *Indian Love* in the Heinemann edition (1905) and *Last Poems: Translations from the Book of Indian Love* in the John Lane U.S. edition of the same year, like her previous books, proved successful, although Hardy was deeply irritated when the book appeared without a preface Heinemann had asked him to contribute. In his biography of Hardy, Martin Seymour Smith argues that Hardy "over-rated" Nicolson because his judgment was "adversely affected," when confronted with 'passionate' poetry written by women. But Hardy's preface was in fact quite restrained, applying no more favorable adjective to Nicolson's verse than "impassioned," and his belief that his imprimatur could boost her sales is belied by languid sales of his own. *Wessex Poems,* reprinted in 1903 after taking five years to sell out its first run of five hundred copies, while in the same year, *The Garden of Kama* was already in its fourth printing.

The popularity of Laurence Hope was something of a problem for the male poets of the day, a period in which poetry was declared by Poet Laureate Sir Alfred Austin to be in something of a "slump." In the June 1907 *Monthly Review* Flecker explored the question of Laurence Hope's success "where most modern poets have failed," namely, in creating for herself "a world of admirers, a multitude of initiants—a Public." "The true cause," he declared, "must be sought in the nature of the feminine—in the appreciation of Laurence Hope by her sex." While women were not "the wild untrammelled creatures of impulse, the primitive and savage beings that Laurence Hope would have them to be," Flecker speculated, "perhaps more of her sex sympathise with this elemental Muse of the whirlwind than would ever care to own or be able to realise the slightest affinity." But, while male critics such as Flecker and Otto Rothfeld were delighted by the thought that the masochistic female slaves of the poems represented the "essence" of femininity, others explained her popularity differently. An anonymous reviewer in *The Academy* (5 August 1905) argued that "Laurence Hope is a man's poet, although femininity is apparent in almost every line; even her delineations of a man's point of view show it. . . . The average Western woman could neither feel nor understand the fire of such a nature."

In any case, the books sold well. Primarily, they appealed to the audience's taste for the exotic. They brought the reader into "a region of native feeling and imagination never yet fully explored," presenting "the wondrous lethal fascination and the 'Inherent Cruelty of Things' in the ancient land of Vishnu" with "the robustness and *abandon* of the eastern bards." Lane emphasized this aspect with advertising circulars warning the reader to "never forget as he reads, that these are the love songs of young Eastern blood, whose laws of conduct were framed to fit *their* temperament, not *ours.*" Not all the reviews were positive, however. One reviewer in *Athenaeum* (2 September 1905) wrote, "to the Western mind such things, though pleasant enough for a while, being exotic, are apt to become a burden if there be not some variety of treatment or thought to save them from dullness." An Indian critic in the *Calcutta Review* railed against "those who indulge a taste for the forbidden, and—indecent, by sheltering behind a misrepresentation of a country their knowledge of which may be summed up in the bare fact that it is the home of elemental passion."

Critics spoke of the passion of Laurence Hope's poems, particularly those in her first volume. Richard Garnett in *The Bookman* (28 September 1905) wrote that her lines were "unique among the poetry of their day for a consuming intensity of passion." Her sincerity was also much discussed, as was her lack of restraint. She was, as Symons wrote in 1905, "one of the strongest personalities in recent English literature." Many thought that she had "overstepped the proper limits," as a review in the *Literary World* (22 January 1904) put it. "These fierce utterances, which are now and then almost the ravings of passion, are the work of a woman now dead," observed *The Times Literary Supplement* (*TLS*) review of *Indian Love* (25 August 1905). Others, however, were intrigued by what Flecker called her "half-scandalous appetite for free speech." "No woman

Title page for Hope's third volume of verse, published one year after her suicide (courtesy of The Lilly Library, Indiana University)

has written lines so full of a strange primeval savagery," observed *The Spectator* in 1905. Her suicide only confirmed the popular perception of "this curiously sincere poet," as Flecker called her. For Hardy, "the tragic circumstances of her death seem but the impassioned closing notes of her impassioned effusions."

New editions of Nicolson's poetry appeared after her death, but only one–a small collection of juvenilia titled *Laurence Hope's Poems* (1907)–included previously unpublished work. The quality of these poems–most of which were written before Nicolson left for India at the age of sixteen–is uneven at best, but they offer some insights into the poet's early attitudes and development. Two illustrated editions of *The Garden of Kama* appeared: the first, titled *Songs from the Garden of Kama* (1908), with photographs of India by Mrs. Eardley Wilmot; and the second, a deluxe "royal quarto," with paintings by Byam Shaw, a fringe member of the Pre-Raphaelite group. In 1922 the Nicolsons' son edited *Selected Poems from the Indian Love Lyrics of Laurence Hope*. After Lane's death Dodd, Mead obtained the American copyright and continued to bring out new and reprinted editions. Some of these included a selection of Shaw illustrations, while another was issued in a cover uniform with the company's edition of Edward FitzGerald's *Rubáiyát of Omar Khayyám*. Dodd, Mead brought out *Complete Love Lyrics, Including India's Love Lyrics, Stars of the Desert, Last Poems* in 1937 and *Selected Love Lyrics, Including India's Love Lyrics, Stars of the Desert, Last Poems* in 1968.

Despite the continued popularity of the poems, little critical work, aside from reviews of the 1909 and 1914 editions, appeared. In the early years a lack of biographical information no doubt inhibited critical analysis, although the inclusion of both Nicolsons in the 1912 supplement to the *Dictionary of National Biography* somewhat rectified this situation. Henry Bruce's 1906 essay in the *East & West,* the only early study able to connect Nicolson's life and work, was not widely available outside of India. Speculative interpretations were offered in essays by H. Pearl Humphry (1905) and Rothfeld (1909), and Austin Johnson contributed a discussion of the poet's work to the *Poetry Review* in 1913. Harold Williams's *Modern English Writers: Being a Study of Imaginative Literature, 1890–1914* (1918) was among the few literary histories of the period to include Nicolson. The critical neglect was already apparent to Johnson, who noted the existence of "a large and enthusiastic band of admirers capable of explaining and justifying their enthusiasm," while at the same time acknowledging that "her name is quite unknown to a large number of those who really care for literature."

Nicolson's legacy has been more inspiring to writers of fiction than to writers of criticism. The most dramatic testimonials to this appeal are the two motion pictures inspired by her work, and the musical adaptations, once "the standby of drawing-room sopranos and, later, of radio tenors," as Stanley J. Kunitz and Howard Haycraft note in *Twentieth Century Authors* (1942). The first motion picture, *Less than the Dust* (1916), which revolves around an orphaned girl, believed to be Hindu, who falls in love with a British Army officer, was Mary Pickford's first movie with the new Artcraft Pictures. Pickford herself, as she noted in her book *Sunshine and Shadow* (1955), thought this movie "incredibly bad," although reviews in *The New York Times* and *Variety* are milder in their criticism, merely citing problems with the scenario and the length of the story. The second motion picture, *The Indian Love Lyrics* (1923), produced in Great Britain by Stoll Pictures and directed by Sinclair Hill, is an exotic story of love and revenge set in medieval India. Among the works of literary fiction inspired by Laurence Hope, the best known is Maugham's "The Colonel's Lady," which was translated to the screen in *Quartet* (1949). A short story by Ted Malone, "The Secret Life of Laurence Hope" (1950), imagines an affair between Nicolson and an Indian prince. *Fate Knows No Tears* (1996), by Australian writer Mary Talbot Cross, is a more respectful effort, combining imaginative reconstruction with substantial historical and biographical research.

Biography:
Lesley Blanch, "Laurence Hope–A Shadow in the Sunlight," in her *Under a Lilac-Bleeding Star: Travels and Travelers* (London: Murray, 1963), pp. 184–208.

References:
Henry Bruce, "A True Indian Poet," *East & West,* 5 (February 1906): 158–166; (March 1906): 240–250;

James Elroy Flecker, "Laurence Hope," *Monthly Review* (June 1907): 164–168;

Thomas Hardy, "Laurence Hope," *Athenaeum* (29 October 1904): 591;

H. Pearl Humphry, "The Work of Laurence Hope," *Acorn,* 1 (1905): 137–147;

Austin Johnson, "The Poetry of Laurence Hope," *Poetry Review,* 3 (July–December 1913): 151–154;

Stanley J. Kunitz and Howard Haycraft, eds., *Twentieth Century Authors: A Biographical Dictionary of Modern Literature* (New York: Wilson, 1942), p. 664;

Otto Rothfeld, "Laurence Hope," in his *Indian Dust* (Oxford: Alden, 1909), pp. 203–216;

Arthur Symons, "The Poetry of Laurence Hope," *Outlook,* 16 (26 August 1905): 261–262;

"Western Interpreters of Eastern Verse," *Calcutta Review,* 1 (April 1904): 478–489;

Harold Williams, *Modern English Writers: Being a Study of Imaginative Literature, 1890–1914* (London: Sidgwick & Jackson, 1918), pp. 142–145.

Papers:
The surviving papers of Laurence Hope are believed to remain in the possession of her grandson, Malcolm P. Nicolson. In the early 1960s an unpublished memoir by her son, Malcolm Josceline Nicolson, was shown to Lesley Blanch, who used material from it in her biographical essay. Subsequent researchers, however, have been denied access to these materials. Two brief cards to Thomas Hardy and an inscribed copy of *Stars of the Desert* are in the collection of Frederic B. Adams, Paris. The Dorset County Museum holds the typescript for Hardy's unpublished introduction to *Indian Love*.

Nora Hopper
(Mrs. Nora Chesson)
(2 January 1871 – 14 or 19 April 1906)

Siobhan Craft Brownson
Winthrop University

BOOKS: *Ballads in Prose,* as Hopper (London: John Lane, Bodley Head / Boston: Roberts, 1894);

Under Quicken Boughs, as Hopper (London: John Lane, Bodley Head / New York: George Richmond, 1896);

Songs of the Morning, as Hopper (London: Richards, 1900);

Aquamarines, as Chesson (London: Richards, 1902);

Mildred and Her Mills and Other Poems, as Chesson (London: Tuck, 1903);

With Louis Wain to Fairyland, as Chesson (London: Tuck, 1904);

The Bell and the Arrow: An English Love Story (London: Laurie, 1905);

Selected Poems, as Chesson, 5 volumes, edited by Wilfred Hugh Chesson (London: Rivers, 1906);

Father Felix's Chronicles, as Chesson, edited by Wilfred Hugh Chesson (London: Unwin, 1907);

O'Brien Butler, *Muirgheis: The First Irish Opera, in Three Acts,* libretto by Hopper, as Chesson, Irish translation by T. O'Donoghue (New York: Breitkopf & Hartel, 1910).

PLAY PRODUCTION: *The Sea Swan,* libretto by Hopper, music by O'Brien Butler, Dublin, Theatre Royal, 7 December 1903.

OTHER: T. E. Donnison, *Old Fairy Legends in New Colours,* contributions by Hopper, as Chesson (London: Tuck, 1903).

A September 1895 article on Nora Hopper in *The Bookman* noted that even the "most Irish of Irish readers" found a reflection of the "essential spirit of their country" in her first book *Ballads in Prose* (1894). Few readers of any nationality today know her work, however, except in connection with her early champion, William Butler Yeats, or her better-known contemporary, Katharine Tynan. Nonetheless, during her lifetime Hopper was a popular writer who composed many poems for such periodicals as *Longman's, Macmillan's,* and *The Yellow Book* that were collected in several volumes. At least in part because of Yeats's interest in her early poetry, nearly all scholars of the period in Irish literature known variously as the Irish Literary Movement, the Celtic Twilight, the Irish Literary Renaissance, or the Celtic Revival devote at least a few paragraphs to her contributions. Because she wrote so copiously for the periodical press, Hopper, especially early in her career, was instrumental in exposing London audiences to what Yeats ultimately called simply "the movement."

Hopper was born in Exeter on 2 January 1871 to Harman Baillie Hopper, an Irishman who was captain of the Thirty-first Bengal Native Infantry, and Caroline Augusta Hopper, née Francis, of Wales. Though known primarily for her romantic Irish subject matter, Hopper lived in London almost all her life. She and her mother moved to the Kensington section of the city after her father's death during her infancy. She began writing as a child, composing plays and fairy romances in her exercise books; her first published poem appeared in the *Family Herald* in 1887. After completing her formal education she studied Icelandic folklore at the British Museum, seeking assistance with translation from Keeper of Printed Books Richard Garnett. In the early 1890s, having read Yeats's *Fairy and Folk Tales of the Irish Peasantry* (1888), she turned her attention to the myths and folklore of Ireland and began to write poetry and short stories based on them. The August 1894 issue of *Macmillan's* included her short story "The Witch of Yell," which combines a contemporary Irish setting with a plot based in Gaelic mysticism and legend. In the October 1894 *Yellow Book* Hopper established the format that she went on to follow in *Ballads in Prose:* a poem followed by a short story. The poem was "The Lament of the Last Leprechaun"; the story, "Aonan-na-Righ," set in "Tir Aelella" (contemporary County Sligo) and based on legends of the eighth-century Viking invasion of Ireland, tells of a Danish king's murderous hatred for the title character, his son by his Irish wife.

Hopper included both pieces in *Ballads in Prose,* which is her best-known collection because of Yeats's enthusiasm for it. Though he never formally reviewed the book, he praised it lavishly in 1895 letters to Tynan; his sister, Susan; and his father. He told Hopper in a 27 January 1895 letter that *Ballads in Prose* was "the most distinguished volume we have had out of Ireland this decade." He especially lauded the stories "Daluan" and "The Gifts of Aodh and Una" and the poems "The Fairy Fiddler" and "The Silk of the Kine": "These have all that strange mystery, that sense of melancholy in which their [*sic*] is no gloom, a sadness as of morning twilight which I find in the legends of the west."

In contrast, contemporary and later critics of *Ballads in Prose* emphasized the derivativeness of Hopper's poetry. In her unsigned review of *Ballads in Prose* in the *Irish Independent* (26 December 1894) Tynan pointedly compared the first two stanzas of Hopper's "The Lament of the Lay Brother" with the first two of Tynan's own "In Iona." In a 20 January 1895 letter to Tynan, Yeats acknowledged that she "was certainly very badly plagiarized in 'the lay brother'"; but he tried to mollify Tynan by suggesting that Hopper had "elected to consider" the more established poet "as a 'document.'" In a letter to his sister on the same day Yeats called the novice poet's adaptations the "plagiarisms of inexperienced enthusiasm." The two poems are similar not only in subject matter—the banishment by St. Columba of cattle from the island of Iona and the resulting sadness of the cattle herd—but also in meter and rhyme. In addition, Hopper's note on the poem in the glossary of *Ballads in Prose* repeats the substance of Tynan's fourth stanza in detailing the legend of Iona.

In the 11 January 1895 *Daily Express* (Dublin) an anonymous reviewer observed of Hopper's "A Connaught Lament": "The rhymes are fascinating in their melody, and an undercurrent of sadness is felt in them all. We fancy we must have seen some of them before." The first two lines, quoted in the review—"I will arise and go hence to the west, / And dig me a grave where the hill-winds call"—echo the first two lines of Yeats's "The Lake Isle of Innisfree": "I will arise and go now, and go to Innisfree, / And a small cabin build there, of clay and wattles made." Among later critics, Gregory A. Schirmer thinks that Hopper's "voice . . . speaks with a kind of authenticity" in "A Connaught Lament," but others have agreed with the *Daily Express* reviewer: Phillip L. Marcus calls attention to the "borrowing" from Yeats, and Ernest Boyd labels the poem "flagrantly imitative."

Title page for Nora Hopper's first book, in which poems alternate with short stories

From August to October 1895 Yeats extolled *Ballads in Prose* in "Irish National Literature," a four-part series he wrote for *The Bookman*. In his first article, on prose writers, he calls Hopper "the one absolute dreamer of Irish literature" and praises the tales in the volume "with hardly a reservation except perhaps that here and there is too much of filmy vagueness, as in visions in the wizard's glass, before the mystical sweeper has swept the clouds away with his broom." Half of the full column he devotes to Hopper consists of a quotation from "The Gifts of Aodh and Una" by which he was "haunted all winter," in which Aodh sacrifices his youth, knowledge, hope, courage, dreams, and heart to the gods to save his land from famine. In the third article, on contemporary Irish poets, Yeats says that Hopper's poetry in her first book has "at all times a beautiful, alluring, unaspiring peace." In the final installment of the series Yeats places *Ballads in Prose* under "Novels and Romances" in his "List of the Best Irish Books."

Yeats found Hopper's second book, *Under Quicken Boughs* (1896), which consists of all poetry, weaker than

though he accepts Yeats's suggestion that most of the volume was composed before *Ballads in Prose*. He finds "The King of Ireland's Son," which was revised from the earlier volume, clumsy and trite, and the rest of the poems overly dependent on Irish clichés and mechanical in execution. Marcus considers the volume "even more derivative than its predecessor," citing the strong resemblance of Hopper's "The Passing of the Sidhe" to Yeats's "The Hosting of the Sidhe."

Some of the poetry in Hopper's second collection justifies these reproaches. The shallow first stanza of "Phyllis and Damon" incites little desire to read the other two:

> Phyllis and Damon met one day:
> (Heigho!)
> Phyllis was sad and Damon grey,
> Tired with treading a separate way.

"The Strangers" has an odd, disjointed meter and an inexplicable rhyme scheme, and poems such as "The Grey Fog" and "The Cuckoo Sings in the Heart of Winter," which deal with the deaths of contemporary rather than mythical lovers, highlight Hopper's over-reliance on "Irishness"—honey-colored hair, wild sweet honey, and names such as Mauryeen and Mavrone. But in "The Dark Man" Hopper displays her ability to tell a story straightforwardly in verse. This tightly worded poem contrasts the dullness of the common folk's "lives' red ashes," their "words galore," with the persona's "blessed pain," worth "all days that a man may live." She convinces the reader that the persona's question, "Rose o' the World, what man would wed / When he might dream of your face instead?" is a rational one and that, for all his pain, the dark man's disability is richly compensated because his "soul's away in a fairy place."

In 1898 Hopper saw her work affirmed in two influential quarters. First, her poetry was recognized by an Irish periodical, *Shan Van Vocht,* which published her "To Sheila ni Gara" in the 7 March 1898 issue. Here the grieving speaker pleads with his dead Sheila to speak to him, "Close though your grave clothes wrap you round." The second momentous occasion for Hopper was Yeats's article "The Poems and Stories of Miss Nora Hopper" in the 24 September *Daily Express*. Though Yeats identified faults that he had been "blind to" during his "first enchantment," he commented that the collection "haunted me as few new books have ever haunted me, for it spoke in strange wayward stories and birdlike little verses of things and of persons I remembered or had dreamed of." Among the faults Yeats noted was the vague sense of place in Hopper's work. Looking back at one of his favorite stories from

Title page for Hopper's second book, a poetry collection that did not fare well with critics

its predecessor. He explained the difference in quality in his introduction to selections from Hopper's works in *A Treasury of Irish Poetry in the English Tongue* (1900) by saying that he supposed the bulk of *Under Quicken Boughs* to have been composed before *Ballads in Prose*. Still, Yeats included two poems from *Under Quicken Boughs* in the anthology, claiming that "Phyllis and Damon" (originally published in the January 1896 issue of *The Yellow Book*) was "perfect in its kind," while "The Dark Man" had "that desire of spiritual beauty and happiness which runs through so much modern true poetry." In his January 1899 *Fortnightly Review* article, "A Group of Celtic Writers," "Fiona Macleod" (William Sharp) contradicted her earlier detractors, saying that her "work is not imitative"; and though he reserved greater acclaim for *Ballads in Prose,* he found in *Under Quicken Boughs* "rememberable poems of the day and hour, of the little day and the brief tragic hour, of common life."

Later critics, however, have found little worthy of approval in the book. Boyd vilifies *Under Quicken Boughs,*

Ballads in Prose, "The Gifts of Aodh and Una," he realized that "Miss Hopper merely describes the Temple of the Heroes as being on an island of the Shannon, and is sometimes even less certain about the places of her legends, though she has much feeling for landscapes; and this uncertainty is, I believe, a defect in her method." Indeed, Hopper's knowledge of Ireland was limited and secondhand, since she had never visited the country. In her remaining works she relied more and more on Irish clichés and set her poems in London or in a generic city rather than in the Irish countryside.

In the acknowledgments in her third collection, *Songs of the Morning* (1900), Hopper thanks the editors of almost twenty magazines for granting permission for her to republish her work. Though London reviewers seem not to have noticed her first two books, *The Academy, The Athenaeum,* and *The Bookman* carried extensive pieces on *Songs of the Morning.* The charge of derivativeness continued to dog Hopper, *The Academy* (24 March 1900) finding suggestions of Dante Gabriel Rossetti in "On the Embankment" and of John Milton in "Kew Gardens." *The Athenaeum* (5 May 1900) remarked that "Miss Hopper's muse is being weakened by over-production" and that her love poems "bear too close a resemblance to each other in theme, treatment, and even imagery." The reviews were, however, largely encouraging, seeing evidence in *Songs of the Morning* of poetic development and potential. *The Bookman* (May 1900) found "signs of a profounder, more individual vision," and *The Academy* and *The Athenaeum* saluted her facility for lyric poetry, reprinting, respectively, "Southernwood" and "Beauty" for special notice.

Few contemporary or later critics, however, had much good to say about the dozen or so poems with Celtic themes in *Songs of the Morning.* *The Academy* found the "mechanical picturesqueness" of the poems unrelieved by the "Irish phrases" and "Gaelic names" scattered throughout them. Boyd notes "how easily denationalised Nora Hopper's poetry became." In "Dirge for a Dead Fairy," for example, except for her names, Aione and "Woman of the Shee," the fairy could be from almost any western folk tradition.

Conventional natural images such as flowers, trees, the moon, sky, and clouds also mar Hopper's love lyrics, such as "If I Had Been a Rose" and "Gipsy Song." But when she has clearly studied a subject, as in "Southernwood," she achieves a memorable sharpness of detail. The poem successfully relies on a contrast between the scents of the rose and the southernwood:

> Gather me, gather. I have dreams to sell.
> The sea is not by any fluted shell
> More faithfully remembered that I keep
> Thoughts of roses, through beguiling sleep
> And the bewildering day. I'll give to him
> Who gathers me more sweetness than he'd dream
> Without me—more than any lily could;
> I that am flowerless, being southernwood

While the theme of the poem, that beauty comes from nature's variety, is not especially original, Hopper renews the thought through a striking use of caesura and detailed visual and olfactory images.

On 5 March 1901 Hopper married the critic Wilfred Hugh Chesson; they had four children, one of whom evidently died in infancy or early childhood. Her next collection, *Aquamarines* (1902), listed the author's name as "Nora Chesson" and was dedicated to her husband. Like those in *Songs of the Morning,* the poems in the volume had been previously published in some twenty periodicals. Little of the poetry deals with Irish mythology; much of it explores more diffuse and generic topics such as life, death, love, nature's course, and time's passing. The conventional imagery and language of these poems—"men's blood" on the feet of the 1800s in "The Old Century" and the "frozen wasp, the starving butterfly" of winter in "Mater Dolorosa: A Winter Song," for example—render them less than memorable.

The volume received little attention, though *The Athenaeum* (19 July 1902) carried a brief notice that offered bland accolades for Hopper's "lively fancy playing sympathetically with the gracious and less solemn aspects of nature." The reviewer also thought that Hopper wrote "charmingly of fairyland" in *Muirgeis,* the play that concludes the book. The play became the libretto of *The Sea Swan,* an opera performed at the Theatre Royal in Dublin on 7 December 1903. Boyd, however, thinks that *Muirgeis* does not redeem Hopper's "desperate attempts at capturing the Irish spirit" in *Aquamarines.*

Hopper ended her writing career with a novel, *The Bell and the Arrow: An English Love Story* (1905). She died of heart failure in April 1906. A notice in the 22 May *Times* (London) listed a dozen people who had joined a committee to raise funds for Hopper's three children because their father was in "delicate health." Wilfred Hugh Chesson edited his wife's five-volume *Selected Poems,* which appeared in 1906. On 31 August 1906 *The Times Literary Supplement* (*TLS*) review of *Selected Poems* called Hopper "a brave woman who made what profit she could out of her talent for the sake of her family" and chided readers "inclined to sneer at a newspaper poet as one who must court publicity too much and write for the applause and profit of the day." Hopper's novel *Father Felix's Chronicles,* edited by Chesson, was published in 1907; it may have been written as early as 1895.

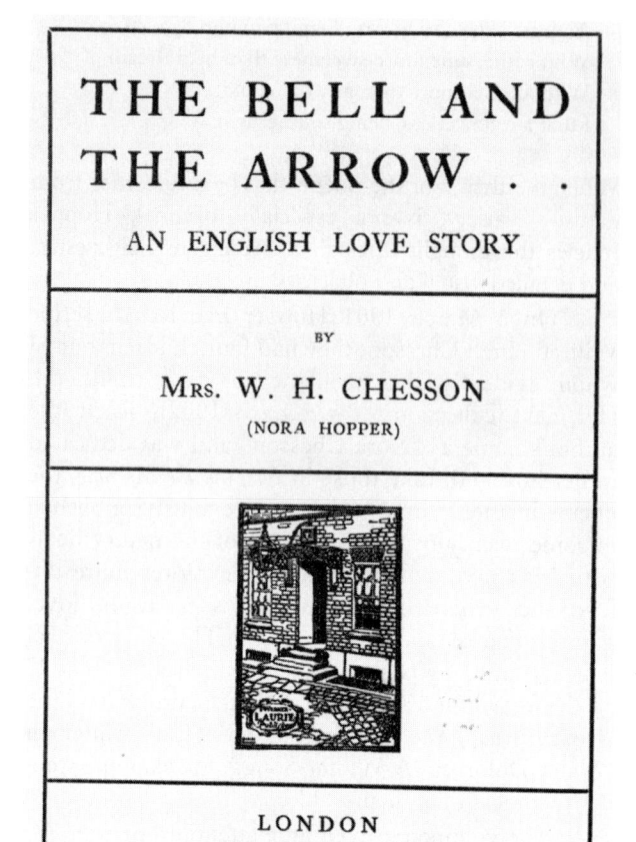

Title page for Hopper's final work, a novel published under her married name (courtesy of The Lilly Library, Indiana University)

Yeats's ultimate opinion of Hopper's later poetry was expressed in a letter to Tynan in late 1906 or early 1907: "our Irish fairyland came to spoil her work." The early poetry, however, continued to receive sporadic attention in Irish verse anthologies through the middle of the twentieth century. John Cooke included six of Hopper's poems in *The Dublin Book of Irish Verse 1728–1909* (1909), among them "The Dark Man," which Yeats had admired in *A Treasury of Irish Poetry in the English Tongue*. The 1958 *Oxford Book of Irish Verse* anthologized her "'Tis I Go Fiddling, Fiddling," but the 1986 edition, *The New Oxford Book of Irish Verse*, does not include any of Hopper's poetry.

Roger McHugh and Maurice Harmon call Hopper "that shameless borrower" from Yeats; they group her with other Irish Literary Revival poets, such as Moira O'Neill and Dora Sigerson Shorter, who "wrote with occasional felicity and with a real sense of song; but their connection with the literary movement or their use of Irish themes or of Irish-English dialect does not seem enough to sustain their reputation as poets of real quality." The *Dictionary of Irish Literature* (1996) assesses Hopper's poetry as "quietly charming and not unpleasantly vapid." Schirmer notes that while Yeats's support did "much to advance Hopper in Dublin literary circles," on the whole "she suffered from her close association with Yeats," since her reputation is rarely considered apart from his criticism of her work. Hopper's early poetry does not withstand comparison with that of Celtic Twilight poets such as Tynan, A.E. (George Russell), nor, above all, her mentor, Yeats. Nor does her later poetry compare well with that of women contemporaries such as "Michael Field" (Katherine Harris Bradley and Edith Emma Cooper) or Charlotte Mew.

Still, it seems unfair to criticize Hopper's work simply because Yeats might have praised it with too much enthusiasm. Yeats had an agenda: to propel the Irish Literary Movement forward. He therefore exploited Hopper's attraction to Gaelic material and did not await confirmation of what he saw as her potential. Furthermore, Hopper lacked the advantage of attentive editing of her collections. Her quickly produced and little-revised work may have been acceptable in periodicals, but the publishers of her books should have forced her to rewrite some of her poems before bringing them out in volume form. Finally, the demands of motherhood and her apparent need to support her family financially, followed by her early death, eliminated the opportunity for the poetic development believed possible for Hopper by contemporary reviewers of *Songs of the Morning*. A judicious selection of her Celtic poetry that eliminated the repetitive images and folktale characters and of her nature poetry that focused on the flowers and other plants she observed so carefully would better reflect her lyric capabilities. Any study of the Irish Renaissance would be incomplete without a reading of Hopper's revitalization of Gaelic legends and folktales in *Ballads in Prose*. While Hopper will always be a minor poet, a balanced view of her accomplishments would recognize the enthusiasm with which she explored the mythology of the Celtic Twilight.

References:

Virginia Blain, Patricia Clements, and Isobel Grundy, "Hopper, Nora (later Chesson)," in their *The Feminist Companion to Literature in English: Women Writers from the Middle Ages to the Present* (New Haven: Yale University Press, 1990), p. 537;

Ernest Boyd, *Ireland's Literary Renaissance* (New York: Knopf, 1922), pp. 194–199;

"Chesson, Nora Hopper," in *Dictionary of Irish Literature*, 2 volumes, edited by Robert Hogan and others, (Westport, Conn.: Greenwood Press, 1996), I: 242;

C. L. Innes, "'A Voice in Directing the Affairs of Ireland,'" in *Irish Writing: Exile and Subversion*, edited by Paul Hyland and Neil Sammells (New York: St. Martin's Press, 1991), pp. 146–152;

Fiona Macleod, "A Group of Celtic Writers," *Fortnightly Review*, new series 385 (January 1899): 34–53;

Phillip L. Marcus, *Yeats and the Beginning of the Irish Renaissance* (Ithaca, N.Y.: Cornell University Press, 1970), pp. 147–157; 267–268;

Roger McHugh and Maurice Harmon, *Short History of Anglo-Irish Literature from its Origins to the Present Day* (Dublin: Wolfhound, 1982; Totowa, N.J.: Barnes & Noble, 1982), pp. 134–135;

Katherine Lyon Mix, *A Study in Yellow: The Yellow Book and Its Contributors* (Lawrence: University of Kansas Press, 1960), pp. 214–215;

"Mrs. Chesson's Poetry," *Times* (London), 31 August 1906, p. 295;

"Nora Hopper," *Bookman*, 8 (September 1895): 163;

D. J. O'Donoghue, *The Poets of Ireland: A Biographical and Bibliographical Dictionary of Irish Writers in English Verse* (Dublin: Hodges Figgis, 1912), p. 203;

Gregory A. Schirmer, *Out of What Began: A History of Irish Poetry in English* (Ithaca, N.Y.: Cornell University Press, 1998), pp. 199–201;

W. B. Yeats, *The Collected Letters of W. B. Yeats*, 3 volumes, edited by John Kelly (Oxford: Clarendon Press, 1986), I: 24, 425–427, 435–436, 440–445; II: 331–332, 335–336;

Yeats, Introduction to selections from Hopper, in *A Treasury of Irish Poetry in the English Tongue*, edited by Stopford A. Brooke and T. W. Rolleston (New York: Macmillan / London: Smith, Elder, 1900), pp. 471–473;

Yeats, "Irish National Literature: Contemporary Irish Poets," *Bookman*, 8 (September 1895): 167–170;

Yeats, "Irish National Literature: Contemporary Prose Writers," *Bookman*, 8 (August 1895): 138–140;

Yeats, "Irish National Literature: A List of the Best Irish Books," *Bookman*, 9 (October 1895): 21–22;

Yeats, *The Letters of W. B. Yeats*, edited by Allan Wade (London: Hart-Davis, 1954), pp. 482–483;

Yeats, "The Poems and Stories of Miss Nora Hopper," *Daily Express* (Dublin), 24 September 1898; republished in *Uncollected Prose by W. B. Yeats*, volume 2: *Reviews, Articles and Other Miscellaneous Prose: 1897–1939*, edited by John P. Frayne and Colton Johnson (New York: Columbia University Press, 1976), pp. 124–128.

Mary Catherine Hume-Rothery

(14 December 1824 – 14 February 1885)

Kathleen McCormack
Florida International University

BOOKS: *A Brief Sketch of the Life, Character, and Religious Opinions of the Late Charles Augustus Tulk* (Boston: Clapp, 1850);

The Bridesmaid, Count Stephen and Other Poems (London: Chapman, 1853);

Normiton, a Dramatic Poem, in Two Parts. With Other Miscellaneous Pieces (London: Parker, 1857);

The Wedding Guests: or, the Happiness of Life, 2 volumes (London: Parker, 1857);

Twelve Obscure Texts of Scripture Illustrated according to the Spiritual Sense (London: Mainwaring, 1861);

Sappho; a Poem (London: Pitman, 1862);

The Golden Rule: and Other Stories for Children (London: Pitman, 1863);

Anti-Mourning (London, 1865);

The Prayer and humble Petition to . . . Queen Victoria, of a Loyal Englishwoman, against a System of Legalized Prostitution (Manchester & London, 1870);

A Letter Addressed to the Right Hon. W. E. Gladstone, and the Other Members of Her Majesty's Government and of Both Houses of Parliament Touching the Contagious Diseases' Acts of 1866 and 1869, Etc. (Manchester: Heywood / London: Simkin, 1870);

Women and Doctors: or, Medical Despotism in England (Manchester: Heywood / London: Grattan, 1871);

The Divine Unity, Trinity, and At-one-ment: A Monograph, by Hume-Rothery and William Hume-Rothery (London: Heywood, 1878);

Swedish Small-pox Statistics' Fraud; The Real Truth of the Matter (Cheltenham, 1882).

Edition: *A Brief Sketch of the Life, Character, and Religious Opinions of Charles Augustus Tulk,* with "Dedication and Historical Outline of the Life of MCH," by Charles Pooley (London: Speirs, 1890).

During the summer of 1853, when Bessie Rayner Parkes was experimenting with writing poetry herself, she recommended Mary Catherine Hume's first volume of poems to a friend who was at the time editing *The Westminster Review.* Marian Evans, later known as George Eliot, had, however, already sampled the passages that appeared in a review in *The Morning Advertiser.* Her reply to Parkes shows complete sincerity if little tact: "Heaven preserve me from reading Miss Hume's poems! . . . I was quite cowed by their first extract and had not courage to proceed." Neither the kind gesture of Parkes nor the reviewer's praise enticed Eliot into noticing *The Bridesmaid, Count Stephen and Other Poems* (1853) in *The Westminster Review.*

Like many events in the life of Mary Catherine Hume, the interest of both Parkes and *The Morning Advertiser* in her first poetry resulted largely from her identity as the daughter of Joseph Hume, the perennial battling Radical member of Parliament. Having just returned from a holiday in Surrey with Evans and other *Westminster Review* connections, Parkes was at the time moving in more-literary circles than Hume, but they both were daughters of M.P.s, close in age, who lived in London and had poetic ambitions. *The Advertiser,* an organ of liberalism, shared many causes with Joseph Hume, and the review of *The Bridesmaid, Count Stephen and Other Poems* leads off by quoting his daughter's prefatory sonnet dedicating the volume to the paternal M.P.

Mary Catherine Hume was born on 14 December 1824 to Joseph and Maria Hume, née Burnley. Although Joseph Hume maintained a seat in Norfolk and made visits to Scotland, his youngest daughter and the rest of the family spent most of their time in their London home on Bryanston Square. Hume positions several of her personae at a window looking out on a London square, and in a poem about a holiday in the Highlands the voice describes herself explicitly as "the city's child." In *Normiton* (1857) her autobiographical character favors living in London because

I love the stirring pulse of life which beats
So bravely through each throbbing artery
Of a great city's organism. There
Life never seems to weary or stagnate,
But works on, ever on, as man must do
Whose life's work lies before him.

Growing up amid urban stimulations, the children of Joseph and Maria Hume learned to value idealism, hard work, and their father's efforts at reform.

Hume's translations reveal training in several languages, especially German, and her poetic allusions demonstrate the scope of her reading, including literature, theology, scripture, and philosophy. During her late teens Hume's education took a unique turn when she began spending time with the large family of Charles Augustus Tulk, another wealthy reforming M.P. A follower of the Swedish philosopher and theologian Emanuel Swedenborg and a widower, Tulk invited his friend's daughter for long visits at his home at Totteridge Park, north of London, almost in Hertfordshire. Hume reports listening to her host sing "the glorious airs of Handel with an expression and a feeling surpassed by few." They read aloud the works not only of Swedenborg but also of William Shakespeare, and the young disciple found Tulk "the most amiable and interesting of companions" with a "great fund of playful humour." Tulk's daughter, Sophia Augusta, became her best friend.

The pious tastes Hume shared with the Tulks, however, seldom made attractive small talk in general society. In Hume's 1857 novel *The Wedding Guests: or, the Happiness of Life*, her character Horace Carysfort labels Florence Forrester's religious preoccupations "trivial." He further demonstrates his inadequacy by dismissing women's attempts to discuss politics. More personally, in a later prose publication, *Twelve Obscure Texts of Scripture Illustrated according to the Spiritual Sense* (1861), a footnote in Hume's own voice describes an occasion on which her discussion of the numerous names applied to God throughout the ages elicited from a companion the comment: "Dear me . . . you do make so much of all these trifles." Even in a London social circle made up of the families of Radical M.P.s, the seriousness of Hume's conversation set her apart from other young people.

When Tulk died in 1849, the loss prompted Hume to begin a memoir of her mentor that, in 1850, became her first publication. Appearing only in the United States, the profile included with its biographical material some dense but clear sections on Tulk's philosophy. Whether writing blank-verse poetry or polemical journalism, Hume always drew on a flowing style that helps render daunting topics readable.

After completing the Tulk memoir in her mid twenties, the young biographer and theologian turned to poetry. Her first volume, *The Bridesmaid, Count Stephen and Other Poems*, treated respectfully by *The Morning Advertiser* but snubbed by George Eliot, contains the two longer poems named in its title, as well as nearly fifty shorter lyrics and narratives that suggest her hard work, linguistic abilities, and continuing devotion to Swedenborgian mysticism. The title poem, in rhymed eight-syllable couplets, affirms the rightness of God's plans through a romantic plot concerning the patient faith of the lonely bridesmaid whose long solitude ends with the return of her lover and their marriage. The title character of "Count Stephen," a mysterious Byronic nobleman, lives aloof in an Austrian mountain setting where wolves roam the wild woods. For three years the protagonist Ivan attempts to puzzle out the Count's history and then, in a dramatic scene in which hungry wolves threaten the characters on the banks of a torrent, discovers that he has found his father. Many of the remaining shorter poems, lyrics and narratives with such titles as "Sunset and Sunrise," "The Only Son of His Mother and She Was a Widow," "Parting," and "Do We Grieve for Him," concern the consolations of solitude and offer spiritual tactics for accepting death. Even in "The Bridal Wreath" the stoic dying daughter calmly welcomes her groom, who turns out to be death himself. The poems depend a good deal on metaphors of sowing and reaping, which Hume favored all her life. They allude to her favorite poets, William Wordsworth and Henry Wadsworth Longfellow, both of whose verses she chose as mottoes for chapters in her novel.

The year after the appearance of her first volume of poetry, Hume went to Norfolk to spend the winter. Her father had become ill in Scotland during the autumn of 1854, and he had made the journey to Burnley Hall, where he prepared for death by gathering his family members about him. During the winter her father lay dying, Hume wrote more poetry, most importantly the two-hundred-line blank-verse drama *Normiton* (1857), as well as dozens of lyrics that appeared two years later in the same volume with the longer poem.

Burnley Hall lies between the Norfolk Broads and the coastline, near the small village of Somerton-on-Sea. On its eastern side the woods of the park yield to cultivated fields, then to a pale brown dune where pools of heather gather in the hollows. Closer to the sea, patches of moss and lichen create a spongy footing threaded by sandy paths that reach to the cliffs. Comfortable but not imposing, the red brick hall itself is of modern construction, although on the edge of the property the woods all but conceal a remnant of a vine-covered Gothic chapel from a more-ancient period. Blending with the green foliage and gray branches of the surrounding trees, this romantic detail, together with the seaside cliffs, contributes to the scenery in *Normiton*.

Hume opens her verse drama with a description of its main setting, a terrace that affords "a magnificent view over the gardens, park, and country beyond, bounded by the sea." In the first scenes, Normiton Cas-

> A BRIEF SKETCH
>
> OF THE
>
> LIFE, CHARACTER, AND RELIGIOUS OPINIONS,
>
> OF THE LATE
>
> CHARLES AUGUSTUS TULK.
>
> ADDRESSED TO
>
> MEMBERS OF THE NEW CHURCH.
>
> BOSTON:
> OTIS CLAPP, 23, SCHOOL STREET.
> 1850.

Title page for Mary Catherine Hume-Rothery's first book, a biography of a wealthy member of Parliament and follower of the Swedish philosopher and theologian Emanuel Swedenborg

tle "is a picturesque turreted building, partly overgrown with ivy." Margaret lives there with her mother and her brother Albert, "the lord of Normiton," who are preparing to welcome Margaret's friend Maud on a visit from London. Prompted by an interval on the cliffs where he has been contemplating infinity, the philosophically inclined Albert reveals his desire for a wife, one who shares his history of mental struggle and who will love him for himself. A few weeks later Albert proposes to Maud, but she points out that her faith in the transcendence of love over death prevents her marrying a nonbeliever because they would be separated in the afterlife. Dejected, Albert walks to the sea cliffs, leaving his room unattended. A fire starts; Normiton burns to the ground; and Albert is blinded.

The second part of the poem opens after several years have tempered Albert's arrogance and restored his sight. He has formed an engagement with his brother-in-law's sister, Olive, and replaced Normiton Castle with a new building. Maud, too, has learned from suffering; indeed, Albert's mother finds her ill in London and brings her to Normiton to recover. When Olive's brother also arrives, he turns out to be the lover Maud has cared for even at the time of Albert's proposal.

Hume's characters, like the author herself, often converse with great earnestness on serious topics. The dialogue of Lord Albert and the morally faultless young-lady characters gets some relief in the lines of Henry Clifford, Margaret's husband, who flippantly regrets that his plan to get Albert and Maud together has failed:

> What so provokes me is, that Maud should spoil
> The matchless match whereon my heart was set,
> 'Twixt two such thorough-bred philosophers
> As would have lifelong furnished me with mirth
> At their expense

In a prefatory note to the poem Hume defends herself against potential accusations that she derives Albert's blindness from the plot of *Aurora Leigh* (1857) by pointing out that she finished *Normiton* before Elizabeth Barrett Browning's poem appeared.

Joseph Hume survived into 1855. Then in February he made his farewells and entered a three-day period during which the bright glare of sunshine on the snow intensified the silence around the deathbed in Burnley Hall. Settings of snow-covered, sunny sand dunes occur in several of the meditations Hume composed during her father's last illness. *Normiton* itself concludes with Maud's certainty that troubles "cannot shut the sunshine from our souls. . . . While we but walk together, hand and heart, / In love which death may grieve, but cannot part!" In "A Shadow in the Pine-Wood" winter and spring join to promise well for a dying man:

> I stand 'neath the pine-wood's sheltering screen
> While the sun-glints come and go
> Upon heather brown and pastures green,
> And broad fields of glittering snow.

Yet, another poem, "Spring Tides," evokes the promise of seasonal renewal in a seaside setting: "Sweep, Spring, over my soul as waves sweep on cliffs." The combinations of sun, snow, and cliffs create fresh, vivid settings for the contemplative themes of the bulk of the lyrics in *Normiton*.

At the time Hume attended her father's decline, she had already published at least a dozen deathbed poems, all of which describe the selfishness of grief that mourns souls gone to a better place. Writing *Normiton*, she sustained these themes even as the death of her adored father tested them. Later in her life she remained active in antimourning causes.

Both of Hume's collections of poetry vary her devotional poems with topical material. In *Normiton* she occasionally inserts a reflection on an event such as the defeat at Sevastopol or the construction of the Crystal Palace. Like Emily Brontë and Christina Rossetti, she lives her religious life partly in her poetry, and like many Victorian women poets, she voices her admiration for Browning, a "sister poet" to whom she dedicates "The Poet's Task and Reward." She writes now and then about travel to Scotland or Switzerland, and in "The Insanity of Emanuel Swedenborg" and "Joseph Hume: A Portrait" she defends her heroes against scornful attacks. But despite variety in settings, occasions, and forms, most of the poems, with preternatural docility, praise patience and faith in a world where all, even death, is for the best.

Twelve days after Joseph Hume's death his family buried him in Kensal Green Cemetery in London. The oldest son, Joseph Burnley, read the memorial poem he had composed in rhymed couplets. Although it concludes with a rhyme of "Hume" and "tomb," it again establishes the family pride. Accustomed to the public's willingness to laugh at Joseph Hume's maladroit political battles, his son laughed back by asserting his father's indifference: "Full often, ere the echo of the jeer had ceased to creep / About St. Stephen's, unto him 'twas nought–he was asleep!"

After her father's death Mary Catherine Hume resumed her literary pursuits. By then in her thirties, she had written many poems and a popular novel, *The Wedding Guests,* featuring weddings and brides without having yet met a suitable partner herself. She believed in a Swedenborgian/Platonic ideal of marriage as a reunion of souls severed at birth and restored to their full unity only through earthly marriage. Because she required a groom who shared these beliefs, they narrowed her choices considerably.

Hume's last long poem, *Sappho* (1862), embodies her tenaciously held ideas about marriage in a form that evokes comparisons with other nineteenth-century poems that place their personae face to face, often in Italy, with a work of art. Hume had first been to Florence in 1849 when her friendship with the Tulks was strongest. With both their fathers dead, she visited her old friend Sophia Augusta Tulk Cottrell, who had married and settled in Italy. The two women visited the artistic venues, both studios and museums, popular with members of the Inglese communities in Fiesole and Bellosguardo which, with Robert Browning and Elizabeth Barrett Browning in residence at Casa Guidi, were at the peak of their social and literary activity.

In *Sappho* two women friends stand before a sculpture representing the ancient poet just before her suicide. Giovanni Dupré places his subject sitting with head bowed and legs crossed, her robe draped about her waist and her lyre at her feet. Hume's Sappho poem differs from those of Felicia Hemans, L.E.L. (Letitia Elizabeth Landon), and Caroline Norton, all of whom make Sappho the speaker and emphasize the pathos of her preparations for a death that will bring peace and indifference after her disappointments in love. In Hume's poem, however, two women, the persona and her friend, view Dupré's statue and soon modify their initial admiration by taking exception to his depiction of the woman as a slave to love rather than as calmly independent. In the tradition of the nineteenth-century woman's literary imagination outlined by Sandra Gilbert and Susan Gubar, the persona challenges John Milton's ideas about marital relations, stating that women are

> Created *not* as his conceit would plan
> The man for God, the woman for the man,
> But male and female both, as equal men
> To know and love and serve their Lord first, then
> Each other as true neighbors.

According to this voice, both women and men should "walk erect and free" so that the woman can "cease to be / His toy or victim." She then describes a dependent wife as a "petted queen" whose husband has a "helpless load to bear / Along life's dusty ways by care." After its initial appearance in *The Intellectual Repository,* an organ of the Swedenborgian New Church, the poem was published the following year in its own volume.

Back from Italy and still living in the family home in Bryanston Square, Hume continued to devote much time to her writing. In addition to *Sappho,* she soon completed two prose works: the formidable *Twelve Obscure Texts of Scripture Illustrated according to the Spiritual Sense* in 1861 and the extremely didactic *The Golden Rule: and Other Stories for Children* two years later. *Twelve Obscure Texts of Scripture* demonstrates the Swedenborgian "science of correspondences" which locates the secondary meanings of words, meanings that diverge entirely from the meaning of "the *letter,* which is the natural finite body of the Word." Heavily footnoted, the introduction argues that material things have standard spiritual significance, for example, the "cup which conveys wine to the mouth corresponds to the external science, or knowledge, which conveys truth to his mind." The children's stories in *The Golden Rule,* replete with lame girls and blind boys, typify Victorian approaches to the moral education of children.

The year after the publication of these widely differing prose works Hume married the Reverend William Rothery. The couple set up housekeeping at 3 Richmond Terrace, Middleton, Manchester. There the new wife underwent the traumatic experience that changed her writing, her thinking, and her way of life. She describes the event in *Women and Doctors: or, Medical Despotism in England* (1871). Becoming pregnant soon after her marriage, she engaged a physician to attend the birth:

> The gentleman who attended me, as above referred to, was about as unobjectionable as I can conceive a male attendant to be; grave, quiet, self-contained, incapable of an offensive–I mean avoidable–offensive–word or act; I was neither young nor specially sensitive, and habituated from the dawn of thought on such a subject to regard a male doctor as indispensable on such occasions. Yet I know that hours elapsed before I recovered from the physical revulsion or arrest of vital action, caused by his first visit to my room. Will anyone tell me that such a suspension of vital action for hours, at such a crisis, can be unattended with danger? Can any one affirm that this very suspension might not be the cause, the instrumental cause, I mean, of the loss of my baby-boy, whom according to the doctor's own verdict, "Ten minutes sooner would have saved!"

Following her infant son's death, she continued for the rest of her life to write and speak against the professionalization of medicine that left women in the care of male physicians. The year afterward she gave birth to a boy who survived and whom they named for his political grandfather: Joseph Hume. Before the boy's birth, the prospective father demonstrated his belief in marital equality by adding his wife's name to his. From 1866 onward they both called themselves Hume-Rothery.

For seven years as a clergyman's wife and a mature, first-time mother, Mary Hume-Rothery wrote only a treatise called *Wheat and Tares; or Christianity versus Orthodoxy,* attributed to both husband and wife. Then, in 1870, two letters, one to Queen Victoria, the other to William Gladstone, took up the same cause. In both letters, Hume-Rothery protests the Contagious Diseases' Act (1864) that outraged so many Victorian feminists. The following year she published *Women and Doctors.*

In these three essays, the earnest, somewhat naive tone of the poetic persona gives way to unsentimental analyses of the conditions of women's lives, including disease, seduction, adultery, and unexpected pregnancies. In the letter to Gladstone, for example, she demands laws that would make "seduction" by either men or women illegal, but would also provide that any subsequent impregnation should constitute a legal marriage. She wants women jurors, women's suffrage, and equal divorce laws concerning adultery. These practical attitudes contrast strongly with the pious stoicism of the characters and voices in her earlier poetic and prose narratives. They also anticipate the style and content of the work of her last ten years: the editing of *The National Anti-Compulsory-Vaccination Reporter.*

In 1873, preparing to take up the cause that defined the rest of their lives, the Hume-Rotherys moved to Cheltenham, where, three years later, William Hume-Rothery went through the legal process of giving up holy orders. From 1874 until Mary Hume-Rothery's death the couple devoted all their time and energy to their effort to gain the repeal of compulsory vaccination. They traveled around England to meetings of their group. They led demonstrations in support of people jailed for refusing to vaccinate their children. They wrote letters to M.P.s in which Mary Hume-Rothery called on her knowledge of her father's milieu to give edge to her attacks on legislative laziness. While her husband assumed the presidency of the organization, Mary Hume-Rothery served as secretary. Between them, they wrote most of the material that appeared in the *Reporter* in their Cheltenham home.

Hume-Rothery's work for the *Reporter* takes a spirited, irreverent, combative tone. One of her old *Bridesmaid* poems, "Dark Days or, Signs of the Times," published over twenty years before, anticipates her activism by betraying an irreverence toward Parliament she will revive in the *Reporter*. The young poet finds little hope for ameliorative legislation because

> In the lofty seats designed
> For wisdom and love to fill
> Sit selfish fools, in terror blind
> Grasping the red sword still.

Her girlhood familiarity with lawmakers permits, if not contempt, at least irreverence in the work of her maturity in which she challenges the decisions of Parliament with a zest unlikely in a woman writer less familiar from an early age with the human frailty of her father's colleagues.

A rare poem from this period, "The Doctors Song" (which, unusually, she contributed to the *Reporter*), repeats the irreverence of "Signs of the Times." In tones of heavy sarcasm, Hume-Rothery, (herself the daughter, as she stresses in *Women and Doctors,* of a member of "the allopathic brotherhood"), places its arrogant assertions in the voice of a group of physicians responding to challenges by organizations such as the Anti-Vaccination League: "We, whose word is law, will set forth plainly / What man may dare to doubt, or may *not* doubt profanely." The collective physicians' voice goes on:

> Doubt that the lark can soar;
> Doubt that man walks on legs;
> Doubt "two and two make four":
> Doubt that a beggar begs;
> Doubt that a Whig loves place, a Tory power or pensions,
> But doubt *not* doctors wise beyond your comprehension.

Hume-Rothery admired Dr. Elizabeth Blackwell, believed that women midwives should replace male accoucheurs, and blamed professionalized male health care for the potential "child murder" of vaccination.

Hume-Rothery cheerfully admits that her attitude toward vaccination proceeds primarily from "intuition." In *Women and Doctors* she observes, "It was not till, somewhat more than four years since, I stood by to see my own baby vaccinated, that the preposterous and unnatural character of the operation flashed upon me by intuition. 'Lacerate the skin of a healthy babe to infuse into its veins matter taken from a suppurating sore!' . . . Maternal instincts are great teachers, and in my case, probably, did more to enlighten my darkness than much reading of many books, unprefaced by their suggestions, might have done." Although she wrote in such personal genres as devotional nonfiction and poetry, Hume-Rothery rarely, if ever, mentions her mother, Maria Burnley. She apparently gained her respect for maternal instinct only after she had borne her own healthy child.

In Cheltenham the Hume-Rotherys had chosen a community where at least forty physicians and surgeons attended the many visitors who came to the spa for its health benefits. As a result of the vaccination legislation, the town at the time had its own vaccination officer as well as a public vaccinator, both of whom lived not far from the Hume-Rotherys. The family had settled in Tivoli, south of the center, an area of comfortable homes set on a gentle slope. After eight years at Merton Lodge, they spent an interval on Lansdown Crescent, then returned to Tivoli Road. They called their new home The Pines, a name justified by a few tall trees in front and a thicker group to the rear arranged in a circle around a pond. In this tranquil setting the former poet and the former clergyman continued their battles against medical despotism.

In 1883, after years of activism and a corresponding number of volumes of the *Reporter,* the woman who vociferously objected to physicians fell terminally ill with breast cancer. She and her husband quickly gave up their activities in the League, and the *Reporter* ceased publication. In December 1884 the cancer spread to her brain. She died on 14 February 1885.

Although not from a specifically feminist stance, the campaign against smallpox vaccination that occupied the last decade of Hume-Rothery's life had its origins in the beliefs she acquired years before at Totteridge Park. During her twenties, Swedenborgian views regarding the equality of souls regardless of their earthly gender prompted her to write poetry, theology, and a popular though decidedly quirky novel. After her marriage she modified this feminism in response to the death of her newborn son and to various acts of Victorian legislation until it culminated in her opposition to a particular form of "medical despotism," compulsory vaccination. Her activism in this cause called for a kind of writing that permitted little poetic creativity.

Following her death a second edition of the Tulk biography appeared, which, by including a short biography "of MCH," revived perceptions of Hume-Rothery as a pious young protégée of Joseph Hume's best friend. In this way, its Swedenborgian author, Charles Pooley, returns Hume-Rothery to the New Church fold that welcomed the poetry she produced during the 1850s: the poetry that expressed her stoic confidence concerning the intimacy between the material and spirit worlds. Hence, while the political Hume-Rothery may interest feminists and historians, and her misguided antivaccination efforts serve as a footnote to medical history, her poetry stimulates interest primarily for its Swedenborgianism, which addresses concerns she shared with other Victorians from spirit rappers to converts to Catholicism. Reading *The Bridesmaid, Normiton,* and *Sappho,* New Church members such as Pooley could find great beauty and consolation in the poetic expressions of their beliefs, despite the ordinariness of the plots, characters, and metaphors through which Hume-Rothery's verses advance these beliefs.

Biography:

Charles Pooley, "Short Introductory Chapter or Historical Outline of the Author's Life," in *A Brief Sketch of the Life, Character, and Religious Opinions of Charles Augustus Tulk* by Mary Catherine Hume (London: Spiers, 1890).

References:

George Eliot, *The George Eliot Letters,* 9 volumes, edited by Gordon S. Haight (New Haven: Yale University Press, 1954–1979);

Sandra Gilbert and Susan Gubar, *The Madwoman in the Attic: The Woman Writer and the Nineteenth-Century Literary Imagination* (New Haven: Yale University Press, 1979);

Joseph Burnley Hume, *Joseph Hume: A Memorial* (London: Parker, 1855).

Violet Jacob

(1 September 1863 – 9 September 1946)

Florence Boos
University of Iowa

BOOKS: *The Bailie Macphee*, by Jacob, as Violet Kennedy-Erskine, and Walter Douglas Campbell (London: Heinemann, 1891);

The Sheep-Stealers (London: Heinemann, 1902; New York: Putnam, 1902);

The Infant Moralist, by Jacob and Lady Helena M. Carnegie (London: Grant, 1903);

The Interloper (London: Heinemann, 1904; New York: Doubleday, Page, 1904);

The Golden Heart and Other Fairy Stories (London: Heinemann, 1904);

Verses (London: Heinemann, 1905);

Irresolute Catherine (London: Murray, 1908);

The History of Aythan Waring (London: Heinemann, 1908; New York: Dutton, 1908);

Stories Told by the Miller (London: Murray, 1909);

The Fortune-Hunters, and Other Stories (London: Murray, 1910);

Flemington (London: Murray, 1911);

Songs of Angus (London: Murray, 1915);

More Songs of Angus and Others (London: Published at the offices of "Country Life" / New York: Scribners, 1918);

Bonnie Joann and Other Poems (London: Murray, 1921);

Tales of My Own Country (London: Murray, 1922);

Two New Poems: Rohallion, The Little Dragon (Edinburgh: Porpoise Press, 1924);

The Northern Lights and Other Poems (London: Murray, 1927);

The Good Child's Year Book (London: Foulis, 1927);

The Lairds of Dun (London: Murray, 1931);

The Scottish Poems of Violet Jacob (Edinburgh & London: Oliver & Boyd, 1944);

The Lum Hat and Other Stories: Last Tales of Violet Jacob, edited by Ronald Garden (Aberdeen: Aberdeen University Press, 1982);

Diaries and Letters from India 1895–1900, edited by Carol Anderson (Edinburgh: Canongate, 1990).

Editions: *Flemington*, edited by Carol Anderson, Association for Scottish Literary Studies annual volumes, no. 24 (Aberdeen: Association for Scottish Literary Studies, 1994);

Flemington; and, Tales from Angus, edited by Anderson, Canongate Classics, no. 83 (Edinburgh: Canongate, 1998).

OTHER: Hans Christian Andersen, *The True Story of My Life*, translated by Mary Howitt, preface by Jacob (London: Routledge, 1926).

Violet Jacob

An important poet and novelist in the Scottish modernist vernacular revival, Violet Jacob was respected by her literary contemporaries for creating some of the finest Scottish literature of her time. In the tradition of James Hogg, Sir Walter Scott, and Robert Louis Stevenson, her short fiction and novels portray passionate conflicts in carefully realized local settings, and her haunting, poetic evocations of northeastern Scottish dialect and characters witness her love of the landscape and culture of the region. New editions of two of her novels appeared in the 1990s, but more editions, a biography, and other correctives to the neglect she suffered in the last half of the twentieth century are long overdue.

Born in Angus on 1 September 1863, Violet Augusta Mary Fredericka Kennedy-Erskine was the second of four children of William Henry Kennedy-Erskine, the eighteenth Laird of Dun, and Catherine Kennedy-Erskine, née Jones, of Carmarthenshire, Wales. Her paternal ancestors, whose history she later detailed in *The Lairds of Dun* (1931), included Sir John Erskine, friend of John Knox and moderator of the General Assembly in 1564, and David Erskine, an eighteenth-century anti-Unionist judge. William Kennedy-Erskine died when Violet was seven.

Educated at home, Violet Kennedy-Erskine spent most of her early life in rural Montrose, and the speech, habits, and modes of thought of the region's people informed much of her work. Her first book, the comic narrative poem *The Bailie McPhee* (1891), was co-authored with Walter Douglas Campbell and included her illustrations.

At thirty-one Kennedy-Erskine married the somewhat younger Arthur Otway Jacob, a lieutenant of the Twentieth Hussars from Maryborough (now Portlaoighise), Ireland. While accompanying him to various brief postings in Britain she gave birth to their only child, Arthur Henry Jacob, in 1895. Shortly thereafter the family moved to Mhow in the Malwa region of central India, where they spent the next four years. Violet Jacob studied Hindi, explored the countryside, volunteered at the military hospital, and observed religious festivals and ceremonies to the extent that the constraints of official British society in India allowed. Jacob never questioned the imperialist premises of the Raj, but she did record in her diaries several instances of British bad behavior. She took an artist's pleasure in the landscape, natural phenomena, and details of Indian life.

Most of Arthur Jacob's subsequent postings were in England, with the exception of a brief assignment in South Africa and two years in Egypt. The family lived for a time in Herefordshire, the setting of several of Violet Jacob's works of fiction, and spent another period in Shropshire, where she became acquainted with the poets A. E. Housman and Hugh MacDiarmid.

While in India, Jacob had begun writing *The Sheep-Stealers* (1902), a novel about two early nineteenth-century Welsh border outlaws and their lovers. It was followed by a children's book, *The Infant Moralist* (1903), co-authored with Lady Helena M. Carnegie and illustrated with Jacob's drawings; *The Interloper* (1904), a novel about love and inheritance set in early-nineteenth-century Scotland dedicated somewhat enigmatically "To An Undying Memory"; and another children's book, *The Golden Heart and Other Fairy Stories* (1904).

Jacob dedicated *Verses* (1905), her first independently written volume of poetry, "To the Ideal Critic" and inscribed the first poem "To H. M. C.," her former co-author Carnegie: "in each other's eyes we seek / And find the thing that each would say." The poems meditate on infinity, love, and life after death, and their language and metric schemes are reminiscent of Alfred Tennyson, Dante Gabriel Rossetti, William Morris, Oscar Wilde, and, to a lesser degree, of Housman, Sappho, A. C. Swinburne, "Michael Field" (Katherine Harris Bradley and Edith Emma Cooper), and W. H. Henley. "The Ballad of Hakon," for example, echoes Morris's Scandinavian poems, and the story told in "The Mill-House" is reminiscent of his "Golden Wings" in *The Defence of Guenevere, and Other Poems* (1858). Other poems—"The Valley of the Kings," "In Lower Egypt," and the concluding nine "Poems of India"—reflect encounters with cultures not her own. "Night in the Plains," the second of the "Poems of India," draws on Jacob's experiences at the hospital in Mhow. More strikingly, "The Distant Temple," the last poem in the sequence, concludes the volume with a wistful expression of homesickness for India, not Scotland or Wales:

> Sound of the temple drum,
> Like distant beating of the march of fate,
> Through the long years your voice is never dumb,
> Calling, at sundown, from the temple gate
> To me, who cannot come.

Jacob followed *Verses* with *Irresolute Catherine* (1908), a novella set in Wales about a woman torn between a prosperous but overbearing cattle merchant and a "man of the soil"; *The History of Aythan Waring* (1908), a novel, also set in the Welsh countryside, about a man falsely accused of murder through the machinations of his stepmother; the children's book *Stories Told by the Miller* (1909); *The Fortune-Hunters, and Other Stories* (1910); and her most complex and best-received novel, *Flemington* (1911), a tale of the Jaco-

Jacob's drawing of an ancient temple on the Malwa plateau in India (from Jacob's Diaries and Letters from India 1895–1900, *edited by Carol Anderson, 1990)*

bite Rebellion in eighteenth-century Scotland. The novelist John Buchan called *Flemington* "the best Scots romance since [Stevenson's] *The Master of Ballantrae* [1889]."

Jacob's attachment to a style of writing that the critic J. H. Millar in 1895 had derisively labeled the "Great Kailyard Movement"–a sentimental and idealized view of Scottish life (*kailyard* means "cabbage patch" in Scots)–appears in the elegiac cadences and varied stanzaic and metrical forms of *Songs of Angus* (1915), her second volume of verse. In his introduction to the book Buchan praises Jacob's use of dialect to express distance, resignation, and irretrievable loss:

> It is the rarest thing, this use of Scots as a living tongue, and perhaps only the exile can achieve it. . . . above all it is a living speech, with the accent of the natural voice, and not a skilful mosaic of robust words. . . . The dialect is Angus, with unfamiliar notes to my Border ear, and in every song there is the sound of the east wind and the rain. . . . The metres are cunningly chosen, and are most artful when they are simplest; and in every case they provide the exact musical counterpart to the thought. Mrs. Jacob . . . has many moods. . . . But in them all are the same clarity and sincerity of vision and clean beauty of phrase.

Jacob celebrates the landscape and environs of Angus in "The Howe o' the Mearns," calls forth the emotions of young men in love in "Tam i' the Kirk," mocks hypocrisy and pretension in "The Beadle o' Drumlee," and offers crafted tributes to youthful idealism and intensity in "The Tod," "The Gowk," and "The Whustlin' Lad." She memorializes complex experiences of loss and estrangement in "The Lang Road" and "The Water Hen"; grieves for dead lovers in "Logie Kirk," "The Jacobie Lass," and "Maggie"; records a mother's vision of her dead child in "The Lost Licht"; and portrays the final reflections of a dying old man in "The Gean-Trees." "Craigo Woods," one of her best elegies, provides an exemplary miniature of her ability to alternate homely concrete details ("braw reid puddock-stules") with elusive suggestions of spiritual presences. An old shepherd recalls

> Craigo Woods, i' the licht o' September sleepin'
>   And the saft mist o' the morn,
> When the hairst climbs to yer feet, an' the sound o' reapin'
>   Comes up frae the stookit corn,
> And the braw reid puddock-stules are like jewels blinkin'
>   And the bramble happs ye baith,
> O what do I see, i' the lang nicht, lyin' an' thinkin'
>   As I see yer wraith–yer wraith?

Cognate shifts of register and lilting onomatopoetic rhythms appear in the monologue "Tam i' the Kirk":

> O Jean, my Jean, when the bell ca's the congregation
> Owre valley an' hill wi' the ding frae its iron mou',
> When a'body's thocts is set on his ain salvation,
>   Mine's set on you. . . .
> He canna sing for the sang that his ain he'rt raises,
> He canna see for the mist that's 'afore his een,
> And a voice drouns the hale o' the psalms an' the paraphrases,
>   Cryin' "Jean, Jean, Jean."

Jacob dedicated *More Songs of Angus and Others* (1918), her third volume of poetry, to the memory of her son, who had been killed in the Battle of the Somme in World War I. Some of her best memorials abandon attempts to find higher purposes in the carnage for simpler and more authentic pleas, as in "Glory":

> But gin ye see my face or gin ye hear me,
>   I daurna' ask, I maunna' seek to ken,
> Though I should dee, wi' sic a glory near me,
>   By nicht or day, come ben, my bairn, come ben!

Similar sentiments are expressed in "Jock, to the First Army," "The Twa Weelums," "The Field by the Lirk o' The Hill," "Montrose," "The Road to Marykirk," and "The Kirk beside the Sands."

Other poems, less overshadowed by the war, include another old man's farewell in "The Last o' the Tinkler" and flytings such as "A Change O' Deils," in which a young woman heeds her grandmother's advice to abandon the "deil" (devil) she knows for another she does not: "a change o' deils is lichtsome, lass!"

In her fourth poetry volume, *Bonnie Joann and Other Poems* (1921), Jacob blurs the boundaries between the living and the dead in her elegies "The Daft Bird" and "Halloween," alternating these recollections with courtship poems such as "Adam" and "The Wise-Like Chap," broadly satiric verses in the tradition of Robert Burns such as "Pride" and "Bailie Bruce," and sympathetic representations of tramps, tinkers, alcoholics, and pregnant servants. In "The Tramp to the Tattie-Dulie" a vagrant envies a scarecrow's free wardrobe and sedentary existence:

> "Yer heid's a neep, yer wame's a sack,
> Yer ill-faured face gars bairnies shak',
> But yet the likes o' you can mak'
>   A livin' frae it,
> Sma' use to me! It isna fair
> For though there's mony wad declare
> That I'm no far ahint ye there,
>   I canna dae it!"

The tramp does not forget to snatch the scarecrow's hat when he departs.

In "The Tinker's Baloo" a tinker's wife sings to her son a wry balladic tribute to his father's theft of a speckled rooster:

> Sleep, an' then, come Sawbath,
>   A feather o' gray ye'll get
> Wi' specklies on it to set i' yer bonnet
>   An' gar ye look brawer yet.
> Sae hide yer heid, my mannie,
>   Haud yer whist, my doo,
> For we'll hae to shift or the sun's i' the lift
>   An' I'm singin' baloo, baloo.

"H. K. G.," who reviewed *Bonnie Joann and Other Poems* for *The Canadian Forum* (September 1922), nullified the praise that Jacob "displays that characteristic Scottish gift to sing of familiar and homely things with freshness and personal insight" by adding the arch pronouncement that "the only hope for the future is for poetry in the English tongue."

The eleven stories in Jacob's next book, *Tales of My Own Country* (1922), evoke timeless qualities in strongly marked characters drawn from every level of the rural Scottish class hierarchy, blending formal elegance and "modernist" detachment with deep respect for the pathos and ironic humor of country life. In *The Northern Lights and Other Poems* (1927) she again presents satires and tributes, such as "Tae Some Lasses" and "John MacFarlane," but the best poems in the volume return to the liminal realms where the dead haunt and comfort the living. In the title poem, for example, a boy sees visions of dead spirits in the "northern lights" that are "past the sicht o' muckle men / And nane but bairns can see." In "The Jaud" an old lady visits the neglected grave of a "fallen woman," where she remembers her rival's beauty with a mixture of admiration and envy:

> "... But lave me tae bide my lane
>   At the fit o' the freendless queyn;
> For oh! wi' envy I'm like tae dee
>   O' the warld she had that was no for me
>   And the kingdom that ne'er was mine!"

In "The Cross-Roads" an outcast haunts a church that had denied him a proper burial and begs a hapless worshiper to

> "... rise and gang tae the kirkyaird heid
>   And plead yer best
> Whaur they wadna bury the ootcast deid
>   For a sad saul spent wi' the weird it's dree'd, and I'll maybe rest!"

In "The Licht Nichts," one of Jacob's most personal lyrics, an unnamed lost child—"ma best, ma bonniest and ma dearest"—had once sung happily "I' the licht nichts o' the year":

VERSES

BY

VIOLET JACOB

(MRS. ARTHUR JACOB)

AUTHOR OF 'THE SHEEP-STEALERS,' 'THE INTERLOPER'

LONDON

WILLIAM HEINEMANN

1905

Title page for Jacob's first poetry collection (courtesy of The Lilly Library, Indiana University)

> Ye were sae glad; ye were aye sae like the laverock
>   Wha's he'rt is i' the lift; ....
> What thocht had you o' the ill-faur'd dairk o' winter
>   But the ingle-neuks o' hame?
> Love lit yer way an' played aboot yer feet,
>   Year in, year oot, the same.
> ....
> But whiles—and whiles—i' the can'lelicht an' the starlicht
>   I'll wauken it tae hear
> The liltin' voice that's singin' doon the braes
>   I' the licht nichts o' the year.

Four years later Jacob dedicated her carefully researched family history, *The Lairds of Dun*, "To the Memory of my Brother, the Nineteenth Laird" (Augustus Kennedy-Erskine died at sea at age forty-two). The book traces the Kennedy-Erskine line from its rise to regional prominence in the fourteenth century to the generation of her grandparents. Among her ancestors were many Royalist and Presbyterian soldiers and several usurpers and murderers. The family's status and fortune declined gradually after the title passed to Alice Erskine, Jacob's great-grandaunt. (Pasted into the front endpapers of Northwestern University's copy of *The Lairds of Dun* is a snapshot of an old woman in a wide-brimmed hat sitting with a dog in front of a large house; it is signed "Violet Jacob and Sammy.") Some of the characters in Jacob's fiction are obviously modeled on her ancestors.

Jacob's husband died in 1936. That year Edinburgh University awarded her an honorary LL.D. She spent the last decade of her life at Marywell House in Kirriemuir, Angus, near her ancestral home. In 1944 the firm of Oliver and Boyd published *The Scottish Poems of Violet Jacob;* wartime paper rationing prevented a companion volume of her short stories. Jacob dedicated the volume "To the Comrade Beyond" (presumably her husband) and added seventeen new poems, including eight elegies for the war dead. In "The Baltic," one of the new poems, a boy tells his dismayed mother that he has seen and heard his father, who is away at sea:

> *"And what did he ca' yon foreign land?"*
> *"He tell'tna its name tae me,*
> *But I doot it's no by the Baltic shore,*
> *For he said there was nae mair sea."*

Jacob's selection and arrangement of her poems highlight the concision and intensity of her work. The volume also brings into sharp relief a few motifs that recur again and again in her poetry: the joys and agonies of courtship, the lost "foreign country" of the past and its environs, and the hopeless yearning to hear a healing word from the dead. Her best poems display these motifs in masterpieces of apparent simplicity and subtle indirection.

A portfolio of Jacob's manuscripts, diaries, drawings, and short stories discovered in the 1970s indicated that she was at work on two novellas, "Banny Firelocks" and "The Lum Hat," when she died on 9 September 1946. The novellas were included in *The Lum Hat and Other Stories: Last Tales of Violet Jacob*, edited by Ronald Garden, in 1982. Her letters, diaries, and watercolor drawings of Indian flora and architecture were edited by Carol Anderson and published in 1990 as *Diaries and Letters from India 1895–1900*. A thorough study of Jacob's life, work, and influence on other aspects of Scottish modernism has yet to appear.

Independent-minded and multiply gifted, Violet Jacob was a "modernist" despite her love of ancestral traditions, for her moral vision of the world was tragic and ironic at its core. Her artfully stylized and psychologically heightened poems and her championship of vernacular forms influenced as well as complemented the work of contemporaries such as Jessie Anderson, Mary Symon, Rachel Annand Taylor, Marion Angus, Bessie MacArthur, and Helen Cruikshank and contributed to the Scottish renaissance associated with MacDiarmid and Lewis Grassic Gibbon. The range and extent of her work make a compelling case for "recuperation" of the woman McDiarmid described as "the most considerable of contemporary vernacular poets." In his introduction to *Songs of Angus* Buchan characterized her as a poet who possessed

> a rare distinction. She writes Scots because what she has to say could not be written otherwise and retain its peculiar quality. . . . Some of us who love the old speech have in our heads or in our note-books an anthology of modern Scots verse. It is a small collection if we would keep it select. To my own edition of this anthology I would add unhesitatingly Mrs. Jacob's "Tam i' the Kirk," and "The Gowk."

Jacob's intense sense of place and critical devotion to Scots culture enabled her to represent that culture with telling authenticity. Her cosmopolitan experiences and her empathetic ear for the special intonations of the regions she visited made her one of the more subtle and distinctive artists of her time.

References:

Florence Boos, "'Oor Location': Victorian Women Poets and the Transition from Rural to Urban Scottish Culture," in *Victorian Urban Settings*, edited by Debra N. Mancoff and D. J. Trela (New York: Garland, 1996), pp. 133–156;

Marion Lochhead, "Neglected or Forgotten: Four Women Novelists," *Library Review*, 25, no. 7 (1976): 251–253;

Hugh McDiarmid, as C. M. Grieve, "Violet Jacob," in his *Contemporary Scottish Studies, First Series* (London: Parsons, 1926).

Papers:

Violet Jacob's manuscripts are in the National Library of Scotland in Edinburgh. Many of her drawings are in the library of the Royal Botanical Gardens, also in Edinburgh.

Eliza Keary

(1827 – 29 August 1918)

Naomi Hetherington
University of Southampton

BOOKS: *Heroes of Asgard and the Giants of Jotunheim; or, The Week and Its Story,* by Keary and Annie Keary, as the author of "Mia and Charlie" and her sister (London: Bogue, 1857); republished as *Christmas Week and Its Stories; or, The Heroes of Asgard* (London: Charles & Henry Clarke, 1860); revised as *The Heroes of Asgard: Tales from Scandinavian Mythology* (London: Macmillan, 1871; New York: Doubleday & McClure, 1898);

Early Egyptian History for the Young; with Descriptions of the Tombs and Monuments, by Keary and Annie Keary, as the author of "Sidney Grey," etc., and her sister (Cambridge: Macmillan, 1861);

Little Wanderlin and Other Fairy Tales, by Keary and Annie Keary (London & Cambridge: Macmillan, 1865);

Little Seal-Skin and Other Poems (London: Bell, 1874);

The Magic Valley; or, Patient Antoine (London: Macmillan, 1877);

Memoir of Annie Keary, by Her Sister (London: Macmillan, 1882);

Cat and Dog Life: Coloured and Other Pictures for Children with Stories by Eliza Keary (London: Marcus Ward, 1882?);

At Home Again (London & New York: Marcus Ward, 1886);

Pets and Playmates (London: Marcus Ward, 1887).

Editions: *The Heroes of Asgard: Tales from Scandinavian Mythology,* edited by M. R. Earle (London: Macmillan, 1905);

Stories of Asgard, edited by John Drinkwater, arranged by Herbert Hayens, John Drinkwater Series for Schools, Standard III (London & Glasgow: Collins' Clear-Type Press, 1924).

OTHER: *Letters of Annie Keary,* edited by Keary (London & Oxford: Christian Knowledge Society, 1883);

A Casket of Pearls: Selections from Holy Scripture, for Morning and Evening, edited by Keary (London: Warne, 1884);

Rays of Light: A Daily Text Book for Divine Guidance, edited by Keary (London: Warne, 1884);

The River of God: A Daily Text Book, compiled by Keary (London: Houlston, 1884);

The Francis Letters by Sir Philip Francis and Other Members of the Family, with a Note on the Junius Controversy by C. F. Keary, 2 volumes, edited by Keary and Beata Francis, introduction by Keary (New York: Dutton / London: Hutchinson, 1901);

"Wild Flowers," "King Fashion," "The Story of Hyacinth and Apollo: The Child, the Sun and the Wind," "Pretty Mouse," "The Moon," "To The Cat at Grandmama's: A Letter," and "Jack Frost," in *Enchanted Tulips and Other Verses for Children,* by Keary, Annie Keary, and Maud Keary (London: Macmillan, 1914), pp. 3–4, 7–8, 15–18, 26–27, 43–44, 49–51, 105–108.

SELECTED PERIODICAL PUBLICATIONS– UNCOLLECTED: "Madeleine's Story," *Blackwood's Magazine,* 149 (January 1891): 103–122; (February 1891): 217–230; (March 1891): 328–344; republished in *Living Age,* 188 (14 February 1891): 406–419; (7 March 1891): 590–599; 189 (18 April 1891): 165–176.

Eliza Keary's sole volume of verse for adults, *Little Seal-Skin and Other Poems,* was published in 1874, when Keary was already middle-aged. Its finest pieces are remarkable for their feminist agenda and their experimentation with verse form; nothing else in Keary's oeuvre is comparable. Before 1874 Keary published exclusively for children; afterward she turned primarily to children's verse and devotional manuals. Her sister, Annie Keary, was a well-known children's writer of the day, and the two collaborated on several projects. Their nephew Charles F. Keary was a creative writer and an early contributor to the *Dictionary of National Biography,* as well as an authority on Scandinavian mythology and prehistory and on English and international medals and

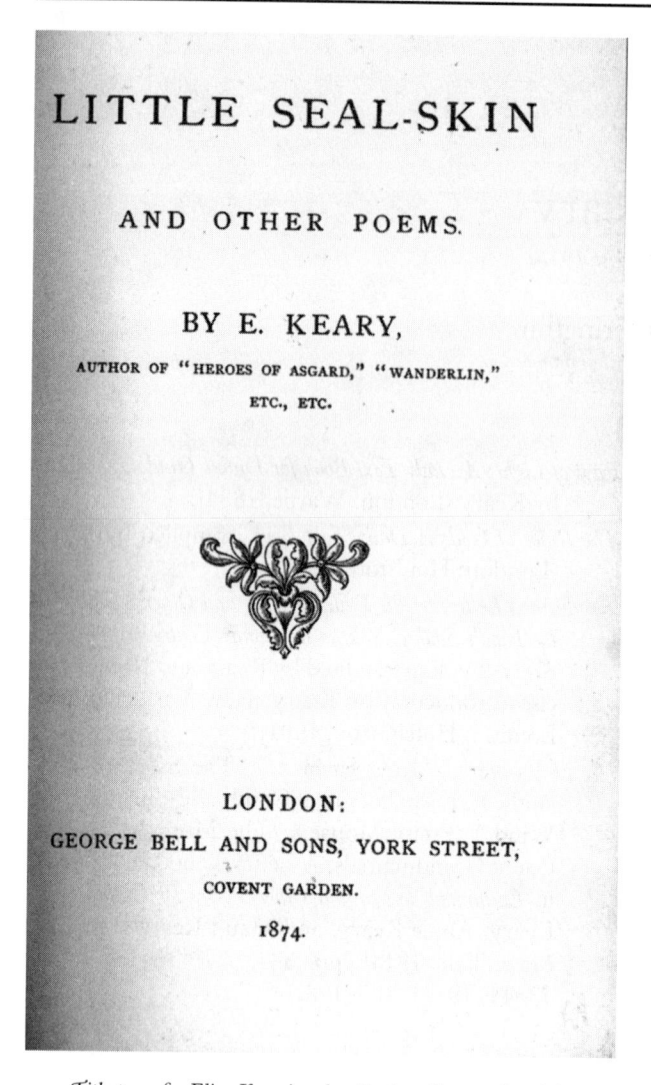

Title page for Eliza Keary's only collection of poetry for adults

coinage. Between 1887 and 1893 he catalogued the English coin collection of the British Museum.

Eliza Harriet Keary was born in Sculcoates, part of the town of Kingston-upon-Hull, the last of seven children of William and Lucy Keary (née Plumer). Her exact date of birth is unknown, but she was baptized on 22 April 1827 by her father, an Anglican minister. In her *Memoir of Annie Keary, by Her Sister* (1882) she remembers Annie as her special playmate, who entertained her with imaginative tales and, later, with works by classical authors that they discovered in their father's library.

When Keary was in her late teens the family moved to Bristol. In 1854 she and Annie moved with their parents to the Kensington section of London. The two sisters continued to live together after their parents died.

Keary's initial publications were co-authored with Annie, who was by then a recognized children's author.

Heroes of Asgard and the Giants of Jotunheim; or, The Week and Its Story (1857) is their most-lasting contribution to the field of children's literature. The first successful interpretation of Norse myths for young readers, it was republished many times and was adapted twice for use in schools in the early twentieth century. The book continues to fascinate readers for its attempt to enliven a pagan worldview while finding a Christian meaning behind the pagan legends. It is structured around the days of Christmas week, with the final story telling of a cosmic battle of heroes and giants in which the chief Norse god, Odin, is told in a vision of the coming of the Christ: "when the worn-out faith of nations shall totter like old men, turn eastward, and behold the light that lighteth every man."

Annie's visit to Egypt in the autumn of 1858 prompted the sisters' next project, *Early Egyptian History for the Young; with Descriptions of the Tombs and Monuments* (1861). The book takes the form of twenty-nine letters from Annie to her nephews, informing them of the history and customs of ancient Egypt while relating a journey up the Nile and visits to ancient sites.

The sisters' *Little Wanderlin and Other Fairy Tales* (1865) is a collection of fables and stories typical of the period in combining fantasy with moral lessons. Most of the tales were originally told to the authors' nephews and nieces, and they include characters Annie had created as a child for her brothers and sisters: *Memoir of Annie Keary, by Her Sister* recalls an early mention of a character in "Little Wanderlin," the fearsome Mrs. Calkill, who rewards good children and punishes naughty ones in her enchanted castle.

In 1869 Keary published two poems for adults in *Macmillan's Magazine:* "Little Seal-Skin" and "The Goose-girl: A Tale of the Year 2009"; they were republished the same year in the Catholic periodicals *Living Age* and *Every Saturday,* respectively. The collection of which "Little Seal-Skin" became the title poem appeared five years later. Some of the pieces are recorded as having been first written for a literary society, the Pen and Pencil Club, Aubrey House. Keary dedicated the volume to her sisters, Lucy and Annie, and Annie's encouragement and contacts appear to have been instrumental in the acceptance of the volume for publication: Reading University's archives include correspondence concerning *Little Seal-Skin and Other Poems,* among which is a letter of introduction from Annie to the publisher, George Bell, on her sister's behalf.

The volume is a curious mixture of fairy tales and conventional piety with more-searching interrogations of gender identity. The title piece places Keary alongside Christina Rossetti in using fantasy as a vehicle for commenting on the position of middle-class women in mid-Victorian society: "Little Seal-Skin" questions the confinement of women to the domestic sphere through

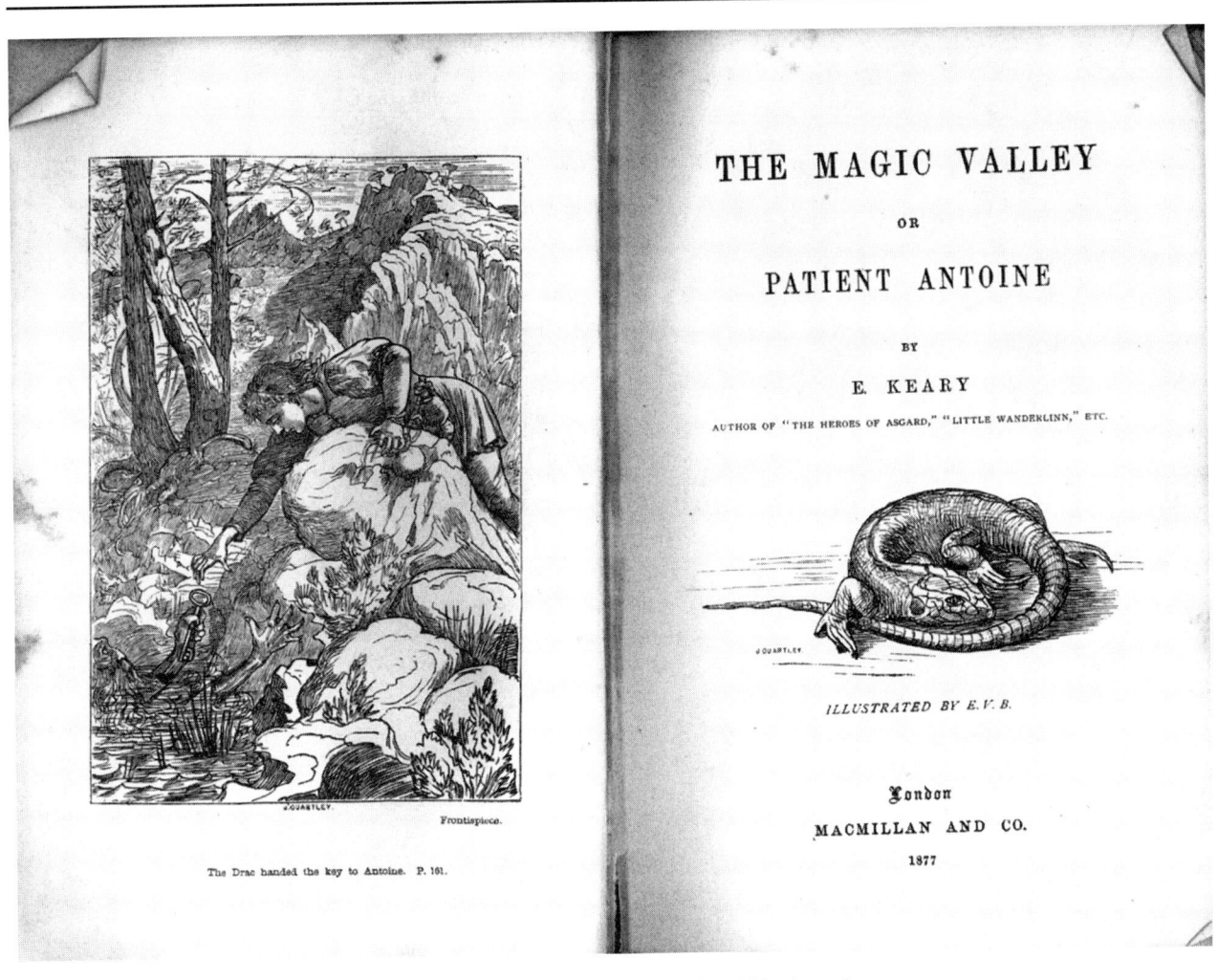

Frontispiece and title page for Keary's first children's novel

an Icelandic legend of seamen and seawomen who shed their sealskins and come ashore once a year. A fisherman finds and hides one seawoman's sealskin, forcing her to live with him as his wife and bear his children. After seven years her misery is so intense that he relents; she deserts her earthly family, slipping back into her sealskin and disappearing into the sea.

"Doctor Emily" provides an alternative role model for women with a female protagonist whose right to practice medicine in a rural community is never questioned. At the time, the issue of admitting women to medical practice was being debated in Parliament. The London School of Medicine for Women was founded by Sophia Jex-Blake the year the book was published; but the opposition Jex-Blake encountered renders "Doctor Emily" a utopian vision. Three months after the book appeared, the senate of the University of London rejected a proposal to open its medical degree to women.

Doctor Emily is presented as a sympathetic and loving figure who gains her authority to practice from aspects of Christ's ministry conventionally associated with femininity: his compassion for the sick and for children. The acute suffering Emily witnesses in her work does not threaten her faith until a colleague discloses his belief in scientific determinism. The poem is a dramatic monologue in which Emily struggles with and finally resolves her doubts through her experience of God's presence. She comes to perceive human labor and, implicitly, her practice, as analogous to Christ's suffering on the cross: "Measureless labour, 'tensest sacrifice, / Price of the very life–." Thus, popular notions of the female temperament as emotional and spiritual and the male as intellectual and rational are used to suggest that medicine is a profession better suited to women, since it demands an innate faith in divine goodness in the face of human misery.

In "Christine and Mary: A Correspondence," the longest poem in the collection, the breakup of a relationship between two women provides the arena for a debate on religious adherence versus free thought. Mary has

Keary's sister, Annie, who co-authored Keary's first three books. Annie Keary died in 1879; Eliza Keary published a memoir of her in 1882 and edited a collection of her letters in 1883.

joined a convent after a sudden conversion experience in which she heard her crucifix sigh, "Behold me." She pledges herself to Christ in a rhetoric of religious and sexual pain and domination:

> let all die, every love in me else,
> If that I have but Thee,
> Bruised, broken beneath Thine agony.

Mary defines humanity as "just / Need, inextinguishable need" of Christ, to be satisfied through the adoration of his crucified form. Christine pleads with Mary not only to return to her love but also to understand holy vows as a form of self-gratification. She describes the Christian deity as "man-magnified," a "projected self seeming to save from misery" but represented by a creed that condemns all but a select few to eternal torture. She advocates, instead, a scientific materialism in which individual death and salvation lose all meaning, and human perfection is achieved in a collective self-consciousness that is made possible by the interconnection of all matter:

> Humanity built up in the obscure
> One, awake to-day perfect, pure,
> A self all-comprehending. I–what am I?
> A link, a cause, a sequence, a transition,
> See how I fall off from myself,–I,–
> A mystery? only the common sound
> Of a note struck that must sound
> At the striking.

Christine's attack on Christianity may owe its urgency to the "Great Convent Case" of 1869, *Saurin* v. *Starr,* in which a former Sister of Mercy from Kingston-upon-Hull, Keary's hometown, sued her convent for £5,000 in damages, claiming a malicious and sustained program of persecution orchestrated by the mother superior and the assistant superior. Sensationalistic coverage of the case in the national press presented the punishments imposed on Susan Saurin for alleged offenses as sadistic and contrasted "unwholesome" monastic life with Protestant family values.

The sexual nature of the previous relationship between Christine and Mary is explicit. They have "been together bodily," and, reminiscing on their love in comparison to her present spiritual communion with Christ, Mary gives Christine an intense description of a female orgasm:

> I remember how life, young, sweet,
> Infinitely tender, from the bud
> Blown complete into flowerhood, yet incomplete
> Thrills to want's pulse, grown up to pain;
> How the heart-beats wax and wane
> Until one meets and fills
> The eternity–for a life say,
> An instant, with only a handful of clay,
> And ecstasy of union that all pain stills,
> And that want satisfies.

Inspiration for Mary's conversion may have come from Keary's travels abroad with Annie in 1871. In the autumn the sisters had called on a former schoolfriend, Elizabeth, who was then mother superior of a Carmelite convent in Paris. Keary's memoir of her sister records two days of intimate conversation and an account of Elizabeth's conversion in "her own words" as a passage "from darkness into light, from spiritual death to spiritual life." Keary acknowledges the reality of Elizabeth's faith but rejects the Catholic doctrines that accompany it: "Whilst she spoke thus simply of what she was experiencing one felt the power of the Spirit in her; when she began to expound the dogmas of her Church, the radiance faded and plain confusion came in." Elsewhere the memoir evokes admiration for Annie's Evangelical piety, which surmounts doubt and depression, suggesting an Evangelical conviction on Keary's part that is at odds with both Christine's and Mary's voices in the poem.

Little Seal-Skin and Other Poems received little attention on its release, and the brief reviews that did appear appraised the author specifically in terms of her gender. In the 25 July 1874 issue of *The Athenaeum* a reviewer compared Keary unfavorably to her more popular contemporary, Jean Ingelow, criticizing Keary's irregular use of rhyme and meter. *The British Quarterly Review* (October 1874) admired the volume, ranking the author alongside Christina Rossetti but favoring the fairy tales and pious sentiments as more suitable for a female author than the more thought-provoking poems in the collection. Such responses may explain why Keary ceased to publish serious poetry for adults.

In 1877 Keary published her first novel for children, *The Magic Valley; or, Patient Antoine*. A full-length fairy tale in which good finally triumphs over evil, it tells the adventures of Antoine, son of a human father and a fairy mother, in a magical land inhabited by fairies and trolls and a white cat who manages the family's accounts.

After Annie's death in 1879 Keary kept house for her nephews, Henry and Charles F. Keary. She never married. In 1882 she published her memoir of her sister, which is the source for most of the available biographical material concerning Keary herself. A year later, at the suggestion of the editor of *The Spectator*, she compiled a collection of Annie's letters to girls who had gone into domestic service from the Home for Young Servants in Bessborough Gardens, an institution in which Annie had taken a great interest.

In 1884 Keary published three pocketbooks of biblical texts with color illustrations: *A Casket of Pearls: Selections from Holy Scripture, for Morning and Evening; Rays of Light: A Daily Text Book for Divine Guidance;* and *The River of God: A Daily Text Book*. These works place her as a female Evangelical writer in offering devotional aids or domestic worship centered on the divine word itself. For the first two she wrote prefaces offering commentaries on the central images of the pearl and the ray of light, respectively, as metaphors for humanity's relationship with God.

In 1886 and 1887 Keary published two lavishly illustrated volumes of children's verse, *At Home Again* and *Pets and Playmates*. *Pets and Playmates* stands out from most children's literature of the day in not attributing human characteristics to animals; instead, it presents them realistically and in idyllic relationships with children, so as to teach the young to care for them and treat them with respect. The book thus accords animals a dignity that is lacking in popular children's novels, such as Anna Sewell's *Black Beauty* (1877) with its talking horses, that tried to elicit sympathy for animals by anthropomorphizing them.

In 1891 Keary published her only short fiction for adults, "Madeleine's Story," in three installments in *Blackwood's Magazine;* it was republished the same year in identical installments in *Living Age*. A mystery story with Gothic and supernatural elements about a Welsh family harboring secrets of alcoholism, mental breakdown, and child abuse, it is written as a series of letters by the title character to her friend Joyce. The two women are about to move in together, and the emotional intimacy and sympathy of their relationship is contrasted to the hasty marriage of Madeleine's sister, Gladys, to a suitor with whom she has little in common.

Ten years later Keary completed *The Francis Letters by Sir Philip Francis and Other Members of the Family, with a Note on the Junius Controversy by C. F. Keary*. The two-volume work, about the great-grandfather of Keary's friend Beata Francis, had been begun by Francis and left unfinished on her death. The appendix, by Keary's nephew Charles, claims that Sir Philip Francis was Junius, the writer of letters during Francis's time in the foreign office that criticized government officials for their policies on trade.

Keary's last published works were seven poems for children in *Enchanted Tulips and Other Verses for Children* (1914), compiled by her grandniece Maud Keary. The volume also includes verses by Annie Keary, along with a greater number of Maud Keary's poems.

Eliza Keary died on 29 August 1918 at the home of her niece Margaret Keary in Torquay, Devon. As was the case with many late-Victorian women poets, her work appeared to die with her. It was revived only in 1996 in *Nineteenth-Century Women Poets: An Oxford Anthology,* edited by Isobel Armstrong, Joseph Bristow, and Cath Sharrock, in which a brief introduction to her life and work accompanies selections from *Little Seal-Skin and Other Poems*. As of 2001, Armstrong's 1999 essay, "Msrepresentation: Codes of Affect and Politics in Nineteenth-Century Women's Poetry," was the only modern critical piece to deal with Keary.

References:

Isobel Armstrong, "Msrepresentation: Codes of Affect and Politics in Nineteenth-Century Women's Poetry," in *Women's Poetry, Late Romantic to Late Victorian: Gender and Genre, 1830–1900,* edited by Armstrong and Virginia Blain (London: Macmillan, 1999), pp. 3–32;

Armstrong, Joseph Bristow, and Cath Sharrock, "Eliza Keary," in *Nineteenth-Century Women Poets: An Oxford Anthology,* edited by Armstrong, Bristow, and Sharrock (Oxford & New York: Clarendon Press, 1996), pp. 458–467; revised (Oxford & New York: Clarendon Press, 1998).

Papers:

Reading University's publishers' archives include a collection of correspondence between Eliza and Annie Keary and George Bell.

May Kendall
(1861 – 1943)

Marion Thain
University of Birmingham

BOOKS: *That Very Mab,* by Kendall and Andrew Lang (London: Longmans, Green, 1885);

Dreams to Sell (London: Longmans, Green, 1887);

From a Garret (London: Longmans, Green, 1887);

Such is Life (London: Longmans, Green, 1889; New York: Longmans, Green, 1892);

White Poppies: A Novel (London: Ward, Lock, Bowden, 1893);

Songs from Dreamland (London: Longmans, Green, 1894);

Turkish Bonds (London: Pearson, 1898);

How the Labourer Lives: A Study of the Rural Labour Problem, by Kendall and Benjamin Seebohm Rowntree (London: Thomas Nelson, 1913).

SELECTED PERIODICAL PUBLICATIONS—UNCOLLECTED: "Pessimism and Thomas Hardy's Poems," *London Quarterly Review,* 91 (April 1899): 223–234;

"A Plea for Asceticism," *London Quarterly Review,* 93 (January 1900): 124–130.

May Kendall is remembered as a poet because of her contribution to social commentary and late-nineteenth-century cultural debates, especially those surrounding issues of science and evolutionary theory. Little is known about Kendall's life. She was born Emma Goldworth Kendall in 1861 in Bridlington, Yorkshire, the daughter of Eliza Goldworth Level Kendall and James Kendall, a Wesleyan minister. She lived in the north of England, in Liverpool and Birmingham, finally settling for most of her life in York.

Kendall's first publication was *That Very Mab,* written with Andrew Lang in 1885. A prose story, the tale concerns the visit of Mab, queen of the fairies, to England. The story is a thinly veiled piece of social criticism, as the fairy, being a visitor, provides a mouthpiece for commenting on some of the absurdities of English society. Fairies had become a suitable topic at the time, for painting in particular and poetry in a smaller way, and Kendall became part of this broader cultural debate.

In Kendall's story, a scientist captures Mab to study her, and the relationship between the two becomes antagonistic. Recognizing her only as a strange butterfly, the scientist shows no heartfelt wonder at her appearance, only a hope that he will get a journal publication out of his encounter. The scientist's son, however, marvels at her, worshiping her as a mystical presence. At the end of the story, however, after he has been educated at Eton, the son sees Mab as his father saw her, just as a strange type of butterfly, not as the magical presence in which he once believed. The point of the story is partly that a scientific style of education destroys our natural capacity for wonder.

That Very Mab introduces themes that are significant in Kendall's later poetry. Sharing the authorship with Lang, one of the leading folklorists of the day, Kendall contrasts a world of fairies and folklore with that of Victorian Britain. Later scholars of the twentieth century would interpret the belief in fairies as a nostalgic reaction to industrialization, urbanization, and the rising faith in science and progress. In the work of Kendall, fairies signify a new domain of knowledge that plays a crucial role in the debate between science and religion. Mab and the fairies seem to represent the realm of the spiritual, which has no place in materialistic science, and which was unacceptable to so many people in a religious context, but for which people still felt the need.

While Kendall's poetry appeared in various magazines during the 1880s, including *Punch* and *Longman's Magazine,* her first volume of poetry, *Dreams to Sell,* appeared in 1887. This volume continues the debate between scientific naturalism and the supernatural. Like *That Very Mab,* the poem "Education's Martyr" is a satire on the figure of the scientific naturalist. Here the male protagonist fails to enjoy beauty and the spiritual effect of nature because he is too busy concentrating on the scientifically specific:

> Yes, all that has been or may be,
> States, beauties, battles, land, and sea,
> The matin songs of larks,
> With glacier, earthquake, avalanche,
> To him were each a separate "branch,"
> And stuff for scoring marks!

Kendall contrasts this epistemology with one based on intuition and appreciation of beauty:

> Ah! happier he who does not know
> The power that makes the Planets go,
> The slaves of Kepler's Laws;
> Who finds not glands in joy or grief,
> Nor, in the blossom and the leaf,
> Seeks for the secret Cause!

Kendall, however, does not reject all science. The language and concepts of evolution are particularly prominent in *Dreams to Sell*. Despite the many ways in which evolutionary theory was unsympathetic to women, women poets claimed evolutionary science as an empowering tool in their fight against Victorian gender ideology. Charles Darwin represented a challenge to the Victorian social order, including gender roles, especially the prevailing belief that women were seen as akin to "mother" nature, while men were associated with the more exalted spiritual realm. With its links between humanity and the animals, evolutionary nature challenged the idea that the genders had a different relationship with nature.

In several poems by Kendall, male narrators confront their own insignificance in the face of evolutionary theory, potentially a great leveler in the gender debate. Kendall's "Lay of the Trilobite," for example, claims that when providence and divine order are reduced to nature's law, no one can claim special status. The poem features an interaction between a character who seems to be a parody of a Romantic poet, and the trilobite. As the human figure wanders in the mountains seeking "Sufficient vague and mighty thought / To fill my mighty mind," he spies the trilobite and muses:

> How wonderful it seemed and right,
> The providential plan,
> That he should be a Trilobite,
> And I should be a Man!

The fossil answers the self-satisfied wanderer by telling him that the faiths upon which he bases his belief in his own superiority are simply "ghosts and dreams," and that he himself is descended from the humble arthropod. The trilobite then questions whether the wanderer is actually any better off than it is. It finds all human achievements to be questionable. After all, the trilobite may be stupid, but it is "free from woe" and much better behaved ("I didn't grumble, didn't steal, / I *never* took to rhyme"). The wanderer goes away much chastised, thinking:

> "I wish our brains were not so good,
> I wish our skulls were thicker,
> I wish that Evolution could
> Have stopped a little quicker;
> For oh, it was a happy plight,
> Of liberty and ease,
> To be a simple Trilobite
> In the Silurian seas!"

This poem clearly highlights the challenge made by evolution to teleology, but it also has implications for the respective status of the sexes. Kendall has destroyed the difference between the creatures, undermining the belief that women were creatures of nature, while men were creatures of spirit.

Title page for May Kendall's first volume of poetry (courtesy of The Lilly Library, Indiana University)

In "The Lower Life," another poem challenging teleology, Kendall's narrator asks whether, although humans have a developed intellect, "Can this atone / For fins or pinions of our own . . . ?" Evolution is not a process of simple amelioration:

> If we have freedom, we lose peace.
> If self-renunciation, cease
> To care for pleasure.

"Is wisdom, then, the only test, / Of lot superlatively blest?," she asks, only to answer: "There have been others." Our age will soon pass, the narrator predicts, and this will leave us questioning, "Are monads so much less than men?" The narrator's conclusion is that:

> This higher life is sold too dear–
> Would I could give a lower sphere.

According to the poem, humans inflate their own importance:

> We weep and waver,
> While Evolution, still the same,
> With knights or pawns pursues the game,
> And shows no favour.

In "Woman's Future" Kendall explicitly explores the reasons for women's sympathetic welcoming of these new ideas. Although witty, the poem does convey a serious message about the relationship between women and evolutionary theory and the possibilities of growth and change. Women no longer have to listen to complacent men who tell them:

> In vain is our ardour: in vain are our sighs:
> Our intellects, bound by a limit decisive,
> To the level of Homer's may never arise.

She also challenges the notion of a God-given order dictating the inferiority of women:

> The laws of the universe, these are our friends,
> Our talents shall rise in a mighty crescendo,
> We trust Evolution to make us amends!

Theories of evolution have freed women from the conviction that they cannot engage in anything outside the limited feminine sphere, and in this newfound freedom, they find the world open to them in a way it has never been before. The middle of Kendall's poem is a diatribe against the "Old Woman" spoken by the liberated and scientific "New Woman":

> You cherish the fleeting, the mere accidental,
> At cost of the True, the Intrinsic, the Free.
> Your feelings, compressed in Society's mangle,
> Are vapid and frivolous, pallid and mean.

Kendall's "New Woman" continues:

> Mere charms superficial, mere feminine graces,
> That fade or that flourish, no more you may prize;
> But the knowledge of Newton will beam from your faces,
> The soul of a Spencer will shine in your eyes.

The "Envoy," the concluding stanza, provides a strong assertion to end the poem:

> Though jealous exclusion may tremble to own us,
> Oh, wait for the time when our brains shall expand!
> When once we're enthroned, you shall never dethrone us–
> The poets, the sages, the seers of the land!

In this poem, and particularly in this final stanza, Kendall is parodying the prevailing fin-de-siècle fear that the future was female, a notion supported by the prevalence of distopian fiction about a world where women had the upper hand. However, many women at the time were producing utopian writings in which they speculated about a future world of sexual equality rather than creating revenge scenarios.

Another significant section of *Dreams to Sell* is "Art," in which Kendall looks at the relationships between art, artist, and audience. "In The Gallery," for example, criticizes the upper classes who appear ridiculous in their refusal to play the game of make-believe involved in the theater experience:

> Even rolling barrels make you blunder–
> These barrels you can *not* hear through!
> Too stupid! When you know 'tis thunder,
> Why should the barrels trouble you?

While the poor in the gallery boo, hiss, and cheer, and engage with the spectacle, those in the pit wrestle with opera glasses that seem to make them "wholly blind."

On a more personal note, the poem "Shakespeare" appears to be an explicit articulation of how Kendall feels she stands in relation to the literary canon and her literary forefathers. Here she voices the view of the minor poet, and rather than being intimidated by the tradition from which she is excluded, she feels liberated in being separated from it. She finds comfort in the status of William Shakespeare precisely because she knows she, unlike the "second-rate great poets," is not in competition with him. Knowing that she can never begin to approach this goal allows her the freedom to experiment:

> Because you are beyond us and above,
> Therefore we need no longer fret
> Our nature's shadowy limit to remove,
> And further in our fancy set
> The bound we baffle love with lingering to regret.

But since the difference is infinite,
Our souls in you may be at peace,
Nor ever weary for their lack of wit,
And from their failings have release.
Our good and evil clash, but you are more than these.

As is usual with these "minor poet" poems, this poem can easily seem like an admission of the poet's own failure; but it can also be read as acknowledging exclusion, finding this a positive attribute, and claiming a different, but not necessarily lesser, goal. Phrases such as "from their failings have release" capture this ambiguity. In fact, the peace found in this poem is the realization that the difference between the poets is "infinite." Kendall does not have to try to be part of the tradition of "great writers"; she can do her own work, which is not necessarily a thing of lesser value.

As a poet, albeit a minor one, Kendall was, at first, celebrated. H. C. Beeching wrote a relatively long review of *Dreams to Sell* in *The Academy* (12 November 1887), singling out the volume as one particularly "marked by literary gift." However, the "reasonable immortality" he prophesied, somewhat paradoxically, for Kendall's poetry did not come to pass. Both Beeching and the anonymous reviewer of the book in *The Athenaeum* (25 February 1888) found Kendall's greatest achievements in her humor and her poems about evolutionary science; her poetry "shows how the theory of evolution is 'taken' by a lady," wrote Beeching. The space devoted to discussing the book, and the praise given, appears to have been elicited at least partly by the assumption that Lang, who wrote a prefatory poem to the volume, was involved with the publication. *The Athenaeum* goes so far as to say that while Kendall's talent should receive independent recognition, "no doubt she owes a great deal, both directly and indirectly, to her versatile and accomplished *collaborateur*."

After this first volume of poetry Kendall published three novels. Her first two novels were "New Woman" fictions. *From a Garret* (1887) shows her interest in the city and its social types, themes also prevalent in her poetry, and *Such is Life* (1889) concerns the life and loves of several characters. The third and final novel, *White Poppies* (1893), is a fairly standard love story in which the hero falls in love with his friend's sister.

In 1894 Kendall's second volume of poetry, *Songs from Dreamland*, was published. The poem "Fairies and the Philologist" reveals again the contrast between science and the realm of fairy tale and myth so prominent in *Dreams to Sell*. The philologist's reaction to the elves and fairies that dance around his pillow at night is to classify them. As with the narrator of "Education's Martyr," science and learning have taken away his sense of wonder. The fairies feel that this objectification does nothing to reflect their real identities, and the implication is that the philologist has not really learned anything about the world through his scientific method. Generally, however, fairies and science do not make much of an appearance in this volume.

The poems in the section "Songs of the City" explore character types of the city and social issues, such as the fantasies of escape of city office workers in "The Phantom Train" or the memories of the suburbs of the passerby in "Arthur Street." "The Ballad of the Flag Painter," which also appears in this section, echoes Kendall's interest in the relationship between art, artist, and audience that she had expressed in *Dreams to Sell*. The poem is narrated by a street artist who paints pictures on the pavement flagstones. This narrator talks about his or her art (the narrator's gender is not disclosed) in relation to that of another much wealthier male artist who graduated from the Royal Academy and paints portraits of royalty. The poem is based on the difference between the position of these two artists, one of whom is in a much more privileged position than the other.

The dichotomy between the portrait painter and the street artist is one of status. His position in the academy and in the aristocracy shows he is firmly situated within the establishment, while the narrator is not. The street artist is literally outside, as well as being metaphorically shut out, excluded from exhibiting in the galleries where the portrait painter's work is held. While his work is permanent, the work of the street artist is transient:

No need of galleries for me,
   My works of art to hold!
Because the new ones, don't you see,
   I paint upon the old.
. . . .
Only–a shower will come some day,
   And spoil my pictures, when
I cannot see them washed away,
   Or paint them in again.

They'll run together, blue and pink,
   And sea and shore and sky,
There'll never be a soul to think
   Of keeping the things dry.

The flags, for me, will stay quite clean.
   But when I'm dead and gone,
His duchesses will smile serene
   Posterity upon.

And so he'll win–but I confess,
   I've very little doubt,
Some of his dukes and duchesses
   Had better be washed out!

Title page for Kendall's second collection of poems, which includes verse on fairies and on art (courtesy of The Lilly Library, Indiana University)

As with "Shakespeare," this poem could reveal Kendall's feelings as a minor writer, in relation to mainstream poetic tradition.

Other poems in *Songs from Dreamland* continue the debate about art in a humorous manner. For example, "A Bonus on Soap" takes as its premise the scenario in which a best-selling book is given away free with the purchase of a certain brand of soap. Physical and mental health are linked in this buying incentive:

> "New lustre on each countenance
> Touched by this soap you'll find;
> This philosophical romance
> Will kindle heart and mind."

The author of the book feels that he has reached the pinnacle of achievement, in being so much a part of so many people's lives:

> I have not lived amiss,
> That I should be so very near
> The nation's heart as this!

Whether this relationship is the finest one between art and audience that can be achieved is debatable. However, it certainly seems a worthy achievement when ironically set against the fate of the book of another author who appears later in the poem. This morose figure claims that "My book wrapped up the soap your book / Was made a bonus on!" The figure of the second author clearly satirizes the idea that literature has a material "use." For his novel has achieved precisely this goal, but in doing so it has relinquished its status as art.

Songs from Dreamland also includes whimsical poems that depict moments, with no explanation as to their significance or political meaning. "In The Drawing Room," for example, focuses on the absence of a central character, a woman, from a room. Kendall carefully conveys the silence and drabness of the space:

> Furniture with the languid mien,
> On which life seems to pall–
> With your insipid grey and green
> And drab, your cheerless wall–
> To think that she has really been
> An hour among you all.

The room grows more gloomy with the woman's absence, and the enforced period of "rest" makes the furniture impassive. Focusing on how dull the room is in her absence is an effective, indirect method of implying her liveliness and vibrancy. While Kendall never describes her and explains the reasons for her absence, she conveys a strong impression of her presence in the room, still warm from her occupation. At the end the narrator sees glimpses of how the occupant enlivens the room:

> I see the dingy curtains stir
> With a faint memory;
> The grand piano dreams of her
> In a drowsy minor key.

Songs from Dreamland, a volume that did not have Lang's backing, was reviewed only briefly and with at best mixed praise. Percy Addleshaw, reviewing the book in *The Academy* on 29 September 1894, this time under the category "minor poetry," sees the volume as "in some measure a disappointment."

Kendall wrote little fiction after *Songs from Dreamland*. During the 1880s and 1890s she published occasional short stories in magazines, particularly *Longman's Magazine*, where Lang also published. Her final fictional book, *Turkish Bonds*, was published in 1898. The book of short stories criticizes the Turks at the time of the

Armenian massacres, and it shows her concerns to be more political than fictional.

The dispiriting lack of interest in her second volume of poetry may well have been part of the reason why Kendall gave up publishing fiction in 1898 in order to concentrate on social work. She published only a few stories and poems between 1927 and 1931, all in *The Cornhill*. While Kendall lived in York, she became actively involved in the philanthropic work of the Rowntrees, a family of entrepreneurs who supported research projects in social welfare. In 1913 she collaborated with Benjamin Seebohm Rowntree on *How the Labourer Lives: A Study of the Rural Labour Problem,* the main aim of which, as stated at the beginning of the study, was to help stop "the steady drift of the population to the towns." The work is a rather sentimental idealization of the beneficial effects of working in the country—for instance, how "work on the land, in constant contact with natural objects and often in comparative isolation, produces a solid strength of character . . ."—but the case studies of the laborers' lives depict their poverty without flinching or patronizing. Kendall wrote these anecdotal studies. Asa Briggs, writing on the work of Seebohm Rowntree in *Social Thought and Social Action* (1961), points out that "There was a pathos in many of the stories which, simply told by May Kendall, were allowed to speak for themselves." Briggs explains that Kendall was responsible for "polishing" Rowntree's style, and "bringing to life" his work. Kendall also helped Rowntree with *The Human Needs of Labour,* published in 1918, although her name was not included on the title page. Briggs describes Kendall as "an 'other-worldly person' who would not accept a salary and always gave loyal and devoted service."

According to Isobel Armstrong, Joseph Bristow, and Cath Sharrock, Kendall, in her later years, "was renowned for her eccentricity, living for many years at 10 Monkgate in a house overrun with cats." The Joseph Rowntree Trust made a grant to pay for her funeral in 1943, after which she was buried in an unmarked grave in York Cemetery.

May Kendall was included as the only woman in the volume of humorous verse in Alfred H. Miles's *The Poets and the Poetry of the Century* (1898). He claims in his introduction to her work that it shows "a sense of humour rarely found in the verse of women." He cites the lack of women included in other collections of humorous verse as evidence of the "often made" contention "that women are distinctly lacking in a sense of humour." It is not clear why Kendall was given this position when other contemporary writers, equally witty, such as May Probyn and Constance Naden, were excluded. In more-recent years, many of the new anthologies of Victorian poetry include Kendall's poetry. She is still seen as a minor writer of humorous verse, but one who uses her wit to bring a fresh light to some of the key cultural debates of the age.

References:

Isobel Armstrong, Joseph Bristow, and Cath Sharrock, eds., *Nineteenth-Century Women Poets: An Oxford Anthology* (Oxford: Clarendon Press, 1996), p. 760;

Asa Briggs, *Social Thought and Social Action: A Study of the Work of Seebohm Rowntree 1871–1954* (London: Longmans, 1961);

Angela Leighton and Margaret Reynolds, *Victorian Women Poets: An Anthology* (Oxford: Blackwell, 1995), p. 627.

Lucy Knox

(9 November 1845 – 10 May 1884)

Kirsten E. Escobar
Baylor University

BOOKS: *Sonnets and Other Poems* (London: Privately printed, 1872; enlarged edition, London: Smith, Elder, 1876);
Four Pictures from a Life and Other Poems (London: Kegan Paul, Trench, 1884).

The daughter of one of Alfred Tennyson's fellow Apostles and Sterling Club intimates, Lucy Knox published two volumes of poems, largely sonnets, in the latter decades of the nineteenth century. Knox's poetry deals with love relationships, the human condition, Christian discipleship, the grandeur of God, the "Woman Question," and relations between Ireland and England. In each of these areas her poems achieve a directness, clarity, and rigor that distinguishes them from the simplistic didacticism of the conventional Victorian "poetess."

Lucy Spring Rice was born on 9 November 1845 at Hither Green, Lewisham, one of ten children and eight daughters of Stephen Edmond Spring Rice, Commissioner of Customs, and Ellen Spring Rice, née Frere. Her father enjoyed lifelong friendships with Tennyson, Thomas Carlyle, and Edward FitzGerald that had begun during his school years at Bury St. Edmunds Grammar School and Trinity College, Cambridge. The poet Sir Henry Taylor was her uncle by marriage, and Aubrey De Vere was her cousin.

Stephen Spring Rice's health began to fail in the late 1850s, and in 1859 he retired from his government position and moved his family to Mount Trenchard, the seat of his father, Thomas Spring Rice, first Baron Monteagle, in County Limerick, Ireland. On 23 August 1866 Lucy Spring Rice married Octavius Newry Knox. They are believed to have had three daughters and a son.

Knox's earliest known publication, a sonnet, appeared in *Macmillan's Magazine* in 1870. Her first collection, *Sonnets and Other Poems,* was privately printed in London in 1872 and sold in Ireland by Foynes and Company. An enlarged edition was published by Smith, Elder and Company in 1876.

The sorrow and loneliness caused by separation from loved ones through death permeate the volume, accounting for more than one-fifth of the poems. The speaker in the first sonnet in the collection, "I have no wealth of grief; no sobs, no tears," avows, "I have a leaden grief" of such staggering weight that tears cannot escape. She asks her listener to remember that "Love was a habit and the grief is new, / So new a thing it has no language yet." Grieving speakers in other poems testify that they honor their lost loved ones by their silence. The central figures of these poems of mourning, such as the speaker in "A Sonnet, which saith that the lost one . . . ," must accept that "God doth erase / And man may not rewrite" a life. The speaker in "Sonnet, which saith that the lost one cannot be made known to those new friends which come after" yearns to reconstruct and preserve a lost life with precision and clarity but finds that memory's picture is "futile, blurred, and faint." In "A Picture" the speaker observes a woman who has exhausted "active grief"; her protracted mourning has left her longing for death. Weary and spent, she passively awaits the coming of night, which will at least end the day and, if she is fortunate, will end her life.

Unlike the poems of bereavement, Knox's nature poems allow the speakers to see in the grave the comforting bosom of Mother Earth ("Epitaph") and the God who "smiles through Nature" ("Song"), connecting all beings "in one mystic chain" ("In a Meadow"). The speaker in "Rejoice Alway" calls children to play and lovers to kiss near the grave that entombs her. The dead speaker retains a vital link to the living through the flowers that grow atop her grave: "I blossom with the May." Nature in Knox's poems is a great, wise, and caring mother, a source of rejuvenation and emotional sustenance. The bucolic retreat, she says in "In a Meadow," allows one to "swift unlearn / Harsh incredulities and dull despair" through the language of field and flower.

Another topic that predominates in *Sonnets and Other Poems* is the faithlessness, betrayal, and inconstancy of male lovers and husbands. "Madge and Her Lovers" may nod approvingly at the dignified suitor who stands aloof from the fawning crowd, but "Lines" recognizes a predator in the suitor whose thoughtless attentions to the youthful speaker turn her "whole bright world into an empty shrine." The suitor is blamed for attracting and then discarding the unsuspecting girl, and Victorian culture is condemned for defining fulfillment for a woman solely in terms of a man's affections.

Other poems look beyond courtship to the realities of married life and assert that the idealized lover dreamed about and longed for will never materialize. At first love's "happy servant" but now its "bitter slave," the wife in "Sonnet: Love's prisoner speaks" bemoans the imperfect creature to whom her life is pledged: he seemed divine, almost worthy of worship, but he has proved to be quite fallible. As the poem concludes, the wife faces a "living death of love which dares not die." The wife in "The Withered Buds of Hope" dreams that she is happy but wakes to remember the discord in her home. The wife in "Ballad" has died of a broken heart. The wife in "A Dedication" hopes for Love's "promise-breathing treasure" to restore her husband's interest in her and in their marriage. Masking her thoughts in the symbolism of a garden, she laments that she cannot give the wreath she is making to her husband, "the Sun," because long ago she gave him the entire garden; the flowers she uses for her wreath are already his. She also grieves that "too seldom hath the Sun shone there," leaving the garden untended and unheeded. He has abandoned the garden after having "marred with rain" and soil the "lilies white"; the garden bears his "stain." The wife concludes her outcry by hoping that love will return to the garden and rejuvenate it. The woman is the garden; she gave herself fully to her husband; and, unless he returns to her, she will wither and go to ruin. She is fixed in place like a garden, while he enjoys the mobility and power of the sun. Such a relationship between husband and wife was the norm in the Victorian marriage: a woman's legal, economic, and social identity were entirely subsumed in her husband's. Repeatedly Knox demonstrates the powerlessness of wives to redress their husband's foibles; in "A Fragment," for example, the speaker cries, "Oh for a voice to speak with and be heard!"

Turning from the abandoned or betrayed lover or wife to the more general set of issues known as the "Woman Question," Knox demands for women the freedom to develop as moral and intellectual beings who would not look for a master, deity, or "Sun" in their husbands. She outlines her vision for reform in such poems as "'Out of the Fulness of the Heart the

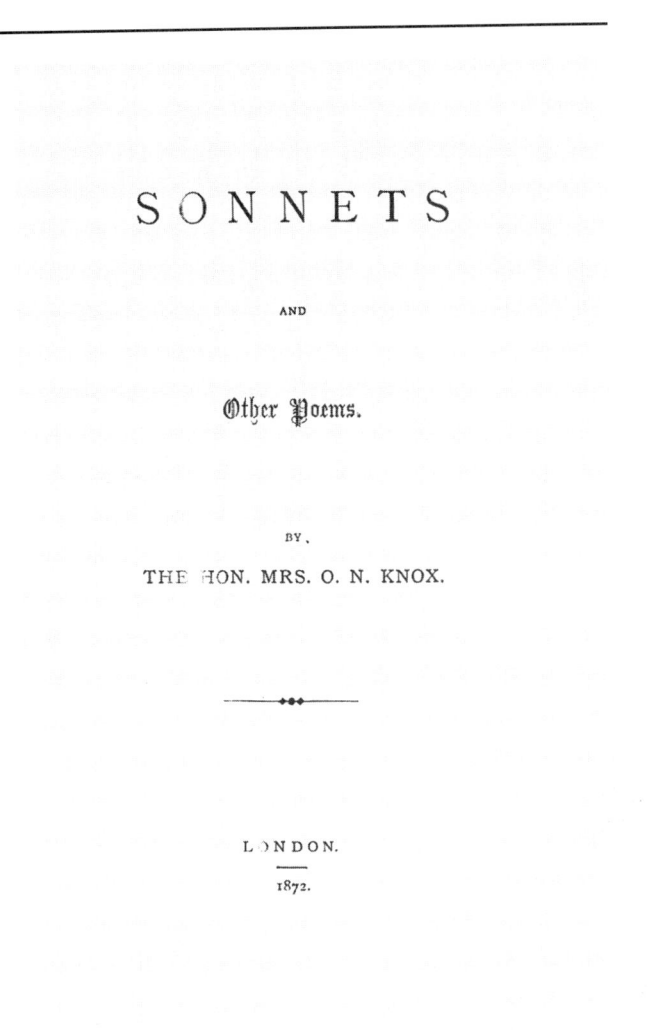

SONNETS

AND

Other Poems.

BY.

THE HON. MRS. O. N. KNOX.

LONDON.
1872.

Title page for Lucy Knox's privately printed first volume of poems, which was republished commercially in 1876

Mouth Speaketh,'" which decries the inadequacy of female education and maintains that God has created women to be capable of discernment, independence, and a life of action. "Woman's Future," one of the poems added for the Smith, Elder edition, addresses England directly: the speaker asks her country, "Who is this woman waiting in the waste, / With empty, fettered hands, and pleading voice?" Echoing Mary Wollstonecraft's *A Vindication of the Rights of Woman* (1792), she argues that female "vanity, weakness, folly" are products of patriarchy that would, under conditions of equality, quickly turn to a "love of Justice, Liberty, and Truth." The woman who "craves a larger life" commands England to acknowledge "aspirant womanhood" and "to leave thy daughter free" to develop her faculties, talents, and abilities to their full potential. Doing so would accomplish "her womanhood not ending, but begun." Moreover, it would make women

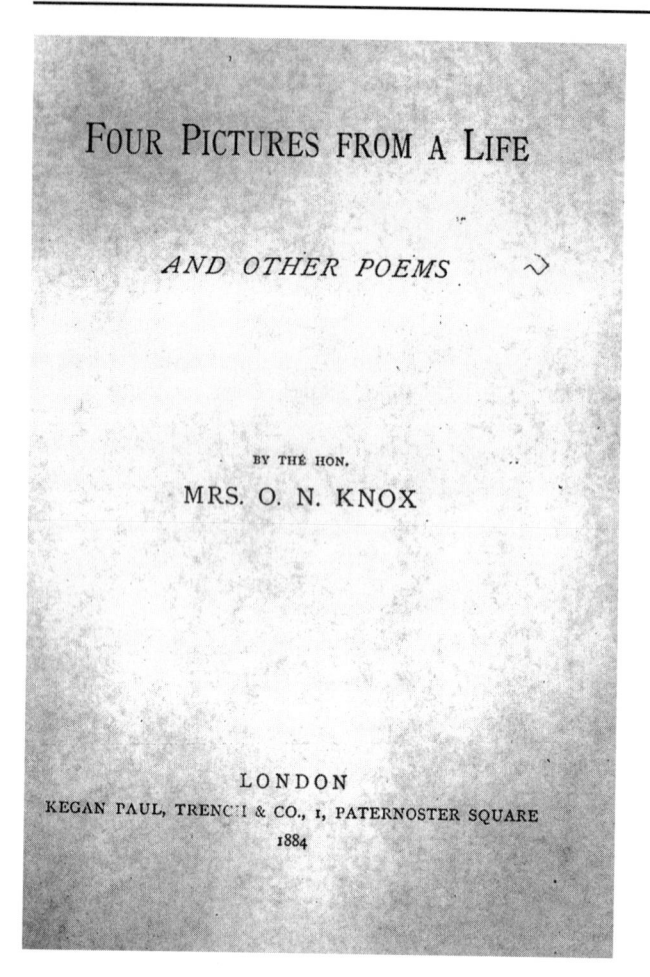

Title page for Knox's second and final poetry collection, which includes her translations from German and Italian

good mothers—also an argument of Wollstonecraft's. As Knox observes in "Sonnet: To a Mother," she "who traineth others must in training be." Ultimately, however, apart from a woman's contribution to others, whether her own children or society at large, she merits an adult identity that she creates and for which she alone is responsible. In "A Wife Answered" the speaker begs God for forgiveness for idolizing her depraved husband. God replies: "Live greatly: raise the Mind and Soul; / The heart shall then arise, / Not maimed, not bound—a perfect whole." God declares against a wife's dissolution in her husband and commands her to love and seek greater, more transcendent realities than romantic love. In "Sonnet: A cry to men" Knox lays at the feet of men responsibility for the working-class women who starve, drudge, faint, and die in the factories and coal mines that have produced England's prosperity and for the sin of prostitution that "discrowns" womanhood.

Knox's calls for reform do not end with the Woman Question poems; she also addresses political issues concerning relations between England and Ireland. In "Sonnet: Lament of the Loyal Irish, 1869" she says that England once "strode on her way with Ireland chained behind" but now "throws toward her sister glances kind." In "Sonnet" Ireland is a "land of sorrow, deeply wronged"; in "Old Irish Lament" it is a country "by familiar friend brought low." "England and Pauperism" attacks the English middle class "for gifts that we abuse" and for the workhouse "used but to pile the poor / In here and there a heap, / Where they may rot unseen."

A final major theme in *Sonnets and Other Poems* is religion. Speakers engage in dialogues with God, asking questions and making observations to which he responds. They beseech God to soothe and calm them. They admonish other people for "foul-weather" belief that only seeks God in calamity, and they admonish themselves for selfish acts that hurt others. In "Epithalamium" Knox says that "the death of self" gives life and in "Trust" that God's grace saves the fallen one who "hast striven in vain" to save himself. In "Song" she notes that "the bud must burst. . . . Before the fruit we see" in Christian maturation, and in "A Lesson of Life" she reminds the reader that the human condition is to face the "dread seclusion" and "void abyss where man is nought." In "To Him Who Was" she defends scientific inquiry, holding that "the God of Truth no search will blame" because "truth alone we seek to see." "Sonnet: The explorer of this world to the explorer of another" draws parallels between natural science and theology: both are forms of exploration. The speaker in "A Sunday Morning," observing a dragonfly that has unwittingly perched on her knee, realizes that God is as incomprehensible to human beings as she is to the insect. Nevertheless, the Christian may rely on God to provide: for a speaker "weary with persistent death" in "I Corinthians III.7" he transforms a withered and shrunken tree into a plant that thrives and blossoms. In "The Noble Army of Martyrs" Knox writes: "Call me to suffer, martyr throng; / I tread the path ye trod. . . . Lead on, through good, to God!"

An anonymous review in the 19 July 1873 issue of *The Spectator* said that Knox's first collection revealed "a very original vein of thoughtfulness" and "a keen eye and a fine hand." While finding her work devoid of the "pettiness" and "prettiness" that characterize the "minor poet," the reviewer nonetheless treated Knox's achievement as lying within the abilities and limitations of the poetess.

Knox contributed several poems to the *Irish Monthly* in 1877. In 1882 T. Hall Caine selected "I have no wealth of grief; no sobs, no tears" from *Sonnets and Other Poems* for inclusion in his anthology *Sonnets of Three Centuries*. He also included poems by Knox's cousin De

Vere and by her father. Yet, while he provided biographical information and comments on the two men, he neglected Knox, not even mentioning the familial ties among the three.

In 1884 Kegan Paul, Trench and Company published Knox's second collection, *Four Pictures from a Life, and Other Poems*. The volume comprises new work by Knox, as well as her translations of sixteen poems from German–fourteen of them by Johann Wolfgang von Goethe–and two from Italian.

In this volume Knox takes a more optimistic view of romance and marriage than she did in *Sonnets and Other Poems*. Speakers proclaim love's delight and rapture; they surrender to "fiery" and "mighty Love"; they relish a reuniting embrace and "clinging lips" that forget "to sever" at Time's bidding ("If We Had Wings"). In contrast to the unhappy wife in "A Dedication" in the earlier volume, here the speaker in a poem of the same title sings joyfully of the beloved who reigns in her heart.

Of the few laudatory poems that Knox included in her two volumes, the only one devoted to a family friend eulogizes Carlyle, who died in 1881. Knox offers her own gratitude as mourners in the poem gather at his "dishonoured grave" to bless him and acknowledge their debt to him. Two sonnets in *Four Pictures from a Life, and Other Poems* bear the title "Beethoven" and are testimonials to the greatness of the composer, whose life she calls a "martyrdom." Several other poems proclaim the grandeur and regenerative powers of music.

Bereavement and its anguish still appear in this volume but subside as poetic themes; only four bereavement poems appear in *Four Pictures from a Life, and Other Poems*. In "Alone" the speaker confesses that she "was like to die" at the deathbed of her mate and now "dares not weep," though she is "heart-sick." But memory eases death's sting in "A Farewell": "YES, we must part," the speaker acknowledges, but declares, "Yet in one soul thou dwellest here / And from one heart thou canst not roam." The bard in "Dying" has departed, but "Great Nature" will immortalize his song by raising others "to sing in his stead." And since "she covered him over / With daisies and buttercups, thyme and white clover," those who seek him will find him not only in the perpetuated song but also in the flora that covers his grave.

While the Woman Question wanes as a theme in the 1884 collection, Knox continues to treat the Irish Question. In "Sonnet: England and Ireland in 1881" she calls on England to face the "gaunt corpses" of Ireland's sons, who died transforming "our sacred homes, your eyesores" into the manors of English landlords. She also expands her political commentary to events such as the Austrian invasion of Italy in the 1860s.

Four Pictures from a Life, and Other Poems was praised by a reviewer in *The Academy* (30 August 1884) for its "distinct merit" and "genuine poetry" but also for its "modesty of aim." This perceived lack of ambition was apparently considered appropriate for a woman. Lucy Knox died on 10 May 1884.

References:

Virginia Blain, Patricia Clements, and Isobel Grundy, *The Feminist Companion to Literature in English* (New Haven: Yale University Press, 1990);

Stephen L. Gwynn, ed., *The Letters and Friendships of Sir Cecil Spring Rice*, 2 volumes (Boston: Houghton Mifflin, 1929);

Cecil Y. Lang and Edgar F. Shannon Jr., eds., *The Letters of Alfred, Lord Tennyson*, 3 volumes (Oxford: Clarendon Press, 1981–1990);

Catherine W. Reilly, *Late Victorian Poetry: 1880–1899* (London: Mansell, 1994);

Clyde de L. Ryals and Kenneth J. Fielding, eds. *The Collected Letters of Thomas and Jane Welsh Carlyle*, volumes 8, 10, 14–17, and 25 (Durham, N.C.: Duke University Press, 1970–1995);

Alfred McKinley Terhune and Annabelle Burdick Terhune, eds., *The Letters of Edward Fitzgerald* (Princeton: Princeton University Press, 1980).

Emily Lawless
(The Hon. Emily Lawless)
(December 1845 – 19 October 1913)

Richard Tobias
University of Pittsburgh

BOOKS: *A Chelsea Householder,* anonymous (3 volumes, London: Sampson Low, 1882; 1 volume, New York: Holt, 1883);

A Millionaire's Cousin (London: Macmillan, 1885; New York: Holt, 1885);

Hurrish: A Study (2 volumes, Edinburgh: Blackwood, 1886; 1 volume, New York: Harper, 1886);

Major Lawrence, F.L.S.: A Novel (3 volumes, London: Murray, 1887; 1 volume, New York: Holt, 1887);

Ireland, by Lawless and Mrs. Arthur Bronson (London: Unwin / New York: Putnam, 1887); republished as *The Story of Ireland* (New York: Putnam / London: Unwin, 1888); revised and enlarged as *Ireland* (London: Unwin, 1912);

Plain Frances Mowbray, and Other Tales (London: Murray, 1889);

With Essex in Ireland: Being Extracts from a Diary Kept in Ireland During the Year 1599 by Mr. Henry Harvey, Sometime Secretary to Robert Devereux, Earl of Essex, with a Preface by John Oliver Maddox, M.A. (London: Smith, Elder, 1890; New York: Lovell, 1890);

Grania: The Story of an Island, 2 volumes (London: Smith, Elder, 1892; New York: Macmillan, 1892);

Maelcho: A Sixteenth Century Narrative (2 volumes, London: Smith, Elder, 1894; 1 volume, New York: Appleton, 1894);

A Colonel of the Empire: From the Private Papers of Mangan O'Driscoll, Late of the Imperial Service of Austria, and a Knight of the Military Order of the Maria Theresa (New York: Appleton, 1895);

Traits and Confidences (London: Methuen, 1898);

Atlantic Rhymes and Rhythms, as E.L. (London & Bungay: Privately printed, 1898);

A Garden Diary: September 1899–September 1900 (London: Methuen, 1901);

Emily Lawless

With the Wild Geese, introduction by Stopford A. Brook (London: Isbister, 1902);

Maria Edgeworth, English Men of Letters (London: Macmillan, 1904; New York: Macmillan, 1904);

The Book of Gilly: Four Months out of a Life (London: Smith, Elder, 1906);

The Point of View (Some Talks and Disputations) (London: Privately printed, 1909);

The Race of Castlebar: Being a Narrative Addressed by Mr. John Bunbury to His Brother, Mr. Theodore Bunbury, Attached to His Britannic Majesty's Embassy at Florence, October 1798, and Now First Given to the World, by Lawless and Shan F. Bullock (London: Murray, 1913);

The Inalienable Heritage and Other Poems, preface by Edith Sichel (London: Privately printed, 1914);

The Poems of Emily Lawless, edited by Padraic Fallon (Dublin: Published for An Chomhairle Ealaion by the Dolmen Press, 1965).

Editions: *Hurrish,* 2 volumes, introduction by Robert Lee Wolff, Ireland, from the Act of Union, 1800, to the Death of Parnell, 1891, no. 71 (New York: Garland, 1979);

With Essex in Ireland, introduction by Wolff, Ireland, from the Act of Union, 1800, to the Death of Parnell, 1891, no. 72 (New York: Garland, 1979);

Grania: The Story of an Island, introduction by Wolff, Ireland, from the Act of Union, 1800, to the Death of Parnell, 1891, no. 73 (New York: Garland, 1979);

Maelcho: A Sixteenth-Century Narrative, introduction by Wolff, Ireland, from the Act of Union, 1800, to the Death of Parnell, 1891, no. 74 (New York: Garland, 1979);

Traits and Confidences, introduction by Wolff, Ireland, from the Act of Union, 1800, to the Death of Parnell, 1891, no. 75 (New York: Garland, 1979);

Hurrish: A Study, introduction by Val Mulkerns (Belfast: Appletree, 1992).

Emily Lawless—listed on the title pages of her books as "The Hon. Emily Lawless"—wrote poetry, novels, a history of Ireland, and articles on entomology. Although she spent her formative years in Ireland and considered herself an Irish patriot, she lived in England most of her adult life. A sense of exile is especially strong in her poems, most of which were published during the last decade of her life.

Lawless was born at Lyons House, County Kildare, the fourth of nine children and eldest daughter of Edward Lawless, third Baron Cloncurry, and Elizabeth Lawless, née Kirwan, a renowned beauty from an ancient west-of-Ireland family. Emily was baptized on 21 December 1845; no record of her birth date exists. Her family belonged to the Ascendancy, the 10 percent of the population that conformed to the Church of Ireland rather than the Roman rite; only a member of that church could vote in elections and serve in the Irish Parliament. As a child and as an adult she spent summers near Castle Hackett, her mother's family home in County Clare. She never learned the Irish language, even though she would have heard Gaelic speakers during those summers in the west of Ireland.

Few schools existed for young women in Ireland, so Lawless was educated at home. As a child she recited passages from Elizabethan dramas for visitors to the family home, but her father thought the material inappropriate for a girl. A possibly autobiographical story in her collection *Traits and Confidences* (1898) is about a child in a large country house who has an intense scientific interest in moths, Lawless's lifelong interest. The girl sneaks out of her house, past the sleeping servants, and opens locked doors to venture out into the night. In 1867 Lawless published an article in an entomology journal that added new information about Irish lepidoptera.

Lawless's father committed suicide in 1869; two of her sisters also killed themselves. After her father's death Lawless and her mother lived in houses on Eaton Terrace and Cadogan Place in the West End of London, which were among the most desirable addresses in the city. They also traveled on the Continent.

Lawless's first two novels, *A Chelsea Householder* (1882) and *A Millionaire's Cousin* (1885), feature young women who live in magnificent London houses, as she did; they also pursue careers as painters, indicating that the author might have thought of such a career. In her first novel a character supports herself by copying the paintings of the masters; later in life Lawless copied Raphael's paintings in a sketchbook that she gave her mother. In both novels women rent houses in Hampshire in imitation of the French Barbizon school of painters, who left Paris to paint in the open air of the countryside.

Lawless's third novel, *Hurrish: A Study* (1886), her first to be set in Ireland, was her most commercially successful work of fiction. The hero's name is Horatio, but the Irish pronounce it "Hurrish." The book is dedicated to the novelist Margaret Oliphant, who gave Lawless early encouragement. Val Mulkerns notes in the introduction to the 1992 Belfast edition of *Hurrish* that Lawless's efforts to "give the actual flavour of the people's speech, with all its Irish derivations, are so vigorous as to be something of an irritation at times." Mulkerns also suggests that the landlord in the novel may be based on Lawless's father.

Hurrish attracted the attention of William Ewart Gladstone, the Whig prime minister who attempted to

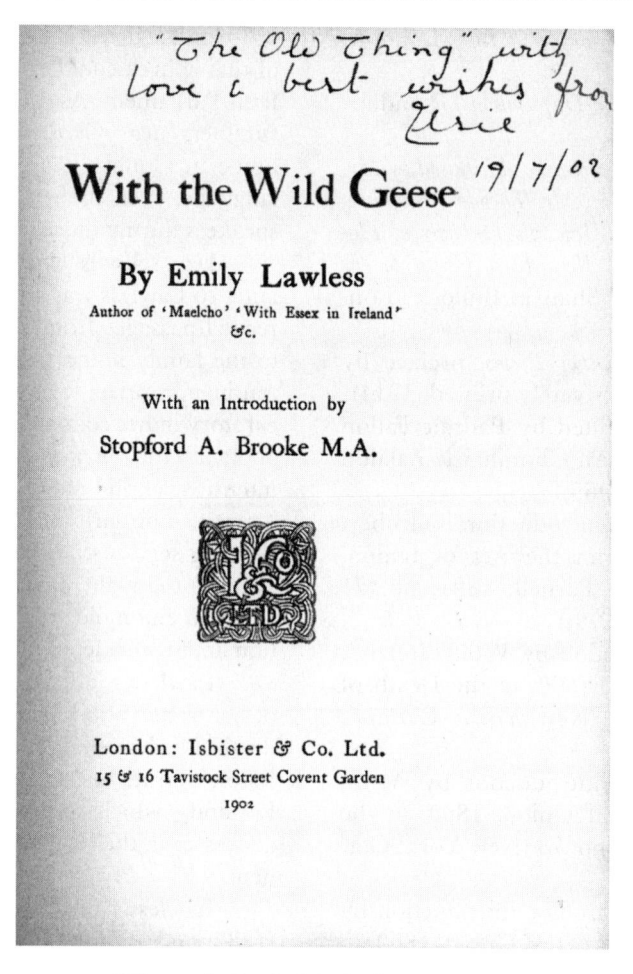

Title page for Lawless's book of poems about the exiled soldiers of County Clare

pass the first Irish Home Rule Bill in 1886 and continued to urge passage of the bill throughout his career. Gladstone quotes from *Hurrish* in his pamphlet *Notes and Queries on the Irish Demands* (1887).

Lawless's *Ireland* (1887) contributed to the debate over Home Rule by making the history of the island known to the English middle class and aristocracy that blocked Gladstone's bill. The work describes English arrogance, misgovernment, and sheer ineptitude in Ireland but also severely criticizes Irish feuding and shows that, given the opportunity, the Irish landgrabbers could be as evil as the absentee English landowners. *Ireland* is a Unionist history, arguing that Ireland is best served by continued association with Great Britain. Gladstone's Home Rule Bill would have kept Ireland in the United Kingdom.

In her novels *With Essex in Ireland* (1890) and *Maelcho* (1894) Lawless creates fearful scenes of English barbarity and Irish instability. The novels also include poetry. *With Essex in Ireland* was published with the date 1599 on the title page and listed Lawless as the editor; many readers, including Gladstone, believed that the book was an authentic Elizabethan travel diary before Lawless admitted her authorship. The narrator is Henry Harvey, poet and secretary to Robert Devereux, Earl of Essex, whom Queen Elizabeth has sent to Ireland to quell Irish unrest and internecine warfare. Harvey writes a hunting ballad, which Essex finds too doleful, and a Shakespearean love sonnet. Harvey is depicted as young and inexperienced, both as a human being and as a poet, and the ballad and the sonnet are close to parody. In 1890 Gladstone sent a note to Smith, Elder, Lawless's publisher, saying that he believed that the novel "constituted a valuable addition to the stores of our historical knowledge." Gladstone also discussed the book with Lawless when he met her in Cannes, France. In *Maelcho* Lawless writes Ossian-like verse about clan history. (The Ossian poems, supposedly heroic epics by an ancient Celtic bard, were fabrications by the eighteenth-century Scottish poet James Macpherson.) Both novels were received well in England and the

United States, but their tone was too Unionist for the Irish literary community.

Critics consider Lawless's 1892 novel *Grania: The Story of an Island* her masterpiece. The novel is set on Inishmaan in the Aran Islands. Grania, the heroine, rejects an offer of marriage from a charming young rogue who seems more interested in her land than in her, and she drowns attempting to bring a priest to the remote island to administer last rites to her half sister, who is dying of tuberculosis. Grania's own lack of religious conviction makes her death heroic, an act of total love. The descriptions of the Irish landscape foreshadow Lawless's poetry.

Lawless never married, and, except for Gladstone, her relative Horace Plunkett, and the historian William E. H. Lecky, she had few male friends. She did, however, have many close friendships with women. Her first two novels end in conventional marriages, but the courtship scenes are, like Jane Austen's, depicted from a distance; scenes in which women share living quarters are much more detailed. After her mother's death in 1895 Lawless shared a house with Lady Sarah Spencer near Gomshall, Surrey, for eight years. Spencer arranged for the private publication of Lawless's first book of poems, *Atlantic Rhymes and Rhythms* (1898). In *A Garden Diary: September 1899–September 1900* (1901), she tells how "we" organized "our" garden: Lawless planned it and supervised the workers, while Spencer admired the results. In the book Lawless, who owned stock in South African mines, enthusiastically supports British colonialism in South Africa even though she raged against it in Ireland. Lawless sometimes took rooms in London to be close to Mary Studd, a friend from the west of Ireland. Her poems addressed to women have the warmth of close friendship that is familiar in much nineteenth-century women's writing.

Lawless's second book of poetry, *With the Wild Geese*, appeared in 1902. "The wild geese" was the name given to the soldiers who left Ireland when, after the Irish defeat at the battle of Aughrim in 1691, they were given the choice of exile or submission to English rule. For the next hundred years these soldiers and their descendants fought on the Continent for France, Spain, and Austria; an estimated 150,000 of them were killed. The men of County Clare marched off to France with the blithe hope of honor, wealth, and adventure, but in the poems they come back as ghosts. In "An Exile's Mother" a mother thanks God that her son is in France rather than in cold Ireland, but the reader knows that the boy is dead. A generalized soldier speaks in many of the poems, longing for the lost homeland as he and his fellows die in stupid wars fought under stupid generals. Lawless's diction in this book, as in all of her poetry, is simple, ordinary human speech, not given to hyperbole or luxuriant word choice. The landscape descriptions in the novels are more "poetic," in conventional terms, than her poems. Although she uses dialect in the novels, she never writes dialect poems; her Irish soldiers speak standard English.

The seascape poems, celebrating the Clare coast from which the soldiers departed, are among the best pieces in the volume. The dominant image throughout is the Atlantic Ocean, the brute force against which human will strives. The dedication of *With the Wild Geese* evokes and apostrophizes the Atlantic as a king:

Spring stamps her signet on our wayward race,
Hers is the charm, hers the elusive grace,
Immortal, changeful, even as thy face,
    King of our hearts.

A deeper glory fills the glad sunshine,
The distance mellows with a hue like wine;
Summer is queen, but Summer too is thin,
    King of our hearts.

Now dimly purple pageants fill the eyes,
Far o'er the plain the mocking vapours rise,
Veiled in autumnal mists thy surface lies,
    King of our hearts.

And still when cliff, when headlands lie a-cold,
And the year's tale of glories is all told,
Still, still thou reignest, even as old,
    King of our hearts.

In contrast to the sea and its force, the Irish bogs signify the history that encumbers the Irish and swallows them. Like the sea, this landscape attracts and repels at once. In "A Tuft of White Bog-Cotton Growing in the Tyrol," which is dated 1886 (Lawless rarely dated her poems), Lawless contrasts Austrian mountain sunshine with darkness of western Ireland, where she has seen the same plant:

Nor here alone exalt that snow-white head,
But in yon western land of sad renown,
Whose only wealth is its forgotten dead,
For never Fortune showed one steadfast frown.
. . . .
Nor Woe but, turning, caught a glad surprise,
Though every tongue conspired to blight renown.

The poems eschew the comfort of religion; the universe is shown as neutral toward human desires. People are victims of chance in a cold, harsh, poor landscape that barely sustains the ignorant popula-

THE
POINT OF VIEW
(SOME TALKS AND DISPUTATIONS)

BY
EMILY LAWLESS, LITT.D.
AUTHOR OF 'WITH THE WILD GEESE,' ETC.

'For with a friend a man . . tosseth his thoughts.'
BACON.

Privately Printed
1909

Title page for Lawless's second book of poetry (courtesy of The Lilly Library, Indiana University)

tion. In "Dirge of the Muster Forest" the woodland speaks about its destruction at the hands of savage English power. The forest advises the "wren, titmouse, robin, fox, and deer" to escape the brutality, but the wolf remains to consume the carrion: "The great grey wolf with scraping claws" will "Lay bare my dead, who died, and died for me." The poem immediately following, "Dirge for All Ireland," allows only a small possibility of genuine human life in the west of Ireland.

Lawless followed *With the Wild Geese* with a biography of the novelist Maria Edgeworth for Macmillan's English Men of Letters series (1904). She was able to draw on her own experiences at Castle Hackett to describe Edgeworth's life in an Ascendancy household in the west of Ireland, where civilization seemed far away and the ways of the local people were mysterious and foreign but attractive.

Lawless's novel *The Book of Gilly: Four Months out of a Life* (1906) is an idyll depicting a perfect education. Gilly is the nine-year-old son of an English mother and an Irish father; the parents have gone to India, leaving him and his four-year-old sister in the care of servants on the family-owned island. The two children are tutored by an Oxford student with a health problem that can be cured by rest in the west of Ireland and a science student from the English midlands. Lawless seems to be looking back to her own education, in which rigorous scientific study was balanced by rock climbing, talks with Irish servants and farmers, and free access to her father's library.

William Linn's dissertation (1971) cites letters in which Lawless refers to poor health; one of her relatives informed him that in the last decade of her life Lawless took heroin to relieve her pain. She wrote most of her verse under these conditions. The poems, however, communicate a dominant will; they demand no pity.

The Point of View (Some Talks and Disputations) (1909), Lawless's second book of poetry, is dedicated to "E. S.," her friend Edith Sichel. The long poem "A Twilight Colloquy" depicts Ireland as under a "load of pain, death, birth." Another poem, "From the Rath," describes the hill fortresses (*raths*) that Irish chieftains built in their seeming eternal clan wars. The poem ends, "What gulfs, what tides of mortal agony, / Sleep in the Past, that huge unplumbed sea?" The speaking voice in the poems, as in the novels, is disinterested. "The End of an Argument" suggests that truth is at neither extreme in a dispute but palpitates somewhere between the two:

Discourse, dispute, grow hot, then calm again,
But whereso'er those disputants do meet
A spirit hovers, a vague shadowy third,
With cold ironic accents, never heard,
Yet in whose silence lurks the essential word.

Lawless died in Gomshall on 19 October 1913; no cause of death is given in her obituary notices. Her friend Sichel wrote the introduction to Lawless's posthumously published book of verse, *The Inalienable Heritage and Other Poems* (1914). In one of the poems in the volume, "The Shadow of the Shore," Ireland is described as a "woman-country":

> Oh, woman-country, weak, yet strangely strong,
> What witchery doth to thy cold skies belong,
> What spells are thine, all other lands apart,
> Which clings so closely, madly to the heart.

Sichel also wrote the 1914 article in *The Nineteenth Century* that is the major source of biographical information about Lawless.

Lawless is a lost poet of the Edwardian Age. Linn devotes only 9 pages—mostly apologetic—to the poems out of the 213 pages of his dissertation; he thinks that she was too ill to concentrate when she wrote them. Linn may be cool to the poetry because he is influenced by the New Criticism: Lawless's poetry lacks the ambiguity, paradox, and complicated image patterns that the New Critics appreciated. Writing in the early 1980s, Betty Webb Brewer finds more to admire in the poems than does Linn, but she is only lukewarm in her praise. Lawless had arrived at her style by the time the first of her four poetry books was published, and she did not change or develop from one volume to the next. She writes in the tradition of William Wordsworth, Alfred Tennyson, and Matthew Arnold, avoiding Pre-Raphaelite ecstasy, detail, and sexuality.

Lawless does not overtly speak as a woman in her poems; although she was writing at a time when women were striving to achieve the vote, no sign of this activity appears in her work. Yet, there is a womanly longing in some of the texts for more freedom and success. Thus, the speaker in "On the Value of Masterpieces" in *The Point of View* "yearns" to write "just one flawless phrase, / To shine a diamond in the unlettered dusk." In "Shall All Then Perish" a speaker talking with a friend compares a passing cloud that leaves no trace to their own efforts as "stumbling pilgrims." The poem concludes that it is enough to have the thought or to write the line, even if it remains unknown.

Emily Lawless's voice in her poetry is that of an aristocrat, a person who knows her own position and feels secure in it. She speaks as an exile, and she should have a new audience in a world where many experience exile and loss.

References:

Betty Webb Brewer, "Emily Lawless: An Irish Writer above All Else," dissertation, University of North Carolina at Chapel Hill, 1982;

Brewer, "'She Was a Part of it': Emily Lawless (1845–1913)," *Eire-Ireland,* 18 (Winter 1983): 119–131;

Mary Elizabeth Grubgeld, "The Poems of Emily Lawless and the Life of the West," *Turn of the Century Women,* 3, no. 2 (1986): 35–41;

Grubgeld, "Private Geographies; Land and Life in the Irish Literary Renaissance: Emily Lawless, George Moore, and J. M. Synge," dissertation, University of Iowa, 1983;

William Linn, "The Life and Works of the Hon. Emily Lawless, First Novelist of the Irish Literary Revival," dissertation, New York University, 1971;

Edith Sichel, "Emily Lawless," *Nineteenth Century,* 76 (July–December 1914): 80–100.

Papers:

The largest collection of Emily Lawless's papers is in the Archbishop Marsh's Library in Dublin. Her correspondence with the Macmillan firm is in the British Library; other collections of her letters are in the University of Glasgow Library, the Bodleian Library of the University of Oxford, the India Office Library and Records in London, and the Hove Central Library.

Amy Levy
(10 November 1861 – 10 September 1889)

Rebecca Shapiro
Westminster College

See also the Levy entry in *DLB 156: British Short-Fiction Writers, 1880–1914: The Romantic Tradition.*

BOOKS: *Xantippe, and Other Verse* (Cambridge: E. Johnson, 1881);
A Minor Poet and Other Verse (London: Unwin, 1884);
The Romance of a Shop (London: Unwin, 1888; Boston: Cupples & Hurd, 1889);
Reuben Sachs: A Sketch (London & New York: Macmillan, 1888);
Miss Meredith (London: Hodder & Stoughton, 1889);
A London Plane-Tree, and Other Verse (London: Unwin, 1889; New York: Stokes, 1890);
A Ballad of Religion and Marriage (N.p.: Privately printed, 1915);
The Complete Novels and Selected Writings of Amy Levy, 1861–1889, edited by Melvyn New (Gainesville: University of Florida Press, 1993).

TRANSLATIONS: Jean Baptiste Pérès, *Historic and Other Doubts; or, The Non-Existence of Napoleon Proved,* translated anonymously by Levy (London: E. W. Allen, 1885);
Yehuda Halevi, "Physician and Poet," and Heinrich Heine, "A Plea," in *Jewish Portraits,* by Lady Katie Magnus (London: Routledge, 1888), pp. 1–31, 45–81.

SELECTED PERIODICAL PUBLICATIONS–UNCOLLECTED: "Ida Grey: A Story of Woman's Sacrifice," *Pelican,* 2 (April 1875): 2;
"Jewish Women and Women's Rights," *Jewish Chronicle,* 17 February 1879, p. 5;
"The Poetry of Christina Rossetti," *Woman's World,* 1 (1888): 178–180.

In her short life Amy Levy was an extraordinarily prolific poet, novelist, essayist, and translator. With the exception of two publications as a teenager, Levy wrote all of her works within a period of ten years. Most of her writing is characterized by alternations of darkness

Amy Levy

and light, pessimism and optimism; there is little joy in her poetry, but there are frequent touches of wry humor and idealism. Edward Wagenknecht believes that "Only the disappointed idealist can suffer such disillusionment as consumes her; the 'realist' has never expected very much." *Weltschmerz*–a word that Levy uses in her 1883 essay "James Thomson: A Minor Poet" (republished in *The Complete Novels and Selected Writings of Amy Levy, 1861–1889,* 1993) to describe Thomson's deeply pessimistic and alienated style and mood–can also be used to characterize her poetry. At the age of twenty-seven, a week after correcting the proofs of her final volume of poetry, she committed suicide. Oscar Wilde wrote in her obituary in his magazine, *The Woman's World:*

> To write thus at six-and-twenty is given to very few.... The loss is the world's, but perhaps not hers. She was never robust; not often actually ill, but seldom well enough to feel life a joy instead of a burden; and her work was not poured out lightly, but drawn drop by drop from the very depth of her own feeling. We may say of it that it was in truth her life's blood.

Amy Levy was born in London on 10 November 1861, the second of the seven children of Lewis Levy, a stockbroker, and Isabelle Levy, née Levin. A precocious child, at thirteen she published the chivalric ballad "Ida Grey: A Story of Woman's Sacrifice" (1875) in *The Pelican,* a short-lived suffragist magazine; the poem shows the influence of Heinrich Heine, whose "Donna Clara" it resembles in meter.

In 1876 Levy enrolled at the Brighton High School for Girls, founded by the feminists Maria and Emily Shirreff in 1871. She developed an intense crush on the headmistress, Edith Creak, a recent graduate of Newnham College, one of the two earliest women's colleges at the University of Cambridge. In February 1879 she wrote a pro-woman-suffrage letter to the newspaper *The Jewish Chronicle* that was published under the headline "Jewish Women and Women's Rights"; it ended with the demand that "those who pay taxes should also have some voice in deciding by whom those taxes should be imposed." In October 1879 Levy became the first Jewish woman to matriculate at Cambridge when she entered Newnham College. While there she began to publish essays and stories in periodicals such as *Victoria Magazine, Temple Bar, Dublin University Magazine,* and *The Cambridge Review.*

Levy also published her first collection of poetry, *Xantippe, and Other Verse* (1881), while she was at Cambridge. Two of the poems, "Run to Death" and the title piece, had been published in periodicals in 1879 and 1880, respectively. Despite a lack of advertising, the entire edition was soon sold out. In the blank-verse dramatic monologue "Xantippe (A Fragment)" Socrates' widow, Xantippe, tells her side of their notoriously troubled relationship to her maids by way of apologizing for her mistreatment of them. Her desire for intellectual stimulation had been met by lack of encouragement and, eventually, by scorn from Socrates. Xantippe took out her resentment on her servants—women who were also oppressed by men. She asks her maids to gather around:

> Come hither, maids; too soundly have ye slept
> That should have watched me; nay, I would not chide—
> Oft I have chidden, yet I would not chide
> In this last hour;—now all should be at peace.

Xantippe says that in her youth she was different from other girls. She had "golden dreams" of knowledge and a voice "That should proclaim the stately mysteries / Of this fair world, and of the holy gods." When her father told her that the much older Socrates was to be her husband, she was repulsed by the philosopher's unkempt and ungainly appearance. But she decided that his greatness must lie in his soul:

> The richest gem lies hidden furthest down,
> And is the dearer for the weary search;
> We grasp the shining shells which strew the shore,
> Yet swift we fling them from us; but the gem
> We keep for aye and cherish....

She saw the throng of young men who gathered around Socrates, listening to his powerful ideas, and she believed that she, too, could be part of that community:

> I, guided by his wisdom and his love,
> Led by his words, and counselled by his care,
> Should lift the shrouding veil from things which be,
> And at the flowing fountain of his soul
> Refresh my thirsting spirit....

Socrates, however, gave his follower Alkibaides a status akin to a feminine partner or lover, a role that by rights should have gone to his wife. Furthermore, Socrates was "Pregnant with noble theories and great thoughts," while Xantippe was "barren." As she carried a wineskin to Socrates and his students, she realized that she and the wineskin were both perceived as utensils for serving men. She became enraged and dashed it to the ground. After this confrontation, Xantippe tells her servants, she evolved into a bitter and angry woman, the shrew the world knows as the wife of Socrates.

The other most important poem in the collection, "Run to Death," is emotional and somewhat overwrought but reveals Levy's distaste for class disparities. It is the story of a gypsy and her baby hunted to exhaustion and death by bored and dissipated French aristocrats, who, after they kill the woman and child, return to their own spoiled and idle women.

Levy left Cambridge in 1881, after her second year, without taking her tripos (final examinations). According to an 1892 memoir of her by the editor and writer Harry Quilter, she then spent some time in Cornwall recovering from an illness. She also traveled to Germany and Switzerland.

Levy published "James Thomson: A Minor Poet" in *The Cambridge Review* in February 1883, a few months after Thomson's death from alcoholism. Levy seems to have felt an affinity for the themes of Thomson's

Levy's parents, Lewis and Isabelle Levin Levy

poetry, in particular his long poem "The City of Dreadful Night" (1880). The subtitle of the essay became the title of her second book, which appeared the next year. In her essay Levy describes a "minor poet" as a "passionately subjective being, with intense eyes fixed on one side of the solid polygon of truth, and realising that one side with a fervour and intensity to which the philosopher with his birdseye view rarely attains." Levy wonders how Thomson's work would have developed had he received more encouragement and artistic nourishment. She says that the "weltschmerz" that characterizes Thomson's work is "modern" and indicative of the burdens of life at the end of the century. She maintains that "The City of Dreadful Night is always standing; ceaselessly one or other human soul visits and revisits the graves of Faith and Hope and Love; ceaselessly in the vast cathedral does the preacher give forth his good tidings to that shadowy congregation, and ever and anon rises up the shrill sound of agonised protest from their midst." Levy concludes by reminding her readers that while few people knew Thomson, those who did not can still draw meaning from his life and work: "To us, who never saw his face nor touched his living hand, his image stands out large and clear, unutterably tragic: the image of a great mind and a great soul thwarted in their development by circumstances; of a nature struggling with itself and Fate; of an existence doomed to bear a twofold burden."

Several poems in Levy's second book, *A Minor Poet and Other Verse* (1884), are republished from *Xantippe, and Other Verse*, but most are new. The mood of the poems is one of darkness and depression. The title poem, a dramatic monologue in iambic pentameter, is an intimate study of the mind of a suicide. The Minor Poet has friends who care about him, but he believes that all people lead solitary lives. He chides his friend Tom Leigh, who prevented him from committing suicide once before:

>   Gentle Tom,
> But you might wag your philosophic tongue
> From morn till eve, and still the thing's the same:
> I am myself, as each man is himself—
> Feels his own pain, joys his own joy, and loves

> With his own love, no other's. Friend, the world
> Is but one man; one man is but the world.

In taking his own life, the poet will be doing the only thing that makes sense to him; he has always been "A blot, a blur, a note / all out of tune in this world's instrument." When he surveys his room and contemplates what he is leaving behind, his gaze stops on his books: because they speak only to him and do not judge him, they, not people, are his true friends. The poet laments leaving these companions—Heine, William Shakespeare, Johann Wolfgang von Goethe, Percy Bysshe Shelley, and one other, who remains nameless but has Walt Whitman-like qualities:

> And one wild singer of to-day, whose song
> Is all aflame with passionate bard's blood
> Lash'd into foam by pain and the world's wrong.
> At least, he has a voice to cry his pain;
> For him, no silent writhing in the dark,
> No muttering of mute lips, no straining out
> Of a weak throat a-choke with pent-up sound,
> A-throb with pent-up passion. . . .

The poet ends by voicing his anger at the inequities in the world; he cannot comprehend why one person has enough food for two, while another cannot eat at all. He is indignant that others are indifferent to injustice and despairs that life is unfair.

In the short piece "To a Dead Poet" the speaker listens to a group of people who are discussing the poet's life:

> I knew not if to laugh or weep;
>   They sat and talked of you—
> 'T was here he sat; 't was this he said!
>   'T was that he used to do.

The speaker grows increasingly dismayed by the superficial and ignorant things that are being said about a person whom they did not know and chooses to honor the poet's memory by saying nothing about him. The poem concludes:

> I, who had never seen your face
>   Perhaps I knew you best.

In "Medea," according to Deborah Epstein Nord, "we have the plaint of another ill-used, apparently monstrous woman. Medea rails against her husband's treachery and betrayal and accuses him of duplicity and ungratefulness, but it is, above all, her sense of foreignness, of being a lusty Colchian in the midst of cold Corinthians that dominates the poem." Medea feels her alienation most acutely after she has been repudiated and discarded by her husband, Jason; she remembers when he was a stranger in her land and was indebted to her for saving his life. She implores him:

> Love, you have not forgot
> The long years passed in this Corinthian home?
> The great love I have borne you through the years?
> Nor that fair time when, in your mighty craft,
> You came, a stranger, to the Colchian shore?
> O strong you were; but not of such a strength
> To have escaped the doom of horrid death,
> Had not I, counting neither loss nor gain,
> Shown you the way to triumph and renown.

Nord remarks that "Levy, the anomalous Jewish woman, surely stands behind the alien and enraged Medea, the stranger in a strange land who is marked in physical type as in temperament."

"Magdalen" is about a prostitute who condemns the man who caused her ruin. Cynthia Scheinberg argues that in this poem Levy "seeks to challenge the common assumption surrounding prostitution and the notions of redemption in Christian society, even as it uses the voice of a Jewish woman to articulate the challenge." The claim that Levy is writing the poem as a Jewish woman challenging the authority of Jesus Christ appears to stretch the range of interpretations of "Magdalen" and is unconvincing.

The speaker of one of the lighter poems, "Sinfonia Eroica," which is dedicated to "Sylvia," remembers a summer afternoon concert that turned into a religious experience when her feelings of love became overpowering. As the concert progresses, her expression of affection follows the structure of a musical composition, gaining in momentum and power and finally reaching a crescendo:

> Then you, the melody, the summer heat,
> Mingled in all my blood and made it wine.
> Straight I forgot the world's great woe and mine;
> My spirit's murky lead grew molten fire;
> Despair itself was rapture.
>   Ever higher,
> Stronger and clearer rose the mighty strain;
> Then sudden fell; then all was still again,
> And I sank back, quivering as one in pain.

The speaker's climax subsides along with the music, and the poem concludes with a sweet tribute to the memory of her love.

In 1885 Levy anonymously translated Jean Baptiste Pérès's pamphlet *Comme quoi Napoleon n'a jamais existe* (1876) as *Historic and Other Doubts; or, The Non-Existence of Napoleon Proved*. While traveling in Italy in 1886 Levy met and became enamored of the novelist and aesthetician Vernon Lee (Violet Paget), dedicating a poem to her, and wrote the essay "The Ghetto at Florence" for

Levy at about seven

The Jewish Chronicle (republished in *The Complete Novels and Selected Writings of Amy Levy, 1861–1889*).

Four years passed between the publication of *A Minor Poet and Other Verse* and Levy's first novel, *The Romance of a Shop* (1888). In the interim she published many essays both in mainstream secular publications and in the Anglo-Jewish press. Beth Zion Lask Abrahams calls 1887 a "barren year" in which Levy published nothing, although Levy's biographer Linda Hunt Beckman has more recently identified a few publications for that year. Melvyn New points out that "her productivity was monumental; at year's end she would have only twenty-two more months to live, but in that span she published, at the least, three short novels, her largest collection of poetry . . . , more than a half-dozen short stories, and several essays." At some point during these years she wrote a short and disturbing poem, *A Ballad of Religion and Marriage*, that was not published until Clement Shorter printed twelve copies in pamphlet form in 1915. The poem takes a negative stance to both its title subjects, using images from the Pentateuch and the New Testament to highlight the inadequacy and anachronistic character of both religion and marriage. The speaker says that she has done what was expected of her, leading a monogamous, dull life, without the promised rewards. She envisions a time when love can be expressed freely and without impediment: "Grant, in a million years at most, / Folk shall be neither pairs nor odd– / Alas! we sha'n't be there to boast / 'Marriage has gone the way of God!'"

Levy's next three books were novels: *The Romance of a Shop,* in which orphaned sisters support themselves by opening a photography business; *Reuben Sachs: A Sketch* (1888), about a Jewish lawyer who chooses a political career over his love for a woman but dies soon after being elected to Parliament; and *Miss Meredith* (1889), a brief, lighthearted potboiler about an English governess who falls in love with the adult son of her aristocratic Italian employers. *Reuben Sachs* was heavily criticized in the Jewish press for its perceived confirmation of anti-Semitic stereotypes; some Gentile reviewers praised it for the same reason.

On 10 September 1889, one week after correcting the proofs of *A London Plane-Tree, and Other Verse* (1889), Levy killed herself by inhaling charcoal fumes in her parents' home at 7 Endsleigh Gardens in Bloomsbury. Some critics believe that her suicide was caused by the negative reaction of the Jewish community to *Reuben Sachs* and to her story "Cohen of Trinity," which appeared in *The Gentleman's Magazine* in May 1889 (republished in *The Complete Novels and Selected Writings of Amy Levy, 1861–1889*) and in which the self-hating Jew Leo Leuniger of *Reuben Sachs* reappears. Others have speculated that she was depressed about the death of her brother Alfred, possibly of syphilis, on 27 May 1887, or that she was afraid that she was about to fall victim to a hereditary form of insanity. But the evidence in her poetry and in testimony from friends such as Richard Garnett of her repeated bouts of clinical depression seems to offer reason enough for her suicide. Three years earlier Levy herself had written an essay for *The Jewish Chronicle*, "Jewish Children" (republished in *The Complete Novels and Selected Writings of Amy Levy, 1861–1889*), in which she said that Jewish parents overindulge their children and that "The Jewish child, descendant of many city-bred ancestors as he is, is apt to be a very complicated little bundle of nerves indeed, to whom woe betide should he meet with unduly rough handling." She ended the article by warning that

The rate of mental and nervous diseases among Jews is deplorably high. That the causes of this melancholy fact are numerous and complicated I do not deny. We are suffering no doubt for the conditions of our past existence; conditions which only our abnormal toughness and vitality have enabled us to survive at all; the comparative smallness of our numbers, our centuries of city life.

Levy's obituary in *The Jewish Chronicle* (16 September 1889) lauded her accomplishments and blamed her death on "a strength of mind far beyond her physical strength . . . combined with over-work." *The New York Times* (22 September 1889) erroneously gave her age as twenty-three and claimed that, had she lived, Levy would have surpassed Emma Lazarus, another Jewish woman writer, in significance.

Dedicated to Levy's friend and literary executrix, Clementina Black, *A London Plane-Tree, and Other Verse* is prefaced by an epigraph from Austin Dobson: "Mine is an urban Muse / And bound / By some strange law to paven ground." The poems are shorter than those in Levy's previous volumes, often no more than twelve lines in length. In this collection Levy largely discards the feminist anger and resentment of *Xantippe, and Other Verse* and *A Minor Poet and Other Verse*, engaging instead in a dialogue with the city and its inhabitants. Levy writes of a grove of trees thriving amid garrets and fog; she depicts the changing appearance of London as the seasons follow one another; and she sings the praises of an omnibus and a newspaper hawker, concluding that a simple urban existence is preferable to life in the country. Levy sees herself as part of a tradition of minor poets in the metropolis; she dedicates "London Poets (In Memoriam)" to her predecessors:

> They trod the streets and squares where I now tread,
> With weary hearts, a little while ago;
> When, thin and grey, and melancholy snow
> Clung to the leafless branches overhead;
> Or when the smoke-veiled sky grew stormy-red
> In autumn; with a re-arisen woe
> Wrestled, what time the passionate spring winds blow;
> And paced scorched stones in summer:–they are dead.
>
> The sorrow of their souls to them did seem
> As real as mine to me, as permanent.
> To-day, it is the shadow of a dream,
> The half-forgotten breath of breezes spent.
> So shall another soothe his woe supreme–
> "No more he comes, who this way came and went."

Several poems in *A London Plane-tree, and Other Verse* seem to portend Levy's suicide. In "The Promise of Sleep" the speaker imagines that the sleep of death will be as gentle as that which comes every night. The speaker of "In the Nower" (*nower* is an archaic expression meaning "nowhere") says: "There is no breath, no sound, no stir, / The drowsy peace to break: / I close my tired eyes–it were / So simple not to wake." In "The End of the Day" the speaker wishes that she could sleep and cease caring:

> And better far than thought I find
> The drowsy blankness of the mind
> More than all joys of soul or sense
> Is this divine indifference;
> Where grief a shadow grows to be,
> And peace a possibility.

"To Vernon Lee" apparently recalls a time when Levy visited Lee in Italy. Lee gives Levy a "snowy black-

Title page for Levy's second book, in which the poems are characterized by a mood of darkness and depression (courtesy of Special Collections, Thomas Cooper Library, University of South Carolina)

Frontispiece and title page for Levy's final book, for which she corrected the proofs one week before committing suicide (courtesy of Special Collections, Thomas Cooper Library, University of South Carolina)

thorn," and Levy responds with a "scarlet blossom." These flowers signify "the gifts the gods had given to each– / Hope unto you, and unto me Despair." New notes that this poem "raises a question that has surrounded Levy ever since her death": that of her sexual orientation. But he concurs with Nord, who says that "It is possible that Levy addressed such poems to women because she was a lesbian, but her conventional love lyrics do not at all give that impression."

Reviewing *A London Plane Tree, and Other Verse* in *The Academy* in (1 February 1890), William Sharp wrote that "its intellectual range is limited, and its expression, sometimes too derivative to be individual." He concluded, however, that "With their few technical shortcomings and their special virtues of sincerity, pathos, grace, and not infrequent delicate beauty, these last utterances of Miss Levy will be welcome to her many friends and admirers."

The second edition of *A Minor Poet and Other Verse*, published in 1891, includes one of the few known photographs of Levy as an adult. In the photograph, taken in Florence in 1889, Levy looks squarely at the camera, appearing weary and grave. E. K. Chambers says of the picture: "There is a face of no special beauty, the brow and eyes burdened with a weight of thought, the lips set as if in some reticence of sorrow." Quilter remembered Levy as a "small, dark girl, of unmistakably Jewish type, with eyes that seemed too large for the delicate features, and far too sad for their youthfulness of line and contour. In its way I had rarely seen a face which was at once so interesting, so intellectual, so beautiful, and alas! so unhappy. . . ." In her memoirs Katharine Tynan described Levy as having a "dreamy" and "charming little Eastern face." An illustration on the title page of the 1884 edition reflects the feeling of estrangement that characterizes the poems: it depicts a woman huddled on the ground next to a well outside a stone building; she is hugging her knees, with her head down. Beside her is a water jug, tipped over and empty.

In 1899 Levy's friend Ada Radford Wallas assessed Levy's poetic oeuvre in *The Academy*. Wallas disagrees with Sharp's criticism of Levy's poetry as derivative, asserting that the influence of Robert Browning and Heine helped her to grow as an artist: "in the manner of this open imitation, there is something scholarly. She makes no claim to Robert Browning's large humanity or Heine's bitter insight, but, nevertheless, her own power is steadily growing under the influence of each." Wallas concludes that because Levy died so young, it is impossible to gauge how great she would have become.

For all of Levy's attempts to write poetry that did not stress her Jewishness, she has been remembered almost exclusively as the author of *Reuben Sachs* and, therefore, as a Jewish writer. She has been most extensively discussed by Jewish scholars, who have debated whether she was a self-hating Jew. Since the 1990s, however, critics such as New, Nord, Scheinberg, and Isobel Armstrong have focused on Levy as a secular poet, which seems to be the approach she would have wanted.

Biography:

Linda Hunt Beckman, *Amy Levy: Her Life and Letters* (Athens: Ohio University Press, 2000).

References:

Beth Zion Lask Abrahams, "Amy Levy and the J. C.," *Jewish Chronicle*, 17 November 1961, p. 13;

Abrahams, "Amy Levy: Poet and Writer," *Anglo-Jewish Association Quarterly*, 6, no. 3 (1960): 11–17;

Isobel Armstrong, *Victorian Poetry: Poetry, Poetics, and Politics* (London: Routledge, 1993), pp. 319, 325, 340, 367, 372, 374–375, 482;

E. K. Chambers, "Poetry and Pessimism," *Westminster Review*, 138 (July–December 1892): 366–376;

Bryan Cheyette, "From Apology to Revolt: Benjamin Farjeon, Amy Levy, and the Post-Emancipation Anglo-Jewish Novel," *Transactions of the Jewish Historical Society of England* (January 1985): 254–265;

Ifor Evans, *English Poetry in the Later Nineteenth Century* (London: Methuen, 1966), pp. 353–354;

Audrey Fay Horton, "Apocalyptic Melancholy: The Poetry of Amy Levy," M.A. thesis, University of South Carolina, 1991;

Linda Hunt, "Amy Levy and 'the Jewish Novel': Representing Jewish Life in the Victorian Period," *Studies in the Novel*, 26 (Fall 1994): 235–253;

Beth Zion Lask, "Amy Levy," *Transactions of the Jewish Historical Society of England*, 11 (22 June 1926): 168–189;

Deborah Epstein Nord, "'Neither Pairs Nor Odd': Female Community in Late Nineteenth-Century London," *Signs: Journal of Women in Culture and Society*, 15 (Summer 1990): 733–754;

Warwick James Price, "Three Forgotten Poetesses," *Forum*, 47 (1912): 361–376;

Harry Quilter, "Amy Levy: A Reminiscence and a Criticism," in his *Preferences in Art, Life, and Literature* (London: Swan Sonnenschein, 1892), pp. 135–149;

Cynthia Scheinberg, "Miriam's Daughters: Women's Poetry and Religious Identity in Victorian England," dissertation, Rutgers University, 1992;

Katharine Tynan, *Twenty-five Years: Reminiscences* (New York: Devin-Adair, 1913), p. 330;

Edward Wagenknecht, "Amy Levy," in his *Daughters of the Covenant: Portraits of Six Jewish Women* (Amherst: University of Massachusetts Press, 1983), pp. 55–93;

Ada Radford Wallas, "The Poetry of Amy Levy," *Academy*, 57 (12 August 1899): 162–163;

Oscar Wilde, "Amy Levy," *Woman's World*, 3 (1890): 51–52.

Papers:

Amy Levy's papers are held by a London financial institution and are not available for inspection.

Annie Matheson
(1853 – 16 March 1924)

Florence Boos
University of Iowa

BOOKS: *The Religion of Humanity and Other Poems* (London: Percival, 1890);

Love's Music, and Other Poems (London: Sampson Low, Marston, 1894);

Love Triumphant, and Other New Poems (London: Innes, 1898);

Selected Poems Old and New (London: Frowde, 1899); republished as *Roses, Loaves, and Old Rhymes* (London: Frowde, 1911; revised and enlarged edition, London: Oxford University Press, 1918);

Snowflakes and Snowdrops. Christmas Rhymes and Valentine Verses for Schoolroom and Nursery (London: Johnson, 1900);

By Divers Paths: The Note-Book of Seven Wayfarers (London: Gay & Hancock, 1909);

The Story of a Brave Child: A Child's Life of Joan of Arc (London: Nelson, 1910);

Leaves of Prose . . . With Two Studies by May Sinclair (London: Swift, 1912);

Florence Nightingale: A Biography (London: Nelson, 1913);

Maytime Songs (London: M. Goschen, 1913);

A Plain Friend (Elizabeth Fry) (London: British Periodicals, 1920);

Our Hero of the Golden Heart. . . . With Biography and Portrait of D. O. Barnett (London: British Periodicals, 1920);

Hal's book for children of all ages . . . (London, 1921).

OTHER: Dinah M. Craik, *John Halifax, Gentleman*, introduction by Matheson (New York: Dodd, Mead, 1900);

George Eliot, *Scenes of Clerical Life*, introduction by Matheson (London: Dent, 1903);

Eliot, *Adam Bede*, introduction by Matheson (London: Dent, 1903);

Eliot, *Silas Marner: The Weaver of Raveloe*, introduction by Matheson (London: Dent, 1903);

Songs of Love and Praise for Home Singing, edited by Matheson (London: Dent, 1907);

Sayings from the Saints, collected by Matheson (London: Eveleigh Nash, 1908);

Annie Matheson

A Day Book for Girls, Chosen and Arranged from the Works of Many Poets and Prose Writers (London: Frowde, 1911);

A Little Book of Courage, compiled by Matheson (London: Gay & Hancock, 1913).

Annie Matheson wrote four volumes of well-received meditative and lyric poetry that appeared in the 1890s, two collections of essays and poems published in 1909 and 1912, and a final retrospective collection of poetry in 1918. She also contributed many essays to contemporary periodicals, including *The Athenaeum, Pall Mall Gazette, Macmillan's Magazine,* and *The Guardian,* and published several biographies for young people. An egalitarian feminist, Matheson wrote poetry in which she explored ecumenical approaches to ethics and spiritual experience, and with her prose she supported reformist schemes for the alleviation of poverty and social injustice.

The frontispieces to *Selected Poems Old and New* (1899) and *Roses, Loaves, and Old Rhymes* (1911) show a slender woman wearing a jacket and cropped hair, but relatively little is known about Matheson's life. She was born in 1853 in Blackheath (now in southeast London), the daughter of Elizabeth Cripps and the Reverend James Matheson, a Congregationalist minister, and her first home was in Oswestry, Shropshire, where she began writing poetry as a girl. She remarks obliquely in her introduction to *Selected Poems Old and New*:

> having nothing else to give, I might in gratitude have entwined the names of London, my birthplace; Oswestry, my first home; Nottingham, always kind to me for my father's sake; New York, Knutsford and Manchester, that long ago helped me to my only years of comparative leisure; and Oxford, the giver of more than can be written.

In her introduction to *The Religion of Humanity and Other Poems* (1890), her first volume, Matheson comments that she had "found a home in the Church," presumably the Church of England, for she refers to "those of us who are Anglicans" in *Leaves of Prose* (1912). She also mentions "brothers and sisters" in "Words and Ways of Children," an essay from *Leaves of Prose,* and dedicates *A Plain Friend* (1920) to "My Brother William Brooklyn Matheson / Tiratahi, Rangomai, New Zealand, 1920." At the time of her death in 1924 at seventy-one, she lived at Honeysuckle Cottage, Maybury Hill, Woking (in Surrey, southwest of London). The writer of her obituary in *The Times* (London) remarked that "her work . . . reflected the fine ardour of her mind, a detachment from materialism, and a childlike confidence of spirit. These qualities, together with a certain charming waywardness of which she herself was usually the first to see the humorous results, won her many friends, by whom she is held in a lasting and tender regard."

Matheson was thirty-seven when she dedicated *The Religion of Humanity and Other Poems* to "My Father and Mother." In her introduction she presents the book as an effort to accommodate readers who sought "fellowship in their search after the ancient answer to the ancient problems" in broadly ethical and ecumenical terms. She also rebuts views that dismiss the validity of theological poetry: "I cannot but hope that heresy and orthodoxy are not so far apart as men suppose, and that schism is in many instances not so much a fact as a misunderstanding."

In the title ode Matheson argues for the deist view that those who act well toward their fellow human beings exhibit a true faith, whatever their formal beliefs. "Sacred" events, by contrast, are hollow if they have no application to present-day life, and the rigid and censorious fall prey to hypocrisy, or even worse:

> the unholy greed
> Of those ill-fathered Pharisees who take
>   His awful Human Name
>   On their smooth lips, and make
> In the clear shining of the Morning Star
>   A little selfish glitter; quick to feed
>   Their vanity on others' sin and need
>   And bitter shame,
> While on the unthinking crowd, of hope forlorn,
> Descends a load too heavy to be borne,
>   Which they, who cast it on them from afar,
> Spurn under foot, nor touch with finger-tips,
>   Clutching at heaven for themselves, and then
>   Damning the souls of half their fellow-men.
> Christ save us from the hell of such a heaven!

Matheson enlivens these echoes of Matthew Arnold's weary cadences in "A Summer Night" with translations from Johann Wolfgang von Goethe and Heinrich Heine, and vigorous poetic denunciations of the poverty that surrounded her. One such denunciation—"A Song for Women," later reprinted by the Women's Protective and Provident League in leaflet form—became one of her best-known works.

> Within a dreary narrow room
>   That looks upon a noisome street,
>   Half fainting with the stifling heat
> A starving girl works out her doom.
>   *Yet not the less in God's sweet air*
>   *The little birds sing free of care,*
>   *And hawthorns blossom everywhere.*
> . . . .
> With envy of the folk who die,
>   Who may at last their leisure take,
>   Whose longed-for sleep none roughly wake,
> Tired hands the restless needle ply.
>   *But far and wide in meadows green*
>   *The golden buttercups are seen,*
>   *And reddening sorrel nods between.*

Modernist ironies emerge from Matheson's stark juxtapositions of the suffocating sweatshop with the emblematic, almost Pre-Raphaelite beauties of "God's sweet air."

Matheson achieves other forms of heightened introspection in the enforced concision of the twenty-five sonnets in *The Religion of Humanity,* which

Our hearts joined company, through wind and wave
And stress of weather, kin for evermore.

In *Love's Music, and Other Poems* (1894), wryly dedicated "To My Publishers, Past and Present...," Matheson comments on religious conventions. In "Pastor Ignotus, His Plea for Cremation," for example, a dramatic monologue in the manner of Robert Browning's "Abt Vogler," the "unknown" pastor denounces "Christian" burial:

What! Do this last disservice?—God forbid!
Let poison lurk beneath my coffin lid
  To work its direful mischief year by year,
  About the human world I hold so dear,
And so dishonour me when I am dead?

Nay! when the Master calls, let cleansing fire
Set free the body of my soul's desire,
  As golden corn uplifts its shining head
  From husk that's slowly burned in earthy bed,
Like to the golden grain and yet unlike!

In some of Matheson's best poems, brief haiku-like lyrics hover between song and tonal meditations. Death comes gently, for example, in "The Snow":

As noiseless as the deepest love I fall,
  As mute and tender and divinely pure;
When sunshine comes, I hide away from all
  In roots that make the coming blossoms sure.

For many a man who must as outcast fare,
  Having no roof, and bidden still move on,
I make a bed where he will lose his care.

In a collection of reviews included at the end of *Love's Music, and Other Poems*, a writer for *The Saturday Review* considered Matheson's "gifts ... more clearly proclaimed in the briefer poems," and another critic, writing for *The Westminster Review*, found "Some of the love songs and ... translations, from Heine and Goethe especially ... worthy of note." A reviewer for *The Literary World* praised *Love's Music* for its "moving impulse of earnestness" and *The St. James's Gazette* found the poems "philosophical and humanitarian."

Matheson prefaced her next book, *Love Triumphant, and Other New Poems* (1898), with an etching of G. F. Watts's painting *Love Triumphant* and inscribed it "to the sorrowful, the downtrodden, the oppressed, and above all, to that religious community whose sufferings are a blot upon our unchristian Christianity ...":

  I am a Jew
Son of the race to whom the Eternal gave,
Not the poor blessings of a slave,

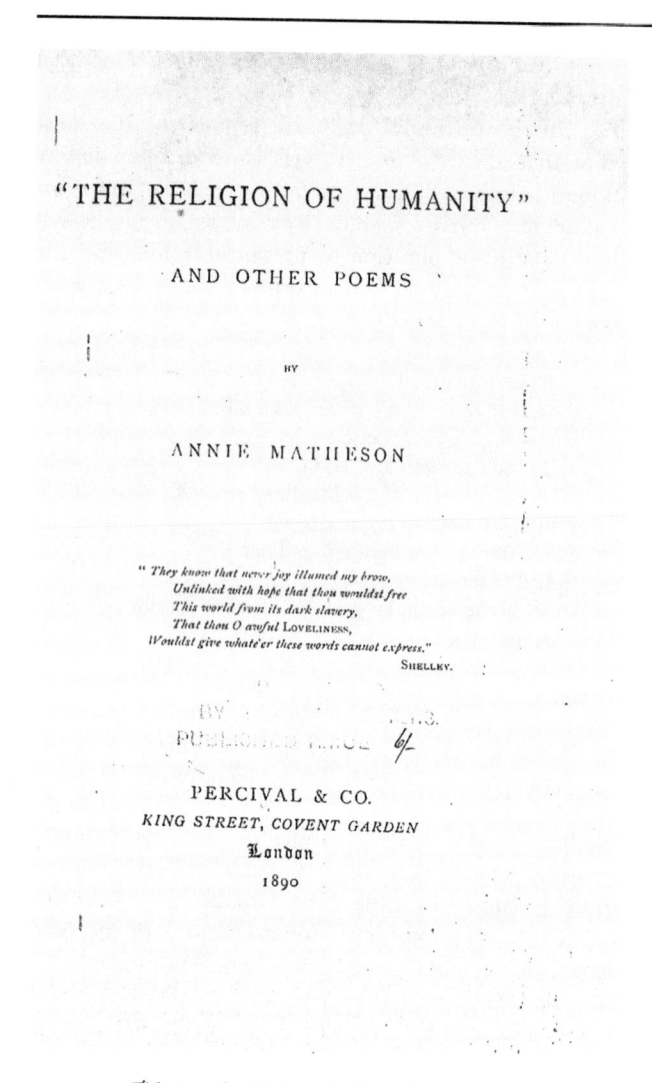

Title page for Matheson's first volume of poetry

include homages to people and antecedents she admired, such as Omar Khayyám, William Wordsworth, Thomas Carlyle, Robert Browning, and George Eliot. In "An Meine Freundin" she also expresses a quasi-Rossettian sense of spiritual union with a fellow voyager and "sister soul":

Sweet recognition, when the soul looks out
  Just for an instant from the unveiled eyes,
  And love in either heart grows rich and wise,
Too glad for fear, too absolute for doubt!
As a ship in mid-ocean tossed about,
  Suddenly sighting with a glad surprise
  Another toiler under the same skies
To the same port, puts all her signals out,
So, when thy life my life's horizon crossed,
  A fellow-voyager to the far shore
Toward which I sailed, but one more strong and brave,
Whose courage had won much my faltering lost;–

> But the fierce chastisement of sons,
>   The elect to pain, the few,
> Chosen and blotted out His world to save
>   In sunless darkness like to Ajalon's!
>   Others, by their false gods,
>   Are beaten with rods,
> But we, who once the sacred mountain trod—
> The kinsmen of the Everlasting God,
>   Are smitten and scourged, and lashed with scorpions!
>   ("Jew to Gentile")

Matheson's artistic interests also reemerge in *Love Triumphant, and Other New Poems*. "Love Triumphant" is also the title of a sketch by Edward Burne-Jones, and Matheson drafted a sonnet in commemoration of Watts, one on the stoic death of the artist Frederick Leighton, and another on Leighton's painting, *Elisha Raising the Son of the Shunammite*. She also evokes *When Adam Delved and Eve Span*, Burne-Jones's beautifully crafted frontispiece for William Morris's *A Dream of John Ball* (1892), in "Labour," a terza-rima ballad:

> It is not labour makes a man a slave;
> Gyves cannot bind a spirit pure and brave;
> But some have bought their freedom with a grave. . . .

More conspicuously conventional objects of Matheson's memorials include Alfred Tennyson, Robert Browning, William Gladstone ("The Great Commoner"), and the queen ("The Year of Rejoicing"). Rather remarkably, she also wrote muckraking poetic denunciations of lethal factory pollution ("Lead-Poisoning. A Dramatic Fragment"), inadequate sewage ("London Water"), and general bourgeois indifference ("Against Social Carelessness"):

> Could we but know how black our murders are,
>   By help ungiven, courageous deeds undone,—
>   If, 'twixt the rising and the setting sun,
> Our lives were doomed to watch them, near and far,
> Those countless souls and bodies that we mar,
>   Locked up in prisons where our gauds are spun. . . .

In "The Priest's Ballad," one of her more explicitly moralistic poems, a beautiful and much-praised woman of means is turned away from heaven, "for the sake of your sister, seven days dead." When she protests that she has no sister, the Gatekeeper scornfully reminds her:

> . . . beautiful work for your dainty wear
> Your sister fashioned; . . . can you dare
>   To whisper to God the cost? . . .
>
> "Such things are hidden"—his sad lip curled—
> "From women like you through all the world—
>   She is Mary Magdalen's guest."

Sent back "to the dark town," the woman seeks "my sister, that she may plead / For the woman who let her die. . . ."

Matheson pays more or less explicit homage to Robert Browning in the poems she characterizes as "dramatic lyrics" ("To 'Carissima,'" "Jew to Gentile," "From the Battle-Field," "The Speculative Monk," "A Musician," and "Meeting and Parting"), but two of the compositions are Debussy-like lyric reveries. In "The Mist" she writes:

> The sun and the dew were so far apart,
>   The world would have said they could never have met,
> But the sun looked down with a burning heart
>   When the earth with the crystal dew was wet;
> So the dew went up in a golden mist—
>   And they kist,
> Till the dew came back at the close of day,
>   In a robe of the colour of amethyst,—
> And a crown of pearls on the green earth lay,
>   Like tears of hope and of wild regret
> That told of an unforgotten tryst,
>   Ere the sun had set.

In "To M. A. M.," an elegy, she writes:

> We miss thee, miss thee, miss thee; ah, and yet
>   At moments when some tender long-sought boon
>   Falls at our feet, then in the solemn noon
> Of joy's great sunlight, like an amulet,
> To wear in secret against worldly fret,
>   The quick thought comes that we shall meet thee soon,
>   Where we shall need no light of sun nor moon,
> And where the love shall neither rise nor set;
> Then swifter, sweeter, nearer, comes belief
> That Love perchance through thee has wrought the gift.

Latent tensions between Matheson's sententious and lyric muses emerged rather ironically in two reviews of *Love Triumphant*. The *Athenaeum* critic believed the volume's author had "a virile mind; she is an Amazon, inspired with a fine fighting enthusiasm for humanitarian causes, and she wields her verse like a sword or spear." The writer's equally enthusiastic colleague at the *St. James Gazette,* however, found her "not one of those women poets who strive to write as men; she has the characteristics of her sex, and is before all things gentle, sympathetic, humane." *The Jewish Chronicle* reviewer felt no such cognitive dissonance: "Jew to Gentile" was spoken by "a liberal soul, as liberal in fact as Miss Matheson herself."

In the preface to *Selected Poems* the slender woman—who looks much younger than forty-six on its frontispiece—calls again for confessional tolerance: "Our faith stands self-condemned if it go not down into the very depths of the social order and of the

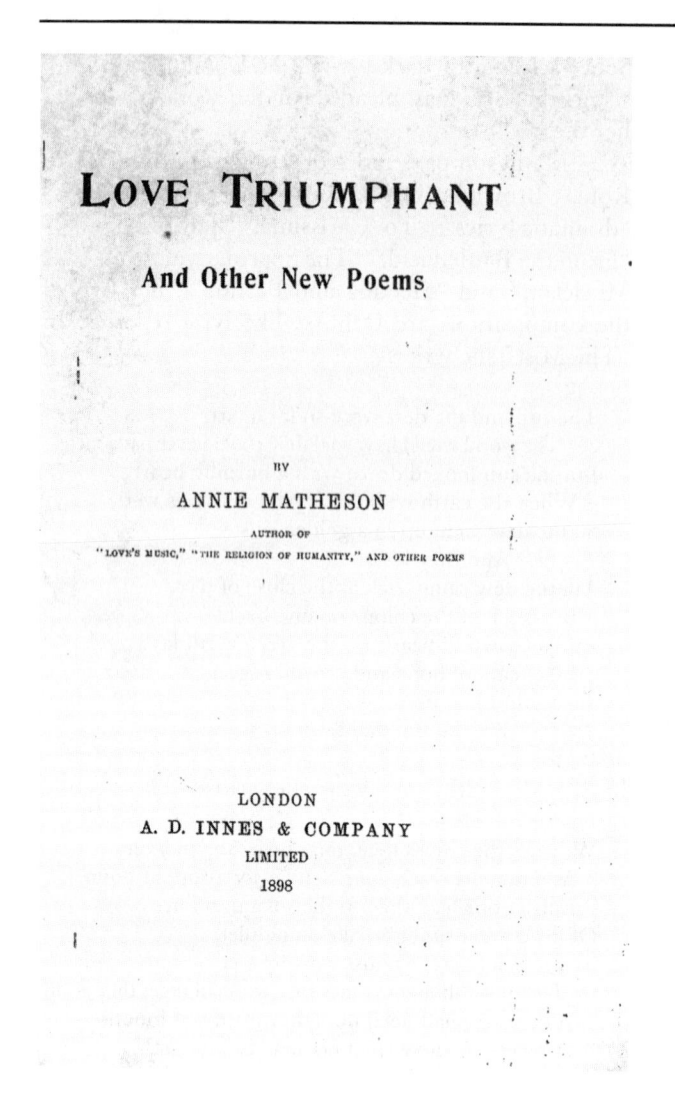

Title page for Matheson's third book of poems

individual lot, with a vital and re-forming power. For do we not believe that Christianity is deeper and wider than any number of ceremonies and opinions?"

Matheson added several new poems and a section of "Earliest Poems (Published Before 1880)" to her selections for this volume, along with two political sonnets on the Dreyfus case. She also included more of her "Christmas songs" in a second printing the next year, newly introduced by Charles Harold Herford, a friend and professor of literature at Manchester University, who praised her as "the familiar poet-friend of a wide circle," and a practitioner of "the catholicity of the mystic, not of the eclectic; that which reads everywhere the symbols of Divine Love. . . . No apostle of Positivism has shown a deeper reverence for humanity, no apostle of the Labour Church a profounder sympathy with toil."

Matheson published her own tribute to the "wide circle" a decade later, in *By Divers Paths: The Note-Book of Seven Wayfarers* (1909), an unusual collection of monthly prose and verse meditations. Her "wayfarers" include Herford, Charles Clement Cotterill, Maude Egerton King, Greville Matheson Macdonald, May Sinclair, and Eleanor Tyrell as well as herself, and an explanation for the book's format appears in its preface (signed "Annie Matheson, Maybury, Woking"):

> [My friends] have at my request, wreathed [my book] about with their beautiful things; for which purpose I have withdrawn rather more than a third of my own pages, in addition to what I had already rejected as too controversial, or elaborate, or heavy. I am encircled now by their more scholarly and piquant leaves—petals that I trust may fashion my boss of tiny things into something that will claim distant kinship with that small yellow-centered flower that grows by the wayside and looks toward the sun.

Her friends' "scholarly and piquant leaves" include a meditation on "Dawn" by Cotterill, author of *Human Justice for Those at the Bottom* (1907); historical and literary place descriptions by Herford; travel narratives by Tyrrell, author of children's books; allegories by the antivivisectionist Macdonald, also the author of *The Ethics of Revolt* (1907), and poems by Sinclair and King, author of *My Book of Songs and Sonnets* (1893). Fourteen more poems and twenty-seven essays comprise Matheson's own contribution to the volume—its "boss of tiny things."

In the traditions of Charles Lamb and Walter Pater, among others, Matheson's prose essays range from whimsical descriptions of cats ("Three White Princesses") to lyrical descriptions of nature and appreciative commentaries on the works of Tennyson, Burne-Jones, Walt Whitman, and Elizabeth and Robert Browning. A personal reflection appears in "Birds," for example, one of the essays for July:

> the window of the room where I slept was wide open and a lamp burning. Perhaps the light had beckoned through the darkness to some homeless little brother that had lost his way. How gladly would I have soothed and comforted the eager, fluttering heart, stroked the soft brown plumage, and mothered the tiny quivering body. But fear stood between us as a dividing angel. The terror of the bird terrified me also, the shirring and swishing of the small wings made music of revolt and anguish, and the swift, violent movements were so blindly bewildering that it seemed, the next instant, they would beat into my face and buffet my eyes. How the vexed soul came there, or whither it vanished, will always remain a mystery; for, while I slipped out of the door to ask

counsel of my more knowledgeable neighbour, the tiny wanderer fled through the window. But a symbol there seemed to be of many a human crisis in which some stormy spirit, communicating its passion to another with a stress of inexplicable moral whirlwind, may find the only kindness in a noiseless flight and silent farewell. . . .

In other essays Matheson's gentle cadences and observant sympathies can arrest the reader's attention in unexpected ways. In "Ghosts," for example, an essay for November, she touches lightly on revenants and the elusive suggestions of transcendence they evoke:

Yet is there food for laughter and for humour, grim or delicate, in our own errant and philistine misuse of the word which marks this higher kinship. That lovely radiant flame within the lamp, that half-veiled vital presence which brings a flash of loveliness to the plainest face, that quickening force of personality which thrills us to the finger-tips—where in the whole sentient universe is there anything more divinely real? Yet the word which names this radiant and throbbing mystery, this ghost that is in man and woman, and that, for aught we know, may step to and fro unseen through the doorways of what men call death—this . . . heir of the undying secret—has lent his royal title to a mere scarecrow peg for grave-clothes, a grotesque . . . simulacrum, a chilly and dissolving shade, a degraded drudge of a word that frightens children and walks in darkness.

In her forty-one essays and ten poems for *Leaves of Prose . . . With Two Studies by May Sinclair* (1912), Matheson returned to her social-critical preoccupations, conjoining reformist ends and literary means in mildly unorthodox ways. In "Sordello at the East End," for example, she finds traces of Browning's poem in the foundation of University Settlement houses, and she seeks antecedents in "Philosophy, Poetry and the Labour Party" of the "desired intercourse between labour and academic knowledge" in works of Whitman, Percy Bysshe Shelley, Elizabeth Barrett Browning, and George Meredith.

In other essays she praises "those hard-working enthusiasts who . . . are doing their best to save the glories of tree and moorland from the hand of the artificial spoiler" ("A Fragment"), and finds such democratic ideals expressed in Christina Rossetti's "Royal Princess" (1863), Dante Gabriel Rossetti's "Burden of Nineveh" (1856), William Morris's *Earthly Paradise* (1868-1870), and Robert Browning's *The Ring and the Book*, as well as Dinah Craik's popular account of the inner life of a tanner in *John Halifax, Gentleman*. Something akin to her beloved Whitman's egalitarianism clearly animated Matheson's ardent conviction that "I have had the high honour of living in the closest intercourse with labouring people, and I know that their lives, which in pathos are ever on the edge of tragedy, often breathe the very spirit of the deepest poetry."

Other essays include a rather unusual study of "The Children in George Eliot's Stories," some introductions Matheson had written for 1903 Dent editions of Eliot's *Scenes of Clerical Life, Silas Marner,* and *Adam Bede,* and appreciations of the poetry of Walter Scott ("The Lady of the Lake," one of Matheson's childhood favorites); Arthur Hugh Clough ("Thrysis in a London Square" and "Forgotten Books V. A Pastoral"); and Elizabeth Barrett Browning ("Memorial to Mrs. Browning," "A Flower for Mrs. Browning's Grave," and "Mrs. Browning as a Social Reformer"). Anticipating the tastes of another fin de siècle, Matheson also finds much to praise in Christina Rossetti's use of symbolism:

the sense of sweet surprise and inevitableness in her cadences, . . . with . . . that just economy of language and metaphor characteristic of what is final and unfathomable in feeling . . . make her appeal . . . wider and more varied . . . while for melody and passion . . . it would not be easy to find a lyrist beside whom one need fear to name her. . . .

A rare glimpse into her personal life appears in Matheson's description of her early desires to write ("Words and Ways of Children"):

there came over her a dumb, passionate desire to embody in these hieroglyphic signs, . . . though she was quite unable to express it in spoken words, some record of a lovely pastoral vision which was haunting her. . . . she can still see in imagination the long, somewhat bare upper room, with its three little white beds, where there came to her the desperate impulse to dash down in lines and circles what she was too shy to express in audible speech, and what, indeed, altogether transcended such possibilities of language as were within her reach. And this shyness was mixed with a scarcely defined belief that this peaceful other-world vision . . . might possibly gain credence if it could only get itself embodied in written symbols; and then how surprised the elders would be who . . . had no idea of the secret treasure which was locked within her memory!

One of the poems Matheson interspersed among the volume's prose essays expresses a recurrent plea for children living in the city to have access to the healing powers of nature ("In Early Autumn"):

> At summer dawn, that makes the world anew
> In primal loveliness of Eden's birth,
> And bathes the blossoms with the heavenly dew
> That gives a daily childhood to the earth,
> *When beauty pierces like a beckoning cry,*
> *Oh, let the children share the earth and sky!*

The essays and poems of *Leaves of Prose* were Matheson's last literary criticisms, ethical musings, and lyric verse.

Moved in her last years by her obvious fondness for children (and perhaps also by publishers' selective readiness to offer such work to women), Matheson turned to the drafting of carefully researched biographies for the young, and her first two subjects, Joan of Arc and Florence Nightingale, reflect her lifelong interest in the actuating power of religious faith.

Matheson addresses her preface to *The Story of a Brave Child: A Child's Life of Joan of Arc* (1910) "To those older people who give this book to the children for whom it was written," and expresses her aim "to stir the imagination of some who in after years will more fully understand" its ideas. She studied original sources and documents with care and drew on them for testimonies and dialogues. She also sketched a plausible social context for Joan's "voices," explaining clearly the issues of succession at stake in the siege of Orleans, and commenting at some length on Joan's peasant childhood and the brutalities and ironies of war. Matheson effectively softened and abbreviated Jeanne d'Arc's betrayal and execution, but she provided in *The Story of a Brave Child* a surprisingly clear, sober, and even harrowing account of a woman-warrior who was *unique en son genre*.

Florence Nightingale: A Biography (1913), Matheson's 374–page historical and scholarly labor of love, appeared five years before Lytton Strachey's scathing portrait of Nightingale's obsessions in *Eminent Victorians* (1918). Matheson summarizes some of the achievements of Nightingale's life in an introductory chapter, and comments pointedly that good children's literature should not be "without interest to people of my generation." Well aware of Nightingale's less attractive traits, she focuses primarily on her motivations and accomplishments, and provides a measured account of Nightingale's tutelage at Kaiserswerth, her campaign to improve sanitation in India, and her efforts to establish public-health nurses for the British poor. She also gave attention to the lives and efforts of Nightingale's collaborators, and interviewed several who were still alive.

In a new edition of *Roses, Loaves, and Old Rhymes* (1918) Matheson reprinted most of the contents of *Selected Poems* but added to them four new poems from her volumes of prose and fourteen "Songs of the People and Sonnets of the Great War." Despite her praise for "the unadorned directness which should characterize songs of the people," World War I blunted Matheson's internationalist and populist ardor, as it did that of many others.

One of her sonnets denounces Irish abstention, for example ("To Ireland, by an English Heretic"), and others praise the involvement of "Courageous, gentle, generous India" ("To India"), or depicts the war as a holy crusade ("To Arms," "Send Us More Men," "For God and Right," "To a Mother Whose Son Fell Fighting for His Country on a Foreign Field"). Only the two sonnets she devotes to "A League of Nations" express tentative hopes for better things:

> Such hell of slaughter must not ever again
> Defile our earth; demoniac sin, withstood,
> Like some old dragon shall be, fangless, bound;
> Nor will their death and wounds be counted vain
> Whose warfare wrought the world's new Brotherhood.

In the last years of her life Matheson edited a series of "Rose and Dragon" biographies for the young and wrote two of them: *Our Hero of the Golden Heart*, a life of Canon Denis Oliver Barnett, and *A Plain Friend*, a biography of Elizabeth Fry.

Matheson's brief but persuasive account in *A Plain Friend* of the ambience of the heroine's Quaker girlhood includes a selection of letters and testimonies from those who knew her, and sketches briefly Fry's efforts to reform conditions at Newgate and the campaigns that followed. In its preface Matheson also recommends "that enchanting volume," William Butler Yeats's *The Secret Rose,* and expresses renewed reformist hopes "that even as obscure runlets feed mighty rivers—[the biographies] may play their part in . . . drawing into closer sympathy of mutual understanding, the different orders of society; restoring to rightful honour the claims alike of manual labour and handicraft and of a really international and popular art."

Lady Elizabeth Balfour, a seasoned advocate of women's suffrage, also added an accompanying foreword to the volume, in which she encourages readers to emulate Fry's challenge to "the barbarous and brutal cruelty that was tolerated in the prisons of that day," and asks rhetorically whether there are not "similar inconsistencies in our own day? . . . is not our prison system nearly as defective? What of the cruelty of solitary confinement, of the orthodox attitude of the gaoler to the prisoner, of the mental vacuity of prison life. . . ?"

An intriguing list of "titles in preparation" for Matheson's series also appeared in the endpapers for *A Plain Friend*. The list includes projected volumes by Matheson herself on "Lincoln's Citizenship," "Comrade Citizens (Florence Nightingale and Lord Herbert)," and "Heroes of Mines and Railways" (with Bertram Pickard), as well as biographies of Thomas More, Henry Fawcett, and the Indian poet "Madame Naidu," and more general studies of "Back to the Land," "The Power of Co-operation," "William Morris and Handicrafts," and "The People's Part in the World-Music." The range of subjects is impressive, especially when one considers again that Matheson conceived the "Rose and Dragon" as a series of volumes for children, but the project apparently died with her in 1924.

During her lifetime Annie Matheson's poetry, songs, meditative compilations, and children's books found many readers, but there is no extant collection of her later poetry, and no biographical account or memoir of her has survived. She was an accomplished poet, essayist, and author of meditative prose, and a careful historical biographer of exemplary lives. Her didactic poetry was vigorous, her lyrics evoked a peaceful spirit, and her personal blend of contemplative aestheticism and Fabian social democracy gave artistic expression to the reformist hopes and ideals of her time.

References:

Isobel Armstrong, Joseph Bristow, and Cath Sharrock, *Nineteenth-Century Women Poets* (Oxford: Clarendon Press, 1996);

Virginia Blain, Patricia Clements, and Isobel Grundy, *The Feminist Companion to Literature in English: Women Writers from the Middle Ages to the Present* (New Haven: Yale University Press, 1990).

Susan Miles
(Ursula Wyllie Roberts)
(16 September 1888 – 12 May 1975)

Becky W. Lewis
University of South Carolina

BOOKS: *The Cause of Purity and Women's Suffrage,* as Roberts (London: Church League for Women's Suffrage, 1912);
Dunch, Adventurers All, a Series of Young Poets Unknown to Fame, no. 18 (Oxford: Blackwell, 1918);
Annotations (London & New York: Oxford University Press, 1922);
Little Mirrors, and Other Studies in Free-Verse (Oxford: Blackwell, 1924);
The Hares, and Other Verses (London: Elkin Mathews, 1925);
Blind Men Crossing a Bridge (London: Constable, 1934; New York: Stokes, 1935);
Rabboni (London: Andrew Dakers, 1942);
News! News! (London: Privately printed, 1943);
Portrait of a Parson (London: Allen & Unwin, 1955);
Lettice Delmar: A Novel in Verse (London: Linden Press, 1958);
A Morsel of Gold and Other Studies (Bedford: Romany Press, 1962);
Epigrams and Jingles (Bedford: Romany Press, 1962);
Rainbows and Other Verses (Bedford: Romany Press, 1962).

OTHER: *Childhood in Verse and Prose,* compiled by Miles (London: Humphrey Milford, Oxford University Press, 1923);
An Anthology of Youth in Verse and Prose, compiled by Miles (London: John Lane, 1925).

Susan Miles (Ursula Wyllie Roberts; photograph by Kamal)

In 1962 "Susan Miles" set up her own publishing company, Romany Press, in Bedford, as she "had a stubborn belief that what she had written was less negligible than contemporary critics would think it." She published three small books of poetry that year; one of them, *A Morsel of Gold and Other Studies,* ends with a list of other writings by Miles that is prefaced by the poignant note "All out of print–." Miles's work never was reprinted, and it is not widely known today. Her poetry merits study, however, for its quiet irony, serious purpose, and psychological insight. Her infatuation with words and experimentation with language place her in the modernist camp. In her time she was popularly known mainly for *Dunch* (1918), her first book of poetry, which deals with her experiences as a pastor's wife in a rural village; her most critically acclaimed work was a novel, *Blind Men Crossing a Bridge* (1934). As a young woman she worked for woman suffrage, and she campaigned all her life for the ordination of women as priests in the Church of England. She was also committed to pacifism. The themes in her poetry reflect her commitment to these ideals.

Miles was born Ursula Wyllie in Meerut, India, on 16 September 1888. She was the youngest of eight children of Lieutenant Colonel Robert John Humphrey Wyllie and Emily Wyllie; her mother was the daughter of Jonathan Holt Titcomb, the first bishop of Rangoon, Burma. Soon after Ursula Wyllie was born, her father settled her mother and the six children who were still living at home in Dorking, south of London, before returning to India. Glimpses of her childhood can be gleaned from poems such as "To My Mother," in which she remembers writing a letter to her mother:

> And Nurse posted it.
> It was mostly crosses and pothooks
> And blots:
> But you liked it.

Miles uses this poignant poem to dedicate *Dunch* to her mother, who will appreciate the book even if "no one else likes it."

Another poem about Miles's childhood, "Catechism," in *A Morsel of Gold and Other Studies,* reveals an early ironic attitude toward organized religion. A "new young Vicar has read aloud a long, dull Lesson," and a girl, Perpetua Ramsey, is praised for her answer to the vicar's questions about it. Perpetua reveals to her friend, who admires how well Perpetua listened to the lesson: "But I didn't know I had been listening. . . . I don't believe I *was* listening" and confesses that she is "baffled by the strangeness / Of Vicars and of Hebrews and her own young mind." When the friend walks on, Perpetua happily dismisses "all life's perplexities" as she looks forward to Sunday tea "With spiced gingerbread, and doughnuts, And hot and buttery / Buns." This iconoclastic view of organized religion permeates Miles's writing throughout her life.

Wyllie was educated at various schools in London, then received private tutoring and attended university extension lectures in Redhill, south of the city. One of her lecturers, the novelist John Cowper Powys, wrote a letter on her behalf when she applied for a scholarship to the University of Cambridge. Her application was turned down. Later in life she completed a degree at London University.

While visiting cousins in Düsseldorf, Germany, in 1908, Wyllie met the Reverend William Corbett Roberts. Fourteen years her senior, Roberts, an Anglican deacon, had become a socialist while studying at the University of Oxford. His first impression of Wyllie, she wrote later in *Portrait of a Parson* (1955), was that she was "conventional and formal–'stuck' was his description." In an unpublished memoir she says that she asked him, "How long do you think it will be before women are ordained?" He was disconcerted by the question, since, even though he considered himself a feminist, the notion of female ordination had never occurred to him. They were married on 13 February 1909 in St. Katharine's Church, Merstham, Surrey, seven months after their initial meeting; they did not take communion during the ceremony, as Wyllie had broken away from the church. She wrote in *Portrait of a Parson* that "however wilful and unworthy his wife was, and however much of a hindrance and an embarrassment at times, his loyalty and his devotion never failed."

The newlyweds moved to Crick, a village in Northamptonshire, where William Roberts was rector. They were out of place in the old-fashioned rural parish: he knew nothing about agriculture, and he disapproved of his parishioners' Low Church form of worship; her youthful exuberance and liberal beliefs were not welcome in the conservative village, nor did she take the trouble to learn the local social customs. An article in the *Northampton Mercury* (29 October 1909), headlined "Crick Choir on Strike–Exit During Service," refers to the "peculiar notions of the Rector, the Rev. W. C. Roberts": when he asked the boys in the choir to leave the church before the sermon, the adult members walked out in sympathy. The last paragraph notes: "Mrs. Roberts, the Rector's wife, by the way, is a pronounced suffragette, and on the occasion of the King's visit to Rugby occupied herself in selling the suffragette paper in Rugby streets." In *Portrait of a Parson* Miles says of the villagers' reaction to her husband:

> it was a slow process, this "getting used" to him. There was a threat to break the Rectory windows one Christmas Eve. . . . on another Sunday the Churchwarden interrupted the Rector with the shout, "that's a lie!"; one morning after a dance in the Rectory club-room every plant in the adjoining conservatory was black and wizened, having been sprayed with weed-killer overnight. . . .

Miles takes on herself the lion's share of the blame for the couple's many blunders in Crick, calling herself "an over-sensitive, shy, ignorant, child-wife, with a conscience that drove her, against the trend of her natural inclinations, into activities that inevitably made for trouble."

In 1912 Ursula Roberts published *The Cause of Purity and Women's Suffrage,* a pamphlet in a series organized by the Church League for Women's Suffrage. She argues that the expansion of the male franchise had led to the establishment of labor unions and, consequently, to higher wages for men; allowing women to vote would give them the power to negotiate for better pay and more

Frontispiece and title page for Miles's third volume of poems (1924), about small moments in the lives of ordinary people

employment options, and so would help to do away with prostitution. She also joined forces with prominent churchwomen such as A. Maude Royden to campaign for the ordination of women in the Church of England, writing letters to the bishop and publishing articles on the subject.

In 1915, tired of trying to promote socialism, feminism, and pacifism in conservative Crick, William Roberts took a position teaching English in St. Stephen's College in Delhi, India for six months. Both "revelled in the life and work in Delhi" and hoped to stay; however, the heat of India was injurious to her health. Her poem "Microcosm" (in *Little Mirrors,* 1924) reflects her Delhi experience. The poem is set in St. Stephen's Hospital. She describes the patients she meets–a "Memsahib" who cries because she has just lost her baby, "a brown baby" who has just lost its mother, a naked child covered with sores and wearing a necklace of yellow marigolds, "babbling of them." For the poet, the child's "unintelligent babble" and display of "now her marigolds, / Now her sores," become "The voice of the unintelligible universe, / Beautiful and appalling."

In 1918 Roberts published *Dunch;* the title is her fictionalized name for Crick. Because she did not want her husband's parishioners to recognize themselves in the poems, she adopted the pseudonym "Susan Miles." She later explained that she chose "Susan" because it was a good, plain name and "Miles" because she happened to be visiting an elderly lady of that name on the day she decided to use a pen name. The twenty-six poems in *Dunch,* most of which are in free verse, depict the lives and thoughts of the people of a rural parish. The title poem celebrates village life by cataloguing aspects of it that the poet likes, such as "the butcher being not 'the butcher,' / But Tom Crisp." It includes vivid thumbnail portraits of the townspeople: for example, Miss Phoebe Underwood, retired schoolmistress,

> . . . now spends her mornings
> Writing Limericks, for competition,
> In praise of cigarettes.

Yet manages to create an atmosphere
In which one thinks instinctively
Of fine, plain needle-work,
Fine, sloped and elegant penmanship,
Samplers and elderberry wine,
Linseed tea,
Skirts worn out round the bottom
By curtseying to quality,
And those other characteristics of an estimable age.

"Dunch" also reveals Miles's sense of humor: she writes of "Dot Fretter, / Who, when the Sunday lesson was on Pharoah's dreams, / Was asked, in introduction, what you sometimes had when you were asleep at night, / And, answered 'Fleas.'"

While "Dunch" depicts a cozy village, the acerbic "A Reaction" illustrates the small-mindedness and unkindness that can be encountered in a rural setting. Miles attacks the triviality of local conversation ("the price of flannelette"), the social obligations that the rector's wife is expected to shoulder ("ask the schoolmaster's wife to tea, / Or the churchwarden's wife to dinner"), the gossips who "chatter / About troubles that tear my heart," men "yelling filth" from the public houses, church members who "hint at hateful things," and the parishioner who, with a "saw-like voice," remarks that the poet "should make 'quite a nice little parson's wife,'" if she "would give up all that silly nonsense about the Vote." One reviewer described Miles in these poems as "an artist—with a scalpel." Other poems in the collection make the reader want to know more about the characters: a curate enjoys gossiping about his day to his elderly aunt; a woman suddenly realizes that she is middle-aged when she has to pack up her belongings to move; a boy carries a bundle of daffodils as if they were the star of Bethlehem.

For the most part, reviewers praised *Dunch*. Katherine Tynan, however, had mixed feelings about the work. Writing in *The Bookman* (June 1918), she called it

a queer book, with qualities. Those who are repelled by the deliberate ugliness of the first part of the book should turn to the later poems. It is difficult to understand how the ugly realism of the village poems—if poems these irregular stanzas can be called—should come from the same hand and mind that produced "Cor Mundum Creavit" or "The Braggart," or any one of a dozen poems towards the end of the book which prove that the writer has gifts of beauty, tenderness, and deep thinking, of which we shall hear again when she has shed her inexorable realism. Yet perhaps there is something to be said for the poet to whom nothing of the stuff of life is common or unclean.

The poems that Tynan praised are written in traditional verse forms rather than in Miles's preferred free verse. They are also more abstract than those in the early part of the book, and they play with religious themes. In "The Braggart" a confident and gay cherry blossom announces that she will never die. In her lonely, fluttering death she has a flash of eternity, and the poet realizes the cherry blossom's boast was true. "Cor Mundum Creavit" (Heart Made Clean) imagines what it would be like to speak to Jesus, "to feel black sin confessed," and to receive the vision of a clean heart. Miles was inspired to write the poem by making her first formal confession at a women's retreat. In 1917 William Roberts became rector of St. George's, Bloomsbury. During this time Miles completed her degree in London University, earning first class honors in Philosophy in 1918. She took a position at Bedford College for Women in Regent's Park in London, coaching students in ethics and philosophy.

She showed promise as a teacher and was encouraged by colleagues; she quit teaching, however, to write her books. Her poem "Grammer" in *Little Mirrors, and Other Studies in Free Verse* (1924) speaks of the inadequacy she felt as a teacher:

All the morning
Students have asked me questions
And I have answered them, fumbling,
Or futilely.
I have said "X is right."
When all that I was in justified in saying
Was: "I do not know that X is wrong."
I have drawn lines
Where probably
No lines should have been drawn;
And I have lumped together in clumsy conglomeration
Facts essentially diverse.
I have, moreover, enunciated platitudes
And dictated dogmas
Which the obedient fountain-pens of misguided young
    women have laboriously inscribed in tidy note-books.

The poem continues in this vein, questioning the necessity of always producing decisive answers. It returns to a memory of a magazine that Wyllie had edited as a ten-year-old and asks, "is the Editer / expected to correct contributors' mistakes / in spelling and grammer?" It ends with the question "Whether life, in answer, must for ever / (Curt and incontrovertible) / Rap out its humiliating and grim affirmative." Miles's poetry shows a strong sensitivity to the complexities, contradictions, and ambivalences of human experience; teaching absolutes to young students did not appeal to her.

Living in Bloomsbury (at 19 Woburn Square, the site of the Courthould Institute Galleries) also gave Miles access to literary London. She went to readings at the Poetry Bookshop on Devonshire Street, recording in her unpublished memoir that "to look at Edith Sitwell was an even more astonishing experience" than hearing Sitwell read and that Siegfried Sassoon was "surprisingly

How pitiless a boy's swift passing seems;
How pitiless the shattering of men's dreams!

A 9 November 1922 review in *The Times Literary Supplement* (*TLS*) (London) called *Annotations* "a collection of brief pieces in which the sheerly poetical quality is seldom looked for and seldom occurs, but which are most vivid and readable records of life."

Miles spent many hours in the reading room of the British Library collecting poems for her anthologies *Childhood in Verse and Prose* (1923) and *An Anthology of Youth in Verse and Prose* (1925). *TLS* for 24 January 1924 called the first anthology "a very considerable success," asserting that "to reckon up the literature which deals with childhood is to touch almost every kind of writing."

Miles published her third volume of poems, *Little Mirrors, and Other Studies in Free-Verse,* in 1924. The book takes as its theme small moments in the lives of ordinary people. In the title poem a woman goes into a restaurant, eats "messily, / A poached egg and piccalilli," and then leaves without paying, telling the waitress that she does not carry a purse because she is afraid of being robbed. She leaves a little mirror behind. The poem ends with the narrator sympathizing with the waitress:

Miles's friend and adviser, the poet Herbert Edward Palmer, in 1927

shy for a poet so renowned." She became close friends with Wilfred Meynell after his wife died. Another poet, Herbert Edward Palmer, helped her to advance her own work by encouraging her to publish. Harold Munro, T. S. Eliot, John Middleton Murry, and Laurence Binyon lived in the parish and gave lectures in the church. While living in London, Miles published poetry in *The London Mercury, The Englishwoman, The New Witness, The Women's Leader, Art and Letters, The Link, Time and Tide, Weekly Westminster, The Observer, The New Age, The New Leader, The Challenge, The Nation, Punch,* and *The Sewanee Review.*

Another collection of Miles's poems, *Annotations,* was published in 1922. One of the most personal poems in the volume, "Grass upon the House-top," is about her brother's eighteen-year-old son, who, infatuated with "aeroplanes," deferred a scholarship to the University of Cambridge to become a flyer in World War I. But his plane crashed, leaving his "body shattered, smashed,– / Shattered and dead." She mourns "the boy who mattered so" and remembers him as a child, safe in "young sleep, still / And dreamless deep," and later his awkward adolescent body "struggling with cricket" and his youthful "glowing modesty" about sex as his "face flamed red." Miles ends the poem:

I cluck my sympathy
And reflect that humanity
May be perhaps dichotomized
Into two classes;
People who carry purses,
And those who swing fat hips
And vanity-bags,
And who, quitting the world,
Leave behind them
Little mirrors
Into which they have reflected
The image
Of a violet-powdered nose.

The "little mirror" has earlier reflected both her image and her small drama. The other thirteen poems in this volume are "little mirrors" of other small moments in time.

In "At the Russian Ballet" a young man earnestly tries to explain the performance to his girlfriend; she, however, merely "snorts and swallows jujubes." The reviewer for *TLS* (27 March 1924) commented that "Her point of view, her quick observation, not any charm in the verse itself, save that it is clear and modestly modern–in a word, her comprehension moves us." A reviewer for *TLS* of 11 December 1924 compared Miles to a nursery-rhyme character, "Mary Martha Merryday," who "Twists her thoughts all round about; / She has the queerest little way / Of seeing life turned inside out."

The twenty-five pieces in Miles's next collection, *The Hares, and Other Verses* (1925), include many nature poems. "The Hares" is about a "shy hare of friendship" and a "wild hare of love" with a "fierce quivering heart," who is betrayed by a "noose . . . fine as a thread." "The Patient Oak" is a study in contrasts. It begins by describing the long-lived tree that, "With its furrowed bark, / Seems a giant stark, / With muscles bared" and ends:

> On the torso stirs,
> Curd-cold, curd-pale,
> A day-old moth,
> Dim-wing'd and frail.

The following poem, "I saw a being yesterday," is about a bird, "lovelier than words can say." Miles describes him as he drinks from the thistle "with needle-tongue. . . . His grace made the humblebees seem gross." Another poem, "Sheep," pictures the animals as "A sullen sea, devoid of grace . . . nibbling their bitter fare."

Miles worked for fourteen years on her 850-page novel *Blind Men Crossing a Bridge*, an epic with a complicated tripartite structure. The novel, about a clergyman's son, his marriage to a rural girl, and their twin children, delves into human suffering brought about by crises of passion, including seduction and thwarted love, tragic passion, illegitimate children, suicide, and wartime deaths.

In her memoir Miles recommends that the novel be read aloud; although it is in prose, many passages display her gift for lyrical descriptions of the natural world:

> They stood beneath the lime whose vivid shoots had pierced George's heart with the brightness of their tips on Easter morning. To-day the floor of the hollow was a mass of fern, spreading forth its newly-opened fronds in tapering, slashed, almost mature growth, flaunting its spore-sheaths. A buzz of young bees on the lime-tree made a medley of melodies. The sweet spices of briar and nutty gorse combined. A brown wren, minute among close leafage, let a fine soft feather fall.

Reviews of the novel were mixed. Graham Greene, writing in *The Spectator* (24 August 1934), was scathing: "Adjectives and metaphors of appalling banality drip from Miss Miles's pen. Miss Miles is nothing if she is not poetic. . . . *Blind Men Crossing a Bridge* is a silly and badly written book." On the other hand, Harold Strauss wrote in *The New York Times* (31 March 1935) that the novel was "the product of a superb imagination which by the depth and power of its concepts and rich proffering of the symbols of life cannot fail to move one." *TLS* for 23 August 1934 called it "an unusual and powerful novel, inspired by a lofty ambition. . . . Miss Miles writes with immense vigour, a stubborn, forcible prose that comes nearest to poetry when it falls into country dialect."

In 1938 Miles and her husband moved to Sutton in Bedfordshire, where he became rector of All Saints Church. During World War II the sixteenth-century rectory became a hostel for refugees from the London blitz. Miles kept a diary that she called "Wartime Journal of a Pacifist"; in the entry for 13 September 1940 she writes, "Bomb fell in Nelson Sq on Monday. No one hurt but all windows smashed and blast terrifying. Bombs on B. Palace, Somerset House, many city churches. Also H. of Lords. Deaths reported to be Jews."

In 1942, Miles published her second novel, *Rabboni* (the Aramaic word for rabbi, meaning teacher). Like *Blind Man Crossing a Bridge*, this novel continues Miles's exploration of human suffering and experimentation with the novel form—most of the second part is written as a play in three acts. It rather obliquely tells the story of a Welsh family destroyed by passions and war. The book received bad reviews because of its inscrutability. Miles comments on the book in her unpublished memoir:

> This work—to describe it as a novel might be misleading—makes demands of a reader which are exorbitant. To get from it what has been put into it he needs to be familiar with the Authorised Version of the Bible, to be ready to hear every paragraph with his mind's ear, to see every happening with his mind's eye, to accept without derision the abrupt transition from archaisms to slang, and, purged of all passions other than pity to receive the catastrophe as inevitable.

In 1943 Miles privately published a small volume titled *News! News!* She dedicated it to "all in the services who have willingly given or risked their lives for their country, and especially to the memory of" her father, her three brothers, and three of her cousins. Because she had been criticized for her free verse on the grounds that it was not poetry, she inserts a defiant note: "These comments do not claim to be poems. The prose in which they are written is divided into lines for the sake of emphasis." The pieces are vignettes about people suffering the ravages of war on the home front, as well as on the battlefield: a woman munitions worker worries about her soldier son, whose death she is hastening by doing her job; a retarded fifteen-year-old dies with "a bayonet stuck through his testicles"; and people take shelter from bombs in Westminster Abbey, "The Shelter under the Arches," where Miles worked with other pacifists:

> Hogarth's pencil, Goya's pencil might have drawn them:
> Rejects from shelters where the less derelict foregather;
> Drunks, dopes, the crazy;
> Old, for the most part;
> Whining their curses through toothless gums;
> Clutching bundles, grimed and hideous;

Miles in old age in front of her home, Romany Cottage, in Bedford

Streets and arches their home;
Red Biddy their nectar;
The copper their dread.
Blackened toe-nails poke through sodden shoe-leather.
Sockless, the old feet sweat, stink, and blister.
Corns, callouses, bunions offend.

In her memoir Miles says that pacifist groups refused to publish *News! News!* because of its bitter cynicism.

Miles's husband died in 1953; two years later she published her memoir of him, *Portrait of a Parson*. The foreword was written by the novelist Storm Jameson, who had admired *Blind Men Crossing a Bridge* and had become a friend of Miles's after reading the work.

In 1958 Miles published a verse novel, *Lettice Delmar;* she had originally written it as a radio play for the British Broadcasting Corporation, but it was never broadcast. *Lettice Delmar* deals with the calamities suffered by the Delmar family during World War I, including thwarted love, rape, abortion, and suicide. When the war breaks out, Lettice's brother is eager to join the army:

Male insistent impulse to seek security through action urges him.
Like some sharp prick,
or some whip lashing him,
the desire to serve his country,
male-bonded, goads him on.
While for his sister, Lettice, war
Dams, rudely and blatantly,
the need *she* knows.
Bitter thwarting,
Hateful thwarting,
In war, for one concerned with personal talent.
Lettice is not drawn towards nursing.

This moving verse drama evokes wartime England with a compelling story, complex characters, and lucid poetry.

In 1962 Miles published a volume of twenty poems, *A Morsel of God and Other Studies,* dedicated to her husband's memory. In the dedication poem she pictures herself as "grizzle-haired," reading old love letters from her husband. As they pass through life together he seems to evolve into seven different lovers, each nobler, deeper, and sweeter than the last, making her as "rich in lovers as a whore." (Palmer cautioned her not to use this line, since it might be misinterpreted as an admission of adultery.) In "The Black Mountains," about the area in Wales where she and her husband had had a vacation home, Miles describes the "vast contorted masses of granite and of feldspar" that remember the "heave and tumult of the earth's ancient convulsions" and compares those convulsions to the passions she suffers:

> Strange that the cloven hills and a barren woman, grey and wrinkled,
> Should know the same tumult in their being,
> The same tearing of their sinews and wrenching of their tendons,
> The same urge, same upheaval, same amazement.

She says that "One object of passion and one alone can stir to rebellion both granite and human flesh / Mountain and woman are linked as brethren in a passionate revulsion from the will of God."

"The Goatherd" describes Sister Thecla, who herds goats as she prays:

> Her blue habit is faded from exposure
> And patched clumsily where thorn and brier have rent it.
> Her veil has a jagged tear, still unmended,
> And on her darned stocking clings a burr.
> Her eyebrows are thick and grizzled.
> On her weather-beaten face a brown mole bristles.

Another nun, "Novice Naomi, shrewish and shrewd," wonders whether Thecla will one day turn into a goat. She says, "Someday I believe we shall see a hoof peeping from beneath her habit / Or a tuft of beard straying on her scapular." But then Naomi has a dream in which she sees Jesus, called

> Scapegoat,
> Dyed scarlet, bound with hyssop, treading the harsh path into the bitter wilderness,
> While behind Him,
> Angular, swarthy, gnarled, and faithful,
> Trudges, limping and alone,
> Lay-sister Thecla.

The title poem–the last piece in the collection–is about an old man who throws his last hope into the garbage can. He dies that night, and when the mysterious "Scavenger" empties the can, "the contents stink vilely on the way to the incinerator." Among the ashes, however, the Scavenger comes "upon a morsel of pure gold / He was not a little pleased. / He set it in His Treasury and it's there still."

Miles spent her final years in Moggerhanger, Bedfordshire, near the old rectory in Sutton, working in a study adorned with the head of a tiger that her father had shot in Bengal. She died on 12 May 1975 and was buried beside her husband in the Sutton churchyard. Her tombstone is engraved, "And she said Rabboni."

References:

Alan Denson, *Herbert Edward Palmer (1880–1961): A Bio-Bibliographical Survey and Calendar of Recordings* (Aberdenshire, Scotland: Oliver Alden, 1994), pp. 37, 53, 98, 174, 176, 178, 182, 185;

Dale A. Johnson, *Women and Religion in Britain and Ireland: An Annotated Bibliography from the Reformation to 1993* (Lanham, Md.: Scarecrow Press, 1995), p. 23.

Papers:

Susan Miles's unpublished memoir and wartime journal are in the Modern Reading Room at the Bodleian Library, University of Oxford; other papers are in the Fawcett Library in London.

Alice Milligan
(14 September 1866 – 13 April 1953)

Eugenie Celeste Martin
Louisiana Tech University

BOOKS: *Glimpses of Erin,* by Milligan and Seaton F. Milligan (London: Ward, Lock, 1888);

A Royal Democrat, as Iris Olkyrn (London: Simpkin, Marshall, Hamilton, Kent, 1892);

Life of Theobald Wolfe Tone (Belfast: Boyd, 1898);

The Last Feast of the Fianna: a dramatic legend (London: Nutt, 1900);

Hero Lays (Dublin: Maunsel, 1908);

The German Plot and Ulster Arms: some reasonable suspicions (Belfast, 1914);

Sons of the Sea Kings, by Milligan and W. H. Milligan (Dublin: Gill, 1914);

Two poems of triumph in death, by Alice Furlong and Milligan (Dublin: Gaelic Press, 1917);

The Dynamite Drummer, by Milligan and William Milligan (Dublin: Lester, 1918);

The Daughter of Donagh: a Cromwellian drama in four acts (Dublin: Lester, 1920);

Two poems (Dublin: Three Candles, 1943);

Poems (Dublin: Gill, 1954).

Collections: *New Songs: A Lyric selection made by AE* (Dublin: O'Donoghue, 1904);

We Sang for Ireland: Poems of Ethna Carbery, Seumas MacManus, and Alice Milligan (Dublin: Gill, 1950 / New York: Devin-Adair, 1950);

Harper of the Only God: A Selection of Poetry by Alice Milligan, edited by Sheila Turner Johnston (Omagh, Ireland: Colourpoint, 1993).

PLAY PRODUCTION: *The Last Feast of the Fianna,* Dublin, Gaiety Theatre, 19 February 1900.

SELECTED PERIODICAL PUBLICATION—UNCOLLECTED: *Shan Van Vocht* (Belfast), edited, with contributions, by Milligan (January 1896–15 November 1897).

Although she was nearly forgotten by the time of her death, Alice Milligan holds a significant place in Irish history. Even before women were granted voting rights in Ireland, Milligan was a respected poet, playwright, and nationalist writer. Sheila Turner Johnston writes of Milligan in her biography, *Alice* (1994), "Ireland became her religion." Indeed, although Milligan was a prolific writer, she was less concerned with preserving her art for posterity than she was determined to fight for Ireland's independence. Most of her poetry was collected and published posthumously. She promoted the knowledge of Irish history, folklore, and language among the Irish themselves, and she made several speaking tours across the country. She was respected by William Butler Yeats, who staged one of her plays in his theater.

Born in Omagh, County Tyrone, Ireland, on 14 September 1866, Alice Letitia Milligan was the third of

Alice Milligan

thirteen children born to Seaton Forrest Milligan and Charlotte Burns Milligan. Milligan's father was a prosperous salesman, and she was reared in affluence in a large house in Omagh where they were among the Protestant elite. Because there were so many children, Alice and her siblings were sent to her grandmother's house each time a new baby was expected. Her great-uncle would take her to the hiring fairs where she would hear the native tongue spoken by the laborers, and it was during these visits Milligan probably developed her appreciation of the Irish language. She also grew to share her father's interest and involvement in Irish archaeology. Milligan and her sisters were not kept behind sheltering doors, as was the case with many Victorian girls, and her parents encouraged individuality rather than conformity.

Milligan began her education at a private school in Omagh, but when her father was promoted, the family moved to Belfast. She wrote one of her most famous poems, "When I Was a Little Girl," about her childhood in Omagh. She writes of the stories that the family nurse told them:

> When after sunny hours,
> At twilight's falling,
> Down through the garden walks
> Came our old nurse calling–
>
> "Come in! for it's growing late,
> And the grass will wet ye!
> Come in! or when it's dark
> The Fenians will get ye."

The Fenians, of whom the nurse was so frightened, were a group of Irish nationalists who were active in the 1860s and who staged an unsuccessful uprising in March of 1867. By the time Milligan was a young child the men who had been involved in the Fenian movement were aging, but the story of their uprising was still in the memories of the Irish people.

In Belfast, Milligan began attending the Methodist College in 1879. Just one year before, the Intermediate Education Act had been passed, allowing both sexes to compete on equal terms in the Intermediate examinations. Milligan performed well in school and began to develop her lifelong interest in Irish matters. Her sisters went on to Germany to continue their education, but she did not want to go so far away from home. Instead, she attended the Ladies' Department of King's College, London in 1886. She did not stay there long, however, returning to Belfast in the summer of 1887. Throughout these years Milligan was writing poetry of a personal nature, and though her writing had not yet taken on much of a political tone, her voice was always eminently Irish.

In the fall of 1887 Milligan moved to Derry, where she took a post as governess at the Ladies' Collegiate School, where she met Marjorie Arthur, a Scot, who became an important friend. Even after leaving the ladies' college, Milligan and Arthur corresponded and visited often. When Arthur met an untimely death in 1892, Milligan wrote many poems about her, including "A Nocturne," "March Violets," "Lyrics in Memory of a Sea Lover," "The White Wave Following," "A Message," and "If This Could Be."

In 1888 Milligan and her father collaborated on a tourism book called *Glimpses of Erin*. At this time she told her parents of her desire to go to Dublin to study the Irish language, and although this life was not what they would have chosen for their fiery redheaded daughter, they consented.

In Dublin, Milligan found her true love, nationalism, and met others who shared her views. She followed closely the career of Charles Stewart Parnell, the nationalist leader of the Home Rule movement, and desperately tried to see him on several occasions. When she finally saw him at a rally in June 1891, she was shocked by his appearance. Parnell had recently suffered political setbacks upon the discovery that he had been carrying on a long-term affair with a mistress and had three children by her. The Catholic Church had turned against him, and his party had asked him to step down, but he had refused. Milligan wrote in her diary, "I will never forget the sad downcast expression–half ashamed as it were, the ghastly pallor of his face–his dark eyes–rather shifty . . . He looked beaten and ashamed." Parnell died four months later. Soon after, Milligan finished her studies in Dublin and returned home to her family.

Milligan, in her mid twenties, began writing poetry on political topics–from singing the praises of ancient Irish heroes to criticizing the Catholic Church for standing against Parnell. In 1892 Milligan completed a novel titled *A Royal Democrat* under the pseudonym Iris Olkyrn, although her identity was well known. In 1893 she was admitted to the Irish Literary Society, the National Literary Society, founded by Yeats and John O'Leary in Dublin in 1892, and in 1895 she was accepted into the newly formed Gaelic League, founded by the Irish nationalist leader Douglas Hyde. In mid 1893 Milligan forged an important friendship with Anna Johnston, whose father, Robert Johnston, was a nationalist leader and member of the 1867 Fenian revolt. Anna Johnston, like Milligan, wrote nationalist poetry and other material, but she wrote under the name of Ethna Carbery. Also in 1893, Milligan befriended Yeats, who was impressed with her work but urged her to try drama. She wrote

Milligan's parents, Seaton Forrest and Charlotte Burns Milligan

her greatest heroic poem that year titled "The Return of Lugh Lamh-Fada." The poem about a half-god, half-human hero of Irish folklore draws a clear comparison to Ireland's situation. Milligan writes:

> And they told how of old that island had been taken,
> And made the prey of plunderers—the mockery of hate,
> The poor of the land by their rightful lords forsaken,
> Appalled by giant tyranny, oppressed by witching fate
> . . . .
> Lugh heard of till his godlike heart was touched with human sorrow,
> And his glad immortal eyes were for the first time wet with tears.

The poem was published in *United Ireland* on 12 May 1893, and it was well received. Milligan was gaining both respect and readership in the nationalist movement.

On 9 February 1894 Milligan was involved in the founding of the Henry Joy McCracken Literary Society, dedicated to Irish history. In 1895 she was elected vice president of the group and gave the inaugural address, which was reprinted in *United Ireland*. Because of the success of the organization, a magazine, *The Northern Patriot,* was launched, and the first issue appeared in October of 1895. Milligan and Carbery were appointed as editors, and though the paper's mission was to report all things Irish, it was to be nonpartisan. Only three months later Milligan and Carbery were removed from their positions as editors, presumably because they did not successfully remain apolitical.

In January of 1896 Milligan and Carbery began publishing their own Irish paper, the *Shan Van Vocht* (The Poor Old Woman), and it soon put *The Northern Patriot* out of business. The motto of the paper was:

> Yes, Ireland shall be free,
> From the centre to the sea
> And hurrah liberty
> Says the Shan Van Vocht.

In addition to editing, Milligan wrote a large portion of the paper. She also organized book-discussion groups, the "Home Reading Circles," based on books she herself selected. Within the pages of her paper Milligan published her story, *Life of Theobald Wolfe Tone* (1898), about one of her favorite Irish heroes who had led a rebellion in 1798. On 6 March 1899 the *Shan Van Vocht* came to an end when a new paper, *The United Irishman,* debuted. Milligan and Carbery gave their list of subscribers to the owner of the new paper.

The demise of the paper allowed Milligan to spend more time lecturing throughout the country on topics of Irish history and the promotion of the nationalist cause. When the old Fenian leader John O'Leary came to stay at her family home during the Belfast Centennial Celebration, some members of her family were angered by this blatantly antiunionist action. Her parents, however, were always tolerant and never condemned her cause.

Milligan became an active member of the Gaelic League, a group that promoted the use of the Irish language. She tried to become fluent in the difficult language and was reasonably successful. In February 1900 Yeats's Irish Literary Theatre staged her play, *The Last Feast of the Fianna*, at the Gaiety Theatre in Dublin. Although Milligan was not able to write the play in the Irish language, she did evoke the Irish heroes of Celtic mythology. The play, only twenty minutes long, was part of a projected trilogy depicting the lives of ancient warriors. The play was fairly well received, but many of the anglicized viewers were ignorant of the myths presented on stage. Milligan regretted the fact that only country people could immediately recognize the characters. Nonetheless, her short hero-plays were staged frequently in Irish festivals.

In 1901 Milligan's friend and partner Carbery married fellow nationalist Seamas McManus and moved away to County Donegal. Before Milligan could visit her, Carbery died quite unexpectedly the next year. Shortly afterward, Milligan's sister Evelyn drowned at the family's summer home at Bangor. These years were bittersweet for Milligan, because at the time of these painful personal events, she was at the height of her popularity.

George Russell, a supporter of young Irish poets, had taken Milligan under his wing, and in 1904 he published a thin volume titled *New Songs*, which included five of her patriotic poems. Four years later Russell edited a book entirely dedicated to Milligan's poetry titled *Hero Lays* (1908), again including only her patriotic and heroic poetry.

After the deaths of her loved ones, Milligan traveled widely on behalf of the Gaelic League, promoting the Irish language and folklore. After demonstrating success in raising funds and in attracting new members, she was appointed to the Coiste Gno, the highest ruling committee of the league, in 1906. However, it would not be long before Milligan's active schedule would be hindered by domestic concerns. Being the only single female daughter still living, Milligan was called upon to nurse her parents, beginning in 1909. She stayed active within Belfast but was unable to travel on short notice.

In 1916 Milligan suffered a series of losses. In January, while she was in London visiting her sick sister, Charlotte Milligan-Fox, their mother died. Milligan-Fox followed in March, and in April her father died. The once noisy family home, bursting with activity, stood quiet and empty. Because she had been away from Irish politics while nursing her sister, she had known nothing of the Easter Uprising of 1916. She was shocked to hear of the Irish nationalist rebellion from her youngest brother, Charles Milligan; however, the effect of it changed her profoundly. The participants of the rebellion were severely punished, and several of Milligan's friends were put to death by the British government on charges of treason.

Milligan as a student at Methodist College in Belfast

One such friend was the traveling teacher and nationalist sympathizer, Roger Casement, whom Milligan had met in 1904 at the home of a mutual friend. Casement had gone to Germany after the beginning of World War I to organize an Irish legion among the prisoners of war, and after failing in his efforts, returned to Ireland on Good Friday 1916 on a German submarine. He was arrested and accused of high treason for consorting with the enemy. In truth, he was trying to stop the transport of arms to the Irish rebels in Dublin in order to halt the uprising. The English public turned on him, and, when secret diaries emerged chronicling his homosexual lifestyle, the courts turned against him, too, and he was executed. In 1916 Milligan wrote her poem "The Man on the Wheel" in his memory:

> A man goes by on a wheel with the rain on his face,
> Against the way of the wind, and he not caring;
> Goes on through the winter night towards a lonesome
>   distant place,
> For his heart is hot with the glow of the ancient hero-
>   daring.

During her stay in England, where she had been caring for her invalid sister, Milligan spent some time in London visiting Irish prisoners. When she returned to

*First page of one of Milligan's diaries, with her sketch of the Irish nationalist leader Charles Stewart Parnell four months before his death
(from Sheila Turner Johnston,* Alice: A Life of Alice Milligan, *1994)*

Ireland at the end of 1917, she continued these visits and wrote poetry, but she was nearing the end of her active career. Now in her fifties, she had no steady income. For a time she returned to England to live with her brother Ernest and his family, but she did not feel at home there, so she and her brother William (who had returned from military service and struggled with alcoholism) moved to Dublin in 1920. They found themselves unwelcome there because William had served in the British military, and the Irish Republican Army told them that if they did not leave immediately, William would be executed. At this point they probably fled to Belfast; however, Milligan continued to take secret trips to visit her old friends in Dublin.

On 7 January 1922 England signed a peace treaty with Ireland, granting universal suffrage to all adults. However, five months later, civil war broke out in Ireland. The event distressed Milligan, inspiring her to write "Till Ferdia Came," a work based on the myth of two Irish heroes who killed each other because of an evil queen. Soon afterward, Milligan and her brother William returned to the home of her brother Ernest in England.

Milligan was glad to be away from tumultuous Ireland, and her brother's children were fond of her, but she missed her home. She and William collaborated on a fairly unsuccessful novel titled *The Dynamite Drummer* in 1918. The main character of the novel is an American who arrives in Northern Ireland and struggles to understand the people there. Shortly after this publication Milligan returned to Omagh with her brother William and his wife and child. She lived with them for several years with little contact with her old friends. She was only allowed to take one more trip to Dublin, to a meeting of the Yeats Academy in 1933. In 1934 William's twenty-six-year-old son died from complications of a stroke, and in 1937 William died. Her family circle was quickly disappearing.

Though she was lonely and in poor circumstances, Milligan was still the only woman asked to sign a leaflet issued by the Northern Council for Unity in January 1938. After William's wife died, Milligan lived alone for a few years. In 1941 the National University of Ireland awarded her with an honorary doctorate. In 1943 a reception was held in Omagh in her honor. She was issued a check as an act of kindness, but it could only go so far to help her circumstances. In 1950 *We Sang for Ireland,* a book of poems that included some of the nationalistic poetry of Carbery, McManus, and Mil-

Milligan in her mid seventies

ligan was published. It was the last time during her life that her poetry would be published in book form.

In 1951 Milligan's youngest brother Charles arranged for her to live with a family named McSwiggin. Charles visited her often until her death on 13 April 1953 in Omagh. Messages of condolence came in from all over Ireland, praising her accomplishments, but few of her fiery contemporaries remained to mourn her. She was buried in the family plot.

After her death Gill and Son published another volume of her poetry titled simply *Poems* (1954), which includes sixty-one poems. In 1993 her biographer Sheila Turner Johnston edited a selection of Milligan's poetry titled *Harper of the Only God,* a more-comprehensive collection.

As a woman writing at a time when women were not allowed much influence, Alice Milligan was a successful defender of the Irish cause. Johnston writes, "She was not one of the giants of the era, but she greatly influenced the landscape across which they marched."

Biography:
Sheila Turner Johnston, *Alice: A Life of Alice Milligan* (Omagh, Ireland: Colourpoint Press, 1994).

Rosa Harriet Newmarch

(18 December 1857 – 9 April 1940)

Lee Anna Maynard
University of South Carolina

BOOKS: *Tchaikovsky: His Life and Works, with Extracts from His Writings, and the Diary of His Tour Abroad in 1888* (London: Richards, 1900; enlarged edition, London: Reeves, 1908);

The Art Songs of Russia: A Lecture (London: Steinway Hall, 1900);

Horæ Amoris: Songs and Sonnets (London: Elkin Mathews, 1903);

Henry J. Wood (London: John Lane, 1904);

Songs to a Singer and Other Verses (London: John Lane, Bodley Head / New York: John Lane, 1906);

Jean Sibelius, A Finnish Composer (Leipzig: Breitkopf & Hartel, 1906);

Bantock's "Omar Khayyam" (London: International Musical Society, 1906);

Poetry and Progress in Russia (London: John Lane, Bodley Head / New York: John Lane, 1907);

Mary Wakefield: A Memoir (London: Kendal, 1912);

The Russian Opera (London: Jenkins, 1914; New York: Dutton, 1914);

The Russian Arts (London: Jenkins, 1916);

The Concert-goer's Library of Descriptive Notes, volume 1: *Symphonies, Overtures, Concertos* (London: Oxford University Press, 1928);

The Concert-goer's Library of Descriptive Notes, volume 2: *Wagnerian excerpts, Symphonic poems and fantasias, marches* (London: Oxford University Press, 1929);

The Concert-goer's Library of Descriptive Notes, volume 3: *Suites and Ballet-Suites for Orchestra, Rhapsodies and Fantasias, Miscellaneous Dances* (London: Oxford University Press, 1930);

The Concert-goer's Library of Descriptive Notes, volume 4: *Symphonies, Overtures, Concertos* (London: Oxford University Press, 1931);

The Concert-goer's Library of Descriptive Notes, volume 5: *Miscellaneous* (London: Oxford University Press, 1938);

Jean Sibelius (Boston: Birchard, 1939; London: Goodwin & Tabb, 1944);

The Music of Czechoslovakia (London: Oxford University Press, 1942);

Rosa Harriet Newmarch

The Concert-goer's Library of Descriptive Notes, volume 6: *Choral Works* (London: Oxford University Press, 1948).

OTHER: *The Devout Russian: A Book of Thoughts and Counsels Gathered from the Saints and Fathers of the Eastern Church and Modern Russian Authors,* compiled with an introduction and biographical notes by Newmarch (London: Jenkins, 1918).

TRANSLATIONS: Hermann Deiters, *Johannes Brahms: A Biographical Sketch,* translated with additions by Newmarch, by J. A. Fuller Maitland (London: Unwin, 1888);

Alfred Habets, *Borodin and Liszt* (London: Digby, Long, 1895);

Six Russian Songs (London: Novello, 1903);

Johann Sebastian Bach, *Cantata for Easter Day,* lyrics by G. Schreck and E. H. Thorne (Leipzig: Breitkopf & Hartel, 1903);

Modeste Tchaikovsky, *The Life & Letters of Peter Ilich Tchaikovsky* (London: John Lane, 1906);

Jean Sibelius, *Six Songs* (London: Frederick Harris, 1907);

Sibelius, *The Captive Queen* (Berlin: Schlesinger, 1907);

Modest Mussorgsky, *Boris Godounov* (London: Chester, 1910);

Sergei Rachmaninoff, *How Fair this Spot* (London: Chester, 1910);

Vincent d'Indy, *César Franck* (London & New York: John Lane, 1910);

Sibelius, *Ukko the Fire-Maker* (Leipzig & London: Breitkopf & Hartel, 1911);

Nicolai Rimsky-Korsakov, *Ivan the Terrible* (Leipzig: Breitkopf & Hartel, 1912);

The Russian Song Books, volumes 1 and 2: *Songs for a Bass Voice* (London: Breitkopf & Hartel, 1912);

Mussorgsky, *Khovanschina* (New York: Ricordi, 1913);

Fourteen Russian Folk-Songs (London: Chester, 1915);

Alexander Gretchaninoff, *The Dreary Steppe,* lyrics by Plestcheiev (London: Chester, 1916);

Russian Songs for British Soldiers (London: Chester, 1916);

Nikolai Karlovich Metner, *Song of the Elves,* lyrics by Johann Wolfgang von Goethe (London: Chester, 1917);

The Russian Song Books, volumes 3 and 4: *Songs for a Soprano Voice* (London: Chester, 1917);

Rimsky-Korsakov, *Night (Picture)* (London: Chester, 1917);

Sergei Nikiforovich Vasilenko, *The Singing Maiden* (London: Chester, 1917);

Theodore Koeneman, *When the King Went Forth to War,* lyrics by M. Konopnitsky (London: Chester, 1918);

Joseph Jongen, *Calm, Beside the Silent Quays* (London: Chester, 1918);

Albert Roussel, *Lovers Divided,* lyrics by H. P. Roché (Paris: Rouart, 1921);

Roussel, *Douze Melodies,* lyrics by Henri de Regnier (Paris: Rouart, 1921);

Leonid Dimitrievitch Malashkin, *Oh, Could I but Express in Song,* lyrics by G. Lishin (London: Chester, 1922);

Vit Novak, *Slovak Songs* (London: Chester, 1923);

Igor Stravinsky, *The Soldier's Tale,* lyrics by Charles-Ferdinand Ramuz (London: Chester, 1924);

Stravinsky, *Trois Histoires Pour Enfants,* lyrics by Ramuz (London: Chester, 1927);

Karel Hoffmeister, *Antonín Dvořák* (London: Bodley Head, 1928);

Roussel, *Jazz at Night,* lyrics by René Dommange (Paris: Durand, 1929);

Leos Janácek, *Festival Mass for Chorus and Orchestra* (Vienna: Universal, 1930);

Frederic Smetana, *The Bartered Bride,* libretto by Karl Sabina (London: Boosey, 1934);

George Frideric Handel, *Five Operatic Choruses* (London: Oxford University Press, 1937);

Pyotr Ilich Tchaikovsky, *The Queen of Spades,* libretto by Modeste Tchaikovsky (New York & London: Schirmer, 1940).

SELECTED PERIODICAL PUBLICATIONS–UNCOLLECTED: "Some New Letters of Tourgeniev," *Atlantic Monthly,* 84 (July–December 1899): 691–705;

"Tchaikovsky and Tolstoi," *Contemporary Review,* 83 (January–June 1903): 112–116, and *Living Age,* seventh series 19 (April–June 1903): 58–63;

"Vassily Verestschagin: War-Painter," *Fortnightly Review,* 81 (January–June 1904): 1011–1018, and *Living Age,* 24 (16 July 1904): 129–136.

During an age when women's participation in the world of classical music was limited, Rosa Harriet Newmarch met, befriended, and wrote about some of the greatest European composers and conductors of her time. Her love of music, talent for writing, and ear for musical composition inform her famous nonpoetical works, but they coalesce in her two volumes of poetry, *Horæ Amoris: Songs and Sonnets* (1903) and *Songs to a Singer and Other Verses* (1906). In many of these poems Newmarch expresses the same emotive power she identifies in the music of Pyotr Ilich Tchaikovsky, Modest Petrovich Mussorgsky, and Henry J. Wood.

Newmarch did not perform music herself, nor did she come from a particularly musical family, but a flair for verbal composition can be traced in her not so distant ancestry. She was born Rosa Harriet Jeaffreson 18 December 1857 in Leamington, Warwick, the daughter of a physician, Samuel Jeaffreson, and the former Sophie Kenney. Rosa's maternal grandfather, who died almost a decade before her birth, was James Kenney, a playwright, whose play *Raising the Wind* (1803) enjoyed success on both sides of the Atlantic. As a result of her grandfather's literary activities, Rosa may well have had greater familiarity with publishing and professional writing than most young Victorian women.

After being educated primarily at home, Jeaffreson entered the Heatherly School of Art in London to study painting. She left school after a time to pursue her literary interests, settling in London in 1880 to work as a contributor to various journals. In 1883 she married Henry Charles Newmarch. In 1895 she published her English

Title pages for Newmarch's two volumes of poems

translation, from a French edition, of a book on Alexsandr Porfiryevich Borodin and Franz Liszt. Newmarch began to succeed as a professional writer in her own right in 1897 with the publication of a series of articles on Tchaikovsky in *The Musician*.

In 1897 Newmarch made the first of what would be many trips to Russia, this time to learn the history of Russian music under the guidance of Vladimir Stassov. Stassov worked officially as the Director of Fine Arts at the Russian Imperial Public Library and tirelessly as a champion of Russian nationalism, especially as expressed in painting and music. "His mission," she writes in *The Russian Opera* (1914), "has been to stimulate the creative faculties of others," and he has given Russia "a revelation of her artistic identity." Identified by Newmarch as "the godfather of the new Russian art," in 1867 Stassov coined the term *Kuchka*, variously translated as the Five, the Mighty Five, the Handful, and the Bunch, to describe the group of Russian composers that formed during the 1860s to pro-

mote and legitimize nationalistic music and to combat the dominance of Western musical forms and conventions. Stassov's ideas and the circle of composers with whom he worked deeply affected the course of Newmarch's career. Two years later, her translation of letters from the Russian novelist Ivan Turgenev to Stassov appeared in *The Atlantic Monthly* magazine. In addition to translating these letters, she provided historical, cultural, and biographical contexts for them, and with this more accessible essay she introduced Stassov to many English readers.

In 1900 the work for which Newmarch is best known today was published–*Tchaikovsky: His Life and Works, with Extracts from His Writings, and the Diary of His Tour Abroad in 1888*. In the preface, she explains why she undertook the biography, six years after the composer's death: "as yet no really adequate biography has appeared. . . . The public interest, especially in England, is steadily increasing, and almost every scrap of information concerning the composer of 'The Pathetic' Symphony is eagerly sought after." Newmarch based part of her text on the papers she had written a few years earlier for *The Musician*, and another section on her extracts from G. Laroche's *The Collected Writings of Tchaikovsky* (1898) which were published in the *Musical Standard*. Another key part of the undertaking was her translation, the first in English, of the composer's diary of his tour abroad in 1888.

Newmarch's treatment of Tchaikovsky's life before he began composing is rather thin and compressed, and she barely explores his personal and other non- or semi-professional relationships. She organizes her project mainly around his compositions and their receptions, both by his teachers and friends and by the public at large. Although deeply influenced by Stassov, Newmarch is not afraid at times to question his viewpoints, especially in the case of Tchaikovsky. Whereas the Russian critic has been quoted as naming Tchaikovsky a sort of honorary sixth member of the Mighty Five, Newmarch writes, "to say that Tchaikovsky is the most accessible and the best known among Russian composers is by no means to say that he is the greatest." While discussing his essentially Russian character and *maladie du siècle*, she also laments the lack of unity in his works and traces his "emotional and romantic despair" to "other times and other lands . . . it echoes Chateaubriand and Byron, not Gogol and Tourgeniev." Furthermore, she criticizes the composer's *Collected Writings*, claiming the volume owes its prestige more to his public personality than to its "intrinsic literary value." Flexing her muscles as a music critic, she advocates a reassessment of one of Tchaikovsky's most famous pieces: "I think we shall never appreciate the true greatness of Tchaikovsky until we have forgotten, for a time, the over-wrought emotion of the *Sixth Symphony* and the fascinating triviality of its musical antithesis, the *Casse-Noisette Suite*. Then perhaps we shall turn with pleasure to the . . . numerous other interesting works of his best and most robust period." In this project, Newmarch is able to combine many of her interests and skills—expert storytelling, sharp musical criticism, and a deep interest in Russian nationalism—to great effect.

Newmarch wrote about Tchaikovsky again in 1903 but returned to the periodical format. In *The Living Age* she describes the first meeting between the composer and Leo Tolstoy and includes excerpts from their subsequent correspondence. She compares the encounter to the initial meetings of Friedrich Schiller and Johann Wolfgang von Goethe, Ludwig van Beethoven and Goethe, Richard Wagner and Franz Liszt, and Johannes Brahms and Tchaikovsky. In playful prose, she explains that while Tolstoy was established but yet mysterious, the composer was relatively new on the scene: "it is not surprising that when this Olympian being descended from his cloud-capped heights and appeared in Tchaikovsky's modest flat, the mere mortal should have owned it to be 'the most flattering moment of his life.'" While Newmarch answers the public clamoring for more details of Tchaikovsky's life with this vignette and the snippets from the letters, she also reveals that "from the personal contact between Tolstoi and Tchaikovsky we can trace no important consequences for the world of music, or of literature."

Newmarch combines her love of music and literature in her first volume of poetry, *Horæ Amoris: Songs and Sonnets*. Even the title of the first section, "In Modo Tristi," explicitly demonstrates Newmarch's self-conscious attempt to merge the musical and the literary, as does the illustration of what is apparently a minor music scale. Many of these first fourteen poems are in a melancholic vein and evoke the language of music. Frequently, birdsongs seem discordant or insufficient. The discord often reflects the listener's unhappiness or dissatisfaction with her love life. In "Song" the speaker's love has left, so "the cuckoo sings less true / And the lark less clearly," and in "Presentiment," the speaker is alone again and hears "the echo of a future requiem" in the "evensong of thrush and linnet." The speaker or listener's ear (in the musical sense of the term) seems to be seriously affected by what is often cast in Newmarch's poetry as the most dire fate: the solitude of desertion and/or of unrequited love. The insufficiency of birdsong to express the complexity of deep human emotions is most evident in "Madrigal," where only the combining of the voices and one-dimensional songs of the blackbird, blue-backed swallow, warbler, nightingale, and lark can come close to three-dimensional human love.

In contrast, the music conceived and performed by humans is able to scale the heights and plumb the depths of the psyche. In "At the Piano," the speaker begs the pianist to "Play me some sober tune of long ago," such as a Lully minuet or a Handel march, "wherein no tides of passion come and go," rather than plunging her "soul again in those dark waters, turbulent and deep, / Of Schumann's anguish." "Modulation," a poem broken, appropriately, into "Major" and "Minor" sections, speaks first of a joy so great that not even "Chopin's sighs" or "Schumann's sorrow" could undo it: "I am so glad, my heart, to-day, / To-day, my heart, I am so glad." The following minor section begins with what is literally a first inversion chord (the first line of the major section as a triad): "My heart, to-day I am so sad." In "To an Instrument," she compares the heart to a musical instrument. Unlike many fine pipe organs and violins, which can be played by a virtuoso who can ultimately be forgotten, almost erased by other fingers on the keys or the strings, the human organ is like the rarest of all instruments, whose strings will break if its only player leaves.

The next section of *Horæ Amoris* is the eponymous thirty-four-poem sonnet sequence. The sonnets chart, more or less chronologically, the course of a relationship from the perspective of a hopeful (and eventually hopeless) lover, and, while the narrator's gender is never disclosed by pronouns, it seems to be a man. Cast often in opposition to the love object's deserting husband, as well as in the role of protector and supporter, the narrator is in love with the despairing and grieving woman who is the subject of the poem. The first sonnet, "Love Among the Ruins," is similar to Robert Browning's poem of the same name. Rather than reciprocal love among architectural ruins, Newmarch describes one-sided love born amidst the ruins of the loved woman's youth, happiness, respectability, and marriage. Her husband has left her, apparently under scandalous circumstances such as excessive gambling debts, and the narrator expresses in several poems that he wishes he could, almost Christlike, assume her sorrows and pains. In a complicating move, in Sonnet Three, the narrator ventures that "Sometimes—not with irreverence—I dare / To wonder if those women who once stood / Afar and watched their Master's agonies, / Knew not the aching grief more hard to bear . . . than His." This friend alone is able to grasp the stupidity and futility of the woman's other friends' advice and gestures ("a fourth vowed needlework alone could keep / a woman's heart from breaking"), but she never seems to fully appreciate him. He makes several comparisons to his situation: to a nurse, who falls in love with her charge and wishes that the child would never grow up; to Tristan, who falls in love with Isolde but is never to have her; to a discharged steward, who is expected to return the keys and hear the confidences of his mistress no more; and to Christ, who also felt "rejected love and useless sacrifice." As the sonnet sequence progresses, he becomes more embittered at the thought of his easy replacement by the erring husband, yet more resigned to this inevitable occurrence.

By Sonnet Twenty-Nine, the narrator begins to see the object of his love as a sort of insensate siren:

The torch that leads one soul to Paradise
Can lure another to the gates of Hell.
When nights are black and wild—so sea-folk tell—
Before the gale the screaming petrel flies
Straight for the beacon, with bewildered eyes,
Trusting where that clear star shines all is well,
And beats about some refuge to compel
Till faint, with broken, baffled plumes it lies.

I, too, have dashed my heart out on the light
Set up to guide another's vessel home.
O well for him whose half-wrecked life shall come,
Drawn by her love, to moorings of great peace,
While storm-winds drive me back into the night
Where no stars rise and darkness does not cease.

Like the petrel, the narrator is bewildered, baffled, and broken by the dawning realization that all of his supposedly selfless energy has been, romantically speaking, misspent, and that regardless of how long he tries, she will never be his safe harbor.

Newmarch's Russian/Eastern European preoccupation makes its first poetic appearance in this sonnet sequence. Sonnet Fifteen, titled "The City of Hope," details a fantastical place where the narrator and the woman could actually be together as lovers. The distinctly Russian flavor of the architecture and scenery make this city of hopeful love exotic, beautiful, and pure: a gold cross and crescent set in blue enamel glow in the sunlight, while ruby, green, and turquoise domes and minarets cast odd shadows on clean, white snow. The speaker's faith that he and the woman are soul mates is reaffirmed in Sonnet Seventeen, "The Symphony (Pyotr Ilych Tchaikovsky)," when both their hands tremble and his eyes are too blurred by tears to see whether she is also crying. He, like Newmarch, seems to believe in the profound emotional and psychological power of great music. In Sonnet Twenty-One, "Tatiana," the speaker narrates an old Russian tale to his friend. Tatiana, who was rejected by Oniegin when single but pursued by him once married, was faithful to her husband, although she still loved Oniegin. Though Oniegin's "pleadings tore her soul in twain," the narrator concludes, "she chose not love, but duty for her doom." The telling includes ambiguities. It is unclear if this story is meant to be a cautionary tale or if it is directed toward the narrator or the object of his affection. The sonnet sequence closes in a similarly equivocal manner, with Sonnet Thirty-Six promisingly titled *Horæ Amoris* (the hours of love), and with some sensuous stanzas, but with the concluding note being that she has deserted or dismissed him.

The final sixteen poems of the volume are collected under the heading "Verses and Translations," and Newmarch's interest in all things Russian or musical, as well as her real talent for painterly description, are apparent. She explores the master artist's "unfathomed" genius in "Rembrandt," and then draws alternately picturesque and dramatic landscapes of her own in "For a Birthday" and "A Tatar Love Letter." Several poems are translations of Russian folk songs, and, in a further confluence of her interests, "St. Vladimir's Day" is dedicated to her teacher and mentor, Stassov. This "name of kings!" is aptly chosen for him, she writes, and he rules the loyalty of "a kingdom of great hearts." He also, she notes, possesses the ability to see young genius before other, duller eyes can.

In 1904 Newmarch published biographies of two prominent figures on the European fine-arts scene, Vassily Verestschagin and Henry J. Wood. While the work on Verestschagin is more akin to a long obituary than an in-depth biography, it is compellingly and dramatically told. The pacifist war painter, whose depictions of the brutality of war stirred violent reactions, was killed when the Russian flagship *Petropavlovsk,* on which he was a passen-

First page of the sheet music for one of the three Russian operas for which Newmarch translated the librettos

ger, struck a mine. Newmarch's abilities as a storyteller and an art critic are both put to admirable use in this essay, which was published in *The Living Age* and *The Fortnightly Review*. She wrote her next book about Wood, a prominent British conductor who in 1895 founded the popular Promenade Concert series (or "Proms") in London. As she discusses in the introduction to her book, Wood was a friend, and she wrote the text while he was still alive, a situation that presented the usual difficulties attendant on writing a biography of a living celebrity. In the book, much as with her earlier work on Tchaikovsky, she keeps the focus on Wood's professional rather than private life. Calling him "our greatest English conductor," she explores his emotional and interpretative conducting style.

Wood's passionate, rubato musical selections and interpretations could well have functioned as a sort of mental soundtrack for Newmarch's second poetic venture, *Songs to a Singer and Other Verses*. Much of this volume, like her first, is pervaded by music and its influence on the emotions. Joining it again are some of her other favorite themes: nature, unrequited love, and Russian folklore and culture. While she does not attempt anything as overtly ambitious as the "Horæ Amoris" sonnet sequence, many of her poems in this book are more sophisticated, with the possible exception of an overuse of a rose motif (e.g., "White Rose or Red?" "The Rose of Song," "Rose of Roses"). Newmarch again employs a tripartite organizational strategy, dividing the volume into "Songs to a Singer," "Other Verses," and "Fragments from 'King Waldemar.'"

Among the thirty-one "songs" in the first section, some are for singers, but many others are instead about singers. While often the singer is a public performer in Newmarch's poems, in "My Birthday" the singer is no celebrated beauty and talent. Rather than the usually dramatic, black and purpled darkness of many of her "minor key" works, the unhappiness and depression of this poem are expressed through bland colors and sounds: the brooding fog, her heart "grey with shadows," her view through "yellow windows / upon a yellow square," and the quiet creaking of her gate. The singer is her friend, whose voice, while unexceptional, is powerful, making "age and fog and sadness . . . long-forgotten things." The sameness of the grays and yellows is interrupted by a reminder of the exciting influences in life, such as music and friendship. Not song but its absence inspires the speaker in "Our Silences." In this more representative poem, Newmarch tells of a great opera star: "The world may have your songs, / Your beauty and your smiles, / The art that moves great throngs, / The manner that beguiles." However, rather than her song touching a chord in the speaker's soul, it is "prefulgent silences," shared with her, which he desires most.

"Song (Russian Style)" and "A Song of Flood Tide" are two of the section's more distinctive poems, in terms of rhyme scheme, rhythm, and structure. "Song" progresses spatially from stanza to stanza: from the heavens to the steppes to the woods to fathoms deep in the ocean and, ultimately and existentially, to death. Each stanza is essentially a couplet, and even further emphasizing the self-contained nature of each stage of descent, there is internal rhyme in each line that rhymes with the other line of the couplet's internal rhyme, such as in "On the steppes warm showers wake flowers Red and blue; / On love's way lie flowers, rare flowers, Shed by you." Perhaps less confusingly, the four stanzas of "A Song of Flood Tide" each consist of three, end-rhyming lines. In a fairly successful attempt to mimic the sound and motion of the tide rushing onto the beach, Newmarch employs lines such as "Like a lover new to blisses, / First earth's garment hem he kisses, / Where the wet beach drags and hisses." This experimenting with rhythm and form would come naturally to a student of Stassov and admirer of *Kuchka* members such as Nicolai Rimsky-Korsakov.

Rather than covering new ground, Newmarch's second section, "Verses," seems to hearken back to the overriding theme of her first poetry volume's central sonnet sequence: loving in vain. "Saint Elizabeth" could well be the name of the *Horæ Amoris* love object–this narrator suggests many situations where St. Elizabeth would show affection, forgiveness, and charity, such as if he were about to expire from a dread disease, or had committed a heinous illegal act, or were a leprous beggar. She repulses him, however, because he, unforgivably, wants her to love him. "Realist to Idealist" echoes more of the sonnet sequence's sentiments, contrasting the male "realist," who urges a woman to "leave your futile shadow-land" and "learn love's actuality," with the female "idealist," who loves and hopes for a man not present. "To a Wanderer" expands on the frustration of a would-be lover spurned for an intangible dream of something better and more exciting, when the only limitless frontier is not geographical but rather emotional–the speaker's own love.

After the generally unrequited love of the eight poems of "Verses," the completely mutual, if doomed, love of Tové and Wolmer in "Fragments from 'King Waldemar'" proves a pleasant juxtaposition. As an original libretto, this section of *Songs to a Singer* would seem to be the pinnacle of Newmarch's creations, if it were to be judged by her own apparent hierarchy. Newmarch communicates the wholeness and completeness of Waldemar and Tové's feelings for each other, and does so most effectively through the characters' use of verbs. To indicate their physical passions, they sing of hearts that "throb," hair that "clings," kisses that "rain," and yellow stars that "pulse and burn," and to illustrate their spiritual connection, they speak of spirits "floating," white peace resting upon souls, and inmost thoughts melting and mingling. In stark contrast, Newmarch depicts the jealous Queen Helvig's destructive potential through the use of descriptors of violence: "sharper than a hunter's knife," "wilder" than the panting of trapped birds, "hotter than the lava-flow / From the riven mountain-side." The King's lover dies of undisclosed causes, and he mourns her to the exclusion of governing or even speaking, except to muse how he might raise a band of specter horsemen to raid the gates of Heaven if God were so cruel as to send Tové there and him to Hell. Newmarch's fragmentary libretto is both readable and engrossing, and it would seem to lend itself easily to staging.

Newmarch provided the English versions of the librettos of at least three major Russian operas, Tchaikovsky's *The Queen of Spades* and Modest Mussorgsky's *Boris Godounov* (1910) and *Khovanschina* (1913). Mussorgsky was another member of the Mighty Five, perhaps the most original, and also the least formally trained. Rimsky-Korsakov completed and orchestrated *Khovanschina* for Mussorgsky in the 1870s.

By the time she published *The Russian Opera* in 1914, Newmarch had a practical, working knowledge of almost every aspect of opera. She considered herself a pioneer in the field of Russian music, and rightly so, especially in terms of dissemination of information to England and America. She dedicates the book to the preeminent bass of the time, Fyodor Shaliapin, and to the memory of their "old friend," Stassov. Shaliapin is the model for many of the illustrations in *The Russian Opera*s donning costumes and makeup for several distinctive roles, including Don Quixote. Newmarch's goal, as these illustrations might indicate, is not to engage in "too much technical analysis," but rather to inform the average opera-goer as to the development of a Russian national opera. She traces its origins back several centuries and devotes entire chapters to especially important or influential composers, such as Michael Ivanovich Glinka, Anton Rubinstein, Mussorgsky, Borodin, César Cui (another member of the *Kuchka*), Rimsky-Korsakov, and Tchaikovsky, among others.

Newmarch's last trip to Russia was in 1915, one year after the publication of her influential book on the country's opera, but her involvement with Russian, English, and Czech music was unremitting. She continued her work as the official program writer to the Queen's Hall Orchestra, which she had begun in 1908, until 1927. In 1926, through her offices and at her urging, Czech composer Leos Janácek visited England. To express his gratitude Janácek dedicated his *Sinfonietta* (1926) to her. In 1928 she published the first of the six-volume *The Concert-goer's Library of Descriptive Notes*.

Newmarch died on 9 April 1940. Her last major work was published two years later: *The Music of Czechoslovakia* is a much more personal text than the generically similar *The Russian Opera*, a tone set by the foreword and introduction that grows only more pronounced as the book progresses. Newmarch dedicates the work to Eduard Benes, who wrote an extremely complimentary foreword. A famous antifascist, Benes served as the Czechoslovak foreign minister from 1918 to 1935 and as the president of that country from 1935 to 1938 and again from 1945 to 1948. He extends to Newmarch the "thanks of the whole Czechoslovak nation for the splendid work" she performed in making their music known in England and elsewhere. He considers that her work demonstrates "that it is worthwhile fighting for the freedom of a nation which gave the world the music of which she here writes with such admiration, love, and understanding." In the introduction Wood writes of the comprehensiveness and insight of Newmarch's final volume:

> she not only knew their language and literature, but was an intimate friend of the leading literary, musical, and political lights of the Bohemian firmament. For many years she had made long sojourns among them, entering into their everyday, care-free loves in such intimacy that their traditions and customs, their aspirations and line of thought, were as an open book to her: indeed her long association with the *people* developed into a very deep and lasting affection for the *arts* of Czechoslovakia.

Wood has mentioned the two most telling and descriptive terms for *The Music of Czechoslovakia*, intimacy and affection. Newmarch's easy relationship with and love for the people and culture of the Czech nation is communicated throughout the book. A particularly humorous and representative example occurs when she is invited to a restaurant in a "typical little Moravian town" to hear an informal group of singers. After several "decorous and solemn" songs, she asks the veterinarian and unofficial leader of the group, "Had they no drinking-songs? No dancing-songs?" He and his friends respond by launching into over two hours of less "ladylike" songs, which Newmarch claims she thoroughly enjoyed.

Rosa Harriet Newmarch has earned a place with the great and influential music critics of the first half of the twentieth century. While her poetry may sometimes lack the good-natured and slyly humorous style of much of her prose, it is certainly an appropriate and true expression of her love of music, human emotions, dramatic potential, and Russian arts and culture.

Letters:

Janácek-Newmarch Correspondence, edited by Zdenka E. Fischmann (Rockville, Md.: Kabel, 1986).

References:

Theodore Baker, "Newmarch, Rosa," revised by Nicolas Slonimsky, in *Baker's Biographical Dictionary of Musicians* (New York: Schirmir, 1992), p. 1302;

Virginia Blain, Patricia Clements, and Isobel Grundy, "Newmarch, Rosa Harriet," in their *Feminist Companion to Literature in English: Women Writers from the Middle Ages to the Present* (New Haven: Yale University Press, 1990), p. 791;

"Newmarch, Rosa," in *New Grove Dictionary of Music and Musicians,* volume 13, edited by Stanley Sadie (London: Macmillan, 1980), pp. 164–165;

"Newmarch, Rosa," in *New Grove Dictionary of Opera,* volume 3, edited by Sadie (London: Macmillan, 1992), pp. 583–584.

Charlotte Grace O'Brien

(23 November 1845 – 3 June 1909)

Lisa Kerr
University of South Carolina

BOOKS: *Light and Shade* (London: Kegan Paul, 1878; New York: Harper, 1878);
A Tale of Venice: A Drama and Lyrics (Dublin: Gill, 1880);
Lyrics (London: Kegan Paul, 1886);
Cahirmoyle, of the Old Home (Limerick: Guy, 1888);
Charlotte Grace O'Brien, Selections from her Writings and Correspondence with Memoir by Stephen Gwynn (Dublin: Maunsel, 1909).

OTHER: H. Haliday Sparling, *Irish Minstrelsy* (London: Scott, 1888);
The Cabinet of Irish Literature, edited by C. A. Read, revised and extended by Katharine Tynan (London: Gresham, 1902);
"Sonnets" and "The River" in *The Dublin Book of Irish Verse: 1728–1909,* edited by John Cooke (Dublin: Hodges, 1909; London: Oxford University Press, 1924);
"Hessy" and "Wicklow" in *Pillars of the House: An Anthology of Verse by Irish Women from 1690 to the Present,* edited by A. A. Kelly (Dublin: Wolfhound, 1987);
Excerpts from "The Feminine Animal" and "Care of the Immigrants" in *Ireland's Women: Writings Past and Present,* edited by Katie Donovan, A. Norman Jeffares, and Brendan Kennelly (New York and London: Norton, 1994).

SELECTED PERIODICAL PUBLICATIONS–
UNCOLLECTED: "The Irish Poor Man," *Nineteenth Century* (December 1880);
"Eighty Years," *Nineteenth Century* (March 1881).

Charlotte Grace O'Brien

Charlotte Grace O'Brien was an energetic and strong-willed Irish political reformer and writer who recorded many of her experiences, both political and personal, in her poetry. O'Brien's poems span the middle ground between traditional, sentimental light verse and modern verse that would characterize the early twentieth century. Writing during a time of literary revival in Ireland, O'Brien never achieved enduring fame as a poet; however, her contribution to nineteenth-century Irish literature is notable. Though her work often concerns stereotypical female topics of the Victorian era–domestic life, love, religion, and nature–much of it is also intellectually and politically charged, engaging social questions and controversies, especially relating to the Irish people.

Before John O'Leary, a Fenian leader, inspired young poets such as William Butler Yeats, Katharine Tynan, and O'Brien's nephew Stephen Gwynn with the words, "There is no great literature without nationality, no great nationality without literature," O'Brien had consistently put this theory into practice. Having completed most of her major works before the death of Irish nationalist leader Charles Parnell in 1891, O'Brien was a direct predecessor of poets of the Irish Renaissance.

O'Brien was born 23 November 1845 at Cahirmoyle in County Limerick to William Smith O'Brien and Lucy Caroline Gabbett, his second wife, whom he had married in 1832. The couple had seven children, five boys and two girls. The O'Briens were wealthy Protestant landlords in Clare County, Ireland, but also members of the native Irish aristocracy, descendants of Brian Boru, conqueror of Viking rule in Ireland. As a ruling family the O'Briens had stood as representatives in Parliament for generations, earning reputations as moderate politicians. O'Brien's father began his career as a conservative but over the years began to assume a more activist voice, calling for Catholic emancipation. He sided with Daniel O'Connell in 1844 in his call for repeal of the union with Britain, and in 1848, O'Brien advocated in a speech at Westminster the overthrow of the legislative body that had oppressed the Irish people for nearly thirty years. After an ill-conceived uprising, he was convicted of treason and exiled to Tasmania. In 1854 he returned to Europe, settling with his family in Brussels, and in 1856, after being fully pardoned, he brought his family home to Ireland. Because of her father's banishment, O'Brien spent part of her young life overseas; however, she considered Clare County and Cahirmoyle Castle, the County Limerick property her father inherited from his maternal grandfather, as her home. She returned there time and again in her life and in her literature.

According to Gwynn, all of the O'Brien children were raised "to use their brains as well as their bodies for play," and in time many of her siblings went to St. Columba's College, near Dublin, and to Trinity College. O'Brien's mother, a gentle, easygoing woman, provided a center for the children's world, but her death in 1861 brought the family cohesion to an end. The father took his children to live in Killiney, near Dublin, for a time, and later O'Brien moved back to Cahirmoyle, completing her education under the guidance of a governess. In 1864 she joined her father at Bangor in Wales, where he died shortly after of heart failure. Like the death of her mother, the loss of her father devastated her, and in time she would exhibit a political ideology and a strong sense of nationalism that mirrored her father's.

In 1866 O'Brien moved in with her brother Edward and his family at Cahirmoyle. When Edward's wife and O'Brien's dear friend, Mary, died two years later, she took charge of the home and children. O'Brien, as well as her brothers and sisters, suffered from hearing loss, and the condition worsened at this time. Because she had always been rough, boyish, and untidy, she also struggled to keep the household in running order.

O'Brien's living habits and attitudes often conflicted with those of her brother, who required order and structure. Relations between the two were difficult at times, despite their obvious love for one another. Not only did Edward view himself as the head of the household, but also he took pleasure in instructing O'Brien about her writing, which she had presumably begun while living at Cahirmoyle. Gwynn writes of the relationship between the siblings: "He had the scholar's instinct developed in excess, he demanded finish, form, all the qualities which she lacked; and she was never enough of an artist to submit even when she raged. She raged without submitting, insisted that her work must be spontaneous, or would be nothing." Perhaps because of her work habits O'Brien did not begin to write seriously and professionally until years later. Even after she started writing O'Brien continued to be distracted by household duties, which would preoccupy her until Edward's remarriage in 1880 and his relocation to London.

In 1878 O'Brien completed and published one novel, *Light and Shade,* a fictionalized account of men involved in the Fenian Uprising of 1867. O'Brien received praise for the book from those who sympathized with the cause. In a letter dated 3 November 1878, Will Upton, a former leader in the Fenian organization, commended her for depicting "peasant life truly without prejudice."

In the two years following the publication of *Light and Shade,* O'Brien faced upheaval again. The children whom she loved dearly were leaving Cahirmoyle for school and Charles, her dearest sibling who lived nearby, passed away in 1879. O'Brien then moved to a small house near Mount Trenchard.

In 1880 O'Brien's first major work that included poetry was published, *A Tale of Venice: A Drama and Lyrics.* The book, which included poems she had written and collected over the years, demonstrates her skills in writing sonnets and ballads as well as her interest in politics. Dedicated to her late brother, the book includes commemorative poems, such as those for Charles and Mary O'Brien, and ones that express her support of the Irish people. In "The Workers for Ireland" and two sonnets

O'Brien as the superintendent of the home for emigrants she operated in Queenstown in 1881–1882

addressed to the prime minister of England, William Ewart Gladstone, she writes of her support for Irish nationalists and her disdain for British interference in Irish affairs. She admired Parnell, and she was increasingly attracted to political life.

In a letter dated 16 February 1881 to Alice Spring Rice, O'Brien confesses that she was becoming "wild" about politics. The next day, in a letter to an unspecified recipient, she wrote, "I have always held that if one could clearly see one's way in a great political question, it is not right to hold back." As she noted in this letter, O'Brien viewed the passage of the Coercion Acts of 1881 and 1882, designed to curtail the civil liberties of agrarian activists, as an "instrument of eviction." In December 1880 and March 1881, she published "The Irish Poor Man" and "Eighty Years" in the journal *Nineteenth Century*. Both articles defended the Irish people against what she called the "vices of slavery" that threatened their lives. She wrote often to *The Pall Mall Gazette*, edited by John Morley, sometimes sending private correspondence to him as well as the public letters that he regularly published.

In the 1880s, with the worsening famine and growing political unrest, Irish emigration became an issue of serious concern. Those who fled the country often did so under inhumane and dangerous conditions. O'Brien's greatest concern was for the young, single women forced to travel to the United States at the risk of their safety. Under typical conditions, single women were not separated from other steerage passengers but lived and slept among men, married couples, and families, sometimes even horses housed with the passengers. In order to reach lavatories at night young women were forced to leave their compartments alone. At times up to five hundred women would be on board a vessel with no female steward to oversee their needs. O'Brien found these circumstances unacceptable.

Although she was still a Protestant, her involvement with emigration reform brought her into close contact with the Catholic Church. She corresponded with and worked alongside Father O'Kennedy, a Catholic priest who shared her concerns for the welfare of Irish immigrants and whom she befriended in 1881. She was also promised by Archbishop Thomas William Croke, whom O'Brien called in a 26 June 1881 letter to Rice "one of the most powerful men in Ireland," that she would have his full support in reform. Although O'Brien did not confess to anyone at the time that she entertained ideas of conversion, she appreciated the power of the Catholic Church in Ireland and the United States and used her connections to the benefit of the emigrants. Her relationships with many members of the Church's hierarchy became personal. For instance, while in the United States on a brief stay, she met and consulted with Bishop Nugent, whom she called one of the greatest men in the United States. She also respected and admired Archbishop John Ireland, the Irish-born leader of the parish of St. Paul in Minnesota, with whom she communicated the rest of her life. During her stays in the United States she was able to remain involved in reform despite the limitations of a disability, which may have been the result of what Gwynn calls a "serious carriage accident" in childhood, and her deafness. Neither kept her from speaking publicly or from entertaining and going out with the friends she made easily.

O'Brien worked to establish an emigration home in Queenstown, Ireland, the major port of embarkation, but when the Catholic Church failed to establish one, in 1881 she founded the home herself. She was able to lodge 105 emigrants at a time at the boardinghouse, and approximately 3,000 people a year stayed there. In establishing the house, she took a good deal of control over Irish traffic on the

Queenstown steamship lines. She could not force the emigrants to travel on one line rather than another, but she was quick to recommend the safest of lines, and the emigrants trusted her word. Realizing her power, Thomas Henry Ismay, the owner of the White Star Lines, agreed to meet with her to discuss her concerns with shipboard conditions.

O'Brien's hard work for others was not achieved without consequence, and by 1882 her health was beginning to fail. She experienced early signs of heart disease, and also began suffering from a tenderness in her right breast. O'Brien wrote to a family member to reassure the rest of the family that she would survive the illness. Living up to her reputation as an optimist, she wrote in a December 1882 letter to her dearest friend in Queenstown, Molly Dickinson: "But in any case this physical fright has done me good. It's rather a blessing to have the shortness of all one's troubles forced on one."

According to Gwynn, O'Brien claimed also that the fear of illness could not match the pain caused by the loss of a loved one that occurred that same year. Although Gwynn includes an 1883 letter from O'Brien to her niece Mary in which O'Brien hints at a "mercenary" betrayal by a loved one, the circumstances surrounding this relationship are clouded. Allegedly, O'Brien had fallen in love with an unnamed person who passed out of her life, leaving her heartbroken. Gwynn offers only one line of explanation in his memoir: "Out of her emigration work had sprung a friendship, which passed into another feeling, and the end was bitter disillusion."

The Queenstown Home closed in 1882, but O'Brien continued to be preoccupied by the plight of the Irish people. Her second volume of poetry, simply titled *Lyrics,* appeared in 1886 and included several political poems that, as Gwynn describes them, belong "to rhetoric rather than to literature." O'Brien operated on the belief that Irish writers could and should write about Ireland in Irish voices. For her the heart of Ireland was represented not only by its politics, but through its people and its natural beauty.

Lyrics continues O'Brien's tradition of commemorative poems. In "Hessy," she praises a young nephew for his sweetness and innocence, and in "Wicklow," she expresses her undying love for the Irish race and for Irish land. *Lyrics* also includes works about the home at Queenstown and her visits to the United States.

O'Brien received praise for the collection. In his December 1888 review in the Catholic nationalist publication *The Irish Monthly,* Father Matthew Russell, a supporter of Irish poets, claimed that O'Brien's sonnet "Liverpool" surpassed her previous ones, including those to Gladstone. He wrote, "Nothing is written as a mere exercise in versification, but in order to express some real feeling of the writer's heart." To demonstrate O'Brien's ability, Russell chose the poem "Deafness: The Past and Present," a poem he claimed achieved literary excellence with its plaintive and well-crafted lines expressing her loss of hearing: "O, bitter loss! all Nature's voices dumb / Oh, loss beyond all loss! about my neck / The children cast their arms; no voices break / Upon my ear; no sounds of laughter come– / Child's laughter, wrought of love, and life, and bliss; / Heedless I leave the rest, had I but this!" O'Brien saw her loss of hearing as the loss of her ability to interact fully with nature and with loved ones. Despite its distinctly Irish voice and timely themes, *Lyrics* did not sell in Ireland, and O'Brien temporarily considered the possibility of selling her collection in the United States. She apparently never followed through with this venture.

In 1887, while she was writing her next volume of poetry, O'Brien converted to Roman Catholicism. By her own account, she was first moved by the acts of faith, humility, and charity she had witnessed among Catholic laymen and clergy while in the United States. In a letter she wrote to her youngest niece, Polly, that year, she professed to have studied the Catholic faith for a long time, through books and the instruction of Father Matthew Russell in Dublin, before finalizing her decision. Once converted, her devotion to the Catholic Church was passionate and reverent. In spite of her conversion, O'Brien continued to support Parnell and his moderate nationalist politics, and she was saddened greatly by his fall from grace in 1890.

In 1888 O'Brien published the last major work of her life, *Cahirmoyle, of the Old Home.* This collection, more than her previously published volumes of poetry, displays thematic unity, with most of the pieces revolving around people and places of her childhood. She devotes individual poems to "The House," "The Old Garden," "The Nursery," "The Study," and "The Drawing Room." In others she praises family members such as "The Father" and "The Mother," commemorating them for their courage and enduring love. She writes of her father as a banished hero: "Outcast because he sought our land's relief, / Exiled from home with every branded thief, / Torn from his love and scarred by insult's knife. / Ah! Father, it was hard such lot to bear." She portrays her mother as loyal and loving: "She stood by that great heart to whom she clave, / Honouring the last and noblest word he gave." Also, a portion of the collection is dedicated to the memory of her ani-

Title page for O'Brien's second book of poems, which includes political and commemorative pieces

mals, including poems to "Old Seal," "Rover," and "The Hedgehogs." Finally, she addresses more abstract subjects in the poems "Dreams," "Absence," and "Farewell."

Though these verses speak of things from O'Brien's childhood, the voice is that of a mature O'Brien. In this collection, she combines forms she has competently mastered with the subjects that have stayed with her all her life. Though somewhat sentimental in nature, these poems are crafted by a more confident imagination. They are the final and most successful tributes to the home, family, and country she loved and to which she devoted her life.

Although most of O'Brien's major published works are volumes of poetry, she also wrote essays, some of which were never printed. Some were unpublished until collected by Gwynn. Two of these essays, "The Feminine Animal" and "The Pain of Solitude," provide windows into O'Brien's state of mind in her later years. In "The Feminine Animal," published in 1890, O'Brien's message seems feminist and Victorian at the same time. For example, O'Brien urges young women to abandon idleness and vanity for "work, cleanliness, truth, modesty, and pure womanhood." While she calls the young women of Ireland to be independent, she also writes that "men are not superior to the mother and child; they are superior to the single woman" who has "failed" to develop herself fully if she has not given birth. Perhaps O'Brien's message is mixed because it is tinged with personal sorrows. As Gwynn observed, O'Brien may have to some degree lamented the absence of marriage and motherhood in her own life. In the essay O'Brien writes, "stores of nerve-passion and mother-love that have never been put to their proper use become as demons to turn in upon her and rend her."

In "The Pain of Solitude," which Gwynn notes he found written on "scraps of creamery accounts and bazaar tickets," some of which are dated 1892, O'Brien continues to reflect on her personal fate as she draws closer to the end of her life. Here she records the misery that plagues a mind in isolation, noting that deafness adds an increased solitude to a life of loneliness, one that ultimately becomes maddening. Her isolation was the cause of the bouts of depression that O'Brien suffered in life: "I should choose death by fire rather than insanity through mental torture."

If these essays are indicators of her mental state, O'Brien seems to have lost her famous spirit and unflagging energy. In the last ten years of her life, O'Brien wrote little, even to family and friends. However, despite her feelings of isolation, she was often in the company of loved ones as well as her beloved pets. She continued to visit the country and to make public appearances. Her last public appearance was in July 1905, when she gave an impromptu speech to a crowd of five thousand at a meeting of the Gaelic League in Abbeyfeale.

During her private time O'Brien continued to make small efforts at writing. She had a hobby collecting riddles and attempted to learn Gaelic. Her last writings were essays that she contributed monthly to *Irish Gardening* as a series titled "The Making of Our Home." O'Brien died on 3 June 1909 at Ardanoir, Foynes, of heart failure.

O'Brien's longtime friend, Father O'Kennedy, gave the eulogy at her funeral, saying to those who gathered: "I need not tell you how kind and good she was; you know it. I need not tell you how noble; that too you know." At her request she was buried in a graveyard at Knockpatrick, overlooking the Shannon River.

In September 1909 *Irish Book Lover* journalist James Coleman correctly predicted that O'Brien would best be remembered for her philanthropic work. He was less accurate in foreseeing the future of O'Brien's literary reputation, believing she would be secured "high rank in the galaxy of high Irish writers." While her work has since been eclipsed by the work of better known pioneers of the Irish Renaissance, Coleman's statement does suggest the respect O'Brien enjoyed during her career.

In the last decades of the twentieth century interest in O'Brien resurfaced. Biographical accounts of her career as an activist and feminist appeared in collections such as Maria Luddy and Mary Cullen's *Women, Power, and Consciousness in 19th Century Ireland* (1995) and Bernadette Whelan's *Clio's Daughters: Essays on Irish Women's History, 1845–1939* (1997). However, without Gwynn's careful record of O'Brien's writing career, which included correspondences and unofficial reviews of her published works, as well as the only comprehensive biography of O'Brien, her place in Irish literature would not have been secured.

Biography:

Charlotte Grace O'Brien, Selections from her Writings and Correspondence, with a Memoir by Stephen Gwynn (Dublin: Maunsel, 1909).

References:

James Coleman, "From South and West," *Irish Book Lover,* 1 (September 1901): 21–22;

Anne Colman, "Charlotte Grace O'Brien," in *Dictionary of Irish Literature: Revised and Expanded Edition,* edited by Robert Hogan (London: Greenwood Press, 1996), pp. 905–906;

M. C. Keogh, "Charlotte Grace O'Brien," *Irish Monthly,* 38 (May 1910): 241–245;

A. O'Connell, "Charlotte Grace O'Brien: 1845–1909," in *Women, Power, and Consciousness in 19th Century Ireland,* edited by Mary Cullen and Maria Luddy (Dublin: Attic, 1995), pp. 231–262;

A. M. O'Donnell, "Good to the Heart's Core, Charlotte Grace O'Brien 1845–1909," in *Clio's Daughters: Essays on Irish Women's History 1845–1939,* edited by Bernadette Whelan (Limerick: University of Limerick, 1997), pp. 1–31;

Richard O'Kennedy, "With the Emigrant," *Irish Monthly,* 38 (May 1910): 661–672;

Father Matthew Russell, "Our Poets: Charlotte Grace O'Brien," *Irish Monthly,* 16 (December 1888): 728–733.

Ellen O'Leary

(22 October 1831 – 15 October 1889)

Rose Novak
Boston College

BOOK: *Lays of Country, Home and Friends* (Dublin: Sealy, Bryers & Walker, 1890).

Ellen O'Leary, an Irish poet, was associated with many of the important leaders of the militant Irish Revolutionary Brotherhood (IRB) and was one of the few poets that the nationalist movement produced. Her brother John was one of its leaders in the 1860s, and when he was arrested and imprisoned and then exiled, O'Leary continued to support nationalist causes and write poetry. Upon his return to Ireland, the brother and sister became active members of several Dublin literary circles dedicated to the revitalization of Irish national literature, and they counted William Butler Yeats as one of their protégés. O'Leary's poems, many published in nationalist newspapers and collected in one posthumous volume, reveal her interest in Irish themes.

Born on 22 October 1831 in Tipperary, Ireland, O'Leary was the only daughter of John O'Leary and his second wife, Margaret Ryan O'Leary. Ellen had two brothers, John, born on 23 July 1830, and Arthur, born on 6 July 1833. Her father was a prosperous merchant who owned a substantial amount of property in Tipperary. When O'Leary's mother died in the mid 1830s, the three children were subsequently reared by their aunt Mary, of whom Ellen later wrote fondly in her poetry. Her father married again in 1841 and had two more children, Mary and Edmund. When he died in 1849 the children inherited a modest income.

Little is known of O'Leary's early life; however, it is likely that she was educated locally. Soon after her father's death, O'Leary began her poetic career at the age of twenty, publishing in such periodicals as *The Commercial Journal* and *The Irishman*. She also traveled with her brothers to Paris and London, keeping house for them while they pursued their studies. The family returned to Dublin in 1858, the same year that James Stephens, a former member of the Young Ireland movement in the 1840s, founded the Irish Revolutionary (later Republican) Brotherhood, a secret-oath-bound

Ellen O'Leary

organization that served as the sister organization to the Fenian Brotherhood in America. The IRB's main objective was to achieve Irish independence from England by physical force. O'Leary and her brothers became closely involved with the group, with Stephens appointing John O'Leary the IRB's financial manager.

In the 1850s and 1860s O'Leary published her verse in Irish nationalist newspapers such as *The Nation*. She usually used the pseudonym "Eily," or sometimes

"Lenel," an anagram of Ellen. She also contributed poetry to *The Irish People,* a newspaper that Stephens had launched in 1863 as a voice for the organization. The verses O'Leary published in *The Irish People* reflect her radical views. For example, the speaker in "The Poor Man's Christmas" (1863) expresses his discontent with the Irish landlord system:

> I'm very sure, if right took place, we'd all have full and plenty,
> The landlords live upon our toil, and leave us bare and empty.
>
> Their lives are one long holiday, through foreign lands they roam,
> Enjoying all earth's pleasures, while we slave for them at home.

In "A Mother's Lament" (1864) a widow mourns the death of her only son in the American Civil War:

> Oh, were it for poor Ireland
> That his young blood was shed,
> Like the brave men of '98
> 'Tis high I'd hold my head;
> He had the good drop in his veins,
> And if he nobly died
> For the old cause and the old land,
> 'Twould be my boast and pride.

"The Emigrants" (1864) describes the plight of those forced by poverty to leave Ireland:

> Five hundred men and women
> In Cork's sweet Cove this night;
> Pent in a close and crowded ship–
> Ill housed, ill clothed, ill fed–
> To sail away at break of day,
> To earn *their daily bread!*

Stephens appointed John an editor of the paper along with Thomas Clarke Luby, one of the IRB's original members, and Charles Joseph Kickham, one of the most successful Irish novelists of the nineteenth century. With these appointments the office of *The Irish People* became in effect the IRB headquarters in Dublin. The literary staff met at John's lodgings every Friday night after the paper went to press to discuss literature, politics, and the progress of the paper. Whenever they came to Dublin from Tipperary, O'Leary and her half sister, Mary, joined the group.

From the time of the IRB's establishment, members were recruited, armed, and drilled, and an armed rising was planned for 1865. By then approximately one hundred thousand men had joined the movement; however, they were poorly equipped. Also, government authorities had put the staff under surveillance and infiltrated the organization with informers. On 15 September 1865 the police broke into the office of *The Irish People* and arrested several IRB men who were on the premises. O'Leary's brother John was arrested later that evening at his lodgings.

A few days later, Kickham, who had avoided arrest along with Stephens and Edward Duffy, one of the top IRB men, sent a note to O'Leary in Tipperary asking her to come to Dublin. She was brought under cover of dark to Sandymount, a Dublin suburb, where she found Stephens in hiding, along with Duffy, Kickham, and Hugh Brophy, one of the original Dublin members of the IRB. Stephens asked her to withdraw IRB money from John's account, but she eventually discovered that the government had ordered the bank's directors not to release any money.

O'Leary describes Stephens in her introduction to *Lays of Country, Home and Friends* (1890): "For myself, believing him at this time to be the right man in the right place, I felt an ardent admiration, had unbounded trust in him, and was willing, under his direction, to do anything for the cause." She discreetly carried messages between Sandymount and Dublin and was apparently not noticed by the police. Some believed that Stephens's wife, however, was identified, and Stephens, Kickham, Duffy, and Brophy were subsequently arrested. When Stephens made plans to break out of jail, O'Leary was the only woman told. After escaping ten days later, Stephens sent O'Leary to Paris on IRB business. Upon her return, she attended her brother's trial, sitting near him throughout the proceedings. John was convicted of treason and sentenced to twenty years. When his verdict was read, reporters noted O'Leary's attempt to conceal her emotions.

The arrests of the leaders of the IRB had damaged the movement but plans continued for a militant uprising. O'Leary remained in Dublin for two years after Stephens's escape. She and Mary actively participated in the Ladies' Committee of the IRB, which collected funds to provide counsel for the prisoners on trial, fed those who were sick, and aided the families of the prisoners. After the outbreak and defeat of the Fenian uprising in 1867, O'Leary returned to her home in Tipperary. She wrote often to her brother, who was in jail.

When a general amnesty was declared in January 1871, John was released from prison on condition of exile, and O'Leary joined him in Antwerp, Belgium, a few weeks after his release. In April, O'Leary returned to Tipperary, while John moved to Paris. She visited her brother often, and he still kept up an active correspondence with his IRB connections in Ireland and the United States.

O'Leary was also deeply religious, a member of the St. Vincent de Paul Society, a Catholic welfare organization, as well as president of the Sacred Heart Society, a devotional group, in Tipperary. She was a favorite of the girls of the nearby convent school. In 1878 the authorities had given her brother permission to return home to Tipperary on family business, and he stayed with O'Leary in her cottage for several months, most of which he spent with his large book collection that his sister had carefully preserved for him.

O'Leary also continued to be politically active. She joined the Ladies Land League when it was formed in 1881 by Anna and Fanny Parnell, sisters of Charles Stewart Parnell. O'Leary was elected as one of its two treasurers and was one of seven officers. The league was one of the first women's political organizations devoted to a nongendered national cause. The Land League of Ireland, formed by Michael Davitt and Parnell, sought radical reform of the Irish land system. The League used legal and quasi-legal action to force the government's hand: boycotts, mass demonstrations, rent strikes, and passive resistance, all of which led the leaders of the Land League to prepare for their arrests. The Ladies Land League sought to provide relief for evicted tenants and legal advice for those resisting eviction. When the group agitated for even more-radical action, Parnell disbanded the league in 1882, a move that angered many members and supporters. In 1885, when her brother's exile ended, O'Leary sold her cottage in Tipperary and moved to Dublin to live with him, bringing with her all of his books, which she called "John's treasures."

Their double income from established property holdings in Tipperary enabled them to enjoy a high standard of living in Dublin. Soon after their arrival the O'Learys became enthusiastic supporters of various nationalist and literary organizations, and they occupied a central place in the Dublin literary scene. In 1885 John presided at meetings of the Young Ireland Society and became a member of the Contemporary Club, where he met the Irish portrait painter John Butler Yeats and his son, William. The informal atmosphere of the club encouraged lively political discourse and created a venue for artists and writers to discuss their work. Women were not allowed membership in the club but were permitted to attend lectures on ladies' night, to publish, and to give readings.

William Butler Yeats first met O'Leary in 1885 when he paid a visit to her home, hoping to speak to her brother. She persuaded him to stay and included him in a game of cards with a few other women. When he lost sixpence, he was compensated with "a glass" of sherry from which it took him several days to recover. In an undated letter to Katharine Tynan, O'Leary described Yeats as "my special and first favourite among our young men."

Once a week, a group of men and women including the poets Tynan, Rosa Mulholland, Rose Kavanagh, and George Russell (later known as AE), and the writers Douglas Hyde and T. W. Rolleston met in the O'Leary parlor for literary discussion. As patrons and sponsors the O'Learys urged these writers to produce prose and poetry that was Irish in content but which transcended sectarianism. John lent Yeats his books hoping to raise the poet's awareness of Irish literature, history, legend, and folklore.

After Yeats moved to London in 1887, the O'Learys corresponded with him regularly, continuing to play major roles in the development of his literary career. By collecting subscriptions, John helped secure the publication in 1889 of Yeats's first book of poetry, *The Wanderings of Oisin*.

Ellen O'Leary was instrumental in bringing about the meeting between Yeats and the woman who would inspire many of his poems, the actress and nationalist leader, Maud Gonne. O'Leary wrote Yeats in January 1889 that she had given "a new lady friend of ours and new convert to love of Ireland" a letter of introduction to his father. In her autobiography, Gonne remembers O'Leary as "a charming little lady with the same aquiline features as her brother, only much softer; she was dressed in very unfashionable clothes which suited her, and which I think she must have bought many years before. . . . there was a curious halo of romance and sadness about her as she presided at the neatly set-out tea table, looking after everyone's wants so quietly, one hardly noticed her."

From 1886 to 1889 O'Leary published her verse in various collections and newspapers. Charles Gavan Duffy, one of the leaders of the Young Ireland movement in the 1840s, reviewed several of her poems for the *Dublin University Review* in December 1886. In his review titled "A Celtic Singer," he called O'Leary a "singer of simple songs true to nature and native feelings" who describes "what she has seen and felt, and whose verses are the outcome of emotions too strong to be repressed." H. H. Sparling's 1887 collection of Irish verse, *Irish Minstrelsy*, included her tribute poem to Edward Duffy, "To God and Ireland True."

The O'Learys also supported the Gaelic Athletic Association (GAA) founded in 1884 to reinvigorate traditional Irish sports such as hurling and gaelic football. O'Leary assisted her brother in his work as literary editor of *The Gael*, the weekly GAA newspaper established in the spring of 1887. The paper published poems, stories, and articles by O'Leary, Yeats, Tynan, Hyde, and Rolleston. In spring 1888 Dublin publisher M. H. Gill and Son published a small anthology, *Poems and Ballads of Young Ireland*, that included a selection of O'Leary's poems as well as verses by Yeats, Hyde, Kavanagh, and Tynan. In 1888 Yeats edited *Fairy and Folk Tales of the Irish Peasantry*, a compilation in which he included her poem "A Legend of Tyrone," a ballad about the legend of a mother's ghost who returns at night to visit and care for her neglected children. The brother and sister also joined the Pan Celtic Society, which was founded in March 1888 as a nonpolitical and nonsectarian group whose membership was limited to those who had published poetry or prose in an Irish magazine or newspaper or who had knowledge of the Irish language. O'Leary contributed several of her poems to its *Lays and Lyrics of the Pan Celtic Society* published in 1889. One of her final compositions, "My Own Galtees," was printed in *The Irish Monthly* in May 1889.

At this stage of O'Leary's career, her poetry favored a more sentimental view of both the political and the personal, reflecting a changed social and political climate in Ireland in general. For example, "A Song for the Gaelic Athletic Clubs" celebrates a moderate cultural nationalism that lacks the violence of her more radical poetry:

> Come forth! come forth! let each man's hand
> Grasp comrade's as a brother,
> By no harsh word let strife be fanned,
> Forbear with one another;
> 'Tis for the right you all unite,
> Then let your watchwords be—
> Courage and truth and stainless youth,
> They'll make old Ireland free.

Her more personal voice is clearer in the poem "Dying in the May," a lament for the death of her half sister Mary:

> Still the hawthorn hedge was shedding
> Its fresh, fragrant, sweet perfume,
> And the primrose outspreading,
> When they bore her to the tomb.

Charles H. Oldham, founder of the Contemporary Club, assisted O'Leary in the publication of her book, *Lays of Country, Home and Friends*. O'Leary had written Tynan on 24 January 1889 that she was collecting her own poems for publication and that she was pleased that Oldham had tactfully refrained from telling her and John about the project until he had gotten subscriptions for £20. She further told Tynan that she and John had wanted to publish a small volume themselves but had found the cost prohibitive.

O'Leary was in ill health even before John's return to Ireland in 1885. She had consulted a Dublin specialist, who diagnosed cancer of the breast and abdomen. Although she had undergone surgery at one time,

O'Leary's father, John O'Leary (from Joseph Denieffe, A Personal Narrative of the Irish Revolutionary Brotherhood, *1969)*

it had been only partially successful, and she experienced several painful relapses between 1885 and 1887. O'Leary had been correcting the proofs for her book when she wrote in a letter to her niece that she had been sick and could not see any beauty or poetry in her verses, though she hoped others would. She was in a hurry to finish the proofs, she explained, so that her brother, who was in Paris, could look them over with Yeats when he visited him in London. She told her niece that Yeats had "a good eye for little verbal alterations and a good ear for harmonious sounds."

John was still in Paris when O'Leary died on 15 October 1889 in Cork, where she was staying with her nephew. On 23 October 1889 Yeats wrote Tynan, asking her about the details of Ellen's death. John had written from Paris telling Yeats that "a horrible calamity has come and the light of my life has gone out." When John arrived in London, he gave Yeats his sister's proof sheets, explaining her request for his corrections. Yeats observed that John was deeply in grief, making constant indirect references to his sister's death but saying nothing definite. He was not able to return to Ireland in time for his sister's funeral.

O'Leary was buried in the family plot in Tipperary. Her death was reported in the *Cork Examiner* on 16 October 1889 and in *The Nation, Nationalist,* and *United Ireland* on 26 October 1889. Tynan published a lengthy obituary in the *Boston Pilot* on 9 November 1889 focusing on O'Leary's heroic nature, patriotism, devotion to her brother, and her central place in the Dublin literary scene. *The Nation* printed excerpts from Tynan's tribute in the 23 November 1889 issue. Yeats also wrote a tribute to her, which was published in the *Boston Pilot* on 28 December 1889.

Oldham, Gonne, and George Sigerson, who was formerly on the staff of *The Irish People,* took over the arrangements for the publication of O'Leary's book. *Lays of Country, Home and Friends* includes a biographical introduction by Rolleston and a reprint of Duffy's 1886 review of her poems. The volume also includes a dedicatory poem by Kavanagh and a selection of Arthur O'Leary's poetry. Yeats published a sympathetic review of the book in the *Boston Pilot* on 18 April 1891. The poet John Todhunter also reviewed the volume in *The Academy* (24 July 1891). He wrote that he was charmed "by its absolute simplicity and absence of literary artifice." It was "racy of the soil" and demonstrated a "stern reticence of feeling," though he wished that the poet had "studied the art of versification more closely." In 1892 a volume of Alfred H. Miles's anthology, *The Poets and Poetry of the Century,* included several of her poems with an introduction by Yeats. Yeats described his friend's poetry as simple, sincere, and passionate. In his tribute to Ellen O'Leary on her death, Yeats wrote that her poetry "had in its mingled austerity and tenderness a very Celtic quality. It was like a rivulet flowing from mountain snows. She was her brother's lifelong friend and fellow-worker."

References:

Marcus Bourke, *John O'Leary: A Study in Irish Separatism* (Tralee, Ireland: Anvil, 1967);

Nancy Cardozo, *Lucky Eyes and a High Heart: The Life of Maud Gonne* (Indianapolis: Bobbs-Merrill, 1978);

Anne Ulry Colman, *Dictionary of Nineteenth Century Irish Women Poets* (Galway, Ireland: Kenny's Bookshop, 1996);

Jane Côté, *Fanny and Anna Parnell: Ireland's Patriot Sisters* (London: Macmillan, 1991);

Joseph Denieffe, *A Personal Narrative of the Irish Revolutionary Brotherhood,* introduction by Seán Ó Lúing (Shannon: Irish University Press, 1969);

John Devoy, *Recollections of an Irish Rebel* (Shannon: Irish University Press, 1969);

R. F. Foster, *W. B. Yeats: A Life,* volume 1: *The Apprentice Mage, 1865–1914* (Oxford: Oxford University Press, 1998);

Michael Kenny, *The Fenians: Photographs and Memorabilia from the National Museum of Ireland* (Dublin: Country House, 1994);

Maud Gonne MacBride, *A Servant of the Queen,* edited by A. Norman Jeffares and Anna McBride White (Gerrards Cross, Ireland: Smythe, 1994);

John O'Leary, *Recollections of Fenians and Fenianism,* 2 volumes (New York: Barnes & Noble, 1969);

Mark F. Ryan, *Fenian Memories,* second edition, edited by T. F. O'Sullivan (Dublin: Gill, 1946);

Margaret Ward, *Maud Gonne: Ireland's Joan of Arc* (London: Pandora, 1990).

Bessie Rayner Parkes
(Madame Belloc)
(16 June 1829 - 23 March 1925)

Constance M. Fulmer
Pepperdine University

BOOKS: *Poems* (London: Chapman, 1852);
Remarks Upon the Education of Girls (London: Chapman, 1854);
Summer Sketches and Other Poems (London, 1854);
Gabriel (London: Chapman, 1856);
The History of Our Cat Aspasia (London, 1856);
Ballads and Songs (London, 1863);
Essays on Women's Work (London: Strahan, 1865);
Vignettes: Twelve Biographical Sketches (London & New York: Strahan, 1866);
La Belle France, as Madame Belloc (London: Strahan, 1868);
Peoples of the World, as Belloc (London & New York: Cassell, Potter & Galpin, 1870);
In a Walled Garden, as Belloc (London: Ward & Downey, 1895);
Historic Nuns, as Belloc (London: Duckworth, 1896);
A Passing World, as Belloc (London: Ward & Downey, 1897);
The Flowing Tide, as Belloc (St. Louis: Herder, 1900);
In Fifty Years, as Belloc (London: Sands, 1904).

OTHER: Mary Merryweather, *Experience of Factory Life*, preface by Parkes (London, 1962).

SELECTED PERIODICAL PUBLICATION–UNCOLLECTED: "Joseph Priestley in Domestic Life," *Contemporary Review* (July–December 1894): 567–579.

Bessie Rayner Parkes

Bessie Rayner Parkes was a poet, feminist, activist, essayist, and journalist. In addition to publishing three volumes of poetry, Parkes played an important part in the beginning years of the women's rights movement in Great Britain. She made her most significant contribution in 1858 when she helped to establish *The English Woman's Journal*. The headquarters of the journal at Langham Place in London became a focal point for those organizing on behalf of women's legal and economic welfare. At least a dozen of Parkes's 135 published poems deal with women's issues.

Parkes was born on 16 June 1829 to Joseph Parkes, a Birmingham solicitor and Unitarian radical, and Elizabeth Priestley Parkes. Her mother's father was Joseph Priestley, the Unitarian theologian, political radical, and scientist who had isolated oxygen as one of the component elements of air. Parkes grew up in a cultivated environment, and from early childhood was associated with the country's leading intellectuals. Her father's friends included Jeremy Bentham, George Grote, John Stuart Mill, William Makepeace Thackeray, and many eminent politicians. Joseph Parkes was a leading figure in the liberal party.

The Parkes family moved back and forth from Birmingham to London but lived largely in London. In her volume *Poems* (1852), Parkes addresses "Dear smoky Birmingham" with the prayer that the efforts of her townsmen will find "a noble power / To cope with and work out each worthy thing." Her father owned three houses in London; the family entertained frequently, attended concerts, and owned an impressive collection of Italian paintings, many of which are now housed at the National Gallery in London.

Parkes taught herself to read and had an early ambition of becoming a poet. Her poem "To Elizabeth Barrett Browning" begins, "I was a child when first I read your books, / And loved you dearly." Parkes started her education at a Unitarian school in Warwickshire and, according to her daughter, described herself as having been "born in the very bosom of Puritan England, and fed daily upon the strict letter of the Scripture from aged lips which I regarded with profound reverence." This knowledge of Scripture informs the rhetoric and subject matter of her poetry.

In 1846 Parkes met Barbara Leigh Smith, later Bodichon, and the two like-minded young women became lifelong friends. In 1847, because Parkes's brother Priestly was ill with consumption, the Parkes family traveled to Hastings, then famous as a seaside health resort, and stayed in a house belonging to Benjamin Leigh Smith, Barbara's father. During those months Parkes and Leigh Smith spent many happy hours together. Parkes's association with Leigh Smith, an accomplished painter, was the most significant relationship of her life as a poet. The impulse and motivation to write, as well as much of the subject matter of Parkes's poems, came from their friendship.

In 1850 Parkes and Leigh Smith traveled unchaperoned through Belgium, Germany, Austria, and Switzerland. In her diary Leigh Smith recorded that they enjoyed sketching and the scenery, but they were also becoming concerned with the issue of oppression. They determined to contribute their efforts to make society more aware of women's need for freedom and education. Upon their return Parkes wrote a poem titled "Home to England" in which she stated, "We stand together on the deck. . . . Glorious lands we leave behind us!" But as they approached England, Parkes realized, "All our heart is wrapt in thee."

Parkes immediately began to work to provide more opportunities for British women and to write poems reflecting her travels with Leigh Smith and their shared enthusiasm for social reform. In "To An Author Who Loved Truth More Than Fame," she writes, "You will not quail beneath the foolish heat, / Nor mourn anathemas you do not fear" but will dare to "write your actions where our sons may see."

Parkes dedicated her first book, *Poems,* to Leigh Smith. In a poem of eleven lines she writes, "If I in the midst of youth should die, in that dark day my greatest strength would be casting my soul on God,—*my work on thee.*" The first several poems in the volume acknowledge the passing of time, the beauties of "great Nature," and the need to work and to share the "impenetrable mystery" which lies behind the tangible. In the poem "Mysteries" she writes, "A deeper meaning, in our utterance lies, / A grander breadth of purpose on our brow. / Is this the Possible held up before us, / In the warm summer of our fitful spring?" This poem sets the tone for all of her verse—conversational, intense, conscious of natural beauty, replete with religious imagery and rhetoric, and somewhat serious and didactic. The meter is consistently iambic but the lines occasionally vary from trimeter to pentameter with the vast majority tetrameter. The stanzas vary in length as do the poems, but most of her poems are no more than two pages.

The subject matter of *Poems* is also characteristic of Parkes's later *Ballads and Songs* (1863). Of the sixty-six poems in *Poems,* ten are addressed to individuals; for example, Parkes gives fervent, humble, and even self-effacing tributes to outstanding women such as fellow poets Adelaide Procter and Elizabeth Barrett Browning, and the physician Elizabeth Blackwell.

Although she ardently supported women in her poems, Parkes also writes about male artists such as in the poem "Giotto, Da Vinci, Titian," or about male literary figures such as Thomas Carlyle, Johann Wolfgang von Goethe, William Shakespeare, Ralph Waldo Emerson, or Francis Bacon. In "The Meeting of Plato and Horace in the Elysian Fields" each man describes his contribution to posterity. Of the sixty-six poems in this first volume, fifteen are about specific places such as "London from Hampstead Heath," "To Birmingham," "Hastings in April," and "London Streets." Two are specifically about flowers—"Marsh Flowers" and "With Primroses." Many allude to delightful experiences involving flowers such as the white convolvulus in "Song," and almost all have a Wordsworthian tone and express reverence for nature. In "Two Artists" she describes a painter like Leigh Smith who says, "Wherever Nature calls will this brave artist speed." The other replies, "And I!—whatever befalls, / Follow like Ganymede!" "Giorgione and Violante" is also about two artists; one is a painter who fears that he loves and worships the glorious face of his model so much that he will lose her.

Parkes also likes to relate balladlike narratives that may or may not allude to personal incidents or friends. "A Ballad of Smuggling Days" tells of Harry, who is searching for smugglers, finds one dead, and then discovers that the dead smuggler is his own brother. Parkes does not often refer to acts of violence or cruelty although she deplores the atrocities of war in "England and Hungary in 1849."

In "The Cloud-Face" she describes a tender face, framed in braids of golden hair, painted on a little cloud. The face is spiritual and seems to be eternal:

> Yet humanly expression'd, full
> Of all that Nature teacheth, Power,
> And grace, and love, and tender joy,
> Unconscious as of any flower.
> Was it some heavenly minister?
> Or memory of mine own, more fair?
> The golden braids were lost in stars,
> The Cloud-face melted into air.

Her poem to Blackwell recalls seeing the struggling woman physician in her "lonely room" and bids her Godspeed on the far shores as she begins a new chapter in New York; Parkes prays daily that "success may crown your brow, / Shedding its glory on your quiet face." In her poems, as well as in her essays, Parkes clearly expresses the difficulty of the task that she and Leigh Smith and their fellow reformers had undertaken and the unlikelihood that their goals could be completely accomplished.

Parkes's second volume of poetry, *Summer Sketches and Other Poems* (1854), consists of only seven poems. The first three are "Lilian's First Letter to Helen," "Lilian's Second Letter to Helen," and "Helen's Answer." Lilian is described as an artist who reads John Keats and John Ruskin. The first letter, which begins "Dear Helen in Smoky town, I Love you well" is dated 13 June. It is thirteen pages long and is written in iambic tetrameter in stanzas of varied length. The second letter is dated July 1853 and is nineteen pages long and, except for two quatrains in iambic pentameter, is also in tetrameter. Lilian actually asks:

> the question which the age demands,
> 'What is a woman's right and fitting sphere?'
> How best she may, with free and willing mind,
> Develope every special genius,
> Retaining and perfecting every charm
> And sweetness sung of old, so, evenpaced,
> Walk in a joint obedience with man,
> And equal freedom of the law of God,
> Up to the height of an immortal hope.

Angela Leighton and Margaret Reynolds, who included "Lilian's Second Letter to Helen" in their 1995 anthology of Victorian women poets, noted that the poem, along with Browning's *Aurora Leigh* (1856), is "one of the few bold attempts to tackle 'the woman question' and it is clearly influenced by the voice of the older writer."

"Helen's Answer" addresses "Dear Lilian," whom she describes as "the glad poet washed in country dew," and rejoices that even "in smoky town" she has been able to read of brave New England women and their movement. She says, "In this great Babel of smoke and noise / I pant I *will* succeed . . . to be a people's poet." She continues, "O how thrice glorious is the time we live in / How ripe in promise and how rich indeed / Thank God I was born now!" and concludes with an echo of Wordsworth's "Composed Upon Westminster Bridge, September 3, 1802": "The darkness falls like dew, all London lies / Like some calm child, asleep. And so good night."

In "To a White Oxalis" she praises the "fair and fragile beauty" of the oxalis that is (perhaps said with irony) like a lady "made more for love than duty." She tells the flower that it is "Set in thy place by Hand divine / As thou fill'st it so I would mine." In "The Duke's Funeral" Parkes tells the Duke of Wellington that "England is mindful of her debt" to him "nor will from age to age forget." The metrical pattern is even more regular than in most of Parkes's poems in that all sixteen stanzas have five lines: each is four lines of iambic tetrameter followed by one of trimeter.

"The Ballad of the King's Daughter" is a story in two parts; each is in iambic tetrameter quatrains—nine in part 1 and seven in part 2. In the poem Parkes tells "How the King's Daughter, having married me a peasant for love, heareth of the death of her only brother, and taketh her little son to the King." The narrator is the peasant; the king's daughter is elegant in bearing and courageous in deed; the appearance of her eyes marks her resemblance and her family ties to her father, her dead brother, and to her little son Walter. She meets her father in her brother's funeral procession and says of her son, "His smile is the dead's, and his eye is your own. . . . I give you my jewel to wear in your crown." The story ends with the lines: "She return'd alone, but her face was white, / And her step as the step of one waked from the dead."

Parkes had met Marian Evans, later George Eliot, in 1851. Parkes introduced Evans to Leigh Smith the next year, and the three women continued to be friends. Eliot and George Henry Lewes followed Parkes's career with interest and often commented on her poems and essays; Lewes reviewed her first volume of poems. Eliot wrote of Parkes's second volume, "I have read through your little book, and have had very sweet tears in my eyes over several passages. As poetry, the 'Ballad of the King's Daughter' seems to me immeasurably the best in the book. But the *thoughts* are everywhere what I love." "The Ballad of the King's Daughter" must have been Parkes's favorite as well as Eliot's since it is the only poem from *Summer Sketches and Other Poems* that is reprinted in *Ballads and Songs*.

During the 1850s Parkes was involved in many activities in addition to writing poetry. She and Leigh Smith were particularly interested in encouraging other women artists. They started the Portfolio Club to exhibit sketches and read poetry, and among the members of the group were Jean Ingelow, Anna Mary Howitt, Christina Rossetti, Dora Greenwell, and Adelaide Procter.

Parkes and Leigh Smith continued to organize and encourage other groups of middle-class women to take united action on behalf of women's rights. In 1853 they were part of a group that called themselves the Committee for the Ladies' Address to their American Sisters on Slavery. Inspired by Harriet Beecher Stowe's *Uncle Tom's Cabin* (1852), they collected 576,000 signatures for their antislavery petition.

During the 1850s Parkes was not only writing poetry but publishing prose pieces such as her 1854 "Remarks on the Education of Girls," an essay that elicited much criticism. On 20 October 1856, when Browning was completing *Aurora Leigh*, she wrote to Isa Blagden that Parkes had "shored her up" as she faced male criticism.

In 1856 Parkes and Leigh Smith were members of the committee of self-consciously feminist women who drew up the petition to Parliament for the Married Women's Property Bill. Among the other members of the committee were writer Anna Jameson, spurred by a sense of injustice at being omitted from her husband's will in 1854; Elizabeth Reid, founder of Bedford College; and poet Mary Howitt. The petition had 24,000 signatures including those of Browning, Elizabeth Gaskell, Harriet Martineau, Geraldine Jewsbury, Jane Welsh Carlyle, and Eliot. All these women were deeply concerned that a career as governess was the only one open to women and that all of a woman's property and money belonged to her husband.

The year 1856 was a productive one for Parkes. In addition to her work toward the Married Women's Property Bill, she published a prose story for children called *The History of Our Cat Aspasia* as well as the series of eighteen poems titled *Gabriel*. Dedicated to Percy Bysshe Shelley "at Easter," Gabriel is indeed like the poet and the angel sent by God whose name he wears, but he also bears many resemblances to the risen Christ as well as to Leigh Smith. Gabriel breathes out the beauty he breathed in, looks for truth, attempts to "wrest the meaning out of life," guards the kingdom of the deer, and like Christ grows in grace with God. In celebration of Easter she writes:

> Let the dead Past be crucified
> The Past for all is full of pain,
> Time shall not slay, nor Death divide,
> Now Christ the Lord hath risen again.
> Tonight within the tomb He sleeps,
> And hides our sinful lives away;
> And all the morrow silent keeps,–
> Arise! Oh glorious Easter Day!
> The anchor's Hope of all this Earth
> The golden April hours will bring;
> Flowers to the woods, to souls new birth,
> And to the heart an inner spring.
> Who loves not Easter? Holiest time
> And radiance of the circling year!

Each of the poems in the slender volume is a different type of tribute to Gabriel. In "To Fidelis" she writes, "Italy gives me peace and health, / Italy gives my poet wealth." By contrast, "England gives me damp and cold, / And winds that drive the winter clouds / Scarce a heart to have or heed, / But evil tongues of scoffing crowds." In the last poem in the volume, Gabriel is like Alfred Tennyson's Hallam in *In Memoriam:* "He stands a type of what our race may be."

In 1858 Parkes made her most significant contribution to women's welfare when she was instrumental in starting *The English Woman's Journal,* championing education and employment for women. In organizing her supporters Parkes said, "if I wish to work especially for women, it is because I am a woman myself, and so able to appreciate their particular troubles." She wanted women to be aware of the many degradations they were suffering and believed that if women were united under the right leadership they could remedy those injustices.

Although Leigh Smith had contributed a large part of the money for the venture, she left the management of *The English Woman's Journal* to Parkes, largely because of a change in her personal situation. On 2 July 1857, Leigh Smith married Eugène Bodichon, a medical doctor and an Algerian of French extraction, and she agreed to spend at least eight months of each year in Algeria and the other four in England.

As the leader of the circle of ardent feminists at Langham Place, Parkes advocated that women needed to understand and meet the challenge of the marketplace. She believed that every young woman should be trained for some trade, and she wrote several articles dealing with women's employment for the journal.

Parkes's collection *Essays on Women's Work* (1865) was a plea for better education and employment opportunities, especially for "surplus" single women. While some women such as Gaskell were working to promote emigration as one solution to the problem, others rallied around Parkes to find ways to train women for the marketplace. Emily Faithfull, writer and activist, and Adelaide Procter, a valued contributor to *The English Woman's Journal,* collaborated with Parkes in establishing the Victoria Press, an enterprise that provided in-service training for women who were seeking employment.

The Victoria Press began in 1860 when Parkes purchased a small press and some type and hired a printer to instruct her and the other women in the craft of printing. She was convinced that women could be trained as compositors. The press took over the printing of *The English Woman's Journal, The Transactions of the Association for the Promotion of a Social Science,* and other projects of particular interest to women.

When the Victoria Press began printing a few tracts, Parkes wrote enthusiastically to Bodichon, "So here are women in the trade at last! One dream of my life!" Every aspect of the press was devoted to furthering women's causes. In 1861 Procter edited a volume called *Victoria Regia,* dedicated with special permission to Queen Victoria. Parkes wrote the poem of dedication: "Victoria Regia!—Never happier name a flower, a woman, or a Queen could claim . . . Victoria Regia! May our blossom hold in Pure white leaves a heart of gold."

A primary purpose of the volume was to provide a showcase for the technical skills of the press. It included essays, poems, and stories by Procter as well as by Blagden, Theodosia Trollope, Jewsbury, Caroline Clive, Dinah Mulock, Anna Jameson, Matilda Hays, Caroline Norton, and Amelia B. Edwards. As a matter of principle, the essays were all signed, because Parkes and her associates had been concerned with women who were still publishing under pseudonyms. In one of the essays in *Women's Work,* Parkes writes, "If editors were ever known to disclose the dread secrets of their dens, they could only give the public an idea of the authoresses whose unsigned names are legion, of their rolls of manuscripts, which are as the sands of the sea."

Procter's death in 1864 was not only a major loss to the women's movement but a grave personal disaster for Parkes. Procter had made a trip to Malvern hoping to recover from tuberculosis but died after being confined to bed for fifteen months. Parkes visited her frequently and was with her on the evening of her death. The two poets worked on a poem of Parkes's about the poetry of Jean Ingelow. Parkes's poem "For Adelaide" indicates that she considered Procter superior to herself as a poet. Parkes says to Procter:

Miniature of Parkes's husband, Louis Belloc (from Marie Belloc Lowndes, I, Too, Have Lived in Arcadia, *1941)*

When, with bent brow and all too anxious heart,
I walk with hurrying step the crowded mart,
And look abroad on men with faithless eyes,
Then do sweet snatches of thy song arise,
And float into my heart like melodies
Down dropping from the far blue deeps of heaven,
Or sweet bells wafted over fields at even.

Even without Procter the Langham Place Circle continued to grow and included many women activists who were working to help others understand the challenges of the marketplace. Many women who had been ill-treated came to Langham Place seeking work, and an employment register was established for the growing demand for shop assistants, clerks, telegraphists, hairdressers, watchmakers, and nurses as well as typesetters.

Another group of women that had offices at Langham Place called themselves the Ladies National Sanitary Association for the Diffusion of Sanitary Knowledge. Parkes supported this group by writing articles explaining how knowledge about sanitation could be disseminated by meetings with mothers and by sharing information through girls' schools. In June 1859 the journal printed her essays titled "The Details of Women's Work in Sanitary Reform" and "Charity as a Portion of the Public Vocation of Women." She and her associates also worked for the repeal of the Contagious Diseases Act. In her poem "My Old House" the narrator is a father who has lost his wife and his precious child to "the Devil of fever." He refuses to accept the possibility that the lack of proper ventilation, bad drains, and the filthy condition of his house had contributed to the illness.

Several of Parkes's poems in her 1852 collection, like those of so many of the women poets of the time, address the "hideous mortality" of infants and children among the poor. Her "London from Hampstead Heath" begins with a description of London as "A noble city and a nation's pride, set in a lovely frame of sloping hills." She then focuses on the sad tragedy of poverty-stricken parents grieving the loss of their only child. Another poem of this type is "Two Scenes of Infancy," which in the first scene describes the newborn son "quietly sleeping on its little couch." A year later he sleeps in his grave. The grieving mother is reminded that she must be as brave as the Old Testament Hannah and take comfort that Jehovah is claiming his own as when in former times the firstborn son "was vow'd unto the Lord."

In each volume of poetry Parkes deals with the role of the poet as if it were a divine mission and addresses the need for faith in God and a humble recognition of his will. In "Voluntaries," written in 1851, the narrator prays, "O Lord, for my labour make me strong." In "Warning" the narrator wants to go to God's right hand or at least to have a Christian deed to lay before his throne. The question in "Earth's Question" is how to lead a meaningful life; the answer is to follow the law of love with the attitude "Not my will but thine!" "The Moors" concludes with "Glory to God who made the Beautiful!" In "The Old Water-Colour Exhibition" she describes the works of artists as "sacrifices on the holy shrine of art to God." In "The Poet's Defense" Plato begs forgiveness for his speech slandering poetry. "The World of Art" describes all true artists as walking on "holy ground."

Parkes's second full-sized volume of poems, *Ballads and Songs*, consists of fifty-three poems of which eight were first published in *Poems* and one in *Summer Sketches and Other Poems*. Although she does not specify to whom it is addressed, the dedication begins, "Those whom these poems may concern / Will each their own true portion know" and concludes, "Dear critic, for whose eyes I wrote the greater part / Take to thyself the book I give, with all my heart." It seems likely that the "dear critic" is Leigh Smith to whom Parkes's first volume of poems was dedicated.

Like the poems of the first volume, several of these later poems are ballads dealing with various tragedies such as "The Black Death." Several are occasional poems such as "New Year's Wishes" for the queen on 31 December 1859; and several are poems of consolation such as "The Palace and the Colliery," which recognizes death as the common denominator. Queen Victoria is the one who commissions "Words of fellow-feeling, deep not loud" for the wives of the dead workers.

Other poems describe the simple beauty of nature, such as "Farmhouse Gardens" where "all sorrow softly melts away, / Dissolving in a rainbow shower," and the narrator, longing "for one long happy day," dreams that she is "a sinless flower." "The Wind Amid the Trees," "At First," "The First Primrose," "Autumn Violets," "The Little Bird," and "Symbols," are all lyrics that proclaim nature's majesties.

Also, as in the 1852 volume, she writes several poems about specific places. "St. Laurence, Undercliff" describes a church beside the sea where the narrator wants to be buried. "The Mersey and the Irwell" deals with an environmental protest describing the changes in the past one hundred years in the air where these two rivers flow; "a vast and filmy veil / Is o'er the landscape drawn" and "Smoke, rising from a thousand fires, / Hides all that past from view." On a more positive note, "The Cathedral" describes a beautiful edifice that God must have framed in the artist's mind who has "wrought / His thoughts divinely into stone."

As in the 1852 volume, there are several poems in this volume that are addressed to individuals such as the one to Robert Burns, written for the anniversary of his birth, 25 January 1859. "King Arthur" recalls the glorious knights, the enchanted spot, the bright armor, and the mystic rites that comprised the charm of Arthur's court. "Robin Hood" describes the time when "Robin stole forth in his quaint forest-fashion" and wishes "we could follow the lesson he teaches."

Parkes includes several love poems. In "Firelight" the lonely narrator is waiting for a love who is coming; in "Absence" the lover says, "I find thee not in sight more dear, / Nor less in absence nigh"; and in "The Dead Love" the bereaved sings "fresh perpetual song" for his lost love. "A Midsummer Night's Dream" features Oberon as *loquitur;* his Fairy Princess has been stolen, and he accuses Nature of having hidden her and describes how lonely his life is without her.

The last two sections of *Ballads and Songs* are titled "Italy," with nine poems, and "Algiers," with two poems. The poems in "Italy" deal with a variety of topics such as Rome, baptized in the blood of Christian men, a Heavenly city; "St. John Lateran," an English mother's son to whom the mother church was raised fifteen hundred years earlier; and "Minerva Medica," dedicated to Blackwell and asking "a helpful blessing" on "Women bent to heal." "Two Graves" honors Mary Wollstonecraft Shelley, who died on 1 February 1851 and sleeps "amidst the heather and the pine," and her husband who died on 8 July 1822 and sleeps "beneath the Roman rose and violets, like his verse divine."

The section "Algiers" is no doubt occasioned by the fact that Algiers was the home of Eugène Bodichon, the husband of Leigh Smith. The first of the poems in this section relates the story of a Christian slave who is working in "this accursed place" waiting for a woman who seems to have forgotten him. He finally sees her on an approaching ship with gold in her hand to purchase his release: "She sprang to shore—but then / Reeling he fell—the ransom came too late!" The other Algerian poem is "Under the Olives" in which a narrator who is seated in a Moorish garden gives a literal and a mythological history of Algeria.

Just as in *Poems* and the other early volumes, several poems throughout *Ballads and Songs* deal explicitly with religious topics. The poem "Peace" makes the point that "All natural things both live and move / In natural peace that is their own," and the poem "Prayer" recommends following the example of "the Godhead's sorrowing Son" who prayed "Father, Thy will, not mine, be done." One of Parkes's poems is based on the Old Testament concept of the creation of separate cities for those who are guilty of accidental murder. The text portrays a slayer who is being pursued by the wrathful Avenger of Blood. The circumstances flash through his mind of his killing the man who was meeting his loved one in a secret tryst; at the last possible moment the slayer leaps through the gate into the city and exclaims, "My life is secure in the law of the Lord!" The poems in this volume indicate that Parkes was always concerned with spiritual matters, but as she grew older she became increasingly devout. Brought up a Unitarian, Parkes converted to Catholicism in 1864.

Three years after becoming a Catholic, Parkes made another life-changing decision. She went with Barbara Bodichon to La Celle St. Cloud, a beautiful village twelve miles from Paris. There she met Louis Belloc, a man trained as a barrister but who had become a semi-invalid after being diagnosed with inflammation of the brain.

Parkes married Belloc on 19 September 1867 at the Catholic Church in Old Spanish Place in London. Three months later she was pregnant; during their brief marriage she had one miscarriage and gave birth to two healthy children. The couple shared five happy years during which they spent most of their time in France. Her husband, never strong, died in 1872, and Parkes eventually returned to England where she said she was "absorbed in responsibilities which left me scant leisure for anything beyond the duties of every hour." She never fully recovered from his death and always had tears in her eyes when she spoke his name.

The Belloc children, Marie Adelaide, later Mrs. Frederic Lowndes, born in 1868, and Joseph Hilaire Pierre, born in 1870, became prolific writers. Marie wrote extensively about her own life, and she was the author of forty-five crime novels. Her memoir, *I, Too, Have Lived in Arcadia* (1941), provides most of the known details about her mother. Hilaire became an essayist, poet, historian, novelist, biographer, and travel writer.

Parkes's last years were uneventful when compared to the first part of her career. She traveled to the United States with Hilaire in 1896 and saw the eastern part of the country. Hilaire remembered that his mother "found it appalling as all English people do."

Parkes continued to write. *In a Walled Garden* (1895) is a collection of twenty essays on varied topics such as "Dorothea Casaubon and George Eliot," "Mary Howitt," and "Dr. Manning of Bayswater." The eleven essays in *A Passing World* (1897) also are of diverse nature such as "The Two Fredericks" and "Franklin's America." In 1896 she wrote *Historic Nuns* about Mary Aikenhead, Catherine M'Aulay, Madame Duchesne, and Mother Seton of Emmettsbury. *The Flowing Tide* (1900) consists of many religious essays such as "Catholicism in France," "The Three Great Cardinals," "The Literature of the Catholic Revival," and "The Little Sisters of the Poor." *In Fifty Years* (1904) is a volume of her collected poems. Bessie Rayner Parkes Belloc died on 23 March 1925.

References:

Daphne Bennett, *Emily Davies and the Liberation of Women: 1830-1921* (London: Deutsch, 1990);

Virginia Blain, Isobel Grundy, and Patricia Clements, *The Feminist Companion to Literature in English* (New Haven: Yale University Press, 1990), p. 833;

Hester Burton, *Barbara Bodichon: 1827-1891* (London: Murray, 1949);

Margaret Foster, *Significant Sisters: The Grassroots of Active Feminism: 1837-1939* (London: Secker & Warburg, 1984);

Pam Hirsch, *Barbara Leigh Smith Bodichon: Feminist, Artist, Rebel* (London: Chatto & Windus, 1998);

Candida Ann Lacey, *Barbara Leigh Smith and the Langham Place Group* (New York: Routledge & Kegan Paul, 1987);

Marie Belloc Lowndes, *I, Too, Have Lived in Arcadia* (London: Macmillan, 1941);

Lowndes, *The Merry Wives of Westminster* (London: Macmillan, 1946);

Lowndes, *A Passing World* (London: Macmillan, 1948);

Lowndes, *Where Love and Friendship Dwelt* (London: Macmillan, 1943);

John P. McCarthy, *Hilaire Belloc: Edwardian Radical* (Indianapolis: Liberty Press, 1978);

J. B. Morton, *Hilaire Belloc: A Memoir* (London: Hollis & Carter, 1955);

Pauline Nestor, *Female Friendships and Communities: Charlotte Brontë, George Eliot, Elizabeth Gaskell* (Oxford: Clarendon, 1985);

Nestor, "A New Departure in Women's Publishing: *The English Woman's Journal* and the *Victoria Magazine*," *Victorian Periodicals Review*, 15 (1982): 93–106;

Joseph W. Reed Jr., *An American Diary: 1857-58* (London: Routledge & Kegan Paul, 1987);

Jane Rendall, *Equal or Different? Women's Politics: 1800-1914* (Oxford: Blackwell, 1987);

Rendall, *The Origins of Modern Feminism: Women in Britain, France, and the United States, 1780-1960* (London: Macmillan, 1985);

Joanne Shattock, *The Oxford Guide to British Women Writers* (London: Oxford University Press, 1993), pp. 330–331;

Elaine Showalter, *A Literature of Their Own: From Charlotte Brontë to Doris Lessing* (London: Virgo Press, 1978);

Robert Speaight, *The Life of Hilaire Belloc* (London: Hollis & Carter, 1957);

James S. Stone, *Emily Faithfull: Victorian Champion of Women's Rights* (Toronto: Meany, 1994);

Ray Strachey, *"The Cause": A Short History of the Women's Movement in Great Britain* (London: Bell, 1928);

Victorian Britain: An Encyclopedia, edited by Sally Mitchell (New York & London: Garland, 1988), p. 576;

A. N. Wilson, *Hilaire Belloc* (London: Hamilton, 1984).

Papers:

A collection of Bessie Rayner Parkes's manuscripts and materials is at Girton College, University of Cambridge.

Dollie Radford

(3 December 1858 – 7 February 1920)

LeeAnne Marie Richardson
Georgia State University

BOOKS: *A Light Load* (London: Elkin Mathews, 1891); republished with designs by Beatrice E. Parsons (London: Elkin Mathews, 1897);
Songs for Somebody (London: Nutt, 1893);
Good Night (London: Nutt, 1895);
Songs and Other Verses (London: John Lane, 1895; Philadelphia: Lippincott, 1895);
One Way of Love: An Idyll (London: Unwin, 1898);
The Poet's Larder and Other Stories (Bristol: Arrowsmith, 1900);
The Young Gardener's Kalendar (London: De La More Press, 1904); republished as *The Young Gardener's Year* (London: De La More Press, 1908);
Sea-Thrift: A Fairy Tale (London: De La More Press, 1904);
In Summer Time: A Little Boy's Dream (Harting: Pear Tree Press, 1905);
A Ballad of Victory and Other Poems (London: Alston Rivers, 1907);
Poems (London: Elkin Mathews, 1910).

PLAY PRODUCTION: *The Ransom*, London, Little Theater, 9 June 1912.

SELECTED PERIODICAL PUBLICATION–UNCOLLECTED: *The Ransom, Poetry Review*, 6 (1915): 117–153.

OTHER: Louis Davis, *The Goose Girl at the Well*, songs by Radford (London: Elkin Mathews, 1906);
William Allingham, *William Allingham: A Diary*, edited by Radford and H. Allingham (London: Macmillan, 1907);
Frances Browne, *Granny's Wonderful Chair and Its Tales of Fairy Times*, introduction by Radford (London: Dent, 1908; New York: Dutton, 1906).

Dollie Radford was a central participant in the vibrant literary, social, and political life of fin de siècle London. Although Radford's name is little known today, her circle included some of the most-celebrated

Dollie Radford

names in turn-of-the-century literature and politics: William Morris, George Bernard Shaw, H. G. Wells, William Butler Yeats, H.D. (Hilda Doolittle), Olive Schreiner, Eleanor Marx and Edward Aveling, Constance and Edward Garnett, Ernest Rhys, Augustine Birrell, Laurence Houseman, John Galsworthy, and D. H. Lawrence. A poet who published books for both adults and children, Radford also has a novel, a verse drama, and several short stories to her credit. Individual poems and stories were published in respected journals, including *The Yellow Book, The Athenaeum, The Nation, The English Review,* and *McClure's.* Radford wrote short Romantic lyric poems for the most part, and her writings for adults bring together the attention to nature that characterizes Wordsworth's poetry with the feminist ideas circulated by the "New Woman" writers of the 1880s and 1890s. Often dismissed as merely "charming," Radford's poems display an undeniable charm–beautiful images, perfect prosody, delightful sounds for the ear–but the sole emphasis on the beauty of her verse obscures other equally important elements of her work. Especially as her career progresses, and as she lives through the end of Victoria's reign, the nascence of literary Modernism, and the horror of World War I, themes of women's emotions, needs, and place in a changing world become more and more prominent.

Dollie Radford, née Caroline Maitland, was born in Worcester on 3 December 1858, daughter of a London West End tailor. She was educated at Queens College, London. Not much else is known of her life before her 1883 marriage to Ernest Radford. Her husband studied at Trinity Hall, Cambridge, and was called to the bar in 1880. In addition, he was a critic who gave lectures on art and architecture; he published a book on Dante Gabriel Rossetti and wrote for *The Pall Mall Gazette,* alongside Oscar Wilde, Rhys and Shaw. Also a poet, he was a member of the "Rhymer's Club," a group of young poets that included Rhys, Yeats, Ernest Dowson, Lionel Johnson, Arthur Symons, and Richard Le Gallienne. Radford's poems appear in both *The Book of the Rhymer's Club* (1892) and *The Second Book of the Rhymer's Club* (1894).

One of these poems, "Song: Oh what know they of harbors," has been published under both Radford's and her husband's name. In Dollie Radford's first book of poetry, *A Light Load* (1891), the contents page reads "Oh, what know they of harbors, by E.R." This poem, however, appears as "'Heart and Home' by Dollie Radford" in the 5 February 1898 issue of *The Living Age.* Perhaps it is best for modern readers to assume, as did *The Nation* reviewer in the 9 December 1897 issue, that "Mrs. Radford represents, with her husband, that rare combination to which the Browning letters are just now directing attention–the marriage of two poets." To exemplify this "rare combination," the reviewer reprinted "Oh what know they of harbors."

This "marriage of two poets" produced three poetic children: Hester, who later became Countess Batthyany, wrote poems and short stories; Margaret published several well-received books of poetry; and Maitland, who was a physician, entered the ranks of published poets when his friends printed a book of his poetry posthumously in 1945. Others of the immediate family were literary as well: Ernest Radford's sister Ada was a writer who published two stories in *The Yellow Book* and wrote several theatricals that the Hammersmith Socialist Society performed as fund-raisers.

That Dollie Radford was the true poet in this "marriage of two poets" is suggested by a poem her husband wrote for her. Karl E. Beckson, in *London in the 1890s: A Cultural History* (1992), reports that Ernest Radford was concerned about the Rhymer's Club's exclusion of women: "Aware of his own slender poetic gifts and those of his colleagues, he wrote a tribute to his more gifted wife, the poet Dollie Radford, in a brief poem titled 'The Book of the Rhymers Club, Vol. II,'" which appeared in his volume of collected verse *Old and New* (1895):

Had you increased our number,
What sweetness might have been
Uprising as from slumber
We bards, in all thirteen,
Amassed this muck and lumber
Sad work without a Queen!

Although she did not achieve her husband's level of fame, Radford is, objectively, the better poet. She has a sureness of touch in her poetic phrasing and a mastery of meter and rhyme that is nowhere represented in Ernest Radford's work, outside of "Oh what know they of harbors."

The "marriage of two poets" is also an appropriate phrase to represent the intermingling of the couple's interests. While it is impossible to know to what extent the two poets collaborated on, or even discussed, their works, it is known–from the memoirs and letters of various members of their wide circle–that the two of them were together at the center of London literary life. According to David Garnett (son of Constance and Edward Garnett) in *The Golden Echo* (1954), "Dollie and Ernest had multitudes of friends and so had their children. At tea-time the drawing-room was always full of poets and poetesses, artists and musicians, and it was seldom that the family sat down to a meal without laying one or two extra places for friends who had dropped in or had to stay on because they were in the middle of an aesthetic discussion which could not be interrupted." Memoirs and diaries by Shaw, Morris, Wells, Rhys, Schreiner, and Edith Lees (wife of Havelock Ellis) all refer to the Radfords, and Lawrence's *Collected Letters* (1962) records his side of his five-year-long correspondence with Dollie Radford.

More important, however, than confirming that they knew famous people is proving what these acquaintances tell about the Radfords personally and politically. Their actions, singly and as a couple, reveal their liberal views on class issues, on religion, on vegetarianism, on sexuality, on literature, and on the nationalist sentiment inspired by World War I. The Radfords were, according to C. E. Wheeler's introduction to *Poems by Maitland Radford* (1945), "much loved members of the Hammersmith group that centered around William Morris." Douglas Goldring, in *South Lodge* (1943), writes that "Dollie and Ernest Radford, a couple of nice vegetarian poets . . . were leading spirits" in "the New Reform Club, the premises of which were in Adelphi Terrace under the flat occupied by Bernard Shaw." Friendly with Eleanor Marx and Aveling, and later Schreiner, Dollie Radford must have had advanced views on women's political and sexual emancipation, because she refused to shun a couple whose union did not involve marriage and she embraced Schreiner's feminist writings. In addition, both Radfords continued to support Wells after the uproar caused by the publication of *Ann Veronica* (1909), when he was "cut" by fellow socialists who were afraid the taint of "free love" would be attached to the party. Schreiner reports in a 1914 letter to Ellis that "dear Dollie Radford" was one of the few friends who would visit her London home during the war, not only because her name was German, but also because her condemnation of the fighting was well known. Radford also remained close to Lawrence throughout the controversies surrounding his novels—even interceding with Wells to mobilize support against the censorship of *The Rainbow* (1915).

Radford seems to have maintained a cheerful outlook despite the anxieties she must have experienced because of the couple's relative poverty, the horrors of World War I she expressed in her letters to Lawrence, and her husband's tragic decline. (Universally described as a brilliant wit in his youth, he spent the last ten years of his life in mental confusion punctuated by moments of clarity.) According to Garnett, "It was impossible not to like her . . . her gay silliness was one of her chief charms, as she was seldom *purely* silly: it was almost always mixed with so much fancy, such sudden spurts of imagination, and so qualified by such little gusts of laughter at herself that one would have had to be a very hard-hearted and humorless person to resist her. . . . She had an intense love of life." Wheeler confirms this assessment: "Dollie radiated a kind of shining peace, and the personal sorrows and trouble that so many brought to her she dissipated or consoled with extraordinary success."

In 1883 Radford saw her first poems in print. Between May and October of that year, a radical "magazine of advanced thought" called *Progress* published nine poems by Caroline Maitland or "C. M." Edited by G. W. Foote and later Aveling (who took over after Foote was imprisoned on blasphemy charges), *Progress* was antimonarchy, anti-imperialist, anticapitalist, antire-

Title page for Radford's second book of poems for adults, which includes some of her best work (courtesy of The Lilly Library, Indiana University)

ligious, and generally anti-establishment. (The front cover featured portraits, in each corner, of Percy Bysshe Shelley, John Stuart Mill, Charles Darwin, and Voltaire.) The politics of the journal reveal the degree to which Radford's politics were radical rather than merely progressive, and it indicates that these ideas were developed early in her life. Her poems take on more complex meanings when the reader remembers that she was associated, throughout her life, with radical political circles.

In 1884 Shaw set to music Radford's lyric poem "She Comes Through the Meadow Yonder," which explores her early themes of love and nature. Writing on 31 March 1884, Shaw identifies both the strength and the defect of her early lyrics: "You will find, on examining the song as it stands, that it is inconclusive—leaves a 'Is that all?' feeling behind it. You seem to have an extraordinary kaleidoscopic talent for stringing all manner of beautiful images and associations harmoniously together, and these, when combined with the pithiness and conclusiveness of an epigram, form perfect songs. But you are neither pithy nor conclusive." His criticism came with encouragement, however. Although he says, "I am not altogether satisfied," it is because "I believe you can do better. A large part of the charm of your verses is their prettiness, and that seems to come so naturally to you that I do not give you much credit for it." Whether or not "prettiness" came naturally to Radford, it is undeniable that her poems are pretty.

In fact, the "prettiness" of her verse is what Radford's reviewers focus on, often to the extent of eclipsing its other aspects. Yeats, in his *Letters to Katharine Tynan* (1953), wrote in late June 1891 that Radford had given him a copy of *A Light Load*. He picks out this stanza from "Out on the Moor"—which also served as headnote to the volume—as the best in the book:

> The love within my heart for thee
>   Before the world was had its birth,
> It is the part God gives to me
>   Of the great wisdom of the earth.

Then, as do many reviewers, Yeats gives with one hand and takes away with the other. "Are they not fine? They have a largeness of thought and feeling, above mere prettiness," he writes, but then adds that they are all "trifling." This opinion was not unanimous, however. In introducing Radford's poems for Alfred Miles's edition of *The Poets and the Poetry of the Century* (1893) Symons writes that these are "lines which any poet might be proud to have written." Moreover, according to Symons, Radford has remedied the inclusiveness of her poetry by this time, for as he notes, "These four lines seem to have something final about them—seem to say concerning the supreme devotion, the sacrament and worship of love, all that needs to be said."

Symons, despite his praise of Radford's conclusiveness, also implicitly judges her in terms similar to Shaw. Like Shaw, he sees her poetic gifts as purely "natural." The terms he uses to praise the poems are grounded in unconscious "nature" rather than conscious poetic craft: *A Light Load*, he writes, "is a book of songs, and the songs are full of instinctive music, which soars naturally. They have the choice, unsought felicity of a nature essentially lyrical. Always finished in style, with the distinction which can never be acquired, they have almost an air of impromptu, and one might imagine the writer to be little conscious of the process by which they have come to be so finished." While scholars do not have access to working notebooks that record Radford's process of composition, it is unlikely that her considerable poetic talents came quite as "naturally" as reviewers assume. Part of the reaction to this volume likely stems from the title: *A Light Load* suggests poems that are "trifling," undemanding, easy, and gentle. This is also true in the sense that these poems, for the most part, express an optimism—a faith in the purity and truth of nature—that cannot be repressed. The poems are centered in a gentle nature: flowers, trees, calm seas—not nature "red in tooth and claw." Loneliness is a theme, and many poems address a "you" who could either be a lover or a Christ figure; the exact valence of the symbol remains unspecified, but the images of a final glorious meeting—and a hopeful waiting for a redeeming figure—allow both interpretations. In her later poetry, it becomes clear that Radford's religion is the religion of Love, not conventional Christianity (a reading supported by her publication in the freethinking *Progress* and her membership in the atheist New Reform Club)—but by making the poems ambiguous, she escapes official censure and garners wider appeal. As a result, Radford gained the reputation of being an unthreatening domestic writer.

A Light Load, however, is more than simply charming. "In the Woods" ("Are your grave eyes graver growing?") tells both her purpose for writing poetry—to lighten the heart—and her model—the Romantic poets who were schooled by nature: "Long ago the poet lingered; / Sun and pale star-beam / Touched his lips, while there he wandered / Summer-time and Spring, / And the mighty woods and river / Taught him how to sing." Symons writes that Radford's lyrics "have not a little of Wordsworth's 'natural magic' of feeling and style—the perfect communion with Nature brings with it the perfect expression." Even so, her style is completely her own. As Symons says, Radford's lyrics—like those of Alfred Tennyson and Heinrich Heine—have "the originality of a single temperament."

Radford expresses anxiety over the problem of being derivative, of being a latter-day Romantic, in "There is no unawakened string": "There is no unawakened string, / No untried note for me to ring, / No new-found song for me to sing." Her sense of belatedness, of being too fatigued to contribute something new, accords with fin de siècle concerns that British culture had reached its apex. The popularity of Max Nordeau's *Degeneration*—first published in English in 1895—attests to this. In the third stanza, Radford parodies the style and subject of a Romantic poem—"My love is young, her face is fair, / The sun-light never leaves her hair, / Her beauty fills me with a prayer"—as if to prove that she knows intimately the form and the style. This parodic rendering only expresses more forcefully her sense that this has all been said before, that she must find her own way. Her poem "What Song Shall I Sing" addresses her other metapoetic concern: the difficulty of combining the work of a poet with the work of a

The home at 32 Well Walk, Hampstead, that Radford shared with her daughter Margaret and where she died (photograph by James Diedrick)

mother. The poem asks "What song shall I sing to you / Now the wee ones are in bed"? It recounts the new songs and new books by new poets, and notes that, because of her time spent with children, "I can sing, these evening times, / Only the children's songs and rhymes." The proper subject of her own poetry is a continued concern.

Radford seems to have found the solution to this problem in the final two poems in the volume, which address the issues circulating around discussions of New Woman fiction: woman's independent emotional life and her position in changing society. In "A Modern Polypheme," the speaker compares herself to the cyclops Polypheme, but "forswear[s] / Thy black emotions" and refuses to be jealous of any Acis who may come along. In this way, the poem rewrites the old myth and, consequently, the old standards of conducting the sexual relationship. Instead of jealousy and violence as the outcome of conflict, she engenders contentment, joy in the moment, and the measure of self-fulfillment she can attain by refusing violence.

The final poem in *A Light Load* is "A Dream of 'Dreams': To Olive Schreiner." Schreiner's first book since her acclaimed feminist novel *The Story of an African Farm* (1883), *Dreams* (1891) was a series of short allegorical and experimental writings on questions of women's emancipation from, and cooperation with, men. While deploring the conditions that currently kept women from sharing life–and love–with men, *Dreams* continually holds out the promise for a future equality. Radford's poem begins "All day I read your book; at Eve / Your dreams into my dark sleep stole" and then describes how Schreiner's vision has entered the dreamer's soul. Like Schreiner's *Dreams,* the poem expresses hope and a sense of something grand waiting just ahead.

In the years following the publication of *A Light Load,* Radford's poetic dreams were deferred, or at least diverted into another channel. "What Song Shall I Sing" narrates Radford's absorption with the duties of motherhood; her next two books, *Songs for Somebody* (1893) and *Good Night* (1895), are children's books. *Songs for Somebody* is a charming twenty-eight page illustrated book, with hand-printed poems incorporated into the pictures. The title page includes the following verse: *Songs for Somebody*–"Which somebody may happily / Read in a quiet nursery / Leaving the garden game and toys / And someone else to make the noise." A drawing of a girl contentedly reading the book shows how poetry is an activity that mother and children can share to their mutual benefit, an activity that provides Radford with a way to be both a good mother and a good poet. *Good Night* is a more substantial book than *Songs for Somebody*. The dimensions are bigger, and although there are approximately the same number of poems, they are longer and more complex than the earlier volume. Meant for older children, this book also has handwritten text, but written in cursive rather than printed.

The narrative of *Good Night* is structured around getting the children to bed, and features a dream-time imagination that empowers children: "A fairy boat with silver sail / And yet no fairy near / Then I must man it all alone / And I myself must steer." Throughout all her writing for children, the power of the imagination is key. This aspect of the children's books is akin to the power of the song in her books for adults: the ability to sing and the gift of hearing poetic music provide hope and courage and strength.

Radford's second book of poems for adults, *Songs and Other Verses* (1895), is much different from *A Light Load*. This volume represents a more mature and realistic vision of a world once idealized. It is an awakening of the dreamer, but not a loss of optimism or spirit. Rather, the poems give the impression of an older wisdom looking at youth and describing the differences. She describes the hardships of her age, recognizes the struggles, and faces each with continued spirit. This volume includes many of Radford's best poems—strong, original, and moving, with the greatest variety in subject and form.

The nature of the difference in this volume is best understood by noting the change in publisher. Elkin Mathews had been Radford's publisher, but when John Lane split his interests from Mathews's in September of 1894, Radford followed Lane. Lane was notorious as the publisher of the "Keynotes" Series (which took its name from the New Woman collection of short stories penned by George Egerton) and *The Yellow Book*. While Radford's poems were not part of the Keynotes Series, Lane still was (in)famous for publishing material such as Grant Allen's *The Woman Who Did* (1895) and other works that threatened the mores of conventional society.

Reviewers place Radford in a tradition completely outside the New Woman and the "unnatural" emotions to which this "strange creature" laid claim. Love and nature remain strong themes in *Songs and Other Verses*, apparently leading reviewers to see these poems as reassuringly conventional. *The Athenaeum* (21 September 1895), in a dual review of *Songs and Other Verses* and Ernest Radford's *Old and New*, seems to have a vested interest in retaining separate masculine and feminine poetic spheres. The review characterizes Ernest's book as "distinctively manly," while Dollie's is "very feminine" and "distinctively womanly." The reviewer in *The Bookman* (January 1896) writes that "There is never an inordinate touch of passion in these little lyrics. . . . The genius is domestic." The criticism implicit in this characterization is evident: "The air and attitude are that of a child, or that of a woman, if you like." The reviewer makes it clear that femininity equals childishness. These poems are "good," the male reviewers say, because they do not threaten conventional notions of women.

It is strange that the poem reviewers hold up as exemplifying Radford's "sweet unpretentious lyrics" (*The Dial*, 1 April 1896), is about unyielding ambition. Nonetheless, *The Bookman* (January 1896) agrees with *The Dial* that in "Because I built my nest so high" these ambitions "become guileless and desires innocent." This poem, however, far from merely embodying sweet innocence, changes the negative connotation of "ambition" when it applies to women and makes striving and seeking *natural* to women. This poem recognizes the possibility for failure when one aims higher than most others:

> Because I built my nest so high,
>   Must I despair
> If a fierce wind, with bitter cry,
> Passes the lower branches by,
>   And mine makes bare?
>
> Because I hung it, in my pride
>   So near the skies,
> Higher than other nests abide,
> Must I lament if far and wide
>   It scattered lies?
>
> I shall but build, and build my best,
>   Till, safety won,
> I hang aloft my new-made nest,
> High as of old, and see it rest
>   As near the sun.

Moreover, the poetic voice iterates that she will not be beaten down. If she fails, she will rebuild, and not any lower than before.

Again, the final poems in this volume represent her greatest departures in theme and form. "A Novice" brings the domestic realm into intimate contact with the bohemian realm of women who transgress: "What is it, in these latter days, / Transfigures my domestic ways, / And round me, as a halo, plays? / My cigarette." She transforms the transgressive connotations of the cigarette (smoking is one of the hallmarks of the rebellious woman) into a heavenly one: the smoke becomes a halo. She takes several stanzas to describe domestic toils: when children misbehave, when servants quit, when the accounts will not balance, when the dinner is burned. The cigarette is her consolation: "For as the smoke curls blue and thin / From my own lips, I first begin / To bathe my tired spirit in / Philosophy." This transgression provides her with an outlet from domestic cares and allows her into the male world of personal privilege and independence. By appropriating the male device, she can imagine "The promised epoch, like a star" shining in the distant future. "If I, in vain, must sit and wait, / To realize our future state, / I shall not be disconsolate, / My cigarette!" The charm of this poem is that it makes its point–that good wives and mothers who dutifully manage all domestic cares still hope for the day when women's rights will be recognized–and does it with so light a touch. By avoiding didacticism, she seduces the reader into agreeing with her view. Here, her "sweetness" and her "charm" serve radical ends.

"From Our Emancipated Aunt in Town" similarly expresses a wish for a new status for women but adds the more complicated question of an older woman's relationship to feminism. In the form of a letter to her nieces, the emancipated aunt writes of the "old ideals blown away" and asks what is to come next. The aunt recognizes that she still clings "to many a worn out tottering thing / Of a convention" and charges her nieces to "face / Our right and wrong, and take your place / As future leaders." It is through poetry that the aunt experiments with the new ideas of modern life: "I, meanwhile, shall still pursue / All that is weird and wild and new, / In song and ballet, / In lecture, drama, verse, and prose." She closes with this admonition not to judge her thus too harshly for not being in the midst of the fray: "Remember she prepares your way, / With many another Aunt to-day."

Radford's next projects were a novel titled *One Way of Love: An Idyll* (1898) and a collection of short stories titled *The Poet's Larder and Other Stories* (1900). These prose works continue exploring the position of women. *One Way of Love* is the story of Sasha, an orphan reared by uncaring relatives. She has a restless sense of longing for she knows not what, and writes both to express and to soothe her emotions. One day she meets Arthur West, falls in love with him, and believes that he is what she has been longing for. The morning after their mutual declaration of love, West leaves. He has been toying with her emotions, enjoying his power to influence her. Sasha goes to London to find him, but discovers that he has all the while been engaged to one of her London friends. Throughout the novel, Sasha's woman friends have called her "The Seeker," and a female artist paints a portrait of her by that name. When Sasha leaves West and her uncle behind to make a new life for herself, however, her friends rename her portrait "Victory." Thus, a woman's "victory" becomes associated with independence from, not attachment to, a man. *One Way of Love* is not quite a New Woman novel, but it is inflected with all of its themes: it features women alone–two young struggling artists, a widow, and an orphan–who form a supportive sisterhood, a community of women. The featured women all express themselves artistically, through paint or pen. The heroine is independent of men at the end, and although the details of her future are not revealed, her friends are certain that she has found success in life.

The title story in *The Poet's Larder* represents a more complicated relationship to the modern woman's movement. In this story of the not-so-modern Doris, who is engaged to marry a thoroughly modern poet, Radford expresses difficulty with the idea of free unions between men and women. When the fiancée finds photos of many women in the poet's larder, she decides "It isn't right." The poet's sister Grace defends her brother, saying, "A poet must have lady friends . . . My dear child, it is part of his education." Doris, however, thinks of the women: "It means disappointment and unhappiness for them–unnecessary suffering." Grace coldly agrees: "people cannot be spared unhappiness and disappointment; the path of development runs beside the path of suffering. . . . You must become a modern; you must see and accept things as they really are."

Despite this admonishment from the modern voice, the story ends with an affirmation of what Grace calls "the old Romantic School": the poet gives up all his ladies so that he can be with his true love. It is troubling, however, that the "true love" accepts and forgives the poet's past transgressions, and that the narrative "forgets" how upsetting the revelation of his actual character was to her.

These works were followed by three books for children, one prose and two poetry. *Sea–Thrift: A Fairy Tale* (1904) thematically shares much in common with *In Summer Time: A Little Boy's Dream* (1905), a collection of poems. Both center on children taken by fairies to magical lands, a journey that both empowers the children with a sphere of autonomous action and relieves them from the dull care of the sickbed (in the former) and the nature-bereft city (in the latter). *The Young Gardener's Kalendar* (1904) is made up of twelve poems, one for each month. Each poem tells the flowers that bloom and the gardening duties that need to be done for each time of year.

A Ballad of Victory and Other Poems (1907) is a small book–only thirty-five pages–and includes only eight new poems. (Two had been previously published in *The Yellow Book* and the rest of the book is comprised of works from *A Light Load* and *Songs and Other Verses*.) "A Ballad of Victory" is the story of a poor and gentle spirit who finds herself passing through a town as she walks steadily toward her goal. The townspeople notice her gentle ways and try

The grave of Radford and her husband, Ernest, in the Churchyard Extension in Hampstead (photograph by James Diedrick)

to tempt her away from her "quest," but she cannot be swayed, either through entreaties to her "tender healing ways" or through offers of luxuries and needed rest: "She turned away with steadfast air, / From all their choice of fair and sweet, / And, as she turned, they saw how bare / And bruiséd were her pilgrim feet." As she goes, the townspeople wonder who she is, where she came from, and where she is going. One woman knows not her name, "Nor whose the bidding she fulfills / But well the roads by which she came"—roads that are harsh and barren and dark. A youth, "With clearer eyes and wiser heart," cries: "Her face and name I know."

> And well the passage of her flight,
> The starless plains she must ascend,
> And well the darkness of the night,
> In which her pilgrimage shall end.
>
> But stronger than the years that roll,
> Than travail past, or yet to be,
> She presses to her hidden goal,
> A crownless, unknown Victory.

Her precise goal is not known, or why she braves hardships, poverty, and bodily pain. She must go there alone, and going there itself is a victory, albeit an unrecognized and uncelebrated one. The poem has much in common with *One Way of Love,* in that the "Victory" is more a feat of endurance than a conquest in the traditional sense. How much this sense of constant endurance and struggle for a distant and underappreciated goal is connected with Radford's sense of her own life struggle is unclear, but Lawrence, in a letter of 27 January 1916, writes: "I like very much the ballad of victory. It makes me think of you."

Poems (1910) is also a volume of collected poems, with roughly twenty new poems. Whereas *Songs and Other Verses* was characterized by *The Athenaeum* as expressing moods "generally touching, often exquisite," the new poems in *Poems* are passionate, powerful, and sometimes violent. Love and nature, as always, are themes; but here, nature can be violent, and the heart of love is despair and pain. The poems are longer, more mature, and much more sad. However, a small poem called simply "Hope" provides the front piece to this volume. Coming even before the Preface, "Hope" is a sort of touchstone to the volume, describing hope as a net or a web "With threads that are strong as steel" that will always catch her and hold her. Unlike previous volumes, here hope is mixed not with loneliness and waiting but with fear and betrayal.

"At Night," a sonnet sequence, pictures a much different aspect of nature than has appeared in previous works. Radford focuses on those who long for love but do not have it, who experience the "great unchannelled floods of misery" of long nights spent without "any word / To save my hope whose wings grow cold and numb." The rebellious anger of the unloved is like the violent actions of the storms when they "drop their torrents down, and leave the scars / Of their fierce passion on the unborn noon." Night is moved by neither lightning strike nor lover's cry. Even her stanza of hope is bitter and insistent. Set in the future tense, she imagines a "plot of barren earth" that will grow one lone flower watered by her tears; the day this flower blooms will be her one day of joy. She repeats "shall" in every line until the shall changes to "must": "Such must there be, oh God, Who made the waste / So bare beneath the Heaven, Who hast spread / The stones upon the path that I must tread, / Who set the thorns through which I may not haste, / The bitter fruits which I must faint to taste, / Such must there be, oh god, Who art o'erhead." In many ways, this stanza of future hope is really just another occasion to relate her current unhappiness. It is a small joy—one day, one flower—that awaits her desperately compelling cry that it "must be so."

"Your Gift" is a demonic parallel to "Ah, bring it not so grudgingly / The gift thou bringest me" from *Songs and Other Verses,* in which she exhorts an unknown someone to "come, and coming do not ask / The answering gift of mine" in order to savor the "joy divine" of giving without expecting anything in return. In "Your Gift" the giver presents her with coldness and cruelty: "You give me to the night" when she feels anguished and alone; "you give me to the wind" which leaves her a "castaway / Unloved and left behind"; "You give me to my grief" that has not even comfort in Heaven because of her "great unbelief." The final two stanzas demonstrate her subtle power, the way she adds to images until they are full to bursting, the way she draws the reader into an extremely intimate and private emotional realm:

> Oh you whose heart is cold,
>   If I should show
> All the waste of my life at your side,
> All the flower of my soul that has died,
>   You would not know
> The gift of gifts you hold.
>
> Oh you whose sleep is dear,
>   And long to take,
> Should you dream how they sicken and die,
> Who are cast from the earth and the sky,
>   You would awake
> And keep your gift for fear.

The barely suppressed violence of these lines, the coldness and rationality of their measures, is chilling and a remarkable achievement of affect.

Radford would likely object to critics trying to read her biography directly into her poetry. In her "Preface" to *Granny's Wonderful Chair* (1906) by Frances Browne, Radford writes that Browne's achievement is praiseworthy because she was able "to realize the world independently of her own personal emotion and needs." Radford writes as if it were an indulgence to let the subjective enter into one's art. Because Browne did not thus indulge herself, "She belonged to the first order of artists. . . . The material with which she tried to deal was Life—apart from herself—a perhaps bigger, and, certainly, a harder piece of work than the subjective expression of a single personality." Having registered Radford's potential objections, however, this new note in her poetry is sounded at the same time her husband's mental health is failing. Garnett observed Radford's husband at home in the years just before 1910: "He was a heavy, tired man, rather corpulent, going bald and with a noble forehead. Usually he seemed only half-awake, and most visitors must have thought him unconscious of the sparkling conversation and bursts of laughter going on all around him. As he lay extended on the sofa, he sometimes actually went to sleep, but more often his eyes, like a cat's, were only half closed, and a faint sardonic smile curled his lip." He would continue to decline and withdraw until his death in 1919. Just two years older than Dollie Radford, his brilliant youth had turned into confused and listless age.

Radford's final published work, *The Ransom* (performed 1912, published in *Poetry Review,* 1915), is a play in verse, and takes up the theme of passion and love. The narrative profiles a woman, Lady Margery, who is in a marriage with a man who is "not unkind," but who lacks any sort of passion. Margery, disregarding social censure, is friendly with all classes and types of people, including Carol—a fallen woman; Robin—a rake; and Martin—a younger man with whom she has fallen in love. He, too, declared his passion for Margery but, engaged to another, deems it necessary to honor the previous commitment. Desperate and unwilling to live without passion, Margery sacrifices herself on the altar of Love. Meanwhile, Martin, realizing his mistake, has waited all night to see Margery as she goes home so that he can tell her he will honor their passion over sterile commitment. Margery, however, has already drunk poison in the wood, so she never passes by his house.

The story is clichéd, but the work expands on Radford's theme of woman's need for passion. It is impossible not to link Garnett's description of Ernest Radford laying extended on the sofa ("Occasionally, he exerted himself to write lectures on architecture or poetry") with the description one of the girls gives of Margery's husband: "Her man is old, and his grey life is lived / Deep in his scholar books; he seldom speaks." Margery has said that "A wife was held more captive by her loneliness / Than any prisoned creature in the world." The world deems her husband a good husband, however, because he provides for her, he is not cruel, and he is well liked. People cannot understand that "one, as rich as she, should seem / To be so striving still for something new!" Again and again, Margery insists that her passionless marriage is not enough. It makes her useless and miserable and empty.

A creative highlight of the poem is in the final act, where a sort of dual Greek chorus enters in a dream sequence induced by Margery's drugged state. In the moments before she dies Margery hears the voice of Love and the complimentary choruses made up of prostitutes on one side and lonely unloved women on the other. They both "are wasted alike in the end" because "Love turns us away from his sight / And we anguish and grope for his light, / Through the wandering prayers of our night." In a letter of 9 April 1915, Lawrence praises this last act: "There is to me something rather terrible in the idea of the chorus of unloved women chanting against the chorus of prostitutes—something really Great in the conception. That is the most splendid part of the play."

Lawrence, however, tells Radford, "you could have made Margery a sterner, more aloof, more completely abstract or generalized figure—as Antigone in a Greek play—so that she is a figure of vengeance as well as love . . . those who know how to love must know how to slay." But Radford, as she demonstrates in "A Modern Polypheme," wants to challenge ideas about human sexual behavior, not reproduce them. By eschewing violence, Radford denies her drama the grandeur associated with Greek tragedy. Lady Margery cannot destroy in the name of love, for she knows too well the misuse of love and thus refuses to continue the pattern.

Underlying the surface of womanly self-sacrifice for the sake of Love, however, are highly controversial premises. A married woman who longs for a relationship outside of her marriage is the heroine, and the audience is meant to admire her. Moreover, her passion is for a younger man, whom she tries to seduce away from a socially legitimized relationship with his fiancée. His clinging to convention is shown to be destructive, misguided, and narrow. Moreover, the sort of physical and emotional passion that Margery not only displays but embraces as woman's true nature is itself subversive, highly critical of accepted notions of womanly behavior. She is definitely no angel in the house. By setting this play in a forest glade and stressing the pastoral, Radford is naturalizing what Victorian sexology deemed "unnatural" in women of her class—a strong, consuming, physical passion. The most-radical device, however, is putting lonely, unloved women (among whose number Lady Margery counts herself) on the same plane with prostitutes. Like the feminists of the 1890s, Radford recovers the victims of unlegitimized passion into a sisterhood of ill-used women, women who do not find fulfillment in life.

The *Bookman* reviewer charged with writing about *Songs and Other Verses* said with authority that for "anything but sweetness you may search Mrs. Radford's verses in vain" (January 1896). To the careful reader of her poetry, however, their politics and power also shine through. Even at the age of fifty-four, when *The Ransom* was first performed, Dollie Radford continued to challenge conventional notions of what women could and should do. Moreover, she cleverly manipulated conventional notions of women's roles to make her feminist points, to naturalize previously unacceptable behavior by women, and to re-envision—through the power of song and the power of nature—the relationship between men and women.

Dollie Radford died on 7 February 1920, in the Hampstead home she shared with her daughter Margaret. She is buried next to Ernest in the Churchyard Extension at Hampstead. Although her poetry fell into obscurity in the years after her death, she is being rediscovered in light of renewed interest in nineteenth-century women writers and fin de siècle culture.

References:

Karl E. Beckson, *London in the 1890s: A Cultural History* (New York: Norton, 1992);

David Garnett, *The Golden Echo* (London: Chatto & Windus, 1954);

Katherine Lyon Mix, *A Study in Yellow: The Yellow Book and Its Contributors* (Lawrence: University of Kansas Press, 1960);

Maitland Radford, *Poems by Maitland Radford: With a Memoir by Some of his Friends* (London: Allen & Unwin, 1945);

Ernest Rhys, *Everyman Remembers* (London: Dent, 1931);

George Bernard Shaw, *Collected Letters,* edited by Dan H. Laurence (New York: Dodd, Mead, 1965);

Arthur Symons, "Mrs. Ernest Radford," in *The Poets and the Poetry of the Century, Vol. 8: "Robert Bridges and Contemporary Poets,"* edited by Alfred H. Miles (London: Hutchinson, 1893), pp. 609–612;

W. B. Yeats, *Letters to Katharine Tynan,* edited by Roger McHugh (New York: McMullen, 1953).

Papers:

Dollie Radford's papers for 1880 to 1920 are held by the William Andrews Clark Memorial Library at the University of California, Los Angeles.

A. Mary F. Robinson
(Madame James Darmesteter, Madame Mary Duclaux)
(27 February 1857 – 9 February 1944)

Cynthia E. Huggins
University of Maine at Machias

BOOKS: *A Handful of Honeysuckle* (London: Kegan Paul, 1878);

The Crowned Hippolytus, translated from Euripides, with New Poems (London: Kegan Paul, Trench, 1881);

Arden, 2 volumes (London: Longmans, Green, 1883; New York: Harper, 1883);

Emily Brontë (London: W. H. Allen, 1883; Boston: Roberts, 1883);

The New Arcadia, and Other Poems (London: Ellis & White, 1884; Boston: Roberts, 1884); republished as *The New Arcadia, Being Idylls of Country Life with Other Poems* (London: Unwin, 1890);

An Italian Garden: A Book of Songs (London: Unwin, 1886; Boston: Roberts, 1897);

Margaret of Angoulême, Queen of Navarre (London: W. H. Allen, 1886; Boston: Roberts, 1887);

Poésies, traduites de l'anglais par James Darmesteter (Paris: Lemerre, 1888);

Songs, Ballads, and a Garden Play (London: Unwin, 1888);

The End of the Middle Ages: Essays and Questions in History (London: Unwin, 1889);

Marguerites du Temps Passé, as Madame James Darmesteter (Paris: Colin, 1891); translated to English by May Tomlinson and republished as *A Medieval Garden* (London: Lawrence & Bullen, 1898);

Retrospect, and Other Poems, as Madame James Darmesteter (London: Unwin, 1893; Boston: Roberts, 1893);

Froissart, as Mary Darmesteter (Paris: Hachette, 1894); translated by E. Frances Poynter (London: Unwin, 1895; New York: Scribners, 1895);

A Life of Ernest Renan, as Madame James Darmesteter (London: Methuen, 1897; Boston: Houghton, Mifflin, 1897); translated to French and republished as *La Vie de Ernest Renan* (Paris: Lévy, 1898);

Grands Ecrivains d'Outre-Manche: Les Brontë-Thackeray-Les Browning-Rossetti (Paris: Lévy, 1901);

A. Mary F. Robinson

The Fields of France: Little Essays in Descriptive Sociology (London: Chapman & Hall, 1903);

The Return to Nature: Songs and Symbols (London: Chapman & Hall, 1904);

La Vie de Emile Duclaux (Laval, France: L. Barnéoud, 1906);

The French Procession: A Pageant of Great Writers (London: Unwin, 1909; New York: Duffield, 1909);

The French Ideal: Pascal, Fénelon and other Essays, as Madame Duclaux (London: Chapman & Hall, 1911; New York: Dutton, 1911);

A Short History of France from Caesar's Invasion to the Battle of Waterloo, as Mary Duclaux (London: Unwin, 1918; New York & London: Putnam, 1918);

Twentieth Century French Writers: Reviews and Reminiscences, as Madame Mary Duclaux (London: Collins, 1919; New York: Scribners, 1920);

Victor Hugo, as Madame Duclaux (London: Constable, 1921; New York: Holt, 1921; Paris: Plon, 1925);

Images and Meditations, as Mary Duclaux (London: Unwin, 1923);

The Life of Racine, as Mary Duclaux (London: Unwin, 1925; New York: Harper, 1926; Paris: Stock, 1939);

Portrait of Pascal, as Mary Duclaux (London: Unwin, 1927; New York: Harper, 1927).

Editions and Collections: *Lyrics Selected from the Works of A. Mary F. Robinson (Madame James Darmesteter)* (New York: Stokes, 1890; London: Unwin, 1891);

The Collected Poems, Lyrical and Narrative of Mary Robinson (Madame Duclaux) (London: Unwin, 1902);

Songs from an Italian Garden, selections from *An Italian Garden,* selected by Thomas B. Mosher (Portland, Me.: Mosher, 1908).

OTHER: Marguerite d'Angoulême, *The Fortunate Lovers, Twenty-seven Novels of the Queen of Navarre,* edited by Robinson (London: Redway, 1887);

"Felicia Hemans," in *The English Poets,* edited by Thomas H. Ward, volume 4 (New York & London: Macmillan, 1894);

James Darmesteter, *English Studies,* translated by Robinson (London: Unwin, 1896);

Elizabeth Barrett Browning, *Casa Guidi Windows,* introduction by Robinson (London & New York: John Lane, 1901);

Marie Sévigné, *Mme. de Sévigné, Textes,* edited by Robinson, as Madame Duclaux (Paris: Plon, 1914);

Robert Browning, *Poèmes de Robert Browning,* introduction by Robinson, as Mary Duclaux (Paris: Grasset, 1922);

Marie Sévigné, *Letters from the Marchioness de Sévigné to Her Daughter, the Countess de Grignan,* introductory essay by Robinson, as Madame Duclaux (London: Spurr & Swift, 1927);

Marie Lenéru, *La Maison Sur le Roc,* preface by Robinson, as Mary Duclaux (Paris: Plon, 1927);

Henriette Renan, *Souvenirs et Impressions: Pologne, Rome, Allemagne, Voyage en Syrie,* introduction by Robinson, as Mary Duclaux (Paris: La Renaissance du Livre, 1930).

SELECTED PERIODICAL PUBLICATIONS—UNCOLLECTED: "Profiles from the French Renaissance," *Magazine of Art,* 8 (1885): "Francis I, Architect and Amateur," 84–88; "Maître Roux," 206–208; "'Le Primatrice,'" 254–255; "Jean Bullant," 298–300; "Pierre Lescot," 394–395; "The Clouets," 477–479; "Philibert Delorme," 506–508;

"Novelists of Naples," *National Review,* 7 (June 1886): 683–697;

"Impressions of Provence," *Contemporary Review,* 62 (November 1892): 647–662;

"Dante Gabriel Rossetti," *Revue de Paris,* 3 (1 June 1896): 550–582;

"Ménage de Poètes–I and II," *Revue de Paris,* 5 (15 September 1898): 295–317; (15 October 1898): 788–817;

"Les Soeurs Brontë–I, II, and III," *Revue de Paris,* 6 (15 December 1899): 831–855; 7 (1 January 1900): 153–171; 7 (15 January 1900): 419–434;

"Thackeray–I and II," *Revue de Paris,* 7 (1 November 1900): 139–165; (15 November 1900): 405–421;

"The youth of Taine," *Fortnightly Review,* 78 (December 1902): 943–961;

"In casa Paget: A retrospect. In memoriam Eugène Lee-Hamilton," *Country Life,* 22 (28 December 1907): 935–937;

"Souvenirs sur Walter Pater," *Revue de Paris,* 32 (15 January 1925): 339–358.

In his introduction to A. Mary F. Robinson's poems in *The Poets and the Poetry of the Nineteenth Century* (1907) Arthur Symons, critic and poet of the Decadent movement, described the writer as the "spoilt child of literature—of two literatures." While this comment might seem an inappropriate remark to include in an otherwise laudatory essay, it was accurate. Robinson was born into a wealthy family and spent her youth in London, immersed in the society of the famous Pre-Raphaelites of the 1880s. Her parents financed the publication of her first book of verse when she was only twenty-one years old, and she then spent the next few years traveling across Europe. Most of Robinson's adult life was spent in France, where she opened her home to the Parisian literary world of the early twentieth century. While most of her nineteenth-century writing was done in English, she spent the last half of her life writing in French, equally at home in both languages.

Robinson was a prolific writer throughout her life—poetry, biographies, reviews, histories, short stories, and a novel—although she is also remembered for the fascinating aspects of her personal life, such as her eight-year relationship with Vernon Lee, her two marriages, and the deep affection felt for her by literary figures such as George Moore and John Addington Symonds. Her only novel was a failure, her histories and biographies have long since been superseded by more recent works, and her poetry has never really been appreciated by contemporary critics. Mary Robinson's literary reputation rests equally on two foundations. Her poetry would not have endured a century after most of it was written if she had not had such a strong, enduring influence on the literary and intellectual culture of her time, in both England and France. On the other hand, she might not have enjoyed such influence had she not been such a talented and prolific writer.

Agnes Mary Frances Robinson was born in Leamington, Warwickshire, on 27 February 1857. She was the elder daughter of George T. Robinson, a wealthy archidiaconal architect for Coventry, Warwicks and later a London banker, and Frances (Sparrow). The family resided briefly in Manchester before settling in London at 84 Gower Street. Mary and her sole sibling, Frances Mabel Robinson, who was younger by one year, were lifelong companions. Mabel, who never married, was for a time one of the most popular of the younger female novelists of the day. Mary wrote poetry from an early age, according to Ruth Van Zuyle Holmes, and she often wrote lines in stress marks only, choosing to wait until later to fill in the words. She was a rather delicate child and spent much of her time in her father's extensive library, reading and educating herself with the help of an occasional governess, until she went to school in Brussels in 1870. Later she studied in Italy and at University College in London, where she spent seven years studying Greek literature.

Robinson's parents were good friends with many writers and were well known in the literary and art worlds of the 1880s and 1890s for their frequent entertaining. Their home became an open house for the painters and writers of the Pre-Raphaelite movement: Moore and Walter Pater met there for the first time, and Robert and Elizabeth Barrett Browning, Henry James, Oscar Wilde, and Thomas Hardy were among those who regularly visited the house on Gower Street. When Robinson came of age in 1878, her parents offered to either have a grand coming-out ball for her or to pay for the private printing of a volume of her verses. Anxious to begin her writing career, Robinson opted for the publication of her first book of poetry, *A Handful of Honeysuckle* (1878), which she dedicated to her parents.

Her book enjoyed considerable success, and literary London soon became interested in this attractive

Robinson's friend and correspondent, the critic and historian John Addington Symonds, whom she met in 1880

young woman poet, so much so that Eric S. Robertson, writing about her in his 1883 book *English Poetesses,* commented that Robinson was a universal topic of conversation and speculation. *A Handful of Honeysuckle,* described by Symons as "so romantic and rococo, so absurd, so inspiriting, so exuberantly poetic," comprises a selection of delicate verse, rather exotic and melancholy at times, self-consciously pretty and poetic at others, suggesting the influence of Algernon Charles Swinburne and Dante Gabriel Rossetti. "Dawn-Angels," for example, is written in five rhymed quatrains of iambic tetrameter. This sweetly lyrical but vague and ambiguous poem opens with "All night I watched awake for morning," until finally the sun rises. "Pale wandering souls" clustered around the moon give way to dawn angels made of "some divine dream elements." "A Pastoral," comprising four quatrains of iambic tetrameter, opens with "Whit Sunday yesterday, / the neighbors met at church to pray." The speaker then remembers that it is May, wanders away, meets a faun, carouses with it, and says goodbye at sunset: "We had forgotten—He and I, / that he was dead, that I must die." While the reviews were predominantly favorable, *The Athenaeum* and the *Saturday Review* cautioned Robinson about the dangers of "artistic affectation," a phrase that was to reappear in reviews of her later work.

Robinson was for a short time the companion of Catherine Symonds's aunt, Arabella North, and also of Vernon Lee (pseudonym of lesbian poet Violet Paget, 1856–1935). Robinson met Lee, possibly through common friends in Florence, some time before 1880, staying with the Pagets in the autumn of that year and then spending December with Lee in Sienna. Several of the poems in *A Handful of Honeysuckle* were addressed to Lee, with whom Robinson maintained a close relationship for eight years. They spent much of their time wandering around Europe together. On the death of Lee's half brother Eugene Lee-Hamilton in 1907, Robinson contributed a memorial article to *Country Life,* which published a picture of Lee and her family at the Pagets' house in Florence around 1880.

In 1880, through Frances Poynter, Robinson met the critic and historian John Addington Symonds, with whom she quickly established a regular and frequent correspondence, in which he analyzed her various works in detail. Although he was married when he met her, Symonds seems to have been quite enamored of Robinson, whom he described in a letter to Lee as "a charming friend in every possible way; a more beautiful & gentle spirit I have never met with. And to get this in combination with her intelligence." When she failed to write to him for some time after their initial introduction, Symonds wrote pitifully to their mutual friend Poynter that seeing him must have broken "the spell of romance." There is a particularly tender note in all his many letters to her in which he repeatedly implores her to visit him in Davos or Venice. When Edmund Gosse chaffed him about rumors he had heard of the many letters passing between them, Symonds replied sheepishly that the reports had been exaggerated.

Although it would perhaps be misleading to view his motivation as jealousy, Symonds disapproved of Lee's strong influence over Robinson. He warned her to stay away from "clever women," and Lee's preoccupation with her own self-interests once prompted Symonds to complain waspishly to Robinson that her friend "becomes more insufferable in her ignorant conceit every day." Although Robinson, who was sixteen years younger than Symonds, does not appear in his memoirs, there was obviously a strong aesthetic and physical attraction between the two friends. In 1881 Robinson dedicated *The Crowned Hippolytus, translated from Euripides, with New Poems* to "My friend J. A. Symonds."

In 1882 Robinson was commissioned to write a biography of Emily Brontë and approached Ellen Nussey, who had been a friend of Charlotte Brontë's, for assistance. Robinson's research efforts for this biography were unusually thorough by Victorian standards—in addition to working with Nussey, she also interviewed many surviving friends of the Brontës and conducted extensive background research. Nussey answered Robinson's lists of questions, offered to correct her manuscript, and lent her some of the many letters which she had received from Charlotte. According to Barbara Whitehead, she was disappointed in Robinson's manuscript itself, insisting that she "did not recognize" the portrait of Emily Brontë. Nussey subsequently insisted on references to herself being cut out and did not want the biography dedicated to her. Nevertheless, in April 1883 Robinson sent her a copy of the book, which was a critical success despite Nussey's disapproval.

Emily Brontë (1883) was the only full-length Victorian biography of the author of *Wuthering Heights* (1847) and is perhaps even more important for having prompted a review by Swinburne, published in *The Athenaeum* on 16 June 1883, an essay considered the most influential critical essay about Emily Brontë of the nineteenth century. As a result of this foray into Brontë scholarship, Robinson was later invited to serve as one of the eleven original vice presidents of the newly formed Brontë Society in 1894. In the company of such well-known literary figures as Augustine Birrell, George Smith, and Peter Bayne, Robinson was the only woman in that otherwise exclusively male group of elected officials.

Arden (1883), Robinson's only novel, was a critical failure, heavily criticized for its weak characterization and implausible plot. Several critics of *Arden,* however, noted the would-be novelist's gift for description, implicitly suggesting that she should stick to writing poetry, a genre in which that particular talent could best be employed.

Robinson returned to verse in 1884 with the publication of *The New Arcadia, and Other Poems,* a book of poems about peasant life that appeared to wildly mixed reviews. Symonds had such high admiration for this volume of songs and ballads that he offered to send a copy to Walt Whitman. The book was strongly criticized in *The Spectator,* however, prompting Symonds to send Robinson a letter of consolation: "I think you are suffering from what success at the beginning always brings—a certain cruel & spiteful reaction—which is also not unjustified." "Tuscan Olives" is the only selection from *The New Arcadia* that was generally well received: "But they are olives always, green or white, / As love is love in torment or delight; / But they are olives, ruffled or at rest, / As love is always love in tears or jest," writes Robinson, in poignant verse reminiscent of *A Handful of Honeysuckle*.

Robinson had also attempted to write realistic social commentary in *The New Arcadia, and Other Poems*, vividly depicting the horrors of rural life. "Tuscan Olives" describes a peasant "bent with age, and hard, / Bruising the grape-skins in a vase of clay" to make his "meagre wine." The fifth stanza opens with "How hot it is! Across the white-hot way / Pale olives stretch towards the blazing street." On 4 October 1884, in one of the harshest reviews, *The Spectator* responded to her efforts by labeling her "an aesthetic pessimist" who depicted rural life in England as a "pestilential inferno." Perhaps realizing that her poetic abilities were not yet sufficiently developed to enable her to address effectively such controversial social issues without losing her audience, Robinson retreated to less graphic and disturbing poetry in her next book.

In 1886 Robinson again achieved critical success with *An Italian Garden: A Book of Songs,* generally considered to be the best of her many poetry collections. The volume includes several wistful lyrics, including the beautiful "Venetian Nocturne." This strange and enigmatic piece opens with "Down the narrow Calle where the moonlight cannot enter." The speaker, walking through the darkness of night, suddenly encounters "All the white Salute towers and domes in moonlit brightness" and wonders, "Ah! could this be Death?" Robinson's second biography, *Margaret of Angoulême, Queen of Navarre* (1886), did not enjoy the critical success of her earlier work on Brontë, but it did not discourage her from taking up biography again later in her career.

Songs, Ballads, and a Garden Play (1888) included more of the Italian ballads and ethereal medieval fantasies at which Robinson seemed to be best and displayed the variety in form and tone that was characteristic of all of her verse. Much of her work is characterized by a nonrepresentational gentleness and sweetness, though Robinson is also capable of much more powerful and analytical insight. A reviewer for *The Athenaeum* (18 April 1891) defined her best qualities as "vague tender melancholy, deep and yet somewhat artificial passion for beauty, grace both natural and skilled, subtle lightness of touch, and a refined use of a special gift of melody." Critics thought most highly of the romantic ballads in *Songs, Ballads, and a Garden Play,* a form to which Robinson returned repeatedly in her later work.

In August 1888, following a brief courtship, Robinson married the French scholar James Darmesteter, professor of Persian in the Collège de France and the Ecole des Hautes Etudes, and editor of *La Revue de Paris*. Darmesteter had seen Robinson's poetry while doing research in India and translated some of the poems into French. The news of their engagement in

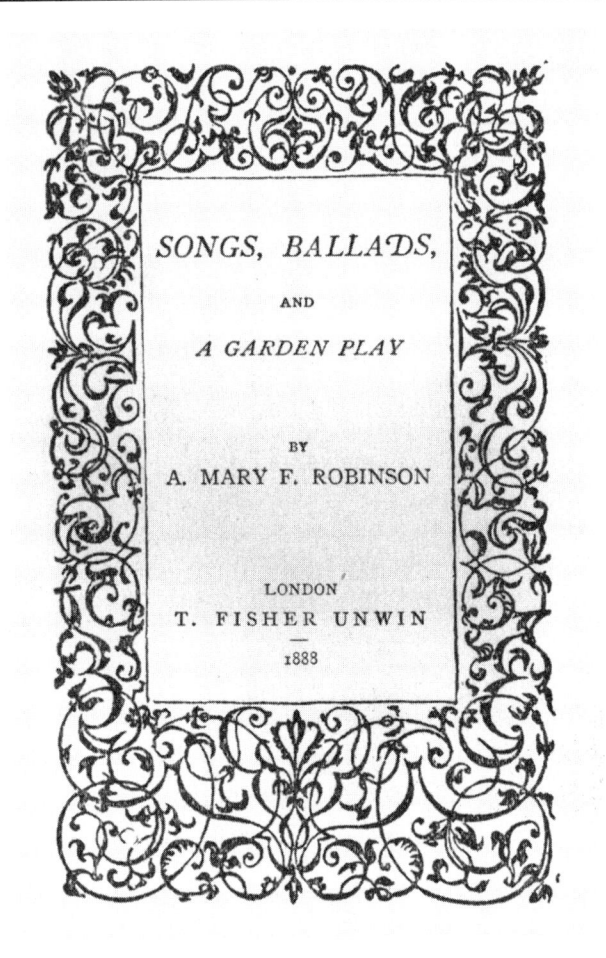

Title page for Robinson's well-received collection of ballads set in Italy and medieval fantasies (courtesy of The Lilly Library, Indiana University)

1887 brought on a nervous and physical collapse in Lee. In a 30 August 1887 letter to her mother, Lee explains, "Last week I received half a sheet of notepaper from Mary telling me that she has engaged herself to marry James Darmesteter, a Jewish professor at the College de France, whom I have seen once . . . and she had then seen *thrice,* including the occasion upon which she asked him (for she says she asked him rather than he her) to marry." Holmes suggests that Lee's extreme reaction to the marriage resulted, at least in part, from the fact that Darmesteter was both a Jew and hunchbacked cripple, but it is difficult to ignore the possibility that Lee had been, and remained, in love with Robinson. It took Lee several years to regain her strength–if indeed she ever did finally recover, for she suffered from physical debility, migraine, and digestive problems for the rest of her life.

Robinson and Darmesteter were both dedicated to bringing about a closer alliance between French and English cultures, and Robinson's salon in Paris soon became a fashionable center of Parisian intellect and

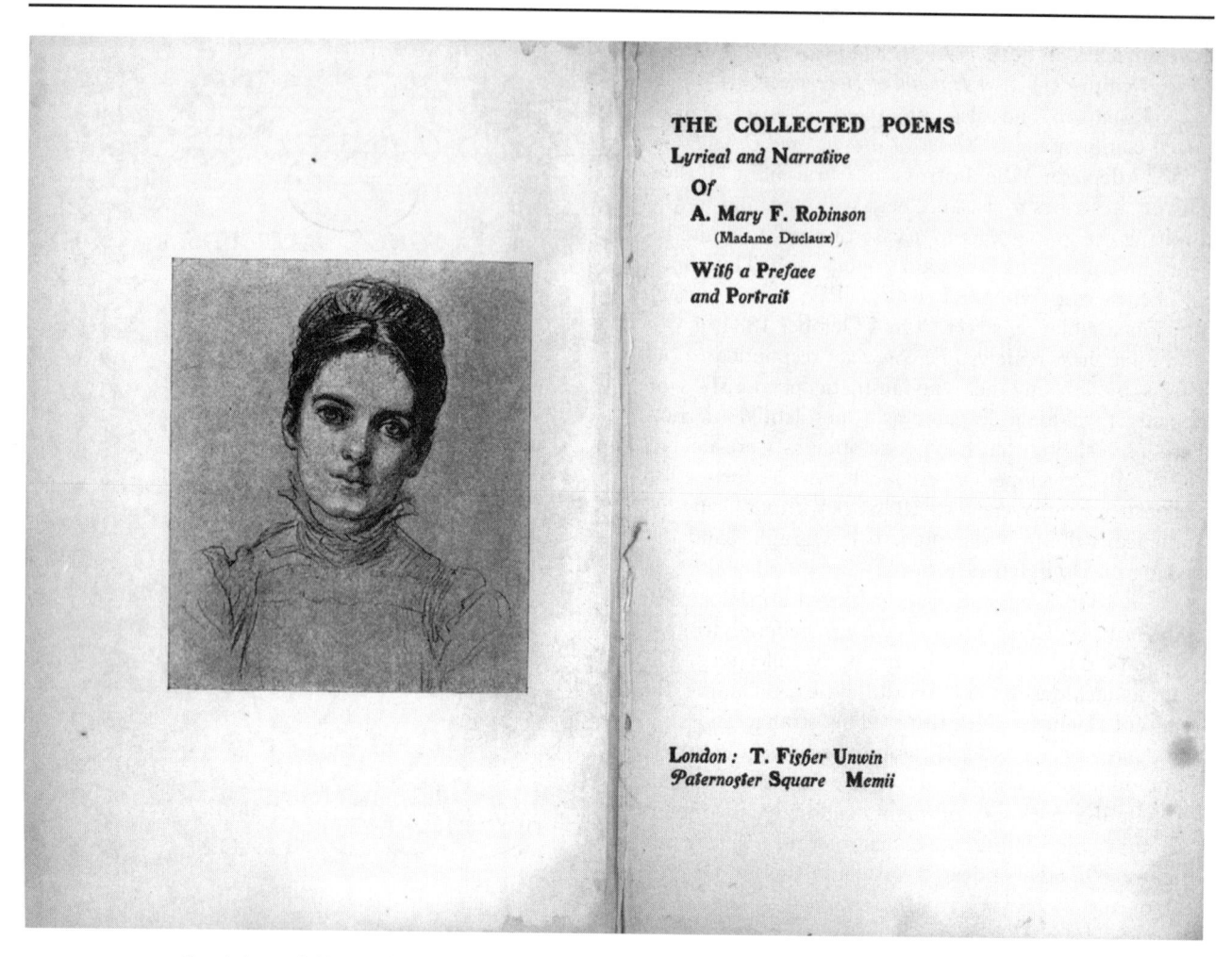

Frontispiece and title page for the collection that includes Robinson's preface about women's affinity for the ballad

culture as the couple played host to—and became intimate friends with—literary figures such as Hippolyte Taine, Ernest Renan, and Gaston Paris. Though an orientalist by vocation, Darmesteter took great interest in literature and founded the *Revue de Paris* shortly before his death. Marriage and the move to France did nothing to impede Robinson's productivity, as she continued to produce a new volume every year or so— *The End of the Middle Ages: Essays and Questions in History* (1889), *Lyrics Selected from the Works of A. Mary F. Robinson (Madame James Darmesteter)* (1890), and *Retrospect, and Other Poems* (1893).

Robinson and Darmesteter sought to promote their writings by translating each other's work. Darmesteter translated Robinson's poems into French as *Poésies* in 1888. Robinson's first work originally written in French was a collection of ten short stories, *Marguerites du Temps Passé* (1891), republished in English as *A Medieval Garden* seven years later. She translated her work on the Brontës, the Brownings, and Thackeray into French for publication in the *Revue de Paris* at the end of the century, and later did some editing in French of writings by Marie de Sévigné, published in 1914 as *Mme. de. Sévigné, Textes Choisis et Commentés par Mme. Duclaux*.

In 1894, with the publication of Anatole France's novel *Le Lys Rouge*, Robinson and Lee became the objects of much gossip, as readers speculated about the identity of one of the novel's main characters, the young Vivian Bell, depicted as a renowned English poetess. This novel, France's first attempt to portray love in modern society, was well received, highly admired by Marcel Proust, among others. The similarities between Robinson, Lee, and the fictional Bell are striking; all were poets, devotees of Tuscan life and art, and comfortable in aristocratic literary circles in both France and Italy. It became generally believed that France had used Robinson, who with James Darmesteter was well known to him, and Lee, whom he probably had met in Italy, to create the composite character of Vivian Bell, thus immortalizing the relationship between Robinson and Lee for subsequent generations of readers.

Robinson circa 1920

Darmesteter's death on 19 October 1894, following a brief illness, proved devastating to Robinson, who was left a widow at the age of thirty-seven. She did not return to England, choosing instead to spend the rest of her life in France and make occasional visits to England and Italy. Symons made the remark a few years later, in 1907, "Perhaps no living English poet, after Swinburne, is nearly so well known abroad. This is partly an accident of circumstance; it is largely a matter of instinctive response. Madame Darmesteter has always been alive to the influence of what is new and significant in foreign literature, and it is but just that her appreciation should be returned." *Froissart* was published in 1894, and a highly acclaimed biography, *A Life of Ernest Renan*, appeared three years later. Robinson was well qualified to write the biography, as her husband had been one of Renan's most distinguished pupils. Robinson also prefaced and translated posthumous work by her late husband, such as his *English Studies* in 1896.

Reviews of *A Life of Ernest Renan* revealed some curious aspects to Robinson's unique position in literature, that of an Englishwoman writing the life of a Frenchman. While Lionel P. Johnson, reviewing for *The Academy* on 20 November 1897, praised the biography as "solid as well as written in measured and musical prose," not all critics were quite so pleased. The reviewer in *The Spectator* (18 December 1897) complained that Robinson's work should not be the final say on the life of Renan; it should be written by a Frenchman who could better understand Renan and his place in literature. Curiously, this same reviewer complained that Robinson's "English is a little stiff and the book seems to have been thought out in French first," perhaps revealing a bit of displeasure with the fact that Robinson, an Englishwoman, had effectively abandoned her native country by electing not to return there after the death of her French husband. A writer for the April 1898 *Sewanee Review* agreed, commenting that since Robinson had learned to write French so well, her English style had been adversely affected, and agreeing that *A Life of Ernest Renan* seems to have been thought out in French. From this point on in her career, Robinson began to devote more and more of her energies to reviewing French literature for English audiences and vice versa, in a continued attempt—first begun early in her marriage to James Darmesteter—to bridge the gap, albeit sometimes unsuccessfully, between the cultures and literatures of the two countries.

In 1901 Robinson married Pierre Emile Duclaux, an eminent French scientist who succeeded Louis Pasteur himself as director of the Pasteur Institute. With Duclaux, a widower with two sons, she moved to a country house near Olmet, in the Cantal region of France. In the autumn of 1901, returning from her annual visit to England, Lee spent six weeks in France. On previous journeys through Paris she had seen Robinson, but the intimacy of their early friendship had never revived. On this occasion Lee went to stay with the Duclaux at their country house near Vic-sur-Cère. She wrote of this visit in a letter to Kit Anstruther-Thomson:

> Getting to know M. Duclaux has been a great delight. I have never met a man so much of a man—so steadfast, single-minded and utterly devoid of all personal or, so to speak, temporal considerations. He is really extraordinary. I was very happy seeing that beautiful country with him. I say *with him*, because charming and intelligent as Mary is, and grateful though I am for her magnanimous fidelity to me, I seem to have absolutely not one fibre in common with her, and nothing comes of our intercourse.

In February 1902 the *Fortnightly Review* published Hannah Lynch's "A. Mary F. Robinson," the only lengthy critical study of Robinson's work. Apparently prompted by the publication of *The Collected Poems, Lyrical and Narrative of Mary Robinson (Madame Duclaux)* (1902), Lynch took the opportunity to write a sweeping review of several of Robinson's major works. She praises Robinson's "depth and quiet intensity" and admires her "finished and delightful style in two languages," while conceding that Robinson's talents clearly lie with poetry rather than prose.

Robinson wrote a preface for the collection, in which she claims that women have a special affinity for the ballad and other popular forms. She argues that the ballad is a special form of poetry for women and valuable for its authenticity of experience:

> Some persons of culture have refused me the right to express myself in those simple forms of popular song which I have loved since childhood and as sincerely as any peasant. If the critics would only believe it, they have come as naturally to me, if less happily, than they came of old to a Lady Wardlaw, a Lady Lindsay, or a Lady Nairn. We women have a privilege in these matters. . . . We have always been the prime makers of ballads and love songs, of anonymous snatches and screeds of popular song. We meet together no longer on Mayday, as of old in Provence, to set the fashion in tensos and sonnets. But some old wife or other, crooning over her fire of sticks, in Scotland or the Val d'Aosta, in Roumania or Gascony, is probably at the beginning of most romantic ballads.

Robinson goes on to argue that "I have never been able to write about what was not known to me and near," although her poems are often set in medieval settings or unidentifiable foreign countries, with a wistful and otherworldly tone.

Robinson then completed a book of historical essays, *The Fields of France,* published in 1903. *The Return to Nature* (1904), her next book of poetry, was dedicated to her second husband, who died suddenly in May of that year. Following Duclaux's death, Robinson devoted herself to her stepchildren, dividing her time between the family estates in the Auvergne and Paris. In 1906, just two years after his death, she published a biography of her husband, *La Vie de Emile Duclaux,* followed by another book of poetry, *Songs from an Italian Garden,* in 1908.

With *The French Procession* (1909), which was dedicated to Lee, and *The French Ideal: Pascal, Fénelon and other Essays* (1911), the focus of Robinson's work shifted from poetry to literary criticism of French writers, French history, and biography. In 1918 came *A Short History of France from Caesar's Invasion to the Battle of Waterloo,* closely followed by *Twentieth Century French Writers* in 1919. In the 1920s she wrote several biographies—Victor Hugo in 1921, Racine in 1925, and Pascal in 1927—all which were well received. She did not abandon poetry altogether, however, and her dedication of *Images and Meditations* (1923) to "Mabel, only sister, dearest friend" mirrored the dedication of Mabel's novel *Disenchantment: An Everyday Story* to Mary in 1886.

In 1939, with World War II threatening, the Duclaux children took Robinson and her sister Mabel to a safe location in Aurillac where they remained through the war. In 1943, at the age of eighty-six, she underwent a successful operation on her eyes for the removal of cataracts. Mary Robinson died a few months later, just prior to her eighty-seventh birthday, on 9 February 1944, and was buried in Aurillac. Though her literary reputation remains uncertain, Robinson will always be remembered for the strong impact that she had, for almost seven full decades, on the literary worlds of both France and England.

Letters:

Mary Duclaux et Maurice Barrès: Lettres Echangées, edited by Daniel Halévy (Paris: Grasset, 1959).

Bibliographies:

Ruth Van Zuyle Holmes, "Mary Duclaux (1857–1944): Primary and Secondary Checklists," *English Literature in Transition, 1880–1920,* 10 (1967): 27–46; 16 (1973): 71–74;

"Agnes Mary Frances Robinson," in *Late Victorian Poetry, 1880–1899: An Annotated Bibliography,* edited by Catherine W. Reilly (London: Mansell, 1994), p. 406.

References:

Phyllis Grosskurth, *John Addington Symonds: A Biography* (London: Longmans, 1964), pp. 223–224, 263;

Peter Gunn, *Vernon Lee: Violet Paget, 1856–1935* (London: Oxford University Press, 1964);

Daniel Halévy, "Les Trois Mary," biographical introduction to *Mary Duclaux et Maurice Barrès: Lettres Echangées* (Paris: Grasset, 1959);

The Letters of John Addington Symonds, volume 2: *1869–1884,* edited by Herbert M. Schueller and Robert L. Peters (Detroit: Wayne State University Press, 1968), p. 584;

Sylvanie Marandon, *L'oeuvre poétique de Mary Robinson* (Bordeaux: Imprimeries Péchade, 1967);

Marandon, "Qui fut Mary Robinson?" *Langues Modernes,* 54 (May–June 1960): 35–41;

John Pollock, "Mary Duclaux," *Contemporary Review,* 1517 (April 1945): 201–208;

Margaret Reynolds, "A. Mary F. Robinson (1857–1944)," in *Victorian Women Poets: An Anthology,* edited by Angela Leighton and Margaret Reynolds (Oxford: Blackwell, 1995), pp. 538–539;

Eric S. Robertson, *English Poetesses* (London: Cassell, 1883);

Arthur Symons, "A. Mary F. Darmesteter," in *The Poets and the Poetry of the Nineteenth Century,* volume 9: *Christina G. Rossetti to Katharine Tynan,* edited by Alfred H. Miles (London: Routledge, 1907), pp. 359–364;

Barbara Whitehead, *Charlotte Brontë and Her "Dearest Nell": The Story of a Friendship* (Otley: Smith Settle, 1993), p. 226.

Christina Rossetti

(5 December 1830 – 29 December 1894)

Mary Arseneau
University of Ottawa

See also the Rossetti entries in *DLB 35: Victorian Poets After 1850,* and *DLB 163: British Children's Writers, 1800–1880.*

BOOKS: *Verses* (London: Privately printed at G. Polidori's, 1847);

Goblin Market and Other Poems (Cambridge & London: Macmillan, 1862);

The Prince's Progress and Other Poems (London: Macmillan, 1866);

Poems (Boston: Roberts, 1866);

Commonplace and Other Short Stories (London: Ellis, 1870; Boston: Roberts, 1870);

Sing-Song: A Nursery Rhyme Book (London: Routledge, 1872; Boston: Roberts, 1872; revised and enlarged edition, London: Macmillan, 1893);

Annus Domini: A Prayer for Each Day of the Year, Founded on a Text of Holy Scripture (Oxford & London: Parker, 1874);

Speaking Likenesses, with Pictures thereof by Arthur Hughes (London: Macmillan, 1874; Boston: Roberts, 1875);

Goblin Market, The Prince's Progress, and Other Poems (London & New York: Macmillan, 1875); republished as *Poems* (Boston: Roberts, 1876);

Seek and Find: A Double Series of Short Studies on the Benedicite (London & Brighton: Society for Promoting Christian Knowledge / New York: Young, 1879);

A Pageant and Other Poems (London: Macmillan, 1880; Boston: Roberts, 1881);

Called to Be Saints: The Minor Festivals Devotionally Studied (London & Brighton: Society for Promoting Christian Knowledge / New York: Young, 1881);

Poems (Boston: Roberts, 1882; enlarged edition, London & New York: Macmillan, 1890);

Letter and Spirit: Notes on the Commandments (London & Brighton: Society for Promoting Christian Knowledge / New York: Young, 1883);

Time Flies: A Reading Diary (London & Brighton: Society for Promoting Christian Knowledge, 1885; Boston: Roberts, 1886);

Christina Rossetti

The Face of the Deep: A Devotional Commentary on the Apocalypse (London & Brighton: Society for Promoting Christian Knowledge / New York: Young, 1892);

Verses: Reprinted from "Called to Be Saints," "Time Flies," "The Face of the Deep" (London & Brighton: Society for Promoting Christian Knowledge / New York: Young, 1893);

New Poems, Hitherto Unpublished or Uncollected, edited by William Michael Rossetti (London & New York: Macmillan, 1896);

Maude: A Story for Girls (London: Bowden, 1897; enlarged edition, Chicago: Stone, 1897);

The Poetical Works of Christina Georgina Rossetti. With Memoir and Notes, &c., edited by William Michael Rossetti (London & New York: Macmillan, 1904);

The Complete Poems of Christina Rossetti: A Variorum Edition, 3 volumes, edited by Rebecca W. Crump (Baton Rouge & London: Louisiana State University Press, 1979–1990).

OTHER: John Francis Waller, ed., *The Imperial Dictionary of Universal Biography,* includes contributions by Rossetti, 3 volumes (London: Mackenzie, 1863).

SELECTED PERIODICAL PUBLICATIONS–
UNCOLLECTED:
POETRY
"Versi" and "L'Incognita," *Bouquet from Marylebone Gardens* (June 1851–January 1852): 175, 216.
FICTION
"Corrispondenza Famigliare," *Bouquet from Marylebone Gardens* (January–July 1852): 120–121, 218–219; (July–December 1852): 14–15, 55–57;
"True in the Main: Two Sketches," *Dawn of Day* (1 May 1882): 57–59; (1 June 1882): 69–70.
NONFICTION
"Dante, an English Classic," *Churchman's Shilling Magazine and Family Treasury,* 2 (1867): 200–205;
"A Harmony on First Corinthians XIII," *New and Old,* 7 (January 1879): 34–39;
"Dante: The Poet Illustrated out of the Poem," *Century,* 27 (1884): 566–573.

Of all Victorian women poets, posterity has been kindest to Christina Rossetti. Her poetry has never disappeared from view, and her reputation, though it suffered a decline in the first half of the twentieth century, has always been preserved to some degree. Critical interest in Rossetti's poetry swelled in the final decades of the twentieth century, a resurgence largely impelled by the emergence of feminist criticism; much of this commentary focuses on gender issues in her poetry and on Rossetti as a woman poet. In Rossetti's lifetime opinion was divided over whether she or Elizabeth Barrett Browning was the greatest female poet of the era; in any case, after Browning's death in 1861 readers and critics saw Rossetti as the older poet's rightful successor. The two poets achieved different kinds of excellence, as is evident in Dante Gabriel Rossetti's comment on his sister, quoted by William Sharp in *The Atlantic Monthly* (June 1895): "She is the finest woman-poet since Mrs. Browning, by a long way; and in artless art, if not in intellectual impulse, is greatly Mrs. Browning's superior." Readers have generally considered Rossetti's poetry less intellectual, less political, and less varied than Browning's; conversely, they have acknowledged Rossetti as having the greater lyric gift, with her poetry displaying a perfection of diction, tone, and form under the guise of utter simplicity.

Rossetti was the youngest child in an extraordinarily gifted family. Her father, the Italian poet and political exile Gabriele Rossetti, immigrated to England in 1824 and established a career as a Dante scholar and teacher of Italian in London. He married the half-English, half-Italian Frances Polidori in 1826, and they had four children in quick succession: Maria Francesca in 1827, Gabriel Charles Dante (famous under the name Dante Gabriel but always called Gabriel by family members) in 1828, William Michael in 1829, and Christina Georgina on 5 December 1830. In 1831 Gabriele Rossetti was appointed to the chair of Italian at the newly opened King's College. The children received their earliest education, and Maria and Christina all of theirs, from their mother, who had been trained as a governess and was committed to cultivating intellectual excellence in her family. Certainly this ambition was satisfied: in addition to Christina's becoming one of the Victorian age's finest poets, Maria was the author of a respected study of Dante, as well as books on religious instruction and Italian grammar and translation; Dante Gabriel distinguished himself as one of the foremost poets and painters of his era; and William was a prolific art and literary critic, editor, and memoirist of the Pre-Raphaelite movement.

Rossetti's childhood was exceptionally happy, characterized by affectionate parental care and the creative companionship of older siblings. In temperament she was most like her brother Dante Gabriel: their father called the pair the "two storms" of the family in comparison to the "two calms," Maria and William. Christina was given to tantrums and fractious behavior, and she fought hard to subdue this passionate temper. Years later, counseling a niece subject to similar outbursts, the mature Christina looked back on the fire now stifled: "You must not imagine, my dear girl, that your Aunt was always the calm and sedate person you now behold. I, too, had a very passionate temper; but I learnt to control it. On one occasion, being rebuked by my dear Mother for some fault, I seized upon a pair of scissors, and ripped up my arm to vent my wrath. I have learnt since to control my feelings–and no doubt you will!" Self-control was, indeed, achieved–perhaps too much so. In his posthumous memoir of his sister that prefaces *The Poetical Works of Christina Georgina Rossetti* (1904) William laments the thwarting of her high spirits: "In innate character she was vivacious, and open to pleasurable impressions; and, during her girlhood, one might readily have supposed that she would develop into a woman of expansive heart, fond of society and diversions, and taking a part in them of more than average brilliancy. What came to pass was of course quite the contrary." As an adult Christina Rossetti was considered by many to be overscrupulous and excessively restrained.

Frances Rossetti read to her children, favoring religious texts such as the Bible, John Bunyan's *The Pilgrim's Progress* (1678), and the writings of St. Augustine, or moralistic tales such as those by Maria Edgeworth. When the children began reading for themselves, however, they generally shunned their mother's edifying selections in favor of the imaginative delights of *The Arabian Nights* or Thomas Keightley's *Fairy Mythology* (1828); later favorites included Sir Walter Scott, Ann Radcliffe, and Matthew Gregory "Monk" Lewis. Until 1836, when the boys began attending day school, the four children were offered similar instruction by their mother; thereafter, only Dante Gabriel and William were formally instructed in classics, mathematics, and sciences. Asked to describe her poetic influences, Rossetti speculated in a 26 March 1884 letter to Edmund Gosse: "If any one thing schooled me in the direction of poetry, it was perhaps the delightful idle liberty to prowl all alone about my grandfather's cottage-grounds some thirty miles from London." At Gaetano Polidori's cottage at Holmer Green she fostered the attention to the minute in nature that marks her poetry; there she also observed the corruptibility and mortality that became keynotes in her work. Her reminiscences in *Time Flies: A Reading Diary* (1885) include reflections on childhood adventures at the cottage: her patient attendance on a strawberry, only to find it blighted before it has fully ripened, and her burial of a dead mouse and later observation of its decay. The visits to Holmer Green ended in 1839 when her grandfather sold the house and moved to London. A great lover of nature, Rossetti nevertheless spent most of her life in the city.

In his memoir William notes that Christina composed her first verse, "Cecilia never went to school / Without her gladiator," before she was old enough to write. Her next attempt was an aborted tale, modeled on *The Arabian Nights*, about a dervish named Hassan; and she wrote her first poem, "To my Mother on her Birthday," when she was eleven. The children produced a family newspaper, "The Hodge-Podge or Weekly Efforts," the first issue of which was dated 20 May 1843, and later a periodical titled "The Illustrated Scrapbook." Christina's early poetic efforts included experiments in lyric, devotional, pastoral, ballad, and fantasy forms.

Caught up in the Tractarian or Oxford Movement when it reached London in the 1840s, the Rossettis shifted from an Evangelical to an Anglo-Catholic orientation, and this outlook influenced virtually all of Christina Rossetti's poetry. She was also influenced by the poetics of the Oxford Movement, as is documented in the annotations and illustrations she added to her copy of John Keble's *The Christian Year* (1827) and in her reading of poetry by Isaac Williams and John Henry Newman. For more than twenty years, beginning in 1843, she worshiped at Christ Church, Albany Street, where services were influenced by the innovations emanating from Oxford. The Reverend William Dodsworth, the priest there until his conversion to Catholicism in 1850, assumed a leading role as the Oxford Movement spread to London. In addition to coming under the religious influence of prominent Tractarians such as Dodsworth, W. J. E. Bennett, Henry W. Burrows, and E. B. Pusey, Rossetti had close personal ties with Burrows and Richard Frederick Littledale, a High Church theologian who became her spiritual adviser. The importance of Rossetti's faith for her life and art can hardly be overstated. More than half of her poetic output is devotional, and the works of her later years in both poetry and prose are almost exclusively so. The inconstancy of human love, the vanity of earthly pleasures, renunciation, individual unworthiness, and the perfection of divine love are recurring themes in her poetry.

Gabriele Rossetti's health collapsed in 1843, leaving him virtually blind and unable to teach. Frances Rossetti returned to her former employment as a daily governess. Maria and William also took employment, Maria as a nursery governess and William in the civil service. Dante Gabriel continued his art studies, while Christina remained at home as a companion to their ailing father. In 1845 she, too, suffered a collapse in health. The breakdown has mystified biographers, some of whom have surmised that the physical symptoms were psychosomatic and rescued Rossetti from having to make a financial contribution to the family by working as a governess like her mother and sister. She was diagnosed as having a heart condition, but another doctor speculated that she was mentally ill, suffering from a kind of religious mania. Her biographer Jan Marsh conjectures that there may have been an attempt at paternal incest: the father's breakdown and the resultant changes in family fortunes leaving a needy patriarch in the daily care of his pubescent daughter, Christina's recurring bouts of depression, her lifelong sense of sinfulness, nightmarish poems about a crocodile devouring his kin, a poetic image of a "clammy fin" repulsively reaching out to her, and the recurring motif of an unnameable secret, Marsh suggests, could be indications of suppressed sexual trauma. Rossetti had bouts of serious illness throughout her life; William insists in his memoir that one cannot understand his sister unless one recognizes that she "was an almost constant and often a sadly-smitten invalid." The morbidity that read-

The End of the Year.

New Year met me somewhat sad;
  Old Year leaves me tired,
Stripped of favourite things I had
  Baulked of much desired:—
Yet farther on my road today
God willing, farther on my way.

New Year coming on apace
  What have you to give me?
Bring you scathe, or bring you grace
Face me with an honest face,
  You shall not deceive me:—
Be it good or ill, be it what you will,
It needs shall help me on my road,
My rugged way to heaven, please God.

13th December 1856.

Page from one of Rossetti's notebooks (from The Family Letters of Christina Georgina Rossetti, *edited by William Michael Rossetti, 1908)*

ers have so often noted in her poetry, William suggests, was attributable to Christina's ill health and the ever-present prospect of early death rather than any innate disposition.

By her sixteenth birthday Christina, who was regarded as the poet in the family, had written more than fifty poems that were transcribed into a notebook by her sister. In 1847 a collection of her poems, titled *Verses,* was privately printed by her grandfather Polidori. As Marsh points out, this private publication, dedicated to her mother, decorously avoided anything resembling public display, but at the same time it constituted a juvenile literary debut in the tradition of other women poets such as Browning and Felicia Hemans. It was circulated among family and friends and was well received. The thirty-nine poems are notably literary in their inspiration, which is traceable to the Gothic writers Radcliffe, Lewis, and Charles Maturin; the English poets George Herbert, George Crabbe, William Blake, Samuel Taylor Coleridge, Percy Bysshe Shelley, John Keats, and Alfred Tennyson; and the Italian poets Dante, Torquato Tasso, and Pietro Metastasio. The first and most striking poem in the collection is "The Dead City," an ambitious 275-line dream vision of a magnificent city, succulent banquet, and voluptuous revelers all turned to stone, the evocative descriptions of which anticipate the Pre-Raphaelite style. Here, as in Rossetti's most famous poem, "Goblin Market" (1862), lusciously described fruits represent the temptations of self-indulgence and pleasure. This genre—a narrative that combines fantasy with moral allegory—was an important one for Rossetti, and she employed it in more-accomplished poems such as "Goblin Market," "From House to Home," "The Prince's Progress," and "A Ballad of Boding," as well as in her tales "Nick," "Hero," and *Speaking Likenesses, with Pictures thereof by Arthur Hughes* (1874). A morbid strain can be seen in many of the poems in the collection: themes of mortality, inconstancy, and corruptibility figure prominently. Although Rossetti's mature style is not fully realized at this point, *Verses* is important as a tangible sign of her commitment to poetry and of her family's recognition of her vocation.

Later in 1847 Dante Gabriel, William, and Christina began a tradition of playing *bouts rimés,* a game in which two of them would race to compose a sonnet conforming to a set of line endings provided by the third. Christina excelled at the exercise, composing sonnets in a matter of minutes. In 1848 she had her first taste of fame when, at Dante Gabriel's instigation, she submitted two of her poems, "Death's Chill Between" and "Heart's Chill Between," to the prestigious literary periodical *The Athenaeum;* their acceptance made her a nationally published poet at seventeen. During this period Dante Gabriel was gathering around him the circle of young men who named themselves the Pre-Raphaelite Brotherhood. Although he assumed that Christina would participate, she was never a member of this artistic and literary group; she even refused to have her work read aloud in her absence at its meetings, on the grounds that such display was unseemly. Nevertheless, her poetry has been described as "Pre-Raphaelite" in its rich and precise natural detail, its use of symbol, its poignancy, and its deliberate medievalism. Later in her career a reviewer in the *Catholic World* (October 1876) called her the "queen of the Preraphaelite school"; but more-recent critics have remarked that the Pre-Raphaelite elements in Rossetti's work have been overemphasized at the expense of proper notice of the Tractarian influences. Certainly, Rossetti was involved in the early days of Pre-Raphaelitism. She sat as Mary for Dante Gabriel's paintings *The Girlhood of Mary Virgin* (1848–1849) and *Ecce Ancilla Domini!* (1850), and her pensive Italianate countenance was a familiar image in the first phase of the movement. The art and poetry of the brotherhood has a strong sacramental element, and Rossetti had more in common with this early manifestation of the Pre-Raphaelite aesthetic than she did with its later developments.

Late in 1849 the Pre-Raphaelite Brotherhood initiated a periodical, *The Germ,* as a vehicle for the members' innovative views on art. Its four issues—dated January to April 1850—provided a venue for seven of Rossetti's poems: "Dreamland," "An End," "Song" ("Oh roses for the flush of youth"), "A Pause of Thought," "A Testimony," "Repining," and "Sweet Death." These publications, which were anonymous in the first issue and pseudonymous thereafter, found an appreciative, though small, audience. The poems, and others composed at this time but not published until later, show that Rossetti had by then attained her mature poetic style, in which pain, loss, and resignation are expressed in diction and images that strike the reader as simple, perfect, and effortless.

One of the Pre-Raphaelite brethren, James Collinson, proposed marriage to Rossetti in 1848. She refused the offer, giving Collinson's recent conversion to Roman Catholicism as the reason. Collinson promptly returned to the Church of England, proposed a second time, and was accepted. Collinson has struck biographers as an unlikely suitor (anecdotes generally portray him as a lackluster sleepyhead), and opinion is mixed as to whether Rossetti was ever in love with him. The engagement ended in the spring of 1850 when Collinson reverted to Catholicism.

In 1850 Rossetti wrote *Maude: A Story for Girls* (1897), a novella that was not published until after her

Rossetti (left) with her sister Maria; her mother, Frances; and her brother Dante Gabriel at Dante Gabriel's home, 16 Cheyne Walk, Chelsea

death. The title character's appearance and personality bear many similarities to accounts of the author, and this work, with its exploration of the tensions among the sometimes incompatible categories of female, poet, and Anglo-Catholic, is usually considered a semi-autobiographical portrait of the adolescent Rossetti. Fifteen-year-old Maude Foster is a poet whose "broken-hearted" verse dwells on themes of suffering, world-weariness, resignation, and religious devotion. Some of Rossetti's important early poems, later published under the titles "Song" ("She sat and sang alway"), "Three Nuns," and "Symbols," are included as Maude's productions, and a *bouts rimés* contest also appears in the narrative. Rossetti returned to this mixing of genres—prose punctuated with poetry—in her devotional works *Called to Be Saints: The Minor Festivals Devotionally Studied* (1881), *Time Flies,* and *The Face of the Deep: A Devotional Commentary on the Apocalypse* (1892). Religious issues play a central role in the story when Maude suffers a spiritual crisis, and Anglo-Catholic practices are described as she discusses with her cousins the heavily symbolic lectern cover they are embroidering, the question of a vocation as a nun, and the Eucharist. The main conflict in the narrative revolves around Maude's experience of the incompatibility of ladylike behavior and poetic achievement. Like the author, Maude is torn between pride in her work and moral qualms about that pride. The heroine's overactive conscience and endless self-recriminations provide considerable insight into Rossetti's own overscrupulous nature.

The family's financial crisis continued, and in 1851 the Rossettis moved from Charlotte Street to Camden Town, where Christina and her mother briefly ran a small day school. A second attempt at establishing a school, this time in Frome, lasted from March 1853 to February 1854, the only period in Rossetti's life when she made her home outside London. When she returned to the city, the family moved to Albany Street. At this point Christina and her mother permanently gave up teaching, and the family lived on William's and Mary's earnings and Frances's modest inherited income. Gabriele Rossetti died on 26 April 1854. For most of her adulthood Christina was financially supported primarily by William, a debt that she made provisions in her will to repay.

Throughout her twenties Rossetti continued to write poetry and prose. Her Italian heritage is apparent in the Italian poems "Versi" and "L'Incognita" and an unfinished epistolary novel, "Corrispondenza [*sic*] Famigliare," which were published in a privately printed periodical, *The Bouquet from Marylebone Gardens* during 1851 and 1852. Attempts at publication in prestigious periodicals such as *Blackwood's* and *Fraser's* in 1854 failed. In a letter of 1 August 1854 to William Edmonstoune Aytoun of *Blackwood's* Rossetti declared: "poetry is with me, not a mechanism, but an impulse and a reality; and . . . I know my aims in writing to be pure, and directed to that which is true and right."

Rossetti has often been depicted as shrinking from worldly concerns, but, in fact, she did engage in humanitarian work. In 1854, during the Crimean War, she volunteered to join Florence Nightingale's nurses but was turned down. Her aunt Eliza Polidori did join Nightingale in Scutari, and Rossetti temporarily took over some of Polidori's district visiting, providing assistance to the sick and poor of the parish. In early 1859 Rossetti began volunteering at the St. Mary Magdalene Penitentiary in Highgate, a charitable institution for the reclamation of "fallen" women. As an "associate" at Highgate, Rossetti was known as "Sister Christina" and wore a habitlike black uniform with a veil. When she was on duty she resided at the penitentiary, probably for a fortnight at a time. By the summer of 1859 Rossetti was devoting a good deal of time to her work at Highgate, and its influence can be seen in her poems about illicit love, betrayal, and illegitimacy, such as "Cousin Kate," "'The Iniquity of the Fathers upon the Children,'" and "From Sunset to Star Rise," though poems composed before the period of her work at Highgate–"An Apple-Gathering," "The Convent Threshold," and "Maude Clare" for instance–demonstrate her prior interest in the fallen woman. "Goblin Market," with its theme of a fallen woman being saved by a "sister," can also be seen as informed by Rossetti's experiences at the St. Mary Magdalene Penitentiary. Her interest in this topic reflects the Victorian concern about prostitution as a social evil; other Pre-Raphaelite treatments of the subject include Dante Gabriel's poem "Jenny," begun in 1847 and revised in 1858–1859 and again in 1870; his unfinished painting *Found* (1854–1881); and William Holman Hunt's *The Awakened Conscience* (1853).

In the 1850s a few of Rossetti's poems were published in anthologies; "Maude Clare" appeared in *Once a Week* (5 November 1859) and the short stories "The Lost Titian" (*The Crayon,* 1856) and "Nick" (*National Magazine,* October 1857). In 1861 she submitted poems to *Macmillan's Magazine,* and Dante Gabriel sent "Goblin Market" to the art critic John Ruskin in the hope that he would recommend it to William Makepeace Thackeray, editor of *The Cornhill.* Ruskin's criticism of Rossetti's masterpiece is infamous. In his letter of 24 January 1861 to Dante Gabriel, Ruskin singled out for criticism the original meter that is now so often praised: he acknowledged the poem's "beauty and power" but asserted that it was unpublishable because it was "so full of quaintnesses and offences," adding,

"Irregular measure . . . is the chief calamity of modern poetry . . . your sister should exercise herself in the severest commonplace of metre until she can write as the public like." Almost simultaneously, Rossetti's poem "Up-hill" was accepted enthusiastically for *Macmillan's* (February 1861), and Alexander Macmillan expressed an interest in seeing more of her work. During 1861 *Macmillan's* published two more of Rossetti's poems: "A Birthday" (April 1861) and "An Apple-Gathering" (August 1861). In June of that year Rossetti took a short vacation in France.

In 1862 the Macmillan firm brought out Rossetti's first commercially published volume of poetry, *Goblin Market and Other Poems.* Although some of the poems had been published in *Macmillan's, Once a Week,* and *The Germ,* and others were included in the manuscript for *Maude,* most were taken from the notebooks in which Rossetti had been writing since the private printing of *Verses* in 1847. Comparisons of the manuscript and printed versions of the poems show that most were not substantially revised. Usually the earliest extant version of a given poem is the fair copy transcribed into the notebook; if Rossetti reworked it in the act of composition, such drafts no longer exist. She often changed a word or two in preparation for publication; where major revisions occurred, they took the form of the deletion of whole stanzas, sometimes reducing a poem by more than half its original length: such is the case with "Maude Clare," "Echo," and "Bitter for Sweet." This tendency to reduce is part of the economy of expression that is a Rossetti trademark, and the result is poetry in which meaning is suggestive rather than explicit. Looking back on her career, Rossetti wrote in an 1888 letter to an unknown clergyman that "Perhaps the nearest approach to a method I can lay claim to was a distinct aim at conciseness; after a while I received a hint from my sister that my love of conciseness tended to make my writing obscure, and I then endeavoured to avoid obscurity as well as diffuseness. In poetics, my elder brother was my acute and most helpful critic." Throughout her career Dante Gabriel not only critiqued her work but also negotiated with publishers, assisted with book design, corrected proofs, and provided illustrations for her publications. As *Goblin Market and Other Poems* was being prepared for the press, he advised on the selection of poems, suggested dividing them into secular and devotional sections, and proposed new titles for some–including the title poem, which was originally called "A Peep at the Goblins." He also provided frontispiece and title-page designs drawn from that poem.

Goblin Market and Other Poems was a critical success, with favorable notices in many periodicals, including *The London Review* (12 April 1862), *The Spectator* (12

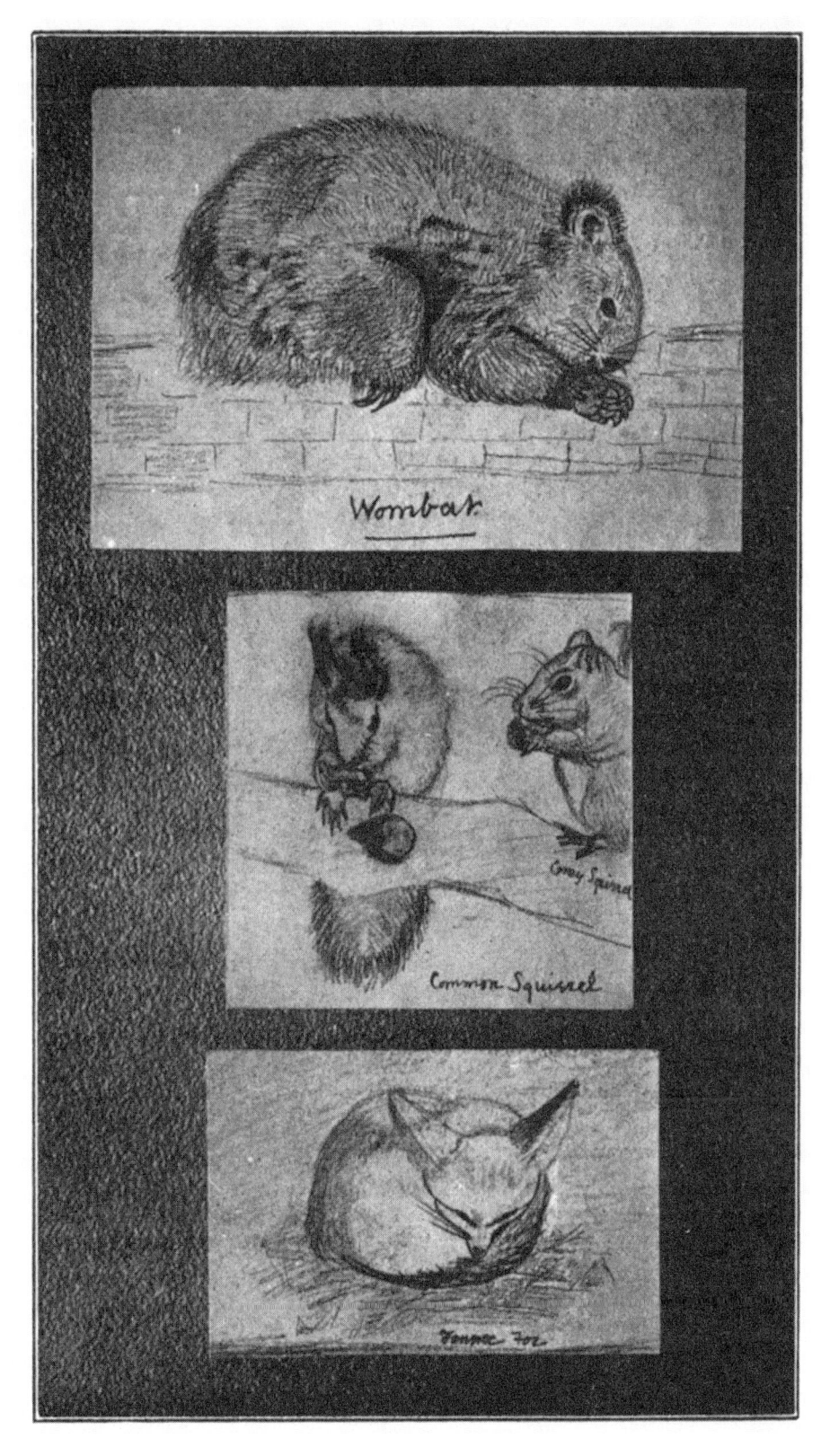

Pencil drawings by Rossetti of animals in the London zoo, circa 1862 (from The Family Letters of Christina Georgina Rossetti, *edited by William Michael Rossetti, 1908)*

April 1862), *The Athenaeum* (26 April 1862), *The Saturday Review* (24 May 1862), *The Eclectic Review* (June 1862), and *The British Quarterly Review* (July 1862). Critics welcomed a fresh and original poetic voice: *The Eclectic Review* hailed "a true and most genuine poet," while *The Athenaeum* remarked that "To read these poems after the laboured and skilful but not original verse which has been issued of late, is like passing from a picture gallery, with its well-feigned semblances of nature, to the real nature out-of-doors which greets us with the waving grass and the pleasant shock of the breeze." "Goblin Market," "Up-hill," "An Apple-Gathering," and "Advent" were frequently singled out for praise.

Today "Goblin Market" remains Rossetti's most discussed poem. Critics have dismissed her protest that she intended no allegorical meaning and have interpreted in various ways her fairy tale of two sisters' responses to the temptation of goblin fruit. Lizzie rejects the luscious fruit as "evil," but Laura purchases it with a lock of her hair and indulges. Afterward she wastes away, pining for more fruit. The goblins refuse to allow Lizzie to purchase fruit to save her sister, try to persuade her to eat with them, then attempt to force the fruit into her mouth. Lizzie escapes and runs home to Laura, who is cured by tasting the juices smeared on her sister's face. The poem ends years later with Laura telling the story to the sisters' offspring; she concludes by saying:

> "For there is no friend like a sister
> In calm or stormy weather;
> To cheer one on the tedious way,
> To fetch one if one goes astray,
> To lift one if one totters down,
> To strengthen whilst one stands."

The suggestiveness of the narrative runs in many directions, and this multivalency is perhaps the most striking quality of the poem. It can be read as a straightforward moral allegory of temptation, indulgence, sacrifice, and redemption. It has also been interpreted as a specifically Christian allegory, with a reenactment of the temptation in the Garden of Eden and a Christ-like offer of redemption through sacrifice—a reading that is encouraged by the Eucharistic diction of Lizzie's greeting, "'Eat me, drink me, love me; / Laura, make much of me.'" Significantly, this Christ is a female one, and feminist readings of "Goblin Market" have often focused on its positive image of sisterhood. Psychoanalytic interpretations have regarded the sisters as two aspects of one psyche and have emphasized the sexuality of the poem, noting both its orality and its lesbian dynamics. Marxist critics have pointed to the poem's separation of the domestic and commercial spheres and to Lizzie and Laura's attempts to do business in a marketplace designed to make women into goods to be exchanged rather than agents in their own right. Critics of many orientations have noted that the sensuality of the fruit, its prohibition to maidens, and its association with nuptial pleasures suggest that Laura's transgression is a sexual one. In this interpretation, Lizzie's climactic redemption of Laura can be seen as a critique of the Victorian cultural understanding of the fallen woman, for here she is not forever lost but is saved by a sister's intervention.

In "Goblin Market" the sisters are endangered by male goblins, and Laura is redeemed through the strength of sisterhood; elsewhere in *Goblin Market and Other Poems,* however, the danger that men pose as sexual predators is not offset by female solidarity. Throughout the volume Rossetti presents a bleak appraisal of gender relations. The flimsiness and inconstancy of romantic love is a recurring theme, as is the treachery of sister against sister in a ruthlessly competitive marriage market. In "Cousin Kate" the unnamed speaker has been seduced by a nobleman and has borne him a son; now she finds herself a discarded "plaything," supplanted by her fair and pure cousin Kate, whom the lord has taken not as a mistress but as his wife. The women in this ballad do not live up to the code of sisterly conduct with which "Goblin Market" concludes. Kate usurps her cousin's position and ensures the latter's status as "an outcast thing"; the speaker accuses Kate of betrayal of female loyalty, but her own moral integrity comes under question in the final stanza when she gloats that while she has borne her former lover a son, her cousin remains barren.

Adversarial women are also depicted in "Noble Sisters," a deftly ambiguous dialogue in which the reader must evaluate the reliability of two speakers with opposed moral viewpoints. Similarly, in "Sister Maude" the reader is asked to consider whose sin is greater: the woman who has taken a lover or her sister, who exposes the illicit union. Other pieces in *Goblin Market and Other Poems* that depict the failure or betrayal of human (as opposed to divine) love and explore women's sexual and economic vulnerability include "At Home," "A Triad," "After Death," "The Hour and the Ghost," "An Apple-Gathering," "Maude Clare," and "The Convent Threshold." These works serve to reinforce the devotional poems' theme of looking to the next life for reward, happiness, and fulfillment. Indeed, with the exception of "A Birthday" and its ecstatic declaration that "the birthday of my life / Is come, my love is come to me," little evidence exists anywhere in the volume that human love is satisfied or satisfying.

The theme of the inconstancy and insufficiency of any love except God's pervades the devotional section. Deferral of satisfaction is constantly advocated, as in "The Convent Threshold," in which the speaker urges her lover to join her in repentance for their "pleasant sin." The speaker's motives are complex, however, for her purpose seems to be the prospect of resuming their "old familiar love" in heaven. Consistently in Rossetti's poetry the concerns of this world are regarded as inconsequential in comparison to the promise of salvation. Throughout her canon, but especially in the devotional poems, biblical image and idiom merge with Rossetti's own voice. Revelation and Ecclesiastes are favorite sources, and the "vanity of vanity" refrain is a recurring motif.

Other pieces reveal some of Rossetti's poetical range: the political subject matter of "In the Round Tower at Jhansi, June 8, 1857"; the social critique of "A Triad"; the banter of "No, Thank You, John"; the whimsical, teasing mystery of "Winter: My Secret"; and the darker, suggestive mystery of poems with enigmatic and unnamed significances, such as "My Dream," "May," and "A Pause of Thought." In a style that has affinities with the Pre-Raphaelite Brotherhood but that she made distinctively her own, Rossetti's precisely drawn natural details assume the weight of suggestive symbolism. For example, in "An Apple-Gathering," in which the speaker finds herself abandoned by Willie and replaced by "Plump Gertrude," the speaker's ill-considered plucking of apple blossoms and the concomitant forfeit of a rich harvest resonates on many levels. Similarly, "Up-hill" and "Symbols" effortlessly evoke profound meaning from the simplest details: an uphill journey toward a place of rest, a flower that blooms and fades, and eggs that fail to hatch. Many poems in *Goblin Market and Other Poems* continue the morbid strain that was so prominent in *Verses*. "Dream-land," "At Home," "Remember," "After Death," "An End," "Song" ("Oh roses for the flush of youth"), "Echo," "A Peal of Bells," "May," "A Pause of Thought," "Shut Out," "Song" ("When I am dead, my dearest"), "Dead Before Death," "Bitter for Sweet," and "Rest" strike the signature Rossetti notes of longing, loss, resignation, and death. In the final two poems in the volume, "Old and New Year Ditties" and "Amen," this loss is met with the promise of fulfillment, expressed in the biblical figures of marriage and the fruitful garden. Critics have noted that Rossetti's volumes are carefully arranged into meaningful sequences, and *Goblin Market and Other Poems* includes many examples of significant continuities among the poems and correlations between the nondevotional and devotional sections.

During the early 1860s Rossetti was often in contact with female artists—including the members of the Portfolio Society, an informal group organized by Barbara Bodichon—and female poets, such as Jean Ingelow and Dora Greenwell. She published poems in the feminist periodicals *The English Woman's Journal* and *Victoria Magazine* and in various anthologies, in addition to making regular appearances in *Macmillan's*. A respiratory complaint led her to spend the winter of 1864–1865 in Hastings, where she began work on her next poetry volume, *The Prince's Progress and Other Poems* (1866).

That Dante Gabriel played a large role in the preparation of the book is evident from the almost daily correspondence between brother and sister, which provides valuable insight into Rossetti's methods and includes some spirited rebuttals to Dante Gabriel's criticisms. Rossetti's letters make it clear that she tried to write to order for the book, which was not her preferred method of composition. In later years she acknowledged in a 20 May 1885 letter to W. Garrett Horder that "Just because poetry *is* a gift . . . I am not surprised to find myself unable to summon it at will and use it according to my choice." According to William Michael Rossetti in *Rossetti Papers 1862 to 1870* (1903), the title poem originated in a suggestion from Dante Gabriel that she "turn a brief dirge-song . . . into that longish narrative, as *pièce de résistance* for a new volume." The Prince's sojourn with the Alchemist gave Rossetti some difficulties, as she explained in a 16 January 1865 letter to Dante Gabriel: "the *Alchemist* makes himself scarce, and I must bide his time." Rossetti was not given to rewriting, and once written, the Alchemist remained unchanged: "He's not precisely the Alchemist I prefigured, but thus he came," she wrote to Dante Gabriel on 30 January, "& thus he must stay: you know my system of work."

In a letter of 10 February she rejected Dante Gabriel's suggestion that she try to write an episode in which the Prince would fight in a tournament, pleading inability, lack of inspiration, and the formidable precedent of Tennyson's two tournaments in *Idylls of the King* (1859). Publication of the volume was delayed for a year, while Rossetti waited for Dante Gabriel's promised illustrations. In May 1865 she, William, and their mother traveled in France, Switzerland, and Italy. That same year she met Robert Browning, who visited her in London and told her about his work in progress, *The Ring and the Book* (1868–1869).

The Prince's Progress and Other Poems was met with mildly favorable reviews. The critic for *The Saturday Review* (23 June 1866) thought that the title poem lacked "subtle suggestion," while the reviewer for *The Reader* (30 June 1866) pronounced it "too long to suit Christina Rossetti's genius for short lyrical thoughts." In a letter of 6 March 1865 to Dante Gabriel Rossetti, Christina Rossetti agreed that "The Prince's Progress" lacked "the special felicity (!) of my *Goblins*." "The Prince's Progress" has never attracted the same inten-

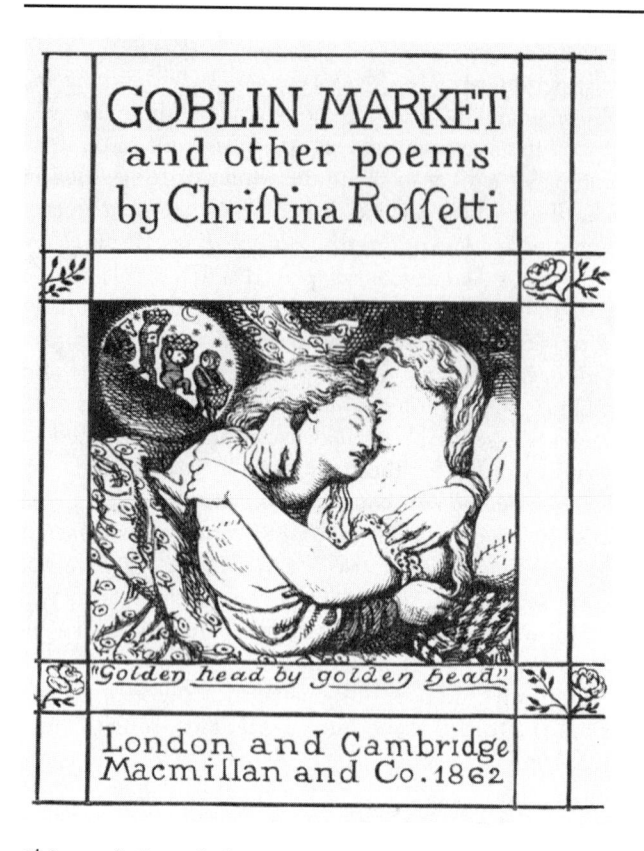

Title page for Rossetti's first commercially published book. The title poem is considered her masterpiece.

sity of critical scrutiny as "Goblin Market" and typically suffers in comparisons with that masterpiece. As the reviewer for the 23 June 1866 issue of *The Athenaeum* observed, the two title poems are similar in that both are allegories of temptation; in "Goblin Market," however, temptation is overcome, while in "The Prince's Progress" it wins out. The Prince procrastinates at great length before setting out to claim his waiting bride. He does not, however, remain true to his purpose, and on his journey he is sidetracked and delayed first by a milkmaid, then by an alchemist, and finally by a circle of ministering females who save him from drowning. When he arrives at his bride's palace, she is dead. The element of spiritual allegory is evident in "The Prince's Progress"; even the title echoes Bunyan's allegorical *The Pilgrim's Progress,* a literary influence from Rossetti's earliest childhood. The pilgrimage of Bunyan's Christian through an emblematic landscape is a topos that Rossetti must have absorbed into her own consciousness, for her poems often depict journeys in which topographical details, such as paths that go uphill or downhill, are morally and spiritually significant. For instance, the easy downhill path of "Amor Mundi" is clearly the way to damnation, while the upward climbs of "Up-hill" and "The Convent Threshold" are made by those who aspire to salvation.

While biblical language and image are pervasive in "The Prince's Progress," the poem also has a fairy-tale quality; the unhappy ending, however, serves to critique the gender roles typical of that genre. Relegated to a passive role, the waiting bride dies because of the Prince's failure to complete his quest in a timely fashion; her fate underlines the dangerous predicament of women waiting to be rescued. Elsewhere in *The Prince's Progress and Other Poems,* however, women engage in lives of active service, deferring satisfaction in this life in favor of the reward promised in the next. In "A Portrait" the sacrifice of "youth," "hope and joy and pleasant ways" for the sake of serving the "poor and stricken" earns the heroine union with the Bridegroom Christ in Paradise. In "A Royal Princess," which originally appeared in *Poems: An Offering to Lancashire* (1863), an anthology published in support of Lancashire textile workers, the title figure realizes that her wealth and privilege are based on the enslavement of others: "Once it came into my heart and whelmed me like a flood, / That these too are men and women, human flesh and blood." The poem ends with the princess's rebellion against the insulation from social concerns to which she has been subject because of her class and gender; echoing the biblical Esther, she risks all in offering herself and her wealth to an angry, hungry mob.

Dante Gabriel was highly critical of a long poem that his sister included in *The Prince's Progress and Other Poems,* "'The Iniquity of the Fathers Upon the Children.'" Responding in a letter of 13 March 1865, Rossetti vigorously defended the woman poet's right to explore indelicate issues such as illegitimacy: "whilst I endorse your opinion of the unavoidable and indeed much-to-be-desired unreality of women's work on many social matters, I yet incline to include within female range such an attempt as this: where the certainly possible circumstances are merely indicated as it were in skeleton, where the subordinate characters perform (and no more) their accessory parts, where the field is occupied by a single female figure whose internal portrait is set forth in her own words.... and whilst it may truly be urged that unless white could be black and Heaven Hell my experience (thank God) precludes me from hers, I yet don't see why 'the Poet mind' should be less able to construct her from its own inner consciousness than a hundred other unknown quantities." The speaker of "'The Iniquity of the Fathers Upon the Children'" lives as a servant in the household of her mother, who so fears social condemnation that she does not acknowledge her illegitimate daughter. Mother and daughter suffer the lifelong consequences of illegitimacy, while the seducer father is absent from the poem and, presumably, free of social stigma. The poem shows the injustice of conventional morality in a patriarchal society and offers the equality of the grave as the only solution.

Typically, Rossetti's poems evince a concern with individual salvation rather than social reform. Writing to Dante Gabriel in April 1870, she declared, "It is not in me, and therefore it will never come out of me, to turn to politics or philanthropy with Mrs Browning: such many-sidedness I leave to a greater than I, and having said my say may well sit silent." *The Prince's Progress and Other Poems* lays great emphasis on the transitoriness of this life, a recurring theme in the Rossetti canon. The lesson to be learned from poems such as "On the Wing," "Beauty is Vain," "The Bourne," "Vanity of Vanities," "Grown and Flown," "A Farm Walk," and "Gone for Ever" is that all earthly things are unreliable, illusory, and passing. Implicitly contrasted with the fleeting quality of this life is the permanence of God and the heavenly reward. With its comparison of human and divine love, "Twice" is a characteristic statement of this theme. The speaker first offers her heart to her lover, who, with a "friendly smile" and "critical eye," sets it aside as "unripe." The speaker then offers the broken heart to God, with the entreaty "Refine with fire its gold, / Purge Thou its dross away." The failure of human love is a keynote in the volume, beginning with the title poem and appearing again in "Jessie Cameron," "The Poor Ghost," "Songs in a Cornfield," "One Day," "A Bird's-Eye View," "Light Love," "On the Wing," "Maggie a Lady," "The Ghost's Petition," "Grown and Flown," and "'The Iniquity of the Fathers Upon the Children.'"

In the autumn of 1866 Rossetti declined an offer of marriage from Charles Bagot Cayley. Cayley had begun studying Italian with her father in 1847, sharing the Rossettis' enthusiasm for Dante and endearing himself to them with his attentive visits during their father's final illness. A hesitant romance probably began to develop between Rossetti and the awkward, absentminded scholar around 1862. Rossetti's reasons for rejecting his proposal can only be surmised. In a note in his edition of *The Family Letters of Christina Georgina Rossetti* (1908) William says that she turned Cayley down "on grounds of religious faith." At the time, William thought that there might be financial obstacles to the union and offered the couple a place in his household; his sister responded on 11 September 1866: "As to money I might be selfish enough to wish that were the only bar, but you see from my point of view it is not.— Now I am at least unselfish enough altogether to deprecate seeing C.B.C. continually (with nothing but mere feeling to offer) to his hamper & discomfort: but, if he *likes* to see me, God knows I like to see him, & any kindness you will show him will only be additional kindness loaded on me." Much is unknown about the relationship between Cayley and Rossetti. In his memoir William notes that "Christina was extremely reticent in all matters in which her affections were deeply engaged" and that "it would have been both indelicate and futile to press her with inquiries, and of several details in the second case [Rossetti's relationship with Cayley]— though important to a close understanding of it—I never was cognizant." Cayley and Rossetti remained close until his death in 1883, and Rossetti served as his literary executor. She declined to have a large packet of her letters to him returned to her, asking that they be destroyed. After Rossetti's death, William found in her desk a series of twenty-one highly personal poems written in Italian. Composed between 1862 and 1868 and titled "Il Rosseggiar dell'Oriente" (The Reddening Dawn), the sequence is generally understood to be addressed to Cayley; it was first published in Rossetti's *New Poems, Hitherto Unpublished or Uncollected* (1896).

In 1867 Rossetti published in *The Churchman's Shilling Magazine* three religious and moralistic stories: "The Waves of this Troublesome World: A Tale of Hastings Ten Years Ago" (April and May 1867), "Some Pros and Cons about Pews" (July 1867), and "A Safe Investment" (November 1867); all were republished in *Commonplace and Other Short Stories* (1870). For this volume Rossetti was persuaded by Dante Gabriel to defect from Macmillan to his publisher, F. S. Ellis. *Commonplace and Other Short Stories* was a commercial failure, though reviewers singled out "The Lost Titian" and the title story, with its Jane Austen-like social comment, for praise.

From 1870 to 1872 Rossetti was dangerously ill, at times apparently near death, with a condition characterized by fever, exhaustion, heart palpitations, stifling sensations, occasional loss of consciousness, violent headaches, palsied hands, and swelling in the neck that made swallowing difficult. Her hair fell out, her skin became discolored, her eyes began to protrude, and her voice changed. After some months her doctors diagnosed a rare thyroid condition, exophthalmic bronchocele, more commonly known as Graves' disease. Although Rossetti recovered, the threat of a relapse always remained. Moreover, the crisis left her appearance permanently altered and her heart weakened.

The reception of Rossetti's collection of stories left Ellis disinclined to publish her next work, a collection of poems for children. *Sing-Song: A Nursery Rhyme Book* was published by Routledge in 1872 and was favorably received; the public was particularly pleased by the illustrations by Arthur Hughes. Some of the poems are primarily edifying, promoting, for instance, patience or good manners; others are memory aids for learning about numbers, time, money, months, and colors. The sound and meter of these little rhymes delight

Charles Bagot Cayley in 1866, the year Rossetti rejected his marriage proposal

the ear, and Rossetti's wit is evident in the playfulness of lines such as "A hill has no leg, but has a foot; / A wine-glass a stem, but not a root." Again nature presents an emblematic aspect, and the phenomena of wind, rain, growth, and death and the alternation of night and day suggest a larger order. Most of the poems are evocative of the security of an ideal childhood, but others modulate into more-serious subject matter in simple and moving explorations of death and loss. Some critics have questioned the appropriateness of these darker themes for the intended audience.

Dante Gabriel had been prone to insomnia for some time and had become dependent on alcohol and chloral in his attempts to sleep. By June 1872 his paranoid belief that there was a conspiracy led by Robert Buchanan, author of "The Fleshly School of Poetry" (1871), to ruin his reputation had become clearly delusional, and he was raving and hearing voices. William concluded that his brother was insane and put him under the care of Dante Gabriel's friend Dr. Thomas Gordon Hake, in whose home he took a large dose of laudanum in an unsuccessful suicide attempt. Cared for by friends, Dante Gabriel made a partial recovery, though he continued his use of alcohol and chloral.

In 1873 Maria Rossetti joined the All Saints' Sisterhood. In March 1874 William married Lucy Brown, daughter of the painter Ford Madox Brown. The combined household of the newly married couple and William's mother, sister, and aunts Charlotte and Eliza Polidori was not a harmonious one.

Following her recovery from Graves' disease Rossetti published the first of her six volumes of devotional prose, *Annus Domini: A Prayer for Each Day of the Year, Founded on a Text of Holy Scripture* (1874). In these devotional writings readers can find explicit statements of themes treated in the poetry of previous decades, and in many instances Rossetti discusses natural and biblical images, virtually glossing favorite poetic symbols. More generally, the devotional prose provides insight into Rossetti's symbolic method, for she repeatedly indicates that this world is to be read as "typical," "suggestive," "emblematical," and "symbolical." *Annus Domini* consists of 366 meditations, each of which includes a passage from scripture followed by a collect beginning with an invocation to Christ. The texts are arranged in the order of their appearance in the Bible, and prayers throughout are intensely Christ-centered; even Old Testament passages prompt an address to Christ.

Rossetti returned to Macmillan for the publication of *Speaking Likenesses* in 1874. The book consists of three tales framed by the dialogue among a storytelling aunt and her nieces. Many readers have noted the sexual implications of the monstrous children in the first tale—boys bristling with hooks, quills, and angles; girls exuding sticky and slimy fluids—and that the predatory games they play amount to a figurative rape. While terror predominates in the first tale, in the second a young child's desire to have a gypsy tea ends in frustration and despair as she fails to master the tasks of lighting a fire and boiling a kettle. The final tale, in which danger and temptation are overcome, rounds out the volume with a happy ending. The influence of Lewis Carroll's *Alice's Adventures in Wonderland* (1865) and *Through the Looking-Glass* (1872) is evident, and Rossetti herself described the work to Dante Gabriel in a letter of 4 May 1874 as "a Christmas trifle, would-be in the *Alice* style, with an eye to the market." The title, Rossetti explained to Macmillan on 27 July 1874, refers to the way the heroines "perpetually encounter 'speaking (literally *speaking*) likenesses' or embodiments or caricatures of themselves or their faults." Ruskin lamented in a 21 January 1875 letter to the publisher Ellis that *Speaking Likenesses* was the worst of the children's books from the previous Christmas season: "How could she or Arthur Hughes sink so low after their pretty nursery rhymes?"

In 1874 Macmillan offered to bring out a new edition of Rossetti's complete poems and inquired after new compositions. On 4 February Rossetti responded, "the possibility of your thinking proper some day to reprint my two volumes, is really gratifying to me as you may suppose; but as to the additional matter, I fear there will be little indeed to offer you. The fire has died out, it seems; and I know of no bellows potent to revive dead coals. I wish I did." In 1875 the idea of a new edition of *Goblin Market and Other Poems* and *Prince's Progress and Other Poems* was taken up again. In a 30 January letter to Macmillan, Rossetti said that she would try to gather new pieces as well as "waifs and strays," poems that had appeared in magazines but had not been published in her collections. In *Goblin Market, The Prince's Progress and Other Poems* (1875) pieces from the previous volumes and thirty-seven new ones are intermingled into a single poetic sequence. Rossetti omitted some poems from the new collection, most notably "A Triad," "Cousin Kate," and "Sister Maude," all of which explore sexual issues. Evidently she did not work under her brother's guidance in preparing the volume, for Dante Gabriel's 3 December 1875 letter addressed the book as a fait accompli. While he conceded that "A Royal Princess" is "too good to omit," he thought it bore the taint of "modern vicious style," a kind of "falsetto muscularity" in part traceable to Elizabeth Barrett Browning's influence. He also perceived this taint in "No, Thank You, John" and, more prominently, in "The Lowest Room," and he lectured his sister that "everything in which this tone appears is utterly foreign to your primary impulses" and warned that she should "rigidly keep guard" against it. Although "The Lowest Room" had been published in *Macmillan's Magazine* in March 1864, Dante Gabriel had prevailed in keeping it out of *The Prince's Progress and Other Poems*. In this extended dialogue between two sisters the younger asks, "Why should not you, why should not I / Attain heroic strength?"–a question at the heart of the poem's engagement with Homeric epic and with women's search for fulfilment in the modern Christian age. The tensions between the sisters, between aspiration and opportunity, and between ambition and resignation are highly charged and never fully resolved. One speaker's hard-won submission–"Not to be first: how hard to learn / That lifelong lesson of the past; / Line graven on line and stroke on stroke; / But, thank God, learned at last"–and acceptance of the "lowest place" are undermined in the final stanza by her anticipation of an inversion of this hierarchy in the heavenly order, where "many last be first." This inversion of earthly and heavenly status appears again in "The Lowest Place," the final poem in the collection. The richness of this well-known lyric comes largely from its curious blend of timidity and temerity, for self-abnegation promises to be rewarded with exaltation, and thus the speaker's humble request is also an audacious one.

In 1876 Rossetti, her mother, and her aunts left William's Euston Square home and moved to Torrington Square, Bloomsbury. In November, Maria died of cancer; Christina's reminiscence in *Time Flies* portrays her death as an example of spiritual confidence and anticipation of salvation. Biographers have often commented on its contrast to Christina's deathbed anguish.

Rossetti's next book, *Seek and Find: A Double Series of Short Studies on the Benedicite* (1879), was published by the Society for Promoting Christian Knowledge (S.P.C.K.), which published the rest of her devotional prose works as well as *Verses* (1893), her collection of devotional poems. *Seek and Find* consists of two series of studies on the Benedicite, a long poem praising a catalogue of God's works that is included in the Book of Common Prayer as an apocryphal addition to the Book of Daniel. The first series of studies in *Seek and Find*, "Creation," contemplates each item in the Benedicite–heavens, waters, the sun, birds, other animals, and human beings–in the context of its creation by providing and discussing scriptural passages that are generally, though not exclusively, from the Old Testament. The second series, "Redemption," considers the same items in relation to Christ and cites mainly New Testament passages.

Like many of Rossetti's poems, her devotional works are double-edged swords of submission and assertion: while they urge obedience to divine will, they also encroach into the traditionally male territories of theological study, biblical exegesis, and spiritual guidance. Similarly, Rossetti's views on gender issues combine the conservative with the radical. Citing biblical teaching on woman's subordination to man, Rossetti had written to the poet Augusta Webster in 1878 that because she believed that "the highest functions are not in this world open to both sexes," she could not sign a petition for women's suffrage. She went on, however, to suggest that suffrage is not enough to protect women's interests and that female representation in Parliament would be more consistent with the aims of the women's movement. She also argued for the heroic possibilities of maternal love and its potential to sweep away "the barrier of sex." It is not uncommon to find such traces of subversiveness in Rossetti's apparently conservative statements on gender roles. An extended discussion of the subject in *Seek and Find* begins with a quite traditional discussion of woman as a lesser light–a moon to

Title page for Rossetti's second commercially published collection of poems

man's sun. But Rossetti then moves from a statement about the feminine lot being one of obedience to a paragraph-long comparison between the feminine role and the position that Christ voluntarily assumed on earth, and she ends with a leveling of gender hierarchies: "one final consolation yet remains to careful and troubled hearts: in Christ there is neither male nor female, for we are all one (Gal.iii.28)."

Biographers have painted an overly simplistic portrait of the middle-aged Rossetti as narrowly conservative, reclusive, and overly pious. Her dedication to Anglo-Catholicism certainly intensified, and it took some odd forms, such as her habit of stooping to pick up stray pieces of paper on the street lest they have the Lord's name printed on them. From 1876, when she moved to Torrington Square, until her final illness Rossetti worshiped at Christ Church, Woburn Square. Mackenzie Bell relates the impression that she made on a fellow member of the congregation: "A friend informs me that towards the close of her life Christina always sat in the very front pew in church. She remained until the very last before leaving the building, and it was evident from her demeanour that even then she strove to avoid ordinary conversation, evidently feeling that it would disturb her mood of mind." Never comfortable socially, by this time she was reluctant to venture beyond her intimate circle of family and friends: she was aware that she possessed a degree of fame, and she felt self-conscious in conversations that bore the aspect of an interview. She also dreaded receiving unsolicited poems from aspiring writers, because she was torn between kindness and honesty regarding the merit of the work. Though increasingly reclusive, however, Rossetti was more politically outspoken in these later years. Critical of slavery, imperialism, and military aggression, she was most passionately committed to the antivivisection movement, at one point breaking with the S.P.C.K. over its publication of a work condoning animal experimentation. She also petitioned for legislation to protect children from prostitution and sexual exploitation by raising the age of consent.

Rossetti's next work, *Called to Be Saints: The Minor Festivals Devotionally Studied,* published in 1881, had been completed by 1876; Macmillan had turned it down under its previous title, "Young Plants and Polished Corners." A devotional accompaniment for the red-letter saints' days, *Called to Be Saints* provides for each day an account of the saint's life, a prayer, an intricate "memorial" in two columns linking the saint's life with biblical texts, and descriptions of the emblem, precious stone, and flower associated with the saint and discussions of their appropriateness. Although biographers have tended to emphasize the narrowing of Rossetti's interests in her later life in that she then wrote in an exclusively devotional vein, one might note that she dealt with a wide array of topics within this framework. In *Called to Be Saints* she ranges from the biblical and hagiographical to the botanical and petrographical.

As her poetic creativity decreased, Rossetti cultivated a modest scholarly impulse. Earlier instances of her scholarly writing include her entries on Italian writers and other celebrities in the *Imperial Dictionary of Universal Biography* (1857–1863); in her article on Petrarch she claims to be a descendant of Laura. In 1867 she had published the first of two articles on Dante, a commendatory piece written in support of Cayley's terza rima translation of *The Divine Comedy* (1851–1855). After attending lectures on *The Divine Comedy* at University College, London, from 1878 to 1880 she wrote a more ambitious article, "Dante: The Poet Illustrated out of the Poem" (1884). In 1882 she considered undertaking literary biographies of Adelaide Proctor and Elizabeth Barrett Browning; and she took a commission and began to research a life of Ann

Radcliffe, but a lack of materials prevented her from completing it. She agreed to trace allusions to Dante, Petrarch, and Giovanni Boccaccio for Alexander Balloch Grosart's scholarly edition of *The Faerie Queene* in *The Complete Works in Verse and Prose of Edmund Spenser* (1882–1884), a project from which she withdrew because of ill health. She spent many afternoons at the British Museum and was a tireless reader of periodicals, including *The Athenaeum*, *Macmillan's Magazine*, *The Saturday Review*, *Blackwood's*, and *The Edinburgh Review*.

Rossetti's research on Petrarch and Dante informs one of the most important poems of her maturity, "*Monna Innominata*," which appeared in her third commercially published poetry collection, *A Pageant and Other Poems* (1880). A sequence of fourteen sonnets—thus subtitled "A Sonnet of Sonnets"—"*Monna Innominata*" draws attention to its links to the medieval amatory tradition both in its prose preface and in the epigraphs from Dante and Petrarch that introduce each sonnet. In his notes in *The Poetical Works of Christina Georgina Rossetti* William Michael Rossetti attested that the introductory prose note was "a blind interposed to draw off attention from the writer in her proper person" and that the sonnet sequence was an "intensely personal" utterance. The subject matter of love deeply felt, reciprocated, and yet unfulfilled is generally taken to refer to Rossetti's relationship with Cayley, but its import is not limited to this context. Recent criticism of "*Monna Innominata*" has explored its complex intertextual operations, particularly its revisionary treatment of the sonnet form, whose gender roles Rossetti deliberately and self-consciously reverses by having the unnamed lady, traditionally the silent object of the male sonneteer's desire, express her love. In doing so, Rossetti is emulating the gender subversion of *Sonnets from the Portuguese* (1850), by Elizabeth Barrett Browning, to whom she refers in her preface as "the Great Poetess of our day and nation."

Although it is not the title poem, "*Monna Innominata*," with its valedictory mode, its questioning of the very possibility of fulfilled desire, and its reappraisal of the sonnet form, sets the tone for *A Pageant and Other Poems*. Rossetti opens the volume with a dedicatory sonnet addressed to her mother, drawing attention both to the expectations raised by the tradition of the genre—"Sonnets are full of love"—and to the preponderance of sonnets in her collection: "and this my tome / Has many sonnets." But in the sonnet sequences that follow—"*Monna Innominata*," "Later Life," "'If thou sayest, behold, we knew it not,'" "The Thread of Life," and "'Behold a Shaking'"— Rossetti veers away from the amatory tradition by dwelling on the love of and aspiration for union with God. These sonnet sequences are complemented by the abundance of multipart poems in the volume, such as "The Months: A Pageant," "Mirrors of Life and Death," and "'All thy works praise Thee, O Lord.' A Processional of Creation," as well as smaller poetic sequences, such as the seasonal sequence "An October Garden," "'Summer is Ended,'" and "Passing and Glassing" and the three Easter poems, "The Descent from the Cross," "'It is finished,'" and "An Easter Carol."

Anticipating the final farewell to youth, beauty, and song in "*Monna Innominata*," in "The Key-note" Rossetti laments "the Winter of my year" and the silencing of "the songs I used to know." Similarly, desire is relinquished in "Till Tomorrow":

Long have I longed, till I am tired
    Of longing and desire;
Farewell my points in vain desired,
    My dying fire;
Farewell all things that die and fail and tire.

By reiteration and accretion the passing months, the progression of seasons, and blooming and fading flowers become poignant and nostalgic symbols of the process of aging. Some poems provide consolation, as when the robin in "The Key-note" "sings thro' Winter's rest" or in the title poem, "The Months: A Pageant," a performance piece consisting of a procession of personifications of the twelve months, where "October" offers comfort: "Nay, cheer up sister. Life is not quite over, / Even if the year has done with corn and clover." But the real movement of the volume is toward relinquishment of love, beauty, Italy, hope, and life itself. The final poems of the nondevotional section return to the seasonal, vegetative cycle. "An October Garden" begins, "In my Autumn garden I was fain / To mourn among my scattered roses," while the next poem, "'Summer is Ended,'" asks if bliss will inevitably end as the rose does, a "Scentless, colourless, . . . meaningless thing." The following poem, "Passing and Glassing," confirms the human analogy readable from "withered roses . . . the fallen peach," and "summer joy that was," saying that "All things that pass / Are woman's looking glass; / They show her how her bloom must fade."

Familiar Rossetti themes are in evidence in the devotional pieces: renounced desire, weariness with this life, the "vanity of vanities" refrain, and God's love for the unworthy supplicant. Rossetti's youthful verses had been called morbid, and death remains a central theme in *A Pageant and Other Poems* but with an altered emphasis. While in earlier verses death was presented in its more-sentimental aspect, often intruding into the frailty of romantic love, in *A Pageant and Other Poems* it is contemplated in a subdued and personal way, as a foreseeable and inevitable event. In the

The house at 30 Torrington Square, London, where Rossetti lived for the last eighteen years of her life

sonnet sequence "Later Life: a Double Sonnet of Sonnets" Rossetti writes, "I have dreamed of Death:—what will it be to die / Not in a dream, but in the literal truth / With all Death's adjuncts ghastly and uncouth." Always doubting her worthiness of salvation, Rossetti imagines her deathbed and acknowledges the possibility that she "May miss the goal at last, may miss a crown." In "The Thread of Life," a sequence of three sonnets, the speaker contemplates the essential and solitary self, aloof from external objects and bound by "inner solitude," and realizes that "I am not what I have nor what I do; / But what I was I am, I am even I." This self, her "sole possession," she offers to God. The relation of the self to the external world is again contemplated in "An Old-World Thicket," which begins with an epigraph from Dante and is obviously engaged with the legacy of Romanticism.

In "'All Thy Works Praise Thee, O Lord.' A Processional of Creation" all aspects of the created world declare God's glory, each according to its nature. In "Spring and Autumn" the two seasons declare, respectively, "I hope,– / And I remember," and these vernal and autumnal attitudes resonate through the volume. In "Later Life" the speaker is "glancing back" on "Lost hopes that leave our hearts upon the rack, / Hopes that were never ours yet seemed to be." The devotional poems trace the yielding of unfulfilled earthly hopes in exchange for the heavenly reward. This life is full of "promise unfulfilled, of everything, / That is puffed vanity and empty talk." Paradoxes abound in "Later Life" as Rossetti writes, "This Life we live is dead for all its breath," "Its very Spring is not indeed like Spring," and she looks for rebirth through "Death who art not Death." The conundrum/insight is reiterated in the pair of sonnets titled "'Behold a Shaking'": "Here life is the beginning of our death, / And death the starting-point whence life ensues; / Surely our life is death, our death is life." The final poems bring a satisfying closure to the volume, looking past the end of this life and ending with a divine embrace in "'Love is as strong as death.'" Though sales were sluggish, *A Pageant and Other Poems* was a critical success: the sonnet sequences, in particular, were praised by reviewers, and *"Monna Innominata"* was compared favorably with *Sonnets from the Portuguese*.

Dante Gabriel Rossetti died in Birchington on Easter Sunday 1882. Christina's commemorative poem, "Birchington Churchyard," was published in *The Athenaeum* (25 April 1882). The following winter she composed her fourth book of devotional prose, *Letter and Spirit: Notes on the Commandments* (1883), in which she considers the Ten Commandments in terms of Christ's two great commandments, to love thy God and thy neighbor. "A Harmony on First Corinthians XIII," first published in the January 1879 issue of *New and Old*, a church magazine, was revised and included as an appendix.

Rossetti's next book, *Time Flies: A Reading Diary*, published in 1885, is both the most readable and the most autobiographical of her devotional works. As the subtitle suggests, the book is diarylike in structure, with daily entries consisting of meditations on religious feast days and saints' days, poetic compositions, or personal reflections and reminiscences. The most often quoted passages are those in which Rossetti describes her experiences of nature and elaborates on the moral and symbolic meaning suggested by them. She regards a spider attempting to escape its own shadow as "a figure of each obstinate impenitent sinner, who having outlived enjoyment remains isolated irretrievably with his own horrible loathsome self." One glimpses Rossetti's affection for God's smallest creatures in the pleasure she took in visiting a garden where she "sat so long and so quietly that a wild garden creature or two made its appearance: a water rat, perhaps, or a water-hunting bird." She goes on, "Few have been my personal experiences of the sort, and this one gratified me." From such encounters she draws parabolic inferences, as in an incident when she spotted a millipede in her bedroom while visiting Alice Boyd and William Bell Scott at Penkill Castle in Ayrshire:

> Towards my co-tenant I felt a sort of good will not inconsistent with an impulse to eject it through the window.
> I stooped and took it up, when in a moment a swarm of baby millepedes occupied my hand in their parent's company.
> Surprised, but resolute, I hurried on, and carried out my scheme successfully; observing the juniors retire into cracks outside the window as adroitly as if they had been centenarians.
> Pondering over this trifle, it seems to me a parable setting forth visibly and vividly the incalculable element in all our actions. I thought to pick up one millepede, and behold! I was transporting a numerous family.

After her mother's death in 1886 Rossetti continued to keep house for her elderly aunts Charlotte and Eliza until their deaths in 1890 and 1893, respectively, while working on a commentary on the Book of Revelation. The last of Rossetti's six devotional studies, *The Face of the Deep: A Devotional Commentary on the Apocalypse,* published in 1892, bears the familiar dedication to her mother, but now "for the first time to her beloved, revered, cherished memory." A substantial work, *The Face of the Deep* consists of wide-ranging, free-association meditations on each verse of Revelation. While some passages engage in traditional exegesis, others are more personally contemplative and address issues of spiritual and moral duty. More important for today's reader, *The Face of the Deep* includes more than two hundred poems; Rossetti combined them with poems from *Called to Be Saints* and *Time Flies* into a volume of devotional poems titled simply *Verses*. Published in 1893 by the S.P.C.K., this collection of 331 religious lyrics was Rossetti's last volume to appear during her lifetime. She undertook extensive revisions and arranged the poems into eight sections that form a double poetic sequence: spiritual progress is traced in terms of the individual's relationship with God in the first four sections and from a universal perspective in the final four. Rossetti's devotional poems have received scant critical attention, but *Verses* enjoyed great popularity and continued to be reprinted well into the twentieth century.

In 1892 Rossetti was diagnosed with breast cancer and underwent a mastectomy that was performed in her own home. The cancer recurred the following year, and after months of acute suffering she died on 29 December 1894. Rossetti had attained fame as a poet and had earned high regard as a spiritual guide; some had even speculated, after Tennyson's death in 1892, that she would make a suitable successor to the laureateship. After her death many articles appeared with personal reminiscences, expressing admiration of her saintliness and assessing her poetry and prose. The sole surviving sibling, William made special efforts to document his sister's life and edit her work. In *New Poems, Hitherto Unpublished or Uncollected* he made available carefully edited and annotated texts of poems from periodicals and anthologies and many unpublished ones, some written late in Rossetti's life and others that she had written earlier but had not

Rossetti's grave in Highgate Cemetery

published presumably because she deemed them either too personal or not up to the standard of her best work. *Maude* appeared in 1897 and *The Poetical Works* in 1904; the latter remained, despite its awkward divisions and arrangement, the standard edition of her poetry until Rebecca W. Crump's *The Complete Poems of Christina Rossetti: A Variorum Edition* (1979–1990), which prompted a modern reassessment of Rossetti's poetry.

While many other women poets are still in the process of being "rediscovered," Rossetti is undergoing a radical revaluation which promises a new appreciation of the complexity and variety of her work. In the century after her death her reputation survived largely on the strength of "Goblin Market" and a handful of lyrics. Her lyric gift has never been doubted, but the unassuming tone and flawless finish of these compositions has sometimes led critics to suggest that their lyric purity is achieved at the expense of intellectual depth and aesthetic complexity. Such assessments have been bolstered by William's description of her as a "casual" and "spontaneous" poet to whom verse came "very easily, without her meditating a possible subject," and without her having to undertake substantial revisions. More recently critics have expressed suspicion of William's reconstruction of his sister's life, his censorship of her letters, and his revisionist editing in the posthumous collections of her poetry.

For several decades after her death Rossetti criticism tended to be narrowly biographical, her mournful lyrics and fantastic allegories being used to construct narratives of agonizing conflict between secular and sacred impulses, renounced love, and repressed passion. In the 1980s a Rossetti renaissance began as feminist critics undertook a reexamination of her poetry, addressing particularly "Goblin Market" and exploring Rossetti's representation of sororal bonds, female creativity, and sexuality and her critique of patriarchal amatory values and gender relations. The trends today run toward a proliferation of critical approaches, many of which recontextualize Rossetti in Victorian culture, and toward critical interest in a wider range of her works, including her fiction, nonfiction, and children's poetry. Critics continue to study Rossetti's response to and influence in a women writers' tradition; also under discussion are gender-conscious models for positioning Rossetti in the mainstream (that is, predominantly male) canon. Christina Rossetti has often been called the greatest Victorian woman poet, but her poetry is increasingly being recognized as among the most beautiful and innovative of the period by either sex.

Letters:

Rossetti Papers 1862 to 1870, edited by William Michael Rossetti (London: Sands, 1903);

The Family Letters of Christina Georgina Rossetti, edited by William Michael Rossetti (London: Brown, Langham, 1908);

Three Rossettis: Unpublished Letters to and from Dante Gabriel, Christina, William, edited by Janet Camp Troxell (Cambridge, Mass.: Harvard University Press, 1937);

The Rossetti-Macmillan Letters, edited by Lona Mosk Packer (Berkeley: University of California Press, 1963);

The Owl and the Rossettis: Letters of Charles A. Howell and Dante Gabriel, Christina, and William Michael Rossetti, edited by C. L. Cline (University Park: Pennsylvania State University Press, 1978);

Christina Rossetti in the Maser Collection, edited by Frederick E. Maser and Mary Louise Jarden Maser (Bryn Mawr, Pa.: Bryn Mawr College Library, 1991);

The Letters of Christina Rossetti, edited by Antony H. Harrison, 3 volumes published, 4 volumes projected (Charlottesville & London: University Press of Virginia, 1997–   ).

Bibliographies:

William E. Fredeman, *Pre-Raphaelitism: A Bibliocritical Study* (Cambridge, Mass.: Harvard University Press, 1965), pp. 176–182;

Fredeman, "Christina Rossetti," in *The Victorian Poets: A Guide to Research*, edited by Frederic E. Faverty (Cambridge, Mass.: Harvard University Press, 1968), pp. 284–293;

Rebecca W. Crump, *Christina Rossetti: A Reference Guide* (Boston: G. K. Hall, 1976);

Jane Addison, "Christina Rossetti Studies, 1974–1991: A Checklist and Synthesis," *Bulletin of Bibliography*, 52 (March 1995): 73–93.

Biographies:

Ellen A. Proctor, *A Brief Memoir of Christina G. Rossetti* (London: Society for Promoting Christian Knowledge, 1895);

Mackenzie Bell, *Christina Rossetti: A Biographical and Critical Study* (Boston: Roberts, 1898);

Mary F. Sandars, *The Life of Christina Rossetti* (London: Hutchinson, 1930);

Eleanor Walter Thomas, *Christina Georgina Rossetti* (New York: Columbia University Press, 1931);

Marya Zaturenska, *Christina Rossetti: A Portrait with a Background* (New York: Macmillan, 1949);

Margaret Sawtell, *Christina Rossetti: Her Life and Religion* (London: Mowbray, 1955);

Lona Mosk Packer, *Christina Rossetti* (Berkeley: University of California Press, 1963);

Georgina Battiscombe, *Christina Rossetti: A Divided Life* (London: Constable, 1981);

Kathleen Jones, *Learning Not to Be First: The Life of Christina Rossetti* (Gloucestershire: Windrush Press, 1991);

Frances Thomas, *Christina Rossetti: A Biography* (London: Virago, 1994);

Jan Marsh, *Christina Rossetti: A Literary Biography* (London: Cape, 1994).

References:

Isobel Armstrong, *Victorian Poetry: Poetry, Poetics and Politics* (London & New York: Routledge, 1993), pp. 344–367;

Mary Arseneau, "Incarnation and Interpretation: Christina Rossetti, the Oxford Movement, and *Goblin Market*," *Victorian Poetry*, 31 (1993): 79–93;

Arseneau, Antony H. Harrison, and Lorraine Janzen Kooistra, eds., *The Culture of Christina Rossetti: Female Poetics and Victorian Contexts* (Athens: Ohio University Press, 1999);

Andrew Belsey and Catherine Belsey, "Christina Rossetti: Sister to the Brotherhood," *Textual Practice*, 2 (1988): 30–50;

Joseph Bristow, ed., *Victorian Women Poets: Emily Brontë, Elizabeth Barrett Browning, Christina Rossetti* (London: Macmillan / New York: St. Martin's Press, 1995);

Jerome Bump, "Hopkins, Christina Rossetti, and Pre-Raphaelitism," *Victorian Newsletter*, 57 (1980): 1–6;

Kathryn Burlinson, "'All Mouth and Trousers': Christina Rossetti's Grotesque and Abjected Bodies," in *Women's Poetry, Late Romantic to Late Victorian: Gender and Genre, 1830–1900*, edited by Isobel Armstrong and Virgina Blain (Houndsmills: Macmillan, 1999), pp. 292–312;

Burlinson, *Christina Rossetti* (Plymouth: Northcote House in association with the British Council, 1998);

Elizabeth Campbell, "Of Mothers and Merchants: Female Economics in Christina Rossetti's *Goblin Market*," *Victorian Studies*, 33 (1990): 393–410;

Mary Wilson Carpenter, "'Eat me, drink me, love me': The Consumable Female Body in Christina Rossetti's *Goblin Market*," *Victorian Poetry*, 29 (1991): 415–434;

Alison Chapman, *The Afterlife of Christina Rossetti* (Houndsmills: Macmillan, 2000; New York: St. Martin's Press, 2000);

Steven Connor, "'Speaking Likenesses': Language and Repetition in Christina Rossetti's *Goblin Market*," *Victorian Poetry*, 22 (1984): 439–448;

Stuart Curran, "The Lyric Voice of Christina Rossetti," *Victorian Poetry*, 9 (1971): 287–299;

Diane D'Amico, *Christina Rossetti: Faith, Gener and Time* (Baton Rouge: Louisiana State University Press, 1999);

D'Amico, "'Equal before God': Christina Rossetti and the Fallen Women of Highgate Penitentiary," in *Gender and Discourse in Victorian Literature and Art*, edited by Antony H. Harrison and Beverly Taylor (De Kalb: Northern Illinois University Press, 1992), pp. 67–83;

Theo Dombrowski, "Dualism in the Poetry of Christina Rossetti," *Victorian Poetry*, 14 (1976): 70–76;

Ifor B. Evans, *English Poetry of the Later Nineteenth Century* (London: Methuen, 1933), pp. 65–80;

Hoxie Neale Fairchild, *Religious Trends in English Poetry IV: 1830–1880* (New York: Columbia University Press, 1957), pp. 302–316;

Barbara Fass, "Christina Rossetti and St. Agnes' Eve," *Victorian Poetry*, 14 (1976): 33–46;

Mary E. Finn, *Writing the Incommensurable: Kierkegaard, Rossetti, and Hopkins* (University Park: Pennsylvania State University Press, 1992);

Barbara Garlick, "Christina Rossetti and the Gender Politics of Fantasy," in *The Victorian Fantasists*, edited by Kath Filmer (Basingstoke: Macmillan, 1991), pp. 133-152;

Pamela K. Gilbert, "'A Horrid Game': Woman as Social Entity in Christina Rossetti's Prose," *English,* 41 (Spring 1992): 1-23;

Sandra Gilbert and Susan Gubar, *The Madwoman in the Attic: The Woman Writer and the Nineteenth-Century Literary Imagination* (New Haven: Yale University Press, 1979), pp. 539-580;

Edmund Gosse, "Christina Rossetti," *Century Magazine,* 46 (June 1893): 211-217;

Eric Griffiths, "The Disappointment of Christina G. Rossetti," *Essays in Criticism,* 47 (April 1997): 107-142;

Lila Hanft, "The Politics of Maternal Ambivalence in Christina Rossetti's *Sing-Song,*" *Victorian Literature and Culture,* 19 (1991): 213-232;

Antony H. Harrison, "Christina Rossetti and the Romantics: Influence and Ideology," in *Influence and Resistance in Nineteenth-Century English Poetry,* edited by G. Kim Blank and Margot K. Louis (London & Basingstoke: Macmillan, 1993), pp. 131-149;

Harrison, "Christina Rossetti and the Sage Discourse of Feminist High Anglicanism," in *Victorian Sages and Cultural Discourse: Renegotiating Gender and Power,* edited by Thais E. Morgan (New Brunswick, N.J.: Rutgers University Press, 1990), pp. 87-104;

Harrison, *Christina Rossetti in Context* (Chapel Hill: University of North Carolina Press, 1988);

Harrison, ed., "Centennial of Christina Rossetti: 1830-1894," *Victorian Poetry,* 32, nos. 3-4 (1994): 201-428;

Constance W. Hassett, "Christina Rossetti and the Poetry of Reticence," *Philological Quarterly,* 65 (1986): 495-514;

Elizabeth K. Helsinger, "Consumer Power and the Utopia of Desire: Christina Rossetti's *Goblin Market,*" *English Literary History,* 58 (1991): 903-933;

Dawn Henwood, "Christian Allegory and Subversive Poetics: Christina Rossetti's *Prince's Progress* Reexamined," *Victorian Poetry,* 35 (1997): 83-94;

Kathleen Hickok, *Representations of Women: Nineteenth-Century British Women's Poetry* (Westport, Conn.: Greenwood Press, 1984), pp. 197-219;

Terrence Holt, "'Men sell not such in any town': Exchange in *Goblin Market,*" *Victorian Poetry,* 28 (1990): 51-67; republished in *Victorian Women Poets: A Critical Reader,* edited by Angela Leighton (London: Blackwell, 1996), pp. 131-147;

Margaret Homans, "Syllables of Velvet: Dickinson, Rossetti, and the Rhetorics of Sexuality," *Feminist Studies,* 11 (1985): 569-593;

Nilda Jimenez, *The Bible and the Poetry of Christina Rossetti: A Concordance* (Westport, Conn.: Greenwood Press, 1979);

David A. Kent, ed., *The Achievement of Christina Rossetti* (Ithaca, N.Y.: Cornell University Press, 1987);

U. C. Knoepflmacher, "Avenging Alice: Christina Rossetti and Lewis Carroll," *Nineteenth-Century Literature,* 41 (1986): 299-328;

Lorraine Janzen Kooistra, "The Jael Who Led the Hosts to Victory: Christina Rossetti and Pre-Raphaelite Book-Making," *Journal of Pre-Raphaelite Studies,* new series 8 (Spring 1999): 50-68;

Sharon Leder and Andrea Abbott, *The Language of Exclusion: The Poetry of Emily Dickinson and Christina Rossetti* (New York: Greenwood Press, 1987);

Angela Leighton, "'Because men made the laws': The Fallen Woman and the Woman Poet," *Victorian Poetry,* 27 (1989): 109-127;

Leighton, *Victorian Women Poets: Writing Against the Heart* (London & New York: Harvester, 1992), pp. 118-163;

Linda E. Marshall, "Mysteries beyond Angels in Christina Rossetti's 'From House to Home,'" in *Women's Poetry, Late Romantic to Late Victorian: Gender and Genre, 1830-1900,* pp. 313-324;

Marshall, "'Transfigured to His Likeness': Sensible Transcendentalism in Christina Rossetti's Goblin Market," *University of Toronto Quarterly,* 63 (1994): 429-450;

Marshall, "What the Dead are Doing Underground: Hades and Heaven in the Writings of Christina Rossetti," *Victorian Newsletter,* 72 (1987): 55-60;

Katherine J. Mayberry, *Christina Rossetti and the Poetry of Discovery* (Baton Rouge: Louisiana State University Press, 1989);

Jerome J. McGann, "Christina Rossetti's Poems: A New Edition and a Revaluation," *Victorian Studies,* 23 (1980): 237-254; republished as "Christina Rossetti's Poems," in *Victorian Women Poets: A Critical Reader,* pp. 97-113;

McGann, "The Religious Poetry of Christina Rossetti," *Critical Inquiry,* 10 (1983): 127-144;

Dorothy Mermin, "The Damsel, the Knight, and the Victorian Woman Poet," *Critical Inquiry,* 13 (1986): 64-80; republished in *Victorian Women Poets: A Critical Reader,* pp. 198-214;

Mermin, "Heroic Sisterhood in *Goblin Market,*" *Victorian Poetry,* 21 (1983) 107-118;

Helena Michie, "'There is no friend like a sister': Sisterhood as Sexual Difference," *English Literary History,* 52 (1989): 401-421;

Ellen Moers, *Literary Women* (Garden City, N.Y.: Doubleday, 1976);

David F. Morrill, "'Twilight is Not Good for Maidens': Uncle Polidori and the Psychodynamics of Vampirism in *Goblin Market*," *Victorian Poetry*, 28 (1990): 1–16;

Kathy Alexis Psomiades, "Feminine and Poetic Privacy in Christina Rossetti's 'Autumn' and 'A Royal Princess,'" *Victorian Poetry*, 31 (1993): 187–202;

Psomiades, "Whose Body? Christina Rossetti and Aestheticist Femininity," in *Women and British Aestheticism*, edited by Psomiades and Talia Schaffer (Charlottesville: University Press of Virginia, 1999), pp. 101–118;

Joan Rees, "Christina Rossetti: Poet," *Critical Quarterly*, 26 (Autumn 1984): 59–72;

Dolores Rosenblum, *Christina Rossetti: The Poetry of Endurance* (Carbondale: Southern Illinois University Press, 1986);

Rosenblum, "Christina Rossetti's Religious Poetry: Watching, Looking, Keeping Vigil," *Victorian Poetry*, 20 (1982): 33–49; republished in *Victorian Women Poets: A Critical Reader*, pp. 114–130;

Linda Schofield, "Displaced and Absent Texts as Contexts for Christina Rossetti's *Monna Innominata*," *Journal of Pre-Raphaelite Studies*, new series 6 (Spring 1997): 38–52;

William Sharp, "Some Reminiscences of Christina Rossetti," *Atlantic Monthly*, 75 (June 1895): 736–749;

Virginia Sickbert, "Christina Rossetti and Victorian Children's Poetry: A Maternal Challenge to the Patriarchal Family," *Victorian Poetry*, 31 (1993): 385–410;

Sharon Smulders, *Christina Rossetti Revisited*, Twayne English Authors Series (New York: Twayne, 1996);

Smulders, "'A Form that Differences': Vocational Metaphors in the Poetry of Christina Rossetti and Gerard Manley Hopkins," *Victorian Poetry*, 29 (1991): 161–173;

Smulders, "Woman's Enfranchisement in Christina Rossetti's Poetry," *Texas Studies in Literature and Language*, 34 (1992): 568–588;

Lionel Stevenson, *The Pre-Raphaelite Poets* (Chapel Hill: University of North Carolina Press, 1972), pp. 78–122;

Deborah Ann Thompson, "Anorexia as a Lived Trope: Christina Rossetti's *Goblin Market*," *Mosaic*, 24 (1991): 89–106;

Winston Weathers, "Christina Rossetti: The Sisterhood of Self," *Victorian Poetry*, 3 (1965): 81–89;

Joel Westerholm, "'I Magnify Mine Office': Christina Rossetti's Authoritative Voice in Her Devotional Prose," *Victorian Newsletter*, 84 (Fall 1993): 11–17.

Papers:

Christina Rossetti's notebooks are held by the British Library; the Bodleian Library, University of Oxford; and the King's School, Canterbury; the contents of the various collections are listed by Rebecca W. Crump in Appendix A, volume 3, of *The Complete Poems of Christina Rossetti: A Variorum Edition* (1990). Significant manuscript collections are also at Princeton University, the University of British Columbia, and Bryn Mawr College. Holograph poems are scattered among various public and private collections, also listed by Crump. Antony H. Harrison notes in his edition of *The Letters of Christina Rossetti* (1997–) that more than 2,100 autograph letters are dispersed in more than one hundred public and private collections. The most substantial collections of letters are at the University of British Columbia, Princeton University, the British Library, the Harry Ransom Research Center of the University of Texas at Austin, the University of Kansas, the New York Public Library, the Wellesley College Library, the Beinecke Library at Yale University, and the Bryn Mawr College Library.

Lady Margaret Sackville
(1881 – 1963)

Whitney Womack
Miami University of Ohio

BOOKS: *Floral Symphony* (Bradford, 1900);
Poems (London & New York: John Lane, 1901);
A Hymn to Dionysus and Other Poems (London: Elkin Mathews, 1905);
Hildris the Queen: A Play in Four Acts (Manchester: Sherratt & Hughes, 1908);
Fairy Tales for Old and Young, by Sackville and Ronald Campbell Macfie (Manchester: Sherratt & Hughes, 1909);
Bertrud and Other Dramatic Poems (Edinburgh: W. Brown, 1911);
Lyrics (London: Herbert & Daniel, 1912);
More Fairy Tales for Old and Young, by Sackville and Macfie (Manchester: Sherratt & Hughes, 1912);
Songs of Aphrodite and Other Poems (London: Elkin Mathews, 1913);
The Career Briefly Set Forth of Mr. Percy Prendergast who Told the Truth (London: Arthur Stockwell, 1914);
The Dream-Pedlar (London: Simpkin, Marshall, Hamilton, Kent, 1914);
The Travelling Companions and Other Stories for Children (London: Simpkin, Marshall, Hamilton, Kent, 1915);
The Pageant of War (London: Simpkin, Marshall, Hamilton, Kent, 1916);
Selected Poems (London: Constable, 1918; New York: Dutton, 1919);
Three Plays for Pacifists (London: Herald, 1919);
Epitaphs (Edinburgh: W. Brown, 1921);
Poems by Margaret Sackville (London: Allen & Unwin, 1923; New York: Dial, 1924);
A Rhymed Sequence (Edinburgh: Porpoise Press, 1924);
Three Fairy Plays (London: Williams & Norgate, 1925);
Collected Dramas. Hildris. Bertrud (London: Allen & Unwin, 1926);
Romantic Ballads (Edinburgh: Porpoise Press, 1927);
100 Little Poems (Edinburgh: Porpoise Press, 1928);
Alicia and the Twilight: A Fantasy (London: W. Gardner, 1928);
Twelve Little Poems (London: E. Lahr for the Red Lion Press, 1931);

Lady Margaret Sackville

Ariadne by the Sea (London: Red Lion Press, 1932);
The Double House and Other Poems (London: Williams & Norgate, 1935);
Mr. Horse's New Shoes (London: Country Life, 1936);
Collected Poems of Lady Margaret Sackville (London: Richard's Press, 1939);
Tom Noodle's Kingdom (London & Edinburgh: Chambers, 1941);
Return to Song and Other Poems (London: Williams & Norgate, 1943);

Paintings and Poems, by Sackville with paintings by Herbert Davis Richter (Leigh-on-Sea: F. Lewis, 1944);

The Lyrical Woodlands, by Sackville with paintings by Lonsdale Ragg (Leigh-on-Sea: F. Lewis, 1945);

Country Scenes and Country Verse (Leigh-on-Sea: F. Lewis, 1945);

Miniatures (Bradford: Beamsley, 1947); second series (Crakye: Guild, 1956);

Tree Music (London: Williams & Norgate, 1947);

Country Verse (Bradford: Beamsley House, 1949);

Quatrains and Other Poems (Llandeilo, Wales: St. Albert's Press, 1960).

OTHER: *A Book of Verse by Living Women,* edited by Sackville (London: Herbert & Daniel, 1910);

Jane Austen, edited by Sackville (London: Herbert & Daniel, 1912);

"Some Aspects of Modern Scottish Literature," in *Essays by Divers Hands; Being the Transactions of the Royal Society of Literature of the United Kingdom,* edited by Sir Francis Younghusband (London: Oxford University Press, 1931), pp. 59–76;

Arthur Row, *The Golden Valley,* foreword by Sackville (London: Row, Clifford, Hereford, 1952);

John Kenneth Gibson Hoffman, *Thanksgiving: Poems,* foreword by Sackville (Crayke: Guild, 1956);

Eric Barry Wilfred Chappelow, *The Tale of Perseus,* foreword by Sackville (Cambridge: Poetry Publication, 1957).

SELECTED PERIODICAL PUBLICATION–UNCOLLECTED: "Sonnet for the Times," *Jongleur* (Spring 1951): 8.

Although she was a popular and prolific writer during the first half of the twentieth century, Lady Margaret Sackville has been all but forgotten by contemporary literary critics. There are no biographies of Sackville, no modern editions of her poems or prose fairy tales, and no selections by her in the major anthologies of British literature and women's literature. The sole critical study devoted to Sackville is a slim volume of laudatory essays collected by her friend Georgina Somerville in 1953, *Harp Aeolian: Commentaries on the Works of Lady Margaret Sackville.* Undoubtedly, a major reason for this critical neglect is that Sackville seems out of step with her age; indeed, John de Lingen in "The Harp Aeolian of a Thousand Strings," in *Harp Aeolian,* claims that she was "born either a century too late, or a couple of generations too early." The latter-day Romanticism of much of her poetry seems to align her more with such earlier poets as Percy Bysshe Shelley, John Keats, Alfred Tennyson, and Christina Rossetti than with the writers of her own generation, including William Butler Yeats, T. S. Eliot, and Virginia Woolf. In addition, the critics in Somerville's *Harp Aeolian* used Sackville as a pawn in a cultural and literary battle. Dallas Kenmare, in "Return to Poetry," positions Sackville as a cultural warrior, fighting against the pernicious influence of modernism: "she has bravely carried the torch of true poetry through all of the fogs and miasmas of the Dark Age of literature." Kenmare contrasts Sackville's traditional sonnets and lyrics with the "ugly hybrid, half prose, half inferior verse" of the modernists. In his epilogue to *Harp Aeolian* the poet Lewis Spence aligns Sackville with the "great tradition" of (premodernist) English poetry: "Her work will remain a part of the victorious performance which began when men of vision first hearkened to the legendary winds of England and turned their intimations into song." Twenty-first-century critics may recover Sackville's works and view them in a larger context, exploring her distinctive poetic voice and complicating this image of her as a reactionary figure. In fact, Sackville's most interesting quality is her ability to weave together elements of Romanticism, Victorianism, Edwardianism, and modernism.

Lady Margaret Sackville was born in 1881 in Buckhurst, Sussex, to Lady Constance Mary Elizabeth Baillie-Cochrane, the daughter of the first Baron Lamington, and the Reverend Reginald Windsor, Baron Buckhurst and later Earl De La Warr. As was common practice for daughters in the nineteenth century, Lady Margaret's exact birth date was not recorded in the family history or *Burke's Peerage.* She was part of an ancient and privileged family; the barony of De La Warr dates back to 1299. Sir Reginald's mother, Lady Elizabeth Sackville, Countess De La Warr, was a favorite of Queen Victoria, who visited the family estate of Buckhurst. One of Lady Elizabeth's daughters was later made the Mistress of the Robes to Queen Victoria. When his mother died in 1870, Sir Reginald assumed the title of Baron Buckhurst; three years later, at the death of his elder brother, Sir Reginald became the seventh Earl De La Warr. He assumed by Royal License the surname Sackville only, in place of the usual Sackville-West.

Lady Margaret Sackville's ancestors include such prominent literary figures as Thomas Sackville, the first Earl of Dorset, who contributed to the *Mirror for Magistrates* and collaborated with Thomas Norton on the blank-verse tragedy *Gorboduc* (first performed in 1651). Queen Elizabeth I raised Thomas Sackville to the peerage in 1567 and presented him with Knole, an estate near Sevenoaks, Kent. Another of Sackville's literary ancestors was Charles Sackville, Lord Buckhurst, the sixth Earl of Dorset, who was a friend of John Dryden

A RHYMED SEQUENCE

by

Lady Margaret Sackville

BROADSHEET
NUMBER EIGHT

PRICE ONE
SHILLING NET

Title page for Sackville's 1924 chapbook, of which only
fifty copies were printed (courtesy of The Lilly
Library, Indiana University)

and patron of other poets. Sackville was also the second cousin of the modernist writer Victoria (Vita) Sackville-West, who was raised at Knole; Vita's grandfather was Lady Margaret's paternal uncle. Sackville-West wrote the novel *The Heir* (1922) as her farewell to her beloved Knole, which she was prevented from inheriting because of her sex. There is no indication, however, that Lady Margaret and Vita, who is perhaps best known today for her relationship with Virginia Woolf, were in close contact.

Little is known of Sackville's formative years. She was the youngest of five siblings: the Honorable Lionel Sackville, the Honorable Gilbert Sackville (later the eighth Earl De La Warr), Lady Edeline Sackville Strickland, Lady Lenore Sackville Griffin, and Lady Margaret Sackville. Her mastery of language, as well as her knowledge of Hellenic culture and Nordic and Celtic myth, indicate that she was well educated, though whether she was sent to school or taught at home is not known. She reportedly began composing poetry at age six, when she dictated the beginning of what she described as a "long Dramatic poem":

She looked at her watch and
   cried "Oh Dear!
It's time to drink poison with
   good cheer."
When all at once she fell on
   the floor
Suffocated. . . .

As a girl Sackville created several "little magazines" that included poems and illustrations by her and neighborhood children; two of these magazines were later collected and published in 1898 by Alexander Meyrick Broadley in *M.S.S. Magazine*.

Sackville's father died in 1896. Two years later Sackville was discovered by Wilfred Scawen Blunt—a poet, traveler, and antiimperialist who wrote passionately in favor of Egyptian, Indian, and Irish independence. With his encouragement, Sackville published her first chapbook of poetry, *Floral Symphony* (1900), at the age of nineteen, marking the beginning of a sixty-year career. Like much of Georgian poetry, these pastoral verses are meditations on the English countryside. C. R. Cammell claims that "her precocity and the renowned Sackville name, illustrious in the annals of English poetry, drew all eyes upon her."

Lady Margaret's second collection, *Poems* (1901), gave readers their first taste of her artistry and variety. *Poems* includes historical poems, such as "The Hellots (Sparta, 500 B.C.)" and "Lorenzo de Medici"; sonnets, such as "Nightfall: Three Sonnets"; and closet dramas, such as "Pan and the Maiden" and "Dreams." In her long piece "The Poet" Sackville describes the process of creative invention, which causes the poet to lose his identity and become merely "a hollow vase, from which men drew / God's wine and nothing further knew." The drama "Pan and the Maiden" reveals Sackville's interest in Hellenic myth and culture, which she later explored in such poems as "The Wooing of Dionysus," "A Hymn to Dionysus," "Tereus," "Songs of Aphrodite," "Orpheus among the Shades," "Syrinx," and "The Pythoness." Kenmare compares these works to those of Sappho, claiming that Sackville's poems seem as if "the priestess of ancient Greece is speaking through a modern English poet." In the monody "The Pythoness" (1913), the speaker is the priestess of the Oracle of Apollo at Dephi. The Pythoness laments her fate:

I am a woman, flesh,
Mortal and incomplete, wrought to endure
One life, to break at last under the weight
Of natural days, soft falling as a pine
Grown old through many seasons yields at last
Beneath its burden of impalpable snow.
. . . .
I live a thousand lives, and yet to live
One life—my own life; that is denied me.

During the next decade of her career, Sackville completed two longer closet dramas: *Hildris the Queen* (1908) and *Bertrud* (1911). De Lingen asserts that these dramas are "reminiscent of the Sagas, and might be of Anglo-Saxon or Scandinavian inspiration." *Hildris the Queen* focuses on several different types of loves and lovers. At the center is the relationship of Queen Hildris and her king; when the king does not sufficiently return Hildris's intense passion, her love turns to bitter hatred. *Bertrud* is a psychological study of Gerta, the mistress of a king, who wrongs and usurps Queen Bertrud. Later, Gerta is overcome with guilt, which manifests itself in a physical illness. On her deathbed, Gerta confesses her crimes and begs forgiveness from Bertrud:

Think you I can be happy
Here as Queen upon a stolen throne
With my evil ever before me? On the road
A beggar, with his love and your forgiveness
I may perchance be happy.

The noble Bertrud accepts; her acceptance, according to de Lingen, allows Bertrud to "transcend herself and win freedom of the soul through generosity in forgiving." Sackville later revised *Bertrud,* cutting much of the archaic language and trimming some of its overblown rhetoric; the volume was republished in 1926 as part of *Collected Dramas. Hildris. Bertrud.*

In 1909 Sackville collaborated with the popular Scottish poet Ronald Campbell Macfie on her first prose publication, *Fairy Tales for Old and Young.* According to Desmond Chapman-Huston in "Should Fairy-Tales Be Told," published in *Harp Aeolian,* Sackville was wise enough to realize that a "genuine fairy-tale" should appeal to readers of all ages. Three years later Sackville and Macfie collaborated again on *More Fairy Tales for Old and Young;* Sackville's admiration for Macfie and appreciation of his support are made clear in the dedication of her 1928 collection *100 Little Poems:* "You have always looked kindly on these verses, and encouraged me to add to their number. So there is no one to whom I can dedicate them more fittingly than you." *The Dream-Pedlar* (1914) is another fairy tale, the story of a wandering peddler on a quest for Beauty; the half-witted boy named Alf, "who's always seeing what other people can't," teaches the peddler that Beauty's mark is all around in the natural world. Sackville's later children's books include *The Travelling Companions and Other Stories for Children* (1915), *Three Fairy Plays* (1925), *Alicia and the Twilight: A Fantasy* (1928), and *Mr. Horse's New Shoes* (1936), a nonsense story in the vein of Lewis Carroll's works. The playful "Rhymed Review" of Sackville's *Three Fairy Plays,* first published in the *Cape Times,* was reprinted in *Harp Aeolian:*

All the works of Margaret Sackville
Have an airy fairy fragrance,
. . . .
Serious-minded, soulful persons,
May not like this lady's writings,
And a decorous crank with whiskers
(Can there still be cranks with whiskers?)
Ones with no imagination
Might consider them untruthful.

The reviewer goes on to claim that Sackville's fans, however, "consider cranks with whiskers / Rather more unreal than fairies." Chapman-Huston asserts that Sackville's fairy tales filled a cultural need in the years surrounding the world wars: "Never has the world needed more an answer to that prayer 'for men who have lost their fairy-lands.' May Lady Margaret help to answer it by writing more fairy tales that will gently lead us back to where we ought to be." He notes, however, that the illustrations accompanying Sackville's fairy tales are "all too often *jejeune,* conventional, even downright bad."

Sackville's somber poems about World War I and its aftermath stand in contrast to her charming fairy tales. Like most of her contemporaries, Sackville was horrified by the reports from the battlefield and deeply lamented the human cost of war. These poems should be read alongside the war poetry of Rupert Brooke, Edward Thomas, Wilfred Owen, Siegfried Sassoon, and Isaac Rosenberg, as well as the lesser-known World War I verses by such women poets as Edith Nesbit, Edith Sitwell, Madeline Ida Bedford, and Rose Macauley. The title poem of her collection *The Pageant of War* (1916) dispels any misconceptions about the glory or gallantry of war. The personified War rides into a town whose roads have been left "starkly white" by the ground "bones of children, bones of men":

He was like Death sitting astride
A pale and neighing horse,
Only he swayed from side to side
Like one glutted in every sense:

His lids were coarse
And overhanging eyes glassy with pride;
There was no trace
Of laughter, tears or pity
In his blue veined, swollen face

And so perforce
He had to wear a mask, lest seeing
The obscene countenance too near,
The heart of every human being
Should sink in loathing and in fear.
And run upon this thing and slay it there.

Frontispiece and title page for the 1939 volume of Sackville's poems

"A Memory" describes the horror of a war-ravaged village, where "In the middle of the street, two corpses lie unburied, / And a bayoneted woman stares in the market-place." "Will Green Corn Grow?" ponders the cultural and environmental consequences of the war:

> Will not green corn grow,
> Where blood has soaked, like rain?
> Corn green, not red
> The blood of all these dead
> Has soaked into the roots, and so
> How shall this corn grow
> Green where red blood was shed?

The poem ends, however, on an optimistic note, describing the new shoots of green corn emerging "From fields soaked through with red, / New life re-born– / This is the miracle of corn." The speakers of "The Question," a poignant poem written between the wars, are the slain soldiers of World War I. The soldiers remind the current generation why they sacrificed their lives and warn them not to engage in another disastrous war:

> Was not our blood sufficient to redeem
>   The world from all these tears? We offered up
> Our lives to save our sons. Now it would seem
>   They too must drain the cup.
>
> Waste not your pity on our scattered dust,
>   We rest secure–but these, our blood, our flesh,
> Our sons–we gave you all our sons in trust–
>   If you betray these living sons we must
>   By you, be slain afresh.

While she did not reject traditional meters or use stream of consciousness as did many of her modernist counterparts, Sackville nonetheless did experiment with form. Her *Epitaphs* (1921), *100 Little Poems,* and *Miniatures* (1947) are comprised of highly concentrated, precise, almost terse poems, which Eva Dobell in "The Poet's Return," in *Harp Aeolian,* effectively describes as "word-cameos," each as "unique and individual as the writer's own signature." De Lingen claims that the poems from these collections are written in "a form of verse which . . . will go down in English literature as distinctly her own, in the sense in which a certain other stanza is Spencer's." Each poem, some comprised of only a single couplet, puts forth a highly concentrated image or thought. In this poem, for example, Sackville focuses on one of her favorite themes, the creative process of the poet:

> How like a chrysalis, the poet brings
> To birth a living rhapsody of wings?
> Who knows from what grey dust of painful thought
> Those iridescent, shining wings were wrought?

In another "miniature," Sackville claims poetry enables readers to transcend the boundaries of time and space:

> Make of my songs a stair whereby to climb
>   From out the close circumference of Time,
> Until the gloom behind these prison-bars
>   Quickens with light of softly falling stars.

"A Masque of Edinburgh" consists of a series of quatrains, each spoken by figures who helped to shape the Scottish city: men of the Bronze Age, Romans, Queen Margaret, Robert the Bruce, James III, Sir John Cochrane, Queen Mary, John Knox, James I, Covenanters, Prince Charlie, and Robert Burns. Robert the Bruce shares his contribution:

> Mine the unshrinking sword: the floods poured down
>   'Raging on Scotland; I the firmer stood,
> And served this famous and disputed crown
>   With great outpouring of heroic blood.

Sackville's epitaphs are all written in first person, leaving the reader to imagine the speaker and his/her life. The following are examples:

> I had a name, a place, who now have none,
> For all I was lies crushed beneath a stone.
> Fame was my Mistress, but a crumbling name
> On a grey stone is all I've had of Fame!

> Humbly I lived but very proudly died:
> Death's chosen! Can you wonder at my pride?–
> Philosophers and Heroes, Saints and Kings,
> He left, but folded *me* beneath his wings.

In *Collected Poems of Lady Margaret Sackville* (1939), she included a note stating that "These should be called Miniature Biographies, rather than Epitaphs, since they attempt to sum up imaginary lives in a few words." While most critics admire Sackville's short verses, Francis Berry in "Lumen Siccum," in *Harp Aeolian,* assumes they are a sign of Sackville's lack of confidence in herself as a writer: "if Lady Margaret Sackville could be persuaded, supported by a proper and deserved confidence in her control over her short poems, to attack either a poem of some length or a series of poems on a single theme . . . then she might compose one of the quite significant poems of our time."

At the time of the publication of her *Collected Poems* Sackville was "well-known to all poetry lovers." In her witty foreword to the volume Sackville reveals her ambivalence about republishing her older poems:

> Like a vain lady, afflicted with a mania for hoarding discarded clothes, who examines her wardrobe on some unoccupied afternoon, curious to rediscover what still hangs stored there, so I, in regard to these poems. She stares bewildered, a little shocked– "Can it be possible," she exclaims, "this gown of ten years back? The frumpy-rag. *I* can't have worn it, *surely*. What *did* I look like." She tries to slip it on. Alas! Gown and figure match no longer. . . . Each batch of garments is a chapter lived by a self which then existed, bearing the same relation to her present self as these over-trimmed, upholstered gowns bear to the crisp, clean-cut unemphatic suit of to-day? And even this suit in a few years time?–Is it too trivial a simile to apply to verse? Yet the same rule, in its degrees, holds. Some gowns, some books, seem never out of fashion; those which blindly reflect the fashion of the moment quickly show their age.

Sackville claims that her humorous poems are the ones that still seem fresh: "I find, in retrospect, the lighter verse less disconcerting than the serious. The tragic mood departs, the black velvet in which we draped ourselves shows as velveteen. Humour is less temperamental. It is solid and unchanging as a family friend." Among these humorous pieces is "The Vicar's Wife and the Faun," a poetic conversation in which each speaker views the other's world as foreign and incomprehensible. When the vicar's wife runs off, the faun is left to wonder what sort of beast a vicar might be:

> Oh! please don't run away.
> Or if you really must, I wish you'd say
> *What* vicars *are*. Oh! dearie me, she's gone
> And I am left to find out alone.
> I'm sure the other fauns won't know or tell
>
> Even if they do. It's a great bore. Ah well!
> Perhaps she made it up. They don't exist,
> They're *myths* . . . and yet I wish I hadn't missed
> Just finding out, as certainly I should–
> There *may* be vicars hiding in the wood!

In "To . . . ," Sackville, with her usual modesty, claims that "No evanescent verse is mine" and imagines a reader sitting down with one of her volumes and exclaiming, "'The pages *still* uncut! / I *meant* to read it once, I *know*.' / Then turning to the fly-leaf: 'But– / Why–that was sixty years ago!'"

Title page for one of the volumes of poems Sackville wrote to accompany paintings by various artists (courtesy of Special Collections, Thomas Cooper Library, University of South Carolina)

Dobell notes that "Too often, after the publication of a Collected Volume of Poems, the poet retires to rest on his laurels; but in Lady Margaret Sackville we have a more generous singer." During the 1940s Sackville wrote three books of poems to accompany others' pictures: *Paintings and Poems* (1944), with pictures by Herbert Davis Richter; *The Lyrical Woodlands* (1945), with pictures by Lonsdale Ragg; and *Country Scenes and Country Verse* (1945), with pictures by various artists, including John Constable and David Cox. These poems, primarily descriptions of pastoral scenes and trees, seem to return to early Georgian verse. Alberta Vickridge's "In Appreciation of the Poems of Lady Margaret Sackville" in *Harp Aeolian* praises the lyric quality of the poems, asserting "You cannot read these poems and not remember their vision in the woods you know. And surely that is the justification and glory of any poem—being remembered, and shedding new light on familiar things and scenes." Dobell claims that *Country Scenes and Country Verse,* published right at the end of World War II, "made its appearance at an appropriate time, for it epitomized in pictures and poems the England we had defended." In her final collection, *Quatrains and Other Poems* (1960), Sackville returns to her "miniatures," which Dobell, editor of the volume, describes as "jewels, each so finely cut and polished by a craftsman's hands."

Sackville, who never married, lived most of her adult life in Edinburgh, Scotland. Her interest in her adopted homeland is clear in her poem "Masque of Edinburgh" and in the essay "Some Aspects of Modern Scottish Literature." First delivered to the Royal Society for Literature of the United Kingdom on 29 October 1930, Sackville's essay promotes Scotland's new literature. She claims that "since I occupy what I may, perhaps, call an amphibious position between the two countries—that is to say, I can breathe in either with equal ease," she is in an ideal position to comment on the current Scottish literary renaissance (linked also to Scotland's political awakening, though she does not address political issues in the essay). British writers and critics, according to Sackville, still equate the Scots with caricatures in *Punch* and Scottish literature with Robert Burns, since modern Scottish literature has "received little in the way of recognition on this side of the border." She goes on to discuss the new voices of Scottish literature, including Neil Gunn, William Jeffrey, Robert Crawford, Marion Angus, Rachel Annand Taylor, and Lewis Spence (who was one of Sackville's admirers and a contributor to *Harp Aeolian*). Many of Sackville's poems appeared in Scottish periodicals, including the *Glasgow Herald* and the *Glasgow Evening News*. Scotland honored Sackville with a bust created by Pittendrigh Macgillivray, the Sculptor Royal of Scotland.

Sackville began her long career in the Edwardian/Georgian period, but in a style and with themes that hearkened back to the Romantics and Victorians. Yet, she lived and wrote throughout the modernist age, and, despite the claims of some of her critics, was not untouched by its literary and cultural transformations. Such collections as *The Pageant of War* and *A Rhymed Sequence* (1924) reveal the ways that Sackville grappled with the same feelings of loss, alienation, and spiritual malaise that haunt the pages of other modernists. The tension that Kenmare and other critics set up between Sackville and the modernists seems to be largely artificial, emerging from a desire to condemn modernism more than from a desire to understand Sackville's oeuvre. Interestingly, Kenmare's claim that modernist poetry is "floundering in a morass of complexity and obscurity, in a belief that such involved diction alone conveys brilliance and profundity of thought" sounds almost identical to the comments of modernist critics of postmodern literature and theory. The most reasoned critical analysis of Sackville comes from Dobell, who rightly asserts that Sackville transcends time and defies easy classification:

> But all through the centuries there have been poets who have worked by themselves, refusing to be fitted into any coterie, and have gone on their way unaffected by the literary fashions of their time. Such a one was William Blake, who assuredly cannot be labelled as belonging to any "School." . . . Among these poets set apart I would number Lady Margaret Sackville. She seems to belong to no century, and to no special group. She combines the rich vocabulary of the Tennysonian era with the grace of the Elizabethan lyric. She can rival the poignant brevity of the epitaphs of the Greek anthology; or paint for us a woodland scene with the Nature poets.

The major obstacle for readers interested in Lady Margaret Sackville is the inaccessibility of her texts. Her chapbooks were published by small presses in limited printings; for example, only 50 copies of *A Rhymed Sequence* and only 250 copies of *Quatrains and Other Poems* were published. The few American libraries that hold Sackville's books generally place them out of circulation, in special collections and rare book rooms. The recovery of Sackville is dependent on the publication of a modern edition of her works, preferably a critical edition that could place her works in their historical and literary context. Until then, Sackville will remain neglected by most readers and literary scholars.

References:

Eva Dobell, ed., *A Poet's Return: Some Later Poems of Lady Margaret Sackville* (Cheltenham: Burrow's Press, 1940);

Dobell, Foreword to *Quatrains and other Poems by Sackville* (Llandeilo, Wales: St. Albert's Press, 1960);

Charles J. Phillips, *History of the Sackville Family* (London: Cassell, 1930);

"Lady Margaret Sackville," in *The Feminist Companion to Literature in English,* edited by Virginia Blain, Isobel Grundy, and Patricia Clements (New Haven: Yale University Press, 1990), p. 937;

Georgina Somerville, ed., *Harp Aeolian: Commentaries on the Works of Lady Margaret Sackville* (Cheltenham: Burrow's Press, 1953).

Papers:

Two letters by Lady Margaret Sackville, one to Francis Berry and one to Thomas Moult, both about literary matters, are held by Washington State University. A letter from Sackville to Lady Cynthia Asquith is in Asquith's papers at Texas Women's University Library. Letters from Sackville to Lorna Keeling (Collard) Horstmann and the foreword for Horstmann's play "The Immortal Rose" are held by the Manuscript Department of The Lilly Library, Indiana University.

Alicia Anne Scott
(Lady John Scott)
(1810 – 12 March 1900)

Susannah Clements
University of South Carolina

BOOK: *Songs and Verses* (Edinburgh: David Douglas, 1904; revised and enlarged, 1911).

In "A Scottish Border Clan" (*Edinburgh Review*, April 1898) Sir Francis Napier, Baron Napier and Ettrick, concluded his discussion of significant Scottish women by mentioning Alicia Anne Scott and her sister, Margaret Campbell, claiming that the two women "joined the faculties of poetical and musical composition with the gift of song, endowments never before united in the person of any one of their predecessors." Although a few of Scott's poems and songs—such as "Ettrick," "Durisdeer," and "The Comin' o' the Spring"—are known to people familiar with Scottish music and literature, her literary reputation rests almost entirely on a single ballad, "Annie Laurie."

Little is known about Alicia Anne Scott's life beyond the information included in the biographical sketch written by her grandniece Margaret Warrender for the 1911 edition of *Songs and Verses* (first published in 1904). Scott was born Alicia Anne Spottiswood in 1810, the eldest of the four children in one of the oldest families in Berwickshire. Her father was John Spottiswood of Spottiswood, and her mother was Helen Wauchope, daughter of the laird of Niddrie-Marischal. She was close to her two brothers, John and Andrew, but she was particularly devoted to her sister, Margaret. Alicia Spottiswood and her siblings were raised with considerable freedom and little restraint. An avid rider and walker, she loved country life and disliked the family's yearly trips to London. She was carefully educated in French, Italian, literature, and drawing, and was also trained in singing and playing the harp. As a child, she often made up tunes and songs and sang to herself for hours. She inherited from her father an interest in botany, geology, and archeology, and from her grandfather Andrew Wauchope she heard stories of the Stuart cause and developed Jacobite leanings. According to Warrender, Alicia Spottiswood was extremely attractive, with

Alicia Anne Scott (from the frontispiece for the 1911 edition of her Songs and Verses*)*

dark curly hair and deep blue eyes. When she grew older, she was not fond of society, and she refused to come out before her sister.

In 1834 Margaret Spottiswood married Sir Hugh Hume Campbell, who had been their friend from childhood. The sisters remained close, and Alicia Spottiswood spent much of her time at her brother-in-law's estate, Marchmont, which was only ten miles from Spottiswood. During one visit to Marchmont, Spottiswood wrote "Annie Laurie." Warrender quotes from a letter to Lord Napier, in which Spottiswood gave an account of how she wrote the song:

> I made the tune very long ago to an absurd ballad, originally Norwegian, I believe, called "Kempie Kaye," and once before I was married I was staying at Marchmont, and fell in with a collection of Allan Cunningham's poetry. I took a fancy to the words of "Annie Laurie," and thought they would go well to the tune I speak of. I didn't quite like the words, however, and I altered the verse, "She's backit like a peacock," to what it is now, and made the third verse ("Like dew on the gowan lying") myself, only for my own amusement; but I was singing it, and Hugh Campbell and my sister Maggy liked it, and I accordingly wrote it down for them.

The Scottish ballad, originally attributed to William Douglas and published in Allan Cunningham's *The Songs of Scotland, Ancient and Modern* (1825), expresses a man's love for a beautiful woman. Spottiswood changed the second verse, which describes Annie's body–including the lines "She's breastit like a swan / She's jimp about the middle"–to a description of her brow, throat, face, and eyes. The third verse, which Spottiswood composed entirely, further develops the description:

> Like dew on the gowan lying
> Is the fa' o' her fairy feet,
> And like winds in summer sighing
> Her voice is low and sweet.
> Her voice is low and sweet,
> And she's a' the world to me,
> And for bonnie Annie Laurie
> I'd lay doun my head and dee!

The song is characteristic of Spottiswood's poetry in its use of her Scottish heritage and the Scots dialect. It was published without her knowledge or permission in 1838, apparently copied when she sent out her music book to be rebound. "Annie Laurie" appeared anonymously as sheet music and was attributed to various poets before her authorship was discovered after the Crimean War (1854–1856), when she gave the manuscript to Lonsdale to publish for the benefit of the widows and orphans of soldiers.

On 16 March 1836 Alicia Spottiswood married Lord John Douglas Montague Scott, the brother of Walter Francis Scott, Duke of Buccleuch and Queensbury and the nephew of Lady Caroline Scott. The couple lived in various places, spending much of their time at Cawston, Lord John's property in Warwickshire, where Alicia Scott felt homesick for Scotland.

Scott's absence from the Scottish countryside inspired many of her ballads, including two of her most frequently anthologized poems, "Durisdeer" and "Ettrick," in which impressions of nature are tied to individuals' emotional states. In "Durisdeer," written shortly after her marriage, Scott's speaker finds the natural setting beautiful but "eerie" because she will no longer meet her dead lover there. The poem ends optimistically, suggesting a future meeting in heaven, but the primary mood is despair. "Ettrick" lacks even a gesture toward optimism. Each of the three stanzas describes how the speaker's emotions change her perceptions of the same natural setting. In the first stanza, nature is bright and beautiful in spring because the speaker is with her love. The second verse acknowledges the shadow of a future death, and in this verse the autumn landscape matches the speaker's sad mood. In the final stanza, the speaker's loved one has died, and nature is dead as well: "The winds were shifting, the storm was waking, / The snow was drifting, my heart was breaking." Nature has become inseparable from the speaker's perspective.

Margaret Campbell died from scarlet fever in 1839, and shortly after her death, Scott wrote two poems to express her grief, introducing one of her primary themes, the loneliness of mourning. Unlike her songs and ballads, they are not written in Scots. "To My Sister in Heaven" describes how Margaret in heaven cannot hear or be moved by her sister's sorrow. Although the lines describing Margaret in life tend to be clichéd and melodramatic, the poem moves into an effective expression of how the speaker misses the sight of her sister in the Scottish countryside. Scott's poetry is at its most powerful when it describes feelings evoked by the natural landscape. Loneliness is also the primary emotion in "Your Voices Are Not Hushed." Written in 1842, three years after her sister's death, the poem expresses Scott's despair and sense of isolation. She is the only person still grieving for her sister, while everyone else talks, laughs, and enjoys the spring.

Scott mourned her sister for the rest of her life, and her preoccupation with loneliness intensified as she faced other tragic events. In 1846 John Spottiswood, the elder of her two brothers, died. The two poems Scott wrote on his death continue to express her absorption with death and isolation.

The poems in Scott's only book, *Songs and Verses*, combine her typically Victorian preoccupation over death, isolation, and the past with her interest in Scottish history, politics, and geography. In the early 1840s, Scott began a friendship and correspondence with Charles Kirkpatrick Sharp, one of the leading authorities on Scottish folklore, family history, and tradition. This correspondence lasted until Sharp's death in 1851 and further inspired Scott's interest in Scotland. According to Warrender, Scott often stated, "I would rather

Letter from Scott describing the composition of her most famous work, the ballad "Annie Laurie" (from The Burial of Lady John Scott, Authoress of "Annie Laurie," *16th March 1900)*

Westruther Kirk, Spottiswood, Berwickshire, Scotland, where Scott is buried

live in a pig-sty in Scotland than in a palace in England." Many of her poems deal with the places and countryside of Scotland. "The Bounds of Cheviot," written in 1858, expresses her desire to return to Scotland and her despair over being away from home:

> Shall I never see the bonnie banks o' Kale again?
> Nor the dark craigs o' Howman Law?
> Nor the green dens o' Chatto, nor Twaeford's mossy stane,
> Nor the birks upon Philogar Shaw?
>   Nae mair! Nae mair!
> I shall never see the bounds o' Cheviot mair!
>
> . . . .
>
> Shall I never wander lanely, when the gloamin' fa's
> And the wild birds flutter to their rest,
> Ower the lang heathery muir, to the bonnie Brunden laws
> Standin' dark against the glitter o' the West?
>   Nae mair! Nae mair!
> I shall never see the bounds o' Cheviot mair!
>
> . . . .
>
> Shall I never win the marches at the Coquet head,
> Thro' the mists and the driftin' snaw?
> Nor the dark doors o' Cottenshope, nor the quiet springs o' Rede,
> Glintin' bright across the Border, far awa?
>   Nae mair! Nae mair!
> I shall never see the bounds o' Cheviot mair!

Scott explained her feelings about the poem in a 15 December 1858 letter to her mother: "The words cannot be dignified by the name of poetry. They are a string of names which I daresay you will hardly be able to get into the tune." In fact, the poem relies on the sounds of names and the dialect rather than elaborate exposition to reveal the speaker's emotion. The repetition of the refrain "Nae mair! Nae mair!" emphasizes her sorrow. Other poems that express her love for the Scottish countryside include "The Comin o' the Spring," "Coming Back to Spottiswood," and "A Ride Over Lammermuir."

Scott also collected items related to the Stuart cause, including pictures, books, and souvenirs. According to Warrender, she even possessed the wedding ring of Charles Stuart, known to his supporters as "Bonnie Prince Charlie" and to his adversaries as the "Young Pretender." She also put together an extensive

SONGS AND VERSES

BY

LADY JOHN SCOTT

'Haud fast by the past'

EDINBURGH: DAVID DOUGLAS
1904

All rights reserved

Title page for the first edition of Scott's only book

collection of Scottish songs and tunes for her brother-in-law, the duke of Buccleuch. Many of the poems in *Songs and Verses* express her enthusiasm for Scottish history and the Stuarts. Among the best of these poems is "Shame on Ye Gallants," in which the speaker chides the Scots who did not support and fight with their prince in 1745, describing him as coming like the dawn to end the Scots' long night of slavery. When she was a child, Scott had spoken to people who had met Charles Stuart face to face, and "Prince Charlie" is the heroic figure in all her Jacobite verse. He is treated most lavishly in "My Prince," which is made more formal than most of her poems by the use of standard English rather than Scots dialect. The refrain—"Oh my Prince, my Prince!"—changes in the last stanza to "Oh my King, my King!" Although he has failed to seize the throne, his followers still see him as their sovereign.

In 1859 Scott's husband became ill and died suddenly. After his death, she stayed increasingly at Spottiswood. Warrender claims that for forty years after Lord John Scott's death, Alicia Scott continued writing journal letters to him, and she refused to move his hats and walking sticks from the hall at Cawston or change anything in his dressing room. As she got older, she dwelt more and more on the past. Many of her later poems describe feelings of remorse for past actions or pain from the loss of loved ones. In 1875 she composed "Written at Thurso," which describes a graveside vigil at night. As the wild winter wind and dark sea match her despair and anguish, the speaker wonders if the deceased is aware of either the wildness of nature or her sorrow and concludes that it is impossible because the dead rest in glory and peace. In the final lines she admits that her dead loved one is mute, and she is completely alone with the howling wind and the sea. In contrast to her earlier poems, "Written at Thurso" depicts nature as an inadequate mediator between the living and the dead.

Scott continued to be inspired by Scottish history, as is evident in one of her best ballads, "There Were Twa Lairds' Sons." Scott explained the source of the poem in a 13 March 1897 letter to James Home: "I am ashamed to say this is a true story. . . . No one ever knew what the two amiable youths quarreled about,—very likely the merits of their respective hawks and hounds. The murder took place in 1611." In the ballad two young men—St. Clair and the laird of Spottiswood's son—go hunting, quarrel, and duel for an unknown reason. Spottiswood kills St. Clair with a hunting knife, and a blood feud between their families nearly results. To prevent further violence, the king orders Spottiswood to give a bag of gold to the St. Clairs and ask their pardon, which the young man does. Spottiswood is forgiven, but the ballad ends with his brooding on how his guilt over his hasty action will haunt him for the rest of his life. Most of the ballad is fast paced and exciting, while the description of guilt is reminiscent of the remorse expressed in Samuel Taylor Coleridge's "The Rime of the Ancient Mariner" (1798), revealing once again Scott's obsession with death and grief.

Scott remained in good health until the late 1890s, when she sprained her ankle and was forced to walk with two canes until her death. Her last poem was "I See Them Not," written in November 1899:

> I see them not; I hear them not;
> Their life on earth is o'er.
> But every day that passes
> I miss them more and more.
>
> Surely if we had parted
> Never to meet again,
> Time would have soothed, and absence dulled,
> This ceaseless bitter pain.

And yet this earth is small,
Age after age has passed
Where could they dwell who hope to rest
In happiness at last!

O slow of heart, were there not thousands fed
On five small loaves of bread?

The last lines suggest a move toward contentment by alluding to Christ's miracle of the loaves and fishes and his desire to provide for the needy, but the abruptness of the lines also evokes an unsettled feeling rather than closure. In 1900 an epidemic of influenza broke out in Spottiswood, and Scott succumbed to the disease on 12 March. She was buried at Westruther Kirk.

Shortly after Scott's death *The Burial of Lady John Scott, Authoress of "Annie Laurie," 16th March 1900,* a poem signed "G.N.N.," was published in a pamphlet, which also included the original version of "Annie Laurie," Scott's version of the song, and a facsimile of a 17 October 1899 letter in which Scott described its composition. *The Burial of Lady John Scott* possesses little literary merit, but it reveals the extent to which Scott's renown rests on the composition of "Annie Laurie."

Aside from "Annie Laurie," most of Scott's poems remained unpublished until after her death, though much of her work was widely circulated in manuscript. In 1904 a volume of Scott's songs and verses was published with a preface by her grandniece Margaret Warrender. Warrender also edited the volume, dividing Scott's poetry into eight different categories: "Places," "Historical," "Jacobite," "Ballads," "Foreign," "Hymns," "Family," and "Personal." For the enlarged 1911 edition Warrender expanded her preface into a biographical sketch, which also includes a selection of Scott's correspondence. She also added a few more poems to the 1911 edition, including "Annie Laurie" and two personal poems.

Alicia Anne Scott's poetry combines her deep love of Scottish history and traditions with her preoccupations with death, isolation, and the past. Her songs were well loved during her lifetime and a few—such as "Think on Me," "Durisdeer," and "Ettrick"—are still popular. No critical writings about her poetry were published during the second half of the twentieth century, and her poetry is rarely republished outside anthologies of Scottish literature. Yet, the growing interest in female and regional poets may spark renewed attention to her verse.

Biography:

Margaret Warrender, "Biographical Sketch," in Scott's *Songs and Verses* (Edinburgh: David Douglas, 1911), pp. 1–102.

Catharine Amy Dawson Scott
(August 1865 – 4 November 1934)

Tonya L. Wertz-Orbaugh
University of South Carolina

BOOKS: *Sappho* (London: Kegan Paul, Trench, 1889);
Idylls of Womanhood (London: Heinemann, 1892);
The Story of Anna Beames (London: Heinemann, 1907);
The Burden (London: Heinemann, 1908; New York: Reynolds, 1908);
Treasure Trove (London: Heinemann, 1909; New York: Duffield, 1909);
The Agony Column (London: Chapman & Hall, 1909);
Madcap Jane; Or, Youth (London: Chapman & Hall, 1910);
Mrs. Noakes, an Ordinary Woman (London: Chapman & Hall, 1911);
Nooks and Corners of Cornwall (London: Glaisher, 1911);
Alice Bland, and The Golden Ball (London: Dent, 1912);
Beyond (London: Glaisher, 1912);
Phoca, and History Repeats Itself (London: Dent, 1912);
Tom, Cousin Mary, and Red Riding Hood (London: Dent, 1912);
The Caddis Worm; Or, Episodes in the Life of Richard and Catherine Blake (London: Hurst & Blackett, 1914);
Wastralls (London: Heinemann, 1918);
Against the Grain (London: Heinemann, 1919); republished as *The Rolling Stone* (New York: Knopf, 1920);
The Headland (London: Heinemann, 1920; New York: Knopf, 1920);
The Haunting (London: Heinemann, 1921; New York: Knopf, 1922);
Bitter Herbs (London: Heinemann, 1923; New York: Knopf, 1923);
They Green Stones; Or, The Cornish Downs (London: Heinemann, 1925); republished as *The Turn of a Day* (New York: Holt, 1925);
The Vampire; A Book of Cornish and Other Stories (London: Holden, 1925);
Blown by the Wind (London: Heinemann, 1926);
From Four Who Are Dead . . . Messages to C. A. Dawson Scott (London: Arrowsmith, 1926);
Kitty Leslie at the Sea (London: Hutchinson, 1927);
Wheal Darkness, by Henry Dawson Lowrey and Scott (London: Hutchinson, 1927);

Catharine Amy Dawson Scott

Oh! Foolish Kitty (London: Selwyn & Blount, 1928);
Is This Wilson? Messages Accredited to Woodrow Wilson, Received by Mrs. C. A. Dawson Scott (New York: Dutton, 1929);
The Sea Princess (London & Liverpool: Philip, 1930);
The House in the Hollow (London: Benn, 1933).

OTHER: *Thirty and One Stories by Thirty and One Authors,* edited by Scott and Ernest Rhys (London: Butterworth, 1923); republished as *31 Stories by Thirty and One Authors* (New York: Appleton, 1923);

Twenty and Three Stories by Twenty and Three Authors, edited by Scott and Rhys (London: Butterworth, 1924; New York: Appleton, 1924);

Old and New Love Stories, edited by Scott and Rhys (London: Holden, 1925); republished as *29 Love Stories, Old and New, by Twenty and Nine Authors* (New York: Appleton, 1925);

Twenty-Seven Humorous Tales, edited by Scott and Rhys (London: Hutchinson, 1926);

28 Humorous Stories, Old and New, by Twenty and Eight Authors, edited by Scott and Rhys (New York: Appleton, 1926);

Tales of Mystery; Startling Stories of the Supernatural, edited by Scott and Rhys (London: Hutchinson, 1927);

26 Mystery Stories, Old and New, by Twenty and Six Authors, edited by Scott and Rhys (New York: Appleton, 1927);

Mainly Horses, edited by Scott and Rhys (New York & London: Appleton, 1929);

26 Adventure Stories, Old and New, by Twenty and Six Authors, edited by Scott and Rhys (New York: Appleton, 1929);

Tales from Far and Near, edited by Scott and Rhys (New York & London: Appleton, 1930);

The Guide to Psychic Knowledge, edited by Scott, 3 volumes (London: Shaw, 1932).

Catharine Amy Dawson Scott is often remembered as the founder of PEN (Poets, Playwrights, Essayists, Editors, Novelists), the international writers' organization. A prolific author, her work includes fiction (adult and children's), poetry, plays, and books on the supernatural. Scott also co-edited with Ernest Rhys, an editor at the Everyman Library, several collections of short stories. These books, such as *Old and New Love Stories* (1925) and *Tales of Mystery; Startling Stories of the Supernatural* (1927) earned Rhys and Scott reputations as discerning editors who recognized not only well-crafted stories but also fresh modern voices. Scott was an engaged member of London's literary scene, often inviting aspiring as well as established writers to tea parties at her home. She lived an unconventional life, supporting herself as a writer and divorcing her husband at a time when such an action was considered scandalous. Toward the end of her life, she lived contentedly in a tent on the coast of her beloved Cornwall, a region that figures largely as the setting in many of her novels. Scott is best known as a novelist, although she also published four collections of poetry: *Sappho* (1889), *Idylls of Womanhood* (1892), *Beyond* (1912), and *Bitter Herbs* (1923). Her poetry is markedly feminist, addressing women's independence and social equality and questioning traditional attitudes toward marriage and women's subservience to men. As a child, Scott said her ambition was to become the Sappho of her age and, indeed, many contemporaries bestowed upon her the nom de guerre "Mrs. Sappho."

Catharine Amy Dawson (she was called Amy by her family) was born in August 1865 to Ebenezer Dawson and Catharine Mason Armstrong Dawson. Two sons followed her birth but both died in infancy. A sister, Ellen ("Nellie") Maude, was born in January 1869. Her paternal relatives were prosperous owners of a pottery works at Plumstead and Dulwich. Both Amy and her sister were born at the family home, Gothic Lodge, in Dulwich, where Ebenezer Dawson managed the pottery works. Despite the family's prosperity, the girls endured an unhappy home life that was shadowed by their mother's alcoholism and physical abuse. Their mother died in 1877, when Dawson and Nellie were ages eleven and seven, respectively. Many years later, Scott's daughter, Marjorie Watts, recalled that her mother had only unhappy childhood memories. In 1878 Ebenezer Dawson married Catherine (Kate) Ancell. Scott later wrote, "She was 21, and I was 12, and we had no point of contact . . . she thought me an undisciplined, self-confident child." Despite these family difficulties, Amy Dawson grew into an intelligent, gifted young girl. At the age of thirteen she was sent to a boarding school run by her step-grandmother, Mrs. Sarah Ancell. She may not have always followed the school's rules, but she demonstrated a talent for storytelling, keeping the other girls enthralled with her own adventurous stories. She also composed poems in her head and recalled her frustration at being denied paper and pencil to write down the lines of verse. Often told to wait until morning, she would naturally forget the lines. One night she shocked the other girls by pricking her arm and writing down a verse in her own blood.

Dawson left Mrs. Ancell's boarding school when she was fifteen to attend the Anglo-German College in Camberwell, where she became interested in geography, fascinated that there was a world to explore outside the boundaries of England. At seventeen, after a brief stay at home, she enrolled in a young ladies' finishing school. There she was dismayed to learn that most of her fellow students had only one goal: marriage. She vowed to avoid marriage at all costs, and this epiphany inspired a poem called "Hypatia," which deals with what she perceived as the problems of marriage. One of her father's friends was so impressed by her poetic talent that he took it upon himself to send a copy of the poem to Robert Browning, asking for his opinion. Browning did respond, commending the young poet's "promise" but observing that the poem was seriously flawed, namely in its "inevitable want . . . of originality–whether of subject or of mode of treatment: nothing here but has been thought and similarly written about before: yet the quality is just what is required nowadays to give distinction to a poem." Despite Browning's criticism of her lack of originality, Dawson was delighted.

Life back at home, however, was anything but encouraging. When she returned from finishing school, the stable world she had known for nineteen years fell apart. Like her late mother, her father had also become an alcoholic, neglecting the family pottery business to the point of financial ruin. He had done little managing of the pottery works for several months, and because no bricks were manufactured to be sold, there was no family income. At the last minute, his eighty-year-old father came to the rescue, but the family was forced to live in vastly reduced financial circumstances.

To help the family, Dawson decided to seek work. She also asked to be called by her given name, Catharine. She found work as a secretary-companion to an elderly man, Professor Jennings, and his daughter Louey. Many years later she reflected, "They paid me what was considered very good wages for a woman–200 [pounds] a year. . . . The old man considered my education unfinished and interested himself in teaching me Greek, Latin and Logic. But he did more than that for me. He had a fairly good library, and he gave me the run of it. I read voraciously–every sort of book." Dawson worked for Jennings until 1889, when he fired her because he disapproved of the attention she drew when *Sappho*, her first book, was published.

From the beginning, *Sappho* was problematic. To find a publisher, Dawson proudly took the manuscript to the premier poetry house at the time, Smith, Elder. They were, however, uninterested in a book of epic poems. Determined to see her book in print, she paid Kegan Paul sixty-four pounds to publish her book.

Arranged in four "books," *Sappho* addresses issues of women's rights. Most reviewers assumed that the book's author was male, referring to "Mr. Dawson" in their essays, many of which praised the poetical skill and imaginative force of the volume. The reviewer for *The Morning Post* commented, "its author has elevation of style, as well as poetical fancy." Few people, however, had the opportunity to read *Sappho* because a fire at the publisher's warehouse destroyed most of the volumes.

Despite such a setback, Dawson's desire to write remained unhampered. When an acquaintance offered her an introduction to publisher William Heinemann, her career began in earnest. Soon she published *Idylls of Womanhood* (1892), stories of women's lives written in verse form, which Dawson later described as evidence of her obsession with feminism. She moved to a flat in London and began earning a living as an author. Her sister, Nellie, joined her although their parents disapproved of the young women living alone in London. Through the friendship with Heinemann, Dawson and Nellie both became part of London's literary scene in the 1890s. In this circle, Dawson met her future husband, a young doctor from Northern Ireland named Horatio Francis Ninian Scott.

"Scottie", as she called him, was educated at Portora Royal School, Ennis Killen, and at Trinity College, Dublin. He was a quiet, conventional man who shocked his family when he became seriously involved with Dawson, a woman of unconventional dress, habits, and ideas. Soon friends referred to the couple as Scottie and Sappho. Despite her negative views on marriage, she married him on 6 June 1896, after Scottie was made a partner in the medical practice attending the royal family. The demands of marriage and family dominated Scott's life for the next several years. She and Scottie had three children: Marjorie, born in December 1898; Christopher, born in March 1901; and Walter (who was nicknamed Toby), born in June 1904. When the children were young, Scott did not write at all, devoting herself to family duties, but she was not idle for long.

When her youngest child was only three years old, Heinemann published Scott's first novel, *The Story of Anna Beames* (1907). The plot centers on quiet and demure Anna, who is seduced by the village playboy. They marry and endure a miserable few months together before Anna dies. Scott addresses the taboo topics of class exploitation as well as domestic violence in this work. Her fiction continually raises what she perceives as the problems that are inherent in marriage, and in many of her novels, powerless women suffer in the male-dominated world.

Not all of Scott's stories end tragically. In *The Burden* (1908) an unappreciated wife unexpectedly embarks on an extramarital affair. Despite her immorality, the heroine changes profoundly as she learns to love herself and others. In creating a woman to admire rather than to condemn, she challenged social attitudes about marriage and adultery.

Morality is also at the crux of the cautionary tale *Treasure Trove* (1909). A woman watches helplessly while her family disintegrates, punished as a result of her own greedy actions. Scott's emphasis on monetary greed reflected her real-life financial woes. Although the family's move from Cowes in July 1909 (where the Scotts had lived since they were first married) to London again offered Scott opportunities to renew and establish literary friendships and connections, it was not a financially sound one. Once again Scott was besieged by money worries.

Despite her lofty dreams to be known as a modern-day Sappho, fiscal necessity rather than divine inspiration fueled Scott's creativity and productivity. She published six novels between 1909 and 1912, including a Cornwall trilogy known as "Some Wives": *The Agony Column* (1909), *Madcap Jane; Or, Youth* (1910), and *Mrs. Noakes, an Ordinary Woman* (1911). All these books depict marriage as a hopeless trap from which women cannot escape. In *The Agony Column* a woman cannot walk away from an unfulfilled marriage, even though she has found her true soul mate. A bored young wife does walk away from her marriage in *Madcap Jane*, but she returns home, presumably having learned her "lesson." Mrs. Noakes, in the novel of the same name, is a saga of a couple's fifty-year marriage, the chief feature of which is Mr. Noakes's drunkenness. All three of the novels are studies in realism, accurately reflecting the complicated situation of early-twentieth-century women bound by their financial dependence upon men.

Although Scott enjoyed publishing successes, Heinemann rejected the novel she considered her best work. Undaunted, she took "Ulalia," set during the reign of Elizabeth I, to the publisher John Murray. The editor was interested but urged her to rewrite the story's tragic ending to a happier one. Frustrated by her desires to earn a living as an author and remain true to her creative instincts, she wrote in her journal:

> My poor *Ulalia*. I have been suffering all this year because publisher after publisher has refused her. They are full of the spirit of commercialism—even William Heinemann, who once could see, says "So tragic is the book, it would never find readers."

In April 1913 the Scotts moved to larger accommodations at The Bank House, 6 King Street, in Southall, where Scottie opened consulting rooms on the lower floor, while the family resided above. Here Scott consorted with literary notables including Violet Hunt, May Sinclair, H. G. Wells, Ford Madox Ford, Ezra Pound, and Charlotte Mew. A year later, she published *The Caddis Worm; Or, Episodes in the Life of Richard and Catherine Blake* (1914), a novel in which a submissive wife uses the circumstances of her husband's betrayal to fuel her metamorphosis into an independent, capable woman.

With the outbreak of World War I, the Scott family left London to live at "Wastehills," a bungalow in Cornwall. Again inspired by her beloved Cornish landscape, Scott began working on the "Cornish Tales," as she called them. The series consisted of five novels that were published over an eight-year period: *Wastralls* (1918); *The Headland* (1920); *The Haunting* (1921); *They Green Stones; Or, The Cornish Downs* (1925); and *Blown by the Wind* (1926). Meanwhile, Scottie joined the army to serve as a medical doctor, while Scott founded the Women's Defence [sic] Relief Corps. The organization's membership grew extensively between 1915 and 1916 until the government-sponsored Women's Land Army and similar groups were formed in mid 1917.

Scott in 1910 with her daughter, Marjorie

By 1917 Scott turned her organizational skills to a more literary-based movement. She founded the To-Morrow Club, the forerunner of PEN. The purpose of the To-Morrow Club was to encourage beginning writers of all types by providing opportunities for them to meet and talk with established authors. Scott knew that she must enlist the support of well-known and well-respected authors if her idea was to succeed, so at the suggestion of one of her literary friends, the novelist J. D. Beresford, she wrote to John Galsworthy, the respected novelist and playwright. He agreed to offer his support to the club, whose weekly meetings featured different topics that were related to writing. Scott was always present, making sure that operations ran smoothly, facilitating the occasionally faltering conversation between a timid unknown and an intimidating "known."

Established writers and authors greeted Scott's plan with enthusiasm. Other early members included Elizabeth Delafield, Louis Golding, Henry Williamson, Stephen Southwold (who also wrote under the pen name Neil Bell), as well as the publisher and founder of Penguin Books, Allen Lane. Speakers at the To-Morrow Club's weekly meetings included luminaries such as Beresford, Ford, Galsworthy, Sinclair, Hunt, T. S. Eliot, George Bernard Shaw, the Sitwells (Edith, Osbert, and Sacheverell), and Sheila Kaye-Smith. In 1919 Scottie was demobilized and found work in London's Chelsea neighborhood. The family bought a spacious home in St. John's Wood, at the corner of Alexandra and Abbey Roads, and To-Morrow Club meetings were often held there. Another novel, *Against the Grain* (1919), published in the United States as *The Rolling Stone* (1920), won critical praise, especially for its realistic portrayal of English village life. The reviewer for *The New York Times Book Review* (8 February 1920) noted that the novel showed "insight and an appreciation of human vagaries. Moreover, it possesses that illusive, unanalyzable quality we call distinction."

Although her writing flourished, all was not well between Scott and Scottie. The couple divorced just one year after Scottie's return home from the war. That same year Scott met Arthur Lynch, the man who became her chief source of emotional support and professional encouragement for the remaining fourteen years of her life.

Lynch was a dilettante who not only served in Irish and British armies but also served time in prison after his arrest for high treason for his activities in the Boer War. A medical doctor trained in Paris and London, Lynch was also a member of Parliament for West Clare and Galway, an electrical engineer, and—most important to Scott—the author of more than twenty-five books. Scott hoped to learn from Lynch how to negotiate a lecture circuit in the United States.

While Scott continued working with the To-Morrow Club, she was reminded of its importance and necessity, especially for fledgling writers. Many writers and journalists from Europe and the United States arrived in London, armed with letters of introduction and aspirations of meeting Scott, whose influence seemed to open doors for novice writers. Marjorie Watts, Scott's daughter, recalls, "In her circle she was judged a serious writer, a woman of letters, with something of value to contribute to the literary scene.... Her house was the centre of a fairly wide group of representatives of all ... branches of writing—editors, sub-editors, publishers, newspaper proprietors or columnists, literary agents, translators, as well as the 'real' writers—novelists, poets, playwrights, historians."

The To-Morrow Club flourished, in 1921 becoming a new organization, PEN (Poets, Playwrights, Essayists, Editors, Novelists). Scott explained her vision for this international group: "the idea is more to draw the nations together—a United States of Europe and America in literature.... I want centres in Paris, New York...." The foundation dinner for PEN was held on 5 October 1921. Forty-four writers and journalists attended and by the evening's end all were PEN members. Galsworthy was elected PEN's first president, and he served in this capacity until 1933. Under Scott's leadership, PEN continued to grow over the next several years.

Throughout the many years during which Scott worked for the organization, she also continued writing and publishing books. Several of the novels in the "Cornish Tales" earned critical notice. A reviewer for *The New York Times Book Review* (28 May 1922) said of *The Haunting*, "Here is an unusually well written story of abundant contrasts, both effective and deeply interesting."

Scott's most complex and best volume of poetry is *Bitter Herbs* (1923). Some poems reek of hopelessness; other poems seethe in anger; while still other poems seem almost to delight in exposing cruel betrayals in love. In "The Knife Grinder," a jealous husband returns home and questions his wife's faithfulness: "Mud on your skirts? / Must have gone far, my Lovely, must be tired, / Tired of the streets." He continues:

> You are all mine!
> A kiss,
> I had your first—last—
> Your bosom swells with this last beat of love!
> "Last, wanton—for we fix it there,
> The knife and I."

The poem becomes more troubling by degrees until the husband's jealous rage erupts into murder. What seems at first to be a couple who are working hard to eke out a living turns into a powerful game of cat and mouse, controller and victim. The reviewer in *The New York Times Book Review* (22 July 1923) commented, "Mrs. Dawson-Scott ... has the dramatic succinctness of Browning; but she is frequently a symbolist in a situation where Browning's method would be a meticulously simulated realism. And this is one of the extraordinary features of her poetry—that symbols are given a reality, that reality is adequately expressed by symbols." Certainly the drama of the situation between husband and wife in "The Knife Grinder" is heightened by the symbolism of the knife as power, especially male power.

The poem "Merry-Begot" is as dramatic as "The Knife-Grinder," but this time the betrayed female exacts revenge. When the wellborn father of her illegitimate child refuses to acknowledge his child, the speaker of this poem becomes enraged. Under cover of night, she steals to the house and levies this curse: "The bat shall heir / Your house of many lights, the lizard slip / Between the stones; / And you shall be / A name / Writ on a stone in the church acre, / Writ at end / Of a long line." The poem abounds in irony: she has borne his child, the "heir," but he refuses to acknowledge his son. Instead, he has married a woman who can produce only money.

Toward the end of her life, Scott became interested in spiritualism and published several books dealing with the supernatural, specifically with communicating with the dead. In *Is This Wilson?* (1929), Scott recounts messages she allegedly "received" from the late United States president Woodrow Wilson. While many viewed such "conversations" with skepticism, Scott's reputation as an author of some distinction worked to her advantage when it came to publishing her "spiritual" works, which were received positively. She followed *Is This Wilson?* with *The Guide to Psychic Knowledge* (1932), three volumes of questions and answers about the afterlife.

The New York Times published Catharine Amy Dawson Scott's obituary on 7 November 1934, the day after she died in London. Although she is identified as a "poet and novelist," and many of her literary and other accomplishments are mentioned, the obituary omits any reference to PEN.

Little published information is available on Catharine Amy Dawson Scott, save a few cursory lines in various bibliographic reference works. In 1987 Watts disregarded her mother's wish that a biography should never be written about her and wrote *Mrs. Sappho: The Life of C. A. Dawson Scott, Mother of International P. E. N.* The title not only pays homage to what may be the strongest aspect of Catharine Amy Dawson Scott's work–her poetry–but also to the issues of women's rights, a current that runs through nearly all of her published works.

Biography:

Marjorie Watts, *Mrs. Sappho: The Life of C. A. Dawson Scott, Mother of International P. E. N.* (London: Duckworth, 1987).

Dora Sigerson Shorter
(16 August 1866 – 6 January 1918)

Deborah A. Logan
Western Kentucky University

BOOKS: *Verses* (London: Elliot Stock, 1893);

The Fairy Changeling and Other Poems (London & New York: John Lane, Bodley Head, 1898);

Ballads and Poems (London: James Bowden, 1899);

My Lady's Slipper, and Other Verses (New York: Dodd, Mead, 1899);

The Father Confessor, Stories of Danger and Death (London & New York: Ward, Lock, 1900);

The Woman Who Went to Hell, and Other Ballads and Lyrics (London: De la More, 1902);

As the Sparks Fly Upward (London: Moring, 1903);

The Country-House Party (London: Hodder & Stoughton, 1905);

The Story and Song of Black Roderick (London: Moring, 1906);

The Collected Poems of Dora Sigerson Shorter (London: Hodder & Stoughton, 1907);

Through Wintry Terrors (London: Cassell, 1907);

The Troubadour and Other Poems (London: Hodder & Stoughton, 1910);

New Poems (Dublin & London: Maunsel, 1912);

Do-Well and Do-Little, A Fairy Tale (London: Cassell, 1913);

Madge Linsey and Other Poems (Dublin & London: Maunsel, 1913);

Comfort the Women. A Prayer in Time of War (London: Privately printed, 1915);

Love of Ireland: Poems and Ballads (Dublin & London: Maunsel, 1916);

An Old Proverb (London: Privately printed, 1916);

Poems of the Irish Rebellion (Edinburgh: Constable, 1916);

Kittie's Toys (Dublin: Gaelic Press, 1917);

The Sad Years (London: Constable, 1918);

A Legend of Glendalough, and Other Ballads (Dublin & London: Maunsel, 1919);

Sixteen Dead Men and Other Poems of Easter Week (New York: Kennerley, 1919); republished as *The Tricolour: Poems of the Irish Revolution* (Dublin: Maunsel & Roberts, 1922);

Dora Sigerson Shorter (courtesy of The Lilly Library, Indiana University)

A Dull Day in London, and Other Sketches (London: Eveleigh Nash, 1920);

New Poems (Dublin & London: Maunsel & Roberts, 1921);

Dora Sigerson Shorter, *The Augustan Books of Poetry* (London: Benn, 1926).

Dora Sigerson Shorter was born in Dublin on 16 August 1866. The eldest daughter of George Sigerson, a surgeon and Gaelic scholar, and Hester Varian Sigerson, a writer, Dora was educated at home in an environment that instilled in her the Republican values that later characterized her poetry. The

Sigerson home was a center for artistic and political culture in Dublin, and her parents' interests thus led to Dora's involvement with the Pan Celtic society in 1888 and to her support of controversial Charles Parnell, who led the fight for Irish home rule in the late nineteenth century.

Another significant influence on Sigerson's early life was William Butler Yeats, a writer whose role in the Irish Literary Renaissance of the period continued to inspire her long after she left Ireland. As a mentor and a colleague, Yeats shared with Sigerson a love for their impoverished and strife-torn country, a desire to recover traditional Celtic culture as a body of lore worthy of artistic legitimation, and a determination to fight for Irish independence through poetic eulogies to the growing list of patriots willing to die for the Irish cause.

What little information is available about Sigerson's life generally includes some reference to her legendary beauty. Only her friend Katharine Tynan is willing to qualify that characterization: "She was full of the *joie de vivre,* despite the hint of tragedy in her beauty." Sigerson's fame, however, rests more with her fiction and poetry than with her appearance. According to her critics, in both fine (she was a skilled painter and sculptor) and literary arts her passion and intensity of expression more than compensated for her lack of formal training. As precocious intellectually as she was politically and artistically, Sigerson's girlhood literary apprenticeship included contributions to the Catholic *Irish Monthly.* Two years after the publication of her first volume of poetry, *Verses* (1893), Sigerson married Clement Shorter, editor of the *Illustrated London News,* and moved to England. By all accounts, the marriage was compatible, and the writer's literary circle expanded to include such figures as Thomas Hardy, A. C. Swinburne, and George Meredith. Shorter's career as a writer was a remarkably prolific one. Yet, the pain of leaving the beloved land of her birth and witnessing from a distance its escalating political conflicts was one she never overcame. As a result, much of her work thematically conveys her longing for a mythical Celtic twilight, the remoteness of which increased dramatically with each Irish freedom fighter's death.

Another key figure in Shorter's poetic development was John O'Leary, a critic who early recognized that the writer's fine poetic abilities suffered from a lack of focus and discipline. O'Leary introduced her to Thomas Percy's *Reliques of Ancient English Poetry* (1765), an influential work on ballads, an ancient style with a combination of lyricism and form that suited Shorter's talent and imagination. More importantly, the association of ballads with folklore, mysticism, and mythology provided the writer with a medium appropriate for the Gaelic themes central to her poetry. Designed to recover Celtic tradition while recording the development of modern Ireland, Shorter's lays and ballads are as timely in their way as her poems eulogizing the Irish patriots massacred in 1916 are in theirs. Although her "undisciplined" style has been compared with that of the young Robert Browning, her simplicity with Oliver Goldsmith, her naiveté with Samuel Taylor Coleridge, and her natural imagery with William Wordsworth, Shorter's poetry is better assessed in terms of her ability to synthesize Celtic, Romantic, and Victorian influences in a modernist perspective. For all her links with a mythical past, Shorter's political sensibility unmistakably casts her as a poet of the modern age.

Shorter's primary themes—Celtic lore, family and gender issues, and Irish politics—are apparent from her first volume of poetry, *Verses* (1893). "The Changeling" depicts a popular folk image in which the narrator's infant has been stolen by fairies who leave a spiritless substitute—bearing a physical resemblance only—in its place. The mother—whose "Future lay cradled asleep" while she prayed that her child would live a full and honorable life under Heaven's protection—finds her reverence insufficient to preserve the child from the fairies who "leave me this changeling child, / Who looked on my tears with a laugh, / And mocked at my prayers." In its demonstration of the conflicts between the paganism of mythology and Shorter's own Catholicism, this early poem evidences modern angst fostered by a worldview in which spirituality grew increasingly remote and difficult to sustain.

Women's mistreatment by careless lovers is another early theme more fully developed later in the poet's lays and ballads. "Man's Discontent" traces the affairs of a man who loves, then leaves, a young girl (budding Spring), a young woman (blooming Summer), a mature woman (colorful Autumn), and a wise, experienced Winter. Perennially irresponsible—each time he "stayed till I grew weary—man's discontent, I ween," careless of the broken hearts he leaves in his wake, he ends life alone, realizing too late how thoughtlessly he has cast aside the precious gift of love: "Thus, having all, I lost all, ere the Winter days had fled."

Similarly, in "A Fairy Prince" Prince Charming promises fairyland but delivers weeds "rank where flowers had been": now, his lover's dreams broken, "Nought but an open grave appears." The theme of disappointed love enacted in "The Awakening," which features a woman whose attempts to remake herself intellectually and physically to please her lover's tastes leave her disillusioned, is more archetypally cast in "Sorrow": "Into my heart, Sorrow, you found a way; / . . . I hushed you till I crushed you / Into rest for all your thorns."

As its title suggests, *The Fairy Changeling and Other Poems* (1898) continues the mythological device with the addition of Gaelic influences through such poems as "Cean Duv Deelish," "Banagher Rhue," and "Death of Gormlaith." Featuring priests and black hounds, spinsters and young maids, this volume treats both pagan holidays, such as "All Hallow's Eve," and the Christmas season in "The Skeleton in the Cupboard." The latter poem is notable for its direct appeal to putting aside family differences and social hypocrisies, "Just this one day in all the year": "No bitter words, no frowning brow, / Disturb the Christmas festal, now / The skeleton's behind the door." Yet, in the end, ". . . useless / Is this pretence of happiness; / The skeleton taps on the door." Published several years after her marriage to Shorter, the author's name is listed as Dora Shorter, beneath which in parentheses is Mrs. Clement Shorter. In subsequent volumes, the poet's name is variously listed as "Dora Sigerson," "Dora Sigerson Shorter," "Mrs. Dora Sigerson Shorter," and "Mrs. Clement Shorter."

The two volumes published in 1899, *Ballads and Poems* (London) and *My Lady's Slipper, and Other Verses* (New York), comprise primarily poems from earlier works compiled into new editions. Prominent imagery in both volumes includes banshees, witches, "Ave Maria," bridals, and roses, which are alternately depicted as faded, blooming, small, white, broken, and wayward.

Also introduced is another Shorter quality—her affinity for animals. A popular anecdote recalls Shorter's girlhood fame resulting from her habit of rescuing stray animals in Dublin and finding homes for them. Thomas Hardy's introduction to her *A Dull Day in London* (1920), a collection of short stories employing animal motifs, observes that her "sympathy with the lower animal creation . . . seems to embrace all animate and inanimate nature." In "A Cry in the World" the "kine," or cattle, cry "piteously" because "Man, man has bereft us and taken our young ones from us," a cry echoed by birds—man has "stolen my nestlings from me"—and sea creatures, ending, significantly, with the piteous weeping of the woman who is mother to the "king of the world." Like the beasts of the field with whom Christ is associated, Mary, too, is deprived of her offspring by the greed and duplicity of man.

"False Dearbhorgil" depicts an Anglo-Norman conflict surrounding a princess whose legendary beauty and amours are reminiscent of those of Helen of Troy. Characterized, like much of Shorter's poetry, as a Gothic romance, this narrative poem—complete with marginal prose glosses—recalls Coleridge's "The Rime of the Ancient Mariner." Also noteworthy in this volume is "The Me Within Thee Blind!" a lengthy narrative about a man who marries a young convent-raised girl. Recalling the issues of faith and man's inhumanity to woman Shorter raises elsewhere, the husband exposes his fragile bride to the harshness of the world. When her love for him dies along with their only child, he seeks her amid scenes of poverty and degradation, locating her at last on her deathbed back in the convent. The wife, who represents the difficulty of maintaining faith—whether in self, in love for another, or in God—in a faithless world, envisions the eternal rest promised to loyal Christians: "Death shall not conquer me, I will not die." But unwilling to simplify these questions for readers in an age of anxiety, Shorter refuses to provide a satisfactory ending: "In my grief," concludes the faithless narrator, "I go from church to church, from clime to clime, / A lone man, haunted by his unbelief."

Although "The Woman Who Went to Hell. An Irish Legend" was published earlier, this unusual poem merited its own slim volume in 1902. The ballad begins with a wedding and the weeping confession of the groom's mother that she had inadvertently made a pact with Satan, who vowed to claim her son's soul on his wedding day. When Satan arrives at Dermod's wedding, the bride, in her unconditional love, offers to serve in Hell for seven years to win back her husband's soul:

> Seven long years did she serve him true
> By the blazing gates of hell,
> And on every soul that entered in
> The tears of her sorrow fell.

Intrigued by her inexhaustible compassion, Satan tricks her into service for another seven years by promising that, when she leaves, she may take with her as many souls as she can carry. She fulfills his conditions, staggering under the immense weight as she attempts to leave Hell, waylaid by Satan in the guise first of the Virgin Mary, then of St. Michael. But in the third visitation, she unhesitatingly discerns the divine from the damned—this time, in no guise, but as

> a Man with face so fair:
> She knelt her down at his wounded feet,
> and she laid her burden there.

The bride then falls asleep for seven days while Christ finishes the harrowing of Hell she began, only to awaken at home in time to witness the wedding of her beloved to a young, fair woman. Fourteen years and seven days in Hell have turned her hair white; but in a moment of epiphany worthy of the occasion, the groom recognizes his true bride and understands how she has suffered for his sake. Unlike Shorter's less-scrupulous

Frontispiece and title page for Shorter's second volume of poetry

male characters, this one rejects the fair young girl in favor of the haggard old woman:

> "I will not marry the fair young girl,
> No woman I wed but this,
> The sweet white rose of her cheek," said he,
> "Shall redden beneath my kiss."

Shorter's novel recasting of the biblical Jacob and Rachel story—with gender roles reversed; of the Virgin Mary's pact with God, the mother's pact with the Devil; of the "true" bride's associations with Christ the redeemer, and of Satan, rather than God, exacting service—is Dantesque in its blending of Catholicism with elements of Celtic myth. The conclusion of the poem, with its recognition of the depth of woman's loyalty matched, although just barely, by Dermod's ethical behavior toward his true wife, is uncharacteristic of the theme of faithlessness underlying Shorter's poetry and prose. On the other hand, in Shorter's world only women, not men, are willing to go to Hell and back for lovers, who are quick to find replacements during their absence.

Also meriting its own volume is "The Story and Song of Black Roderick" (1906). Featuring a distinctive border engraving on each page—symbolic of a more luxurious era in publishing history, this work offers a prose narrative that frequently shifts to the more lyrical ballad form, "lest thou [readers] grow weary of my prose." Although similar to "The Woman Who Went to Hell" in theme and plot, the focus, as the title indicates, is more on the man who is redeemed by woman's faith than on the redeemer herself. The narrator's opening lines—"This is the story of Black Earl Roderick, the story and the song of his pride and of his humbling; of the bitterness of his heart, and of the love that came to it at last; of his threatened destruction, and the strange and wonderful way of his salvation"—demonstrate the blending in this tale of Arthurian conventions and Celtic superstition with the Christian idea of salvation.

A fierce and implacable warrior, Roderick grudgingly agrees to marry the daughter of an enemy clan leader solely to promote peace among the warring clans. He takes his bride-in-name-only back to his castle and shuns her; she grows pale and ill under his mistreatment, wandering the moors alone in despair. Finding her dead of grief, a remorseful Roderick realizes too late that the faith and love the bride represents are lost to him forever. One of most intriguing features of this tale is its vivid rendering of the bride's reactions to her physical death and to her ascension to heaven, where, like Dante Gabriel Rossetti's "Blessed Damozel," she went "to the golden bar of heaven, and, leaning forth, looked down upon the earth." Her compassion for the man who has wronged her is such that she petitions Mary, Christ, and God to let her leave Heaven. She then strives with the Nameless One for Roderick's soul—serving two seven-year terms in Hell before leaving and also performing a Christ-like harrowing of Hell. Despite its obvious similarities to "The Woman Who Went to Hell," the innovativeness of "Black Roderick" resides in its effective interplays between prose (story) and poetry (song), Christian and pagan, and man's faithlessness and woman's sacrifice.

Shorter's most comprehensive volume of poems is *The Collected Poems* (1907). George Meredith's introduction suggests that the poet's work should be read with "some consideration of the Celtic mind" while taking into account Shorter's preference for ballads, "which are rather in disfavour now." Meredith defines "the Celtic mind" as "fantastical, remote, divorced from reality"; yet, he reminds readers that although poetic symbolism "swallows Reality, . . . Reality is read through it." Shorter's Celtic mind, in other words, is as perfectly suited to poetic symbolism as her lyricism is to the musical demands of the ballad form. Meredith's focus on musicality—Swinburne, he writes, is an "unrivalled instrumentalist"—challenges critics who respond only to rigid metrics and stilted rhyme schemes, forgetting that the most ancient roots of poetry are more musical than mathematical. Shorter possesses "the art of compression and progression" and an intensity of imagination best expressed through verse in which lyricism is not sacrificed to form.

Along with many of the poems and themes already discussed, those in *The Collected Poems* range from the mythical to the modern. "Jeanne Bras" addresses a Victorian issue. A woman's sleep is disturbed by a desperate knocking and calling at her door. Her daughter pleads for protection from wind and rain, but Jeanne cruelly rejects her child—"I had a child, but she left me long ago. . . . The child I bore I shall curse with dying breath." As the narrative unfolds, the women's dialogue reveals that the daughter is an unmarried mother returning home in disgrace, seeking sanctuary with her mother. The daughter begs,

> A priest! a priest, I pray you bring to me;
> Unchurched and unshriven am I. . . .
> . . . A priest! A priest! My little dying boy!
> Unchristened and unholy he lies.

But appeals neither to her maternalism nor to Christian compassion move Jeanne from her self-righteousness, and she goes back to bed; she finds both corpses on her doorstep the next morning. Shorter typically employs the themes of another era—here, the fallen woman—but also typically she adds an unconventional resolution. In this poem, Jeanne Bras is compelled to roam through sleepless nights, calling to the daughter and grandchild she has wronged, tormented by a guilt that will not be expiated: no rest, at night or in old age, is permitted her. Whatever the historical setting, the poet seems resigned to the inevitability that the most serious breaches of faith are often committed by those who are closest to one; yet, Shorter also exacts a degree of suffering from those whose hypocrisy has tragic consequences.

A conventional personification of Ireland, Kathleen ni Houlihan appears throughout Shorter's works in various guises—a queen, a lady, a peasant maid—and under several names. "Kathleen's Charity" depicts a beautiful young woman whose hard work, love for the world, and devotion to the sick, the old, the poor, and the orphaned compels her to give until there is nothing left to give but tears of compassion. Alternatively, "Lady Kathleen," recalling Alfred Tennyson's Mariana and the Lady of Shalott, is imprisoned in a tower where she waits for her absent lover, weeping and spinning "for love's sweet sake." Although compelled to remain in the tower in order to preserve her beauty, Kathleen decides that active love, rather than passive waiting, is what makes a woman beautiful; therefore, she leaves to seek her lover. Much to the fairies' amusement, the spell breaks: Kathleen is transformed into an old woman and, as a result, rejected by her lover. The narrative concludes,

> But ah, for woman whose heart is strong,
> To weary never and love too long!
> And what is life to a heart denied?
> Fair Lady Kathleen drooped and died.

But this poem is no conventional romance; understood in terms of its history, its Celtic roots, and its struggle for independence in the modern world, Ireland—or Lady Kathleen—grows tired of waiting for unrequited love, for unfulfilled promises, for permission to leave her cultural prison and assume her rightful place in the world. But in Shorter's view, Irish independence means more than mere freedom from English rule; her poems can hardly be characterized as invectives against British imperialism. Instead, like others associated with the Irish Literary Renaissance, Shorter favors an approach to independence that works from within, one that begins by honoring that which is most native to this culture—Gaelicism, for example—and by reclaiming that which has been lost through generations of political oppression. Kathleen's lover is the Irish people, who have left her alone so long they no longer recognize her, who have forgotten her worth, and who reject her in her shabbiness in favor of less substantial values. The fairies, then, represent British rule, which sees in Kathleen's rejection by her own kind the cultural divisiveness essential to maintaining political oppression. Seen through the lens of this conflict, Shorter's lays and ballads assume deeper relevance than innocuous romances: for her, the betrayal of the legacy of Ireland and the failure to fight for its recovery is the most insidious faithlessness of all.

Another sort of cultural validation is revealed in "The Flight of the Wild Geese," in which the birds represent freedom fighters—"Wrapt in the darkness of the night, / Gathering in silence on the shore" pursued by wolfhounds. Each howl of the hounds is answered by the banshee's screams—traditionally heralding death—as these fugitive patriots become exiles from the land for which they are pledged to die: "Wild geese with fierce eyes, deathless hope in your hearts, / Stretching your strong white wings eager for your flight."

Gender issues are also more than a literary device for Shorter, and some poems convey her struggle to free herself from the Victorian constraints dictating women's lives well into the twentieth century. The narrator of "A Vagrant Heart" rails against a fate resulting solely from her gender:

O to be a woman! to be left to pique and pine,
When the winds are out and calling to this vagrant heart of mine.
. . . .
There is danger on the waters—there is joy where dangers be—
Alas! to be a woman and the nomad's heart in me.

But instead of danger and adventure, she is offered a cloth to sew and "little fashions" and "petty passions" about which to "chatter, chatter, chatter." Though Shorter was at the forefront of London's literary set, "The Vagrant Heart" suggests the poet's frustration with English social propriety, which compelled her to conform with empty social rituals as the price of respectability.

Although many of Shorter's themes are laced with an existential despair about the darker side of human existence—unanswered questions, philosophical conundrums, and religious doubt—her poems also reflect a psychological resiliency, implying that, even in the face of the greatest hopelessness, for her giving up is never an option. "The Lone of Soul," for example, asserts that "The world has many lovers," but she loves best he who

stands alone
Torn by the passions of his own strange heart,
Stoned by continual wreckage of his dreams,
He in the crowd for ever is apart.

On a more transcendent note, "I Am The World" acknowledges the tragedies and challenges of the human condition while balancing individual responsibility with acceptance of one's fate. "I am the world," the narrator asserts, "I am the dawn . . . the changing colours of the tree . . . the melancholy of the sea: / I am the world." Conveying a remarkable identification of self with the Divine, the poet asks, "Am I not one with all the things that be? . . . All that my ears can hear, or eyes can see." But this identification is not based on an egoism implied by the insistent "I am": rather, it is grounded in an interconnectedness with the natural world and in its tradition as a cross-cultural referent to God. At death,

I shall arise, and like a shooting star
Slip from my place;
So lingering see the old world from afar
Revolve in space.
And know more things than all the wise may know
Till all be done;
Till One shall come who, breathing on the stars,
Blows out the sun.

Children's roles in these profound issues evoke varying responses in the poet. The father in "The Heritage" seeks to comfort his weeping infant by pointing out all the remarkable gifts of nature that comprise his human birthright. Ending with an appeal to "God's high paradise" as the reward at life's conclusion, "he sought the skies, / And there despairing saw—unnumbered worlds." The conflict between the celebration of life in this poem and the despair engendered by the incomprehensible vastness of creation suggests that comfort, if found at all, is as illusory and fantastic as the bedtime stories told to weeping children.

"The Enemies," the final work in *The Collected Poems,* employs one of Shorter's favorite images, birds, as a symbol for a free spirit diminished by life's difficulties. "I could have sung as sweet as any lark," but the strifes of living, "a grey and stinging throng, . . . / Did blind my eyes and hush my song in tears. . . . They sting my soul unto its overthrow." To many of her contemporaries, these words, placed so strategically at the conclusion of a volume in which she clearly did sing "as sweet as any lark," seemed prophetic.

Madge Linsey and Other Poems (1913) more fully develops the poet's concern with gender inequities expressed in "The Vagrant Heart." The title character of "The Sister" questions a sailor, a hunter, and a soldier about the joys of their occupations, which are forbidden to her as a woman. Their response is less than encouraging:

> "Then seek some solitary place beneath a cyprus tree,
> And dig a grave both wide and long, O! dig it wide and deep
> To hold a woman's restless heart and hush her soul to sleep."

"The Two Laws" exposes the inequities of a social code based on a sexual double standard—one protecting the squire's son and the other condemning the peasant-serving maid. After their illicit union, he rides off in search of more adventure, while she "crouched" in the streets, "Thrust out from her father's door" like the daughter of Jeanne Bras. He marries a "lady of high degree" and kisses his son and legitimate heir; but the fallen woman "had no smile for the little babe / Who lay by her side so cold." Although theirs is the prior claim, this mother and child are permanent outcasts according to society's inequitable moral code.

The title poem of the volume, "Madge Linsey, or the Three Souls," also depicts a fallen woman, although she is less victim than aggressor. Young and strong, Madge's beauty inspires men's lust and women's derision. She lacks both a mother "to point her path softly" and a sister for companionship. Left alone with a cruel father, Madge's environment conspires to turn her into a fallen woman:

> Who taught her right or wrong? See there her teacher grows—
> Switch of the hazel tree, branch of the thorn.
> Power of her father's arm full of wrath falling sore
> Bruising the child's young soul tenderly born.

Loved by two men—Ben, who prays for her, and John, who strives to win her from her destructive path—Madge leaves her village after being "left forlorn." Hardened by communal rejection and her father's abuse, she is indifferent to John's devotion to her:

> Into the whirling pool followed he after her,
> Drank glass for glass with her, shared sin for sin,
> Fought for her, slaved for her, went down to hell for her.
> There in its agonies strove he to win.

Years later, Ben—still a prudent bachelor—brings his Thanksgiving offering of food to the church altar and is met there by John with his unique offering—Madge Linsey's soul: "Here is my offering, here my good harvesting, / Lord! I have brought it thee, safe from the snare." Ben in his sanctimonious cowardice fails to understand the magnitude of the events being enacted; pitying John, he offers to pray for him, too, an offer that John rejects:

> "Into the depth I went," cried John the gardener, . . .
> Pawned my own soul her faint spirit to win.
> Now I but bear her up, up from the whirling pool
> Over the brim of it to Heaven's gate,
> Hold to her, cling to her, ere I slip back again,
> Pray for her wounded soul early and late."

Although "Madge Linsey" is notable for reversing the genders of worthy and unworthy lovers of Shorter's earlier poems, the poem also recalls the issues of religious hypocrisy raised by "Jeanne Bras." John sacrifices his life and his afterlife to save the soul of a woman of "faint spirit"; yet, no heavenly reward is forthcoming for his sacrifice. Nor is Ben moved by the spirit of compassion any more than he has been touched by a genuine engagement with life; in love and death, he stands aloof in his untested faith. The despair Shorter conveys in this poem demonstrates that the real danger of the "grey and stinging throng" resides in its cumulative effects and in the doubts engendered by God's seeming indifference to human effort.

Death is a primary theme in this volume. In "The West Wind" the "east is as a voice / That calls me from my sleeping," a voice of divine spirit summoning her to another realm. In contrast, the west wind is "full of ghostly laughter . . . dim shades and shadows . . . phantom sighing; / Where lost dear voices speak, / To hurt me with their crying." Similarly, the changing seasons of "Spring and Autumn" feature a narrator, "lone" and "weary," waiting in the churchyard "Where sleep my dead . . . / I hear a voice that calls, 'Come to us.'"

Shorter responds to the shattering events of World War I in "An Old Proverb." Privately printed in a limited edition, the poem's harsh imagery, short, choppy lines, and brittle diction suggest the modern enactment of an ancient theme of war: "It will be all the same in a Thousand Years." The poet's lifelong grappling to reconcile the realities of life with abstract philosophical issues is here brought to focus on "Payment of blood and tears, / Horrors we dare not name." The cyclical pattern of war throughout human history emphasizes that nothing has been learned from the troubled past of the world:

> What is the value then
> To all those sleeping men?

It will be all the same,
Passion and grief and blame,
This in the years to be,
My God, the tragedy!

But for Shorter, the tragedies of World War I were overshadowed by those occurring in Ireland, and the volume inspired by the execution of Irish rebels during Easter week, 1916, serves as the crowning and final poetic achievement of her life. Published in New York in 1919 as *Sixteen Dead Men and Other Poems of Easter Week* and in Dublin in 1922 as *The Tricolour: Poems of the Irish Revolution*, this collection is presented, according to the editor, as "a sacred obligation to one who broke her heart over Ireland." Rightly anticipating her impending death, Shorter spent the final weeks of her life composing a dedication to the "tricolour" and arranging the poems for printing. Shorter's final legacy to Ireland dedicates the work of her life to the land she never left in spirit. All profits from this and earlier writings were to support the construction of a monument she herself designed and sculpted to mark the graves of the men killed at the Easter massacre.

"The Tricolour," a prose introduction to this collection, deals less with the flag of a nation than with a set of values—"Labour," "Idealism," and "Peace"—each "shot down" along with the men representing the values. The Easter of 1916 was one of death, not resurrection, prompting Shorter to make a powerful analogy with Christ:

> Who will take it upon himself to crucify Labour, since Christ was the Son of a carpenter; Idealism, for Christ was an idealist; Peace, for did not Christ our Lord say "Blessed are the peace-makers, for they shall be called the children of God?"

The appeal to Christian values claimed by both sides in this struggle reinforces the religious underpinnings of a conflict still unresolved nearly a century after Shorter's death. But an even more powerful image for readers of her poetry is that of an old woman kneeling in Dublin's war-torn "danger zone," praying over her rosary beads for a victorious revolution. Like Kathleen ni Houlihan, she comes "out of poverty and misery from some dark corner of the slums," a woman "without fear of death, who mourned for nobody, for whom nobody would mourn." Like Shorter's many depictions of Kathleen, the woman is transformed by this act from an aged crone to one "beautiful in the tricolour of faith, hope, and love." That the woman lay dead only hours later still clutching her rosary signifies not failure but a "brave, unconquered heart."

Kathleen is, of course, a primary theme in *The Tricolour*; she is an ancient symbol brought insistently into

SIXTEEN DEAD MEN
AND OTHER POEMS OF EASTER WEEK

BY

DORA SIGERSON SHORTER

NEW YORK
MITCHELL KENNERLEY
MCMXIX

Title page for Shorter's volume commemorating the Irish rebels who were executed by the British after the Easter Rising in Dublin in 1916

the modern age by the increasing mobilization of freedom fighters. Dublin's burning ruins become a "Sacred Fire" to "make thee warm once more, Kathleen, to bid thee live again." "They Did Not See Thy Face" is about those unwilling to fight for Kathleen, a true glimpse of whom prevents one from doing less than dying for love of her. As revolutionary fervor grows, Kathleen in "The Queen" assumes her rightful role: "Out through the ruins of her home, she walked as would a queen. / Ni Houlihan, Ni Houlihan, she came a splendid queen."

Juxtaposed with the mystical tradition surrounding Kathleen are the poems "Sixteen Dead Men," "Conscription," "A Catholic to His Ulster Brother," "The Young Volunteer," "The Prisoner," "The Story Without End," and "The Dead Soldier." The sharpening edge of revolutionary excitement—in the poet's terms, a resurrection growing out of the Easter week deaths—prompts the return from exile of "The Wild Geese" of earlier poems, while "Ourselves Alone" has become better known as *Sinn Fein Amhain*.

Although Shorter's political commentary focused on celebrating Irish Nationalism, rarely on criticizing the British, "Empire Building" is unmistakably anti-British in sentiment, only thinly disguising the two nations as "John" and "Kate": "Somehow I never liked you, John, your ways were crude: / Your smile was pharisaical, your manners rude." More boldly, the British presence in Ireland amounts to rape: John "loved to make a spectacle of her, / Because she never liked you, John, since you / To her sweet garden forced your rough way through." The fanciful nursery rhyme "Kittie's Toys" offers a more taunting example: "When Johnny gets a whacking, a whacking, a whacking, / When Johnny gets a whacking, I think he'll let me be."

A romantic legend worthy of Shorter's poetic themes surrounds accounts of her final illness and rapid decline. The popular idea that the events and aftermath of Easter 1916 broke her heart and caused her death seems overwrought; yet, according to Tynan, who contributed "Dora Sigerson: A Tribute and Some Memories" to Shorter's *The Sad Years* (1918), the poet herself attributed her end "to her intense and isolated suffering over the events following Easter week, 1916, in Dublin. . . . She broke her heart over it all; and so she died, as she would have chosen to die, for love of the Dark Rosaleen." Perhaps Shorter's frustration over the passive role assigned to her as a woman manifests itself in the idea that her death vicariously contributed to the cause of Irish freedom. But, fortunately for literary history, Shorter was no Maud Gonne; and her finest dedication to "the Dark Rosaleen," *The Tricolour,* speaks enduringly and compellingly of the struggle that continues long after her death.

References:

Evelyn A. Hanley, "Dora Sigerson Shorter: Late Victorian Romantic," *Victorian Poetry,* 3 (1965): 223–234;

In Memoriam Dora Sigerson (N.p.: Privately printed, 1923);

William Butler Yeats, *Collected Letters,* volume 1, *1865–1895,* edited by John Kelley and Eric Domville (Oxford: Clarendon Press, 1986).

Papers:

The Manuscript Department of the library at Trinity College, Dublin, holds notebooks, manuscripts, and letters in the Papers of Dora Sigerson Shorter. Letters can also be found at the National Library of Ireland, including those to T. Dawson and Mary Thompson.

Flora Thompson

(5 December 1876 – 21 May 1947)

John Ferns
McMaster University

BOOKS: *Bog-Myrtle and Peat* (London: Philip Allan, 1921);

Guide to Liphook, by Thompson and others (Liphook, 1925);

Lark Rise (London & New York: Oxford University Press, 1939);

Over to Candleford (London & New York: Oxford University Press, 1941);

Candleford Green (London & New York: Oxford University Press, 1943);

Lark Rise To Candleford: A Trilogy (London & New York: Oxford University Press, 1945);

Still Glides the Stream (London & New York: Oxford University Press, 1948);

A Country Calendar and Other Writings, edited by Margaret Lane (Oxford & New York: Oxford University Press, 1979); republished in part as *Heatherley* (Oxford: Clio Press, 1991);

The Peverel Papers: A Yearbook of the Countryside, edited by Julian Shuckburgh (London, Melbourne, Auckland & Johannesburg: Century, 1986);

The Lark Rise Recipe Book, compiled by Mary Norwak (Devizes: Selecta, 1986).

The Edwardian-Georgian writer Flora Thompson is much better known as a chronicler of rural life than she is as a poet. Her only volume of poetry, *Bog-Myrtle and Peat* (1921), brought her brief renown, but her success as a poet was not sustained. Instead, she developed her prose writing about rural life, enjoying considerable success with the trilogy *Lark Rise To Candleford* (1939–1943) in the last years of her life.

Flora Jane Timms was born at Juniper Hill (called Lark Rise in *Lark Rise To Candleford*), Oxfordshire, on 5 December 1876 to Albert and Emma (Dibber) Timms. A stonemason, who had had aspirations to become a sculptor, Albert Timms was originally from Oxford, where his family had been publicans. Emma Timms was a local woman who had been a nursemaid. Their lives are sensitively described in *Lark Rise* (1939), the first volume of the trilogy, in

Flora Thompson

which Flora appears as Laura. The sibling to whom Flora felt closest, her brother Edwin (Edmund in *Lark Rise*), was born in 1878.

Flora Timms began school in Cottisford, Oxfordshire, in 1880 and started work in the post office at Fringford (Candleford Green in her trilogy) in 1891 at the age of fourteen. Sometime after the celebrations of Queen Victoria's Diamond Jubilee on 22 June 1897, Flora left Fringford for a temporary job elsewhere, possibly at Hatfield Peverel in Essex. In September 1898, at the age of twenty-one, she settled in Grayshott, Hampshire, and took a job in the post office. She later remembered seeing two well-known local residents, George Bernard Shaw and Sir Arthur Conan Doyle. At first she lodged with the postmaster and his family, the Chapmans, but Walter Chapman's strange behavior, including arguments with his wife and sneaking into Flora's bedroom at night on the pretext of fearing burglars, caused Flora to change her lodgings in March 1899. (About two years later Chapman murdered his wife.)

On 3 January 1903 Flora Timms married John Thompson, a fellow postal worker, at St. Mary's Church, Twickenham. They made their first home in Winton, a suburb of Bournemouth, where Flora Thompson gave birth to their first two children: Winifred Grace "Diana" on 24 October 1903 and Henry Basil Thompson on 6 October 1909. Flora Thompson's first success as a writer came in February 1911, when she won a competition in *The Ladies Companion* for an essay on Jane Austen. She won another *Ladies Companion* competition in July of the same year with an essay on William Shakespeare's heroines, and in 1912 the magazine published her short story "The Toft Cup." Her first payment for her writing was from *The Literary Monthly* for a critical essay on Dr. Ronald Campbell Macfie's ode on the sinking of the *Titanic*. Macfie visited Thompson, and they began a literary correspondence that continued until Macfie's death in 1931. He likely encouraged her to write poetry. In "To Ronald Campbell Macfie," the ten-line dedicatory poem in *Bog-Myrtle and Peat,* Thompson contrasts their respective poetic subjects. Macfie's are "the moors, the billowy seas, / Tall mountains and blue distances"; whereas,

> Mine is a cottage garden, set
> With marigold and mignonette,
> And all the wilding things that dare,
> Without a gardener's fostering care.
> Yet very well-content I rest
> In my obscure, sequestered nest;
> For from my cottage garden I
> Can see your cloud-peaks pierce the sky!

In a sense these lines define Thompson's position in poetry and prose. She wrote from a perspective of being in immediate and intimate contact with the natural world as well as the world that literature opens.

The first real tragedy in Thompson's life occurred in April 1916, when her brother Edwin was killed in action in Belgium during World War I. He had enlisted in the military during the Boer War (1899–1902), immigrated to Canada afterward, and was serving with a Canadian regiment at the time of his death. In August 1916 the Thompson family moved from Bournemouth to Liphook, close to Grayshott, where Flora Thompson had worked from 1898 to 1903, and their second son, Peter Redmond, was born in Liphook on 19 October 1918. She was delighted to return to the area she called "Heatherley" in her prose writings.

During this time she wrote many of her *Bog-Myrtle and Peat* poems and began writing prose works on nature and rural life. In 1920 Thompson wrote six stories for *The Catholic Fireside,* and in 1921 the same journal published her "Out of Doors," a series of nature articles about the New Forest. In that same year, with the publication of *Bog-Myrtle and Peat,* photographs of Thompson appeared on the back page of *The Daily Mirror* (London) for 3 March 1921, while a review-interview headed "Woman Of Letters. Village Postmistress Poetess. Her First Volume" appeared in the *Daily Chronicle* for 2 March. Calling Thompson's "slim volume" a work of "considerable merit," the reviewer-interviewer described Thompson as "a busy mother and housewife, as well as postmistress and poet," and also stated that "Mrs. Thompson's poems are well-written and show much promise. They bear traces of her having laboriously built up her technique upon the models of the greater poets. . . . The publishers had no idea as to what sort of person Mrs. Thompson was, and her work has been taken entirely on its merits." Thompson's own comments on her poetry writing in the interview offer a helpful introduction to *Bog-Myrtle and Peat.* "I started writing little things long ago," she told her interviewer, thus placing her poetic beginnings in the Victorian-Edwardian period. She also said that she found "time for a good deal of reading. Francis Thompson and Robert Browning are my favourites, but I don't like Swinburne"–literary tastes that establish her as an Edwardian-Georgian poet emerging from the Victorian poetic tradition.

In *The Englishman's Flora* (1955) Geoffrey Grigson described bog myrtle as "A useful as well as a sweetly resinous shrub. It provided faggots for the cloam oven, it kept fleas away, and highlanders slept on flea-proof beds of the Bog Myrtle, it was put to good use to repel moths, it gave a yellow dye; and more important, it was one of those plants which gave a flavouring to ale or beer before the popularisation of hops." He added that "Where it is locally dominant, for instance in parts of the wet, sandy basin of the New Forest, it sends out a delicious fragrance, especially in the flowering months of April and May." Thompson's title pairing of *Bog-Myrtle and Peat* suggests, at least, a color contrast and establishes imagistically the method of moving between love and nature that directs the book. *Bog-Myrtle and Peat* comprises twenty-four short poems typical of the Edwardian-Georgian mode of verse. They are traditional, not modernist, in form, and although a poem or two shows that Thompson was aware that World War I had taken place, the style of her poetry is not affected by the war, as was that of combatant poets such as Wilfred Owen.

Thompson's "Home Thoughts From The Desert" is reminiscent of Robert Browning's "Home Thoughts From Abroad" (1845). Her homesick speaker recalls her love of Hampshire from the perspective of "desert sand and heat," naming Hampshire places (Bratley Down, Dudman's Lea, and the Isle of Wight) in the first three of the four four-and-a-half-line stanzas. The final half-line refrain of these stanzas is "In Hampshire now!"–which changes in the final stanza to the nostalgic, "Ah, Hampshire dear!" The opening stanza best reveals Thompson's descriptive ability as an observer and evoker of nature:

> In Hampshire now, the woods are brown,
>   The heath-sands tawny-gold with rain;
> The mist lies blue on Bratley Down,
>   The firelight flecks the window pane–
>   In Hampshire now!

In the final stanza the speaker smells "the good smoke of burning peat" which draws in the title of the book. Another poem in the book, "When Swallows Fly," is reminiscent of "Home Thoughts From The Desert" since the speaker thinks of a lover who is away in a desert country, "midst the desert sands and heat."

"Flood Time" is filled with Edwardian-Georgian sentimentality. The opening seven-line stanza describes the setting honestly, without imposing human emotions on inanimate objects, but it ends ominously and with an echo of Samuel Taylor Coleridge's "The Rime of the Ancient Mariner" (1798):

> The floods are out at Welborough:
> The encroaching waters creep and moan;
> One gaunt old willow stands alone,
> Reflected in a steely glass;
> And lanes, where we were wont to pass,
> And fields where children used to play,
> Are water, water all the way.

The second ten-line stanza depicts a painful circumstance:

> The floods are out at Welborough:
> The house is hushed, the curtain drawn;
> The women watch from dusk to dawn,
> Because a little child has gone
> To walk the meadows all alone.
> I search alway, but find him not;
> Only a drowned forget-me-not
> Mimicks the azure of his eyes;
> Beyond the mist, a curlew cries
> O, tell me, sad bird, where he lies!

Thompson in her early twenties

By drawing an analogy between the drowned boy's eyes and then speaking to the curlew as if expecting a reply, the speaker employs pathetic fallacy in a manner that the modernists rejected. "Flood Time" is a poem in the Edwardian-Georgian mode rather than a modernist poem. Though her book was published just a year before T. S. Eliot's major modernist poem *The Waste Land* (1922), Thompson was working outside the literary circles in which Eliot and the other modernists were moving. As she told the interviewer for the *Daily Chronicle:* "No one helped me, and I have carried on my passion for literature quite alone. In fact, I sometimes think I must be the most isolated of women who write poetry."

"The Airman" is one of the few poems in the book that engages the modern world, which is, nonetheless, treated in an Edwardian-Georgian rather than a modernist poetic manner. Thus the flier "fluttering against the sky" is "Shooting vast spaces like a bolt of gold, / So swift, so bold. / 'Till men's cold hearts kindled to pride to view, / What Man dared do!"

"Heather" was written for Thompson's Grayshott friend Annie Symonds around 1899, not long after

Thompson had moved to the "Heatherley" area. Rather like the opening poem, in which Thompson contrasts Macfie's preferences to her own, this poem seems to contrast Thompson's natural preference to Symonds's in two parallel stanzas. Thompson's love of the "Heatherley" area becomes clear:

> You talk of pale primroses,
> Of frail and fragrant posies,
>   The cowslip and the cuckoo-
>   flower, that scent the spring-time lea.
>   But give to me the heather,
>   The honey-scented heather,
>   The glowing gypsy heather–
>   That is the flower for me!

Stanza 2 repeats the pattern. Symonds loves "alleys," "valleys," and the "sea," while Thompson prefers "the moorland / The noble purple moorland, / The free, far-stretching moorland."

Written in seven octosyllabic couplets, "May Moonlight" is another romantic descriptive nature poem. The third line–"Along the shore, beneath the trees"–echoes rather strongly a line in William Wordsworth's "Daffodils" (1804)–"Beside the lake, beneath the trees." To contrast Thompson's description of moonlight with D. H. Lawrence's handling of the same image in the "Moony" chapter of *Women in Love* (1921) again brings out the difference between her Edwardian-Georgian sensibility and that of a modernist.

In "Cuckoo" the bird's springtime call invites the speaker to return to childhood:

> "Come out! Come out!" it seems to say,
> "O, cast your work and books away;
> "For this one day forget the pain
> "Of life and be a child again–
>   Cuckoo! Cuckoo!"

In a similar vein, "April" and "If We Were Young Together" are romantic love poems that demonstrate how Thompson favored nature description and simple techniques of parallelism, repetition, terminal half lines, and rhyme to obtain her poetic effects.

"Ocean Malignant" is tragic. In the opening stanza "the first cave-man" names the ocean "Mother of our Race." In stanza 2, though, Thompson focuses on the malignancy of the ocean:

> No Mother, but a Mistress; crafty, vain,
> She loves to lure man down to caverns dim,
> And there for nine days hold high sport with him,
>   Entwining with dank weeds his sodden hair,
>   Then fling his carrion back to Earth again,
> So cruel false! But fair–Ah, God, how fair!

"The Egoist" is perhaps a criticism of romantic transcendentalism:

> I am a rose, a dragon's wing,
> The flame-clad Autumn and the Spring.
> I am an aloe tree in bloom;
> A cypress waving o'er a tomb;
> A pond with lilies at the brink;
> A well where thirsty Arabs drink;
> A snow-peak on a mountain high;
> A rainbow in an April sky;
> A vintage ere the grapes are trod,
> I am the sun, and stars, and God!

While the speaker of the poem expresses the transcendentalist view that all living things are united in one universal godhead, the title of the poem suggests the possibility that Thompson was critical of the speaker's egocentrism.

Awareness of the recent war appears in "Flight At Sunset," in which Thompson's contemplation of an airplane–"At eve I saw man's aerial steed, celestial dragonfly, / Slough off its tetherings of earth, and mount into the sky"–prompts thoughts about human greatness and human insignificance, as if the airplane were on a holy mission to seek

> Pardon to plead for all the sins our age must answer for–
> For Love made desolate by Hate, Beauty laid waste by War.
> One instant, at the Golden Gate, before Heaven's topaz wall,
> Hung Man, immeasurable great, yet infinitely small!

"The Land Girl's Song" is another of the poems that reveal Thompson's awareness of World War I. Land girls were young women recruited to do farmwork in the absence of young men who were at the front. Thompson's poem is a balladlike love song reminiscent of Wordsworth's "The Solitary Reaper" (1807) and John Keats's "La Belle Dame Sans Merci" (1820). While the land girl reaps, she sings a summoning love song that she hopes will charm her lover:

> "O, come to-day, and poppies will spring,
>   Poppies will spring, poppies will spring,
>   With their blood-red blossoms I'll crown thee king
>   And the spell that I weave and the song that I sing
>   Shall hold thee captive for ever!"

The repeated reference to poppies with their "blood-red blossoms" suggests the poppy fields of Flanders, where many young men fought and died, held there "captive for ever!"

Although the speaker of "August Again" speaks of a lover rather than a brother, the poem possibly expresses the grief that Thompson felt at the loss of her brother in the war, a death that, according to Thompson's daughter, broke her mother's heart. The poem begins,

> The heather flings her purple robe
>   Once more upon the hill;
> Beneath a shivering aspen-tree
>   My love lies cold and still;–
> Ah, very deep my Love must sleep,
>   On that far Flemish plain,
> If he does not know that heath-bells blow
>   On the Hampshire hills again!

Edwin Timms died "On that far Flemish plain."

Flora Thompson's poem "Moments of Vision" is a reply to the pessimism of Thomas Hardy's *Moments of Vision* (1917). Referring to Hardy as "That master among men / Who hold this life a cramping cage, / The grave our goal," Thompson finds the answer to his fatalism in "the scent / Of hedgerows sweet with rain" and "children's happy laughter," which fill her with "Some blessed Hope," of which she thinks Hardy in his general philosophy is "unaware."

"You Have Forgotten Our Cave," the longest poem in the book, is a romantic love fantasy that is also the least successful poem in the volume. The speaker of the poem is a woman who addresses her lover, who she says has forgotten the time when they broke away from their tribe and lived together in a cave:

> You pillowed your head on my knee, in the fitful firelight glow,
> And, guttural, slow, and uncouth, I shaped our wild speech into song;
> Of Gurth and the Thunderer's wrath; of Edda the Fair and Goddell;
> And of two who escaped from their tribe, and lived on the sea-shore alone.

These lines are the least saccharine in a poem redolent with adolescent fantasy.

"Garden Fires" is a characteristic Edwardian-Georgian poem that wistfully combines realistic nature description with a sense of transience, ending

> And men shall make such fires,
>   And warm Spring winds blow free,
> When all the great desires
>   Which rend the heart of me
>   Shall dwindle into dust,
>   For Time is just!

Along the same line, "Wild-Thyme" is in Thompson's characteristic vein of Edwardian-Georgian nostalgia, beginning and ending with the lines, "A scent of wild-thyme on the air / Can bear one back to days afar." Presumably, "A scent of wild-thyme" in rural Hampshire transported the poet in imagination back to earlier days in rural Oxfordshire.

Thompson in the kitchen of her home in Liphook, Hampshire, in 1921, the year her only volume of poetry, Bog-Myrtle and Peat, *was published*

"A Villanelle of Spring" shows Thompson's ability to handle a familiar late-Victorian form. The final stanza gathers the two lines that have been repeated throughout the poem:

> Hark to the swallows twittering!
>   *They're* mending their old nests with clay;
> *I* sing a villanelle of Spring,
> Of primrose dells where throstles sing!

The penultimate poem in the volume, "The Earthly Paradises," seems to concern Thompson's poetic mentor Macfie. In this poem Thompson's principal poetic interests in love and the rural world come together. She prefers "harps of earth" to the "gold harps" of heaven and continues:

Thompson's grave in Longcross Cemetery, Dartmouth, Devonshire

When I am old,
Give me for heaven a little house set on a heath;
The blue hills behind; the blue sea before.
The brick floors scoured crimson, the flagstones like snow;
The brass taps and candlesticks like gold,
And there, in my soft grey gown between the holly-hocks,
Upon a day of days I would welcome an old poet;
And pour him tea, and walk on the heath, and talk the sun down;
And then by the wood fire he should read me the poems of his passionate youth,
And make new ones praising friendship above love!

The final poem of *Bog-Myrtle and Peat*, "To One In Prison," is addressed to an idealized "poet-hero, poet-king, likely again Macfie." It begins with the lines:

Had I the power to match my love,
Not Beatrice herself should be
Hymned higher unto heaven than thee!

In the same year that she published *Bog-Myrtle and Peat* Thompson also made her true beginning as a writer of nature prose. In 1922 she began publishing "The Peverel Papers," a series of nature notes about the Liphook area, in *The Catholic Fireside,* and from 1923 through 1925 she wrote an article a month for the magazine, either in "The Peverel Papers" series or in "The Fireside Reading Circle," a series she started in 1923. In 1925 she helped to write the *Guide to Liphook,* ended "The Fireside Reading Circle" series, and began The Peverel Society with a friend, Mildred Humble-Smith. The society was a post-office writers' group that published *The Peverel Monthly.* The last of "The Peverel Papers" appeared in December 1927.

In July 1926 the Thompsons bought Woolmer Gate, a house at Griggs Green near Liphook, and a year later John Thompson was appointed postmaster at Dartmouth in Devon. He moved there in November 1927, and Flora, Diana, and Peter joined him a year later once Woolmer Gate was sold. (Their other son, Basil, had gone to Queensland, Australia, in February 1926.)

In her 1921 interview Thompson mentioned, "At present I have got a novel in hand. Of course, the central subject is a girl, and it is rather autobiographical. It is almost impossible for one to get away from oneself." The novel she mentioned may be *Gates of Eden,* which was serialized in *The Peverel Monthly* in 1928, but has not been published in book form.

In the late 1930s Thompson published several stories in magazines, including "An Oxfordshire Hamlet in the Eighties" (*The National Review*, August 1937), which was the germ of *Lark Rise*. *Lark Rise* was accepted by Oxford University Press in 1938 and published in March 1939. It was a critical success, and Thompson soon began to write *Over to Candleford* (1941).

John Thompson had retired from the post office in 1935 at the age of sixty-one, and in 1940 the Thompsons moved to a house called Lauriston in Brixham, just up the coast from Dartmouth. Their son Peter, who had joined the Merchant Navy, was lost at sea from an Atlantic convoy in September 1941. Flora Thompson soon disbanded The Peverel Society, but she continued writing, finishing *Candleford Green*, which appeared in January 1943. During 1944 she wrote *Heatherley*, about her time in Grayshott between 1898 and 1903, but did not submit it for publication. It was eventually published posthumously in *A Country Calendar and Other Writings* (1979). By August 1946 Thompson had completed *Still Glides the Stream*, which appeared posthumously in 1948. Having suffered from heart trouble since her son's death in 1941, Thompson died on the evening of 21 May 1947 at the age of seventy. Her husband died the following year at seventy-four. The Thompsons' daughter, Diana, became her mother's literary executor.

In 1957 Margaret Lane published a biographical essay on Flora Thompson in *The Cornhill Magazine*. Twenty-two years later she expanded the essay as an introduction to *A Country Calendar and Other Writings*, which comprises selections from "The Peverel Papers," poems from *Bog-Myrtle and Peat*, and *Heatherley*, published for the first time. In May 1976 the centenary of Flora Thompson's birth was celebrated in Liphook, which has since honored her with a plaque (1978) and a bust by Philip Jackson (1981).

Flora Thompson's Edwardian-Georgian poems are principally concerned with love and nature. When compared to the evocative descriptions of rural life in *Lark Rise to Candleford*, *Bog-Myrtle and Peat* is a minor work. Thompson's strength was as a poetic prose writer rather than as a formal poet.

References:

Christine G. Bloxham, *The World of Flora Thompson* (Oxford: Dugdale, 1998);

Margaret Lane, *Flora Thompson* (London: Murray, 1976);

Gillian Lindsay, *Flora Thompson: The Story of the Lark Rise Writer* (London: Hale, 1990);

Anne Mallinson, *Flora Thompson: Literary Walks* (N.p.: East Hampshire District Council, n.d.);

Mary Norwak, *The Lark Rise Recipe Book* (Devizes: Selecta, 1986);

W. R. Trotter, *The Hilltop Writers* (Bramshott & Liphook: Bramshott and Liphook Preservation Society, 1996);

John Owen Smith, *On the Trail of Flora Thompson: Heatherley to Peverel, Grayshott to Griggs Green* (Headley Down: John Owen Smith, 1997).

Papers:

Flora Thompson's papers are held by the Harry Ransom Humanities Research Center at the University of Texas at Austin.

Katharine Tynan

(23 January 1861 – 2 April 1931)

Michele Martinez
Trinity College

See also the Tynan entry in *DLB 153: Late-Victorian and Edwardian British Novelists, First Series.*

BOOKS: *Louise de la Vallière and Other Poems* (London: Kegan Paul, Trench, 1885);
Shamrocks (London: Kegan Paul, Trench, 1887);
The Land I Love Best (Woking & London: Unwin, 1890);
Ballads and Lyrics (London: Kegan Paul, Trench, Trübner, 1891);
A Nun, Her Friends, and her Order: Being a sketch of the life of Mother Mary Xaveria Fallon (London: Kegan Paul, Trench, Trübner, 1891);
A Cluster of Nuts: Being Sketches Among My Own People (London: Lawrence & Bullen, 1894);
Cuckoo Songs (London: Elkin Mathews, 1894; Boston: Copeland & Day, 1894);
Christmas Verses, by Probyn and Tynan (London, 1895);
An Isle in the Water (London: Black, 1895);
The Land of Mist and Mountain (London: Unwin, 1895);
Miracle Plays: Our Lord's Coming and Childhood (London: Bodley Head, 1895; Chicago: Stone & Temple, 1895);
The Way of a Maid (New York: Dodd, Mead, 1895);
A Lover's Breast-Knot (London: Elkin Mathews, 1896);
Oh, What a Plague is Love (London: Black, 1896);
O'Grady of Trinity: A Story of Irish University Life (London: Lawrence & Bullen, 1896; Chicago: McClurg, 1900);
The Handsome Brandons (London: Blackie, 1898; Chicago: McClurg, 1900);
The Wind in the Trees: A Book of Country Verse (London: Richards, 1898);
The Dear Irish Girl (London: Smith, Elder, 1899; Chicago: McClurg, 1899);
Led By a Dream, and Other Stories (London, 1899);
She Walks in Beauty (London: Smith, Elder, 1899; Chicago: McClurg, 1900);
The Adventures of Carlo (London: Blackie, 1900);
A Daughter of the Fields (London: Smith, Elder, 1900; Chicago: McClurg, 1901);
Her Father's Daughter (New York: Benziger, 1901);

Katharine Tynan

Poems (London: Lawrence & Bullen, 1901);
That Sweet Enemy (Philadelphia: Lippincott, 1901);
Three Fair Maids; or, The Burkes of Derrymore (London: Blackie, 1901);
A Union of Hearts (London: Nisbet, 1901);
A Girl of Galway (London: Blackie, 1902);
The Golden Lily (New York: Benziger, 1902);
The Great Captain (New York: Benziger, 1902);
The Handsome Quaker and Other Stories (London: Bullen, 1902);
A King's Woman (London: Hurst & Blackett, 1902);
Love of Sisters (London: Smith, Elder, 1902);
The Queen's Page (New York: Benziger, 1902);
Dick Pentreath (London: Smith, Elder, 1903; Chicago: McClurg, 1906);

The Honorable Molly (London: Smith, Elder, 1903);

A Red, Red Rose (London: Nash, 1903);

The French Wife (London: White, 1904);

Judy's Lovers (London: White, 1904);

Julia (London: Smith, Elder, 1904; Chicago: McClurg, 1905);

A Daughter of Kings (London: Nash, 1905; New York: Benziger, 1905);

For the White Rose (New York: Benziger, 1905);

Fortune's Favourite (London: White, 1905);

Innocencies: A Book of Verse (London: Bullen; Dublin: Maunsel, 1905);

The Luck of the Fairfaxes (London: Collins, 1905);

The Adventures of Alicia (London: White, 1906);

A Book of Memory: The Birthday Book of the Blessed Dead (London: Hodder & Stoughton, 1906);

For Maisie (London: Hodder & Stoughton, 1906; Chicago: McClurg, 1907);

A Little Book for John O'Mahony's Friends (Petersfield: Pear Tree Press, 1906; Portland, Me.: Mosher, 1909);

A Little Book for Mary Gill's Friends (Petersfield: Pear Tree Press, 1906);

A Little Book of Courtesies (London: Dent, 1906);

The Story of Bawn (London: Smith, Elder, 1906; Chicago: McClurg, 1907);

The Yellow Domino and Other Stories (London: White, 1906);

Her Ladyship (London: Smith, Elder, 1907; Chicago: McClurg, 1908);

A Little Book of XXIV Carols (Portland, Me.: Mosher, 1907);

The Rhymed Life of St. Patrick (London: Burns & Oates, 1907);

The Story of Our Lord for Children (Dublin: Sealy, Bryers & Walker, 1907);

Twenty-One Poems, selected by William Butler Yeats (Dundrum, Ireland: Dun Emer Press, 1907);

Adveniat Regnum Tuum (Mallowfield: Privately printed, 1908);

Experiences: Poems (London: Bullen, 1908);

Father Mathew (London: Macdonald & Evans, 1908; New York: Benziger, 1908);

Four Years Old: Song, words by Tynan, music by Herman Lohr (London: Chappell, 1908);

The House of the Crickets (London: Smith, Elder, 1908);

The Lost Angel (London: Milne, 1908; Philadelphia: Lippincott, 1908);

Mary Gray (London: Cassell, 1908);

Men and Maids; or, The Lovers' Way (Dublin: Sealy, Bryers & Walker, 1908);

The Book of Flowers, by Tynan and Frances Maitland (London: Smith, Elder, 1909);

Cousins and Others: Tales (London: Laurie, 1909);

Her Mother's Daughter (London: Smith, Elder, 1909);

Ireland (London: Black, 1909);

Kitty Aubrey (London: Nisbet, 1909);

Lauds (London: Cedar Press, 1909);

Peggy, the Daughter (London: Cassell, 1909);

Betty Carew (London: Smith, Elder, 1910);

The Dearest of All (Portland, Me.: Mosher, 1910);

Freda (New York: Cassell, 1910);

The House of the Secret (London: Clarke, 1910);

Paradise Farm (New York: Duffield, 1911); republished as *Mrs. Pratt of Paradise Farm* (London: Smith, Elder, 1913);

Princess Katharine (New York: Duffield, 1911);

New Poems (London: Sidgwick & Jackson, 1911);

The Story of Cecilia (London: Smith, Elder, 1911; New York: Benziger, 1911);

The Story of Clarice (London, 1911);

Heart o' Gold; or, The Little Princess (London: Patridge, 1912);

Honey, My Honey (London: Smith, Elder, 1912);

Rose of the Garden (London: Constable, 1912; Indianapolis: Bobbs-Merrill, 1913);

Irish Poems (London: Sidgwick & Jackson, 1913; New York: Benziger, 1914);

A Mésailliance (New York: Duffield, 1913);

A Midsummer Rose (London: Smith, Elder, 1913);

Out in the World (London, 1913);

Twenty-Five Years: Reminiscences (London: Smith, Elder, 1913; New York: Devin-Adair, 1913);

The Daughter of the Manor (London: Blackie, 1914);

The Flower of Peace: A Collection of the Devotional Poetry of Katharine Tynan (London: Burns & Oates, 1914; New York: Scribners, 1915);

John Bulteel's Daughters (London: Smith, Elder, 1914);

A Little Radiant Girl (London: Blackie, 1914);

Lover's Meetings (London: Laurie, 1914);

Molly, My Heart's Delight (London: Smith, Elder, 1914);

A Shameful Inheritance (London, 1914);

Countrymen All: A Collection of Tales (London: Maunsel, 1915);

The Curse of Castle Eagle (New York: Duffield, 1915);

Flower of Youth: Poems in War-Time (London: Sidgwick & Jackson, 1915);

The House of the Foxes (London: Smith, Elder, 1915);

Men Not Angels and Other Tales (London: Burns & Oates, 1915; New York: Kennedy, 1915);

Since I First Saw Your Face (London: Hutchinson, 1915);

The Squire's Sweetheart (London: Ward, Lock, 1915);

The Holy War (London: Sidgwick & Jackson, 1916);

John-A-Dreams (London: Smith, Elder, 1916);

Lord Edward: A Study in Romance (London: Smith, Elder, 1916);

Margery Dawe (London: Blackie, 1916);

The Middle Years (London: Constable, 1916);

The Web of Fraulein (London: Hodder & Stoughton, 1916);

The West Wind (London: Constable, 1916);

Kit (London: Smith, Elder, 1917);

Late Songs (London: Sidgwick & Jackson, 1917);

Miss Mary (London: Murray, 1917);

The Rattlesnake (London: Ward, Lock, 1917);

Herb o' Grace: Poems in War-Time (London: Sidgwick & Jackson, 1918);

Katharine Tynan's Book of Irish History (Dublin: Educational Company of Ireland, 1918);

Miss Gascoigne (London: Murray, 1918);

My Love's But a Lassie (London: Ward, Lock, 1918);

Love of Brothers (London: Constable, 1919);

The Man from Australia (London: Collins, 1919);

The Years of the Shadow (London: Constable, 1919);

Denys the Dreamer (London: Collins, 1920; New York: Benziger, 1921);

The Great Captain: A Story of the Days of Sir Walter Raleigh (New York: Benziger, 1920);

The House (London: Collins, 1920);

Sally Victrix (London: Collins, 1921);

The Second Wife; together with A July Rose (London: Murray, 1921);

Evensong (Oxford: Blackwell, 1922);

The House of the Bogs (London: Ward, Lock, 1922);

A Mad Marriage (London: Collins, 1922);

The Wandering Years (London: Constable, 1922);

White Ladies (London: Nash & Grayson, 1922);

The Child at Prayer (London: Burns & Oates, 1923);

Mary Beaudesert, V. S. (London: Collins, 1923);

Pat, the Adventurer (London: Ward, Lock, 1923);

They Loved Greatly (London: Nash & Grayson, 1923);

The Golden Rose (London: Nash & Grayson, 1924);

The House of Doom (London: Nash & Grayson, 1924);

Memories (London: Nash & Grayson, 1924);

Wives (London: Hurst & Blackett, 1924);

Dear Lady Bountiful (London: Ward, Lock, 1925);

Life in the Occupied Area (London: Hutchinson, 1925);

Miss Phipps (London: Ward, Lock, 1925);

The Moated Grange (London: Collins, 1925); republished as *The Night of Terror* (London: Collins, 1932);

The Briar Bush Maid (London: Ward, Lock, 1926);

A Dog Book (London: Hutchinson, 1926);

The Heiress of Wyke (London: Ward, Lock, 1926);

The Infatuation of Peter (London: Collins, 1926);

The Face in the Picture (London: Ward, Lock, 1927);

Haroun of London (London: Collins, 1927);

The Respectable Lady (London: Collins, 1927; New York: Appleton, 1928);

Twilight Songs (Oxford: Blackwell, 1927);

The Wild Adventure (London: Ward, Lock, 1927);

Bitha's Wonderful Year (London: Oxford University Press, 1928);

Castle Perilous (London: Ward, Lock, 1928);

The House in the Forest (London: Ward, Lock, 1928);

Lover of Women (London: Collins, 1928);

Pat the Adventurer (London: Ward, Lock, 1928);

Remembrance, music by Frederick Keel, words by Tynan (London: Cramer, 1928);

A Fine Gentleman (London: Ward, Lock, 1929);

The Most Charming Family (London: Ward, Lock, 1929);

The Rich Man (London: Collins, 1929);

The River (London: Collins, 1929);

The Admirable Simmons (London: Ward, Lock, 1930);

Denise the Daughter (London: Ward, Lock, 1930);

Grayson's Girl (London: Collins, 1930);

The Playground (London: Ward, Lock, 1930);

Delia's Orchard (London: Ward, Lock, 1931);

The Forbidden Way (London: Collins, 1931);

Katharine Tynan (London: Benn, 1931);

A Lonely Maid (London: Ward, Lock, 1931);

Philippa's Lover (London: Ward, Lock, 1931);

A Red, Red Rose (London: Ward, Lock, 1931);

The Other Man (London: Ward, Lock, 1932);

The Pitiful Lady (London: Ward, Lock, 1932);

Connor's Wood (London: Collins, 1933);

An International Marriage (London: Ward, Lock, 1933);

The House of Dreams (London: Ward, Lock, 1934);

A Lad Was Born (London: Collins, 1934);

The Summer Aeroplane (London: Weidenfeld & Nicolson, 1975);

Kitty at School and College (Dublin: Educational Company of Ireland, n.d.).

Editions and Collections: *Collected Poems* (London: Macmillan, 1930);

Twenty-Four Poems, edited by Pamela Hinkson (London: Benn, 1931);

The Poems of Katharine Tynan, edited, with an introduction, by Monk Gibbon (Dublin: Figgis, 1963).

OTHER: *Poems and Ballads of Young Ireland,* includes poems by Tynan (Dublin: M. H. Gill, 1888);

Irish Love Songs, selected by Tynan (London: Unwin, 1892);

Lionel Johnson, *Poems,* introduction by Tynan (Portland, Me.: Mosher, 1904);

The Cabinet of Irish Literature, edited by C. A. Read, revised and greatly extended by Tynan, 4 volumes (London: Gresham, 1905);

Edmund Leamy, *By the Barrow River and Other Stories,* foreword by Tynan (Dublin: Sealy, Bryers & Walker, 1907);

Anne Manning, *Mary Powell* and *Deborah's Diary,* introduction by Tynan (London: Everyman's Library, 1908);

The Poems of Henry Wadsworth Longfellow, 1823–1866, introduction by Tynan (London: Dent, 1909); published as *Longfellow's Poems* (New York: Dutton, 1909; enlarged and expanded, 1960);

"St. Martin's Summer," in *The Press Album,* edited by Thomas Catling (London: Murray, 1909), p. 33;

Edith Ivor Parry, *In the Garden of Childhood,* introduction by Tynan (London: Routledge, 1913; New York: Dutton, 1913);

The Wild Harp, a Selection from Irish Poetry (London: Sidgwick & Jackson, 1913);

Dora Sigerson Shorter, *The Sad Years,* introduction by Tynan (London: Constable, 1918);

Frank Mathew, *A Book of Songs,* foreword by Tynan (London: Elkin Mathews, 1925);

Michael Walsh, *Brown Earth and Green: Poems,* foreword by Tynan (Dublin: Talbot Press, 1929).

SELECTED PERIODICAL PUBLICATIONS–UNCOLLECTED: "Three Young Poets," *Irish Monthly,* 15 (March 1887): 166–167;

Review of William Butler Yeats's *The Wanderings of Oisin, Irish Times,* 4 March 1889, p. 6;

"William Butler Yeats," *Magazine of Poetry,* 1 (October 1889): 454;

"W. B. Yeats," *Bookman,* 5 (October 1893): 13–14;

"William Butler Yeats," *Sketch,* 4 (29 November 1893): 256;

"The Literary Revival in Ireland," *New Outlook,* 49 (30 June 1894): 1189–1191;

"The Poetry of Christina Rossetti," *Bookman,* 5 (December 1894): 78;

"London Letters," *Literary World* (26 January 1895): 24;

Review of *A Book of Irish Verse, Daily Express* (London), 21 March 1895;

"Mr. Yeats's Poems," *Spectator,* 76 (25 January 1896): 136–137;

"The Neglect of Irish Writers," *Catholic World,* 87 (April 1908): 83–92;

"Santa Christina," *Bookman,* 41 (January 1912): 186;

"The Poetry of James Stephens," *Journal of English Studies,* 7: 2 (September 1912 – January 1913): 98;

"Recent Irish Poetry," *Studies,* 6 (June 1917): 200–211;

Review of *Per Amica Silentia Lunae, Studies,* 7 (March 1918): 188–189;

Review of William Butler Yeats's "Wild Swans at Coole," in "A Strayed Poet," *Bookman,* 56 (May 1919): 18–19;

"Personal Memories of John Butler Yeats," *Double Dealer,* 4 (July 1922): 8–15.

Katharine Tynan was the most prolific and widely read Irish woman writer of the late-nineteenth and early-twentieth century. From 1885 to her death in 1931, Tynan's poetry appeared in the major Irish, English, and American periodicals and was published in seventeen individual volumes and several collected editions. A friend and colleague of the young William Butler Yeats, Tynan played a prominent part in the formation of the Irish Literary Revival, which she described in her colorful and controversial memoirs. While her nature and devotional poetry reflect a close study of English writers–Henry Vaughan, Richard Crashaw, early William Blake, and the Rossettis–she was one of the first Revival poets to popularize Celtic legends (translated from the Irish by Samuel Ferguson and Clarence Mangan) and to position herself in an Anglo-Catholic tradition of poetry. After her marriage and the birth of her children in the 1890s, Tynan developed a poetics of motherhood distinct from the cloistered reserve of her esteemed rival Christina Rossetti and crucial to her popularity as an elegist during World War I. While Tynan seldom brought to her poetry the metaphysical or political complexities of her time, such as Dante Gabriel Rossetti or William Butler Yeats had, she frequently composed graceful lyrics, capturing singular features of the Irish landscape, her sorrows and joys as a mother, and the consolation of her faith.

Katharine Tynan was born 23 January 1861, the fourth daughter and one of eleven children of Andrew and Elizabeth Tynan. Her father, Andrew Cullen Tynan, the son of a Catholic mother and Protestant father, was a prosperous tenant farmer and entrepreneur in County Dublin, where he raised cattle for contracts with the armies of England and Ireland. Tynan's mother, Elizabeth Reily Cullen, who was an invalid, brought her children up to be Catholics. In 1868 Andrew Tynan moved his family from the city of Dublin to a country house called Whitehall in Clondalkin, County Dublin. Katharine's memoirs, *Twenty-Five Years: Reminiscences* (1913) and *Memories* (1924), affectionately portray her father as an intelligent, hardworking, passionate Irishman who preferred the lively company of his daughter to that of his frequently ailing wife. According to Tynan's memoirs, her familial affections centered on her father after her eldest sister Mary died in 1868 from a sudden illness. Katharine's younger sister, the novelist Norah Tynan O'Mahony, recalls that Katharine had been a studious girl sheltered from household worries and that as a successful author Tynan contributed financial support to her large family.

At the age of six, Tynan suffered from eye ulcers that for two years left her nearly blind. After receiving treatment from a Dublin doctor, she regained some of her eyesight, but was left bespectacled and severely shortsighted for the rest of her life. In her memoirs Tynan rarely mentions her visual impairment, but in a

Title page for Tynan's second book, which established her as an important voice in the emerging Irish literary revival

poem published in 1922, "The Purblind Praises the Lord," she claims that the disability gave her spiritual insight and enhanced her poetic gifts. Despite the challenges that partial blindness presented, it actually had little effect upon her literary output. Tynan published more than two hundred books, including volumes of poetry, novels, memoirs, and anthologies. She also produced hundreds of reviews, interviews, and articles. Extensive diaries (upon which her memoirs are based) were made available to the public after the death of Tynan's only daughter, Pamela Hinkson, in 1982.

Tynan left Whitehall for three years (1871–1874) to attend boarding school in Drogheda at the Dominican Convent of St. Catherine of Siena. Tynan's brief and happy convent education proved formative in her intellectual and spiritual life, producing subjects for her first volume, *Louise de la Vallière and Other Poems* (1885), and her first prose work, *A Nun, Her Friends, and her Order: Being a sketch of the life of Mother Mary Xaveria Fallon* (1891). Although Tynan never considered becoming a nun, Catholicism informed and shaped her poems, eventually gaining for her a loyal readership in Ireland and England. Tynan's verse captured the attention of contemporary devotional writers, including Christina Rossetti, Wilfrid and Alice Meynell, Lionel Johnson, and Gerard Manley Hopkins.

After leaving Siena Convent, Tynan returned to Whitehall, where she assumed the role of an aspiring writer. Her father encouraged her reading of English novels and poetry as well as introduced her to the Irish nationalist verse of his youth. In the 1840s her father had been a supporter of Young Ireland, a group of journalists and poets who, in a daily newspaper called *The Nation,* called for the repeal of Ireland's union with England. Tynan's earliest girlhood memories recall her father's favorite street songs and ballads commemorating the men who fought in the struggle for independence. Foremost in the battle were the Fenians, members of a radical political organization with designs on parliamentary power and affilated with the Irish Republican Brotherhood (IRB), the militant faction later to become the Irish Republican Army (IRA). *The Nation* also published poetry by Samuel Ferguson and Clarence Mangan, writers who brought Celtic legends and Irish-language poetry into circulation as part of a nationalist project. Tynan's father appears not to have been directly involved with the Fenians or the IRB but rather passed on to his daughter a passionate commitment to the nationalist cause.

In Tynan's teens and early twenties, the largely fractious Fenian leaders celebrated by the Young Irelanders were overshadowed by the rise to power of Charles Stewart Parnell, an Irish Protestant landlord and parlimentary advocate for Home Rule. Parnell gained popularity for his ability to consolidate protests and legal recourse on behalf of Irish tenant farmers and make interventions on their behalf as an Irish member of the English Parliament. When Parnell and others were imprisoned for inciting boycotts and some violence in 1881, many Irishwomen, such as Parnell's sisters Fanny and Anna, took charge of land-reform agitation. As a tenant farmer himself, Andrew Tynan supported Katharine's involvement in the Ladies' Land League, formed by Anna Parnell in 1881. Katharine Tynan worked in the League's Dublin office on a letter-writing campaign and visited jailed political prisoners, such as Michael Davitt and Charles Parnell himself.

Tynan claims to have written her first poem in 1878 and seen it printed in a Dublin "penny paper" sometime in the early 1880s. Her first paid publication, a ballad called "The Legend of the Sorrowful Mother," appeared in the 1881 issue of *The Irish Monthly,* a periodical under the editorship of Father Matthew Russell, S. J., whom she called a "priest-editor." The narrative poem, written in two parts with a short prologue, recounts the story of a Germanic queen, stricken with grief over the illness of her baby and consoled by a visitation from the "Mother of the Lord." Father Russell published twenty-seven of Tynan's poems in *The Irish Monthly* and introduced her enthusiastically to Dublin's literary establishment. In this first flush of her poetic career, Tynan also published articles and poems in the literary section of the *The Gael*, a nationalist journal, edited by the Young Irelander poet John O'Leary and his sister Ellen. She also contributed poems to the *Dublin University Review* and *Hibernia*. Through Father Russell and the O'Learys, Tynan became close friends with the poets Rose Kavanagh and Dora Sigerson Shorter, with whom she also collaborated.

Tynan secured connections with London publishers by sending out a constant stream of poems and reviews to periodicals and made her first significant visit to London in 1884. Guided by the Reverend Henry Stuart Fagan, a Norfolk parson and Home Rule sympathizer with ties to the publishing establishment, Tynan met Wilfrid and Alice Meynell, a poet and co-editor of the *Weekly Register* and *Merry England,* who became Tynan's close friend for forty years. On this same visit to London, Tynan met Lady and Oscar Wilde, who later published some of Tynan's prose sketches in the journal *Woman's World*. With a financial subsidy from her father and Wilfrid Meynell's mediation with the London publisher Kegan Paul, Tynan's first book of poems *Louise de la Vallière and Other Poems* was accepted and printed in June 1885.

Louise de la Vallière and Other Poems was widely reviewed in London and Dublin, receiving the modest praise of "promise" from *The Athenaeum* (25 July 1885) and wholehearted endorsements from Irish periodicals. The volume's success prompted Kegan Paul to issue a second edition and inspired the twenty-year-old, unpublished Yeats to desire Tynan's company. The book begins with the title poem, "Louise de la Vallière," a dramatic monologue spoken by Louis XIV's young, estranged mistress. Forced to enter a Carmelite sisterhood by her scandalized family, Louise confesses her gothic fears of the convent and mourns her lost innocence. The poem shares subject matter with Christina Rossetti's earlier lyric "Soeur Louise de la Misericorde," but Tynan's detailed interest in the duchess's psychology distinguishes it from Rossetti's. While Rossetti's lyric laments the vanity of Louise, Tynan's Louise vacillates between feelings of despair and hope promised by her thought that God will welcome her to his house: "I am but this, a broken reed that He / Hath bound with His strong fingers tenderly. / Lord! where Thy Father's many mansions shine, / Wilt Thou not keep a last least place for me?" Echoing Rossetti's lyric, "The Lowest Place," in the final line, Tynan transforms Rossettian despair into hope, through a domestic fantasy of heaven and a benevolent father. Many of her early poems resolve in this way and establish Tynan as a poet of domestic harmony and religious piety.

The poems from *Louise de la Vallière and Other Poems* favored most by Tynan's reviewers have Irish subject matter and announce her place in a nationalist poetic tradition. The dramatic monologue "Waiting" recounts the legend of the Irish warrior Fionn Mac Cumhail, who, with his comrades, slumbers in a Donegal cavern, waiting for the appropriate moment to rise up and defend Ireland in her hour of need. Tynan's use of this particular Irish legend evokes the 1798 uprisings of the Fenian army, which derived its name from the legend of Fionn and his warrior-like readiness to fight. Tynan's choice to employ this historically overdetermined legend impressed Yeats, who may have been inspired by her to draw upon the Fenian cycle for his first significant contribution to the Irish renaissance, *The Wanderings of Oisin* (1889). Two other poems in the volume also have nationalist overtones. "The Flight of the Wild Geese" is a lament for the Irish soldiers, who, after the Williamite conquest, left Ireland to take service in foreign armies. A feminized, abandoned "Eire" speaks mournfully as she watches the horizon for sons unlikely to return. "The Dead Patriot: The Late A. M. Sullivan" is a eulogy for Alexander Martin Sullivan, editor of the nationalist daily *The Nation* and eloquent M.P. who advocated Home Rule. Tynan's choices of subject matter in these three poems reflect her political allegiances and interest in Irish mythology and history prior to her friendship with Yeats. Yet, *Louise de la Vallière and Other Poems* is not solely an "Irish" work. Imitations of Pre-Ralphaelite verse and Crashavian lyrics are largely unsuccessful, the work of a young apprentice.

In *Twenty-Five Years: Reminiscences* Tynan states that Dante Gabriel Rossetti's *Poems* (1870) was the first book she bought with her earnings as a writer, suggesting that he had been a major influence upon her poetry. Pleased with the reception of her first volume, Tynan sent a copy to Rossetti's brother William Michael, who remarked in a letter that her "volume appears . . . on the whole to be more indicative of an influence from my sister's work than my brother's." After receiving a copy of *Louise de La Vallière and Other Poems* from the author, Christina Rossetti sent Tynan a letter expressing admiration for her "poetic gifts" and adding "beyond all gifts I account *graces,* and therefore the piety of your work fills me with hopes far beyond any to be raised by music of diction." In this statement Rossetti, who devoted herself in her later years solely to religious poetry, encouraged Tynan to work in a similar vein. In the autumn of 1885 Tynan visited Rossetti at her home in

Torrington Square, London, and in her memoirs writes of preparing "to meet her as a saint." Tynan's detailed account of their meeting dispels this idea, providing one of the most vivid descriptions of Rossetti by someone outside the family. Her "short serviceable skirts of iron grey tweed and stout boots" were a "species of mortification" in Tynan's eyes, yet Rossetti's generous conversation and sense of humor made Tynan believe that she was "not really at all nun-like." The stories surrounding Rossetti—that she would not allow herself to marry a man of a different faith—prompted Tynan to speculate that Rossetti wrote melancholy poetry because "romantic love must have stayed with her to the end." In an article written for *The Bookman* a year before Rossetti's death in 1894, Tynan characterizes her work as "the poetry of the mystics," which "ranges itself by the raptures of St. Teresa and the burning heart of Crashaw."

Tynan herself captures not so much the mysticism as the absolute certainty of belief in her devotional poetry. Poems such as "A Tired Heart" or "The Dead Christ" present speakers who talk with God and reaffirm their faith by observing God's work in nature. Writing in 1916, Ernest A. Boyd observed that Tynan was unique among the group of Revivalist poets because she gave literary expression to her Catholicism: "her verse voices that naïve faith, that complete surrender to the simpler emotions of wonder and pity, which characterize the religious experiences of the plain man." At her finest, Tynan's poems resemble Blake's songs of childhood innocence and piety. While still showing signs of a young poet learning her craft in *Louise de la Vallière and Other Poems*, "An Answer" and "A Bird's Song" approach the Rossettian harmony of poetic line and soul found in her later poetry. The best of Tynan's devotional verse was later collected and published in an anthology, *The Flower of Peace* (1914). An epigraph from Vaughan's "Peace" prepares the reader for Tynan's visions of, in Vaughan's words, "a Countrie / Far beyond the stars / . . . There above noise, and danger."

Tynan's popular success and connections to the London literary world drew other Dublin writers to Whitehall, where she and her family were known to be congenial hosts. When Yeats first met Tynan in 1885, he was four years younger and consumed with literary ambition. He was brought to Tynan's home by Charles Hubert Oldham, founder of the *Dublin University Review* and publisher of Yeats's first verse drama. As their correspondence of the late 1880s demonstrates, Yeats and Tynan became great friends and shared the conviction that Celtic legend and folklore were integral to a revival of Irish literature. In a letter dated 27 April 1887, Yeats wrote: "I feel more and more that we shall have a school of Irish poetry—founded on Irish myth and history—a neo-romantic movement." Tynan admittedly shared Yeats's enthusiasm and responded favorably to his close attention to her work. Some have speculated that Yeats thought of proposing marriage to Tynan, but neither her published memoirs nor his letters hint that there was ever any romantic interest between them.

The friendship with Yeats also led to Tynan's close association with Yeats's sisters, Elizabeth (Lolly) and Lilly, as well as with their father, the artist John Butler Yeats, who in 1886 painted Tynan's portrait, which is now at the Municipal Gallery of Modern Art, Dublin. Tynan gives a long account of John Yeats in *Memories,* recalling that he took great care with her portrait and exhibited it at the Royal Hibernian Academy in 1887. A watercolor portrait of Tynan rendered by Yeats in 1888 is reported by Richard Finneran in his biography of W. B. Yeats but remains untraced. As Tynan herself recounts in her published memoirs, John Yeats's studio was the gathering place for other Anglo-Irish poets of his son's acquaintance, notably the art student and poet AE (George Russell) and Douglas Hyde, the scholar and translator of Irish legends, who would become the first president of the Irish Free State. Until she left for England in 1893, these writers frequented Tynan's home at Whitehall. She developed a strong friendship with AE, who would prove to be a lifelong friend, editing Tynan's *Collected Poems* in 1930 and cherishing her "natural gift for song."

In June 1886 Oldham published Yeats's verse drama *Mosada,* which Tynan reviewed in the *Irish Monthly* of March 1887. The review announces the arrival of "a new singer in Erin" about whom "great things may be prophesied." Yeats himself had begun to establish his reputation as a literary critic, and in three different journals—*The Gael,* the *Irish Fireside Review,* and *Truth*—he reviewed Tynan's second volume, *Shamrocks* (1887). In his mixture of praise and criticism, he upholds the author as an important figure in a nascent Irish literary revival. In all three reviews, Yeats contrasts *Shamrocks* with her first volume and praises Tynan's discovery of a new voice: "in the finding [of] her nationality she has found also herself, and written many pages of great truthfulness and simplicity." Yeats's personal investment in Tynan's success is expressed privately in a letter: "I feel almost as anxious about it as if it were my own book."

Shamrocks comprises poems on various subjects—nature, motherhood, and religion, but the title and green covers emphasize the verse on Irish legends. The three major Irish poems in the volume, "The Pursuit of Diarmuid and Grainne," "The Fate of King Fergus," and "The Story of Aibhric," are based on Celtic sources that had recently been published in translation by Gaelic revivalist writers. Like Tynan's earlier poem "Waiting," "The Pursuit of Diarmuid and Grainne" is a

Fenian legend based on the translation by Samuel Ferguson. Tynan may have been the first poet after Ferguson to treat the story in English, and her version is a seven-part narrative in quatrains, recounting the flight of two lovers from the vengeful King Fionn. Also from the Fenian cycle is Tynan's "The Story of Aibhric," a dramatic lyric based on the legend of Lir's children, who were transformed into swans by a witch. "The Fate of King Fergus" is from an Ulster legend about a prince who was born so disfigured that his mother kept the kingdom free of mirrors. Oblivious to his appearance, Fergus tries to woo a young woman for his queen. Upon seeing his reflection in her frightened eyes, he flees into the woods never to be seen again. In all three poems Tynan versifies the Irish rather blandly without embellishing the psychology of the characters nor enriching the formal qualities of poetic form. The use of Irish legend was actually a short-lived development in Tynan's career, one that earned her a position among the Irish poetry Revivalists but would not secure the esteem of critics.

In his *Fireside* review of *Shamrocks,* Yeats also commented upon the improvement of Tynan's lyrics in general, perceiving in them not the "metaphors of things," but the "things themselves." His favorite poem was "The Heart of a Mother," a dramatic monologue uttered by a woman anxious for news of her son lost at sea. He commends Tynan for eschewing the Pre-Raphaelite imitations found in her first volume and discovering a way to express her religion through descriptions of nature. In the *Fireside* review he praises "St. Francis to the Birds" as the "most faultless poem in the book," an opinion Yeats repeats in a letter to Tynan. A Catholic saint known particularly for his love of animals, St. Francis of Assisi preached that men and creatures were all children of God. Yeats identified Tynan's affectionate personality with this saint and used the term "Franciscan" to describe the heartfelt piety and formal precision of her best verse. In a letter to Tynan, Yeats apologized for "fault-finding" in his review of *Louise de la Vallière* but felt that "a peculiar kind of tenderness" had newly emerged in *Shamrocks.* Yeats's critical assessment recognizes the formula for Tynan's future success as an Irish Catholic poet.

The year 1887 also marks the beginning of Tynan's publishing career in the United States. On the advice of her friend Rosa Mulholland, Tynan had articles accepted to the *Providence Sunday Journal,* edited by Alfred Williams, and later the *Boston Pilot.* Yeats also contributed to these journals but later wrote that reviewing proved a distraction from his real calling as a playwright and poet. Tynan, however, found that journalism and her newfound occupation of keeping a diary were worthwhile and lucrative occupations, ones that developed into her prolific, but to her mind less-satisfying, career as a novelist.

At the end of 1887 the Yeats family moved from Dublin to London, and with this separation the two writers struck up a lively, intimate correspondence. Yeats's share of letters were collected by Roger McHugh and published in 1953. The letters are a record of Yeats's side of their friendship, namely, his commitment to forging an aesthetic continuous with a Celtic past as well as his own keen interest in Tynan's poetic productivity and success. Yeats sent drafts of his poems for her perusal, including "The Lake Isle of Innisfree," and kept Tynan informed about reviews of her work in London. Through the mail they worked on what has been considered the first major collaborative work of the Irish renaissance, *Poems and Ballads of Young Ireland* (1888).

The verse anthology was undertaken by the circle of poets who congregated at the home of John O'Leary, the former Fenian chief and editor of *The Gael,* and his sister Ellen, also a contributing poet. In the spirit of nationalism, the volume is dedicated to O'Leary and the Young Irelanders Society. Yeats contributed four poems to the volume, and Tynan, three: "The Grave of Michael Dwyer," "Shameen Dhu," and "Papist and Puritan." Yeats was pleased with the reception of the book by London critics and tells Tynan that "Shameen Dhu" and "Michael Dwyer" had been singled out as noteworthy contributions. All three poems address Ireland's troubled history. "Shameen Dhu" is one of Tynan's few poems written in dialect and recounts the story of a young man evicted from his farm by an intolerant landlord. "Michael Dwyer" is an elegy for a Fenian leader, who, after the failed uprising of 1798, was transported to Australia, where he later died in a penal colony. Both poems reflect Tynan's Land League activism and her sympathy for Fenian exiles, such as O'Leary. "Papist and Puritan" is a narrative about a Protestant boy in love with a Catholic girl, whom he plans to marry. The poem ends with the boy's decision to marry the girl, without hinting at the consequences. Tynan's optimism may reflect the religious tolerance of her own family. Her father was the product of an interfaith marriage, and Tynan herself later married a Protestant.

In the spring of 1889 a visit with the Meynells in London for four months yielded new acquaintances in political and literary circles. In May at a party hosted by Sir Charles and Lady Russell, Tynan met her hero, Parnell, whose warmth and praise of her poetry earned him an indelible place in her affections. In December 1890 Parnell was deserted by the majority of the Irish Parliamentary Party and the Catholic Church for his affair with Katharine O'Shea, the wife of an Irish M.P.

Title page for Tynan's critically acclaimed third volume of poetry, which includes many of her best-known poems

Parnell's fall caused a rift among his nationalist supporters and Tynan's circle of friends. His death in 1891 created violent divisions in Ireland between Parnell supporters and "anti-Parnellites." Tynan and Yeats were openly Parnellite and their sympathies were made known under fire in criticism of their poetry.

According to biographers Marilyn Gaddis Rose and Ann Connerton Fallon, Tynan had few political opinions and a weak understanding of history. While Tynan's memoirs and poetry only provide sketches and impressions of the events of her time, she held strong political views and lent her support to liberal causes, particularly the feminist movement both before and after World War I. In May 1889 Alice Meynell brought Tynan to the first Women Writer's Dinner in London, where the poets Amy Levy, Mathilde Blind, and Graham Tomson (Mrs. Marriott Watson) were in attendance. Tynan also met the radical journalist and novelist Mona Caird and the fellow Parnellite poet Emily Hickey. In April 1914, on the verge of World War I, Tynan traveled to Rome at the invitation of her friend Lady Aberdeen to report for *Westminster Magazine* on the International Women's Congress. In the attempt to uphold her reputation as a liberal but modest woman writer, Tynan's memoirs downplay her feminist activities and emphasize the domestic values of a British middle-class woman, content with her lot as a mother of three and a successful writer. Like her contemporary Virginia Woolf, Tynan never speculates on the political implications of her friendships with English M.P.s or Irish radicals. Tynan's impressions of active feminists suggest that, while not herself an agitator, she supported the enfranchisment of women and admired those women who compromised their reputations in the cause.

The years 1889 to 1893 were productive ones for Yeats and Tynan, and their influence upon one another was at its height. Yeats was busy editing a collection of Irish fairy and folklore for Camelot Classics and writing poetry reviews. In November 1889 he began addressing his letters to "Katey" and dedicated *The Stories from Carleton* to her. Yeats informed Tynan about favorable reviews of her poems published in London newspapers and expressed his keen interest in her forthcoming volumes. On the eve of Tynan's publication of her third volume, *Ballads and Lyrics,* in 1891 and a biography of Mother Mary Xaveria Fallon that same year, Yeats wrote that while the prose work was competent, it could not compete with her verse. In his review published in *The Evening Herald* (2 January 1892), Yeats called *Ballads and Lyrics* "a thoroughly Irish book, springing straight from the Celtic mind and pouring itself out in soft Celtic music." He singles out as striking "The Children of Lir," a narrative in alexandrines based on the four children of Lir transformed into swans. In lines that Yeats applauded, the poem captures the beauty and melancholy of the Irish landscape and the loneliness of the swans:

> Dews are in the clear air, and the roselight paling,
> Over sands and sedges shines the evening star,
> And the moon's disc lonely high in heaven is sailing,
> Silvered all the spear-heads of the rushes are,
> Housed warm are all things as the night grows colder,
> Water-fowl and sky-fowl dreamless in the nest;
> But the swans go drifting, drooping wing and shoulder
> Cleaving the still water where the fishes are.

Ballads and Lyrics was considered Tynan's strongest volume to date and includes several of the poems for which she is best known. In addition to "The Childen of Lir," "Sheeps and Lambs" is probably Tynan's most anthologized work. Yeats commented that it has "the *naïveté* of mediaeval song . . . a product quite as much of art as of impulse." Like Blake's "The Lamb," Tynan's lyric transforms a pastoral motif into an epiphany. The poem was set to music by the Scottish composer Sir Hugh Roberton and popularized as a song, "All in the April Evening."

In 1892 Tynan edited a second anthology of poetry, *Irish Love Songs,* for Camelot Classics. She apparently solicited advice from Yeats, for in a letter dated 2 March 1892, he advised her to include poems by Thomas Davis and others. He also suggested a couple of his own poems from *The Wanderings of Oisin,* which duly appear near the end of the volume. Featuring a frontispiece drawing of James Clarence Mangan, the anthology consists mostly of nineteenth-century translations of Gaelic verse. Tynan singles out Edward Walsh and Samuel Ferguson as the best translator–poets of love songs. The last third of the volume is comprised of translations and lyrics contributed by her own circle, including two by herself. In the preface, Tynan suggests that the rise and fall of poetry in Ireland is intimately linked with the country's politics: "there seems no doubt that the Jacobite movement stirred into life the poetry with which the early years of the eighteenth-century in Ireland were so rich." Yeats, in his own introduction to *A Book of Irish Verse: Selected from Modern Writers* (1895), makes the similar observation that politics gives an "oratorical vehemence" to some Irish writers. He adds that the best poets transcend politics in the perfection of their craft.

In October 1893 Tynan published a reminiscence about her friendship with Yeats in *The Bookman.* By this time he was already a public figure in London, having published widely as a reviewer, co-authored a book on Blake, and been acclaimed as the author of a drama *The Countess Kathleen* (1892). He was involved in the Theosophical Society, the National Literary Society in Dublin, and London's The Rhymer's Club, which published anthologies of contributions by its members. Tynan's *Bookman* article contrasts the sociability of Yeats with the image of a solitary Irish bard, walking through the countryside and inspiring nationalist sentiment in those he meets. Anticipating a long, successful career for her friend, Tynan calls him unique among the writers of his day. One year later, in *The Bookman,* Yeats is less flattering about the poetry produced by his Dublin friends, including Tynan. In "Irish National Literature III: Contemporary Irish Poets" Yeats reiterates his earlier observation that Tynan's poetry improved after her first volume because she studied the Irish translators and was freed from the "bondage of imitation of contemporary English poets." Reserving his highest praise for AE, Yeats concludes that Tynan's work possesses simplicity and tenderness but lacks the passion of the Gaelic poets. This judgment is one that AE himself later modifies in his introduction to Tynan's *Collected Poems,* praising the "shy beauty" and sublimated energy that characterizes some of her later work.

In her memoirs, Tynan is silent about the occasion of meeting her future husband, Henry Albert Hinkson, son of a Protestant family from Rathmines, a suburb of Dublin. Hinkson earned his B.A. in classics from Trinity College in 1887 and in 1888 won a scholarship to pursue his M.A., which he was awarded in 1890. During his years as a student, he published several books, including *Dublin Verses By Members of Trinity College* (1895). Tynan probably met Hinkson through T. W. Rolleston or John Todhunter, both of whom contributed to this volume as well as to Yeats's anthology, *A Book of Irish Verse.* In 1891 Tynan seems to have confessed her interest in Hinkson to Yeats, who then consulted a schoolfellow about his character. In May 1893 Tynan agreed to marry Hinkson, and they decided to leave Ireland for London and a new lease on her career. The marriage took place at the London home of Alice and Wilfrid Meynell in Palace Court, and the Hinksons moved near the Meynells in Ealing, where they started a family. Hinkson worked as a classics tutor and published several novels until he decided to pursue law. He was called to the bar of the Inner Temple in January 1902.

The Hinksons lived in London for nineteen years, during which time Tynan wrote regularly for *The Independent, The Sketch,* and *Illustrated London News.* She took great pride in becoming the author of the "Wares of Autolycus" column for the *Pall Mall Gazette,* whose editor, Henry Cust, she admired for his recruitment of women writers and the work of the best new poets. Her increasing fame as a journalist and her friendship with the sociable Meynells led to Tynan's acquaintance with other Catholic poets whose work she reviewed and admired in print, particularly Francis Thompson and Lionel Johnson.

In 1894 Tynan produced the first works published under her married name, Katharine Tynan Hinkson: a volume of poetry, *Cuckoo Songs,* and a prose anthology, *A Cluster of Nuts: Sketches Among My Own People.* Perhaps because she was so well known by her maiden name, Tynan did not continue to use "Hinkson" for future volumes of poetry. In the meantime, Yeats had undertaken the work for a new anthology, *A Book of Irish Verse: Selected from Modern Writers* (1895), and he included five poems by "Mrs. Hinkson." Though he chose several of her most popular poems, Yeats wrote in his introduction that her poetry lacks reverie and speculation. This remark might be taken as censorious, if Tynan herself had not admitted that her poetry possessed limited range. In the introductory poem to *Ballads and Lyrics* called "Apologia," she writes:

> Here in my book there will be found
> No gleanings from a foreign ground:
> The quiet thoughts of one whose feet
> Have scarcely left her green retreat;
> A little dew, a little scent,
> A little measure of content,
> A robin's song, perchance to stir
> Some heart-untravelled traveller.

The Hinksons had five children, three of whom survived into adulthood: Theobald Henry (Toby), Giles Aylmer (Pat), and Pamela Mary. While her second memoir, *The Middle Years* (1916), records mainly happy memories of being a mother and active writer, Tynan's poetry of the mid to late 1890s describes many of the darker moments. Sometime in 1895–1896, a son Godfrey was born and died in infancy. Another baby, unnamed in the memoirs, died a few years later. Tynan's children were a source of great joy and pride to her. During World War I, both sons served in Irish forces on the fronts of Palestine and France and survived without physical harm. After the war Toby remained on active duty abroad, returning to Ireland in 1921 briefly to marry. He and his wife then moved to British East Africa. Tynan's second son, Pat, was part of the Army of Occupation in the Rhineland and his stories of the war and its aftermath are recounted in Tynan's third memoir, *The Wandering Years* (1922). Pat eventually returned to Ireland but moved back to England with his mother and sister after his father's death in 1919. Tynan's daughter remained her constant companion until her death. Hinkson herself published collections of sketches about Ireland as well as reminiscences about her mother's life. She edited a small collection of Tynan's verse in 1931 and was the executor of Tynan's literary estate upon her death.

Between 1894 and 1901 Tynan published *Cuckoo Songs* (1894), *A Lover's Breast-Knot* (1896), *The Wind in the Trees: A Book of Country Verse* (1898), and *Poems* (1901). These volumes depart from her earlier collections in their focus on themes of married love, motherhood, and the grief of losing two infants. *Cuckoo Songs* features a dedication "to my dearest friend, my husband" and a woodcut title page, featuring a woman with her lute, by the illustrator Laurence Houseman. The subjects of the volume range among the elegiac, devotional, and pastoral, reflecting Tynan's grief over losing Parnell and her friend the Irish poet Frances Wynne, as well as solace in religion, and her happiness in marriage. *A Lover's Breast-Knot* is a sequence of lyrics that addresses various aspects of love, drawing upon the conventional language of flowers and birds to convey her sentiments.

The mostly lighthearted poems darken with the lyric "Love Lies Bleeding," which is dedicated to her son Godfrey and conveys her intense physical feelings of the child's absence. "Holy Innocents" is a consolation poem that imagines a heavenly place for her infants. *The Wind in the Trees: A Book of Country Verse* continues the elegiac and pastoral modes of her previous two volumes and is organized according to the seasons beginning with January and ending in December. She writes about gardening and the peace that the activity brings. "Love Lies Bleeding" clearly refers to the death of Godfrey. The flower represents the wound that remains planted in the heart of the poet.

In subject matter *Poems* evolves from the previous volumes, presenting the wonder of children as they come to know the world and a mother's feelings as her children grow independent from her. There are poems on the beauty of an infant's hair ("Toby's Hair"), a child's grief over the departure of a nanny ("The New Nurse"), and the beauty of a mother's body as she breast-feeds her child ("Maternity"). The poem "Immortality" is a first-person lyric describing the power a woman feels after giving birth:

> "So I have sunk my roots in earth
> Since that my pretty boys had birth;
> And fear no more the grave and gloom,
> I, with the centuries to come."

Innocencies (1905) continues the themes of maternity but in a darker vein. "The Dead Child," "Without You," and "The Sick Child" reflect upon the feelings of helplessness and loss that haunt a woman after her child has died. "The Doves" is a throwback to Yeats's moody lyrics of the 1890s, in which the sounds of birds remind the melancholy speaker of time passing.

In 1894 Tynan moved to Notting Hill; she moved back to Ealing in 1898. In her memoirs she recalls several literary visitors to her home, vacations in Ireland, and the impact of the Boer War on English and Irish society. In recounting Queen Victoria's visit to Dublin in April 1900, she is moved by "this old, old mother of her people" who had lost so many sons in South Africa. Tynan's colorful visits to Ireland, however, were hardly vacations. Tynan recalls being exhausted by the work of revising the second edition of the anthology, *The Cabinet of Irish Literature,* which originally appeared in 1880 and was edited by Charles Read. Tynan expanded the three-volume anthology of prose and poetry to four, in part, by adding seventy-one women writers from the seventeenth to nineteenth centuries. Tynan's anthology made women writers an integral part of an Irish national tradition at the turn of a new century.

The Hinksons' frequent visits to Ireland for rural pleasures prompted them to seek new environs for their family, and in 1907 they moved to several locations in southern England–Chipperfield, Southborough, Tunbridge Wells–before finally settling in a Surrey village. In *The Middle Years* Tynan remarks that she had begun to suffer from violent headaches and white flashes, which made her wonder about her future as a writer. She felt haunted by doubts about whether her poetry mattered anymore, noting the "swing of the pendulum toward material prosperity and away from spiritual things." Tynan never mentions meeting any of the modernist poets working in England at this time, but senses that a new aesthetic has made her poetry "profitless."

If Tynan had despaired that her poetic career was on the wane, she must have felt heartened by Yeats's renewed interest in her poetry. In 1907 he and his sisters, who ran the shop at Dun Emer Press, published *Twenty-One Poems by Katharine Tynan* in a limited edition. The majority of the selections are from *Poems* and *Innocencies,* and Yeats includes the poems, "Sheep and Lambs" and "The Children of Lir," that established Tynan's reputation. In the following year Tynan followed up the Blakean allusion in *Innocencies* by publishing *Experiences* (1908), a collection that she considered to be one of her best books. Returning to Irish subjects, Tynan writes autobiographically about her father, who died in 1906, and about living away from Ireland. "A Memory," "For Your Sake," and "Everything That I Made" commemorate her father's piety, industry, and support of her work. In "'Tis Hot To-day in London,'" Tynan assumes the voice of an Irish émigré. "At Euston Station" and "The Common" reflect Tynan's own acclimatization to English life. In the first version of "Gorse," which she revised three times over the next twenty years, Tynan calls forth the golden brilliance and sensuality of a London common in high summer. The second version, published in *Irish Poems* (1913), is dedicated to "W. B. Yeats, who taught me." The loosely pentameter lines of the first version are expanded to fourteen, perhaps in imitation of "The Lake Isle of Innisfree." The speaker relishes the beauty of the furze-covered common but disavows the landscape as "not mine." In the final version, published in *Twilight Songs* (1927), the poet removes the dedication and situates herself contentedly among the gorse, which in its brightness at night "apes the sun." The poem has mellowed into mediocrity in the last version, lacking the spirit of the first and the reverie of the second. To a certain degree, the poem's evolution reflects the scattered efflorescence of Tynan's poetry, which from volume to volume tends to be uneven in quality.

Experiences was followed by *Lauds* (1909) and *New Poems* (1911), the last volumes published before Tynan and her family moved back to Ireland. In 1912 Henry Hinkson was appointed a resident magistrate in Ireland, and the family moved first to Dalkey, Killiney Bay, then to a house called Clarebeg situated near the Irish Sea in Shankill, County Dublin. Tynan was enthusiastic about the move, even though her two boys, Toby and Pat, stayed in England to attend school. The return to Ireland, however, occurred on the eve of civil war, with the workers' strikes, led by Michael Collins, in 1913, and the Easter Uprising three years later. In her memoirs Tynan tries to maintain a neutral tone about these events but seems subtly to support them. Her memoirs chronicle the significant rise in urban poverty, as well as the new spirit of commercialism, which James Joyce made his subjects in *Dubliners* (1914) and later *Ulysses* (1922). In her first year back in Dublin, Tynan became acquainted with members of a new poetry movement, led by her friend AE. The new circle included Padraic Colum, James Stephens, Joseph Campbell, and Seamus O'Sullivan, less-brilliant lights on the horizon of the Celtic Twilight, according to Yeats, but consolidating the conception of a nationalist literature, nonetheless.

One year after returning to Ireland, Tynan published three works that staked out her place in the emergent Irish poetry scene. In the introduction to a new anthology, *The Wild Harp, a Selection from Irish Poetry* (1913), Tynan claims that her selections capture "for English ears" the sounds of a "wild music" innate to Irish poetry. She includes recent poetry by AE and his contemporaries as well as the "fruits" of Yeats and work by a new young poet named James Joyce. Although she excluded herself from the anthology, Tynan's own collection, *Irish Poems,* appeared in the same year. Each poem in the volume is dedicated to friends past and present, and attempts to forge connections in Tynan's life in England and Ireland. Despite the distinguished list of dedicatees, many of the devotional and elegiac poems are rather formulaic and conventional in their use of meter or imagery. The poem "Shanganagh," dedicated to Mrs. Rowan Hamilton and named for her "castle," may be the exception. Its seemingly lighthearted diction carries a note of ominousness as a child plays on the shore of a swirling river: "Laughs the darling river, hurrying, dancing onward. / Sorrow she knows of maybe, the bird's or the bee's, / Or some butterfly weary, its wings dropped downward, / Caught in a swirling eddy, drowned in her seas." The river, as it turns out, is in Heaven, and the child, guarded by angels, plays there awaiting his mother.

The publication of *Twenty-Five Years: Reminiscences* caused some consternation among Tynan's friends,

Title page for Tynan's fourth collection of poems, published a year after her marriage to Henry Albert Hinkson

including Yeats, for the memoir liberally quotes from private letters without the permission of the authors. Yeats wrote to her that she "had not been very indiscreet" and that he would liked "to have improved the letters." Tynan uses Yeats's correspondence again in her second memoir, *The Middle Years* (1916), having asked his permission in advance. Instead of letting the corrections serve as copy, however, she places them in footnotes and defends her action by saying that his emendations reminded her of their happy collaborations in their youth. Yeats's fame may have prompted Tynan's indiscretion, or perhaps she was sending him a sign that he should remember the early days of his poetic development. Her articles on Yeats from this period suggest that he had "strayed" from his poetic ideals into a murky world of mysticism. Yeats and Tynan met once more before her death. In a story recounted by Tynan's daughter Pamela, the two poets met in Dublin at one of AE's afternoon tea parties, where Tynan and Yeats, both nearly blind, arrived "looking at a blur of indistinguishable faces." Upon recognizing Tynan, Hinkson recalls, Yeats sat down beside her and said, "Katharine, who are all these people?"

In 1913 the Hinksons moved to Castlebar, County Mayo, where Henry was assigned a position as magistrate. The family anxiously watched the country prepare for England's declaration of war on Germany. Irish volunteer forces were fully mobilized, and Tynan's sons were eager to sign up (Pat was too young to join the 1st Dublin Battalion initially, but later got his chance). As the death and casualty tolls rose, Dublin was transformed into a scene of triage and training for men serving the Allies as well as a battleground for unionist and IRA forces.

Tynan wrote her poetry in the cause of the Allies, raising funds for the Dublin Castle Red Cross Hospital from the proceeds of a poem "The Flower of Youth." Instead of being moved by the birth of a "terrible beauty" in Ireland as Yeats was, she made the return of maimed and shell-shocked soldiers the new subject for her poetry. "The Flower of Youth" had originally been published in an autumn 1914 *Spectator* and drew letters from readers all over the British Isles. With horrific reports of casualties on the battlefield making their way to the homefront, the poem offers comfort for those whose sons died in terror:

> Oh, if the sonless mothers weeping,
> And widowed girls could look inside
> The glory that hath them in keeping
> Who went to the Great War and died,
> They would rise and put their mourning off,
> And say: "Thank God, he has enough!"

Tynan has been criticized for sentimentalizing death and offering a false justification for the war's purpose. Yet the poem appeals to readers, who, struggling with the immediacy of loss, remained strong in their Christian faith.

Flower of Youth: Poems in War-Time (1915) is comprised mostly of elegies, commemorating individuals and offering consolation through images of peace in heaven. Some of the poems possess a degree of irony unseen before in Tynan's verse. "A Girl's Song," "'Mid the Piteous Heaps of Dead," and "To R. A. A." are pathetic pieces, certainly, but also they reflect upon the senselessness of violence and the ways in which the cycles of nature can obliterate any evidence of human suffering. The poems in *The Holy War* (1916), *Late Songs* (1917), and *Herb o' Grace: Poems in War-Time* (1918) reflect the concern of the Georgian poets, whose formal verse and pastoralism evoke lost visions of peace.

In the collections of verse published between 1914 and 1918, Tynan revives the use of floral motifs from *A Lover's Breast-Knot* to offer poetic balms for English and Irish mourners. Many of the poems in these volumes represent soldiers as "boys" and their cause as a "Great Crusade." Even her starkest images of the wounded, such as "The Broken Soldier" in *The Holy War,* suggest that God is immanent within them: "The broken soldier sings and whistles day to dark; / He's but the remnant of a man, maimed and half-blind, / But the soul they could not harm goes singing like the lark, / Like the incarnate Joy that will not be confined." Tynan may have gathered such a startlingly positive view of a solider's faith from her friendship with a soldier-poet, Frances Ledwidge, whom she met in 1913. Tynan had reviewed his first published volume, *Songs of Peace* (1914), and in *The Years of the Shadow* (1919) she printed several of the letters and poems that he addressed to her from France. Ledwidge's nostalgia for Ireland and optimism reflect his own way of coping with the misery, and Tynan's mentoring friendship gave him hope for his own career as a poet. Ledwidge was killed in action in June 1917 and had written movingly to Tynan on one of his final days.

In *The Years of the Shadow,* Tynan writes of visiting Dublin with her daughter in the aftermath of the Easter Uprising of 1916. She muses on the fact that her radical Fenian position had mellowed over the years due to the congenial period of her life raising three children in England and to her friendships with Anglo-Irish gentry and reformers, such as George Wyndham and the Lord and Lady Aberdeen. Viewing the conflict between England and Ireland as a "tragedy," Tynan is particularly astute on how the bigotry between English and Irish, and later Protestants and Catholics, manifests quickly in young children and is perpetrated in the next generation.

In 1919, one year after the Armistice, Henry Hinkson died suddenly, leaving his wife and daughter without a home or pension. The title of Tynan's postwar memoir, *The Wandering Years* (1922), aptly describes her state of dislocation until 1927. Although she sustained her family's livelihood with her pen, Tynan at age fifty-eight came to think of novel writing, or "pot-boiling" in her own phrase, as her most-reliable source of income, though she took little pride in this employment. Before settling in a house back in London, Tynan and her daughter traveled to Scotland, Italy, and Germany, writing articles and another book of memoirs, on the effects of the war on the people of Europe. *Evensong* (1922) and *Twilight Songs* (1927) reflect the poet's yearning for her youth, the "old country" of Ireland before the wars, and a heavenly afterlife that re-creates it. The poem "Curfew" from *Evensong* is unusual in its reflection upon Ireland as a "sad country" torn by civil strife, even after independence. The blackbird, usually ebullient in her poems, sings "his maddest song" and "plucks Death by the beard."

AE included the opening poem of *Twilight Songs,* "The Old Country," for his *Collected Poems* of Tynan published the year before her death. Addressed to her dead father, "The Old Country" exemplifies Tynan's lyric powers, or in AE's phrase, "the shapeliness of architecture" into which her memories and affections are poured:

> As I go home at the end of the day, the old road,
> Through the enchanted country full of my dreams,
> By the dim hills, the pellucid o'er-arching sky,
> Home to the West, full of great clouds and the sunset,
> Past the cattle that stand in rich grass to the knees,
> It is not I who go home: it is not I.

The poet is not "I" because she is no longer young. Like Yeats's Aengus wandering in the green shades, Tynan sees her older self as lost among "strange faces" where "no one knows me." The paradise of the enchanted country is carried within her imagination in the form of a twilight song, and as the shadows lengthen she looks forward to the "strange country" that she hopes will be heaven. *Twilight Songs* is rich in this landscape of memory and the desire for death. The last poem in the volume is the third of three Christmas carols called "The Thorns." The subject is not Christ's crown, however, but Mary's heart pierced by the loss of her child. At the end of her long eventful life, Tynan's deepest sadness remained the loss of her two infants.

In his introduction to the *Collected Poems,* AE characterizes Tynan as "the earliest singer in that awakening of our imagination which has been spoken of as the Irish Renaissance. . . . To the majority of my countrymen the symbols she uses are keys to a sanctuary they often enter." AE accords Tynan a special place at the origins of a literary movement, which, under the influence of the Symbolists, had evolved into a kind of mystic brotherhood. Yet, Tynan maintained a distance from this development, plotting instead a different course. In the poem "Thanksgiving" she reflects on her art: "I thank God when I kneel to pray / That mine is still the middle way, / Set in a safe and sweet estate / Between the little and the great." In choosing not to create a hieratic or political art, Tynan's poetry of domesticity, piety, and nature offered a position of tolerance and sympathy to her strife-ridden nation. Moreover, Tynan's "middle way" freed her to pursue the life of a professional writer, providing financial support for her family and participating in the literary cultures of Dublin and London.

Biography:

Marilyn Gaddis Rose, *Katharine Tynan* (Lewisburg, Pa.: Bucknell University Press, 1974).

References:

K. R. Alspach, "The Poetry of Katharine Tynan Hinkson," *Ireland America Review,* 4 (1940): 121–126;

Ernest A. Boyd, *Ireland's Literary Renaissance* (New York: John Lane, 1916);

Joan Montgomery Byles, *War, Women, and Poetry, 1914–1945* (Newark: University of Delaware Press, 1995);

Anne Ulry Colman, *Dictionary of Nineteenth-Century Irish Women Poets* (Galway: Kenny's Bookshop, 1996), pp. 219–229;

Fred D. Crawford, *British Poets of the Great War* (London & Toronto: Associated University Presses, 1988);

Diane D'Amico, "Saintly Singer or Tanagra Figurine? Christina Rossetti through the Eyes of Katharine Tynan and Sara Teasdale," *Victorian Poetry,* 32 (Autumn–Winter 1994): 387–407;

Ann Connerton Fallon, *Katharine Tynan* (Boston: Twayne, 1979);

R. F. Foster, *W. B. Yeats: A Life,* volume 1: *The Apprentice Mage* (Oxford: Oxford University Press, 1997);

Pamela Hinkson, "The Friendship of Yeats and Katharine Tynan, I: Early Days of the Irish Literary Revival," *Fortnightly,* 174 (October 1953): 255;

Hinkson, "The Friendship of Yeats and Katharine Tynan, II: Later Days of the Irish Literary Movement," *Fortnightly,* 174 (November 1953): 327;

Carolyn Holdsworth, "'Shelley Plain': Yeats and Katharine Tynan," *Yeats Annual,* 2 (1983): 59–92;

C. L. Innes, *Woman and Nation in Irish Literature and Society, 1880–1935* (London: Harvester Wheatsheaf, 1993);

Nosheen Khan, *Women's Poetry of the First World War* (Hemel Hempstead: Harvester Wheatsheaf, 1988);

James J. McFadden, "William Butler Yeats at Katharine Tynan's Home, Whitehall," *Yeats: An Annual of Critical and Textual Studies,* 8 (1990): 206–242;

Norreys Jephson O'Conor, *Changing Ireland: Literary Backgrounds of the Irish Free State, 1889–1922* (Cambridge, Mass.: Harvard University Press, 1924);

Norah Tynan O'Mahony, "Katharine Tynan's Girlhood," *Irish Monthly,* 59 (June 1931): 358–368;

Catherine Reilly, ed., *Scars upon My Heart: Women's Poetry and Verse of the First World War* (London: Virago, 1992);

Yeats, "Irish National Literature III," *Bookman* (July–October 1895); republished in *Uncollected Prose by W. B. Yeats,* edited by John P. Frayne And Colton Johnson, 2 volumes (London: Macmillan, 1970), I: 375–382;

Yeats, Letter to the editor of *The Daily Express* (27 February 1895); republished in *The Letters of W. B. Yeats,* edited by Allan Wade (New York: Macmillan, 1955), p. 248;

Yeats, *Letters to Katharine Tynan,* edited by Roger MacHugh (New York: McMullen, 1953);

Yeats, "Miss Tynan's New Book," *Irish Fireside,* 9 July 1887; republished in *Uncollected Prose,* I: 119–122;

Yeats, "Mr. Lionel Johnson and Certain Irish Poets," *Daily Express* (27 August 1898); republished in *Uncollected Prose,* II: 116–117.

Papers:

On her death in 1982 Pamela Hinkson, Katharine Tynan's daughter, bequeathed her mother's literary estate to the Right Reverend Richard Hanson and Canon Anthony Hanson D.D., sons of Sir Philip Hanson, Tynan's friend and the private secretary to George Wyndham. The archive, which includes typewritten manuscripts of her poems, novels, and an unpublished 429-page volume of reminiscences written in 1930, is housed in Newman House, 86, St. Stephen's Green, Dublin. Other holdings of Tynan's letters include the University of Southern Illinois at Carbondale, Special Collections, Morris Library; the University of Texas at Austin, Harry Ransom Humanities Research Center Library; University College, Dublin; the National Library of Ireland; the Central Catholic Library, Merrion Square, Dublin; and the University of Manchester.

Evelyn Underhill

(6 December 1875 – 15 June 1941)

James Whitlark
Texas Tech University

A Bar-Lamb's Ballad Book (London: Kegan Paul, Trench, Trübner, 1902);

The Grey World (London: Heinemann, 1904); republished as *The Gray World* (New York: Century, 1904);

The Miracles of Our Lady Saint Mary Brought Out of Divers Tongues and Newly Set Forth in English (London: Heinemann, 1905; New York: Dutton, 1906);

The Lost Word (London: Heinemann, 1907);

The Column of Dust (London: Methuen, 1909);

Mysticism: A Study in the Nature and Development of Man's Spiritual Consciousness (London: Methuen, 1911; New York: Dutton, 1911; revised edition, London: Methuen, 1930; New York: Dutton, 1930);

The Path of Eternal Wisdom: A Mystical Commentary on the Way of the Cross, as John Cordelier (London: Watkins, 1911);

The Spiral Way: Being Meditations Upon the Fifteen Mysteries of the Soul's Ascent, as Cordelier (London: Watkins, 1912; revised, 1922);

A Franciscan Mystic of the Thirteenth Century: The Blessed Angela of Foligno, British Society of Franciscan Studies, extra series no. 1 (Aberdeen: Aberdeen University Press, 1912);

Immanence: A Book of Verses (London: Dent, 1912; New York: Dutton, 1912);

The Mystic Way: A Psychological Study in Christian Origins (London: Dent, 1913; New York: Dutton, 1913);

Practical Mysticism: A Little Book for Normal People (London: Dent, 1914; New York: Dutton, 1914);

Mysticism and War (London: Watkins, 1915);

Ruysbroeck (London: Bell, 1915);

Theophanies: A Book of Verses (London: Dent, 1916; New York: Dutton, 1916);

Jacopone da Todi: Poet and Mystic, 1228–1306: A Spiritual Biography (London: Dent, 1919; New York: Dutton, 1919);

The Essentials of Mysticism and Other Essays (London: Dent, 1920; New York: Dutton, 1920);

The Life of the Spirit and the Life of To-Day (London: Methuen, 1922; New York: Dutton, 1922);

Evelyn Underhill

The Mystics of the Church (London: Clarke, 1925; New York: Doran, 1926);

Concerning the Inner Life (London: Methuen, 1926; New York: Dutton, 1926);

Prayer (London: YWCA, 1926);

A Franciscan Poet: Jacopone da Todi (London, 1926);

Man and the Supernatural (London: Methuen, 1927; New York: Dutton, 1928);

Life as Prayer (Edinburgh: United Free Church of Scotland, 1927?);

The Teacher's Vocation (London: St. Christopher's, 1928);

The House of the Soul (London: Methuen, 1929; New York: Dutton, 1930);

Worship (London: Mowbray, 1929; New York: Harper, 1937);

The Philosophy of Contemplation (Cheltenham: Burrow, 1930);

The Inside of Life (London: Mowbray, 1931);

The Golden Sequence: A Fourfold Study of the Spiritual Life (London: Methuen, 1932; New York: Dutton, 1933);

Mixed Pasture: Twelve Essays and Addresses (London: Methuen, 1933; New York: Longmans, Green, 1933);

The School of Charity: Meditations on the Christian Creed (London & New York: Longmans, Green, 1934);

What Is Mysticism? (London: Mowbray, 1936);

Education and the Spirit of Worship (London: Headly, 1937);

The Spiritual Life: Four Broadcast Talks (London: Hodder & Stoughton, 1937; New York & London: Harper, 1937);

The Parish Priest and the Life of Prayer (London: Mowbray, 1937);

The Mystery of Sacrifice: A Meditation on the Liturgy (London & New York: Longmans, Green, 1938);

A Meditation on Peace (London: Fellowship of Reconciliation, 1939);

A Service of Prayer for Use in War-time (London: Church Literature Association, 1939);

Spiritual Life in Wartime (London: Christian Literature Association, 1939);

Abba: Meditations on the Lord's Prayer (London & New York: Longmans, Green, 1940);

The Church and War (London: Anglican Pacifist Fellowship, 1940);

The Fruits of the Spirit (London & New York: Longmans, Green, 1942);

Light of Christ: Addresses Given at the House of Retreat, Pleshey, in May, 1932 (London & New York: Longmans, Green, 1944);

Collected Papers of Evelyn Underhill, edited by Lucy Menzies (London & New York: Longmans, Green, 1946); republished as *Life as Prayer and Other Writings of Evelyn Underhill* (Harrisburg, Pa.: Morehouse, 1991);

Meditations and Prayers (London & New York: Longmans, Green, 1949);

Shrines and Cities of France and Italy, edited by Menzies (London & New York: Longmans, Green, 1949);

Fragments from an Inner Life: The Notebooks of Evelyn Underhill (Harrisburg, Pa.: Morehouse, 1993).

Editions and Collections: *Evelyn Underhill,* Benn's Augustan Books of Poetry (London: Benn, 1932);

The Wisdom of Evelyn Underhill: An Anthology from Her Writings, edited by John Stobbart (London: Mowbray, 1951);

An Anthology of the Love of God from the Writings of Evelyn Underhill, edited by Lucy Menzies and Lumsden Barkway (London: Mowbray, 1953; New York: McKay, 1954);

The Mount of Purification (London: Longmans, 1960);

Selections from the Writings of Evelyn Underhill (Nashville: Upper Room, 1961);

The Evelyn Underhill Reader, edited by T. S. Kepler (Nashville: Abingdon, 1962);

Lent with Evelyn Underhill: Selections from her Writings, edited by G. P. Mellick Belshaw (London: Mowbray, 1964; New York: Morehouse-Barlow, 1964);

Evelyn Underhill: Modern Guide to the Ancient Quest for the Holy, edited, with an introduction, by Dana Greene (Albany: State University of New York Press, 1988);

Evelyn Underhill on Prayer, edited by Tony Castle, Christian Spirituality Series (London: Marshall Pickering, 1989);

The Ways of the Spirit, edited, with an introduction, by Grace Adolphsen Brame (New York: Crossroad, 1990);

Daily Readings with a Modern Mystic: Selections from the Writings of Evelyn Underhill, edited by Delroy Oberg (Mystic, Conn.: Twenty-third Publications, 1992);

Given to God, edited by Oberg (London: Darton, Longman & Todd, 1992);

Heaven a Dance: An Evelyn Underhill Anthology, edited by Brenda Blanch and Stuart Blanch (Chicago: Triangle, 1992);

The Soul's Delight: Selected Writings of Evelyn Underhill, edited, with an introduction, by Keith Beasley-Topliffe (Nashville: Upper Room, 1998).

OTHER: *One Hundred Poems of Kabir,* translated by Underhill and Rabindranath Tagore (London: India Society, 1914); republished as *Songs of Kabir* (New York: Macmillan, 1916);

Jan van Ruysbroeck, *The Adornment of the Spiritual Marriage. The Sparkling Stone. The Book of Supreme Truth,* translated by C. A. Wynschenck, edited, with an introduction, by Underhill (London: Dent, 1916; New York: Dutton, 1916);

Caroline F. E. Spurgeon, *The Training for the Combatant: An Address Delivered for the Fight for Right Movement,* includes a note by Underhill (London: Dent, 1916);

Walter Hilton, *The Scale of Perfection,* introduction by Underhill (London: Watkins, 1923);

A Book of Contemplation, the Which Is Called The Cloud of Unknowing in the Which a Soul Is Oned with God, edited, with an introduction, by Underhill (London: Watkins, 1934);

Eucharistic Prayers from the Ancient Liturgies, edited by Underhill (London & New York: Longmans, Green, 1939).

SELECTED PERIODICAL PUBLICATION—UNCOLLECTED: "A Defence of Magic," *Fortnightly Review,* 88 (November 1907): 763–764.

Since 1988 Evelyn Underhill has been commemorated in the Episcopalian Calendar, the closest that denomination comes to canonization. She was the first woman to lecture on religion at Oxford University and the first laywoman to lead retreats in the Anglican Church, opportunities that arose because of her books on mysticism. Their reputation still keeps in print her religious poetry (despite its no-longer fashionable style). Indeed, during her lifetime, her fame probably was a significant factor in the decision by Ernest Benn Limited to reprint in 1932 some of her devotional lyrics as part of its Augustan Books of Poetry series. Her verses are less appreciated in their own right than as part of her vision of psychological development toward mysticism. She herself abandoned writing poetry, saying that it was too easy. Poetry, nonetheless, was her primary avenue to the aesthetic, and coupled with the social work she did in the slums, it formed, she believed, a foundation for the highest level of human activity: the mystical, or the perception of ultimate reality.

Evelyn Underhill was born on 6 December 1875, the only child of Alice Lucy Ironmonger and Arthur (later Sir Arthur) Underhill. Her family soon moved from her birthplace, Wolverhampton, to London, where she was educated privately until she was thirteen years old. From 1888 to 1891 she attended Sandgate House near Folkestone. Despite her later devotion to religion, her family was not especially pious, aside from one uncle who became an Anglican priest. Nonetheless, at age sixteen she was confirmed on 11 March 1892 at Christ Church, Folkestone, and took her first communion at St. Paul's, Sandgate, on Easter Sunday. Presaging another of her future interests, she won first prize in a short-story competition conducted by *Hearth and Home* magazine that same year.

Underhill's father was a barrister of Lincoln's Inn who spent as much of his time as possible at the Royal Cruising Club that he founded. Comparably, her poetry sometimes turns from the limitations of earthly law to the freedom of ceaseless exploration, imaged as sailing. According to Margaret Cropper, her parents' motives for sending Underhill to boarding school from 1885 to 1891 may have included a desire for more leisure to enjoy their ship, the *Amoretta.* From 1888 onward, however, she joined them there during vacations. Among their frequent guests was Underhill's eventual husband, Hubert Stuart Moore, who became a specialist in marine law.

Following boarding school, she attended King's College, London, studying botany, Latin, French, Italian, philosophy, and history. A less formal but equally important component of her education was an annual trip to Europe, a practice she and her mother began in 1898. Viewing Roman Catholic art, particularly during visits to Italy, enhanced Underhill's appreciation of that faith, and her growing admiration of it fills her letters to Moore, who was much less entranced by it. Consequently, her thoughts of marrying him and of converting ran counter to one another; both thus progressed slowly while theology largely occupied her time.

The earliest of her books, the amateurish *A Bar-Lamb's Ballad Book* (1902), however, was not religious scholarship but an imitation of Sir William Gilbert's *The "Bab" Ballads* (1869). Even in that first book, nonetheless, she occasionally slips into religious allusions, as in the poem "Jones v. Lock," where an infant, cheated at law by his older siblings, "homeward riding in his little pram / Allowed his Nurse to call him 'Martyred lamb!'" The playfulness with which Underhill likens this silly baby to Christ in his trial and martyrdom as sacrificial Lamb of God is intriguing. Throughout her life her sense of humor always tempered her otherwise overwhelming piety. At this period, her modernist theology was close to Unitarian, with Jesus no more than a conventional symbol, so she did not worry that her humor was slightly tinged with blasphemy. (The book also satirizes law but with sufficient gentleness so that her lawyer friend Moore was willing to draw the linocut that decorates the volume.)

Her ruminations about religion take more direct form in her next book, the novel *The Grey World* (1904), dedicated to Alice Herbert, wife of J. A. Herbert. J. A. Herbert was the keeper of manuscripts at the British Museum and Underhill's collaborator on the book *Illuminated Manuscripts* (1911), which was published under Herbert's name. The protagonist of *The Grey World* becomes a medievalist illuminator of books, but his story derives from sources in the Oriental as well as the Occidental past. He is at first the ghost of a London slum child, who "flung out the whole force of his poor little spirit in a prayer to some Force which he dreaded but knew not, for a return, at any price, to the excitements and uncertainties of life." Reborn as Willie Hopkinson, he can recall his ghostly existence, which makes him think of both worlds—spectral and material—as equally gray and unreal.

Although reference to the protagonist's "prayer" is perhaps a concession to Christianity, the rest of his

Underhill; her mother, Alice Lucy Underhill, née Ironmonger; her father, Arthur Underhill; and two unidentified sailors on the family yacht, Amoretta

experience seems Eastern: the maya, or unreality of life, the frustrated desires of wandering ghosts (as in Buddhist myth), the impersonal divine "Force," and his reincarnation. Nurtured by a mother who expects him to be a poet, he grows up wondering "if he were really a little boy as everybody seemed to think, or only some sort of tiny insect"—an allusion to the Chinese Taoist Chuang Tsu, who wondered if he were actually a butterfly. Willie joins an ecumenical organization whose members include a "Shintoist" and "several Buddhists." This orientalism is typical of fin-de-siècle narratives, as is the presentation of art as a kind of religion and meaningful life as being derived from work at traditional crafts. (In becoming a bookbinder Willie follows an art that Underhill herself practiced with some success, one of her works being purchased by the Hungarian Museum for its collection.)

In another convention of the Aesthetic period, *The Grey World* has an "effeminate" protagonist. In a meeting likened to "the first page of a romance," he is drawn to Stephen Miller as by a "magnet": "it was a case of love at first sight, a phenomenon rather absurdly supposed to occur only between persons of opposite sex." Stephen eventually transfers his affection to Willie's sister Pauline (portrayed as a more materialistic, less suitable companion than Willie). At first Willie hears of the engagement with "disgust," but then, from a desire to imitate his friend, Willie becomes engaged to a similarly inappropriate young woman. To his great relief, she soon breaks the engagement and, after a trip to Italy, he settles near an anchoress, with whom he may share chastely a life that fuses the spiritual and artistic. He enunciates Underhill's most persistent theme: poets and mystics "all speak a different language, but what they are trying to say is substantially the same"—they are devoted to eternal, divine Beauty.

Preoccupied by this idea, Underhill approached engagement to Moore with doubts. She turned from writing her first scholarly book, *The Miracles of Our Lady Saint Mary Brought Out of Divers Tongues and Newly Set Forth in English* (1905), to composing her most scathing satire on heterosexuality, *The Lost Word* (1907). The novel tells of Paul Vickery, a name that evokes both *vicar* (indicative of his ecclesiastical forebears) and Paul Valéry, a poet who tried unsuccessfully to give up his art for a more normal existence. Valéry's marriage followed his artistic crisis by several years, but Underhill's Paul is a master builder who loses his ability to represent the Absolute because he marries. "The Word which he sought and lost had been Spiritual Chastity." As the epigraph to a chapter, she quotes the poet Arthur Symons: "To love a woman is, for an artist, to change his religion." To avoid this apostasy, rather than seek a wife (who also loses her artistic gift through wedlock), Paul should have been content with his "bond" to Mason Rogers, a relationship that he happily views as that between "master and . . . slave."

Imagery from freemasonry permeates the book, probably a residue of Underhill's brief membership in the Hermetic Society of the Golden Dawn (1904–1905), which had historic ties to the Masonic Order. Like Underhill, Paul loses his literal faith in Christianity through familiarity with historical criticism and science. Masonic initiation, however, brings his spirit into the "Graal-city"–a place he later loses when he contemplates marriage and the saints place him on trial for betraying them.

Despite all the concerns expressed in that book, at age thirty-two Underhill finally married Moore in 1907, ushering in not the complaisance that *The Lost Word* predicts but her most agonized, yet productive, period. She was greatly disturbed by Moore's vetoing her plan to join the Catholic Church. There is reason to think that she might eventually have convinced him, for the first Easter after their marriage he sent flowers to her favorite convent. In September 1907, however, Pope Pius X's encyclical *Pascendi Dominici Gregis* caused her to abandon all thought of conversion. That papal decree condemned modernists for attempting to unite science and religion in controversial ways. Underhill's primary interest in Catholicism was precisely in that modernism, which she had gleaned from the writings of George Tyrrell and Maud Petre.

By then she knew that she could not find a substitute religion as an artisan or as a member of an esoteric society. She became a religious exile, a situation she explores powerfully in *The Column of Dust* (1909), the only one of her narratives to have the developed plot and characterization expected of a novel. The book explores a paradox she first enunciated in her article "A Defence of Magic," published in the *Fortnightly Review* (November 1907), that occultism might prepare the way for conversion to "true" (in other words, mystical) Christianity. In *The Column of Dust* Constance Tyrrel summons a spirit, who first manifests as that column and then possesses her. Through their interactions (the union of finite and eternal) they manage to wake from their respective dreams of earthly and spectral life and to attain a love that transports them to the celestial presence of "the Real." The best parts of the book involve Constance's communion with the possessing spirit, whose eternal gaze transfigures ordinary events and leads her to glimpse their numinous qualities. The gaze also becomes a vehicle for Underhill's wit, as when the spirit perceives an average British church to be without spirituality. Finding no help from established religion, Constance works out her own salvation by sacrificing her life nursing her dangerously infectious daughter.

Constance is a much stronger character than either Willie or Paul, though she shares their tendencies toward homophile bonding. She is "of those women for whom the crucial encounter and the overmastering appeal must always come from one of her own sex." Consequently, she falls in love with Muriel Vince. Obstacles to their relationship include a difference in social class and Constance's various secrets: her being possessed by an extraterrestrial spirit, her eventually acquiring the "Holy Graal" (which she keeps in her cupboard), and her being an unwed mother. Not desiring a husband but wanting offspring, she mated without even inquiring the name of her daughter's begetter.

Constance is but one member of an eccentric cast. The novel also features an Egyptian priestess who sacrifices a cat to her husband's ghost; her wealthy followers, who play at asceticism; and a former poet who becomes a "Graal" keeper. More than merely an amusing satire, however, *The Column of Dust* lays out a partly original scheme of deliverance from the wasteland it ridicules. According to this scheme, one need not accept conventional sexual orientation or orthodox faith. Salvation comes from "selfless adoration," which can be learned by following such controversial activities as ritual magic and fornication to their ultimate results.

Even more significant than *The Column of Dust* was Underhill's next book, *Mysticism: A Study in the Nature and Development of Man's Spiritual Consciousness* (1911), which brought her acclaim. As the first large, popularly accessible work on that subject, it moved mysticism from the category of medieval superstition to what Abraham Maslow later considered it–a peak experience in human development. Underhill interprets mysticism as a crowning achievement coming at the conclusion of each historical period of human accomplishment: "When science, politics, literature, and the arts–the domination and the ordering of life–have risen to their height and produced their greatest works, the mystic comes to the front, snatches the torch and carries it on."

Like those other activities, spiritual experiences arise through effort and discipline. Underhill particularly notes their similarity to poetry in often involving a hypnotic use of rhythmical language to reach the unconscious. According to the first edition of *Mysticism,* because trance can be induced by such means, spirituality is largely subject to the human will. In the twelfth

Being equivocal, *Mysticism* could be read as relatively friendly to both Catholic and Protestant Christianity, a reconciliation of Christian faith with the latest in philosophy, comparative religions, and psychology; Underhill's reticence in some matters raised doubts, however. For instance, William Inge, the author of *Christian Mysticism* (1899), refrained from criticizing her tome publicly but wrote to her publisher that the book was inept philosophically and perhaps incompatible with belief in a transcendent deity. This criticism upset Underhill, who spoke privately of Inge as "the old wretch." On such key points as whether a self exists, *Mysticism* shows that Underhill was aware of many philosophical problems (which she mentions in the notes) but deliberately chose to ignore them in the main text. The popular success of the book owes much to her restraint; her later books inevitably address the vital issues she glosses over in *Mysticism* and are consequently more controversial than that earlier work.

Indicative of her fear of writing more directly about Christianity, her subsequent two books, *The Path of Eternal Wisdom: A Mystical Commentary on the Way of the Cross* (1911) and *The Spiral Way: Being Meditations Upon the Fifteen Mysteries of the Soul's Ascent* (1912), appeared under the nom de plume John Cordelier. This caution was reasonable, for the next major scholarly work to bear her name, *The Mystic Way: A Psychological Study in Christian Origins* (1913), generated controversy. In *Mysticism* her prying into the minds of Catholic saints had not bothered Protestant readers, who had no devotion to them, nor British Catholics, who were pleased that a nominal Protestant was fairly reverent to their heroes. For her to psychoanalyze Jesus, however, was more upsetting. Underhill presents him as the supreme mystic, a status that is significantly less exalted than Christian orthodoxy posits. Furthermore, following historical criticism, she presumes that the words of Jesus in the Bible were "put into his mouth" by the evangelists who shaped his legend into a myth. After reading the book, her longtime friend Arthur Machen said he could not consider her a Christian any longer.

Since it shows that Jesus was not for Underhill spiritually unique, *The Mystic Way* illuminates the volume that directly preceded it, *Immanence: A Book of Verses* (1912), her first collection of devotional poetry. One poem from the collection, "Madonna and Child, with Donor," for example, speaks of "The Son of God, the soul," as if each person shared inherently in the divine quality of Jesus rather than needing him as savior. Similarly, "Transcendence" mentions "some new avatar," implying more than one divine incarnation, an idea (like the word *avatar* itself) more Hindu than Christian. Consequently, when in the poem "Celestial Beauty" Underhill attributes "Deity" to Jesus, she presumably

Underhill at fifteen

edition, published in 1930, she regrets that she had not emphasized the importance of grace—in other words, the mystic's dependence on the supernatural. Nevertheless, she did not completely revise her book and really just updated her opinions.

In her first edition she takes seriously the vitalism of Henri-Louis Bergson, from which perspective mysticism appears to have emerged naturally as the universe evolved through progressive levels of complexity until it became not merely sentient but divine. By 1930 Bergson was passé, and Underhill had come closer to Christian orthodoxy, even (according to vague references in her letters) perhaps having during the 1920s some experiences of the presence of Christ. Nonetheless, in all editions *Mysticism* differs from Christian orthodoxy in a subtle yet significant way. According to Underhill, Catholic imagery offers a way of contacting "the Real" through the unconscious, but she did not necessarily mean to suggest that she thought the imagery was objectively true. She leaves the issue open and is never clear whether her later sensing Christ's spiritual presence made her believe the Gospel accounts of him, which Bergson repeatedly questioned.

Underhill and Hubert Stuart Moore on their wedding day in 1907

means no more than that he has found within himself a potential common to all humanity. The verses proclaim deity to be a beauty that has as its "twin brother Pain" and that reveals life beyond death. In other words, intense sensation, whether pleasant or unpleasant, may shatter complaisance and open the mystic to the Eternal.

Like *Mysticism, Immanence* is divided between two aspects of the divine: God's manifestation in the world (represented by the poem "Immanence" and the section following it) and God's transcending the physical (evoked through "Transcendence" and many of the other poems that precede it). The central poem of the collection is "The Idol," about the place of worship in uniting immanence and transcendence. Its speaker dreams herself a worshiped idol, but angels complain that the devout better deserve to be worshiped than the idol. Presumably, devotion is a paradoxical activity that opens humanity to the divine within each person but only to the extent that each devotee humbly imagines the divine to be elsewhere. Although (like *Mysticism*) *Immanence* ends with divine transcendence, Underhill's emphasis in both books is more on God's immanence–

the title she chose for that volume of poetry. Indeed, even her concluding poem, "Transcendence," not only concerns God as hidden–"the sheltering darkness" in which the spheres spin–but also as immanent in his avatars. The last line of the poem resolves the contrasting themes of divine proximity and distance by envisioning a time when humanity comes home to God.

Although Underhill wrote verse for much of her life, *Immanence* comes particularly from the period when she was discovering her own version of Christianity. In autobiographical terms the most important poem in the collection is "The Uxbridge Road." In verses redolent of Rudyard Kipling's unorthodox religious ballads, the poem describes a 1907 experience she had after spending four days at St. Mary of the Angels, a convent of French nuns at Southampton. She was walking away on Notting Hill when she "saw the hidden Spirit's thrust; saw the race fulfil / The spiral of its steep Ascent predestined of the Will." This evolutionary image of human "Ascent" is particularly modernist, while "Will" as a synonym for God seems Schopenhauerian. Her prose account of the event reads, "The day after I came away, a good deal shaken but unconvinced I was 'converted' quite suddenly once and for all by an overpowering vision which had really no specific Christian element but yet convinced me that the Catholic religion was true." Her being "converted" to Catholicism by a vision with "no specific Christian element" may sound like a contradiction. Nonetheless, for her Catholicism meant using Catholic art and rituals as ways of touching reality through the unconscious. Thus, she places *converted* in quotation marks to show that she was using the term in an idiosyncratic manner (the truth of Catholicism being to her in the effectiveness of its practices, not in its doctrines).

Other poems express spiritual stages comparable to those in her fictions. As does *The Grey World* and *The Lost Word*, "Two Carols" retreats into an idealized Middle Ages. "The Liberated Hosts," like *The Grey World* and *The Column of Dust,* concerns the companionship of living and dead. Comparable to *The Lost Word,* "La Cathedrale Engloutie" uses Masonic imagery to describe how true religion has sunk to secret depths.

Although undermined by clichés, *Immanence* showed enough poetic merit (and religious acumen) to lead to Underhill collaborating with the Nobel Prize–winning poet Rabindranath Tagore on *One Hundred Poems of Kabir* (1914), a translation of poems misattributed to the fifteenth-century mystical poet. Her other books from around the same time, *Practical Mysticism: A Little Book for Normal People* (1914) and *Mysticism and War* (1915), evidence her concern to show that her subject had pragmatic value in helping the British summon the spirituality to persevere during World War I. The war came home to her quite literally when her neighbor's house was bombed, as was Lincoln's Inn. Moore joined the hospital board and designed artificial limbs, while Underhill at first became busier than usual with her social work and from 1916 onward labored in the intelligence branch of the Admiralty. As a prank, indicative both of her sense of humor and perhaps also of a growing disenchantment with militarism, she invented a nonexistent African country as well as a guidebook for it, which she submitted to her superiors.

Appearing during the war, her second book of poetry, *Theophanies: A Book of Verses* (1916), implicitly or (in its last group of poems) explicitly has that conflict as its context. At that time the title of her poem "In Patria" presumably made readers first assume that it was about the defense of England; instead, however, it declares God to be the true home, requiring no struggle: "whilst we are, from thee we cannot fall." Comparably, while others were looking in Revelation for signs that World War I would bring an end to the world, her poem "Apocalypse" condemns that book of the Bible for its vengefulness. Rather, in the song of a skylark she hears intimations that God will tell "His vengeful hosts their fury to withhold."

The poems often express a restlessness probably induced by the strains and restraints Underhill felt during the wartime years. Typical in this regard is "Continuous Voyage," which imagines eternity as endless sailing, or "Dynamic Love," which visualizes God not as a static "Unmoved Mover" but as a "surging torrent." Sometimes this restlessness has sexual overtones: "For Love is time, succession, ardour, change; / It is the holy thrust of living things / That seeks a consummation, and enlace / Some fragment of the All in each fecund embrace / Whence life again flows forth upon its endless chase." Underhill's use of "All" suggests that living constitutes a divine collectivity of which each person is a part.

The final six poems in the collection voice generally conventional attitudes about war. "The Naval Reserve" and "The Return" imagine the loyal ghosts of veterans floating home. "England and the Soldier," "Any Englishwoman," and "Non-combatants" invoke the sleepless anguish of grieving for those soldiers. "The Dreamer in War-Time" defends visionary pursuits in the midst of a war. Underhill contends that mystical poetry requires reading courageously the dark "unfinished scroll / Where dying hands have written plain / The passion of the soul." The last poem of the volume, "Invocation," apologizes for her "failure." Such concluding humility is, of course, conventional, but given that the poem marks the finale of her poetic career, it may perhaps be taken seriously. A few experiments in free verse show that she was not entirely isolated from the changing currents in poetry, but she never produced an original poetic style. Furthermore, when in 1932 Benn published a collection of her poems, almost all were from her first volume, as if the second marked a decline. Another reason she may have eventually felt dissatisfied with *Theophanies* is that she later became an ardent pacifist, and she may have felt the subtle resistance to militarism in the volume was too easily missed by readers.

By 1917 Underhill had not only abandoned poetry but also her painful exile from established religion. Perhaps because the death of her Catholic friend Ethel Barker severed an important tie with Rome, she rejoined the Anglican Church. She had not become completely settled in that faith, however. The Catholic Modernist Baron Friedrich von Hügel, who repeatedly complained that she was little more than a deist, served as her spiritual adviser from 1921 until his death in 1925. The 1921 Upton lectures that she delivered at Oxford were not at an Anglican school but at the Unitarian-affiliated Manchester College.

Underhill with her spiritual director, Anglican bishop Walter Frere, in 1938

Published as *The Life of the Spirit and the Life of To-Day* (1922), these lectures argue: "If we exclude those merely degraded and pathological theories which have resulted from too exclusive a study of degenerate minds, we find that the current conception of the psyche . . . was anticipated by Plotinus, when he said in the Fourth Ennead, that every soul has something of the lower life for purposes of the body and of the higher for the purposes of the Spirit, and yet constitutes a unity: an unbroken series of ascending values and powers of response, from the levels of merely physical and mainly unconscious life to those of the self-determining and creative consciousness." Underhill's conception of the self as a continuum is at least more sophisticated than her previous, rather cursory formulations of it. Moreover, that continuum suits well the evolutionary underpinnings of her theology, according to which (as she proclaimed in one of these lectures) "sin is conservatism or atavism." Instead of evil being a falling away from Edenic perfection, it is a failure to strive forward. Whereas previously she had somewhat naively assumed that spiritual progress resulted from the will, she now understood it as coming from the poetic imagination: "I go on to the law of Reversed Effort. . . . The pull of imaginative desire, not the push of desperate effort, serves us best."

Like her books that precede and follow *The Life of the Spirit and the Life of To-Day,* the lectures are ecumenical, finding the same spiritual path in "Hindu, Buddhist, Egyptian, Greek, Alexandrian, Moslem and Christian" faiths. Comparably, in a 1930 essay reprinted in *Mixed Pasture: Twelve Essays and Addresses* (1933), she states: "It is never the genuine mystic who talks about 'dead forms.' He can reach out, through every religious form, to that Eternal Reality which it conveys." In *Worship* (1929) she remarks: "It has been pointed out to me that I have failed to denounce the shortcomings of Judaism with Christian thoroughness, that I have left almost unnoticed primitive and superstitious elements which survive in Catholic and Orthodox worship, that I have not emphasized as I should the liturgic and sacramental shortcomings of the Protestant sects." Despite such criticism of her tolerance, she continued to see the many faiths as paths to the same goal. What she most esteemed in von Hügel was not his more sectarian thought but his Modernism. Thus, in *Worship* she comments, "As Von Hügel said of Eucharistic devotions, whatever their theological credentials may be, they have contributed to the formation of 'saints, and great saints.'" Thus from von Hügel himself, the one who was trying to make her more orthodox, she found justification that doctrines—"the theological credentials"—might well be doubted while one follows the practices. Despite von Hügel's efforts, she remained relatively true to what had been her antisectarian motto when she was eighteen: "Be noble men of noble deeds, For love is holier than creeds."

After von Hügel's death she accepted Walter Frere, Bishop of Truro, as her spiritual director, though she also consulted Dom John Chapman, a Benedictine abbot. During this period she began leading retreats, giving radio broadcasts, and acting as the spiritual director of others. She belonged to many Anglican committees, including one revising the prayer book, and opposed the ordination of women, because she felt a female clergy would be a major obstacle to reunion with Roman Catholicism. Frere inspired her to study Russian Orthodoxy, which led to her joining the Fellowship of St. Alban and St. Sergius in early 1935. Nonetheless, by 1932 her principal director had become the Anglican Reginald Somerset Ward. He had sacrificed his pastorate to travel and give retreats. He was one influence toward her pacifism, as was also her reading of Aldous Huxley's pamphlet *What Are You Going to Do About It?* (1936). That year she joined the Peace Pledge Union, and, in 1939, the Anglican Pacifist Fellowship. Despite a mortal respiratory ailment, in the winter of 1940–1941 she composed "Postscript," a final pacifist tract. She died that summer on 15 June 1941.

Author of more than forty books, Underhill's primary literary contribution was to bring greater public notice to a host of visionary voices, including Angela of Foligno, John Ruysbroeck, Jacopone da Todi, Al Ghazzalli, Jacob Boehme, Catherine of Genoa, Catherine of Sienna, Meister Eckhart, John of the Cross, and whatever anonymous poet she mistook for Kabir. She alludes to many of them not only in each scholarly work, but also in her fiction and poetry. She influenced Thomas Merton, Alan Watts, and Charles Williams. That such mystical works as *The Cloud of Unknowing* now often find their way into medieval literature courses may owe something to her writings. Her poetic reputation has dimmed, but her argument that poetry and mysticism explore the same reality made the latter seem more familiar and encouraged such poets as T. S. Eliot to investigate the numinous. Popularized by her, the status of mysticism rose from an obsolete relic of monasticism to a respectable element of modern culture. As her writing matured, she moved away from a Victorian assumption that flesh must be sacrificed to spirit. Instead, she turned more and more to a balance between the two that anticipated New Age holism while she remained close enough to Christianity to become a virtual saint to the Episcopal Church of America.

Letters:

The Letters of Evelyn Underhill, edited, with an introduction, by Charles Williams (London & New York: Longmans, Green, 1943).

Biographies:

Margaret Cropper, *Evelyn Underhill* (New York: Longmans, Green, 1958);

Christopher J. R. Armstrong, *Evelyn Underhill (1875–1941): An Introduction to Her Life and Writings* (Grand Rapids, Mich.: Eerdmans, 1975);

Armstrong, *Evelyn Underhill,* Masters of Prayer (London: Church Information Office, 1986);

Dana Greene, *Evelyn Underhill: Artist of the Infinite Life* (New York: Crossroad, 1990).

References:

A. M. Allchin and Michael Ramsey, *Evelyn Underhill: Two Centenary Essays* (Oxford: SLG, 1977); enlarged as *Evelyn Underhill: Anglican Mystic: Eight Letters of Evelyn Underhill & Essays by A. M. Ramsay & A. M. Allchin* (Oxford: SLG, 1996);

Arthur Underhill, *Change and Decay: The Recollections and Reflections of an Octogenarian Bencher* (London: Butterworth, 1938).

Papers:

The largest collection of Evelyn Underhill's personal papers, consisting of sixty-two items, is in the King's College Archives, London. Other depositories include the May Sinclair Collection at the University of Pennsylvania, Philadelphia (fourteen letters); the St. Andrews University Archives, St. Andrews, Scotland (fifty-three letters); and the Fawcett Library, City of London Polytechnic, London (one letter).

Helen Waddell

(31 May 1889 – 5 March 1965)

Susan T. Harrington
University of Maryland Eastern Shore

BOOKS: *The Spoiled Buddha: A Play in Two Acts* (Dublin: Talbot Press, 1919; London: Unwin, 1919);

The Fairy Ring (London: Arnold, 1921);

The Wandering Scholars (London: Constable, 1927; New York: Holt, 1927);

The Abbé Prévost: A Play in a Prologue and Three Acts (Bungay: Privately printed, 1931; London: Constable, 1933);

A Book of Medieval Latin for Schools (London: Constable, 1931);

Peter Abelard (London: Constable, 1933; New York: Holt, 1933);

New York City (Newtown, U.K.: Davis, 1935);

Poetry in the Dark Ages (Glasgow: Jackson, 1948; New York: Barnes & Noble, 1948);

Stories from Holy Writ (London: Constable, 1949; New York: Macmillan, 1950).

Editions and Collections: *Songs of the Wandering Scholars* (London: Folio Society, 1982);

Between Two Eternities: A Helen Waddell Anthology, edited by Felicitas Corrigan (London: SPCK, 1993).

PLAY PRODUCTIONS: *The Spoiled Buddha,* Belfast, Grand Opera House, February 1915;

The Abbé Prévost, London, Arts Theatre, 19 May 1935.

OTHER: William F. Marshall, *Ballads & Verses from Tyrone,* introduction by Waddell (Dublin: Talbot Press, 1929);

The Blecheley Diary of the Reverend William Cole, M. A., F. S. A., 1765-67, introduction by Waddell (London: Constable, 1931);

William Cole, *A Journal of My Journey to Paris in the Year 1765,* edited by Francis Griffin Stokes, introduction by Waddell (London: Constable, 1931);

George Saintsbury, *Shakespeare,* with an appreciation by Waddell (Cambridge: Cambridge University Press, 1934; New York: Macmillan, 1934).

Helen Waddell

TRANSLATIONS: *Lyrics from the Chinese* (London: Constable, 1913; Boston & New York: Houghton Mifflin, 1915);

Mediaeval Latin Lyrics (London: Constable, 1929; New York: Smith, 1930);

Abbé Prévost, *The History of the Chevalier des Grieux and of Manon Lescaut* (London: Constable, 1931; New York: Smith, 1931); republished as *Manon Lescaut* (New York: Dutton, 1935);

Marcel Aymé, *The Hollow Field* (London: Constable, 1933);

Beasts and Saints (London: Constable, 1934; New York: Holt, 1934);

The Desert Fathers (Vitae Patrum) (London: Constable, 1936; New York: Holt, 1936);

A French Soldier Speaks (London: Constable, 1941);

Sulpicius Severus, "Cyrenaica in the Fifth Century," translated by Waddell, in *Queen Mary's Book for India* (London: Harrap, 1943);

Lament for Damon: Translated from Epitaphium Damonis of John Milton (London: Privately printed, 1943);

David Holbrock, ed., *Plucking the Rushes: An Anthology of Chinese Poetry in Translations,* by Arthur Waley, Ezra Pound, and Waddell (London: Heinemann Educational, 1968);

More Latin Lyrics: from Virgil to Milton, edited and with an introduction by Dame Felicitas Corrigan (London: Gollancz, 1976; New York: Norton, 1977).

SELECTED PERIODICAL PUBLICATION–UNCOLLECTED: "John of Salisbury," *Essays and Studies,* 13 (1928): 28–51.

At her death in 1965, Helen Waddell's nephew, Mayne Waddell, wrote a letter to Helen's sister, Meg Waddell Martin, describing his aunt as "perhaps the greatest woman-scholar" of the early half of the twentieth century. Twenty-one years later, critic Molly Tibbs called her "the most distinguished woman of her generation." Waddell's work ranged from translations of poetry to plays, novels, short stories, and fairy tales. Perhaps her greatest contributions were her idiomatic translations of secular and religious Latin lyrics, from Virgil in 119 B.C. to John Milton in 1623. In addition, Waddell produced a distinguished study of medieval writers, especially those of the seventh to the twelfth centuries, the *vagantes,* or wandering scholars, men who left the monasteries and became teachers, poets, and entertainers. The best known of these scholars was Peter Abelard, a teacher, theologian, and independent thinker famous throughout medieval Europe. According to Waddell, whether major philosophers like Abelard or mere lapidary poets, these *vagantes* reinvigorated literature. Waddell helped revise the view of the medieval world as "the Dark Ages" to a more positive perception as a time of vigorous literary activity.

Helen Jane Waddell was born in Tokyo, Japan, on 31 May 1889, the youngest of ten children of an Irish Presbyterian missionary, Hugh Waddell, and his wife, Jenny Martin Waddell, who died when Helen was two. At the age of ten, Helen was taken home to Belfast by her father, who died within the year, leaving Helen and the other children in the care of a stepmother, Martha Waddell. In Belfast, Helen first attended the Victoria School for Girls, then Queen's College, where in 1911 she earned her Bachelor of Arts degree with distinction. In 1912 she received her Master of Arts degree from Queen's College with a thesis titled *John Milton the Epicurist.* The man who evaluated her thesis, Professor George Saintsbury, commented, "For appreciation of literature and power of expressing that appreciation it would be hard to find a superior to her." In 1914, when a cousin offered to send her to Oxford for doctoral study at his expense, the youthful Helen dutifully chose to remain at home in Belfast to take care of her then-ailing stepmother.

Meanwhile, Waddell was already making her debut in the literary world with the publication of her *Lyrics from the Chinese* (1913), a forty-page translation of Chinese odes written between the seventh and the twelfth centuries B.C. Because she did not know Chinese, Waddell had to base her versions on the work of two other translators, James Legge, who produced his *Chinese Classic* in the 1840s, and the Reverend William Jennings, who started his work in 1891. Legge himself had translated his poems into prose from Latin, while Jennings, who in contrast to Legge knew Chinese quite well, translated the lyrics into a metrical version. According to one critic, Legge's translations were full of archaisms–what Waddell herself called his "awful and literal prose." One critic noted that this feature may have been encouraged in part by the grand tradition of Chinese scholarship itself, which stifled the works themselves, making the lyrics "too much commented on by revered ancients." Waddell bypassed the problem of literality by making good English poems her greatest priority.

Whereas both Legge and Jennings had translated all the original odes, Waddell distilled from the 305 poems in the original a selection of only 36 poems; sometimes she used only part of a poem. The results are translations that sometimes differ rather markedly from the originals. For example, one titled "780 B.C.: Jacques Bonhomme complains of the useless stars" is from a much longer poem and it is clearly not written by anyone called Jacques Bonhomme. Despite the departures Waddell makes from the original texts, critic James Douglas acclaimed her as "a new and powerful poet" and Professor Gregory Smith, her adviser at Queen's College, called her translations "exceptional." The translations were reviewed by, among others, the well-known Irish poet George Russell (AE) and they were much discussed in Dublin. In 1968, along with translations by Arthur Waley and Ezra Pound, some of these poems were anthologized by David Holbrook, editor of the newly formed Poetry Book Society. During the same time as the publication of her *Lyrics from the Chinese,* Waddell also embarked on her first play, *The Spoiled Buddha* (1919), which her eldest brother, Sam, produced at the Grand Opera House in Belfast in 1915. Dealing with what

Waddell and her sister Meg in 1906

Waddell's biographer Dame Felicitas Corrigan calls "the problem of human passion entangling the life of the spirit," the play concerns the fall of Buddha from grace when he becomes sexually attracted to a woman.

During this period Waddell wrote a novel in the manner of Jane Austen and Ivy Compton-Burnett titled *Discipline,* but it was never published. Written at the time when the British Parliament decided to grant some women over thirty the right to vote, the novel concerns a woman who divorces her husband because he regards her as inferior. According to Saintsbury, the book was rejected by publishers because of its "suffragettery." Also at this time, Waddell wrote articles for several newspapers and magazines as well as children's Bible stories for the Presbyterian publication, *Daybreak*.

In 1920, when her stepmother died, Waddell was able to return to her studies. At the age of thirty-one, she entered Somerville College, Oxford, where she was given the opportunity to deliver lectures to undergraduates. Her eight-lecture series on Saturdays in the fall semester of 1921 on "The Mime in the Middle Ages" was considered among the best ever heard at Oxford. Nevertheless, she found that as a lecturer she was unable to earn enough money to sustain herself and that she had little or no time for research. In June 1922, jeopardizing the possibility of earning a doctorate, she left Oxford for London, where she was to spend the rest of her life. She briefly taught at Bedford College in London from 1922 to 1923.

Before her departure, Waddell had applied for the Susette Taylor traveling scholarship. Competing successfully against many applicants, Waddell was awarded the two-year grant, and in 1923 she traveled to Paris to study the medieval wandering scholars. The resulting work, *The Wandering Scholars* (1927), challenged the accepted theory that English drama originated exclusively in the liturgical mystery and morality plays. Instead, in *The Wandering Scholars* Waddell proposes that English drama arose from secular roots. She asserts that this secular tradition even continued through the time of William Shakespeare, perpetuated in the intrigue and murder of the Jacobean and Elizabethan dramas as well as the acceptance of farce and tales of "bawdry." Furthermore, as Waddell points out, these wandering scholars (or goliards) enabled humanism to survive the Middle Ages; they produced poetry of unparalleled freshness and beauty. These qualities, she says, were earned largely through the scholars' studies of antiquity. Whether in the form of love songs, spring songs, or drinking songs, such poetry was accessible to all Europeans because it was written in Latin, which was, as she noted, "not only the language of literature, of the Church, of the law-courts, of all educated men, but of ordinary correspondence: the language in which a student will write home for a pair of boots."

By the time Waddell returned to London in 1925, the two-year term of the fellowship was almost over. She stopped by the offices of Constable, the publisher that had printed her *Lyrics from the Chinese* twelve years earlier. While applying for work as a manuscript reader, she met the director, Otto Kyllmann, who read the almost-completed manuscript of *The Wandering Scholars* immediately. He was eager to publish it. Kyllmann was to become one of Waddell's greatest friends and benefactors, offering her a staff position as literary adviser in 1932. Eighteen years earlier, another benefactor, the Reverend George Pritchard Taylor, a Presbyterian missionary in India and a Queen's College graduate, had asked Waddell to accept an allowance of £80 a year so that she could buy books. She accepted the offer but reduced the amount to £60.

The Wandering Scholars was well received by most critics. Commenting on the book, the famous English poet Walter de la Mare said in a letter to Kyllmann, "She writes about poetry absolutely unknown to me, in a fashion that is itself poetry." In 1928 Waddell received the A. C. Benson Silver Medal from the Royal Society of Literature for *The Wandering Scholars*. The medal had been rarely bestowed, and never before to a woman. The book was also commercially successful, and she received many invitations to speak at colleges and on the BBC.

The years 1924 to 1934 were the most productive of Waddell's life. She now counted as friends some of England's most important literary figures, including Julian Huxley, the British biologist and author, as well as the famous dramatist George Bernard Shaw, who recognized her brilliance and originality. The best-known people in England sought her company, including the prime minister, Stanley Baldwin, and Queen Mary. Though she received many offers, especially at this time, Waddell never married.

In 1929, at the age of forty, she published *Medieval Latin Lyrics,* a translation from the Latin of poems composed by the wandering scholars in the years 1150 to 1250. Some of the poems are by anonymous writers, but a few are by such well-known figures as Boethius, the Roman philosopher and statesman, and Alcuin, the English scholar and ecclesiastic. The book also includes three poems by Abelard. In addition, the collection includes twenty-seven translations of *Carmina Burana,* thirteenth-century songs from the monastery of Benedictbeuern (from which 'Burana' is derived). One of the best-known medieval anthologies, the manuscript consists of many love and drinking songs. Before the publication of *Medieval Latin Lyrics,* few of these songs had been known either to scholars or to the public. In 1937, German composer Carl Orff made *Carmina Burana* the centerpiece of his famous oratorio. *Medieval Latin Lyrics* was generally well received with one reviewer commenting that Waddell possessed "the most important of all the translator's qualifications—a sympathy with her material." The English composer Gustav Holst also set several of the poems in the book to music and based the libretto of his chamber opera, *The Wandering Scholar* (1929), on Waddell's translations. On the other hand, a well-known Cambridge medieval scholar, George Gordon Coulton, wrote a review in *The Times* (London) in 1930 criticizing her work. He repeated his opposition a year later in a letter to *The Observer,* to which Waddell responded publicly. Later, however, in a personal letter to Waddell, Coulton admitted that it was "hard . . . for an old man . . . one nearing the end of his work, not to feel jealous . . . It was my own reputation that was challenged."

In 1931 Waddell translated Abbé Prévost's *The History of the Chevalier des Grieux and of Manon Lescaut* (1731) into eighteenth-century English prose and followed it with a play, *The Abbé Prévost.* Also in 1931 Waddell published *A Book of Medieval Latin for Schools.* This book was a collection of excerpts, both poetry and prose, which Waddell said represented the kind of material she would have liked to have translated when she was learning Latin, rather than the traditional Julius Caesar. Brevity and lightheartedness characterize most selections; few are more than twenty-eight lines, and they concern topics such as sleeping out of doors, overworked students, the apostle Peter, and the arrival of spring. Like the much longer *The Wandering Scholars* and *Medieval Lyrics,* this small work was well received. In a letter to Waddell (published later in Woolf's *Death of the Moth,* 1942), Virginia Woolf commented, "A purr of content and anticipation rose from half the armchairs in England." According to Monica Blackett, a friend and Waddell biographer, *A Book of Medieval Latin for Schools* continued to sell well decades after its release.

In 1926 Waddell had started working on a novel based on the life of Abelard, and in 1933 *Peter Abelard* was published. One of her most successful works, the novel was eventually translated into nine languages. *Beasts and Saints,* a translation of Latin fables from the fourth to the end of the twelfth century, was published in 1934. The following year Waddell traveled to New York City to receive an honorary doctorate from Columbia University. Then, in 1936, she published *The Desert Fathers (Vitae Patrum),* a study of fourth-century ascetics who sought spiritual truth in the desert.

In 1939, at the outset of World War II, Waddell, against the advice of her friends, purchased a large and unmanageable house in London. In November 1944 her house was bombed, and she was almost killed. During the bombing she sat up in bed as soon as she felt the hit; a substantial piece of ceiling missed her head and landed on the pillow. Even before war was officially declared, Waddell was under no illusions about the desperate situation facing England. She found expression for her feelings of dread through the creation of one of the few original poems she wrote, a poem from April 1939 titled "Earth Said to Death." Quoting Milton in a letter to her sister Meg in September 1939, she commented, "I think far more than in 1914, people feel that they are fighting 'principalities and powers and the rulers of darkness'."

The immediate effect of the twin burdens of caring for her house and trying to survive the war made Waddell postpone plans to publish a projected biography of John of Salisbury. Salisbury was an English philosopher, humanist, and Latinist and Abelard's best-known pupil. Instead, she turned back to medieval lyrics. According to Corrigan, Waddell said many of the poems evoked parallels to the suffering of England and Europe, especially a fragment by Alcuin lamenting the Lombard occupation of Rome.

Waddell turned her art of translation to political and human use. When Adolf Hitler invaded Poland in 1939, she sent a cable to President Franklin D. Roosevelt expressing her consternation and followed up by publishing in *The Nineteenth Century* a free translation into English of a poem called "The White Eagle," a popular, patriotic Polish song based on a toast by Kornel Ujejski, poet, patriot, and prophet. When she was asked how she translated a song in a language she did not know, she responded that she picked up the rhythm while it was being sung and that a friend told her the meaning. Waddell also became involved in resistance activities. When France fell to Hitler in 1940, Waddell got in touch with the Free French headquarters in London. Finding "something to do for France," she translated the manuscript of a young man in the French Resistance, Guy Robin, into a series for *The Nineteenth Century,* a periodical she was then editing, and in 1941, into a book titled *A French Soldier Speaks* (using the name Jacques as a pseudonym for Robin). In 1943 her translation of the French soldier's insight into the war brought Waddell a request from General Charles de Gaulle to translate his speech at Tunis. According to Blackett, de Gaulle considered Waddell's translation better than his original speech.

Waddell's third important literary accomplishment of the war years was a translation from the Latin of Milton's poem *Epitaphium Damonis*. In 1638 Milton had lost his dearest friend, Charles Diodati, and mourned him in a pastoral elegy. She found that the traditional, impersonal form of the elegy, in which Milton expresses his grief at Diodati's death through mourning a fictional shepherd named Damon, itself "became a kind of liturgy that releases emotion even while it controls it." Far from cramping her emotionally or technically, translating *Epitaphium Damonis* into English enabled Waddell to find expression for her own grief at the death of her nephew, George Martin, who died in the war at the age of twenty-three. Dedicated to Martin, *Lament for Damon* was published privately for family and friends in 1943. When World War II ended in 1945, like many Londoners, Waddell said she felt fatigue rather than exhilaration. She was also unable to recover the spirit and delight in living that she felt ten years earlier.

Waddell, receiving an honorary degree at Columbia University on 3 June 1935, with (left to right) the Archbishop of St. Louis, John Glennon, President Nicholas Murray Butler of Columbia, and Henry A. Wallace, Secretary of Agriculture

After the war Waddell produced the last book published under her name, *Stories from Holy Writ* (1949), a reprint of some Bible stories she had written for children thirty years earlier. In Glasgow in 1947, she also carried out what was to be her final major literary project–the W. P. Ker Eighth Memorial Lecture titled "Poetry in the Dark Ages." Noting that the title of the lecture should have been "Latin Poetry in the Dark Ages," Waddell argued in favor of Rome's demise as a political power so that its legend, rather than its decadence, could inspire Europe. According to Waddell, it was Rome's poetry, not its laws, that the people of the Middle Ages remembered, and this poetry, translated and reinvigorated by medieval clerics, assured that Western literary and historical development could follow a continuous tradition from antiquity to the present.

As was the case with many of Waddell's translations, the audience members at the Ker Lecture were unfamiliar with most of the medieval poems she quoted, ones that she had translated during the war years. In 1976 the lyrics were published posthumously by Corrigan in a volume titled *More Latin Lyrics*. The book consists of Waddell's previously unpublished translations of poetry, translations from languages other than Latin, and previously unpublished original poetry. *More Latin Lyrics* also included an undated preface to this book, which was planned but not brought to fruition because of the war.

The 1976 collection of Latin lyrics, compared to her earlier compilations, includes more religious poetry. Although there are six new poems from *Carmina Burana*, the collection also includes nine poems written by saints. The tone of the poems is also considerably more somber than in her earlier books; one by Alcuin, for example, mourns the absence of one whose love his mind cherishes "with its whole desiring." Waddell's own poems of this period are likewise dark, especially her prophetic evocation of death in "Earth Said to Death" (1939) and her ironic juxtaposition of quotations from the New Testament against the rhetoric of war in "Hitler Speaks" (1940). Even the earlier poems in this volume are somber, including "New York City" (1935), written as a result of her visit to New York to receive a degree of D. Litt. In this poem, perhaps ironically, she compares the skyscrapers of New York to the roofs of Notre Dame in Paris. She also contrasts the Babylonish lust for money exemplified by the modish skyscrapers and expensive cars with the human compassion offered by Bellevue Hospital, a "house of light . . . for the sick and dying." A poem opening with the line "I stood within the empty House of Life," probably written when she was at Queen's University, also strikes a characteristically pessimistic note, evoking youth waiting for life, life which steals away even as it arrives. Like these poems that she wrote herself, Waddell's translations in *More Latin Lyrics* also reveal a common thread. In this case, the translations here most closely resemble the technique of her 1913 work, *Lyrics from the Chinese*. Exercising the same kind of freedom as in that book, in which she sometimes translated only parts of poems, here she sometimes uses part of a poem and then translates another part as though it were an entirely new poem. Clearly, in translating works from other languages, Waddell felt that she could justify creating a new poem in order to sustain the spirit of the older literature. To illustrate Waddell's approach, Corrigan cites Edward Fitzgerald's comment, "Better a live sparrow than a stuffed eagle."

In 1949, as Waddell turned sixty, her output slowed to letters, tributes, and translations of single poems published in *The Times*. She began to complain of severe forgetfulness. Even her letters to her sister Meg became sporadic. Although in 1955 the BBC recorded an interview with her based on an earlier paper titled "The Art of Translation," it became increasingly clear that Waddell was most likely suffering from Alzheimer's disease. By 1957 she failed to recognize even those closest to her. She never knew about the death of Kyllmann in 1958. On 5 March 1965 Helen Waddell died of pneumonia in a nursing home.

Although a few critics maintain that Waddell's output never equaled her prodigious talents, all agree that she contributed much to literature. Probably most significant are her Chinese and medieval Latin translations, what her obituary writer in *The Times* called her "poet's gift of translation." Commenting on her translations of Latin poetry in particular, *The Times* writer asserts that "few have interpreted so well its poetic impulse, or captured with so haunting an effect [its] tenderness and passion." Moreover, for the entire forty years of her writing life, Waddell retained the ability to capture and transmit the lyrical spirit of her originals. In so doing, she enabled new generations to experience the immediacy and intensity of the classics. Healing a gap that had hitherto existed between scholarship and aesthetics, Waddell made it possible for her audience to encounter the originals in all their directness and spontaneity. Through injecting the freshness of ancient poetry into the present, she achieved her aim of making readers comprehend and grasp the classical past and thereby renew their imagination.

Biographies:

Monica Blackett, *The Mark of the Maker: A Portrait of Helen Waddell* (London: Constable, 1973);

Felicitas Corrigan, *Helen Waddell: A Biography* (London: Gollancz, 1986).

References:

Arthur Cooper, "Englishing the Earliest Chinese Poems," *Agenda,* 20 (1982): 54–59;

Molly Tibbs, "Helen Waddell, A Thwarted Life," *Contemporary Review,* 248 (April 1986): 221–222.

Anna Louisa Walker
(Mrs. Harry Coghill)
(circa 1836 – 7 July 1907)

Bettina Tate Pedersen
California State University, Northridge

BOOKS: *Leaves from the Backwoods,* anonymous (Montreal: John Lovell, 1861);
A Canadian Heroine: A Novel, as the author of *Leaves from the Backwoods,* 3 volumes (London: Tinsley, 1873);
Plays for Children (London & New York, 1876 [i.e., 1875]);
Against Her Will, 3 volumes (London: Tinsley, 1877);
Lady's Holm, 3 volumes (London: Tinsley, 1878);
Hollywood, 3 volumes (London: Tinsley, 1880);
Two Rival Lovers: A Novel, 3 volumes (London: White, 1881);
Oak and Maple: English and Canadian Verses, as Mrs. Harry Coghill (London: Kegan Paul, Trench, Trübner, 1890);
The Trials of Mary Bloom: A Staffordshire Story, as Coghill (London: Hutchinson, 1894).

OTHER: Margaret Oliphant, *The Autobiography and Letters of Mrs. M. O. W. Oliphant,* edited and arranged by Walker, as Mrs. Harry Coghill (Edinburgh & London: Blackwood, 1899; New York: Dodd, Mead, 1899).

SELECTED PERIODICAL PUBLICATION–UNCOLLECTED: "The Vicar of Moor Edge," *Leisure Hour* (1895).

The two volumes of poetry published by Anna Louisa Walker (later Mrs. Harry Coghill) represent the smaller portion of her literary output, which also includes five "triple-decker" (three-volume) novels, a book of children's plays, a novella, and her edition of her cousin Margaret Oliphant's autobiography and letters. Walker's occasionally sentimental, frequently religious and didactic verse ranks her among the minor English poets, but her contribution to Canada's nascent national literature during the few years she lived in that country gives her poetry some historical importance.

Scholarly consensus puts the date of Walker's birth at around 1836. She was born in Staffordshire to Robert Walker, a civil engineer, and Anna Walker. As a girl Walker moved with her parents and two older sisters, Isabella and Frances, to Canada, where her father had been hired to work on the construction of the Grand Trunk Railway. They lived at first in Pointe de Levy (today Lévis-Lauzon), Quebec, then followed the westward progress of the railroad to Sarnia, Ontario, where they settled in 1858. The three sisters established a private school there for young ladies. In a biographical sketch of Walker in his *Canadian Hymns and Hymn Writers* (1908), A. Wylie Mahon quotes a former pupil of the sisters who described them as "very English, very dignified, and somewhat exclusive, but . . . excellent teachers, especially in the departments of history and English literature. Anna was the youngest and best looking of the three sisters. At times her face had a pensive and somewhat dreamy expression. Her manner was gentle and sweet." Walker's sisters died after a few years, and the school was closed.

Walker had been writing poetry since she was a teenager, and while working as a schoolteacher she had had some of it printed in Canadian periodicals. In 1861 she gathered the poems into *Leaves from the Backwoods,* which appeared anonymously; it was published by subscription in Montreal by John Lovell, one of the two foremost Canadian publishers of the nineteenth century. The subscription list comprised 150 names from Canada, the United States, and England, and many subscribers requested multiple copies.

Leaves from the Backwoods is divided into three sections: "The Dear," "Miscellaneous Poems," and "Leaves from the Wayside." The verse throughout is nostalgic, largely religious, and often didactic. The nostalgia is expressed in a longing for childhood, for

England, for lost loved ones and friends, and for happier times. Walker generally closes her poems by directing the reader to acknowledge God's hand in the events depicted.

The epigram from William Shakespeare's *As You Like It* (1600) with which Walker precedes "The Dear" encapsulates the tenor and theme of the first part of the volume: "And this our life, exempt from public haunt, / Finds tongues in trees, books in the running brooks; / Sermons in stones, and good in everything." The first poem, "Christmas Midnight Chimes," asks the bells to "Wake in each heart a joy as great, as pure as childhood's own" and "With softened distance-mellowed tone, fall on the listening ear / Of him, whom rolling seas divide from all he holds most dear; / Let the loved voices of his home, come mingled with your peal."

In contrast to the joyfulness of "Christmas Midnight Chimes," nearly half of the thirty-two poems in "The Dear" deal with death or other forms of bereavement. In "Dead" the speaker muses about keeping the beloved deceased alive in memory, then acknowledges the reality of the loss, and is ultimately comforted by the prospect of a reunion in the hereafter: "Dead? no! thou'rt living yet– / Distant, but we *shall* meet again, / And heart be read by faithful heart, / When love more closely draws his chain, / Round friends forever met." "The Bridal," however, offers no religious consolation in the face of death: "See! they fade, the flowers ye bring, / For the bride, to-morrow; / Little fragrance they shall fling, / Round the bride, to-morrow; / Cast them forth, and bring, instead, / Yew, that mourneth for the dead, / Twine dark ivy overhead, / For the bride, to-morrow." "Visions" also faces loss without recourse to religious optimism:

> I have dreamt of a home in a changeless clime,
> Where nought that we loved was the spoil of Time;
> Where the summer breezes' gentle wings
> Brought to our dwelling all lovely things;
> And life was bliss on that happy shore–
> I've dreamt;–but I see the bright vision no more.
> I dream no more of a golden age,–
> I have learned a lesson from life's dark page;
> Flowers may bud, and bloom, and die;
> Storms may darken the summer sky;
> But not in skies, or in withering flowers,
> Is the saddest change;–for that change is ours
> Day by day, as our life glides past,
> Something must leave us that graced the last;
> Some rose of hope, from its stem is shed;
> Some bud of fancy, falls pale and dead;
> Till nought is left, but the scentless bloom
> That memory plants by affection's tomb.

Walker closes "The Dear" with two poems that reflect on the plight of the poor, a typical middle-class Victorian preoccupation. In "Autumn" the speaker criticizes praise of "autumn's charms" in view of the season's effects on the homeless: "I shudder to my inmost heart, / To hear the bitter blast sweep by, / And think of frail and shivering forms / Beneath this wintry sky; / Of childhood and of helpless age, / That begs its bread from door to door / Amid this Autumn's tempest's rage; / God shield the homeless poor!" "Christmas Carol" evinces a biting sarcasm:

> Two children singing in the street
> With plaintive voice, low and sweet,
> A simple strain, so soft and clear,
> That many a passer stayed to hear,
> And smiled or sighed to note their rhyme
> In honour of the Christmas time.
> "We are wanderers, wanderers ever,
> No friends, no home have we,
> We sleep beside the river,
> Or 'neath the spreading tree;
> We have not kindred faces
> Our winter days to cheer,
> Yet, we wish you a merry Christmas,
> And a prosperous New Year!
> We see, through many a window,
> The gleaming firelight shine,
> Shine on us, poor and friendless,
> Yet why should we repine?
> We know that He who seeth
> The poor, our cry will hear,
> So we wish you a merry Christmas,
> And a prosperous New Year!"

The poems expressing nostalgia for England include "To an Oriole. Seen May, 1861," which likens the bird to an exile and Canada, with its "cold shores," to a "living tomb"; the speaker urges the oriole to return to its "land of flowers," since "Home, home alone is blest!" "The Evening Walk" begins by praising the Canadian woods as a "rustic palace" with "arching boughs that . . . Mock man's laborious tracery, and show / A mightier Architect–no windows throw, / Though stained with loveliest hues, a light so pure, / So cool, so chaste, as, through the fluttering screen, / Steals down upon the flowers, and lends them grace." Those flowers, however, are contrasted with "our English flowers . . . fair" whose "familiar faces stir our hearts"; the Canadian flowers are "unnatural . . . Strange to our eyes, and speechless to our hearts." The preference of the speaker in "Flowers" for the English flowers is even stronger: "Oh, bring me, bring me flowers, from my own dear land again . . . the flowers, I ever loved the best, . . . My eyes grow dim with unshed tears, the tears of vain regret, / Oh, flowers of home, in many a dream, your bright forms haunt me yet, / But never, never more amid your beauties may I stand, / Or lay ye on my heart again, gems of my fatherland!"

Seven of the first ten poems in part 2, "Miscellaneous Poems," address the "woman question"; Walker's position on the issue is conservative. The speaker of "Ianthe," the opening poem, is a virgin who throws herself into the sea to appease the gods and save her village: "O father! friends beloved! if any be / most fit to die in such a cause, 'tis I: / Thou knowest, Father, I have ever led / A simple innocent life, nor once have failed / To bring my daily offering to the gods." The following poem, "Joan of Arc," also depicts a virgin who dies in the service of her country; here, however, the woman's sacrifice is dishonored by betrayal, imprisonment, torture, forced confession, and execution. Both poems end abruptly, without moralizing commentary.

In "Women's Rights" Walker attacks feminists who denigrate the domestic sphere:

> You cannot rob us of the rights we cherish,
> Nor turn our thoughts away
> From the bright picture of a "Woman's Mission"
> Our hearts portray.
> We claim to dwell, in quiet and seclusion,
> Beneath the household roof,–
> From the great world's harsh strife, and jarring voices,
> To stand aloof;–
> Not in a dreamy and inane abstraction
> To sleep our life away,
> But, gathering up the brightness of home sunshine,
> To deck our way.
> As humble plants by country hedgerows growing,
> That treasure up the rain,
> And yield in odours, ere the day's declining,
> The gift again;
> So let us, unobtrusive and unnoticed,
> But happy none the less,
> Be privileged to fill the air around us
> With happiness;
> To live, unknown beyond the cherished circle
> Which we can bless and aid;
> To die, and not a heart that does not love us
> Know where we're laid.

In "The Ballad Singer" a wandering female balladeer esteems above all a "beautiful home" full of love: "There peeps from the windows bright / A spirit of heartfelt joy, / And winter and summer, and day and night, / It blesses the household with calm delight, / And pleasures that never cloy; / 'Tis the pure home love that hallows the spot, / And sheds its light o'er that peaceful cot." In "Home" the speaker represents all women who have allowed ambition to lure them out into the world: "when the goal approaches, and our eyes / Greet, bright, and almost won, the wished-for prize, / Still, half regretful, turn our thoughts again / To homes we left that glittering prize to gain, / Fondly recalling fireside pleasures fled, / And joys, o'er which long years a glory shed." In "The Old Wife" the title figure is honored by her husband for "the records of her faithful love," including "My solace in each hour of need, / My anchor that no storm could move; / For me each day of care she bore, / For me and mine the tears she shed; / Rememb'ring all, I can but pour / A thousand blessings on her head." "Song. Respectfully Dedicated to the 'Women's Rights' Convention" catalogues the accomplishments of women as soldiers, wits, scholars, artists, and poets, then turns to an ironically ardent rejection of domesticity:

> Home affections! peaceful hours!
> Fireside joys, that once were ours;
> Vain delusions! meant to keep
> Women's souls from loftier sweep,
> We have cast you all away.
> Husbands, children, what are they?

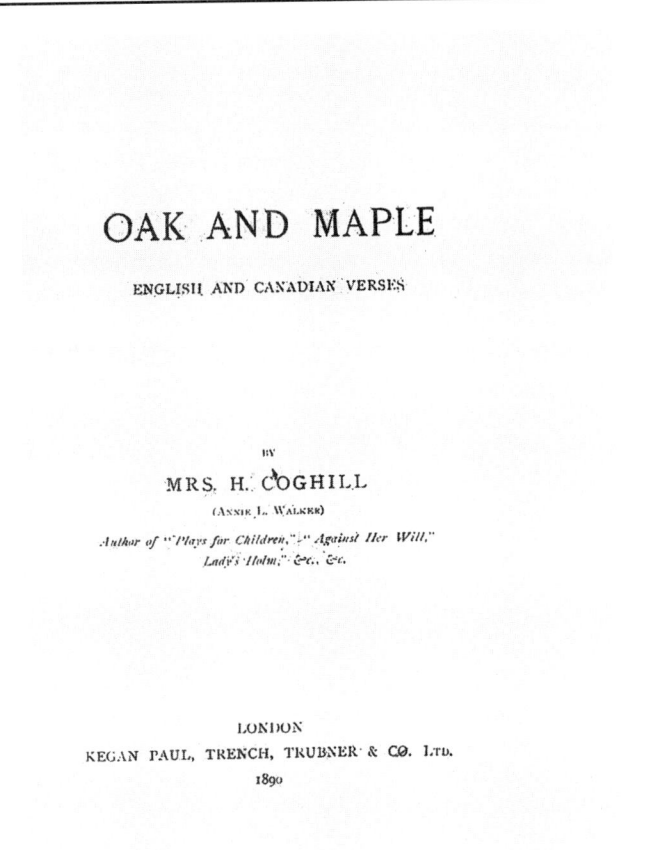

Title page for Anna Louisa Walker's second volume of poetry, published to assert her authorship after she learned that a poem from her first volume had been republished without her permission and attributed to someone else

Ours no more each household task,
Injured Women's Rights we ask!

Other poems treat a variety of themes. "A Ballad" deals with infanticide from the point of view of the victim: "Mother, here in the forest / You left me to starve and die, / And here, where my bones are bleaching, / Your lifeless corpse must lie; / But now, the gates of Heaven / May open to let you in, / For true and hearty repentance / Has washed away your sin." In "Genius" Walker says that intellectuals will be "blest, trebly blest, if in each dangerous hour / Religion guides them with her ray divine." In "Clarissa Harlowe. A Small Picture, by Landseer, in the Vernon Collection" art has a didactic function: "Thus, after years of absence, vivid, and pure and bright, / She, in some hour of dreaming, rises before my sight; / Thus Art, with magic pencil, sketching a vision fair, / Preaches of faith and patience, faith that can quell despair."

In "Lines to a Friend. March, 1859" Walker acknowledges the virtues of her new home: "I would have had you see to-day, my friend, / How beauteously our Canada can vie / With our still dearer England, in the charm / Of sky and lake and river." She likens Canada to more exotic reaches of the British Empire: "I could have dreamt, the genii of the lamp / Had heaped the waters with the costly freight / Of jewels, for Aladdin's matchless pile. / Long stood I on the shore, and could not tear / My feasted eyes from such a lovely scene, / Till the clear waters 'gan be tinged with gold, / And, slowly, slowly, westward sank the sun." In "A Forest Legend" she describes the aurora borealis, "those northern gleams that throw, / When all the hills are white with snow, / O'er earth and sky their rainbow glow, / Yet fade and leave it night." Longing for England is, however, keenly expressed in several other poems, such as "The Islander's Song of Home":

Oh, give me back my home!
Brightly may shine
The land to which we roam—
It is not mine.
Give me the hills again!
The glorious hills,
Whose fragrant breath the soul
With rapture fills.
Give me the sounding sea!
Its hollow roar,
Dear beyond words to me,
Give me once more.
I wake amid the night,
All is so still;
Oh! could its murmured voice
The silence fill!

Or dreaming, I behold
The tall ships glide,
With white and tapering masts,
O'er the blue tide.
These are the sights I see
Where'er I roam;
Nought has such charms for me—
Give me my home!

The final poem in part 2 reiterates this theme:

It is not that I cannot see
In other lands the brave and good,
Nor that I hold all right to be
Engirt by thy surrounding flood;
Let other lands be great and fair,
And other skies more clear than thine,
Yet, not for all of rich or rare,
Would I exchange the rays that shine
Bright with the favouring smile of God
Upon thy throne, thy church, thy sod.
Heart cherished home! no length of years
Divorces that sweet name from thee;
One changeless love my bosom bears,—
Star of the Ocean! 'tis for thee.
. . . .
While from afar I see thee shine,
My heart's devotion shall be thine!

The eleven poems in part 3, "Leaves from the Wayside," are religious. The volume ends with "Life's Pilgrims," an Italian sonnet that instructs a silent sojourner to rejoice and give thanks, keeping heaven and worship around God's eternal throne in view.

Shortly after the publication of *Leaves from the Backwoods* Walker and her parents returned to England; her parents soon died. In the spring of 1865 Walker wrote to introduce herself to her second cousin, Oliphant, who was then living in Paris. In her autobiography Oliphant recalled: "I heard for the first time of our afterwards so familiar and beloved cousin Annie, in reality a second cousin, whom I had never seen, but who wrote introducing herself to me, with some literary aspirations, taking at that time the shape of poetry, against which I remember I advised her, suggesting a novel instead." The two women first met after Oliphant returned to her home in Windsor in December; according to Oliphant, "Cousin Annie, whom I did not know before, drifted towards me almost as soon as I came to Windsor, and as she was an orphan without a home, stayed with me for a number of years." In the narrative Walker wrote to link Oliphant's autobiography and letters, she describes herself as Oliphant's "intimate and housekeeper." While living with Oliphant, Walker published five novels—*A Canadian*

Heroine (1873), *Against Her Will* (1877), *Lady's Holm* (1878), *Hollywood* (1880), and *Two Rival Lovers* (1881)–and *Plays for Children* (1875). She remained with Oliphant until her marriage to a wealthy widower, Harry Coghill of Coghurst, on 29 January 1884.

In 1890 Walker published her second volume of poetry, *Oak and Maple: English and Canadian Verses*, listing herself on the title page as "Mrs. H. Coghill." In the preface she related that her motivation for publishing the work was the discovery that her poem "The Night Cometh," from *Leaves from the Backwoods*, had been used as a hymn text without her permission and attributed to someone else:

> Cares and anxieties, and the swiftly-accomplished loss of all those who had had pleasure in my doings, had swept the book and its contents almost out of my mind, when I was startled one day by seeing some verses of my own printed among those to be sung at a great temperance meeting. I asked whence they came, and was told "from Moody and Sankey's Hymn-book." I borrowed a copy of Messrs. Moody and Sankey's collection, and there, slightly altered, set to a tune which is not, certainly, strikingly beautiful, and attributed to somebody I never heard of, were my poor verses, beginning, "Work, for the night is coming."

Most of the forty-seven poems in *Oak and Maple* are repeated from *Leaves from the Backwoods;* twelve are new. "A Lament for Books" bemoans the rise of literary criticism. "Old Letters" reflects on the memories aroused by touching the letters of deceased friends and loved ones:

> I cannot touch them with a careless hand,
> I cannot view them with a careless eye;
> There spells the shades of love and youth command,
> And bind the present to the days gone by.
> I touch them with a reverent hand, and see!
> What shadowy forms around me seem to rise;
> Gentle and fair, and oh, how dear to me
> Are those familiar forms, those friendly eyes.

"Love" is a religious poem:

> Child of the everlasting love,
> Sweet inmate of our world of pain,
> By thee life's deepest pulses move,
> From thee our souls new courage gain;
> With varying aspect, steadfast mind,
> Thee ever by our path we find.
> . . . .
> And age goes creeping on its way,
> A grey-haired spouse, a tottering dame–
> Changed is their world, and changed are they,
> Thou, only thou, art still the same;
> Youth's joy, life's solace, age's friend,
> Heaven's self thy mission shall not end.

"Song of the Willow" tells of a woman longing for suicide; "Wedded and Widowed" is about a wife's bereavement and the lonely life that awaits her. The penultimate piece in *Oak and Maple,* "In the Canadian Woods," is one of Coghill's longest and best poems. A five-part ode in rhyming couplets of iambic pentameter, with three inserted lays of a different meter and rhyme scheme, it evinces the Romantic themes of nature's beauty and soothing power. The speaker reminds readers that when nothing else can heal a wounded spirit, nature can:

> Oh! in such moments when no mortal nigh
> Reads the wild misery in the tearless eye,
> And when no human voice, however dear,
> May dare to break upon the conflict drear,
> Then the deep gorge, the ever-flowing stream,
> The cloud-flecked heavens, calm as an infant's dream,
> Have subtler ways to reach the troubled heart
> Than man's most boasted wisdom can impart,
> And softening still as still their charms increase,
> The pain grows less, and yields almost to peace.

Furthermore, nature is egalitarian in sharing its bounty; all people, regardless of class, stand on an equal footing before it:

> Oh, perfect Nature! thus to hear and see,
> To feel the beauties that attend on thee,
> This is a boon that all alike may share,
> Free as the flowing tide, th' encircling air.
> Th' enchantress Art for some may spread her store,
> To others, Wisdom yields her costly lore;
> To some Ambition's glittering prizes fall,
> Wealth, Honour, Health, and Love are not for all;
> *Thou* greet'st alone, with equal aspect mild,
> Earth's greatest monarch or the cotter's child.

The volume closes with "The Last Evening," a reflection on the passing of life and the inexorable process of change:

> That hour is past; the silent stream
> Bears other boats upon their way;
> But we and ours are like a dream
> That faded in the Autumn day.
> Parting, and change, and death! We read
> No dark previsions on that sky;
> No shrouded griefs with silent tread
> Upon the waters passed us by.
> And yet not God Himself could call
> That bright day from the vanished past,
> Nor gather up the links, whose fall
> Has made that evening hour the last.

After *Oak and Maple*, the only original works Coghill published were a novella, *The Trials of Mary Bloom: A Stafforsdhire Story* (1894), and a short story, "The Vicar of Moor Edge," in the London periodical *Leisure Hour* in 1895. Her husband died in 1897. Oliphant died the same year, leaving Coghill and a niece with authority over her papers. Coghill saw *The Autobiography and Letters of Mrs. M. O. W. Oliphant* to publication in 1899. The consensus among critics is that Coghill was responsible for establishing Oliphant's conservative reputation by sanitizing the text of the autobiography. Coghill died in Bath on 7 July 1907.

References:

Vineta Colby and Robert A. Colby, *The Equivocal Virtue: Mrs. Oliphant and the Victorian Literary Market Place* (New York: Archon, 1966);

William A. Guerry, "Mrs. Oliphant," *Sewanee Review*, 8 (January 1900): 64–72;

Elisabeth Jay, Introduction to *The Autobiography and Letters of Mrs. Margaret Oliphant: The Complete Text*, edited by Jay (Oxford & New York: Oxford University Press, 1990);

Laurie Langbauer, Foreword to *The Autobiography of Mrs. Oliphant, Arranged and Edited by Mrs. Harry Coghill* (Chicago & London: University of Chicago Press, 1988);

A. Wylie Mahon, *Canadian Hymns and Hymn Writers* (St. Andrews-by-the-Sea, N.B., 1908);

Bettina Tate Pedersen, "Regional and Female National Selves in the Fiction of Post-Confederation Canadian Women Writers, 1867–1900," dissertation, University of Illinois at Urbana-Champaign, 1997;

Merryn Williams, *Margaret Oliphant: A Critical Biography* (London: Macmillan, 1986).

Anna Letitia Waring

(19 April 1823 – 10 May 1910)

Crys Armbrust
University of South Carolina

BOOKS: *Hymns and Meditations* (London: Gilpin, 1850; enlarged edition, London: Cash, 1852; enlarged again, London: Cash / Dublin: McGlashan & Gilpin / Edinburgh: Menzies, 1854; enlarged again, London: Bennett / Edinburgh: Menzies, 1858; Philadelphia: Association of Friends for the Diffusion of Religious and Useful Knowledge, 1859; enlarged again, London: Bennett / Edinburgh: Menzies, 1860; Boston: Dutton, 1863; enlarged again, London: Bennett, 1863; enlarged again, London: Strahan, 1870; enlarged again, London: Daldy, Isbister, 1878; enlarged again, London: Shaw, 1883);

"What can't be cured must be endured"; or, Christian patience and forebearance in practice (London: Nisbet, 1854);

"Early to Bed, and early to rise, Makes a man healthy, wealthy and wise"; or, Early Rising, a natural, social, and religious duty, as the author of "What can't be cured must be endured" (Northampton: Abel & Sons / London: Nisbet, 1856);

Additional Hymns (London: Bennett, 1858);

Lizzie Weston's Mission (Boston: American Tract Society, 1864);

The Wasted Grain and Other Poems (Leominster: Orphans' Printing Press, 1867).

OTHER: *Days of Remembrance: A Memorial Calendar,* compiled by Waring (Dublin: Hodges, 1886).

SELECTED PERIODICAL PUBLICATIONS–UNCOLLECTED: "Dwelling in Safety," *Sunday Magazine,* 7 (1 November 1870): 128;

"A Song of Allegiance," *Sunday Magazine,* 7 (1 June 1871): 529;

"Mercy before Sacrifice," *Sunday Magazine,* 7 (1 September 1871): 749.

The literary remains of Anna Letitia Waring are comparatively few for an author whose works were consistently before the reading public for more than sixty years. Her reputation rests largely on a single volume, *Hymns and Meditations,* first published in 1850 and enlarged several times during her career; she is best known today for the hymn that begins "Father, I know that all my life / Is portioned out for me," a metrical paraphrase of Psalm 31:15. She garnered a large readership in both Britain and the United States, and her verse evoked powerful emotions in its readers and praise from critics. In the introduction to the eighth edition of *Hymns and Meditations* (1863), the Right Reverend F. D. Huntington, Episcopal bishop of central New

Anna Letitia Waring

York, categorized the work as "a class of devotional writings having a peculiar ministry and a peculiar value," indicating Waring's evangelical working- and lower-middle-class readership. On stylistic grounds Huntington praises Waring's pure "tone of spiritual feeling," her "inventive thought," her "fine discriminations in the application of terms," her "delicate shades of imaginative coloring," and her "certain reserve and self-command in the use of fancy."

Waring was born on 19 April 1823 in Plas-y-Velin, Neath, Glamorganshire, Wales, one of seven children born to Elijah and Deborah Waring. Waring's father was known for his refined literary tastes and dedication to social reform. He had become a journalist after relocating in 1810 from his native Hampshire to Wales, where he had campaigned vigorously for parliamentary reform in *The Cambrian Visitor* (1813), a journal he founded and edited. Later he published a biography of his friend Iolo Morganwg (Edward Williams), *Recollections and Anecdotes of Edward Williams, the Bard of Glamorgan* (1850). Waring's mother appears to have been supportive of her daughter's literary productions; Waring's biographer Mary S. Talbot records an extract from an 1842 letter from the mother to her sister in Hampshire: "Anna Letitia is a beautiful writer in prose. I do not know any one who can more originally or tersely express herself on any subject she chooses to descant." Waring was the niece of the hymn writer Samuel Miller Waring, whose *Sacred Melodies* (1826) exerted a powerful influence on her religious outlook and literary work.

Life in the Waring household was rarely uneventful; many guests enjoyed the hospitality of Waring's father, whom she described to Talbot as "full of sympathy for all in distress or need." An example is given in an anecdote Waring told Talbot: "One day he [our father] brought home two New Zealand chiefs who were being exhibited in the town. He had asked them to spend a week with us, thinking they must suffer a great deal in the confinement of their lives." The children contributed to the genial atmosphere of the household, devising comic entertainments and writing humorous nonsense prose and verse. Anna Waring's interest in verse was nurtured during visits in the 1830s to the Hampshire home of her aunt Sarah Waring, who had published two volumes of nature poetry and a biographical sketch of the Swedish botanist Carolus Linnaeus.

In 1840 Anna Waring decided to leave the Society of Friends (Quakers), to which her family had belonged for generations, and join the Church of England. Her resolve to do so was strengthened by her reading of a document left behind by her uncle Samuel, who had died in 1827, in which he said that he had converted to Anglicanism because he felt a need for the sacraments; Waring had the same need. Her family acquiesced in her decision, and after much self-examination she was baptized by the Reverend Anthony Crowdy on 15 May 1842 at the Parish Church of St. Martin's, Winnall, Winchester. Following her conversion, Waring undertook an in-depth study of the Scriptures, even learning Hebrew so that she could read the Old Testament in the original language. She also made a daily practice of reading from the Hebrew Psalter.

Waring's career as an author began in 1850 with the publication of *Hymns and Meditations* by the Quaker bookseller and publisher Charles Gilpin of London. The octavo volume, which was priced inexpensively at two shillings sixpence, included nineteen poems. All of the verses are paraphrases of biblical texts; the most memorable ones are taken from the Psalms, such as "Father, I know that all my life," "In Heavenly Love abiding," and "Go not far from me, O my God." Waring's vision of sin is terrible, but it is accompanied by the promise of salvation by a merciful Supreme Being. Divine revelation, stoic resignation, and spiritual redemption figure in each of the poems. Enlarged editions of the book were brought out by other publishers in 1852 and 1854.

The popularity Waring attained with *Hymns and Meditations* was increased by the publication of two prose tracts, *"What can't be cured must be endured"; or, Christian patience and forebearance in practice* (1854) and *"Early to Bed, and early to rise, Makes a man healthy, wealthy and wise"; or, Early Rising, a natural, social, and religious duty* (1856). These works are typical of the instructional and improvement tract literature that was produced throughout the Victorian period and targeted at working-class audiences.

In 1858 Gilpin's successor, Alfred William Bennett, published Waring's second volume of poetry under the title *Additional Hymns*. The fourteen poems in the book are in the same vein as those in her first volume and were incorporated into *Hymns and Meditations*, beginning with the eighth edition in 1860. These later editions of *Hymns and Meditations* were published in the twelvemo and sixteenmo formats, pocket-sized volumes that were cheap to produce and convenient for buyers to carry. Equally important in furthering Waring's reputation were the popular hymnbooks in which some of her poems achieved wide circulation, most notably the *Leeds Hymn Book* (1853), the American Unitarian *Hymn Book for Church and Home* (1868), and James Martineau's *Hymns of Praise and Prayer* (1873). Martineau's 4 April 1873 letter to Waring, requesting permission to include her poems in his collection, is quoted by Talbot; it is indicative of the way many readers felt about her: "With memory of long-standing spiritual obligations to you, he writes to you not as an entire stranger: for, in truth, the quiet hours of sympathy in thought, which may be given by true heart words, like yours, are of more avail to unite the distant, than ordinary intercourse to make friends of the near."

In the 1860s Waring began taking an active part in the temperance and prison-reform movements, an involvement that continued for the rest of her life. Two works of the period reflect her interest in reform issues: *Lizzie Weston's Mission,* a prose tract, was published in Boston in 1864 by the American Tract Society; *The Wasted Grain and Other Poems* was published in 1867 by the Orphans' Printing Press in Leominster, Herefordshire.

Waring's entrance into mainstream publishing came in 1870, when Alexander Strahan published the eleventh enlarged edition of *Hymns and Meditations.* Waring's appearance in Strahan's list put her in the company of such authors as Alfred Tennyson, Anthony Trollope, and William Ewart Gladstone. The association also gave Waring the opportunity to publish her poems in Strahan's sevenpenny monthly, *The Sunday Magazine,* which had an estimated readership of ninety thousand. Between 1870 and 1883 the Strahan firm and its successor, Dalby, Isbister and Company, published four more editions of the work. In 1883 Daldy, Isbister dropped *Hymns and Meditations* from its list; but the work was taken up by the Society for Promoting Christian Knowledge, which continued to publish it until long after Waring's death.

Waring's only other publication was a compilation of scriptural texts, *Days of Remembrance: A Memorial Calendar* (1886), published in Dublin. From the 1890s until her death she wrote poetry only for private circulation among her friends. Talbot includes some of these poems in an appendix to her biography of Waring.

Waring spent her last years in Bristol, where she visited inmates in Horfield Prison and was active in the Discharged Prisoners Aid Society. According to Talbot, "In her own conversation there were no conventional sayings, no vain repetitions; each thought came slowly, clothed in graphic and appropriate language. There was always an extraordinary directness of approach in all her dealings with her fellows, and her gravity of manner had in it no sternness. Those who knew her well took much delight in the fund of merry quiet humour which lay concealed under her grave demeanour." Waring died on 10 May 1910 after a brief illness. At her request, most of her letters and many of her unpublished verses were destroyed after her death.

References:

Alfred H. Miles, *The Sacred Poets of the Nineteenth Century,* 12 volumes (London: Routledge, 1906), XI: 387–396;

Mary S. Talbot, *In Remembrance of Anna Letitia Waring* (London: Society for Promoting Christian Knowledge, 1911).

Rosamund Marriott Watson
(Graham R. Tomson)
(6 October 1860 – 29 December 1911)

Linda K. Hughes
Texas Christian University

BOOKS: *Tares,* anonymous (London: Kegan Paul, Trench, 1884); republished as *Tares: A Book of Verses,* as Marriott Watson (Portland, Me.: Mosher, 1898);

Daisy Days, by Watson, as Tomson; Edith Nesbit; Carl Otta; Robert Ellice Mack; and Agnes M. Clausen (New York: Dutton, 1888);

The Bird-Bride: A Volume of Ballads and Sonnets, as Graham R. Tomson (London: Longmans, Green, 1889);

A Summer Night, and Other Poems, as Tomson (London: Methuen, 1891); republished as *A Summer Night and Other Poems,* as Marriott Watson (London: John Lane / Chicago: Way & Williams, 1895);

The Patch-Work Quilt, as Tomson (London: Nister / New York: Dutton, 1891);

Vespertilia, and Other Verses, as Watson (London: John Lane / Chicago: Way & Williams, 1895);

The Art of the House, as Watson (London: Bell, 1897; New York: Macmillan, 1897);

Old Books, Fresh Flowers, as Tomson (Gouverneur, N.Y.: Privately printed at the Adirondack Press, 1899);

An Island Rose, as Watson (London: Nister, 1900);

After Sunset, as Watson (London & New York: John Lane, 1904);

The Heart of a Garden, as Watson (London: Moring, 1906; Philadelphia: Jacobs, 1906;

The Poems of Rosamund Marriott Watson (London: John Lane, 1912).

OTHER: *Ballades and Rondeaus, Chants Royal, Sestinas, Villanelles, Etc.,* edited by Gleeson White, contributions by Watson (London & New York: Walter Scott, 1887);

Ballads of the North Countrie, edited, with introduction and notes, as Tomson (London: Walter Scott, 1888; New York: White & Allen, 1888); abridged and republished as *Border Ballads,* Canterbury Poets series (London & Newcastle-on-Tyne: Walter Scott, 1888; New York & London: White & Allen, 1888);

Ballads of Books, edited by Andrew Lang, contributions by Watson (London & New York: Longmans, Green, 1888);

"Ballad of Pentyre Town," in *Sea-Music: An Anthology of Poems and Passages Descriptive of the Sea,* edited by Elizabeth A. Sharp (London: Walter Scott, 1888);

Selections from the Greek Anthology, edited by Watson, as Tomson (London: Walter Scott / New York & Toronto: Gage, 1889);

Concerning Cats: A Book of Poems by Many Authors, edited by Watson, as Tomson (London: Unwin, 1892);

"Omar Khayyám," in *The Rubáiyát of Omar Khayyám,* translated by Edward FitzGerald (Philadelphia: Coates, 1898);

Mother Goose Nursery Tales, contributions by Watson (London: Nister, 1898; New York: Burt, n.d.);

The H. G. Wells Calendar: A Quotation from the Works of H. G. Wells for Every Day in the Year, edited by Watson (London: Palmer, 1911); republished as *Great Thoughts from H. G. Wells* (New York: Dodge, 1912).

SELECTED PERIODICAL PUBLICATIONS–UNCOLLECTED: "'Mariage de Convenance.–After!' (*Orchardson*)," as R. Armytage, *Academy* (12 June 1886): 415;

"Beauty, from the Historical Point of View," as Tomson, *Woman's World,* 2 (July 1889): 454–459; and 2 (August 1889): 536–541;

"The Ballad of Tonio Manzi," as Tomson, *Scribner's,* 7 (January 1890): 53–54;

"Procris," as Tomson, *Universal Review,* 7 (May & June 1890): 79–92, 226–237;

"At the Sign of the Golden Bird," as Tomson, *Macmillan's Magazine,* 63 (December 1890): 136–141;

Review of *A Minor Poet,* by Amy Levy, as Tomson, *Illustrated London News* (21 November 1891): 667;

"My Kinsman's Portrait," as Tomson, *Speaker* (8 October 1892): 440–441;

Review of *Poems* and *The Rhythm of Life,* by Alice Meynell, as Tomson, *Academy* (21 January 1893): 53–54;

"The Bailiff's Daughter," as Tomson, *Independent* (22 June 1893): 26–28;

"In the Down Country," as Tomson, *Magazine of Art,* 17 (1894): 206–211.

In singling out the most telling feature of poems by Rosamund Marriott Watson, William Archer settled on their intimidating "correctness": "Without metaphor or exaggeration of any sort, Mrs. Marriott-Watson has achieved an astonishing correctness of style and perfection of technique. 'Achieved' is perhaps not the right word; this sense of form is a thing innate, constitutional." Archer referred chiefly to her lyrics; the American editor Edmund Clarence Stedman, who included her work in his *Victorian Anthology* (1895), linked quite different traits to her ballads. In an 1895 letter to Robert Bridges he wrote, "The Armytage-Tomson-Watson sequence is interesting. Well, a woman who can write such ballads has a right to be her own mistress–to touch Life, one may say, at as many points as she cares for?"

Technical control fused with imaginative and erotic flight (Stedman's "sequence" refers to the poet's second adulterous elopement from marriage) informs the career of Watson and her significance for the nineteenth and twentieth centuries. A notable exponent of aestheticism and decadence, she contributed to seven volumes of *The Yellow Book* and published with John Lane at The Bodley Head. If she insisted (like her mentor Andrew Lang) on Tennysonian plangency of sound and rhythmic subtleties, she participated in avant-garde poetics in impressionist poems on urban streets and gardens or landscape's atmospheric effects; ballads of revenants, monsters, and feys; an array of French verse forms; and defiantly agnostic lyrics. Other elements in her poetry adumbrate women's literary modernism: her experimentation with free verse and chiselled images, her revisions of fairy tale and myth, and her adoption (like H.D.) of male decadence for poems articulating transgressive female desire. Her biographical importance derives as well from her friendships with Lang, Thomas Hardy, Henry James, and H. G. Wells and from her participation in a women writers network that included Alice Meynell, Mathilde Blind, Amy Levy, Elizabeth Pennell, Katharine Tynan, and Violet Hunt. Her admission of broken marriage and divorce as subjects of poetry and her unstable nom de plume also illuminate the role of gender in poetic careers and anticipate twentieth-century feminist issues.

In a 1905 letter to Nora Hopper–in one of only three extant paragraphs of autobiography–she overcame her characteristic reticence to describe her early childhood:

> It is so difficult to write things about oneself, & I don't feel as if I had anything interesting to tell. I was born in London, & have read poetry and written verse ever since I can remember. I had naturally rather a lonely childhood as all my brothers & sisters were so far older than myself. From my father, who was a very brilliant personality, an ardent bibliophile, (& a very graceful verse-writer) I owe a fairly wide acquaintance with prose & poetry, more especially poetry, in which he had a fine taste. He had a large & well-chosen library in which I spent my happiest hours.

Rosamund Ball was born in Hackney on 6 October 1860, the youngest of five children of Benjamin Williams Ball, an accountant, and Sylvia Good Ball, who had their daughter baptized in the Anglican Church. As

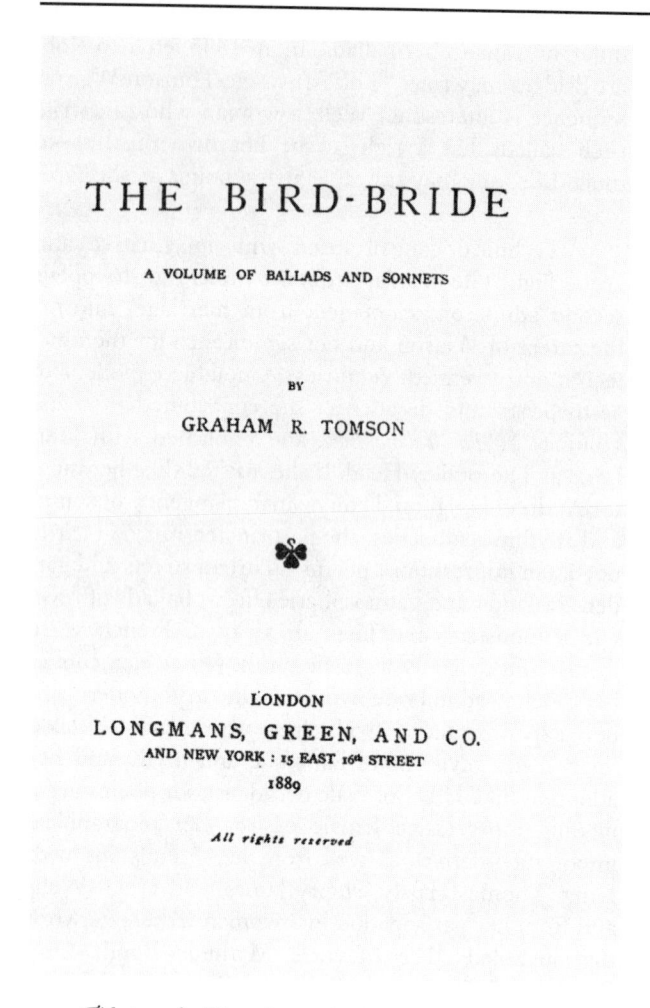

Title page for Watson's second volume, published under the pseudonym she derived from the name of her husband, painter Arthur Graham Tomson

an adult she was fluent in French and had some knowledge of German and classical literature, but how she came by this learning, and whether she traveled during childhood, is unknown. Her 1905 letter mentions only wide reading in her father's library and the influence on her own work of Jean Ingelow, Algernon Swinburne, Dante Gabriel Rossetti and Christina Rossetti, and William Morris.

When Ball was thirteen, her mother died of uterine cancer at age fifty-five, leaving "Rose" (her name in family circles) more solitary than ever, and perhaps giving her the opportunity to develop unconventional views. If artistic ambition originated with her father, the bank clerk and amateur poet, it descended both to Ball and her older brother, Wilfrid Williams Ball, who was trained as an accountant but attended art school after hours, winning praise from James McNeill Whistler in the early 1880s for his work in watercolor. Wilfrid seems to have pursued his artistic career against the wishes of his father, who excised all mention of this son from his will; this background may explain Ball comment to Hopper: "my dearest ambition was to become a painter; but, as an art education did not come within the range of practical politics, I had to give up the idea."

Instead, Ball followed, at first, a far more conventional course. During her childhood the family relocated to Wandsworth, another center of accountants and stockbrokers but a step up from Hackney. By 1874, the year of his wife's death, Benjamin Ball had risen to the position of secretary of a bank. His youngest daughter speedily developed into a beauty who dazzled through her wit and learning as well as physical presence. Her attractions, and the improved social contacts afforded by her father's rise in profession, led to what must have seemed a brilliant marriage on 9 September 1879. Her husband, George Francis Armytage, seven years her senior, had been born in Tasmania but had attended Jesus College, Cambridge, where his most distinguished accomplishment was on the river (he rowed in the University Boat in 1874) rather than in examination halls. In addition to athletic physique he possessed sufficient wealth to ensure that he and his wife could live a life of independent leisure. That Rosamund's own family recognized the disparity between their fortunes and those of their son-in-law is evident in the marriage registry, where Benjamin Ball, momentarily forgetting his salaried position at the bank, signed himself "gentleman" in imitation of Rosamund's new father-in-law.

The couple settled in Surbiton, not far from Hampton Court and Kingston-upon-Thames. Despite what seem in retrospect their disparate interests, the couple appears to have been happy at first, and Rosamund gave birth to Eulalie Georgina on 26 June 1880 and to Daphne on 29 September 1884. The young Mrs. Armytage did not neglect her literary interests, continuing to write poetry and publishing a signed article (as "Mrs. G. Armytage"), "Modern Dress," in the September 1883 *Fortnightly Review,* anticipating her later fashion column for W. E. Henley in the *Scots Observer.* If this article was her first signed publication, it appeared too late for her father to read; he had died in August, willing the only copy of his original poems to Rosamund. The next year her debut volume, *Tares,* appeared anonymously under the Kegan Paul, Trench imprint.

A slender work comprising fifteen poems, *Tares* might derive its title from Sir Thomas Browne's *Religio Medici* (1643): "Not picked from the leaves of any author, but bred amongst the weeds and tares of mine own brain"—boastful and modest at once, a coupling that characterized her dealings in the literary marketplace all her life. *Tares* reflects wide reading (writers such as Horace, François Villon, John Milton, and Johann Wolfgang von Goethe) and—despite what may be the title's boast—direct borrowing from Robert Browning, Alfred Tennyson, and Ingelow. Her poem "Eidothe?," for example, is Browningesque in its representation of a couple who briefly attain union ("one hour our souls were one") before their love unravels due to "Chance and the world's cult," a conventionality that "stifled the spirit-birth." If Rosamund Armytage borrowed, however, she also innovated. "Old Pauline" echoes the form and matter of Tennyson's "Rizpah" (1880) but explores a mother's loss of her daughter rather than a son to the city and its lures. "Beyond" borrows from Ingelow's "Divided" (1863)—"divided" is the first word of "Beyond"—but merges the theme of sundered lovers with a glancing, evasive tone by turns cynical and bored, its speaker perhaps articulating a legitimate union now broken beyond repair, perhaps regretting an omitted opportunity for illicit passion, and concluding that "real" love is a needful self-deception:

> The tender light of illusion
> Shines unsullied for aye, through the dusk of my life's dim room,
> Only a glimmer; nay, but say, only a beacon,
> Pallid, but steady and pure, as the sacred lamp in a tomb.

While she shows less technical "correctness" here than in later work, attesting to incomplete development, she could also be expressing a willingness to break poetic rules in the interests of experimentation. The little booklet was briefly reviewed in the 21 March 1885 *Academy,* which noted the poet's modest pretensions and "lugubrious" vision but detected genuine talent as well:

> The technical quality of the verse seems to us to be distinctly high. Condensed, forcible, even vigorous, exact, and often masterful is the handling of words in this little book. Higher than such merit, high as it must be considered, is the strong vein of poetic feeling. If this is the book of a young writer, we have no hesitation in saying that it is work of the greatest promise.

The recurrent note of disillusionment and uncoupling in *Tares* (in his 1893 *Rambles in Books* Charles F. Blackburn noted that the five letters of its title "form also the word 'tears'") may reflect the downward spiral of the Armytage marriage. Though in much of 1884 she was pregnant with the daughter born in September, the couple began to quarrel over her habit of being seen publicly riding in other men's carriages in South Kensington. Unable to resolve their differences, they obtained a legal separation in January 1885, when Daphne was not yet four months old; Armytage agreed to pay Rosamund an allowance of £500 a year "so long as she lived a virtuous life," as a report in *News of the World* noted (6 February 1887). She moved in with her married sister, Sylvia Lewis, from whose house she continued to publish poems mocking the permanence or fulfillment of marriage, most notably in "'Mariage de Convenance.—After!' (*Orchardson*)," signed R. Armytage in the 12 June 1886 *Academy*. This poem defends an eloping adulteress, blaming disparities in age and economic power rather than the errant woman:

> Small wonder that she fled
>   To love and laughter,
> To Life's full swirl and stir,
> Though years must bring to her
>   Even a bitterer,
>   More sordid, "After"—
> . . . .
> A woman rashly bought,
> Ambition coldly sought,
> Passion and Greed—have wrought
>   This desolation.

Certainly, by June 1886 she was finding her own consolation in "love and laughter" with Arthur Graham Tomson, son of a bank manager and himself a landscape painter who could provide a window onto the profession from which she had been barred as a girl. Born in Chelmsford, Essex, Tomson had studied art in Düsseldorf and by 1886 was exhibiting at the Royal Academy and Grosvenor Gallery, soon affiliating himself with the New English Art Club founded that year. He was in many ways a quiet man, according to Pennell, "given to . . . melancholy"; but Pennell also calls him "one of the best friends in the world" and a "spirited revolutionary." This defiance of tradition was soon evident. In October 1886 the lovers eloped to Cornwall and George Armytage filed for divorce, which he obtained, along with custody of their two daughters, in August 1887. By then Rosamund was seven months pregnant; on 21 September she and Arthur married, and on 29 October their son Graham was born in Abinger.

"Graham R. Tomson," however, the name under which she enjoyed her greatest success as a writer, debuted even earlier, in the 9 December 1886 issue of *The Independent* (New York), with "Ballade of the Fair Sorceress." She in fact published under all three poetic signatures (R. Armytage, Graham R. Tomson, and Rosamund Marriott Watson) in *The Independent,* one of several periodicals in the United States—including *Atlantic Monthly, Harper's,* and especially *Scribner's*—to which she regularly contributed. As she remarked to Hopper, "the American periodicals were first and kindest to a quite unknown versifier." Audiences in the United States also tended to accord her more stature as a poet

Frontispiece, with Arthur Tomson's portrait of the author in her garden, and title page for her second poetry volume

than in England; not surprisingly, the majority of her surviving papers are housed in U.S. collections.

Periodicals in the United States also led to her introduction to English audiences. On receiving a submission to *Harper's New Monthly Magazine* from Graham R. Tomson in 1887, Andrew Lang, then British editor, was so impressed that he announced the arrival of a new poet in his monthly column ("At the Sign of the Ship") in *Longman's Magazine*. Her work was immediately marked for inclusion in an important document of aestheticism, *Ballades and Rondeaus, Chants Royal, Sestinas, Villanelles, Etc.*, edited by Gleeson White (1887), reprinted several times in the 1890s. Twelve of her poems appeared in this collection, which also featured work by Austin Dobson, Henley, Lang, and Edmund Gosse. Her translation of Joseph Boulmier, as well as an original poem, also appeared in Lang's *Ballads of Books* in 1888. Overnight Tomson had become a recognized poet with entrée to important literary circles. All along it was assumed, however, that Graham R. Tomson was "Mr. Graham R. Tomson" (so-named in White's and Lang's volumes), a convenient screen for a poet whose divorce had been reported in weekly papers. Only after Lang exchanged a few letters with the new poet and invited "him" to dine at the Savile Club was Rosamund forced to reveal her identity. By then, however, the entrée had been secured.

Lang's influence can be discerned in Tomson's technique (he corrected imperfect rhymes and irregularities in poems she sent to him) and her interest in romantic lore and eighteenth-century settings, fostered as well by the acquaintance she had formed with Dobson. Lang also helped her with several book projects, including her edition of *Border Ballads* (1888), for which Lang wrote the notes—despite assertions to the contrary on the title page, her edition of *Selections from the Greek Anthology* (1889, to which Lang contributed translations)—and her first signed volume of poems, *The Bird-Bride: A Volume of Ballads and Sonnets*, published in 1889 by Longmans, Green (for which Lang served as literary adviser).

Tomson was not merely a Lang disciple. As if to make up for time lost as Rosamund Armytage, she embarked on a whirlwind of publishing and social contacts from 1887 to 1889, often in directions uncongenial to Lang's conservative tastes. She and Arthur attended Socialist Party gatherings and hosted occasional meetings at the home (complete with studio) into which they moved in early 1888: Number 20, St. John's Wood Road. Here they also entertained an array of literary, artistic, and feminist acquaintances, including Oscar Wilde, Hardy, Walter Sickert, Levy, Blind, Mona Caird, George Bernard Shaw, William and Elizabeth Sharp, and Americans Joseph and Elizabeth Pennell, Louise Chandler Moulton, and Harold Frederic. In 1889 Hardy nominated her for membership in the Society of Authors and arranged for her to sit beside him at the 3 July 1889 dinner. In late May of that year, she attended the inaugural dinner of the Literary Ladies, founded specifically to promote opportunities for women writers; and it was around this time that she began regularly seeing Elizabeth Pennell, who quickly became her closest friend.

Tomson was also writing prolifically, publishing signed poems, art criticism, and essays (including the two-part "Beauty, from the Historical Point of View" in Wilde's *Woman's World*); penning the introduction for her edition of the Greek Anthology; and inaugurating her witty fashion column for Henley in the *Scots Observer*, which Pennell later termed "a poem with a stately measure in frocks and hats, a flowing rhythm in every frill and furbelow." It was amid this flurry of activity that *The Bird-Bride: A Volume of Ballads and Sonnets* appeared in April 1889.

This book represented a clear advance over *Tares* in range and technique. The volume was divided into five sections—ballads, sonnets, verses, translations, and a cluster of fixed French verse forms (the last mostly reprinted from Gleeson White's 1887 collection)—and the emotional register ranges from violent passion to wistful yearning to the hard-edged skepticism of "The Smile of All-Wisdom" (which sees precisely nothing behind the veil of death) or humor of "The Optimist." The ballads' compressed diction and fluid rhythms introduce a distinctive note in her poetry, the evocation of liminal beings recognizably human but strangely alien, whose orbit outside conventional social settings enabled her to explore otherwise indecorous material.

Both "Ballad of the Bird-Bride" and "Le Mauvais Larron" explore almost feral women who exceed conventional norms of bourgeois womanhood. More suggestive in biographical terms, perhaps, they narrate marital flight, the wresting away of children, and the sundering of lovers. The husband's cry for his alienated children in "Ballad of Bird-Bride" ("Of the wild wind's kin though ye surely be, / Are ye not of my kin too?") seems especially resonant for a woman whose own daughters were wrested away with the divorce decree granted their father. In her introduction to *Border Ballads* she argued that ballads represent humanity minus the veneer of civilization, suggesting that they articulate passions censored in confessional lyrics. If in their use of "literary" Scots dialect these ballads seem dated, in other respects they are the freshest work in the volume and anticipate twentieth-century feminist rewriting of fairy tales.

Even in her lyrics, however, erotic and family relations are contingent rather than stable. In the sonnet "To-Day," inscribed to her husband, Tomson celebrates their newfound happiness in love but tropes it as a narrow green isthmus between "two bitter seas," while in "The Flight of Nicolete," a ballade drawn from the medieval French tale popularized by Walter Pater and Swinburne, Nicolete flees from home to seek her lover. These contingent relationships consort with the larger theme of transience, as in "Scythe Song," in which the susurrous refrain enacts the motion of the scythe that cuts down life in its path: "Hush! the Scythe says, where, ah where?" (Lang was so impressed that he published the poem in his column in *Longman's* [September 1887] after paying her the compliment of imitating it in a poem of his own.) In its review of *The Bird-Bride* the *Scots Observer* (4 May 1889) remarked that "There is more than a reminiscence of Messrs. Lang and Austin Dobson, and we are also here and there reminded of Jean Ingelow"; the review might also have pointed to the influence of Dante Gabriel Rossetti's ballads on "Ballad of Pentyre Town" or of "The Blessed Damozel" on "Hereafter," of Christina Rossetti's fairy tales on the delightful "Fairies' Valediction" and "Fairies' Cobbler," and of William Morris's socialist songs on "Hymn to Labour" and "On the Road." The bookish poems and fixed verse forms inspired by Lang and Dobson are unmemorable, and the anti-Semitic reference to a "swart Hebrew's wares" in "My Aster Plate" mar the volume. There is, however, a great deal to praise. In 1889 Tomson had not merely achieved "correctness" in her meters and rhymes but, at times, such command over diction as to achieve the effect of inevitability, in cadences at once sure and evocatively subtle. As Wilde declared in *Woman's World* in 1889, "She is one of our most artistic workers in poetry, and treats language as a fine material." If *The Bird-Bride* sold badly (fewer than two hundred copies), it enhanced her reputation among other writers; and Robert Gittings argues that the title poem also left its trace on canonical literature in Tess's vision of "weird Arctic birds" in Hardy's *Tess of the D'Urbervilles* (1891).

As the 1890s opened Tomson was involved in *Art Weekly*, the new periodical targeted at working artists that Arthur Tomson founded and co-edited. Though short-lived, this endeavor gave her firsthand experience in editing and may have inspired her own decision in late 1892 to accept the editorship of a woman's magazine. Meanwhile she was submitting a series of Greek-inspired mythological pieces to *Universal Review* ("Marpessa," "Procris," and "Helle in Hades") that further explored themes of sundered families and failed marriages, perhaps suggesting a period of reflection and catharsis. She was also becoming known as a brilliant hostess at her Sunday afternoon gatherings, the flavor of which is suggested by C. Lewis Hind in his introduction to Stephen Phillips's *Christ in Hades* (1917):

> John Lane and I first met at the house of our friends Mr. and Mrs. Graham R. Tomson in St. John's Wood. . . . Under the inspiration of 'Graham R. Tomson's' dark eyes and winning manner I heard Oscar Wilde make one of his best impromptus. It was the time of the Japanese fan craze, and Madame was engaged in decorating the wall of the drawing-room with them. Oscar was announced. 'Oh, Mr. Wilde,' she said, 'you are just in time to help me arrange these fans.' 'Madame,' he replied, his vast smile broadening, 'They should not be arranged; they should occur.' There I heard Harold Frederic perform, with astonishing success, the feat of singing folk-songs and eating bread and butter at the same moment; there I actually saw my idol, Andrew Lang, write the best part of an article, standing, or rather lolling against the window sash, chattering languidly as he wrote, the paper, when it suited him, resting on the window-pane . . . .

Soon Tomson was planning two more volumes of poems. Just as *The Bird-Bride* was quickly followed in 1889 by *Selections from the Greek Anthology* (a bid for the status of learned woman of letters as well as poet), so she was working in mid 1891 on a second collection of poems, *A Summer Night, and Other Poems* (1891), and *Concerning Cats: A Book of Poems by Many Authors* (1892), which capitalized on the cat's domestic as well as decadent associations. Both projects reflected her partnership with Arthur: the frontispiece to *A Summer Night* was an impressionistic painting of her in the garden at Number 20, St. John's Wood Road, and *Concerning Cats* was illustrated by him.

More than a third of the thirty-four poems in *A Summer Night* debuted in the columns of Henley's *National Observer*, which also first published Meynell's *Rhythm of Life* (1893) and Rudyard Kipling's *Barrack-Room Ballads* (1892). Tomson's sonnet, "To My Cat," had appeared next to Yeats's "Lake Isle of Innisfree" in the 13 December 1890 issue. With *A Summer Night* Tomson announced herself eminently contemporary: she consigned seven supernatural poems to the back of the volume, suppressed her narrative mythological poems from the *Universal Review*, and emphasized impressionist landscapes and urban lyrics as well as other decadent material akin to that of Rhymers' Club poets (if also reflecting kinship with the lyrics of Meynell and Christina Rossetti). Paterian intensity in life is celebrated in "Chimaera," which opens with the effects of gaslight on stone and pavement and articulates female desire:

> The dim grass stirs with your footstep,
>   The blue dusk throbs with your smile;
> I and the world of glory
>   Are one for a little while.

"The Last Fairy" uses romance lore but is written in free verse and sounds the theme of the alienated outcast. Before veering into a conventional lament for lost Arcady, "South Coast Idyl" opens with lines anticipating Imagism: "Beneath these sun-warmed pines among the heather, / A white goat, bleating, strains his hempen tether, / A purple stain dreams on the broad blue plain." "Reveille" adopts the restraint, economy, and vividness of Rossetti while admitting a decadent touch in a disturbing image of growing grass viewed from within the grave. Poems exploring lost connections, deviant sexuality, and rage are usually cast as ballads, but these, too, are inflected by decadent content. "A Ballad of the Were-Wolf" takes up a familiar Decadent image but assigns the role of beast to a woman who performs the subordinate role of wife by day, marauding wolf who steals the couple's two children by night.

The book was favorably reviewed, *Black and White* pronouncing that "Mrs. Tomson holds, perhaps, the very highest rank among poetesses of English birth." Diverse reviewers, however, identified different excellences. *The National Observer* in a 16 January 1892 review (perhaps merely plumping for poems published in its pages or reflecting Henley's tastes) singled out her impressionist urbanscapes and "dismissed . . . her essays in romance." Reviewing the book for *The Independent* (18 February 1892), Louise Chandler Moulton thought "In the Rain," "The House of Dream," "Reveille," and a few other lyrics her most representative work in the volume, as well as "The Moor Girl's Well" and "Ballad of the Willow Pool" (neither of them, she felt, as fine as "Le Mauvais Larron"). William Watson in the *Academy* (9 January 1892) and *The Speaker* reviewer–most likely John Davidson–insisted on the importance of her supernatural poems. According to the 16 January 1892 review in *The Speaker*, "'The Moor Girl's Well' and the terrible 'Ballad of the Were-Wolf,' are the best things in these eight volumes . . . and among the best poems that have been published this year . . . the latter will never be forgotten."

Tomson was at the high point of her career. *Concerning Cats,* which included three of her own poems alongside those of Gosse and Théophile Gautier, was well reviewed in 1892. In June of that year she chaired the annual Literary Ladies dinner as president. While continuing to publish signed reviews and poems in leading periodicals she was also making forays into prose fiction. "At the Sign of the Golden Bird," a romance representing a poet's origins in elusive beauty that can never entirely be grasped, appeared in the 1890 volume of *Macmillan's Magazine*. Additional short stories dealing with inheritance, love triangles, and elopement appeared in *The Speaker* and *The Independent* (New York) in 1892 and 1893. At this time she and Pennell also became "patronesses" of J. M. Barrie's cricket team, the Allahakbarries, whose practice grounds were at the Tomson home (Arthur was a team member) and the *National Observer* office.

There was cause, however, for tension with Henley. In March 1892 Tomson told him that she was abandoning the fashion column to assume the editorship of *Sylvia's Journal*, a woman's magazine. This new job gave her the chance to promote writers in whom she believed (especially women) and to keep her name, posted prominently on the masthead, before the public. Her first issue appeared in Christmas 1892; thereafter the magazine adopted strategies parallel to *Woman's World* as edited by Wilde. Tomson introduced lavish visual illustration (especially by R. Anning Bell, a black and white artist whose career she advanced), greater coverage of poetry and books, a garden column that was also the story of a woman gardener making her way in a man's world, and a series of articles on women's colleges. The poet Nora Hopper also appeared in the journal, which also published a series of feminist literary criticism by Katharine Tynan.

In 1893–1894 Tomson became active in another women's network, the "Wares of Autolycus" in the *Pall Mall Gazette*, written by a different woman each night. Though the column eventually became associated with Meynell, who initially wrote on Friday nights, it may owe its name to Tomson, who had written under the signature "Autolycus" in *Art Weekly* and *Sylvia's Journal*. Tomson's own contributions to the column, a series of Thursday night articles on interior decoration, were later collected as *The Art of the House* in 1897.

Tomson's personal life was once again becoming more complicated, however. She had a mesmerizing effect on people, as a *Boston Herald* reporter testified in an 1890 interview: "Mrs. Tomson . . . at once attracted me by an indescribable charm of manner, in which gentleness and sweetness were strongly blended. A tall, slight, brown-haired woman, with large gray eyes, that at times seemed to be deep hazel, and a striking individuality pervading her carriage, manner, and dress, the artistic largely dominating the latter, is a summary of what my first impression was of this very attractive woman." She appears never to have relied on her physical beauty to advance professionally, and indeed Lang had recognized her talent with no assistance from her physical charms. She flirted with editors such as T. Fisher Unwin and John Lane in correspondence but appears to have rebuffed an advance from Hardy in October of 1892 after a sustained but discreet flirtation. Michael Millgate suggests that Nichola Pine-Avon in Hardy's *Pursuit of the Well-Beloved*, serialized in *The Illustrated London News* from 1 October to 17 December 1892, was drawn in part from Tomson.

Sexual temptation materialized in another quarter for her, in the person of H. B. Marriott Watson, another Allahakbarrie (and Barrie's good friend) who practiced cricket at the Tomson home and, as one of Henley's "regatta," attended the Pennells' Thursday night "at-homes" also frequented by the Tomsons. Watson, the son of an Anglican clergyman, was born in Australia, attended university at Christ Church, New Zealand (distinguishing himself as a classics scholar), and immigrated to London to pursue a writing career since his lack of faith precluded church preferment. Tall, handsome, and ebullient where Arthur Tomson was quiet and melancholic, Watson had published several short stories about illicit passion in the *National Observer* by the early 1890s. In "The House of Dishonour" (3 October 1891), for example, a married man who falls in love with another woman defends his "great sin that was my happiness." According to the only extant account of the affair, which composer Cyril Scott attributes to Louisa Stevenson (widow to "Bob" Stevenson, Robert Louis Stevenson's cousin), Rosamund initiated the affair. The disruptions to her personal life and to her husband Arthur and young son "Tommy" (then around seven) are not documented but can easily be imagined; the disruptions to her professional life left a clearer trail. After doing so much to develop *Sylvia's Journal* into an imaginative voice for female aestheticism, she suddenly threw it over in the first quarter of 1894. A new volume of poems, *After Sunset*, was announced by publishers Elkins Mathews and John Lane in 1893 and again in 1894 but never materialized. Soon she also discarded the name "Graham R. Tomson" and the symbolic capital she had worked hard to associate with it.

In June 1894 Arthur Tomson inscribed in the presentation copy of *The Bird-Bride*, which his estranged wife had dedicated to him in 1889, these lines from her poem "To-night":

The dawn draws near to bid us both resign
Our storm-worn shallop to the tide-wave's might:
   Yet this, a little while, was mine and thine–
One green vine-garland plucked in Fate's despite.

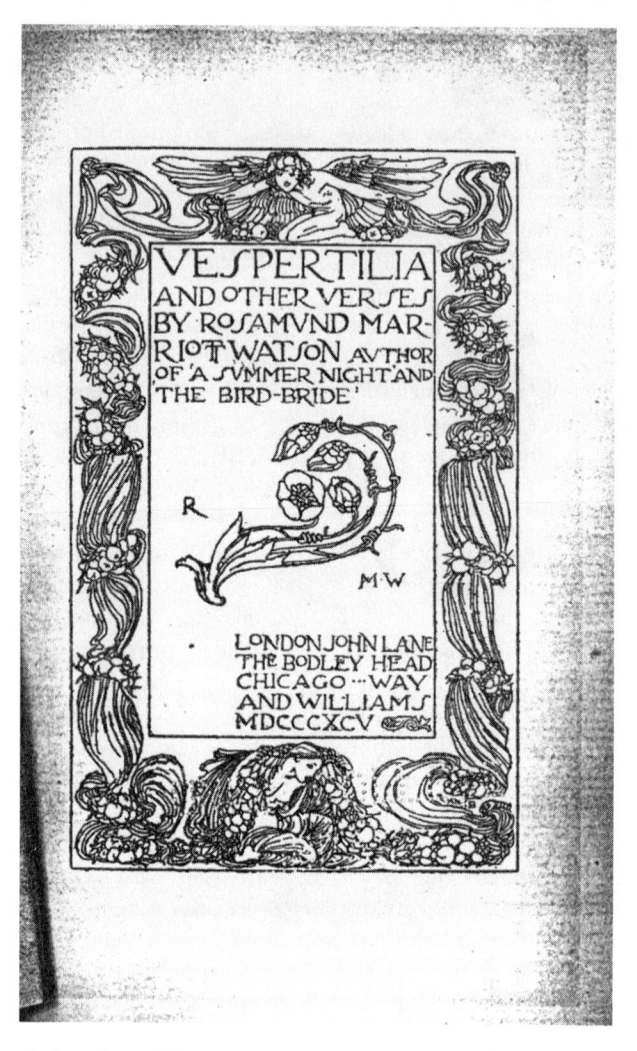

Title page for the collection of poems Watson published shortly after she left Tomson for H. B. Marriott Watson

By July she had moved in with Watson in Westminster, though it took Arthur Tomson a year to summon the resolve to file a divorce petition. The publishing world could not quite keep pace with this revolution in domestic arrangements, and Rosamund's first publication in *The Yellow Book*–"Vespertilia" (January 1895)–appeared under the signature "Graham R. Tomson." By the fifth volume of *The Yellow Book* she was Rosamund Marriott Watson and remained so the rest of her life, though she and H. B. never married. Later in 1895 John Lane republished *A Summer Night* in new boards, with the frontispiece of the poet by Arthur Tomson excised and a new title page inserted; the same year Lane also published *Vespertilia, and Other Verses,* dedicated "To Alice Meynell . . . in Sincere Admiration and Friendship."

Vespertilia expanded more than it extended interests evident in earlier volumes. New urban poems included "Song of London" and "Nocturn," but these rarely went beyond 1891 poems such as "Of the Earth, Earthy."

Other poems invoked Pater, while "Quern of the Giants" and "Walpurgis" reprised the female fury articulated in poems of 1889 and 1891; "Quern" was an effective socialist romance as well. As in *Tares,* the predominant themes were death, disillusionment, and the failure of love, though a small cluster of lyrics celebrated love and desire (sometimes by encapsulating a love song within a death song). Though poetic convention and the pressures of the literary marketplace are certainly factors, the failure of her second marriage, her rediscovery of love in an extramarital affair, and her succeeding divorce help explain her increased preoccupation in 1895 with dying love, renewed desire, and the resurfacing of past emotional connections in the present.

Watson's title poem merges details from Roman Britain and natural description with the decadent theme of the revenant and a representation of erotic failure. A Roman woman who followed her lover to England and died in the strange, misty island seeks not blood but love to live again, but the narrator, invested in sentimental fidelity to the memory of his dead sweetheart, vows that he can never give his heart again. "Open Sesame" is similarly skeptical about love, its direct language and rhythms anticipating modernist work: "Joy in the fleeting glimpse, the vain endeavour, / Tho' Almost meadows flower by the gates of Never." The volume could have been stronger had Marriott Watson eliminated less original work. At times she resorted to what now seems mere prettiness of language for its own sake, as in "Sheep-Bells" or "City of Dream." The recycling of ballads on shipwrecks or lyrics on inescapable aging such as "The Isle of Voices" may, however, function to defuse and disperse poems that might otherwise seem too recognizably related to volatile personal experience.

The new volume was well received, with the *National Observer* (18 January 1896) laying particular stress on its modernity and technical finish. Some of the new professional problems she now faced, however, were evident. Only Norman Gale in *The Academy* (30 November 1895) even mentioned her as author of other verses under another name; *The Independent* (New York) neither betrayed familiarity with her identity nor acknowledged her as a frequent contributor in its 6 February 1896 review: "There is a smack of sophisticated honey, none the less sweet for being cleverly adulterated, in these highly colored flowers—artificial flowers. It is an acquired taste, but not a bad one, by which the nectar of such honeyed words is brewed and liked. We plead guilty to a fondness for it." In her 1905 letter to Nora Hopper, Marriott Watson contended that she had always been happy in her literary career; but from 1895 onward her recognition, sphere of activity, and agency steadily diminished, though she was to develop new literary friendships and continue to be regarded by selected literary insiders as a gifted poet.

Meantime, there were other immediate sources of pleasure. On her own birthday in 1895 she gave birth to Richard Marriott Watson ("Dick" to his parents, an inside joke because H. B. had published a novel that year on highwayman Richard Ryder titled *Galloping Dick*). This child evidently resembled his mother in looks and linguistic gifts, and though the impression may be due in part to the survival of letters naming him but not her other three children, he seems to have been especially beloved. Dick was a frequent point of reference in her letters to Albert Bigelow Paine in the United States or H. G. and Catherine Wells, close friends of the Watsons (originating with H. B.'s "discovery" of Wells and recommendation of his work to Henley). Poems such as "The Golden Feather," first published in the 27 May 1897 *Independent,* then in her 1903 volume, also introduce a new note of affectionate maternal observation into her poems.

Scott alleges that discord and near-ruptures after the couple's elopement required Louisa Stevenson to act as peacemaker before the couple settled into harmonious, profound love for each other. Since H. B. requested that their personal papers be burned on his death, there is no evidence to confirm Scott's account. What remains is a record relatively placid, even increasingly conventional, of domestic and professional life. In autumn 1895 the family settled in Heathfield Cottage, a roomy house with large grounds ideal for gardening (Rosamund boasted of six thousand bulbs in her garden in January 1898), in Chiswick. They were still close enough to central London to maintain professional contacts, and Rosamund and H. B. often appeared at Henry Harland's afternoon gatherings, rubbing shoulders with James, Gosse, and the poets Arthur Symons and Charlotte Mew.

Watson continued to place poems in *The Yellow Book, Pall Mall Magazine,* and periodicals in the United States. In 1897 she collected her "Wares of Autolycus" columns on interior decoration, retroactively stamping the "Autolycus" contributions with her (new) name just when the column was becoming exclusively identified with Meynell. She tried a children's novel, *An Island Rose,* in 1900. Set in Carisbrooke Castle on the Isle of Wight during the English Civil War, it is memorable only for its concluding paragraph in which the heroine declares she will marry but never change her name (perhaps reflecting its author's rueful conclusions on practice to the contrary). More promisingly, she began a series of meditative columns on gardening in 1901. Appearing in the *Daily Mail,* the new mass circulation daily owned by Alfred Harmsworth, and the short-lived but significant *New Liberal Review,* the columns were later collected, along with poems, in *The Heart of a Garden,* published in 1906.

William Archer included Watson among genuine, if "minor," poets in his 1902 *Poets of the Younger Generation,* identifying her technical finish as a preeminent trait. She was clearly proud that he included her work (along with the poetry of Meynell and Margaret Woods) in his 12 March 1902 lecture on "Poetesses of Culture" at the Women's Department, King's College, University of London; for she took care to enclose a copy of the lecture announcement to her publisher John Lane. As with the earlier volume planned in 1893 and 1894, however, she was curiously uncertain about a new volume still called *After Sunset*. First pressuring Lane to proceed with publication in January 1902, she then postponed the volume indefinitely a month later.

Watson's lack of confidence may reflect increasingly precarious health. When he met her for the first time in 1901, Scott reports, the formerly willowlike Rosamund was "enormous" if "queen-like in . . .

Title page for Watson's posthumous collection

impressiveness. Her stoutness was not due to gluttonous habits, but to a complaint known to obstetricians." This statement may refer to the earliest signs of the uterine cancer that took her life a decade later. She herself mentioned other causes of distress in her 31 March 1903 letter to Bigelow Paine, whose books she and Dick read with such delight: the pressures of work and, more seriously, a protracted nervous breakdown.

After Sunset is weaker than the previous volumes. The good poems in it are disproportionately few compared to lyrics hackneyed in thought and diction, and several show a marked narrowing of perspective on the world (though perhaps reflecting a nascent modernism committed to the artist's alienation). Poems are repeatedly set in the garden, the locus of much of her time in Chiswick, and her thought seems cloistered, too, returning again and again to the loss of youth, the momentary resurgence of youth amidst spring's renewal, and approaching death. "D'Outre Tombe" is the volume's best work, another love song cloaked in a death song:

> I with the dead, and you among the living,
> In separate camps we sojourn, unallied;
> Life is unkind and Death is unforgiving,
> And both divide.

Her freshest note, however, is to be found in a concluding cluster of children's poems. "'Where Neither Moth nor Rust Doth Corrupt,'" for example, is a passionate love lyric uttered by a mother to her young son as she contemplates their divergent paths in later life. The delicacy and sensuous detail with which the infant is described are especially deft, and the concluding apostrophe to the beloved child may indicate the depth of Watson's own passion for her son. *After Sunset* was praised in *The Athenaeum* (14 November 1903) as the work of a genuine poet (in contrast to better-known names), but the review was written by her dear friend Vernon Rendall, who had assumed the position of editor in 1901. In general the volume had little impact on her reputation, neither harming nor substantially enhancing it. It was to be the last volume of poems she published during her lifetime.

After her nervous breakdown in late 1902 and early 1903 Watson struggled on, but her health caused the family to leave London for the village of Shere in the Surrey Downs, which they knew from Allahakbarries matches played there in the early 1890s. They settled in Orchard Cottage in late 1904, letting their lease of Heathfield Cottage in Chiswick lapse by October 1905. In place of the expansive Chiswick garden on which she had lavished so much care and based many of her poems and essays, she spent leisure moments in the modest patch of green behind the house. In his *More Authors and I* (1922) Hind recalled seeing her there, sitting in her garden "ostensibly shelling peas, but . . . really making a poem."

Bad health also forced Watson to give up full-time journalism. She dropped reviews of fiction when she became a regular reviewer for *The Athenaeum* (succeeding Edith Nesbit in the post) to focus on children's literature, interior decoration, furniture, and poetry. In 1906 she gathered her gardening poems and essays together into *The Heart of a Garden,* illustrated with photographs (most of them evidently her own). Apart from her continuing delight in family, friends, and the making of verses, however, her story is one of illness and decline: after a hysterectomy in December 1910 to remove a cancerous uterus, she had about a year to live. As she worsened H. B. frantically appealed to Lane to publish her collected poems, which he thought would strengthen her will to live. The volume was planned for February 1912 but came too late. She died at Vachery Cottage, Shere, on 29 December 1911, just before midnight, and she was buried in St. James

Churchyard in Shere. H. B. was so prostrated by grief that he was unable to attend the funeral and later resorted to spiritualism (in which both had dabbled in her last years) to contact her after death. The defiant agnostic was seen out of the world with a conventional Anglican funeral.

As posthumous volume, *The Poems of Rosamund Marriott Watson* (1912), included the contents of all of her prior volumes plus "Marpessa" (first published in the 1889 *Universal Review*) and new poems in a section titled "The Lamp and the Lute," which included poems from *Heart of a Garden* and those dedicated to friends, "The Haunted Palace" to Henry James and "Two Songs" to Thomas Hardy. In "The Lamp and the Lute" she recovered much of the grace and charm of her 1890s volumes, with their glancing rhythms and mellifluous diction; if it includes little experimentation and some poems that fall below her general average, several demonstrate her continuing vitality as a poet. Perhaps the burden of life-threatening illness overcame her customary reticence, or perhaps personal revelation was simply a last phase of development in her work; but many of these poems seem expressive, even confessional, dealing with everything from lost beauty and youth or continuing friendships to her literary fame relative to her husband's, as in "The Low Road": "'Tis you shall have a golden throne and laurels in your hair, / And castled courts, but let me keep / My leafy haunt where woods are deep."

Juxtaposed to such confessions of diminishment are poems that exult in identifying with what is wild and free, whether the starling that others consider a "rogue" but whose caprices derive from a heart full of joy ("The Starling"); the open ocean and wandering sea mew whose "soul" was decreed "in this poor earth of mine" ("Thalassa"); or the wild rooks who sail home at night ("The Magic Carpet"). To the end, too, she repudiated, in "The Earthly Paradise," the prospect of "the radiant white-winged throng / That wanders where the Heavenly gardens are" in favor of the song-thrush's ecstatic earthly voice:

> Infinite solace falls with every note,
> And dead dreams flower again the while he sings,
> My Angel with the throbbing speckled throat
> And dim brown wings.

The most original poem, though, is "To a Child," notable for its honest directness in anticipating the fearful nightmares that a mother's bodily decay after death might inspire in her child. Part of the poem's power derives from adopting the diction of sentimental babyhood ("pattering . . . feet," "happy meadows") and counterpointing it with the physical horror of death and the dying mother's alienation from childhood innocence.

The Times (London) obituary on 2 January 1912 pronounced that Watson's poetry titled "her to rank highly among the numerous 'minor poets'–to use an inevitable phrase–of the last two decades," while Vernon Rendall's obituary in *The Athenaeum* (6 January 1912) praised her for merging "gifts of technique which mark the scrupulous artist" with "a sense of passion and wistfulness that are all her own." Her name was kept before the public not only through H. B.'s work (his 1913 novel, *Rosalind in Arden,* twice quotes Rosamund's verse in the course of the story) but also by the popularity of art songs by Scott, who set music to fifteen of her lyrics. She left her trace as well on the work of Hardy, in the lyric "An Old Likeness (Remembering R.T.)" and on William Butler Yeats in his autobiography, which narrates her elopement with H. B., though without citing her name.

Watson continued to figure in literary histories and anthologies well into the twentieth century. She has always been ranked among the best poets contributing to *The Yellow Book*. In his *The Renaissance of the Nineties* (1911) W. B. Blaikie Murdoch classed her with Ernest Dowson and John Gray; Harold Williams grouped her with Arthur Symons, John Davidson, Dowson, Laurence Binyon, and Yeats in *Modern English Writers* (1918); and in her 1960 study of *The Yellow Book,* Katherine Lyon Mix termed her the best of that periodical's women poets. In his *The Eighteen Nineties* (1927) Holbrook Jackson considered her work second-tier, behind originals such as A. E. Housman or Meynell, but–in company with Nesbit and Michael Field–above the level achieved by Symons, Richard Le Gallienne, or Gray. Gradually, however, memory of her work lapsed except among Hardy scholars such as Michael Millgate, whose 1973 essay in *Notes & Queries* was the first substantive work on Watson following Mix's.

With renewed interest in Victorian women poets, the relation of aestheticism to early modernism, and the role of women in the literary marketplace and canon formation, her work is again being anthologized and studied. Though when faced with illness and professional burdens in later years she sometimes retreated to conventional forms, themes, and life experiences, Watson is an important figure for her sheer command of poetic craft; for her anticipation of modernist work by women; for the boldness of her lyrics and ballads; for her verve as "Graham R. Tomson" in negotiating the literary marketplace; and for the price in reputation she paid when "Graham R. Tomson" became Rosamund Marriott Watson.

References:

William Archer, "Mrs. Marriott-Watson," in his *Poets of the Younger Generation* (London & New York: John Lane, 1902), pp. 469-480;

Marysa Demoor, "Women Poets as Critics in the Athenaeum: Ungendered Anonymity Unmasked," *Nineteenth Century Prose,* 24 (1997): 51-71;

Linda K. Hughes, "'Fair Hymen Holdeth Hid a World of Woes': Myth and Marriage in Poems by Graham R. Tomson," *Victorian Poetry,* 32 (1994): 97-120;

Hughes, "A Female Aesthete at the Helm: *Sylvia's Journal* and 'Graham R. Tomson,' 1893-1894," *Victorian Periodicals Review,* 29 (Summer 1996): 173-192;

Hughes, "Feminizing Decadence: Poems by Graham R. Tomson," in *Women and British Aestheticism,* edited by Talia Schaffer and Kathy Alexis Psomiades (Charlottesville: University Press of Virginia, 1999), pp. 119-138;

Hughes, "A Fin-de-Siècle Beauty and the Beast: Configuring the Body in Works by Graham R. Tomson (Rosamund Marriott Watson)," *Tulsa Studies in Women's Literature,* 14 (Spring 1995): 95-121;

Richard Le Gallienne, "Woman-Poets of the Day," *English Illustrated Magazine,* 11 (April 1894): 649-657;

Michael Millgate, *Thomas Hardy: A Biography* (New York: Random House, 1982);

Millgate, "Thomas Hardy and Rosamund Tomson," *Notes & Queries* (July 1973): 253-255;

Katherine Lyon Mix, *A Study in Yellow: The Yellow Book and Its Contributors* (Lawrence: University of Kansas Press, 1960);

Elizabeth Robins Pennell, *Nights: Rome and Venice in the Aesthetic Eighties, London and Paris in the Fighting Nineties,* second edition (Philadelphia & London: Lippincott, 1916);

Talia Schaffer, *The Forgotten Female Aesthetes: Literary Culture in Late-Victorian England* (Charlottesville: University Press of Virginia, 2000);

Cyril Scott, *My Years of Indiscretion* (London: Mills & Boon, 1924), pp. 74-77;

Ana I. Parejo Vadillo, "New Women Poets and the Culture of the *Salon* at the *fin de siècle*," *Woman: A Cultural Review,* 10 (1999): 22-34;

John Lawrence Waltman, "The Early London Journals of Elizabeth Robins Pennell," dissertation, University of Texas at Austin, 1976, pp. 384-457.

Papers:

The John Lane papers at the Harry Ransom Humanities Research Center, University of Texas at Austin, comprise the principal archive of Rosamund Marriott Watson's correspondence and include, as well, letters of Arthur Tomson and H. B. Marriott Watson. The Louise Chandler Moulton and Pennell papers at the Library of Congress and the Gordon Ray papers at the Pierpont Morgan Library in New York City also include significant materials.

Lucy Webling
(Lucy Betty MacRaye)
(30 August 1877 – 6 December 1952)

and

Peggy Webling
(Arthur Weston)
(1 January 1871 – 27 June 1949)

Jeanie Grant Moore
University of Wisconsin at Oshkosh

BOOKS: *Poems and Stories,* by Lucy and Peggy Webling (Toronto: McLean, 1896?);

Blue Jay, by Peggy Webling (London: Heinemann, 1906);

The Story of Virginia Perfect, by Peggy Webling (London: Methuen, 1909); republished as *Virginia Perfect* (London: Methuen, 1911);

A Spirit of Mirth, by Peggy Webling (London: Methuen, 1910; New York: Dutton, 1911);

Felix Christie, by Peggy Webling (London: Methuen, 1912);

The Pearl Stringer, by Peggy Webling (London: Methuen, 1913);

A Sketch of John Ruskin, by Peggy Webling (London: Baines & Scarsbrook, 1914);

Edgar Chirrup, by Peggy Webling (New York: Putnam, 1915);

Boundary House, by Peggy Webling (London: Hutchinson, 1916);

Guests of the Heart, by Peggy Webling (London: Baines & Scarsbrook, 1917);

In Our Street, by Peggy Webling (London: Hutchinson, 1918);

Saints and their Stories, by Peggy Webling (London: Nisbet, 1919; New York: Stokes, 1920);

The Scent Shop, by Peggy Webling (London: Hutchinson, 1919);

Verses to Men, by Peggy Webling (London: Privately published, 1919);

Comedy Corner, by Peggy Webling (London: Hutchinson, 1920);

*Lucy Webling, as Little Lord Fauntleroy, in 1888
(photograph by Elliott & Fry)*

The Fruitless Orchard, by Peggy Webling (London: Hutchinson, 1922);

The Life of Isobel Erne, by Peggy Webling (London: Hutchinson, 1922);

Peggy: The Story of One Score Years and Ten, by Peggy Webling (London: Hutchinson, 1924);

The Amber Merchant, by Peggy Webling (London: Hutchinson, 1925);

Anna Maria, by Peggy Webling (London: Hutchinson, 1927);

Strange Enchantment, by Peggy Webling (London: Hutchinson, 1929);

One Way Street, by Lucy Webling, as Lucy Betty MacRaye (London: Hutchinson, 1933);

Aspidistra's Career, by Peggy Webling (London: Hutchinson, 1936);

Opal Screens, by Peggy Webling (London: Hutchinson, 1937);

Centre Stage, by Lucy Webling, as Lucy Betty MacRaye (London: Hutchinson, 1938);

Young Laetitia, by Peggy Webling (London: Hutchinson, 1939).

PLAY PRODUCTIONS (Peggy Webling): *Westward Ho!,* Manchester, Gaiety Theatre, February 1913;

Frankenstein: An Adventure in the Macabre, Portcawl, Wales, December 1927; London, Little Theatre, February 1930;

Reprieve, Nottingham, July 1931.

Sisters Lucy and Peggy Webling acted professionally at early ages, and their dramatic presentations brought them into contact with famous figures of the late nineteenth-century literary, artistic, and political world. As young adults they published a book together that included poems by Lucy and short stories by Peggy. Lucy continued her acting career and eventually wrote two novels. Peggy, by far the more prolific of the two, turned her full attention to writing and produced several novels, an autobiography, essays, another volume of poetry, adaptations for the stage, and a series of news articles and short stories for a variety of London publications.

Peggy was born on 1 January 1871 and Lucy on 30 August 1877 to Robert James and Maria Webling. They had four older sisters. Lucy and Peggy spent most of their childhood near Kensington Gardens, London, in a house in Wellington Terrace, where their father also kept a jewelry and silver shop. In her autobiography Peggy describes her father as "hard to live with" but "just and generous," "high-minded," and "liberal"—even "revolutionary"—in political belief. Peggy saves her highest praise for her mother: "Her encouragement, her goodness, her sympathy have been the joy of Home." Both parents are credited with being ahead of their time in their gentle treatment of their children. Several of the daughters demonstrated various talents: for instance, Ethel, the eldest, studied at the Slade School at University College and became an artist, with portraits of her sisters exhibited at the Royal Academy. Josephine and Rosalind, the second and fourth daughters, acted with their younger sisters, Lucy and Peggy.

Peggy's theatrical career began as "Moth" in a private production of William Shakespeare's *Love's Labour's Lost* when she was eight years old. Her sister Ethel's friend, daughter of the former leader of the Irish party in the House of Commons, Justin McCarthy, assembled a group of friends to perform the play for specially invited audiences. Perhaps this production, along with their own private family performances, inspired Maria Webling to create a public program in which three of her daughters would give recitations for a fee. She booked Steinway Hall, printed tickets, and advertised with bills and newspaper notices; more than six hundred people attended on 29 October 1879 to hear Josephine, Rosalind, and Peggy recite the poetry of John Keats and Henry Wadsworth Longfellow, and the nonsense verse of Edward Lear. The evening—a stunning success prompting rave reviews in *The Daily Telegraph, The Times* (London), and *Punch*—initiated a wave of popular performances over the next few years. The program became increasingly sophisticated: the sisters developed their acting skills, learned scenes from Shakespeare, and engaged a professional designer to make their costumes. There followed several public performances, such as a benefit for the National Orphan Home on 19 July 1880, and, in 1882, a rendition of *School for Scandal* by Josephine and Peggy at Fancy Fair in Knightsbridge. As it became fashionable to have the little Weblings recite, Peggy and her family had an entrée into elite London homes, where they were introduced to luminaries of the time: Robert Browning, Mark Twain, Oliver Wendell Holmes, Ellen Terry, Lily Langtry, and the Wilde brothers, Oscar and Willie. They gave a special performance for the Prince and Princess of Wales on 23 June 1882 at a private home in Bradford. One of their most significant meetings was with the essayist/critic John Ruskin, who invited them to stay at his country home, Brantwood, in Coniston for the summer months. He became interested in their education, sometimes informally tutoring them, and he often wrote them affectionate letters, sent little gifts, and even composed poems for them. The girls were not formally educated, but they received instruction at home from their parents, and, sporadically, from teachers hired by friends for their own children. All of the performing daughters regularly took music and dancing lessons.

Lucy had been too young to participate in the early recitations of her sisters, but she joined them at the age of three. When she was nine years old, she was chosen for the title role in the touring production of Frances Hodgson Burnett's *Little Lord Fauntleroy* (1886). Peggy played the role of Dick, an American shoeblack, and the sisters set off with their mother for two tours, lasting six months each. When they returned, Lucy took on the role in another Burnett play, *Nixie* (1890), in Edward Terry's theater in the Strand. Lucy herself received high praise for her work, but the play was less successful than *Little Lord Fauntleroy*.

When Peggy was nineteen, she and her sister Josephine stayed for a year with their father's younger brother and his family in Brantford, in western Ontario. This initial Canadian stay, which lasted over a year, and a later acting tour of Canada, significantly affected Peggy's work; some of her later novels are set entirely in Canada; in others, her British characters leave their country to make a Canadian tour. During their first stay, the sisters did only a few recitations, so they had time to absorb the culture and the beautiful Canadian landscape; Peggy's mixed feelings about Canada and its residents, including her relatives, appear throughout her work. Two meetings at a fair in Canada also played important roles in Peggy's life. The first was with an acrobat, a configuration of whom often appears in Peggy's novels. Second, she met the Canadian Pauline Johnson, a poet and performer. Pauline's father was a Mohawk chief, and she used her great grandfather's name, Tekahionwake, as her stage name. Johnson wrote a poem about Peggy and she influenced Peggy's poetry; she also provided theatrical contacts. While in Canada, Peggy wrote her first short story, which was published in the fall of 1890 in *The Expositor,* the daily newspaper in Brantford.

Peggy and Josephine left Canada for a brief, unproductive stay in New York, where their mother and Lucy had come to join them. Discouraged by the difficulty of arranging dramatic engagements in the United States, Peggy and her sisters returned to England. They were hardly more successful at home, where they went on tour "working the hydros," a reference to hydropathic health establishments that sometimes provided entertainment for their guests; the only remuneration was by voluntary contribution from the audience. Afterward, back in London, Lucy

Peggy Webling at age twenty

appeared on stage several times, including a performance as Midge in Edward Terry's production of *Uncle Mike* (1892). Peggy began training as a journalist and continued to write short stories, publishing them in *The Sun* and the magazine *Merry-Go-Round.* The dramatic careers of the Webling sisters were revitalized by Peggy's sudden inspiration to write a brief entertainment called a *commediata.* Titled "An April Jest," the playlet bore the name "Arthur Weston" as its author; Peggy had chosen a pseudonym, partly out of a sense of fun and partly out of fear of failure. She need not have worried, for performances were successful, and they sparked a new interest in going on tour once again. At this same time, their Canadian friend, Johnson, came to London to publish a book, *The White Wampum* (1895); she urged them to return to Canada and arranged for a theatrical agent to assist them.

On this second Canadian trip Lucy joined her sisters Peggy and Rosalind in the presentation of dramatic evenings: the program consisted of scenes from Shakespeare, songs and dances by Lucy and Rosalind, "An April Jest," and another commediata by Peggy, titled "Britannia." Lasting three years (1895–1897) their tours took them from Toronto to Vancouver, down the west coast of California, back through the midwestern states, and up through Canada once again. They played small towns and large cities in various venues: little halls, opera houses, theaters, hotel dining rooms, church halls, and even the Kootenay mining camps. Their shows were highly successful, and the "Misses Sisters Webling Company," as they were called on the circuit, became well known across the provinces.

Peggy and Lucy had written poems as children, and they decided to put their more recent efforts together into one volume for publication; R. G. McLean of Toronto published *Poems and Stories* (1896?), which included poems by Lucy and short stories by Peggy. The stories are precursors of Peggy's later novels, set both in Britain and in Canada. Lucy's poems are rhythmic and romantic, but not distinguished by striking language or images. They reflect her Canadian experience: at times they paint an idyllic picture of Canadian beauty, and at others they express a nostalgic longing for Britain. In "A Canadian River Song" the softness of language and the rhythm of the lines suggest the lazy sensual experience of drifting along in a lover's canoe:

> I can hear the sighing breeze
> In the silver willow trees,
> Oh, the summer days of sunshine
> And the sky's unfathomed blue;
> See your dripping blade sun-kissed
> And the turning of your wrist,
> As I lie and fall a-dreaming
> And we drift in your canoe.

There is a richness in the description of the Canadian lake, the fading sun, and the evening hours; the sensuous description of the canoe ride and the surroundings throughout several stanzas ultimately suggests a lover's interlude as the canoe drifts: "lying still is the paddle."

Lucy's love poems sometimes evince emotion, even though they are often flawed by trite language. Many of her poems are infused with Victorian sentimentality, but at other times, she begins to treat significant themes. In "A Lesson in Love," for instance, Cupid instructs a young man on the way to win his love. First, he must simply love her, and, second, he must love her as an equal:

> Cupid answered, "Take no heed,
>   There's no need,
> For she's beside you, not above you,
> And soon your kiss shall tell her this,
>   Sweet, my sweet,–I love you.

Throughout the poem Cupid's advice outlines a respectful relationship on both sides. She explores new possibilities in male/female relationships and, in doing so, informs men of women's feelings and needs.

Back in England in 1898, the sisters took up residence with their family at 124 The Grove in Hammersmith. Lucy continued her stage career, acting with several well-known companies. Peggy proposed to a new London weekly that she write a series of articles on Canada. Two of her stories appeared in print before the publication ceased. She then became a regular staff member of another weekly, *M.A.P.*, or *Mostly About People,* for which she wrote theatrical notes and interviews, as well as short stories. Her first interview was with Vesta Tilley, a male impersonator. For the English pieces she used her own name, Peggy Webling, but for the Canadian tales she once again used the pseudonym, Arthur Weston. She also wrote for *Era,* a weekly publication, and worked for the *Morning Leader* in London before it became a part of the *Daily News.*

Along with her own touring experience, the interviews with actors and "show people" that Peggy conducted in this period provided valuable background for her novels, which almost invariably reflect the theatrical world. For example, the main character in her first novel, *Blue Jay* (1906), is a Canadian acrobat who eventually develops his own fantastic flying act. Peggy professed to like "simple people"–the acrobats, jugglers, and magicians she interviewed–better than stage actors, and that simplicity is extolled in Blue Jay's character. The book also owes much to Peggy's experience in Canada, where she met many performers. Ethel Webling painted a watercolor for the cover of the book, which received much praise but did not sell particularly well.

Peggy continued writing novels; all are somewhat formulaic, with repetitive plot devices and characters; the acrobat and the Canadian tour are regular features. Many well-crafted descriptive passages depict the Canadian landscape. Her perception of character is often astute, although the books are sometimes marred by typically unenlightened nineteenth-century views of ethnicity. Her essays, collected in a volume titled *Guests of the Heart* (1917), are somewhat mawkish allegories. Peggy's novel *Edgar Chirrup* (1915), one of her own favorites, was written for her sister Lucy about the British acting world.

While Peggy was writing her first novels, Lucy was on the London stage in such plays as *The Only Way* in William Haviland's company. In 1909 Lucy married Walter Jackson McRea, an actor who used the stage name Walter MacRaye. The couple lived in Canada and had two children: a daughter, Peggy, who died in infancy, and a son, Louis Drummond MacRaye, born in 1915 in London, Ontario. Lucy left

Canada and her husband in 1926 and returned to England with her son to live in Hammersmith near her family. Under the name Lucy Betty MacRaye she wrote two novels in the 1930s, which, like those of her sister, had theatrical settings. Her first novel, *One Way Street* (1933), abjured the social judgment placed on unwed mothers. Whereas Lucy's novels demonstrate at least a potential for more sophisticated writing than that of her sister, Peggy's poems surpass those Lucy published, perhaps partly because Lucy's were written at an earlier age. After having several novels accepted for publication, Peggy privately published a volume of poems, *Verses to Men* (1919).

In *Verses to Men* Webling uses a woman's voice that alternately confronts, analyzes, criticizes, and praises men. Although not as directly didactic as conduct books, through which women had been instructed by men for centuries, the poems as a whole have much that could be instructive to men about women. Divided into four sections, the poems span a wide range of male/female relationships and openly address several issues, often from a point of view that is decidedly feminist.

Throughout the first section of poems, Webling employs humor in a variety of ways to achieve differing effects. Sometimes the poems do not convey a serious message but simply entertain, as does "Four Young Men"; an amusing turn at the end of the poem reveals the identity of the lads who have completely captivated her: the Four Musketeers. A similar twist occurs in "To Nicholas." Not far into the poem the reader begins to recognize the familiar trope of unrequited love:

> We met, you smiled, I don't upbraid,
>   Upbraid,
> But still I know you only played,
>   Idly played.
> We tossed the ball with laugh and jest,
>   Foolish jest,
> Touched hands, by chance, and all the rest–
>   All the rest!

The accusation of betrayal follows in the same vein: "You smiled again, on her you smiled / She smiled / With just the same old games beguiled. . . ." The metaphors of childish play create nostalgia for a youthful love, but these are actually literal references that constitute another meaning, as the last lines of the poem reveal. She will forgive him:

> For I am old, but you and she,
>   You and she,
> Are very young–both under three,
>   Under three.

Lucy Webling dressed as a nun and Peggy Webling as a friar for one of the professional dramatic recitals in which they appeared

The childhood allusions prove appropriate for the three-year-old Nicholas. The structure of the poem, with a repetition at the end of each line, not only creates playfulness, but it also makes the poem a performance, as it suggests a childish repetition, even a dialogue between an adult and a child.

Peggy often uses satire; for example, in "To a Poet," whose work is more like prose, she criticizes the poet himself and his lack of creativity. In the short dramatic monologue "To an Artist," she leaves no doubt about her views of modern abstract painting; she speaks to herself about several possible images that might be represented, but she cannot determine the significance and concludes the painting must be hung upside down. A final comment to the painter furthers the point:

> In other words:–"Dear Mr. Browne,
> I saw your picture when in town.
> Now is it London in a fog?
> Oh, no, I've found the catalogue–
> 'Futurist Portrait of a Frog.'"

A satiric tone also infuses her playful exploration of theories of evolution, resulting in some of her most humorous poetic moments. Two lovers journey from age to age, beginning as bubbles, then stones, then eventually fungi, as they work their way to the vegetable stage:

> Let us recall that luscious place,
> The melting dew, the azure sky,
> The silence and the round embrace—
> *Two perfect pumpkins*—you and I!

The pumpkin/lovers, progenitors of all other vegetables, eventually evolve to human status, but they do not lose all traces of the evolutionary past: the male partner is affectionately called a cucumber—a phallic image appropriate to the sexual invitation at the end of the poem:

> O, happy fate! We've met again,
> We're just the same, heart, brain and will,
> My cucumber! Most cool of men!
> O, take me! I'm a turnip still!

Accompanied by a drawing by Leo Bates, "The Lover's Evolution" occupies the first place in this book of verses. The first stanzas can be read as direct messages to men, suggesting that relationships—and men—are capable of evolution and that her book itself will be part of the journey of discovery:

> How gladly will I turn the page
> That tells me of the "how" and "when,"
> Before the neolithic age
> And men were unevolved as men.
> If you will help me in the search
> To find ourselves, just you and me:
> You'll never leave me in the lurch?
> Turn back the volume—let us see!

Although "The Lover's Evolution" creates great fun at the expense of Darwin's theory, the comedy neither registers an objection to it nor purports to be a serious discussion of it. Rather, evolutionary theory becomes an amusing vehicle for exploring relationships between men and women.

While retaining the humor of her lighter poems, other pieces aim their messages to men forthrightly from a feminist perspective. She uses different tones of humor, ranging from light to heavily sarcastic, to address issues of patriarchy. She attacks the ultimate iconic patriarch in "The Victorian Papa," establishing a mock-epic tone in the quatrain that begins the poem:

> I sing the Victorian Papa,
>   I chant upon his pyre—
> Gone, like a dim and twinkling star,
>   Gone, like the wealth of Tyre.

As she moves into the central body of the poem she uses rhyming couplets, producing a rather singsongy rhythm that embellishes the humor of the piece:

> Hear me proclaim, in tones Gregorian,
> In ancient days, called mid-Victorian,
> There dwelt within the British islands,
> Revered from Cornwall to the Highlands
> A Person who, without apology,
> We place within the realm's hagiology.

The strategy is effective, for she manages, in a style similar to that of George Gordon, Lord Byron in *Don Juan*, to satirize social types and society itself. She shrewdly points out that "Papa" is most powerful in the domestic sphere:

> His "House" was the domestic mansion,
> And there he ruled, firm, autocratic,
> Calm, but rarely diplomatic.

A petty tyrant, "Papa" rarely smiles, unless his dinner particularly pleases him; then he might even be "merry / (A splendid judge of port and sherry)" and begin to tell stories to his captive audience. His wife is afraid to contradict him (she is "Cophetua's Bride become a matron"). He controls his daughters' lives until they are "'given away' in marriage." Webling's quotation marks surrounding "given away" indicate her awareness that the process objectifies these women.

Peggy's own father can be glimpsed here: she remarks that he controlled their "intellectual outlook" in the fields of art, religion, and politics. On the other hand, his views in these areas do not seem to fit the mold of the specific type of Victorian Papa she attacks. In contrast to the "Episcopalian" Papa in the poem, her father did not hold any particular religious beliefs and preferred not to impose religion on his children. "Papa" is "a bullet-headed Tory" who looks "down upon the masses / From out the lofty middle classes"; he sees the lower classes as victims of socialist "marauders." Whereas the poetic Papa would reject all "reforming / Or new ideas would send him storming," Peggy's own father was politically liberal, attending, in fact, those socialist meetings condemned by the Papa of the poem. This patriarch has a wider-reaching significance than would a personal re-creation of her own father: Peggy perceptively recognizes that "Papa" is a middle-class "institution" who shapes the lives of all women. The last lines of the poem—again, in quatrain form—suggest that he is a vanishing type, but she also implies an awareness that this is a wishful vision of the future:

Josephine, Rosalind, Lucy, and Peggy Webling

I chant the Victorian Papa,
    Who fell without a stab,
And, arm in arm, with "dear Mama,"
    Fled, in a hansom cab!
. . . .
I see the Victorian Papa,
    Dead, gone, with all his kith,
Lost in the bygone days afar,
    A dream—a tale—a myth!

While a day may come when the Victorian Papa is as remote as the figures of the epics she invokes, she is aware that the patriarchy he embodies has not yet been exorcised. In "Consistent Man," for instance, she makes the point that a woman's life is never her own. The "consistent man" is seen at the center of his own universe, demanding his own priority from each of the women in his life, no matter what her relationship to him. From his wife, for instance, he demands first allegiance, but he does not expect his mother to show that same preference toward her husband: his mother's first allegiance should be to him, her son. The same is true for his sisters, whose first duties should be to their brother, and his daughters, whose first loyalty should be to their father. The consistent man is consistent in two ways: in considering himself the central figure in each of his relationships with the females in his life, and, second, in being inconsistent in the expectations of the different, male-oriented roles women play. This poem may have been inspired by a childhood story from one of the moralistic books that Peggy and her sisters detested; they termed them "Goody-goody books." The life story of a girl named "Gertrude" illustrated the way women's lives were controlled by the men in their lives: their fathers, their husbands, their sons, and even their grandsons.

The dominance of men in women's lives is reversed in "Man's Inspiration: (And the Cause of Women's Lack of It)," albeit in a traditional way. Peggy again uses rhyming couplets, this time to take a humorous approach to male writers and their accomplishments, proposing that women have always inspired them. Dante's Beatrice and Petrarch's Laura, Homer's Helen, Lord Byron's loves, and even John Milton's Eve are examples of female figures of influence. Less predictable is the swipe she takes at men themselves for their incapacity to reciprocate:

> A being who can thus affect her,
> She has but Man, and though he's teasing,
> Provocative and very pleasing,
> He's not a being (does he know it?)
> To turn a woman to a poet....
> . . . .
> In brief, he'll never, never tire her,
> But don't expect him to inspire her.

She does reverse the sentiment, however, in two short poems, "Woman's Advantage Over Man" and "Another on the Same Theme." In both she proposes that men deserve the glory they have received for all of their accomplishments, but they cannot experience the bliss that women enjoy when they are loved by men.

Despite such adulation, she paints a more-realistic picture in two amusing poems about male/female relationships: "To My First Love" and "Ode to a Husband (An Attempt to Write When Inspired by His Presence)." "First Love" consists of two sections, each consisting of seventeen rhyming couplets. In the first, the female speaker describes a man she had loved twenty years earlier. She directly addresses him as she recalls for him his youth: as a young man his interests had lain in art, literature, nature, and liberal politics. Most importantly, he loved her and wanted to marry her. The second section recounts a more recent meeting: he is now "forty-two or three," and the "flashing laughing eyes" have now turned "dull":

> "Spectacles were quite a boon,"
> You said, and polished, with a smile,
> Your glasses, blinking all the while.

Not just physically old, he is old in outlook and has lost his idealism and his love of nature and of art. She strains to catch a glimpse of anything that remains of his old self, but she cannot:

> I could not catch, from first to last,
> One far, faint echo of the Past.
> For nothing you have done to prove
> The promise of your early love—
> Except that you would married be
> But (thank the Lord!) 'tis not to me.

The humor masks neither the rather devastating critique of this man nor the larger social satire, for he is a typical male who has succumbed to an economic system that has suppressed his values. The image of his dull blinking eyes demonstrates the striking loss of beauty, but the dullness also indicates his incapability of seeing the world in the way he once had done, in the way that the speaker still values it.

Virginia Woolf's most famous pronouncement—the need of a room of one's own—is also clearly foreshadowed in the second poem, "Ode to a Husband (An Attempt to Write When Inspired by His Presence)." The ironic subtitle recalls the inability of men to inspire women in "Man's Inspiration (And the Cause of Woman's Lack of It)." In "Ode to a Husband" the sarcasm in the reference to inspiration becomes clear as the duties of a wife and the preeminence of a husband are a detriment to creativity. This poem is almost a performative piece, and as such, it perhaps owes the most to Peggy's theatrical background. In this monologue spoken by a married woman, there are two voices: the voice of the poet who speaks to her husband idealistically through the lines of a love poem she is composing, and the voice of the wife who interrupts herself through a series of asides as she tends to her husband's needs.

The poem begins with a poem-within-a-poem that will be interrupted by the entrance of a husband:

> "Beloved, when I take my pen
> To write my thoughts of thee,
> All other wise and fearless men,
> However great they be—"
> (Is that my husband at the gate?
> Well, Thomas, you are rather late).

As the poem progresses, the voices begin to contradict one another: the parenthetical comments about and to the husband belie the romantic picture created by the poetry:

> "The star of love arose—" (What's that?
> Oh, Thomas, but you're wet!
> There's quite a pool upon the mat,
> I see you're dripping yet).
> "The star of love—" (You needn't shout,
> I'll come and get the dry things out).

Poetically elevated as he is, this "star of love" is in actuality a demanding, dripping mess. She glorifies his strength, but in reality he is not strong at all: he is humanly getting a cold. When she praises his sense of duty in her poem, their actual conversation reveals that she, in fact, has done his duty, although he will take credit for it:

> "To ev'ry duty thou dost fly,
>   And fond affection seek"
> (I wrote your Mother, by the bye,
>   Her birthday is next week,
> You know how happy she will be
> In saying you reminded me).

The wife creates an illusionary husband in the poem, but it also becomes clear that she contributes to the creation of an illusion about him in their lives. By the last stanza, the boundaries between the two worlds blur as the poetic blends with the real. Significantly, the poem is lost as it dissolves into real life:

> "O husband, let me end my rhyme
>   In proof of love for thee
> By saying this—" (it's feeding time!)
> "Beloved, thou shalt see—"
>   (Your dinner, Thomas, in a trice,
>   And how I *pray* you'll find it nice!)

This poem establishes a clear need for a room of one's own, as it demonstrates a woman caught in a vicious cycle. The female speaker creates an illusion on two levels and both are problematic. On the poetic level, her writing extols her husband and creates a version of him that contradicts reality; the fact that she chooses him as the focus of her own art demonstrates the way her circumstances have enclosed her. On the level of reality, it is her husband who is the destroyer of her work; she struggles to keep the two worlds separate, but she cannot. The art that romanticizes him is sacrificed for him, but her creativity will presumably continue to construct an illusion in the "real" world. This dramatic monologue is amusing in its seemingly good spirit, but it offers a serious look at male/female relationships, as well as the difficult position of the female writer.

"To a Boy of Long Ago," another poem using style in a deceptive way, is the sole selection in the second section, titled "Poems in Another Vein." The simplistic language in rhyming couplets appears to create a naive portrait of a pastoral scene:

> How wonderful it is to see
> The first buds on the dark ash tree:
> How wonderful it is to hear
> The cuckoo calling far and near.

Each of the first eight couplets (constituting nearly half the poem) begins with "How wonderful," "More wonderful," or "Most wonderful." A surfeit of wonder and sweetness culminates in her reference to God: "Most wonderful it is to prove, By all these wonders, God is love."

The origin of the type of satire and the style found in "To a Boy of Long Ago" perhaps lies in the loathed "Goody-goody books" mentioned earlier. Well-meaning Victorian friends gave these books to the children, partly because they felt the girls' theatrical experiences might taint their moral characters. Guests at a party were once shocked when Lucy said that she "hated morals." The Webling parents clearly

Rosalind, Peggy, and Lucy Webling in Britannia, *a patriotic sketch they performed on their tour of Canada from 1895 to 1897*

taught their children ethical values, but the daughters were allowed more freedom of thought than typical Victorian children. This freedom is reflected in the later work of both women, especially in their liberal attitudes toward sexual relationships. An example is the poem at hand, "To a Boy Long Ago," in which Peggy's broad-minded views of premarital sex are evident. In her novel *One Way Street* Lucy also interrogates Victorian mores as she decries the double standards that make unwed mothers social outcasts. The "Goody-goody books" perhaps contributed another element to this poem as well: the employment of deliberately simple language and singsong rhythms in the service of satire. Peggy recalls a particularly maudlin poem from one of these books; another dimension of "To a Boy of Long Ago" becomes apparent when comparing it to the original and rewritten versions of the "Goody-goody" poem:

> Mother, guide my little steps
>   Gently while you can,
> Guide me up the hill of life

> Till I grow a man.
> Mother, when I grow a man,
>   Good, and strong, and brave,
> I'll lead my Mother down the hill
>   Kindly to the grave.

As children, the sisters wrote a parody of the poem, using a female version of the same voice to satirize the sentimentality:

> Mother, guide my little steps
>   Harshly while you can,
> Kick me up the hill of life
>   Till I wed a man.
> Mother, when I wed a man,
>   Stout, and rich, and brave,
> I'll trot my Mother down the hill
>   Quickly to the grave.

Their adaptation shows an early ability to create a sickeningly sweet surface that masks conflicting meanings; in "To a Boy of Long Ago" the description of nature seems simple in its beauty:

> From hand of His there flutters forth
> The little, blue-winged, timid moth:
> He paints the harebell in the dell;
> He hides the scarlet pimpernel.

In among the flowers there is the implication of a sexual experience to which God himself has led these lovers:

> He led us to the water's edge,
> And there we found among the sedge
> A wild forget-me-not—His care
> And loving thought had planted there.

Peggy asserts in "To a Boy of Long Ago" that both God and Nature sanction sex. The female speaker addresses a man she had known as a youth, persuading him that their relationship, which society would regard as illicit, was as innocent, natural, and beautiful as the flowers she describes; moreover, their experience was God's design:

> A perfect hour for you and me
> He gave—remember, e'er you smile,
> If it is worth our Father's while
> To care for all the living things
> That creep, or fly with tiny wings,
> It surely pleases Him to joy
> A little girl and little boy?

In this poem her appeal for sexual pleasure without guilt is implicitly made to the social order as a whole.

In the "Verses in Memoriam" section Webling examines her own feelings as she acknowledges the important men in her life, such as her father or the artist Henry Page. Sometimes her poems are straightforward messages of love, as in the last section of the volume, "Japanese Love Letters." Her satiric poetry of the first section, usually written in rhyming couplets or quatrains, markedly contrasts these love poems. Each written to a Japanese man, these seven poems evidence a strong Asian influence. Although the poems do not conform to the structure of Haiku, they share some of its elements: a simple, unadorned style and images from the natural world that express an internal emotion. The most-successful of this group is "To a Painter," in which she combines natural images with representations of a Japanese painting:

> The whole of Heaven I saw
> In a sweep of your brush's blue;
> The sunny surface of the sea
> In a fish you drew
> For me.
>
> The bloom of almond I felt
> With colour and perfume blent,
> The happy Springtime still to be,
> In a blossom you sent
> To me.
>
> The sound of music I heard,
> And murmuring streams awoke,
> With caged son-birds all set free,
> In a word you spoke
> To me.

In the longer lines the female speaker gathers images from the external world and then compresses them in the last line of each verse, "To me," in a way that internalizes them.

The last section rounds out the range of messages sent to men in the volume as it speaks to the possibility of straightforward romantic relationships. Perhaps more than any other factor, Peggy Webling's directness distinguishes her work in a period when women were not rewarded for directness. The openness of her ideas about sex and relationships is refreshing, partly because of the way she communicates them to men, whether they reside within the poem or act as its audience—or both. Overall, her poems tell men about themselves, about the way women feel about them, and about the way women feel about themselves.

As Peggy continued to write novels, she also retained her connections with the stage. She wrote an adaptation of Charles Kingsley's *Westward Ho!* (1855) that was performed in 1913. In 1927 she embarked on a project that eventually secured a place for her in the annals of motion-picture history: she adapted Mary Shelley's *Frankenstein* (1818) for the stage. While Peggy's *Frankenstein: An Adventure in the Macabre* was not the first dramatization of the novel, it was significant, for it was ultimately used as a basis for the screenplay of the 1931 *Frankenstein* movie starring Boris Karloff. The idea for the adaptation came about when a friend of Peggy's, Hamilton Deane, was playing Dracula in a 1927 London stage production. Inspired by the success of the play and the current vogue of the horror genre, Peggy created her three-act play, *Frankenstein: An Adventure in the Macabre,* as a comparison piece to *Dracula*. It premiered in December 1927 in Portcawl, a small town in Wales. In tandem with *Dracula, Frankenstein* toured for two years with Hamilton Deane playing the major roles in both productions. Peggy continued to revise the piece as it traveled, and in February 1930 *Frankenstein* opened at the Little Theatre in London's West End. Although the reviews were not especially good, Peggy is credited with emphasizing significant aspects of Shelley's tale. For instance, she was one of the first to recognize and dramatize the doppelgänger element in the story: many of her characters noticeably reflect one another, and, most important, the "creature" of Shelley's novel takes on the name of his creator as Peggy calls them both Frankenstein. Convinced that *Frankenstein* could successfully follow *Dracula* to Broadway, an American producer commissioned John Balderston to join Peggy in revising her script for the American stage. Balderston made major revisions in Peggy's play, but before the production materialized, Universal Studios purchased the rights to both scripts for $20,000. The movie, produced by Carl Laemmle Jr. at Universal, premiered in New York City on 4 December 1931. Although the screenplay differed greatly from Peggy's original dramatization, skeletal elements remained, and she received a film credit and 1 percent of the gross earnings.

The lives of Peggy and Lucy Webling remain obscure. Their significance lies, therefore, not in their influence, but in their contemporary contributions to a feminist view of the Victorian and Edwardian world.

References:

Virginia Blain, Patricia Clements, and Isobel Grundy, *The Feminist Companion to Literature in English: Women Writers from the Middle Ages to the Present* (New Haven & London: Yale University Press, 1990), p. 1142;

Steven Earl Forry, *Hideous Progenies: Dramatizations of Frankenstein from Mary Shelley to the Present* (Philadelphia: University of Pennsylvania Press, 1990), pp. 90–99;

David J. Skal, *The Monster Show: A Cultural History of Horror* (New York & London: Norton, 1993), pp. 97–108.

Title page for the Weblings' only collaborative book, which includes poems by Lucy and short stories by Peggy

Papers:

Letters, theatrical documents, an unpublished manuscript by Peggy Webling titled "The Story of a Pen: A Book for Would-be Writers," and other material relating to the Webling family are privately held by Dorian Gieseler Greenbaum, the great-granddaughter of Josephine Webling.

Augusta Webster

(30 January 1837 – 5 September 1894)

Kathleen Hickok
Iowa State University

See also the Webster entry in *DLB 35: Victorian Poets After 1850.*

BOOKS: *Blanche Lisle, and Other Poems,* as Cecil Home (Cambridge & London: Macmillan, 1860);
Lilian Gray, a Poem, as Home (London: Smith, Elder, 1864);
Lesley's Guardians, as Home, 3 volumes (London & Cambridge: Macmillan, 1864);
Dramatic Studies (London & Cambridge: Macmillan, 1866);
A Woman Sold and Other Poems (London & Cambridge: Macmillan, 1867);
Portraits (London & Cambridge: Macmillan, 1870; enlarged, London & New York: Macmillan, 1893);
The Auspicious Day (London: Macmillan, 1872);
Yu-Pe-Ya's Lute: A Chinese Tale in English Verse (London: Macmillan, 1874);
Disguises, A Drama (London: Kegan Paul, 1879);
A Housewife's Opinions (London: Macmillan, 1879);
A Book of Rhyme (London: Macmillan, 1881);
In a Day, A Drama (London: Kegan Paul, Trench, 1882);
Daffodil and the Croäxaxicans: A Romance of History (London: Macmillan, 1884);
The Sentence, a Drama (London: Unwin, 1887);
Selections from the Verse of Augusta Webster (London: Macmillan, 1893);
Mother and Daughter, an Uncompleted Sonnet-Sequence, edited by William Michael Rossetti (London & New York: Macmillan, 1895).

PLAY PRODUCTION: *In a Day,* London, Terry Theatre, matinee, summer 1890.

OTHER: *Parliamentary Franchise for Women Ratepayers,* a pamphlet (London: printed by John Bale for the Central Committee of the National Society for Women's Suffrage, 1878).

TRANSLATIONS: *The Prometheus Bound of Aeschylus,* edited by Thomas Webster (London & Cambridge: Macmillan, 1866);

Augusta Webster

The Medea of Euripides (London & Cambridge: Macmillan, 1868).

SELECTED PERIODICAL PUBLICATION – UNCOLLECTED: "The Brissons," as Home, *Macmillan's Magazine* (November 1861): 60-64.

Augusta Webster was chiefly a dramatic, narrative, and lyric poet of the late nineteenth century. Her many extended dramatic monologues, featuring both male and female speakers, compare favorably with dramatic monologues by Robert Browning, and her melancholy sonnets and renunciatory verse narratives resemble poems by Christina Rossetti. Webster's plays in blank verse explore characters and plots ranging from historical and religious traditions to classical drama and Elizabethan theater; she translated plays by Aeschylus and Euripides into English verse.

Webster also wrote in prose, including an adult novel, a children's fantasy, and many social and political essays concerning women's rights and responsibilities. Her most persistent—and frequently interrelated—themes in all these various genres were women and marriage, innocence and betrayal, religious faith and doubt. In addition to her work as a writer, Webster found time to campaign for women's suffrage and to serve on the London School Board.

Julia Augusta Davies was born on 30 January 1837 in Poole, Dorset, to naval officer (later vice admiral) George Davies and Julia Augusta Hume. Her mother's father, Joseph Hume, had traveled in Romantic circles that included William Godwin, William Hazlitt, and Charles Lamb; in 1812 he had published a blank-verse translation of Dante's *Inferno*, and in 1841 "A Search into the Old Testament." Knowledge of the Godwin connection may have helped legitimize for Webster the feminist philosophy she adopted later in life. Association with Hume may have sparked his granddaughter's interest in classical and modern languages and in religious themes. Ostensibly to help a younger brother, Augusta Davies studied Greek, taking a particular interest in Greek drama. She also learned French, Italian, and Spanish. In her early twenties, she spent a few months in Paris and Geneva.

Her father held several coast-guard commands, including Banff and Penzance; Augusta spent much of her early childhood on various islands and ships, including the *Griper*, which was berthed in Chichester Harbor. This youthful experience with the sea probably accounts for the recurrence of sea imagery in Webster's poetry. Commander Davies was distinguished for rescuing shipwreck victims. One such shipwreck, in January 1851 off the coast of Cornwall, Webster subsequently described in a suspenseful short piece for *Macmillan's Magazine* (November 1861), titled "The Brissons" for the sister islands on which the ship had foundered. Shipwreck stories were frequent and popular in the nineteenth century; this vivid piece by Webster, in which a daring rescue is attempted as onlookers alternately cheer and shriek, recalls the climactic shipwreck scene in *David Copperfield* (1849-1850) by Charles Dickens.

In 1851 the Davies family moved to Cambridge, where George Davies was appointed chief constable, and Augusta began attending classes at the Cambridge School of Art. In 1860 she embarked upon her poetic career with *Blanche Lisle, and Other Poems*, published under the name "Cecil Home." Despite the masculine pseudonym, Webster was recognized in Cambridge as the author of the book, which, though poetically undistinguished, was well received. It includes mostly melancholy lyrics and narratives of bereavement, romantic misunderstanding and loss, humbled pride, and wronged innocence—poems of courtship and love gone wrong.

The title poem, "Blanche Lisle," is in four sections: "Reveries," "Together," "The Old Year's Last Midnight," and "Floating On." The orphaned heroine, Blanche, in "Reveries" is reminiscent of Alfred Tennyson's "Mariana" (1830):

All things are dreary, to what end is youth?
   I that am young yet feel so tired and old;
Oh, languid life, and hast thou not in truth
   In all thy dross one little grain of gold?
All things are dreary, all things are a dream.

In part 2 Blanche's lover has come after all; he makes her promise that if he should die, she would never wed another. Part 3 opens in a ruined chapel, the family burial place, to which Blanche has come seeking a vision of the future. The imagery is reminiscent of John Keats's "Eve of St. Agnes" (1820). She has a vision, indeed, of her dead forbears, including her parents, who beckon her to join them. She discovers her own coffin, with herself in it dead, still young. She screams, the vision disappears, she swoons, and she is found near death in the morning. She is nursed back to life by her lover and the last section begins. In part 4 the lover has betrayed her, and Blanche pines away to death in typical Victorian poetic fashion.

Alongside conventional poems such as this one, Webster also included in *Blanche Lisle, and Other Poems* a few overtly political pieces—for example, "Song of the Septembriseurs," representing French peasants' justifiable anger just prior to the French Revolution. Other original pieces include the shipwreck and drowning narratives "Margaret Beneath the Waves," and "Once Lovers," and "The Killarney Snake," based on an Irish legend.

In 1863 Augusta married Thomas Webster, a fellow (and later law lecturer) at Trinity College, Cambridge, and a practicing solicitor there. The couple had one daughter, their only child. Webster's next two publications, both appearing in 1864 shortly after her marriage, chiefly concern the difficulties and complexities of forming happy marital unions. This concern becomes so much Webster's lifelong central theme as to raise the question of whether her own marriage was problematic, or, alternatively, whether her many representations of failed attempts to marry for love are in contrast with her own situation. It is impossible now to discover which came first, her feminist commitment to combatting the forces that prevent women from fulfilling their intellectual, emotional, and social potential, or her recognition of the powerlessness of many women at the most crucial juncture of their lives—contracting a suitable and happy marriage.

Lilian Gray (1864) is a narrative poem portraying both social and personal causes of heartbreaking mismatched marriages, including class differences, financial difficulties, poor timing, scheming mothers, lovers' quarrels and misunderstandings, hasty decision making, and fateful accidents. The narrator, Margaret Aubrey, tells her younger sister, who is at sixteen happily betrothed, a sad story explaining why Margaret has never married (and probably never will). The one man she loves and could ever love made a hasty commitment to a simple, yet delicate, rural girl named Lilian Gray. In good conscience and according to the dictates of honor, he cannot jilt her for Margaret, even though he now realizes a more-mature love that he has for Margaret, and even though he has grown estranged from Lilian. The narrator prevails upon the young man to do the right thing—he marries Lilian, they have a child, and Lilian dies before the fragile child is two years old. Margaret cannot imagine ever renewing her relationship to her former suitor, even though he, she, and the child are all devastated because she cannot and will not do so. Throughout Webster's work, innocence betrayed cannot be restored.

Lesley's Guardians (1864) takes up the marriage plot in a three-volume novel, the only adult novel Webster ever published. In a signed copy of this book, addressed to poet Jean Ingelow "with A. W.'s very kind regards," Webster pronounced *Lesley's Guardians* to be "one of my earliest failures." The book turns on a melodramatic false marriage plot, set partly in France. Lesley, called Desirée in France, is an art student trying to reconcile her career aspirations with the cultural expectation that she will marry and have children, thenceforth pursuing art only as an avocation or accomplishment. She falls in love, and a false marriage is promulgated upon her; for two years she is unable to consider another marriage because Louis, the scoundrel who tricked her into believing she was legally married to him when she was not, is still alive and still trying to claim her affections. When marriage to Louis finally becomes possible, Lesley/Desirée can by no means imagine accepting it. Louis then kills himself, and in the end Lesley settles for an unromantic but companionate marriage with Maurice, a kindly older man, one of her self-appointed "guardians" of the title.

The plot of *Lesley's Guardians* is melodramatic, but the characters are sympathetic, the narrative is fast-paced, the dialogue is natural, and the secondary characters are well drawn, especially the women. Stephanie, Louis's fiancée, tries to develop romantic feelings for Louis in the context of a marriage arranged by their families for financial stability—a delicate personal challenge in the Victorian "marriage market," as Webster repeatedly called it. Lesley's cousins Eloisa and Octavia are not equally able or inclined to cultivate the marriageable woman's accomplishments, demeanor, and destiny—yet Eloisa cannot escape this fate even though it does not suit her. Marion Raymond, a young widow, having lost her chance at a happy marriage, rescues a poor relation and her children and makes a home for them instead.

Lesley abandons the name Desirée and becomes instead Mrs. Maurice. At the end of the novel Marion, who had hoped to marry Maurice herself, paces the terrace alone in the September moonlight, while Maurice and Lesley sit on the porch telling each other of their happiness. The irony of this ending is double: a stable marriage has been achieved by the heroine at last, yet half a dozen lives have been harmed, lost, or ruined in the bargain, including Lesley's.

Lilian Gray and *Lesley's Guardians* were the last books Webster published under the Cecil Home pseudonym. Later, in an essay in the *Examiner* titled "The Novel-Making Trade," Webster reveals her opinion that women's novels are—excepting those by Jane Austen, Charlotte Brontë, and George Eliot—"light literature." (With this opinion George Eliot herself concurred, writing in the *Westminster Review* [October 1856] to condemn "silly novels by lady novelists.") Webster regarded novel making as a "trade" similar to nursing, which middle-class girls might take up, "much as their sisters of the working-classes set up a mangle. . . . It is not strange that women should thus rush into the one remunerative profession available; it is not strange that many of them should find in it only disappointment and failure," as she herself evidently did.

These three early books—*Blanche Lisle*, *Lilian Gray*, and *Lesley's Guardians*—are generally regarded as apprenticeship works, published before Webster found the voice and mode that best suited her. Her gift was not primarily for narrative, whether in poetry or in prose, but for drama—dramatic monologues and verse plays.

In preparation for a new, more-dramatic phase of her writing career, Webster spent several years studying and translating the Greek plays *Prometheus Bound* (1866) and *Medea* (1868) into English verse. A writer for *The Illustrated London News* considered it "astonishing how a certain poetic majesty, for which the original is remarkable, discloses itself in the choral portions and the monologues" of her *Prometheus Bound*. Webster's husband, who was well educated in classics, assisted her and edited the first of the two translations. Webster's philosophy of translating poetry, she explained later in "The Translation of Poetry," an essay for the *Examiner* that was later collected in *A Housewife's Opinions* (1879), was to preserve the spirit of the translated piece by keeping as close as possible to a literal translation; in this goal she seems to have succeeded. Two periodicals that were to support Webster's work during her entire subsequent career, the *Athenaeum* and the *Westminster Review*, likewise praised the *Medea* translation. The reviewer for the *Athenaeum* noted "how closely and correctly she has reproduced the original, expressing its full force and delicate shades of meaning line for line, and almost word for word," while the writer in the *Westminster Review* remarked, "We really do not know where to find another translation in which the spirit is rendered with such fidelity and beauty."

In addition to her classical apprenticeship, Webster was probably also reading recent work by her two strongest contemporary influences, Robert Browning and Christina Rossetti, particularly Browning's *Men and Women* (1855) and *Dramatis Personae* (1864) and Rossetti's *Goblin Market and Other Poems* (1862) and *The Prince's Progress* (1866). Other evident influences on Webster's work are Tennyson (*Poems*, 1842), and Elizabeth Barrett Browning (*Poems*, 1844, and *Aurora Leigh*, 1857), as well as Robert Browning's earlier volume, *Dramatic Lyrics and Romances* (1845).

The poetry for which Webster is most remembered today appeared over a period of five years: *Dramatic Studies* (1866), *A Woman Sold and Other Poems* (1867), and *Portraits* (1870). The poems in these three books, which have been repeatedly compared with the work of major Victorian poets, include the most successful poetry of Webster's career.

Dramatic Studies consists of eight dramatic monologues of varying length, and establishes the range and thematics of Webster's work in that genre. The first two poems, "A Preacher" and "A Painter," resemble Robert Browning's characteristic idiom, syntax, and tone, and recall his self-revelatory speakers. The preacher in Webster's poem struggles with both religious doubt and self-doubt—a recurrent theme in her work. His biblical text, "Lest that by any means / When I have preached to others I myself / Should be a castaway," introduces the "castaway" theme that appears in a different context in *Portraits*. Like Webster's other successful dramatic monologues, this poem creates a convincing psychological portrait of a conflicted speaker, in this case a successful preacher who cannot believe in his own sermons. Echoing Tennyson's "There lives more faith in honest doubt, / Believe me, than in half the creeds" (*In Memoriam*, 1850), Webster's preacher concludes, "Better to doubt and be perplexed in soul / Because thy truth seems many and not one, /

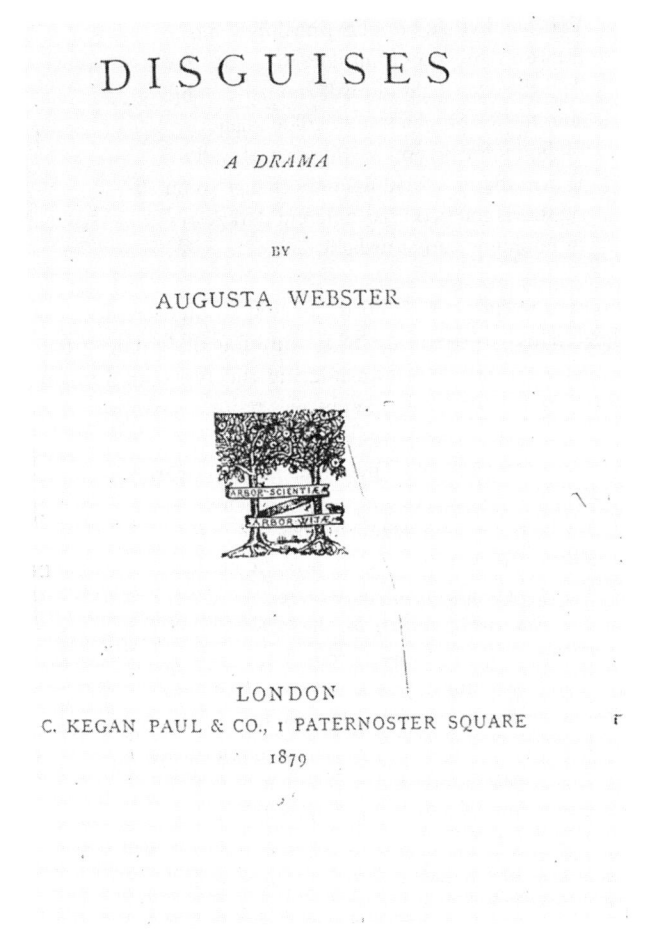

Title page for Webster's verse drama set in the Elizabethan era

Than cease to seek Thee, even through reverence, / In the fulness and minuteness of thy truth." As was usually the case, Webster's speaker is less cynical than Browning's comparable speakers, such as the ones in "The Bishop Orders His Tomb at St. Praxed's Church" (1845) or "Bishop Blougram's Apology" (1855).

The speaker in "The Painter" owes something of his difficult situation and his philosophy of art to Browning's 1855 monologues, "Andrea del Sarto" and "Fra Lippo Lippi" as well as to Elizabeth Barrett Browning's long verse novel about a woman artist, *Aurora Leigh*. Like Andrea del Sarto, Webster's painter has a wife who creates both his inspiration and his limitations—he must pander to popular taste to earn enough money to support his family. Like Browning's frustrated artist monk, Fra Lippo Lippi, Webster's painter confirms the validity of his unrecognized gift:

All the world is beauty. We know that
We painters, we whom God shows how to see.
We have beauty ours, we take it where we go.
Aye my wise critics, rob me of my bread,

> You can do that, but of my birthright, no.
> Imprison me away from skies and seas
> And the open sight of earth and her rich life
> And the lesson of a face or golden hair:
> I'll find it for you on a whitewashed wall
> Where the slow shadows only change so much
> As shows the street has different darknesses
> At noontime and at twilight.

Remembering that Webster herself studied art, it is not far-fetched to assume she is thinking of female artists and writers as well. Considering the representation of women in popular art, Webster's painter says:

> Ah well I am a poor man and must earn—
> And little dablets of a round-faced blonde,
> Or pretty pert brunette who drops her fan,
> Or else the kind the public, save the mark,
> Calls poem-like, ideal, and the rest—
> I have a sort of aptness for the style—
> A buttercup or so made prominent
> To point a moral, how youth fades like grass
> Or some such wisdom, a lace handkerchief
> Or broidered hem mapped out as if one meant
> To give a seamstress patterns—that's to show
> How "conscientious," that's the word, one is—
> And a girl dying, crying, marrying, what you will,
> With a blue-light tint about her—these will sell.

This verse is a good description of the popular novel or melancholy poem's typical heroine, just the sort of characterization present in Webster's early productions as Cecil Home. "A Painter" shows what she hoped to avoid by turning to more-dramatic poetry.

Like Browning's poet heroine Aurora Leigh, Webster's painter worries about his critics. Some will complain that he has not studied enough to dare to offer his work to the world. The work is good, and he is proud of it, but it is not yet his best; without recognition and encouragement from the world, he does not know how he will ever bring forth his most original work. Here Webster draws on Browning's characteristic theme of success and failure, and upon her own experiences of failure with her earlier work. The poem concludes with a turn toward domesticity as Ruth, the painter's wife, appears after putting the children to bed. Unlike Andrea del Sarto's Lucrezia, Ruth does not fly away but remains to comfort her husband and to offer supportive criticism. He greets her:

> Ah love, you come in time to chase some thoughts
> I do not care to dwell on. Come, stand there
> And criticise my picture. It has failed
> Of course—I always fail. Yet on the whole
> I think the world would praise it were I known.

The painter can accept the impossibility of perfectly achieving his artistic vision, but he indicts the custom of lionizing established artists while disregarding worthy newcomers as partly responsible for his plight. Though the speaker of this poem is male, the concerns he expresses are equally—perhaps even more—applicable to women.

The third and fourth monologues in *Dramatic Studies,* "Jeanne D'Arc" and "Sister Annunciata," introduce the strong religious theme that runs through Webster's work. The human challenge is to renounce worldly satisfaction through courage and faith in exchange for self-mastery, confidence in God's benevolence, and often a martyr's death. Encouraged by visions of St. Margaret and St. Catherine, Jeanne D'Arc faces her immolation bravely:

> My God, I thank Thee who hast chosen me
> To be Thy messenger to drive them forth;
> And, since my death was destined with the mission,
> Lord of my life, I thank Thee for my death.

Similarly, the novice nun Sister Annunciata (formerly called Eva), after a terrible all-night struggle, renounces her former lover's entreaty that she sustain a vision of heaven in which they will be reunited. Webster's renunciatory religious poems are the ones that most reflect the influence of Christina Rossetti, whose poem "The Convent Threshold" (1862), for example, relates a similar situation to "Sister Annunciata." Eva's struggle is long and agonizing (the poem runs fifty-nine pages), but she is ultimately rewarded with mystical visions and an early death. As in Rossetti's "The World" (1862), such speakers in Webster's work develop a horror of earthly temptation and strive continually to give themselves to God. The religious poems of Webster typically present a yearning for quiescence and for release from the torturous and deceptive hope of romantic love, thus uniting two of her major themes: women and marriage, and religious faith and doubt.

In a metaphor typical of women writers of the nineteenth century, Eva compares herself to a caged bird that wishes to fly free. Remembering her naive decision to enter a convent in order to escape the constraints of a woman's life, she recalls:

> What knew I of vocation? I was galled
> By the bird-snare fetters round me, longed to fly
> On wild young wings towards the freer Heaven;
> And, seeing that the cage hung on the tree
> Was higher than the nest upon the ground,
> Said sometimes, "Yet at least if I were there,"
> Because I so might reach a purer sky
> And breath untainted air; but most of all
> Because I longed to soar.

The connection between the three major themes of Webster's work is clear: women in the nineteenth century were so fettered by the necessity of marriage and so powerless to affect the process of matchmaking that they often found their innocent confidence betrayed by more worldly others—fathers, mothers, suitors, and seducers. One plausible response they could make was to renounce the joys of life, which seemed so impossible to obtain, and to take consolation in doing God's will and waiting patiently for a heavenly reward. This impulse toward religious consolation parallels Christina Rossetti's personal vision and poetics.

The anguished male speaker in "With the Dead," also from *Dramatic Studies,* has forfeited this spiritual alternative, as Webster's male speakers often do. He betrayed a band of Christians, including his beloved Lucilla, to the Romans, who then tortured and executed them; consequently the speaker has, according to legend, spent fifteen centuries groping in darkness, seeking his way out of the catacombs where the martyred Lucilla rests in peace. He committed the crime not, like Browning's pagan speaker "Cleon" (1855), because he could not welcome the new religion, but because he was jealous of Glaucon, his Christian rival for Lucilla's affections. Although once a year he is offered a chance to convert to Christianity and rest beside Lucilla, whom he loves, and Glaucon, her companion, whom he hates, he continues to make the wrong choice and to suffer because of it.

In contrast to the religious themes of these three poems, two other short monologues in *Dramatic Studies* address social issues of the period. "Too Late" resembles the poem of the same title in Browning's *Dramatis Personae* and perhaps also the title poem of Rossetti's *The Prince's Progress.* In all three, the dilatory and self-indulgent male speaker rebukes himself for delaying in speaking his feelings and reuniting with his beloved, who meanwhile has perished. "By the Looking-Glass" is spoken by a homely spinster who regards her image in the mirror and regrets the opportunities that her lack of beauty has denied her: dancing, admirers, love, marriage, and children. She goes to sleep at last, hoping that sleep will "Let self and this sadness of self leave me free, / Lost in the peace of the night." Here, as elsewhere, Webster points to the emptiness of life for those women the Victorians called "redundant," women for whom there would be no husband, women who feminists like Webster thought should be offered other outlets for their energies than endlessly waiting for the husband-suitor who "will not come," as Tennyson's Mariana laments.

"Snow Waste," the eighth poem in *Dramatic Studies,* was considered by Webster's contemporaries to be particularly striking. It is a fantastical study of human guilt, akin to Browning's "Porphyria's Lover" in *Madhouse Cells* (1849) or Samuel Taylor Coleridge's "The Rime of the Ancient Mariner" (1798). In "Snow Waste" a mood of psychological desolation and emotional frigidity is set by the speaker's description of the scene "mid a waste of snow / Where never sun looked down nor silvering moon, / But far around the silent skies were grey." The speaker describes a fearful figure, seemingly more dead than alive, who stumbles through the snow waste with two figures dragging after him, "two forms that seemed of flesh / But blue with the first clutchings of their deaths / Fixed rigid in the death-pang, glassy-eyed, / Turning towards him each a vacant gaze." Like the Ancient Mariner, this figure tells his sad tale to the speaker, who responds with horror. The spectres are the figure's wife and her brother, who died of the plague, but whose deaths are on his conscience because of his jealous rage at their close but innocent relationship. Like the speaker in "With the Dead," this figure has created his doom by his own actions. He has cursed the sun and banished light, life, and love from his universe rather than share his wife with her brother. The figure speaks in a monotone, devoid of feeling; correspondingly, the rhyme scheme is unusual—the same rhyme for eight long monotonous lines per stanza:

> I know if I one pang could make
> Of sorrow in me, if my heart could ache
> One moment for the memories I spake,
> The spell that is upon me now might break,
> And I might with a sudden anguish shake
> The numbness from it and perceive it wake,
> And these be no more bound here for my sake
> But slumber calmly in their silent lake.

Both the spectre of the wife and the shadow of her brother attempt to evoke such feeling in the snow waste figure, but without success. He recounts having thrown their two bodies in the lake, "And slept such quiet sleep as children know. / But I awakened in this waste of snow / Where evermore gnawed by quick cold I go." Like the speaker in "With the Dead," this man's rigidity, his inability or refusal to feel and choose rightly, prevent the resolution of his psychological pain. However, "The Snow Waste" is more effective than "With the Dead," because of the imaginative representation of the haunted man's inner struggle and the eerie wasteland in which it occurs.

Dramatic Studies was well received by the *Saturday Review,* the *Athenaeum,* and other periodicals. Recognizing the dramatic intent of Webster's newest work, the writer for the *Eclectic Review* declared, "She possesses a power of dramatic strength no woman has evidenced since Joanna Baillie; a mastery of passion, a dissection

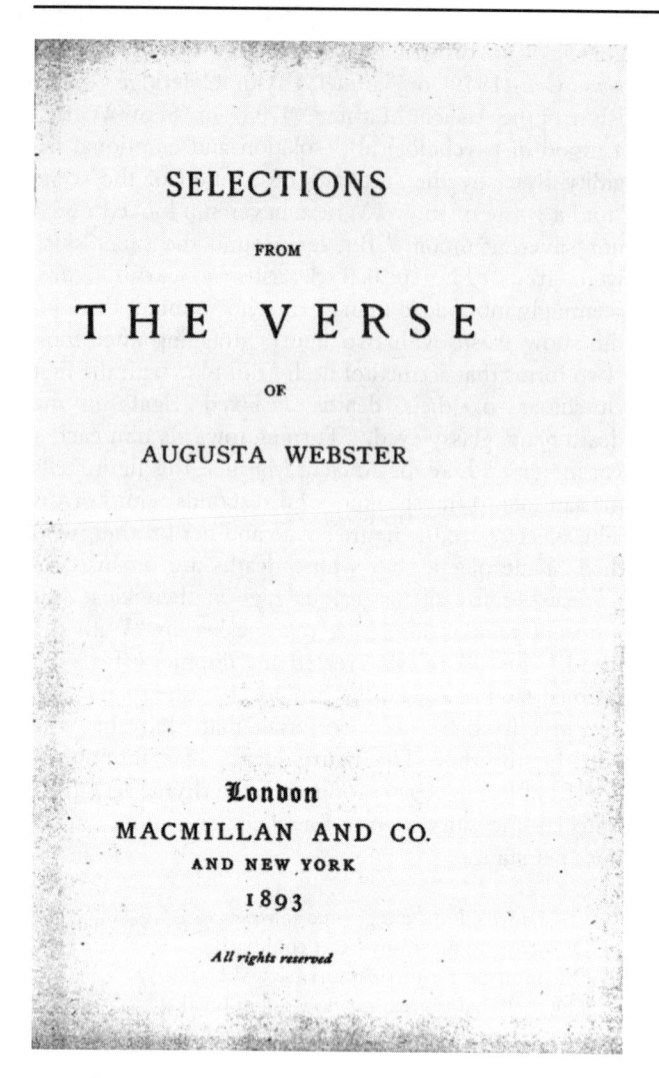

Title page for the last book Webster published in her lifetime. It includes six previously unpublished poems.

and description of its moods, which show her to be profound in the ways and workings of souls." The reviewer for the *Westminster Review* (October 1866) also compared her with other women poets, commenting, "Mrs. Webster shows not only originality, but what is nearly as rare, trained intellect and self-command."

Only one year later, *A Woman Sold and Other Poems* appeared and was equally acclaimed. A reviewer in the *Leader* initiated a continuing debate about the "masculinity" of Webster's verse when he wrote in response to *A Woman Sold and Other Poems,* "Since Mrs. Barrett Browning, no woman has written half such good poetry as Mrs. Webster. She combines in her verse the fulness and vigour of a matured masculine mind, with the ever-recurring tenderness of expression, the sweet impassioned emotional touches, which can only be communicated by the heart of the highly-gifted woman." Indeed, the title poem, which is in the form of two dramatic dialogues, includes strong language about the marriage market—spoken by the betrayed suitor Lionel to his beloved Eleanor Vaughan:

> That you were bought like any lower thing
> Our Croesus fancies, like the horse that won
> The Derby last, the picture of the year,
> The best bred pointer, or the costliest ring;
> You bought by such a buyer, a cold fool. . . .
> A man past youth and practised out of tune
> For loving should not haggle at the price
> When he buys girlhood, blushes, sentiment,
> Grace, innocence, aye even piety
> And taste in decking churches, such fawn eyes
> As yours are, Eleanor, and such a bloom
> Of an unfingered peach just newly ripe.
> Aye, when a modest woman sells herself
> Like an immodest one, she should not find
> A niggard at the cheque book.

Later, Lionel pleads with Eleanor to reconsider, employing caged bird imagery to make his point:

> You'll pine to love as a caged sparrow pines
> To fly, you'll tear and break your useless wings
> With beating at the bars, or else you'll mope
> In obstinate tired stillness; you'll not thrive
> On caged birds' food and sing.

Eleanor promises to wait for Lionel, but she does not wait, and the prophecy comes true. As Lady Boycott, she confides in a friend that she is

> wearier than the worn drudge
> Who toils past woman's strength the hard day through
> And cowers at evening to the drunken boor
> Who strikes her with a curse because she's his
> And that's his right upon her—wearier
> Because my labour was to love against
> The longings and the loathings of my heart,
> Because the price I earned was only smiles
> And too familiar fondlings. Ah! he had
> His rights upon me.

Here Webster alludes to the sexual duties of the woman sold—tolerating the husband's "condescending husbandly caress / [that] made me feel so abject and so false." This frankness about wife beating and married women's sexual obligations was unusual in the nineteenth century, unusual coming from a woman writer, and unusual to be found in poetry. Other poems in this volume—notably "The Heiress's Wooer," "A Mother's Cry," and the long blank verse narrative "Lota"—address courtship and marriage issues but none so brutally as "A Woman Sold." "Lota" seems to have derived certain plot details, characters, and class issues from *Aurora Leigh*. Like Elizabeth Barrett Browning, who believed, "If a woman ignores these wrongs, then may women as a sex continue to suffer them," Webster purposely set out to reveal the truth about marriage and sexuality in nineteenth-century England.

In contrast to these realistic social poems, the volume also included medieval and Pre-Raphaelite poems, reminiscent of those by Dante Gabriel Rossetti and William Morris, such as "The River," "Dreaming," and the long poem "Fairies' Chatter." The title of "Fairies' Chatter" belies the serious philosophical content of this piece. Like the prose and verse fairy tales of Christina Rossetti, "Fairies' Chatter" is more a fable than a children's story. A mortal and a fairy fall in love, and the fairy must choose whether to sacrifice her innocence and freedom for the sorrows of human life and the promise of heaven. Fairies tell the story, and the resolution of the conflict must be inferred by the human reader. This piece was Webster's first published attempt at the fairy story/fable genre. "Anno Domini," another long poem in this volume, addresses Victorian doubt and faith through dramatic monologues spoken by biblical figures Bartimaeus and Judas.

Portraits, her third book of poetry in five years, secured Webster's reputation as a dramatic poet. Webster was explicitly compared with Robert Browning and Morris in the *Westminster Review* (1 April 1870) and with Elizabeth Barrett Browning in the *Examiner* (21 May 1870). H. Buxton Forman wrote in *Our Living Poets* (1871), "I have more than once seen claimed for her the first place among the women-poets of England." *Portraits* was so successful that it was republished in 1893 with additional poems; it consists of twelve dramatic monologues, including two that are highly regarded today: "A Castaway" and "Circe."

"A Castaway" continues the frank tone of "A Woman Sold," which had compared women who married for money to prostitutes. The speaker of "A Castaway" is not an accusatory male, however, but a high-class prostitute speaking about her forced life choices and their devastating consequences. "A Castaway" was immediately compared with Dante Gabriel Rossetti's 1870 poem "Jenny," in which a male customer compares the sleeping prostitute Jenny with his own innocent cousin Nell. Rossetti's poetry was often attacked by reviewers for its sexual subject matter. For a woman writer such as Webster to publish a poem in which a prostitute justifies herself and her actions was quite daring. Critic Mackenzie Bell believed that Webster's "delineation of Woman's heart in the most appalling condition of Woman's life" in "A Castaway" may have been "too painful. . . . Were it not for the tender pity which inspires this poem as a whole some of the bitter things that fall from the lips of the lost girl would be too terrible and too daring for poetic art," he wrote in *The Poets and the Poetry of the Century* (1892).

Eulalie, the "lost girl," recounts her own personal history; she went from being an innocent English girl to an orphan, a governess, a housemaid, a seduced woman, a Magdalen penitent, an unmarried pregnant girl, a bereaved mother, and finally a kept woman. Protected by the sexual double standard, her lover has shunned Eulalie; her married brother refuses to admit her existence to his sheltered wife; and not one respectable woman has offered assistance. She has no skills, no protection, and no reputation or "character." She has been cast by circumstances into the role of prostitute and kept there by "the prudent world / that will not have the flawed soul prank itself / with a hoped second virtue, will not have / the woman fallen once lift up herself. . . . . . / lest she should fall again." In reflecting on this career and its causes and effects, Eulalie indicts the entire Victorian system of economics, class, education, marriage, sexuality, and religion.

The "castaway" emerges as a sympathetic and believable character, who can declare at one moment, "I have looked coolly on my what and why, / and I accept myself" and later cry out "No help! no help! no help! / How could it be? It was too late long since – / even at the first too late. Whose blame is that? / There are some kindly people in the world, / but what can they do? If one hurls oneself / into a quicksand, what can be the end, / but that one sinks and sinks?" Later, she says, "I could laugh outright . . . or else, / for I feel near it, roll on the ground and sob." The poem ends as a female visitor arrives: "Most welcome, dear: one gets so moped alone." "A Castaway" is a tour de force and the single most effective and enduring poem Webster ever wrote.

Like "A Castaway," "Circe" is also a dramatic monologue in which a despised and feared female figure—in this case the classic femme fatale of Greek myth—has an opportunity to present her case, while it remains believable that she is musing in private rather than directly addressing society. The poem opens with highly sexualized imagery: "The sun drops luridly into the west; / darkness has raised her arms to draw him down / before the time, not waiting as of wont / till he has come to her behind the sea." This initial sexual desire is reinforced by storm and sea imagery, while Circe yearns for romance, life, and love, for an honorable and passionate consort who will be a match for her. Meanwhile she preys on lesser men, visitors to her island, whose bestial nature she reveals by turning them into pigs, snakes, apes, dogs, and other animals. Circe's isolated situation somewhat resembles that of the secluded, idealized Victorian wife:

> What fate is mine who, far apart from pains
> and fears and turmoils of the cross-grained world,
> dwell, like a lonely god, in a charmed isle,
> where I am first and only, and, like one
> who should love poisonous savours more than mead,
> long for a tempest on me and grow sick
> of rest and of divine free carelessness!

Though Victorian reviewers sidestepped these qualities, "Circe" is notable for its sensuality and its fierce female voice. The *English Independent and Free Church Advocate* wrote of *Portraits*, Mrs. Webster "has a daring genius. . . . But her daring is not rashness; she justifies her enterprise by its success. There is an air of reality and a deep sense of seriousness in these poems."

Among the other poems in this volume, "A Soul in Prison" and "The Manuscript of Saint Alexius" are religious studies of doubt and faith, self-discipline and renunciation. "Medea in Athens" revisits Aeschylus but with less success than Webster achieves in "Circe." "The Happiest Girl in the World" and "Coming Home" are male and female monologues of youthful joy and optimism. Uncharacteristically, the speakers' hopes are not dashed within these two poems, but their placement in the same volume with monologues of older, disillusioned speakers makes their optimism appear ironic and emphasizes the naivete of their innocent hopes. "A Dilettante," "Tired," and "In an Almshouse" offer a critique of Victorian economics, middle-class respectability, and the meaningless bustle of modern life. In "Faded" (added in 1893), an aging woman comes to terms with her changed appearance and her consequent devaluation by society. "An Inventor" addresses again the dilemma of the painter in *Dramatic Studies*.

Taken as a body of work, *Dramatic Studies*, *A Woman Sold and Other Poems*, and *Portraits* constitute a remarkable achievement; 1870 was the halcyon year of Webster's literary career. Her decision not to capitalize words at the beginning of lines in *Portraits* was considered eccentric and prosaic in 1870, but it has given these poems a more-modern look and feel than many comparable nineteenth-century pieces. The *Examiner* reviewer summarized her achievement: "It is long since we encountered a volume of short miscellaneous pieces which would bear reading a second time. Many of those now before us, however, can be perused again and again with increasing pleasure. Whole lines cling to the memory as only the 'winged words' of genius can do, and refuse to be cast out of the chambers of the brain." Whereas the *Westminster Review* concluded, "we do not expect Mrs. Webster to be popular all at once; but if she only remains true to herself she will most assuredly take a higher rank as a poet than any woman has yet done," the *Examiner* ended by suggesting "that Mrs. Webster would do well to attempt a play. Her genius is essentially dramatic, and we think that she could scarcely fail to succeed."

Webster and her husband moved to London in 1870, where he established a law practice and she turned her attention to municipal and national politics. She published a large number of essays, many with a feminist perspective, in the *Examiner;* one of these, "Parliamentary Franchise for Women Ratepayers," was published separately in 1878 as a pamphlet in support of suffrage for women. Webster remained confident that women's suffrage would be approved, in spite of the six parliamentary defeats of the proposal that she witnessed in her lifetime.

Other *Examiner* essays were collected in 1878 and published in a volume titled *A Housewife's Opinions,* addressing many current social issues. For example, Webster deplored educational customs that emphasized silly "accomplishments" for girls, and she called for opening English universities to women seeking degrees. She recommended classes in domestic economy for girls and women. She suggested that children's literature, toys, and games should be made more challenging and interesting, and less didactic. She advocated dress reform for women, including abandoning the custom of wearing formal mourning garb. Of course, she deplored matrimony as a means of livelihood. She defended the virtue of unconventional modern women against attacks by critics such as Eliza Lynn Linton, who wrote for the *Saturday Review*.

Webster also defended the dignity of servants, favored cooperative housekeeping, and called for protective labor legislation for working-class women and children. In an 1880 *Athenaeum* essay, Theodore Watts-Dunton ranked Webster as a moral leader alongside George Eliot, Frances Power Cobbe, and Lady Charlotte Elliot. Webster ran for the London School Board in November 1879 and won by nearly four thousand votes; she served from 1879 to 1882 and was returned for a second three-year term in 1885. In the *Dictionary of National Biography* (1899), Elizabeth Lee described Webster's school-board career: "Mrs. Webster was a working rather than a talking member of the board. She was anxious to popularise education by bringing old endowments into close contact with elementary schools, and she anticipated the demand that, as education is a national necessity, it should also be a national charge. . . . Her leanings were frankly democratic, but in the heat of controversy her personality rendered her attractive even to her most vigorous opponents."

Meanwhile, Webster persevered in her literary career, turning her attention to writing in forms other than the dramatic monologue, particularly verse drama. Her first play to be published, *The Auspicious Day* (1872), dramatizes the tragic fate of an accused witch, an innocent young woman around whom hysteria mounts until she is betrayed, made a scapegoat, and finally stoned to death, scarcely believing any longer in her own innocence. As in all Webster's plays, the classical unities of time, place, and action are observed, and once the plot has been set into motion, the play moves swiftly and inexorably to its horrifying conclusion.

In 1874 she published *Yu-Pe-Ya's Lute: A Chinese Tale in English Verse*. Ostensibly an English rendering of a French version of a Chinese story, this poem seems rather to turn upon Victorian issues such as the rewards of cross-class friendships, the virtue of respecting one's parents even when their dictates and needs interfere with one's own fulfillment, and the consolatory bonds of romantic friendship between persons of the same sex (in this instance, men). The prince Yu-Pe-Ya tells his peasant friend Tse-Ky, from whom he is separated:

> thou hast won
> My closest heart thy lover. If the sun
> Who presently with his unwelcome glow
> Will save the kindly night and see me go
> To life that knows thee not, see thee remain
> A drudge among these wilds, yet not in vain
> Have we two met who never more shall be
> As though the other were not. Far from thee
> I shall remember, "Would he praise or chide?"
> Thou in the toilsome days, and lone beside
> The old folks dozing, weary with their age,
> In winter evenings, brooding o'er the page
> Thou hast forgot to turn, wilt think, "Ah well,
> The world holds one who knows me." We shall tell
> Our counted years from now, as women do,
> From when their firstborn came.

The two men were brought together across class differences by their mutual love of music, signified by the lute of the title. Webster acknowledged in the preface, "I need hardly say that I am responsible for all that may be considered nineteenth century. . . . The time of action is placed in an epoch so vague and so remote that it has no date, or rather it comes back into the present of every day human nature."

Webster's next published work, another play, was a romantic comedy, set in a seemingly Elizabe-

MOTHER & DAUGHTER

AN UNCOMPLETED SONNET-SEQUENCE

BY THE LATE
AUGUSTA WEBSTER

WITH AN INTRODUCTORY NOTE BY
WILLIAM MICHAEL ROSSETTI

To which are added Seven (her only other) Sonnets

London
MACMILLAN AND CO.
AND NEW YORK
1895

The Right of Translation and Reproduction is Reserved

Title page for Webster's volume of poems about her love for her daughter, published posthumously by her husband, Thomas

than world and titled *Disguises* (1879). Critics have compared it to William Shakespeare's *As You Like It* (1599) and *A Winter's Tale* (1610–1611). Like *Yu-Pe-Ya's Lute, Disguises* has a democratic theme: it suggests that peasants and queens may be equals in mind and spirit. The play raises the question: who is more free—aristocrats who have marital obligations they must fulfill, or peasants who can choose their own life mates? Perhaps because it resembled a Shakespearean play, and Shakespearean revivals were a popular staple of British theater in the nineteenth century, *Disguises* was well received. A writer for the *Scotsman* declared it "by far the most important contribution made to this department of English literature in recent years."

A Book of Rhyme, the slender volume of lyrics that appeared in 1881, resembles Webster's much-earlier work. The book consists mostly of melancholy poems of lost love, lost youth, and lost dreams. It includes several anxious war poems, "The Wind's Tidings in August 1870" and "No News from the War," as well as a poignant dramatic monologue,

"Poulain the Prisoner," which is reminiscent of George Gordon, Lord Byron's "The Prisoner of Chillon" (1816). This volume is most notable because it introduced into English poetry the verse form known in Italy as "stornelli" and in England as "rispetti" or "risputti," a form subsequently adopted by A. Mary F. Robinson and William Sharp. Webster had become interested in this form, originally a type of Italian peasant song, when she spent time in Italy between London school-board terms recovering from a bout of ill health. In *A Book of Rhyme,* the form is employed in a sequence of nostalgic seasonal lyrics. "The Daughter" is a representative example, perhaps written with Webster's own daughter in mind:

> Go forth, my darling, in the wreath and veil;
>   My hand shall place them for thee; so goodbye.
> Thou hast Love's rose, and tend it without fail;
>   It withers, dear, if lovers let it lie.
> Go, my own singing bird, and be his now;
> And I am more than half as glad as thou.
>   Ah me! the singing birds that were our own
>   Fly forth and mate: and 'tis long life alone.

In their delicacy and tone, these graceful little poems resemble the lyric verse of Alice Meynell, Robert Bridges, and other turn-of-the-century poets. The writer for the *Westminster Review* declared that Webster's stornelli were "each a little study, carved like a gem by a skillful master-hand."

In a Day (1882) was the only one of Webster's plays to be produced. In the summer of 1890 it received one matinee performance at Terry Theatre in London, with Webster's grown daughter in the lead role, Klydone. Like *The Auspicious Day,* this play is a classical tragedy showing that "in a day" everything in one's life can change completely. As the play opens, Klydone is a slave soon to be freed and permitted to marry her master, Myron. Before her emancipation, however, Myron is falsely accused of treason. Under Roman law, slaves must be questioned under conditions of torture if their testimony is to be accepted. Klydone begs Myron to allow her to endure the interrogation, and ultimately he does. However, Klydone cannot maintain her composure under torture. She is made to testify against Myron; he forgives her, and both commit suicide. The point is partly that unfounded accusations can ruin a good man, partly that slavery is an unconscionable condition, and partly that innocent girls cannot be expected to be strong in extraordinary circumstances. Myron's teacher Olymnios counsels him thus:

> Forgive her, Myron: thou hadst spoiled the girl,
> Thou and thy mother, in whose soft controls
> She hath not known so much ungentle need
> As to walk northwards with the wind in her face.
> Blame me who, fool, because she is my child,
> Thought she should be some such brave paragon
> As courage makes some women, and love some;
> Who, fool, believed her for her eagerness,
> Put her unproved, unpractised, to the touch,
> And found her, what? a wincing mindless babe,
> A crouching thing distraught by pain, and faithless.

Olymnios also commits suicide. Klydone's failure is similar to that of the accused witch in *The Auspicious Day* who is persuaded to admit what she has not done. Both women are innocents who are tricked into betraying themselves and their loved ones.

Webster's last play, *The Sentence* (1887), portrays Caligula, the notoriously cruel Roman emperor, and two women who are also tricked into betraying themselves and those they love. Lelia is the good woman—a gentle, trusting, vulnerable wife and mother—who kills herself over her husband's betrayal. Aeonia is the bad woman, the foil for Caligula. She betrays her lover Stellio, Lelia's husband, either for power (Caligula offers her the empress's throne) or to save Stellio from infamy; she herself hardly knows which. Both Aeonia and Stellio are outwitted by the vengeful emperor, whose innocent love for Lelia is represented as the motivation for his turning evil when she is driven to her death. The innocent children of Aeonia and Stellio point up the corruption of the adults. The play ends with these children kissing their dying father, who calls out for his wife and children as he dies. Aeonia is imprisoned for life, a punishment Caligula deems worse than the death with which he has threatened her. In the end, Caligula's absolute power and his egotism reign supreme. Like *The Auspicious Day* and *In a Day, The Sentence* is deeply pessimistic, even fatalistic. Once events are set in action, nothing can save the unwitting characters.

William Michael Rossetti praised *The Sentence,* calling it "one of the masterpieces of European drama." He actually admired all four of Webster's plays. In an 1895 introduction to *Mother and Daughter* he wrote:

> *The Auspicious Day* is in a marked degree a capable and bold performance. The other three dramas are all so excellent that it might almost count as a matter of individual preference to choose between them—*In a Day* being the most compactly poetical, *Disguises* the most romantic, and full of high perception and sympathy in character and incident. But to me *The Sentence* appears the one supreme thing.

High critical opinion of the plays did not survive Mrs. Webster's death, nor have they been reprinted. Their fatalism and their removal from Victorian culture may account for the lack of continued interest they have received.

In 1884 Webster began to write anonymous reviews of poetry for the *Athenaeum* alongside her friend Watts-Dunton. Though her opinions were generally accepted by the periodical's readership, all reviews were anonymous, and she did not develop an identifiable voice as a critic. According to Marysa Demoor, the central question in Webster's reviews was always "whether the person producing the verse is a poet or not, whether what lies before her is genuine poetry or not."

Also in 1884 Webster published a prose fantasy for children, somewhat on the order of Lewis Carroll's *Alice in Wonderland* (1865), titled *Daffodil and the Croäxaxicans: A Romance of History* (1884). Daffodil is a human child who tumbles into a magical world below the surface of a nearby pond. In this fantasy world all the characters are frogs except Daffodil. The story is a satire on royal and aristocratic hierarchies and protocols, with some effective whimsy but not much sense of purpose. The plot dissolves into lengthy and complex marriage eligibility problems. Daffodil, like Alice, is to be promoted to queen, but she prefers being eaten by a boa constrictor to marrying (at age twelve) a dissolute, violent, and crazy old frog. She escapes the pond just in the nick of time. The descriptions of the frog palace and Daffodil's acquisition of the frog language, Croäxaxican, are amusing, but the book is much too long for children and is not illustrated.

The last book Webster published in her lifetime was *Selections from the Verse of Augusta Webster* (1893), which includes six previously uncollected poems from *Cornhill Magazine,* the *English Illustrated Magazine,* and *Good Words.* Augusta Webster died at Kew, London on 5 September 1894. In her *Athenaeum* obituary Watts-Dunton predicted that Webster's reputation would not survive the nineteenth century: "Poetic immortality is . . . a relative term. Enough, then, for the memory of the lady we have just lost that during her own life her pathetic picture of the 'Castaway' has touched a heart here and there, and that among these hearts was Robert Browning's."

Unknown to Watts-Dunton in 1894, one more original book was yet to appear from Augusta Webster. In 1895 her husband published *Mother and Daughter, an Uncompleted Sonnet-Sequence,* with an introduction by William Michael Rossetti. The twenty-seven intimate sonnets in that volume express varying moods and personal experiences of motherhood. Webster's daughter was by this time in her mid twenties, but the poems are mainly in the present tense, with the daughter still a child; they were perhaps written over a period of years to record and preserve Webster's feelings as a mother. The following sonnet gives an idea of the overall character of the volume.

> Sometimes, as young things will, she vexes me,
>   Wayward, or too unheeding, or too blind.
>   Like aimless birds that, flying on a wind,
> Strike slant against their own familiar tree;
> Like venturous children pacing with the sea,
>   That turn but when the breaker spurts behind
>   Outreaching them with spray: she in such kind
> Is borne against some fault, or does not flee.
> And so, may be, I blame her for her wrong,
>   And she will frown and lightly plead her part,
>   And then I bid her go. But 'tis not long:
>   Then comes she lip to ear and heart to heart.
> And thus forgiven her love seems newly strong,
>   And, oh my penitent, how dear thou art!

Rossetti explained, "Nothing could be more genuine than these Sonnets. A Mother is expressing her love for a Daughter—her reminiscences, anxieties, and hopeful anticipations." It seems a fitting close to her poetic career.

Christina Rossetti admired Webster's poetry greatly, though she disagreed with her on the question of suffrage for women; the two occasionally exchanged private letters on the subject. Christina Rossetti considered Webster second only to Elizabeth Barrett Browning. In *The Poets and the Poetry of the Century,* Mackenzie Bell asserted that "all the other women poets of England must yield to her in that quality which, as it is generally deemed the specially masculine quality, is called virility." In the 1899 *DNB,* Lee summarized Webster's career: "Mrs. Webster's verse entitles her to a high place among English poets. She used with success the form of the dramatic monologue. She often sacrificed beauty to strength, but she possessed much metrical skill and an ear for melody. Some of her lyrics deserve a place in every anthology of modern English poetry. Many of her poems treat entirely or incidentally of questions specially affecting women."

As Watts-Dunton predicted, Webster's reputation faded early in the twentieth century, though in 1929 Vita Sackville-West, writing in *The Eighteen Seventies,* could still admire Webster's forthrightness about delicate subjects and the overall feminist tenor of her social and literary concerns. Webster's work experienced a revival of interest in the 1990s, as feminist critics began to explore both women's poetry, and Victorian genres like the dramatic monologue, the closet drama, and the social essay, with renewed interest. Augusta Webster is recognized chiefly for the psychological and social accuracy and the persistent feminism of her dramatic monologues.

References:

Isobel Armstrong, *Victorian Poetry: Poetry, Poetics and Politics* (London & New York: Routledge, 1993), pp. 373–375;

Susan Brown, "Determined Heroines: George Eliot, Augusta Webster, and Closet Drama by Victorian Women," *Victorian Poetry,* 33 (Spring 1995): 89–109;

Brown, "Economical Representations: Dante Gabriel Rossetti's 'Jenny,' Augusta Webster's 'A Castaway,' and the Campaign against the Contagious Diseases Acts," *Victorian Review,* 17 (Summer 1991): 78–95;

Thomas Collins and Vivienne Rundle, eds., *The Broadview Anthology of Victorian Poetry and Poetic Theory* (Ontario: Broadview Press, 1999), pp. 1010–1028;

Marysa Demoor, "Power in Petticoats: Augusta Webster's Poetry, Political Pamphlets, and Poetry Reviews," in *Voices of Power: Co-Operation and Conflict in English Language and Literatures,* edited by Marc Maufort and Jean Pierre van Noppen (Liege, Belgium: Belgian Association of Anglists in Higher Education, 1997), pp. 133–140;

Kathleen Hickok, "'Intimate Egoism': Reading and Evaluating Noncanonical Poetry by Women," *Victorian Poetry,* 33 (Spring 1995): 13–30;

Hickok, *Representations of Women: Nineteenth-Century British Women's Poetry* (Westport, Conn.: Greenwood Press, 1984); pp. 10, 48, 58–60, 76–77, 84–88, 111–113, 128, 131, 199, 232;

Angela Leighton, "'Because Men Made the Laws': The Fallen Woman and the Woman Poet," in *New Feminist Discourse: Critical Essays on Theories and Texts,* edited by Isobel Armstrong (London & New York: Routledge, 1992), pp. 342–360;

Leighton, *Victorian Women Poets: Writing against the Heart* (London & Charlottesville: University Press of Virginia, 1992), pp. 164–201;

Leighton and Margaret Reynolds, eds., *Victorian Women Poets: An Anthology* (Oxford: Blackwell, 1995), pp. 417–450;

Dorothy Mermin, *Godiva's Ride: Women of Letters in England, 1830–1880* (Bloomington: Indiana University Press, 1993), pp. 79–80.

Anna Wickham
(Edith Alice Mary Harper)
(1884 – 30 April 1947)

Ann Vickery
Macquarie University

BOOKS: *The Seasons: A Speaking Tableaux for Girls,* as Edith Harper (Sydney: Printed by W. A. Pepperday, 1902);

Wonder Eyes: A Journey to Slumbertown, as Harper (Sydney: Printed by W. A. Pepperday, 1903);

Songs of John Oland (London: Privately printed, Women's Printing Society, 1911);

The Contemplative Quarry (London: Poetry Bookshop, 1915; New York: Harcourt, Brace, 1921);

The Man with a Hammer: Verses (London: Richards, 1916);

The Contemplative Quarry, and the Man with a Hammer, introduction by Louis Untermeyer (New York: Harcourt, Brace, 1921);

The Little Old House (London: Poetry Bookshop, 1921);

Anna Wickham, edited by John Gawsworth, Richards' Shilling Selection from Edwardian Poets (London: Richards, 1936).

Editions and Collections: *Selected Poems,* edited by David Garnett (London: Chatto & Windus, 1971);

The Writings of Anna Wickham: Free Woman and Poet, edited by R. D. Smith (London: Virago, 1984).

OTHER: Geoffrey, Count Potocki de Montalk, *Dreams,* introduction by Wickham (London: Columbia Press, 1932);

John Gawsworth, ed., *Edwardian Poetry,* contributions by Wickham (London: Richards, 1936);

Gawsworth, ed., *Neo-Georgian Poetry 1936–1937,* contributions by Wickham (London: Richards, 1937);

Gawsworth, ed., *Fifty Years of Modern Verse: An Anthology,* contributions by Wickham (London: Secker, 1938).

SELECTED PERIODICAL PUBLICATIONS–
UNCOLLECTED: "The Spirit of the Lawrence Women: A Posthumous Memoir," *Texas Quarterly,* 9 (Autumn 1966): 33–50;

"I & My Genius," *Women's Review,* 5 (March 1986): 16–20.

Anna Wickham

One of the most politically forthright women poets of the early twentieth century, Anna Wickham focused in her work on the difficulties of balancing the demands of marriage, motherhood, and a literary career. Writing in both free and rhymed verse, she published in a diverse range of places from *Poetry: A Magazine of Verse* to *The Liberator*. This variety, along with the fact that she remained unaligned with any poetic movement, has made her work difficult to frame critically. After committing suicide in 1947, Wickham was largely forgotten until a comprehensive collection of her poetry and prose appeared in 1984. Since then, there has been a resurgence of interest in her writing.

Wickham was born Edith Alice Mary Harper in Wimbledon in 1884; her exact date of birth is unknown. She was the only surviving child—a brother had been stillborn—of Geoffrey Harper, a piano repairman, and Alice Harper, née Whelan. When Edith was eighteen months old, her mother ran away with her to Australia. There Alice Harper contracted pneumonia, and Edith was placed in an institution. By the time the authorities informed Geoffrey Harper of their whereabouts and he had arranged their return to England, Edith was two and a half.

Harper became the focus of her father's literary ambitions. A failed novelist, he encouraged Harper to write her first poem at age four. When Harper was five, a rival piano business set up shop nearby, and the family immigrated to Australia in search of better prospects. In Marysborough, Queensland, Geoffrey Harper managed a music shop with two branches in nearby towns, and Alice taught elocution. Harper attended the local convent school, where the nuns encouraged her singing. A visiting English musician, Seymour Dicker, was so impressed by her voice that he offered to take her on tour as a child singer.

After a year or two in Marysborough the family moved to Brisbane, where Geoffrey Harper became a piano tuner and repairman in a large music shop; Alice Harper, having discovered that she possessed clairvoyant powers, set up business as "Madame Reprah" (Harper spelled backwards), a physiognomist and character reader. One evening the ten-year-old Harper was walking with her father in Wickham Terrace, stopping between two churches out of which hymn-singing blared; in that emotionally charged atmosphere, at his urging, she promised him that she would become a poet. Geoffrey began showing his daughter's compositions to fellow workers, as well as to people he met in bars or on the street; the popular Australian poet Brunton Stephens told him that Harper would be a poet if she had enough pain, "a condition you can hardly wish her since you are her father."

Alice Harper was successful enough in her business to send her daughter to an expensive girls' boarding school. At seventeen Edith Harper wrote two plays, *The Seasons: A Speaking Tableaux for Girls* (1902) and *Wonder Eyes: A Journey to Slumbertown* (1903). In 1904, with her parents' encouragement, Harper moved back to London, where she auditioned for and won a scholarship to Beerbohm Tree's Academy of Acting. She also took singing lessons. At a lecture by George Bernard Shaw she met William Ray, a freelance reporter. Feeling alone and alienated, she became engaged to him. Ray introduced her to his friend Patrick Hepburn, a thirty-two-year-old solicitor and amateur astronomer, and a romantic triangle was formed. In 1905 Harper went to Paris and entered the master singing class of Jean de Reszke. Despite the prospect of a promising singing career, she returned to England and married Hepburn in the fall of 1906. They were happy in their new home in Bloomsbury for six months; then Alice Harper came to visit them. The always-difficult mother-daughter relationship produced intense quarrels. Patrick Hepburn took his pregnant wife sailing to distract her from the problems her mother was causing; but the boat capsized, causing her to go into premature labor. The baby, a girl, lived for only a few minutes. Edith later suffered a miscarriage and was pregnant again when her mother finally went back to Australia, sending back a cable, "Luck in thirds."

This pregnancy resulted in the birth of a son, James, in 1908. For a year Edith Hepburn enthusiastically took up the role of motherhood, joining the School for Mothers and taking other women's sick babies into her own nursery. But she began to desire greater intellectual and artistic stimulation. She still sang occasionally at the Lyceum Club and began writing verses to the superintendent of the school, Emily Colles. The family moved to 49 Downshire Hill, Hampstead, where a second son, John, was born in 1909. Their neighbors included the novelists David Garnett and D. H. Lawrence, both of whom had long conversations with Hepburn and later promoted her work. She established a salon in her home that included music and lectures on women's suffrage. All the while she continued to write poetry. Her husband resented the attention she was giving to these intellectual pursuits, and a series of arguments and reconciliations ensued.

Exhausted from looking after a young family and attending to herself intellectually, Hepburn took a vacation with her father, visiting Ceylon and southern India. In 1911 she had her first volume of poetry, *Songs*, printed privately under the pseudonym John Oland; the name was taken from the Jenolan Caves in Australia, which she had visited with her friend, the cellist May Mukle. The volume includes "The Town Dirge," a lament for the death of a child, and the contrasting "Song of the Young John," which expresses the joy of motherhood:

How all my senses thrill to the dear treasure,
Till I must weep for sweet excess of pleasure.

The apple-blossomy king
Is lord of this new spring,

Edith Harper (seated on ground) with her mother, Alice Harper, née Whelan (center); her father, Geoffrey Harper; and her Aunt Beat in Australia in 1900

He is the spirit of young joy,
My little yellow-headed boy.

"Outline" suggests that the maternal body is merely the husk for the accommodation of the soul, the man the woman will bear.

Many poems in the volume express a desire to escape from bourgeois life, with what she calls in "Illusion" its "little boxes of straight built towns." "Divorce" includes the refrain, "I smother in the house in the valley below, / Let me out to the night, let me go, let me go." In "Song of the Low-Caste Wife" the speaker asks her husband for "that greatest glory, / A little growth":

Am I your mate because I share your bed?
Go then, find each day a new mate outside your house.
I am your mate if I can share your vision.
Have you no vision king-descended?
Come share mine!
Will you give me this, for your son?
O scion of kings!

Patrick Hepburn was impervious to such pleas and remonstrated against his wife's poetic flights. When she suggested in 1913 that she might publish a second volume of poems, a battle ensued, and he ejected her from the house. Outside, she recited her poem "Nervous Prostration," which ends:

I married a man of the Croydon class
When I was twenty-two.
And I vex him, and he bores me
Till we don't know what to do!
And I sit in this ordered house,
I feel I must sob or shriek,
To force a man of the Croydon class
To live, or to love, or to speak!

Patrick Hepburn was unmoved. Believing that her desire to be a poet was a symptom of mental illness, he enlisted the aid of her mother to have her committed to an asylum. After six weeks she was sent home for a "probationary month." The incarceration merely energized her poetic drive, resulting in some eighty poems. "The Tired Man," one of her most anthologized poems, was written soon after she returned home. A few days later she took *Songs* to Harold Monro at the Poetry Bookshop and asked, "Have you any free rhythms?" Realizing that she meant free verse, he replied, "We've all been trying to write them."

After reading *Songs* Monro asked Hepburn for more poems, and he and his partner, Alida Klementaski, published nine of her poems, including "The Tired Man," "The Cherry-Blossom Wand," "Gift to a Jade," "Self-Analysis," and "Susannah in the Morning," in their journal *Poetry and Drama* (June 1914); the issue also carried critical essays by Ford Madox Hueffer, Edward Thomas, T. E. Hulme, and F. S. Flint, as well as poetry by Maurice Hewlett and John Gould Fletcher. It was an impressive debut. Hepburn's poems appeared regularly in newspapers throughout 1914, and she became a familiar figure at the Poetry Bookshop readings.

In 1915 the Poetry Bookshop published Hepburn's second volume of poems, *The Contemplative Quarry,* which included the pieces from *Poetry and Drama*. For this book she used the pseudonym "Anna Wickham," derived from Anne, her father's nickname for her, and from Wickham Terrace in Brisbane, where she had vowed to fulfill her father's hopes and become a poet.

The speaker of the poems in *The Contemplative Quarry* is a woman who is her own person. "Gift to a Jade" ends, "At that cold moralist I hotly hurled, / His perfect pure symmetrical small world." In "The Slighted Lady" a beautiful woman turns from her cold husband to a young, romantic lover. "Susannah in the Morning" revises the story in the Book of Susanna in the Apocrypha of the attempted seduction of Susanna by a pair of elders, who, when they are refused, claim that they saw her committing adultery with another man. In Wickham's version the "chaste and good" Susanna finds herself responding to her attacker, surprising him with the passion that lies behind her "shaded eyes." When he leaves, she is invigorated: "To the high night I fling my prayer: / Master of chariots drive me in the air!"

Wickham takes up overtly feminist issues in the volume. Having once torn off her own whalebone corset stays at a concert, she cautions in "Artificiality" against their "rotting" of women's bodies. Gender constraints are flung aside: "I will be neither man nor woman," she writes in "The Revolt of Wives," "I will be just a human."

Wickham also reflects on questions of poetic form. In "The Egoist" she argues that "A faulty rhyme may . . . hold a perfect imperfection of its own" and that "It was as fit for one man's thoughts to trot in iambs, as it is for me, / Who lives not in the horse-age, but in the days of aeroplanes, to write my rhythms free." Despite this disavowal, several of the poems follow a traditional rhyme scheme.

In 1916 Grant Richards published *The Man with a Hammer: Verses,* the largest collection of Wickham's poetry up to that time. Continuing to treat feminist themes, she contrasts the moral integrity of a "fallen woman" to the hypocrisy of a married man. "The Viper" vilifies a pimp who views pregnancy as fitting punishment for a prostitute. Many poems describe the intimacy of the relationship between mother and child, but others show that maternal love can be a form of bondage. While women alone may nurture their sons and husbands to higher attainment, creativity is beyond the feminine. "The Angry Women" states, "There is the sexless part of me that is my mind" while "A Woman in Bed" finishes with the line: "I hide my breast beneath a workman's shirt, / And hunt the perfect phrase." Many of Wickham's poems are humorous; in "Prayer on Sunday," Wickham's sharp criticism is turned on both others and herself:

> God send a higher courage
> For to cut straight and clean!
> God send a juster language,
> To state the things I mean!
> Here is such random thinking
> Such sloth, such slime, such fog,
> I see an old cow sinking
> Deep, in a pitchy bog!

Wickham addressed several poems in *The Man with a Hammer* to Anita Brackenbury, a friend and neighbor who helped her with the book. In the same year Wickham assisted another friend, Carmel Haden Guest, with the *Princess Marie-José's Children's Book,* which was published to help Belgian children suffering from World War I.

Wickham's third son, Richard, was born in 1917, and a fourth, George, was born in December 1919. By 1917 Wickham had begun publishing in little magazines in the United States, ranging from the formally experimental *Poetry: A Magazine of Verse* to those directed to social change such as *The Liberator*. As the war came to an end, the family moved to a better-appointed house at Parliament Hill in Hampstead.

In addition to publishing Wickham's work in his magazine, *The Chapbook,* Monro published her fourth collection, *The Little Old House* (1921) through the Poetry Bookshop. Although written a few years earlier, the poem "On the Day They Took Down the Grille" reflects Wickham's current feeling of domestic calm. "I have made peace with my true-love," she writes. Artistic frustration is exchanged for mute submission:

> Tell me some henbird sings upon her tree
> And I will raise a natural melody
> But if male singing is by God preferred
> I will learn silence from the nobler bird.

Other poems similarly bring politics into the private realm. "Stateswoman and the House" suggests that social order begins in the home, with the mistress setting the example for her servants. Tidiness, too, is associated with control. In contrast, a growing number of poems refer to a fairy world, with its delicate but more-removed wildness of spirit.

Impressed by Wickham's work, New York poet and critic Louis Untermeyer convinced Harcourt Brace to publish a combined American edition of *The Contemplative Quarry* and *The Man with a Hammer*. This volume appeared in 1921 with an additional poem, "Note on Method":

> Here is no sacrificial I,
> Here are more I's than yet were in one human,
> Here I reveal our common mystery:
> I give you woman.
> Let it be so for our old world's relief
> I give you *woman*, and my method's brief.

In his introduction Untermeyer wrote of the small group of women appraising themselves without fear of male contempt or condescension: "Searchers like May Sinclair, Virginia Woolf, Rebecca West, Willa Cather and Dorothy Richardson are working in a prose that illuminates their experiments. In poetry, a regiment of young women are recording an even more vigorous self-examination. The most typical, and in many ways the best of these seekers and singers is Anna Wickham." The volume was a success, and Wickham's reputation escalated.

In her private life, however, Wickham was grieving over the loss of four-year-old Richard, who died of septic scarlet fever—just as he was thought to be out of danger. Although almost always fatal, this fact offered Wickham no reassurance of her capabilities as a parent; she believed instead that her son's death was a judgment for letting poetry divert attention from her family. Taking her eldest son, James, with her, she left in early January 1922 for a five-month visit to Paris. While several of Wickham's poems appeared in little magazines over the following two years, another poetry collection did not appear for fourteen years.

In France, Wickham joined the expatriate circle of writers, artists, and publishers that included Sylvia Beach, Natalie Barney, Bob McAlmon, Djuna Barnes,

Wickham's husband, Patrick Hepburn, in his Royal Navy Air Service uniform during World War I

Griffin Barry, Berenice Abbott, Beatrice Hastings, Nina Hamnett, Tommy Earp, Ezra Pound, George Slocombe, and Aleister Crowley. Earp fought a duel with Van Loo, the art dealer, in the Luxembourg Gardens over some real or imagined slight to Anna (although the swords were only made of wood).

When she returned from Paris, Wickham tried to conform to conventional domestic expectations, but she was still drawn to the world beyond the home. She regularly met artists such as Augustus John and Hamnett at the Fitzroy Tavern and encouraged young writers, including the unknown teenager Stephen Spender. She was also friends with Catharine Amy Dawson Scott, the founder of the international writer's group PEN. She gave poetry readings and was involved in charitable and political activities.

Throughout the rest of the decade Wickham returned frequently to Paris, often attending Barney's salon in rue Jacob. She corresponded with Barney from 1926 to 1937; in these letters she tested new poems such as "New Eve," "Lament of the Red Knight," and "Da Capo." She also filled them with passionate entreaty, her thoughts on poetics, and literary intrigue. The letters provided Wickham with a necessary but private outlet for her writing and reveal a developing mature poetic voice.

In 1926 Patrick had obtained a legal separation from his wife. Wickham and the children stayed first in Hampstead and then at Alida Klemantaski's house in Bloomsbury. In 1928 the family reunited. After a five-year gap in publication a couple of Wickham's poems appeared in two periodicals that catered to her specific tastes: *The London Aphrodite* (October 1928), a short-lived, irreverent magazine run by Australians Jack Lindsay and P. R. Stephenson, and *The Sackbut* (November 1928 and November 1929), which had musical leanings. Personal circumstances, however, again halted Wickham's publishing. Taking his annual walking tour of the Lake District, Patrick fell and died of exposure on Christmas Day 1929. Wickham's poem "The Homecoming" had uncannily predicted this event in 1921.

Patrick's death left the family in straitened circumstances, and Wickham was forced to take in lodgers. A notice hung in the hall:

Tour Bourgeoise 68 Parliament Hill, N.W.3
ANNA WICKHAM'S
Stabling for Poets Painters and their Executives
Saddle your Pegasus here
Creative Moods respected Meals at all Hours.

During the early 1930s Dylan Thomas and Malcolm Lowry were visitors. In 1935 Lucie Delarue Mardrus's translations of Wickham's poetry appeared—much to Wickham's pleasure—in *Edition des Poèmes Choisis de Lucie Delarue-Mardrus*. Wickham began writing various prose pieces again. In "Prelude to a Spring Clean," an unfinished autobiography that she began in the spring of 1935, Wickham struggled with her ambivalent feelings toward Hepburn and her parents, as well as her frustrated ambitions. Around the same time, Wickham wrote "The Spirit of the Lawrence Women," part memoir and part critique. In it she separates the friend she knew from the man who wrote so portentously on the page. She decries Lawrence's exaltation of male fertility (or creativity) over female fertility, pointing out that his representation of women sexualizes them at the expense of their intellectual capacity. In contrast, she believes the creative consciousness of the artist to be bisexual, such that "There is a marriage in the house of the soul."

In 1936 poet and admirer John Gawsworth edited a fifth collection of Wickham's poetry, titled *Anna Wickham*, which came out as one of the Shilling Selections from Edwardian Poets. One of the poems, "In the House of the Soul," explicitly recalls Wickham's debate with Lawrence. Subtitled "Harlequin and a Woman under One Skin," it presents the act of poetry as produced out of a mutually supportive relationship between the quiet wife of "Control" and the imaginative "I," the mime and "master of surprises." Many poems in this volume recall the energy of her first three books. "Mare Bred from Pegasus," for example, is one of her most powerful poems. Referring to both her father's favorite pony and Hepburn's love of the stars, Wickham rages against aesthetic and domestic taming:

For God's sake, stand off from me:
There's a brood mare here going to kick like hell
With a mad up-rising of energy;
And where the wreck will end who'll tell?
She'll splinter the stable and eat a groom.
For God's sake, give me room;
Give my will room.

Another poem, "The Sick Assailant," effectively broaches the subject of domestic violence from the perspective of the perpetrator. The poem begins, "I hit her in the face because she loved me," and ends decrying the woman's "sticky irritating patience."

Toward the end of 1936 Wickham began sending a series of spirited poems on postcards to Barney. In titling them "Des Cartes à L'Amazone" she was alluding to the writer Rémy de Gourmont's letters to Barney, *Lettres à L'Amazone* (1923) as well as to the split between mind and body espoused by the philosopher René Descartes. Although Wickham's poetry appeared in many anthologies in the United States throughout the 1920s and early 1930s, her reputation—like Charlotte Mew's—had suffered from not being included in British anthologies such as the *Georgian Poetry* series edited by Edward Marsh (only two women were ever published in the five volumes). In the mid to late 1930s, however, Gawsworth featured Wickham's work in three anthologies: *Edwardian Poetry* (1936), *Neo-Georgian Poetry* (1937), and *Fifty Years of Modern Verse* (1938). In 1938 Wickham gathered signatures and sent a cable to the Friends of the Library of Chicago, honoring the memory of Harriet Monroe, who had died the year before. In June of that year she helped organize a group of seven feminists who called themselves The League for the Protection of the Imagination of Women. Their slogan was "World's Management by Entertainment." The British Broadcasting Corporation contracted her to take part in a television program on 3 September 1939, but the program was canceled because of the declaration of war.

While all three of her sons left home for military duty, Wickham remained alone in Parliament Hill. During the war her house was bombed and several of her manuscripts and most of her letters from Barney were destroyed. After the war, in April 1946, *Picture Post* ran a story on her titled "The Poet Landlady." In November she wrote to Barney, "I have nothing worthy of you. I hope to do something that I can send to you soon. Pray for me." On the last day of the following April, Wickham hanged herself, leaving a poem rather than a suicide note:

> I hung myself
> I was unconscious on the floor
> The rope slipped
> There'll be no hanging more.
> I've not the strength to take my life
> By rope or bane or knife–
> I am iced with terror
> At the sure doom
> Of my long pride and error.

James and John were away; George had returned home, and he was the one who found her. She had been depressed because she felt that her sons no longer needed her. Nervous exhaustion, a bitterly cold winter, nagging bronchitis, and the loss of her clothing coupons earlier that day may have been contributing factors.

Wickham left behind more than one thousand unpublished poems. A few were collected in *Selected Poems* (1971). The extensive 1984 Virago collection, *The Writings of Anna Wickham: Free Woman and Poet*, drew a new reading public to her work. Edited by R. D. Smith and with a preface by Wickham's son James, the collection features selections from all her books as well as previously unpublished poetry and prose. Soon after its publication Wickham's writing appeared in several groundbreaking anthologies of women's writing and feminist criticism of the modernist period. Given her cross-cultural background, her work is also featured in anthologies of both Australian and English poetry. In 1991 the complete version of "Prelude to a Spring Clean" was published in French translation.

Throughout her writing Anna Wickham explores issues of sexuality, class, and culture. In examining the complex, often ambivalent identity of a woman juggling a multitude of roles, her poetry remains topical. A full recovery and reappraisal of her work remains to be done.

References:
Lionel Birch, "The Poet Landlady," *Picture Post* (27 April 1946): 23–25;
Carmel Haden Guest, ed., *Princess Marie-José's Children's Book* (London: Cassell, 1916);

Wickham with her sons James and John in 1915

James Hepburn, "Anna Wickham," *Women's Review*, 7 (May 1986): 41;
Jennifer Vaughan Jones, "The Poetry and Place of Anna Wickham, 1910–1930," dissertation, University of Wisconsin, 1994.

Papers:
Collections of Anna Wickham's manuscripts and correspondence are in the British Library; the Bibliothèque Ste. Geneviève, Paris (Fonds Littéraire Jacques Doucet); The Lilly Library, Indiana University, Bloomington; State University of New York at Buffalo (Poetry/Rare Books Collection); the University of Reading; and the Harry Ransom Humanities Research Center, University of Texas at Austin.

Margaret L. Woods
(20 November 1855 – 1 December 1945)

Martha S. Vogeler
California State University, Fullerton

BOOKS: *A Village Tragedy* (London: Bentley, 1887; New York: Holt, 1888);

Lyrics, (Oxford: Daniel, 1888; Portland, Me.: T. B. Mosher, 1906); enlarged as *Lyrics and Ballads* (London: Bentley, 1889);

Esther Vanhomrigh, 3 volumes (London: Murray, 1891; New York: Hovendon, 1891);

The Vagabonds (London: Smith, Elder, 1894; New York & London: Macmillan, 1894);

Songs (Oxford: Daniel, 1896);

Wild Justice (London: Smith, Elder, 1896);

Aëromancy, and Other Poems (London: Elkin Mathews, 1896);

Weeping Ferry, and other Stories (London & New York: Longmans, Green, 1898);

Sons of the Sword: A Romance of the Peninsular War (London: Heinemann, 1901; New York: McClure, Phillips, 1901);

The Princess of Hanover (London: Duckworth, 1902; New York: Holt, 1903);

The King's Revoke: An Episode in the Life of Patrick Dillon (London: Smith, Elder, 1905; New York: Dutton, 1906);

The Invader (London: Heinemann, 1907; New York & London: Harper, 1907);

Poems, Old and New (London: Macmillan, 1907);

Pastels under the Southern Cross (London: Smith, Elder, 1911);

The Collected Poems of Margaret L. Woods (London & New York: John Lane, 1914);

"Come unto these Yellow Sands" (London & New York: John Lane, 1914);

The Return, and Other Poems (London & New York: John Lane, 1921);

A Poet's Youth (London & Sydney: Chapman & Dodd, 1923; New York: Boni & Liveright, 1923);

The Spanish Lady (London: Cape, 1927).

OTHER: "Tennyson and Bradley (Dean of Westminster)," in *Tennyson and His Friends,* edited by Hallam, Lord Tennyson (London: Macmillan, 1912), pp. 175-185;

Margaret L. Woods

"Swift, Stella, and Vanessa," in *Essays by Divers Hands, being the Transactions of the Royal Society of Literature,* second series, volume 32 (London: Milford, 1914), pp. 185-214;

"Finisterre," in *The Book of the Homeless (Le livre des sans-foyer),* edited by Edith Wharton (London: Macmillan, 1916; New York: Scribners, 1916), pp. 43-44, 26-27;

Henry G. Woods, *Christianity and War*, introduction by Margaret L. Woods (London: Scott, 1916);

A Scallop Shell of Quiet, introduction by Woods (Oxford: Blackwell, 1917);

"Henry Daniel and His Home," in *Memorials of C. H. O. Daniel with a Bibliography of the Press, 1845–1915*, edited by Falconer Madan (Oxford: Oxford University Press, 1921), pp. 22–31;

A. G. Bradley, with contributions by Lady Birchenough and Mrs. Robert Noel, *Our Centenarian Grandfather, 1790–1890*, preface by Woods (London: John Bale, Sons & Danielsson, 1922);

"Ballads," in *Essays by Divers Hands, being the Transactions of the Royal Society of Literature*, third series, volume 6 (London: Milford, 1926), pp. 25–42;

Essays by Divers Hands, being the Transactions of the Royal Society of Literature, third series, volume 7, introduction by Woods (London: Milford, 1927), pp. v–xv;

"Matthew Arnold," in *Essays and Studies by Members of the English Association*, edited by Sir Herbert Warren (Oxford: Clarendon Press, 1929), pp. 7–19;

"The Poets of the 'Eighties," in *The Eighteen-Eighties: Essays by Fellows of the Royal Society of Literature*, edited by Walter de la Mare (Cambridge: Cambridge University Press, 1930), pp. 1–15;

The Writers' Club Anthology, introduction by Woods (Oxford: Blackwell, 1932).

SELECTED PERIODICAL PUBLICATIONS–
UNCOLLECTED:
POETRY
"On the Step," *London Mercury*, 11 (January 1925): 233–234;

"Maisie and the Broken Man (Monte Carlo)," *London Mercury*, 26 (September 1932): 391–392.

NONFICTION
"Supermanity and the Superwoman, by a Subter-Woman," *Nineteenth Century and After*, 68 (September 1910): 532–535;

"Shelley at Tan-yr-allt," *Nineteenth Century and After*, 70 (November 1911): 890–903;

"Poetry: And Women Poets as Artists," *Fortnightly Review*, 100 (August 1913): 230–235;

"Mrs Humphry Ward: A Sketch from Memory," *Quarterly Review*, 234 (July 1920): 147–160;

"Poetry and the Prosaics," *Fortnightly Review*, 121 (June 1924): 809–819;

"Oxford in the 'Seventies," *Fortnightly Review*, new series 150 (July–September 1941): 276–282.

Margaret L. Woods's obituary in *The Times* (London, 4 December 1945) called her "one of the most distinguished women writers of her day." Her poems, essays, and stories appeared in leading periodicals, and her books were widely reviewed. She was said to resemble a well-known portrait of Percy Bysshe Shelley, and George Gissing saw genius in her face. Quoted in *The Times* obituary, her daughter-in-law, Viola Woods, asserted she "knew nothing about what she wrote, it simply came through," and she herself once declared in a letter to E. W. Scripture that her shorter works arose from "the subliminal" but that completing them required "the critical understanding."

Margaret Louisa Bradley was born in Rugby, Warwicks, on 20 November 1855, to Marian (née Philpot) and George Granville Bradley. Daisy, as she was called by her intimates, fit comfortably in her family's world of culture and achievement. All four of her sisters and one of her two brothers became writers. In her childhood her father was headmaster of Marlborough College, and in her essay "Matthew Arnold" (1929) she recalls him reciting–"almost chanting"–verse by Arnold, who had been a pupil under him at Rugby. She also heard Alfred Tennyson, a great friend of the family, intone his verses, on one occasion, she writes in "Tennyson and Bradley (Dean of Westminster)" (1912), reducing her to tears by their sadness. Her own earliest lyrics, which survive in "The Miscellany," the Bradley family magazine, derive some of their pronounced meter and their melancholy from these two poets. In one issue of "The Miscellany" her uncle A. C. Bradley, the Shakespeare critic, named Tennyson's *In Memoriam* (1850) and Arnold's "Thyrsis" (1866) as examples of the "elegiac nature" of modern literature.

Arnold's poem gained new significance for Daisy after her father became master of University College, Oxford, in 1870, and together they rode on nearby Boars Hill, a locale in "Thyrsis" and "The Scholar-Gipsy" (1853). The movement to establish women's colleges at the university came too late to benefit her significantly, but she attended the first lecture held under its auspices. The serious reading of history she began at this time informed some of her later fiction and dramatic poetry. Her literary aspirations were nurtured by contemporaries at Oxford, notably Arnold's niece, Mary Augusta Arnold, who became Mrs. Humphry Ward in 1872, and Rhoda Broughton, already well known for her fiction and for wit that Bradley thought keener than Oscar Wilde's. Wilde invited her to his "Beauty Parties" and in the 23 May 1885 issue of the *Dramatic Review* called her a "charming Lady Percy" in a production by the university Dramatic Club of William Shakespeare's *Henry IV*. Marriage in 1879 to the Reverend Henry G. Woods, fellow and bursar of Trinity College, Oxford, widened her circle, bringing into it his friend Henry Daniel, fellow and later provost of Worcester College, and some of the

Title page for the volume that includes Woods's poem "The Gondola of London"

writers whose works Daniel printed on his handpress. In 1881 Daniel included a lyric by her in *The Garland of Rachel,* an anthology of verses he printed to honor his daughter's first birthday. The volume was noticed at the time, because among its sixteen other contributors were such authors as Andrew Lang, Robert Bridges, Lewis Carroll, and Edmund Gosse. In her thirty-two rhyming couplets Woods imagines her own infant son, Gilbert, asking about the mysteries of the nursery:

> Rachel! Tell me what you know,
> Tell me where the shadows go;
> For before I'm sent to sleep
> I can watch them run and creep,
> Rock and spring and fly and fall
> On the ceiling and the wall,
> Troops of shadows at their games
> Dancing to the dancing flames.

Colin Franklin, in his *Poets of the Daniel Press* (1988), dismisses the poem as "vacuous and inconsequential," an assessment that perhaps ignores the playful nature of the volume.

Yet, the figure of the child recurs in some of the weakest of Woods's later poetry, though not always in so mundane a context as the nursery, for Woods had a fondness for abstractions that derived in part from Shelley. They abound in *Lyrics,* a volume that Daniel printed in 1888. One poem, "The Earth Angel," speaks of a child as "Beloved spirit, whom the angels miss," coming from the realm of Time with a tenderness bought by tears of dead men. Equally portentous and obscure, "'Again I Saw Another Angel,'" depicts an apocalyptic dream vision and asks how often "angels of the whirlwind" shall "sow / Fierce seed the children take for wheat." The speaker in "The Song of the Lute Player" announces his readiness to express and share the listener's unexplained sorrow: "Light though it be, soon to depart, / I'll sing it weeping." And in "A Ballade of the Night" the "quiet darkness" provides the "toiling earth" with "time to weep."

Only 125 copies of *Lyrics* were printed, each with an initial letter designed by Daniel's wife, Emily, showing a meadow and distant Oxford spires. A year before the book began to be seen on the tables of Woods's friends, the firm of Richard Bentley and Son, acting on Broughton's recommendation, brought out her first novel, *A Village Tragedy.* It is the story of a simple Oxfordshire girl who drowns herself after finding no sympathy when the father of her infant dies before he can arrange their marriage. Henry James and Robert Browning admired the book for reasons best articulated by Wilde in his November 1887 review for *Women's World*: its realism was that "of the artist, not of the reporter." The Positivist Frederic Harrison noted in his glowing review in *Nineteenth Century* (February 1889) that the novel was illuminated by her *Lyrics,* which he had been given as a family friend. He was especially impressed by "To the Forgotten Dead," which celebrates those who, in her words, had by "renunciation and laborious years" helped to "lay the deep foundations of our race." Comparing her idea of a corporate benevolent humanity to that of George Eliot in her "O May I Join the Choir Invisible" (1867), which the Positivists were using in their worship of Humanity, he called for a wider distribution of Woods's "dainty little volume," which occurred later in the year when Bentley paid the author £50 to publish an enlarged edition, *Lyrics and Ballads.*

Of these early poems, the best known is a Petrarchan sonnet, "Genius Loci," which Sir Arthur Quiller-Couch reprinted in his *Oxford Book of English Verse 1250–1900* (1900). The octave queries the value of a poetic shepherd "singing on" since the gods have departed from Helicon. The sestet affirms the possibility of "some nameless power of Nature" straying into "these broad fields in May," where ordinary shepherds will not recognize the "gift divine." Similarly set in the Oxford countryside, "Twilight" sounds a happier note, apparently alluding to the poet's marriage, but the vague melancholy of the early verse persists. An unnamed speaker, lost in reverie with a companion by a river in the "grey and silent eve," muses on the thought of dreaming there again in the future, when memory will transmute "all Time's store, / Till the sad years exult and deem they bore / Only the long, long love 'twixt thee and me."

To the reviewer in *The Spectator* (13 July 1889), the most-successful works in the volume were the ballads. They show that for all her love of the serenely pastoral, she was capable of portraying stirring action: "Young Windebank" tells of the proud death at Merton College of a Royalist martyr; and in "At the Barricade" a fearless Parisian woman in 1870 confronts the Versailles troops alone. The achievement of two other ballads is undercut by their derivative nature. Tennyson's voice can be heard too insistently in "The Ballad of King Hjorward's Death," and Byron's in "The Ballad of King Rameses." The variety of her work impressed reviewers, and Robert Bridges, as knowledgeable as anyone about verse forms, complimented her in a letter (1 February 1889) on "doing some rare and difficult things as well as possible."

With the election of her husband as president of Trinity College, Oxford, in 1887 and their relocation from rooms in Holywell Street to the new President's Lodgings at Trinity, her duties as a hostess increased. She could not welcome all her guests with the same genuine warmth as she did the young William Rothenstein, who had come from his Paris studio to sketch Oxford worthies, or the future historian H. A. L. Fisher, then a brilliant undergraduate who later married a cousin of hers and remained a lifelong friend and adviser on issues of scholarship. Occasionally she spoke to groups on literature and women's role in society, and she took some part in Trinity's London mission, though with nothing like the zeal for philanthropy of Mrs. Humphry Ward. She opposed woman suffrage, though without joining her friend's campaign against it. In her "Poetry: And Women Poets as Artists" (*Fortnightly Review*, August 1913), however, she anticipates contemporary feminism, citing Sappho's community of women as an example of a society in which feminine genius could flourish. Her own strategy for coping with the demands of her position at the university was to retreat whenever she could: to Wales, where the family had a summer cottage, or to France, or even just to the house she and her husband built on Boars Hill. During these years she was pursuing the scholarship that went into her next two novels, *Esther Vanhomrigh* (1891), about the ill-fated lover of Jonathan Swift, and *The Vagabonds* (1894), about circus people.

That prosody and verse forms continued to interest her is evident in three volumes of her work that appeared in 1896. Daniel printed *Songs,* including eight verses from periodicals and the 1888 volume as well as six new poems. The new poems are composed in short, rhymed stanzas, and as exercises on the familiar lyrical themes of love and nature they are competent but unremarkable. Many embody emotions from her own experiences, such as the birth of her second son, Maurice, in 1882.

Aëromancy, and Other Poems (1896) is more varied than *Songs* but similar in that it was designed to appeal to lovers of fine press editions of poetry. It was the fourth volume in the Shilling Garland Series of Elkin Mathews, a London bookseller who sold Daniel's work at inflated prices in his Vigo Street bookshop. Woods was recruited for the series by its editor, the poet Laurence Binyon, who remembered trudging up to Boars Hill to discuss verse with her during his undergraduate years at Trinity. As reported by James G. Nelson in *Elkin Mathews: Publisher to Yeats, Joyce, Pound* (1989), Binyon privately said "Aëromancy" was "a little odd" as the title poem in her volume, but "perhaps none the worse for that." The word originally meant "prophecy" but had come to signify witchcraft done in the air, which is how Woods uses it. In her collected poems the work bears the less esoteric title "Oxford Bells," which points to its central image, the "iron tongues" in the "aery tiers of clustered pinnacles" of the university, whose sound summons the ghosts of dead scholars. They warn the living of dangers awaiting them and cry, "Away! Away!," which echoes the poet's admonition in "The Scholar-Gipsy" to "fly our paths, our feverish contact fly!" While Arnold's speaker deplores "this strange disease of modern life," however, Woods's phantom scholars condemn its opposite, the cloistered academic existence. At the same time her poem, like Arnold's, recalls joyous occasions of the past, notably her summer morning visits to the garden of Rhoda Broughton and her sister Ellinor Newcome, neighbors in Holywell Street.

"Aëromancy" is written largely in stanzas of terza rima. The remaining eight poems in the volume employ other verse forms and evoke other moods: for example, there are complex rhyme patterns in "The Child Alone," a Blakean song about a little girl's imaginative role-playing, and the mood is one of exhilaration; whereas in "The Mariners Sleep by the Sea," rhyme and the repetition of words simulate the soothing lapping of waves on the shore. The short lines and many feminine rhymes of "Weep No More" owe much to

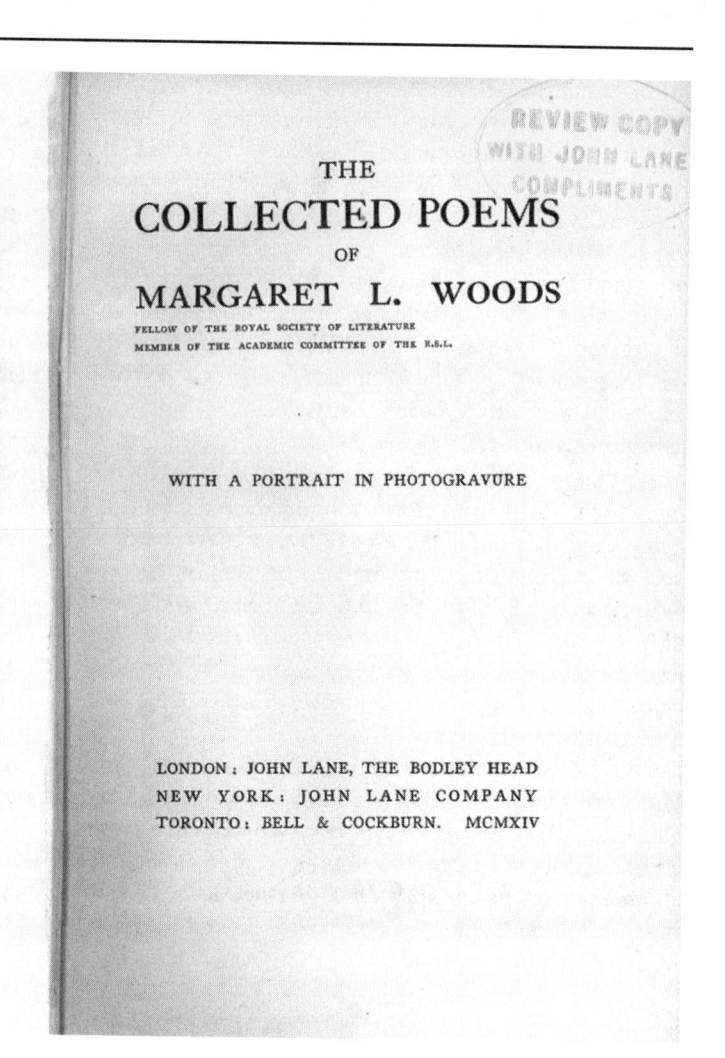

Frontispiece and title page for a retrospective volume of Woods's poetry

Shakespeare's songs. The reviewer in the *Saturday Review* (17 July 1897) rightly praised the "word music" in the volume, and the reviewer for *Academy* (12 September 1896) with equal justification complained about its "obscurities." Its select audience was apparently satisfied, however, and the book received a second printing.

Wild Justice (1896), the third book in Woods's annus mirabilis, is an ambitious and powerful tragic drama set in a troubled family's home on a bleak island off the Welsh coast. It tells of a plot against the life of a vicious tyrant by his long-suffering wife and grown children. Their plan goes awry, causing his death but also that of a son and daughter. The widow expresses her grief and guilt in passionate lines about grim destiny, some of which anticipate speeches in John Millington Synge's *Riders to the Sea* (1903). Not meant for the stage, Woods's dramatic poem features strong set pieces of different moods and meters: for example, a moving lyric, "Sleep we must, but when to slumber?"; the anguished blank-verse speeches of those waiting to learn the outcome of the murder; and a harrowing ballad in which the mother in her coffin is tormented by the sounds of her wailing children.

In 1897 Woods's husband resigned the presidency of Trinity, giving as his reason the injurious effect of Oxford on his wife's health. She suffered from sciatica, but more relevant was her desire to escape university demands on her time. In two 1898 letters to Rothenstein she spoke of having "wasted half a lifetime" in "that circle of Purgatory." Significantly, her last book to appear during the Oxford years was *Weeping Ferry, and other Stories* (1898), a work that did not require the sustained attention of a novel or verse drama. She disliked North Wales and Hertfordshire, where her husband served successive parishes. With their third child, Gabriel, in school by 1900, they were free to spend long periods in Spain, which she depicted in the *Cornhill Magazine,* and in St. Jean-de-Luz near the Pyrenees, the subject of other essays and setting for *Sons of the Sword: A Romance of the Peninsular War* (1901).

European history informed her next poetic drama, *The Princess of Hanover* (1902). As in *Wild Justice*, in *The Princess of Hanover* Woods employed various poetic forms: the ballad, choric song, and declamatory blank verse. Her characters—the Hanoverian Elector; his wife; his son, George (the future king of England); and George's estranged wife—naturally speak a more stately language than the family in *Wild Justice*. The Electress, for example, informed of her daughter-in-law's unwillingness to leave Hanover, exclaims:

> Thou'lt not be Queen of England?
> No, for by Heaven that needs a royal heart!
> What were it to be Queen of England? Answer,
> Shade of the illustrious dead, answer Elizabeth!

Not content with looking back to Queen Elizabeth, Woods clearly means the reader to think of the recently dead Victoria when the Electress describes the homage a monarch can expect even in old age:

> A sea of worshipping eyes, a ripple of hands
> Claiming you with the old rapture, lifting you
> To the height of their hearts' throne, yours as in youth,
> Yours on through age to death. . . .

The preface to *The Princess of Hanover* embodies an important statement of the author's belief that the sounds of words are all-important in poetry, and hence eye rhymes are usually an "absurdity." She endorses Robert Bridges's theory that stress rather than the mechanical measuring of syllables should determine scansion, and deems the idea insufficiently noticed though it had been before the public since the appearance of his treatise on John Milton's prosody in 1889. The reviewer in *The Times Literary Supplement* (*TLS*, 14 November 1902) thought few would object to the principle but found that her drama carried it "strangely far." Bridges was naturally pleased to have his work endorsed, expressing this sentiment in a 28 October 1902 letter to Woods, and Thomas Hardy, another experimenter in verse forms, named *The Princess of Hanover* as the most interesting book he had read that year in *Academy and Literature* (6 December 1902).

Early in the new century Woods set two of her most successful poems in Westminster Abbey. "The Builders" commemorates the special service held there for colonial troops in London for the coronation of King Edward VII. Addressing the abbey itself, the poet asks: "On what dost thou dream, solitary all the night long, / Immense, dark, alone, shrine of a world?" She likens the edifice to "a brand consumed and blackened of fire, / In the fierce heart of London" and imagines it inhabited by phantoms of the workers who created it, their "tenuous hands" clinging to the "carven crumbling / Work that they wrought ere they lay in forgotten graveyards." Most readers of *The Cornhill*, where the poem first appeared in December 1902, would have known that her father had been in charge of the abbey since becoming dean of Westminster in 1882. He had contributed an historical chapter to the immensely popular 1890 guidebook of the abbey by her sisters Mabel Charlotte Bradley (later married to Sir Henry Birchenough) and Emily Tennyson Bradley (later the wife of Alexander Murray Smith, whose father, the publisher George Smith, owned *The Cornhill*). In the year "The Builders" appeared, Emily Bradley published her learned *Roll-Call of Westminster Abbey*, biographical sketches of the persons buried or honored within its walls. She began the book with Woods's poem on the "forgotten dead," revised to include a new stanza on the "remembered dead."

Dean Bradley's long association with the abbey was inevitably the theme of "The Passing Bell," the elegy Woods wrote after his death in March 1903. It is a long, carefully structured poem of irregular, unrhymed stanzas, each including at least one line of Latin text to enhance its reverential tone and liturgical power. The imagery moves from the darkness and silence of the empty abbey to the light of the stars and the sound of the great bell, and, like many English elegies, from death to transcendence. After spectral voices insist on the loneliness and finality of death, the tolling of the bell in the tower marks the return of the dead man's soul to the Heavenly Father as his years fall into the "infinite Past," "feeding the heart of the world." To indicate its importance in her canon Woods placed this elegy, followed by "The Builders," at the beginning of both her later collections: *Poems, Old and New* in 1907 and *The Collected Poems of Margaret L. Woods* in 1914.

One of the most penetrating reviews of the 1914 volume was by the American critic Stuart P. Sherman in *The Nation* (7 May 1914). Headed "A Well-bred Poet Who Sings of the Well-Bred Clan," it pointed out that the author sounded "no note of revolt" and was "intensely English." The latter characteristic made especially gratifying her husband's appointment as master of the temple in 1904, and their move to its historic grounds off Fleet Street, in London, once the haunt of the Knights Templars and more recently of writers such as Samuel Johnson, Oliver Goldsmith, and Charles Lamb. Her new home inspired several poems about London. In "High Tide on the Victoria Embankment," published in *The Cornhill Magazine* (January 1910) and in *The Collected Poems of Margaret L. Woods* the nearby Thames figures as a great road from the sea to the city, its tide whispering "Hail" to the builders of Empire residing there as well as to the workers toiling at their metaphoric looms, blind to the "woof tremendous" of

Vine Cottage
Thursley.
Godalming

July 8. '35.

R. L. Mégroz Esq

Dear Sir — I am pleased you should choose the first three sections of "High Tide on the Victoria Embankment" for your Anthology. So far as I am concerned I will of course let you have it without paying a fee. I will write to the Bodley Head (Lane) & ask them to give favorable consideration to an application from you. I shall be pleased to have the Anthology, when it appears —

Yrs faithfully
Margaret L. Woods.

Letter from Woods to Rodolphe Louis Mégroz about the selection of one of her poems for an anthology he was editing

the city. In contrast to the solemn tone and irregular meter of that poem, "The Gondola of London," published in *Poems, Old and New,* is a jaunty dramatic monologue, evocative of Robert Browning, in which a happy lover in a hansom cab speaks to his lady:

> Ever the hurrying faces pass,
> Phantom-dim through a rain-blurred glass.
> Which of the swarm will heed if warm
> Here a venturous arm enwind you?

In *The Bookman* (January 1914) Edward Thomas judged this poem "probably the best" in the collection, but he confessed in a 2 November 1907 letter to a friend that the poet interested him "not at all." Hardy, however, in a letter to Woods (19 October 1907) praised her work because it seemed to "insist upon a poet's privilege of originality in presentation," a feature, he added, that "mostly shocks reviewers" (19 October 1907 letter to Woods). As if to bear him out, the reviewer in *TLS* (28 November 1907) hoped that the irregular line lengths and the lack of rhyme in "The Builders" and "The Passing Bell" would not become fashionable.

In these London years, Woods published two dissimilar novels. *The King's Revoke: An Episode in the Life of Patrick Dillon* (1905), about Spain under Joseph Bonaparte, is overburdened with historical detail; whereas *The Invader* (1907) in part forsakes realism to portray the inner conflicts of a member of the first generation of women at Oxford, perhaps experienced to some degree by Woods herself. Her heroine is hypnotized in her student days by a friend who promises relief from sleeplessness induced by overwork. Instead, she becomes intermittently possessed by an alternate personality, presumably that of a seductively beautiful ancestor whom she physically resembles. When the "invader" continues to intrude after her marriage, she repudiates her responsibilities to her husband, an Oxford don, and their child, escaping to a freer, more sexually exciting life, until the return of her authentic self brings such remorse that she commits suicide. Unwilling or unable to deal with the full implications of the story, some reviewers—for example, those for *TLS* (10 May 1907) and *The Bookman* (June 1907)—concentrated on the realism of the Oxford setting and the role of hypnotism, then much in the news.

Woods returned to the subject of hypnotism to establish a connection between it and rhyme in the essay "Poetry and the Prosaics" (*Fortnightly Review,* June 1924). Just as rhythmic repetition of speech might induce the hypnotic state, so, she argued, rhyme, assonance, and alliteration enable the poet to bypass the "rational Self" and reach "that mysterious Self" within. The "Prosaics," or modern poets who believe that the language of poetry and of prose are identical, miss this opportunity. As an example of their "dullness" she quotes the second and third lines of "The Love Song of J. Alfred Prufrock" (1917), apparently forgetting that the opening lines of her own poem, "Under the Lamp," written in 1913, anticipate other passages in T. S. Eliot's work:

> Under the lamp
> In the midnight lonely
> Desolation
> Of the flaring street—
> Illumination
> To exhibit only
> The obscene pavement's horrible slime,
> Spittle of smokers, foulness of feet
> That have stayed their tramp,
> Their everlasting journey for a time.

But Eliot (who wrote his Harvard dissertation on the philosopher F. H. Bradley, Woods's uncle) was interested in the psychological, she in the moral. In place of Eliot's self-conscious couple shrinking from sexuality, she introduces a London streetwalker and her customer, a gentleman ("By diverse ways to this one way come!"). In the grip of "primal powers," the man closes his soul to the prayer of his mother, and it mysteriously finds its way into the soul of a poor youth, reading on his mean bed; he "immediately / Knows there is light somewhere, somewhere a friend" and is saved from the urban evil around him.

Woods's fondness for the supernatural in literature found a more fitting expression in her stories for children. In one of her best, *"Come unto These Yellow Sands"* (1915), fairies play amusing tricks on a scientifically minded couple who refuse to credit their existence. But in poems not meant for children the magical can seem intrusive. Her attraction to the ballad may be in part explained by the prominence of the mysterious in this genre, though she did not stress this characteristic in her lecture on the history of the ballad for the Royal Society of Literature in 1926. Her war poems are full of the inexplicable. In "The First Battle of Ypres," from *The Return, and Other Poems* (1921), ghosts of English soldiers arise from the past and attain the victory, an episode she said came from German prisoners' accounts of the battle, not from the angels of Mons story. "Finisterre," her contribution to Edith Wharton's *The Book of the Homeless (Le livre des sans-foyer),* an anthology sold to raise money for refugee relief in 1916, ends with a ship bearing wounded souls to Avalon. Wharton used the image three years later in her poetic eulogy to Theodore Roosevelt, who had written an introduction to *The Book of the Homeless.* Two poems by Woods about postwar life, "On the Step" and "Maisie and the Broken Man"–which appeared in *The London Mercury* in January 1925 and September 1932, respectively–concern dead women who manifest their presence to the living. Conventional Christian supernatural imagery is also featured in "Good Friday Night," a poem affirming the "new mystery" of the Resurrection that she read on BBC radio.

Woods's last novels are *A Poet's Youth* (1923), on William Wordsworth and Annette Vallon, and *The Spanish Lady* (1927), about the Duke of Wellington–both competent but uninspired historical fiction. The nonfiction of her later years includes essays from a visit to South Africa, lectures on literature for an American speaking tour before the war, an introduction to sermons by her husband published after his death in 1915, an eyewitness report on Wharton's war refugee centers in France, and introductions to two anthologies of poetry by unknown women whom she selflessly encouraged. Her last home was Vine Cottage in the quiet Surrey village of Thursley, chosen because H. A. L. Fisher and his family lived nearby. It was also accessible to London, where until the early 1930s she faithfully attended meetings of the Academic Committee of the Royal Society of Literature, to which she had been elected in 1913, at the time a singular honor for a woman. As an active member of the society she remained informed about literary trends and writers coming to the fore until well into her old age. Before her death at age ninety, on 1 December 1945, her own name had been long forgotten. The innovative stress and verse patterns in her work that had led Bridges to consult her on prosody had come to seem commonplace. The melancholy in so much of her verse had gone out of style. But for anyone today interested in the evolution of poetic forms, fictional treatment of historical events, and insights into late Victorian university and literary life, her publications should place her among the "remembered dead."

References:
W. L. Courtney, *The Feminine Note in Fiction* (London: Chapman & Hall, 1904), pp. 137–155;

James G. Nelson, *Elkin Mathews: Publisher to Yeats, Joyce, Pound* (Madison: University of Wisconsin, 1989);

Mary C. Sturgeon, "Margaret L. Woods," in *Studies of Contemporary Poets,* revised and enlarged edition (New York: Dodd, Mead, 1916), pp. 301–326.

Papers:
The Margaret L. Woods Papers are at Bodleian Library, Oxford University. Other papers may be found in the C. H. O. Daniel Papers, Worcester College, Oxford University; the Henry Woods Papers, Trinity College, Oxford University; and the William Rothenstein Papers, Houghton Library, Harvard University.

Checklist of Further Readings

Armstrong, Isobel. *Victorian Poetry: Poetry, Poetics, and Politics.* London & New York: Routledge, 1993.

Armstrong and Virginia Blain, eds. *Women's Poetry, Late Romantics to Late Victorians: Gender and Genre, 1830–1900.* New York: St. Martin's Press, 1999.

Ball, Patricia M. *The Heart's Events: The Victorian Poetry of Relationships.* London: Athlone, 1976.

Beckson, Karl. *Aesthetes and Decadents of the 1890's: An Anthology of British Poetry and Prose.* New York: Vintage, 1966.

Bethune, George W., ed. *The British Female Poets With Biographical and Critical Notices.* Philadelphia: Lindsay & Blakiston, 1848.

Bivona, Daniel. *Desire and Contradiction: Imperial Visions and Domestic Debates in Victorian Literature.* Manchester: Manchester University Press, 1990.

Breen, Jennifer, ed. *Victorian Women Poets 1830–1901: An Anthology.* London: Dent, 1994.

Bryans, E. L. "Characteristics of Women's Poetry," *Dark Blue,* 2 (1871): 484.

Christ, Carol. "Victorian Masculinity and the Angel in the House," in *A Widening Sphere: Changing Roles of Victorian Women,* edited by Martha Vicinus. Bloomington & London: Indiana University Press, 1977.

Claridge, Laura, and Elizabeth Langland, eds. *Out of Bounds: Male Writers and Gender(ed) Criticism.* Amherst: University of Massachusetts Press, 1990.

Cooper, Helen M., Adrienne Auslander Munich, and Susan Merril Squier, eds. *Arms and the Woman: War, Gender, and Literary Representation.* Chapel Hill & London: University of North Carolina Press, 1989.

Cross, Nigel. *The Common Writer: Life in Nineteenth-Century Grub Street.* Cambridge: Cambridge University Press, 1985.

David, Deirdre. *Intellectual Women and Victorian Patriarchy.* London: Macmillan, 1987.

De Shazer, Mary K. *Inspiring Women: Re-Imagining the Muse.* Oxford & New York: Pergamon, 1989.

Du Plessis, Rachel Blau. "Rewriting the Rose: Women, Poetry and the Canon," in *Margin to Mainstream: The Broadening of the American Literary Canon,* edited by Eugene A. Bolt Jr. and Constance D. Harsh. Philadelphia: Philomathean Society Press, 1992.

Ezell, Margaret J. M. *Writing Women's Literary History.* Baltimore & London: Johns Hopkins University Press, 1993.

Faderman, Lillian. *Surpassing the Love of Men: Romantic Friendship and Love between Women from the Renaissance to the Present.* New York: Morrow, 1981.

Gilbert, Sandra M., and Susan Gubar. *The Madwoman in the Attic: The Woman Writer and the Nineteenth-Century Literary Imagination.* New Haven: Yale University Press, 1979.

Gilmour, Robin. *The Victorian Period: The Intellectual and Cultural Context of English Literature, 1830–1890.* London: Longman, 1993.

Gubar, Susan. "'The Blank Page' and Issues of Female Creativity," *Critical Inquiry,* 8 (1981): 243–263.

Gubar. "Sapphistries," *Signs,* 10 (1984): 43–62.

Hickok, Kathleen. *Representations of Women: Nineteenth-Century British Women's Poetry.* Westport, Conn.: Greenwood Press, 1984.

Homans, Margaret. *Bearing the Word: Language and Female Experience in Nineteenth-Century Women's Writing.* Chicago: University of Chicago Press, 1986.

Kaplan, Cora, ed. *Salt and Bitter and Good: Three Centuries of English and American Women Poets.* New York: Paddington, 1975.

Krishnamurti, G., ed. *Women Writers of the 1890's.* London: H. Sotheran, 1991.

Landow, George. *Victorian Types, Victorian Shadows: Biblical Typology in Victorian Literature, Art, and Thought.* Boston & London: Routledge & Kegan Paul, 1980.

Leighton, Angela. *Victorian Women Poets: Writing against the Heart.* Charlottesville: University Press of Virginia, 1992.

Leighton and Margaret Reynolds, eds. *Victorian Women Poets: An Anthology.* Oxford: Blackwell, 1995.

Levine, Philippa. *Feminist Lives in Victorian England: Private Roles and Public Commitment.* Oxford: Blackwell, 1990.

McGregor, O. R. *Divorce in England: A Centenary Study.* London: Heinemann, 1957.

Mermin, Dorothy. *Godiva's Ride: Women of Letters in England, 1830–1880.* Bloomington: Indiana University Press, 1993.

Mix, Katharine Lyon. *A Study in Yellow: The Yellow Book and Its Contributors.* London: Constable, 1960; Lawrence: University of Kansas Press, 1960.

Moers, Ellen. *Literary Women.* New York: Doubleday, 1976.

Montefiore, Jan. *Feminism and Poetry: Language, Experience, Identity in Women's Writing.* London: Pandora, 1987.

Parrinder, Patrick. *Authors and Authority: A Study of English Literary Criticism and Its Relation to Culture, 1750–1900.* London: Routledge & Kegan Paul, 1977.

Robertson, Eric S. *English Poetesses: A Series of Critical Biographies, with Illustrative Extracts.* London: Cassell, 1883.

Rose, Jonathan. *The Edwardian Temperament, 1895–1919.* Athens: Ohio University Press, 1986.

Ross, Marlon B. *The Contours of Masculine Desire: Romanticism and the Rise of Women's Poetry.* New York: Oxford University Press, 1989.

Rowton, Frederic. *The Female Poets of Great Britain.* Facsimile of the 1853 edition, with an introduction by Marilyn L. Williamson. Detroit: Wayne State University Press, 1980.

Showalter, Elaine. "Women Writers and the Double Standard," in *Woman in Sexist Society: Studies in Power and Powerlessness,* edited by Vivian Gornick and Barbara K. Moran. New York: Basic Books, 1971, pp. 323–343.

Stephenson, Glennis, and Shirley Neuman, eds. *ReImagining Women: Representations of Women in Culture.* Toronto: University of Toronto Press, 1993.

Stodart, Mary Ann. *Female Writers: Thoughts on Their Proper Sphere and on Their Powers of Usefulness.* London: Seeley & Burnside, 1842.

Swindells, Julia. *Victorian Writing and Working Women: The Other Side of Silence.* Cambridge: Polity Press, 1985.

Tennyson, G. B. *Victorian Devotional Poetry: The Tractarian Mode.* Cambridge, Mass.: Harvard University Press, 1981.

Wharton, Grace and Philip. *The Queens of Society.* New York: Harper, 1860.

Williams, Jane. *The Literary Women of England.* London: Saunders, Otley, 1861.

Contributors

Crys Armbrust	*University of South Carolina*
Mary Arseneau	*University of Ottawa*
Florence Boos	*University of Iowa*
Ashley Brown	*University of South Carolina*
Siobhan Craft Brownson	*Winthrop University*
Susannah Clements	*University of South Carolina*
Kirsten E. Escobar	*Baylor University*
John Ferns	*McMaster University*
Roslyn Reso Foy	*University of New Orleans*
Constance M. Fulmer	*Pepperdine University*
Susan T. Harrington	*University of Maryland Eastern Shore*
John C. Hawley	*Santa Clara University*
Naomi Hetherington	*University of Southampton*
Kathleen Hickok	*Iowa State University*
Chris Hopkins	*Sheffield Hallam University*
Cynthia E. Huggins	*University of Maine at Machias*
Linda K. Hughes	*Texas Christian University*
Linda A. Julian	*Furman University*
Lisa Kerr	*University of South Carolina*
Becky W. Lewis	*University of South Carolina*
Deborah A. Logan	*Western Kentucky University*
Ed Madden	*University of South Carolina*
Eugenie Celeste Martin	*Louisiana Tech University*
Michele Martinez	*Trinity College*
Edward Marx	*Kyoto University*
Lee Anna Maynard	*University of South Carolina*
Kathleen McCormack	*Florida International University*
Jeanie Grant Moore	*University of Wisconsin at Oshkosh*
Rose Novak	*Boston College*
Bettina Tate Pedersen	*California State University, Northridge*
Amanda Jo Pettit	*University of South Carolina*
LeeAnne Marie Richardson	*Georgia State University*
Rebecca Shapiro	*Westminster College*
Alpana Sharma	*Wright State University*
Marion Thain	*University of Birmingham*

Contributors

Richard Tobias	*University of Pittsburgh*
Ann Vickery	*Macquarie University*
Martha S. Vogeler	*California State University, Fullerton*
Tonya L. Wertz-Orbaugh	*University of South Carolina*
James Whitlark	*Texas Tech University*
Michelle L. Whitney	*University of South Carolina*
Whitney Womack	*Miami University of Ohio*

Cumulative Index

Dictionary of Literary Biography, Volumes 1-240
Dictionary of Literary Biography Yearbook, 1980-1999
Dictionary of Literary Biography Documentary Series, Volumes 1-19
Concise Dictionary of American Literary Biography, Volumes 1-7
Concise Dictionary of British Literary Biography, Volumes 1-8
Concise Dictionary of World Literary Biography, Volumes 1-4

Cumulative Index

DLB before number: *Dictionary of Literary Biography*, Volumes 1-240
Y before number: *Dictionary of Literary Biography Yearbook*, 1980-1999
DS before number: *Dictionary of Literary Biography Documentary Series*, Volumes 1-19
CDALB before number: *Concise Dictionary of American Literary Biography*, Volumes 1-7
CDBLB before number: *Concise Dictionary of British Literary Biography*, Volumes 1-8
CDWLB before number: *Concise Dictionary of World Literary Biography*, Volumes 1-4

A

Aakjær, Jeppe 1866-1930 .... DLB-214
Abbey, Edwin Austin 1852-1911 .... DLB-188
Abbey, Maj. J. R. 1894-1969 .... DLB-201
Abbey Press DLB-49
The Abbey Theatre and Irish Drama, 1900-1945 .... DLB-10
Abbot, Willis J. 1863-1934 .... DLB-29
Abbott, Jacob 1803-1879 .... DLB-1
Abbott, Lee K. 1947- DLB-130
Abbott, Lyman 1835-1922 .... DLB-79
Abbott, Robert S. 1868-1940 .... DLB-29, 91
Abe Kōbō 1924-1993 .... DLB-182
Abelard, Peter circa 1079-1142? DLB-115, 208
Abelard-Schuman DLB-46
Abell, Arunah S. 1806-1888 .... DLB-43
Abell, Kjeld 1901-1961 .... DLB-214
Abercrombie, Lascelles 1881-1938 ...... DLB-19
Aberdeen University Press Limited DLB-106
Abish, Walter 1931- DLB-130, 227
Ablesimov, Aleksandr Onisimovich 1742-1783 .... DLB-150
Abraham à Sancta Clara 1644-1709 ..... DLB-168
Abrahams, Peter 1919- DLB-117, 225; CDWLB-3
Abrams, M. H. 1912- DLB-67
Abrogans circa 790-800 .... DLB-148
Abschatz, Hans Aßmann von 1646-1699 .... DLB-168
Abse, Dannie 1923- DLB-27
Abutsu-ni 1221-1283 .... DLB-203
Academy Chicago Publishers DLB-46
Accius circa 170 B.C.-circa 80 B.C. DLB-211
Accrocca, Elio Filippo 1923- DLB-128
Ace Books DLB-46
Achebe, Chinua 1930- DLB-117; CDWLB-3
Achtenberg, Herbert 1938- DLB-124
Ackerman, Diane 1948- DLB-120
Ackroyd, Peter 1949- DLB-155, 231
Acorn, Milton 1923-1986 .... DLB-53
Acosta, Oscar Zeta 1935?- DLB-82

Acosta Torres, José 1925- DLB-209
Actors Theatre of Louisville DLB-7
Adair, Gilbert 1944- DLB-194
Adair, James 1709?-1783? DLB-30
Adam, Graeme Mercer 1839-1912 .... DLB-99
Adam, Robert Borthwick II 1863-1940 ... DLB-187
Adame, Leonard 1947- DLB-82
Adameșteanu, Gabriel 1942- DLB-232
Adamic, Louis 1898-1951 .... DLB-9
Adams, Abigail 1744-1818 .... DLB-200
Adams, Alice 1926-1999 .... DLB-234, Y-86
Adams, Bertha Leith (Mrs. Leith Adams, Mrs. R. S. de Courcy Laffan) 1837?-1912 .... DLB-240
Adams, Brooks 1848-1927 .... DLB-47
Adams, Charles Francis, Jr. 1835-1915 .... DLB-47
Adams, Douglas 1952- Y-83
Adams, Franklin P. 1881-1960 .... DLB-29
Adams, Hannah 1755-1832 .... DLB-200
Adams, Henry 1838-1918 .... DLB-12, 47, 189
Adams, Herbert Baxter 1850-1901 .... DLB-47
Adams, J. S. and C. [publishing house] DLB-49
Adams, James Truslow 1878-1949 .... DLB-17; DS-17
Adams, John 1735-1826 .... DLB-31, 183
Adams, John 1735-1826 and Adams, Abigail 1744-1818 .... DLB-183
Adams, John Quincy 1767-1848 .... DLB-37
Adams, Léonie 1899-1988 .... DLB-48
Adams, Levi 1802-1832 .... DLB-99
Adams, Samuel 1722-1803 .... DLB-31, 43
Adams, Sarah Fuller Flower 1805-1848 .... DLB-199
Adams, Thomas 1582 or 1583-1652 ..... DLB-151
Adams, William Taylor 1822-1897 .... DLB-42
Adamson, Sir John 1867-1950 .... DLB-98
Adcock, Arthur St. John 1864-1930 ...... DLB-135
Adcock, Betty 1938- DLB-105
"Certain Gifts" DLB-105
Adcock, Fleur 1934- DLB-40
Addison, Joseph 1672-1719 ... DLB-101; CDBLB-2
Ade, George 1866-1944 .... DLB-11, 25

Adeler, Max (see Clark, Charles Heber)
Adonias Filho 1915-1990 .... DLB-145
Advance Publishing Company DLB-49
Ady, Endre 1877-1919 ...... DLB-215; CDWLB-4
AE 1867-1935 .... DLB-19; CDBLB-5
Ælfric circa 955-circa 1010 .... DLB-146
Aeschines circa 390 B.C.-circa 320 B.C. DLB-176
Aeschylus 525-524 B.C.-456-455 B.C. DLB-176; CDWLB-1
Afro-American Literary Critics: An Introduction DLB-33
After Dinner Opera Company Y-92
Agassiz, Elizabeth Cary 1822-1907 ...... DLB-189
Agassiz, Louis 1807-1873 .... DLB-1, 235
Agee, James 1909-1955 .... DLB-2, 26, 152; CDALB-1
The Agee Legacy: A Conference at the University of Tennessee at Knoxville Y-89
Aguilera Malta, Demetrio 1909-1981 .... DLB-145
Ai 1947- DLB-120
Aichinger, Ilse 1921- DLB-85
Aidoo, Ama Ata 1942- DLB-117; CDWLB-3
Aiken, Conrad 1889-1973 .... DLB-9, 45, 102; CDALB-5
Aiken, Joan 1924- DLB-161
Aikin, Lucy 1781-1864 .... DLB-144, 163
Ainsworth, William Harrison 1805-1882 .. DLB-21
Aistis, Jonas 1904-1973 ..... DLB-220; CDWLB-4
Aitken, George A. 1860-1917 .... DLB-149
Aitken, Robert [publishing house] DLB-49
Akenside, Mark 1721-1770 .... DLB-109
Akins, Zoë 1886-1958 .... DLB-26
Aksahov, Sergei Timofeevich 1791-1859 .... DLB-198
Akutagawa, Ryūnsuke 1892-1927 .... DLB-180
Alabaster, William 1568-1640 .... DLB-132
Alain de Lille circa 1116-1202/1203 ...... DLB-208
Alain-Fournier 1886-1914 .... DLB-65
Alanus de Insulis (see Alain de Lille)
Alarcón, Francisco X. 1954- DLB-122
Alarcón, Justo S. 1930- DLB-209
Alba, Nanina 1915-1968 .... DLB-41

369

Cumulative Index   DLB 240

Albee, Edward 1928- DLB-7; CDALB-1
Albert the Great circa 1200-1280 .... DLB-115
Albert, Octavia 1853-ca. 1889 .... DLB-221
Alberti, Rafael 1902-1999 .... DLB-108
Albertinus, Aegidius circa 1560-1620 .... DLB-164
Alcaeus born circa 620 B.C. DLB-176
Alcott, Bronson 1799-1888 .... DLB-1, 223
Alcott, Louisa May 1832-1888
    ... DLB-1, 42, 79, 223, 239; DS-14; CDALB-3
Alcott, William Andrus 1798-1859 .... DLB-1
Alcuin circa 732-804 .... DLB-148
Alden, Beardsley and Company DLB-49
Alden, Henry Mills 1836-1919 .... DLB-79
Alden, Isabella 1841-1930 .... DLB-42
Alden, John B. [publishing house] DLB-49
Aldington, Richard
    1892-1962 .... DLB-20, 36, 100, 149
Aldis, Dorothy 1896-1966 .... DLB-22
Aldis, H. G. 1863-1919 .... DLB-184
Aldiss, Brian W. 1925- DLB-14
Aldrich, Thomas Bailey
    1836-1907 .... DLB-42, 71, 74, 79
Alegría, Ciro 1909-1967 .... DLB-113
Alegría, Claribel 1924- DLB-145
Aleixandre, Vicente 1898-1984 .... DLB-108
Aleksandravičius, Jonas (see Aistis, Jonas)
Aleksandrov, Aleksandr Andreevich
    (see Durova, Nadezhda Andreevna)
Aleramo, Sibilla 1876-1960 .... DLB-114
Alexander, Cecil Frances 1818-1895 ..... DLB-199
Alexander, Charles 1868-1923 .... DLB-91
Alexander, Charles Wesley
    [publishing house] DLB-49
Alexander, James 1691-1756 .... DLB-24
Alexander, Lloyd 1924- DLB-52
Alexander, Sir William, Earl of Stirling
    1577?-1640 .... DLB-121
Alexie, Sherman 1966- DLB-175, 206
Alexis, Willibald 1798-1871 .... DLB-133
Alfred, King 849-899 .... DLB-146
Alger, Horatio, Jr. 1832-1899 .... DLB-42
Algonquin Books of Chapel Hill DLB-46
Algren, Nelson
    1909-1981 ..... DLB-9; Y-81, Y-82; CDALB-1
Allan, Andrew 1907-1974 .... DLB-88
Allan, Ted 1916- DLB-68
Allbeury, Ted 1917- DLB-87
Alldritt, Keith 1935- DLB-14
Allen, Ethan 1738-1789 .... DLB-31
Allen, Frederick Lewis 1890-1954 .... DLB-137
Allen, Gay Wilson 1903-1995 ..... DLB-103; Y-95
Allen, George 1808-1876 .... DLB-59
Allen, George [publishing house] DLB-106
Allen, George, and Unwin Limited DLB-112
Allen, Grant 1848-1899 .... DLB-70, 92, 178
Allen, Henry W. 1912- Y-85

Allen, Hervey 1889-1949 .... DLB-9, 45
Allen, James 1739-1808 .... DLB-31
Allen, James Lane 1849-1925 .... DLB-71
Allen, Jay Presson 1922- DLB-26
Allen, John, and Company DLB-49
Allen, Paula Gunn 1939- DLB-175
Allen, Samuel W. 1917- DLB-41
Allen, Woody 1935- DLB-44
Allende, Isabel 1942- DLB-145; CDWLB-3
Alline, Henry 1748-1784 .... DLB-99
Allingham, Margery 1904-1966 .... DLB-77
Allingham, William 1824-1889 .... DLB-35
Allison, W. L. [publishing house] DLB-49
The *Alliterative Morte Arthure and the Stanzaic
    Morte Arthur* circa 1350-1400 .... DLB-146
Allott, Kenneth 1912-1973 .... DLB-20
Allston, Washington 1779-1843 ...... DLB-1, 235
Almon, John [publishing house] DLB-154
Alonzo, Dámaso 1898-1990 .... DLB-108
Alsop, George 1636-post 1673 .... DLB-24
Alsop, Richard 1761-1815 .... DLB-37
Altemus, Henry, and Company DLB-49
Altenberg, Peter 1885-1919 .... DLB-81
Altolaguirre, Manuel 1905-1959 .... DLB-108
Aluko, T. M. 1918- DLB-117
Alurista 1947- DLB-82
Alvarez, A. 1929- DLB-14, 40
Alver, Betti 1906-1989 ..... DLB-220; CDWLB-4
Amadi, Elechi 1934- DLB-117
Amado, Jorge 1912- DLB-113
Ambler, Eric 1909-1998 .... DLB-77
American Conservatory Theatre DLB-7
American Fiction and the 1930s DLB-9
American Humor: A Historical Survey
    East and Northeast
    South and Southwest
    Midwest
    West DLB-11
The American Library in Paris Y-93
American News Company DLB-49
The American Poets' Corner: The First
    Three Years (1983-1986) Y-86
American Publishing Company DLB-49
American Stationers' Company DLB-49
American Sunday-School Union DLB-49
American Temperance Union DLB-49
American Tract Society DLB-49
The American Trust for the
    British Library Y-96
The American Writers Congress
    (9-12 October 1981) Y-81
The American Writers Congress: A Report
    on Continuing Business Y-81
Ames, Fisher 1758-1808 .... DLB-37
Ames, Mary Clemmer 1831-1884 .... DLB-23
Amiel, Henri-Frédéric 1821-1881 .... DLB-217
Amini, Johari M. 1935- DLB-41

Amis, Kingsley 1922-1995
    ...... DLB-15, 27, 100, 139, Y-96; CDBLB-7
Amis, Martin 1949- DLB-194
Ammianus Marcellinus
    circa A.D. 330-A.D. 395 .... DLB-211
Ammons, A. R. 1926- DLB-5, 165
Amory, Thomas 1691?-1788 .... DLB-39
Anania, Michael 1939- DLB-193
Anaya, Rudolfo A. 1937- DLB-82, 206
Ancrene Riwle circa 1200-1225 .... DLB-146
Andersch, Alfred 1914-1980 .... DLB-69
Andersen, Benny 1929- DLB-214
Anderson, Alexander 1775-1870 .... DLB-188
Anderson, Frederick Irving 1877-1947 ... DLB-202
Anderson, Margaret 1886-1973 .... DLB-4, 91
Anderson, Maxwell 1888-1959 .... DLB-7, 228
Anderson, Patrick 1915-1979 .... DLB-68
Anderson, Paul Y. 1893-1938 .... DLB-29
Anderson, Poul 1926- DLB-8
Anderson, Robert 1750-1830 .... DLB-142
Anderson, Robert 1917- DLB-7
Anderson, Sherwood
    1876-1941 ..... DLB-4, 9, 86; DS-1; CDALB-4
Andreae, Johann Valentin 1586-1654 .... DLB-164
Andreas Capellanus
    flourished circa 1185 .... DLB-208
Andreas-Salomé, Lou 1861-1937 .... DLB-66
Andres, Stefan 1906-1970 .... DLB-69
Andreu, Blanca 1959- DLB-134
Andrewes, Lancelot 1555-1626 ..... DLB-151, 172
Andrews, Charles M. 1863-1943 .... DLB-17
Andrews, Miles Peter ?-1814 .... DLB-89
Andrian, Leopold von 1875-1951 .... DLB-81
Andrić, Ivo 1892-1975 ...... DLB-147; CDWLB-4
Andrieux, Louis (see Aragon, Louis)
Andrus, Silas, and Son DLB-49
Andrzejewski, Jerzy 1909-1983 .... DLB-215
Angell, James Burrill 1829-1916 .... DLB-64
Angell, Roger 1920- DLB-171, 185
Angelou, Maya 1928- DLB-38; CDALB-7
Anger, Jane flourished 1589 .... DLB-136
Angers, Félicité (see Conan, Laure)
Anglo-Norman Literature in the Development
    of Middle English Literature DLB-146
The *Anglo-Saxon Chronicle* circa 890-1154 .. DLB-146
The "Angry Young Men" DLB-15
Angus and Robertson (UK) Limited DLB-112
Anhalt, Edward 1914- DLB-26
Anners, Henry F. [publishing house] DLB-49
Annolied between 1077 and 1081 .... DLB-148
Annual Awards for *Dictionary of Literary Biography*
    Editors and Contributors Y-98, Y-99
Anselm of Canterbury 1033-1109 .... DLB-115
Anstey, F. 1856-1934 .... DLB-141, 178
Anthony, Michael 1932- DLB-125
Anthony, Piers 1934- DLB-8

370

Anthony, Susanna 1726-1791..........DLB-200

Antin, David 1932- DLB-169

Antin, Mary 1881-1949..........DLB-221; Y-84

Anton Ulrich, Duke of Brunswick-Lüneburg
1633-1714.....................DLB-168

Antschel, Paul (see Celan, Paul)

Anyidoho, Kofi 1947- DLB-157

Anzaldúa, Gloria 1942- DLB-122

Anzengruber, Ludwig 1839-1889 ....DLB-129

Apess, William 1798-1839 ....DLB-175

Apodaca, Rudy S. 1939- DLB-82

Apollonius Rhodius third century B.C....DLB-176

Apple, Max 1941- DLB-130

Appleton, D., and Company DLB-49

Appleton-Century-Crofts..............DLB-46

Applewhite, James 1935- DLB-105

Applewood Books DLB-46

Apuleius circa A.D. 125-post A.D. 164
..................DLB-211; CDWLB-1

Aquin, Hubert 1929-1977 ....DLB-53

Aquinas, Thomas 1224 or 1225-1274 ....DLB-115

Aragon, Louis 1897-1982...............DLB-72

Aralica, Ivan 1930- DLB-181

Aratus of Soli
circa 315 B.C.-circa 239 B.C.....DLB-176

Arbasino, Alberto 1930- DLB-196

Arbor House Publishing Company.......DLB-46

Arbuthnot, John 1667-1735 ....DLB-101

Arcadia House.......................DLB-46

Arce, Julio G. (see Ulica, Jorge)

Archer, William 1856-1924 ....DLB-10

Archilochhus
mid seventh century B.C.E........DLB-176

The Archpoet circa 1130?-?..........DLB-148

Archpriest Avvakum (Petrovich)
1620?-1682...................DLB-150

Arden, John 1930- DLB-13

Arden of Faversham....................DLB-62

Ardis Publishers........................Y-89

Ardizzone, Edward 1900-1979.........DLB-160

Arellano, Juan Estevan 1947- DLB-122

The Arena Publishing Company.........DLB-49

Arena Stage DLB-7

Arenas, Reinaldo 1943-1990 ....DLB-145

Arensberg, Ann 1937- Y-82

Arghezi, Tudor 1880-1967...DLB-220; CDWLB-4

Arguedas, José María 1911-1969 ......DLB-113

Argueta, Manilio 1936- DLB-145

Arias, Ron 1941- DLB-82

Arishima, Takeo 1878-1923...........DLB-180

Aristophanes circa 446 B.C.-circa 386 B.C.
..................DLB-176; CDWLB-1

Aristotle 384 B.C.-322 B.C.
..................DLB-176; CDWLB-1

Ariyoshi Sawako 1931-1984 ....DLB-182

Arland, Marcel 1899-1986.............DLB-72

Arlen, Michael 1895-1956 .... DLB-36, 77, 162

Armah, Ayi Kwei 1939- ... DLB-117; CDWLB-3

Armantrout, Rae 1947- DLB-193

Der arme Hartmann ?-after 1150.......DLB-148

Armed Services Editions DLB-46

Armstrong, Martin Donisthorpe
1882-1974....................DLB-197

Armstrong, Richard 1903- DLB-160

Arndt, Ernst Moritz 1769-1860 ....DLB-90

Arnim, Achim von 1781-1831 ....DLB-90

Arnim, Bettina von 1785-1859...........DLB-90

Arnim, Elizabeth von (Countess Mary
Annette Beauchamp Russell)
1866-1941....................DLB-197

Arno Press..........................DLB-46

Arnold, Edward [publishing house]......DLB-112

Arnold, Edwin 1832-1904 ....DLB-35

Arnold, Edwin L. 1857-1935 ....DLB-178

Arnold, Matthew
1822-1888..........DLB-32, 57; CDBLB-4

Preface to *Poems* (1853) DLB-32

Arnold, Thomas 1795-1842............DLB-55

Arnott, Peter 1962- DLB-233

Arnow, Harriette Simpson 1908-1986......DLB-6

Arp, Bill (see Smith, Charles Henry)

Arpino, Giovanni 1927-1987 ....DLB-177

Arreola, Juan José 1918- DLB-113

Arrian circa 89-circa 155 ....DLB-176

Arrowsmith, J. W. [publishing house] ...DLB-106

The Art and Mystery of Publishing:
Interviews Y-97

Arthur, Timothy Shay
1809-1885............DLB-3, 42, 79; DS-13

The Arthurian Tradition and
Its European Context DLB-138

Artmann, H. C. 1921- DLB-85

Arvin, Newton 1900-1963 ....DLB-103

Asch, Nathan 1902-1964..........DLB-4, 28

Ascham, Roger 1515 or 1516-1568......DLB-236

Ash, John 1948- DLB-40

Ashbery, John 1927- DLB-5, 165; Y-81

Ashbridge, Elizabeth 1713-1755........DLB-200

Ashburnham, Bertram Lord
1797-1878....................DLB-184

Ashendene Press DLB-112

Asher, Sandy 1942- Y-83

Ashton, Winifred (see Dane, Clemence)

Asimov, Isaac 1920-1992..........DLB-8; Y-92

Askew, Anne circa 1521-1546 ....DLB-136

Aspazija 1865-1943 ....DLB-220; CDWLB-4

Asselin, Olivar 1874-1937 ....DLB-92

The Association of American Publishers.....Y-99

Astley, William (see Warung, Price)

Asturias, Miguel Angel
1899-1974............DLB-113; CDWLB-3

Atheneum Publishers...................DLB-46

Atherton, Gertrude 1857-1948..... DLB-9, 78, 186

Athlone Press........................DLB-112

Atkins, Josiah circa 1755-1781 ....DLB-31

Atkins, Russell 1926- DLB-41

Atkinson, Louisa 1834-1872 ....DLB-230

The Atlantic Monthly Press...............DLB-46

Attaway, William 1911-1986............DLB-76

Atwood, Margaret 1939- DLB-53

Aubert, Alvin 1930- DLB-41

Aubert de Gaspé, Phillipe-Ignace-François
1814-1841......................DLB-99

Aubert de Gaspé, Phillipe-Joseph
1786-1871......................DLB-99

Aubin, Napoléon 1812-1890 ....DLB-99

Aubin, Penelope
1685-circa 1731..................DLB-39

Preface to *The Life of Charlotta
du Pont* (1723) DLB-39

Aubrey-Fletcher, Henry Lancelot (see Wade, Henry)

Auchincloss, Louis 1917- DLB-2; Y-80

Auden, W. H. 1907-1973...DLB-10, 20; CDBLB-6

Audio Art in America: A Personal Memoir...Y-85

Audubon, John Woodhouse
1812-1862.....................DLB-183

Auerbach, Berthold 1812-1882 ....DLB-133

Auernheimer, Raoul 1876-1948.........DLB-81

Augier, Emile 1820-1889 ....DLB-192

Augustine 354-430...................DLB-115

Responses to Ken Auletta Y-97

Aulus Cellius
circa A.D. 125-circa A.D. 180? DLB-211

Austen, Jane
1775-1817............DLB-116; CDBLB-3

Auster, Paul 1947- DLB-227

Austin, Alfred 1835-1913................DLB-35

Austin, Jane Goodwin 1831-1894 ....DLB-202

Austin, Mary 1868-1934 ..... DLB-9, 78, 206, 221

Austin, William 1778-1841..............DLB-74

Australie (Emily Manning)
1845-1890.....................DLB-230

Author-Printers, 1476–1599............DLB-167

Author Websites Y-97

Authors and Newspapers Association DLB-46

Authors' Publishing Company DLB-49

Avallone, Michael 1924-1999.............Y-99

Avalon Books........................DLB-46

Avancini, Nicolaus 1611-1686 ....DLB-164

Avendaño, Fausto 1941- DLB-82

Averroëó 1126-1198..................DLB-115

Avery, Gillian 1926- DLB-161

Avicenna 980-1037...................DLB-115

Avison, Margaret 1918- DLB-53

Avon Books.........................DLB-46

Avyžius, Jonas 1922-1999 ....DLB-220

Awdry, Wilbert Vere 1911-1997 ....DLB-160

Awoonor, Kofi 1935- DLB-117

Ayckbourn, Alan 1939- DLB-13

Aymé, Marcel 1902-1967...............DLB-72

Cumulative Index

Aytoun, Sir Robert 1570-1638 .... DLB-121
Aytoun, William Edmondstoune 1813-1865 .... DLB-32, 159

B

B. V. (see Thomson, James)
Babbitt, Irving 1865-1933 .... DLB-63
Babbitt, Natalie 1932- DLB-52
Babcock, John [publishing house] DLB-49
Babits, Mihály 1883-1941 ... DLB-215; CDWLB-4
Babrius circa 150-200 .... DLB-176
Baca, Jimmy Santiago 1952- DLB-122
Bache, Benjamin Franklin 1769-1798 ..... DLB-43
Bacheller, Irving 1859-1950 .... DLB-202
Bachmann, Ingeborg 1926-1973 .... DLB-85
Bačinskaitė-Bučienė, Salomėja (see Neris, Salomėja)
Bacon, Delia 1811-1859 .... DLB-1
Bacon, Francis 1561-1626 .... DLB-151, 236; CDBLB-1
Bacon, Sir Nicholas circa 1510-1579 ..... DLB-132
Bacon, Roger circa 1214/1220-1292 ..... DLB-115
Bacon, Thomas circa 1700-1768 .... DLB-31
Bacovia, George 1881-1957 .... DLB-220; CDWLB-4
Badger, Richard G., and Company DLB-49
Bage, Robert 1728-1801 .... DLB-39
Bagehot, Walter 1826-1877 .... DLB-55
Bagley, Desmond 1923-1983 .... DLB-87
Bagley, Sarah G. 1806-1848 .... DLB-239
Bagnold, Enid 1889-1981 ..... DLB-13, 160, 191
Bagryana, Elisaveta 1893-1991 .... DLB-147; CDWLB-4
Bahr, Hermann 1863-1934 .... DLB-81, 118
Bailey, Abigail Abbot 1746-1815 ...... DLB-200
Bailey, Alfred Goldsworthy 1905- DLB-68
Bailey, Francis [publishing house] DLB-49
Bailey, H. C. 1878-1961 .... DLB-77
Bailey, Jacob 1731-1808 .... DLB-99
Bailey, Paul 1937- DLB-14
Bailey, Philip James 1816-1902 .... DLB-32
Baillargeon, Pierre 1916-1967 .... DLB-88
Baillie, Hugh 1890-1966 .... DLB-29
Baillie, Joanna 1762-1851 .... DLB-93
Bailyn, Bernard 1922- DLB-17
Bainbridge, Beryl 1933- DLB-14, 231
Baird, Irene 1901-1981 .... DLB-68
Baker, Augustine 1575-1641 .... DLB-151
Baker, Carlos 1909-1987 .... DLB-103
Baker, David 1954- DLB-120
Baker, Herschel C. 1914-1990 .... DLB-111
Baker, Houston A., Jr. 1943- DLB-67
Baker, Nicholson 1957- DLB-227
Baker, Samuel White 1821-1893 .... DLB-166
Baker, Thomas 1656-1740 .... DLB-213
Baker, Walter H., Company ("Baker's Plays") DLB-49

The Baker and Taylor Company DLB-49
Balaban, John 1943- DLB-120
Bald, Wambly 1902- DLB-4
Balde, Jacob 1604-1668 .... DLB-164
Balderston, John 1889-1954 .... DLB-26
Baldwin, James 1924-1987 ...... DLB-2, 7, 33; Y-87; CDALB-1
Baldwin, Joseph Glover 1815-1864 .... DLB-3, 11
Baldwin, Louisa (Mrs. Alfred Baldwin) 1845-1925 .... DLB-240
Baldwin, Richard and Anne [publishing house] DLB-170
Baldwin, William circa 1515-1563 ...... DLB-132
Bale, John 1495-1563 .... DLB-132
Balestrini, Nanni 1935- DLB-128, 196
Balfour, Sir Andrew 1630-1694 .... DLB-213
Balfour, Arthur James 1848-1930 ..... DLB-190
Balfour, Sir James 1600-1657 .... DLB-213
Ballantine Books DLB-46
Ballantyne, R. M. 1825-1894 .... DLB-163
Ballard, J. G. 1930- DLB-14, 207
Ballard, Martha Moore 1735-1812 ..... DLB-200
Ballerini, Luigi 1940- DLB-128
Ballou, Maturin Murray 1820-1895 .... DLB-79, 189
Ballou, Robert O. [publishing house] DLB-46
Balzac, Honoré de 1799-1855 .... DLB-119
Bambara, Toni Cade 1939- DLB-38, 218; CDALB-7
Bamford, Samuel 1788-1872 .... DLB-190
Bancroft, A. L., and Company DLB-49
Bancroft, George 1800-1891 ..... DLB-1, 30, 59
Bancroft, Hubert Howe 1832-1918 ... DLB-47, 140
Bandelier, Adolph F. 1840-1914 .... DLB-186
Bangs, John Kendrick 1862-1922 ..... DLB-11, 79
Banim, John 1798-1842 .... DLB-116, 158, 159
Banim, Michael 1796-1874 .... DLB-158, 159
Banks, Iain 1954- DLB-194
Banks, John circa 1653-1706 .... DLB-80
Banks, Russell 1940- DLB-130
Bannerman, Helen 1862-1946 .... DLB-141
Bantam Books DLB-46
Banti, Anna 1895-1985 .... DLB-177
Banville, John 1945- DLB-14
Banville, Théodore de 1823-1891 ...... DLB-217
Baraka, Amiri 1934- DLB-5, 7, 16, 38; DS-8; CDALB-1
Barańczak, Stanisław 1946- DLB-232
Baratynsky, Evgenii Abramovich 1800-1844 .... DLB-205
Barbauld, Anna Laetitia 1743-1825 .... DLB-107, 109, 142, 158
Barbeau, Marius 1883-1969 .... DLB-92
Barber, John Warner 1798-1885 .... DLB-30
Bàrberi Squarotti, Giorgio 1929- DLB-128
Barbey d'Aurevilly, Jules-Amédée 1808-1889 .... DLB-119

Barbier, Auguste 1805-1882 .... DLB-217
Barbilian, Dan (see Barbu, Ion)
Barbour, John circa 1316-1395 .... DLB-146
Barbour, Ralph Henry 1870-1944 ...... DLB-22
Barbu, Ion 1895-1961 ...... DLB-220; CDWLB-4
Barbusse, Henri 1873-1935 .... DLB-65
Barclay, Alexander circa 1475-1552 ..... DLB-132
Barclay, E. E., and Company DLB-49
Bardeen, C. W. [publishing house] DLB-49
Barham, Richard Harris 1788-1845 ..... DLB-159
Barich, Bill 1943- DLB-185
Baring, Maurice 1874-1945 .... DLB-34
Baring-Gould, Sabine 1834-1924 .... DLB-156, 190
Barker, A. L. 1918- DLB-14, 139
Barker, Arthur, Limited DLB-112
Barker, George 1913-1991 .... DLB-20
Barker, Harley Granville 1877-1946 ...... DLB-10
Barker, Howard 1946- DLB-13, 233
Barker, James Nelson 1784-1858 .... DLB-37
Barker, Jane 1652-1727 .... DLB-39, 131
Barker, Lady Mary Anne 1831-1911 .... DLB-166
Barker, William circa 1520-after 1576 ... DLB-132
Barkov, Ivan Semenovich 1732-1768 .... DLB-150
Barks, Coleman 1937- DLB-5
Barlach, Ernst 1870-1938 .... DLB-56, 118
Barlow, Joel 1754-1812 .... DLB-37
The Prospect of Peace (1778) DLB-37
Barnard, John 1681-1770 .... DLB-24
Barne, Kitty (Mary Catherine Barne) 1883-1957 .... DLB-160
Barnes, A. S., and Company DLB-49
Barnes, Barnabe 1571-1609 .... DLB-132
Barnes, Djuna 1892-1982 .... DLB-4, 9, 45
Barnes, Jim 1933- DLB-175
Barnes, Julian 1946- DLB-194; Y-93
Barnes, Margaret Ayer 1886-1967 .... DLB-9
Barnes, Peter 1931- DLB-13, 233
Barnes, William 1801-1886 .... DLB-32
Barnes and Noble Books DLB-46
Barnet, Miguel 1940- DLB-145
Barney, Natalie 1876-1972 .... DLB-4
Barnfield, Richard 1574-1627 .... DLB-172
Baron, Richard W., Publishing Company DLB-46
Barr, Amelia Edith Huddleston 1831-1919 .... DLB-202, 221
Barr, Robert 1850-1912 .... DLB-70, 92
Barral, Carlos 1928-1989 .... DLB-134
Barrax, Gerald William 1933- DLB-41, 120
Barrès, Maurice 1862-1923 .... DLB-123
Barrett, Eaton Stannard 1786-1820 ..... DLB-116
Barrie, J. M. 1860-1937 ..... DLB-10, 141, 156; CDBLB-5
Barrie and Jenkins DLB-112
Barrio, Raymond 1921- DLB-82

372

Barrios, Gregg 1945- DLB-122	Beagle, Peter S. 1939- Y-80	Belknap, Jeremy 1744-1798 ....DLB-30, 37
Barry, Philip 1896-1949............ DLB-7, 228	Beal, M. F. 1937- Y-81	Bell, Adrian 1901-1980 ....DLB-191
Barry, Robertine (see Françoise)	Beale, Howard K. 1899-1959............DLB-17	Bell, Clive 1881-1964.................... DS-10
Barse and Hopkins......................DLB-46	Beard, Charles A. 1874-1948 ....DLB-17	Bell, George, and Sons.................DLB-106
Barstow, Stan 1928- DLB-14, 139	A Beat Chronology: The First Twenty-five Years, 1944-1969...................DLB-16	Bell, Gertrude Margaret Lowthian 1868-1926......................DLB-174
Barth, John 1930- DLB-2, 227	Periodicals of the Beat Generation........DLB-16	Bell, James Madison 1826-1902..........DLB-50
Barthelme, Donald 1931-1989 .... DLB-2, 234; Y-80, Y-89	The Beats in New York City DLB-237	Bell, Madison Smartt 1957- DLB-218
Barthelme, Frederick 1943- Y-85	The Beats in the West DLB-237	Bell, Marvin 1937- DLB-5
Bartholomew, Frank 1898-1985.........DLB-127	Beattie, Ann 1947- DLB-218; Y-82	Bell, Millicent 1919- DLB-111
Bartlett, John 1820-1905 ....DLB-1, 235	Beattie, James 1735-1803 ....DLB-109	Bell, Quentin 1910-1996 ....DLB-155
Bartol, Cyrus Augustus 1813-1900 ....DLB-1, 235	Beatty, Chester 1875-1968..............DLB-201	Bell, Robert [publishing house] DLB-49
Barton, Bernard 1784-1849 ....DLB-96	Beauchemin, Nérée 1850-1931 ....DLB-92	Bell, Vanessa 1879-1961 .... DS-10
Barton, John ca. 1610-1675 ....DLB-236	Beauchemin, Yves 1941- DLB-60	Bellamy, Edward 1850-1898 ....DLB-12
Barton, Thomas Pennant 1803-1869.....DLB-140	Beaugrand, Honoré 1848-1906 ....DLB-99	Bellamy, John [publishing house]........DLB-170
Bartram, John 1699-1777 ....DLB-31	Beaulieu, Victor-Lévy 1945- DLB-53	Bellamy, Joseph 1719-1790..............DLB-31
Bartram, William 1739-1823 ....DLB-37	Beaumont, Francis circa 1584-1616 and Fletcher, John 1579-1625 .... DLB-58; CDBLB-1	La Belle Assemblée 1806-1837 ....DLB-110
Basic Books DLB-46	Beaumont, Sir John 1583?-1627.........DLB-121	Bellezza, Dario 1944-1996 ....DLB-128
Basille, Theodore (see Becon, Thomas)	Beaumont, Joseph 1616-1699...........DLB-126	Belloc, Hilaire 1870-1953 .... DLB-19, 100, 141, 174
Bass, Rick 1958- DLB-212	Beauvoir, Simone de 1908-1986 .... DLB-72; Y-86	Belloc, Madame (see Parkes, Bessie Rayner)
Bass, T. J. 1932- Y-81	Becher, Ulrich 1910- DLB-69	Bellonci, Maria 1902-1986..............DLB-196
Bassani, Giorgio 1916- DLB-128, 177	Becker, Carl 1873-1945 ....DLB-17	Bellow, Saul 1915- DLB-2, 28; Y-82; DS-3; CDALB-1
Basse, William circa 1583-1653 ....DLB-121	Becker, Jurek 1937-1997................DLB-75	Belmont Productions...................DLB-46
Bassett, John Spencer 1867-1928 ....DLB-17	Becker, Jurgen 1932- DLB-75	Bels, Alberts 1938- DLB-232
Bassler, Thomas Joseph (see Bass, T. J.)	Beckett, Samuel 1906-1989 ....DLB-13, 15, 233; Y-90; CDBLB-7	Belševica, Vizma 1931- DLB-232; CDWLB-4
Bate, Walter Jackson 1918-1999 ..... DLB-67, 103	Beckford, William 1760-1844 ....DLB-39	Bemelmans, Ludwig 1898-1962..........DLB-22
Bateman, Christopher [publishing house] DLB-170	Beckham, Barry 1944- DLB-33	Bemis, Samuel Flagg 1891-1973 ....DLB-17
Bateman, Stephen circa 1510-1584 ......DLB-136	Becon, Thomas circa 1512-1567 ....DLB-136	Bemrose, William [publishing house] DLB-106
Bates, H. E. 1905-1974...........DLB-162, 191	Becque, Henry 1837-1899 ....DLB-192	Ben no Naishi 1228?-1271? DLB-203
Bates, Katharine Lee 1859-1929 ....DLB-71	Beddoes, Thomas 1760-1808...........DLB-158	Benchley, Robert 1889-1945 ....DLB-11
Batiushkov, Konstantin Nikolaevich 1787-1855......................DLB-205	Beddoes, Thomas Lovell 1803-1849 .....DLB-96	Bencúr, Matej (see Kukučin, Martin)
Batsford, B. T. [publishing house] DLB-106	Bede circa 673-735 ....DLB-146	Benedetti, Mario 1920- DLB-113
Battiscombe, Georgina 1905- DLB-155	Beecher, Catharine Esther 1800-1878 ......DLB-1	Benedictus, David 1938- DLB-14
The Battle of Maldon circa 1000 ....DLB-146	Beecher, Henry Ward 1813-1887 ..... DLB-3, 43	Benedikt, Michael 1935- DLB-5
Baudelaire, Charles 1821-1867 ....DLB-217	Beer, George L. 1872-1920 ....DLB-47	Benediktov, Vladimir Grigor'evich 1807-1873 ....DLB-205
Bauer, Bruno 1809-1882 ....DLB-133	Beer, Johann 1655-1700 ....DLB-168	Benét, Stephen Vincent 1898-1943.................DLB-4, 48, 102
Bauer, Wolfgang 1941- DLB-124	Beer, Patricia 1919-1999 ....DLB-40	Benét, William Rose 1886-1950 ....DLB-45
Baum, L. Frank 1856-1919 ....DLB-22	Beerbohm, Max 1872-1956 .... DLB-34, 100	Benford, Gregory 1941- Y-82
Baum, Vicki 1888-1960.................DLB-85	Beer-Hofmann, Richard 1866-1945 ....DLB-81	Benjamin, Park 1809-1864......... DLB-3, 59, 73
Baumbach, Jonathan 1933- Y-80	Beers, Henry A. 1847-1926 ....DLB-71	Benjamin, S. G. W. 1837-1914 ....DLB-189
Bausch, Richard 1945- DLB-130	Beeton, S. O. [publishing house] DLB-106	Benlowes, Edward 1602-1676 ....DLB-126
Bausch, Robert 1945- DLB-218	Bégon, Elisabeth 1696-1755 ....DLB-99	Benn Brothers Limited DLB-106
Bawden, Nina 1925- DLB-14, 161, 207	Behan, Brendan 1923-1964 ....DLB-13, 233; CDBLB-7	Benn, Gottfried 1886-1956 ....DLB-56
Bax, Clifford 1886-1962 ....DLB-10, 100	Behn, Aphra 1640?-1689 ....DLB-39, 80, 131	Bennett, Arnold 1867-1931 .... DLB-10, 34, 98, 135; CDBLB-5
Baxter, Charles 1947- DLB-130	Behn, Harry 1898-1973 ....DLB-61	Bennett, Charles 1899-1995..............DLB-44
Bayer, Eleanor (see Perry, Eleanor)	Behrman, S. N. 1893-1973............ DLB-7, 44	Bennett, Emerson 1822-1905............DLB-202
Bayer, Konrad 1932-1964 ....DLB-85	Belaney, Archibald Stansfeld (see Grey Owl)	Bennett, Gwendolyn 1902- DLB-51
Baynes, Pauline 1922- DLB-160	Belasco, David 1853-1931 ....DLB-7	Bennett, Hal 1930- DLB-33
Baynton, Barbara 1857-1929 ....DLB-230	Belford, Clarke and Company...........DLB-49	Bennett, James Gordon 1795-1872 ......DLB-43
Bazin, Hervé 1911-1996.................DLB-83	Belinksy, Vissarion Grigor'evich 1811-1848 ....DLB-198	Bennett, James Gordon, Jr. 1841-1918.....DLB-23
Beach, Sylvia 1887-1962...........DLB-4; DS-15	Belitt, Ben 1911- DLB-5	Bennett, John 1865-1956 ....DLB-42
Beacon Press DLB-49		
Beadle and Adams....................DLB-49		Bennett, Louise 1919- DLB-117; CDWLB-3

Benni, Stefano 1947- DLB-196	Bertrand, Louis "Aloysius" 1807-1841 .... DLB-217	*Biographia Brittanica* DLB-142
Benoit, Jacques 1941- DLB-60	Besant, Sir Walter 1836-1901 ...... DLB-135, 190	Biographical Documents I Y-84
Benson, A. C. 1862-1925 .... DLB-98	Bessette, Gerard 1920- DLB-53	Biographical Documents II............... Y-85
Benson, E. F. 1867-1940 .... DLB-135, 153	Bessie, Alvah 1904-1985............... DLB-26	Bioren, John [publishing house] DLB-49
Benson, Jackson J. 1930- DLB-111	Bester, Alfred 1913-1987............... DLB-8	Bioy Casares, Adolfo 1914- DLB-113
Benson, Robert Hugh 1871-1914 .... DLB-153	Besterman, Theodore 1904-1976 ...... DLB-201	Bird, Isabella Lucy 1831-1904 .... DLB-166
Benson, Stella 1892-1933 .... DLB-36, 162	The Bestseller Lists: An Assessment......... Y-84	Bird, Robert Montgomery 1806-1854 ... DLB-202
Bent, James Theodore 1852-1897........DLB-174	Bestuzhev, Aleksandr Aleksandrovich (Marlinsky) 1797-1837 .... DLB-198	Bird, William 1888-1963 .... DLB-4; DS-15
Bent, Mabel Virginia Anna ?-? DLB-174		Birken, Sigmund von 1626-1681 .... DLB-164
Bentham, Jeremy 1748-1832........DLB-107, 158	Bestuzhev, Nikolai Aleksandrovich 1791-1855..................... DLB-198	Birney, Earle 1904- DLB-88
Bentley, E. C. 1875-1956 .... DLB-70	Betham-Edwards, Matilda Barbara (see Edwards, Matilda Barbara Betham-)	Birrell, Augustine 1850-1933 .... DLB-98
Bentley, Phyllis 1894-1977 .... DLB-191		Bisher, Furman 1918- DLB-171
Bentley, Richard [publishing house]..... DLB-106	Betjeman, John 1906-1984 .... DLB-20; Y-84; CDBLB-7	Bishop, Elizabeth 1911-1979............ DLB-5, 169; CDALB-6
Benton, Robert 1932- and Newman, David 1937- DLB-44	Betocchi, Carlo 1899-1986 .... DLB-128	Bishop, John Peale 1892-1944 ...... DLB-4, 9, 45
Benziger Brothers DLB-49	Bettarini, Mariella 1942- DLB-128	Bismarck, Otto von 1815-1898......... DLB-129
Beowulf circa 900-1000 or 790-825 .... DLB-146; CDBLB-1	Betts, Doris 1932- DLB-218; Y-82	Bisset, Robert 1759-1805 .... DLB-142
	Beùkoviù, Matija 1939- DLB-181	Bissett, Bill 1939- DLB-53
Berent, Wacław 1873-1940............ DLB-215	Beveridge, Albert J. 1862-1927 .... DLB-17	Bitzius, Albert (see Gotthelf, Jeremias)
Beresford, Anne 1929- DLB-40	Beverley, Robert circa 1673-1722 ...... DLB-24, 30	Bjørnvig, Thorkild 1918- DLB-214
Beresford, John Davys 1873-1947.............DLB-162, 178, 197	Bevilacqua, Alberto 1934- DLB-196	Black, David (D. M.) 1941- DLB-40
"Experiment in the Novel" (1929) DLB-36	Bevington, Louisa Sarah 1845-1895..... DLB-199	Black, Walter J. [publishing house]....... DLB-46
Beresford-Howe, Constance 1922- DLB-88	Beyle, Marie-Henri (see Stendhal)	Black, Winifred 1863-1936............ DLB-25
Berford, R. G., Company............. DLB-49	Białoszewski, Miron 1922-1983 .... DLB-232	The Black Aesthetic: Background DS-8
Berg, Stephen 1934- DLB-5	Bianco, Margery Williams 1881-1944 ... DLB-160	Black Theaters and Theater Organizations in America, 1961-1982: A Research List DLB-38
Bergengruen, Werner 1892-1964 .... DLB-56	Bibaud, Adèle 1854-1941 .... DLB-92	
Berger, John 1926- DLB-14, 207	Bibaud, Michel 1782-1857 .... DLB-99	Black Theatre: A Forum [excerpts]....... DLB-38
Berger, Meyer 1898-1959................ DLB-29	Bibliographical and Textual Scholarship Since World War II................. Y-89	Blackamore, Arthur 1679-? DLB-24, 39
Berger, Thomas 1924- DLB-2; Y-80		Blackburn, Alexander L. 1929- Y-85
Berkeley, Anthony 1893-1971............ DLB-77	Bichsel, Peter 1935- DLB-75	Blackburn, Paul 1926-1971.........DLB-16; Y-81
Berkeley, George 1685-1753 .... DLB-31, 101	Bickerstaff, Isaac John 1733-circa 1808.... DLB-89	Blackburn, Thomas 1916-1977........... DLB-27
The Berkley Publishing Corporation DLB-46	Biddle, Drexel [publishing house]........ DLB-49	Blackmore, R. D. 1825-1900 .... DLB-18
Berlin, Lucia 1936- DLB-130	Bidermann, Jacob 1577 or 1578-1639 .... DLB-164	Blackmore, Sir Richard 1654-1729 ...... DLB-131
Bernal, Vicente J. 1888-1915 .... DLB-82		Blackmur, R. P. 1904-1965............. DLB-63
Bernanos, Georges 1888-1948 .... DLB-72	Bidwell, Walter Hilliard 1798-1881 .... DLB-79	Blackwell, Basil, Publisher DLB-106
Bernard, Harry 1898-1979 .... DLB-92	Bienek, Horst 1930- DLB-75	Blackwood, Algernon Henry 1869-1951 ....DLB-153, 156, 178
Bernard, John 1756-1828 .... DLB-37	Bierbaum, Otto Julius 1865-1910 .... DLB-66	
Bernard of Chartres circa 1060-1124? ... DLB-115	Bierce, Ambrose 1842-1914? DLB-11, 12, 23, 71, 74, 186; CDALB-3	Blackwood, Caroline 1931-1996 .....DLB-14, 207
Bernard of Clairvaux 1090-1153 .... DLB-208		Blackwood, William, and Sons, Ltd. DLB-154
Bernard Silvestris flourished circa 1130-1160 .... DLB-208	Bigelow, William F. 1879-1966......... DLB-91	*Blackwood's Edinburgh Magazine* 1817-1980 .... DLB-110
	Biggle, Lloyd, Jr. 1923- DLB-8	
Bernari, Carlo 1909-1992...............DLB-177	Bigiaretti, Libero 1905-1993............DLB-177	Blades, William 1824-1890............ DLB-184
Bernhard, Thomas 1931-1989 .... DLB-85, 124; CDWLB-2	Bigland, Eileen 1898-1970............. DLB-195	Blaga, Lucian 1895-1961 .... DLB-220
	Biglow, Hosea (see Lowell, James Russell)	Blagden, Isabella 1817?-1873 .... DLB-199
Bernstein, Charles 1950- DLB-169	Bigongiari, Piero 1914- DLB-128	Blair, Eric Arthur (see Orwell, George)
Berriault, Gina 1926-1999 .... DLB-130	Billinger, Richard 1890-1965 .... DLB-124	Blair, Francis Preston 1791-1876 .... DLB-43
Berrigan, Daniel 1921- DLB-5	Billings, Hammatt 1818-1874 .... DLB-188	Blair, James circa 1655-1743 .... DLB-24
Berrigan, Ted 1934-1983 .... DLB-5, 169	Billings, John Shaw 1898-1975 .... DLB-137	Blair, John Durburrow 1759-1823 .... DLB-37
Berry, Wendell 1934- DLB-5, 6, 234	Billings, Josh (see Shaw, Henry Wheeler)	Blais, Marie-Claire 1939- DLB-53
Berryman, John 1914-1972 .... DLB-48; CDALB-1	Binding, Rudolf G. 1867-1938 .... DLB-66	Blaise, Clark 1940- DLB-53
Bersianik, Louky 1930- DLB-60	Bingham, Caleb 1757-1817 .... DLB-42	Blake, George 1893-1961 .... DLB-191
Berthelet, Thomas [publishing house] DLB-170	Bingham, George Barry 1906-1988 ..... DLB-127	Blake, Lillie Devereux 1833-1913... DLB-202, 221
Berto, Giuseppe 1914-1978.............DLB-177	Bingham, Sallie 1937- DLB-234	Blake, Nicholas 1904-1972 .... DLB-77 (see Day Lewis, C.)
Bertolucci, Attilio 1911- DLB-128	Bingley, William [publishing house]..... DLB-154	
Berton, Pierre 1920- DLB-68	Binyon, Laurence 1869-1943 .... DLB-19	

Blake, William
1757-1827.......DLB-93, 154, 163; CDBLB-3

The Blakiston Company...............DLB-49

Blandiana, Ana 1942-......DLB-232; CDWLB-4

Blanchot, Maurice 1907-.............DLB-72

Blanckenburg, Christian Friedrich von
1744-1796......................DLB-94

Blaser, Robin 1925-................DLB-165

Blaumanis, Rudolfs 1863-1908.........DLB-220

Bledsoe, Albert Taylor 1809-1877......DLB-3, 79

Bleecker, Ann Eliza 1752-1783..........DLB-200

Blelock and Company.................DLB-49

Blennerhassett, Margaret Agnew
1773-1842......................DLB-99

Bles, Geoffrey [publishing house]........DLB-112

Blessington, Marguerite, Countess of
1789-1849.....................DLB-166

The Blickling Homilies circa 971........DLB-146

Blind, Mathilde 1841-1896............DLB-199

Blish, James 1921-1975.................DLB-8

Bliss, E., and E. White
[publishing house].................DLB-49

Bliven, Bruce 1889-1977..............DLB-137

Blixen, Karen 1885-1962..............DLB-214

Bloch, Robert 1917-1994..............DLB-44

Block, Lawrence 1938-...............DLB-226

Block, Rudolph (see Lessing, Bruno)

Blondal, Patricia 1926-1959.............DLB-88

Bloom, Harold 1930-.................DLB-67

Bloomer, Amelia 1818-1894............DLB-79

Bloomfield, Robert 1766-1823..........DLB-93

Bloomsbury Group....................DS-10

Blotner, Joseph 1923-................DLB-111

Blount, Thomas 1618?-1679...........DLB-236

Bloy, Léon 1846-1917................DLB-123

Blume, Judy 1938-...................DLB-52

Blunck, Hans Friedrich 1888-1961.......DLB-66

Blunden, Edmund 1896-1974...DLB-20, 100, 155

Blundeville, Thomas 1522?-1606.......DLB-236

Blunt, Lady Anne Isabella Noel
1837-1917.....................DLB-174

Blunt, Wilfrid Scawen 1840-1922....DLB-19, 174

Bly, Nellie (see Cochrane, Elizabeth)

Bly, Robert 1926-....................DLB-5

Blyton, Enid 1897-1968...............DLB-160

Boaden, James 1762-1839..............DLB-89

Boas, Frederick S. 1862-1957..........DLB-149

The Bobbs-Merrill Archive at the
Lilly Library, Indiana University........Y-90

Boborykin, Petr Dmitrievich 1836-1921..DLB-238

The Bobbs-Merrill Company...........DLB-46

Bobrov, Semen Sergeevich
1763?-1810.....................DLB-150

Bobrowski, Johannes 1917-1965........DLB-75

The Elmer Holmes Bobst Awards in Arts
and Letters......................Y-87

Bodenheim, Maxwell 1892-1954.......DLB-9, 45

Bodenstedt, Friedrich von 1819-1892....DLB-129

Bodini, Vittorio 1914-1970.............DLB-128

Bodkin, M. McDonnell 1850-1933.......DLB-70

Bodley, Sir Thomas 1545-1613.........DLB-213

Bodley Head........................DLB-112

Bodmer, Johann Jakob 1698-1783.......DLB-97

Bodmershof, Imma von 1895-1982......DLB-85

Bodsworth, Fred 1918-................DLB-68

Boehm, Sydney 1908-.................DLB-44

Boer, Charles 1939-....................DLB-5

Boethius circa 480-circa 524............DLB-115

Boethius of Dacia circa 1240-?..........DLB-115

Bogan, Louise 1897-1970............DLB-45, 169

Bogarde, Dirk 1921-..................DLB-14

Bogdanovich, Ippolit Fedorovich
circa 1743-1803.................DLB-150

Bogue, David [publishing house].........DLB-106

Böhme, Jakob 1575-1624..............DLB-164

Bohn, H. G. [publishing house].........DLB-106

Bohse, August 1661-1742..............DLB-168

Boie, Heinrich Christian 1744-1806......DLB-94

Bok, Edward W. 1863-1930.......DLB-91; DS-16

Boland, Eavan 1944-..................DLB-40

Boldrewood, Rolf
(Thomas Alexander Browne)
1826?-1915.....................DLB-230

Bolingbroke, Henry St. John, Viscount
1678-1751.....................DLB-101

Böll, Heinrich
1917-1985........DLB-69; Y-85; CDWLB-2

Bolling, Robert 1738-1775..............DLB-31

Bolotov, Andrei Timofeevich
1738-1833.....................DLB-150

Bolt, Carol 1941-.....................DLB-60

Bolt, Robert 1924-1995............DLB-13, 233

Bolton, Herbert E. 1870-1953...........DLB-17

Bonaventura........................DLB-90

Bonaventure circa 1217-1274..........DLB-115

Bonaviri, Giuseppe 1924-.............DLB-177

Bond, Edward 1934-..................DLB-13

Bond, Michael 1926-.................DLB-161

Boni, Albert and Charles
[publishing house].................DLB-46

Boni and Liveright....................DLB-46

Bonner, Marita 1899-1971.............DLB-228

Bonner, Paul Hyde 1893-1968.......... DS-17

Bonner, Sherwood (see McDowell, Katharine
Sherwood Bonner)

Robert Bonner's Sons.................DLB-49

Bonnin, Gertrude Simmons (see Zitkala-Ša)

Bonsanti, Alessandro 1904-1984........DLB-177

Bontemps, Arna 1902-1973..........DLB-48, 51

The Book Arts Press at the University
of Virginia......................Y-96

The Book League of America...........DLB-46

Book Publishing Accounting: Some Basic
Concepts........................Y-98

Book Reviewing in America: I..............Y-87

Book Reviewing in America: II............. Y-88

Book Reviewing in America: III............Y-89

Book Reviewing in America: IV............Y-90

Book Reviewing in America: V.............Y-91

Book Reviewing in America: VI............Y-92

Book Reviewing in America: VII............Y-93

Book Reviewing in America: VIII...........Y-94

Book Reviewing in America and the
Literary Scene....................Y-95

Book Reviewing and the
Literary Scene................Y-96, Y-97

Book Supply Company...............DLB-49

The Book Trade History Group...........Y-93

The Booker Prize......................Y-96

Address by Anthony Thwaite,
Chairman of the Booker Prize Judges
Comments from Former Booker
Prize Winners....................Y-86

Boorde, Andrew circa 1490-1549.......DLB-136

Boorstin, Daniel J. 1914-..............DLB-17

Booth, Franklin 1874-1948............DLB-188

Booth, Mary L. 1831-1889.............DLB-79

Booth, Philip 1925-....................Y-82

Booth, Wayne C. 1921-...............DLB-67

Booth, William 1829-1912.............DLB-190

Borchardt, Rudolf 1877-1945...........DLB-66

Borchert, Wolfgang 1921-1947......DLB-69, 124

Borel, Pétrus 1809-1859...............DLB-119

Borges, Jorge Luis
1899-1986........DLB-113; Y-86; CDWLB-3

Börne, Ludwig 1786-1837..............DLB-90

Bornstein, Miriam 1950-..............DLB-209

Borowski, Tadeusz
1922-1951............DLB-215; CDWLB-4

Borrow, George 1803-1881......DLB-21, 55, 166

Bosch, Juan 1909-...................DLB-145

Bosco, Henri 1888-1976...............DLB-72

Bosco, Monique 1927-................DLB-53

Bosman, Herman Charles 1905-1951....DLB-225

Boston, Lucy M. 1892-1990...........DLB-161

Boswell, James
1740-1795.........DLB-104, 142; CDBLB-2

Boswell, Robert 1953-................DLB-234

Bote, Hermann
circa 1460-circa 1520...............DLB-179

Botev, Khristo 1847-1876..............DLB-147

Botta, Anne C. Lynch 1815-1891.........DLB-3

Botto, Ján (see Krasko, Ivan)

Bottome, Phyllis 1882-1963............DLB-197

Bottomley, Gordon 1874-1948...........DLB-10

Bottoms, David 1949-............DLB-120; Y-83

Bottrall, Ronald 1906-................DLB-20

Bouchardy, Joseph 1810-1870..........DLB-192

Boucher, Anthony 1911-1968............DLB-8

Boucher, Jonathan 1738-1804...........DLB-31

Boucher de Boucherville, George 1814-1894. . . . . DLB-99

Boudreau, Daniel (see Coste, Donat)

Bourassa, Napoléon 1827-1916. . . . . DLB-99

Bourget, Paul 1852-1935 . . . . DLB-123

Bourinot, John George 1837-1902. . . . . . . DLB-99

Bourjaily, Vance 1922- DLB-2, 143

Bourne, Edward Gaylord 1860-1908 . . . . DLB-47

Bourne, Randolph 1886-1918. . . . . DLB-63

Bousoño, Carlos 1923- DLB-108

Bousquet, Joë 1897-1950. . . . . DLB-72

Bova, Ben 1932- Y-81

Bovard, Oliver K. 1872-1945 . . . . DLB-25

Bove, Emmanuel 1898-1945. . . . . DLB-72

Bowen, Elizabeth 1899-1973. . . . . DLB-15, 162; CDBLB-7

Bowen, Francis 1811-1890 . . . . . . DLB-1, 59, 235

Bowen, John 1924- DLB-13

Bowen, Marjorie 1886-1952 . . . . DLB-153

Bowen-Merrill Company DLB-49

Bowering, George 1935- DLB-53

Bowers, Bathsheba 1671-1718. . . . . DLB-200

Bowers, Claude G. 1878-1958 . . . . DLB-17

Bowers, Edgar 1924- DLB-5

Bowers, Fredson Thayer 1905-1991 . . . . DLB-140; Y-91

Bowles, Paul 1910-1999 . . . . . DLB-5, 6, 218; Y-99

Bowles, Samuel III 1826-1878 . . . . DLB-43

Bowles, William Lisles 1762-1850 . . . . . . DLB-93

Bowman, Louise Morey 1882-1944 . . . . . DLB-68

Boyd, James 1888-1944 . . . . DLB-9; DS-16

Boyd, John 1919- DLB-8

Boyd, Thomas 1898-1935 . . . . DLB-9; DS-16

Boyd, William 1952- DLB-231

Boyesen, Hjalmar Hjorth 1848-1895 . . . . DLB-12, 71; DS-13

Boyle, Kay 1902-1992 . . . . . DLB-4, 9, 48, 86; Y-93

Boyle, Roger, Earl of Orrery 1621-1679. . . DLB-80

Boyle, T. Coraghessan 1948- DLB-218; Y-86

Božić, Mirko 1919- DLB-181

Brackenbury, Alison 1953- DLB-40

Brackenridge, Hugh Henry 1748-1816. . . . . DLB-11, 37

Brackett, Charles 1892-1969. . . . . DLB-26

Brackett, Leigh 1915-1978 . . . . DLB-8, 26

Bradburn, John [publishing house] DLB-49

Bradbury, Malcolm 1932-2000. . . . . . DLB-14, 207

Bradbury, Ray 1920- DLB-2, 8; CDALB-6

Bradbury and Evans. DLB-106

Braddon, Mary Elizabeth 1835-1915. . . . . .DLB-18, 70, 156

Bradford, Andrew 1686-1742 . . . . . . DLB-43, 73

Bradford, Gamaliel 1863-1932 . . . . DLB-17

Bradford, John 1749-1830. . . . . DLB-43

Bradford, Roark 1896-1948 . . . . DLB-86

Bradford, William 1590-1657. . . . . . . DLB-24, 30

Bradford, William III 1719-1791 . . . . . DLB-43, 73

Bradlaugh, Charles 1833-1891 . . . . DLB-57

Bradley, David 1950- DLB-33

Bradley, Ira, and Company DLB-49

Bradley, J. W., and Company DLB-49

Bradley, Katherine Harris (see Field, Michael)

Bradley, Marion Zimmer 1930-1999 . . . . . . DLB-8

Bradley, William Aspenwall 1878-1939 . . . . DLB-4

Bradshaw, Henry 1831-1886 . . . . DLB-184

Bradstreet, Anne 1612 or 1613-1672 . . . . . . DLB-24; CDABL-2

Bradūnas, Kazys 1917- DLB-220

Bradwardine, Thomas circa 1295-1349 . . . . DLB-115

Brady, Frank 1924-1986. . . . . DLB-111

Brady, Frederic A. [publishing house] DLB-49

Bragg, Melvyn 1939- DLB-14

Brainard, Charles H. [publishing house] . . DLB-49

Braine, John 1922-1986 . DLB-15; Y-86; CDBLB-7

Braithwait, Richard 1588-1673 . . . . DLB-151

Braithwaite, William Stanley 1878-1962. . . . . DLB-50, 54

Braker, Ulrich 1735-1798 . . . . DLB-94

Bramah, Ernest 1868-1942 . . . . DLB-70

Branagan, Thomas 1774-1843 . . . . DLB-37

Branch, William Blackwell 1927- DLB-76

Branden Press. DLB-46

Branner, H.C. 1903-1966. . . . . DLB-214

Brant, Sebastian 1457-1521. . . . . .DLB-179

Brassey, Lady Annie (Allnutt) 1839-1887. . . . . DLB-166

Brathwaite, Edward Kamau 1930- DLB-125; CDWLB-3

Brault, Jacques 1933- DLB-53

Braun, Matt 1932- DLB-212

Braun, Volker 1939- DLB-75

Brautigan, Richard 1935-1984 . . . . DLB-2, 5, 206; Y-80, Y-84

Braxton, Joanne M. 1950- DLB-41

Bray, Anne Eliza 1790-1883 . . . . DLB-116

Bray, Thomas 1656-1730 . . . . DLB-24

Brazdžionis, Bernardas 1907- DLB-220

Braziller, George [publishing house] DLB-46

The Bread Loaf Writers' Conference 1983 . . . Y-84

Breasted, James Henry 1865-1935 . . . . . . DLB-47

Brecht, Bertolt 1898-1956 . . . . .DLB-56, 124; CDWLB-2

Bredel, Willi 1901-1964 . . . . DLB-56

Bregendahl, Marie 1867-1940. . . . . DLB-214

Breitinger, Johann Jakob 1701-1776 . . . . . DLB-97

Bremser, Bonnie 1939- DLB-16

Bremser, Ray 1934- DLB-16

Brennan, Christopher 1870-1932 . . . . DLB-230

Brentano, Bernard von 1901-1964 . . . . . . DLB-56

Brentano, Clemens 1778-1842 . . . . DLB-90

Brentano's. DLB-49

Brenton, Howard 1942- DLB-13

Breslin, Jimmy 1929-1996 . . . . DLB-185

Breton, André 1896-1966. . . . . DLB-65

Breton, Nicholas circa 1555-circa 1626. . . DLB-136

The Breton Lays 1300-early fifteenth century DLB-146

Brewer, Luther A. 1858-1933. . . . . .DLB-187

Brewer, Warren and Putnam DLB-46

Brewster, Elizabeth 1922- DLB-60

Breytenbach, Breyten 1939- DLB-225

Bridge, Ann (Lady Mary Dolling Sanders O'Malley) 1889-1974 . . . . DLB-191

Bridge, Horatio 1806-1893. . . . . DLB-183

Bridgers, Sue Ellen 1942- DLB-52

Bridges, Robert 1844-1930 . . . . DLB-19, 98; CDBLB-5

The Bridgewater Library DLB-213

Bridie, James 1888-1951 . . . . DLB-10

Brieux, Eugene 1858-1932 . . . . DLB-192

Brigadere, Anna 1861-1933 . . . . DLB-220

Bright, Mary Chavelita Dunne (see Egerton, George)

Brimmer, B. J., Company. DLB-46

Brines, Francisco 1932- DLB-134

Brink, André 1935- DLB-225

Brinley, George, Jr. 1817-1875 . . . . DLB-140

Brinnin, John Malcolm 1916-1998 . . . . . . DLB-48

Brisbane, Albert 1809-1890 . . . . DLB-3

Brisbane, Arthur 1864-1936. . . . . DLB-25

British Academy. DLB-112

The British Critic 1793-1843 . . . . DLB-110

The British Library and the Regular Readers' Group Y-91

British Literary Prizes. Y-98

The British Review and London Critical Journal 1811-1825 . . . . DLB-110

British Travel Writing, 1940-1997 . . . DLB-204

Brito, Aristeo 1942- DLB-122

Brittain, Vera 1893-1970. . . . . DLB-191

Brizeux, Auguste 1803-1858. . . . . .DLB-217

Broadway Publishing Company. DLB-46

Broch, Hermann 1886-1951 . . . . .DLB-85, 124; CDWLB-2

Brochu, André 1942- DLB-53

Brock, Edwin 1927- DLB-40

Brockes, Barthold Heinrich 1680-1747 . . . DLB-168

Brod, Max 1884-1968. . . . . DLB-81

Brodber, Erna 1940- DLB-157

Brodhead, John R. 1814-1873 . . . . DLB-30

Brodkey, Harold 1930-1996 . . . . DLB-130

Brodsky, Joseph 1940-1996 . . . . Y-87

Broeg, Bob 1918- DLB-171

Brøgger, Suzanne 1944- DLB-214

Brome, Richard circa 1590-1652 . . . . DLB-58

Brome, Vincent 1910- DLB-155

Bromfield, Louis 1896-1956 . . . . DLB-4, 9, 86

DLB 240   Cumulative Index

Bromige, David 1933- DLB-193
Broner, E. M. 1930- DLB-28
Bronk, William 1918-1999............DLB-165
Bronnen, Arnolt 1895-1959...........DLB-124
Brontë, Anne 1820-1849 ....DLB-21, 199
Brontë, Charlotte 1816-1855 ......DLB-21, 159, 199; CDBLB-4
Brontë, Emily 1818-1848 ......DLB-21, 32, 199; CDBLB-4
Brook, Stephen 1947- DLB-204
Brook Farm 1841-1847 ....DLB-223
Brooke, Frances 1724-1789..........DLB-39, 99
Brooke, Henry 1703?-1783..............DLB-39
Brooke, L. Leslie 1862-1940 ....DLB-141
Brooke, Margaret, Ranee of Sarawak 1849-1936......................DLB-174
Brooke, Rupert 1887-1915 ....DLB-19, 216; CDBLB-6
Brooker, Bertram 1888-1955...........DLB-88
Brooke-Rose, Christine 1923- DLB-14, 231
Brookner, Anita 1928- DLB-194; Y-87
Brooks, Charles Timothy 1813-1883.......DLB-1
Brooks, Cleanth 1906-1994 ....DLB-63; Y-94
Brooks, Gwendolyn 1917-2000 ....DLB-5, 76, 165; CDALB-1
Brooks, Jeremy 1926- DLB-14
Brooks, Mel 1926- DLB-26
Brooks, Noah 1830-1903.........DLB-42; DS-13
Brooks, Richard 1912-1992 ....DLB-44
Brooks, Van Wyck 1886-1963.................DLB-45, 63, 103
Brophy, Brigid 1929-1995 ....DLB-14
Brophy, John 1899-1965 ....DLB-191
Brossard, Chandler 1922-1993 ....DLB-16
Brossard, Nicole 1943- DLB-53
Broster, Dorothy Kathleen 1877-1950 ....DLB-160
Brother Antoninus (see Everson, William)
Brotherton, Lord 1856-1930 ....DLB-184
Brougham and Vaux, Henry Peter Brougham, Baron 1778-1868 ....DLB-110, 158
Brougham, John 1810-1880 ....DLB-11
Broughton, James 1913-1999.............DLB-5
Broughton, Rhoda 1840-1920 ....DLB-18
Broun, Heywood 1888-1939 ....DLB-29, 171
Brown, Alice 1856-1948..............DLB-78
Brown, Bob 1886-1959 ....DLB-4, 45
Brown, Cecil 1943- DLB-33
Brown, Charles Brockden 1771-1810 .... DLB-37, 59, 73; CDALB-2
Brown, Christy 1932-1981.............DLB-14
Brown, Dee 1908- Y-80
Brown, Frank London 1927-1962 ....DLB-76
Brown, Fredric 1906-1972 ....DLB-8
Brown, George Mackay 1921-1996 .... DLB-14, 27, 139
Brown, Harry 1917-1986 ....DLB-26
Brown, Larry 1951- DLB-234

Brown, Marcia 1918- DLB-61
Brown, Margaret Wise 1910-1952........DLB-22
Brown, Morna Doris (see Ferrars, Elizabeth)
Brown, Oliver Madox 1855-1874 ....DLB-21
Brown, Sterling 1901-1989 ....DLB-48, 51, 63
Brown, T. E. 1830-1897 ....DLB-35
Brown, Thomas Alexander (see Boldrewood, Rolf)
Brown, William Hill 1765-1793 ....DLB-37
Brown, William Wells 1814-1884 ....DLB-3, 50, 183
Browne, Charles Farrar 1834-1867 ....DLB-11
Browne, Frances 1816-1879 ....DLB-199
Browne, Francis Fisher 1843-1913........DLB-79
Browne, Howard 1908-1999 ....DLB-226
Browne, J. Ross 1821-1875 ....DLB-202
Browne, Michael Dennis 1940- DLB-40
Browne, Sir Thomas 1605-1682 ....DLB-151
Browne, William, of Tavistock 1590-1645 ....DLB-121
Browne, Wynyard 1911-1964 ....DLB-13, 233
Browne and Nolan...................DLB-106
Brownell, W. C. 1851-1928.............DLB-71
Browning, Elizabeth Barrett 1806-1861 ....DLB-32, 199; CDBLB-4
Browning, Robert 1812-1889 ....DLB-32, 163; CDBLB-4
Introductory Essay: *Letters of Percy Bysshe Shelley* (1852) DLB-32
Brownjohn, Allan 1931- DLB-40
Brownson, Orestes Augustus 1803-1876 ....DLB-1, 59, 73
Bruccoli, Matthew J. 1931- DLB-103
Bruce, Charles 1906-1971 ....DLB-68
John Edward Bruce: Three Documents....DLB-50
Bruce, Leo 1903-1979 ....DLB-77
Bruce, Mary Grant 1878-1958 ....DLB-230
Bruce, Philip Alexander 1856-1933 ....DLB-47
Bruce Humphries [publishing house] DLB-46
Bruce-Novoa, Juan 1944- DLB-82
Bruckman, Clyde 1894-1955 ....DLB-26
Bruckner, Ferdinand 1891-1958 ....DLB-118
Brundage, John Herbert (see Herbert, John)
Brutus, Dennis 1924- DLB-117, 225; CDWLB-3
Bryan, C. D. B. 1936- DLB-185
Bryant, Arthur 1899-1985 ....DLB-149
Bryant, William Cullen 1794-1878 ..... DLB-3, 43, 59, 189; CDALB-2
Bryce Echenique, Alfredo 1939- DLB-145; CDWLB-3
Bryce, James 1838-1922............DLB-166, 190
Bryden, Bill 1942- DLB-233
Brydges, Sir Samuel Egerton 1762-1837 ..DLB-107
Bryskett, Lodowick 1546?-1612 ....DLB-167
Buchan, John 1875-1940 .... DLB-34, 70, 156
Buchanan, George 1506-1582 ....DLB-132
Buchanan, Robert 1841-1901 ....DLB-18, 35

"The Fleshly School of Poetry and Other Phenomena of the Day" (1872), by Robert Buchanan DLB-35
"The Fleshly School of Poetry: Mr. D. G. Rossetti" (1871), by Thomas Maitland (Robert Buchanan) DLB-35
Buchman, Sidney 1902-1975 ....DLB-26
Buchner, Augustus 1591-1661..........DLB-164
Büchner, Georg 1813-1837 .. DLB-133; CDWLB-2
Bucholtz, Andreas Heinrich 1607-1671 ...DLB-168
Buck, Pearl S. 1892-1973...DLB-9, 102; CDALB-7
Bucke, Charles 1781-1846 ....DLB-110
Bucke, Richard Maurice 1837-1902........DLB-99
Buckingham, Joseph Tinker 1779-1861 and Buckingham, Edwin 1810-1833 ....DLB-73
Buckler, Ernest 1908-1984.............DLB-68
Buckley, William F., Jr. 1925- DLB-137; Y-80
Buckminster, Joseph Stevens 1784-1812 ....DLB-37
Buckner, Robert 1906- DLB-26
Budd, Thomas ?-1698 ....DLB-24
Budrys, A. J. 1931- DLB-8
Buechner, Frederick 1926- Y-80
Buell, John 1927- DLB-53
Bufalino, Gesualdo 1920-1996..........DLB-196
Buffum, Job [publishing house] DLB-49
Bugnet, Georges 1879-1981 ....DLB-92
Buies, Arthur 1840-1901 ....DLB-99
Building the New British Library at St Pancras Y-94
Bukowski, Charles 1920-1994....DLB-5, 130, 169
Bulatović, Miodrag 1930-1991 ....DLB-181; CDWLB-4
Bulgarin, Faddei Venediktovich 1789-1859 ....DLB-198
Bulger, Bozeman 1877-1932............DLB-171
Bullein, William between 1520 and 1530-1576 ....DLB-167
Bullins, Ed 1935- DLB-7, 38
Bulwer, John 1606-1656 ....DLB-236
Bulwer-Lytton, Edward (also Edward Bulwer) 1803-1873 ....DLB-21
"On Art in Fiction "(1838)...............DLB-21
Bumpus, Jerry 1937- Y-81
Bunce and Brother...................DLB-49
Bunner, H. C. 1855-1896 ....DLB-78, 79
Bunting, Basil 1900-1985..............DLB-20
Buntline, Ned (Edward Zane Carroll Judson) 1821-1886......................DLB-186
Bunyan, John 1628-1688......DLB-39; CDBLB-2
Burch, Robert 1925- DLB-52
Burciaga, José Antonio 1940- DLB-82
Bürger, Gottfried August 1747-1794.......DLB-94
Burgess, Anthony 1917-1993 ....DLB-14, 194; CDBLB-8
The Anthony Burgess Archive at the Harry Ransom Humanities Research Center Y-98

Cumulative Index

Anthony Burgess's 99 Novels:
An Opinion Poll....................Y-84
Burgess, Gelett 1866-1951 .... DLB-11
Burgess, John W. 1844-1931 .... DLB-47
Burgess, Thornton W. 1874-1965 .... DLB-22
Burgess, Stringer and Company......... DLB-49
Burick, Si 1909-1986................. DLB-171
Burk, John Daly circa 1772-1808 .... DLB-37
Burk, Ronnie 1955- DLB-209
Burke, Edmund 1729?-1797 .... DLB-104
Burke, James Lee 1936- DLB-226
Burke, Kenneth 1897-1993 .... DLB-45, 63
Burke, Thomas 1886-1945 .... DLB-197
Burlingame, Edward Livermore
1848-1922 .... DLB-79
Burnet, Gilbert 1643-1715............. DLB-101
Burnett, Frances Hodgson
1849-1924 .... DLB-42, 141; DS-13, 14
Burnett, W. R. 1899-1982 .... DLB-9, 226
Burnett, Whit 1899-1973 and
Martha Foley 1897-1977 .... DLB-137
Burney, Fanny 1752-1840............. DLB-39
Dedication, *The Wanderer* (1814)......... DLB-39
Preface to *Evelina* (1778) DLB-39
Burns, Alan 1929- DLB-14, 194
Burns, John Horne 1916-1953 .... Y-85
Burns, Robert 1759-1796...... DLB-109; CDBLB-3
Burns and Oates..................... DLB-106
Burnshaw, Stanley 1906- DLB-48
Burr, C. Chauncey 1815?-1883 .... DLB-79
Burr, Esther Edwards 1732-1758 .... DLB-200
Burroughs, Edgar Rice 1875-1950 .... DLB-8
Burroughs, John 1837-1921 .... DLB-64
Burroughs, Margaret T. G. 1917- DLB-41
Burroughs, William S., Jr. 1947-1981 ..... DLB-16
Burroughs, William Seward 1914-1997
.... DLB-2, 8, 16, 152, 237; Y-81, Y-97
Burroway, Janet 1936- DLB-6
Burt, Maxwell Struthers
1882-1954 .... DLB-86; DS-16
Burt, A. L., and Company DLB-49
Burton, Hester 1913- DLB-161
Burton, Isabel Arundell 1831-1896...... DLB-166
Burton, Miles (see Rhode, John)
Burton, Richard Francis
1821-1890 .... DLB-55, 166, 184
Burton, Robert 1577-1640 .... DLB-151
Burton, Virginia Lee 1909-1968......... DLB-22
Burton, William Evans 1804-1860 ...... DLB-73
Burwell, Adam Hood 1790-1849 .... DLB-99
Bury, Lady Charlotte 1775-1861 .... DLB-116
Busch, Frederick 1941- DLB-6, 218
Busch, Niven 1903-1991............... DLB-44
Bushnell, Horace 1802-1876 ....DS-13
Bussieres, Arthur de 1877-1913......... DLB-92
Butler, Charles ca. 1560-1647 .... DLB-236

Butler, Guy 1918- DLB-225
Butler, E. H., and Company............ DLB-49
Butler, Josephine Elizabeth 1828-1906 ... DLB-190
Butler, Juan 1942-1981................. DLB-53
Butler, Octavia E. 1947- DLB-33
Butler, Pierce 1884-1953............. DLB-187
Butler, Robert Olen 1945- DLB-173
Butler, Samuel 1613-1680.......... DLB-101, 126
Butler, Samuel 1835-1902......... DLB-18, 57, 174
Butler, William Francis 1838-1910 ...... DLB-166
Butor, Michel 1926- DLB-83
Butter, Nathaniel [publishing house].....DLB-170
Butterworth, Hezekiah 1839-1905 .... DLB-42
Buttitta, Ignazio 1899- DLB-114
Butts, Mary 1890-1937............... DLB-240
Buzzati, Dino 1906-1972...............DLB-177
Byars, Betsy 1928- DLB-52
Byatt, A. S. 1936- DLB-14, 194
Byles, Mather 1707-1788 .... DLB-24
Bynneman, Henry
[publishing house] DLB-170
Bynner, Witter 1881-1968 .... DLB-54
Byrd, William circa 1543-1623.........DLB-172
Byrd, William II 1674-1744 .... DLB-24, 140
Byrne, John Keyes (see Leonard, Hugh)
Byron, George Gordon, Lord
1788-1824.......... DLB-96, 110; CDBLB-3
Byron, Robert 1905-1941 .... DLB-195

C

Caballero Bonald, José Manuel
1926- DLB-108
Cabañero, Eladio 1930- DLB-134
Cabell, James Branch 1879-1958....... DLB-9, 78
Cabeza de Baca, Manuel 1853-1915..... DLB-122
Cabeza de Baca Gilbert, Fabiola
1898- DLB-122
Cable, George Washington
1844-1925 ....DLB-12, 74; DS-13
Cable, Mildred 1878-1952 .... DLB-195
Cabrera, Lydia 1900-1991 .... DLB-145
Cabrera Infante, Guillermo
1929- DLB-113; CDWLB-3
Cadell [publishing house] DLB-154
Cady, Edwin H. 1917- DLB-103
Caedmon flourished 658-680.......... DLB-146
Caedmon School circa 660-899 .... DLB-146
Cafés, Brasseries, and Bistros DS-15
Cage, John 1912-1992 .... DLB-193
Cahan, Abraham 1860-1951....... DLB-9, 25, 28
Cain, George 1943- DLB-33
Cain, James M. 1892-1977 .... DLB-226
Caird, Mona 1854-1932............... DLB-197
Čaks, Aleksandrs
1901-1950 .... DLB-220; CDWLB-4
Caldecott, Randolph 1846-1886........ DLB-163

Calder, John (Publishers), Limited DLB-112
Calderón de la Barca, Fanny
1804-1882 .... DLB-183
Caldwell, Ben 1937- DLB-38
Caldwell, Erskine 1903-1987 .... DLB-9, 86
Caldwell, H. M., Company DLB-49
Caldwell, Taylor 1900-1985.............DS-17
Calhoun, John C. 1782-1850 .... DLB-3
Călinescu, George 1899-1965 .... DLB-220
Calisher, Hortense 1911- DLB-2, 218
A Call to Letters and an Invitation
to the Electric Chair,
by Siegfried Mandel............... DLB-75
Callaghan, Mary Rose 1944- DLB-207
Callaghan, Morley 1903-1990 .... DLB-68
Callahan, S. Alice 1868-1894 ....DLB-175,221
Callaloo Y-87
Callimachus circa 305 B.C.-240 B.C......DLB-176
Calmer, Edgar 1907- DLB-4
Calverley, C. S. 1831-1884............. DLB-35
Calvert, George Henry 1803-1889..... DLB-1, 64
Calvino, Italo 1923-1985 .... DLB-196
Cambridge, Ada 1844-1926 .... DLB-230
Cambridge Press DLB-49
Cambridge Songs (Carmina Cantabrigensia)
circa 1050...................... DLB-148
Cambridge University Press...........DLB-170
Camden, William 1551-1623 ....DLB-172
Camden House: An Interview with
James Hardin...................... Y-92
Cameron, Eleanor 1912- DLB-52
Cameron, George Frederick
1854-1885 .... DLB-99
Cameron, Lucy Lyttelton 1781-1858 .... DLB-163
Cameron, Peter 1959- DLB-234
Cameron, William Bleasdell 1862-1951... DLB-99
Camm, John 1718-1778................ DLB-31
Camon, Ferdinando 1935- DLB-196
Campana, Dino 1885-1932 .... DLB-114
Campbell, Bebe Moore 1950- DLB-227
Campbell, Gabrielle Margaret Vere
(see Shearing, Joseph, and Bowen, Marjorie)
Campbell, James Dykes 1838-1895 ..... DLB-144
Campbell, James Edwin 1867-1896 ..... DLB-50
Campbell, John 1653-1728 .... DLB-43
Campbell, John W., Jr. 1910-1971 .... DLB-8
Campbell, Roy 1901-1957 .... DLB-20, 225
Campbell, Thomas 1777-1844 ...... DLB-93, 144
Campbell, William Wilfred 1858-1918 ... DLB-92
Campion, Edmund 1539-1581 .... DLB-167
Campion, Thomas
1567-1620.......... DLB-58, 172; CDBLB-1
Camus, Albert 1913-1960............. DLB-72
The Canadian Publishers' Records
Database Y-96
Canby, Henry Seidel 1878-1961........ DLB-91
Candelaria, Cordelia 1943- DLB-82

Candelaria, Nash 1928- DLB-82
Canetti, Elias
    1905-1994 ....DLB-85, 124; CDWLB-2
Canham, Erwin Dain 1904-1982........DLB-127
Canitz, Friedrich Rudolph Ludwig von
    1654-1699 ....DLB-168
Cankar, Ivan 1876-1918..... DLB-147; CDWLB-4
Cannan, Gilbert 1884-1955 .... DLB-10, 197
Cannan, Joanna 1896-1961 ....DLB-191
Cannell, Kathleen 1891-1974.............DLB-4
Cannell, Skipwith 1887-1957 ....DLB-45
Canning, George 1770-1827...........DLB-158
Cannon, Jimmy 1910-1973 ....DLB-171
Cano, Daniel 1947- DLB-209
Cantú, Norma Elia 1947- DLB-209
Cantwell, Robert 1908-1978 ....DLB-9
Cape, Jonathan, and Harrison Smith
    [publishing house] DLB-46
Cape, Jonathan, Limited DLB-112
Čapek, Karel 1890-1938 ....DLB-215; CDWLB-4
Capen, Joseph 1658-1725................DLB-24
Capes, Bernard 1854-1918..............DLB-156
Capote, Truman 1924-1984
    ..... DLB-2, 185, 227; Y-80, Y-84; CDALB-1
Caproni, Giorgio 1912-1990 ....DLB-128
Caragiale, Mateiu Ioan 1885-1936.......DLB-220
Cardarelli, Vincenzo 1887-1959.........DLB-114
Cárdenas, Reyes 1948- DLB-122
Cardinal, Marie 1929- DLB-83
Carew, Jan 1920- DLB-157
Carew, Thomas 1594 or 1595-1640.....DLB-126
Carey, Henry circa 1687-1689-1743.......DLB-84
Carey, M., and Company DLB-49
Carey, Mathew 1760-1839........... DLB-37, 73
Carey and Hart DLB-49
Carlell, Lodowick 1602-1675...........DLB-58
Carleton, William 1794-1869..........DLB-159
Carleton, G. W. [publishing house].......DLB-49
Carlile, Richard 1790-1843 .... DLB-110, 158
Carlyle, Jane Welsh 1801-1866 ....DLB-55
Carlyle, Thomas
    1795-1881 ....DLB-55, 144; CDBLB-3
"The Hero as Man of Letters: Johnson,
    Rousseau, Burns" (1841) [excerpt] DLB-57
The Hero as Poet. Dante;
    Shakspeare (1841)..................DLB-32
Carman, Bliss 1861-1929...............DLB-92
Carmina Burana circa 1230 ....DLB-138
Carnero, Guillermo 1947- DLB-108
Carossa, Hans 1878-1956...............DLB-66
Carpenter, Humphrey 1946- DLB-155
The Practice of Biography III: An Interview
    with Humphrey Carpenter Y-84
Carpenter, Stephen Cullen ?-1820?.......DLB-73
Carpentier, Alejo
    1904-1980 ....DLB-113; CDWLB-3
Carrier, Roch 1937- DLB-53

Carrillo, Adolfo 1855-1926 ....DLB-122
Carroll, Gladys Hasty 1904- DLB-9
Carroll, John 1735-1815...............DLB-37
Carroll, John 1809-1884 ....DLB-99
Carroll, Lewis
    1832-1898...... DLB-18, 163, 178; CDBLB-4
The Lewis Carroll Centenary Y-98
Carroll, Paul 1927- DLB-16
Carroll, Paul Vincent 1900-1968.........DLB-10
Carroll and Graf Publishers DLB-46
Carruth, Hayden 1921- DLB-5, 165
Carryl, Charles E. 1841-1920 ....DLB-42
Carson, Anne 1950- DLB-193
Carswell, Catherine 1879-1946 ....DLB-36
Cărtărescu, Mirea 1956- DLB-232
Carter, Angela 1940-1992 .... DLB-14, 207
Carter, Elizabeth 1717-1806 ....DLB-109
Carter, Henry (see Leslie, Frank)
Carter, Hodding, Jr. 1907-1972 ....DLB-127
Carter, John 1905-1975 ....DLB-201
Carter, Landon 1710-1778 ....DLB-31
Carter, Lin 1930- Y-81
Carter, Martin 1927-1997.... DLB-117; CDWLB-3
Carter, Robert, and Brothers............DLB-49
Carter and Hendee DLB-49
Cartwright, John 1740-1824............DLB-158
Cartwright, William circa 1611-1643.....DLB-126
Caruthers, William Alexander 1802-1846...DLB-3
Carver, Jonathan 1710-1780..............DLB-31
Carver, Raymond
    1938-1988 .... DLB-130; Y-84, Y-88
First Strauss "Livings" Awarded to Cynthia
    Ozick and Raymond Carver
    An Interview with Raymond Carver Y-83
Cary, Alice 1820-1871 ....DLB-202
Cary, Joyce 1888-1957....DLB-15, 100; CDBLB-6
Cary, Patrick 1623?-1657 ....DLB-131
Casey, Juanita 1925- DLB-14
Casey, Michael 1947- DLB-5
Cassady, Carolyn 1923- DLB-16
Cassady, Neal 1926-1968 .... DLB-16, 237
Cassell and Company DLB-106
Cassell Publishing Company DLB-49
Cassill, R. V. 1919- DLB-6, 218
Cassity, Turner 1929- DLB-105
Cassius Dio circa 155/164-post 229......DLB-176
Cassola, Carlo 1917-1987..............DLB-177
The Castle of Perseverance circa 1400-1425..DLB-146
Castellano, Olivia 1944- DLB-122
Castellanos, Rosario
    1925-1974 ....DLB-113; CDWLB-3
Castillo, Ana 1953- DLB-122, 227
Castillo, Rafael C. 1950- DLB-209
Castlemon, Harry (see Fosdick, Charles Austin)
Čašule, Kole 1921- DLB-181
Caswall, Edward 1814-1878............DLB-32

Catacalos, Rosemary 1944- DLB-122
Cather, Willa
    1873-1947 ....DLB-9, 54, 78; DS-1; CDALB-3
Catherine II (Ekaterina Alekseevna), "The Great,"
    Empress of Russia 1729-1796 ....DLB-150
Catherwood, Mary Hartwell 1847-1902 ...DLB-78
Catledge, Turner 1901-1983 ....DLB-127
Catlin, George 1796-1872.........DLB-186, 189
Cato the Elder 234 B.C.-149 B.C........DLB-211
Cattafi, Bartolo 1922-1979.............DLB-128
Catton, Bruce 1899-1978 ....DLB-17
Catullus circa 84 B.C.-54 B.C.
    ....DLB-211; CDWLB-1
Causley, Charles 1917- DLB-27
Caute, David 1936- DLB-14, 231
Cavendish, Duchess of Newcastle,
    Margaret Lucas 1623-1673.........DLB-131
Cawein, Madison 1865-1914............DLB-54
Caxton, William [publishing house] DLB-170
The Caxton Printers, Limited DLB-46
Cayrol, Jean 1911- DLB-83
Cecil, Lord David 1902-1986 ....DLB-155
Cela, Camilo José 1916- Y-89
Celan, Paul 1920-1970........ DLB-69; CDWLB-2
Celati, Gianni 1937- DLB-196
Celaya, Gabriel 1911-1991 ....DLB-108
A Celebration of Literary Biography........Y-98
Céline, Louis-Ferdinand 1894-1961.......DLB-72
The Celtic Background to Medieval English
    Literature DLB-146
Celtis, Conrad 1459-1508 ....DLB-179
Center for Bibliographical Studies and
    Research at the University of
    California, Riverside.................Y-91
The Center for the Book in the Library
    of Congress.....................Y-93
Center for the Book Research Y-84
Centlivre, Susanna 1669?-1723 ....DLB-84
The Century Company................DLB-49
Cernuda, Luis 1902-1963 ....DLB-134
Cervantes, Lorna Dee 1954- DLB-82
Chaadaev, Petr Iakovlevich
    1794-1856 ....DLB-198
Chacel, Rosa 1898- DLB-134
Chacón, Eusebio 1869-1948 ....DLB-82
Chacón, Felipe Maximiliano 1873-?.......DLB-82
Chadwyck-Healey's Full-Text Literary Databases:
    Editing Commercial Databases of
    Primary Literary Texts...............Y-95
Challans, Eileen Mary (see Renault, Mary)
Chalmers, George 1742-1825............DLB-30
Chaloner, Sir Thomas 1520-1565 .....DLB-167
Chamberlain, Samuel S. 1851-1916.......DLB-25
Chamberland, Paul 1939- DLB-60
Chamberlin, William Henry 1897-1969....DLB-29
Chambers, Charles Haddon 1860-1921 ...DLB-10
Chambers, María Cristina (see Mena, María Cristina)
Chambers, Robert W. 1865-1933 ....DLB-202

Cumulative Index

Chambers, W. and R. [publishing house] DLB-106
Chamisso, Albert von 1781-1838 .... DLB-90
Champfleury 1821-1889 .... DLB-119
Chandler, Harry 1864-1944 .... DLB-29
Chandler, Norman 1899-1973 .... DLB-127
Chandler, Otis 1927- DLB-127
Chandler, Raymond 1888-1959 .... DLB-226; DS-6; CDALB-5
Raymond Chandler Centenary Tributes from Michael Avallone, James Ellroy, Joe Gores, and William F. Nolan Y-88
Channing, Edward 1856-1931 .... DLB-17
Channing, Edward Tyrrell 1790-1856 .... DLB-1, 59, 235
Channing, William Ellery 1780-1842 .... DLB-1, 59, 235
Channing, William Ellery II 1817-1901 .... DLB-1, 223
Channing, William Henry 1810-1884 .. DLB-1, 59
Chaplin, Charlie 1889-1977 .... DLB-44
Chapman, George 1559 or 1560-1634 .... DLB-62, 121
Chapman, John DLB-106
Chapman, Olive Murray 1892-1977 ..... DLB-195
Chapman, R. W. 1881-1960 .... DLB-201
Chapman, William 1850-1917 .... DLB-99
Chapman and Hall DLB-106
Chappell, Fred 1936- DLB-6, 105
"A Detail in a Poem" DLB-105
Chappell, William 1582-1649 .... DLB-236
Charbonneau, Jean 1875-1960 .... DLB-92
Charbonneau, Robert 1911-1967 .... DLB-68
Charles, Gerda 1914- DLB-14
Charles, William [publishing house] DLB-49
Charles d'Orléans 1394-1465 .... DLB-208
Charley (see Mann, Charles)
Charteris, Leslie 1907-1993 .... DLB-77
Chartier, Alain circa 1385-1430 .... DLB-208
Charyn, Jerome 1937- Y-83
Chase, Borden 1900-1971 .... DLB-26
Chase, Edna Woolman 1877-1957 ...... DLB-91
Chase, Mary Coyle 1907-1981 .... DLB-228
Chase-Riboud, Barbara 1936- DLB-33
Chateaubriand, François-René de 1768-1848 .... DLB-119
Chatterton, Thomas 1752-1770 .... DLB-109
Essay on Chatterton (1842), by Robert Browning DLB-32
Chatto and Windus DLB-106
Chatwin, Bruce 1940-1989 .... DLB-194, 204
Chaucer, Geoffrey 1340?-1400 .... DLB-146; CDBLB-1
Chauncy, Charles 1705-1787 .... DLB-24
Chauveau, Pierre-Joseph-Olivier 1820-1890 .... DLB-99
Chávez, Denise 1948- DLB-122
Chávez, Fray Angélico 1910- DLB-82

Chayefsky, Paddy 1923-1981 ..... DLB-7, 44; Y-81
Cheesman, Evelyn 1881-1969 .... DLB-195
Cheever, Ezekiel 1615-1708 .... DLB-24
Cheever, George Barrell 1807-1890 ...... DLB-59
Cheever, John 1912-1982 ...... DLB-2, 102, 227; Y-80, Y-82; CDALB-1
Cheever, Susan 1943- Y-82
Cheke, Sir John 1514-1557 .... DLB-132
Chelsea House DLB-46
Chênedollé, Charles de 1769-1833 ..... DLB-217
Cheney, Ednah Dow 1824-1904 ..... DLB-1, 223
Cheney, Harriet Vaughn 1796-1889 ..... DLB-99
Chénier, Marie-Joseph 1764-1811 ...... DLB-192
Chernyshevsky, Nikolai Gavrilovich 1828-1889 .... DLB-238
Cherry, Kelly 1940 .... Y-83
Cherryh, C. J. 1942- Y-80
Chesebro', Caroline 1825-1873 .... DLB-202
Chesney, Sir George Tomkyns 1830-1895 .... DLB-190
Chesnut, Mary Boykin 1823-1886 ...... DLB-239
Chesnutt, Charles Waddell 1858-1932 .... DLB-12, 50, 78
Chesson, Mrs. Nora (see Hopper, Nora)
Chester, Alfred 1928-1971 .... DLB-130
Chester, George Randolph 1869-1924 ... DLB-78
The Chester Plays circa 1505-1532; revisions until 1575 .... DLB-146
Chesterfield, Philip Dormer Stanhope, Fourth Earl of 1694-1773 .... DLB-104
Chesterton, G. K. 1874-1936 ...DLB-10, 19, 34, 70, 98, 149, 178; CDBLB-6
Chettle, Henry circa 1560-circa 1607 .... DLB-136
Chew, Ada Nield 1870-1945 .... DLB-135
Cheyney, Edward P. 1861-1947 .... DLB-47
Chiara, Piero 1913-1986 .... DLB-177
Chicano History DLB-82
Chicano Language DLB-82
Child, Francis James 1825-1896 ... DLB-1, 64, 235
Child, Lydia Maria 1802-1880 .... DLB-1, 74
Child, Philip 1898-1978 .... DLB-68
Childers, Erskine 1870-1922 .... DLB-70
Children's Book Awards and Prizes DLB-61
Children's Illustrators, 1800-1880 ...... DLB-163
Childress, Alice 1920-1994 .... DLB-7, 38
Childs, George W. 1829-1894 .... DLB-23
Chilton Book Company DLB-46
Chin, Frank 1940- DLB-206
Chinweizu 1943- DLB-157
Chitham, Edward 1932- DLB-155
Chittenden, Hiram Martin 1858-1917 .... DLB-47
Chivers, Thomas Holley 1809-1858 ...... DLB-3
Cholmondeley, Mary 1859-1925 .... DLB-197
Chopin, Kate 1850-1904... DLB-12, 78; CDALB-3
Chopin, Rene 1885-1953 .... DLB-92
Choquette, Adrienne 1915-1973 .... DLB-68

Choquette, Robert 1905- DLB-68
Chrétien de Troyes circa 1140-circa 1190 .... DLB-208
Christensen, Inger 1935- DLB-214
The Christian Publishing Company DLB-49
Christie, Agatha 1890-1976 .... DLB-13, 77; CDBLB-6
Christine de Pizan circa 1365-circa 1431 .... DLB-208
Christus und die Samariterin circa 950 ...... DLB-148
Christy, Howard Chandler 1873-1952 ... DLB-188
Chulkov, Mikhail Dmitrievich 1743?-1792 .... DLB-150
Church, Benjamin 1734-1778 .... DLB-31
Church, Francis Pharcellus 1839-1906 .... DLB-79
Church, Peggy Pond 1903-1986 .... DLB-212
Church, Richard 1893-1972 .... DLB-191
Church, William Conant 1836-1917 ..... DLB-79
Churchill, Caryl 1938- DLB-13
Churchill, Charles 1731-1764 .... DLB-109
Churchill, Winston 1871-1947 .... DLB-202
Churchill, Sir Winston 1874-1965 .... DLB-100; DS-16; CDBLB-5
Churchyard, Thomas 1520?-1604 ...... DLB-132
Churton, E., and Company DLB-106
Chute, Marchette 1909-1994 .... DLB-103
Ciardi, John 1916-1986 .... DLB-5; Y-86
Cibber, Colley 1671-1757 .... DLB-84
Cicero 106 B.C.-43 B.C. DLB-211, CDWLB-1
Cima, Annalisa 1941- DLB-128
Čingo, Živko 1935-1987 .... DLB-181
Cioran, E. M. 1911-1995 .... DLB-220
Čipkus, Alfonsas (see Nyka-Niliūnas, Alfonsas)
Cirese, Eugenio 1884-1955 .... DLB-114
Cīrulis, Jānis (see Bels, Alberts)
Cisneros, Sandra 1954- DLB-122, 152
City Lights Books DLB-46
Cixous, Hélène 1937- DLB-83
Clampitt, Amy 1920-1994 .... DLB-105
Clancy, Tom 1947- DLB-227
Clapper, Raymond 1892-1944 .... DLB-29
Clare, John 1793-1864 .... DLB-55, 96
Clarendon, Edward Hyde, Earl of 1609-1674 .... DLB-101
Clark, Alfred Alexander Gordon (see Hare, Cyril)
Clark, Ann Nolan 1896- DLB-52
Clark, C. E. Frazer Jr. 1925- DLB-187
Clark, C. M., Publishing Company DLB-46
Clark, Catherine Anthony 1892-1977 .... DLB-68
Clark, Charles Heber 1841-1915 .... DLB-11
Clark, Davis Wasgatt 1812-1871 .... DLB-79
Clark, Eleanor 1913- DLB-6
Clark, J. P. 1935- DLB-117; CDWLB-3
Clark, Lewis Gaylord 1808-1873 ... DLB-3, 64, 73
Clark, Walter Van Tilburg 1909-1971 .... DLB-9, 206

Clark, William (see Lewis, Meriwether)

Clark, William Andrews Jr. 1877-1934 . . . DLB-187

Clarke, Austin 1896-1974. . . . . DLB-10, 20

Clarke, Austin C. 1934- DLB-53, 125

Clarke, Gillian 1937- DLB-40

Clarke, James Freeman
 1810-1888 . . . . .DLB-1, 59, 235

Clarke, Lindsay 1939- DLB-231

Clarke, Marcus 1846-1881. . . . . .DLB-230

Clarke, Pauline 1921- DLB-161

Clarke, Rebecca Sophia 1833-1906 . . . . . . .DLB-42

Clarke, Robert, and Company DLB-49

Clarkson, Thomas 1760-1846 . . . . .DLB-158

Claudel, Paul 1868-1955 . . . . .DLB-192

Claudius, Matthias 1740-1815 . . . . .DLB-97

Clausen, Andy 1943- DLB-16

Clawson, John L. 1865-1933 . . . . .DLB-187

Claxton, Remsen and Haffelfinger DLB-49

Clay, Cassius Marcellus 1810-1903. . . . . . .DLB-43

Cleage, Pearl 1948- DLB-228

Cleary, Beverly 1916- DLB-52

Cleary, Kate McPhelim 1863-1905 . . . . . .DLB-221

Cleaver, Vera 1919- and
 Cleaver, Bill 1920-1981. . . . . .DLB-52

Cleland, John 1710-1789. . . . . .DLB-39

Clemens, Samuel Langhorne (Mark Twain)
 1835-1910 . . . . .DLB-11, 12, 23, 64, 74,
  186, 189; CDALB-3

Mark Twain on Perpetual Copyright Y-92

Clement, Hal 1922- DLB-8

Clemo, Jack 1916- DLB-27

Clephane, Elizabeth Cecilia
 1830-1869 . . . . .DLB-199

Cleveland, John 1613-1658 . . . . .DLB-126

Cliff, Michelle 1946- DLB-157; CDWLB-3

Clifford, Lady Anne 1590-1676. . . . . .DLB-151

Clifford, James L. 1901-1978 . . . . .DLB-103

Clifford, Lucy 1853?-1929. . . . . DLB-135, 141, 197

Clifton, Lucille 1936- DLB-5, 41

Clines, Francis X. 1938- DLB-185

Clive, Caroline (V) 1801-1873. . . . . .DLB-199

Clode, Edward J. [publishing house] DLB-46

Clough, Arthur Hugh 1819-1861 . . . . .DLB-32

Cloutier, Cécile 1930- DLB-60

Clouts, Sidney 1926-1982 . . . . .DLB-225

Clutton-Brock, Arthur 1868-1924 . . . . .DLB-98

Coates, Robert M. 1897-1973. . . . . . .DLB-4, 9, 102

Coatsworth, Elizabeth 1893- DLB-22

Cobb, Charles E., Jr. 1943- DLB-41

Cobb, Frank I. 1869-1923 . . . . .DLB-25

Cobb, Irvin S. 1876-1944 . . . . .DLB-11, 25, 86

Cobbe, Frances Power 1822-1904 . . . . . . .DLB-190

Cobbett, William 1763-1835 . . . . .DLB-43, 107

Cobbledick, Gordon 1898-1969 . . . . .DLB-171

Cochran, Thomas C. 1902- DLB-17

Cochrane, Elizabeth 1867-1922 . . . . . .DLB-25, 189

Cockerell, Sir Sydney 1867-1962 . . . . .DLB-201

Cockerill, John A. 1845-1896. . . . . .DLB-23

Cocteau, Jean 1889-1963 . . . . .DLB-65

Coderre, Emile (see Jean Narrache)

Coe, Jonathan 1961- DLB-231

Coetzee, J. M. 1940- DLB-225

Coffee, Lenore J. 1900?-1984. . . . . .DLB-44

Coffin, Robert P. Tristram 1892-1955. . . . . .DLB-45

Coghill, Mrs. Harry (see Walker, Anna Louisa)

Cogswell, Fred 1917- DLB-60

Cogswell, Mason Fitch 1761-1830 . . . . .DLB-37

Cohen, Arthur A. 1928-1986 . . . . .DLB-28

Cohen, Leonard 1934- DLB-53

Cohen, Matt 1942- DLB-53

Colbeck, Norman 1903-1987 . . . . .DLB-201

Colden, Cadwallader 1688-1776 . . . . . .DLB-24, 30

Colden, Jane 1724-1766 . . . . .DLB-200

Cole, Barry 1936- DLB-14

Cole, George Watson 1850-1939 . . . . . . .DLB-140

Colegate, Isabel 1931- DLB-14, 231

Coleman, Emily Holmes 1899-1974 . . . . . . .DLB-4

Coleman, Wanda 1946- DLB-130

Coleridge, Hartley 1796-1849 . . . . .DLB-96

Coleridge, Mary 1861-1907 . . . . .DLB-19, 98

Coleridge, Samuel Taylor
 1772-1834 . . . . .DLB-93, 107; CDBLB-3

Coleridge, Sara 1802-1852. . . . . .DLB-199

Colet, John 1467-1519 . . . . .DLB-132

Colette 1873-1954 . . . . .DLB-65

Colette, Sidonie Gabrielle (see Colette)

Colinas, Antonio 1946- DLB-134

Coll, Joseph Clement 1881-1921 . . . . .DLB-188

Collier, John 1901-1980. . . . . .DLB-77

Collier, John Payne 1789-1883. . . . . .DLB-184

Collier, Mary 1690-1762 . . . . .DLB-95

Collier, P. F. [publishing house] DLB-49

Collier, Robert J. 1876-1918. . . . . .DLB-91

Collin and Small DLB-49

Collingwood, W. G. 1854-1932. . . . . .DLB-149

Collins, An floruit circa 1653. . . . . .DLB-131

Collins, Isaac [publishing house] DLB-49

Collins, Merle 1950- DLB-157

Collins, Mortimer 1827-1876 . . . . .DLB-21, 35

Collins, Tom (see Furphy, Joseph)

Collins, Wilkie
 1824-1889 . . . . . . .DLB-18, 70, 159; CDBLB-4

Collins, William 1721-1759 . . . . .DLB-109

Collins, William, Sons and Company DLB-154

Collis, Maurice 1889-1973 . . . . .DLB-195

Collyer, Mary 1716?-1763? DLB-39

Colman, Benjamin 1673-1747 . . . . .DLB-24

Colman, George, the Elder 1732-1794. . . . .DLB-89

Colman, George, the Younger
 1762-1836 . . . . .DLB-89

Colman, S. [publishing house] DLB-49

Colombo, John Robert 1936- DLB-53

Colquhoun, Patrick 1745-1820 . . . . .DLB-158

Colter, Cyrus 1910- DLB-33

Colum, Padraic 1881-1972. . . . . .DLB-19

Columella fl. first century A.D. DLB-211

Colvin, Sir Sidney 1845-1927 . . . . .DLB-149

Colwin, Laurie 1944-1992 . . . . DLB-218; Y-80

Comden, Betty 1919- and
 Green, Adolph 1918- DLB-44

Come to Papa Y-99

Comi, Girolamo 1890-1968 . . . . .DLB-114

The Comic Tradition Continued
 [in the British Novel] DLB-15

Commager, Henry Steele 1902-1998. . . . . .DLB-17

The Commercialization of the Image of
 Revolt, by Kenneth Rexroth DLB-16

Community and Commentators: Black
 Theatre and Its Critics DLB-38

Commynes, Philippe de
 circa 1447-1511 . . . . .DLB-208

Compton-Burnett, Ivy 1884?-1969 . . . . . . .DLB-36

Conan, Laure 1845-1924. . . . . .DLB-99

Concord History and Life DLB-223

Concord Literary History of a Town DLB-223

Conde, Carmen 1901- DLB-108

Conference on Modern Biography Y-85

Congreve, William
 1670-1729 . . . . .DLB-39, 84; CDBLB-2

Preface to *Incognita* (1692) DLB-39

Conkey, W. B., Company. DLB-49

Conn, Stewart 1936- DLB-233

Connell, Evan S., Jr. 1924- DLB-2; Y-81

Connelly, Marc 1890-1980 . . . . DLB-7; Y-80

Connolly, Cyril 1903-1974 . . . . .DLB-98

Connolly, James B. 1868-1957. . . . . DLB-78

Connor, Ralph 1860-1937 . . . . .DLB-92

Connor, Tony 1930- DLB-40

Conquest, Robert 1917- DLB-27

Conrad, John, and Company DLB-49

Conrad, Joseph
 1857-1924 . . . .DLB-10, 34, 98, 156; CDBLB-5

Conroy, Jack 1899-1990 . . . . Y-81

Conroy, Pat 1945- DLB-6

The Consolidation of Opinion: Critical
 Responses to the Modernists. DLB-36

Consolo, Vincenzo 1933- DLB-196

Constable, Archibald, and Company DLB-154

Constable, Henry 1562-1613. . . . . .DLB-136

Constable and Company Limited DLB-112

Constant, Benjamin 1767-1830. . . . . .DLB-119

Constant de Rebecque, Henri-Benjamin de
 (see Constant, Benjamin)

Constantine, David 1944- DLB-40

Constantin-Weyer, Maurice 1881-1964. . . .DLB-92

Contempo Caravan: Kites in a Windstorm . . . Y-85

A Contemporary Flourescence of Chicano
 Literature Y-84

Cumulative Index

Continental European Rhetoricians,
   1400-1600. . . . . DLB-236

The Continental Publishing Company. . . . DLB-49

Conversations with Editors Y-95

Conversations with Publishers I: An Interview
   with Patrick O'Connor Y-84

Conversations with Publishers II: An Interview
   with Charles Scribner III Y-94

Conversations with Publishers III: An Interview
   with Donald Lamm Y-95

Conversations with Publishers IV: An Interview
   with James Laughlin. Y-96

Conversations with Rare Book Dealers I: An
   Interview with Glenn Horowitz Y-90

Conversations with Rare Book Dealers II: An
   Interview with Ralph Sipper Y-94

Conversations with Rare Book Dealers
   (Publishers) III: An Interview with
   Otto Penzler. Y-96

The Conversion of an Unpolitical Man,
   by W. H. Bruford DLB-66

Conway, Moncure Daniel
   1832-1907. . . . . DLB-1, 223

Cook, David C., Publishing Company. . . . DLB-49

Cook, Ebenezer circa 1667-circa 1732. . . . . DLB-24

Cook, Edward Tyas 1857-1919 . . . . DLB-149

Cook, Eliza 1818-1889 . . . . DLB-199

Cook, Michael 1933- DLB-53

Cooke, George Willis 1848-1923 . . . . DLB-71

Cooke, Increase, and Company DLB-49

Cooke, John Esten 1830-1886 . . . . DLB-3

Cooke, Philip Pendleton 1816-1850 . . . . DLB-3, 59

Cooke, Rose Terry 1827-1892 . . . . DLB-12, 74

Cook-Lynn, Elizabeth 1930- DLB-175

Coolbrith, Ina 1841-1928 . . . . DLB-54, 186

Cooley, Peter 1940- DLB-105

"Into the Mirror" DLB-105

Coolidge, Clark 1939- DLB-193

Coolidge, George [publishing house] DLB-49

Coolidge, Susan (see Woolsey, Sarah Chauncy)

Cooper, Anna Julia 1858-1964 . . . . DLB-221

Cooper, Edith Emma (see Field, Michael)

Cooper, Giles 1918-1966 . . . . DLB-13

Cooper, J. California 19??- DLB-212

Cooper, James Fenimore
   1789-1851. . . . . DLB-3, 183; CDALB-2

Cooper, Kent 1880-1965 . . . . DLB-29

Cooper, Susan 1935- DLB-161

Cooper, Susan Fenimore 1813-1894. . . . . DLB-239

Cooper, William [publishing house] DLB-170

Coote, J. [publishing house] DLB-154

Coover, Robert 1932- DLB-2, 227; Y-81

Copeland and Day DLB-49

Ćopić, Branko 1915-1984. . . . . DLB-181

Copland, Robert 1470?-1548 . . . . DLB-136

Coppard, A. E. 1878-1957 . . . . DLB-162

Coppée, François 1842-1908 . . . . DLB-217

Coppel, Alfred 1921- Y-83

Coppola, Francis Ford 1939- DLB-44

Copway, George (Kah-ge-ga-gah-bowh)
   1818-1869 . . . . DLB-175, 183

Corazzini, Sergio 1886-1907 . . . . DLB-114

Corbett, Richard 1582-1635 . . . . DLB-121

Corbière, Tristan 1845-1875. . . . . DLB-217

Corcoran, Barbara 1911- DLB-52

Cordelli, Franco 1943- DLB-196

Corelli, Marie 1855-1924 . . . . DLB-34, 156

Corle, Edwin 1906-1956. . . . . Y-85

Corman, Cid 1924- DLB-5, 193

Cormier, Robert 1925- DLB-52; CDALB-6

Corn, Alfred 1943- DLB-120; Y-80

Cornford, Frances 1886-1960 . . . . DLB-240

Cornish, Sam 1935- DLB-41

Cornish, William circa 1465-circa 1524 . . DLB-132

Cornwall, Barry (see Procter, Bryan Waller)

Cornwallis, Sir William, the Younger
   circa 1579-1614 . . . . DLB-151

Cornwell, David John Moore (see le Carré, John)

Corpi, Lucha 1945- DLB-82

Corrington, John William 1932- DLB-6

Corrothers, James D. 1869-1917. . . . . DLB-50

Corso, Gregory 1930- DLB-5, 16, 237

Cortázar, Julio 1914-1984. . . .DLB-113; CDWLB-3

Cortéz, Carlos 1923- DLB-209

Cortez, Jayne 1936- DLB-41

Corvinus, Gottlieb Siegmund
   1677-1746 . . . . DLB-168

Corvo, Baron (see Rolfe, Frederick William)

Cory, Annie Sophie (see Cross, Victoria)

Cory, William Johnson 1823-1892. . . . . . . DLB-35

Coryate, Thomas 1577?-1617. . . . . . . DLB-151, 172

Ćosić, Dobrica 1921- DLB-181; CDWLB-4

Cosin, John 1595-1672 . . . . DLB-151, 213

Cosmopolitan Book Corporation DLB-46

Costain, Thomas B. 1885-1965 . . . . DLB-9

Coste, Donat 1912-1957 . . . . DLB-88

Costello, Louisa Stuart 1799-1870. . . . . . DLB-166

Cota-Cárdenas, Margarita 1941- DLB-122

Cotten, Bruce 1873-1954 . . . . DLB-187

Cotter, Joseph Seamon, Sr. 1861-1949 . . . . DLB-50

Cotter, Joseph Seamon, Jr. 1895-1919 . . . . DLB-50

Cottle, Joseph [publishing house] DLB-154

Cotton, Charles 1630-1687. . . . . DLB-131

Cotton, John 1584-1652 . . . . DLB-24

Cotton, Sir Robert Bruce 1571-1631. . . . . DLB-213

Coulter, John 1888-1980 . . . . DLB-68

Cournos, John 1881-1966. . . . . DLB-54

Courteline, Georges 1858-1929 . . . . DLB-192

Cousins, Margaret 1905-1996 . . . . DLB-137

Cousins, Norman 1915-1990 . . . . DLB-137

Couvreur, Jessie (see Tasma)

Coventry, Francis 1725-1754 . . . . DLB-39

Dedication, *The History of Pompey
   the Little* (1751) DLB-39

Coverdale, Miles 1487 or 1488-1569 . . . . DLB-167

Coverly, N. [publishing house] DLB-49

Covici-Friede DLB-46

Coward, Noel 1899-1973 . . . . . DLB-10; CDBLB-6

Coward, McCann and Geoghegan. DLB-46

Cowles, Gardner 1861-1946. . . . . DLB-29

Cowles, Gardner "Mike" Jr.
   1903-1985 . . . . DLB-127, 137

Cowley, Abraham 1618-1667. . . . . . DLB-131, 151

Cowley, Hannah 1743-1809. . . . . DLB-89

Cowley, Malcolm
   1898-1989 . . . . DLB-4, 48; Y-81, Y-89

Cowper, William 1731-1800. . . . . . . DLB-104, 109

Cox, A. B. (see Berkeley, Anthony)

Cox, James McMahon 1903-1974 . . . . . . .DLB-127

Cox, James Middleton 1870-1957 . . . . . . .DLB-127

Cox, Leonard ca. 1495-ca. 1550. . . . . . . DLB-236

Cox, Palmer 1840-1924 . . . . DLB-42

Coxe, Louis 1918-1993 . . . . DLB-5

Coxe, Tench 1755-1824 . . . . DLB-37

Cozzens, Frederick S. 1818-1869 . . . . DLB-202

Cozzens, James Gould
   1903-1978. . . . . DLB-9; Y-84; DS-2; CDALB-1

James Gould Cozzens–A View from Afar Y-97

James Gould Cozzens Case Re-opened Y-97

James Gould Cozzens: How to Read Him . . . Y-97

Cozzens's *Michael Scarlett*. Y-97

Crabbe, George 1754-1832. . . . . DLB-93

Crace, Jim 1946- DLB-231

Crackanthorpe, Hubert 1870-1896. . . . . . DLB-135

Craddock, Charles Egbert (see Murfree, Mary N.)

Cradock, Thomas 1718-1770 . . . . DLB-31

Craig, Daniel H. 1811-1895 . . . . DLB-43

Craik, Dinah Maria 1826-1887. . . . . . DLB-35, 136

Cramer, Richard Ben 1950- DLB-185

Cranch, Christopher Pearse 1813-1892 . DLB-1, 42

Crane, Hart 1899-1932. . . . . DLB-4, 48; CDALB-4

Crane, R. S. 1886-1967. . . . . DLB-63

Crane, Stephen
   1871-1900. . . . . . . DLB-12, 54, 78; CDALB-3

Crane, Walter 1845-1915. . . . . DLB-163

Cranmer, Thomas 1489-1556 . . . . . DLB-132, 213

Crapsey, Adelaide 1878-1914 . . . . DLB-54

Crashaw, Richard 1612 or 1613-1649 . . . DLB-126

Craven, Avery 1885-1980 . . . . .DLB-17

Crawford, Charles 1752-circa 1815 . . . . . DLB-31

Crawford, F. Marion 1854-1909. . . . . DLB-71

Crawford, Isabel Valancy 1850-1887 . . . . DLB-92

Crawley, Alan 1887-1975 . . . . DLB-68

Crayon, Geoffrey (see Irving, Washington)

Creamer, Robert W. 1922- DLB-171

Creasey, John 1908-1973 . . . . DLB-77

Creative Age Press DLB-46

Creech, William [publishing house] DLB-154

Creede, Thomas [publishing house] DLB-170	Cruse, Mary Anne 1825?-1910 . . . . .DLB-239	**D**
Creel, George 1876-1953 . . . . .DLB-25	Cruz, Victor Hernández 1949- DLB-41	
Creeley, Robert 1926- . . . DLB-5, 16, 169; DS-17	Csokor, Franz Theodor 1885-1969 . . . . . . .DLB-81	Dabit, Eugène 1898-1936 . . . . .DLB-65
Creelman, James 1859-1915 . . . . .DLB-23	Csoóri, Sándor 1930- DLB-232; CDWLB-4	Daborne, Robert circa 1580-1628 . . . . .DLB-58
Cregan, David 1931- DLB-13	Cuala Press DLB-112	Dąbrowska, Maria
Creighton, Donald Grant 1902-1979 . . . . . .DLB-88	Cullen, Countee	1889-1965 . . . . DLB-215; CDWLB-4
Cremazie, Octave 1827-1879 . . . . .DLB-99	1903-1946 . . . . .DLB-4, 48, 51; CDALB-4	Dacey, Philip 1939- DLB-105
Crémer, Victoriano 1909?- DLB-108	Culler, Jonathan D. 1944- DLB-67	"Eyes Across Centuries: Contemporary
Crescas, Hasdai circa 1340-1412? DLB-115	Cullinan, Elizabeth 1933- DLB-234	Poetry and 'That Vision Thing,'" DLB-105
Crespo, Angel 1926- DLB-134	The Cult of Biography	Dach, Simon 1605-1659 . . . . .DLB-164
Cresset Press DLB-112	Excerpts from the Second Folio Debate:	Daggett, Rollin M. 1831-1901 . . . . .DLB-79
Cresswell, Helen 1934- DLB-161	"Biographies are generally a disease of English Literature" – Germaine Greer,	D'Aguiar, Fred 1960- DLB-157
Crèvecoeur, Michel Guillaume Jean de	Victoria Glendinning, Auberon Waugh,	Dahl, Roald 1916-1990 . . . . .DLB-139
1735-1813 . . . . .DLB-37	and Richard Holmes Y-86	Dahlberg, Edward 1900-1977 . . . . .DLB-48
Crewe, Candida 1964- DLB-207	Cumberland, Richard 1732-1811 . . . . .DLB-89	Dahn, Felix 1834-1912 . . . . .DLB-129
Crews, Harry 1935- DLB-6, 143, 185	Cummings, Constance Gordon	Dal', Vladimir Ivanovich (Kazak Vladimir
Crichton, Michael 1942- Y-81	1837-1924 .DLB-174	Lugansky) 1801-1872 . . . . .DLB-198
A Crisis of Culture: The Changing Role	Cummings, E. E.	Dale, Peter 1938- DLB-40
of Religion in the New Republic DLB-37	1894-1962 . . . . .DLB-4, 48; CDALB-5	Daley, Arthur 1904-1974 . . . . .DLB-171
Crispin, Edmund 1921-1978 . . . . .DLB-87	Cummings, Ray 1887-1957 . . . . .DLB-8	Dall, Caroline Healey 1822-1912 . . . . .DLB-1, 235
Cristofer, Michael 1946- DLB-7	Cummings and Hilliard DLB-49	Dallas, E. S. 1828-1879 . . . . .DLB-55
Crnjanski, Miloš	Cummins, Maria Susanna	From *The Gay Science* (1866) DLB-21
1893-1977 . . . . .DLB-147; CDWLB-4	1827-1866 . . . . .DLB-42	The Dallas Theater Center DLB-7
Crocker, Hannah Mather 1752-1829 . . . . .DLB-200	Cumpián, Carlos 1953- DLB-209	D'Alton, Louis 1900-1951 . . . . .DLB-10
Crockett, David (Davy)	Cunard, Nancy 1896-1965 . . . . .DLB-240	Daly, Carroll John 1889-1958 . . . . .DLB-226
1786-1836 . . . . .DLB-3, 11, 183	Cundall, Joseph [publishing house] DLB-106	Daly, T. A. 1871-1948 . . . . .DLB-11
Croft-Cooke, Rupert (see Bruce, Leo)	Cuney, Waring 1906-1976 . . . . .DLB-51	Damon, S. Foster 1893-1971 . . . . .DLB-45
Crofts, Freeman Wills 1879-1957 . . . . .DLB-77	Cuney-Hare, Maude 1874-1936 . . . . .DLB-52	Damrell, William S. [publishing house] DLB-49
Croker, John Wilson 1780-1857 . . . . .DLB-110	Cunningham, Allan 1784-1842 . . . . .DLB-116, 144	Dana, Charles A. 1819-1897 . . . . .DLB-3, 23
Croly, George 1780-1860 . . . . .DLB-159	Cunningham, J. V. 1911- DLB-5	Dana, Richard Henry, Jr.
Croly, Herbert 1869-1930 . . . . .DLB-91	Cunningham, Peter F.	1815-1882 . . . . .DLB-1, 183, 235
Croly, Jane Cunningham 1829-1901 . . . . . .DLB-23	[publishing house] DLB-49	Dandridge, Ray Garfield DLB-51
Crompton, Richmal 1890-1969 . . . . .DLB-160	Cunquiero, Alvaro 1911-1981 . . . . .DLB-134	Dane, Clemence 1887-1965 . . . . .DLB-10, 197
Cronin, A. J. 1896-1981 . . . . .DLB-191	Cuomo, George 1929- Y-80	Danforth, John 1660-1730 . . . . .DLB-24
Cros, Charles 1842-1888 . . . . .DLB-217	Cupples, Upham and Company DLB-49	Danforth, Samuel, I 1626-1674 . . . . .DLB-24
Crosby, Caresse 1892-1970 . . . . .DLB-48	Cupples and Leon DLB-46	Danforth, Samuel, II 1666-1727 . . . . .DLB-24
Crosby, Caresse 1892-1970	Cuppy, Will 1884-1949 . . . . .DLB-11	Dangerous Years: London Theater,
and Crosby, Harry	Curiel, Barbara Brinson 1956- DLB-209	1939-1945 . . . . .DLB-10
1898-1929 . . . . .DLB-4; DS-15	Curll, Edmund [publishing house] DLB-154	Daniel, John M. 1825-1865 . . . . .DLB-43
Crosby, Harry 1898-1929 . . . . .DLB-48	Currie, James 1756-1805 . . . . .DLB-142	Daniel, Samuel 1562 or 1563-1619 . . . . . . .DLB-62
Crosland, Camilla Toulmin	Currie, Mary Montgomerie Lamb Singleton,	Daniel Press DLB-106
(Mrs. Newton Crosland)	Lady Currie	Daniells, Roy 1902-1979 . . . . .DLB-68
1812-1895 .DLB-240	(see Fane, Violet)	Daniels, Jim 1956- DLB-120
Cross, Gillian 1945- DLB-161	*Cursor Mundi* circa 1300 . . . . .DLB-146	Daniels, Jonathan 1902-1981 . . . . .DLB-127
Cross, Victoria 1868-1952 . . . . .DLB-135, 197	Curti, Merle E. 1897- DLB-17	Daniels, Josephus 1862-1948 . . . . .DLB-29
Crossley-Holland, Kevin 1941- DLB-40, 161	Curtis, Anthony 1926- DLB-155	Danilevsky, Grigorii Petrovich
Crothers, Rachel 1878-1958 . . . . .DLB-7	Curtis, Cyrus H. K. 1850-1933 . . . . .DLB-91	1829-1890 .DLB-238
Crowell, Thomas Y., Company DLB-49	Curtis, George William	Dannay, Frederic 1905-1982 and
Crowley, John 1942- Y-82	1824-1892 . . . . .DLB-1, 43, 223	Manfred B. Lee 1905-1971 . . . . .DLB-137
Crowley, Mart 1935- DLB-7	Curzon, Robert 1810-1873 . . . . .DLB-166	Danner, Margaret Esse 1915- DLB-41
Crown Publishers .DLB-46	Curzon, Sarah Anne 1833-1898 . . . . .DLB-99	Danter, John [publishing house] DLB-170
Crowne, John 1641-1712 . . . . .DLB-80	Cushing, Harvey 1869-1939 . . . . .DLB-187	Dantin, Louis 1865-1945 . . . . .DLB-92
Crowninshield, Edward Augustus	Custance, Olive (Lady Alfred Douglas)	Danzig, Allison 1898-1987 . . . . .DLB-171
1817-1859 .DLB-140	1874-1944 .DLB-240	D'Arcy, Ella circa 1857-1937 . . . . .DLB-135
Crowninshield, Frank 1872-1947 . . . . .DLB-91	Cynewulf circa 770-840 . . . . .DLB-146	Darke, Nick 1948- DLB-233
Croy, Homer 1883-1965 . . . . .DLB-4	Czepko, Daniel 1605-1660 . . . . .DLB-164	Darley, Felix Octavious Carr 1822-1888 . .DLB-188
Crumley, James 1939- DLB-226; Y-84	Czerniawski, Adam 1934- DLB-232	

Cumulative Index

Darley, George 1795-1846 . . . . DLB-96

Darmesteter, Madame James
(see Robinson, A. Mary F.)

Darwin, Charles 1809-1882 . . . . .DLB-57, 166

Darwin, Erasmus 1731-1802. . . . . DLB-93

Daryush, Elizabeth 1887-1977. . . . . DLB-20

Dashkova, Ekaterina Romanovna
(née Vorontsova) 1743-1810 . . . . DLB-150

Dashwood, Edmée Elizabeth Monica de la Pasture
(see Delafield, E. M.)

Daudet, Alphonse 1840-1897 . . . . DLB-123

d'Aulaire, Edgar Parin 1898- and
d'Aulaire, Ingri 1904- DLB-22

Davenant, Sir William 1606-1668 . . . DLB-58, 126

Davenport, Guy 1927- DLB-130

Davenport, Marcia 1903-1996 . . . . DS-17

Davenport, Robert ?-? DLB-58

Daves, Delmer 1904-1977. . . . . DLB-26

Davey, Frank 1940- DLB-53

Davidson, Avram 1923-1993 . . . . DLB-8

Davidson, Donald 1893-1968. . . . . DLB-45

Davidson, John 1857-1909 . . . . DLB-19

Davidson, Lionel 1922- DLB-14

Davidson, Robyn 1950- DLB-204

Davidson, Sara 1943- DLB-185

Davie, Donald 1922- DLB-27

Davie, Elspeth 1919- DLB-139

Davies, Sir John 1569-1626 . . . . .DLB-172

Davies, John, of Hereford 1565?-1618 . . . DLB-121

Davies, Peter, Limited DLB-112

Davies, Rhys 1901-1978 . . . . DLB-139, 191

Davies, Robertson 1913- DLB-68

Davies, Samuel 1723-1761. . . . . DLB-31

Davies, Thomas 1712?-1785 . . . . . . DLB-142, 154

Davies, W. H. 1871-1940 . . . . .DLB-19, 174

Daviot, Gordon 1896?-1952 . . . . DLB-10
(see also Tey, Josephine)

Davis, Arthur Hoey (see Rudd, Steele)

Davis, Charles A. 1795-1867. . . . . DLB-11

Davis, Clyde Brion 1894-1962 . . . . DLB-9

Davis, Dick 1945- DLB-40

Davis, Frank Marshall 1905-? DLB-51

Davis, H. L. 1894-1960 . . . . DLB-9, 206

Davis, John 1774-1854 . . . . DLB-37

Davis, Lydia 1947- DLB-130

Davis, Margaret Thomson 1926- DLB-14

Davis, Ossie 1917- DLB-7, 38

Davis, Paxton 1925-1994 . . . . Y-94

Davis, Rebecca Harding 1831-1910 . . DLB-74, 239

Davis, Richard Harding 1864-1916
. . . . DLB-12, 23, 78, 79, 189; DS-13

Davis, Samuel Cole 1764-1809 . . . . DLB-37

Davis, Samuel Post 1850-1918 . . . . DLB-202

Davison, Peter 1928- DLB-5

Davydov, Denis Vasil'evich
1784-1839. . . . . DLB-205

Davys, Mary 1674-1732 . . . . DLB-39

Preface to *The Works of
Mrs. Davys* (1725) DLB-39

DAW Books DLB-46

Dawson, Ernest 1882-1947. . . . . DLB-140

Dawson, Fielding 1930- DLB-130

Dawson, Sarah Morgan 1842-1909 . . . . . DLB-239

Dawson, William 1704-1752. . . . . DLB-31

Day, Angel flourished 1583-1599 . . . . DLB-167, 236

Day, Benjamin Henry 1810-1889 . . . . DLB-43

Day, Clarence 1874-1935 . . . . DLB-11

Day, Dorothy 1897-1980 . . . . DLB-29

Day, Frank Parker 1881-1950 . . . . DLB-92

Day, John circa 1574-circa 1640 . . . . DLB-62

Day, John [publishing house] DLB-170

Day, The John, Company DLB-46

Day Lewis, C. 1904-1972 . . . . DLB-15, 20
(see also Blake, Nicholas)

Day, Mahlon [publishing house]. DLB-49

Day, Thomas 1748-1789. . . . . DLB-39

Dazai Osamu 1909-1948 . . . . DLB-182

Deacon, William Arthur 1890-1977 . . . . . DLB-68

Deal, Borden 1922-1985. . . . . DLB-6

de Angeli, Marguerite 1889-1987 . . . . DLB-22

De Angelis, Milo 1951- DLB-128

De Bow, James Dunwoody Brownson
1820-1867 . . . . DLB-3, 79

de Bruyn, Günter 1926- DLB-75

de Camp, L. Sprague 1907- DLB-8

De Carlo, Andrea 1952- DLB-196

De Casas, Celso A. 1944- DLB-209

Dechert, Robert 1895-1975. . . . . DLB-187

Dee, John 1527-1608 or 1609 . . . . . DLB-136, 213

Deeping, George Warwick 1877-1950 . . . DLB 153

Defoe, Daniel
1660-1731. . . . . . . DLB-39, 95, 101; CDBLB-2

Preface to *Colonel Jack* (1722) DLB-39

Preface to *The Farther Adventures of
Robinson Crusoe* (1719) DLB-39

Preface to *Moll Flanders* (1722). DLB-39

Preface to *Robinson Crusoe* (1719) DLB-39

Preface to *Roxana* (1724) DLB-39

de Fontaine, Felix Gregory 1834-1896 . . . . DLB-43

De Forest, John William 1826-1906 . . DLB-12, 189

DeFrees, Madeline 1919- DLB-105

"The Poet's Kaleidoscope: The Element
of Surprise in the Making of
the Poem" DLB-105

DeGolyer, Everette Lee 1886-1956 . . . . . DLB-187

de Graff, Robert 1895-1981 . . . . Y-81

de Graft, Joe 1924-1978 . . . . .DLB-117

De Heinrico circa 980? DLB-148

Deighton, Len 1929- DLB-87; CDBLB-8

DeJong, Meindert 1906-1991 . . . . DLB-52

Dekker, Thomas
circa 1572-1632 . . . . . DLB-62, 172; CDBLB-1

Delacorte, Jr., George T. 1894-1991 . . . . . DLB-91

Delafield, E. M. 1890-1943. . . . . DLB-34

Delahaye, Guy 1888-1969 . . . . DLB-92

de la Mare, Walter
1873-1956. . . . . . DLB-19, 153, 162; CDBLB-6

Deland, Margaret 1857-1945 . . . . DLB-78

Delaney, Shelagh 1939- DLB-13; CDBLB-8

Delano, Amasa 1763-1823 . . . . DLB-183

Delany, Martin Robinson 1812-1885 . . . . . DLB-50

Delany, Samuel R. 1942- DLB-8, 33

de la Roche, Mazo 1879-1961 . . . . DLB-68

Delavigne, Jean François Casimir
1793-1843 . . . . DLB-192

Delbanco, Nicholas 1942- DLB-6, 234

Del Castillo, Ramón 1949- DLB-209

De León, Nephtal 1945- DLB-82

Delgado, Abelardo Barrientos 1931- DLB-82

Del Giudice, Daniele 1949- DLB-196

De Libero, Libero 1906-1981 . . . . DLB-114

DeLillo, Don 1936- DLB-6, 173

de Lisser H. G. 1878-1944 . . . . .DLB-117

Dell, Floyd 1887-1969. . . . . DLB-9

Dell Publishing Company DLB-46

delle Grazie, Marie Eugene 1864-1931 . . . . DLB-81

Deloney, Thomas died 1600 . . . . DLB-167

Deloria, Ella C. 1889-1971 . . . . .DLB-175

Deloria, Vine, Jr. 1933- DLB-175

del Rey, Lester 1915-1993 . . . . DLB-8

Del Vecchio, John M. 1947- DS-9

Del'vig, Anton Antonovich 1798-1831 . . . DLB-205

de Man, Paul 1919-1983. . . . . DLB-67

DeMarinis, Rick 1934- DLB-218

Demby, William 1922- DLB-33

Deming, Philander 1829-1915 . . . . DLB-74

Deml, Jakub 1878-1961. . . . . DLB-215

Demorest, William Jennings 1822-1895 . . . DLB-79

De Morgan, William 1839-1917 . . . . DLB-153

Demosthenes 384 B.C.-322 B.C. DLB-176

Denham, Henry [publishing house] DLB-170

Denham, Sir John 1615-1669 . . . . DLB-58, 126

Denison, Merrill 1893-1975 . . . . DLB-92

Denison, T. S., and Company DLB-49

Dennery, Adolphe Philippe 1811-1899. . . DLB-192

Dennie, Joseph 1768-1812. . . . . . DLB-37, 43, 59, 73

Dennis, John 1658-1734 . . . . DLB-101

Dennis, Nigel 1912-1989 . . . . .DLB-13, 15, 233

Denslow, W. W. 1856-1915. . . . . DLB-188

Dent, J. M., and Sons DLB-112

Dent, Tom 1932-1998 . . . . DLB-38

Denton, Daniel circa 1626-1703 . . . . DLB-24

DePaola, Tomie 1934- DLB-61

Department of Library, Archives, and Institutional
Research, American Bible Society Y-97

De Quille, Dan 1829-1898 . . . . DLB-186

De Quincey, Thomas
1785-1859. . . . . DLB-110, 144; CDBLB-3

"Rhetoric" (1828; revised, 1859) [excerpt]..........................DLB-57
Derby, George Horatio 1823-1861 ....DLB-11
Derby, J. C., and Company............DLB-49
Derby and Miller....................DLB-49
De Ricci, Seymour 1881-1942..........DLB-201
Derleth, August 1909-1971.........DLB-9; DS-17
The Derrydale Press DLB-46
Derzhavin, Gavriil Romanovich 1743-1816 ....DLB-150
Desaulniers, Gonsalve 1863-1934 ....DLB-92
Desbordes-Valmore, Marceline 1786-1859 ....DLB-217
Deschamps, Emile 1791-1871..........DLB-217
Deschamps, Eustache 1340?-1404.......DLB-208
Desbiens, Jean-Paul 1927- DLB-53
des Forêts, Louis-Rene 1918- DLB-83
Desiato, Luca 1941- DLB-196
Desnica, Vladan 1905-1967............DLB-181
DesRochers, Alfred 1901-1978..........DLB-68
Desrosiers, Léo-Paul 1896-1967.........DLB-68
Dessì, Giuseppe 1909-1977 ....DLB-177
Destouches, Louis-Ferdinand (see Céline, Louis-Ferdinand)
De Tabley, Lord 1835-1895 ....DLB-35
Deutsch, André, Limited DLB-112
Deutsch, Babette 1895-1982 ....DLB-45
Deutsch, Niklaus Manuel (see Manuel, Niklaus)
Deveaux, Alexis 1948- DLB-38
The Development of the Author's Copyright in Britain DLB-154
The Development of Lighting in the Staging of Drama, 1900-1945 ....DLB-10
"The Development of Meiji Japan" DLB-180
De Vere, Aubrey 1814-1902 ....DLB-35
Devereux, second Earl of Essex, Robert 1565-1601 ....DLB-136
The Devin-Adair Company............DLB-46
De Vinne, Theodore Low 1828-1914 ....DLB-187
De Voto, Bernard 1897-1955 ....DLB-9
De Vries, Peter 1910-1993 ....DLB-6; Y-82
Dewdney, Christopher 1951- DLB-60
Dewdney, Selwyn 1909-1979 ....DLB-68
Dewey, Thomas B. 1915-1981..........DLB-226
DeWitt, Robert M., Publisher DLB-49
DeWolfe, Fiske and Company DLB-49
Dexter, Colin 1930- DLB-87
de Young, M. H. 1849-1925 ....DLB-25
Dhlomo, H. I. E. 1903-1956 .... DLB-157, 225
Dhuoda circa 803-after 843 ....DLB-148
The Dial 1840-1844 ....DLB-223
The Dial Press......................DLB-46
Diamond, I. A. L. 1920-1988 ....DLB-26
Dibble, L. Grace 1902-1998............DLB-204
Dibdin, Thomas Frognall 1776-1847 .....DLB-184
Di Cicco, Pier Giorgio 1949- DLB-60

Dick, Philip K. 1928-1982 ....DLB-8
Dick and Fitzgerald DLB-49
Dickens, Charles 1812-1870 ....DLB-21, 55, 70, 159, 166; CDBLB-4
Dickey, James 1923-1997 ....DLB-5, 193; Y-82, Y-93, Y-96; DS-7, DS-19; CDALB-6
James Dickey Tributes.................Y-97
The Life of James Dickey: A Lecture to the Friends of the Emory Libraries, by Henry Hart Y-98
Dickey, William 1928-1994..............DLB-5
Dickinson, Emily 1830-1886 ...DLB-1; CDWLB-3
Dickinson, John 1732-1808 ....DLB-31
Dickinson, Jonathan 1688-1747 ....DLB-24
Dickinson, Patric 1914- DLB-27
Dickinson, Peter 1927- DLB-87, 161
Dicks, John [publishing house].........DLB-106
Dickson, Gordon R. 1923- DLB-8
Dictionary of Literary Biography Yearbook Awards ..Y-92, Y-93, Y-97, Y-98, Y-99
The Dictionary of National Biography........DLB-144
Didion, Joan 1934- DLB-2, 173, 185; Y-81, Y-86; CDALB-6
Di Donato, Pietro 1911- DLB-9
Die Fürstliche Bibliothek Corvey Y-96
Diego, Gerardo 1896-1987..............DLB-134
Digges, Thomas circa 1546-1595.........DLB-136
The Digital Millennium Copyright Act: Expanding Copyright Protection in Cyberspace and Beyond Y-98
Dillard, Annie 1945- Y-80
Dillard, R. H. W. 1937- DLB-5
Dillingham, Charles T., Company DLB-49
The Dillingham, G. W., Company DLB-49
Dilly, Edward and Charles [publishing house]................DLB-154
Dilthey, Wilhelm 1833-1911 ....DLB-129
Dimitrova, Blaga 1922- ...DLB-181; CDWLB-4
Dimov, Dimitr 1909-1966 ....DLB-181
Dimsdale, Thomas J. 1831?-1866 ....DLB-186
Dinescu, Mircea 1950- DLB-232
Dinesen, Isak (see Blixen, Karen)
Dingelstedt, Franz von 1814-1881 ....DLB-133
Dintenfass, Mark 1941- Y-84
Diogenes, Jr. (see Brougham, John)
Diogenes Laertius circa 200............DLB-176
DiPrima, Diane 1934- DLB-5, 16
Disch, Thomas M. 1940- DLB-8
Disney, Walt 1901-1966 ....DLB-22
Disraeli, Benjamin 1804-1881 ....DLB-21, 55
D'Israeli, Isaac 1766-1848 ....DLB-107
Ditlevsen, Tove 1917-1976 ....DLB-214
Ditzen, Rudolf (see Fallada, Hans)
Dix, Dorothea Lynde 1802-1887......DLB-1, 235
Dix, Dorothy (see Gilmer, Elizabeth Meriwether)
Dix, Edwards and Company............DLB-49

Dix, Gertrude circa 1874-?.............DLB-197
Dixie, Florence Douglas 1857-1905 ......DLB-174
Dixon, Ella Hepworth 1855 or 1857-1932...............DLB-197
Dixon, Paige (see Corcoran, Barbara)
Dixon, Richard Watson 1833-1900.......DLB-19
Dixon, Stephen 1936- DLB-130
Dmitriev, Ivan Ivanovich 1760-1837 .....DLB-150
Dobell, Bertram 1842-1914 ....DLB-184
Dobell, Sydney 1824-1874..............DLB-32
Dobie, J. Frank 1888-1964..............DLB-212
Döblin, Alfred 1878-1957 ..... DLB-66; CDWLB-2
Dobson, Austin 1840-1921 ....DLB-35, 144
Doctorow, E. L. 1931- DLB-2, 28, 173; Y-80; CDALB-6
Documents on Sixteenth-Century Literature DLB-167, 172
Dodd, Anne [publishing house].........DLB-154
Dodd, Mead and Company............DLB-49
Dodd, William E. 1869-1940............DLB-17
Doderer, Heimito von 1896-1968 ....DLB-85
Dodge, B. W., and Company DLB-46
Dodge, Mary Abigail 1833-1896 ....DLB-221
Dodge, Mary Mapes 1831?-1905 ....DLB-42, 79; DS-13
Dodge Publishing Company DLB-49
Dodgson, Charles Lutwidge (see Carroll, Lewis)
Dodsley, R. [publishing house] DLB-154
Dodsley, Robert 1703-1764 ....DLB-95
Dodson, Owen 1914-1983...............DLB-76
Dodwell, Christina 1951- DLB-204
Doestricks, Q. K. Philander, P. B. (see Thomson, Mortimer)
Doheny, Carrie Estelle 1875-1958........DLB-140
Doherty, John 1798?-1854..............DLB-190
Doig, Ivan 1939- DLB-206
Doinaş, Ştefan Augustin 1922- DLB-232
Domínguez, Sylvia Maida 1935- DLB-122
Donahoe, Patrick [publishing house]......DLB-49
Donald, David H. 1920- DLB-17
The Practice of Biography VI: An Interview with David Herbert Donald Y-87
Donaldson, Scott 1928- DLB-111
Doni, Rodolfo 1919- DLB-177
Donleavy, J. P. 1926- DLB-6, 173
Donnadieu, Marguerite (see Duras, Marguerite)
Donne, John 1572-1631 ....DLB-121, 151; CDBLB-1
Donnelley, R. R., and Sons Company.....DLB-49
Donnelly, Ignatius 1831-1901 ....DLB-12
Donohue and Henneberry..............DLB-49
Donoso, José 1924-1996 ....DLB-113; CDWLB-3
Doolady, M. [publishing house].........DLB-49
Dooley, Ebon (see Ebon)
Doolittle, Hilda 1886-1961 ....DLB-4, 45
Doplicher, Fabio 1938- DLB-128

Cumulative Index

Dor, Milo 1923- DLB-85
Doran, George H., Company.......... DLB-46
Dorgelès, Roland 1886-1973........... DLB-65
Dorn, Edward 1929-1999............... DLB-5
Dorr, Rheta Childe 1866-1948........ DLB-25
Dorris, Michael 1945-1997............DLB-175
Dorset and Middlesex, Charles Sackville,
    Lord Buckhurst, Earl of 1643-1706....DLB-131
Dorst, Tankred 1925- DLB-75, 124
Dos Passos, John 1896-1970
    .... DLB-4, 9; DS-1, DS-15; CDALB-5
John Dos Passos: Artist................... Y-99
John Dos Passos: A Centennial
    Commemoration Y-96
Dostoevsky, Fyodor 1821-1881 .... DLB-238
Doubleday and Company DLB-49
Dougall, Lily 1858-1923............... DLB-92
Doughty, Charles M.
    1843-1926 .... DLB-19, 57, 174
Douglas, Lady Alfred (see Custance, Olive)
Douglas, Gavin 1476-1522 .... DLB-132
Douglas, Keith 1920-1944 .... DLB-27
Douglas, Norman 1868-1952 .... DLB-34, 195
Douglass, Frederick
    1817?-1895..... DLB-1, 43, 50, 79; CDALB-2
Douglass, William circa 1691-1752....... DLB-24
Dourado, Autran 1926- DLB-145
Dove, Arthur G. 1880-1946 .... DLB-188
Dove, Rita 1952- DLB-120; CDALB-7
Dover Publications DLB-46
Doves Press DLB-112
Dowden, Edward 1843-1913 .... DLB-35, 149
Dowell, Coleman 1925-1985 .... DLB-130
Dowland, John 1563-1626 ....DLB-172
Downes, Gwladys 1915- DLB-88
Downing, J., Major (see Davis, Charles A.)
Downing, Major Jack (see Smith, Seba)
Dowriche, Anne
    before 1560-after 1613 ....DLB-172
Dowson, Ernest 1867-1900......... DLB-19, 135
Doxey, William [publishing house] DLB-49
Doyle, Sir Arthur Conan
    1859-1930 ...DLB-18, 70, 156, 178; CDBLB-5
Doyle, Kirby 1932- DLB-16
Doyle, Roddy 1958- DLB-194
Drabble, Margaret
    1939- DLB-14, 155, 231; CDBLB-8
Drach, Albert 1902- DLB-85
Dragojević, Danijel 1934- DLB-181
Drake, Samuel Gardner 1798-1875...... DLB-187
The Dramatic Publishing Company...... DLB-49
Dramatists Play Service DLB-46
Drant, Thomas early 1540s?-1578 ...... DLB-167
Draper, John W. 1811-1882............ DLB-30
Draper, Lyman C. 1815-1891........... DLB-30
Drayton, Michael 1563-1631 .... DLB-121

Dreiser, Theodore 1871-1945
    ....DLB-9, 12, 102, 137; DS-1; CDALB-3
Dresser, Davis 1904-1977 .... DLB-226
Drewitz, Ingeborg 1923-1986.......... DLB-75
Drieu La Rochelle, Pierre 1893-1945 ..... DLB-72
Drinker, Elizabeth 1735-1807 .... DLB-200
Drinkwater, John
    1882-1937................DLB-10, 19, 149
Droste-Hülshoff, Annette von
    1797-1848 .... DLB-133; CDWLB-2
The Drue Heinz Literature Prize
    Excerpt from "Excerpts from a Report
    of the Commission," in David
    Bosworth's *The Death of Descartes*
    An Interview with David Bosworth...... Y-82
Drummond, William, of Hawthornden
    1585-1649 .... DLB-121, 213
Drummond, William Henry
    1854-1907..................... DLB-92
Druzhinin, Aleksandr Vasil'evich
    1824-1864 .... DLB-238
Dryden, Charles 1860?-1931 ....DLB-171
Dryden, John
    1631-1700...... DLB-80, 101, 131; CDBLB-2
Držić, Marin
    circa 1508-1567 ....DLB-147; CDWLB-4
Duane, William 1760-1835............. DLB-43
Dubé, Marcel 1930- DLB-53
Dubé, Rodolphe (see Hertel, François)
Dubie, Norman 1945- DLB-120
Dubois, Silvia 1788 or 1789?-1889 ...... DLB-239
Du Bois, W. E. B.
    1868-1963 ....DLB-47, 50, 91; CDALB-3
Du Bois, William Pène 1916-1993 .... DLB-61
Dubrovina, Ekaterina Oskarovna
    1846-1913 .... DLB-238
Dubus, Andre 1936-1999 .... DLB-130
Ducange, Victor 1783-1833 .... DLB-192
Du Chaillu, Paul Belloni 1831?-1903 .... DLB-189
Ducharme, Réjean 1941- DLB-60
Dučić, Jovan 1871-1943 .....DLB-147; CDWLB-4
Duck, Stephen 1705?-1756 .... DLB-95
Duckworth, Gerald, and Company
    Limited....................... DLB-112
Duclaux, Madame Mary (see Robinson, A. Mary F.)
Dudek, Louis 1918- DLB-88
Duell, Sloan and Pearce DLB-46
Duerer, Albrecht 1471-1528 ....DLB-179
Duff Gordon, Lucie 1821-1869 .... DLB-166
Dufferin, Helen Lady, Countess of Gifford
    1807-1867...................... DLB-199
Duffield and Green..................... DLB-46
Duffy, Maureen 1933- DLB-14
Dufief, Nicholas Gouin 1776-1834 ...... DLB-187
Dugan, Alan 1923- DLB-5
Dugard, William [publishing house].....DLB-170
Dugas, Marcel 1883-1947............. DLB-92
Dugdale, William [publishing house] DLB-106
Duhamel, Georges 1884-1966 .... DLB-65

Dujardin, Edouard 1861-1949 .... DLB-123
Dukes, Ashley 1885-1959.............. DLB-10
Dumas, Alexandre *père* 1802-1870 .....DLB-119, 192
Dumas, Alexandre *fils* 1824-1895 .... DLB-192
Dumas, Henry 1934-1968 .... DLB-41
du Maurier, Daphne 1907-1989 .... DLB-191
Du Maurier, George 1834-1896.....DLB-153, 178
Dunbar, Paul Laurence
    1872-1906....... DLB-50, 54, 78; CDALB-3
Dunbar, William
    circa 1460-circa 1522 ..... DLB-132, 146
Duncan, Norman 1871-1916 .... DLB-92
Duncan, Quince 1940- DLB-145
Duncan, Robert 1919-1988 ....DLB-5, 16, 193
Duncan, Ronald 1914-1982 .... DLB-13
Duncan, Sara Jeannette 1861-1922 ...... DLB-92
Dunigan, Edward, and Brother DLB-49
Dunlap, John 1747-1812 .... DLB-43
Dunlap, William 1766-1839 .... DLB-30, 37, 59
Dunn, Douglas 1942- DLB-40
Dunn, Harvey Thomas 1884-1952 .... DLB-188
Dunn, Stephen 1939- DLB-105
"The Good, The Not So Good".... DLB-105
Dunne, Finley Peter 1867-1936....... DLB-11, 23
Dunne, John Gregory 1932- Y-80
Dunne, Philip 1908-1992 .... DLB-26
Dunning, Ralph Cheever 1878-1930 ...... DLB-4
Dunning, William A. 1857-1922..........DLB-17
Dunsany, Lord (Edward John Moreton
    Drax Plunkett, Baron Dunsany)
    1878-1957............ DLB-10, 77, 153, 156
Duns Scotus, John circa 1266-1308 ..... DLB-115
Dunton, John [publishing house] DLB-170
Dunton, W. Herbert 1878-1936........ DLB-188
Dupin, Amantine-Aurore-Lucile (see Sand, George)
Durand, Lucile (see Bersianik, Louky)
Duranti, Francesca 1935- DLB-196
Duranty, Walter 1884-1957 .... DLB-29
Duras, Marguerite 1914-1996........... DLB-83
Durfey, Thomas 1653-1723 .... DLB-80
Durova, Nadezhda Andreevna
    (Aleksandr Andreevich Aleksandrov)
    1783-1866 .... DLB-198
Durrell, Lawrence 1912-1990
    .... DLB-15, 27, 204; Y-90; CDBLB-7
Durrell, William [publishing house]...... DLB-49
Dürrenmatt, Friedrich
    1921-1990 ....DLB-69, 124; CDWLB-2
Duston, Hannah 1657-1737............ DLB-200
Dutt, Toru 1856-1877................ DLB-240
Dutton, E. P., and Company DLB-49
Duvoisin, Roger 1904-1980 .... DLB-61
Duyckinck, Evert Augustus
    1816-1878..................... DLB-3, 64
Duyckinck, George L. 1823-1863......... DLB-3
Duyckinck and Company DLB-49
Dwight, John Sullivan 1813-1893..... DLB-1, 235

Dwight, Timothy 1752-1817 ....DLB-37
Dybek, Stuart 1942- DLB-130
Dyer, Charles 1928- DLB-13
Dyer, Sir Edward 1543-1607 ....DLB-136
Dyer, George 1755-1841 ....DLB-93
Dyer, John 1699-1757 ....DLB-95
Dyk, Viktor 1877-1931................DLB-215
Dylan, Bob 1941- DLB-16

E

Eager, Edward 1911-1964 ....DLB-22
Eames, Wilberforce 1855-1937 ....DLB-140
Earle, Alice Morse 1853-1911 ....DLB-221
Earle, James H., and Company DLB-49
Earle, John 1600 or 1601-1665 ....DLB-151
Early American Book Illustration,
  by Sinclair Hamilton DLB-49
Eastlake, William 1917-1997 .....DLB-6, 206
Eastman, Carol ?- DLB-44
Eastman, Charles A. (Ohiyesa)
  1858-1939 ....DLB-175
Eastman, Max 1883-1969 ....DLB-91
Eaton, Daniel Isaac 1753-1814 ....DLB-158
Eaton, Edith Maude 1865-1914........DLB-221
Eaton, Winnifred 1875-1954 ....DLB-221
Eberhart, Richard 1904- DLB-48; CDALB-1
Ebner, Jeannie 1918- DLB-85
Ebner-Eschenbach, Marie von
  1830-1916 ....DLB-81
Ebon 1942- DLB-41
E-Books Turn the Corner Y-98
Ecbasis Captivi circa 1045 ....DLB-148
Ecco Press DLB-46
Eckhart, Meister circa 1260-circa 1328 ...DLB-115
The Eclectic Review 1805-1868 ....DLB-110
Eco, Umberto 1932- DLB-196
Edel, Leon 1907-1997 ....DLB-103
Edes, Benjamin 1732-1803..............DLB-43
Edgar, David 1948- DLB-13, 233
Edgeworth, Maria
  1768-1849 ....DLB-116, 159, 163
The Edinburgh Review 1802-1929.........DLB-110
Edinburgh University Press............DLB-112
The Editor Publishing Company.........DLB-49
Editorial Statements..................DLB-137
Edmonds, Randolph 1900- DLB-51
Edmonds, Walter D. 1903-1998 ....DLB-9
Edschmid, Kasimir 1890-1966...........DLB-56
Edwards, Amelia Anne Blandford
  1831-1892 ....DLB-174
Edwards, Edward 1812-1886............DLB-184
Edwards, James [publishing house] DLB-154
Edwards, Jonathan 1703-1758 ....DLB-24
Edwards, Jonathan, Jr. 1745-1801 .....DLB-37
Edwards, Junius 1929- DLB-33

Edwards, Matilda Barbara Betham
  1836-1919 ....DLB-174
Edwards, Richard 1524-1566 ....DLB-62
Edwards, Sarah Pierpont 1710-1758......DLB-200
Effinger, George Alec 1947- DLB-8
Egerton, George 1859-1945.............DLB-135
Eggleston, Edward 1837-1902 ....DLB-12
Eggleston, Wilfred 1901-1986 ....DLB-92
Eglītis, Anšlavs 1906-1993............DLB-220
Ehrenstein, Albert 1886-1950 ....DLB-81
Ehrhart, W. D. 1948- DS-9
Ehrlich, Gretel 1946- DLB-212
Eich, Günter 1907-1972 ....DLB-69, 124
Eichendorff, Joseph Freiherr von
  1788-1857 ....DLB-90
Eifukumon'in 1271-1342 ....DLB-203
1873 Publishers' Catalogues DLB-49
Eighteenth-Century Aesthetic
  Theories DLB-31
Eighteenth-Century Philosophical
  Background..........................DLB-31
Eigner, Larry 1926-1996 ....DLB-5, 193
Eikon Basilike 1649 ....DLB-151
Eilhart von Oberge
  circa 1140-circa 1195...............DLB-148
Einhard circa 770-840 ....DLB-148
Eiseley, Loren 1907-1977 ....DS-17
Eisenreich, Herbert 1925-1986 ....DLB-85
Eisner, Kurt 1867-1919 ....DLB-66
Eklund, Gordon 1945- Y-83
Ekwensi, Cyprian
  1921- DLB-117; CDWLB-3
Elaw, Zilpha circa 1790-? DLB-239
Eld, George [publishing house] DLB-170
Elder, Lonne III 1931- DLB-7, 38, 44
Elder, Paul, and Company DLB-49
The Electronic Text Center and the Electronic
  Archive of Early American Fiction at the
  University of Virginia Library Y-98
Eliade, Mircea 1907-1986....DLB-220; CDWLB-4
Elie, Robert 1915-1973................DLB-88
Elin Pelin 1877-1949........DLB-147; CDWLB-4
Eliot, George
  1819-1880 ....DLB-21, 35, 55; CDBLB-4
Eliot, John 1604-1690 ....DLB-24
Eliot, T. S.
  1888-1965 ......DLB-7, 10, 45, 63; CDALB-5
T. S. Eliot Centennial Y-88
Eliot's Court Press...................DLB-170
Elizabeth I 1533-1603 ....DLB-136
Elizabeth of Nassau-Saarbrücken
  after 1393-1456 ....DLB-179
Elizondo, Salvador 1932- DLB-145
Elizondo, Sergio 1930- DLB-82
Elkin, Stanley 1930-1995....DLB-2, 28, 218; Y-80
Elles, Dora Amy (see Wentworth, Patricia)
Ellet, Elizabeth F. 1818?-1877.........DLB-30
Elliot, Ebenezer 1781-1849..........DLB-96, 190

Elliot, Frances Minto (Dickinson)
  1820-1898 ....DLB-166
Elliott, Charlotte 1789-1871 ....DLB-199
Elliott, George 1923- DLB-68
Elliott, Janice 1931- DLB-14
Elliott, Sarah Barnwell 1848-1928 .....DLB-221
Elliott, Thomes and Talbot DLB-49
Elliott, William 1788-1863............DLB-3
Ellis, Alice Thomas (Anna Margaret Haycraft)
  1932- DLB-194
Ellis, Edward S. 1840-1916 ....DLB-42
Ellis, Frederick Staridge
  [publishing house]..................DLB-106
The George H. Ellis Company DLB-49
Ellis, Havelock 1859-1939.............DLB-190
Ellison, Harlan 1934- DLB-8
Ellison, Ralph
  1914-1994 ...DLB-2, 76, 227; Y-94; CDALB-1
Ellmann, Richard 1918-1987 ......DLB-103; Y-87
Ellroy, James 1948- DLB-226
Elyot, Thomas 1490?-1546 ....DLB-136
Emanuel, James Andrew 1921- DLB-41
Emecheta, Buchi 1944- DLB-117; CDWLB-3
The Emergence of Black Women Writers ...DS-8
Emerson, Ralph Waldo 1803-1882
  ....DLB-1, 59, 73, 183, 223; CDALB-2
Ralph Waldo Emerson in 1982............Y-82
Emerson, William 1769-1811............DLB-37
Emerson, William 1923-1997............Y-97
Emin, Fedor Aleksandrovich
  circa 1735-1770 ....DLB-150
Empedocles fifth century B.C...........DLB-176
Empson, William 1906-1984.............DLB-20
Enchi Fumiko 1905-1986................DLB-182
"Encounter with the West"............DLB-180
The End of English Stage Censorship,
  1945-1968..........................DLB-13
Ende, Michael 1929-1995 ....DLB-75
Endō Shūsaku 1923-1996 ....DLB-182
Engel, Marian 1933-1985...............DLB-53
Engels, Friedrich 1820-1895...........DLB-129
Engle, Paul 1908- DLB-48
English, Thomas Dunn 1819-1902 ......DLB-202
English Composition and Rhetoric (1866),
  by Alexander Bain [excerpt] DLB-57
The English Language: 410 to 1500 .....DLB-146
Ennius 239 B.C.-169 B.C...............DLB-211
Enright, D. J. 1920- DLB-27
Enright, Elizabeth 1909-1968..........DLB-22
Epic and Beast Epic..................DLB-208
Epictetus circa 55-circa 125-130.........DLB-176
Epicurus 342/341 B.C.-271/270 B.C......DLB-176
Epps, Bernard 1936- DLB-53
Epstein, Julius 1909- and
  Epstein, Philip 1909-1952 ....DLB-26
Equiano, Olaudah
  circa 1745-1797 ....DLB-37, 50; DWLB-3

Olaudah Equiano and Unfinished Journeys: The Slave-Narrative Tradition and Twentieth-Century Continuities, by Paul Edwards and Pauline T. Wangman DLB-117

Eragny Press.................... DLB-112

Erasmus, Desiderius 1467-1536 .... DLB-136

Erba, Luciano 1922- DLB-128

Erdrich, Louise 1954- DLB-152, 175, 206; CDALB-7

Erichsen-Brown, Gwethalyn Graham (see Graham, Gwethalyn)

Eriugena, John Scottus circa 810-877 .... DLB-115

Ernst, Paul 1866-1933 .... DLB-66, 118

Ershov, Petr Pavlovich 1815-1869 ...... DLB-205

Erskine, Albert 1911-1993 .... Y-93

Erskine, John 1879-1951........... DLB-9, 102

Erskine, Mrs. Steuart ?-1948.......... DLB-195

Ertel', Aleksandr Ivanovich 1855-1908 .... DLB-238

Ervine, St. John Greer 1883-1971 .... DLB-10

Eschenburg, Johann Joachim 1743-1820... DLB-97

Escoto, Julio 1944- DLB-145

Esdaile, Arundell 1880-1956.......... DLB-201

Eshleman, Clayton 1935- DLB-5

Espriu, Salvador 1913-1985 .... DLB-134

Ess Ess Publishing Company DLB-49

Essex House Press DLB-112

Essop, Ahmed 1931- DLB-225

Esterházy, Péter 1950- DLB-232; CDWLB-4

Estes, Eleanor 1906-1988 .... DLB-22

Estes and Lauriat DLB-49

Estleman, Loren D. 1952- DLB-226

Eszterhas, Joe 1944- DLB-185

Etherege, George 1636-circa 1692 .... DLB-80

Ethridge, Mark, Sr. 1896-1981 .... DLB-127

Ets, Marie Hall 1893- DLB-22

Etter, David 1928- DLB-105

Ettner, Johann Christoph 1654-1724 .... DLB-168

Eupolemius flourished circa 1095....... DLB-148

Euripides circa 484 B.C.-407/406 B.C. DLB-176; CDWLB-1

Evans, Augusta Jane 1835-1909 .... DLB-239

Evans, Caradoc 1878-1945 .... DLB-162

Evans, Charles 1850-1935 .... DLB-187

Evans, Donald 1884-1921............ DLB-54

Evans, George Henry 1805-1856 .... DLB-43

Evans, Hubert 1892-1986............ DLB-92

Evans, M., and Company............ DLB-46

Evans, Mari 1923- DLB-41

Evans, Mary Ann (see Eliot, George)

Evans, Nathaniel 1742-1767 .... DLB-31

Evans, Sebastian 1830-1909 .... DLB-35

Evaristi, Marcella 1953- DLB-233

Everett, Alexander Hill 1790-1847 ...... DLB-59

Everett, Edward 1794-1865........ DLB-1, 59, 235

Everson, R. G. 1903- DLB-88

Everson, William 1912-1994 ..... DLB-5, 16, 212

Ewart, Gavin 1916-1995............. DLB-40

Ewing, Juliana Horatia 1841-1885 ... DLB-21, 163

The Examiner 1808-1881............. DLB-110

Exley, Frederick 1929-1992 ....DLB-143; Y-81

von Eyb, Albrecht 1420-1475 .... DLB-179

Eyre and Spottiswoode............... DLB-106

Ezera, Regīna 1930- DLB-232

Ezzo ?-after 1065................... DLB-148

F

Faber, Frederick William 1814-1863 ..... DLB-32

Faber and Faber Limited.............. DLB-112

Faccio, Rena (see Aleramo, Sibilla)

Fagundo, Ana María 1938- DLB-134

Fair, Ronald L. 1932- DLB-33

Fairfax, Beatrice (see Manning, Marie)

Fairlie, Gerard 1899-1983............. DLB-77

Fallada, Hans 1893-1947............. DLB-56

Fancher, Betsy 1928- Y-83

Fane, Violet 1843-1905............... DLB-35

Fanfrolico Press DLB-112

Fanning, Katherine 1927 .... DLB-127

Fanshawe, Sir Richard 1608-1666 ...... DLB-126

Fantasy Press Publishers............... DLB-46

Fante, John 1909-1983 ....DLB-130; Y-83

Al-Farabi circa 870-950 .... DLB-115

Farabough, Laura 1949- DLB-228

Farah, Nuruddin 1945- ... DLB-125; CDWLB-3

Farber, Norma 1909-1984 .... DLB-61

Farigoule, Louis (see Romains, Jules)

Farjeon, Eleanor 1881-1965 .... DLB-160

Farley, Harriet 1812-1907............ DLB-239

Farley, Walter 1920-1989............. DLB-22

Farmborough, Florence 1887-1978 ...... DLB-204

Farmer, Penelope 1939- DLB-161

Farmer, Philip José 1918- DLB-8

Farnaby, Thomas 1575?-1647.......... DLB-236

Farningham, Marianne (see Hearn, Mary Anne)

Farquhar, George circa 1677-1707........ DLB-84

Farquharson, Martha (see Finley, Martha)

Farrar, Frederic William 1831-1903 ..... DLB-163

Farrar and Rinehart DLB-46

Farrar, Straus and Giroux............. DLB-46

Farrell, J. G. 1935-1979............... DLB-14

Farrell, James T. 1904-1979 ... DLB-4, 9, 86; DS-2

Fast, Howard 1914- DLB-9

Faulkner, George [publishing house] DLB-154

Faulkner, William 1897-1962 ....DLB-9, 11, 44, 102; DS-2; Y-86; CDALB-5

William Faulkner Centenary Y-97

"Faulkner 100–Celebrating the Work," University of South Carolina, Columbia.. Y-97

Impressions of William Faulkner Y-97

Faulkner and Yoknapatawpha Conference, Oxford, Mississippi Y-97

Faulks, Sebastian 1953- DLB-207

Fauset, Jessie Redmon 1882-1961........ DLB-51

Faust, Irvin 1924- DLB-2, 28, 218; Y-80

Fawcett, Edgar 1847-1904............ DLB-202

Fawcett, Millicent Garrett 1847-1929 .... DLB-190

Fawcett Books...................... DLB-46

Fay, Theodore Sedgwick 1807-1898..... DLB-202

Fearing, Kenneth 1902-1961........... DLB-9

Federal Writers' Project DLB-46

Federman, Raymond 1928- Y-80

Fedorov, Innokentii Vasil'evich (see Omulevsky, Innokentii Vasil'evich)

Feiffer, Jules 1929- DLB-7, 44

Feinberg, Charles E. 1899-1988 ....DLB-187; Y-88

Feind, Barthold 1678-1721 .... DLB-168

Feinstein, Elaine 1930- DLB-14, 40

Feiss, Paul Louis 1875-1952 ....DLB-187

Feldman, Irving 1928- DLB-169

Felipe, Léon 1884-1968.............. DLB-108

Fell, Frederick, Publishers.............. DLB-46

Felltham, Owen 1602?-1668........ DLB-126, 151

Fels, Ludwig 1946- DLB-75

Felton, Cornelius Conway 1807-1862.. DLB-1, 235

Fenn, Harry 1837-1911............... DLB-188

Fennario, David 1947- DLB-60

Fenner, Dudley 1558?-1587? DLB-236

Fenno, Jenny 1765?-1803 .... DLB-200

Fenno, John 1751-1798 .... DLB-43

Fenno, R. F., and Company DLB-49

Fenoglio, Beppe 1922-1963..............DLB-177

Fenton, Geoffrey 1539?-1608.......... DLB-136

Fenton, James 1949- DLB-40

Ferber, Edna 1885-1968 .... DLB-9, 28, 86

Ferdinand, Vallery III (see Salaam, Kalamu ya)

Ferguson, Sir Samuel 1810-1886......... DLB-32

Ferguson, William Scott 1875-1954 ...... DLB-47

Fergusson, Robert 1750-1774 .... DLB-109

Ferland, Albert 1872-1943............ DLB-92

Ferlinghetti, Lawrence 1919- DLB-5, 16; CDALB-1

Fermor, Patrick Leigh 1915- DLB-204

Fern, Fanny (see Parton, Sara Payson Willis)

Ferrars, Elizabeth 1907- DLB-87

Ferré, Rosario 1942- DLB-145

Ferret, E., and Company DLB-49

Ferrier, Susan 1782-1854............. DLB-116

Ferril, Thomas Hornsby 1896-1988..... DLB-206

Ferrini, Vincent 1913- DLB-48

Ferron, Jacques 1921-1985 .... DLB-60

Ferron, Madeleine 1922- DLB-53

Ferrucci, Franco 1936- DLB-196

Fetridge and Company................ DLB-49

Feuchtersleben, Ernst Freiherr von
  1806-1849 .... DLB-133
Feuchtwanger, Lion 1884-1958 .... DLB-66
Feuerbach, Ludwig 1804-1872 .... DLB-133
Feuillet, Octave 1821-1890 .... DLB-192
Feydeau, Georges 1862-1921 .... DLB-192
Fichte, Johann Gottlieb 1762-1814 .... DLB-90
Ficke, Arthur Davison 1883-1945 .... DLB-54
Fiction Best-Sellers, 1910-1945 .... DLB-9
Fiction into Film, 1928-1975: A List of Movies
  Based on the Works of Authors in
  British Novelists, 1930-1959 .... DLB-15
Fiedler, Leslie A. 1917- DLB-28, 67
Field, Barron 1789-1846 .... DLB-230
Field, Edward 1924- DLB-105
Field, Michael
  (Katherine Harris Bradley [1846-1914]
  and Edith Emma Cooper
  [1862-1913]) DLB-240
"The Poetry File" DLB-105
Field, Eugene
  1850-1895 .... DLB-23, 42, 140; DS-13
Field, John 1545?-1588 .... DLB-167
Field, Marshall, III 1893-1956 .... DLB-127
Field, Marshall, IV 1916-1965 .... DLB-127
Field, Marshall, V 1941- DLB-127
Field, Nathan 1587-1619 or 1620 .... DLB-58
Field, Rachel 1894-1942 .... DLB-9, 22
A Field Guide to Recent Schools of American
  Poetry Y-86
Fielding, Helen 1958- DLB-231
Fielding, Henry
  1707-1754 .... DLB-39, 84, 101; CDBLB-2
"Defense of Amelia" (1752) DLB-39
From The History of the Adventures of
  Joseph Andrews (1742) DLB-39
Preface to Joseph Andrews (1742) DLB-39
Preface to Sarah Fielding's The Adventures
  of David Simple (1744) DLB-39
Preface to Sarah Fielding's Familiar Letters
  (1747) [excerpt] DLB-39
Fielding, Sarah 1710-1768 .... DLB-39
Preface to The Cry (1754) DLB-39
Fields, Annie Adams 1834-1915 .... DLB-221
Fields, James T. 1817-1881 .... DLB-1, 235
Fields, Julia 1938- DLB-41
Fields, Osgood and Company DLB-49
Fields, W. C. 1880-1946 .... DLB-44
Fifty Penguin Years Y-85
Figes, Eva 1932- DLB-14
Figuera, Angela 1902-1984 .... DLB-108
Filmer, Sir Robert 1586-1653 .... DLB-151
Filson, John circa 1753-1788 .... DLB-37
Finch, Anne, Countess of Winchilsea
  1661-1720 .... DLB-95
Finch, Robert 1900- DLB-88
Findley, Timothy 1930- DLB-53
Finlay, Ian Hamilton 1925- DLB-40

Finley, Martha 1828-1909 .... DLB-42
Finn, Elizabeth Anne (McCaul)
  1825-1921 .... DLB-166
Finney, Jack 1911-1995 .... DLB-8
Finney, Walter Braden (see Finney, Jack)
Firbank, Ronald 1886-1926 .... DLB-36
Firmin, Giles 1615-1697 .... DLB-24
First Edition Library/Collectors'
  Reprints, Inc. Y-91
Fischart, Johann
  1546 or 1547-1590 or 1591 .... DLB-179
Fischer, Karoline Auguste Fernandine
  1764-1842 .... DLB-94
Fischer, Tibor 1959- DLB-231
Fish, Stanley 1938- DLB-67
Fishacre, Richard 1205-1248 .... DLB-115
Fisher, Clay (see Allen, Henry W.)
Fisher, Dorothy Canfield 1879-1958 ... DLB-9, 102
Fisher, Leonard Everett 1924- DLB-61
Fisher, Roy 1930- DLB-40
Fisher, Rudolph 1897-1934 .... DLB-51, 102
Fisher, Steve 1913-1980 .... DLB-226
Fisher, Sydney George 1856-1927 .... DLB-47
Fisher, Vardis 1895-1968 .... DLB-9, 206
Fiske, John 1608-1677 .... DLB-24
Fiske, John 1842-1901 .... DLB-47, 64
Fitch, Thomas circa 1700-1774 .... DLB-31
Fitch, William Clyde 1865-1909 .... DLB-7
FitzGerald, Edward 1809-1883 .... DLB-32
Fitzgerald, F. Scott 1896-1940
  .... DLB-4, 9, 86, 219; Y-81, Y-92;
              DS-1, 15, 16; CDALB-4
F. Scott Fitzgerald Centenary
  Celebrations Y-96
F. Scott Fitzgerald Inducted into the American
  Poets' Corner at St. John the Divine;
  Ezra Pound Banned Y-99
"F. Scott Fitzgerald: St. Paul's Native Son
  and Distinguished American Writer":
  University of Minnesota Conference,
  29-31 October 1982 .... Y-82
First International F. Scott Fitzgerald
  Conference Y-92
Fitzgerald, Penelope 1916- DLB-14, 194
Fitzgerald, Robert 1910-1985 .... Y-80
Fitzgerald, Thomas 1819-1891 .... DLB-23
Fitzgerald, Zelda Sayre 1900-1948 .... Y-84
Fitzhugh, Louise 1928-1974 .... DLB-52
Fitzhugh, William circa 1651-1701 .... DLB-24
Flagg, James Montgomery 1877-1960 .... DLB-188
Flanagan, Thomas 1923- Y-80
Flanner, Hildegarde 1899-1987 .... DLB-48
Flanner, Janet 1892-1978 .... DLB-4
Flannery, Peter 1951- DLB-233
Flaubert, Gustave 1821-1880 .... DLB-119
Flavin, Martin 1883-1967 .... DLB-9
Fleck, Konrad
  (flourished circa 1220) DLB-138
Flecker, James Elroy 1884-1915 ...... DLB-10, 19

Fleeson, Doris 1901-1970 .... DLB-29
Fleißer, Marieluise 1901-1974 ...... DLB-56, 124
Fleming, Abraham 1552?-1607 .... DLB-236
Fleming, Ian 1908-1964 ... DLB-87, 201; CDBLB-7
Fleming, Paul 1609-1640 .... DLB-164
Fleming, Peter 1907-1971 .... DLB-195
Fletcher, Giles, the Elder 1546-1611 ..... DLB-136
Fletcher, Giles, the Younger
  1585 or 1586-1623 .... DLB-121
Fletcher, J. S. 1863-1935 .... DLB-70
Fletcher, John (see Beaumont, Francis)
Fletcher, John Gould 1886-1950 .... DLB-4, 45
Fletcher, Phineas 1582-1650 .... DLB-121
Flieg, Helmut (see Heym, Stefan)
Flint, F. S. 1885-1960 .... DLB-19
Flint, Timothy 1780-1840 .... DLB-73, 186
Flores-Williams, Jason 1969- DLB-209
Florio, John 1553?-1625 .... DLB-172
Fo, Dario 1926- Y-97
Foix, J. V. 1893-1987 .... DLB-134
Foley, Martha (see Burnett, Whit, and Martha Foley)
Folger, Henry Clay 1857-1930 .... DLB-140
Folio Society DLB-112
Follen, Charles 1796-1840 .... DLB-235
Follen, Eliza Lee (Cabot) 1787-1860 .... DLB-1, 235
Follett, Ken 1949- DLB-87; Y-81
Follett Publishing Company DLB-46
Folsom, John West [publishing house] DLB-49
Folz, Hans
  between 1435 and 1440-1513 .... DLB-179
Fontane, Theodor
  1819-1898 .... DLB-129; CDWLB-2
Fontes, Montserrat 1940- DLB-209
Fonvisin, Denis Ivanovich
  1744 or 1745-1792 .... DLB-150
Foote, Horton 1916- DLB-26
Foote, Mary Hallock
  1847-1938 .... DLB-186, 188, 202, 221
Foote, Samuel 1721-1777 .... DLB-89
Foote, Shelby 1916- DLB-2, 17
Forbes, Calvin 1945- DLB-41
Forbes, Ester 1891-1967 .... DLB-22
Forbes, Rosita 1893?-1967 .... DLB-195
Forbes and Company DLB-49
Force, Peter 1790-1868 .... DLB-30
Forché, Carolyn 1950- DLB-5, 193
Ford, Charles Henri 1913- DLB-4, 48
Ford, Corey 1902-1969 .... DLB-11
Ford, Ford Madox
  1873-1939 .... DLB-34, 98, 162; CDBLB-6
Ford, J. B., and Company DLB-49
Ford, Jesse Hill 1928-1996 .... DLB-6
Ford, John 1586-? DLB-58; CDBLB-1
Ford, R. A. D. 1915- DLB-88
Ford, Richard 1944- DLB-227
Ford, Worthington C. 1858-1941 .... DLB-47

Fords, Howard, and Hulbert DLB-49
Foreman, Carl 1914-1984 . . . . DLB-26
Forester, C. S. 1899-1966 . . . . DLB-191
Forester, Frank (see Herbert, Henry William)
Forman, Harry Buxton 1842-1917 . . . . . . DLB-184
Fornés, María Irene 1930- DLB-7
Forrest, Leon 1937-1997 . . . . DLB-33
Forster, E. M.
    1879-1970 . . . . DLB-34, 98, 162, 178, 195;
    DS-10; CDBLB-6
Forster, Georg 1754-1794 . . . . DLB-94
Forster, John 1812-1876 . . . . DLB-144
Forster, Margaret 1938- DLB-155
Forsyth, Frederick 1938- DLB-87
Forten, Charlotte L. 1837-1914 . . . . . . DLB-50, 239
Charlotte Forten: Pages from
    her Diary DLB-50
Fortini, Franco 1917- DLB-128
Fortune, Mary ca. 1833-ca. 1910 . . . . DLB-230
Fortune, T. Thomas 1856-1928 . . . . DLB-23
Fosdick, Charles Austin 1842-1915 . . . . . . DLB-42
Foster, Genevieve 1893-1979 . . . . DLB-61
Foster, Hannah Webster 1758-1840 . . . DLB-37, 200
Foster, John 1648-1681 . . . . DLB-24
Foster, Michael 1904-1956 . . . . DLB-9
Foster, Myles Birket 1825-1899 . . . . DLB-184
Foulis, Robert and Andrew / R. and A.
    [publishing house] DLB-154
Fouqué, Caroline de la Motte
    1774-1831 . . . . DLB-90
Fouqué, Friedrich de la Motte
    1777-1843 . . . . DLB-90
Four Seas Company DLB-46
Four Winds Press DLB-46
Fournier, Henri Alban (see Alain-Fournier)
Fowler and Wells Company DLB-49
Fowles, John
    1926- DLB-14, 139, 207; CDBLB-8
Fox, John, Jr. 1862 or 1863-1919 . . . DLB-9; DS-13
Fox, Paula 1923- DLB-52
Fox, Richard K. [publishing house] DLB-49
Fox, Richard Kyle 1846-1922 . . . . DLB-79
Fox, William Price 1926- DLB-2; Y-81
Foxe, John 1517-1587 . . . . DLB-132
Fraenkel, Michael 1896-1957 . . . . DLB-4
France, Anatole 1844-1924 . . . . DLB-123
France, Richard 1938- DLB-7
Francis, C. S. [publishing house] DLB-49
Francis, Convers 1795-1863 . . . . DLB-1, 235
Francis, Dick 1920- DLB-87
Francis, Sir Frank 1901-1988 . . . . DLB-201
Francis, Jeffrey, Lord 1773-1850 . . . . DLB-107
François 1863-1910 . . . . DLB-92
François, Louise von 1817-1893 . . . . DLB-129
Franck, Sebastian 1499-1542 . . . . DLB-179
Francke, Kuno 1855-1930 . . . . DLB-71

Frank, Bruno 1887-1945 . . . . DLB-118
Frank, Leonhard 1882-1961 . . . . DLB-56, 118
Frank, Melvin (see Panama, Norman)
Frank, Waldo 1889-1967 . . . . DLB-9, 63
Franken, Rose 1895?-1988 . . . . . . DLB-228, Y-84
Franklin, Benjamin
    1706-1790 . . . . DLB-24, 43, 73, 183; CDALB-2
Franklin, James 1697-1735 . . . . DLB-43
Franklin, Miles 1879-1954 . . . . DLB-230
Franklin Library DLB-46
Frantz, Ralph Jules 1902-1979 . . . . DLB-4
Franzos, Karl Emil 1848-1904 . . . . DLB-129
Fraser, G. S. 1915-1980 . . . . DLB-27
Fraser, Kathleen 1935- DLB-169
Frattini, Alberto 1922- DLB-128
Frau Ava ?-1127 . . . . DLB-148
Fraunce, Abraham 1558?-1592 or 1593 . . DLB-236
Frayn, Michael 1933- DLB-13, 14, 194
Frederic, Harold
    1856-1898 . . . . DLB-12, 23; DS-13
Freeling, Nicolas 1927- DLB-87
Freeman, Douglas Southall
    1886-1953 . . . . DLB-17; DS-17
Freeman, Legh Richmond 1842-1915 . . . . . DLB-23
Freeman, Mary E. Wilkins
    1852-1930 . . . . DLB-12, 78, 221
Freeman, R. Austin 1862-1943 . . . . DLB-70
Freidank circa 1170-circa 1233 . . . . DLB-138
Freiligrath, Ferdinand 1810-1876 . . . . DLB-133
Frémont, John Charles 1813-1890 . . . . . . DLB-186
Frémont, John Charles 1813-1890 and
    Frémont, Jessie Benton 1834-1902 . . . DLB-183
French, Alice 1850-1934 . . . . DLB-74; DS-13
French Arthurian Literature DLB-208
French, David 1939- DLB-53
French, Evangeline 1869-1960 . . . . DLB-195
French, Francesca 1871-1960 . . . . DLB-195
French, James [publishing house] DLB-49
French, Samuel [publishing house] DLB-49
Samuel French, Limited DLB-106
Freneau, Philip 1752-1832 . . . . DLB-37, 43
Freni, Melo 1934- DLB-128
Freshfield, Douglas W. 1845-1934 . . . . DLB-174
Freytag, Gustav 1816-1895 . . . . DLB-129
Fried, Erich 1921-1988 . . . . DLB-85
Friedman, Bruce Jay 1930- DLB-2, 28
Friedrich von Hausen circa 1171-1190 . . . DLB-138
Friel, Brian 1929- DLB-13
Friend, Krebs 1895?-1967? DLB-4
Fries, Fritz Rudolf 1935- DLB-75
Fringe and Alternative Theater in
    Great Britain DLB-13
Frisch, Max
    1911-1991 . . . . DLB-69, 124; CDWLB-2
Frischlin, Nicodemus 1547-1590 . . . . DLB-179
Frischmuth, Barbara 1941- DLB-85

Fritz, Jean 1915- DLB-52
Froissart, Jean circa 1337-circa 1404 . . . . . DLB-208
Fromentin, Eugene 1820-1876 . . . . DLB-123
Frontinus circa A.D. 35-A.D. 103/104 . . . DLB-211
Frost, A. B. 1851-1928 . . . . DLB-188; DS-13
Frost, Robert
    1874-1963 . . . . DLB-54; DS-7; CDALB-4
Frothingham, Octavius Brooks
    1822-1895 . . . . DLB-1
Froude, James Anthony
    1818-1894 . . . . DLB-18, 57, 144
Fruitlands 1843-1844 . . . . DLB-223
Fry, Christopher 1907- DLB-13
Fry, Roger 1866-1934 . . . . DS-10
Fry, Stephen 1957- DLB-207
Frye, Northrop 1912-1991 . . . . DLB-67, 68
Fuchs, Daniel 1909-1993 . . . . . DLB-9, 26, 28; Y-93
Fuentes, Carlos 1928- DLB-113; CDWLB-3
Fuertes, Gloria 1918- DLB-108
Fugard, Athol 1932- DLB-225
The Fugitives and the Agrarians:
    The First Exhibition Y-85
Fujiwara no Shunzei 1114-1204 . . . . DLB-203
Fujiwara no Tameaki 1230s?-1290s? DLB-203
Fujiwara no Tameie 1198-1275 . . . . DLB-203
Fujiwara no Teika 1162-1241 . . . . DLB-203
Fulbecke, William 1560-1603? DLB-172
Fuller, Charles H., Jr. 1939- DLB-38
Fuller, Henry Blake 1857-1929 . . . . DLB-12
Fuller, John 1937- DLB-40
Fuller, Margaret (see Fuller, Sarah)
Fuller, Roy 1912-1991 . . . . DLB-15, 20
Fuller, Samuel 1912- DLB-26
Fuller, Sarah 1810-1850
    . . . . . DLB-1, 59, 73, 183, 223, 239; CDALB-2
Fuller, Thomas 1608-1661 . . . . DLB-151
Fullerton, Hugh 1873-1945 . . . . DLB-171
Fullwood, William flourished 1568 . . . . . DLB-236
Fulton, Alice 1952- DLB-193
Fulton, Len 1934- Y-86
Fulton, Robin 1937- DLB-40
Furbank, P. N. 1920- DLB-155
Furman, Laura 1945- Y-86
Furness, Horace Howard
    1833-1912 . . . . DLB-64
Furness, William Henry
    1802-1896 . . . . DLB-1, 235
Furnivall, Frederick James
    1825-1910 . . . . DLB-184
Furphy, Joseph
    (Tom Collins) 1843-1912 . . . . DLB-230
Furthman, Jules 1888-1966 . . . . DLB-26
Furui Yoshikichi 1937- DLB-182
Fushimi, Emperor 1265-1317 . . . . DLB-203
Futabatei, Shimei
    (Hasegawa Tatsunosuke)
    1864-1909 . . . . DLB-180

The Future of the Novel (1899), by
  Henry James...................DLB-18
Fyleman, Rose 1877-1957.............DLB-160

G

Gadda, Carlo Emilio 1893-1973........DLB-177
Gaddis, William 1922-1998.........DLB-2, Y-99
Gág, Wanda 1893-1946..............DLB-22
Gagarin, Ivan Sergeevich 1814-1882.....DLB-198
Gagnon, Madeleine 1938-............DLB-60
Gaine, Hugh 1726-1807..............DLB-43
Gaine, Hugh [publishing house].........DLB-49
Gaines, Ernest J.
  1933-......DLB-2, 33, 152; Y-80; CDALB-6
Gaiser, Gerd 1908-1976..............DLB-69
Galarza, Ernesto 1905-1984............DLB-122
Galaxy Science Fiction Novels...........DLB-46
Gale, Zona 1874-1938............DLB-9, 228, 78
Galen of Pergamon 129-after 210.......DLB-176
Gales, Winifred Marshall 1761-1839.....DLB-200
Gall, Louise von 1815-1855............DLB-133
Gallagher, Tess 1943-.........DLB-120, 212
Gallagher, Wes 1911-..............DLB-127
Gallagher, William Davis 1808-1894......DLB-73
Gallant, Mavis 1922-...............DLB-53
Gallegos, María Magdalena 1935-.....DLB-209
Gallico, Paul 1897-1976...........DLB-9, 171
Galloway, Grace Growden 1727-1782....DLB-200
Gallup, Donald 1913-..............DLB-187
Galsworthy, John 1867-1933
  .....DLB-10, 34, 98, 162; DS-16; CDBLB-5
Galt, John 1779-1839...............DLB-99, 116
Galton, Sir Francis 1822-1911..........DLB-166
Galvin, Brendan 1938-...............DLB-5
Gambit..........................DLB-46
Gamboa, Reymundo 1948-...........DLB-122
Gammer Gurton's Needle.............DLB-62
Gan, Elena Andreevna (Zeneida R-va)
  1814-1842.....................DLB-198
Gannett, Frank E. 1876-1957..........DLB-29
Gaos, Vicente 1919-1980.............DLB-134
García, Andrew 1854?-1943...........DLB-209
García, Lionel G. 1935-.............DLB-82
García, Richard 1941-..............DLB-209
García-Camarillo, Cecilio 1943-.......DLB-209
García Lorca, Federico 1898-1936......DLB-108
García Márquez, Gabriel
  1928-.........DLB-113; Y-82; CDWLB-3
Gardam, Jane 1928-........DLB-14, 161, 231
Garden, Alexander circa 1685-1756......DLB-31
Gardiner, Margaret Power Farmer
  (see Blessington, Marguerite, Countess of)
Gardner, John
  1933-1982.........DLB-2; Y-82; CDALB-7
Garfield, Leon 1921-1996............DLB-161
Garis, Howard R. 1873-1962...........DLB-22

Garland, Hamlin 1860-1940..DLB-12, 71, 78, 186
Garneau, Francis-Xavier 1809-1866......DLB-99
Garneau, Hector de Saint-Denys
  1912-1943.....................DLB-88
Garneau, Michel 1939-..............DLB-53
Garner, Alan 1934-................DLB-161
Garner, Hugh 1913-1979.............DLB-68
Garnett, David 1892-1981.............DLB-34
Garnett, Eve 1900-1991..............DLB-160
Garnett, Richard 1835-1906...........DLB-184
Garrard, Lewis H. 1829-1887..........DLB-186
Garraty, John A. 1920-..............DLB-17
Garrett, George
  1929-...........DLB-2, 5, 130, 152; Y-83
Fellowship of Southern Writers..........Y-98
Garrett, John Work 1872-1942.........DLB-187
Garrick, David 1717-1779..........DLB-84, 213
Garrison, William Lloyd
  1805-1879........DLB-1, 43, 235; CDALB-2
Garro, Elena 1920-1998..............DLB-145
Garth, Samuel 1661-1719.............DLB-95
Garve, Andrew 1908-...............DLB-87
Gary, Romain 1914-1980.............DLB-83
Gascoigne, George 1539?-1577.........DLB-136
Gascoyne, David 1916-...............DLB-20
Gaskell, Elizabeth Cleghorn
  1810-1865.......DLB-21, 144, 159; CDBLB-4
Gaspey, Thomas 1788-1871............DLB-116
Gass, William H. 1924-...........DLB-2, 227
Gates, Doris 1901-.................DLB-22
Gates, Henry Louis, Jr. 1950-.........DLB-67
Gates, Lewis E. 1860-1924...........DLB-71
Gatto, Alfonso 1909-1976............DLB-114
Gault, William Campbell 1910-1995.....DLB-226
Gaunt, Mary 1861-1942..........DLB-174, 230
Gautier, Théophile 1811-1872.........DLB-119
Gauvreau, Claude 1925-1971..........DLB-88
The *Gawain*-Poet
  flourished circa 1350-1400........DLB-146
Gay, Ebenezer 1696-1787.............DLB-24
Gay, John 1685-1732.............DLB-84, 95
Gayarré, Charles E. A. 1805-1895........DLB-30
Gaylord, Charles [publishing house].....DLB-49
Gaylord, Edward King 1873-1974.......DLB-127
Gaylord, Edward Lewis 1919-.........DLB-127
Geda, Sigitas 1943-................DLB-232
Geddes, Gary 1940-................DLB-60
Geddes, Virgil 1897-................DLB-4
Gedeon (Georgii Andreevich Krinovsky)
  circa 1730-1763.................DLB-150
Gee, Maggie 1948-.................DLB-207
Geßner, Salomon 1730-1788..........DLB-97
Geibel, Emanuel 1815-1884...........DLB-129
Geiogamah, Hanay 1945-............DLB-175
Geis, Bernard, Associates..............DLB-46
Geisel, Theodor Seuss 1904-1991...DLB-61; Y-91

Gelb, Arthur 1924-.................DLB-103
Gelb, Barbara 1926-................DLB-103
Gelber, Jack 1932-................DLB-7, 228
Gelinas, Gratien 1909-..............DLB-88
Gellert, Christian Füerchtegott
  1715-1769.....................DLB-97
Gellhorn, Martha 1908-1998.........Y-82, Y-98
Gems, Pam 1925-..................DLB-13
Genet, Jean 1910-1986............DLB-72; Y-86
Genevoix, Maurice 1890-1980..........DLB-65
Genovese, Eugene D. 1930-..........DLB-17
Gent, Peter 1942-..................Y-82
Geoffrey of Monmouth
  circa 1100-1155.................DLB-146
George, Henry 1839-1897.............DLB-23
George, Jean Craighead 1919-.........DLB-52
George, W. L. 1882-1926.............DLB-197
George III, King of Great Britain and Ireland
  1738-1820.....................DLB-213
George V. Higgins to Julian Symons........Y-99
Georgslied 896?....................DLB-148
Gerber, Merrill Joan 1938-...........DLB-218
Gerhardie, William 1895-1977..........DLB-36
Gerhardt, Paul 1607-1676............DLB-164
Gérin, Winifred 1901-1981............DLB-155
Gérin-Lajoie, Antoine 1824-1882........DLB-99
German Drama 800-1280.............DLB-138
German Drama from Naturalism
  to Fascism: 1889-1933............DLB-118
German Literature and Culture from Charlemagne
  to the Early Courtly Period
  ....DLB-148; CDWLB-2
German Radio Play, The.............DLB-124
German Transformation from the Baroque
  to the Enlightenment, The..........DLB-97
The Germanic Epic and Old English
  Heroic Poetry: *Widsith, Waldere,*
  and *The Fight at Finnsburg*..........DLB-146
Germanophilism, by Hans Kohn........DLB-66
Gernsback, Hugo 1884-1967........DLB-8, 137
Gerould, Katharine Fullerton
  1879-1944.....................DLB-78
Gerrish, Samuel [publishing house]......DLB-49
Gerrold, David 1944-................DLB-8
The Ira Gershwin Centenary.............Y-96
Gerson, Jean 1363-1429..............DLB-208
Gersonides 1288-1344................DLB-115
Gerstäcker, Friedrich 1816-1872........DLB-129
Gerstenberg, Heinrich Wilhelm von
  1737-1823.....................DLB-97
Gervinus, Georg Gottfried
  1805-1871.....................DLB-133
Geston, Mark S. 1946-...............DLB-8
Al-Ghazali 1058-1111................DLB-115
Gibbings, Robert 1889-1958...........DLB-195
Gibbon, Edward 1737-1794............DLB-104
Gibbon, John Murray 1875-1952........DLB-92
Gibbon, Lewis Grassic (see Mitchell, James Leslie)

Gibbons, Floyd 1887-1939 . . . . DLB-25	Giudici, Giovanni 1924- DLB-128	Gogarty, Oliver St. John 1878-1957 . . . DLB-15, 19
Gibbons, Reginald 1947- DLB-120	Giuliani, Alfredo 1924- DLB-128	Gogol, Nikolai Vasil'evich 1809-1852 . . . DLB-198
Gibbons, William ?-? DLB-73	Glackens, William J. 1870-1938 . . . . DLB-188	Goines, Donald 1937-1974 . . . . DLB-33
Gibson, Charles Dana 1867-1944 . . . . DLB-188; DS-13	Gladstone, William Ewart 1809-1898 . . . . DLB-57, 184	Gold, Herbert 1924- DLB-2; Y-81
Gibson, Graeme 1934- DLB-53	Glaeser, Ernst 1902-1963 . . . . DLB-69	Gold, Michael 1893-1967 . . . . DLB-9, 28
Gibson, Margaret 1944- DLB-120	Glancy, Diane 1941- DLB-175	Goldbarth, Albert 1948- DLB-120
Gibson, Margaret Dunlop 1843-1920 . . . . . DLB-174	Glanville, Brian 1931- DLB-15, 139	Goldberg, Dick 1947- DLB-7
Gibson, Wilfrid 1878-1962 . . . . DLB-19	Glapthorne, Henry 1610-1643? DLB-58	Golden Cockerel Press DLB-112
Gibson, William 1914- DLB-7	Glasgow, Ellen 1873-1945 . . . . DLB-9, 12	Golding, Arthur 1536-1606 . . . . DLB-136
Gide, André 1869-1951 . . . . DLB-65	Glasier, Katharine Bruce 1867-1950 . . . . . DLB-190	Golding, Louis 1895-1958 . . . . DLB-195
Giguère, Diane 1937- DLB-53	Glaspell, Susan 1876-1948 . . . . . . DLB-7, 9, 78, 228	Golding, William 1911-1993 . . . . . DLB-15, 100; Y-83; CDBLB-7
Giguère, Roland 1929- DLB-60	Glass, Montague 1877-1934 . . . . DLB-11	Goldman, Emma 1869-1940 . . . . DLB-221
Gil de Biedma, Jaime 1929-1990 . . . . DLB-108	Glassco, John 1909-1981 . . . . DLB-68	Goldman, William 1931- DLB-44
Gil-Albert, Juan 1906- DLB-134	Glauser, Friedrich 1896-1938 . . . . DLB-56	Goldring, Douglas 1887-1960 . . . . DLB-197
Gilbert, Anthony 1899-1973 . . . . DLB-77	F. Gleason's Publishing Hall DLB-49	Goldsmith, Oliver 1730?-1774 . . . . DLB-39, 89, 104, 109, 142; CDBLB-2
Gilbert, Sir Humphrey 1537-1583 . . . . . . DLB-136	Gleim, Johann Wilhelm Ludwig 1719-1803 . . . . DLB-97	Goldsmith, Oliver 1794-1861 . . . . DLB-99
Gilbert, Michael 1912- DLB-87	Glendinning, Victoria 1937- DLB-155	Goldsmith Publishing Company DLB-46
Gilbert, Sandra M. 1936- DLB-120	The Cult of Biography Excerpts from the Second Folio Debate: "Biographies are generally a disease of English Literature" Y-86	Goldstein, Richard 1944- DLB-185
Gilchrist, Alexander 1828-1861 . . . . DLB-144		Gollancz, Sir Israel 1864-1930 . . . . DLB-201
Gilchrist, Ellen 1935- DLB-130		Gollancz, Victor, Limited DLB-112
Gilder, Jeannette L. 1849-1916 . . . . DLB-79	Glinka, Fedor Nikolaevich 1786-1880 . . . . DLB-205	Gombrowicz, Witold 1904-1969 . . . . DLB-215; CDWLB-4
Gilder, Richard Watson 1844-1909 . . . DLB-64, 79	Glover, Richard 1712-1785 . . . . DLB-95	
Gildersleeve, Basil 1831-1924 . . . . DLB-71	Glück, Louise 1943- DLB-5	Gómez-Quiñones, Juan 1942- DLB-122
Giles of Rome circa 1243-1316 . . . . DLB-115	Glyn, Elinor 1864-1943 . . . . DLB-153	Gomme, Laurence James [publishing house] DLB-46
Giles, Henry 1809-1882 . . . . DLB-64	Gnedich, Nikolai Ivanovich 1784-1833 . . . DLB-205	
Gilfillan, George 1813-1878 . . . . DLB-144	Gobineau, Joseph-Arthur de 1816-1882 . . . . DLB-123	Goncharov, Ivan Aleksandrovich 1812-1891 . . . . DLB-238
Gill, Eric 1882-1940 . . . . DLB-98		
Gill, Sarah Prince 1728-1771 . . . . DLB-200	Godber, John 1956- DLB-233	Goncourt, Edmond de 1822-1896 . . . . . . DLB-123
Gill, William F., Company DLB-49	Godbout, Jacques 1933- DLB-53	Goncourt, Jules de 1830-1870 . . . . DLB-123
Gillespie, A. Lincoln, Jr. 1895-1950 . . . . . . DLB-4	Goddard, Morrill 1865-1937 . . . . DLB-25	Gonzales, Rodolfo "Corky" 1928- DLB-122
Gilliam, Florence ?-? DLB-4	Goddard, William 1740-1817 . . . . DLB-43	González, Angel 1925- DLB-108
Gilliatt, Penelope 1932-1993 . . . . DLB-14	Godden, Rumer 1907-1998 . . . . DLB-161	Gonzalez, Genaro 1949- DLB-122
Gillott, Jacky 1939-1980 . . . . DLB-14	Godey, Louis A. 1804-1878 . . . . DLB-73	Gonzalez, Ray 1952- DLB-122
Gilman, Caroline H. 1794-1888 . . . . . . DLB-3, 73	Godey and McMichael DLB-49	Gonzales-Berry, Erlinda 1942- DLB-209
Gilman, Charlotte Perkins 1860-1935 . . . DLB-221	Godfrey, Dave 1938- DLB-60	"Chicano Language" DLB-82
Gilman, W. and J. [publishing house] DLB-49	Godfrey, Thomas 1736-1763 . . . . DLB-31	González de Mireles, Jovita 1899-1983 . . . . DLB-122
Gilmer, Elizabeth Meriwether 1861-1951 . . DLB-29	Godine, David R., Publisher DLB-46	
Gilmer, Francis Walker 1790-1826 . . . . DLB-37	Godkin, E. L. 1831-1902 . . . . DLB-79	González-T., César A. 1931- DLB-82
Gilroy, Frank D. 1925- DLB-7	Godolphin, Sidney 1610-1643 . . . . DLB-126	Goodbye, Gutenberg? A Lecture at the New York Public Library, 18 April 1995, by Donald Lamm Y-95
Gimferrer, Pere (Pedro) 1945- DLB-134	Godwin, Gail 1937- DLB-6, 234	
Gingrich, Arnold 1903-1976 . . . . DLB-137	Godwin, M. J., and Company DLB-154	Goodis, David 1917-1967 . . . . DLB-226
Ginsberg, Allen 1926-1997 . . . . DLB-5, 16, 169, 237; CDALB-1	Godwin, Mary Jane Clairmont 1766-1841 . . . . DLB-163	Goodison, Lorna 1947- DLB-157
		Goodman, Paul 1911-1972 . . . . DLB-130
Ginzburg, Natalia 1916-1991 . . . . DLB-177	Godwin, Parke 1816-1904 . . . . DLB-3, 64	The Goodman Theatre DLB-7
Ginzkey, Franz Karl 1871-1963 . . . . DLB-81	Godwin, William 1756-1836 . . . . . . DLB-39, 104, 142, 158, 163; CDBLB-3	Goodrich, Frances 1891-1984 and Hackett, Albert 1900-1995 . . . . DLB-26
Gioia, Dana 1950- DLB-120		
Giono, Jean 1895-1970 . . . . DLB-72	Preface to St. Leon (1799) DLB-39	Goodrich, Samuel Griswold 1793-1860 . . . . DLB-1, 42, 73
Giotti, Virgilio 1885-1957 . . . . DLB-114	Goering, Reinhard 1887-1936 . . . . DLB-118	
Giovanni, Nikki 1943- DLB-5, 41; CDALB-7	Goes, Albrecht 1908- DLB-69	Goodrich, S. G. [publishing house] DLB-49
Gipson, Lawrence Henry 1880-1971 . . . . . DLB-17	Goethe, Johann Wolfgang von 1749-1832 . . . . DLB-94; CDWLB-2	Goodspeed, C. E., and Company DLB-49
Girard, Rodolphe 1879-1956 . . . . DLB-92		Goodwin, Stephen 1943- Y-82
Giraudoux, Jean 1882-1944 . . . . DLB-65	Goetz, Curt 1888-1960 . . . . DLB-124	Googe, Barnabe 1540-1594 . . . . DLB-132
Gissing, George 1857-1903 . . . . . DLB-18, 135, 184	Goffe, Thomas circa 1592-1629 . . . . DLB-58	Gookin, Daniel 1612-1687 . . . . DLB-24
The Place of Realism in Fiction (1895) DLB-18	Goffstein, M. B. 1940- DLB-61	Gordimer, Nadine 1923- DLB-225; Y-91

Gordon, Adam Lindsay 1833-1870 . . . . . .DLB-230	Grahame, Kenneth 1859-1932 . . . . DLB-34, 141, 178	Greene, Asa 1789-1838 . . . . .DLB-11
Gordon, Caroline 1895-1981 . . . . DLB-4, 9, 102; DS-17; Y-81	Grainger, Martin Allerdale 1874-1941 . . . . .DLB-92	Greene, Belle da Costa 1883-1950. . . . . . .DLB-187
Gordon, Giles 1940- DLB-14, 139, 207	Gramatky, Hardie 1907-1979. . . . . .DLB-22	Greene, Benjamin H. [publishing house] DLB-49
Gordon, Helen Cameron, Lady Russell 1867-1949 . . . . .DLB-195	Grand, Sarah 1854-1943 . . . . DLB-135, 197	Greene, Graham 1904-1991 . . . . DLB-13, 15, 77, 100, 162, 201, 204; Y-85, Y-91; CDBLB-7
Gordon, Lyndall 1941- DLB-155	Grandbois, Alain 1900-1975. . . . . .DLB-92	
Gordon, Mary 1949- DLB-6; Y-81	Grandson, Oton de circa 1345-1397 . . . . .DLB-208	Greene, Robert 1558-1592. . . . . DLB-62, 167
Gordone, Charles 1925-1995. . . . . .DLB-7	Grange, John circa 1556-? DLB-136	Greene, Robert Bernard (Bob) Jr. 1947- DLB-185
Gore, Catherine 1800-1861 . . . . .DLB-116	Granich, Irwin (see Gold, Michael)	
Gore-Booth, Eva 1870-1926. . . . . .DLB-240	Granovsky, Timofei Nikolaevich 1813-1855 . . . . .DLB-198	Greenhow, Robert 1800-1854 . . . . .DLB-30
Gores, Joe 1931- DLB-226	Grant, Anne MacVicar 1755-1838. . . . . . .DLB-200	Greenlee, William B. 1872-1953 . . . . . . .DLB-187
Gorey, Edward 1925- DLB-61	Grant, Duncan 1885-1978 . . . . DS-10	Greenough, Horatio 1805-1852. . . . . . .DLB-1, 235
Gorgias of Leontini circa 485 B.C.-376 B.C. DLB-176	Grant, George 1918-1988 . . . . .DLB-88	Greenwell, Dora 1821-1882. . . . . DLB-35, 199
Görres, Joseph 1776-1848. . . . . .DLB-90	Grant, George Monro 1835-1902 . . . . . . .DLB-99	Greenwillow Books DLB-46
Gosse, Edmund 1849-1928 . . . . . DLB-57, 144, 184	Grant, Harry J. 1881-1963. . . . . .DLB-29	Greenwood, Grace (see Lippincott, Sara Jane Clarke)
Gosson, Stephen 1554-1624. . . . . .DLB-172	Grant, James Edward 1905-1966. . . . . .DLB-26	Greenwood, Walter 1903-1974 . . . . . . DLB-10, 191
The Schoole of Abuse (1579) DLB-172	Grass, Günter 1927- . . . DLB-75, 124; CDWLB-2	Greer, Ben 1948- DLB-6
Gotlieb, Phyllis 1926- DLB-88	Grasty, Charles H. 1863-1924. . . . . .DLB-25	Greflinger, Georg 1620?-1677 . . . . .DLB-164
Go-Toba 1180-1239. . . . . .DLB-203	Grau, Shirley Ann 1929- DLB-2, 218	Greg, W. R. 1809-1881 . . . . .DLB-55
Gottfried von Straßburg died before 1230 . . . . DLB-138; CDWLB-2	Graves, John 1920- Y-83	Greg, W. W. 1875-1959 . . . . .DLB-201
Gotthelf, Jeremias 1797-1854 . . . . .DLB-133	Graves, Richard 1715-1804 . . . . .DLB-39	Gregg, Josiah 1806-1850 . . . . DLB-183, 186
Gottschalk circa 804/808-869. . . . . .DLB-148	Graves, Robert 1895-1985 . . . DLB-20, 100, 191; DS-18; Y-85; CDBLB-6	Gregg Press DLB-46
Gottsched, Johann Christoph 1700-1766. . . . . .DLB-97	Gray, Alasdair 1934- DLB-194	Gregory, Isabella Augusta Persse, Lady 1852-1932 . . . . .DLB-10
Götz, Johann Nikolaus 1721-1781 . . . . .DLB-97	Gray, Asa 1810-1888 . . . . .DLB-1, 235	Gregory, Horace 1898-1982 . . . . .DLB-48
Goudge, Elizabeth 1900-1984 . . . . .DLB-191	Gray, David 1838-1861 . . . . .DLB-32	Gregory of Rimini circa 1300-1358 . . . . . .DLB-115
Gould, Wallace 1882-1940 . . . . .DLB-54	Gray, Simon 1936- DLB-13	Gregynog Press DLB-112
Govoni, Corrado 1884-1965 . . . . .DLB-114	Gray, Thomas 1716-1771. . . . . .DLB-109; CDBLB-2	Greiffenberg, Catharina Regina von 1633-1694 . . . . .DLB-168
Gower, John circa 1330-1408. . . . . .DLB-146	Grayson, Richard 1951- DLB-234	
Goyen, William 1915-1983 . . . . . DLB-2, 218; Y-83	Grayson, William J. 1788-1863 . . . . .DLB-3, 64	Grenfell, Wilfred Thomason 1865-1940 . . . . .DLB-92
Goytisolo, José Augustín 1928- DLB-134	The Great Bibliographers Series Y-93	
Gozzano, Guido 1883-1916 . . . . .DLB-114	The Great Modern Library Scam Y-98	Gress, Elsa 1919-1988 . . . . .DLB-214
Grabbe, Christian Dietrich 1801-1836. . . .DLB-133	The Great War and the Theater, 1914-1918 [Great Britain] .DLB-10	Greve, Felix Paul (see Grove, Frederick Philip)
Gracq, Julien 1910- DLB-83		Greville, Fulke, First Lord Brooke 1554-1628 . . . . DLB-62, 172
Grady, Henry W. 1850-1889. . . . . .DLB-23	The Great War Exhibition and Symposium at the University of South Carolina Y-97	
Graf, Oskar Maria 1894-1967 . . . . .DLB-56	Grech, Nikolai Ivanovich 1787-1867 . . . . .DLB-198	Grey, Sir George, K.C.B. 1812-1898 . . . . .DLB-184
Graf Rudolf between circa 1170 and circa 1185 . . .DLB-148	Greeley, Horace 1811-1872 . . . . DLB-3, 43, 189	Grey, Lady Jane 1537-1554 . . . . .DLB-132
	Green, Adolph (see Comden, Betty)	Grey Owl 1888-1938. . . . . DLB-92; DS-17
Grafton, Richard [publishing house] DLB-170	Green, Anna Katharine 1846-1935 . . . . DLB-202, 221	Grey, Zane 1872-1939 . . . . .DLB-9, 212
Grafton, Sue 1940- DLB-226		Grey Walls Press .DLB-112
Graham, George Rex 1813-1894. . . . . .DLB-73	Green, Duff 1791-1875. . . . . .DLB-43	Griboedov, Aleksandr Sergeevich 1795?-1829 . . . . .DLB-205
Graham, Gwethalyn 1913-1965. . . . . .DLB-88	Green, Elizabeth Shippen 1871-1954 . . . . .DLB-188	
Graham, Jorie 1951- DLB-120	Green, Gerald 1922- DLB-28	Grier, Eldon 1917- DLB-88
Graham, Katharine 1917- DLB-127	Green, Henry 1905-1973 . . . . .DLB-15	Grieve, C. M. (see MacDiarmid, Hugh)
Graham, Lorenz 1902-1989 . . . . .DLB-76	Green, Jonas 1712-1767 . . . . .DLB-31	Griffin, Bartholomew flourished 1596. . . .DLB-172
Graham, Philip 1915-1963 . . . . .DLB-127	Green, Joseph 1706-1780 . . . . .DLB-31	Griffin, Gerald 1803-1840 . . . . .DLB-159
Graham, R. B. Cunninghame 1852-1936 . . . . DLB-98, 135, 174	Green, Julien 1900-1998 . . . . DLB-4, 72	Griffith, Elizabeth 1727?-1793 . . . . DLB-39, 89
	Green, Paul 1894-1981 . . . . DLB-7, 9; Y-81	Preface to *The Delicate Distress* (1769) DLB-39
Graham, Shirley 1896-1977 . . . . .DLB-76	Green, T. and S. [publishing house] DLB-49	Griffith, George 1857-1906 . . . . .DLB-178
Graham, Stephen 1884-1975 . . . . .DLB-195	Green, Thomas Hill 1836-1882. . . . . .DLB-190	Griffiths, Ralph [publishing house] DLB-154
Graham, W. S. 1918- DLB-20	Green, Timothy [publishing house] DLB-49	Griffiths, Trevor 1935- DLB-13
Graham, William H. [publishing house] . . .DLB-49	Greenaway, Kate 1846-1901 . . . . .DLB-141	Griggs, S. C., and Company DLB-49
Graham, Winston 1910- DLB-77	Greenberg: Publisher DLB-46	Griggs, Sutton Elbert 1872-1930 . . . . .DLB-50
	Green Tiger Press .DLB-46	Grignon, Claude-Henri 1894-1976 . . . . . .DLB-68
		Grigorovich, Dmitrii Vasil'evich 1822-1899 . . . . .DLB-238

Cumulative Index

Grigson, Geoffrey 1905- DLB-27
Grillparzer, Franz
   1791-1872 .... DLB-133; CDWLB-2
Grimald, Nicholas
   circa 1519-circa 1562 .... DLB-136
Grimké, Angelina Weld 1880-1958 ... DLB-50, 54
Grimké, Sarah Moore 1792-1873 .... DLB-239
Grimm, Hans 1875-1959 .... DLB-66
Grimm, Jacob 1785-1863 .... DLB-90
Grimm, Wilhelm
   1786-1859............. DLB-90; CDWLB-2
Grimmelshausen, Johann Jacob Christoffel von
   1621 or 1622-1676 ..... DLB-168; CDWLB-2
Grimshaw, Beatrice Ethel 1871-1953 ..... DLB-174
Grindal, Edmund 1519 or 1520-1583..... DLB-132
Griswold, Rufus Wilmot 1815-1857.... DLB-3, 59
Grosart, Alexander Balloch 1827-1899 ... DLB-184
Gross, Milt 1895-1953 .... DLB-11
Grosset and Dunlap DLB-49
Grossman, Allen 1932- DLB-193
Grossman Publishers DLB-46
Grosseteste, Robert circa 1160-1253..... DLB-115
Grosvenor, Gilbert H. 1875-1966 .... DLB-91
Groth, Klaus 1819-1899 .... DLB-129
Groulx, Lionel 1878-1967.............. DLB-68
Grove, Frederick Philip 1879-1949 .... DLB-92
Grove Press DLB-46
Grubb, Davis 1919-1980 .... DLB-6
Gruelle, Johnny 1880-1938............ DLB-22
von Grumbach, Argula
   1492-after 1563?................DLB-179
Grymeston, Elizabeth
   before 1563-before 1604........... DLB-136
Gryphius, Andreas
   1616-1664........... DLB-164; CDWLB-2
Gryphius, Christian 1649-1706......... DLB-168
Guare, John 1938- DLB-7
Guerra, Tonino 1920- DLB-128
Guest, Barbara 1920- DLB-5, 193
Guèvremont, Germaine 1893-1968 ...... DLB-68
Guidacci, Margherita 1921-1992 .... DLB-128
Guide to the Archives of Publishers, Journals,
   and Literary Agents in North American
   Libraries......................... Y-93
Guillén, Jorge 1893-1984 .... DLB-108
Guilloux, Louis 1899-1980............ DLB-72
Guilpin, Everard
   circa 1572-after 1608?............. DLB-136
Guiney, Louise Imogen 1861-1920...... DLB-54
Guiterman, Arthur 1871-1943 .... DLB-11
Günderrode, Caroline von 1780-1806 .... DLB-90
Gundulić, Ivan 1589-1638 ...DLB-147; CDWLB-4
Gunn, Bill 1934-1989 .... DLB-38
Gunn, James E. 1923- DLB-8
Gunn, Neil M. 1891-1973 .... DLB-15
Gunn, Thom 1929- DLB-27; CDBLB-8
Gunnars, Kristjana 1948- DLB-60

Günther, Johann Christian
   1695-1723..................... DLB-168
Gurik, Robert 1932- DLB-60
Gustafson, Ralph 1909- DLB-88
Gütersloh, Albert Paris 1887-1973 .... DLB-81
Guthrie, A. B., Jr. 1901-1991 .... DLB-6, 212
Guthrie, Ramon 1896-1973 .... DLB-4
The Guthrie Theater DLB-7
Guthrie, Thomas Anstey
   (see Anstey, FC)
Gutzkow, Karl 1811-1878.............. DLB-133
Guy, Ray 1939- DLB-60
Guy, Rosa 1925- DLB-33
Guyot, Arnold 1807-1884............... DS-13
Gwynne, Erskine 1898-1948 .... DLB-4
Gyles, John 1680-1755 .... DLB-99
Gysin, Brion 1916- DLB-16

H

H.D. (see Doolittle, Hilda)
Habington, William 1605-1654 .... DLB-126
Hacker, Marilyn 1942- DLB-120
Hackett, Albert (see Goodrich, Frances)
Hacks, Peter 1928- DLB-124
Hadas, Rachel 1948- DLB-120
Hadden, Briton 1898-1929............. DLB-91
Hagedorn, Friedrich von 1708-1754 ..... DLB-168
Hagelstange, Rudolf 1912-1984 .... DLB-69
Haggard, H. Rider
   1856-1925 .... DLB-70, 156, 174, 178
Haggard, William 1907-1993 .... Y-93
Hahn-Hahn, Ida Gräfin von
   1805-1880 .... DLB-133
Haig-Brown, Roderick 1908-1976........ DLB-88
Haight, Gordon S. 1901-1985.......... DLB-103
Hailey, Arthur 1920- DLB-88; Y-82
Haines, John 1924- DLB-5, 212
Hake, Edward flourished 1566-1604 .... DLB-136
Hake, Thomas Gordon 1809-1895....... DLB-32
Hakluyt, Richard 1552?-1616.......... DLB-136
Halas, František 1901-1949 .... DLB-215
Halbe, Max 1865-1944................ DLB-118
Haldane, J. B. S. 1892-1964 .... DLB-160
Haldeman, Joe 1943- DLB-8
Haldeman-Julius Company DLB-46
Haldone, Charlotte 1894-1969.......... DLB-191
Hale, E. J., and Son.................. DLB-49
Hale, Edward Everett
   1822-1909 ....DLB-1, 42, 74, 235
Hale, Janet Campbell 1946- DLB-175
Hale, Kathleen 1898- DLB-160
Hale, Leo Thomas (see Ebon)
Hale, Lucretia Peabody 1820-1900...... DLB-42
Hale, Nancy
   1908-1988 ...... DLB-86; DS-17; Y-80, Y-88

Hale, Sarah Josepha (Buell)
   1788-1879....................DLB-1, 42, 73
Hale, Susan 1833-1910............... DLB-221
Hales, John 1584-1656 .... DLB-151
Halévy, Ludovic 1834-1908........... DLB-192
Haley, Alex 1921-1992....... DLB-38; CDALB-7
Haliburton, Thomas Chandler
   1796-1865..................... DLB-11, 99
Hall, Anna Maria 1800-1881 .... DLB-159
Hall, Donald 1928- DLB-5
Hall, Edward 1497-1547 .... DLB-132
Hall, James 1793-1868 ....DLB-73, 74
Hall, Joseph 1574-1656 .... DLB-121, 151
Hall, Radclyffe 1880-1943 .... DLB-191
Hall, Samuel [publishing house] DLB-49
Hall, Sarah Ewing 1761-1830 .... DLB-200
Hallam, Arthur Henry 1811-1833 ..... DLB-32
On Some of the Characteristics of Modern
   Poetry and On the Lyrical Poems of
   Alfred Tennyson (1831) DLB-32
Halleck, Fitz-Greene 1790-1867 .... DLB-3
Haller, Albrecht von 1708-1777 .... DLB-168
Halliday, Brett (see Dresser, Davis)
Halliwell-Phillipps, James Orchard
   1820-1889 .... DLB-184
Hallmann, Johann Christian
   1640-1704 or 1716? DLB-168
Hallmark Editions DLB-46
Halper, Albert 1904-1984.............. DLB-9
Halperin, John William 1941- DLB-111
Halstead, Murat 1829-1908 .... DLB-23
Hamann, Johann Georg 1730-1788....... DLB-97
Hamburger, Michael 1924- DLB-27
Hamilton, Alexander 1712-1756 .... DLB-31
Hamilton, Alexander 1755?-1804........ DLB-37
Hamilton, Cicely 1872-1952.........DLB-10, 197
Hamilton, Edmond 1904-1977 .... DLB-8
Hamilton, Elizabeth 1758-1816......DLB-116, 158
Hamilton, Gail (see Corcoran, Barbara)
Hamilton, Gail (see Dodge, Mary Abigail)
Hamilton, Hamish, Limited DLB-112
Hamilton, Ian 1938- DLB-40, 155
Hamilton, Janet 1795-1873 .... DLB-199
Hamilton, Mary Agnes 1884-1962.......DLB-197
Hamilton, Patrick 1904-1962 ....DLB-10, 191
Hamilton, Virginia 1936- DLB-33, 52
Hammett, Dashiell
   1894-1961 .... DLB-226; DS-6; CDALB-5
The Glass Key and Other Dashiell Hammett
   Mysteries Y-96
Dashiell Hammett: An Appeal in *TAC*...... Y-91
Hammon, Jupiter 1711-died between
   1790 and 1806 .... DLB-31, 50
Hammond, John ?-1663 .... DLB-24
Hamner, Earl 1923- DLB-6
Hampson, John 1901-1955............. DLB-191
Hampton, Christopher 1946- DLB-13

Handel-Mazzetti, Enrica von 1871-1955 ...DLB-81
Handke, Peter 1942- DLB-85, 124
Handlin, Oscar 1915- DLB-17
Hankin, St. John 1869-1909............DLB-10
Hanley, Clifford 1922- DLB-14
Hanley, James 1901-1985 ....DLB-191
Hannah, Barry 1942- DLB-6, 234
Hannay, James 1827-1873 ....DLB-21
Hansberry, Lorraine
 1930-1965 ....DLB-7, 38; CDALB-1
Hansen, Martin A. 1909-1955.........DLB-214
Hansen, Thorkild 1927-1989..........DLB-214
Hanson, Elizabeth 1684-1737.........DLB-200
Hapgood, Norman 1868-1937..........DLB-91
Happel, Eberhard Werner 1647-1690 ....DLB-168
The Harbinger 1845-1849 ....DLB-223
Harcourt Brace Jovanovich DLB-46
Hardenberg, Friedrich von (see Novalis)
Harding, Walter 1917- DLB-111
Hardwick, Elizabeth 1916- DLB-6
Hardy, Thomas
 1840-1928 ....DLB-18, 19, 135; CDBLB-5
"Candour in English Fiction" (1890) DLB-18
Hare, Cyril 1900-1958...............DLB-77
Hare, David 1947- DLB-13
Hargrove, Marion 1919- DLB-11
Häring, Georg Wilhelm Heinrich
 (see Alexis, Willibald)
Harington, Donald 1935- DLB-152
Harington, Sir John 1560-1612 ....DLB-136
Harjo, Joy 1951- DLB-120, 175
Harkness, Margaret (John Law)
 1854-1923 ....DLB-197
Harley, Edward, second Earl of Oxford
 1689-1741 ....DLB-213
Harley, Robert, first Earl of Oxford
 1661-1724 ....DLB-213
Harlow, Robert 1923- DLB-60
Harman, Thomas flourished 1566-1573 ...DLB-136
Harness, Charles L. 1915- DLB-8
Harnett, Cynthia 1893-1981 ....DLB-161
Harper, Edith Alice Mary (see Wickham, Anna)
Harper, Fletcher 1806-1877 ....DLB-79
Harper, Frances Ellen Watkins
 1825-1911 ....DLB-50, 221
Harper, Michael S. 1938- DLB-41
Harper and Brothers DLB-49
Harpur, Charles 1813-1868............DLB-230
Harraden, Beatrice 1864-1943 ....DLB-153
Harrap, George G., and Company
 Limited DLB-112
Harriot, Thomas 1560-1621 ....DLB-136
Harris, Alexander 1805-1874 ....DLB-230
Harris, Benjamin ?-circa 1720 ....DLB-42, 43
Harris, Christie 1907- DLB-88
Harris, Frank 1856-1931 ....DLB-156, 197

Harris, George Washington
 1814-1869 ....DLB-3, 11
Harris, Joel Chandler
 1848-1908 ....DLB-11, 23, 42, 78, 91
Harris, Mark 1922- DLB-2; Y-80
Harris, Wilson 1921- DLB-117; CDWLB-3
Harrison, Mrs. Burton
 (see Harrison, Constance Cary)
Harrison, Charles Yale 1898-1954........DLB-68
Harrison, Constance Cary 1843-1920....DLB-221
Harrison, Frederic 1831-1923 ....DLB-57, 190
"On Style in English Prose" (1898).......DLB-57
Harrison, Harry 1925- DLB-8
Harrison, James P., Company DLB-49
Harrison, Jim 1937- Y-82
Harrison, Mary St. Leger Kingsley
 (see Malet, Lucas)
Harrison, Paul Carter 1936- DLB-38
Harrison, Susan Frances 1859-1935........DLB-99
Harrison, Tony 1937- DLB-40
Harrison, William 1535-1593 ....DLB-136
Harrison, William 1933- DLB-234
Harrisse, Henry 1829-1910 ....DLB-47
Harryman, Carla 1952- DLB-193
Harsdörffer, Georg Philipp 1607-1658....DLB-164
Harsent, David 1942- DLB-40
Hart, Albert Bushnell 1854-1943.........DLB-17
Hart, Anne 1768-1834 ....DLB-200
Hart, Elizabeth 1771-1833 ....DLB-200
Hart, Julia Catherine 1796-1867..........DLB-99
The Lorenz Hart Centenary Y-95
Hart, Moss 1904-1961..................DLB-7
Hart, Oliver 1723-1795 ....DLB-31
Hart-Davis, Rupert, Limited DLB-112
Harte, Bret 1836-1902
 .... DLB-12, 64, 74, 79, 186; CDALB-3
Harte, Edward Holmead 1922- DLB-127
Harte, Houston Harriman 1927- DLB-127
Hartlaub, Felix 1913-1945 ....DLB-56
Hartleben, Otto Erich 1864-1905 ....DLB-118
Hartley, L. P. 1895-1972 ....DLB-15, 139
Hartley, Marsden 1877-1943 ....DLB-54
Hartling, Peter 1933- DLB-75
Hartman, Geoffrey H. 1929- DLB-67
Hartmann, Sadakichi 1867-1944 ....DLB-54
Hartmann von Aue
 circa 1160-circa 1205....DLB-138; CDWLB-2
Harvey, Gabriel 1550?-1631 ...DLB-167, 213, 236
Harvey, Jean-Charles 1891-1967.........DLB-88
Harvill Press Limited.................DLB-112
Harwood, Lee 1939- DLB-40
Harwood, Ronald 1934- DLB-13
Hašek, Jaroslav 1883-1923...DLB-215; CDWLB-4
Haskins, Charles Homer 1870-1937 ......DLB-47
Haslam, Gerald 1937- DLB-212
Hass, Robert 1941- DLB-105, 206

Hastings, Michael 1938- DLB-233
Hatar, Győző 1914- DLB-215
The Hatch-Billops Collection DLB-76
Hathaway, William 1944- DLB-120
Hauff, Wilhelm 1802-1827 ....DLB-90
A Haughty and Proud Generation (1922),
 by Ford Madox Hueffer DLB-36
Haugwitz, August Adolph von
 1647-1706.....................DLB-168
Hauptmann, Carl 1858-1921........DLB-66, 118
Hauptmann, Gerhart
 1862-1946 ....DLB-66, 118; CDWLB-2
Hauser, Marianne 1910- Y-83
Havel, Václav 1936- DLB-232; CDWLB-4
Havergal, Frances Ridley 1836-1879 .....DLB-199
Hawes, Stephen 1475?-before 1529 ......DLB-132
Hawker, Robert Stephen 1803-1875 ....DLB-32
Hawkes, John
 1925-1998 ....DLB-2, 7, 227; Y-80, Y-98
John Hawkes: A Tribute Y-98
Hawkesworth, John 1720-1773 ....DLB-142
Hawkins, Sir Anthony Hope (see Hope, Anthony)
Hawkins, Sir John 1719-1789.......DLB-104, 142
Hawkins, Walter Everette 1883-? DLB-50
Hawthorne, Nathaniel
 1804-1864 ....DLB-1, 74, 183, 223; CDALB-2
Hawthorne, Nathaniel 1804-1864 and
 Hawthorne, Sophia Peabody
 1809-1871 ....DLB-183
Hawthorne, Sophia Peabody
 1809-1871 ....DLB-183, 239
Hay, John 1835-1905..........DLB-12, 47, 189
Hayashi, Fumiko 1903-1951 ....DLB-180
Haycox, Ernest 1899-1950 ....DLB-206
Haycraft, Anna Margaret (see Ellis, Alice Thomas)
Hayden, Robert
 1913-1980 ....DLB-5, 76; CDALB-1
Haydon, Benjamin Robert
 1786-1846 ....DLB-110
Hayes, John Michael 1919- DLB-26
Hayley, William 1745-1820.........DLB-93, 142
Haym, Rudolf 1821-1901 ....DLB-129
Hayman, Robert 1575-1629..............DLB-99
Hayman, Ronald 1932- DLB-155
Hayne, Paul Hamilton 1830-1886...DLB-3, 64, 79
Hays, Mary 1760-1843 ....DLB-142, 158
Hayward, John 1905-1965..............DLB-201
Haywood, Eliza 1693?-1756 ....DLB-39
From the Dedication, *Lasselia* (1723) DLB-39
From *The Tea-Table* *DLB-39*
From the Preface to *The Disguis'd
 Prince* (1723)....................DLB-39
Hazard, Willis P. [publishing house] DLB-49
Hazlitt, William 1778-1830 ....DLB-110, 158
Hazzard, Shirley 1931- Y-82
Head, Bessie
 1937-1986 ....DLB-117, 225; CDWLB-3
Headley, Joel T. 1813-1897 ...DLB-30, 183; DS-13

Heaney, Seamus 1939- DLB-40; Y-95; CDBLB-8

Heard, Nathan C. 1936- DLB-33

Hearn, Lafcadio 1850-1904 ...... DLB-12, 78, 189

Hearn, Mary Anne (Marianne Farningham, Eva Hope) 1834-1909 .... DLB-240

Hearne, John 1926- DLB-117

Hearne, Samuel 1745-1792 .... DLB-99

Hearne, Thomas 1678?-1735 .... DLB-213

Hearst, William Randolph 1863-1951 .... DLB-25

Hearst, William Randolph, Jr. 1908-1993 .... DLB-127

Heartman, Charles Frederick 1883-1953 .... DLB-187

Heath, Catherine 1924- DLB-14

Heath, Roy A. K. 1926- DLB-117

Heath-Stubbs, John 1918- DLB-27

Heavysege, Charles 1816-1876 .... DLB-99

Hebbel, Friedrich 1813-1863. .... DLB-129; CDWLB-2

Hebel, Johann Peter 1760-1826. .... DLB-90

Heber, Richard 1774-1833 .... DLB-184

Hébert, Anne 1916- DLB-68

Hébert, Jacques 1923- DLB-53

Hecht, Anthony 1923- DLB-5, 169

Hecht, Ben 1894-1964 .... DLB-7, 9, 25, 26, 28, 86

Hecker, Isaac Thomas 1819-1888 .... DLB-1

Hedge, Frederic Henry 1805-1890 ..... DLB-1, 59

Hefner, Hugh M. 1926- DLB-137

Hegel, Georg Wilhelm Friedrich 1770-1831 .... DLB-90

Heidish, Marcy 1947- Y-82

Heißenbüttel, Helmut 1921-1996 .... DLB-75

Heike monogatari DLB-203

Hein, Christoph 1944- ... DLB-124; CDWLB-2

Hein, Piet 1905-1996 .... DLB-214

Heine, Heinrich 1797-1856 ... DLB-90; CDWLB-2

Heinemann, Larry 1944- DS-9

Heinemann, William, Limited DLB-112

Heinesen, William 1900-1991. .... DLB-214

Heinlein, Robert A. 1907-1988 .... DLB-8

Heinrich Julius of Brunswick 1564-1613. .... DLB-164

Heinrich von dem Türlîn flourished circa 1230 .... DLB-138

Heinrich von Melk flourished after 1160 .... DLB-148

Heinrich von Veldeke circa 1145-circa 1190 .... DLB-138

Heinrich, Willi 1920- DLB-75

Heinse, Wilhelm 1746-1803 .... DLB-94

Heinz, W. C. 1915- DLB-171

Heiskell, John 1872-1972. .... DLB-127

Hejinian, Lyn 1941- DLB-165

Heliand circa 850 .... DLB-148

Heller, Joseph 1923-1999 .... DLB-2, 28, 227; Y-80, Y-99

Heller, Michael 1937- DLB-165

Hellman, Lillian 1906-1984 ..... DLB-7, 228; Y-84

Hellwig, Johann 1609-1674. .... DLB-164

Helprin, Mark 1947- Y-85; CDALB-7

Helwig, David 1938- DLB-60

Hemans, Felicia 1793-1835 .... DLB-96

Hemingway, Ernest 1899-1961
..... DLB-4, 9, 102, 210; Y-81, Y-87, Y-99; DS-1, DS-15, DS-16; CDALB-4

The Hemingway Centenary Celebration at the JFK Library Y-99

Ernest Hemingway: A Centennial Celebration Y-99

The Ernest Hemingway Collection at the John F. Kennedy Library Y-99

Ernest Hemingway's Reaction to James Gould Cozzens Y-98

Ernest Hemingway's Toronto Journalism Revisited: With Three Previously Unrecorded Stories Y-92

Falsifying Hemingway Y-96

Hemingway: Twenty-Five Years Later. Y-85

Not Immediately Discernible . . . but Eventually Quite Clear: The *First Light* and *Final Years* of Hemingway's Centenary Y-99

Second International Hemingway Colloquium: Cuba Y-98

Hémon, Louis 1880-1913. .... DLB-92

Hempel, Amy 1951- DLB-218

Hemphill, Paul 1936- Y-87

Hénault, Gilles 1920- DLB-88

Henchman, Daniel 1689-1761 .... DLB-24

Henderson, Alice Corbin 1881-1949 ..... DLB-54

Henderson, Archibald 1877-1963 ...... DLB-103

Henderson, David 1942- DLB-41

Henderson, George Wylie 1904- DLB-51

Henderson, Zenna 1917-1983. .... DLB-8

Henisch, Peter 1943- DLB-85

Henley, Beth 1952- Y-86

Henley, William Ernest 1849-1903 ..... DLB-19

Henning, Rachel 1826-1914 .... DLB-230

Henningsen, Agnes 1868-1962. .... DLB-214

Henniker, Florence 1855-1923 .... DLB-135

Henry, Alexander 1739-1824 .... DLB-99

Henry, Buck 1930- DLB-26

Henry VIII of England 1491-1547. ..... DLB-132

Henry of Ghent circa 1217-1229 - 1293 .... DLB-115

Henry, Marguerite 1902-1997 .... DLB-22

Henry, O. (see Porter, William Sydney)

Henry, Robert Selph 1889-1970 .... DLB-17

Henry, Will (see Allen, Henry W.)

Henryson, Robert 1420s or 1430s-circa 1505 .... DLB-146

Henschke, Alfred (see Klabund)

Hensley, Sophie Almon 1866-1946 ..... DLB-99

Henson, Lance 1944- DLB-175

Henty, G. A. 1832?-1902 .... DLB-18, 141

Hentz, Caroline Lee 1800-1856 .... DLB-3

Heraclitus flourished circa 500 B.C. DLB-176

Herbert, Agnes circa 1880-1960. .... DLB-174

Herbert, Alan Patrick 1890-1971 .... DLB-10, 191

Herbert, Edward, Lord, of Cherbury 1582-1648 .... DLB-121, 151

Herbert, Frank 1920-1986 ..... DLB-8; CDALB-7

Herbert, George 1593-1633 .. DLB-126; CDBLB-1

Herbert, Henry William 1807-1858 .... DLB-3, 73

Herbert, John 1926- DLB-53

Herbert, Mary Sidney, Countess of Pembroke (see Sidney, Mary)

Herbert, Zbigniew 1924-1998 .... DLB-232; CDWLB-4

Herbst, Josephine 1892-1969 .... DLB-9

Herburger, Gunter 1932- DLB-75, 124

Hercules, Frank E. M. 1917-1996 .... DLB-33

Herder, Johann Gottfried 1744-1803 ..... DLB-97

Herder, B., Book Company DLB-49

Heredia, José-María de 1842-1905 ....DLB-217

Herford, Charles Harold 1853-1931 .... DLB-149

Hergesheimer, Joseph 1880-1954 ..... DLB-9, 102

Heritage Press. DLB-46

Hermann the Lame 1013-1054 .... DLB-148

Hermes, Johann Timotheus 1738-1821. .... DLB-97

Hermlin, Stephan 1915-1997 .... DLB-69

Hernández, Alfonso C. 1938- DLB-122

Hernández, Inés 1947- DLB-122

Hernández, Miguel 1910-1942 .... DLB-134

Hernton, Calvin C. 1932- DLB-38

Herodotus circa 484 B.C.-circa 420 B.C.
.... DLB-176; CDWLB-1

Heron, Robert 1764-1807 .... DLB-142

Herr, Michael 1940- DLB-185

Herrera, Juan Felipe 1948- DLB-122

Herrick, E. R., and Company DLB-49

Herrick, Robert 1591-1674. .... DLB-126

Herrick, Robert 1868-1938. ....DLB-9, 12, 78

Herrick, William 1915- Y-83

Herrmann, John 1900-1959 .... DLB-4

Hersey, John 1914-1993 ... DLB-6, 185; CDALB-7

Hertel, François 1905-1985. .... DLB-68

Hervé-Bazin, Jean Pierre Marie (see Bazin, Hervé)

Hervey, John, Lord 1696-1743 .... DLB-101

Herwig, Georg 1817-1875 .... DLB-133

Herzog, Emile Salomon Wilhelm (see Maurois, André)

Hesiod eighth century B.C. DLB-176

Hesse, Hermann 1877-1962 .... DLB-66; CDWLB-2

Hessus, Helius Eobanus 1488-1540 ......DLB-179

Hewat, Alexander circa 1743-circa 1824. .. DLB-30

Hewitt, John 1907- DLB-27

Hewlett, Maurice 1861-1923 .... DLB-34, 156

Heyen, William 1940- DLB-5

Heyer, Georgette 1902-1974. ....DLB-77, 191

Heym, Stefan 1913- DLB-69
Heyse, Paul 1830-1914 ....DLB-129
Heytesbury, William
   circa 1310-1372 or 1373............DLB-115
Heyward, Dorothy 1890-1961............DLB-7
Heyward, DuBose 1885-1940 .... DLB-7, 9, 45
Heywood, John 1497?-1580?...........DLB-136
Heywood, Thomas
   1573 or 1574-1641................DLB-62
Hibbs, Ben 1901-1975 ....DLB-137
Hichens, Robert S. 1864-1950..........DLB-153
Hickey, Emily 1845-1924 ....DLB-199
Hickman, William Albert 1877-1957 ......DLB-92
Hidalgo, José Luis 1919-1947..........DLB-108
Hiebert, Paul 1892-1987 ....DLB-68
Hieng, Andrej 1925- DLB-181
Hierro, José 1922- DLB-108
Higgins, Aidan 1927- DLB-14
Higgins, Colin 1941-1988 ....DLB-26
Higgins, George V.
   1939-1999 .... DLB-2; Y-81, Y-98, Y-99
George V. Higgins to Julian Symons Y-99
Higginson, Thomas Wentworth
   1823-1911 ....DLB-1, 64
Highwater, Jamake 1942?- DLB-52; Y-85
Hijuelos, Oscar 1951- DLB-145
Hildegard von Bingen 1098-1179........DLB-148
Das Hildesbrandslied
   circa 820 ....DLB-148; CDWLB-2
Hildesheimer, Wolfgang
   1916-1991 ....DLB-69, 124
Hildreth, Richard 1807-1865 ...DLB-1, 30, 59, 235
Hill, Aaron 1685-1750 ....DLB-84
Hill, Geoffrey 1932- DLB-40; CDBLB-8
Hill, George M., Company DLB-49
Hill, "Sir" John 1714?-1775.............DLB-39
Hill, Lawrence, and Company,
   Publishers DLB-46
Hill, Leslie 1880-1960 ....DLB-51
Hill, Susan 1942- DLB-14, 139
Hill, Walter 1942- DLB-44
Hill and Wang.......................DLB-46
Hillberry, Conrad 1928- DLB-120
Hillerman, Tony 1925- DLB-206
Hilliard, Gray and Company............DLB-49
Hills, Lee 1906- DLB-127
Hillyer, Robert 1895-1961 ....DLB-54
Hilton, James 1900-1954 ....DLB-34, 77
Hilton, Walter died 1396...............DLB-146
Hilton and Company...................DLB-49
Himes, Chester 1909-1984.... DLB-2, 76, 143, 226
Hindmarsh, Joseph [publishing house].... DLB-170
Hine, Daryl 1936- DLB-60
Hingley, Ronald 1920- DLB-155
Hinojosa-Smith, Rolando 1929- DLB-82
Hinton, S. E. 1948- CDALB-7

Hippel, Theodor Gottlieb von
   1741-1796 ....DLB-97
Hippocrates of Cos flourished circa 425 B.C.
   .... DLB-176; CDWLB-1
Hirabayashi, Taiko 1905-1972..........DLB-180
Hirsch, E. D., Jr. 1928- DLB-67
Hirsch, Edward 1950- DLB-120
Hoagland, Edward 1932- DLB-6
Hoagland, Everett H., III 1942- DLB-41
Hoban, Russell 1925- DLB-52
Hobbes, Thomas 1588-1679 ....DLB-151
Hobby, Oveta 1905- DLB-127
Hobby, William 1878-1964 ....DLB-127
Hobsbaum, Philip 1932- DLB-40
Hobson, Laura Z. 1900- DLB-28
Hobson, Sarah 1947- DLB-204
Hoby, Thomas 1530-1566..............DLB-132
Hoccleve, Thomas
   circa 1368-circa 1437..............DLB-146
Hochhuth, Rolf 1931- DLB-124
Hochman, Sandra 1936- DLB-5
Hocken, Thomas Morland
   1836-1910 ....DLB-184
Hodder and Stoughton, Limited DLB-106
Hodgins, Jack 1938- DLB-60
Hodgman, Helen 1945- DLB-14
Hodgskin, Thomas 1787-1869 ....DLB-158
Hodgson, Ralph 1871-1962 ....DLB-19
Hodgson, William Hope
   1877-1918 .... DLB-70, 153, 156, 178
Hoe, Robert III 1839-1909 ....DLB-187
Hoeg, Peter 1957- DLB-214
Højholt, Per 1928- DLB-214
Hoffenstein, Samuel 1890-1947 ....DLB-11
Hoffman, Charles Fenno 1806-1884 ....DLB-3
Hoffman, Daniel 1923- DLB-5
Hoffmann, E. T. A.
   1776-1822 ....DLB-90; CDWLB-2
Hoffman, Frank B. 1888-1958..........DLB-188
Hoffman, William 1925- DLB-234
Hoffmanswaldau, Christian Hoffman von
   1616-1679 ....DLB-168
Hofmann, Michael 1957- DLB-40
Hofmannsthal, Hugo von
   1874-1929 .... DLB-81, 118; CDWLB-2
Hofstadter, Richard 1916-1970 ....DLB-17
Hogan, Desmond 1950- DLB-14
Hogan, Linda 1947- DLB-175
Hogan and Thompson DLB-49
Hogarth Press DLB-112
Hogg, James 1770-1835 .... DLB-93, 116, 159
Hohberg, Wolfgang Helmhard Freiherr von
   1612-1688 ....DLB-168
von Hohenheim, Philippus Aureolus
   Theophrastus Bombastus (see Paracelsus)
Hohl, Ludwig 1904-1980...............DLB-56
Holbrook, David 1923- DLB-14, 40

Holcroft, Thomas 1745-1809..... DLB-39, 89, 158
Preface to *Alwyn* (1780) DLB-39
Holden, Jonathan 1941- DLB-105
"Contemporary Verse Story-telling" DLB-105
Holden, Molly 1927-1981 ....DLB-40
Hölderlin, Friedrich 1770-1843 DLB-90; CDWLB-2
Holiday House DLB-46
Holinshed, Raphael died 1580...........DLB-167
Holland, J. G. 1819-1881................DS-13
Holland, Norman N. 1927- DLB-67
Hollander, John 1929- DLB-5
Holley, Marietta 1836-1926..............DLB-11
Hollinghurst, Alan 1954- DLB-207
Hollingsworth, Margaret 1940- DLB-60
Hollo, Anselm 1934- DLB-40
Holloway, Emory 1885-1977...........DLB-103
Holloway, John 1920- DLB-27
Holloway House Publishing Company....DLB-46
Holme, Constance 1880-1955 ....DLB-34
Holmes, Abraham S. 1821?-1908 ....DLB-99
Holmes, John Clellon 1926-1988..... DLB-16, 237
"Four Essays on the Beat Generation".....DLB-16
Holmes, Mary Jane 1825-1907 ..... DLB-202, 221
Holmes, Oliver Wendell
   1809-1894 .... DLB-1, 189, 235; CDALB-2
Holmes, Richard 1945- DLB-155
The Cult of Biography
   Excerpts from the Second Folio Debate:
   "Biographies are generally a disease of
   English Literature" Y-86
Holmes, Thomas James 1874-1959 ......DLB-187
Holroyd, Michael 1935- DLB-155
Holst, Hermann E. von 1841-1904 ....DLB-47
Holt, Henry, and Company DLB-49
Holt, John 1721-1784 ....DLB-43
Holt, Rinehart and Winston DLB-46
Holtby, Winifred 1898-1935 ....DLB-191
Holthusen, Hans Egon 1913- DLB-69
Hölty, Ludwig Christoph Heinrich
   1748-1776.......................DLB-94
Holub, Miroslav
   1923-1998............DLB-232; CDWLB-4
Holz, Arno 1863-1929................DLB-118
Home, Henry, Lord Kames
   (see Kames, Henry Home, Lord)
Home, John 1722-1808 ....DLB-84
Home, William Douglas 1912- DLB-13
Home Publishing Company DLB-49
Homer circa eighth-seventh centuries B.C.
   .... DLB-176; CDWLB-1
Homer, Winslow 1836-1910 ....DLB-188
Homes, Geoffrey (see Mainwaring, Daniel)
Honan, Park 1928- DLB-111
Hone, William 1780-1842 .... DLB-110, 158
Hongo, Garrett Kaoru 1951- DLB-120
Honig, Edwin 1919- DLB-5
Hood, Hugh 1928- DLB-53

Cumulative Index

Hood, Mary 1946- DLB-234
Hood, Thomas 1799-1845 .... DLB-96
Hook, Theodore 1788-1841 .... DLB-116
Hooker, Jeremy 1941- DLB-40
Hooker, Richard 1554-1600............ DLB-132
Hooker, Thomas 1586-1647............. DLB-24
Hooper, Johnson Jones 1815-1862 ..... DLB-3, 11
Hope, Anthony 1863-1933......... DLB-153, 156
Hope, Christopher 1944- DLB-225
Hope, Eva (see Hearn, Mary Anne)
Hope, Laurence (Adela Florence
  Cory Nicolson) 1865-1904......... DLB-240
Hopkins, Ellice 1836-1904 .... DLB-190
Hopkins, Gerard Manley
  1844-1889 .... DLB-35, 57; CDBLB-5
Hopkins, John (see Sternhold, Thomas)
Hopkins, John H., and Son............. DLB-46
Hopkins, Lemuel 1750-1801............. DLB-37
Hopkins, Pauline Elizabeth 1859-1930.... DLB-50
Hopkins, Samuel 1721-1803 .... DLB-31
Hopkinson, Francis 1737-1791.......... DLB-31
Hopper, Nora (Mrs. Nora Chesson)
  1871-1906..................... DLB-240
Hoppin, Augustus 1828-1896........... DLB-188
Hora, Josef 1891-1945 ..... DLB-215; CDWLB-4
Horace 65 B.C.-8 B.C...... DLB-211; CDWLB-1
Horgan, Paul 1903-1995......DLB-102, 212; Y-85
Horizon Press DLB-46
Hornby, C. H. St. John 1867-1946 ...... DLB-201
Hornby, Nick 1957- DLB-207
Horne, Frank 1899-1974............... DLB-51
Horne, Richard Henry (Hengist)
  1802 or 1803-1884................. DLB-32
Hornung, E. W. 1866-1921 .... DLB-70
Horovitz, Israel 1939- DLB-7
Horton, George Moses 1797?-1883?...... DLB-50
Horváth, Ödön von 1901-1938 ..... DLB-85, 124
Horwood, Harold 1923- DLB-60
Hosford, E. and E. [publishing house] DLB-49
Hoskens, Jane Fenn 1693-1770? DLB-200
Hoskyns, John 1566-1638.............. DLB-121
Hosokawa Yūsai 1535-1610 .... DLB-203
Hostovský, Egon 1908-1973 .... DLB-215
Hotchkiss and Company DLB-49
Hough, Emerson 1857-1923 .... DLB-9, 212
Houghton, Stanley 1881-1913 .... DLB-10
Houghton Mifflin Company............. DLB-49
Household, Geoffrey 1900-1988......... DLB-87
Housman, A. E. 1859-1936 ... DLB-19; CDBLB-5
Housman, Laurence 1865-1959 .... DLB-10
Houwald, Ernst von 1778-1845 .... DLB-90
Hovey, Richard 1864-1900............. DLB-54
Howard, Donald R. 1927-1987 .... DLB-111
Howard, Maureen 1930- Y-83
Howard, Richard 1929- DLB-5

Howard, Roy W. 1883-1964 .... DLB-29
Howard, Sidney 1891-1939 .... DLB-7, 26
Howard, Thomas, second Earl of Arundel
  1585-1646 .... DLB-213
Howe, E. W. 1853-1937............. DLB-12, 25
Howe, Henry 1816-1893 .... DLB-30
Howe, Irving 1920-1993............... DLB-67
Howe, Joseph 1804-1873 .... DLB-99
Howe, Julia Ward 1819-1910 .... DLB-1, 189, 235
Howe, Percival Presland 1886-1944..... DLB-149
Howe, Susan 1937- DLB-120
Howell, Clark, Sr. 1863-1936.......... DLB-25
Howell, Evan P. 1839-1905 .... DLB-23
Howell, James 1594?-1666 .... DLB-151
Howell, Soskin and Company DLB-46
Howell, Warren Richardson
  1912-1984 .... DLB-140
Howells, William Dean 1837-1920
  ....DLB-12, 64, 74, 79, 189; CDALB-3
Introduction to Paul Laurence Dunbar,
  Lyrics of Lowly Life (1896) DLB-50
Howitt, Mary 1799-1888 .... DLB-110, 199
Howitt, William 1792-1879 and
  Howitt, Mary 1799-1888 .... DLB-110
Hoyem, Andrew 1935- DLB-5
Hoyers, Anna Ovena 1584-1655 .... DLB-164
Hoyos, Angela de 1940- DLB-82
Hoyt, Henry [publishing house] DLB-49
Hoyt, Palmer 1897-1979 .... DLB-127
Hrabal, Bohumil 1914-1997 .... DLB-232
Hrabanus Maurus 776?-856 .... DLB-148
Hronský, Josef Cíger 1896-1960 .... DLB-215
Hrotsvit of Gandersheim
  circa 935-circa 1000 .... DLB-148
Hubbard, Elbert 1856-1915 .... DLB-91
Hubbard, Kin 1868-1930 .... DLB-11
Hubbard, William circa 1621-1704....... DLB-24
Huber, Therese 1764-1829............. DLB-90
Huch, Friedrich 1873-1913............. DLB-66
Huch, Ricarda 1864-1947.............. DLB-66
Huck at 100: How Old Is
  Huckleberry Finn?................. Y-85
Huddle, David 1942- DLB-130
Hudgins, Andrew 1951- DLB-120
Hudson, Henry Norman 1814-1886 ..... DLB-64
Hudson, Stephen 1868?-1944........... DLB-197
Hudson, W. H. 1841-1922......DLB-98, 153, 174
Hudson and Goodwin DLB-49
Huebsch, B. W. [publishing house] DLB-46
Oral History: B. W. Huebsch............. Y-99
Hueffer, Oliver Madox 1876-1931 ...... DLB-197
Hugh of St. Victor circa 1096-1141 ..... DLB-208
Hughes, David 1930- DLB-14
Hughes, Dusty 1947- DLB-233
Hughes, John 1677-1720 .... DLB-84
Hughes, Langston 1902-1967
  ....DLB-4, 7, 48, 51, 86, 228; CDALB-5

Hughes, Richard 1900-1976 .... DLB-15, 161
Hughes, Ted 1930-1998.............. DLB-40, 161
Hughes, Thomas 1822-1896 .... DLB-18, 163
Hugo, Richard 1923-1982 .... DLB-5, 206
Hugo, Victor 1802-1885.......DLB-119, 192, 217
Hugo Awards and Nebula Awards......... DLB-8
Hull, Richard 1896-1973 .... DLB-77
Hulme, T. E. 1883-1917................ DLB-19
Hulton, Anne ?-1779?................. DLB-200
Humboldt, Alexander von 1769-1859 .... DLB-90
Humboldt, Wilhelm von 1767-1835 ...... DLB-90
Hume, David 1711-1776 .... DLB-104
Hume, Fergus 1859-1932 .... DLB-70
Hume, Sophia 1702-1774 .... DLB-200
Hume-Rothery, Mary Catherine
  1824-1885 .... DLB-240
Humishuma (see Mourning Dove)
Hummer, T. R. 1950- DLB-120
Humorous Book Illustration............. DLB-11
Humphrey, Duke of Gloucester
  1391-1447 .... DLB-213
Humphrey, William 1924-1997 .. DLB-6, 212, 234
Humphreys, David 1752-1818 .... DLB-37
Humphreys, Emyr 1919- DLB-15
Huncke, Herbert 1915-1996............ DLB-16
Huneker, James Gibbons 1857-1921..... DLB-71
Hunold, Christian Friedrich
  1681-1721..................... DLB-168
Hunt, Irene 1907- DLB-52
Hunt, Leigh 1784-1859........DLB-96, 110, 144
Hunt, Violet 1862-1942 ....DLB-162, 197
Hunt, William Gibbes 1791-1833........ DLB-73
Hunter, Evan 1926- Y-82
Hunter, Jim 1939- DLB-14
Hunter, Kristin 1931- DLB-33
Hunter, Mollie 1922- DLB-161
Hunter, N. C. 1908-1971 .... DLB-10
Hunter-Duvar, John 1821-1899 .... DLB-99
Huntington, Henry E. 1850-1927....... DLB-140
Huntington, Susan Mansfield
  1791-1823..................... DLB-200
Hurd and Houghton DLB-49
Hurst, Fannie 1889-1968 .... DLB-86
Hurst and Blackett DLB-106
Hurst and Company DLB-49
Hurston, Zora Neale
  1901?-1960........... DLB-51, 86; CDALB-7
Husson, Jules-François-Félix (see Champfleury)
Huston, John 1906-1987 .... DLB-26
Hutcheson, Francis 1694-1746 .... DLB-31
Hutchinson, R. C. 1907-1975 .... DLB-191
Hutchinson, Thomas 1711-1780...... DLB-30, 31
Hutchinson and Company
  (Publishers) Limited.............. DLB-112
Hutton, Richard Holt 1826-1897 .... DLB-57
von Hutton, Ulrich 1488-1523..........DLB-179

Huxley, Aldous 1894-1963
.........DLB-36, 100, 162, 195; CDBLB-6
Huxley, Elspeth Josceline
1907-1997 .... DLB-77, 204
Huxley, T. H. 1825-1895 ....DLB-57
Huyghue, Douglas Smith 1816-1891......DLB-99
Huysmans, Joris-Karl 1848-1907........DLB-123
Hwang, David Henry 1957- DLB-212, 228
Hyde, Donald 1909-1966 and
Hyde, Mary 1912- DLB-187
Hyman, Trina Schart 1939- DLB-61

I

Iavorsky, Stefan 1658-1722 ....DLB-150
Iazykov, Nikolai Mikhailovich
1803-1846 ....DLB-205
Ibáñez, Armando P. 1949- DLB-209
Ibn Bajja circa 1077-1138 ....DLB-115
Ibn Gabirol, Solomon
circa 1021-circa 1058.............DLB-115
Ibuse, Masuji 1898-1993 ....DLB-180
Ichijō Kanera
(see Ichijō Kaneyoshi)
Ichijō Kaneyoshi (Ichijō Kanera)
1402-1481 ....DLB-203
The Iconography of Science-Fiction Art DLB-8
Iffland, August Wilhelm 1759-1814.......DLB-94
Ignatow, David 1914-1997..............DLB-5
Ike, Chukwuemeka 1931- DLB-157
Ikkyū Sōjun 1394-1481 ....DLB-203
Iles, Francis
(see Berkeley, Anthony)
The Illustration of Early German Literar
Manuscripts, circa 1150-circa 1300 ...DLB-148
Illyés, Gyula 1902-1983 .....DLB-215; CDWLB-4
Imbs, Bravig 1904-1946................DLB-4
Imbuga, Francis D. 1947- DLB-157
Immermann, Karl 1796-1840 ....DLB-133
Inchbald, Elizabeth 1753-1821 ....DLB-39, 89
Inge, William 1913-1973 ......DLB-7; CDALB-1
Ingelow, Jean 1820-1897 ....DLB-35, 163
Ingersoll, Ralph 1900-1985 ....DLB-127
The Ingersoll Prizes Y-84
Ingoldsby, Thomas
(see Barham, Richard Harris)
Ingraham, Joseph Holt 1809-1860.........DLB-3
Inman, John 1805-1850 ....DLB-73
Innerhofer, Franz 1944- DLB-85
Innis, Harold Adams 1894-1952 ....DLB-88
Innis, Mary Quayle 1899-1972 ....DLB-88
Inō Sōgi 1421-1502 ....DLB-203
Inoue Yasushi 1907-1991 ....DLB-181
International Publishers Company DLB-46
Interviews:
Anastas, Benjamin Y-98
Bank, Melissa Y-98
Bernstein, Harriet Y-82

Bosworth, David Y-82
Burnshaw, Stanley....................Y-97
Carpenter, Humphrey............Y-84, Y-99
Carver, Raymond Y-83
Donald, David Herbert Y-87
Ellroy, James........................Y-91
Greenfield, George...................Y-91
Griffin, Bryan Y-81
Guilds, John Caldwell Y-92
Higgins, George V...................Y-98
Hoban, Russell......................Y-90
Holroyd, Michael....................Y-99
Horowitz, Glenn Y-90
Jenkinson, Edward B..................Y-82
Jenks, Tom Y-86
Kaplan, Justin......................Y-86
Krug, Judith........................Y-82
Lamm, Donald.......................Y-95
Laughlin, James Y-96
Mailer, Norman.....................Y-97
Manchester, William Y-85
McCormack, Thomas Y-98
Mellen, Joan........................Y-94
Mooneyham, Lamarr..................Y-82
O'Connor, Patrick..............Y-84, Y-99
Ozick, Cynthia......................Y-83
Penzler, Otto Y-96
Plimpton, George....................Y-99
Potok, Chaim........................Y-84
Prescott, Peter S. Y-86
Rabe, David.........................Y-91
Reid, B. L. Y-83
Reynolds, Michael..............Y-95, Y-99
Schlafly, Phyllis Y-82
Schroeder, Patricia.................Y-99
Scribner, Charles III Y-94
Sipper, Ralph.......................Y-94
Weintraub, Stanley Y-82
Editors, Conversations with Y-95
Irving, John 1942- DLB-6; Y-82
Irving, Washington 1783-1859
..............DLB-3, 11, 30, 59, 73, 74,
183, 186; CDALB-2
Irwin, Grace 1907- DLB-68
Irwin, Will 1873-1948 ....DLB-25
Isherwood, Christopher
1904-1986 ....DLB-15, 195; Y-86
The Christopher Isherwood Archive,
The Huntington Library.............Y-99
Ishiguro, Kazuo 1954- DLB-194
Ishikawa Jun 1899-1987 ....DLB-182
The Island Trees Case: A Symposium on
School Library Censorship
An Interview with Judith Krug
An Interview with Phyllis Schlafly
An Interview with Edward B. Jenkinson

An Interview with Lamarr Mooneyham
An Interview with Harriet Bernstein......Y-82
Islas, Arturo 1938-1991 ....DLB-122
Issit, Debbie 1966- DLB-233
Ivanišević, Drago 1907-1981 ....DLB-181
Ivaska, Astrīde 1926- DLB-232
Ivers, M. J., and Company DLB-49
Iwaniuk, Wacław 1915- DLB-215
Iwano, Hōmei 1873-1920...............DLB-180
Iwaszkiewicz, Jarosław 1894-1980 ....DLB-215
Iyayi, Festus 1947- DLB-157
Izumi, Kyōka 1873-1939 ....DLB-180

J

Jackmon, Marvin E. (see Marvin X)
Jacks, L. P. 1860-1955 ....DLB-135
Jackson, Angela 1951- DLB-41
Jackson, Charles 1903-1968...........DLB-234
Jackson, Helen Hunt
1830-1885 ....DLB-42, 47, 186, 189
Jackson, Holbrook 1874-1948 ....DLB-98
Jackson, Laura Riding 1901-1991 ....DLB-48
Jackson, Shirley
1916-1965 ....DLB-6, 234; CDALB-1
Jacob, Naomi 1884?-1964 ....DLB-191
Jacob, Piers Anthony Dillingham
(see Anthony, Piers)
Jacob, Violet 1863-1946..............DLB-240
Jacobi, Friedrich Heinrich 1743-1819......DLB-94
Jacobi, Johann Georg 1740-1841 ....DLB-97
Jacobs, George W., and Company DLB-49
Jacobs, Harriet 1813-1897 ....DLB-239
Jacobs, Joseph 1854-1916..............DLB-141
Jacobs, W. W. 1863-1943 ....DLB-135
Jacobsen, Jørgen-Frantz 1900-1938 ......DLB-214
Jacobson, Dan 1929- DLB-14, 207, 225
Jacobson, Howard 1942- DLB-207
Jacques de Vitry circa 1160/1170-1240 ...DLB-208
Jæger, Frank 1926-1977 ....DLB-214
Jaggard, William [publishing house] DLB-170
Jahier, Piero 1884-1966 ....DLB-114
Jahnn, Hans Henny 1894-1959 .....DLB-56, 124
Jakes, John 1932- Y-83
James, Alice 1848-1892 ....DLB-221
James, C. L. R. 1901-1989 ....DLB-125
James, George P. R. 1801-1860.........DLB-116
James, Henry 1843-1916
......DLB-12, 71, 74, 189; DS-13; CDALB-3
James, John circa 1633-1729 ....DLB-24
James, M. R. 1862-1936...........DLB-156, 201
James, Naomi 1949- DLB-204
James, P. D. 1920- ...DLB-87; DS-17; CDBLB-8
James VI of Scotland, I of England
1566-1625 ....DLB-151, 172
*Ane Schort Treatise Conteining Some Revlis
and Cautelis to Be Obseruit and Eschewit
in Scottis Poesi* (1584) DLB-172

Cumulative Index

James, Thomas 1572?-1629 .... DLB-213
James, U. P. [publishing house] DLB-49
James, Will 1892-1942 .... DS-16
Jameson, Anna 1794-1860........... DLB-99, 166
Jameson, Fredric 1934- DLB-67
Jameson, J. Franklin 1859-1937 .... DLB-17
Jameson, Storm 1891-1986............. DLB-36
Jančar, Drago 1948- DLB-181
Janés, Clara 1940- DLB-134
Janevski, Slavko 1920- ... DLB-181; CDWLB-4
Janvier, Thomas 1849-1913 .... DLB-202
Jaramillo, Cleofas M. 1878-1956........ DLB-122
Jarman, Mark 1952- DLB-120
Jarrell, Randall 1914-1965 . DLB-48, 52; CDALB-1
Jarrold and Sons DLB-106
Jarry, Alfred 1873-1907................. DLB-192
Jarves, James Jackson 1818-1888 .... DLB-189
Jasmin, Claude 1930- DLB-60
Jaunsudrabiņš, Jānis 1877-1962......... DLB-220
Jay, John 1745-1829 .... DLB-31
Jean de Garlande (see John of Garland)
Jefferies, Richard 1848-1887 .... DLB-98, 141
Jeffers, Lance 1919-1985............... DLB-41
Jeffers, Robinson
  1887-1962.......... DLB-45, 212; CDALB-4
Jefferson, Thomas
  1743-1826......... DLB-31, 183; CDALB-2
Jégé 1866-1940 .... DLB-215
Jelinek, Elfriede 1946- DLB-85
Jellicoe, Ann 1927- DLB-13, 233
Jemison, Mary circa 1742-1833......... DLB-239
Jenkins, Elizabeth 1905- DLB-155
Jenkins, Robin 1912- DLB-14
Jenkins, William Fitzgerald (see Leinster, Murray)
Jenkins, Herbert, Limited DLB-112
Jennings, Elizabeth 1926- DLB-27
Jens, Walter 1923- DLB-69
Jensen, Johannes V. 1873-1950......... DLB-214
Jensen, Merrill 1905-1980.............. DLB-17
Jensen, Thit 1876-1957 .... DLB-214
Jephson, Robert 1736-1803............. DLB-89
Jerome, Jerome K. 1859-1927 .... DLB-10, 34, 135
Jerome, Judson 1927-1991............. DLB-105
Jerrold, Douglas 1803-1857 .... DLB-158, 159
Jesse, F. Tennyson 1888-1958........... DLB-77
Jewel, John 1522-1571................. DLB-236
Jewett, John P., and Company DLB-49
Jewett, Sarah Orne 1849-1909 ....DLB-12, 74, 221
The Jewish Publication Society......... DLB-49
Jewitt, John Rodgers 1783-1821 .... DLB-99
Jewsbury, Geraldine 1812-1880 .... DLB-21
Jewsbury, Maria Jane 1800-1833 .... DLB-199
Jhabvala, Ruth Prawer 1927- DLB-139, 194
Jiménez, Juan Ramón 1881-1958 .... DLB-134
Joans, Ted 1928- DLB-16, 41

Jōha 1525-1602..................... DLB-203
Johannis de Garlandia (see John of Garland)
John, Errol 1924-1988 .... DLB-233
John, Eugenie (see Marlitt, E.)
John of Dumbleton
  circa 1310-circa 1349 .... DLB-115
John of Garland (Jean de Garlande, Johannis de
  Garlandia) circa 1195-circa 1272 .... DLB-208
Johns, Captain W. E. 1893-1968 .... DLB-160
Johnson, Mrs. A. E. ca. 1858-1922...... DLB-221
Johnson, Amelia (see Johnson, Mrs. A. E.)
Johnson, B. S. 1933-1973 .... DLB-14, 40
Johnson, Benjamin [publishing house] DLB-49
Johnson, Benjamin, Jacob, and
  Robert [publishing house] DLB-49
Johnson, Charles 1679-1748 .... DLB-84
Johnson, Charles R. 1948- DLB-33
Johnson, Charles S. 1893-1956........ DLB-51, 91
Johnson, Denis 1949- DLB-120
Johnson, Diane 1934- Y-80
Johnson, Dorothy M. 1905–1984....... DLB-206
Johnson, E. Pauline (Tekahionwake)
  1861-1913 ....DLB-175
Johnson, Edgar 1901-1995 .... DLB-103
Johnson, Edward 1598-1672........... DLB-24
Johnson, Fenton 1888-1958 .... DLB-45, 50
Johnson, Georgia Douglas 1886-1966 .... DLB-51
Johnson, Gerald W. 1890-1980 .... DLB-29
Johnson, Greg 1953- DLB-234
Johnson, Helene 1907-1995 .... DLB-51
Johnson, Jacob, and Company DLB-49
Johnson, James Weldon
  1871-1938................ DLB-51; CDALB-4
Johnson, John H. 1918- DLB-137
Johnson, Joseph [publishing house] DLB-154
Johnson, Linton Kwesi 1952- DLB-157
Johnson, Lionel 1867-1902 .... DLB-19
Johnson, Nunnally 1897-1977 .... DLB-26
Johnson, Owen 1878-1952 .... Y-87
Johnson, Pamela Hansford 1912- DLB-15
Johnson, Pauline 1861-1913 .... DLB-92
Johnson, Ronald 1935-1998 .... DLB-169
Johnson, Samuel 1696-1772 ... DLB-24; CDBLB-2
Johnson, Samuel
  1709-1784 ....DLB-39, 95, 104, 142, 213
Johnson, Samuel 1822-1882 .... DLB-1
Johnson, Susanna 1730-1810 .... DLB-200
Johnson, Terry 1955- DLB-233
Johnson, Uwe 1934-1984 ..... DLB-75; CDWLB-2
Johnston, Annie Fellows 1863-1931 ...... DLB-42
Johnston, Basil H. 1929- DLB-60
Johnston, David Claypole 1798?-1865 ... DLB-188
Johnston, Denis 1901-1984............. DLB-10
Johnston, Ellen 1835-1873 .... DLB-199
Johnston, George 1913- DLB-88
Johnston, Sir Harry 1858-1927..........DLB-174

Johnston, Jennifer 1930- DLB-14
Johnston, Mary 1870-1936 .... DLB-9
Johnston, Richard Malcolm 1822-1898 ... DLB-74
Johnstone, Charles 1719?-1800?......... DLB-39
Johst, Hanns 1890-1978 .... DLB-124
Jolas, Eugene 1894-1952 .... DLB-4, 45
Jones, Alice C. 1853-1933............. DLB-92
Jones, Charles C., Jr. 1831-1893......... DLB-30
Jones, D. G. 1929- DLB-53
Jones, David 1895-1974 .. DLB-20, 100; CDBLB-7
Jones, Diana Wynne 1934- DLB-161
Jones, Ebenezer 1820-1860 .... DLB-32
Jones, Ernest 1819-1868............... DLB-32
Jones, Gayl 1949- DLB-33
Jones, George 1800-1870 .... DLB-183
Jones, Glyn 1905- DLB-15
Jones, Gwyn 1907- DLB-15, 139
Jones, Henry Arthur 1851-1929......... DLB-10
Jones, Hugh circa 1692-1760 .... DLB-24
Jones, James 1921-1977........DLB-2, 143; DS-17
James Jones Papers in the Handy Writers'
  Colony Collection at the University of
  Illinois at Springfield Y-98
The James Jones Society................ Y-92
Jones, Jenkin Lloyd 1911- DLB-127
Jones, John Beauchamp 1810-1866...... DLB-202
Jones, LeRoi (see Baraka, Amiri)
Jones, Lewis 1897-1939................ DLB-15
Jones, Madison 1925- DLB-152
Jones, Major Joseph
  (see Thompson, William Tappan)
Jones, Marie 1955- DLB-233
Jones, Preston 1936-1979 .... DLB-7
Jones, Rodney 1950- DLB-120
Jones, Sir William 1746-1794 .... DLB-109
Jones, William Alfred 1817-1900 .... DLB-59
Jones's Publishing House DLB-49
Jong, Erica 1942- DLB-2, 5, 28, 152
Jonke, Gert F. 1946- DLB-85
Jonson, Ben
  1572?-1637 .... DLB-62, 121; CDBLB-1
Jordan, June 1936- DLB-38
Joseph and George Y-99
Joseph, Jenny 1932- DLB-40
Joseph, Michael, Limited DLB-112
Josephson, Matthew 1899-1978 .... DLB-4
Josephus, Flavius 37-100 ....DLB-176
Josiah Allen's Wife (see Holley, Marietta)
Josipovici, Gabriel 1940- DLB-14
Josselyn, John ?-1675 .... DLB-24
Joudry, Patricia 1921- DLB-88
Jovine, Giuseppe 1922- DLB-128
Joyaux, Philippe (see Sollers, Philippe)
Joyce, Adrien (see Eastman, Carol)
Joyce, James
  1882-1941 ... DLB-10, 19, 36, 162; CDBLB-6

400

James Joyce Centenary: Dublin, 1982 . . . . Y-82	Karadžić, Vuk Stefanović 1787-1864 . . . . DLB-147; CDWLB-4	Kemelman, Harry 1908- DLB-28
James Joyce Conference Y-85	Karamzin, Nikolai Mikhailovich 1766-1826 . . . . DLB-150	Kempe, Margery circa 1373-1438 . . . . DLB-146
A Joyce (Con)Text: Danis Rose and the Remaking of *Ulysses* Y-97	Karinthy, Frigyes 1887-1938 . . . . DLB-215	Kempner, Friederike 1836-1904 . . . . DLB-129
The New *Ulysses* Y-84	Karsch, Anna Louisa 1722-1791 . . . . DLB-97	Kempowski, Walter 1929- DLB-75
Jozsef, Attila 1905-1937 . . . . . DLB-215; CDWLB-4	Kasack, Hermann 1896-1966 . . . . DLB-69	Kendall, Claude [publishing company] DLB-46
Judd, Orange, Publishing Company DLB-49	Kasai, Zenzō 1887-1927 . . . . DLB-180	Kendall, Henry 1839-1882 . . . . DLB-230
Judd, Sylvester 1813-1853 . . . . DLB-1	Kaschnitz, Marie Luise 1901-1974 . . . . DLB-69	Kendall, May 1861-1943 . . . . DLB-240
Judith circa 930 . . . . DLB-146	Kassák, Lajos 1887-1967 . . . . DLB-215	Kendell, George 1809-1867 . . . . DLB-43
Julian of Norwich 1342-circa 1420 . . . . DLB-1146	Kaštelan, Jure 1919-1990 . . . . DLB-147	Kenedy, P. J., and Sons DLB-49
Julius Caesar 100 B.C.-44 B.C. DLB-211; CDWLB-1	Kästner, Erich 1899-1974 . . . . DLB-56	Kenkō circa 1283-circa 1352 . . . . DLB-203
June, Jennie (see Croly, Jane Cunningham)	Katenin, Pavel Aleksandrovich 1792-1853 . . . . DLB-205	Kennan, George 1845-1924 . . . . DLB-189
Jung, Franz 1888-1963 . . . . DLB-118	Kattan, Naim 1928- DLB-53	Kennedy, Adrienne 1931- DLB-38
Jünger, Ernst 1895- DLB-56; CDWLB-2	Katz, Steve 1935- Y-83	Kennedy, John Pendleton 1795-1870 . . . . . . DLB-3
Der jüngere Titurel circa 1275 . . . . DLB-138	Kauffman, Janet 1945- DLB-218; Y-86	Kennedy, Leo 1907- DLB-88
Jung-Stilling, Johann Heinrich 1740-1817 . . . . DLB-94	Kauffmann, Samuel 1898-1971 . . . . DLB-127	Kennedy, Margaret 1896-1967 . . . . DLB-36
Justice, Donald 1925- Y-83	Kaufman, Bob 1925- DLB-16, 41	Kennedy, Patrick 1801-1873 . . . . DLB-159
Juvenal circa A.D. 60-circa A.D. 130 . . . . DLB-211; CDWLB-1	Kaufman, George S. 1889-1961 . . . . DLB-7	Kennedy, Richard S. 1920- DLB-111
The Juvenile Library (see Godwin, M. J., and Company)	Kavanagh, P. J. 1931- DLB-40	Kennedy, William 1928- DLB-143; Y-85
	Kavanagh, Patrick 1904-1967 . . . . DLB-15, 20	Kennedy, X. J. 1929- DLB-5
K	Kawabata, Yasunari 1899-1972 . . . . DLB-180	Kennelly, Brendan 1936- DLB-40
Kacew, Romain (see Gary, Romain)	Kaye-Smith, Sheila 1887-1956 . . . . DLB-36	Kenner, Hugh 1923- DLB-67
Kafka, Franz 1883-1924 . . . . . . DLB-81; CDWLB-2	Kazin, Alfred 1915-1998 . . . . DLB-67	Kennerley, Mitchell [publishing house] DLB-46
Kahn, Roger 1927- DLB-171	Keane, John B. 1928- DLB-13	Kenny, Maurice 1929- DLB-175
Kaikō Takeshi 1939-1989 . . . . DLB-182	Keary, Annie 1825-1879 . . . . DLB-163	Kent, Frank R. 1877-1958 . . . . DLB-29
Kaiser, Georg 1878-1945 . . . . DLB-124; CDWLB-2	Keary, Eliza 1827-1918 . . . . DLB-240	Kenyon, Jane 1947-1995 . . . . DLB-120
Kaiserchronik circca 1147 . . . . DLB-148	Keating, H. R. F. 1926- DLB-87	Keough, Hugh Edmund 1864-1912 . . . . . DLB-171
Kaleb, Vjekoslav 1905- DLB-181	Keats, Ezra Jack 1916-1983 . . . . DLB-61	Keppler and Schwartzmann DLB-49
Kalechofsky, Roberta 1931- DLB-28	Keats, John 1795-1821 . . . . DLB-96, 110; CDBLB-3	Ker, John, third Duke of Roxburghe 1740-1804 . . . . DLB-213
Kaler, James Otis 1848-1912 . . . . DLB-12	Keble, John 1792-1866 . . . . DLB-32, 55	Ker, N. R. 1908-1982 . . . . DLB-201
Kames, Henry Home, Lord 1696-1782 . . . . DLB-31, 104	Keckley, Elizabeth 1818?-1907 . . . . DLB-239	Kerlan, Irvin 1912-1963 . . . . DLB-187
Kamo no Chōmei (Kamo no Nagaakira) 1153 or 1155-1216 . . . . DLB-203	Keeble, John 1944- Y-83	Kern, Jerome 1885-1945 . . . . DLB-187
Kamo no Nagaakira (see Kamo no Chōmei)	Keeffe, Barrie 1945- DLB-13	Kerner, Justinus 1776-1862 . . . . DLB-90
Kampmann, Christian 1939-1988 . . . . . . DLB-214	Keeley, James 1867-1934 . . . . DLB-25	Kerouac, Jack 1922-1969 . . . DLB-2, 16, 237; DS-3; CDALB-1
Kandel, Lenore 1932- DLB-16	W. B. Keen, Cooke and Company DLB-49	The Jack Kerouac Revival Y-95
Kanin, Garson 1912-1999 . . . . DLB-7	Keillor, Garrison 1942- Y-87	"Re-meeting of Old Friends": The Jack Kerouac Conference Y-82
Kant, Hermann 1926- DLB-75	Keith, Marian 1874?-1961 . . . . DLB-92	Kerouac, Jan 1952-1996 . . . . DLB-16
Kant, Immanuel 1724-1804 . . . . DLB-94	Keller, Gary D. 1943- DLB-82	Kerr, Charles H., and Company DLB-49
Kantemir, Antiokh Dmitrievich 1708-1744 . . . . DLB-150	Keller, Gottfried 1819-1890 . . . . DLB-129; CDWLB-2	Kerr, Orpheus C. (see Newell, Robert Henry)
Kantor, MacKinlay 1904-1977 . . . . DLB-9, 102	Kelley, Edith Summers 1884-1956 . . . . DLB-9	Kesey, Ken 1935- DLB-2, 16, 206; CDALB-6
Kanze Kōjirō Nobumitsu 1435-1516 . . . . DLB-203	Kelley, Emma Dunham ?-? DLB-221	Kessel, Joseph 1898-1979 . . . . DLB-72
Kanze Motokiyo (see Zeimi)	Kelley, William Melvin 1937- DLB-33	Kessel, Martin 1901- DLB-56
Kaplan, Fred 1937- DLB-111	Kellogg, Ansel Nash 1832-1886 . . . . DLB-23	Kesten, Hermann 1900- DLB-56
Kaplan, Johanna 1942- DLB-28	Kellogg, Steven 1941- DLB-61	Keun, Irmgard 1905-1982 . . . . DLB-69
Kaplan, Justin 1925- DLB-111	Kelly, George 1887-1974 . . . . DLB-7	Key and Biddle DLB-49
The Practice of Biography V: An Interview with Justin Kaplan Y-86	Kelly, Hugh 1739-1777 . . . . DLB-89	Keynes, Sir Geoffrey 1887-1982 . . . . DLB-201
Kaplinski, Jaan 1941- DLB-232	Kelly, Piet and Company DLB-49	Keynes, John Maynard 1883-1946 . . . . DS-10
Kapnist, Vasilii Vasilevich 1758?-1823 . . . DLB-150	Kelly, Robert 1935- DLB-5, 130, 165	Keyserling, Eduard von 1855-1918 . . . . . . DLB-66
	Kelman, James 1946- DLB-194	Khan, Ismith 1925- DLB-125
	Kelmscott Press DLB-112	Khaytov, Nikolay 1919- DLB-181
	Kemble, E. W. 1861-1933 . . . . DLB-188	Khemnitser, Ivan Ivanovich 1745-1784 . . . . DLB-150
	Kemble, Fanny 1809-1893 . . . . DLB-32	Kheraskov, Mikhail Matveevich 1733-1807 . . . . DLB-150

Khomiakov, Aleksei Stepanovich
1804-1860 .... DLB-205

Khristov, Boris 1945- DLB-181

Khvoshchinskaia, Nadezhda Dmitrievna
1824-1889 .... DLB-238

Khvostov, Dmitrii Ivanovich
1757-1835 .... DLB-150

Kidd, Adam 1802?-1831 .... DLB-99

Kidd, William [publishing house] DLB-106

Kidder, Tracy 1945- DLB-185

Kiely, Benedict 1919- DLB-15

Kieran, John 1892-1981 .... DLB-171

Kiggins and Kellogg DLB-49

Kiley, Jed 1889-1962 .... DLB-4

Kilgore, Bernard 1908-1967 .... DLB-127

Killens, John Oliver 1916- DLB-33

Killigrew, Anne 1660-1685 .... DLB-131

Killigrew, Thomas 1612-1683 .... DLB-58

Kilmer, Joyce 1886-1918 .... DLB-45

Kilroy, Thomas 1934- DLB-233

Kilwardby, Robert circa 1215-1279 .... DLB-115

Kimball, Richard Burleigh 1816-1892 ... DLB-202

Kincaid, Jamaica 1949-
.... DLB-157, 227; CDALB-7; CDWLB-3

King, Charles 1844-1933 .... DLB-186

King, Clarence 1842-1901 .... DLB-12

King, Florence 1936- Y-85

King, Francis 1923- DLB-15, 139

King, Grace 1852-1932 .... DLB-12, 78

King, Harriet Hamilton 1840-1920 ..... DLB-199

King, Henry 1592-1669 .... DLB-126

King, Solomon [publishing house] DLB-49

King, Stephen 1947- DLB-143; Y-80

King, Susan Petigru 1824-1875 .... DLB-239

King, Thomas 1943- DLB-175

King, Woodie, Jr. 1937- DLB-38

Kinglake, Alexander William
1809-1891 .... DLB-55, 166

Kingsley, Charles
1819-1875 .... DLB-21, 32, 163, 178, 190

Kingsley, Henry 1830-1876 .... DLB-21, 230

Kingsley, Mary Henrietta 1862-1900 .... DLB-174

Kingsley, Sidney 1906- DLB-7

Kingsmill, Hugh 1889-1949 .... DLB-149

Kingsolver, Barbara
1955- DLB-206; CDALB-7

Kingston, Maxine Hong
1940- DLB-173, 212; Y-80; CDALB-7

Kingston, William Henry Giles
1814-1880 .... DLB-163

Kinnan, Mary Lewis 1763-1848 .... DLB-200

Kinnell, Galway 1927- DLB-5; Y-87

Kinsella, Thomas 1928- DLB-27

Kipling, Rudyard 1865-1936
.... DLB-19, 34, 141, 156; CDBLB-5

Kipphardt, Heinar 1922-1982 .... DLB-124

Kirby, William 1817-1906 .... DLB-99

Kircher, Athanasius 1602-1680 .... DLB-164

Kireevsky, Ivan Vasil'evich 1806-1856 ... DLB-198

Kireevsky, Petr Vasil'evich 1808-1856 ... DLB-205

Kirk, Hans 1898-1962 .... DLB-214

Kirk, John Foster 1824-1904 .... DLB-79

Kirkconnell, Watson 1895-1977 .... DLB-68

Kirkland, Caroline M.
1801-1864 .... DLB-3, 73, 74; DS-13

Kirkland, Joseph 1830-1893 .... DLB-12

Kirkman, Francis [publishing house] DLB-170

Kirkpatrick, Clayton 1915- DLB-127

Kirkup, James 1918- DLB-27

Kirouac, Conrad (see Marie-Victorin, Frère)

Kirsch, Sarah 1935- DLB-75

Kirst, Hans Hellmut 1914-1989 .... DLB-69

Kiš, Danilo 1935-1989 ..... DLB-181; CDWLB-4

Kita Morio 1927- DLB-182

Kitcat, Mabel Greenhow 1859-1922 ..... DLB-135

Kitchin, C. H. B. 1895-1967 .... DLB-77

Kittredge, William 1932- DLB-212

Kiukhel'beker, Vil'gel'm Karlovich
1797-1846 .... DLB-205

Kizer, Carolyn 1925- DLB-5, 169

Klabund 1890-1928 .... DLB-66

Klaj, Johann 1616-1656 .... DLB-164

Klappert, Peter 1942- DLB-5

Klass, Philip (see Tenn, William)

Klein, A. M. 1909-1972 .... DLB-68

Kleist, Ewald von 1715-1759 .... DLB-97

Kleist, Heinrich von
1777-1811 .... DLB-90; CDWLB-2

Klinger, Friedrich Maximilian
1752-1831 .... DLB-94

Klíma, Ivan 1931- DLB-232; CDWLB-4

Kliushnikov, Viktor Petrovich
1841-1892 .... DLB-238

Oral History Interview with Donald S.
Klopfer Y-97

Klopstock, Friedrich Gottlieb
1724-1803 .... DLB-97

Klopstock, Meta 1728-1758 .... DLB-97

Kluge, Alexander 1932- DLB-75

Knapp, Joseph Palmer 1864-1951 .... DLB-91

Knapp, Samuel Lorenzo 1783-1838 ..... DLB-59

Knapton, J. J. and P.
[publishing house] DLB-154

Kniazhnin, Iakov Borisovich
1740-1791 .... DLB-150

Knickerbocker, Diedrich (see Irving, Washington)

Knigge, Adolph Franz Friedrich Ludwig,
Freiherr von 1752-1796 .... DLB-94

Knight, Charles, and Company DLB-106

Knight, Damon 1922- DLB-8

Knight, Etheridge 1931-1992 .... DLB-41

Knight, John S. 1894-1981 .... DLB-29

Knight, Sarah Kemble 1666-1727 .... DLB-24, 200

Knight-Bruce, G. W. H. 1852-1896 ..... DLB-174

Knister, Raymond 1899-1932 .... DLB-68

Knoblock, Edward 1874-1945 .... DLB-10

Knopf, Alfred A. 1892-1984 .... Y-84

Knopf, Alfred A. [publishing house] DLB-46

Knorr von Rosenroth, Christian
1636-1689 .... DLB-168

"Knots into Webs: Some Autobiographical
Sources," by Dabney Stuart DLB-105

Knowles, John 1926- DLB-6; CDALB-6

Knox, Frank 1874-1944 .... DLB-29

Knox, John circa 1514-1572 .... DLB-132

Knox, John Armoy 1850-1906 .... DLB-23

Knox, Lucy 1845-1884 .... DLB-240

Knox, Ronald Arbuthnott 1888-1957 .... DLB-77

Knox, Thomas Wallace 1835-1896 ..... DLB-189

Kobayashi Takiji 1903-1933 .... DLB-180

Kober, Arthur 1900-1975 .... DLB-11

Kobiakova, Aleksandra Petrovna
1823-1892 .... DLB-238

Kocbek, Edvard 1904-1981 ... DLB-147; CDWB-4

Koch, Howard 1902- DLB-26

Koch, Kenneth 1925- DLB-5

Kōda, Rohan 1867-1947 .... DLB-180

Koenigsberg, Moses 1879-1945 .... DLB-25

Koeppen, Wolfgang 1906-1996 .... DLB-69

Koertge, Ronald 1940- DLB-105

Koestler, Arthur 1905-1983 ...... Y-83; CDBLB-7

Kohn, John S. Van E. 1906-1976 and
Papantonio, Michael 1907-1978 ..... DLB-187

Kokoschka, Oskar 1886-1980 .... DLB-124

Kolb, Annette 1870-1967 .... DLB-66

Kolbenheyer, Erwin Guido
1878-1962 .... DLB-66, 124

Kolleritsch, Alfred 1931- DLB-85

Kolodny, Annette 1941- DLB-67

Kol'tsov, Aleksei Vasil'evich
1809-1842 .... DLB-205

Komarov, Matvei circa 1730-1812 ...... DLB-150

Komroff, Manuel 1890-1974 .... DLB-4

Komunyakaa, Yusef 1947- DLB-120

Koneski, Blaže 1921-1993 .... DLB-181; CDWLB-4

Konigsburg, E. L. 1930- DLB-52

Konparu Zenchiku 1405-1468? DLB-203

Konrád, György 1933- DLB-232; CDWLB-4

Konrad von Würzburg
circa 1230-1287 .... DLB-138

Konstantinov, Aleko 1863-1897 .... DLB-147

Konwicki, Tadeusz 1926- DLB-232

Kooser, Ted 1939- DLB-105

Kopit, Arthur 1937- DLB-7

Kops, Bernard 1926?- DLB-13

Kornbluth, C. M. 1923-1958 .... DLB-8

Körner, Theodor 1791-1813 .... DLB-90

Kornfeld, Paul 1889-1942 .... DLB-118

Kosinski, Jerzy 1933-1991 .... DLB-2; Y-82

Kosmač, Ciril 1910-1980 .... DLB-181

Kosovel, Srečko 1904-1926 . . . . DLB-147
Kostrov, Ermil Ivanovich 1755-1796 . . . . . DLB-150
Kotzebue, August von 1761-1819 . . . . DLB-94
Kotzwinkle, William 1938- DLB-173
Kovačić, Ante 1854-1889 . . . . DLB-147
Kovič, Kajetan 1931- DLB-181
Kozlov, Ivan Ivanovich 1779-1840 . . . . DLB-205
Kraf, Elaine 1946- Y-81
Kramer, Jane 1938- DLB-185
Kramer, Mark 1944- DLB-185
Kranjčević, Silvije Strahimir 1865-1908 . . . DLB-147
Krasko, Ivan 1876-1958 . . . . DLB-215
Krasna, Norman 1909-1984 . . . . DLB-26
Kraus, Hans Peter 1907-1988 . . . . DLB-187
Kraus, Karl 1874-1936 . . . . DLB-118
Krauss, Ruth 1911-1993 . . . . DLB-52
Kreisel, Henry 1922- DLB-88
Krestovsky V. (see Khvoshchinskaia, Nadezhda Dmitrievna)
Krestovsky, Vsevolod Vladimirovich 1839-1895 . . . . DLB-238
Kreuder, Ernst 1903-1972 . . . . DLB-69
Krėvė-Mickevičius, Vincas 1882-1954 . . . . DLB-220
Kreymborg, Alfred 1883-1966 . . . . DLB-4, 54
Krieger, Murray 1923- DLB-67
Krim, Seymour 1922-1989 . . . . DLB-16
Kristensen, Tom 1893-1974 . . . . DLB-214
Krleža, Miroslav 1893-1981 . . DLB-147; CDWLB-4
Krock, Arthur 1886-1974 . . . . DLB-29
Kroetsch, Robert 1927- DLB-53
Kross, Jaan 1920- DLB-232
Krúdy, Gyula 1878-1933 . . . . DLB-215
Krutch, Joseph Wood 1893-1970 . . . . . DLB-63, 206
Krylov, Ivan Andreevich 1769-1844 . . . . . DLB-150
Kubin, Alfred 1877-1959 . . . . DLB-81
Kubrick, Stanley 1928-1999 . . . . DLB-26
Kudrun circa 1230-1240 . . . . DLB-138
Kuffstein, Hans Ludwig von 1582-1656 . . . . DLB-164
Kuhlmann, Quirinus 1651-1689 . . . . DLB-168
Kuhnau, Johann 1660-1722 . . . . DLB-168
Kukol'nik, Nestor Vasil'evich 1809-1868 . . . . DLB-205
Kukučín, Martin 1860-1928 . . . . DLB-215; CDWLB-4
Kumin, Maxine 1925- DLB-5
Kuncewicz, Maria 1895-1989 . . . . DLB-215
Kundera, Milan 1929- DLB-232; CDWLB-4
Kunene, Mazisi 1930- DLB-117
Kunikida, Doppo 1869-1908 . . . . DLB-180
Kunitz, Stanley 1905- DLB-48
Kunjufu, Johari M. (see Amini, Johari M.)
Kunnert, Gunter 1929- DLB-75
Kunze, Reiner 1933- DLB-75
Kupferberg, Tuli 1923- DLB-16
Kurahashi Yumiko 1935- DLB-182

Kureishi, Hanif 1954- DLB-194
Kürnberger, Ferdinand 1821-1879 . . . . . . DLB-129
Kurz, Isolde 1853-1944 . . . . DLB-66
Kusenberg, Kurt 1904-1983 . . . . DLB-69
Kushchevsky, Ivan Afanas'evich 1847?-1876 . . . . DLB-238
Kushner, Tony 1956- DLB-228
Kuttner, Henry 1915-1958 . . . . DLB-8
Kyd, Thomas 1558-1594 . . . . DLB-62
Kyffin, Maurice circa 1560?-1598 . . . . DLB-136
Kyger, Joanne 1934- DLB-16
Kyne, Peter B. 1880-1957 . . . . DLB-78
Kyōgoku Tamekane 1254-1332 . . . . DLB-203

L

L. E. L. (see Landon, Letitia Elizabeth)
Laberge, Albert 1871-1960 . . . . DLB-68
Laberge, Marie 1950- DLB-60
Labiche, Eugène 1815-1888 . . . . DLB-192
Labrunie, Gerard (see Nerval, Gerard de)
La Capria, Raffaele 1922- DLB-196
Lacombe, Patrice (see Trullier-Lacombe, Joseph Patrice)
Lacretelle, Jacques de 1888-1985 . . . . DLB-65
Lacy, Ed 1911-1968 . . . . DLB-226
Lacy, Sam 1903- DLB-171
Ladd, Joseph Brown 1764-1786 . . . . DLB-37
La Farge, Oliver 1901-1963 . . . . DLB-9
Laffan, Mrs. R. S. de Courcy (see Adams, Bertha Leith)
Lafferty, R. A. 1914- DLB-8
La Flesche, Francis 1857-1932 . . . . DLB-175
Laforge, Jules 1860-1887 . . . . DLB-217
Lagorio, Gina 1922- DLB-196
La Guma, Alex 1925-1985 . . . . DLB-117, 225; CDWLB-3
Lahaise, Guillaume (see Delahaye, Guy)
Lahontan, Louis-Armand de Lom d'Arce, Baron de 1666-1715? DLB-99
Laing, Kojo 1946- DLB-157
Laird, Carobeth 1895- Y-82
Laird and Lee DLB-49
Lalić, Ivan V. 1931-1996 . . . . DLB-181
Lalić, Mihailo 1914-1992 . . . . DLB-181
Lalonde, Michèle 1937- DLB-60
Lamantia, Philip 1927- DLB-16
Lamartine, Alphonse de 1790-1869 . . . . . . DLB-217
Lamb, Lady Caroline 1785-1828 . . . . DLB-116
Lamb, Charles 1775-1834 . . . . . . DLB-93, 107, 163; CDBLB-3
Lamb, Mary 1764-1874 . . . . DLB-163
Lambert, Betty 1933-1983 . . . . DLB-60
Lamming, George 1927- . . . DLB-125; CDWLB-3
L'Amour, Louis 1908-1988 . . . . . . DLB-206; Y-80
Lampman, Archibald 1861-1899 . . . . DLB-92
Lamson, Wolffe and Company DLB-49

Lancer Books DLB-46
Landesman, Jay 1919- and Landesman, Fran 1927- DLB-16
Landolfi, Tommaso 1908-1979 . . . . DLB-177
Landon, Letitia Elizabeth 1802-1838 . . . . . DLB-96
Landor, Walter Savage 1775-1864 . . . . DLB-93, 107
Landry, Napoléon-P. 1884-1956 . . . . DLB-92
Lane, Charles 1800-1870 . . . . DLB-1, 223
Lane, John, Company DLB-49
Lane, Laurence W. 1890-1967 . . . . DLB-91
Lane, M. Travis 1934- DLB-60
Lane, Patrick 1939- DLB-53
Lane, Pinkie Gordon 1923- DLB-41
Laney, Al 1896-1988 . . . . DLB-4, 171
Lang, Andrew 1844-1912 . . . . . . DLB-98, 141, 184
Langevin, André 1927- DLB-60
Langgässer, Elisabeth 1899-1950 . . . . DLB-69
Langhorne, John 1735-1779 . . . . DLB-109
Langland, William circa 1330-circa 1400 . . . . DLB-146
Langton, Anna 1804-1893 . . . . DLB-99
Lanham, Edwin 1904-1979 . . . . DLB-4
Lanier, Sidney 1842-1881 . . . . DLB-64; DS-13
Lanyer, Aemilia 1569-1645 . . . . DLB-121
Lapointe, Gatien 1931-1983 . . . . DLB-88
Lapointe, Paul-Marie 1929- DLB-88
Larcom, Lucy 1824-1893 . . . . DLB-221
Lardner, John 1912-1960 . . . . DLB-171
Lardner, Ring 1885-1933 . . . . . . DLB-11, 25, 86, 171; DS-16; CDALB-4
Lardner 100: Ring Lardner Centennial Symposium Y-85
Lardner, Ring, Jr. 1915- DLB-26
Larkin, Philip 1922-1985 . . . . . DLB-27; CDBLB-8
La Roche, Sophie von 1730-1807 . . . . DLB-94
La Rocque, Gilbert 1943-1984 . . . . DLB-60
Laroque de Roquebrune, Robert (see Roquebrune, Robert de)
Larrick, Nancy 1910- DLB-61
Larsen, Nella 1893-1964 . . . . DLB-51
La Sale, Antoine de circa 1386-1460/1467 . . . . DLB-208
Lasker-Schüler, Else 1869-1945 . . . . . DLB-66, 124
Lasnier, Rina 1915- DLB-88
Lassalle, Ferdinand 1825-1864 . . . . DLB-129
Latham, Robert 1912-1995 . . . . DLB-201
Lathrop, Dorothy P. 1891-1980 . . . . DLB-22
Lathrop, George Parsons 1851-1898 . . . . . DLB-71
Lathrop, John, Jr. 1772-1820 . . . . DLB-37
Latimer, Hugh 1492?-1555 . . . . DLB-136
Latimore, Jewel Christine McLawler (see Amini, Johari M.)
Latymer, William 1498-1583 . . . . DLB-132
Laube, Heinrich 1806-1884 . . . . DLB-133
Laud, William 1573-1645 . . . . DLB-213
Laughlin, James 1914-1997 . . . . DLB-48

Cumulative Index

James Laughlin Tributes..................Y-97
Conversations with Publishers IV:
 An Interview with James Laughlin.......Y-96
Laumer, Keith 1925- DLB-8
Lauremberg, Johann 1590-1658........DLB-164
Laurence, Margaret 1926-1987..........DLB-53
Laurentius von Schnüffis 1633-1702.....DLB-168
Laurents, Arthur 1918- DLB-26
Laurie, Annie (see Black, Winifred)
Laut, Agnes Christiana 1871-1936.......DLB-92
Lauterbach, Ann 1942- DLB-193
Lautreamont, Isidore Lucien Ducasse, Comte de 1846-1870...................DLB-217
Lavater, Johann Kaspar 1741-1801.......DLB-97
Lavin, Mary 1912-1996 ....DLB-15
Law, John (see Harkness, Margaret)
Lawes, Henry 1596-1662 ....DLB-126
Lawless, Anthony (see MacDonald, Philip)
Lawless, Emily (The Hon. Emily Lawless) 1845-1913 DLB-240
Lawrence, D. H. 1885-1930
  .....DLB-10, 19, 36, 98, 162, 195; CDBLB-6
Lawrence, David 1888-1973............DLB-29
Lawrence, Jerome 1915- and
 Lee, Robert E. 1918-1994..........DLB-228
Lawrence, Seymour 1926-1994 ....Y-94
Lawrence, T. E. 1888-1935 ....DLB-195
Lawson, George 1598-1678 ....DLB-213
Lawson, Henry 1867-1922 ....DLB-230
Lawson, John ?-1711.................DLB-24
Lawson, John Howard 1894-1977 .....DLB-228
Lawson, Louisa Albury 1848-1920......DLB-230
Lawson, Robert 1892-1957............DLB-22
Lawson, Victor F. 1850-1925 ....DLB-25
Layard, Sir Austen Henry 1817-1894.....................DLB-166
Layton, Irving 1912- DLB-88
LaZamon flourished circa 1200 ....DLB-146
Lazarević, Laza K. 1851-1890..........DLB-147
Lazarus, George 1904-1997 ....DLB-201
Lazhechnikov, Ivan Ivanovich 1792-1869......................DLB-198
Lea, Henry Charles 1825-1909..........DLB-47
Lea, Sydney 1942- DLB-120
Lea, Tom 1907- DLB-6
Leacock, John 1729-1802.............DLB-31
Leacock, Stephen 1869-1944 ....DLB-92
Lead, Jane Ward 1623-1704 ....DLB-131
Leadenhall Press....................DLB-106
Leakey, Caroline Woolmer 1827-1881...DLB-230
Leapor, Mary 1722-1746..............DLB-109
Lear, Edward 1812-1888 ......DLB-32, 163, 166
Leary, Timothy 1920-1996............DLB-16
Leary, W. A., and Company DLB-49
Léautaud, Paul 1872-1956 ....DLB-65
Leavitt, David 1961-................DLB-130

Leavitt and Allen DLB-49
Le Blond, Mrs. Aubrey 1861-1934.......DLB-174
le Carré, John 1931- DLB-87; CDBLB-8
Lécavelé, Roland (see Dorgeles, Roland)
Lechlitner, Ruth 1901- DLB-48
Leclerc, Félix 1914- DLB-60
Le Clézio, J. M. G. 1940- DLB-83
Lectures on Rhetoric and Belles Lettres (1783), by Hugh Blair [excerpts] DLB-31
Leder, Rudolf (see Hermlin, Stephan)
Lederer, Charles 1910-1976 ....DLB-26
Ledwidge, Francis 1887-1917 ....DLB-20
Lee, Dennis 1939- DLB-53
Lee, Don L. (see Madhubuti, Haki R.)
Lee, George W. 1894-1976............DLB-51
Lee, Harper 1926- DLB-6; CDALB-1
Lee, Harriet (1757-1851) and
 Lee, Sophia (1750-1824)............DLB-39
Lee, Laurie 1914-1997 ....DLB-27
Lee, Li-Young 1957- DLB-165
Lee, Manfred B. (see Dannay, Frederic, and Manfred B. Lee)
Lee, Nathaniel circa 1645-1692 ....DLB-80
Lee, Sir Sidney 1859-1926 ....DLB-149, 184
Lee, Sir Sidney, "Principles of Biography," in *Elizabethan and Other Essays*..........DLB-149
Lee, Vernon 1856-1935 ....DLB-57, 153, 156, 174, 178
Lee and Shepard.....................DLB-49
Le Fanu, Joseph Sheridan 1814-1873............DLB-21, 70, 159, 178
Leffland, Ella 1931- Y-84
le Fort, Gertrud von 1876-1971........DLB-66
Le Gallienne, Richard 1866-1947 ....DLB-4
Legaré, Hugh Swinton 1797-1843...DLB-3, 59, 73
Legaré, James M. 1823-1859 ....DLB-3
The Legends of the Saints and a Medieval Christian Worldview..............DLB-148
Léger, Antoine-J. 1880-1950 ....DLB-88
Le Guin, Ursula K. 1929- DLB-8, 52; CDALB-6
Lehman, Ernest 1920- DLB-44
Lehmann, John 1907- DLB-27, 100
Lehmann, John, Limited..............DLB-112
Lehmann, Rosamond 1901-1990 ....DLB-15
Lehmann, Wilhelm 1882-1968..........DLB-56
Leiber, Fritz 1910-1992..................DLB-8
Leibniz, Gottfried Wilhelm 1646-1716 ...DLB-168
Leicester University Press DLB-112
Leigh, W. R. 1866-1955...............DLB-188
Leinster, Murray 1896-1975 ....DLB-8
Leisewitz, Johann Anton 1752-1806 ......DLB-94
Leitch, Maurice 1933- DLB-14
Leithauser, Brad 1943- DLB-120
Leland, Charles G. 1824-1903 ....DLB-11
Leland, John 1503?-1552 ....DLB-136
Lemay, Pamphile 1837-1918 ....DLB-99

Lemelin, Roger 1919- DLB-88
Lemercier, Louis-Jean-Népomucène 1771-1840......................DLB-192
Le Moine, James MacPherson 1825-1912 ....DLB-99
Lemon, Mark 1809-1870 ....DLB-163
Le Moyne, Jean 1913- DLB-88
Lemperly, Paul 1858-1939 ....DLB-187
L'Engle, Madeleine 1918- DLB-52
Lennart, Isobel 1915-1971 ....DLB-44
Lennox, Charlotte 1729 or 1730-1804 ....DLB-39
Lenox, James 1800-1880..............DLB-140
Lenski, Lois 1893-1974...............DLB-22
Lenz, Hermann 1913-1998............DLB-69
Lenz, J. M. R. 1751-1792.............DLB-94
Lenz, Siegfried 1926- DLB-75
Leonard, Elmore 1925- DLB-173, 226
Leonard, Hugh 1926- DLB-13
Leonard, William Ellery 1876-1944 ......DLB-54
Leonowens, Anna 1834-1914.......DLB-99, 166
LePan, Douglas 1914- DLB-88
Lepik, Kalju 1920-1999 ....DLB-232
Leprohon, Rosanna Eleanor 1829-1879...DLB-99
Le Queux, William 1864-1927 ....DLB-70
Lermontov, Mikhail Iur'evich 1814-1841 ....DLB-205
Lerner, Max 1902-1992 ....DLB-29
Lernet-Holenia, Alexander 1897-1976.....DLB-85
Le Rossignol, James 1866-1969 ....DLB-92
Lescarbot, Marc circa 1570-1642 ....DLB-99
LeSeur, William Dawson 1840-1917 .....DLB-92
LeSieg, Theo. (see Geisel, Theodor Seuss)
Leskov, Nikolai Semenovich 1831-1895..DLB-238
Leslie, Doris before 1902-1982.........DLB-191
Leslie, Eliza 1787-1858 ....DLB-202
Leslie, Frank 1821-1880 ....DLB-43, 79
Leslie, Frank, Publishing House........DLB-49
Leśmian, Bolesław 1878-1937..........DLB-215
Lesperance, John 1835?-1891...........DLB-99
Lessing, Bruno 1870-1940 ....DLB-28
Lessing, Doris 1919- DLB-15, 139; Y-85; CDBLB-8
Lessing, Gotthold Ephraim 1729-1781............DLB-97; CDWLB-2
Lettau, Reinhard 1929- DLB-75
Letter from Japan..................Y-94, Y-98
Letter from London Y-96
Letter to [Samuel] Richardson on *Clarissa* (1748), by Henry Fielding DLB-39
A Letter to the Editor of *The Irish Times* Y-97
Lever, Charles 1806-1872.............DLB-21
Lever, Ralph ca. 1527-1585 ....DLB-236
Leverson, Ada 1862-1933.............DLB-153
Levertov, Denise 1923-1997 ....DLB-5, 165; CDALB-7
Levi, Peter 1931- DLB-40

Levi, Primo 1919-1987................DLB-177
Levien, Sonya 1888-1960...............DLB-44
Levin, Meyer 1905-1981........DLB-9, 28; Y-81
Levine, Norman 1923- DLB-88
Levine, Philip 1928- DLB-5
Levis, Larry 1946- DLB-120
Levy, Amy 1861-1889............DLB-156, 240
Levy, Benn Wolfe 1900-1973......DLB-13; Y-81
Lewald, Fanny 1811-1889..............DLB-129
Lewes, George Henry 1817-1878.....DLB-55, 144
"Criticism In Relation To
  Novels" (1863)....................DLB-21
The Principles of Success in Literature
  (1865) [excerpt]...................DLB-57
Lewis, Agnes Smith 1843-1926..........DLB-174
Lewis, Alfred H. 1857-1914..........DLB-25, 186
Lewis, Alun 1915-1944.............DLB-20, 162
Lewis, C. Day (see Day Lewis, C.)
Lewis, C. S.
  1898-1963......DLB-15, 100, 160; CDBLB-7
Lewis, Charles B. 1842-1924............DLB-11
Lewis, Henry Clay 1825-1850............DLB-3
Lewis, Janet 1899-1999 .... Y-87
Lewis, Matthew Gregory
  1775-1818................ DLB-39, 158, 178
Lewis, Meriwether 1774-1809 and
  Clark, William 1770-1838.......DLB-183, 186
Lewis, Norman 1908- DLB-204
Lewis, R. W. B. 1917- DLB-111
Lewis, Richard circa 1700-1734..........DLB-24
Lewis, Sinclair
  1885-1951......DLB-9, 102; DS-1; CDALB-4
Sinclair Lewis Centennial Conference....... Y-85
Lewis, Wilmarth Sheldon 1895-1979.....DLB-140
Lewis, Wyndham 1882-1957............DLB-15
Lewisohn, Ludwig 1882-1955 ...DLB-4, 9, 28, 102
Leyendecker, J. C. 1874-1951 ....DLB-188
Lezama Lima, José 1910-1976...........DLB-113
Libbey, Laura Jean 1862-1924...........DLB-221
The Library of America................DLB-46
The Licensing Act of 1737..............DLB-84
Lichfield, Leonard I [publishing house] ...DLB-170
Lichtenberg, Georg Christoph 1742-1799 ..DLB-94
The Liddle Collection Y-97
Lieb, Fred 1888-1980.................DLB-171
Liebling, A. J. 1904-1963.........DLB-4, 171
Lieutenant Murray (see Ballou, Maturin Murray)
Lighthall, William Douw 1857-1954......DLB-92
Lilar, Françoise (see Mallet-Joris, Françoise)
Lili'uokalani, Queen 1838-1917.........DLB-221
Lillo, George 1691-1739................DLB-84
Lilly, J. K., Jr. 1893-1966.............DLB-140
Lilly, Wait and Company...............DLB-49
Lily, William circa 1468-1522..........DLB-132
Limited Editions Club.................DLB-46
Limón, Graciela 1938- DLB-209

Lincoln and Edmands DLB-49
Lindesay, Ethel Forence
  (see Richardson, Henry Handel)
Lindsay, Alexander William, Twenty-fifth Earl
  of Crawford 1812-1880............DLB-184
Lindsay, Sir David circa 1485-1555......DLB-132
Lindsay, Jack 1900- Y-84
Lindsay, Lady (Caroline Blanche Elizabeth Fitzroy
  Lindsay) 1844-1912................DLB-199
Lindsay, Vachel 1879-1931 ....DLB-54; CDALB-3
Linebarger, Paul Myron Anthony
  (see Smith, Cordwainer)
Link, Arthur S. 1920-1998.............DLB-17
Linn, John Blair 1777-1804...............DLB-37
Lins, Osman 1924-1978................DLB-145
Linton, Eliza Lynn 1822-1898...........DLB-18
Linton, William James 1812-1897.......DLB-32
Lintot, Barnaby Bernard
  [publishing house]................DLB-170
Lion Books DLB-46
Lionni, Leo 1910-1999.................DLB-61
Lippard, George 1822-1854............DLB-202
Lippincott, J. B., Company DLB-49
Lippincott, Sara Jane Clarke 1823-1904 ...DLB-43
Lippmann, Walter 1889-1974 ....DLB-29
Lipton, Lawrence 1898-1975 ....DLB-16
Liscow, Christian Ludwig 1701-1760......DLB-97
Lish, Gordon 1934- DLB-130
Lisle, Charles-Marie-René Leconte de
  1818-1894.......................DLB-217
Lispector, Clarice
  1925-1977 ....DLB-113; CDWLB-3
A Literary Archaeologist Digs On: A Brief
  Interview with Michael Reynolds by
  Michael Rogers.................... Y-99
The Literary Chronicle and Weekly Review
  1819-1828.......................DLB-110
Literary Documents: William Faulkner
  and the People-to-People Program Y-86
Literary Documents II: *Library Journal*
  Statements and Questionnaires from
  First Novelists...................... Y-87
Literary Effects of World War II
  [British novel]....................DLB-15
Literary Prizes [British] DLB-15
Literary Research Archives: The Humanities
  Research Center, University of Texas ... Y-82
Literary Research Archives II: Berg Collection
  of English and American Literature of
  the New York Public Library Y-83
Literary Research Archives III:
  The Lilly Library Y-84
Literary Research Archives IV:
  The John Carter Brown Library........ Y-85
Literary Research Archives V:
  Kent State Special Collections.......... Y-86
Literary Research Archives VI: The Modern
  Literary Manuscripts Collection in the
  Special Collections of the Washington
  University Libraries Y-87
Literary Research Archives VII:
  The University of Virginia Libraries Y-91

Literary Research Archives VIII:
  The Henry E. Huntington Library...... Y-92
Literary Research Archives IX:
  Special Collections at Boston University.. Y-99
The Literary Scene and Situation and ... Who
  (Besides Oprah) Really Runs American
  Literature?........................ Y-99
Literary Societies.................Y-98, Y-99
"Literary Style" (1857), by William
  Forsyth [excerpt] DLB-57
Literatura Chicanesca: The View From
  Without..........................DLB-82
Literature at Nurse, or Circulating Morals (1885),
  by George Moore DLB-18
Littell, Eliakim 1797-1870...............DLB-79
Littell, Robert S. 1831-1896..............DLB-79
Little, Brown and Company DLB-49
Little Magazines and Newspapers DS-15
The Little Review 1914-1929.............. DS-15
Littlewood, Joan 1914- DLB-13
Lively, Penelope 1933- DLB-14, 161, 207
Liverpool University Press DLB-112
The Lives of the Poets...................DLB-142
Livesay, Dorothy 1909- DLB-68
Livesay, Florence Randal 1874-1953 ......DLB-92
"Living in Ruin," by Gerald Stern.......DLB-105
Livings, Henry 1929-1998...............DLB-13
Livingston, Anne Howe 1763-1841 ... DLB-37, 200
Livingston, Myra Cohn 1926-1996.......DLB-61
Livingston, William 1723-1790 ....DLB-31
Livingstone, David 1813-1873..........DLB-166
Livingstone, Douglas 1932-1996........DLB-225
Livy 59 B.C.-A.D. 17.......DLB-211; CDWLB-1
Liyong, Taban lo (see Taban lo Liyong)
Lizárraga, Sylvia S. 1925- DLB-82
Llewellyn, Richard 1906-1983...........DLB-15
Lloyd, Edward [publishing house].......DLB-106
Lobel, Arnold 1933- DLB-61
Lochridge, Betsy Hopkins (see Fancher, Betsy)
Locke, David Ross 1833-1888........DLB-11, 23
Locke, John 1632-1704 .... DLB-31, 101, 213
Locke, Richard Adams 1800-1871........DLB-43
Locker-Lampson, Frederick
  1821-1895....................DLB-35, 184
Lockhart, John Gibson
  1794-1854 ....DLB-110, 116 144
Lockridge, Ross, Jr. 1914-1948 ....DLB-143; Y-80
Locrine and Selimus.....................DLB-62
Lodge, David 1935- DLB-14, 194
Lodge, George Cabot 1873-1909.........DLB-54
Lodge, Henry Cabot 1850-1924 ....DLB-47
Lodge, Thomas 1558-1625 ....DLB-172
From *Defence of Poetry* (1579)............DLB-172
Loeb, Harold 1891-1974 ....DLB-4
Loeb, William 1905-1981 ....DLB-127
Lofting, Hugh 1886-1947...............DLB-160
Logan, Deborah Norris 1761-1839 ......DLB-200

Logan, James 1674-1751 .... DLB-24, 140
Logan, John 1923- DLB-5
Logan, Martha Daniell 1704?-1779 ...... DLB-200
Logan, William 1950- DLB-120
Logau, Friedrich von 1605-1655........ DLB-164
Logue, Christopher 1926- DLB-27
Lohenstein, Daniel Casper von
   1635-1683 .... DLB-168
Lomonosov, Mikhail Vasil'evich
   1711-1765 .... DLB-150
London, Jack
   1876-1916..... DLB-8, 12, 78, 212; CDALB-3
The London Magazine 1820-1829........ DLB-110
Long, H., and Brother DLB-49
Long, Haniel 1888-1956............... DLB-45
Long, Ray 1878-1935 .... DLB-137
Longfellow, Henry Wadsworth
   1807-1882........ DLB-1, 59, 235; CDALB-2
Longfellow, Samuel 1819-1892.......... DLB-1
Longford, Elizabeth 1906- DLB-155
Longinus circa first century DLB-176
Longley, Michael 1939- DLB-40
Longman, T. [publishing house]........ DLB-154
Longmans, Green and Company DLB-49
Longmore, George 1793?-1867.......... DLB-99
Longstreet, Augustus Baldwin
   1790-1870..................... DLB-3, 11, 74
Longworth, D. [publishing house] DLB-49
Lonsdale, Frederick 1881-1954.......... DLB-10
A Look at the Contemporary Black Theatre
   Movement DLB-38
Loos, Anita 1893-1981 ..... DLB-11, 26, 228; Y-81
Lopate, Phillip 1943- Y-80
López, Diana
   (see Isabella, Ríos)
López, Josefina 1969- DLB-209
Loranger, Jean-Aubert 1896-1942........ DLB-92
Lorca, Federico García 1898-1936 ...... DLB-108
Lord, John Keast 1818-1872 .... DLB-99
The Lord Chamberlain's Office and Stage
   Censorship in England............ DLB-10
Lorde, Audre 1934-1992 .... DLB-41
Lorimer, George Horace 1867-1939 ..... DLB-91
Loring, A. K. [publishing house]........ DLB-49
Loring and Mussey................... DLB-46
Lorris, Guillaume de (see *Roman de la Rose*)
Lossing, Benson J. 1813-1891.......... DLB-30
Lothar, Ernst 1890-1974............... DLB-81
Lothrop, D., and Company DLB-49
Lothrop, Harriet M. 1844-1924 .... DLB-42
Loti, Pierre 1850-1923 .... DLB-123
Lotichius Secundus, Petrus 1528-1560 .... DLB-179
Lott, Emeline ?-?.................... DLB-166
Louisiana State University Press Y-97
The Lounger, no. 20 (1785), by Henry
   Mackenzie DLB-39
Lounsbury, Thomas R. 1838-1915....... DLB-71

Louÿs, Pierre 1870-1925.............. DLB-123
Lovelace, Earl 1935- DLB-125; CDWLB-3
Lovelace, Richard 1618-1657 .... DLB-131
Lovell, Coryell and Company DLB-49
Lovell, John W., Company DLB-49
Lover, Samuel 1797-1868 .... DLB-159, 190
Lovesey, Peter 1936- DLB-87
Lovinescu, Eugen
   1881-1943 .... DLB-220; CDWLB-4
Lovingood, Sut
   (see Harris, George Washington)
Low, Samuel 1765-? DLB-37
Lowell, Amy 1874-1925 .... DLB-54, 140
Lowell, James Russell 1819-1891
   .... DLB-1, 11, 64, 79, 189, 235; CDALB-2
Lowell, Robert
   1917-1977 .... DLB-5, 169; CDALB-7
Lowenfels, Walter 1897-1976 .... DLB-4
Lowndes, Marie Belloc 1868-1947 .... DLB-70
Lowndes, William Thomas 1798-1843... DLB-184
Lownes, Humphrey [publishing house] ... DLB-170
Lowry, Lois 1937- DLB-52
Lowry, Malcolm 1909-1957 ... DLB-15; CDBLB-7
Lowther, Pat 1935-1975 .... DLB-53
Loy, Mina 1882-1966 .... DLB-4, 54
Lozeau, Albert 1878-1924 .... DLB-92
Lubbock, Percy 1879-1965 .... DLB-149
Lucan A.D. 39-A.D. 65................ DLB-211
Lucas, E. V. 1868-1938 .... DLB-98, 149, 153
Lucas, Fielding, Jr. [publishing house] DLB-49
Luce, Clare Booth 1903-1987 .... DLB-228
Luce, Henry R. 1898-1967 .... DLB-91
Luce, John W., and Company DLB-46
Lucian circa 120-180................. DLB-176
Lucie-Smith, Edward 1933- DLB-40
Lucilius circa 180 B.C.-102/101 B.C..... DLB-211
Lucini, Gian Pietro 1867-1914 .... DLB-114
Lucretius circa 94 B.C.-circa 49 B.C.
   .... DLB-211; CDWLB-1
Luder, Peter circa 1415-1472 .... DLB-179
Ludlum, Robert 1927- Y-82
Ludus de Antichristo circa 1160 .... DLB-148
Ludvigson, Susan 1942- DLB-120
Ludwig, Jack 1922- DLB-60
Ludwig, Otto 1813-1865 .... DLB-129
Ludwigslied 881 or 882................ DLB-148
Luera, Yolanda 1953- DLB-122
Luft, Lya 1938- DLB-145
Lugansky, Kazak Vladimir
   (see Dal', Vladimir Ivanovich)
Lukács, György
   1885-1971............ DLB-215; CDWLB-4
Luke, Peter 1919- DLB-13
Lummis, Charles F. 1859-1928......... DLB-186
Lupton, F. M., Company DLB-49
Lupus of Ferrières
   circa 805-circa 862 .... DLB-148

Lurie, Alison 1926- DLB-2
Lustig, Arnošt 1926- DLB-232
Luther, Martin 1483-1546 ... DLB-179; CDWLB-2
Luzi, Mario 1914- DLB-128
L'vov, Nikolai Aleksandrovich
   1751-1803..................... DLB-150
Lyall, Gavin 1932- DLB-87
Lydgate, John circa 1370-1450 .... DLB-146
Lyly, John circa 1554-1606......... DLB-62, 167
Lynch, Patricia 1898-1972 .... DLB-160
Lynch, Richard flourished 1596-1601 ... DLB-172
Lynd, Robert 1879-1949............... DLB-98
Lyon, Matthew 1749-1822 .... DLB-43
Lysias circa 459 B.C.-circa 380 B.C...... DLB-176
Lytle, Andrew 1902-1995........... DLB-6; Y-95
Lytton, Edward
   (see Bulwer-Lytton, Edward)
Lytton, Edward Robert Bulwer
   1831-1891....................... DLB-32

M

Maass, Joachim 1901-1972 .... DLB-69
Mabie, Hamilton Wright 1845-1916 ..... DLB-71
Mac A'Ghobhainn, Iain (see Smith, Iain Crichton)
MacArthur, Charles 1895-1956 ..... DLB-7, 25, 44
Macaulay, Catherine 1731-1791 .... DLB-104
Macaulay, David 1945- DLB-61
Macaulay, Rose 1881-1958 .... DLB-36
Macaulay, Thomas Babington
   1800-1859 .... DLB-32, 55; CDBLB-4
Macaulay Company................... DLB-46
MacBeth, George 1932- DLB-40
Macbeth, Madge 1880-1965 .... DLB-92
MacCaig, Norman 1910-1996 .... DLB-27
MacDiarmid, Hugh
   1892-1978.............. DLB-20; CDBLB-7
MacDonald, Cynthia 1928- DLB-105
MacDonald, George 1824-1905.... DLB-18, 163, 178
MacDonald, John D. 1916-1986...... DLB-8; Y-86
MacDonald, Philip 1899?-1980 .... DLB-77
Macdonald, Ross (see Millar, Kenneth)
MacDonald, Wilson 1880-1967 .... DLB-92
Macdonald and Company (Publishers) .. DLB-112
MacEwen, Gwendolyn 1941- DLB-53
Macfadden, Bernarr 1868-1955 ...... DLB-25, 91
MacGregor, John 1825-1892 .... DLB-166
MacGregor, Mary Esther (see Keith, Marian)
Machado, Antonio 1875-1939 .... DLB-108
Machado, Manuel 1874-1947 .... DLB-108
Machar, Agnes Maule 1837-1927 ...... DLB-92
Machaut, Guillaume de
   circa 1300-1377 .... DLB-208
Machen, Arthur Llewelyn Jones
   1863-1947 .... DLB-36, 156, 178
MacInnes, Colin 1914-1976 .... DLB-14
MacInnes, Helen 1907-1985 .... DLB-87

Mačiulis, Jonas (see Maironis, Jonas)
Mack, Maynard 1909- DLB-111
Mackall, Leonard L. 1879-1937.........DLB-140
MacKaye, Percy 1875-1956.............DLB-54
Macken, Walter 1915-1967.............DLB-13
Mackenzie, Alexander 1763-1820.......DLB-99
Mackenzie, Alexander Slidell
 1803-1848......................DLB-183
Mackenzie, Compton 1883-1972.....DLB-34, 100
Mackenzie, Henry 1745-1831...........DLB-39
Mackenzie, William 1758-1828.........DLB-187
Mackey, Nathaniel 1947- DLB-169
Mackey, Shena 1944- DLB-231
Mackey, William Wellington
 1937- DLB-38
Mackintosh, Elizabeth (see Tey, Josephine)
Mackintosh, Sir James 1765-1832......DLB-158
Maclaren, Ian (see Watson, John)
Macklin, Charles 1699-1797............DLB-89
MacLean, Katherine Anne 1925- DLB-8
Maclean, Norman 1902-1990...........DLB-206
MacLeish, Archibald 1892-1982
 ....DLB-4, 7, 45, 228; Y-82; CDALB-7
MacLennan, Hugh 1907-1990...........DLB-68
MacLeod, Alistair 1936- DLB-60
Macleod, Fiona (see Sharp, William)
Macleod, Norman 1906-1985............DLB-4
Mac Low, Jackson 1922- DLB-193
Macmillan and Company..............DLB-106
The Macmillan Company..............DLB-49
Macmillan's English Men of Letters,
 First Series (1878-1892)............DLB-144
MacNamara, Brinsley 1890-1963........DLB-10
MacNeice, Louis 1907-1963.........DLB-10, 20
MacPhail, Andrew 1864-1938...........DLB-92
Macpherson, James 1736-1796.........DLB-109
Macpherson, Jay 1931- DLB-53
Macpherson, Jeanie 1884-1946.........DLB-44
Macrae Smith Company..............DLB-46
MacRaye, Lucy Betty (see Webling, Lucy)
Macrone, John [publishing house].......DLB-106
MacShane, Frank 1927-1999...........DLB-111
Macy-Masius........................DLB-46
Madden, David 1933- DLB-6
Madden, Sir Frederic 1801-1873........DLB-184
Maddow, Ben 1909-1992..............DLB-44
Maddux, Rachel 1912-1983.....DLB-234; Y-93
Madgett, Naomi Long 1923- DLB-76
Madhubuti, Haki R. 1942- DLB-5, 41; DS-8
Madison, James 1751-1836.............DLB-37
Madsen, Svend Åge 1939- DLB-214
Maeterlinck, Maurice 1862-1949........DLB-192
Mafūz, Najīb 1911- Y-88
Magee, David 1905-1977..............DLB-187
Maginn, William 1794-1842........DLB-110, 159

Magoffin, Susan Shelby 1827-1855......DLB-239
Mahan, Alfred Thayer 1840-1914........DLB-47
Maheux-Forcier, Louise 1929- DLB-60
Mahin, John Lee 1902-1984............DLB-44
Mahon, Derek 1941- DLB-40
Maikov, Vasilii Ivanovich 1728-1778.....DLB-150
Mailer, Norman 1923-
 ....DLB-2, 16, 28, 185; Y-80, Y-83;
 DS-3; CDALB-6
Maillart, Ella 1903-1997...............DLB-195
Maillet, Adrienne 1885-1963...........DLB-68
Maillet, Antonine 1929- DLB-60
Maillu, David G. 1939- DLB-157
Maimonides, Moses 1138-1204........DLB-115
Main Selections of the Book-of-the-Month
 Club, 1926-1945..................DLB-9
Main Trends in Twentieth-Century Book
 Clubs..........................DLB-46
Mainwaring, Daniel 1902-1977.........DLB-44
Mair, Charles 1838-1927..............DLB-99
Maironis, Jonas
 1862-1932..............DLB-220; CDWLB-4
Mais, Roger 1905-1955.....DLB-125; CDWLB-3
Major, Andre 1942- DLB-60
Major, Charles 1856-1913.............DLB-202
Major, Clarence 1936- DLB-33
Major, Kevin 1949- DLB-60
Major Books........................DLB-46
Makemie, Francis circa 1658-1708......DLB-24
The Making of Americans Contract...........Y-98
The Making of a People, by
 J. M. Ritchie....................DLB-66
Maksimović, Desanka
 1898-1993..............DLB-147; CDWLB-4
Malamud, Bernard 1914-1986
 ......DLB-2, 28, 152; Y-80, Y-86; CDALB-1
Mălăncioiu, Ileana 1940- DLB-232
Malerba, Luigi 1927- DLB-196
Malet, Lucas 1852-1931...............DLB-153
Mallarmé, Stéphane 1842-1898........DLB-217
Malleson, Lucy Beatrice (see Gilbert, Anthony)
Mallet-Joris, Françoise 1930- DLB-83
Mallock, W. H. 1849-1923..........DLB-18, 57
 "Every Man His Own Poet; or,
 The Inspired Singer's Recipe
 Book" (1877)....................DLB-35
Malone, Dumas 1892-1986............DLB-17
Malone, Edmond 1741-1812..........DLB-142
Malory, Sir Thomas
 circa 1400-1410 - 1471....DLB-146; CDBLB-1
Malraux, André 1901-1976............DLB-72
Malthus, Thomas Robert
 1766-1834................DLB-107, 158
Maltz, Albert 1908-1985..............DLB-102
Malzberg, Barry N. 1939- DLB-8
Mamet, David 1947- DLB-7
Mamin, Dmitrii Narkisovich 1852-1912..DLB-238
Manaka, Matsemela 1956- DLB-157

Manchester University Press..........DLB-112
Mandel, Eli 1922- DLB-53
Mandeville, Bernard 1670-1733........DLB-101
Mandeville, Sir John
 mid fourteenth century............DLB-146
Mandiargues, André Pieyre de 1909- ...DLB-83
Manea, Morman 1936- DLB-232
Manfred, Frederick 1912-1994...DLB-6, 212, 227
Manfredi, Gianfranco 1948- DLB-196
Mangan, Sherry 1904-1961............DLB-4
Manganelli, Giorgio 1922-1990.........DLB-196
Manilius fl. first century A.D..........DLB-211
Mankiewicz, Herman 1897-1953.......DLB-26
Mankiewicz, Joseph L. 1909-1993........DLB-44
Mankowitz, Wolf 1924-1998..........DLB-15
Manley, Delarivière 1672?-1724......DLB-39, 80
 Preface to The Secret History, of Queen Zarah,
 and the Zarazians (1705)............DLB-39
Mann, Abby 1927- DLB-44
Mann, Charles 1929-1998................Y-98
Mann, Heinrich 1871-1950........DLB-66, 118
Mann, Horace 1796-1859.........DLB-1, 235
Mann, Klaus 1906-1949..............DLB-56
Mann, Mary Peabody 1806-1887.......DLB-239
Mann, Thomas 1875-1955....DLB-66; CDWLB-2
Mann, William D'Alton 1839-1920......DLB-137
Mannin, Ethel 1900-1984..........DLB-191, 195
Manning, Emily (see Australie)
Manning, Marie 1873?-1945............DLB-29
Manning and Loring..................DLB-49
Mannyng, Robert
 flourished 1303-1338................DLB-146
Mano, D. Keith 1942- DLB-6
Manor Books........................DLB-46
Mansfield, Katherine 1888-1923........DLB-162
Manuel, Niklaus circa 1484-1530......DLB-179
Manzini, Gianna 1896-1974............DLB-177
Mapanje, Jack 1944- DLB-157
Maraini, Dacia 1936- DLB-196
March, William 1893-1954............DLB-9, 86
Marchand, Leslie A. 1900-1999........DLB-103
Marchant, Bessie 1862-1941...........DLB-160
Marchenko, Anastasia Iakovlevna
 1830-1880......................DLB-238
Marchessault, Jovette 1938- DLB-60
Marcinkevičius, Justinas 1930- DLB-232
Marcus, Frank 1928- DLB-13
Marden, Orison Swett 1850-1924.......DLB-137
Marechera, Dambudzo 1952-1987......DLB-157
Marek, Richard, Books...............DLB-46
Mares, E. A. 1938- DLB-122
Margulies, Donald 1954- DLB-228
Mariani, Paul 1940- DLB-111
Marie de France flourished 1160-1178....DLB-208
Marie-Victorin, Frère 1885-1944........DLB-92

Marin, Biagio 1891-1985 .... DLB-128
Marincovič, Ranko 1913- DLB-147; CDWLB-4
Marinetti, Filippo Tommaso 1876-1944 .... DLB-114
Marion, Frances 1886-1973 .... DLB-44
Marius, Richard C. 1933-1999 .... Y-85
Markevich, Boleslav Mikhailovich 1822-1884 .... DLB-238
Markfield, Wallace 1926- DLB-2, 28
Markham, Edwin 1852-1940 ...... DLB-54, 186
Markle, Fletcher 1921-1991 ...... DLB-68; Y-91
Marlatt, Daphne 1942- DLB-60
Marlitt, E. 1825-1887 .... DLB-129
Marlowe, Christopher 1564-1593 .... DLB-62; CDBLB-1
Marlyn, John 1912- DLB-88
Marmion, Shakerley 1603-1639 .... DLB-58
Der Marner before 1230-circa 1287 .... DLB-138
Marnham, Patrick 1943- DLB-204
The *Marprelate Tracts* 1588-1589 ..... DLB-132
Marquand, John P. 1893-1960 ...... DLB-9, 102
Marqués, René 1919-1979 .... DLB-113
Marquis, Don 1878-1937 .... DLB-11, 25
Marriott, Anne 1913- DLB-68
Marryat, Frederick 1792-1848 ...... DLB-21, 163
Marsh, Capen, Lyon and Webb DLB-49
Marsh, George Perkins 1801-1882 ..... DLB-1, 64
Marsh, James 1794-1842 .... DLB-1, 59
Marsh, Narcissus 1638-1713 .... DLB-213
Marsh, Ngaio 1899-1982 .... DLB-77
Marshall, Edison 1894-1967 .... DLB-102
Marshall, Edward 1932- DLB-16
Marshall, Emma 1828-1899 .... DLB-163
Marshall, James 1942-1992 .... DLB-61
Marshall, Joyce 1913- DLB-88
Marshall, Paule 1929- DLB-33, 157, 227
Marshall, Tom 1938- DLB-60
Marsilius of Padua circa 1275-circa 1342 .... DLB-115
Mars-Jones, Adam 1954- DLB-207
Marson, Una 1905-1965 .... DLB-157
Marston, John 1576-1634 .... DLB-58, 172
Marston, Philip Bourke 1850-1887 ..... DLB-35
Martens, Kurt 1870-1945 .... DLB-66
Martial circa A.D. 40-circa A.D. 103 .... DLB-211; CDWLB-1
Martien, William S. [publishing house] ... DLB-49
Martin, Abe (see Hubbard, Kin)
Martin, Catherine ca. 1847-1937 .... DLB-230
Martin, Charles 1942- DLB-120
Martin, Claire 1914- DLB-60
Martin, Jay 1935- DLB-111
Martin, Johann (see Laurentius von Schnüffis)
Martin, Thomas 1696-1771 .... DLB-213
Martin, Violet Florence (see Ross, Martin)

Martin du Gard, Roger 1881-1958 .... DLB-65
Martineau, Harriet 1802-1876 ..... DLB-21, 55, 159, 163, 166, 190
Martínez, Demetria 1960- DLB-209
Martínez, Eliud 1935- DLB-122
Martínez, Max 1943- DLB-82
Martínez, Rubén 1962- DLB-209
Martone, Michael 1955- DLB-218
Martyn, Edward 1859-1923 .... DLB-10
Marvell, Andrew 1621-1678 .... DLB-131; CDBLB-2
Marvin X 1944- DLB-38
Marx, Karl 1818-1883 .... DLB-129
Marzials, Theo 1850-1920 .... DLB-35
Masefield, John 1878-1967 ... DLB-10, 19, 153, 160; CDBLB-5
Mason, A. E. W. 1865-1948 .... DLB-70
Mason, Bobbie Ann 1940- DLB-173; Y-87; CDALB-7
Mason, William 1725-1797 .... DLB-142
Mason Brothers DLB-49
Massey, Gerald 1828-1907 .... DLB-32
Massey, Linton R. 1900-1974 .... DLB-187
Massinger, Philip 1583-1640 .... DLB-58
Masson, David 1822-1907 .... DLB-144
Masters, Edgar Lee 1868-1950 .... DLB-54; CDALB-3
Mastronardi, Lucio 1930-1979 .... DLB-177
Matevski, Mateja 1929- ... DLB-181; CDWLB-4
Mather, Cotton 1663-1728 .... DLB-24, 30, 140; CDALB-2
Mather, Increase 1639-1723 .... DLB-24
Mather, Richard 1596-1669 .... DLB-24
Matheson, Annie 1853-1924 .... DLB-240
Matheson, Richard 1926- DLB-8, 44
Matheus, John F. 1887- DLB-51
Mathews, Cornelius 1817?-1889 ...... DLB-3, 64
Mathews, Elkin [publishing house] DLB-112
Mathews, John Joseph 1894-1979 ...... DLB-175
Mathias, Roland 1915- DLB-27
Mathis, June 1892-1927 .... DLB-44
Mathis, Sharon Bell 1937- DLB-33
Matković, Marijan 1915-1985 .... DLB-181
Matoš, Antun Gustav 1873-1914 .... DLB-147
Matsumoto Seichō 1909-1992 .... DLB-182
The Matter of England 1240-1400 ...... DLB-146
The Matter of Rome early twelfth to late fifteenth century DLB-146
Matthew of Vendôme circa 1130-circa 1200 .... DLB-208
Matthews, Brander 1852-1929 .... DLB-71, 78; DS-13
Matthews, Jack 1925- DLB-6
Matthews, Victoria Earle 1861-1907 .... DLB-221
Matthews, William 1942-1997 .... DLB-5
Matthiessen, F. O. 1902-1950 .... DLB-63
Matthiessen, Peter 1927- DLB-6, 173

Maturin, Charles Robert 1780-1824 ...... DLB-178
Maugham, W. Somerset 1874-1965 ..... DLB-10, 36, 77, 100, 162, 195; CDBLB-6
Maupassant, Guy de 1850-1893 .... DLB-123
Mauriac, Claude 1914-1996 .... DLB-83
Mauriac, François 1885-1970 .... DLB-65
Maurice, Frederick Denison 1805-1872 .... DLB-55
Maurois, André 1885-1967 .... DLB-65
Maury, James 1718-1769 .... DLB-31
Mavor, Elizabeth 1927- DLB-14
Mavor, Osborne Henry (see Bridie, James)
Maxwell, Gavin 1914-1969 .... DLB-204
Maxwell, H. [publishing house] DLB-49
Maxwell, John [publishing house] DLB-106
Maxwell, William 1908- DLB-218; Y-80
May, Elaine 1932- DLB-44
May, Karl 1842-1912 .... DLB-129
May, Thomas 1595 or 1596-1650 ...... DLB-58
Mayer, Bernadette 1945- DLB-165
Mayer, Mercer 1943- DLB-61
Mayer, O. B. 1818-1891 .... DLB-3
Mayes, Herbert R. 1900-1987 .... DLB-137
Mayes, Wendell 1919-1992 .... DLB-26
Mayfield, Julian 1928-1984 .... DLB-33; Y-84
Mayhew, Henry 1812-1887 ...... DLB-18, 55, 190
Mayhew, Jonathan 1720-1766 .... DLB-31
Mayne, Ethel Colburn 1865-1941 .... DLB-197
Mayne, Jasper 1604-1672 .... DLB-126
Mayne, Seymour 1944- DLB-60
Mayor, Flora Macdonald 1872-1932 ..... DLB-36
Mayröcker, Friederike 1924- DLB-85
Mazrui, Ali A. 1933- DLB-125
Mažuranić, Ivan 1814-1890 .... DLB-147
Mazursky, Paul 1930- DLB-44
McAlmon, Robert 1896-1956 .... DLB-4, 45; DS-15
McArthur, Peter 1866-1924 .... DLB-92
McBride, Robert M., and Company DLB-46
McCabe, Patrick 1955- DLB-194
McCaffrey, Anne 1926- DLB-8
McCarthy, Cormac 1933- DLB-6, 143
McCarthy, Mary 1912-1989 .... DLB-2; Y-81
McCay, Winsor 1871-1934 .... DLB-22
McClane, Albert Jules 1922-1991 .... DLB-171
McClatchy, C. K. 1858-1936 .... DLB-25
McClellan, George Marion 1860-1934 .... DLB-50
McCloskey, Robert 1914- DLB-22
McClung, Nellie Letitia 1873-1951 ...... DLB-92
McClure, Joanna 1930- DLB-16
McClure, Michael 1932- DLB-16
McClure, Phillips and Company DLB-46
McClure, S. S. 1857-1949 .... DLB-91
McClurg, A. C., and Company DLB-49
McCluskey, John A., Jr. 1944- DLB-33

McCollum, Michael A. 1946 .... Y-87

McConnell, William C. 1917- DLB-88

McCord, David 1897-1997.............DLB-61

McCorkle, Jill 1958- DLB-234; Y-87

McCorkle, Samuel Eusebius
1746-1811 ....DLB-37

McCormick, Anne O'Hare 1880-1954 ....DLB-29

Kenneth Dale McCormick Tributes Y-97

McCormick, Robert R. 1880-1955 ....DLB-29

McCourt, Edward 1907-1972............DLB-88

McCoy, Horace 1897-1955 ....DLB-9

McCrae, John 1872-1918...............DLB-92

McCullagh, Joseph B. 1842-1896.........DLB-23

McCullers, Carson
1917-1967 ..... DLB-2, 7, 173, 228; CDALB-1

McCulloch, Thomas 1776-1843..........DLB-99

McDonald, Forrest 1927- DLB-17

McDonald, Walter 1934- DLB-105, DS-9

"Getting Started: Accepting the Regions
You Own—or Which Own You,"....DLB-105

McDougall, Colin 1917-1984............DLB-68

McDowell, Katharine Sherwood Bonner
1849-1883 ....DLB-202, 239

McDowell, Obolensky.................DLB-46

McEwan, Ian 1948- DLB-14, 194

McFadden, David 1940- DLB-60

McFall, Frances Elizabeth Clarke
(see Grand, Sarah)

McFarlane, Leslie 1902-1977 ....DLB-88

McFee, William 1881-1966 ....DLB-153

McGahern, John 1934- DLB-14, 231

McGee, Thomas D'Arcy 1825-1868 ......DLB-99

McGeehan, W. O. 1879-1933 .... DLB-25, 171

McGill, Ralph 1898-1969................DLB-29

McGinley, Phyllis 1905-1978.........DLB-11, 48

McGinniss, Joe 1942- DLB-185

McGirt, James E. 1874-1930 ....DLB-50

McGlashan and Gill..................DLB-106

McGough, Roger 1937- DLB-40

McGrath, John 1935- DLB-233

McGrath, Patrick 1950- DLB-231

McGraw-Hill DLB-46

McGuane, Thomas 1939- DLB-2, 212; Y-80

McGuckian, Medbh 1950- DLB-40

McGuffey, William Holmes 1800-1873 ....DLB-42

McHenry, James 1785-1845............DLB-202

McIlvanney, William 1936- DLB-14, 207

McIlwraith, Jean Newton 1859-1938......DLB-92

McIntosh, Maria Jane 1803-1878 ....DLB-239

McIntyre, James 1827-1906 ....DLB-99

McIntyre, O. O. 1884-1938 ....DLB-25

McKay, Claude 1889-1948 .... DLB-4, 45, 51, 117

The David McKay Company DLB-49

McKean, William V. 1820-1903 ....DLB-23

McKenna, Stephen 1888-1967 ....DLB-197

The McKenzie Trust Y-96

McKerrow, R. B. 1872-1940 ....DLB-201

McKinley, Robin 1952- DLB-52

McKnight, Reginald 1956- DLB-234

McLachlan, Alexander 1818-1896........DLB-99

McLaren, Floris Clark 1904-1978 ....DLB-68

McLaverty, Michael 1907- DLB-15

McLean, John R. 1848-1916 ....DLB-23

McLean, William L. 1852-1931...........DLB-25

McLennan, William 1856-1904...........DLB-92

McLoughlin Brothers..................DLB-49

McLuhan, Marshall 1911-1980 ....DLB-88

McMaster, John Bach 1852-1932.........DLB-47

McMurtry, Larry
1936- ... DLB-2, 143; Y-80, Y-87; CDALB-6

McNally, Terrence 1939- DLB-7

McNeil, Florence 1937- DLB-60

McNeile, Herman Cyril 1888-1937 ....DLB-77

McNickle, D'Arcy 1904-1977....... DLB-175, 212

McPhee, John 1931- DLB-185

McPherson, James Alan 1943- DLB-38

McPherson, Sandra 1943- Y-86

McWhirter, George 1939- DLB-60

McWilliams, Carey 1905-1980 ....DLB-137

Mda, Zakes 1948- DLB-225

Mead, L. T. 1844-1914 ....DLB-141

Mead, Matthew 1924- DLB-40

Mead, Taylor ?- DLB-16

Meany, Tom 1903-1964 ....DLB-171

Mechthild von Magdeburg
circa 1207-circa 1282 ....DLB-138

Medieval French Drama DLB-208

Medieval Travel Diaries DLB-203

Medill, Joseph 1823-1899 ....DLB-43

Medoff, Mark 1940- DLB-7

Meek, Alexander Beaufort 1814-1865......DLB-3

Meeke, Mary ?-1816? DLB-116

Meinke, Peter 1932- DLB-5

Mejia Vallejo, Manuel 1923- DLB-113

Melanchthon, Philipp 1497-1560 ....DLB-179

Melançon, Robert 1947- DLB-60

Mell, Max 1882-1971...............DLB-81, 124

Mellow, James R. 1926-1997 ....DLB-111

Mel'nikov, Pavel Ivanovich 1818-1883 ...DLB-238

Meltzer, David 1937- DLB-16

Meltzer, Milton 1915- DLB-61

Melville, Elizabeth, Lady Culross
circa 1585-1640..................DLB-172

Melville, Herman
1819-1891 ....DLB-3, 74; CDALB-2

Memoirs of Life and Literature (1920),
by W. H. Mallock [excerpt] DLB-57

Mena, María Cristina 1893-1965....DLB-209, 221

Menander 342-341 B.C.-circa 292-291 B.C.
.... DLB-176; CDWLB-1

Menantes (see Hunold, Christian Friedrich)

Mencke, Johann Burckhard
1674-1732 ....DLB-168

Mencken, H. L. 1880-1956
.... DLB-11, 29, 63, 137, 222; CDALB-4

Mencken and Nietzsche: An Unpublished
Excerpt from H. L. Mencken's *My Life
as Author and Editor*................. Y-93

Mendelssohn, Moses 1729-1786..........DLB-97

Mendes, Catulle 1841-1909............DLB-217

Méndez M., Miguel 1930- DLB-82

Mens Rea (or Something) Y-97

The Mercantile Library of New York Y-96

Mercer, Cecil William (see Yates, Dornford)

Mercer, David 1928-1980 ....DLB-13

Mercer, John 1704-1768................DLB-31

Meredith, George
1828-1909.... DLB-18, 35, 57, 159; CDBLB-4

Meredith, Louisa Anne 1812-1895 ..DLB-166, 230

Meredith, Owen
(see Lytton, Edward Robert Bulwer)

Meredith, William 1919- DLB-5

Mergerle, Johann Ulrich
(see Abraham à Sancta Clara)

Mérimée, Prosper 1803-1870.......DLB-119, 192

Merivale, John Herman 1779-1844 ....DLB-96

Meriwether, Louise 1923- DLB-33

Merlin Press........................DLB-112

Merriam, Eve 1916-1992................DLB-61

The Merriam Company DLB-49

Merrill, James 1926-1995 ..... DLB-5, 165; Y-85

Merrill and Baker DLB-49

The Mershon Company DLB-49

Merton, Thomas 1915-1968 ....DLB-48; Y-81

Merwin, W. S. 1927- DLB-5, 169

Messner, Julian [publishing house] DLB-46

Mészöly, Miklós 1921- DLB-232

Metcalf, J. [publishing house]............DLB-49

Metcalf, John 1938- DLB-60

The Methodist Book Concern..........DLB-49

Methuen and Company...............DLB-112

Meun, Jean de (see *Roman de la Rose*)

Mew, Charlotte 1869-1928 ....DLB-19, 135

Mewshaw, Michael 1943- Y-80

Meyer, Conrad Ferdinand 1825-1898....DLB-129

Meyer, E. Y. 1946- DLB-75

Meyer, Eugene 1875-1959..............DLB-29

Meyer, Michael 1921- DLB-155

Meyers, Jeffrey 1939- DLB-111

Meynell, Alice 1847-1922...........DLB-19, 98

Meynell, Viola 1885-1956 ....DLB-153

Meyrink, Gustav 1868-1932 ....DLB-81

Mézières, Philipe de circa 1327-1405 .....DLB-208

Michael, Ib 1945- DLB-214

Michaëlis, Karen 1872-1950 ....DLB-214

Michaels, Leonard 1933- DLB-130

Micheaux, Oscar 1884-1951 ....DLB-50

Michel of Northgate, Dan circa 1265-circa 1340 .... DLB-146
Micheline, Jack 1929-1998 .... DLB-16
Michener, James A. 1907?-1997 .... DLB-6
Micklejohn, George circa 1717-1818 .... DLB-31
Middle English Literature: An Introduction DLB-146
The Middle English Lyric DLB-146
Middle Hill Press DLB-106
Middleton, Christopher 1926- DLB-40
Middleton, Richard 1882-1911 .... DLB-156
Middleton, Stanley 1919- DLB-14
Middleton, Thomas 1580-1627 .... DLB-58
Miegel, Agnes 1879-1964 .... DLB-56
Miežalaitis, Eduardas 1919-1997 .... DLB-220
Mihailović, Dragoslav 1930- DLB-181
Mihalić, Slavko 1928- DLB-181
Mikhailov, A. (see Sheller, Aleksandr Konstantinovich)
Mikhailov, Mikhail Larionovich 1829-1865 .... DLB-238
Miles, Josephine 1911-1985 .... DLB-48
Miles, Susan (Ursula Wyllie Roberts) 1888-1975 .... DLB-240
Miliković, Branko 1934-1961 .... DLB-181
Milius, John 1944- DLB-44
Mill, James 1773-1836 .... DLB-107, 158
Mill, John Stuart 1806-1873 .... DLB-55, 190; CDBLB-4
Millar, Andrew [publishing house] DLB-154
Millar, Kenneth 1915-1983 .... DLB-2, 226; Y-83; DS-6
Millay, Edna St. Vincent 1892-1950 .... DLB-45; CDALB-4
Millen, Sarah Gertrude 1888-1968 ...... DLB-225
Miller, Arthur 1915- DLB-7; CDALB-1
Miller, Caroline 1903-1992 .... DLB-9
Miller, Eugene Ethelbert 1950- DLB-41
Miller, Heather Ross 1939- DLB-120
Miller, Henry 1891-1980 .... DLB-4, 9; Y-80; CDALB-5
Miller, Hugh 1802-1856 .... DLB-190
Miller, J. Hillis 1928- DLB-67
Miller, James [publishing house] DLB-49
Miller, Jason 1939- DLB-7
Miller, Joaquin 1839-1913 .... DLB-186
Miller, May 1899- DLB-41
Miller, Paul 1906-1991 .... DLB-127
Miller, Perry 1905-1963 .... DLB-17, 63
Miller, Sue 1943- DLB-143
Miller, Vassar 1924-1998 .... DLB-105
Miller, Walter M., Jr. 1923- DLB-8
Miller, Webb 1892-1940 .... DLB-29
Millhauser, Steven 1943- DLB-2
Millican, Arthenia J. Bates 1920- DLB-38
Milligan, Alice 1866-1953 .... DLB-240

Mills and Boon DLB-112
Milman, Henry Hart 1796-1868 .... DLB-96
Milne, A. A. 1882-1956 ..... DLB-10, 77, 100, 160
Milner, Ron 1938- DLB-38
Milner, William [publishing house] DLB-106
Milnes, Richard Monckton (Lord Houghton) 1809-1885 .... DLB-32, 184
Milton, John 1608-1674 .... DLB-131, 151; CDBLB-2
Miłosz, Czesław 1911- ... DLB-215; CDWLB-4
Minakami Tsutomu 1919- DLB-182
Minamoto no Sanetomo 1192-1219 ..... DLB-203
The Minerva Press DLB-154
Minnesang circa 1150-1280 .... DLB-138
Minns, Susan 1839-1938 .... DLB-140
Minor Illustrators, 1880-1914 .... DLB-141
Minor Poets of the Earlier Seventeenth Century DLB-121
Minton, Balch and Company DLB-46
Mirbeau, Octave 1848-1917 .... DLB-123, 192
Mirk, John died after 1414? DLB-146
Miron, Gaston 1928- DLB-60
A Mirror for Magistrates DLB-167
Mishima Yukio 1925-1970 .... DLB-182
Mitchel, Jonathan 1624-1668 .... DLB-24
Mitchell, Adrian 1932- DLB-40
Mitchell, Donald Grant 1822-1908 .... DLB-1; DS-13
Mitchell, Gladys 1901-1983 .... DLB-77
Mitchell, James Leslie 1901-1935 ...... DLB-15
Mitchell, John (see Slater, Patrick)
Mitchell, John Ames 1845-1918 .... DLB-79
Mitchell, Joseph 1908-1996 .... DLB-185; Y-96
Mitchell, Julian 1935- DLB-14
Mitchell, Ken 1940- DLB-60
Mitchell, Langdon 1862-1935 .... DLB-7
Mitchell, Loften 1919- DLB-38
Mitchell, Margaret 1900-1949 .. DLB-9; CDALB-7
Mitchell, S. Weir 1829-1914 .... DLB-202
Mitchell, W. O. 1914- DLB-88
Mitchison, Naomi Margaret (Haldane) 1897-1999 .... DLB-160, 191
Mitford, Mary Russell 1787-1855 ... DLB-110, 116
Mitford, Nancy 1904-1973 .... DLB-191
Mittelholzer, Edgar 1909-1965 .... DLB-117; CDWLB-3
Mitterer, Erika 1906- DLB-85
Mitterer, Felix 1948- DLB-124
Mitternacht, Johann Sebastian 1613-1679 .... DLB-168
Miyamoto, Yuriko 1899-1951 .... DLB-180
Mizener, Arthur 1907-1988 .... DLB-103
Mo, Timothy 1950- DLB-194
Modern Age Books DLB-46
"Modern English Prose" (1876), by George Saintsbury DLB-57

The Modern Language Association of America Celebrates Its Centennial Y-84
The Modern Library DLB-46
"Modern Novelists – Great and Small" (1855), by Margaret Oliphant DLB-21
"Modern Style" (1857), by Cockburn Thomson [excerpt] DLB-57
The Modernists (1932), by Joseph Warren Beach DLB-36
Modiano, Patrick 1945- DLB-83
Moffat, Yard and Company DLB-46
Moffet, Thomas 1553-1604 .... DLB-136
Mohr, Nicholasa 1938- DLB-145
Moix, Ana María 1947- DLB-134
Molesworth, Louisa 1839-1921 .... DLB-135
Möllhausen, Balduin 1825-1905 ...... DLB-129
Molnár, Ferenc 1878-1952 .... DLB-215; CDWLB-4
Molnár, Miklós (see Mészöly, Miklós)
Momaday, N. Scott 1934- DLB-143, 175; CDALB-7
Monkhouse, Allan 1858-1936 .... DLB-10
Monro, Harold 1879-1932 .... DLB-19
Monroe, Harriet 1860-1936 .... DLB-54, 91
Monsarrat, Nicholas 1910-1979 ...... DLB-15
Montagu, Lady Mary Wortley 1689-1762 .... DLB-95, 101
Montague, C. E. 1867-1928 .... DLB-197
Montague, John 1929- DLB-40
Montale, Eugenio 1896-1981 .... DLB-114
Montalvo, José 1946-1994 .... DLB-209
Monterroso, Augusto 1921- DLB-145
Montesquiou, Robert de 1855-1921 ..... DLB-217
Montgomerie, Alexander circa 1550?-1598 .... DLB-167
Montgomery, James 1771-1854 ..... DLB-93, 158
Montgomery, John 1919- DLB-16
Montgomery, Lucy Maud 1874-1942 .... DLB-92; DS-14
Montgomery, Marion 1925- DLB-6
Montgomery, Robert Bruce (see Crispin, Edmund)
Montherlant, Henry de 1896-1972 ..... DLB-72
The Monthly Review 1749-1844 ...... DLB-110
Montigny, Louvigny de 1876-1955 ..... DLB-92
Montoya, José 1932- DLB-122
Moodie, John Wedderburn Dunbar 1797-1869 .... DLB-99
Moodie, Susanna 1803-1885 .... DLB-99
Moody, Joshua circa 1633-1697 .... DLB-24
Moody, William Vaughn 1869-1910 .... DLB-7, 54
Moorcock, Michael 1939- DLB-14, 231
Moore, Catherine L. 1911- DLB-8
Moore, Clement Clarke 1779-1863 ...... DLB-42
Moore, Dora Mavor 1888-1979 .... DLB-92
Moore, George 1852-1933 .... DLB-10, 18, 57, 135
Moore, Lorrie 1957- DLB-234
Moore, Marianne 1887-1972 .... DLB-45; DS-7; CDALB-5

Moore, Mavor 1919- DLB-88	Morris, James Humphrey (see Morris, Jan)	Moxon, Joseph [publishing house].......DLB-170
Moore, Richard 1927- DLB-105	Morris, Jan 1926- DLB-204	Mphahlele, Es'kia (Ezekiel) 1919- DLB-125; CDWLB-3
Moore, T. Sturge 1870-1944 ....DLB-19	Morris, Lewis 1833-1907...............DLB-35	Mrożek, Sławomir 1930- ..DLB-232; CDWLB-4
Moore, Thomas 1779-1852 ....DLB-96, 144	Morris, Margaret 1737-1816............DLB-200	Mtshali, Oswald Mbuyiseni 1940- DLB-125
Moore, Ward 1903-1978 ....DLB-8	Morris, Richard B. 1904-1989...........DLB-17	Mucedorus.........................DLB-62
Moore, Wilstach, Keys and Company DLB-49	Morris, William 1834-1896 .... DLB-18, 35, 57, 156, 178, 184; CDBLB-4	Mudford, William 1782-1848 ....DLB-159
Moorehead, Alan 1901-1983...........DLB-204	Morris, Willie 1934-1999................ Y-80	Mueller, Lisel 1924- DLB-105
Moorhouse, Geoffrey 1931- DLB-204	Morris, Wright 1910-1998 ....DLB-2, 206, 218; Y-81	Muhajir, El (see Marvin X)
The Moorland-Spingarn Research Center......................DLB-76	Morrison, Arthur 1863-1945.... DLB-70, 135, 197	Muhajir, Nazzam Al Fitnah (see Marvin X)
Moorman, Mary C. 1905-1994 ....DLB-155	Morrison, Charles Clayton 1874-1966.....DLB-91	Mühlbach, Luise 1814-1873............DLB-133
Mora, Pat 1942- DLB-209	Morrison, Toni 1931- DLB-6, 33, 143; Y-81, Y-93; CDALB-6	Muir, Edwin 1887-1959........ DLB-20, 100, 191
Moraga, Cherríe 1952- DLB-82	Morrow, William, and Company DLB-46	Muir, Helen 1937- DLB-14
Morales, Alejandro 1944- DLB-82	Morse, James Herbert 1841-1923 ....DLB-71	Muir, John 1838-1914 ....DLB-186
Morales, Mario Roberto 1947- DLB-145	Morse, Jedidiah 1761-1826..............DLB-37	Muir, Percy 1894-1979 ....DLB-201
Morales, Rafael 1919- DLB-108	Morse, John T., Jr. 1840-1937 ....DLB-47	Mujū Ichien 1226-1312 ....DLB-203
Morality Plays: *Mankind* circa 1450-1500 and *Everyman* circa 1500...............DLB-146	Morselli, Guido 1912-1973 ....DLB-177	Mukherjee, Bharati 1940- DLB-60, 218
Morante, Elsa 1912-1985................DLB-177	Mortimer, Favell Lee 1802-1878 ....DLB-163	Mulcaster, Richard 1531 or 1532-1611..............DLB-167
Morata, Olympia Fulvia 1526-1555......DLB-179	Mortimer, John 1923- DLB-13; CDBLB-8	Muldoon, Paul 1951- DLB-40
Moravia, Alberto 1907-1990 ....DLB-177	Morton, Carlos 1942- DLB-122	Müller, Friedrich (see Müller, Maler)
Mordaunt, Elinor 1872-1942 ....DLB-174	Morton, H. V. 1892-1979 ....DLB-195	Müller, Heiner 1929-1995.............DLB-124
Mordovtsev, Daniil Lukich 1830-1905 ...DLB-238	Morton, John P., and Company DLB-49	Müller, Maler 1749-1825 ....DLB-94
More, Hannah 1745-1833 .... DLB-107, 109, 116, 158	Morton, Nathaniel 1613-1685 ....DLB-24	Muller, Marcia 1944- DLB-226
More, Henry 1614-1687 ....DLB-126	Morton, Sarah Wentworth 1759-1846.....DLB-37	Müller, Wilhelm 1794-1827 ....DLB-90
More, Sir Thomas 1477 or 1478-1535................DLB-136	Morton, Thomas circa 1579-circa 1647 ....DLB-24	Mumford, Lewis 1895-1990 ....DLB-63
Moreno, Dorinda 1939- DLB-122	Moscherosch, Johann Michael 1601-1669......................DLB-164	Munby, A. N. L. 1913-1974............DLB-201
Morency, Pierre 1942- DLB-60	Moseley, Humphrey [publishing house]...............DLB-170	Munby, Arthur Joseph 1828-1910........DLB-35
Moretti, Marino 1885-1979 ....DLB-114	Möser, Justus 1720-1794 ....DLB-97	Munday, Anthony 1560-1633 .... DLB-62, 172
Morgan, Berry 1919- DLB-6	Mosley, Nicholas 1923- DLB-14, 207	Mundt, Clara (see Mühlbach, Luise)
Morgan, Charles 1894-1958 .... DLB-34, 100	Moss, Arthur 1889-1969 ....DLB-4	Mundt, Theodore 1808-1861 ....DLB-133
Morgan, Edmund S. 1916- DLB-17	Moss, Howard 1922-1987 ....DLB-5	Munford, Robert circa 1737-1783.........DLB-31
Morgan, Edwin 1920- DLB-27	Moss, Thylias 1954- DLB-120	Mungoshi, Charles 1947- DLB-157
Morgan, John Pierpont 1837-1913.......DLB-140	The Most Powerful Book Review in America [*New York Times Book Review*]........... Y-82	Munk, Kaj 1898-1944 ....DLB-214
Morgan, John Pierpont, Jr. 1867-1943 ....DLB-140	Motion, Andrew 1952- DLB-40	Munonye, John 1929- DLB-117
Morgan, Robert 1944- DLB-120	Motley, John Lothrop 1814-1877 ....DLB-1, 30, 59, 235	Munro, Alice 1931- DLB-53
Morgan, Sydney Owenson, Lady 1776?-1859...............DLB-116, 158	Motley, Willard 1909-1965 .... DLB-76, 143	Munro, George [publishing house] DLB-49
Morgner, Irmtraud 1933- DLB-75	Mott, Lucretia 1793-1880...............DLB-239	Munro, H. H. 1870-1916 ....DLB-34, 162; CDBLB-5
Morhof, Daniel Georg 1639-1691 ....DLB-164	Motte, Benjamin Jr. [publishing house] ...DLB-154	Munro, Neil 1864-1930 ....DLB-156
Mori, Ōgai 1862-1922 ....DLB-180	Motteux, Peter Anthony 1663-1718.......DLB-80	Munro, Norman L. [publishing house] DLB-49
Móricz, Zsigmond 1879-1942..........DLB-215	Mottram, R. H. 1883-1971..............DLB-36	Munroe, James, and Company DLB-49
Morier, James Justinian 1782 or 1783?-1849................DLB-116	Mount, Ferdinand 1939- DLB-231	Munroe, Kirk 1850-1930...............DLB-42
Mörike, Eduard 1804-1875 ....DLB-133	Mouré, Erin 1955- DLB-60	Munroe and Francis....................DLB-49
Morin, Paul 1889-1963 ....DLB-92	Mourning Dove (Humishuma) between 1882 and 1888?-1936 .... DLB-175, 221	Munsell, Joel [publishing house] DLB-49
Morison, Richard 1514?-1556 ....DLB-136	Movies from Books, 1920-1974 ....DLB-9	Munsey, Frank A. 1854-1925 ....DLB-25, 91
Morison, Samuel Eliot 1887-1976.......DLB-17	Mowat, Farley 1921- DLB-68	Munsey, Frank A., and Company........DLB-49
Morison, Stanley 1889-1967 ....DLB-201	Mowbray, A. R., and Company, Limited......................DLB-106	Murakami Haruki 1949- DLB-182
Moritz, Karl Philipp 1756-1793 ....DLB-94	Mowrer, Edgar Ansel 1892-1977 ....DLB-29	Murav'ev, Mikhail Nikitich 1757-1807....DLB-150
Moriz von Craûn circa 1220-1230.........DLB-138	Mowrer, Paul Scott 1887-1971 ....DLB-29	Murdoch, Iris 1919-1999......DLB-14, 194, 233; CDBLB-8
Morley, Christopher 1890-1957..........DLB-9	Moxon, Edward [publishing house]......DLB-106	Murdoch, Rupert 1931- DLB-127
Morley, John 1838-1923 .... DLB-57, 144, 190		Murfree, Mary N. 1850-1922 .... DLB-12, 74
Morris, George Pope 1802-1864 ....DLB-73		Murger, Henry 1822-1861...............DLB-119
		Murger, Louis-Henri (see Murger, Henry)

Murner, Thomas 1475-1537 . . . . .DLB-179
Muro, Amado 1915-1971 . . . . DLB-82
Murphy, Arthur 1727-1805. . . . . DLB-89, 142
Murphy, Beatrice M. 1908- DLB-76
Murphy, Dervla 1931- DLB-204
Murphy, Emily 1868-1933 . . . . DLB-99
Murphy, John, and Company DLB-49
Murphy, John H., III 1916- DLB-127
Murphy, Richard 1927-1993. . . . . DLB-40
Murray, Albert L. 1916- DLB-38
Murray, Gilbert 1866-1957. . . . . DLB-10
Murray, John [publishing house] DLB-154
Murry, John Middleton 1889-1957. . . . . . DLB-149
"The Break-Up of the Novel" (1922) DLB-36
Murray, Judith Sargent 1751-1820 . . . .DLB-37, 200
Murray, Pauli 1910-1985 . . . . DLB-41
Musäus, Johann Karl August 1735-1787 . . . DLB-97
Muschg, Adolf 1934- DLB-75
The Music of *Minnesang* DLB-138
Musil, Robert
  1880-1942 . . . . DLB-81, 124; CDWLB-2
Muspilli circa 790-circa 850 . . . . DLB-148
Musset, Alfred de 1810-1857 . . . . . .DLB-192, 217
Mussey, Benjamin B., and Company DLB-49
Mutafchieva, Vera 1929- DLB-181
Mwangi, Meja 1948- DLB-125
Myers, Frederic W. H. 1843-1901 . . . . . . DLB-190
Myers, Gustavus 1872-1942 . . . . DLB-47
Myers, L. H. 1881-1944 . . . . DLB-15
Myers, Walter Dean 1937- DLB-33
Mykolaitis-Putinas, Vincas 1893-1967 . . . DLB-220
Myles, Eileen 1949- DLB-193

N

Na Prous Boneta circa 1296-1328. . . . . . . DLB-208
Nabl, Franz 1883-1974 . . . . DLB-81
Nabokov, Vladimir 1899-1977
  . . . . .DLB-2; Y-80, Y-91; DS-3; CDALB-1
The Vladimir Nabokov Archive
  in the Berg Collection Y-91
Nabokov Festival at Cornell Y-83
Nádaši, Ladislav (see Jégé)
Naden, Constance 1858-1889. . . . . DLB-199
Nadezhdin, Nikolai Ivanovich
  1804-1856 . . . . DLB-198
Naevius circa 265 B.C.-201 B.C. DLB-211
Nafis and Cornish. DLB-49
Nagai, Kafū 1879-1959 . . . . DLB-180
Naipaul, Shiva 1945-1985. . . . . . . .DLB-157; Y-85
Naipaul, V. S. 1932-
  . . . . DLB-125, 204, 207; Y-85;
                                   CDBLB-8; CDWLB-3
Nakagami Kenji 1946-1992 . . . . DLB-182
Nakano-in Masatada no Musume (see Nijō, Lady)
Nałkowska, Zofia 1884-1954 . . . . DLB-215
Nancrede, Joseph [publishing house] DLB-49

Naranjo, Carmen 1930- DLB-145
Narezhny, Vasilii Trofimovich
  1780-1825. . . . . DLB-198
Narrache, Jean 1893-1970. . . . . DLB-92
Nasby, Petroleum Vesuvius (see Locke, David Ross)
Nash, Eveleigh [publishing house] DLB-112
Nash, Ogden 1902-1971 . . . . DLB-11
Nashe, Thomas 1567-1601? DLB-167
Nast, Conde 1873-1942 . . . . DLB-91
Nast, Thomas 1840-1902 . . . . DLB-188
Nastasijević, Momčilo 1894-1938. . . . . . . DLB-147
Nathan, George Jean 1882-1958. . . . . DLB-137
Nathan, Robert 1894-1985. . . . . DLB-9
The National Jewish Book Awards. Y-85
The National Theatre and the Royal
  Shakespeare Company: The
  National Companies DLB-13
Natsume, Sōseki 1867-1916 . . . . DLB-180
Naughton, Bill 1910- DLB-13
Navarro, Joe 1953- DLB-209
Naylor, Gloria 1950- DLB-173
Nazor, Vladimir 1876-1949 . . . . DLB-147
Ndebele, Njabulo 1948- DLB-157
Neagoe, Peter 1881-1960 . . . . DLB-4
Neal, John 1793-1876 . . . . DLB-1, 59
Neal, Joseph C. 1807-1847 . . . . DLB-11
Neal, Larry 1937-1981 . . . . DLB-38
The Neale Publishing Company DLB-49
Nebel, Frederick 1903-1967 . . . . DLB-226
Neely, F. Tennyson [publishing house] . . . DLB-49
Negoițescu, Ion 1921-1993. . . . . DLB-220
Negri, Ada 1870-1945. . . . . DLB-114
"The Negro as a Writer," by
  G. M. McClellan DLB-50
"Negro Poets and Their Poetry," by
  Wallace Thurman DLB-50
Neidhart von Reuental
  circa 1185-circa 1240 . . . . DLB-138
Neihardt, John G. 1881-1973 . . . . DLB-9, 54
Neilson, John Shaw 1872-1942 . . . . DLB-230
Neledinsky-Meletsky, Iurii Aleksandrovich
  1752-1828. . . . . DLB-150
Nelligan, Emile 1879-1941 . . . . DLB-92
Nelson, Alice Moore Dunbar 1875-1935 . . DLB-50
Nelson, Kent 1943- DLB-234
Nelson, Thomas, and Sons [U.K.] DLB-106
Nelson, Thomas, and Sons [U.S.]. DLB-49
Nelson, William 1908-1978 . . . . DLB-103
Nelson, William Rockhill 1841-1915 . . . . . DLB-23
Nemerov, Howard 1920-1991 . . . . .DLB-5, 6; Y-83
Németh, László 1901-1975 . . . . DLB-215
Nepos circa 100 B.C.-post 27 B.C. DLB-211
Nėris, Salomėja
  1904-1945 . . . . DLB-220; CDWLB-4
Nerval, Gerard de 1808-1855 . . . . DLB-217
Nesbit, E. 1858-1924 . . . . .DLB-141, 153, 178
Ness, Evaline 1911-1986. . . . . DLB-61

Nestroy, Johann 1801-1862 . . . . DLB-133
Neugeboren, Jay 1938- DLB-28
Neukirch, Benjamin 1655-1729 . . . . DLB-168
Neumann, Alfred 1895-1952 . . . . DLB-56
Neumann, Ferenc (see Molnár, Ferenc)
Neumark, Georg 1621-1681 . . . . DLB-164
Neumeister, Erdmann 1671-1756 . . . . . . DLB-168
Nevins, Allan 1890-1971. . . . . .DLB-17; DS-17
Nevinson, Henry Woodd 1856-1941. . . . DLB-135
The New American Library. DLB-46
New Approaches to Biography: Challenges
  from Critical Theory, USC Conference
  on Literary Studies, 1990. . . . . Y-90
New Directions Publishing Corporation . . DLB-46
A New Edition of *Huck Finn* Y-85
New Forces at Work in the American Theatre:
  1915-1925 . . . . DLB-7
New Literary Periodicals:
  A Report for 1987 . . . . Y-87
New Literary Periodicals:
  A Report for 1988 . . . . Y-88
New Literary Periodicals:
  A Report for 1989 . . . . Y-89
New Literary Periodicals:
  A Report for 1990 . . . . Y-90
New Literary Periodicals:
  A Report for 1991 . . . . Y-91
New Literary Periodicals:
  A Report for 1992 . . . . Y-92
New Literary Periodicals:
  A Report for 1993 . . . . Y-93
The New Monthly Magazine
  1814-1884 . . . . DLB-110
The New Variorum Shakespeare. Y-85
A New Voice: The Center for the Book's First
  Five Years Y-83
The New Wave [Science Fiction] DLB-8
New York City Bookshops in the 1930s and 1940s:
  The Recollections of Walter Goldwater . . Y-93
Newbery, John [publishing house] DLB-154
Newbolt, Henry 1862-1938 . . . . DLB-19
Newbound, Bernard Slade (see Slade, Bernard)
Newby, Eric 1919- DLB-204
Newby, P. H. 1918- DLB-15
Newby, Thomas Cautley
  [publishing house] DLB-106
Newcomb, Charles King 1820-1894. . . DLB-1, 223
Newell, Peter 1862-1924. . . . . DLB-42
Newell, Robert Henry 1836-1901 . . . . DLB-11
Newhouse, Samuel I. 1895-1979. . . . . . . .DLB-127
Newman, Cecil Earl 1903-1976 . . . . .DLB-127
Newman, David (see Benton, Robert)
Newman, Frances 1883-1928 . . . . Y-80
Newman, Francis William 1805-1897. . . . DLB-190
Newman, John Henry
  1801-1890 . . . . DLB-18, 32, 55
Newman, Mark [publishing house] DLB-49
Newmarch, Rosa Harriet 1857-1940. . . . . DLB-240
Newnes, George, Limited. DLB-112

Newsome, Effie Lee 1885-1979 ....DLB-76
Newspaper Syndication of American
    Humor DLB-11
Newton, A. Edward 1864-1940 ....DLB-140
Nexø, Martin Andersen 1869-1954 ......DLB-214
Nezval, Vítěslav
    1900-1958 ....DLB-215; CDWLB-4
Ngugi wa Thiong'o
    1938- DLB-125; CDWLB-3
Niatum, Duane 1938- DLB-175
The *Nibelungenlied* and the *Klage*
    circa 1200 ....DLB-138
Nichol, B. P. 1944- DLB-53
Nicholas of Cusa 1401-1464 ....DLB-115
Nichols, Beverly 1898-1983...........DLB-191
Nichols, Dudley 1895-1960 ....DLB-26
Nichols, Grace 1950- DLB-157
Nichols, John 1940- Y-82
Nichols, Mary Sargeant (Neal) Gove
    1810-1884 ....DLB-1
Nichols, Peter 1927- DLB-13
Nichols, Roy F. 1896-1973...........DLB-17
Nichols, Ruth 1948- DLB-60
Nicholson, Edward Williams Byron
    1849-1912 ....DLB-184
Nicholson, Norman 1914- DLB-27
Nicholson, William 1872-1949.........DLB-141
Ní Chuilleanáin, Eiléan 1942- DLB-40
Nicol, Eric 1919- DLB-68
Nicolai, Friedrich 1733-1811 ....DLB-97
Nicolas de Clamanges circa 1363-1437 ...DLB-208
Nicolay, John G. 1832-1901 and
    Hay, John 1838-1905 ....DLB-47
Nicolson, Adela Florence Cory (see Hope, Laurence)
Nicolson, Harold 1886-1968 ....DLB-100, 149
Nicolson, Nigel 1917- DLB-155
Niebuhr, Reinhold 1892-1971 .....DLB-17; DS-17
Niedecker, Lorine 1903-1970.........DLB-48
Nieman, Lucius W. 1857-1935..........DLB-25
Nietzsche, Friedrich
    1844-1900 ....DLB-129; CDWLB-2
Nievo, Stanislao 1928- DLB-196
Niggli, Josefina 1910- Y-80
Nightingale, Florence 1820-1910 ....DLB-166
Nijō, Lady (Nakano-in Masatada no Musume)
    1258-after 1306 ....DLB-203
Nijō Yoshimoto 1320-1388 ....DLB-203
Nikolev, Nikolai Petrovich
    1758-1815 ....DLB-150
Niles, Hezekiah 1777-1839 ....DLB-43
Nims, John Frederick 1913-1999 ....DLB-5
Nin, Anaïs 1903-1977..........DLB-2, 4, 152
1985: The Year of the Mystery:
    A Symposium Y-85
The 1997 Booker Prize Y-97
The 1998 Booker Prize Y-98
Niño, Raúl 1961- DLB-209
Nissenson, Hugh 1933- DLB-28

Niven, Frederick John 1878-1944.........DLB-92
Niven, Larry 1938- DLB-8
Nixon, Howard M. 1909-1983 ....DLB-201
Nizan, Paul 1905-1940................DLB-72
Njegoš, Petar II Petrović
    1813-1851 ....DLB-147; CDWLB-4
Nkosi, Lewis 1936- DLB-157
"The No Self, the Little Self, and the Poets,"
    by Richard Moore................DLB-105
Nobel Peace Prize
The 1986 Nobel Peace Prize: Elie Wiesel Y-86
The Nobel Prize and Literary Politics Y-86
Nobel Prize in Literature
The 1982 Nobel Prize in Literature:
    Gabriel García Márquez Y-82
The 1983 Nobel Prize in Literature:
    William Golding..................Y-83
The 1984 Nobel Prize in Literature:
    Jaroslav Seifert...................Y-84
The 1985 Nobel Prize in Literature:
    Claude Simon Y-85
The 1986 Nobel Prize in Literature:
    Wole Soyinka Y-86
The 1987 Nobel Prize in Literature:
    Joseph Brodsky...................Y-87
The 1988 Nobel Prize in Literature:
    Najīb Mahfūz Y-88
The 1989 Nobel Prize in Literature:
    Camilo José Cela.................Y-89
The 1990 Nobel Prize in Literature:
    Octavio Paz.....................Y-90
The 1991 Nobel Prize in Literature:
    Nadine Gordimer Y-91
The 1992 Nobel Prize in Literature:
    Derek Walcott...................Y-92
The 1993 Nobel Prize in Literature:
    Toni Morrison Y-93
The 1994 Nobel Prize in Literature:
    Kenzaburō Ōe...................Y-94
The 1995 Nobel Prize in Literature:
    Seamus Heaney..................Y-95
The 1996 Nobel Prize in Literature:
    Wisława Szymborska Y-96
The 1997 Nobel Prize in Literature:
    Dario Fo Y-97
The 1998 Nobel Prize in Literature:
    José Saramago Y-98
The 1999 Nobel Prize in Literature:
    Günter Grass....................Y-99
Nodier, Charles 1780-1844 ....DLB-119
Noel, Roden 1834-1894 ....DLB-35
Nogami, Yaeko 1885-1985 ....DLB-180
Nogo, Rajko Petrov 1945- DLB-181
Nolan, William F. 1928- DLB-8
Noland, C. F. M. 1810?-1858 ....DLB-11
Noma Hiroshi 1915-1991 ....DLB-182
Nonesuch Press DLB-112
Noonan, Robert Phillipe (see Tressell, Robert)
Noonday Press....................DLB-46
Noone, John 1936- DLB-14
Nora, Eugenio de 1923- DLB-134

Nordan, Lewis 1939- DLB-234
Nordbrandt, Henrik 1945- DLB-214
Nordhoff, Charles 1887-1947..........DLB-9
Norman, Charles 1904-1996 ....DLB-111
Norman, Marsha 1947- Y-84
Norris, Charles G. 1881-1945 ....DLB-9
Norris, Frank
    1870-1902 ....DLB-12, 71, 186; CDALB-3
Norris, Leslie 1921- DLB-27
Norse, Harold 1916- DLB-16
Norte, Marisela 1955- DLB-209
North, Marianne 1830-1890 ....DLB-174
North Point Press DLB-46
Nortje, Arthur 1942-1970.............DLB-125
Norton, Alice Mary (see Norton, Andre)
Norton, Andre 1912- DLB-8, 52
Norton, Andrews 1786-1853 ....DLB-1, 235
Norton, Caroline 1808-1877 ....DLB-21, 159, 199
Norton, Charles Eliot 1827-1908 ...DLB-1, 64, 235
Norton, John 1606-1663 ....DLB-24
Norton, Mary 1903-1992.............DLB-160
Norton, Thomas (see Sackville, Thomas)
Norton, W. W., and Company DLB-46
Norwood, Robert 1874-1932 ....DLB-92
Nosaka Akiyuki 1930- DLB-182
Nossack, Hans Erich 1901-1977 ......DLB-69
Not Immediately Discernible . . . but Eventually
    Quite Clear: The *First Light* and *Final Years*
    of Hemingway's Centenary Y-99
A Note on Technique (1926), by
    Elizabeth A. Drew [excerpts].........DLB-36
Notker Balbulus circa 840-912..........DLB-148
Notker III of Saint Gall circa 950-1022 ...DLB-148
Notker von Zweifalten ?-1095..........DLB-148
Nourse, Alan E. 1928- DLB-8
Novak, Slobodan 1924- DLB-181
Novak, Vjenceslav 1859-1905.........DLB-147
Novalis 1772-1801 ....DLB-90; CDWLB-2
Novaro, Mario 1868-1944............DLB-114
Novás Calvo, Lino 1903-1983 ....DLB-145
"The Novel in [Robert Browning's] 'The Ring and
    the Book'" (1912), by Henry James ...DLB-32
The Novel of Impressionism,
    by Jethro Bithell DLB-66
Novel-Reading: *The Works of Charles Dickens,
    The Works of W. Makepeace Thackeray*
    (1879), by Anthony Trollope DLB-21
Novels for Grown-Ups Y-97
The Novels of Dorothy Richardson (1918),
    by May Sinclair DLB-36
Novels with a Purpose (1864), by
    Justin M'Carthy DLB-21
Noventa, Giacomo 1898-1960..........DLB-114
Novikov, Nikolai
    Ivanovich 1744-1818................DLB-150
Novomeský, Laco 1904-1976..........DLB-215
Nowlan, Alden 1933-1983 ....DLB-53
Noyes, Alfred 1880-1958.............DLB-20

Noyes, Crosby S. 1825-1908 .... DLB-23
Noyes, Nicholas 1647-1717 .... DLB-24
Noyes, Theodore W. 1858-1946 .... DLB-29
N-Town Plays circa 1468 to early
    sixteenth century................ DLB-146
Nugent, Frank 1908-1965............... DLB-44
Nugent, Richard Bruce 1906- DLB-151
Nušić, Branislav
    1864-1938 ....DLB-147; CDWLB-4
Nutt, David [publishing house]........ DLB-106
Nwapa, Flora 1931-1993.... DLB-125; CDWLB-3
Nye, Bill 1850-1896 .... DLB-186
Nye, Edgar Wilson (Bill) 1850-1896... DLB-11, 23
Nye, Naomi Shihab 1952- DLB-120
Nye, Robert 1939- DLB-14
Nyka-Niliūnas, Alfonsas 1919- DLB-220

O

Oakes Smith, Elizabeth 1806-1893 .... DLB-1, 239
Oakes, Urian circa 1631-1681 .... DLB-24
Oakley, Violet 1874-1961 .... DLB-188
Oates, Joyce Carol 1938- ...DLB-2, 5, 130; Y-81
Ōba Minako 1930- DLB-182
Ober, Frederick Albion 1849-1913 ..... DLB-189
Ober, William 1920-1993................Y-93
Oberholtzer, Ellis Paxson 1868-1936 ..... DLB-47
Obradović, Dositej 1740?-1811......... DLB-147
O'Brien, Charlotte Grace 1845-1909 .... DLB-240
O'Brien, Edna 1932- ... DLB-14, 231; CDBLB-8
O'Brien, Fitz-James 1828-1862 .... DLB-74
O'Brien, Flann (see O'Nolan, Brian)
O'Brien, Kate 1897-1974................ DLB-15
O'Brien, Tim
    1946- DLB-152; Y-80; DS-9; CDALB-7
O'Casey, Sean 1880-1964..... DLB-10; CDBLB-6
Occom, Samson 1723-1792............. DLB-175
Ochs, Adolph S. 1858-1935 .... DLB-25
Ochs-Oakes, George Washington
    1861-1931 .... DLB-137
O'Connor, Flannery 1925-1964
    .... DLB-2, 152; Y-80; DS-12; CDALB-1
O'Connor, Frank 1903-1966 .... DLB-162
Octopus Publishing Group............ DLB-112
Oda Sakunosuke 1913-1947 .... DLB-182
Odell, Jonathan 1737-1818 .... DLB-31, 99
O'Dell, Scott 1903-1989 .... DLB-52
Odets, Clifford 1906-1963 ....DLB-7, 26
Odhams Press Limited DLB-112
Odoevsky, Aleksandr Ivanovich
    1802-1839 .... DLB-205
Odoevsky, Vladimir Fedorovich
    1804 or 1803-1869................ DLB-198
O'Donnell, Peter 1920- DLB-87
O'Donovan, Michael (see O'Connor, Frank)
O'Dowd, Bernard 1866-1953 .... DLB-230
Ōe Kenzaburō 1935- DLB-182; Y-94

O'Faolain, Julia 1932- DLB-14, 231
O'Faolain, Sean 1900- DLB-15, 162
Off Broadway and Off-Off Broadway DLB-7
Off-Loop Theatres DLB-7
Offord, Carl Ruthven 1910- DLB-76
O'Flaherty, Liam 1896-1984....DLB-36, 162; Y-84
Ogilvie, J. S., and Company........... DLB-49
Ogilvy, Eliza 1822-1912 .... DLB-199
Ogot, Grace 1930- DLB-125
O'Grady, Desmond 1935- DLB-40
Ogunyemi, Wale 1939- DLB-157
O'Hagan, Howard 1902-1982 .... DLB-68
O'Hara, Frank 1926-1966 ..... DLB-5, 16, 193
O'Hara, John
    1905-1970...... DLB-9, 86; DS-2; CDALB-5
John O'Hara's Pottsville Journalism......... Y-88
O'Hegarty, P. S. 1879-1955 .... DLB-201
Okara, Gabriel 1921- DLB-125; CDWLB-3
O'Keeffe, John 1747-1833 .... DLB-89
Okes, Nicholas [publishing house].......DLB-170
Okigbo, Christopher
    1930-1967 .... DLB-125; CDWLB-3
Okot p'Bitek 1931-1982 .... DLB-125; CDWLB-3
Okpewho, Isidore 1941- DLB-157
Okri, Ben 1959- DLB-157, 231
Olaudah Equiano and Unfinished Journeys:
    The Slave-Narrative Tradition and
    Twentieth-Century Continuities, by
    Paul Edwards and Pauline T.
    Wangman DLB-117
Old English Literature:
    An Introduction DLB-146
Old English Riddles
    eighth to tenth centuries.......... DLB-146
Old Franklin Publishing House DLB-49
Old German Genesis and Old German Exodus
    circa 1050-circa 1130 .... DLB-148
Old High German Charms and
    Blessings........... DLB-148; CDWLB-2
The Old High German Isidor
    circa 790-800 .... DLB-148
The Old Manse DLB-223
Older, Fremont 1856-1935............ DLB-25
Oldham, John 1653-1683 .... DLB-131
Oldman, C. B. 1894-1969............. DLB-201
Olds, Sharon 1942- DLB-120
Olearius, Adam 1599-1671 .... DLB-164
O'Leary, Ellen 1831-1889 .... DLB-240
Oliphant, Laurence 1829?-1888 ..... DLB-18, 166
Oliphant, Margaret 1828-1897 ..... DLB-18, 190
Oliver, Chad 1928- DLB-8
Oliver, Mary 1935- DLB-5, 193
Ollier, Claude 1922- DLB-83
Olsen, Tillie 1912 or 1913-
    .... DLB-28, 206; Y-80; CDALB-7
Olson, Charles 1910-1970........ DLB-5, 16, 193
Olson, Elder 1909- DLB-48, 63
Omotoso, Kole 1943- DLB-125

Omulevsky, Innokentii Vasil'evich
    1836 or 1837-1883 .... DLB-238
On Learning to Write.................. Y-88
Ondaatje, Michael 1943- DLB-60
O'Neill, Eugene 1888-1953 .... DLB-7; CDALB-5
Eugene O'Neill Memorial Theater
    Center DLB-7
Eugene O'Neill's Letters: A Review......... Y-88
Onetti, Juan Carlos
    1909-1994 ....DLB-113; CDWLB-3
Onions, George Oliver 1872-1961 ...... DLB-153
Onofri, Arturo 1885-1928 .... DLB-114
O'Nolan, Brian 1911-1966 .... DLB-231
Opie, Amelia 1769-1853 ....DLB-116, 159
Opitz, Martin 1597-1639.............. DLB-164
Oppen, George 1908-1984 .... DLB-5, 165
Oppenheim, E. Phillips 1866-1946....... DLB-70
Oppenheim, James 1882-1932 .... DLB-28
Oppenheimer, Joel 1930-1988 .... DLB-5, 193
Optic, Oliver (see Adams, William Taylor)
Oral History: B. W. Huebsch Y-99
Oral History Interview with Donald S.
    Klopfer........................ Y-97
Orczy, Emma, Baroness 1865-1947 ...... DLB-70
Origo, Iris 1902-1988................ DLB-155
Orlovitz, Gil 1918-1973 .... DLB-2, 5
Orlovsky, Peter 1933- DLB-16
Ormond, John 1923- DLB-27
Ornitz, Samuel 1890-1957 .... DLB-28, 44
O'Rourke, P. J. 1947- DLB-185
Orten, Jiří 1919-1941 .... DLB-215
Ortese, Anna Maria 1914- DLB-177
Ortiz, Simon J. 1941- DLB-120, 175
Ortnit and Wolfdietrich circa 1225-1250.... DLB-138
Orton, Joe 1933-1967 .... DLB-13; CDBLB-8
Orwell, George
    1903-1950 ...... DLB-15, 98, 195; CDBLB-7
The Orwell Year Y-84
(Re-)Publishing Orwell.................. Y-86
Ory, Carlos Edmundo de 1923- DLB-134
Osbey, Brenda Marie 1957- DLB-120
Osbon, B. S. 1827-1912............... DLB-43
Osborn, Sarah 1714-1796 .... DLB-200
Osborne, John 1929-1994..... DLB-13; CDBLB-7
Osgood, Herbert L. 1855-1918.......... DLB-47
Osgood, James R., and Company DLB-49
Osgood, McIlvaine and Company...... DLB-112
O'Shaughnessy, Arthur 1844-1881 ...... DLB-35
O'Shea, Patrick [publishing house]....... DLB-49
Osipov, Nikolai Petrovich
    1751-1799 .... DLB-150
Oskison, John Milton 1879-1947 ....DLB-175
Osler, Sir William 1849-1919 .... DLB-184
Osofisan, Femi 1946- DLB-125; CDWLB-3
Ostenso, Martha 1900-1963 .... DLB-92
Ostrauskas, Kostas 1926- DLB-232

Ostriker, Alicia 1937- DLB-120	Page, Louise 1955- DLB-233	Parizeau, Alice 1930- DLB-60
Osundare, Niyi 1947- DLB-157; CDWLB-3	Page, P. K. 1916- DLB-68	Parke, John 1754-1789................DLB-31
Oswald, Eleazer 1755-1795..............DLB-43	Page, Thomas Nelson 1853-1922 ....DLB-12, 78; DS-13	Parker, Dorothy 1893-1967.......DLB-11, 45, 86
Oswald von Wolkenstein 1376 or 1377-1445 ....DLB-179	Page, Walter Hines 1855-1918 ....DLB-71, 91	Parker, Gilbert 1860-1932 ....DLB-99
Otero, Blas de 1916-1979.............DLB-134	Paget, Francis Edward 1806-1882 ....DLB-163	Parker, J. H. [publishing house]..........DLB-106
Otero, Miguel Antonio 1859-1944........DLB-82	Paget, Violet (see Lee, Vernon)	Parker, James 1714-1770................DLB-43
Otero, Nina 1881-1965 ....DLB-209	Pagliarani, Elio 1927- DLB-128	Parker, John [publishing house]..........DLB-106
Otero Silva, Miguel 1908-1985 ....DLB-145	Pain, Barry 1864-1928............DLB-135, 197	Parker, Matthew 1504-1575.............DLB-213
Otfried von Weißenburg circa 800-circa 875?................DLB-148	Pain, Philip ?-circa 1666.................DLB-24	Parker, Theodore 1810-1860.........DLB-1, 235
Otis, Broaders and Company DLB-49	Paine, Robert Treat, Jr. 1773-1811.........DLB-37	Parker, William Riley 1906-1968 ....DLB-103
Otis, James (see Kaler, James Otis)	Paine, Thomas 1737-1809.....DLB-31, 43, 73, 158; CDALB-2	Parkes, Bessie Rayner (Madame Belloc) 1829-1925 ....DLB-240
Otis, James, Jr. 1725-1783...............DLB-31	Painter, George D. 1914- DLB-155	Parkman, Francis 1823-1893 ....DLB-1, 30, 183, 186, 235
Ottaway, James 1911- DLB-127	Painter, William 1540?-1594...........DLB-136	Parks, Gordon 1912- DLB-33
Ottendorfer, Oswald 1826-1900 ....DLB-23	Palazzeschi, Aldo 1885-1974 ....DLB-114	Parks, Tim 1954- DLB-231
Ottieri, Ottiero 1924- DLB-177	Paley, Grace 1922- DLB-28, 218	Parks, William 1698-1750 ....DLB-43
Otto-Peters, Louise 1819-1895..........DLB-129	Palfrey, John Gorham 1796-1881...DLB-1, 30, 235	Parks, William [publishing house]........DLB-49
Otway, Thomas 1652-1685..............DLB-80	Palgrave, Francis Turner 1824-1897 ....DLB-35	Parley, Peter (see Goodrich, Samuel Griswold)
Ouellette, Fernand 1930- DLB-60	Palmer, Joe H. 1904-1952 ....DLB-171	Parmenides late sixth-fifth century B.C..........DLB-176
Ouida 1839-1908.................DLB-18, 156	Palmer, Michael 1943- DLB-169	Parnell, Thomas 1679-1718 ....DLB-95
Outing Publishing Company............DLB-46	Paltock, Robert 1697-1767 ....DLB-39	Parnicki, Teodor 1908-1988 ....DLB-215
Outlaw Days, by Joyce Johnson DLB-16	Paludan, Jacob 1896-1975 ....DLB-214	Parr, Catherine 1513?-1548.............DLB-136
Overbury, Sir Thomas circa 1581-1613..................DLB-151	Pan Books Limited DLB-112	Parrington, Vernon L. 1871-1929 .....DLB-17, 63
The Overlook Press.................DLB-46	Panama, Norman 1914- and Frank, Melvin 1913-1988 ....DLB-26	Parrish, Maxfield 1870-1966 ....DLB-188
Overview of U.S. Book Publishing, 1910-1945 ....DLB-9	Panaev, Ivan Ivanovich 1812-1862 ......DLB-198	Parronchi, Alessandro 1914- DLB-128
Ovid 43 B.C.-A.D. 17 ......DLB-211; CDWLB-1	Panaeva, Avdot'ia Iakovlevna 1820-1893 ....DLB-238	Parton, James 1822-1891...............DLB-30
Owen, Guy 1925- DLB-5	Pancake, Breece D'J 1952-1979 ....DLB-130	Parton, Sara Payson Willis 1811-1872 ....DLB-43, 74, 239
Owen, John 1564-1622 ....DLB-121	Panduro, Leif 1923-1977 ....DLB-214	Partridge, S. W., and Company DLB-106
Owen, John [publishing house] DLB-49	Panero, Leopoldo 1909-1962...........DLB-108	Parun, Vesna 1922- DLB-181; CDWLB-4
Owen, Peter, Limited..................DLB-112	Pangborn, Edgar 1909-1976..............DLB-8	Pasinetti, Pier Maria 1913- DLB-177
Owen, Robert 1771-1858.........DLB-107, 158	"Panic Among the Philistines": A Postscript, An Interview with Bryan Griffin........Y-81	Pasolini, Pier Paolo 1922- DLB-128, 177
Owen, Wilfred 1893-1918 ....DLB-20; DS-18; CDBLB-6	Panizzi, Sir Anthony 1797-1879 ....DLB-184	Pastan, Linda 1932- DLB-5
The Owl and the Nightingale circa 1189-1199 ....DLB-146	Panneton, Philippe (see Ringuet)	Paston, George (Emily Morse Symonds) 1860-1936.................DLB-149, 197
Owsley, Frank L. 1890-1956 ....DLB-17	Panshin, Alexei 1940- DLB-8	The Paston Letters 1422-1509............DLB-146
Oxford, Seventeenth Earl of, Edward de Vere 1550-1604 ....DLB-172	Pansy (see Alden, Isabella)	Pastorius, Francis Daniel 1651-circa 1720 ....DLB-24
Ozerov, Vladislav Aleksandrovich 1769-1816 ....DLB-150	Pantheon Books...................DLB-46	Patchen, Kenneth 1911-1972 ....DLB-16, 48
Ozick, Cynthia 1928- DLB-28, 152; Y-82	Papadat-Bengescu, Hortensia 1876-1955 ....DLB-220	Pater, Walter 1839-1894 ....DLB-57, 156; CDBLB-4
First Strauss "Livings" Awarded to Cynthia Ozick and Raymond Carver An Interview with Cynthia Ozick Y-83	Papantonio, Michael (see Kohn, John S. Van E.)	Aesthetic Poetry (1873) DLB-35
	Paperback Library.................DLB-46	Paterson, A. B. "Banjo" 1864-1941 ......DLB-230
P	Paperback Science Fiction DLB-8	Paterson, Katherine 1932- DLB-52
	Paquet, Alfons 1881-1944 ....DLB-66	Patmore, Coventry 1823-1896 ....DLB-35, 98
Pace, Richard 1482?-1536.............DLB-167	Paracelsus 1493-1541.................DLB-179	Paton, Alan 1903-1988 ....DS-17
Pacey, Desmond 1917-1975 ....DLB-88	Paradis, Suzanne 1936- DLB-53	Paton, Joseph Noel 1821-1901...........DLB-35
Pack, Robert 1929- DLB-5	Páral, Vladimír, 1932- DLB-232	Paton Walsh, Jill 1937- DLB-161
Packaging Papa: *The Garden of Eden* Y-86	Pardoe, Julia 1804-1862................DLB-166	Patrick, Edwin Hill ("Ted") 1901-1964...DLB-137
Padell Publishing Company.............DLB-46	Paredes, Américo 1915-1999 ....DLB-209	Patrick, John 1906-1995.................DLB-7
Padgett, Ron 1942- DLB-5	Pareja Diezcanseco, Alfredo 1908-1993...DLB-145	Pattee, Fred Lewis 1863-1950 ....DLB-71
Padilla, Ernesto Chávez 1944- DLB-122	Parents' Magazine Press...............DLB-46	Pattern and Paradigm: History as Design, by Judith Ryan..........DLB-75
Page, L. C., and Company............DLB-49	Parise, Goffredo 1929-1986 ....DLB-177	Patterson, Alicia 1906-1963............DLB-127
	Parisian Theater, Fall 1984: Toward A New Baroque....................Y-85	Patterson, Eleanor Medill 1881-1948......DLB-29

Patterson, Eugene 1923- DLB-127
Patterson, Joseph Medill 1879-1946 ...... DLB-29
Pattillo, Henry 1726-1801 .... DLB-37
Paul, Elliot 1891-1958 .... DLB-4
Paul, Jean (see Richter, Johann Paul Friedrich)
Paul, Kegan, Trench, Trubner and
  Company Limited DLB-106
Paul, Peter, Book Company DLB-49
Paul, Stanley, and Company Limited DLB-112
Paulding, James Kirke 1778-1860 ... DLB-3, 59, 74
Paulin, Tom 1949- DLB-40
Pauper, Peter, Press DLB-46
Pavese, Cesare 1908-1950 .... DLB-128, 177
Pavić, Milorad 1929- DLB-181; CDWLB-4
Pavlov, Konstantin 1933- DLB-181
Pavlov, Nikolai Filippovich 1803-1864 .... DLB-198
Pavlova, Karolina Karlovna 1807-1893 .... DLB-205
Pavlović, Miodrag
  1928- DLB-181; CDWLB-4
Paxton, John 1911-1985 .... DLB-44
Payn, James 1830-1898 .... DLB-18
Payne, John 1842-1916 .... DLB-35
Payne, John Howard 1791-1852 .... DLB-37
Payson and Clarke DLB-46
Paz, Octavio 1914-1998 .... Y-90, Y-98
Pazzi, Roberto 1946- DLB-196
Peabody, Elizabeth Palmer 1804-1894 . DLB-1, 223
Peabody, Elizabeth Palmer
  [publishing house] DLB-49
Peabody, Oliver William Bourn
  1799-1848 .... DLB-59
Peace, Roger 1899-1968 .... DLB-127
Peacham, Henry 1578-1644? DLB-151
Peacham, Henry, the Elder
  1547-1634 .... DLB-172, 236
Peachtree Publishers, Limited DLB-46
Peacock, Molly 1947- DLB-120
Peacock, Thomas Love 1785-1866 ... DLB-96, 116
Pead, Deuel ?-1727 .... DLB-24
Peake, Mervyn 1911-1968 .... DLB-15, 160
Peale, Rembrandt 1778-1860 .... DLB-183
Pear Tree Press DLB-112
Pearce, Philippa 1920- DLB-161
Pearson, H. B. [publishing house] DLB-49
Pearson, Hesketh 1887-1964 .... DLB-149
Pechersky, Andrei (see Mel'nikov, Pavel Ivanovich)
Peck, George W. 1840-1916 .... DLB-23, 42
Peck, H. C., and Theo. Bliss
  [publishing house] DLB-49
Peck, Harry Thurston 1856-1914 ..... DLB-71, 91
Peden, William 1913-1999 .... DLB-234
Peele, George 1556-1596 .... DLB-62, 167
Pegler, Westbrook 1894-1969 .... DLB-171
Pekić, Borislav 1930-1992 ... DLB-181; CDWLB-4
Pellegrini and Cudahy DLB-46
Pelletier, Aimé (see Vac, Bertrand)

Pemberton, Sir Max 1863-1950 .... DLB-70
de la Peña, Terri 1947- DLB-209
Penfield, Edward 1866-1925 .... DLB-188
Penguin Books [U.K.] DLB-112
Penguin Books [U.S.] DLB-46
Penn Publishing Company DLB-49
Penn, William 1644-1718 .... DLB-24
Penna, Sandro 1906-1977 .... DLB-114
Pennell, Joseph 1857-1926 .... DLB-188
Penner, Jonathan 1940- Y-83
Pennington, Lee 1939- Y-82
Pepys, Samuel
  1633-1703 .... DLB-101, 213; CDBLB-2
Percy, Thomas 1729-1811 .... DLB-104
Percy, Walker 1916-1990 ...... DLB-2; Y-80, Y-90
Percy, William 1575-1648 .... DLB-172
Perec, Georges 1936-1982 .... DLB-83
Perelman, Bob 1947- DLB-193
Perelman, S. J. 1904-1979 .... DLB-11, 44
Perez, Raymundo "Tigre" 1946- DLB-122
Peri Rossi, Cristina 1941- DLB-145
Perkins, Eugene 1932- DLB-41
Perkoff, Stuart Z. 1930-1974 .... DLB-16
Perley, Moses Henry 1804-1862 .... DLB-99
Permabooks DLB-46
Perovsky, Aleksei Alekseevich
  (Antonii Pogorel'sky) 1787-1836 .... DLB-198
Perri, Henry 1561-1617 .... DLB-236
Perrin, Alice 1867-1934 .... DLB-156
Perry, Bliss 1860-1954 .... DLB-71
Perry, Eleanor 1915-1981 .... DLB-44
Perry, Henry (see Perri, Henry)
Perry, Matthew 1794-1858 .... DLB-183
Perry, Sampson 1747-1823 .... DLB-158
Persius A.D. 34-A.D. 62 .... DLB-211
Perutz, Leo 1882-1957 .... DLB-81
Pesetsky, Bette 1932- DLB-130
Pestalozzi, Johann Heinrich 1746-1827 .... DLB-94
Peter, Laurence J. 1919-1990 .... DLB-53
Peter of Spain circa 1205-1277 .... DLB-115
Peterkin, Julia 1880-1961 .... DLB-9
Peters, Lenrie 1932- DLB-117
Peters, Robert 1924- DLB-105
"Foreword to Ludwig of Baviria" DLB-105
Petersham, Maud 1889-1971 and
  Petersham, Miska 1888-1960 .... DLB-22
Peterson, Charles Jacobs 1819-1887 ...... DLB-79
Peterson, Len 1917- DLB-88
Peterson, Levi S. 1933- DLB-206
Peterson, Louis 1922-1998 .... DLB-76
Peterson, T. B., and Brothers DLB-49
Petitclair, Pierre 1813-1860 .... DLB-99
Petrescu, Camil 1894-1957 .... DLB-220
Petronius circa A.D. 20-A.D. 66
  .... DLB-211; CDWLB-1

Petrov, Aleksandar 1938- DLB-181
Petrov, Gavriil 1730-1801 .... DLB-150
Petrov, Valeri 1920- DLB-181
Petrov, Vasilii Petrovich 1736-1799 ..... DLB-150
Petrović, Rastko
  1898-1949 .... DLB-147; CDWLB-4
Petruslied circa 854? DLB-148
Petry, Ann 1908-1997 .... DLB-76
Pettie, George circa 1548-1589 .... DLB-136
Peyton, K. M. 1929- DLB-161
Pfaffe Konrad flourished circa 1172 ..... DLB-148
Pfaffe Lamprecht flourished circa 1150 .. DLB-148
Pfeiffer, Emily 1827-1890 .... DLB-199
Pforzheimer, Carl H. 1879-1957 .... DLB-140
Phaedrus circa 18 B.C.-circa A.D. 50 .... DLB-211
Phaer, Thomas 1510?-1560 .... DLB-167
Phaidon Press Limited DLB-112
Pharr, Robert Deane 1916-1992 .... DLB-33
Phelps, Elizabeth Stuart 1815-1852 ...... DLB-202
Phelps, Elizabeth Stuart 1844-1911 .... DLB-74, 221
Philander von der Linde
  (see Mencke, Johann Burckhard)
Philby, H. St. John B. 1885-1960 .... DLB-195
Philip, Marlene Nourbese 1947- DLB-157
Philippe, Charles-Louis 1874-1909 ...... DLB-65
Philips, John 1676-1708 .... DLB-95
Philips, Katherine 1632-1664 .... DLB-131
Phillipps, Sir Thomas 1792-1872 .... DLB-184
Phillips, Caryl 1958- DLB-157
Phillips, David Graham 1867-1911 ..... DLB-9, 12
Phillips, Jayne Anne 1952- Y-80
Phillips, Robert 1938- DLB-105
"Finding, Losing, Reclaiming: A Note
  on My Poems" DLB-105
Phillips, Sampson and Company DLB-49
Phillips, Stephen 1864-1915 .... DLB-10
Phillips, Ulrich B. 1877-1934 .... DLB-17
Phillips, Wendell 1811-1884 .... DLB-235
Phillips, Willard 1784-1873 .... DLB-59
Phillips, William 1907- DLB-137
Phillpotts, Adelaide Eden (Adelaide Ross)
  1896-1993 .... DLB-191
Phillpotts, Eden 1862-1960 ... DLB-10, 70, 135, 153
Philo circa 20-15 B.C.-circa A.D. 50 ..... DLB-176
Philosophical Library DLB-46
Phinney, Elihu [publishing house] DLB-49
Phoenix, John (see Derby, George Horatio)
PHYLON (Fourth Quarter, 1950),
  The Negro in Literature:
  The Current Scene DLB-76
Physiologus circa 1070-circa 1150 ...... DLB-148
Piccolo, Lucio 1903-1969 .... DLB-114
Pickard, Tom 1946- DLB-40
Pickering, William [publishing house] DLB-106
Pickthall, Marjorie 1883-1922 .... DLB-92
Pictorial Printing Company DLB-49

Piercy, Marge 1936- DLB-120, 227
Pierro, Albino 1916- DLB-128
Pignotti, Lamberto 1926- DLB-128
Pike, Albert 1809-1891 ....DLB-74
Pike, Zebulon Montgomery
    1779-1813 ....DLB-183
Pillat, Ion 1891-1945 ....DLB-220
Pilon, Jean-Guy 1930- DLB-60
Pinckney, Eliza Lucas 1722-1793 ....DLB-200
Pinckney, Josephine 1895-1957 ....DLB-6
Pindar circa 518 B.C.-circa 438 B.C.
    .... DLB-176; CDWLB-1
Pindar, Peter (see Wolcot, John)
Pineda, Cecile 1942- DLB-209
Pinero, Arthur Wing 1855-1934 ....DLB-10
Pinget, Robert 1919-1997...............DLB-83
Pinnacle Books.........................DLB-46
Piñon, Nélida 1935- DLB-145
Pinsky, Robert 1940- Y-82
Robert Pinsky Reappointed Poet Laureate ... Y-98
Pinter, Harold 1930- DLB-13; CDBLB-8
Piontek, Heinz 1925- DLB-75
Piozzi, Hester Lynch [Thrale]
    1741-1821 ....DLB-104, 142
Piper, H. Beam 1904-1964................DLB-8
Piper, Watty DLB-22
Pirckheimer, Caritas 1467-1532.........DLB-179
Pirckheimer, Willibald 1470-1530 ......DLB-179
Pisar, Samuel 1929- Y-83
Pisemsky, Aleksai Feofilaktovich
    1821-1881 ....DLB-238
Pitkin, Timothy 1766-1847 ....DLB-30
The Pitt Poetry Series: Poetry Publishing
    Today Y-85
Pitter, Ruth 1897- DLB-20
Pix, Mary 1666-1709 ....DLB-80
Pixerécourt, René Charles Guilbert de
    1773-1844 ....DLB-192
Plaatje, Sol T. 1876-1932 ....DLB-125, 225
Plante, David 1940- Y-83
Platen, August von 1796-1835 ....DLB-90
Plath, Sylvia
    1932-1963 ....DLB-5, 6, 152; CDALB-1
Plato circa 428 B.C.-348-347 B.C.
    .... DLB-176; CDWLB-1
Plato, Ann 1824?-?...................DLB-239
Platon 1737-1812 ....DLB-150
Platt and Munk Company...............DLB-46
Plautus circa 254 B.C.-184 B.C.
    .... DLB-211; CDWLB-1
Playboy Press.........................DLB-46
Playford, John [publishing house] DLB-170
Plays, Playwrights, and Playgoers DLB-84
Playwrights on the Theater DLB-80
Der Pleier flourished circa 1250.........DLB-138
Plenzdorf, Ulrich 1934- DLB-75
Plessen, Elizabeth 1944- DLB-75

Pletnev, Petr Aleksandrovich
    1792-1865 ....DLB-205
Pliekšāne, Elza Rozenberga (see Aspazija)
Pliekšāns, Jānis (see Rainis, Jānis)
Plievier, Theodor 1892-1955.............DLB-69
Plimpton, George 1927- DLB-185
Pliny the Elder A.D. 23/24-A.D. 79......DLB-211
Pliny the Younger
    circa A.D. 61-A.D. 112 ....DLB-211
Plomer, William
    1903-1973 ....DLB-20, 162, 191, 225
Plotinus 204-270.......... DLB-176; CDWLB-1
Plume, Thomas 1630-1704 ....DLB-213
Plumly, Stanley 1939- DLB-5, 193
Plumpp, Sterling D. 1940- DLB-41
Plunkett, James 1920- DLB-14
Plutarch
    circa 46-circa 120....... DLB-176; CDWLB-1
Plymell, Charles 1935- DLB-16
Pocket Books..........................DLB-46
Poe, Edgar Allan
    1809-1849 ......DLB-3, 59, 73, 74; CDALB-2
Poe, James 1921-1980 ....DLB-44
The Poet Laureate of the United States
    Statements from Former Consultants
    in Poetry Y-86
Pogodin, Mikhail Petrovich
    1800-1875 ....DLB-198
Pogorel'sky, Antonii
    (see Perovsky, Aleksei Alekseevich)
Pohl, Frederik 1919- DLB-8
Poirier, Louis (see Gracq, Julien)
Poláček, Karel 1892-1945 ... DLB-215; CDWLB-4
Polanyi, Michael 1891-1976............DLB-100
Pole, Reginald 1500-1558 ....DLB-132
Polevoi, Nikolai Alekseevich
    1796-1846 ....DLB-198
Polezhaev, Aleksandr Ivanovich
    1804-1838 ....DLB-205
Poliakoff, Stephen 1952- DLB-13
Polidori, John William 1795-1821 ......DLB-116
Polite, Carlene Hatcher 1932- DLB-33
Pollard, Alfred W. 1859-1944 ....DLB-201
Pollard, Edward A. 1832-1872...........DLB-30
Pollard, Graham 1903-1976.............DLB-201
Pollard, Percival 1869-1911 ....DLB-71
Pollard and Moss.....................DLB-49
Pollock, Sharon 1936- DLB-60
Polonsky, Abraham 1910-1999 ....DLB-26
Polotsky, Simeon 1629-1680 ....DLB-150
Polybius circa 200 B.C.-118 B.C. DLB-176
Pomialovsky, Nikolai Gerasimovich
    1835-1863 ....DLB-238
Pomilio, Mario 1921-1990.............DLB-177
Ponce, Mary Helen 1938- DLB-122
Ponce-Montoya, Juanita 1949- DLB-122
Ponet, John 1516?-1556................DLB-132

Poniatowski, Elena
    1933- DLB-113; CDWLB-3
Ponsard, François 1814-1867..........DLB-192
Ponsonby, William [publishing house] ... DLB-170
Pontiggia, Giuseppe 1934- DLB-196
Pony Stories.........................DLB-160
Poole, Ernest 1880-1950 ....DLB-9
Poole, Sophia 1804-1891 ....DLB-166
Poore, Benjamin Perley 1820-1887 ....DLB-23
Popa, Vasko 1922-1991..... DLB-181; CDWLB-4
Pope, Abbie Hanscom 1858-1894 ....DLB-140
Pope, Alexander
    1688-1744 ......DLB-95, 101, 213; CDBLB-2
Popov, Mikhail Ivanovich
    1742-circa 1790 ....DLB-150
Popović, Aleksandar 1929-1996 ....DLB-181
Popular Library......................DLB-46
Porete, Marguerite ?-1310 ....DLB-208
Porlock, Martin (see MacDonald, Philip)
Porpoise Press DLB-112
Porta, Antonio 1935-1989 ....DLB-128
Porter, Anna Maria 1780-1832 .....DLB-116, 159
Porter, David 1780-1843 ....DLB-183
Porter, Eleanor H. 1868-1920 ....DLB-9
Porter, Gene Stratton (see Stratton-Porter, Gene)
Porter, Henry ?-?.....................DLB-62
Porter, Jane 1776-1850............DLB-116, 159
Porter, Katherine Anne 1890-1980
    ...... DLB-4, 9, 102; Y-80; DS-12; CDALB-7
Porter, Peter 1929- DLB-40
Porter, William Sydney
    1862-1910 ....DLB-12, 78, 79; CDALB-3
Porter, William T. 1809-1858 ....DLB-3, 43
Porter and Coates DLB-49
Portillo Trambley, Estela 1927-1998 ....DLB-209
Portis, Charles 1933- DLB-6
Posey, Alexander 1873-1908 ....DLB-175
Postans, Marianne circa 1810-1865 .....DLB-166
Postl, Carl (see Sealsfield, Carl)
Poston, Ted 1906-1974 ....DLB-51
Potekhin, Aleksei Antipovich 1829-1908..DLB-238
Potok, Chaim 1929- DLB-28, 152
A Conversation with Chaim Potok Y-84
Potter, Beatrix 1866-1943 ....DLB-141
Potter, David M. 1910-1971............DLB-17
Potter, Dennis 1935-1994 ....DLB-233
The Harry Potter Phenomenon............Y-99
Potter, John E., and Company...........DLB-49
Pottle, Frederick A. 1897-1987 ..... DLB-103; Y-87
Poulin, Jacques 1937- DLB-60
Pound, Ezra 1885-1972
    ....DLB-4, 45, 63; DS-15; CDALB-4
Poverman, C. E. 1944- DLB-234
Povich, Shirley 1905-1998.............DLB-171
Powell, Anthony 1905- DLB-15; CDBLB-7

Cumulative Index

Dawn Powell, Where Have You Been All Our Lives?.................... Y-97
Powell, John Wesley 1834-1902....... DLB-186
Powell, Padgett 1952- DLB-234
Powers, J. F. 1917-1999............. DLB-130
Pownall, David 1938- DLB-14
Powys, John Cowper 1872-1963........ DLB-15
Powys, Llewelyn 1884-1939........... DLB-98
Powys, T. F. 1875-1953........... DLB-36, 162
Poynter, Nelson 1903-1978........... DLB-127
The Practice of Biography: An Interview with Stanley Weintraub.............. Y-82
The Practice of Biography II: An Interview with B. L. Reid.................. Y-83
The Practice of Biography III: An Interview with Humphrey Carpenter........... Y-84
The Practice of Biography IV: An Interview with William Manchester............ Y-85
The Practice of Biography VI: An Interview with David Herbert Donald......... Y-87
The Practice of Biography VII: An Interview with John Caldwell Guilds........ Y-92
The Practice of Biography VIII: An Interview with Joan Mellen................ Y-94
The Practice of Biography IX: An Interview with Michael Reynolds............ Y-95
Prados, Emilio 1899-1962............ DLB-134
Praed, Mrs. Caroline (see Praed, Rosa)
Praed, Rosa (Mrs. Caroline Praed) 1851-1935..................... DLB-230
Praed, Winthrop Mackworth 1802-1839 .. DLB-96
Praeger Publishers................. DLB-46
Praetorius, Johannes 1630-1680...... DLB-168
Pratolini, Vasco 1913-1991..........DLB-177
Pratt, E. J. 1882-1964.............. DLB-92
Pratt, Samuel Jackson 1749-1814..... DLB-39
Preciado Martin, Patricia 1939- DLB-209
Preface to *The History of Romances* (1715), by Pierre Daniel Huet [excerpts]........ DLB-39
Préfontaine, Yves 1937- DLB-53
Prelutsky, Jack 1940- DLB-61
Premisses, by Michael Hamburger..... DLB-66
Prentice, George D. 1802-1870....... DLB-43
Prentice-Hall...................... DLB-46
Prescott, Orville 1906-1996......... Y-96
Prescott, William Hickling 1796-1859............ DLB-1, 30, 59, 235
The Present State of the English Novel (1892), by George Saintsbury............... DLB-18
Prešeren, Francè 1800-1849............ DLB-147; CDWLB-4
Preston, Margaret Junkin 1820-1897.... DLB-239
Preston, May Wilson 1873-1949....... DLB-188
Preston, Thomas 1537-1598........... DLB-62
Price, Reynolds 1933- DLB-2, 218
Price, Richard 1723-1791............ DLB-158
Price, Richard 1949- Y-81
Prideaux, John 1578-1650............ DLB-236
Priest, Christopher 1943- DLB-14, 207

Priestley, J. B. 1894-1984 .... DLB-10, 34, 77, 100, 139; Y-84; CDBLB-6
Primary Bibliography: A Retrospective...... Y-95
Prime, Benjamin Young 1733-1791....... DLB-31
Primrose, Diana floruit circa 1630...... DLB-126
Prince, F. T. 1912- DLB-20
Prince, Nancy Gardner 1799-?........ DLB-239
Prince, Thomas 1687-1758........ DLB-24, 140
Pringle, Thomas 1789-1834........... DLB-225
Printz, Wolfgang Casper 1641-1717..... DLB-168
Prior, Matthew 1664-1721............ DLB-95
Prisco, Michele 1920- DLB-177
Pritchard, William H. 1932- DLB-111
Pritchett, V. S. 1900-1997....... DLB-15, 139
Probyn, May 1856 or 1857-1909....... DLB-199
Procter, Adelaide Anne 1825-1864... DLB-32, 199
Procter, Bryan Waller 1787-1874 .... DLB-96, 144
Proctor, Robert 1868-1903........... DLB-184
Producing Dear Bunny, Dear Volodya: The Friendship and the Feud........................ Y-97
The Profession of Authorship: Scribblers for Bread................. Y-89
Prokopovich, Feofan 1681?-1736....... DLB-150
Prokosch, Frederic 1906-1989........ DLB-48
The Proletarian Novel............... DLB-9
Pronzini, Bill 1943- DLB-226
Propertius circa 50 B.C.-post 16 B.C. DLB-211; CDWLB-1
Propper, Dan 1937- DLB-16
Prose, Francine 1947- DLB-234
Protagoras circa 490 B.C.-420 B.C........DLB-176
Proud, Robert 1728-1813............. DLB-30
Proust, Marcel 1871-1922............ DLB-65
Prynne, J. H. 1936- DLB-40
Przybyszewski, Stanislaw 1868-1927..... DLB-66
Pseudo-Dionysius the Areopagite floruit circa 500..................... DLB-115
Public Domain and the Violation of Texts.... Y-97
The Public Lending Right in America Statement by Sen. Charles McC. Mathias, Jr. PLR and the Meaning of Literary Property Statements on PLR by American Writers............. Y-83
The Public Lending Right in the United Kingdom Public Lending Right: The First Year in the United Kingdom.................... Y-83
The Publication of English Renaissance Plays................ DLB-62
Publications and Social Movements [Transcendentalism]................ DLB-1
Publishers and Agents: The Columbia Connection...................... Y-87
Publishing Fiction at LSU Press............ Y-87
The Publishing Industry in 1998: Sturm-und-drang.com................ Y-98
The Publishing Industry in 1999.......Y-99
Pückler-Muskau, Hermann von 1785-1871.....................DLB-133
Pufendorf, Samuel von 1632-1694..... DLB-168
Pugh, Edwin William 1874-1930....... DLB-135

Pugin, A. Welby 1812-1852........... DLB-55
Puig, Manuel 1932-1990.....DLB-113; CDWLB-3
Pulitzer, Joseph 1847-1911.......... DLB-23
Pulitzer, Joseph, Jr. 1885-1955..... DLB-29
Pulitzer Prizes for the Novel, 1917-1945.... DLB-9
Pulliam, Eugene 1889-1975...........DLB-127
Purchas, Samuel 1577?-1626.......... DLB-151
Purdy, Al 1918- DLB-88
Purdy, James 1923- DLB-2, 218
Purdy, Ken W. 1913-1972   ....DLB-137
Pusey, Edward Bouverie 1800-1882...... DLB-55
Pushkin, Aleksandr Sergeevich 1799-1837..................... DLB-205
Pushkin, Vasilii L'vovich 1766-1830 .... DLB-205
Putnam, George Palmer 1814-1872.....DLB-3, 79
Putnam, Samuel 1892-1950............ DLB-4
G. P. Putnam's Sons [U.K.]......... DLB-106
G. P. Putnam's Sons [U.S.]......... DLB-49
A Publisher's Archives: G. P. Putnam....... Y-92
Puzo, Mario 1920-1999............... DLB-6
Pyle, Ernie 1900-1945............... DLB-29
Pyle, Howard 1853-1911 .... DLB-42, 188; DS-13
Pym, Barbara 1913-1980 ......DLB-14, 207; Y-87
Pynchon, Thomas 1937- DLB-2, 173
Pyramid Books...................... DLB-46
Pyrnelle, Louise-Clarke 1850-1907...... DLB-42
Pythagoras circa 570 B.C.-?..........DLB-176

Q

Quad, M. (see Lewis, Charles B.)
Quaritch, Bernard 1819-1899......... DLB-184
Quarles, Francis 1592-1644.......... DLB-126
The Quarterly Review 1809-1967...... DLB-110
Quasimodo, Salvatore 1901-1968...... DLB-114
Queen, Ellery (see Dannay, Frederic, and Manfred B. Lee)
The Queen City Publishing House...... DLB-49
Queneau, Raymond 1903-1976......... DLB-72
Quennell, Sir Peter 1905-1993..... DLB-155, 195
Quesnel, Joseph 1746-1809............ DLB-99
The Question of American Copyright in the Nineteenth Century
  Preface, by George Haven Putnam
  The Evolution of Copyright, by Brander Matthews
  Summary of Copyright Legislation in the United States, by R. R. Bowker
  Analysis of the Provisions of the Copyright Law of 1891, by George Haven Putnam
  The Contest for International Copyright, by George Haven Putnam
  Cheap Books and Good Books, by Brander Matthews.......... DLB-49
Quiller-Couch, Sir Arthur Thomas 1863-1944 ....DLB-135, 153, 190
Quin, Ann 1936-1973............. DLB-14, 231
Quincy, Samuel, of Georgia ?-?......... DLB-31
Quincy, Samuel, of Massachusetts 1734-1789..................... DLB-31

418

Quinn, Anthony 1915- DLB-122
Quinn, John 1870-1924 ....DLB-187
Quiñónez, Naomi 1951- DLB-209
Quintana, Leroy V. 1944- DLB-82
Quintana, Miguel de 1671-1748
   A Forerunner of Chicano Literature ..DLB-122
Quintillian
   circa A.D. 40-circa A.D. 96 ....DLB-211
Quintus Curtius Rufus fl. A.D. 35 ....DLB-211
Quist, Harlin, Books DLB-46
Quoirez, Françoise (see Sagan, Françoise)

R

R-va, Zeneida (see Gan, Elena Andreevna)
Raabe, Wilhelm 1831-1910 ....DLB-129
Raban, Jonathan 1942- DLB-204
Rabe, David 1940- DLB-7, 228
Raboni, Giovanni 1932- DLB-128
Rachilde 1860-1953 ....DLB-123, 192
Racin, Kočo 1908-1943 ....DLB-147
Rackham, Arthur 1867-1939 ....DLB-141
Radauskas, Henrikas
   1910-1970 ....DLB-220; CDWLB-4
Radcliffe, Ann 1764-1823 ....DLB-39, 178
Raddall, Thomas 1903- DLB-68
Radford, Dollie 1858-1920 ....DLB-240
Radichkov, Yordan 1929- DLB-181
Radiguet, Raymond 1903-1923 ....DLB-65
Radishchev, Aleksandr Nikolaevich
   1749-1802 ....DLB-150
Radnóti, Miklós
   1909-1944 ....DLB-215; CDWLB-4
Radványi, Netty Reiling (see Seghers, Anna)
Rahv, Philip 1908-1973 ....DLB-137
Raich, Semen Egorovich 1792-1855 .....DLB-205
Raičković, Stevan 1928- DLB-181
Raimund, Ferdinand Jakob 1790-1836 ....DLB-90
Raine, Craig 1944- DLB-40
Raine, Kathleen 1908- DLB-20
Rainis, Jānis 1865-1929 ....DLB-220; CDWLB-4
Rainolde, Richard
   circa 1530-1606 ....DLB-136, 236
Rakić, Milan 1876-1938 .....DLB-147; CDWLB-4
Rakosi, Carl 1903- DLB-193
Ralegh, Sir Walter
   1554?-1618 ....DLB-172; CDBLB-1
Ralin, Radoy 1923- DLB-181
Ralph, Julian 1853-1903 ....DLB-23
Ramat, Silvio 1939- DLB-128
Rambler, no. 4 (1750), by Samuel Johnson
   [excerpt] DLB-39
Ramée, Marie Louise de la (see Ouida)
Ramírez, Sergío 1942- DLB-145
Ramke, Bin 1947- DLB-120
Ramler, Karl Wilhelm 1725-1798 ....DLB-97
Ramon Ribeyro, Julio 1929- DLB-145
Ramos, Manuel 1948- DLB-209

Ramous, Mario 1924- DLB-128
Rampersad, Arnold 1941- DLB-111
Ramsay, Allan 1684 or 1685-1758 ....DLB-95
Ramsay, David 1749-1815 ....DLB-30
Ramsay, Martha Laurens 1759-1811 .....DLB-200
Ranck, Katherine Quintana 1942- DLB-122
Rand, Avery and Company DLB-49
Rand, Ayn 1905-1982 ....DLB-227; CDALB-7
Rand McNally and Company DLB-49
Randall, David Anton 1905-1975 ....DLB-140
Randall, Dudley 1914- DLB-41
Randall, Henry S. 1811-1876 ....DLB-30
Randall, James G. 1881-1953 ....DLB-17
The Randall Jarrell Symposium:
   A Small Collection of Randall Jarrells
   Excerpts From Papers Delivered at the
   Randall Jarrel Symposium Y-86
Randolph, A. Philip 1889-1979 ....DLB-91
Randolph, Anson D. F.
   [publishing house] DLB-49
Randolph, Thomas 1605-1635 .....DLB-58, 126
Random House DLB-46
Ranlet, Henry [publishing house] DLB-49
Ransom, Harry 1908-1976 ....DLB-187
Ransom, John Crowe
   1888-1974 ....DLB-45, 63; CDALB-7
Ransome, Arthur 1884-1967 ....DLB-160
Raphael, Frederic 1931- DLB-14
Raphaelson, Samson 1896-1983 ....DLB-44
Rashi circa 1040-1105 ....DLB-208
Raskin, Ellen 1928-1984 ....DLB-52
Rastell, John 1475?-1536 ....DLB-136, 170
Rattigan, Terence
   1911-1977 ....DLB-13; CDBLB-7
Rawlings, Marjorie Kinnan 1896-1953
   ....DLB-9, 22, 102; DS-17; CDALB-7
Rawlinson, Richard 1690-1755 ....DLB-213
Rawlinson, Thomas 1681-1725 ....DLB-213
Raworth, Tom 1938- DLB-40
Ray, David 1932- DLB-5
Ray, Gordon Norton 1915-1986 ....DLB-103, 140
Ray, Henrietta Cordelia 1849-1916 ......DLB-50
Raymond, Ernest 1888-1974 ....DLB-191
Raymond, Henry J. 1820-1869 ......DLB-43, 79
Michael M. Rea and the Rea Award for the
   Short Story Y-97
Reach, Angus 1821-1856 ....DLB-70
Read, Herbert 1893-1968 ....DLB-20, 149
Read, Herbert, "The Practice of Biography," in
   *The English Sense of Humour and
   Other Essays* DLB-149
Read, Martha Meredith DLB-200
Read, Opie 1852-1939 ....DLB-23
Read, Piers Paul 1941- DLB-14
Reade, Charles 1814-1884 ....DLB-21
Reader's Digest Condensed Books DLB-46
Readers Ulysses Symposium Y-97

Reading, Peter 1946- DLB-40
Reading Series in New York City Y-96
The Reality of One Woman's Dream:
   The de Grummond Children's
   Literature Collection Y-99
Reaney, James 1926- DLB-68
Rebhun, Paul 1500?-1546 ....DLB-179
Rèbora, Clemente 1885-1957 ....DLB-114
Rebreanu, Liviu 1885-1944 ....DLB-220
Rechy, John 1934- DLB-122; Y-82
The Recovery of Literature:
   Criticism in the 1990s: A Symposium Y-91
Redding, J. Saunders 1906-1988 ......DLB-63, 76
Redfield, J. S. [publishing house] DLB-49
Redgrove, Peter 1932- DLB-40
Redmon, Anne 1943- Y-86
Redmond, Eugene B. 1937- DLB-41
Redpath, James [publishing house] DLB-49
Reed, Henry 1808-1854 ....DLB-59
Reed, Henry 1914- DLB-27
Reed, Ishmael
   1938- DLB-2, 5, 33, 169, 227; DS-8
Reed, Rex 1938- DLB-185
Reed, Sampson 1800-1880 ....DLB-1, 235
Reed, Talbot Baines 1852-1893 ....DLB-141
Reedy, William Marion 1862-1920 ....DLB-91
Reese, Lizette Woodworth 1856-1935 .....DLB-54
Reese, Thomas 1742-1796 ....DLB-37
Reeve, Clara 1729-1807 ....DLB-39
   Preface to *The Old English Baron* (1778) DLB-39
   The Progress of Romance (1785) [excerpt] DLB-39
Reeves, James 1909-1978 ....DLB-161
Reeves, John 1926- DLB-88
"Reflections: After a Tornado,"
   by Judson Jerome DLB-105
Regnery, Henry, Company DLB-46
Rehberg, Hans 1901-1963 ....DLB-124
Rehfisch, Hans José 1891-1960 ....DLB-124
Reich, Ebbe Kløvedal 1940- DLB-214
Reid, Alastair 1926- DLB-27
Reid, B. L. 1918-1990 ....DLB-111
The Practice of Biography II:
   An Interview with B. L. Reid Y-83
Reid, Christopher 1949- DLB-40
Reid, Forrest 1875-1947 ....DLB-153
Reid, Helen Rogers 1882-1970 ....DLB-29
Reid, James ?-? DLB-31
Reid, Mayne 1818-1883 ....DLB-21, 163
Reid, Thomas 1710-1796 ....DLB-31
Reid, V. S. (Vic) 1913-1987 ....DLB-125
Reid, Whitelaw 1837-1912 ....DLB-23
Reilly and Lee Publishing Company DLB-46
Reimann, Brigitte 1933-1973 ....DLB-75
Reinmar der Alte
   circa 1165-circa 1205 ....DLB-138
Reinmar von Zweter
   circa 1200-circa 1250 ....DLB-138

Cumulative Index

Reisch, Walter 1903-1983 . . . . DLB-44

Reizei Family DLB-203

Remarks at the Opening of "The Biographical Part of Literature" Exhibition, by William R. Cagle Y-98

Remarque, Erich Maria 1898-1970 . . . . DLB-56; CDWLB-2

Remington, Frederic 1861-1909 . . . . DLB-12, 186, 188

Reminiscences, by Charles Scribner Jr. DS-17

Renaud, Jacques 1943- DLB-60

Renault, Mary 1905-1983 . . . . Y-83

Rendell, Ruth 1930- DLB-87

Rensselaer, Maria van Cortlandt van 1645-1689 . . . . DLB-200

Repplier, Agnes 1855-1950 . . . . DLB-221

Representative Men and Women: A Historical Perspective on the British Novel, 1930-1960 . . . . DLB-15

Research in the American Antiquarian Book Trade Y-97

Reshetnikov, Fedor Mikhailovich 1841-1871 . . . . DLB-238

Rettenbacher, Simon 1634-1706 . . . . DLB-168

Reuchlin, Johannes 1455-1522 . . . . DLB-179

Reuter, Christian 1665-after 1712 . . . . DLB-168

Revell, Fleming H., Company DLB-49

Reuter, Fritz 1810-1874 . . . . DLB-129

Reuter, Gabriele 1859-1941 . . . . DLB-66

Reventlow, Franziska Gräfin zu 1871-1918 . . . . DLB-66

Review of Reviews Office DLB-112

Review of [Samuel Richardson's] Clarissa (1748), by Henry Fielding DLB-39

The Revolt (1937), by Mary Colum [excerpts] DLB-36

Rexroth, Kenneth 1905-1982 . . . . DLB-16, 48, 165, 212; Y-82; CDALB-1

Rey, H. A. 1898-1977 . . . . DLB-22

Reynal and Hitchcock DLB-46

Reynolds, G. W. M. 1814-1879 . . . . DLB-21

Reynolds, John Hamilton 1794-1852 . . . . DLB-96

Reynolds, Sir Joshua 1723-1792 . . . . DLB-104

Reynolds, Mack 1917- DLB-8

A Literary Archaelogist Digs On: A Brief Interview with Michael Reynolds by Michael Rogers Y-99

Reznikoff, Charles 1894-1976 . . . . DLB-28, 45

Rhett, Robert Barnwell 1800-1876 . . . . . . DLB-43

Rhode, John 1884-1964 . . . . DLB-77

Rhodes, James Ford 1848-1927 . . . . DLB-47

Rhodes, Richard 1937- DLB-185

Rhys, Jean 1890-1979
. . . . . DLB-36, 117, 162; CDBLB-7; CDWLB-3

Ricardo, David 1772-1823 . . . . DLB-107, 158

Ricardou, Jean 1932- DLB-83

Rice, Elmer 1892-1967 . . . . DLB-4, 7

Rice, Grantland 1880-1954 . . . . DLB-29, 171

Rich, Adrienne 1929- DLB-5, 67; CDALB-7

Richard de Fournival 1201-1259 or 1260 . . . . DLB-208

Richard, Mark 1955- DLB-234

Richards, David Adams 1950- DLB-53

Richards, George circa 1760-1814 . . . . . . DLB-37

Richards, Grant [publishing house] DLB-112

Richards, I. A. 1893-1979 . . . . DLB-27

Richards, Laura E. 1850-1943 . . . . DLB-42

Richards, William Carey 1818-1892 . . . . DLB-73

Richardson, Charles F. 1851-1913 . . . . . . DLB-71

Richardson, Dorothy M. 1873-1957 . . . . . DLB-36

Richardson, Henry Handel (Ethel Florence Lindesay Robertson) 1870-1946 . . . . DLB-197, 230

Richardson, Jack 1935- DLB-7

Richardson, John 1796-1852 . . . . DLB-99

Richardson, Samuel 1689-1761 . . . . DLB-39, 154; CDBLB-2

Introductory Letters from the Second Edition of Pamela (1741) DLB-39

Postscript to [the Third Edition of] Clarissa (1751) DLB-39

Preface to the First Edition of Pamela (1740) DLB-39

Preface to the Third Edition of Clarissa (1751) [excerpt] DLB-39

Preface to Volume 1 of Clarissa (1747) DLB-39

Preface to Volume 3 of Clarissa (1748) DLB-39

Richardson, Willis 1889-1977 . . . . DLB-51

Riche, Barnabe 1542-1617 . . . . DLB-136

Richepin, Jean 1849-1926 . . . . DLB-192

Richler, Mordecai 1931- DLB-53

Richter, Conrad 1890-1968 . . . . DLB-9, 212

Richter, Hans Werner 1908- DLB-69

Richter, Johann Paul Friedrich 1763-1825 . . . . DLB-94; CDWLB-2

Rickerby, Joseph [publishing house] DLB-106

Rickword, Edgell 1898-1982 . . . . DLB-20

Riddell, Charlotte 1832-1906 . . . . DLB-156

Riddell, John (see Ford, Corey)

Ridge, John Rollin 1827-1867 . . . . DLB-175

Ridge, Lola 1873-1941 . . . . DLB-54

Ridge, William Pett 1859-1930 . . . . DLB-135

Riding, Laura (see Jackson, Laura Riding)

Ridler, Anne 1912- DLB-27

Ridruejo, Dionisio 1912-1975 . . . . DLB-108

Riel, Louis 1844-1885 . . . . DLB-99

Riemer, Johannes 1648-1714 . . . . DLB-168

Rifbjerg, Klaus 1931- DLB-214

Riffaterre, Michael 1924- DLB-67

Riggs, Lynn 1899-1954 . . . . DLB-175

Riis, Jacob 1849-1914 . . . . DLB-23

Riker, John C. [publishing house] DLB-49

Riley, James 1777-1840 . . . . DLB-183

Riley, John 1938-1978 . . . . DLB-40

Rilke, Rainer Maria 1875-1926 . . . . DLB-81; CDWLB-2

Rimanelli, Giose 1926- DLB-177

Rimbaud, Jean-Nicolas-Arthur 1854-1891 . . . . DLB-217

Rinehart and Company DLB-46

Ringuet 1895-1960 . . . . DLB-68

Ringwood, Gwen Pharis 1910-1984 . . . . . DLB-88

Rinser, Luise 1911- DLB-69

Ríos, Alberto 1952- DLB-122

Ríos, Isabella 1948- DLB-82

Ripley, Arthur 1895-1961 . . . . DLB-44

Ripley, George 1802-1880 . . . . . DLB-1, 64, 73, 235

The Rising Glory of America: Three Poems DLB-37

The Rising Glory of America: Written in 1771 (1786), by Hugh Henry Brackenridge and Philip Freneau DLB-37

Riskin, Robert 1897-1955 . . . . DLB-26

Risse, Heinz 1898- DLB-69

Rist, Johann 1607-1667 . . . . DLB-164

Ristikivi, Karl 1912-1977 . . . . DLB-220

Ritchie, Anna Mowatt 1819-1870 . . . . DLB-3

Ritchie, Anne Thackeray 1837-1919 . . . . . DLB-18

Ritchie, Thomas 1778-1854 . . . . DLB-43

Rites of Passage [on William Saroyan] Y-83

The Ritz Paris Hemingway Award Y-85

Rivard, Adjutor 1868-1945 . . . . DLB-92

Rive, Richard 1931-1989 . . . . DLB-125, 225

Rivera, Marina 1942- DLB-122

Rivera, Tomás 1935-1984 . . . . DLB-82

Rivers, Conrad Kent 1933-1968 . . . . DLB-41

Riverside Press DLB-49

Rivington, Charles [publishing house] . . . DLB-154

Rivington, James circa 1724-1802 . . . . DLB-43

Rivkin, Allen 1903-1990 . . . . DLB-26

Roa Bastos, Augusto 1917- DLB-113

Robbe-Grillet, Alain 1922- DLB-83

Robbins, Tom 1936- Y-80

Roberts, Charles G. D. 1860-1943 . . . . . . DLB-92

Roberts, Dorothy 1906-1993 . . . . DLB-88

Roberts, Elizabeth Madox 1881-1941 . . . . DLB-9, 54, 102

Roberts, James [publishing house] DLB-154

Roberts, Kenneth 1885-1957 . . . . DLB-9

Roberts, Michèle 1949- DLB-231

Roberts, Ursula Wyllie (see Miles, Susan)

Roberts, William 1767-1849 . . . . DLB-142

Roberts Brothers DLB-49

Robertson, A. M., and Company DLB-49

Robertson, Ethel Florence Lindesay (see Richardson, Henry Handel)

Robertson, William 1721-1793 . . . . DLB-104

Robins, Elizabeth 1862-1952 . . . . DLB-197

Robinson, A. Mary F. (Madame James Darmesteter, Madame Mary Duclaux) 1857-1944 . . . . DLB-240

Robinson, Casey 1903-1979 . . . . DLB-44

Robinson, Edwin Arlington 1869-1935 . . . . .DLB-54; CDALB-3	Rosa, João Guimarães 1908-1967. . . . . . .DLB-113	Rowson, Susanna Haswell circa 1762-1824 . . . . DLB-37, 200
Robinson, Henry Crabb 1775-1867 . . . . . . DLB-107	Rosales, Luis 1910-1992 . . . . .DLB-134	Roy, Camille 1870-1943 . . . . .DLB-92
Robinson, James Harvey 1863-1936 . . . . . .DLB-47	Roscoe, William 1753-1831 . . . . .DLB-163	Roy, Gabrielle 1909-1983 . . . . .DLB-68
Robinson, Lennox 1886-1958 . . . . .DLB-10	Danis Rose and the Rendering of *Ulysses* Y-97	Roy, Jules 1907- DLB-83
Robinson, Mabel Louise 1874-1962. . . . . . .DLB-22	Rose, Reginald 1920- DLB-26	The G. Ross Roy Scottish Poetry Collection at the University of South Carolina Y-89
Robinson, Marilynne 1943- DLB-206	Rose, Wendy 1948- DLB-175	
Robinson, Mary 1758-1800 . . . . .DLB-158	Rosegger, Peter 1843-1918 . . . . .DLB-129	The Royal Court Theatre and the English Stage Company. DLB-13
Robinson, Richard circa 1545-1607 . . . . . .DLB-167	Rosei, Peter 1946- DLB-85	
Robinson, Therese 1797-1870. . . . . . .DLB-59, 133	Rosen, Norma 1925- DLB-28	The Royal Court Theatre and the New Drama. DLB-10
Robison, Mary 1949- DLB-130	Rosenbach, A. S. W. 1876-1952. . . . . .DLB-140	
Roblès, Emmanuel 1914-1995 . . . . .DLB-83	Rosenbaum, Ron 1946- DLB-185	The Royal Shakespeare Company at the Swan Y-88
Roccatagliata Ceccardi, Ceccardo 1871-1919 . . . . .DLB-114	Rosenberg, Isaac 1890-1918 . . . . .DLB-20, 216	Royall, Anne 1769-1854. . . . . .DLB-43
	Rosenfeld, Isaac 1918-1956 . . . . .DLB-28	The Roycroft Printing Shop DLB-49
Roche, Billy 1949- DLB-233	Rosenthal, M. L. 1917-1996. . . . . .DLB-5	Royde-Smith, Naomi 1875-1964 . . . . .DLB-191
Rochester, John Wilmot, Earl of 1647-1680 . . . . .DLB-131	Rosenwald, Lessing J. 1891-1979. . . . . . . .DLB-187	Royster, Vermont 1914- DLB-127
	Ross, Alexander 1591-1654. . . . . .DLB-151	Royston, Richard [publishing house]. DLB-170
Rock, Howard 1911-1976 . . . . .DLB-127	Ross, Harold 1892-1951 . . . . .DLB-137	Różewicz, Tadeusz 1921- DLB-232
Rockwell, Norman Perceval 1894-1978. . .DLB-188	Ross, Leonard Q. (see Rosten, Leo)	Ruark, Gibbons 1941- DLB-120
Rodgers, Carolyn M. 1945- DLB-41	Ross, Lillian 1927- DLB-185	Ruban, Vasilii Grigorevich 1742-1795. . . .DLB-150
Rodgers, W. R. 1909-1969 . . . . .DLB-20	Ross, Martin 1862-1915. . . . . .DLB-135	Rubens, Bernice 1928- DLB-14, 207
Rodríguez, Claudio 1934-1999 . . . . .DLB-134	Ross, Sinclair 1908- DLB-88	Rudd and Carleton DLB-49
Rodríguez, Joe D. 1943- DLB-209	Ross, W. W. E. 1894-1966 . . . . .DLB-88	Rudd, Steele (Arthur Hoey Davis) DLB-230
Rodríguez, Luis J. 1954- DLB-209	Rosselli, Amelia 1930-1996 . . . . .DLB-128	Rudkin, David 1936- DLB-13
Rodriguez, Richard 1944- DLB-82	Rossen, Robert 1908-1966. . . . . .DLB-26	Rudolf von Ems circa 1200-circa 1254 . . .DLB-138
Rodríguez Julia, Edgardo 1946- DLB-145	Rossetti, Christina 1830-1894 . . .DLB-35, 163, 240	Ruffin, Josephine St. Pierre 1842-1924 . . . . .DLB-79
Roe, E. P. 1838-1888 . . . . .DLB-202	Rossetti, Dante Gabriel 1828-1882 . . . . DLB-35; CDBLB-4	
Roethke, Theodore 1908-1963 . . . . .DLB-5, 206; CDALB-1		Ruganda, John 1941- DLB-157
	Rossner, Judith 1935- DLB-6	Ruggles, Henry Joseph 1813-1906. . . . . . .DLB-64
Rogers, Jane 1952- DLB-194	Rostand, Edmond 1868-1918 . . . . .DLB-192	Ruiz de Burton, María Amparo 1832-1895 . . . . .DLB-209, 221
Rogers, Pattiann 1940- DLB-105	Rosten, Leo 1908-1997 . . . . .DLB-11	
Rogers, Samuel 1763-1855 . . . . .DLB-93	Rostenberg, Leona 1908- DLB-140	Rukeyser, Muriel 1913-1980 . . . . .DLB-48
Rogers, Will 1879-1935 . . . . .DLB-11	Rostopchina, Evdokiia Petrovna 1811-1858 . . . . .DLB-205	Rule, Jane 1931- .DLB-60
Rohmer, Sax 1883-1959 . . . . .DLB-70		Rulfo, Juan 1918-1986. . . . . . .DLB-113; CDWLB-3
Roiphe, Anne 1935- Y-80	Rostovsky, Dimitrii 1651-1709 . . . . .DLB-150	Rumaker, Michael 1932- DLB-16
Rojas, Arnold R. 1896-1988 . . . . .DLB-82	Rota, Bertram 1903-1966. . . . . .DLB-201	Rumens, Carol 1944- DLB-40
Rolfe, Frederick William 1860-1913 . . . . .DLB-34, 156	Bertram Rota and His Bookshop. Y-91	Rummo, Paul-Eerik 1942- DLB-232
	Roth, Gerhard 1942- DLB-85, 124	Runyon, Damon 1880-1946 . . . . . DLB-11, 86, 171
Rolland, Romain 1866-1944 . . . . .DLB-65	Roth, Henry 1906?-1995 . . . . .DLB-28	Ruodlieb circa 1050-1075. . . . . .DLB-148
Rolle, Richard circa 1290-1300 - 1340. . . .DLB-146	Roth, Joseph 1894-1939 . . . . .DLB-85	Rush, Benjamin 1746-1813 . . . . .DLB-37
Rölvaag, O. E. 1876-1931 . . . . .DLB-9, 212	Roth, Philip 1933- DLB-2, 28, 173; Y-82; CDALB-6	Rush, Rebecca 1779-? DLB-200
Romains, Jules 1885-1972 . . . . .DLB-65		Rushdie, Salman 1947- DLB-194
Roman, A., and Company. DLB-49	Rothenberg, Jerome 1931- DLB-5, 193	Rusk, Ralph L. 1888-1962 . . . . .DLB-103
Roman de la Rose: Guillaume de Lorris 1200 to 1205-circa 1230, Jean de Meun 1235-1240-circa 1305 . . . . .DLB-208	Rothschild Family DLB-184	Ruskin, John 1819-1900 . . . . . . DLB-55, 163, 190; CDBLB-4
	Rotimi, Ola 1938- DLB-125	
	Routhier, Adolphe-Basile 1839-1920 . . . . .DLB-99	Russ, Joanna 1937- DLB-8
Romano, Lalla 1906- DLB-177	Routier, Simone 1901-1987 . . . . .DLB-88	Russell, B. B., and Company. DLB-49
Romano, Octavio 1923- DLB-122	Routledge, George, and Sons. DLB-106	Russell, Benjamin 1761-1845 . . . . .DLB-43
Romero, Leo 1950- DLB-122	Roversi, Roberto 1923- DLB-128	Russell, Bertrand 1872-1970. . . . . .DLB-100
Romero, Lin 1947- DLB-122	Rowe, Elizabeth Singer 1674-1737 . . . . .DLB-39, 95	Russell, Charles Edward 1860-1941 . . . . . .DLB-25
Romero, Orlando 1945- DLB-82	Rowe, Nicholas 1674-1718 . . . . .DLB-84	Russell, Charles M. 1864-1926 . . . . .DLB-188
Rook, Clarence 1863-1915 . . . . .DLB-135	Rowlands, Samuel circa 1570-1630 . . . . . .DLB-121	Russell, George William (see AE)
Roosevelt, Theodore 1858-1919 . . . . . DLB-47, 186	Rowlandson, Mary circa 1637-circa 1711 . . . . .DLB-24, 200	Russell, Countess Mary Annette Beauchamp (see Arnim, Elizabeth von)
Root, Waverley 1903-1982 . . . . .DLB-4		
Root, William Pitt 1941- DLB-120	Rowley, William circa 1585-1626 . . . . . . .DLB-58	Russell, R. H., and Son DLB-49
Roquebrune, Robert de 1889-1978 . . . . . . .DLB-68	Rowse, A. L. 1903-1997 . . . . .DLB-155	Russell, Willy 1947- DLB-233

Rutebeuf flourished 1249-1277 . . . . DLB-208
Rutherford, Mark 1831-1913 . . . . DLB-18
Ruxton, George Frederick 1821-1848 . . . DLB-186
Ryan, Michael 1946- Y-82
Ryan, Oscar 1904- DLB-68
Ryga, George 1932- DLB-60
Rylands, Enriqueta Augustina Tennant
 1843-1908 . . . . DLB-184
Rylands, John 1801-1888 . . . . DLB-184
Ryleev, Kondratii Fedorovich
 1795-1826 . . . . DLB-205
Rymer, Thomas 1643?-1713 . . . . DLB-101
Ryskind, Morrie 1895-1985 . . . . DLB-26
Rzhevsky, Aleksei Andreevich
 1737-1804 . . . . DLB-150

S

The Saalfield Publishing Company DLB-46
Saba, Umberto 1883-1957 . . . . DLB-114
Sábato, Ernesto 1911- DLB-145; CDWLB-3
Saberhagen, Fred 1930- DLB-8
Sabin, Joseph 1821-1881 . . . . DLB-187
Sacer, Gottfried Wilhelm 1635-1699 . . . . DLB-168
Sachs, Hans 1494-1576 . . . . . . DLB-179; CDWLB-2
Sack, John 1930- DLB-185
Sackler, Howard 1929-1982 . . . . DLB-7
Sackville, Lady Margaret 1881-1963 . . . . DLB-240
Sackville, Thomas 1536-1608 . . . . DLB-132
Sackville, Thomas 1536-1608
 and Norton, Thomas 1532-1584 . . . . . DLB-62
Sackville-West, Edward 1901-1965 . . . . . DLB-191
Sackville-West, V. 1892-1962 . . . . DLB-34, 195
Sadlier, D. and J., and Company DLB-49
Sadlier, Mary Anne 1820-1903 . . . . DLB-99
Sadoff, Ira 1945- DLB-120
Sadoveanu, Mihail 1880-1961 . . . . DLB-220
Sáenz, Benjamin Alire 1954- DLB-209
Saenz, Jaime 1921-1986 . . . . DLB-145
Saffin, John circa 1626-1710 . . . . DLB-24
Sagan, Françoise 1935- DLB-83
Sage, Robert 1899-1962 . . . . DLB-4
Sagel, Jim 1947- DLB-82
Sagendorph, Robb Hansell 1900-1970 . . . DLB-137
Sahagún, Carlos 1938- DLB-108
Sahkomaapii, Piitai (see Highwater, Jamake)
Sahl, Hans 1902- DLB-69
Said, Edward W. 1935- DLB-67
Saigyō 1118-1190 . . . . DLB-203
Saiko, George 1892-1962 . . . . DLB-85
St. Dominic's Press DLB-112
Saint-Exupéry, Antoine de 1900-1944 . . . . DLB-72
St. John, J. Allen 1872-1957 . . . . DLB-188
St. Johns, Adela Rogers 1894-1988 . . . . . DLB-29
The St. John's College Robert Graves Trust . . Y-96
St. Martin's Press DLB-46

St. Omer, Garth 1931- DLB-117
Saint Pierre, Michel de 1916-1987 . . . . . . DLB-83
Sainte-Beuve, Charles-Augustin
 1804-1869 . . . . DLB-217
Saints' Lives DLB-208
Saintsbury, George 1845-1933 . . . . . . DLB-57, 149
Saiokuken Sōchō 1448-1532 . . . . DLB-203
Saki (see Munro, H. H.)
Salaam, Kalamu ya 1947- DLB-38
Šalamun, Tomaž 1941- . . . DLB-181; CDWLB-4
Salas, Floyd 1931- DLB-82
Sálaz-Marquez, Rubén 1935- DLB-122
Salemson, Harold J. 1910-1988 . . . . DLB-4
Salinas, Luis Omar 1937- DLB-82
Salinas, Pedro 1891-1951 . . . . DLB-134
Salinger, J. D.
 1919- DLB-2, 102, 173; CDALB-1
Salkey, Andrew 1928- DLB-125
Sallust circa 86 B.C.-35 B.C.
 . . . . DLB-211; CDWLB-1
Salt, Waldo 1914- DLB-44
Salter, James 1925- DLB-130
Salter, Mary Jo 1954- DLB-120
Saltus, Edgar 1855-1921 . . . . DLB-202
Saltykov, Mikhail Evgrafovich
 1826-1889 . . . . DLB-238
Salustri, Carlo Alberto (see Trilussa)
Salverson, Laura Goodman 1890-1970 . . . DLB-92
Samain, Albert 1858-1900 . . . . DLB-217
Sampson, Richard Henry (see Hull, Richard)
Samuels, Ernest 1903-1996 . . . . DLB-111
Sanborn, Franklin Benjamin
 1831-1917 . . . . DLB-1, 223
Sánchez, Luis Rafael 1936- DLB-145
Sánchez, Philomeno "Phil" 1917- DLB-122
Sánchez, Ricardo 1941-1995 . . . . DLB-82
Sánchez, Saúl 1943- DLB-209
Sanchez, Sonia 1934- DLB-41; DS-8
Sand, George 1804-1876 . . . . DLB-119, 192
Sandburg, Carl
 1878-1967 . . . . DLB-17, 54; CDALB-3
Sanders, Ed 1939- DLB-16
Sandoz, Mari 1896-1966 . . . . DLB-9, 212
Sandwell, B. K. 1876-1954 . . . . DLB-92
Sandy, Stephen 1934- DLB-165
Sandys, George 1578-1644 . . . . DLB-24, 121
Sangster, Charles 1822-1893 . . . . DLB-99
Sanguineti, Edoardo 1930- DLB-128
Sanjōnishi Sanetaka 1455-1537 . . . . DLB-203
Sansay, Leonora ?-after 1823 . . . . DLB-200
Sansom, William 1912-1976 . . . . DLB-139
Santayana, George
 1863-1952 . . . . DLB-54, 71; DS-13
Santiago, Danny 1911-1988 . . . . DLB-122
Santmyer, Helen Hooven 1895-1986 . . . . . . Y-84
Sanvitale, Francesca 1928- DLB-196

Sapidus, Joannes 1490-1561 . . . . DLB-179
Sapir, Edward 1884-1939 . . . . DLB-92
Sapper (see McNeile, Herman Cyril)
Sappho circa 620 B.C.-circa 550 B.C.
 . . . . DLB-176; CDWLB-1
Saramago, José 1922- Y-98
Sardou, Victorien 1831-1908 . . . . DLB-192
Sarduy, Severo 1937- DLB-113
Sargent, Pamela 1948- DLB-8
Saro-Wiwa, Ken 1941- DLB-157
Saroyan, William
 1908-1981 . . . . . DLB-7, 9, 86; Y-81; CDALB-7
Sarraute, Nathalie 1900-1999 . . . . DLB-83
Sarrazin, Albertine 1937-1967 . . . . DLB-83
Sarris, Greg 1952- DLB-175
Sarton, May 1912-1995 . . . . DLB-48; Y-81
Sartre, Jean-Paul 1905-1980 . . . . DLB-72
Sassoon, Siegfried
 1886-1967 . . . . DLB-20, 191; DS-18
Siegfried Loraine Sassoon:
 A Centenary Essay
 Tributes from Vivien F. Clarke and
 Michael Thorpe Y-86
Sata, Ineko 1904- DLB-180
Saturday Review Press DLB-46
Saunders, James 1925- DLB-13
Saunders, John Monk 1897-1940 . . . . . . DLB-26
Saunders, Margaret Marshall
 1861-1947 . . . . DLB-92
Saunders and Otley DLB-106
Savage, James 1784-1873 . . . . DLB-30
Savage, Marmion W. 1803?-1872 . . . . DLB-21
Savage, Richard 1697?-1743 . . . . DLB-95
Savard, Félix-Antoine 1896-1982 . . . . DLB-68
Savery, Henry 1791-1842 . . . . DLB-230
Saville, (Leonard) Malcolm 1901-1982 . . . DLB-160
Sawyer, Ruth 1880-1970 . . . . DLB-22
Sayers, Dorothy L.
 1893-1957 . . . . DLB-10, 36, 77, 100; CDBLB-6
Sayle, Charles Edward 1864-1924 . . . . . . DLB-184
Sayles, John Thomas 1950- DLB-44
Sbarbaro, Camillo 1888-1967 . . . . DLB-114
Scalapino, Leslie 1947- DLB-193
Scannell, Vernon 1922- DLB-27
Scarry, Richard 1919-1994 . . . . DLB-61
Schaefer, Jack 1907-1991 . . . . DLB-212
Schaeffer, Albrecht 1885-1950 . . . . DLB-66
Schaeffer, Susan Fromberg 1941- DLB-28
Schaff, Philip 1819-1893 . . . . DS-13
Schaper, Edzard 1908-1984 . . . . DLB-69
Scharf, J. Thomas 1843-1898 . . . . DLB-47
Schede, Paul Melissus 1539-1602 . . . . DLB-179
Scheffel, Joseph Viktor von 1826-1886 . . . DLB-129
Scheffler, Johann 1624-1677 . . . . DLB-164
Schelling, Friedrich Wilhelm Joseph von
 1775-1854 . . . . DLB-90
Scherer, Wilhelm 1841-1886 . . . . DLB-129

Scherfig, Hans 1905-1979................DLB-214

Schickele, René 1883-1940...............DLB-66

Schiff, Dorothy 1903-1989...............DLB-127

Schiller, Friedrich
    1759-1805 ....DLB-94; CDWLB-2

Schirmer, David 1623-1687..............DLB-164

Schlaf, Johannes 1862-1941..............DLB-118

Schlegel, August Wilhelm 1767-1845......DLB-94

Schlegel, Dorothea 1763-1839............DLB-90

Schlegel, Friedrich 1772-1829...........DLB-90

Schleiermacher, Friedrich 1768-1834.....DLB-90

Schlesinger, Arthur M., Jr. 1917-   DLB-17

Schlumberger, Jean 1877-1968............DLB-65

Schmid, Eduard Hermann Wilhelm
    (see Edschmid, Kasimir)

Schmidt, Arno 1914-1979.................DLB-69

Schmidt, Johann Kaspar (see Stirner, Max)

Schmidt, Michael 1947-..................DLB-40

Schmidtbonn, Wilhelm August
    1876-1952 ....DLB-118

Schmitz, James H. 1911-.................DLB-8

Schnabel, Johann Gottfried
    1692-1760 ....DLB-168

Schnackenberg, Gjertrud 1953-..........DLB-120

Schnitzler, Arthur
    1862-1931.........DLB-81, 118; CDWLB-2

Schnurre, Wolfdietrich 1920-1989........DLB-69

Schocken Books..........................DLB-46

Scholartis Press........................DLB-112

Scholderer, Victor 1880-1971............DLB-201

The Schomburg Center for Research
    in Black Culture DLB-76

Schönbeck, Virgilio (see Giotti, Virgilio)

Schönherr, Karl 1867-1943...............DLB-118

Schoolcraft, Jane Johnston 1800-1841....DLB-175

School Stories, 1914-1960...............DLB-160

Schopenhauer, Arthur 1788-1860..........DLB-90

Schopenhauer, Johanna 1766-1838.........DLB-90

Schorer, Mark 1908-1977.................DLB-103

Schottelius, Justus Georg 1612-1676.....DLB-164

Schouler, James 1839-1920...............DLB-47

Schrader, Paul 1946-....................DLB-44

Schreiner, Olive
    1855-1920 ....DLB-18, 156, 190, 225

Schroeder, Andreas 1946-................DLB-53

Schubart, Christian Friedrich Daniel
    1739-1791 ....DLB-97

Schubert, Gotthilf Heinrich 1780-1860...DLB-90

Schücking, Levin 1814-1883..............DLB-133

Schulberg, Budd 1914-   DLB-6, 26, 28; Y-81

Schulte, F. J., and Company.............DLB-49

Schulz, Bruno 1892-1942....DLB-215; CDWLB-4

Schulze, Hans (see Praetorius, Johannes)

Schupp, Johann Balthasar 1610-1661.....DLB-164

Schurz, Carl 1829-1906..................DLB-23

Schuyler, George S. 1895-1977........DLB-29, 51

Schuyler, James 1923-1991...........DLB-5, 169

Schwartz, Delmore 1913-1966........DLB-28, 48

Schwartz, Jonathan 1938-   Y-82

Schwartz, Lynne Sharon 1939-........DLB-218

Schwarz, Sibylle 1621-1638.............DLB-164

Schwerner, Armand 1927-1999..........DLB-165

Schwob, Marcel 1867-1905..............DLB-123

Sciascia, Leonardo 1921-1989..........DLB-177

Science Fantasy........................DLB-8

Science-Fiction Fandom and Conventions...DLB-8

Science-Fiction Fanzines: The Time
    Binders DLB-8

Science-Fiction Films..................DLB-8

Science Fiction Writers of America and the
    Nebula Awards DLB-8

Scot, Reginald circa 1538-1599.........DLB-136

Scotellaro, Rocco 1923-1953............DLB-128

Scott, Alicia Anne (Lady John Scott)
    1810-1900 ....DLB-240

Scott, Catharine Amy Dawson
    1865-1934 ....DLB-240

Scott, Dennis 1939-1991................DLB-125

Scott, Dixon 1881-1915.................DLB-98

Scott, Duncan Campbell 1862-1947.......DLB-92

Scott, Evelyn 1893-1963.............DLB-9, 48

Scott, F. R. 1899-1985.................DLB-88

Scott, Frederick George 1861-1944......DLB-92

Scott, Geoffrey 1884-1929..............DLB-149

Scott, Harvey W. 1838-1910.............DLB-23

Scott, Lady Jane (see Scott, Alicia Anne)

Scott, Paul 1920-1978..............DLB-14, 207

Scott, Sarah 1723-1795.................DLB-39

Scott, Tom 1918-   DLB-27

Scott, Sir Walter 1771-1832
    ......DLB-93, 107, 116, 144, 159; CDBLB-3

Scott, Walter, Publishing
    Company Limited....................DLB-112

Scott, William Bell 1811-1890..........DLB-32

Scott, William R. [publishing house]...DLB-46

Scott-Heron, Gil 1949-.................DLB-41

Scribe, Eugene 1791-1861...............DLB-192

Scribner, Arthur Hawley 1859-1932....DS-13, 16

Scribner, Charles 1854-1930..........DS-13, 16

Scribner, Charles, Jr. 1921-1995........Y-95

Reminiscences DS-17

Charles Scribner's Sons DLB-49; DS-13, 16, 17

Scripps, E. W. 1854-1926...............DLB-25

Scudder, Horace Elisha 1838-1902....DLB-42, 71

Scudder, Vida Dutton 1861-1954.........DLB-71

Scupham, Peter 1933-...................DLB-40

Seabrook, William 1886-1945............DLB-4

Seabury, Samuel 1729-1796..............DLB-31

Seacole, Mary Jane Grant 1805-1881.....DLB-166

The Seafarer circa 970...............DLB-146

Sealsfield, Charles (Carl Postl)
    1793-1864 ....DLB-133, 186

Sears, Edward I. 1819?-1876............DLB-79

Sears Publishing Company DLB-46

Seaton, George 1911-1979...............DLB-44

Seaton, William Winston 1785-1866......DLB-43

Secker, Martin [publishing house]......DLB-112

Secker, Martin, and Warburg Limited ...DLB-112

Second-Generation Minor Poets of the
    Seventeenth Century DLB-126

Sedgwick, Arthur George 1844-1915......DLB-64

Sedgwick, Catharine Maria
    1789-1867 ....DLB-1, 74, 183, 239

Sedgwick, Ellery 1872-1930.............DLB-91

Sedley, Sir Charles 1639-1701..........DLB-131

Seeberg, Peter 1925-1999...............DLB-214

Seeger, Alan 1888-1916.................DLB-45

Seers, Eugene (see Dantin, Louis)

Segal, Erich 1937-   Y-86

Šegedin, Petar 1909-...................DLB-181

Seghers, Anna 1900-1983 ....DLB-69; CDWLB-2

Seid, Ruth (see Sinclair, Jo)

Seidel, Frederick Lewis 1936-   Y-84

Seidel, Ina 1885-1974..................DLB-56

Seifert, Jaroslav
    1901-1986.......DLB-215; Y-84; CDWLB-4

Seigenthaler, John 1927-...............DLB-127

Seizin Press...........................DLB-112

Séjour, Victor 1817-1874...............DLB-50

Séjour Marcou et Ferrand, Juan Victor
    (see Séjour, Victor)

Sekowski, Jósef-Julian, Baron Brambeus
    (see Senkovsky, Osip Ivanovich)

Selby, Bettina 1934-...................DLB-204

Selby, Hubert, Jr. 1928-............DLB-2, 227

Selden, George 1929-1989...............DLB-52

Selden, John 1584-1654.................DLB-213

Selected English-Language Little Magazines
    and Newspapers [France, 1920-1939] ...DLB-4

Selected Humorous Magazines
    (1820-1950).......................DLB-11

Selected Science-Fiction Magazines and
    Anthologies.......................DLB-8

Selenić, Slobodan 1933-1995............DLB-181

Self, Edwin F. 1920-...................DLB-137

Self, Will 1961-.......................DLB-207

Seligman, Edwin R. A. 1861-1939........DLB-47

Selimović, Meša
    1910-1982 ....DLB-181; CDWLB-4

Selous, Frederick Courteney
    1851-1917 ....DLB-174

Seltzer, Chester E. (see Muro, Amado)

Seltzer, Thomas [publishing house]......DLB-46

Selvon, Sam 1923-1994......DLB-125; CDWLB-3

Semmes, Raphael 1809-1877..............DLB-189

Senancour, Etienne de 1770-1846 ....DLB-119

Sendak, Maurice 1928-..................DLB-61

Seneca the Elder
    circa 54 B.C.-circa A.D. 40 ....DLB-211

Seneca the Younger
    circa 1 B.C.-A.D. 65 ....DLB-211; CDWLB-1

Cumulative Index   DLB 240

Senécal, Eva 1905- DLB-92
Sengstacke, John 1912- DLB-127
Senior, Olive 1941- DLB-157
Senkovsky, Osip Ivanovich
   (Józef-Julian Sekowski, Baron Brambeus)
   1800-1858..................... DLB-198
Šenoa, August 1838-1881 .... DLB-147; CDWLB-4
"Sensation Novels" (1863), by
   H. L. Manse..................... DLB-21
Sepamla, Sipho 1932- DLB-157, 225
Seredy, Kate 1899-1975 .... DLB-22
Sereni, Vittorio 1913-1983 .... DLB-128
Seres, William [publishing house]........DLB-170
Serling, Rod 1924-1975................ DLB-26
Serote, Mongane Wally 1944- ... DLB-125, 225
Serraillier, Ian 1912-1994 .... DLB-161
Serrano, Nina 1934- DLB-122
Service, Robert 1874-1958 .... DLB-92
Sessler, Charles 1854-1935............ DLB-187
Seth, Vikram 1952- DLB-120
Seton, Elizabeth Ann 1774-1821 .... DLB-200
Seton, Ernest Thompson
   1860-1942............ DLB-92; DS-13
Setouchi Harumi 1922- DLB-182
Settle, Mary Lee 1918- DLB-6
Seume, Johann Gottfried 1763-1810 ..... DLB-94
Seuse, Heinrich 1295?-1366 ....DLB-179
Seuss, Dr. (see Geisel, Theodor Seuss)
The Seventy-fifth Anniversary of the Armistice:
   The Wilfred Owen Centenary and
   the Great War Exhibit
   at the University of Virginia Y-93
Severin, Timothy 1940- DLB-204
Sewall, Joseph 1688-1769 .... DLB-24
Sewall, Richard B. 1908- DLB-111
Sewell, Anna 1820-1878 .... DLB-163
Sewell, Samuel 1652-1730............. DLB-24
Sex, Class, Politics, and Religion [in the
   British Novel, 1930-1959] DLB-15
Sexton, Anne 1928-1974 ... DLB-5, 169; CDALB-1
Seymour-Smith, Martin 1928-1998...... DLB-155
Sgorlon, Carlo 1930- DLB-196
Shaara, Michael 1929-1988................ Y-83
Shabel'skaia, Aleksandra Stanislavovna
   1845-1921 .... DLB-238
Shadwell, Thomas 1641?-1692......... DLB-80
Shaffer, Anthony 1926- DLB-13
Shaffer, Peter 1926- DLB-13, 233; CDBLB-8
Shaftesbury, Anthony Ashley Cooper,
   Third Earl of 1671-1713............ DLB-101
Shairp, Mordaunt 1887-1939 .... DLB-10
Shakespeare, Nicholas 1957- DLB-231
Shakespeare, William
   1564-1616.......... DLB-62, 172; CDBLB-1
The Shakespeare Globe Trust Y-93
Shakespeare Head Press.............. DLB-112
Shakhovskoi, Aleksandr Aleksandrovich
   1777-1846..................... DLB-150

Shange, Ntozake 1948- DLB-38
Shapiro, Karl 1913- DLB-48
Sharon Publications DLB-46
Sharp, Margery 1905-1991........... DLB-161
Sharp, William 1855-1905 .... DLB-156
Sharpe, Tom 1928- DLB-14, 231
Shaw, Albert 1857-1947 .... DLB-91
Shaw, George Bernard
   1856-1950........DLB-10, 57, 190, CDBLB-6
Shaw, Henry Wheeler 1818-1885 .... DLB-11
Shaw, Joseph T. 1874-1952........... DLB-137
Shaw, Irwin
   1913-1984 ..... DLB-6, 102; Y-84; CDALB-1
Shaw, Mary 1854-1929............... DLB-228
Shaw, Robert 1927-1978 .... DLB-13, 14
Shaw, Robert B. 1947- DLB-120
Shawn, William 1907-1992 .... DLB-137
Shay, Frank [publishing house]......... DLB-46
Shchedrin, N. (see Saltykov, Mikhail Evgrafovich)
Shea, John Gilmary 1824-1892......... DLB-30
Sheaffer, Louis 1912-1993 .... DLB-103
Shearing, Joseph 1886-1952 .... DLB-70
Shebbeare, John 1709-1788 .... DLB-39
Sheckley, Robert 1928- DLB-8
Shedd, William G. T. 1820-1894 .... DLB-64
Sheed, Wilfrid 1930- DLB-6
Sheed and Ward [U.S.]................ DLB-46
Sheed and Ward Limited [U.K.] DLB-112
Sheldon, Alice B. (see Tiptree, James, Jr.)
Sheldon, Edward 1886-1946............. DLB-7
Sheldon and Company................ DLB-49
Sheller, Aleksandr Konstantinovich
   1817-1875 .... DLB-238
Shelley, Mary Wollstonecraft 1797-1851
   ....DLB-110, 116, 159, 178; CDBLB-3
Shelley, Percy Bysshe
   1792-1822...... DLB-96, 110, 158; CDBLB-3
Shelnutt, Eve 1941- DLB-130
Shenstone, William 1714-1763 .... DLB-95
Shepard, Clark and Brown............. DLB-49
Shepard, Ernest Howard 1879-1976 ..... DLB-160
Shepard, Sam 1943- DLB-7, 212
Shepard, Thomas I, 1604 or 1605-1649 ... DLB-24
Shepard, Thomas II, 1635-1677 .... DLB-24
Shepherd, Luke
   flourished 1547-1554 .... DLB-136
Sherburne, Edward 1616-1702 .... DLB-131
Sheridan, Frances 1724-1766......... DLB-39, 84
Sheridan, Richard Brinsley
   1751-1816............... DLB-89; CDBLB-2
Sherman, Francis 1871-1926............ DLB-92
Sherman, Martin 1938- DLB-228
Sherriff, R. C. 1896-1975 ....DLB-10, 191, 233
Sherry, Norman 1935- DLB-155
Sherry, Richard 1506-1551 or 1555 ..... DLB-236
Sherwood, Mary Martha 1775-1851 ..... DLB-163

Sherwood, Robert 1896-1955..........DLB-7, 26
Shevyrev, Stepan Petrovich
   1806-1864 .... DLB-205
Shiel, M. P. 1865-1947 .... DLB-153
Shiels, George 1886-1949............. DLB-10
Shiga, Naoya 1883-1971 .... DLB-180
Shiina Rinzō 1911-1973 .... DLB-182
Shikishi Naishinnō 1153?-1201 .... DLB-203
Shillaber, Benjamin Penhallow
   1814-1890 .... DLB-1, 11, 235
Shimao Toshio 1917-1986 .... DLB-182
Shimazaki, Tōson 1872-1943 .... DLB-180
Shine, Ted 1931- DLB-38
Shinkei 1406-1475.................... DLB-203
Ship, Reuben 1915-1975............... DLB-88
Shirer, William L. 1904-1993........... DLB-4
Shirinsky-Shikhmatov, Sergii Aleksandrovich
   1783-1837 .... DLB-150
Shirley, James 1596-1666 .... DLB-58
Shishkov, Aleksandr Semenovich
   1753-1841 .... DLB-150
Shockley, Ann Allen 1927- DLB-33
Shōno Junzō 1921- DLB-182
Shore, Arabella 1820?-1901 and
   Shore, Louisa 1824-1895 .... DLB-199
Short, Peter [publishing house].........DLB-170
Shorter, Dora Sigerson 1866-1918 ..... DLB-240
Shorthouse, Joseph Henry 1834-1903 .... DLB-18
Shōtetsu 1381-1459 .... DLB-203
Showalter, Elaine 1941- DLB-67
Shulevitz, Uri 1935- DLB-61
Shulman, Max 1919-1988............. DLB-11
Shute, Henry A. 1856-1943 .... DLB-9
Shuttle, Penelope 1947- DLB-14, 40
Sibbes, Richard 1577-1635 .... DLB-151
Sibiriak, D. (see Mamin, Dmitrii Narkisovich)
Siddal, Elizabeth Eleanor 1829-1862 .... DLB-199
Sidgwick, Ethel 1877-1970.............DLB-197
Sidgwick and Jackson Limited DLB-112
Sidney, Margaret (see Lothrop, Harriet M.)
Sidney, Mary 1561-1621 .... DLB-167
Sidney, Sir Philip
   1554-1586 .... DLB-167; CDBLB-1
An Apologie for Poetrie (the Olney
   edition, 1595, of Defence of Poesie) DLB-167
Sidney's Press...................... DLB-49
Sierra, Rubén 1946- DLB-122
Sierra Club Books DLB-49
Siger of Brabant circa 1240-circa 1284 ... DLB-115
Sigourney, Lydia Huntley
   1791-1865..........DLB-1, 42, 73, 183, 239
Silkin, Jon 1930- DLB-27
Silko, Leslie Marmon 1948- DLB-143, 175
Silliman, Benjamin 1779-1864 .... DLB-183
Silliman, Ron 1946- DLB-169
Silliphant, Stirling 1918- DLB-26
Sillitoe, Alan 1928- DLB-14, 139; CDBLB-8

424

Silman, Roberta 1934- DLB-28	Skácel, Jan 1922-1989 ....DLB-232	Smith, Charlotte 1749-1806 ....DLB-39, 109
Silva, Beverly 1930- DLB-122	Skalbe, Kārlis 1879-1945 ....DLB-220	Smith, Chet 1899-1973 ....DLB-171
Silverberg, Robert 1935- DLB-8	Skármeta, Antonio 1940- DLB-145; CDWLB-3	Smith, Cordwainer 1913-1966............DLB-8
Silverman, Kenneth 1936- DLB-111	Skavronsky, A. (see Danilevsky Grigorii Petrovich)	Smith, Dave 1942- DLB-5
Simak, Clifford D. 1904-1988 ....DLB-8	Skeat, Walter W. 1835-1912 ....DLB-184	Smith, Dodie 1896- DLB-10
Simcoe, Elizabeth 1762-1850 ....DLB-99	Skeffington, William [publishing house].................DLB-106	Smith, Doris Buchanan 1934- DLB-52
Simcox, Edith Jemima 1844-1901 ....DLB-190	Skelton, John 1463-1529 ....DLB-136	Smith, E. E. 1890-1965 ....DLB-8
Simcox, George Augustus 1841-1905 .....DLB-35	Skelton, Robin 1925- DLB-27, 53	Smith, Elder and Company............DLB-154
Sime, Jessie Georgina 1868-1958 ....DLB-92	Škėma, Antanas 1910-1961 ....DLB-220	Smith, Elihu Hubbard 1771-1798.........DLB-37
Simenon, Georges 1903-1989 ......DLB-72; Y-89	Skinner, Constance Lindsay 1877-1939 ....DLB-92	Smith, Elizabeth Oakes (Prince) (see Oakes Smith, Elizabeth)
Simic, Charles 1938- DLB-105	Skinner, John Stuart 1788-1851 ....DLB-73	Smith, Eunice 1757-1823 ....DLB-200
"Images and 'Images,'" DLB-105	Skipsey, Joseph 1832-1903..............DLB-35	Smith, F. Hopkinson 1838-1915 ....DS-13
Simionescu, Mircea Horia 1928- DLB-232	Skou-Hansen, Tage 1925- DLB-214	Smith, George D. 1870-1920 ....DLB-140
Simmel, Johannes Mario 1924- DLB-69	Škvorecký, Josef 1924- DLB-232; CDWLB-4	Smith, George O. 1911-1981 ....DLB-8
Simmes, Valentine [publishing house] DLB-170	Slade, Bernard 1930- DLB-53	Smith, Goldwin 1823-1910 ....DLB-99
Simmons, Ernest J. 1903-1972 ....DLB-103	Slamnig, Ivan 1930- DLB-181	Smith, H. Allen 1907-1976 ....DLB-11, 29
Simmons, Herbert Alfred 1930- DLB-33	Slančeková, Božena (see Timrava)	Smith, Harrison, and Robert Haas [publishing house].................DLB-46
Simmons, James 1933- DLB-40	Slater, Patrick 1880-1951 ....DLB-68	Smith, Harry B. 1860-1936 ....DLB-187
Simms, William Gilmore 1806-1870 ....DLB-3, 30, 59, 73	Slaveykov, Pencho 1866-1912 ....DLB-147	Smith, Hazel Brannon 1914- DLB-127
Simms and M'Intyre DLB-106	Slaviček, Milivoj 1929- DLB-181	Smith, Henry circa 1560-circa 1591......DLB-136
Simon, Claude 1913- DLB-83; Y-85	Slavitt, David 1935- DLB-5, 6	Smith, Horatio (Horace) 1779-1849 ......DLB-116
Simon, Neil 1927- DLB-7	Sleigh, Burrows Willcocks Arthur 1821-1869 ....DLB-99	Smith, Horatio (Horace) 1779-1849 and James Smith 1775-1839 ....DLB-96
Simon and Schuster DLB-46	A Slender Thread of Hope: The Kennedy Center Black Theatre Project DLB-38	Smith, Iain Crichton 1928- DLB-40, 139
Simons, Katherine Drayton Mayrant 1890-1969 ....Y-83		Smith, J. Allen 1860-1924 ....DLB-47
Simović, Ljubomir 1935- DLB-181	Slesinger, Tess 1905-1945 ....DLB-102	Smith, J. Stilman, and Company DLB-49
Simpkin and Marshall [publishing house]................DLB-154	Slick, Sam (see Haliburton, Thomas Chandler)	Smith, Jessie Willcox 1863-1935 ....DLB-188
Simpson, Helen 1897-1940...............DLB-77	Sloan, John 1871-1951 ....DLB-188	Smith, John 1580-1631 ....DLB-24, 30
Simpson, Louis 1923- DLB-5	Sloane, William, Associates DLB-46	Smith, Josiah 1704-1781 ....DLB-24
Simpson, N. F. 1919- DLB-13	Small, Maynard and Company DLB-49	Smith, Ken 1938- DLB-40
Sims, George 1923- DLB-87; Y-99	Small Presses in Great Britain and Ireland, 1960-1985 ....DLB-40	Smith, Lee 1944- DLB-143; Y-83
Sims, George Robert 1847-1922...DLB-35, 70, 135		Smith, Logan Pearsall 1865-1946 ....DLB-98
Sinán, Rogelio 1904- DLB-145	Small Presses I: Jargon Society............Y-84	Smith, Mark 1935- Y-82
Sinclair, Andrew 1935- DLB-14	Small Presses II: The Spirit That Moves Us Press Y-85	Smith, Michael 1698-circa 1771 ....DLB-31
Sinclair, Bertrand William 1881-1972 .....DLB-92		Smith, Pauline 1882-1959 ....DLB-225
Sinclair, Catherine 1800-1864 ....DLB-163	Small Presses III: Pushcart Press...........Y-87	Smith, Red 1905-1982 ....DLB-29, 171
Sinclair, Jo 1913-1995 ....DLB-28	Smart, Christopher 1722-1771 ....DLB-109	Smith, Roswell 1829-1892 ....DLB-79
Sinclair, Lister 1921- DLB-88	Smart, David A. 1892-1957 ....DLB-137	Smith, Samuel Harrison 1772-1845 ....DLB-43
Sinclair, May 1863-1946 ....DLB-36, 135	Smart, Elizabeth 1913-1986 ....DLB-88	Smith, Samuel Stanhope 1751-1819 ......DLB-37
Sinclair, Upton 1878-1968 ......DLB-9; CDALB-5	Smedley, Menella Bute 1820?-1877 ......DLB-199	Smith, Sarah (see Stretton, Hesba)
Sinclair, Upton [publishing house].......DLB-46	Smellie, William [publishing house].....DLB-154	Smith, Sarah Pogson 1774-1870 ....DLB-200
Singer, Isaac Bashevis 1904-1991 ....DLB-6, 28, 52; Y-91; CDALB-1	Smiles, Samuel 1812-1904 ....DLB-55	Smith, Seba 1792-1868................DLB-1, 11
	Smiley, Jane 1949- DLB-227, 234	Smith, Stevie 1902-1971 ....DLB-20
Singer, Mark 1950- DLB-185	Smith, A. J. M. 1902-1980 ....DLB-88	Smith, Sydney 1771-1845...............DLB-107
Singmaster, Elsie 1879-1958 ....DLB-9	Smith, Adam 1723-1790 ....DLB-104	Smith, Sydney Goodsir 1915-1975........DLB-27
Sinisgalli, Leonardo 1908-1981 ....DLB-114	Smith, Adam (George Jerome Waldo Goodman) 1930- DLB-185	Smith, Sir Thomas 1513-1577 ....DLB-132
Siodmak, Curt 1902- DLB-44		Smith, W. B., and Company DLB-49
Sîrbu, Ion D. 1919-1989................DLB-232	Smith, Alexander 1829-1867 ....DLB-32, 55	Smith, W. H., and Son DLB-106
Siringo, Charles A. 1855-1928.........DLB-186	"On the Writing of Essays" (1862) DLB-57	Smith, Wendell 1914-1972..............DLB-171
Sissman, L. E. 1928-1976 ....DLB-5	Smith, Amanda 1837-1915.............DLB-221	Smith, William flourished 1595-1597 ....DLB-136
Sisson, C. H. 1914- DLB-27	Smith, Betty 1896-1972 ....Y-82	Smith, William 1727-1803 ....DLB-31
Sitwell, Edith 1887-1964...... DLB-20; CDBLB-7	Smith, Carol Sturm 1938- Y-81	A General Idea of the College of Mirania (1753) [excerpts] DLB-31
Sitwell, Osbert 1892-1969 ....DLB-100, 195	Smith, Charles Henry 1826-1903 ....DLB-11	

Cumulative Index

Smith, William 1728-1793 .... DLB-30
Smith, William Gardner 1927-1974 .... DLB-76
Smith, William Henry 1808-1872 .... DLB-159
Smith, William Jay 1918- DLB-5
Smithers, Leonard [publishing house] DLB-112
Smollett, Tobias
  1721-1771 .... DLB-39, 104; CDBLB-2
Dedication, *Ferdinand Count
  Fathom* (1753) DLB-39
Preface to *Ferdinand Count Fathom* (1753) ... DLB-39
Preface to *Roderick Random* (1748) DLB-39
Smythe, Francis Sydney 1900-1949 ..... DLB-195
Snelling, William Joseph 1804-1848 ..... DLB-202
Snellings, Rolland (see Touré, Askia Muhammad)
Snodgrass, W. D. 1926- DLB-5
Snow, C. P.
  1905-1980 .... DLB-15, 77; DS-17; CDBLB-7
Snyder, Gary 1930- DLB-5, 16, 165, 212, 237
Sobiloff, Hy 1912-1970 .... DLB-48
The Society for Textual Scholarship and
  TEXT Y-87
The Society for the History of Authorship,
  Reading and Publishing Y-92
Soffici, Ardengo 1879-1964 .... DLB-114
Sofola, 'Zulu 1938- DLB-157
Solano, Solita 1888-1975 .... DLB-4
Soldati, Mario 1906-1999 .... DLB-177
Šoljan, Antun 1932-1993 .... DLB-181
Sollers, Philippe 1936- DLB-83
Sollogub, Vladimir Aleksandrovich
  1813-1882 .... DLB-198
Solmi, Sergio 1899-1981 .... DLB-114
Solomon, Carl 1928- DLB-16
Solway, David 1941- DLB-53
Solzhenitsyn and America Y-85
Somerville, Edith Œnone 1858-1949 .... DLB-135
Somov, Orest Mikhailovich
  1793-1833 .... DLB-198
Sønderby, Knud 1909-1966 .... DLB-214
Song, Cathy 1955- DLB-169
Sono Ayako 1931- DLB-182
Sontag, Susan 1933- DLB-2, 67
Sophocles 497/496 B.C.-406/405 B.C.
  ....DLB-176; CDWLB-1
Šopov, Aco 1923-1982 .... DLB-181
Sørensen, Villy 1929- DLB-214
Sorensen, Virginia 1912-1991 .... DLB-206
Sorge, Reinhard Johannes 1892-1916 .... DLB-118
Sorrentino, Gilbert 1929- DLB-5, 173; Y-80
Sotheby, James 1682-1742 .... DLB-213
Sotheby, John 1740-1807 .... DLB-213
Sotheby, Samuel 1771-1842 .... DLB-213
Sotheby, Samuel Leigh 1805-1861 ..... DLB-213
Sotheby, William 1757-1833 .... DLB-93, 213
Soto, Gary 1952- DLB-82
Sources for the Study of Tudor and Stuart
  Drama DLB-62

Souster, Raymond 1921- DLB-88
The *South English Legendary* circa thirteenth-fifteenth
  centuries DLB-146
Southerland, Ellease 1943- DLB-33
Southern, Terry 1924-1995 .... DLB-2
Southern Illinois University Press Y-95
Southern Writers Between the Wars DLB-9
Southerne, Thomas 1659-1746 .... DLB-80
Southey, Caroline Anne Bowles
  1786-1854 .... DLB-116
Southey, Robert 1774-1843 ...... DLB-93, 107, 142
Southwell, Robert 1561?-1595 .... DLB-167
Southworth, E. D. E. N. 1819-1899 ..... DLB-239
Sowande, Bode 1948- DLB-157
Sowle, Tace [publishing house] DLB-170
Soyfer, Jura 1912-1939 .... DLB-124
Soyinka, Wole
  1934- DLB-125; Y-86, Y-87; CDWLB-3
Spacks, Barry 1931- DLB-105
Spalding, Frances 1950- DLB-155
Spark, Muriel 1918- ... DLB-15, 139; CDBLB-7
Sparke, Michael [publishing house] DLB-170
Sparks, Jared 1789-1866 .... DLB-1, 30, 235
Sparshott, Francis 1926- DLB-60
Späth, Gerold 1939- DLB-75
Spatola, Adriano 1941-1988 .... DLB-128
Spaziani, Maria Luisa 1924- DLB-128
Special Collections at the University of Colorado
  at Boulder Y-98
The Spectator 1828- DLB-110
Spedding, James 1808-1881 .... DLB-144
Spee von Langenfeld, Friedrich
  1591-1635 .... DLB-164
Speght, Rachel 1597-after 1630 .... DLB-126
Speke, John Hanning 1827-1864 .... DLB-166
Spellman, A. B. 1935- DLB-41
Spence, Catherine Helen 1825-1910 ..... DLB-230
Spence, Thomas 1750-1814 .... DLB-158
Spencer, Anne 1882-1975 .... DLB-51, 54
Spencer, Charles, third Earl of Sunderland
  1674-1722 .... DLB-213
Spencer, Elizabeth 1921- DLB-6, 218
Spencer, George John, Second Earl Spencer
  1758-1834 .... DLB-184
Spencer, Herbert 1820-1903 .... DLB-57
  "The Philosophy of Style" (1852) DLB-57
Spencer, Scott 1945- Y-86
Spender, J. A. 1862-1942 .... DLB-98
Spender, Stephen 1909-1995 .. DLB-20; CDBLB-7
Spener, Philipp Jakob 1635-1705 ...... DLB-164
Spenser, Edmund
  circa 1552-1599 .... DLB-167; CDBLB-1
Envoy from *The Shepheardes Calender* DLB-167
"The Generall Argument of the
  Whole Booke," from
  The Shepheardes Calender DLB-167
"A Letter of the Authors Expounding
  His Whole Intention in the Course

of this Worke: Which for that It Giueth
  Great Light to the Reader, for the Better
  Vnderstanding Is Hereunto Annexed,"
  from *The Faerie Qveene* (1590) DLB-167
"To His Booke," from
  The Shepheardes Calender (1579) DLB-167
"To the Most Excellent and Learned Both
  Orator and Poete, Mayster Gabriell Haruey,
  His Verie Special and Singular Good Frend
  E. K. Commendeth the Good Lyking of
  This His Labour, and the Patronage of
  the New Poete," from
  The Shepheardes Calender DLB-167
Sperr, Martin 1944- DLB-124
Spicer, Jack 1925-1965 .... DLB-5, 16, 193
Spielberg, Peter 1929- Y-81
Spielhagen, Friedrich 1829-1911 .... DLB-129
"Spielmannsepen" (circa 1152-circa 1500) .. DLB-148
Spier, Peter 1927- DLB-61
Spillane, Mickey 1918- DLB-226
Spinrad, Norman 1940- DLB-8
Spires, Elizabeth 1952- DLB-120
Spitteler, Carl 1845-1924 .... DLB-129
Spivak, Lawrence E. 1900- DLB-137
Spofford, Harriet Prescott
  1835-1921 ....DLB-74, 221
Spring, Howard 1889-1965 .... DLB-191
Squibob (see Derby, George Horatio)
Squier, E. G. 1821-1888 .... DLB-189
Stacpoole, H. de Vere 1863-1951 .... DLB-153
Staël, Germaine de 1766-1817 ....DLB-119, 192
Staël-Holstein, Anne-Louise Germaine de
  (see Staël, Germaine de)
Stafford, Jean 1915-1979 ....DLB-2, 173
Stafford, William 1914-1993 .... DLB-5, 206
Stage Censorship: "The Rejected Statement"
  (1911), by Bernard Shaw [excerpts] ... DLB-10
Stallings, Laurence 1894-1968 ....DLB-7, 44
Stallworthy, Jon 1935- DLB-40
Stampp, Kenneth M. 1912- DLB-17
Stănescu, Nichita 1933-1983 .... DLB-232
Stanev, Emiliyan 1907-1979 .... DLB-181
Stanford, Ann 1916- DLB-5
Stangerup, Henrik 1937-1998 .... DLB-214
Stanitsky, N. (see Panaeva, Avdot'ia Iakovlevna)
Stankevich, Nikolai Vladimirovich
  1813-1840 .... DLB-198
Stanković, Borisav ("Bora")
  1876-1927 ....DLB-147; CDWLB-4
Stanley, Henry M. 1841-1904 ... DLB-189; DS-13
Stanley, Thomas 1625-1678 .... DLB-131
Stannard, Martin 1947- DLB-155
Stansby, William [publishing house] DLB-170
Stanton, Elizabeth Cady 1815-1902 ...... DLB-79
Stanton, Frank L. 1857-1927 .... DLB-25
Stanton, Maura 1946- DLB-120
Stapledon, Olaf 1886-1950 .... DLB-15
Star Spangled Banner Office DLB-49
Stark, Freya 1893-1993 .... DLB-195

Starkey, Thomas circa 1499-1538 . . . . . . .DLB-132
Starkie, Walter 1894-1976 . . . . .DLB-195
Starkweather, David 1935- DLB-7
Starrett, Vincent 1886-1974 . . . . .DLB-187
The State of Publishing Y-97
Statements on the Art of Poetry DLB-54
Stationers' Company of London, The DLB-170
Statius circa A.D. 45-A.D. 96 . . . . .DLB-211
Stead, Robert J. C. 1880-1959 . . . . .DLB-92
Steadman, Mark 1930- DLB-6
The Stealthy School of Criticism (1871), by
 Dante Gabriel Rossetti DLB-35
Stearns, Harold E. 1891-1943 . . . . .DLB-4
Stedman, Edmund Clarence 1833-1908 . . .DLB-64
Steegmuller, Francis 1906-1994 . . . . .DLB-111
Steel, Flora Annie 1847-1929 . . . . . . .DLB-153, 156
Steele, Max 1922- Y-80
Steele, Richard
 1672-1729 . . . . .DLB-84, 101; CDBLB-2
Steele, Timothy 1948- DLB-120
Steele, Wilbur Daniel 1886-1970 . . . . .DLB-86
Steere, Richard circa 1643-1721 . . . . .DLB-24
Stefanovski, Goran 1952- DLB-181
Stegner, Wallace 1909-1993 . . . . .DLB-9, 206; Y-93
Stehr, Hermann 1864-1940 . . . . .DLB-66
Steig, William 1907- DLB-61
Stein, Gertrude 1874-1946
 . . . . . . .DLB-4, 54, 86, 228; DS-15; CDALB-4
Stein, Leo 1872-1947 . . . . .DLB-4
Stein and Day Publishers DLB-46
Steinbeck, John
 1902-1968 . . . .DLB-7, 9, 212; DS-2; CDALB-5
John Steinbeck Research Center Y-85
Steiner, George 1929- DLB-67
Steinhoewel, Heinrich 1411/1412-1479 . . .DLB-179
Steloff, Ida Frances 1887-1989 . . . . .DLB-187
Stendhal 1783-1842 . . . . .DLB-119
Stephen Crane: A Revaluation Virginia
 Tech Conference, 1989 . . . . Y-89
Stephen, Leslie 1832-1904 . . . . .DLB-57, 144, 190
Stephen Vincent Benét Centenary Y-97
Stephens, A. G. 1865-1933 . . . . .DLB-230
Stephens, Alexander H. 1812-1883 . . . . . . .DLB-47
Stephens, Alice Barber 1858-1932 . . . . . . .DLB-188
Stephens, Ann 1810-1886 . . . . .DLB-3, 73
Stephens, Charles Asbury 1844?-1931 . . . . .DLB-42
Stephens, James 1882?-1950 . . . .DLB-19, 153, 162
Stephens, John Lloyd 1805-1852 . . . . . . .DLB-183
Stephens, Michael 1946- DLB-234
Sterling, George 1869-1926 . . . . .DLB-54
Sterling, James 1701-1763 . . . . .DLB-24
Sterling, John 1806-1844 . . . . .DLB-116
Stern, Gerald 1925- DLB-105
Stern, Gladys B. 1890-1973 . . . . .DLB-197
Stern, Madeleine B. 1912- DLB-111, 140
Stern, Richard 1928- DLB-218; Y-87

Stern, Stewart 1922- DLB-26
Sterne, Laurence
 1713-1768 . . . . .DLB-39; CDBLB-2
Sternheim, Carl 1878-1942 . . . . .DLB-56, 118
Sternhold, Thomas ?-1549 and
 John Hopkins ?-1570 . . . . .DLB-132
Steuart, David 1747-1824 . . . . .DLB-213
Stevens, Henry 1819-1886 . . . . .DLB-140
Stevens, Wallace 1879-1955 . . . .DLB-54; CDALB-5
Stevenson, Anne 1933- DLB-40
Stevenson, D. E. 1892-1973 . . . . .DLB-191
Stevenson, Lionel 1902-1973 . . . . .DLB-155
Stevenson, Robert Louis
 1850-1894 . . . . . . .DLB-18, 57, 141, 156, 174;
   DS-13; CDBLB-5
"On Style in Literature:
 Its Technical Elements" (1885) DLB-57
Stewart, Donald Ogden
 1894-1980 . . . . .DLB-4, 11, 26
Stewart, Dugald 1753-1828 . . . . .DLB-31
Stewart, George, Jr. 1848-1906 . . . . .DLB-99
Stewart, George R. 1895-1980 . . . . .DLB-8
Stewart, Maria W. 1803?-1879 . . . . .DLB-239
Stewart, Randall 1896-1964 . . . . .DLB-103
Stewart and Kidd Company DLB-46
Stickney, Trumbull 1874-1904 . . . . .DLB-54
Stieler, Caspar 1632-1707 . . . . .DLB-164
Stifter, Adalbert
 1805-1868 . . . . .DLB-133; CDWLB-2
Stiles, Ezra 1727-1795 . . . . .DLB-31
Still, James 1906- DLB-9
Stirner, Max 1806-1856 . . . . .DLB-129
Stith, William 1707-1755 . . . . .DLB-31
Stock, Elliot [publishing house] DLB-106
Stockton, Frank R.
 1834-1902 . . . . .DLB-42, 74; DS-13
Stoddard, Ashbel [publishing house] DLB-49
Stoddard, Charles Warren
 1843-1909 . . . . .DLB-186
Stoddard, Elizabeth 1823-1902 . . . . .DLB-202
Stoddard, Richard Henry
 1825-1903 . . . . .DLB-3, 64; DS-13
Stoddard, Solomon 1643-1729 . . . . .DLB-24
Stoker, Bram
 1847-1912 . . . . . . .DLB-36, 70, 178; CDBLB-5
Stokes, Frederick A., Company DLB-49
Stokes, Thomas L. 1898-1958 . . . . .DLB-29
Stokesbury, Leon 1945- DLB-120
Stolberg, Christian Graf zu 1748-1821 . . . . .DLB-94
Stolberg, Friedrich Leopold Graf zu
 1750-1819 . . . . .DLB-94
Stone, Herbert S., and Company DLB-49
Stone, Lucy 1818-1893 . . . . .DLB-79, 239
Stone, Melville 1848-1929 . . . . .DLB-25
Stone, Robert 1937- DLB-152
Stone, Ruth 1915- DLB-105
Stone, Samuel 1602-1663 . . . . .DLB-24
Stone, William Leete 1792-1844 . . . . .DLB-202

Stone and Kimball DLB-49
Stoppard, Tom
 1937- DLB-13, 233; Y-85; CDBLB-8
Playwrights and Professors DLB-13
Storey, Anthony 1928- DLB-14
Storey, David 1933- DLB-13, 14, 207
Storm, Theodor 1817-1888 . . .DLB-129; CDWLB-2
Story, Thomas circa 1670-1742 . . . . .DLB-31
Story, William Wetmore 1819-1895 . . .DLB-1, 235
Storytelling: A Contemporary Renaissance . . . Y-84
Stoughton, William 1631-1701 . . . . .DLB-24
Stow, John 1525-1605 . . . . .DLB-132
Stowe, Harriet Beecher 1811-1896
 . . . . . .DLB-1, 12, 42, 74, 189, 239; CDALB-3
Stowe, Leland 1899- DLB-29
Stoyanov, Dimitr Ivanov (see Elin Pelin)
Strabo 64 or 63 B.C.-circa A.D. 25 . . . . . .DLB-176
Strachey, Lytton 1880-1932 . . . . . .DLB-149; DS-10
Strachey, Lytton, Preface to Eminent
 Victorians DLB-149
Strahan, William [publishing house] DLB-154
Strahan and Company DLB-106
Strand, Mark 1934- DLB-5
The Strasbourg Oaths 842 . . . . .DLB-148
Stratemeyer, Edward 1862-1930 . . . . .DLB-42
Strati, Saverio 1924- DLB-177
Stratton and Barnard DLB-49
Stratton-Porter, Gene
 1863-1924 . . . . .DLB-221; DS-14
Straub, Peter 1943- Y-84
Strauß, Botho 1944- DLB-124
Strauß, David Friedrich 1808-1874 . . . . . .DLB-133
The Strawberry Hill Press DLB-154
Streatfeild, Noel 1895-1986 . . . . .DLB-160
Street, Cecil John Charles (see Rhode, John)
Street, G. S. 1867-1936 . . . . .DLB-135
Street and Smith .DLB-49
Streeter, Edward 1891-1976 . . . . .DLB-11
Streeter, Thomas Winthrop 1883-1965 . . .DLB-140
Stretton, Hesba 1832-1911 . . . . .DLB-163, 190
Stribling, T. S. 1881-1965 . . . . .DLB-9
Der Stricker circa 1190-circa 1250 . . . . . . .DLB-138
Strickland, Samuel 1804-1867 . . . . .DLB-99
Stringer, Arthur 1874-1950 . . . . .DLB-92
Stringer and Townsend DLB-49
Strittmatter, Erwin 1912- DLB-69
Strniša, Gregor 1930-1987 . . . . .DLB-181
Strode, William 1630-1645 . . . . .DLB-126
Strong, L. A. G. 1896-1958 . . . . .DLB-191
Strother, David Hunter 1816-1888 . . . . .DLB-3
Strouse, Jean 1945- DLB-111
Stuart, Dabney 1937- DLB-105
Stuart, Jesse 1906-1984 . . . . .DLB-9, 48, 102; Y-84
Stuart, Lyle [publishing house] DLB-46
Stuart, Ruth McEnery 1849?-1917 . . . . . .DLB-202

Stubbs, Harry Clement (see Clement, Hal)

Stubenberg, Johann Wilhelm von 1619-1663................ DLB-164

Studio.................... DLB-112

The Study of Poetry (1880), by Matthew Arnold.............. DLB-35

Sturgeon, Theodore 1918-1985..... DLB-8; Y-85

Sturges, Preston 1898-1959........... DLB-26

"Style" (1840; revised, 1859), by Thomas de Quincey [excerpt]....... DLB-57

"Style" (1888), by Walter Pater......... DLB-57

Style (1897), by Walter Raleigh [excerpt].................... DLB-57

"Style" (1877), by T. H. Wright [excerpt].................... DLB-57

"Le Style c'est l'homme" (1892), by W. H. Mallock................. DLB-57

Styron, William 1925- DLB-2, 143; Y-80; CDALB-6

Suárez, Mario 1925- DLB-82

Such, Peter 1939- DLB-60

Suckling, Sir John 1609-1641?...... DLB-58, 126

Suckow, Ruth 1892-1960........... DLB-9, 102

Sudermann, Hermann 1857-1928....... DLB-118

Sue, Eugène 1804-1857.............. DLB-119

Sue, Marie-Joseph (see Sue, Eugène)

Suetonius circa A.D. 69-post A.D. 122... DLB-211

Suggs, Simon (see Hooper, Johnson Jones)

Sui Sin Far (see Eaton, Edith Maude)

Suits, Gustav 1883-1956.... DLB-220; CDWLB-4

Sukenick, Ronald 1932- DLB-173; Y-81

Suknaski, Andrew 1942- DLB-53

Sullivan, Alan 1868-1947 .... DLB-92

Sullivan, C. Gardner 1886-1965........ DLB-26

Sullivan, Frank 1892-1976 .... DLB-11

Sulte, Benjamin 1841-1923.......... DLB-99

Sulzberger, Arthur Hays 1891-1968..... DLB-127

Sulzberger, Arthur Ochs 1926- DLB-127

Sulzer, Johann Georg 1720-1779 .... DLB-97

Sumarokov, Aleksandr Petrovich 1717-1777................... DLB-150

Summers, Hollis 1916- DLB-6

A Summing Up at Century's End Y-99

Sumner, Charles 1811-1874 .... DLB-235

Sumner, Henry A. [publishing house] DLB-49

Surtees, Robert Smith 1803-1864 .... DLB-21

A Survey of Poetry Anthologies, 1879-1960................. DLB-54

Surveys: Japanese Literature, 1987-1995................. DLB-182

Sutherland, Efua Theodora 1924-1996................. DLB-117

Sutherland, John 1919-1956 .... DLB-68

Sutro, Alfred 1863-1933 .... DLB-10

Svendsen, Hanne Marie 1933- DLB-214

Swados, Harvey 1920-1972 .... DLB-2

Swain, Charles 1801-1874............ DLB-32

Swallow Press.................. DLB-46

Swan Sonnenschein Limited.......... DLB-106

Swanberg, W. A. 1907- DLB-103

Swenson, May 1919-1989.............. DLB-5

Swerling, Jo 1897- DLB-44

Swift, Graham 1949- DLB-194

Swift, Jonathan 1667-1745....... DLB-39, 95, 101; CDBLB-2

Swinburne, A. C. 1837-1909.......... DLB-35, 57; CDBLB-4

Swineshead, Richard floruit circa 1350 .... DLB-115

Swinnerton, Frank 1884-1982 .... DLB-34

Swisshelm, Jane Grey 1815-1884 .... DLB-43

Swope, Herbert Bayard 1882-1958....... DLB-25

Swords, T. and J., and Company DLB-49

Swords, Thomas 1763-1843 and Swords, James ?-1844.............. DLB-73

Sykes, Ella C. ?-1939 ....DLB-174

Sylvester, Josuah 1562 or 1563-1618 .... DLB-121

Symonds, Emily Morse (see Paston, George)

Symonds, John Addington 1840-1893 ....DLB-57, 144

"Personal Style" (1890) DLB-57

Symons, A. J. A. 1900-1941 .... DLB-149

Symons, Arthur 1865-1945 ......DLB-19, 57, 149

Symons, Julian 1912-1994 ..... DLB-87, 155; Y-92

Julian Symons at Eighty Y-92

Symons, Scott 1933- DLB-53

A Symposium on *The Columbia History of the Novel* Y-92

Synge, John Millington 1871-1909............ DLB-10, 19; CDBLB-5

Synge Summer School: J. M. Synge and the Irish Theater, Rathdrum, County Wiclow, Ireland Y-93

Syrett, Netta 1865-1943 ....DLB-135, 197

Szabó, Lőrinc 1900-1957 .... DLB-215

Szabó, Magda 1917- DLB-215

Szymborska, Wisława 1923- DLB-232, Y-96; CDWLB-4

T

Taban lo Liyong 1939?- DLB-125

Tabucchi, Antonio 1943- DLB-196

Taché, Joseph-Charles 1820-1894 .... DLB-99

Tachihara Masaaki 1926-1980 .... DLB-182

Tacitus circa A.D. 55-circa A.D. 117 .... DLB-211; CDWLB-1

Tadijanović, Dragutin 1905- DLB-181

Tafdrup, Pia 1952- DLB-214

Tafolla, Carmen 1951- DLB-82

Taggard, Genevieve 1894-1948 .... DLB-45

Taggart, John 1942- DLB-193

Tagger, Theodor (see Bruckner, Ferdinand)

Taiheiki late fourteenth century DLB-203

Tait, J. Selwin, and Sons............ DLB-49

Tait's Edinburgh Magazine 1832-1861 ..... DLB-110

The Takarazaka Revue Company.......... Y-91

Talander (see Bohse, August)

Talese, Gay 1932- DLB-185

Talev, Dimitr 1898-1966 .... DLB-181

Taliaferro, H. E. 1811-1875 .... DLB-202

Tallent, Elizabeth 1954- DLB-130

TallMountain, Mary 1918-1994........ DLB-193

Talvj 1797-1870................. DLB-59, 133

Tamási, Áron 1897-1966 .... DLB-215

Tammsaare, A. H. 1878-1940........... DLB-220; CDWLB-4

Tan, Amy 1952- DLB-173; CDALB-7

Tandori, Dezső 1938- DLB-232

Tanner, Thomas 1673/1674-1735....... DLB-213

Tanizaki Jun'ichirō 1886-1965 .... DLB-180

Tapahonso, Luci 1953- DLB-175

The Mark Taper Forum............ DLB-7

Taradash, Daniel 1913- DLB-44

Tarbell, Ida M. 1857-1944 .... DLB-47

Tardivel, Jules-Paul 1851-1905.......... DLB-99

Targan, Barry 1932- DLB-130

Tarkington, Booth 1869-1946 .... DLB-9, 102

Tashlin, Frank 1913-1972.............. DLB-44

Tasma (Jessie Couvreur) 1848-1897 .... DLB-230

Tate, Allen 1899-1979........DLB-4, 45, 63; DS-17

Tate, James 1943- DLB-5, 169

Tate, Nahum circa 1652-1715........... DLB-80

Tatian circa 830.................... DLB-148

Taufer, Veno 1933- DLB-181

Tauler, Johannes circa 1300-1361 ....DLB-179

Tavčar, Ivan 1851-1923 ....DLB-147

Taverner, Richard ca. 1505-1575 .... DLB-236

Taylor, Ann 1782-1866 .... DLB-163

Taylor, Bayard 1825-1878 .... DLB-3, 189

Taylor, Bert Leston 1866-1921 .... DLB-25

Taylor, Charles H. 1846-1921 .... DLB-25

Taylor, Edward circa 1642-1729 .... DLB-24

Taylor, Elizabeth 1912-1975 .... DLB-139

Taylor, Henry 1942- DLB-5

Taylor, Sir Henry 1800-1886.......... DLB-32

Taylor, Jane 1783-1824............. DLB-163

Taylor, Jeremy circa 1613-1667 .... DLB-151

Taylor, John 1577 or 1578 - 1653 .... DLB-121

Taylor, Mildred D. ? - DLB-52

Taylor, Peter 1917-1994 ..... DLB-218; Y-81, Y-94

Taylor, Susie King 1848-1912 .... DLB-221

Taylor, William, and Company......... DLB-49

Taylor-Made Shakespeare? Or Is "Shall I Die?" the Long-Lost Text of Bottom's Dream?..... Y-85

Teasdale, Sara 1884-1933.............. DLB-45

Telles, Lygia Fagundes 1924- DLB-113

Temple, Sir William 1628-1699 .... DLB-101

Temrizov, A. (see Marchenko, Anastasia Iakovlevna)

Tench, Watkin ca. 1758-1833........... DLB-230

Tenn, William 1919- DLB-8

Tennant, Emma 1937- DLB-14

Tenney, Tabitha Gilman 1762-1837 .... DLB-37, 200
Tennyson, Alfred 1809-1892 .... DLB-32; CDBLB-4
Tennyson, Frederick 1807-1898......... DLB-32
Tenorio, Arthur 1924- DLB-209
Tepliakov, Viktor Grigor'evich 1804-1842 .... DLB-205
Terence circa 184 B.C.-159 B.C. or after DLB-211; CDWLB-1
Terhune, Albert Payson 1872-1942........ DLB-9
Terhune, Mary Virginia 1830-1922 .... DS-13, DS-16
Terry, Megan 1932- DLB-7
Terson, Peter 1932- DLB-13
Tesich, Steve 1943-1996 .... Y-83
Tessa, Delio 1886-1939 .... DLB-114
Testori, Giovanni 1923-1993........ DLB-128, 177
Tey, Josephine 1896?-1952 .... DLB-77
Thacher, James 1754-1844............. DLB-37
Thackeray, William Makepeace 1811-1863 ... DLB-21, 55, 159, 163; CDBLB-4
Thames and Hudson Limited DLB-112
Thanet, Octave (see French, Alice)
Thatcher, John Boyd 1847-1909 .... DLB-187
Thaxter, Celia Laighton 1835-1894...... DLB-239
Thayer, Caroline Matilda Warren 1785-1844 .... DLB-200
The Theatre Guild................. DLB-7
The Theater in Shakespeare's Time DLB-62
Thegan and the Astronomer flourished circa 850................ DLB-148
Thelwall, John 1764-1834 .... DLB-93, 158
Theocritus circa 300 B.C.-260 B.C....... DLB-176
Theodorescu, Ion N. (see Arghezi, Tudor)
Theodulf circa 760-circa 821 .... DLB-148
Theophrastus circa 371 B.C.-287 B.C..... DLB-176
Theriault, Yves 1915-1983.............. DLB-88
Thério, Adrien 1925- DLB-53
Theroux, Paul 1941- DLB-2, 218; CDALB-7
Thesiger, Wilfred 1910- DLB-204
They All Came to Paris................. DS-16
Thibaudeau, Colleen 1925- DLB-88
Thielen, Benedict 1903-1965........... DLB-102
Thiong'o Ngugi wa (see Ngugi wa Thiong'o)
Third-Generation Minor Poets of the Seventeenth Century.............. DLB-131
This Quarter 1925-1927, 1929-1932 .... DS-15
Thoma, Ludwig 1867-1921 .... DLB-66
Thoma, Richard 1902- DLB-4
Thomas, Audrey 1935- DLB-60
Thomas, D. M. 1935- ..DLB-40, 207; CDBLB-8
D. M. Thomas: The Plagiarism Controversy Y-82
Thomas, Dylan 1914-1953 ....DLB-13, 20, 139; CDBLB-7
The Dylan Thomas Celebration Y-99

Thomas, Edward 1878-1917 .... DLB-19, 98, 156, 216
Thomas, Frederick William 1806-1866...DLB-202
Thomas, Gwyn 1913-1981 .... DLB-15
Thomas, Isaiah 1750-1831........ DLB-43, 73, 187
Thomas, Isaiah [publishing house] DLB-49
Thomas, Johann 1624-1679........... DLB-168
Thomas, John 1900-1932................ DLB-4
Thomas, Joyce Carol 1938- DLB-33
Thomas, Lorenzo 1944- DLB-41
Thomas, R. S. 1915- DLB-27; CDBLB-8
Thomasîn von Zerclære circa 1186-circa 1259................ DLB-138
Thomasius, Christian 1655-1728........ DLB-168
Thompson, Daniel Pierce 1795-1868..... DLB-202
Thompson, David 1770-1857............ DLB-99
Thompson, Dorothy 1893-1961 .... DLB-29
Thompson, Flora 1876-1947 .... DLB-240
Thompson, Francis 1859-1907 .... DLB-19; CDBLB-5
Thompson, George Selden (see Selden, George)
Thompson, Henry Yates 1838-1928 ..... DLB-184
Thompson, Hunter S. 1939- DLB-185
Thompson, Jim 1906-1977 .... DLB-226
Thompson, John 1938-1976............ DLB-60
Thompson, John R. 1823-1873 .... DLB-3, 73
Thompson, Lawrance 1906-1973 .... DLB-103
Thompson, Maurice 1844-1901 ...... DLB-71, 74
Thompson, Ruth Plumly 1891-1976 ..... DLB-22
Thompson, Thomas Phillips 1843-1933 ... DLB-99
Thompson, William 1775-1833 ....DLB-158
Thompson, William Tappan 1812-1882 .... DLB-3, 11
Thomson, Edward William 1849-1924....DLB-92
Thomson, James 1700-1748 .... DLB-95
Thomson, James 1834-1882 .... DLB-35
Thomson, Joseph 1858-1895........... DLB-174
Thomson, Mortimer 1831-1875......... DLB-11
Thoreau, Henry David 1817-1862 .... DLB-1, 183, 223; CDALB-2
The Thoreauvian Pilgrimage: The Structure of an American Cult.................. DLB-223
Thorpe, Adam 1956- DLB-231
Thorpe, Thomas Bangs 1815-1878 ..... DLB-3, 11
Thorup, Kirsten 1942- DLB-214
Thoughts on Poetry and Its Varieties (1833), by John Stuart Mill DLB-32
Thrale, Hester Lynch (see Piozzi, Hester Lynch [Thrale])
Thubron, Colin 1939- DLB-204, 231
Thucydides circa 455 B.C.-circa 395 B.C. DLB-176
Thulstrup, Thure de 1848-1930 .... DLB-188
Thümmel, Moritz August von 1738-1817 .... DLB-97
Thurber, James 1894-1961 .....DLB-4, 11, 22, 102; CDALB-5
Thurman, Wallace 1902-1934..........DLB-51

Thwaite, Anthony 1930- DLB-40
The Booker Prize
Address by Anthony Thwaite, Chairman of the Booker Prize Judges Comments from Former Booker Prize Winners Y-86
Thwaites, Reuben Gold 1853-1913....... DLB-47
Tibullus circa 54 B.C.-circa 19 B.C. DLB-211
Ticknor, George 1791-1871 ... DLB-1, 59, 140, 235
Ticknor and Fields.................... DLB-49
Ticknor and Fields (revived) DLB-46
Tieck, Ludwig 1773-1853 .... DLB-90; CDWLB-2
Tietjens, Eunice 1884-1944 .... DLB-54
Tilney, Edmund circa 1536-1610 ...... DLB-136
Tilt, Charles [publishing house]........ DLB-106
Tilton, J. E., and Company DLB-49
Time and Western Man (1927), by Wyndham Lewis [excerpts]................. DLB-36
Time-Life Books DLB-46
Times Books DLB-46
Timothy, Peter circa 1725-1782 .... DLB-43
Timrava 1867-1951 .... DLB-215
Timrod, Henry 1828-1867 .... DLB-3
Tindal, Henrietta 1818?-1879 .... DLB-199
Tinker, Chauncey Brewster 1876-1963 ... DLB-140
Tinsley Brothers DLB-106
Tiptree, James, Jr. 1915-1987 .... DLB-8
Tišma, Aleksandar 1924- DLB-181
Titus, Edward William 1870-1952 .... DLB-4; DS-15
Tiutchev, Fedor Ivanovich 1803-1873 .... DLB-205
Tlali, Miriam 1933- DLB-157, 225
Todd, Barbara Euphan 1890-1976....... DLB-160
Tofte, Robert 1561 or 1562-1619 or 1620......... DLB-172
Toklas, Alice B. 1877-1967............... DLB-4
Tokuda, Shūsei 1872-1943............. DLB-180
Tolkien, J. R. R. 1892-1973 .... DLB-15, 160; CDBLB-6
Toller, Ernst 1893-1939............... DLB-124
Tollet, Elizabeth 1694-1754 .... DLB-95
Tolson, Melvin B. 1898-1966 .... DLB-48, 76
Tolstoy, Aleksei Konstantinovich 1817-1875 .... DLB-238
Tolstoy, Leo 1828-1910.............. DLB-238
Tom Jones (1749), by Henry Fielding [excerpt] DLB-39
Tomalin, Claire 1933- DLB-155
Tomasi di Lampedusa, Giuseppe 1896-1957 .... DLB-177
Tomlinson, Charles 1927- DLB-40
Tomlinson, H. M. 1873-1958 ... DLB-36, 100, 195
Tompkins, Abel [publishing house]....... DLB-49
Tompson, Benjamin 1642-1714 .... DLB-24
Tomson, Graham R. (see Watson, Rosamund Marriott)
Ton'a 1289-1372 .... DLB-203
Tondelli, Pier Vittorio 1955-1991 .... DLB-196

Tonks, Rosemary 1932- DLB-14, 207
Tonna, Charlotte Elizabeth 1790-1846 ... DLB-163
Tonson, Jacob the Elder
 [publishing house] DLB-170
Toole, John Kennedy 1937-1969 .... Y-81
Toomer, Jean 1894-1967 .. DLB-45, 51; CDALB-4
Tor Books. DLB-46
Torberg, Friedrich 1908-1979 .... DLB-85
Torrence, Ridgely 1874-1950 .... DLB-54
Torres-Metzger, Joseph V. 1933- DLB-122
Toth, Susan Allen 1940- Y-86
Tottell, Richard [publishing house]. DLB-170
"The Printer to the Reader," (1557)
 by Richard Tottell DLB-167
Tough-Guy Literature DLB-9
Touré, Askia Muhammad 1938- DLB-41
Tourgée, Albion W. 1838-1905 .... DLB-79
Tournemir, Elizaveta Sailhas de (see Tur, Evgeniia)
Tourneur, Cyril circa 1580-1626 .... DLB-58
Tournier, Michel 1924- DLB-83
Tousey, Frank [publishing house] DLB-49
Tower Publications. DLB-46
Towne, Benjamin circa 1740-1793 ...... DLB-43
Towne, Robert 1936- DLB-44
The Townely Plays fifteenth and sixteenth
 centuries. DLB-146
Townshend, Aurelian
 by 1583-circa 1651 .... DLB-121
Toy, Barbara 1908- DLB-204
Tracy, Honor 1913- DLB-15
Traherne, Thomas 1637?-1674. .... DLB-131
Traill, Catharine Parr 1802-1899 .... DLB-99
Train, Arthur 1875-1945. .... DLB-86; DS-16
The Transatlantic Publishing Company... DLB-49
The Transatlantic Review 1924-1925 .... DS-15
The Transcendental Club 1836-1840. ... DLB-223
Transcendentalism DLB-223
Transcendentalists, American.............. DS-5
A Transit of Poets and Others: American
 Biography in 1982 .... Y-82
transition 1927-1938 .... DS-15
Translators of the Twelfth Century: Literary Issues
 Raised and Impact Created DLB-115
Travel Writing, 1837-1875 .... DLB-166
Travel Writing, 1876-1909 .... DLB-174
Travel Writing, 1910-1939 .... DLB-195
Traven, B. 1882? or 1890?-1969? DLB-9, 56
Travers, Ben 1886-1980 .... DLB-10, 233
Travers, P. L. (Pamela Lyndon)
 1899-1996 .... DLB-160
Trediakovsky, Vasilii Kirillovich
 1703-1769 .... DLB-150
Treece, Henry 1911-1966. .... DLB-160
Trejo, Ernesto 1950- DLB-122
Trelawny, Edward John
 1792-1881 .... DLB-110, 116, 144
Tremain, Rose 1943- DLB-14

Tremblay, Michel 1942- DLB-60
Trends in Twentieth-Century
 Mass Market Publishing DLB-46
Trent, William P. 1862-1939 .... DLB-47
Trescot, William Henry 1822-1898 .... DLB-30
Tressell, Robert (Robert Phillipe Noonan)
 1870-1911 .... DLB-197
Trevelyan, Sir George Otto
 1838-1928 .... DLB-144
Trevisa, John circa 1342-circa 1402 .... DLB-146
Trevor, William 1928- DLB-14, 139
Trierer Floyris circa 1170-1180 .... DLB-138
Trillin, Calvin 1935- DLB-185
Trilling, Lionel 1905-1975 .... DLB-28, 63
Trilussa 1871-1950 .... DLB-114
Trimmer, Sarah 1741-1810 .... DLB-158
Triolet, Elsa 1896-1970................ DLB-72
Tripp, John 1927- DLB-40
Trocchi, Alexander 1925- DLB-15
Troisi, Dante 1920-1989............... DLB-196
Trollope, Anthony
 1815-1882 .... DLB-21, 57, 159; CDBLB-4
Trollope, Frances 1779-1863. .... DLB-21, 166
Trollope, Joanna 1943- DLB-207
Troop, Elizabeth 1931- DLB-14
Trotter, Catharine 1679-1749 .... DLB-84
Trotti, Lamar 1898-1952 .... DLB-44
Trottier, Pierre 1925- DLB-60
Troubadours, *Trobairitz*, and Trouvères .. DLB-208
Troupe, Quincy Thomas, Jr. 1943- DLB-41
Trow, John F., and Company. DLB-49
Trowbridge, John Townsend 1827-1916 . DLB-202
Truillier-Lacombe, Joseph-Patrice
 1807-1863. .... DLB-99
Trumbo, Dalton 1905-1976 .... DLB-26
Trumbull, Benjamin 1735-1820 .... DLB-30
Trumbull, John 1750-1831 .... DLB-31
Trumbull, John 1756-1843 .... DLB-183
Truth, Sojourner 1797?-1883 .... DLB-239
Tscherning, Andreas 1611-1659 ...... DLB-164
Tsubouchi, Shōyō 1859-1935. .... DLB-180
Tucholsky, Kurt 1890-1935 .... DLB-56
Tucker, Charlotte Maria
 1821-1893 .... DLB-163, 190
Tucker, George 1775-1861 .... DLB-3, 30
Tucker, James 1808?-1866? DLB-230
Tucker, Nathaniel Beverley 1784-1851..... DLB-3
Tucker, St. George 1752-1827 .... DLB-37
Tuckerman, Henry Theodore 1813-1871.. DLB-64
Tumas, Juozas (see Vaižgantas)
Tunis, John R. 1889-1975.......... DLB-22, 171
Tunstall, Cuthbert 1474-1559.......... DLB-132
Tuohy, Frank 1925- DLB-14, 139
Tupper, Martin F. 1810-1889 .... DLB-32
Tur, Evgeniia 1815-1892 .... DLB-238
Turbyfill, Mark 1896- DLB-45

Turco, Lewis 1934- Y-84
Turgenev, Aleksandr Ivanovich
 1784-1845....................... DLB-198
Turgenev, Ivan Sergeevich 1818-1883 ... DLB-238
Turnball, Alexander H. 1868-1918 ..... DLB-184
Turnbull, Andrew 1921-1970.......... DLB-103
Turnbull, Gael 1928- DLB-40
Turner, Arlin 1909-1980 .... DLB-103
Turner, Charles (Tennyson)
 1808-1879....................... DLB-32
Turner, Ethel 1872-1958 .... DLB-230
Turner, Frederick 1943- DLB-40
Turner, Frederick Jackson
 1861-1932 .... DLB-17, 186
Turner, Joseph Addison 1826-1868 ..... DLB-79
Turpin, Waters Edward 1910-1968 ..... DLB-51
Turrini, Peter 1944- DLB-124
Tutuola, Amos 1920-1997 ...DLB-125; CDWLB-3
Twain, Mark (see Clemens, Samuel Langhorne)
Tweedie, Ethel Brilliana
 circa 1860-1940 .... DLB-174
The 'Twenties and Berlin, by Alex Natan . DLB-66
Twysden, Sir Roger 1597-1672. .... DLB-213
Tyler, Anne
 1941- DLB-6, 143; Y-82; CDALB-7
Tyler, Mary Palmer 1775-1866. .... DLB-200
Tyler, Moses Coit 1835-1900.......... DLB-47, 64
Tyler, Royall 1757-1826 .... DLB-37
Tylor, Edward Burnett 1832-1917 .... DLB-57
Tynan, Katharine 1861-1931 ...... DLB-153, 240
Tyndale, William circa 1494-1536...... DLB-132

U

Uchida, Yoshika 1921-1992 ....CDALB-7
Udall, Nicholas 1504-1556 .... DLB-62
Ugrešić, Dubravka 1949- DLB-181
Uhland, Ludwig 1787-1862............. DLB-90
Uhse, Bodo 1904-1963................. DLB-69
Ujević, Augustin ("Tin") 1891-1955......DLB-147
Ulenhart, Niclas flourished circa 1600 ... DLB-164
Ulibarrí, Sabine R. 1919- DLB-82
Ulica, Jorge 1870-1926 .... DLB-82
Ulivi, Ferruccio 1912- DLB-196
Ulizio, B. George 1889-1969 .... DLB-140
Ulrich von Liechtenstein
 circa 1200-circa 1275 .... DLB-138
Ulrich von Zatzikhoven
 before 1194-after 1214 .... DLB-138
Ulysses, Reader's Edition................. Y-97
Unaipon, David 1872-1967............ DLB-230
Unamuno, Miguel de 1864-1936 .... DLB-108
Under, Marie 1883-1980 ... DLB-220; CDWLB-4
Under the Microscope (1872), by
 A. C. Swinburne DLB-35
Underhill, Evelyn 1875-1941 .... DLB-240
Ungaretti, Giuseppe 1888-1970 .... DLB-114
Unger, Friederike Helene 1741-1813 ..... DLB-94

United States Book Company DLB-49	Valente, José Angel 1929- DLB-108	Vazov, Ivan 1850-1921 ..... DLB-147; CDWLB-4
Universal Publishing and Distributing Corporation DLB-46	Valenzuela, Luisa 1938- ... DLB-113; CDWLB-3	Véa Jr., Alfredo 1950- DLB-209
	Valeri, Diego 1887-1976 .... DLB-128	Vega, Janine Pommy 1942- DLB-16
The University of Iowa Writers' Workshop Golden Jubilee Y-86	Valerius Flaccus fl. circa A.D. 92 .... DLB-211	Veiller, Anthony 1903-1965 .... DLB-44
	Valerius Maximus fl. circa A.D. 31 ...... DLB-211	Velásquez-Trevino, Gloria 1949- DLB-122
The University of South Carolina Press Y-94	Valesio, Paolo 1939- DLB-196	Veley, Margaret 1843-1887 .... DLB-199
University of Wales Press DLB-112	Valgardson, W. D. 1939- DLB-60	Velleius Paterculus circa 20 B.C.-circa A.D. 30 .... DLB-211
University Press of Kansas Y-98	Valle, Víctor Manuel 1950- DLB-122	
University Press of Mississippi Y-99	Valle-Inclán, Ramón del 1866-1936 ..... DLB-134	Veloz Maggiolo, Marcio 1936- DLB-145
"The Unknown Public" (1858), by Wilkie Collins [excerpt] DLB-57	Vallejo, Armando 1949- DLB-122	Vel'tman Aleksandr Fomich 1800-1870 .... DLB-198
	Vallès, Jules 1832-1885 .... DLB-123	
Uno, Chiyo 1897-1996 .... DLB-180	Vallette, Marguerite Eymery (see Rachilde)	Venegas, Daniel ?-? DLB-82
Unruh, Fritz von 1885-1970 .... DLB-56, 118	Valverde, José María 1926-1996 .... DLB-108	Venevitinov, Dmitrii Vladimirovich 1805-1827 .... DLB-205
Unspeakable Practices II: The Festival of Vanguard Narrative at Brown University Y-93	Van Allsburg, Chris 1949- DLB-61	Vergil, Polydore circa 1470-1555 .... DLB-132
Unsworth, Barry 1930- DLB-194	Van Anda, Carr 1864-1945 .... DLB-25	Veríssimo, Erico 1905-1975 .... DLB-145
Unt, Mati 1944- DLB-232	van der Post, Laurens 1906-1996 ...... DLB-204	Verlaine, Paul 1844-1896 .... DLB-217
The Unterberg Poetry Center of the 92nd Street Y Y-98	Van Dine, S. S. (see Wright, Williard Huntington)	Verne, Jules 1828-1905 .... DLB-123
	Van Doren, Mark 1894-1972 .... DLB-45	Verplanck, Gulian C. 1786-1870 .... DLB-59
Unwin, T. Fisher [publishing house] DLB-106	van Druten, John 1901-1957 .... DLB-10	Very, Jones 1813-1880 .... DLB-1
Upchurch, Boyd B. (see Boyd, John)	Van Duyn, Mona 1921- DLB-5	Vian, Boris 1920-1959 .... DLB-72
Updike, John 1932- DLB-2, 5, 143, 218, 227; Y-80, Y-82; DS-3; CDALB-6	Van Dyke, Henry 1852-1933 ..... DLB-71; DS-13	Viazemsky, Petr Andreevich 1792-1878 .... DLB-205
	Van Dyke, Henry 1928- DLB-33	
	Van Dyke, John C. 1856-1932 .... DLB-186	Vicars, Thomas 1591-1638 .... DLB-236
John Updike on the Internet Y-97	van Gulik, Robert Hans 1910-1967 ...... DS-17	Vickers, Roy 1888?-1965 .... DLB-77
Upīts, Andrejs 1877-1970 .... DLB-220	van Itallie, Jean-Claude 1936- DLB-7	Vickery, Sukey 1779-1821 .... DLB-200
Upton, Bertha 1849-1912 .... DLB-141	Van Loan, Charles E. 1876-1919 .... DLB-171	Victoria 1819-1901 .... DLB-55
Upton, Charles 1948- DLB-16	Van Rensselaer, Mariana Griswold 1851-1934 .... DLB-47	Victoria Press DLB-106
Upton, Florence K. 1873-1922 .... DLB-141		Vidal, Gore 1925- DLB-6, 152; CDALB-7
Upward, Allen 1863-1926 .... DLB-36	Van Rensselaer, Mrs. Schuyler (see Van Rensselaer, Mariana Griswold)	Vidal, Mary Theresa 1815-1873 .... DLB-230
Urban, Milo 1904-1982 .... DLB-215		Viebig, Clara 1860-1952 .... DLB-66
Urista, Alberto Baltazar (see Alurista)	Van Vechten, Carl 1880-1964 .... DLB-4, 9	Viereck, George Sylvester 1884-1962 .... DLB-54
Urquhart, Fred 1912- DLB-139	van Vogt, A. E. 1912- DLB-8	
Urrea, Luis Alberto 1955- DLB-209	Vanbrugh, Sir John 1664-1726 .... DLB-80	Viereck, Peter 1916- DLB-5
Urzidil, Johannes 1896-1976 .... DLB-85	Vance, Jack 1916?- DLB-8	Viets, Roger 1738-1811 .... DLB-99
The Uses of Facsimile Y-90	Vančura, Vladislav 1891-1942 .... DLB-215; CDWLB-4	Viewpoint: Politics and Performance, by David Edgar DLB-13
Usk, Thomas died 1388 .... DLB-146		
Uslar Pietri, Arturo 1906- DLB-113	Vane, Sutton 1888-1963 .... DLB-10	Vigil-Piñon, Evangelina 1949- DLB-122
Ussher, James 1581-1656 .... DLB-213	Vanguard Press DLB-46	Vigneault, Gilles 1928- DLB-60
Ustinov, Peter 1921- DLB-13	Vann, Robert L. 1879-1940 .... DLB-29	Vigny, Alfred de 1797-1863 .... DLB-119, 192, 217
Uttley, Alison 1884-1976 .... DLB-160	Vargas Llosa, Mario 1936- DLB-145; CDWLB-3	
Uz, Johann Peter 1720-1796 .... DLB-97		Vigolo, Giorgio 1894-1983 .... DLB-114
	Varley, John 1947- Y-81	The Viking Press DLB-46
V	Varnhagen von Ense, Karl August 1785-1858 .... DLB-90	Vilde, Eduard 1865-1933 .... DLB-220
Vac, Bertrand 1914- DLB-88		Vilinskaia, Maria Aleksandrovna (see Vovchok, Marko)
Vācietis, Ojārs 1933-1983 .... DLB-232	Varnhagen von Ense, Rahel 1771-1833 .... DLB-90	
Vaičiulaitis, Antanas 1906-1992 .... DLB-220	Varro 116 B.C.-27 B.C. DLB-211	Villanueva, Alma Luz 1944- DLB-122
Vaculík, Ludvík 1926- DLB-232	Vasiliu, George (see Bacovia, George)	Villanueva, Tino 1941- DLB-82
Vaičiūnaite, Judita 1937- DLB-232	Vásquez, Richard 1928- DLB-209	Villard, Henry 1835-1900 .... DLB-23
Vail, Laurence 1891-1968 .... DLB-4	Vásquez Montalbán, Manuel 1939- DLB-134	Villard, Oswald Garrison 1872-1949 .... DLB-25, 91
Vailland, Roger 1907-1965 .... DLB-83	Vassa, Gustavus (see Equiano, Olaudah)	
Vaižgantas 1869-1933 .... DLB-220	Vassalli, Sebastiano 1941- DLB-128, 196	Villarreal, Edit 1944- DLB-209
Vajda, Ernest 1887-1954 .... DLB-44	Vaughan, Henry 1621-1695 .... DLB-131	Villarreal, José Antonio 1924- DLB-82
Valdés, Gina 1943- DLB-122	Vaughan, Thomas 1621-1666 .... DLB-131	Villaseñor, Victor 1940- DLB-209
Valdez, Luis Miguel 1940- DLB-122	Vaughn, Robert 1592?-1667 .... DLB-213	Villegas de Magnón, Leonor 1876-1955 .... DLB-122
Valduga, Patrizia 1953- DLB-128	Vaux, Thomas, Lord 1509-1556 .... DLB-132	Villehardouin, Geoffroi de circa 1150-1215 .... DLB-208

Cumulative Index

Villemaire, Yolande 1949- DLB-60
Villena, Luis Antonio de 1951- DLB-134
Villiers, George, Second Duke
   of Buckingham 1628-1687 .... DLB-80
Villiers de l'Isle-Adam, Jean-Marie Mathias
   Philippe-Auguste, Comte de
   1838-1889 .... DLB-123, 192
Villon, François 1431-circa 1463?...... DLB-208
Vine Press..................... DLB-112
Viorst, Judith ?- DLB-52
Vipont, Elfrida (Elfrida Vipont Foulds,
   Charles Vipont) 1902-1992 .... DLB-160
Viramontes, Helena María 1954- DLB-122
Virgil 70 B.C.-19 B.C...... DLB-211; CDWLB-1
Vischer, Friedrich Theodor 1807-1887 .. DLB-133
Vitruvius circa 85 B.C.-circa 15 B.C..... DLB-211
Vitry, Philippe de 1291-1361 .... DLB-208
Vivanco, Luis Felipe 1907-1975........ DLB-108
Viviani, Cesare 1947- DLB-128
Vivien, Renée 1877-1909 .... DLB-217
Vizenor, Gerald 1934- DLB-175, 227
Vizetelly and Company DLB-106
Voaden, Herman 1903- DLB-88
Voß, Johann Heinrich 1751-1826........ DLB-90
Voigt, Ellen Bryant 1943- DLB-120
Vojnović, Ivo 1857-1929.....DLB-147; CDWLB-4
Volkoff, Vladimir 1932- DLB-83
Volland, P. F., Company DLB-46
Vollbehr, Otto H. F.
   1872?-1945 or 1946 .... DLB-187
Vologdin (see Zasodimsky, Pavel Vladimirovich)
Volponi, Paolo 1924- DLB-177
von der Grün, Max 1926- DLB-75
Vonnegut, Kurt 1922-
   .... DLB-2, 8, 152; Y-80; DS-3; CDALB-6
Voranc, Prežihov 1893-1950 .... DLB-147
Vovchok, Marko 1833-1907.......... DLB-238
Voynich, E. L. 1864-1960............ DLB-197
Vroman, Mary Elizabeth
   circa 1924-1967 .... DLB-33

W

Wace, Robert ("Maistre")
   circa 1100-circa 1175 .... DLB-146
Wackenroder, Wilhelm Heinrich
   1773-1798 .... DLB-90
Wackernagel, Wilhelm 1806-1869 ..... DLB-133
Waddell, Helen 1889-1965 .... DLB-240
Waddington, Miriam 1917- DLB-68
Wade, Henry 1887-1969............. DLB-77
Wagenknecht, Edward 1900- DLB-103
Wagner, Heinrich Leopold 1747-1779..... DLB-94
Wagner, Henry R. 1862-1957 .... DLB-140
Wagner, Richard 1813-1883.......... DLB-129
Wagoner, David 1926- DLB-5
Wah, Fred 1939- DLB-60
Waiblinger, Wilhelm 1804-1830 .... DLB-90

Wain, John
   1925-1994 ...DLB-15, 27, 139, 155; CDBLB-8
Wainwright, Jeffrey 1944- DLB-40
Waite, Peirce and Company........... DLB-49
Wakeman, Stephen H. 1859-1924 ..... DLB-187
Wakoski, Diane 1937- DLB-5
Walahfrid Strabo circa 808-849 .... DLB-148
Walck, Henry Z. DLB-46
Walcott, Derek
   1930- DLB-117; Y-81, Y-92; CDWLB-3
Waldegrave, Robert [publishing house] ...DLB-170
Waldman, Anne 1945- DLB-16
Waldrop, Rosmarie 1935- DLB-169
Walker, Alice 1900-1982 .... DLB-201
Walker, Alice
   1944- DLB-6, 33, 143; CDALB-6
Walker, Annie Louisa (Mrs. Harry Coghill)
   circa 1836-1907 .... DLB-240
Walker, George F. 1947- DLB-60
Walker, John Brisben 1847-1931 .... DLB-79
Walker, Joseph A. 1935- DLB-38
Walker, Margaret 1915- DLB-76, 152
Walker, Ted 1934- DLB-40
Walker and Company DLB-49
Walker, Evans and Cogswell Company... DLB-49
Wallace, Alfred Russel 1823-1913 ...... DLB-190
Wallace, Dewitt 1889-1981 and
   Lila Acheson Wallace 1889-1984.... DLB-137
Wallace, Edgar 1875-1932 .... DLB-70
Wallace, Lew 1827-1905............. DLB-202
Wallace, Lila Acheson
   (see Wallace, Dewitt, and Lila Acheson Wallace)
Wallant, Edward Lewis
   1926-1962 .... DLB-2, 28, 143
Waller, Edmund 1606-1687 .... DLB-126
Walpole, Horace 1717-1797......DLB-39, 104, 213
Preface to the First Edition of
   The Castle of Otranto (1764)........... DLB-39
Preface to the Second Edition of
   The Castle of Otranto (1765)........... DLB-39
Walpole, Hugh 1884-1941 .... DLB-34
Walrond, Eric 1898-1966............ DLB-51
Walser, Martin 1927- DLB-75, 124
Walser, Robert 1878-1956 .... DLB-66
Walsh, Ernest 1895-1926 .... DLB-4, 45
Walsh, Robert 1784-1859 .... DLB-59
Walters, Henry 1848-1931 .... DLB-140
Waltharius circa 825................ DLB-148
Walther von der Vogelweide
   circa 1170-circa 1230 .... DLB-138
Walton, Izaak
   1593-1683 .... DLB-151, 213; CDBLB-1
Wambaugh, Joseph 1937- DLB-6; Y-83
Wand, Alfred Rudolph 1828-1891...... DLB-188
Waniek, Marilyn Nelson 1946- DLB-120
Wanley, Humphrey 1672-1726......... DLB-213
Warburton, William 1698-1779 .... DLB-104
Ward, Aileen 1919- DLB-111

Ward, Artemus (see Browne, Charles Farrar)
Ward, Arthur Henry Sarsfield (see Rohmer, Sax)
Ward, Douglas Turner 1930- DLB-7, 38
Ward, Mrs. Humphry 1851-1920 ...... DLB-18
Ward, Lynd 1905-1985 .... DLB-22
Ward, Lock and Company DLB-106
Ward, Nathaniel circa 1578-1652........ DLB-24
Ward, Theodore 1902-1983........... DLB-76
Wardle, Ralph 1909-1988 .... DLB-103
Ware, Henry, Jr. 1794-1843 .... DLB-235
Ware, William 1797-1852........... DLB-1, 235
Waring, Anna Letitia 1823-1910 ....DLB-240
Warne, Frederick, and Company [U.K.].. DLB-106
Warne, Frederick, and Company [U.S.] ... DLB-49
Warner, Anne 1869-1913............. DLB-202
Warner, Charles Dudley 1829-1900 ..... DLB-64
Warner, Marina 1946- DLB-194
Warner, Rex 1905- DLB-15
Warner, Susan 1819-1885 ..... DLB-3, 42, 239
Warner, Sylvia Townsend
   1893-1978..................DLB-34, 139
Warner, William 1558-1609...........DLB-172
Warner Books DLB-46
Warr, Bertram 1917-1943............ DLB-88
Warren, John Byrne Leicester (see De Tabley, Lord)
Warren, Lella 1899-1982 .... Y-83
Warren, Mercy Otis 1728-1814 ..... DLB-31, 200
Warren, Robert Penn 1905-1989
   ....DLB-2, 48, 152; Y-80, Y-89; CDALB-6
Warren, Samuel 1807-1877 .... DLB-190
Die Wartburgkrieg circa 1230-circa 1280... DLB-138
Warton, Joseph 1722-1800.........DLB-104, 109
Warton, Thomas 1728-1790........DLB-104, 109
Warung, Price (William Astley)
   1855-1911 .... DLB-230
Washington, George 1732-1799 .... DLB-31
Wassermann, Jakob 1873-1934 .... DLB-66
Wasserstein, Wendy 1950- DLB-228
Wasson, David Atwood 1823-1887 ... DLB-1, 223
Watanna, Onoto (see Eaton, Winnifred)
Waterhouse, Keith 1929- DLB-13, 15
Waterman, Andrew 1940- DLB-40
Waters, Frank 1902-1995..........DLB-212; Y-86
Waters, Michael 1949- DLB-120
Watkins, Tobias 1780-1855 .... DLB-73
Watkins, Vernon 1906-1967 .... DLB-20
Watmough, David 1926- DLB-53
Watson, James Wreford (see Wreford, James)
Watson, John 1850-1907 .... DLB-156
Watson, Rosamund Marriott
   (Graham R. Tomson) 1860-1911.... DLB-240
Watson, Sheila 1909- DLB-60
Watson, Thomas 1545?-1592 .... DLB-132
Watson, Wilfred 1911- DLB-60
Watt, W. J., and Company DLB-46

Watten, Barrett 1948- DLB-193
Watterson, Henry 1840-1921 ....DLB-25
Watts, Alan 1915-1973................DLB-16
Watts, Franklin [publishing house] DLB-46
Watts, Isaac 1674-1748...............DLB-95
Waugh, Alec 1898-1981 ....DLB-191
Waugh, Auberon 1939- DLB-14, 194
The Cult of Biography
 Excerpts from the Second Folio Debate:
 "Biographies are generally a disease of
 English Literature" Y-86
Waugh, Evelyn
 1903-1966 ......DLB-15, 162, 195; CDBLB-6
Way and Williams....................DLB-49
Wayman, Tom 1945- DLB-53
We See the Editor at Work Y-97
Weatherly, Tom 1942- DLB-41
Weaver, Gordon 1937- DLB-130
Weaver, Robert 1921- DLB-88
Webb, Beatrice 1858-1943 and
 Webb, Sidney 1859-1947 ....DLB-190
Webb, Frank J. ?-?...................DLB-50
Webb, James Watson 1802-1884.........DLB-43
Webb, Mary 1881-1927................DLB-34
Webb, Phyllis 1927- DLB-53
Webb, Walter Prescott 1888-1963.........DLB-17
Webbe, William ?-1591................DLB-132
Webber, Charles Wilkins 1819-1856?....DLB-202
Webling, Lucy (Lucy Betty MacRaye)
 1877-1952 ....DLB-240
Webling, Peggy (Arthur Weston)
 1871-1949 ....DLB-240
Webster, Augusta 1837-1894 ....DLB-35, 240
Webster, Charles L., and Company DLB-49
Webster, John
 1579 or 1580-1634?...... DLB-58; CDBLB-1
John Webster: The Melbourne
 Manuscript Y-86
Webster, Noah 1758-1843 ... DLB-1, 37, 42, 43, 73
Weckherlin, Georg Rodolf 1584-1653....DLB-164
Wedekind, Frank
 1864-1918 ....DLB-118; CDBLB-2
Weeks, Edward Augustus, Jr.
 1898-1989 ....DLB-137
Weeks, Stephen B. 1865-1918 ....DLB-187
Weems, Mason Locke 1759-1825 .. DLB-30, 37, 42
Weerth, Georg 1822-1856 ....DLB-129
Weidenfeld and Nicolson DLB-112
Weidman, Jerome 1913-1998 ....DLB-28
Weiß, Ernst 1882-1940 ....DLB-81
Weigl, Bruce 1949- DLB-120
Weinbaum, Stanley Grauman 1902-1935 ...DLB-8
Weintraub, Stanley 1929- DLB-111
The Practice of Biography: An Interview
 with Stanley Weintraub Y-82
Weise, Christian 1642-1708.............DLB-168
Weisenborn, Gunther 1902-1969 ....DLB-69, 124
Weiss, John 1818-1879.................DLB-1

Weiss, Peter 1916-1982 ....DLB-69, 124
Weiss, Theodore 1916- DLB-5
Weisse, Christian Felix 1726-1804........DLB-97
Weitling, Wilhelm 1808-1871 ....DLB-129
Welch, James 1940- DLB-175
Welch, Lew 1926-1971?................DLB-16
Weldon, Fay 1931- DLB-14, 194; CDBLB-8
Wellek, René 1903-1995 ....DLB-63
Wells, Carolyn 1862-1942...............DLB-11
Wells, Charles Jeremiah circa 1800-1879...DLB-32
Wells, Gabriel 1862-1946 ....DLB-140
Wells, H. G.
 1866-1946 ... DLB-34, 70, 156, 178; CDBLB-6
Wells, Helena 1758?-1824 ....DLB-200
Wells, Robert 1947- DLB-40
Wells-Barnett, Ida B. 1862-1931 .....DLB-23, 221
Welty, Eudora 1909-
 .... DLB-2, 102, 143; Y-87; DS-12; CDALB-1
Eudora Welty: Eye of the Storyteller.........Y-87
Eudora Welty Newsletter Y-99
Eudora Welty's Ninetieth Birthday Y-99
Wendell, Barrett 1855-1921..............DLB-71
Wentworth, Patricia 1878-1961 ....DLB-77
Wentworth, William Charles
 1790-1872 ....DLB-230
Werder, Diederich von dem 1584-1657 ..DLB-164
Werfel, Franz 1890-1945 ....DLB-81, 124
Werner, Zacharias 1768-1823 ....DLB-94
The Werner Company DLB-49
Wersba, Barbara 1932- DLB-52
Wescott, Glenway 1901- DLB-4, 9, 102
Wesker, Arnold 1932- DLB-13; CDBLB-8
Wesley, Charles 1707-1788...............DLB-95
Wesley, John 1703-1791...............DLB-104
Wesley, Mary 1912- DLB-231
Wesley, Richard 1945- DLB-38
Wessels, A., and Company DLB-46
Wessobrunner Gebet circa 787-815 ....DLB-148
West, Anthony 1914-1988................DLB-15
West, Dorothy 1907-1998 ....DLB-76
West, Jessamyn 1902-1984 ....DLB-6; Y-84
West, Mae 1892-1980..................DLB-44
West, Nathanael
 1903-1940 ....DLB-4, 9, 28; CDALB-5
West, Paul 1930- DLB-14
West, Rebecca 1892-1983 ....DLB-36; Y-83
West, Richard 1941- DLB-185
West and Johnson DLB-49
Westcott, Edward Noyes 1846-1898.....DLB-202
The Western Messenger 1835-1841 ....DLB-223
Western Publishing Company...........DLB-46
Western Writers of America Y-99
The Westminster Review 1824-1914........DLB-110
Weston, Arthur (see Webling, Peggy)
Weston, Elizabeth Jane circa 1582-1612 ..DLB-172

Wetherald, Agnes Ethelwyn 1857-1940....DLB-99
Wetherell, Elizabeth (see Warner, Susan)
Wetherell, W. D. 1948- DLB-234
Wetzel, Friedrich Gottlob 1779-1819......DLB-90
Weyman, Stanley J. 1855-1928 .....DLB-141, 156
Wezel, Johann Karl 1747-1819 ....DLB-94
Whalen, Philip 1923- DLB-16
Whalley, George 1915-1983 ....DLB-88
Wharton, Edith 1862-1937
 ..... DLB-4, 9, 12, 78, 189; DS-13; CDALB-3
Wharton, William 1920s?- Y-80
"What You Lose on the Swings You Make Up
 on the Merry-Go-Round"..............Y-99
Whately, Mary Louisa 1824-1889........DLB-166
Whately, Richard 1787-1863 ....DLB-190
From Elements of Rhetoric (1828;
 revised, 1846) DLB-57
What's Really Wrong With Bestseller Lists ..Y-84
Wheatley, Dennis Yates 1897-1977 ....DLB-77
Wheatley, Phillis
 circa 1754-1784 ....DLB-31, 50; CDALB-2
Wheeler, Anna Doyle 1785-1848?......DLB-158
Wheeler, Charles Stearns 1816-1843...DLB-1, 223
Wheeler, Monroe 1900-1988............DLB-4
Wheelock, John Hall 1886-1978 ....DLB-45
Wheelwright, J. B. 1897-1940 ....DLB-45
Wheelwright, John circa 1592-1679......DLB-24
Whetstone, George 1550-1587 ....DLB-136
Whetstone, Colonel Pete (see Noland, C. F. M.)
Whicher, Stephen E. 1915-1961 ....DLB-111
Whipple, Edwin Percy 1819-1886......DLB-1, 64
Whitaker, Alexander 1585-1617 ....DLB-24
Whitaker, Daniel K. 1801-1881..........DLB-73
Whitcher, Frances Miriam
 1812-1852 ....DLB-11, 202
White, Andrew 1579-1656..............DLB-24
White, Andrew Dickson 1832-1918 ......DLB-47
White, E. B. 1899-1985 ....DLB-11, 22; CDALB-7
White, Edgar B. 1947- DLB-38
White, Edmund 1940- DLB-227
White, Ethel Lina 1887-1944............DLB-77
White, Henry Kirke 1785-1806 ....DLB-96
White, Horace 1834-1916 ....DLB-23
White, Phyllis Dorothy James (see James, P. D.)
White, Richard Grant 1821-1885 ....DLB-64
White, T. H. 1906-1964 ....DLB-160
White, Walter 1893-1955 ....DLB-51
White, William, and Company..........DLB-49
White, William Allen 1868-1944.......DLB-9, 25
White, William Anthony Parker
 (see Boucher, Anthony)
White, William Hale (see Rutherford, Mark)
Whitechurch, Victor L. 1868-1933 ....DLB-70
Whitehead, Alfred North 1861-1947.....DLB-100
Whitehead, James 1936- Y-81
Whitehead, William 1715-1785 ......DLB-84, 109

Whitfield, James Monroe 1822-1871 ..... DLB-50	Wilder, Billy 1906- DLB-26	Williams, Sherley Anne 1944-1999 ...... DLB-41
Whitfield, Raoul 1898-1945 .... DLB-226	Wilder, Laura Ingalls 1867-1957......... DLB-22	Williams, T. Harry 1909-1979 ....DLB-17
Whitgift, John circa 1533-1604......... DLB-132	Wilder, Thornton 1897-1975........DLB-4, 7, 9, 228; CDALB-7	Williams, Tennessee 1911-1983 ..... DLB-7; Y-83; DS-4; CDALB-1
Whiting, John 1917-1963 .... DLB-13	Thornton Wilder Centenary at Yale Y-97	Williams, Terry Tempest 1955- DLB-206
Whiting, Samuel 1597-1679 .... DLB-24	Wildgans, Anton 1881-1932........... DLB-118	Williams, Ursula Moray 1911- DLB-160
Whitlock, Brand 1869-1934 .... DLB-12	Wiley, Bell Irvin 1906-1980 .... DLB-17	Williams, Valentine 1883-1946 .... DLB-77
Whitman, Albert, and Company DLB-46	Wiley, John, and Sons DLB-49	Williams, William Appleman 1921- DLB-17
Whitman, Albery Allson 1851-1901..... DLB-50	Wilhelm, Kate 1928- DLB-8	Williams, William Carlos
Whitman, Alden 1913-1990 .... Y-91	Wilkes, Charles 1798-1877 .... DLB-183	1883-1963 ..... DLB-4, 16, 54, 86; CDALB-4
Whitman, Sarah Helen (Power) 1803-1878..................... DLB-1	Wilkes, George 1817-1885 .... DLB-79	Williams, Wirt 1921- DLB-6
Whitman, Walt 1819-1892........ DLB-3, 64, 224; CDALB-2	Wilkins, John 1614-1672 .... DLB-236	Williams Brothers..................... DLB-49
Whitman Publishing Company DLB-46	Wilkinson, Anne 1910-1961 .... DLB-88	Williamson, Henry 1895-1977 .... DLB-191
Whitney, Geoffrey 1548 or 1552?-1601.. DLB-136	Wilkinson, Eliza Yonge 1757-circa 1813.................. DLB-200	Williamson, Jack 1908- DLB-8
Whitney, Isabella flourished 1566-1573 .. DLB-136	Wilkinson, Sylvia 1940- Y-86	Willingham, Calder Baynard, Jr. 1922-1995 .... DLB-2, 44
Whitney, John Hay 1904-1982.......... DLB-127	Wilkinson, William Cleaver 1833-1920... DLB-71	Williram of Ebersberg circa 1020-1085 ... DLB-148
Whittemore, Reed 1919-1995........... DLB-5	Willard, Barbara 1909-1994............ DLB-161	Willis, Nathaniel Parker 1806-1867 .....DLB-3, 59, 73, 74, 183; DS-13
Whittier, John Greenleaf 1807-1892............ DLB-1; CDALB-2	Willard, Emma 1787-1870............. DLB-239	Willkomm, Ernst 1810-1886 .... DLB-133
Whittlesey House................... DLB-46	Willard, Frances E. 1839-1898........... DLB-221	Willumsen, Dorrit 1940- DLB-214
Who Runs American Literature?........... Y-94	Willard, L. [publishing house] DLB-49	Wilmer, Clive 1945- DLB-40
Whose *Ulysses?* The Function of Editing...... Y-97	Willard, Nancy 1936- DLB-5, 52	Wilson, A. N. 1950- DLB-14, 155, 194
Wickham, Anna (Edith Alice Mary Harper) 1884-1947..................... DLB-240	Willard, Samuel 1640-1707............. DLB-24	Wilson, Angus 1913-1991 ......DLB-15, 139, 155
Wicomb, Zoë 1948- DLB-225	Willeford, Charles 1919-1988 .... DLB-226	Wilson, Arthur 1595-1652 .... DLB-58
Wideman, John Edgar 1941- DLB-33, 143	William of Auvergne 1190-1249........ DLB-115	Wilson, August 1945- DLB-228
Widener, Harry Elkins 1885-1912 ...... DLB-140	William of Conches circa 1090-circa 1154 .... DLB-115	Wilson, Augusta Jane Evans 1835-1909... DLB-42
Wiebe, Rudy 1934- DLB-60	William of Ockham circa 1285-1347 .... DLB-115	Wilson, Colin 1931- DLB-14, 194
Wiechert, Ernst 1887-1950 .... DLB-56	William of Sherwood 1200/1205-1266/1271 .... DLB-115	Wilson, Edmund 1895-1972............ DLB-63
Wied, Martina 1882-1957.............. DLB-85	The William Chavrat American Fiction Collection at the Ohio State University Libraries Y-92	Wilson, Effingham [publishing house] ... DLB-154
Wiehe, Evelyn May Clowes (see Mordaunt, Elinor)	Williams, A., and Company............ DLB-49	Wilson, Ethel 1888-1980 .... DLB-68
Wieland, Christoph Martin 1733-1813.... DLB-97	Williams, Ben Ames 1889-1953 .... DLB-102	Wilson, F. P. 1889-1963 .... DLB-201
Wienbarg, Ludolf 1802-1872 .... DLB-133	Williams, C. K. 1936- DLB-5	Wilson, Harriet 1827/1828?-1863?... DLB-50, 239
Wieners, John 1934- DLB-16	Williams, Chancellor 1905- DLB-76	Wilson, Harry Leon 1867-1939 .... DLB-9
Wier, Ester 1910- DLB-52	Williams, Charles 1886-1945 ....DLB-100, 153	Wilson, John 1588-1667................ DLB-24
Wiesel, Elie 1928- DLB-83; Y-86, 87; CDALB-7	Williams, Denis 1923-1998............DLB-117	Wilson, John 1785-1854................ DLB-110
Wiggin, Kate Douglas 1856-1923........ DLB-42	Williams, Emlyn 1905- DLB-10, 77	Wilson, John Dover 1881-1969 .... DLB-201
Wigglesworth, Michael 1631-1705 ...... DLB-24	Williams, Garth 1912-1996 .... DLB-22	Wilson, Lanford 1937- DLB-7
Wilberforce, William 1759-1833........ DLB-158	Williams, George Washington 1849-1891 .... DLB-47	Wilson, Margaret 1882-1973 .... DLB-9
Wilbrandt, Adolf 1837-1911 .... DLB-129	Williams, Heathcote 1941- DLB-13	Wilson, Michael 1914-1978 .... DLB-44
Wilbur, Richard 1921- DLB-5, 169; CDALB-7	Williams, Helen Maria 1761-1827 ...... DLB-158	Wilson, Mona 1872-1954 .... DLB-149
Wild, Peter 1940- DLB-5	Williams, Hugo 1942- DLB-40	Wilson, Robley 1930- DLB-218
Wilde, Lady Jane Francesca Elgee 1821?-1896..................... DLB-199	Williams, Isaac 1802-1865 .... DLB-32	Wilson, Romer 1891-1930 .... DLB-191
Wilde, Oscar 1854-1900 ....DLB-10, 19, 34, 57, 141, 156, 190; CDBLB-5	Williams, Joan 1928- DLB-6	Wilson, Thomas 1524-1581....... DLB-132, 236
	Williams, John A. 1925- DLB-2, 33	Wilson, Woodrow 1856-1924 .... DLB-47
	Williams, John E. 1922-1994 .... DLB-6	Wimsatt, William K., Jr. 1907-1975 ..... DLB-63
"The Critic as Artist" (1891) DLB-57	Williams, Jonathan 1929- DLB-5	Winchell, Walter 1897-1972............ DLB-29
From "The Decay of Lying" (1889) DLB-18	Williams, Miller 1930- DLB-105	Winchester, J. [publishing house]........ DLB-49
"The English Renaissance of Art" (1908)..................... DLB-35	Williams, Nigel 1948- DLB-231	Winckelmann, Johann Joachim 1717-1768 .... DLB-97
"L'Envoi" (1882) DLB-35	Williams, Raymond 1921- DLB-14, 231	Winckler, Paul 1630-1686 .... DLB-164
Wilde, Richard Henry 1789-1847...... DLB-3, 59	Williams, Roger circa 1603-1683 .... DLB-24	Wind, Herbert Warren 1916- DLB-171
Wilde, W. A., Company DLB-49	Williams, Rowland 1817-1870 .... DLB-184	Windet, John [publishing house] DLB-170
	Williams, Samm-Art 1946- DLB-38	Windham, Donald 1920- DLB-6
		Wing, Donald Goddard 1904-1972 .....DLB-187
		Wing, John M. 1844-1917 ....DLB-187

Wingate, Allan [publishing house] DLB-112
Winnemucca, Sarah 1844-1921 . . . . .DLB-175
Winnifrith, Tom 1938- DLB-155
Winning an Edgar Y-98
Winsloe, Christa 1888-1944 . . . . .DLB-124
Winslow, Anna Green 1759-1780 . . . . . . .DLB-200
Winsor, Justin 1831-1897. . . . . .DLB-47
John C. Winston Company. DLB-49
Winters, Yvor 1900-1968 . . . . .DLB-48
Winterson, Jeanette 1959- DLB-207
Winthrop, John 1588-1649 . . . . .DLB-24, 30
Winthrop, John, Jr. 1606-1676. . . . . .DLB-24
Winthrop, Margaret Tyndal 1591-1647 . .DLB-200
Winthrop, Theodore 1828-1861 . . . . .DLB-202
Wirt, William 1772-1834 . . . . .DLB-37
Wise, John 1652-1725 . . . . .DLB-24
Wise, Thomas James 1859-1937 . . . . .DLB-184
Wiseman, Adele 1928- DLB-88
Wishart and Company DLB-112
Wisner, George 1812-1849 . . . . .DLB-43
Wister, Owen 1860-1938 . . . . DLB-9, 78, 186
Wister, Sarah 1761-1804 . . . . .DLB-200
Wither, George 1588-1667 . . . . .DLB-121
Witherspoon, John 1723-1794 . . . . .DLB-31
Withrow, William Henry 1839-1908. . . . . .DLB-99
Witkacy (see Witkiewicz, Stanisław Ignacy)
Witkiewicz, Stanisław Ignacy
  1885-1939 . . . . .DLB-215; CDWLB-4
Wittig, Monique 1935- DLB-83
Wodehouse, P. G.
  1881-1975 . . . . . .DLB-34, 162; CDBLB-6
Wohmann, Gabriele 1932- DLB-75
Woiwode, Larry 1941- DLB-6
Wolcot, John 1738-1819. . . . . .DLB-109
Wolcott, Roger 1679-1767 . . . . .DLB-24
Wolf, Christa 1929- DLB-75; CDWLB-2
Wolf, Friedrich 1888-1953. . . . . .DLB-124
Wolfe, Gene 1931- DLB-8
Wolfe, John [publishing house] DLB-170
Wolfe, Reyner (Reginald)
  [publishing house] DLB-170
Wolfe, Thomas
  1900-1938 . . . . DLB-9, 102, 229; Y-85;
     DS-2, DS-16; CDALB-5
The Thomas Wolfe Collection at the University
  of North Carolina at Chapel Hill Y-97
Fire at Thomas Wolfe Memorial Y-98
The Thomas Wolfe Society. Y-97
Wolfe, Tom 1931- DLB-152, 185
Wolfenstein, Martha 1869-1906 . . . . .DLB-221
Wolff, Helen 1906-1994 . . . . Y-94
Wolff, Tobias 1945- DLB-130
Wolfram von Eschenbach
  circa 1170-after 1220 . . . .DLB-138; CDWLB-2
Wolfram von Eschenbach's Parzival:
  Prologue and Book 3. . . . . .DLB-138
Wolker, Jiří 1900-1924 . . . . .DLB-215

Wollstonecraft, Mary
  1759-1797 . . . . . . .DLB-39, 104, 158; CDBLB-3
Wondratschek, Wolf 1943- DLB-75
Wood, Anthony à 1632-1695 . . . . .DLB-213
Wood, Benjamin 1820-1900 . . . . .DLB-23
Wood, Charles 1932- DLB-13
Wood, Mrs. Henry 1814-1887 . . . . .DLB-18
Wood, Joanna E. 1867-1927 . . . . .DLB-92
Wood, Sally Sayward Barrell Keating
  1759-1855 . . . . .DLB-200
Wood, Samuel [publishing house] DLB-49
Wood, William ?-? DLB-24
The Charles Wood Affair:
  A Playwright Revived Y-83
Woodberry, George Edward
  1855-1930 . . . . .DLB-71, 103
Woodbridge, Benjamin 1622-1684 . . . . . . .DLB-24
Woodcock, George 1912-1995 . . . . .DLB-88
Woodhull, Victoria C. 1838-1927 . . . . . . .DLB-79
Woodmason, Charles circa 1720-? DLB-31
Woodress, Jr., James Leslie 1916- DLB-111
Woods, Margaret L. 1855-1945 . . . . .DLB-240
Woodson, Carter G. 1875-1950. . . . . .DLB-17
Woodward, C. Vann 1908-1999 . . . . .DLB-17
Woodward, Stanley 1895-1965 . . . . .DLB-171
Wooler, Thomas 1785 or 1786-1853 . . . . .DLB-158
Woolf, David (see Maddow, Ben)
Woolf, Leonard 1880-1969 . . . . . .DLB-100; DS-10
Woolf, Virginia 1882-1941
  . . . . .DLB-36, 100, 162; DS-10; CDBLB-6
Woolf, Virginia, "The New Biography," New York
  Herald Tribune, 30 October 1927 . . . . .DLB-149
Woollcott, Alexander 1887-1943 . . . . .DLB-29
Woolman, John 1720-1772. . . . . .DLB-31
Woolner, Thomas 1825-1892 . . . . .DLB-35
Woolrich, Cornell 1903-1968 . . . . .DLB-226
Woolsey, Sarah Chauncy 1835-1905 . . . . .DLB-42
Woolson, Constance Fenimore
  1840-1894 . . . . DLB-12, 74, 189, 221
Worcester, Joseph Emerson
  1784-1865 . . . . .DLB-1, 235
Worde, Wynkyn de [publishing house]. . .DLB-170
Wordsworth, Christopher 1807-1885 . . . .DLB-166
Wordsworth, Dorothy 1771-1855 . . . . . . .DLB-107
Wordsworth, Elizabeth 1840-1932 . . . . . . .DLB-98
Wordsworth, William
  1770-1850 . . . . .DLB-93, 107; CDBLB-3
Workman, Fanny Bullock 1859-1925 . . . .DLB-189
The Works of the Rev. John Witherspoon
  (1800-1801) [excerpts]. DLB-31
A World Chronology of Important Science
  Fiction Works (1818-1979) DLB-8
World Publishing Company DLB-46
World War II Writers Symposium at the University
  of South Carolina, 12–14 April 1995 . . . . Y-95
Worthington, R., and Company DLB-49
Wotton, Sir Henry 1568-1639 . . . . .DLB-121
Wouk, Herman 1915- Y-82; CDALB-7
Wreford, James 1915- DLB-88

Wren, Sir Christopher 1632-1723 . . . . . . .DLB-213
Wren, Percival Christopher 1885-1941. . .DLB-153
Wrenn, John Henry 1841-1911. . . . . .DLB-140
Wright, C. D. 1949- DLB-120
Wright, Charles 1935- DLB-165; Y-82
Wright, Charles Stevenson 1932- DLB-33
Wright, Frances 1795-1852 . . . . .DLB-73
Wright, Harold Bell 1872-1944 . . . . .DLB-9
Wright, James
  1927-1980 . . . . .DLB-5, 169; CDALB-7
Wright, Jay 1935- DLB-41
Wright, Louis B. 1899-1984 . . . . .DLB-17
Wright, Richard
  1908-1960 . . . . .DLB-76, 102; DS-2; CDALB-5
Wright, Richard B. 1937- DLB-53
Wright, Sarah Elizabeth 1928- DLB-33
Wright, Willard Huntington ("S. S. Van Dine")
  1888-1939 . . . . DS-16
Writers and Politics: 1871-1918,
  by Ronald Gray DLB-66
Writers and their Copyright Holders:
  the WATCH Project. Y-94
Writers' Forum Y-85
Writing for the Theatre,
  by Harold Pinter DLB-13
Wroth, Lawrence C. 1884-1970 . . . . .DLB-187
Wroth, Lady Mary 1587-1653. . . . . .DLB-121
Wurlitzer, Rudolph 1937- DLB-173
Wyatt, Sir Thomas circa 1503-1542 . . . . .DLB-132
Wycherley, William
  1641-1715 . . . . .DLB-80; CDBLB-2
Wyclif, John
  circa 1335-31 December 1384. . . . . . .DLB-146
Wyeth, N. C. 1882-1945 . . . . .DLB-188; DS-16
Wylie, Elinor 1885-1928 . . . . .DLB-9, 45
Wylie, Philip 1902-1971. . . . . .DLB-9
Wyllie, John Cook 1908-1968. . . . . .DLB-140
Wyman, Lillie Buffum Chace
  1847-1929 . . . . .DLB-202
Wymark, Olwen 1934- DLB-233
Wynne-Tyson, Esmé 1898-1972 . . . . .DLB-191

X

Xenophon circa 430 B.C.-circa 356 B.C. DLB-176

Y

Yasuoka Shōtarō 1920- DLB-182
Yates, Dornford 1885-1960 . . . . DLB-77, 153
Yates, J. Michael 1938- DLB-60
Yates, Richard
  1926-1992 . . . . DLB-2, 234; Y-81, Y-92
Yau, John 1950- DLB-234
Yavorov, Peyo 1878-1914 . . . . .DLB-147
The Year in Book Publishing Y-86
The Year in Book Reviewing and the Literary
  Situation Y-98
The Year in British Drama Y-99
The Year in British Fiction Y-99
The Year in Children's
  Books Y-92–Y-96, Y-98, Y-99
The Year in Children's Literature Y-97
The Year in Drama Y-82–Y-85, Y-87–Y-96

The Year in Fiction... Y-84–Y-86, Y-89, Y-94–Y-99
The Year in Fiction: A Biased View Y-83
The Year in Literary Biography Y-83–Y-98
The Year in Literary Theory Y-92–Y-93
The Year in London Theatre Y-92
The Year in the Novel Y-87, Y-88, Y-90–Y-93
The Year in Poetry Y-83–Y-92, Y-94–Y-99
The Year in Short Stories Y-87
The Year in the Short Story Y-88, Y-90–Y-93
The Year in Texas Literature Y-98
The Year's Work in American Poetry Y-82
The Year's Work in Fiction: A Survey Y-82
Yearsley, Ann 1753-1806 .... DLB-109
Yeats, William Butler 1865-1939 ... DLB-10, 19, 98, 156; CDBLB-5
Yep, Laurence 1948- DLB-52
Yerby, Frank 1916-1991 .... DLB-76
Yezierska, Anzia 1880-1970 .... DLB-28, 221
Yolen, Jane 1939- DLB-52
Yonge, Charlotte Mary 1823-1901 .... DLB-18, 163
The York Cycle circa 1376-circa 1569 ... DLB-146
A Yorkshire Tragedy DLB-58
Yoseloff, Thomas [publishing house] DLB-46
Young, Al 1939- DLB-33
Young, Arthur 1741-1820 .... DLB-158
Young, Dick 1917 or 1918 - 1987 .... DLB-171
Young, Edward 1683-1765 .... DLB-95
Young, Francis Brett 1884-1954 .... DLB-191
Young, Gavin 1928- DLB-204
Young, Stark 1881-1963 ...... DLB-9, 102; DS-16

Young, Waldeman 1880-1938 .... DLB-26
Young, William [publishing house] DLB-49
Young Bear, Ray A. 1950- DLB-175
Yourcenar, Marguerite 1903-1987 .... DLB-72; Y-88
"You've Never Had It So Good," Gusted by "Winds of Change": British Fiction in the 1950s, 1960s, and After DLB-14
Yovkov, Yordan 1880-1937 ..DLB-147; CDWLB-4

Z

Zachariä, Friedrich Wilhelm 1726-1777 ... DLB-97
Zagajewski, Adam 1945- DLB-232
Zagoskin, Mikhail Nikolaevich 1789-1852 .... DLB-198
Zajc, Dane 1929- DLB-181
Zālīte, Māra 1952- DLB-232
Zamora, Bernice 1938- DLB-82
Zand, Herbert 1923-1970 .... DLB-85
Zangwill, Israel 1864-1926 .....DLB-10, 135, 197
Zanzotto, Andrea 1921- DLB-128
Zapata Olivella, Manuel 1920- DLB-113
Zasodimsky, Pavel Vladimirovich 1843-1912 .... DLB-238
Zebra Books DLB-46
Zebrowski, George 1945- DLB-8
Zech, Paul 1881-1946 .... DLB-56
Zeidner, Lisa 1955- DLB-120
Zeidonis, Imants 1933- DLB-232
Zeimi (Kanze Motokiyo) 1363-1443 ..... DLB-203
Zelazny, Roger 1937-1995 .... DLB-8
Zenger, John Peter 1697-1746 ...... DLB-24, 43
Zepheria DLB-172

Zesen, Philipp von 1619-1689 .... DLB-164
Zhukovsky, Vasilii Andreevich 1783-1852 .... DLB-205
Zieber, G. B., and Company DLB-49
Ziedonis, Imants 1933- CDWLB-4
Zieroth, Dale 1946- DLB-60
Zigler und Kliphausen, Heinrich Anshelm von 1663-1697 .... DLB-168
Zimmer, Paul 1934- DLB-5
Zinberg, Len (see Lacy, Ed)
Zindel, Paul 1936- DLB-7, 52; CDALB-7
Zingref, Julius Wilhelm 1591-1635 ...... DLB-164
Zinnes, Harriet 1919- DLB-193
Zinzendorf, Nikolaus Ludwig von 1700-1760 .... DLB-168
Zitkala-Ša 1876-1938 .... DLB-175
Zīverts, Mārtiņš 1903-1990 .... DLB-220
Zlatovratsky, Nikolai Nikolaevich 1845-1911 .... DLB-238
Zola, Emile 1840-1902 .... DLB-123
Zolla, Elémire 1926- DLB-196
Zolotow, Charlotte 1915- DLB-52
Zschokke, Heinrich 1771-1848 .... DLB-94
Zubly, John Joachim 1724-1781 .... DLB-31
Zu-Bolton II, Ahmos 1936- DLB-41
Zuckmayer, Carl 1896-1977 ...... DLB-56, 124
Zukofsky, Louis 1904-1978 .... DLB-5, 165
Zupan, Vitomil 1914-1987 .... DLB-181
Župančič, Oton 1878-1949 ...DLB-147; CDWLB-4
zur Mühlen, Hermynia 1883-1951 .... DLB-56
Zweig, Arnold 1887-1968 .... DLB-66
Zweig, Stefan 1881-1942 .... DLB-81, 118

ISBN 0-7876-4657-1